W9-CPN-991

THE OXFORD ENCYCLOPEDIA OF
THE BIBLE AND GENDER
STUDIES

Julia M. O'Brien

EDITOR IN CHIEF

VOLUME 1

ASI—MUJ

OXFORD

UNIVERSITY PRESS

OXFORD
UNIVERSITY PRESS

Oxford University Press is a department of the
University of Oxford. It furthers the University's objective
of excellence in research, scholarship, and education
by publishing worldwide.

Oxford   New York
Auckland   Cape Town   Dar es Salaam   Hong Kong   Karachi
Kuala Lumpur   Madrid   Melbourne   Mexico City   Nairobi
New Delhi   Shanghai   Taipei   Toronto

With offices in
Argentina   Austria   Brazil   Chile   Czech Republic   France   Greece
Guatemala   Hungary   Italy   Japan   Poland   Portugal   Singapore
South Korea   Switzerland   Thailand   Turkey   Ukraine   Vietnam

Oxford is a registered trademark of Oxford University Press
in the UK and certain other countries.

Published in the United States of America by
Oxford University Press
198 Madison Avenue, New York, NY 10016
www.oup.com

Library of Congress Cataloging-in-Publication Data
The Oxford encyclopedia of the Bible and gender studies / Julia O'Brien, editor in chief.
2 volumes   cm
Includes bibliographical references and index.
ISBN 978-0-19-020488-4 (v. 1 : alk. paper)—ISBN 978-0-19-020489-1 (v. 2 : alk. paper)—
ISBN 978-0-19-983699-4 (set : alk. paper)   1. Bible and feminism—Encyclopedias.
2. Women in the Bible—Encyclopedias.
I. O'Brien, Julia M., editor.
    BS680.W7O94   2014
    220.8'3053—dc23   2014028030

1 3 5 7 9 8 6 4 2

Printed in the United States of America on acid-free paper

Editorial and Production Staff

CONTENTS

LIST OF ARTICLES

Series Introduction

The Oxford Encyclopedias of the Bible

The importance of the Bible cannot be overstated. For Jews and Christians, it is the supremely authoritative text, which has guided and inspired them for some two thousand years. It has also profoundly affected Western culture, influencing not just religious belief and practice, but also the arts, literature, law, politics, and many other fields. In the last century especially, it has also had an impact on cultures worldwide, and scholars, writers, and artists from those cultures have in turn influenced the interpretation of the Bible everywhere.

Several years ago, when editors at Oxford University Press and I discussed producing a new biblical encyclopedia, we first thought along traditional lines: a comprehensive, up-to-date multivolume reference work that would provide a wide audience with comprehensive information about everything in the Bible and about the Bible. We wanted to do this in part because our online reference tool, *Oxford Biblical Studies Online*, needed constant feeding, and in part because it had been almost twenty years since such a work had been produced. As we began to work on the early stages of the project, however, we began to think more creatively. This was prompted in part by the appearance of just such a comprehensive dictionary, and also by our experience in producing some entries for the website. We realized that the amount of effort necessary to duplicate what was already available, about, say, every minor Levite in the book of Chronicles, would not be proportionate to the result, and in many such cases there was little or nothing new to be said.

Biblical studies, however, is not static: new discoveries, new approaches, new insights make the discipline of biblical interpretation dynamic, and it is difficult to communicate these developments in the format of a comprehensive encyclopedia of the Bible. So, we changed the template: instead of a collection of relatively brief articles even on important topics, we decided to produce The Oxford Encyclopedias of the Bible in two-volume sets, each of which is devoted to a particular subject or approach. Within each set, entries several thousand words long explore specific topics in depth.

The cumulative result is a monumental reference work, consisting of more than a dozen volumes containing hundreds of comprehensive essays by scholars from many countries and with a wide variety of perspectives. The simultaneous publication of the articles in these sets in *Oxford Biblical Studies Online* enhances their use and reach. It makes them accessible to scholars and students in a wide variety of places, and it enables us to revise entries on a regular basis. As a whole then, the series is a worthy addition to the innumerable distinguished reference works produced by Oxford University Press, both as printed books and, more and more, in digital format.

Michael D. Coogan
General Editor

PREFACE

Gender-critical exploration of biblical literature remains a relatively new enterprise. Building on and encompassing the work of nineteenth- and twentieth-century feminist scholarship and more recent queer studies, biblically focused gender studies seeks to advance the scholarly conversation by systematically exploring the ways in which gender is constructed in the diverse texts, cultures, and readers that constitute "the world of the Bible."

As the first major encyclopedia of its kind, *The Oxford Encyclopedia of the Bible and Gender Studies* reflects the interdisciplinary and emergent nature of this discipline. It includes not only the work of established and newer biblical scholars but also the contributions of contemporary gender theorists, classicists, archaeologists, and ancient historians whose work bears upon our understandings of the biblical material. The work of New Testament scholars who consult Greek and Roman texts as background to early Christian literature, for example, appears alongside the contributions of those whose primary fields are Greek and Roman literature. Ancient Near Eastern conceptions of the gender of deities are explored both by those specializing in Mesopotamian literature and by those who read Hebrew Bible texts in light of ancient Near Eastern texts. Among entries and within them, the insights of experts who often work in isolation from one another come into fruitful and at times challenging dialogue.

As the Topical Outline of Contents indicates, the *Encyclopedia* includes various types of entries. (1) Substantive entries are devoted to gender theory. Entries such as "Sexuality," "Heteronormativity/Heterosexism," and "Gender" provide an overview of major theorists and key questions within the larger academic discourse on gender, offering readers an entry into the vocabulary and perspectives of this field. (2) Entries focused on history and method identify key moments in the development of biblically focused gender criticism and offer suggestions for future research. Contributions on womanist criticism, intersectional studies, queer readings, historical-critical approaches, and third-wave feminism, for example, not only survey the history of each endeavor but also offer the author's own analysis and insights. (3) Several important entries focus on topics that span the Jewish and Christian canons, such as "Creation," "Canon/Canonicity/Canonization," and "Authors of Biblical Books." (4) The majority of entries investigate the social and ideological dimensions of gender-related topics within specific areas of study. For example, the nature of marriage and divorce in the cultures of the ancient Mediterranean is explored in the following subentries under "Marriage and Divorce":

Ancient Near East
Hebrew Bible
Greek World
Roman World
New Testament
Early Judaism
Early Church

The nonanalogous nature of these seven areas warrants explanation. The inclusion of canonical/confessional categories (Hebrew Bible, New Testament, Early Judaism, Early Church) alongside those marked by chronology/geography (Ancient Near East, Greek world, Roman world) might suggest that the editors have privileged biblical materials (and the confessional communities that preserved them) over noncanonical materials or have chosen to isolate biblical texts from the contexts in which they emerged; it might be seen as denying, for example, that the Hebrew Bible is an ancient Near Eastern document and that Early Judaism developed within the Roman world.

These impressions, however, run contrary to the logic underlying the project's structure. Our intent is to provide multiple paths by which readers can enter the rich conversation offered here. A reader who comes to the work concerned only with the apostle Paul, for example, will be immersed in the world of Greek and Roman thought not only by the entries devoted to Paul but also by cross-references to entries on Greek and Roman conceptions of masculinity/femininity and same-sex relations. Readers who turn first to entries in the areas of the Greek and Roman worlds will be pointed to related entries in New Testament literature and Early Judaism.

The division of topics into these seven areas of study also reflects the discipline-specific character of standard academic training. Most scholars now conducting gender studies have been trained to work with particular texts, periods, and regions and within academic communities shaped by distinctive assumptions. Hebrew Bible scholars who treat ancient Near Eastern materials as "background," for example, often approach Assyrian texts differently than Assyriologists for whom the same texts are "foreground." The editorial team intentionally sought experts from various disciplines who would approach gender in the ancient Mediterranean from various perspectives to the issues. We wanted readers of the *Encyclopedia* to encounter not only up-to-date *information* about the ancient world but also a discussion of the *methodological and perspectival issues* that emerge in the course of studying gender.

For these reasons, the editorial team considers the resulting overlap and tension among entries a strength of the project. Because each entry reflects the perspectives of the author as well as the disciplinary assumptions and proclivities that inform his or her approach, readers will benefit from reading both *across* the seven areas and *within* a single area. For example, reading across areas reveals that the Greek practice of pederasty is assessed differently by New Testament scholars and classical Greek scholars. Conversely, reading within the area of the Hebrew Bible alone demonstrates the methodological pluralism of contemporary biblical studies: some scholars emphasize ancient Near Eastern studies whereas others emphasize archaeology, literary studies, social sciences, or contemporary critical theory. Reading all the entries within an area also offers the reader a snapshot of the current state of gender studies in that area: for example, the *Encyclopedia* includes fewer entries related to the ancient Near East than those related to the New Testament, not by design but as a reflection of the current status of research.

The editorial team is proud to bring this engaging and important work to the attention of a wider public. We believe that the *Encyclopedia* builds upon the pioneering work of others and helps guide and encourage further gendered engagements of the Bible.

Julia M. O'Brien
Editor in Chief

ABBREVIATIONS USED IN THIS WORK

// or ‖	parallel passages
§	section
Acts	Acts of the Apostles
Add Dan	Additions to Daniel
Add Esth	Additions to Esther
Amos	Amos
ANE	ancient Near East
ASV	American Standard Version
b.	Babylonian Talmud
Bar	Baruch
2 Bar.	*2 Baruch*
Barn.	*Barnabas*
B.C.E.	Before the Common Era (= B.C.)
Bel	Bel and the Dragon
c.	century
ca.	circa
CAD	*The Assyrian Dictionary of the Oriental Institute of the University of Chicago* (Chicago, 1956)
CD	Cairo Genizah, *Damascus Document*
C.E.	Common Era (= A.D.)
cf.	*confer,* compare
ch./chs.	chapter/chapters
1–2 Chr	1–2 Chronicles
Col	Colossians
col./cols.	column/columns
cont.	continued

1–2 Cor	1–2 Corinthians
d.	died
Dan	Daniel
Deut	Deuteronomy
DH	Deuteronomistic History
Did.	*Didache*
DSS	Dead Sea Scrolls
Dtr	Deuteronomist
Eccl	Ecclesiastes
ed.	editor (pl., eds), edition
1 En.	*1 Enoch*
Eng.	English
Eph	Ephesians
Ep Jer	Letter of Jeremiah
1–2 Esd	1–2 Esdras
Esth	Esther
Exod	Exodus
Ezek	Ezekiel
Ezra	Ezra
4 Ezra	*4 Ezra*
f.	feminine
frag.	fragment
Gal	Galatians
Gen	Genesis
Gk.	Greek
Gos. Mary	*Gospel of Mary*
Gos. Phil.	*Gospel of Philip*
Gos. Thom.	*Gospel of Thomas*
Hab	Habakkuk
Hag	Haggai
HB	Hebrew Bible
Heb	Hebrews
Heb.	Hebrew (biblical citations and language)
Hos	Hosea
Isa	Isaiah

Jas	James
Jdt	Judith
Jer	Jeremiah
Job	Job
Joel	Joel
John	John
1–2–3 John	1–2–3 John
Jonah	Jonah
Jos. Asen.	*Joseph and Aseneth*
Josh	Joshua
Jub.	*Jubilees*
Jude	Jude
Judg	Judges
1–2 Kgs	1–2 Kings
KJV	King James Version
Lam	Lamentations
Lat.	Latin
LGBTQIA	Lesbian, gay, bisexual, transgender, queer, intersex, asexual (and/or ally)
Lev	Leviticus
lit.	literally
Luke	Luke
LXX	Septuagint
m.	masculine
m.	Mishnah
1–2 Macc	1–2 Maccabees
3–4 Macc	3–4 Maccabees
Mal	Malachi
Mark	Mark
Matt	Matthew
Mic	Micah
Midr.	*Midrash*
ms/mss	manuscript/manuscripts
MT	Masoretic Text
NA 27	*Novum Testamentum Graece,* Nestle-Aland, 27th ed.

NAB	New American Bible
Nah	Nahum
NAS	New American Standard Version
n.d.	no date
NEB	New English Bible
Neh	Nehemiah
neu.	neuter
NIV	New International Version
NJB	New Jerusalem Bible
NJPS	Tanakh: The Holy Scriptures: The New JPS Translation according to the Traditional Hebrew Text
NKJB	New King James Bible
n.p.	no place
NRSV	New Revised Standard Version
NT	New Testament
Num	Numbers
Obad	Obadiah
Odes	*Odes of Solomon*
OG	Old Greek
OL	Old Latin
OT	Old Testament
P.	Papyrus
p./pp.	page/pages
1–2 Pet	1–2 Peter
Phil	Philippians
Phlm	Philemon
PN	personal name
Pr Azar	Prayer of Azariah
Pr Man	Prayer of Manasseh
Prov	Proverbs
Ps(s)	Psalm(s)
Ps 151	Psalm 151
Pss. Sol.	*Psalms of Solomon*
Q	*Quelle*, a hypothetical source used by Matthew and Luke

Q (preceded by numeral)	Qumran
r.	reigned
Rev	Revelation
rev.	revised
Rom	Romans
RSV	Revised Standard Version
Ruth	Ruth
1–2 Sam	1–2 Samuel
Sg Three	Song of the Three Young Men
Sib. Or.	*Sibylline Oracles*
Sir	Sirach
Song	Song of Solomon
SP	Samaritan Pentateuch
supp.	Supplement
Sus	Susanna
Syr.	Syriac
t.	Tosefta
Tg(s).	Targum(s); Targumic
1–2 Thess	1–2 Thessalonians
1–2 Tim	1–2 Timothy
Titus	Titus
Tob	Tobit
v./vv.	verse/verses
vol./vols.	volume/volumes
Vulg.	Vulgate
Wis	Wisdom of Solomon
y.	Jerusalem Talmud
Zech	Zechariah
Zeph	Zephaniah

THE OXFORD ENCYCLOPEDIA OF
THE BIBLE AND GENDER STUDIES

Asian/Asian American Interpretation

Addressing what constitutes Asian/Asian American interpretation is an arduous task, and perhaps an impossible one because of the heterogeneity of practitioners and the fluidity of contexts. Nonetheless, the collective identity of the Asian/Asian American in biblical interpretation has been conceived of as a response to the hegemony or parochialism of Western interpretation. Given the minority position of Asians and Asian Americans in geopolitics and in society, the modifier "Asian/Asian American" signifies the ethnicity of interpreter, the particularity of context, and the partiality of interpretation. Thus, "Asian/Asian American" is not merely a cultural and geographical identifier but also a social and political designator (Foskett and Kuan, 2006, p. xiii). Recognizing that there are many dangers in mapping Asian/Asian American interpretation owing to the political nature of geographical and demographical divisions, this article will begin with brief descriptions of biblical interpretation conducted in different regions of Asia and in the United States. Then it will introduce different approaches to interpretation that demonstrate Asian/Asian American interpretation as it has emerged as a discourse within the discipline of biblical interpretation or biblical studies. Finally, hermeneutical issues in Asian/Asian American interpretation that intersect with gender studies will be addressed.

Interpretation in Asia. The descriptions below do not represent the totality of biblical interpretation in a particular region but make an attempt to grasp the characteristics of Asian biblical interpretation, which is in conversation with Asian cultural religious traditions or sociopolitical realities. Although the continent of Asia includes the Middle East, the countries of Central Asia, a large part of Russia, and a portion of the Pacific Islands, this discussion will limit its scope to East Asia, South Asia, Southeast Asia, and North America. Even limiting the discussion of Asian/Asian American interpretation within these demarcated regions, it should be acknowledged that "Asian" and "Asian American" refer to multiple peoples and diverse cultures and histories. Not only do geographical and geopolitical situatedness and social formation distinguish Asians and Asian Americans, but Asia itself is heterogeneous. Even in a single country with a presumably homogeneous population like India, there are a multitude of indigenous people.

East Asia. East Asian biblical interpretation generally addresses cross-textual and cross-cultural issues on the one hand and liberative concerns on the other. East Asian interpretation cannot be discussed without considering the tremendous influence of Chinese culture, in which sacred texts of Confucianism, Taoism, and Buddhism were produced. When the Bible was first translated into Chinese at the beginning of the nineteenth century, enculturation figured significantly in its interpretation. As China has been the site of continuation and contestation of Western imperialism, nationalism, communism, modernization, and globalization, the Bible has functioned along with the aforementioned sacred texts as a sacred text promoting not only personal and spiritual but also moral and social formation. Yet these canonical traditions in the other sacred texts, which biblical interpretation engages with, may be viewed as patriarchal and elitist. In addition, ordinary people, especially women and the marginalized, find that stories such as legends and folk tales provoke dialogical imagination—a creative hermeneutical process that seeks to negotiate complexities and contradictions in the encounter of two different worlds, the Bible and Asia (Kwok, 2005, pp. 38–39).

On the other hand, *minjung* (literally, "the mass of the people") theology emerged as a Christian response to political oppression, economic exploitation, and social injustice, witnessing *minjung* as the subject of history in South Korea. This theology regards the social biography of Asians as the text of *minjung* hermeneutics, along with the biblical text produced by the people (*minjung*) in biblical times. However, the political exigencies of the 1970s did not allow *minjung* theologians to consider adequately the most oppressed group under Japanese or Western colonialism, patriarchal social structure, and the Confucian family structure—that is, women among *minjung*.

South Asia. As in China, the translation of the Bible into vernacular languages and the incorporation of Indian religious concepts and methods in biblical interpretation played an important role in the development of South Asian interpretation. The multireligious and multiethnic formation of Indian society facilitated interreligious and pluralist Indian readings of the Bible. In Indian theology and biblical interpretation, Jesus is represented as a moral and social reformer (Ram Mohan Roy), *avatara* (a manifestation of God, Vengal Chakkarai), or as a liberator (Stanley J. Samartha). In *Waters of Fire* (1988), Sister Vandana's interpretation focuses on the symbolism

of water in the Gospel of John and in Hindu traditions, particularly the Upanishad, and seeks to dialogue with Hindu religiosity and spirituality. Yet as the scriptures and theologies of Indian religions, including those of Christianity, have legitimized male domination over women, the need for a new vision of biblical interpretation is advocated by oppressed minorities such as tribals (Soares-Prabhu in Sugirtharajah, 2006) and Dalits.

In spite of the significance of Indian interpretation in its history and practice, India is not the sole representative of South Asia. While there may be other diverse readers of the Bible that scholarship fails to recognize, R. S. Sugirtharajah is a prominent Sri Lankan scholar who, although located in the United Kingdom, nonetheless positions himself "between and betwixt cultures and countries and engage[s] in a processual hermeneutic" (1998, p. 109). From that location, his contribution to Asian biblical interpretation, particularly in conjunction with postcolonial criticism, is extensive.

Southeast Asia. Since the population in Southeast Asia is much more diverse than that of East and South Asia in terms of race and ethnicity, culture, religion, and language, Southeast Asia shows most clearly how "Asian" and "Asian American" flounder as concepts that suggest any type of uniformity with regard to interpretive identities and practices. If there is something almost all Southeast Asian countries have in common, it is the experience of colonization, which can become a costly source and contested site of liberation or postcolonial biblical interpretation. Yet Christians constitute a small percentage of the population, and the Bible most often appears in the languages of colonizers. The scarcity of Bible-reading communities makes biblical interpretation from the region largely inaccessible and unavailable (Chia in Foskett and Kuan, 2006, p. 46). Therefore, biblical interpretation in Southeast Asia is quite a recent development, and it is even harder to find the voice of women in biblical interpretation. In such a circumstance, the task of biblical interpretation as a local endeavor might be to engage with indigenous cultures and religions. Such interpretation also would not only engage people who are marginalized in society and excluded in religious systems but also pursue solidarity with Asian *minjung* and women.

Interpretation in Asian America. The collectivity assigned to Asians is also applied to Asian descendants in the United States. Despite their immense diversity in terms of ethnicity, language, generation, and class as well as in their relations to the homeland and the dominant American culture, they have been essentialized as a monolithic group by the dominant culture. Furthermore, the title "model minority" attached to Asian Americans reinforces racialization and ethnicization by controlling racial dynamics among minority groups. Being conscious of this forced reality, Asian American interpreters find a subjectivity that emerges from "complex and contested processes of differentiation and renegotiation of discourses" (Ling, 1997, p. 325). The consequence of this is that Asian American interpreters tend to strategically take an "essentialist" position to politicize their marginalized subjectivity as a group movement, while mutually acknowledging their respective power positions and differences of identity. A similar tactic can also be seen in feminist practice. Hence, Asian American interpreters utilize the unified category of Asian American as a strategic device to collaboratively resist Eurocentric bias in biblical studies. Nevertheless, this strategic unification does not occur without cultural complication. A frontier for Asian American biblical scholarship, in parallel to specifically Asian contexts, is to promote more particularity in Asian American biblical scholarship within the presumed whole of Asian American identities.

Identifying "Asian American." A variety of concepts for self-identification have been employed. While later generations of Asian immigrants tend to assimilate into American culture, the experience of earlier generations may be described in terms of liminality. Other interpreters highlight the creative and constructive aspect of in-betweenness in being neither Asian nor American. The hyphen between Asian and American is often discussed as symbolizing such in-betweenness (Wan in Foskett and Kuan, 2006). It is even argued that persons at the margins stand not only between the two worlds but also beyond them. While hybridity may also describe the status of in-betweenness, some Asian American interpreters employ the concept of hybridity to intentionally disrupt the homogeneity of Asian Americans and the convention of rational either/or choices. Moreover, the interpreter's construction of liminal cultural identity promotes intertextual hybridity, where interpretive moves refuse the fixed boundaries between the biblical material, texts from Asian American culture, and contemporary theory (Yamada in Foskett and Kuan, 2006).

Forming "Asian American." Although who Asian Americans are and what Asian Americans do are fundamental issues, the question of "how" to make sense of "Asian American" in Asian American biblical interpretation demands attention. Tat-siong Benny Liew suggests legitimizing Asian American biblical hermeneutics through "an inventive tradition of citation, or of reference" rather than seeking authenticity through racial/ethnic or cultural identity (2008, p. 7). The repeated practice of such citation will not only form and transform the tradition of Asian American biblical hermeneutics but also cause a "re-vision" of the field of biblical hermeneutics, in which Western interpretation is positioned as historically and mistakenly presuming universal value. Instead of biblical interpretation consisting merely of the effort to find (original) meaning in a biblical text, it becomes a way of using the biblical text to illuminate how meaning and its accompanying power are produced through interpretation. This proposal by Liew more constructively addresses what counts as "Asian American" than the prevailing discussion of the cultural identity of Asian Americans does, in that it promotes the agency and discursive power of Asian American interpretation not by describing what it is but by suggesting how to make it. Given the Asian/Asian American emphasis on the performative quality of interpretation within and against the power structure that produces knowledge, therefore, Asian/Asian American interpretation is understood as a discourse rather than methodology.

Place of gender in "Asian American" hermeneutics. Whether one seeks sophisticated and wide-ranging cultural definitions for Asian and Asian American or focuses on how to make meaning, sense, and reality through discursive practice or production of interpretation, it is crucial that any advance in Asian and Asian American hermeneutics take seriously the category of gender. The identity politics of Asia and America often pass over women, who are marginalized by racial discrimination, cultural norms, and gender stereotypes at multiple levels. The immigration history of Asians bears witness to how Asian men have been suppressed by the dominant white American culture, but have also struggled with their invisibility by making women invisible. Here the construction of gender operates both within and outside Asian American communities: first, Asian American men are feminized by the dominant culture; second, Asian American women are oppressed not only by racialization but also by the Asian and Asian American patriarchal system. Thus, although "Asian American" may be considered a racial/ethnic label, the problem of gender is inherent in what constitutes Asian American, whether the term refers to the subject, object, or practice of interpretation. The concept is further troubled by how gender is marked when issues of sexuality such as queer and transgender are involved in biblical interpretation. In addition, these others in gender and sexuality have been silenced among racial/ethnic others and have had neither power nor text from which to produce knowledge and make tradition. Asian American women and other minorities may be suspicious of forming both their cultural identity as Asian American readers and the tradition of Asian American biblical interpretation.

Interpretive Approaches. Just as the racial/ethnic notions of "Asian" or "Asian American" cannot be adequately understood apart from the factor of gender, so methodologies, approaches, and discourse employed in Asian American biblical interpretation are informed by and intersect with gender studies in multiple ways. It should be noted that approaches introduced here—cultural hermeneutics, cultural studies, liberation hermeneutics, and postcolonial interpretation—are not mutually exclusive, but can overlap in the practice of interpretation.

Cultural hermeneutics. One of the prevalent approaches in Asian and Asian American interpretation is represented by contextual readings of the Bible, particularly in the form of cross-cultural or cross-textual interpretation. This can be seen in the comparative analysis of the history of religion, as in the Western comparative analysis of Near Eastern and Mediterranean religions within traditional historical criticism. Khiok-Khng Yeo deals with the issue of Chinese ancestor worship, which was condemned by Western missionaries, through examining the rhetorical hermeneutics of 1 Corinthians 8 (in Sugirtharajah, 2006, pp. 371–385). Although by finding correlation between the Bible and Asian traditions he makes the Bible more culturally accessible, his cross-cultural interpretation also challenges existing Chinese social order and policies. Another comparative analysis of religious texts, which is called the "vernacular reading," appropriates ancient Asian reading practices such as Sanskritic or Brahmanic traditions (Sugirtharajah, 1998). However, given different understandings of scripture in religious traditions, comparative analysis or cross-textual engagement is not a simple matter. Additionally, these scriptures are not only viewed as sacred but also as ideological products.

From a gender-critical perspective, both Asian religious texts and the Bible, as well as their canonical interpretations, are vulnerable to criticism because of their logocentric and elitist tendencies. In addition, the formation and use of the texts have excluded and marginalized women and other minorities. While cross-scriptural interpretation is usually conducted by elite males, others may find rich resources for alternative cross-cultural interpretation in dialogue with folk religions such as shamanism, which does not have sacred texts and has been practiced mostly by women and common people. Some vernacular readings adopt the method of storytelling, that is, the retelling of old stories instead of the rereading of old texts (Melanchthon, 2010, pp. 117–118). However, such approaches are often dismissed in biblical interpretation because of their lack of methodological rigor.

Cultural studies. Cultural hermeneutics has been reformulated in the Asian American context by employing methodological and theoretical frameworks borrowed from cultural studies. Asian American biblical interpretation in this mode critically engages with the text, interpretation, and interpreter in an interdisciplinary manner. The main issue in cultural studies is to move toward a system that engages the production of truth and the construction of reality. In this regard, biblical interpretation intersects with Asian studies, postcolonial studies, gender studies, and so forth. Examples of such an interdisciplinary undertaking are displayed in Liew's interpretations of a variety of New Testament texts.

Critical research on how Asian and Asian American women have been silenced in the process of national and cultural identity formation in contestation with Western masculinity can challenge existing Asian and Asian American biblical interpretation, which concentrates on race/ethnicity at the expense of gender. Asian and Asian American feminist interpretation can benefit from Western feminist theory in advocating for women's identity and agency in the face of the patriarchal language system. However, Asian and Asian American feminist interpretation is also aware of feminism's tendency to essentialize women's experience and its accompanying failure to represent the third-world woman's experience. In this regard postcolonial feminist theory is a useful tool to address the interlocking problem of gender and race in Asian/Asian American interpretation.

Suspicion of the heavy use of theory may arise on the part of some Asian readers, who acknowledge that the experience of colonialism influences their identity formation and thus take a critical stance toward Western theory. There are examples, however, of critical theory that is distinctly Asian or a modification of Western modes of thought with Asian interests. Using Western theory and method is inescapable and can even be considered a witting tool, used by the colonized when they try to "write back and work against colonial assumptions, representations, and ideologies" (Sugirtharajah, 1998, p. x). The Filipino Jeepney hermeneutics is one such venture, demonstrating the capacity to transform tools of mass destruction into resources for life (as in the writings of Revelation E. Velunta). Thus while

cultural studies is not just an Asian American interpretive mode of discourse, it may be utilized by Asian interpreters in a more critical manner.

Liberation hermeneutics. Given the experience of colonization and oppressive social structures among the majority of Asian peoples, liberation constitutes an important context for Asians' reading of the Bible. Readings of Indian Dalits, Japanese Burakumin, Korean *minjung*, indigenous people, and Asian women are motivated by the liberative impulse, which emphasizes freedom from bondage and oppression. The Bible plays a crucial role in empowering people to participate in the process of struggle. For example, Korean *minjung* biblical hermeneutics rereads the Exodus, the prophets' messages, and the Jesus movement in the present context in which people suffer from oppression and the concomitant struggle for liberation (Kim, 1981). According to Ahn Byung-Mu, the *ochlos* (crowd) in the Gospel of Mark do not merely constitute the background of Jesus's ministry but bear witness to the Jesus event. Mark describes Jesus as siding with the *minjung*. Jesus is the Messiah mainly in the sense that he struggles together with the suffering *minjung* on the frontline of the advent of God's kingdom (in Sugirtharajah, 2006).

Similarly, Dhyanchand Carr proposes a biblical paradigm for Dalit theology through interpreting the Gospel of Matthew from an Indian perspective. Matthew appears to affirm God's preference toward the socially ostracized and stigmatized people, who are identified with the untouchables, those outside the traditional social system of caste (Carr, 2009, p. 82). In the Dalit reading, Jesus is perceived as a "truly dalit deity" (Premnath in Foskett and Kuan, 2006, p. 7). In this Dalitness of Jesus, the Dalits recognize the goal of liberation, the realization of full humanness and full divinity. Among the Dalits, the 80 million women in India are multiply oppressed, not only by the social systems of patriarchy, caste, and class but also by androcentric Christian theology and dogma. Thus, the sociocultural, political, and economic reality of Dalit women and their experience ordain the hermeneutical starting point and provide its goal of survival and liberation. Dalit women's hermeneutics is a significant move/movement in Asian biblical interpretation in that it attempts to destabilize any oppressive systems—whether Christian or traditional religions—and their texts, which legitimize the subordination of women (Melanchthon, 2010).

Postcolonial interpretation. Asian liberation hermeneutics holds a diversity of viewpoints regarding biblical authority, Christology, and the oppressed. For Asians, the Bible is the Word of God in the living community, but the texts that legitimize domination and violence over women and minorities are questioned. Jesus can be a *minjung* or Dalit; even a *minjung* is the Messiah. Liberation is not only for the poor but for those multiply oppressed in terms of gender, caste, class, and ethnicity. Some liberation hermeneutics overlap with postcolonial criticism in that they are concerned with the aftermath of liberation. The appropriation of postcolonialism especially sheds light on Asian feminist interpretation. This interpretation provides insights into the role of gender and sexuality in the ongoing struggle of the postcolonial Asian situation, in which resistance to colonialism and struggle for liberation are facilitated by the nationalistic impulse. However, anticolonial discourse often duplicates hegemonic colonial values by retaining cultural identity and superiority through the justification of women's domesticity. Not only is the conflict between genders in view, but competition between masculinities is also displayed. Imperial and anticolonial masculinities attempt to control women's sexuality according to their own respective desires: the desire of imperial masculinity for the colonized to be territorially/sexually dispossessed, on the one hand, and the desire of anticolonial masculinity for sexual/territorial repossession from whiteness and white civilization, on the other hand (Gandhi, 1998, pp. 98–99). Jean K. Kim's reading of the Gospel of John in the context of Korean nationalist movements testifies that this struggle between masculinities sacrifices women (Kim, 2004).

Although the practitioners of these interpretive approaches are predominantly males, the above discussion suggests some ways to strengthen and expand Asian/Asian American interpretation by positively incorporating gender as a category or con-

sciousness in each approach. Women's religious experience and practice can be a text along with (or against) Asian and Christian scriptures (cultural hermeneutics). Asian women's reality and struggle for liberation become sources for refurbishing *minjung* or Dalit theology (liberation hermeneutics). Asian and Asian American women can write back to both colonial/imperial and androcentric/patriarchal discourse in biblical interpretation (cultural studies and postcolonial interpretation).

Hermeneutical Issues. While there are a variety of hermeneutical issues raised in Asian and Asian American interpretation, this entry focuses on analysis of how gender and sexuality are constructed in and through biblical interpretive work rather than introducing the traditional feminist approach to women characters in the Bible (Kinukawa, 1994; Satoko, 2002).

Cultural identity and gender. In the Asian American context, cultural identity is a predominant issue, challenging the dominant culture and disrupting the hegemonic mode of Anglo-Eurocentric interpretation. This issue not only covers a variety of experiences such as immigration, exile, and diaspora but also becomes even more complicated by multigenerational, multiracial, and adoption experiences. A common approach is to discover one's cultural identity by engaging with characters in biblical stories who are analogous to Asian Americans. Focusing on the politics of identity, Uriah Y. Kim's inter(con)textual readings of the stories of Josiah and Uriah the Hittite not only lead Asian Americans to find themselves in these stories demonstrating Israel's identity struggle but also make the text a site of struggle for his own identity and for Asian American collective identity (in Foskett and Kuan, 2006). Liew similarly employs the concept of yin-yang as the basic forces of life bound together in tension to understand the identity of Asian Americans and interpret the Bible. Reading with yin-yang eyes, a contradictory look, helps negotiate his multiple identity in contradiction to, and functioning to disrupt, the normative authority of the Bible (Liew, 2008).

Yet for Gale Yee, a third-generation Chinese American, there was nothing that culturally identified her as Asian other than her name and face, and thus she claims, "Yin/Yang is not me." Yet her identity is forced to be constructed as an Asian based on her appearance. She in turn inscribes her own Asian American identity in reading the story of Yael in Judges 4–5 with the story of the Chinese woman warrior Fa Mulan, while interrogating the role of gender in contestation of forming one's identity as "foreign" (in Foskett and Kuan, 2006).

As seen in these few examples, Asian American male and female interpreters inter(con)textually read both biblical materials and their experiences, which are the sites of struggle for cultural identity. In many cases, however, the category of gender is subsumed under the identification of race/ethnicity, while in fact race and gender ideologies are inextricably encoded in the process of identity formation. In this regard, Mai-Anh Le Tran's postcolonial feminist reading of narratives of Lot's wife, Ruth, and Tô Thị is distinct in its attentiveness to the intersection of gender and race. Her cross-textual reading engages simultaneously with these two biblical stories and with traditional Vietnamese folklore concentrating on common motif of a pillar. By juxtaposing these stories, she deconstructs the normative narratives, which have functioned to inscribe domination and subordination on women in ancient and contemporary societies. Moreover, Tran's reading demonstrates how gender representations are distorted in the patriarchal symbolic system as represented by "sin" and "redemption." Her reading overcomes the limitation of feminist theory by arguing that this is the genderizing and racializing language that reveals "interstructured forms of subordination" and that sustains both ancient and contemporary "patriarchal/kyriarchal and ethnocentric/imperialistic ideologies" (in Foskett and Kuan, 2006, p. 135).

Asian women's experience and body. Another hermeneutical issue that can be explored in the intersection of gender and race/ethnicity is the body. Many Asian American interpreters acknowledge that their bodies are a readable text upon which social reality is inscribed, as they often experience the body in which the racist rule of the dominant culture is engraved. Memory plays a significant role in this regard. Yamada's reading of Genesis 2–3 implies that the earlier generation of Japanese Americans' experience of shame in the internment camps was inscribed on the bodies and on the identity of the third generation in the form of memory. It is a memory of "human survival in the midst of a life of adversity" (in Foskett and Kuan, 2006, p. 175).

While "memory is a powerful tool in resisting institutionally sanctioned forgetfulness," for multiply oppressed Asian women it is "inscribed on the body, on one's most private self, on one's sexuality" (Kwok, 2005, pp. 37, 77–78). Asian women's conception of body is distant from the French feminist discourse of body, which approaches the female body by focusing on a woman's own individualist sexuality or sexual freedom. In contrast, for many Asian women, the colonized body speaks a language not only of poverty, exploitation, and violence but also of resistance, healing, and hope. Therefore, memory is not only a sign of life but life itself: it is hope for the continuation of life (Song, 1979, p. 144).

Asian women's biblical interpretation, therefore, is a life-affirming reading in the commitment to communal survival and healing, as represented by the hermeneutics of *salim*, which means in Korean "making things alive," "mending broken things," "feeding everybody," and "creating peace, health, and abundant living." Thus the hermeneutics of *salim* is a life-centered and relation-oriented Bible reading practice. In employing *salim* hermeneutics, Seong Hee Kim recalls Korean women's experiences in their colonial and postcolonial history and identifies the way that women read biblical stories by using dialogical imagination and inspiring reciprocal healing and well-being. Similarly, "hermeneutics of compassion in detachment," proposed by Hyun Ju Bae, highlights the faith community's "art of friendship" with both people today and the written text(s) in creative dialogue and interaction, while taking a critical stance against the oppressive function and use of the Bible. This hermeneutics, rooted in the multireligious and multiscriptural context of Asia, is best evoked by the image of "dancing around life." When a person dances, she attunes her body to the rhythm of life, while all human faculties participate in the movement of the body.

Dalit women's biblical hermeneutics values alternative sources in reading the Bible, such as feeling, wisdom, and the heart, womb, and body. Like Korean feminist readers, Dalit women's interpretation advocates on behalf of their own silenced voices and seeks the transformation of life in all its wholeness, which means celebrating plurality, diversity, mutuality, and partnership (Melanchthon, 2010, pp. 113–114).

Although C. S. Song is not a biblical scholar, his reading of biblical stories with rich stories of Asian people, which embody their suffering, evokes powerful female/feminine images regarding life and hope. A young Vietnamese woman, who has just lost her husband in the midst of cruel war, "looks down at the seed coming to life" (Song, 1979, pp. 127). This instinctive feeling for the seed in the womb, which in turn signifies the seed of hope, becomes a lens for interpreting the story of Sarah, Isaiah's prophecy to King Ahaz, the birth of Jesus Christ, and the birth of Cain. This hope is an outlook on salvation, which is grasped by the experience of life in the mother's womb.

Feminization of Asian America. While the characters and images of women in the Bible, which come to life through Asian women's experience, are embodied, life-centered, and interdependent, another potential hermeneutical issue in Asian and Asian American interpretation in the intersection of gender and race/ethnicity is the feminization of Asian America. The competing desires of imperial and anticolonial masculinities, as discussed above, produce competing anxieties, since the imperial man defines himself by emasculating the colonized man: the colonized land is colonizable because it lacks real men. As Western colonization was facilitated by constructing the image of the East as feminine, in the history of Asian immigration the racialization of Asians in the United States has been reinforced by constructing "Asian men" as powerless and thus harmless. In this way, Asian men are distinguished from other minorities like African Americans, Hispanics, and Native Americans. Alongside this feminization of Asian men, Asian women were "ultrafeminized," being represented as desirable sexual partners who are willing to serve and please (Ling, 1997).

In this Asian American context, the author of this entry reads the body of Jesus represented in the Gospel of Mark as feminized in contrast to the Roman imperial construction of the body. Moreover, this feminized body, along with the bodies of the silenced and passive colonized subjects, resists the dominant discourse of the body. Asian/Asian American interpretation, therefore, furthers feminist interpretation. This is not only about female or feminine, because Asian and Asian American males represent the most feminized sexual identities among males in North American culture as well as in the scheme of Orientalism. Can Asian bodies be a cultural text that is cross-read with the Bible? In this regard, Asian/Asian American interpretation is a discursive space where other issues of sexuality such as queer and transgender could be both compelling and complicated (Liew, 2009).

Looking Forward. While Asian/Asian American interpretation is heterogeneous and fluid, it constitutes a discourse that decenters the universalizing discourse of Anglo-Eurocentric biblical interpretation in multiple ways. First, it claims that other Asian scriptures and the Bible are equally authoritative for or inspire lives. Second, it resists the use of the Bible and biblical interpretation to colonize and oppress Asian people. Third, in order to disrupt the hegemonic discourse and practice of biblical interpretation, Asian American interpreters apply identity politics and reinvent the tradition of biblical hermeneutics, focusing on the production of meaning and power. Last, it writes back to the dominant culture, which racializes and feminizes Asians and Asian Americans and provides the normative script regarding gender and sexuality. In envisioning the future of Asian/Asian American interpretation, a reconsideration of gender and sexuality in its discourse and practice will reinforce the ethos of liberation and decolonization. In this regard, a promising move can be made by *minjung* or Dalit interpretations from Asian and Asian American feminist perspectives, which affirm and transform life and celebrate its mutuality and plurality.

[*See also* Intersectional Studies; *and* Postcolonial Approaches.]

BIBLIOGRAPHY

Bae, Hyun Ju. "Dancing around Life: An Asian Woman's Perspective." *Ecumenical Review* 56 (2004): 390–403.

Brock, Rita Nakashima. "Dusting the Bible on the Floor: A Hermeneutics of Wisdom." In *Searching the Scriptures: A Feminist Introduction*, vol. 1, edited by Elisabeth Schüssler Fiorenza, pp. 164–175. New York: Crossroad, 1993.

Carr, Dhyanchand. "Dalit Theology Is Biblical and It Makes the Gospel Relevant." In *A Reader in Dalit Theology*, edited by Arvind P. Nirmal, pp. 71–83. Chennai: Gurukul Lutheran Theological College and Research Institute, 2009.

Foskett, Mary F., and Jeffrey Kah-Jin Kuan, eds. *Ways of Being, Ways of Reading: Asian American Biblical Interpretation*. Saint Louis, Mo.: Chalice, 2006.

Gandhi, Leela. *Postcolonial Theory: A Critical Introduction*. New York: Columbia University Press, 1998.

Kim, Jean K. *Woman and Nation: An Intercontextual Reading of the Gospel of John from a Postcolonial Feminist Perspective*. Boston: Brill Academic, 2004.

Kim, Seong Hee. *Mark, Women and Empire: A Korean Postcolonial Perspective*. Sheffield, U.K.: Sheffield Phoenix Press, 2010.

Kim, Yong Bock, ed. *Minjung Theology: People as the Subjects of History*. Singapore: Commission on Theological Concerns, Christian Conference of Asia, 1981.

Kinukawa, Hisako. *Women and Jesus in Mark: A Japanese Feminist Perspective*. Maryknoll, N.Y.: Orbis, 1994.

Kwok, Pui-lan. *Discovering the Bible in the Non-Biblical World*. Maryknoll, N.Y.: Orbis, 1995.

Kwok, Pui-lan. *Postcolonial Imagination and Feminist Theology*. Louisville, KY.: Westminster John Knox, 2005.

Lee, Archie C. C. "Cross-Textual Hermeneutics and Identity in a Multi-Scriptural Asia." In *Christian Theology in Asia*, edited by Sebastian C. H. Kim, pp. 179–204. New York: Cambridge University Press, 2008.

Liew, Tat-siong Benny. *What Is Asian American Biblical Hermeneutics? Reading the New Testament*. Honolulu: University of Hawai'i Press, 2008.

Liew, Tat-siong Benny. "Queering Closets and Perverting Desires: Cross-Examining John's Engendering and Transgendering Word across Different Worlds." In *They Were All Together in One Place? Toward Minority Biblical Criticism*, edited by Randall C. Bailey, Tat-siong Benny Liew, and Fernando F. Segovia, pp. 251–288. Atlanta: Society of Biblical Literature, 2009.

Liew, Tat-siong Benny, and Gale A. Yee, eds. *The Bible in Asian America*. Semeia 90/91. Atlanta: Society of Biblical Literature, 2002.

Ling, Jinqi. "Identity Crisis and Gender Politics: Reappropriating Asian American Masculinity." In *An Interethnic Companion to Asian American Literature*, edited by King-Kok Cheung, pp. 311–337. New York: Cambridge University Press, 1997.

Melanchthon, Monica J. "Dalit Women and the Bible: Hermeneutical and Methodological Reflections." In *Hope Abundant: Third World and Indigenous Women's Theology*, edited by Kwok Pui-lan, pp. 103–122. Maryknoll, N.Y.: Orbis, 2010.

Patte, Daniel, ed. *Global Bible Commentary*. Nashville, Tenn.: Abingdon, 2004.

Rebera, Ranjini Wickramaratne. "The Syrophoenician Woman: A South Asian Feminist Perspective." In *A Feminist Companion to Mark*, edited by Amy-Jill Levine, pp. 101–110. Sheffield, U.K.: Sheffield Academic Press, 2001.

Satoko, Yamaguchi. *Mary and Martha: Women in the World of Jesus*. Maryknoll, N.Y.: Orbis, 2002.

Song, Choan-Seng. *Third-Eye Theology: Theology in Formation in Asian Settings*. Maryknoll, N.Y.: Orbis, 1979.

Sugirtharajah, R. S. *Asian Biblical Hermeneutics and Postcolonialism: Contesting the Interpretations*. Maryknoll, N.Y.: Orbis, 1998.

Sugirtharajah, R. S., ed. *Voices from the Margin: Interpreting the Bible in the Third World*. 3d ed. Maryknoll, N.Y.: Orbis, 2006.

Yee, Gale. "'She Stood in Tears Amid the Alien Corn'": Ruth, the Perpetual Foreigner and Model Minority." In *They Were All Together in One Place? Toward Minority Biblical Criticism*, edited by Randall C. Bailey, Tat-siong Benny Liew, and Fernando F. Segovia, pp. 119–140. Atlanta: Society of Biblical Literature, 2009.

Jin Young Choi

AUTHORS OF BIBLICAL BOOKS

To question the gender of the authors of biblical books seems both fantastic and revisionist given that the available history on the Bible states that only men authored these books. That the Bible centers the experience of men, treats women as second-class humans, and remains irredeemably sexist should be common knowledge for most persons. The fact that a *woman*, or perhaps more tempting, *women*, contributed some aspect of the development of the Bible may not reveal marked differences between those portions of the Bible and others developed by men, but while women's contribution may not radically change the content of the Bible, knowledge of women's contribution can alter the way that content is read and interpreted. The absence of incontrovertible evidence proving female authorship of specific books of the Bible does not rule out the need for thinking and reflection upon the gender of authors of the Bible.

Examination of the processes of text production reveals that the closed system of a single author creating texts for consumption by an audience oversimplifies scribal functions and excludes critical considerations in thinking about the development of texts. Because the authors of the vast majority of the books of the Bible remain largely unknown, the notion of "author" with respect to the Bible is a highly fraught enterprise. This reality need not suggest an easy process of conjuring up female authors, because the mostly pseudonymous texts of the Bible are unable to hold together the idea of originally composed textual material, let alone the concept of a single author. This means that interrogating the authorship of biblical texts requires investigating various levels of composition and textual activity. And yet the gender concerns are not simply settled by the discovery of biological female author/s. The concerns of gender go beyond biology to the gendered voice/s that appear/s in the Bible.

Literacy among Women. Since all biblical books that claim an author identify only men as authors, it can be easily assumed that the Bible reflects the general culture where women did no writing. The historical record indicates greater levels of writing competence than the Bible enables readers to believe existed in the ancient world. The Egyptians depict the goddess Seshat as the inventor of writing, portraying her with a stylus in her hand and the title "Mistress of the House of Books." Seshat stands next to the Egyptian god Thoth as part of the pair that inventories conquered treasure and the details of the pharaoh's rule. Although a goddess, "Seshat" reads more as a title (Female Scribe) rather than a name indicating that scribes were mostly men. However, while no evidence of female scribes in Egypt exists, women seemed to have varying levels of competence with writing-like tools used in painting or cosmetic applications.

In Sumer, Enheduanna, the daughter of King Sargon of Agade (2334–2290 B.C.E), wrote poems and other texts. A priestess in the Sumerian kingdom, Enheduanna is the first acknowledged female author in literature. Her hymn compositions extol the virtues of her father's conquests and those of the goddess Inanna. Enheduanna attains writing skills from her place in the temple where scribes were educated to function in the service of the religion and state.

Evidence of female literacy in cultures adjacent to ancient Israel suggests that similar forms of literacy may have occurred in Israel. Queens Jezebel and Esther provide the only indication of women writing in the Old Testament. Both these queens issue official documents in their own hand in performance of their functions in elite society (1 Kgs 21:8; Esth 9:29). Presumably, based upon the evidence from surrounding cultures, a woman could be educated to write and therefore the picture of queens writing documents is plausible. These portrayals, though, offer limited evidence of the ability of women to author texts beyond routine documents, since Esther relies upon scribes to pen the king's decree (Esth 8:8–9).

The Greco-Roman world reveals more textual activity among women. Female-authored texts dating as early as 600 B.C.E occur in Greece. Both Plato (ca. 428–ca. 348 B.C.E) and Pythagoras (ca. 570–495 B.C.E) admit to having female students. Pythagoras's daughter Myia and Theano, possibly his wife or daughter, wrote several letters and treatises still in existence. Both girls and boys received some form of formal education in Greco-Roman society. Girls could possibly learn to read and write but were not likely taught the advanced skills of rhetoric and mathematics primarily because they were generally married at the age when these subjects were taught to boys. Although the societal norms make it quite possible for women to author texts in the Greco-Roman world, no evidence of women writing exists in the New Testament and no book can be easily attributed to women. Among early Christian texts, the *Apocryphal Acts* possibly contains female-authored texts given their provenance among a group that included elite women with the necessary education to write these texts. Stevan Davies posits that the

Acts of Paul and Thecla is authored by a woman, reasoning that the violent depictions of actions against Thecla represent a sexually chaste woman's hyperbolic critique of men and their sexual intentions.

Women's Books. Dismissing women's authorship of biblical books for lack of evidence of female scribes too easily settles the presumption that the authors are men. In many instances, no evidence supports a man as the author except the masculinist notion of writing as an exclusively male domain. The absence of author identity makes consideration of the content of books possible and necessary. That authors of different genders can produce the voice of a gender not their own remains a given reality, but too often the assumption of what may appear to be the women's voice in biblical texts is assigned to male authorship without sufficient attention to the possibilities of women authors. The following books suggest the potential for women authors.

Song of Solomon. The Song of Solomon (Heb. Song of Songs) offers the rare opportunity of reading the unmediated words from a female protagonist in the Bible. In fact, 53 percent of the words in the book can be attributed to a single female voice with additional amounts from the chorus of women. The woman's perspectives, her preoccupations, and her desires frame the book, offering a bias toward the female viewpoint unmatched in any single book of the Bible. Shelomo Dov Goitein, who believes a woman composed the Song, observes the female bias in the preference for the mother's house over any mention of the father's house, seven appeals to the Daughters of Zion with only two mentions of the man's friends, and five other references to daughters or young women. This preponderance of detail from a woman's perspective marks a decided shift in both the gender balance in biblical texts as well as the gender performances in these texts. The woman in Song takes the initiative in the relationship (Song 3:1), disregards social conventions (Song 8:1–2), speaks with self-assurance (Song 1:5), embraces her sexuality in a healthy manner (Song 8:10), and questions the authority of men (Song 8:8–10). Such a portrayal can either reflect a woman's standpoint or that of a man comfortable with shifting the prevailing gender assumptions.

Determining the gender of the author of the Song of Solomon based upon the female bias in the book remains an uncertain enterprise. The nature of the book as a collection of love poems may indicate female authorship given the evidence of women composing songs both in ancient Israel and the surrounding cultures. As a collection of love poems, though, the Song exhibits a level of incoherence making it possible to regard only some of the poetry in the book as composed by women rather than the entire collection. Although she regards the book as a unity, J. Cheryl Exum remains unconvinced of the possibility of female composition in the Song. Exum notes that in the exchanges between the woman and the man, the woman quotes the man's words, but he does not return the favor. Further, she points to the reinscription of patriarchal culture and the control of the woman's sexuality by men despite the seeming independence of the woman. In the end, the evidence for a woman as author of the Song rests upon the dominant woman's voice that emerges in the text.

Ruth. The survival of two widowed women in a time of famine sets the backdrop for the book of Ruth. The book examines women's relationships with other women as well as with men and offers a view that differs from the rivalry among women common in Genesis. Ruth and Naomi's relationship questions the presumptions of male culture, particularly regarding childbearing. Fokkelein van Dijk-Hemmes offers that Naomi's speech to Ruth and Orpah presents childbearing as a path to survival rather than childbearing being in the interests of men (Ruth 1:11–13). Similarly, she sees the women overturning the men's wish to Boaz (4:11–12) in Naomi's favor (4:17), placing Naomi in a greater role than the father. The style of the text, its storytelling quality, as well as its ironies, which eventually place the women in the foremost position, all point to women's culture as its source and to the possibility of a female author.

The Yahwist. Most scholars accept the composite nature of the Pentateuch and regard the Yahwist (the "J" author posited by the Documentary Hypothesis) as a significant contributor to its development.

Debates about the date, texts, and the origins of the Yahwist persist in the scholarship. Harold Bloom unsettles the presumption of the male identity of the Yahwist by suggesting a female rival to the Court Historian who was responsible for the development of 2 Samuel. Locating her as an educated elite member of the post-Solomonic court, Bloom regards her as a theological historian who tells the story of the ancestors with an eye to developments that begin to emerge at the end of Solomon's reign and continue thereafter. Bloom points to the concern for the fate of women under polygamy, the portrayals of God unencumbered by constraints, and the several ironic turns in the story as evidence of women's storytelling abilities. He acknowledges the idea of a female Yahwist to be a fiction, but a fiction similar to those of other historical authors held by readers and critics. Nonetheless, one can only imagine who those authors were despite the available historical detail. For Bloom positing a female Yahwist is more than a fanciful gimmick; it is a thoughtful engagement with a body of texts that defies the traditional classifications and presumptions. From this perspective, Bloom draws attention to the marked difference between the writing of the Yahwist and other Pentateuchal sources. Such differences possibly point not only to a different cultural location for the author but also for the presumed gender.

Hebrews. Among the contenders for the authorship of Hebrews stand Priscilla or Prisca, a close friend of Paul and a member of the community at Rome, who together with her husband, Aquilla, offers leadership in the community (Acts 18). Priscilla's name appears before her husband in letters from Paul and others (Rom 16:32; 2 Tim 4:19). As a woman of means, she most likely possesses the education necessary to compose the text. In 1900 Adolf Harnack proposes Priscilla as the obvious answer to the puzzle as to why the name of an influential apostolic teacher of high rank and associated with Paul would be withheld from the text. Building on Harnack's thesis, Ruth Hoppin notes the self-deprecating apology (Heb 13:22) as likely coming from a woman writing instructions to a largely male audience. Hoppin views the character of Hebrews with its concern for

the sufferings of Jesus and its emphasis on his humanity, along with the mention of women's role in the resurrection, and the intrigues relating to Moses and the pharaoh's daughter, as a woman's concern. While the evidence for Priscilla's authorship remains absent, the claim that the masculine form of διηγούμενον ("should I say," 11:32) eliminates a female author ignores the real possibility of a woman writing pseudonymously as a man. In addition, the strong objections that develop in the early Christian community to women's leadership in later years open the space for a plausible case that a female author would assume a male identity in order to pen Hebrews.

Women's Compositions. The question of the gender of the authors of biblical texts creates the corresponding effect of focusing intently on the final text products and thereby privileging those with the skills of reading and writing as well as access to the forms of production that ensure the development of texts. With regard to the Bible, this form of investigation inevitably will exclusively reveal men. Expanding the question of text authorship to incorporate composition includes other voices and contributions normally overlooked. Biblical texts, for the most part, are composite works made up of material compiled from both oral and written sources. However, these sources and the gender of their composers go unacknowledged as long as the attention remains on the agent responsible for the creation of the final form of texts. Several unacknowledged nonliterary sources that make up written texts belong to women and represent what can be regarded as the women's voice. Women's creative literacy initially exists in oral form and appears later in texts through the work of men who control the processes of writing. Such oral activity represents the traditions of women in their culture and in places where women are free to develop their own customs.

The Bible generally locates women's cultural productions in songs and poems. These literary traditions appear as songs composed and used by women in various life settings on occasions and are associated with women characters in texts. These songs represent spaces where women's creativity flourish and women contribute to the life of the community. Women sing songs on various occasions such as victories after battle, birth, and death. While no actual fragments of laments exist that could be directly attributed to women, the Bible points to women leading acts of lament (Jer 9:17, 20) even though it appears that men would join in these acts (2 Chr 35:25). In addition, women function as entertainers singing, dancing, and at times playing instruments (Judg 21:21; Isa 23:16). Performing these roles in these social spaces provides women the opportunity to compose songs that make their way into the texts produced by men.

Women's leadership in victory songs after battles appears commonplace (Judg 5:28). These short pithy songs offer time for celebration of the champion warrior as in the case of David (1 Sam 18:6–7) or the LORD (Exod 15:20–21). Whether spontaneous compositions or not, such victory songs reflect the authentic voice of women even though the final version of the narrative may obscure this. Athalya Brenner notes that the shape of Exodus 15 places Moses as the author of the song at the Sea with Miriam echoing his composition, when the song may more likely be Miriam's composition. She bases her position on the common use of the verb 'nh (literally "answered" but translated as "sang") in Exodus 15:21, Judges 5:29, and 1 Samuel 18:7. This verb hints at a more spontaneous response from the women who lead the victory songs rather than a studied composition. However, the more technical verb śyr ("to sing") introduces Moses's words in Exodus 15:1. The verb here indicates a subsequent attribution to Moses instead of the more spontaneous response from Miriam. The feminine singular verb form watāśar ("sang") in Judges 5:1 makes "and Barak" seem as a later inclusion designed so that Deborah shares credit of the song with Barak. This apparent addition presents further evidence of the reduction of women's creative contributions. Whether an earlier and perhaps shorter version of Deborah's Song exists remains uncertain. Undoubtedly, the song in its current form reflects the remarkable feats of a woman warrior, Jael, and sings her praises in the forms used for victorious male heroes (Judg 5:24–27). The song's concerns with the impact of the defeat of Sisera upon his mother, the response of the court ladies, and the mention of women as victims and spoils of war offer a striking gender insight (Judg 28:30) that could possibly come from a woman. That Deborah's Song and the accompanying narrative in chapter 4 place women in superior positions to men reveals a different conception of gender positioning and power than that characterized in most of the Bible.

Birth songs reveal another space of women's creativity. The risks involved in childbearing coupled with the demands to produce male heirs serve as the occasion for poetic songs of various lengths. From Eve's outburst on the birth of her son (Gen 4:1) to the series of utterances that frame the names of Rachel and Leah's sons at their birth (Gen 29:31–30:24), women express victory at times of birth over circumstances that could cause either physical or social death. The women's words to Naomi on the birth of Oded function like a birth song (Ruth 4:14), since they recognize the moment as a victory for Naomi and Ruth over their dire circumstances. Although not stated as a song but a prayer, the poetic structure of Hannah's word on the birth of Samuel suggests it as a song of praise (1 Sam 2:1–10). The song moves from concerns that connect with Hannah's story as a bullied secondary wife unable to bear children (vv. 2–5) to more general and nationalist concerns (vv. 6–10). This movement reflects the cooptation of a birth song composed by a woman into the national religious and political order where men serve. Hannah's redemption from distress forms the basis for shaping Samuel's birth as the marker for Israel's future redemption. The final form of 1 Samuel effects this movement so smoothly that it serves as an example for Luke's nativity narratives (Luke 2). By expanding an original woman's composition on the birth of her son, the male-centered text reduces women only to bearers of the national saviors while erasing their other creative contributions.

The Voice of Gender. The quest for women authors in the Bible may not produce clear evidence of women writing biblical texts but it unsettles the presuppositions about the gender of authors in ways that require consideration of the gendered voice in biblical texts. Yet identifying gendered voices remains a slippery task given the fluidity of gender. While voice can exist independent of gendered bodies, such voice participates in and reflects the gender assumptions of the culture. Insisting on the androcentric nature of the Bible, Elisabeth Schüssler Fiorenza remarks that since women writers participate in patriarchy as much as men they may not produce substantially different texts. Schüssler Fiorenza foregrounds here the masculinist ideology of the Bible and thereby sets up the space for gender critique of those texts. At best, this critique enables discovery of the spaces where the masculinist view yields to another perspective or at least spaces where such views are moderated, as in the case of the gospels of Mark and John that offer different conceptions of discipleship and community from texts like the Pastoral Epistles.

The notion of gendered voice suggests that gender contains essentialist qualities. While essentialism remains a troublesome concept for some, others regard it as a necessary tool to avoid acquiescing to the default male position. What female voice looks like in the Bible is uncertain given the male control of the production of the Bible. Hélène Cixous's notion of *l'ecriture feminine* means that women-produced texts do not fit seamlessly into the Bible or simply are not included or else they should be self-evident. Cixous understands such writing by women to be writing with the body (sexts = sex and text) in a way that transcends the phallocentricism of male-produced texts and should be clearly different in their style and language. Cixous's idea of sexts draws attention to texts that appear to fit easily into the Bible but at the same time occupy that space awkwardly. No pure form of *l'ecriture feminine* exists in the Bible since texts are at best dual gendered, resulting in the women's voice, both original women's composition and otherwise, being transmitted through the male pen. The presence of women's voices in the Bible emerges most often disembodied from real women. While such voices draw attention to women's culture, creative traditions, and perspectives, these voices do not always represent authoritative sources of women's experiences.

The search for the gender of authors in the Bible can easily participate in the binarism of gender and ignores what Judith Butler regards as gender performances. Despite its androcentric nature, aspects of the Bible break out of the singularity of the male perspective to embrace the female viewpoint; at other times these gender categories are so blurred as to be indistinct, as in the case of Deborah's Song. Anticipating that gender writes its exclusive experiences and worldviews, nothing else reifies gender in ways that result in the easy dismissal of the idea of women writers or conflate representations of women with real women. The fluidity of gender enables authors to transcend their biology and perform gender in ways other than those culturally prescribed. Such fluidity of gender opens the possibility to conceive not only of women writing biblical texts pseudonymously as men but also to conceive of men who (to adapt Cixous here to mean sexuality and text) sext biblical texts in transgressive ways. Such possibilities leave room to interrogate the gender performances of authors of books such as the grisly book of Judges and the pornographic aspects of the books of Jeremiah, Ezekiel, and Hosea.

[*See also* Education, *subentries on* Ancient Near East, Hebrew Bible, *and* New Testament; Gender; *and* Masculinity and Femininity, *subentry* Hebrew Bible.]

BIBLIOGRAPHY

Brenner, Athalya. *A Feminist Companion to Ruth.* Sheffield, U.K.: Sheffield Academic Press, 1993a.

Brenner, Athalya, ed. *Feminist Companion to the Song of Songs.* Sheffield, U.K.: JSOT Press, 1993b.

Brenner, Athalya, and Fokkelein van Dijk-Hemmes. *On Gendering Texts: Female and Male Voices in the Hebrew Bible.* Leiden, The Netherlands: E. J. Brill, 1993.

Davies, Stevan. *The Revolt of the Widows: The Social World of the Apocryphal Acts.* Carbondale: Southern Illinois University Press, 1980.

Exum, J. Cheryl. *Fragmented Women: Feminist (Sub)versions of Biblical Narratives.* Valley Forge, Pa.: Trinity, 1993.

Exum, J. Cheryl. *Song of Songs: A Commentary.* Louisville, Ky.: Westminster John Knox, 2005.

Hoppin, Ruth. *Priscilla: Author of the Epistles to the Hebrews and Other Essays.* New York: Exposition, 1969.

Hoppin, Ruth. *Priscilla's Letter: Finding the Author of the Epistle to the Hebrews.* Fort Bragg, Calif.: Lost Coast, 1997.

Kraemer, Ross. "Women's Authorship of Jewish and Christian Literature in the Greco-Roman World." In *Women Like This: New Perspectives on Jewish Women in the Greco-Roman World,* edited by Amy-Jill Levine, pp. 221–242. Atlanta: Scholars Press, 1991.

Lefkowitz, Mary R. "Did Ancient Women Write Novels?" In *Women Like This: New Perspectives on Jewish Women in the Greco-Roman World,* edited by Amy-Jill Levine, pp. 199–219. Atlanta: Scholars Press, 1991.

Rosenberg, David, and Harold Bloom. *The Book of J.* New York: Grove Weidenfeld, 1990.

Schüssler Fiorenza, Elisabeth, *In Memory of Her: A Feminist Theological Reconstruction of Christian Origins.* New York: Crossroad, 1984.

Steed Vernyl Davidson

C

CANON/CANONICITY/CANONIZATION

Theological scholarship typically defines a canon as "the corpus of scriptural writings that is considered authoritative and standard for defining and determining 'orthodox' religious beliefs and practices" (Sanders, 1992). In such a definition the only canon in sight is that of the Bible. As distinct from this, scholars in humanist and social sciences often use the term canon in a wider sense and may, for instance, refer to the Western canon, the philosophical canon, canons of sociology or of cultural heritage, ethnic canons, and so on (e.g., Goody, 1998; Guillory, 1993; Hallberg, 1984). This broader concept resonates with a line of comparative religious scholarship studying scripture across religious traditions (e.g., Henderson, 1991; Levering, 1989; Smith, 1993). Gender studies have been sensitive to canons and canonicity in this wider sense (Reed, 2006). Still, much scholarship on gender and the Bible seems to have remained influenced by the narrower definition and is thereby still affected by the power discourse that surrounds the biblical canon (and other strong, authoritative canons).

We would use a wider concept of canon: "A *canon* denotes an identifiable collection (of texts, authors, rules, dogma, artifacts, action, etc.), which is recognized by an identifiable community as superb, authoritative, classical, etc." (cf. Stordalen, 2012, pp. 20–27).

The salient points in this definition are the canonical corpus, a canonical group, and the authority ascribed to the canon. A textual canon may have different characteristics—closed or open, textually fixed or not—but to qualify as a canon it should be recognizable as a collection to its users. The authority ascribed to the canon may be of different quality and intensity. Following this definition, *canonization* names the process in which the canonical body attains its authority, and *canonicity* denotes the status and authority ascribed to the canon. A key point in our apprehension of canonicity was formulated by Wilfred Cantwell Smith (1993, p. 18). Canonicity is not a function of particular characteristics of the canonical collection, such as its quality, high age, closure, ability to produce commentaries, and so forth. Rather, canonicity is a product of human activity: scripture is something that the canonical community *does*.

We propose that a study of practices attached to biblical canons through this generative lens may prove to be important for a broad spectrum of humanist and social science scholarship, especially when studied in relation to gender, since both categories are so deeply anchored in social practices. Biblical canons are more formalized and more explicitly documented than many other canons, which may render them convenient spaces for in-depth case studies in a humanist attempt to understand typical ecologies of canons.

Feminists and the Canon. Feminists have had an uneasy relationship with established canons of the past—not only the biblical canon but also the canons of philosophy, literature, music, and film, as well as other religious canons. The canon may in itself be seen as the root of the problem of continuing patriarchy: canons tend to symbolize current social structures, and so canonized writings often endorse and reinforce the subordination or at least secondary status of women and the primacy of men. Canons represent and promote institutional power. To dismantle such power and overturn patriarchy, feminists have often found it necessary to de-canonize or remove the canon. Most canons have canonized texts (and commentaries) written by men and reflecting male perspectives and experiences. In so doing they render women's talent, creativity, achievements, perspectives, and experiences invisible. This has been another reason why female emancipation often has seen canons as problematic.

The problem with such an understanding of canon, which is heavily colored by the case of the biblical canon, is that it tends to (implicitly) perpetuate an attitude toward the canon as something rather fixed and eternal. The risks with such an assumption are many. First, it is a misconception that the Bible is fixed. Jewish, Catholic, Christian Orthodox, and Protestant Bibles include different books (see below). The wide variety of manuscripts available means that publishers of the Bible have to make harsh choices with regard to which textual variants to follow. More importantly, the presumed canonicity of the original is transferred to the translations, so that ancient, medieval, and early modern ways of translating gendered/sexual terminology easily become bestowed with a certain authority that current philology would deem unwarranted.

A second risk of such an implicit assumption that canon is by nature patriarchal and fixed is that one's own views of which texts are must-reads within an academic discipline or other cultural areas evade critical scrutiny and remain unrecognized. Even in the most canon-critical gender studies departments, to pass exams, every student has to read and know books on reading lists prepared by the faculty in the various subject areas. To create a reading list is an act of canonization (Bourdieu, 1993, p. 32). Since canonization is about deciding which texts or social expressions are the most important, or most representative, we simply cannot avoid creating canons. A world without distinctions is a chaotic world. Perhaps textual canons have become more important than ever, as tools of navigation in today's global world culture where other distinctions (gender, national, cultural, etc.) are increasingly dismantled. We need representative symbols as never before.

Since canonization is a cultural process that takes place whether we like it or not, it is important to analyze and discuss such processes and the effects they have in terms of gender. As noted by feminist historians, such processes historically have marginalized women's expressions. When a text or corpus of texts has achieved canonical status, it begins to function in a way that is regulative, normative, and authoritative for further textual production (Lyons, 2002). This process naturalizes the exclusion of those expressions that were not included in the canon in the first place and makes such processes of exclusion seem reasonable and permanent. To analyze canon and canonization in a gender-critical perspective implies the analysis of all these levels: the processes of canonization and also the canonicity; how the end-product, the canon, functions as a norm; interventions, subversions, and critiques of existing canons; and canon supplements, additions, and suggested "improvements" (e.g., by including women).

Third, even within a canonized list, works included and excluded will vary. In the biblical canon, some books are more popular in some periods and almost forgotten in others (see below). There emerges what we would call canonical reading practices, which are no less influential for the actual use of the canon than the canonical writings themselves.

Fourth, what the canon actually says is constantly renegotiated, sometimes by way of confirming or revising canonical commentary to the scriptures. Feminist exegesis of the Bible is a good case in point. After the transformation of the content of the Bible carried out by feminist interpreters, it is no longer clear that there were only male leaders and apostles in early Christianity (Brooten, 1977), that God is described exclusively in male terms (Løland, 2008), or that the Exodus and Revelation narratives of liberation are liberating for all believers (Brenner, 1994; Pippin, 1992).

Hence, the assumption that canonicity always implies something fixed and patriarchal that is irreconcilable with feminism cannot be upheld. We return to some of these points later.

A Canonical Approach to Gender Is Transhistorical. Gender studies at large have often had a contemporary focus. How to understand and describe the world here and now has been more important than dealing with a past that has often been seen as oppressive. The past is seen more as a chapter that should be closed. Needless to say, this has not been the perspective of historical feminist/queer studies, but they do not constitute the main bulk of gender studies, and their results are often not incorporated into the wider field of gender studies—to its disadvantage: the ability to cope with time, future, and change is lost in gender studies if we relinquish the past altogether. To study processes of canonization, then, is a way of learning how to persist through cultural change.

Biblical gender studies at large have not operated with canonicity as analytical category, and "canon" has for the most part been taken at face value as referring to the existing biblical canon. In this overview, we demonstrate this tendency in the work of several scholars and offer alternative modes of interpretation.

Feminist exegetes have investigated the history of the early Christian movement (Schüssler Fiorenza, 1983) and identified important female leaders. We note, however, that early Christian female leaders may not have written very much, or their texts—and definitely the texts attributed to them—never made it into the biblical canon (although they may have been part of social canons in their groups at the time); hence such research may profit from broader interdisciplinary comparison.

Comparison between the early Christian period and, for example, the Enlightenment illumines the issues faced by gender-critical studies of the biblical canon. For the Enlightenment period, we can compare texts authored by women that did not make it into the various canons with texts that were canonized and trace the influence of the former on the latter—and often vice versa. We can trace how quotes or ideas from the letters of various noblewomen who corresponded with notable male philosophers can be found in the publications of the latter—usually without reference. One case in point is Descartes (Owesen, 2010), but there are many others. In contrast, for the early Christian period, "historical reconstruction" consists in extrapolating historical women from the existing biblical text, which in most likelihood is written by men and with the assistance of some slightly later sources that attest to some impact and memory of these women—all to be read in light of indirect literary evidence and archaeological material attesting to everyday life in the period. In this period, for example, we have the text of John Chrysostom but not the responses of Olympias, who sponsored his work (Clark, 1999, pp. 37–38).

Such transhistorical comparison demonstrates the canon's fluid boundaries with regard to gender agency. They suggest that women's thoughts were most likely included in canonical texts without being explicitly recognized as such. They also suggest that the biblical canons had a wider social context in which canonical boundaries, impulses, and influences would have been very different from those reflected in the biblical corpus and ancient ecclesiastical interpretation of it (Horsfield, 2013).

Gender and genre. The concept of canon was much discussed in American literary criticism in the 1990s. A key concern was the value of a multicultural society and how it was (not) reflected in the "Introduction to the Western Canon" courses at liberal arts colleges. Allan Bloom's *The Closing of the American Mind* (Bloom, 1987) itself canonized in the reading lists of such courses, sparked a debate on what place the Western canon could still occupy in the curricula of multicultural, multigendered societies and universities. The debates reached a stalemate around the turn of the millennium, when American culture shifted toward a more conservative stance.

Critical discussions of canon and canonicity, both literary and religious, were paradoxically seen as undermining Western values.

Because access to text production has always been class contingent, women's main means of expression have often been letters, pamphlets, painting, and poems—media less often preserved than the erudite philosophical treatises written by elite males. The analysis of gender in canon formations, therefore, must include considerations of media, class, and genre, as well as investigation of the processes of canonization and the gendered effects of canons. Although some of this work has been undertaken, there are still countless historical women whose interactions, interventions, and subversions of cultural canons remain to be analyzed and brought to attention. Such work could help feminism understand itself better as a historical phenomenon in need of facing its own canons and its own historically contingent and vulnerable position.

Alternative strategies. Instead of simply avoiding or denying canons and canonicity, feminist and gender-critical scholars have developed several strategies turning the construction, deconstruction, or criticism of the canon into a key academic endeavor.

One strategy has been to recuperate forgotten women writers and artists; to incorporate women into the various canons; or to create new, altogether female-friendly canons (Wollstonecraft, 1789). This has been a popular approach in the case of Hebrew Bible characters such as Sarah, Rebecca, Esther, Ruth, Deborah, Huldah, and Miriam.

Another strategy is to take a material approach, analyzing how access to literacy, writing, reading materials (a more limited good in Antiquity and the Middle Ages than today), and distribution channels largely determined whose ideas were preserved for posterity. A material approach also questions how the notion of the fixity of the biblical canon, as a specific number of books included within one book cover, can be deconstructed or dismantled. What is considered "biblical canon" in Judaism and in Catholic, Orthodox, and Protestant Christianity is actually from a material point of view three different collections.

As mentioned previously, they differ in the texts they exclude as well as the ones they include: Mishnah and Talmud function as canon in Judaism, akin to the role of the liturgy in Eastern Orthodoxy and tradition in Roman Catholicism. Most significantly, the order and structure of the canon vary, with great consequences for the understanding of biblical gender in the history of interpretation (Fischer et al., 2011, p. 20). The way a particular canon is structured shapes how the women who are presented within the canon are framed. Are they given a prominent position, for example, at the beginning and end, or are they more hidden in the middle? For example, the Roman Catholic Bible (*Jerusalem Bible*) includes not only the book of Judith, which is attributed to a woman, but also the Book of Sirach, a book of "wisdom" with myriad misogynist statements. Unique to Christian Bibles are not only normative statements that silence women's speaking in assemblies (1 Tim) but also descriptions of women as public speakers, as leaders, patrons, and apostles (Acts, Pauline letters). The Introduction to the encyclopedia *The Bible and Women* (Fischer et al., 2011, pp. 15–20), itself a project in de- and re-canonization, highlights that Christianity labels "Historical books" those writings that the Hebrew canon deems "Prophets." By separating the Former and Latter Prophets, the Christian canon makes the texts describing female prophets less prominent than does the Jewish canon. This point is argued on the basis of Klara Butting's work, which demonstrates how the prophetic figures Deborah (Judg 4–5) and Huldah (2 Kgs 22) frame the "Former Prophets." Butting argues that this *inclusio* influences the understanding of prophecy as a gendered phenomenon, suggesting that all references to "prophets" between these two bookends must be understood as referring to "men and women prophets" (Fischer et al., 2011, pp. 19–20).

Even within a single version of the Bible, questions of content arise. Is the version to be read as a material book or as it was actually received via oral tradition, reading conventions, canonical commentary, and general use? For example, although the Vulgate (a key Latin Roman Catholic Bible) may have been "canon" in the medieval period, the public only knew a narrow range of "highlights" that were cited repeatedly in sermons and liturgies. The learned biblical audience of the monasteries, on the contrary, often read biblical literature as part of the *pagina sacra*, which included also the *Glossa Ordinaria*, a huge compendium of philological and philosophical commentary gleaned from patristic writings especially from Late Antiquity. Gender critical studies might fruitfully study the distribution of male and female literary characters in the selected highlights and the *Glossa Ordinaria* as compared with the Bible as a whole. To our knowledge such study has not been done; we suspect that stories of Mary the Mother of Jesus, Mary Magdalene, and some other female characters were so popular with medieval, chiefly illiterate audiences that they may have perceived the Bible as more female-friendly than do modern readers of the written text. We also suspect that the *Glossa* is dominated by philosophical dogmatics in which biblical female characters find comparatively less resonance.

A third strategy employed by feminist and gender-critical scholars is the transformation of the canon's content. The use of feminist exegesis for such an explicit program of canonical transformation can be traced back to the 1970s; antecedents can be traced to earlier feminist biblical scholarship and even earlier gender-critical interpretations of the Bible carried out by nonscholars (e.g., Elizabeth Cady Stanton, Margaret Fell, and others). This critical engagement with canonical content and its various possibilities of meaning and signification is important and is ongoing. Denise Buell states: "All feminist biblical interpreters call for some kinds of transformations, within Judaism or Christianity, within academic practices, or in the ways that biblical interpretation relates to wider moral, social, or ethical norms in contemporary situations" (Buell, forthcoming). Her essay goes on to explore in more detail the ways feminist biblical interpreters have approached the meaning and significance of canons.

Another alternative strategy for dealing with the patriarchal canon is to deconstruct the perception that it is closed, treating the notion of a closed canon more as a symptom or *result* of the sociocultural process of canonization than as a fixed reality. Such an approach necessarily addresses the social forces that enforce a closed canon. Elisabeth Schüssler Fiorenza (1994, p. 8) has urgently called for the opening of the canon: "Feminist biblical scholarship cannot remain within the limits drawn by the established canon. Rather it must transgress them for the sake of a different theological self-understanding and historical imagination." She argues that the emergence of a canon is always embedded in structures of power. Earliest Christianity saw a high involvement of women and religious writings written by or attributed to women, but the gendered struggles between different strands of Christianity over leadership and power in the fourth century led to the closure of the Christian canon. Feminist research over the past forty years has well documented that canonization went hand in hand with the imperialization of the church in the fourth century, a process that also led to a reduction of female participation in the leadership of early Christian communities (Horsfield, 2013; Schüssler Fiorenza, 1994). The closing of the Christian (New Testament) canon excluded women's traditions and female-authored or -attributed books (Schüssler Fiorenza, 2011, p. 27). Transgressing canonical boundaries in search of gender in earliest Christianity requires, on the one hand, treating texts that express a more balanced gender ideology as sacred scriptures and, on the other hand, halting the continued reception of misogynous texts. Following her lead, many of Schüssler Fiorenza's colleagues and students have investigated early Christian writings without privileging canonical writings over noncanonical ones. They simply assume, as Buell points out, that "the Bible as a literary canon was the result of a process of centuries of use, interpretation, negotiation, and debate" (Buell [forthcoming]).

Impact, content, and material form. Despite the importance of this historical scholarship, we would stress that it is the finished text as received in the canonical reading (and not the more or less hidden history behind it) that continues to exercise cultural influence today. Yet, the canon continues to evolve even after the fixation of its material content. The

Bible as material object continues to be read, cited, printed, and now also digitalized, and the consequences of its ongoing transformation have not yet been sufficiently considered by gender-critical biblical scholarship.

A material approach raises questions about the reception of feminist exegesis (or lack thereof) within broader biblical scholarship and popular culture. The possible ongoing marginalization of insights from gender-critical exegesis may reflect the material streams and practices of scholarship. Women in Western culture were not full legal subjects until the twentieth century. Few were remembered in the official historiographies or as interpreters of the Bible. Nevertheless, some women did read and interpret the Bible and became focal points for traditions, since they defied the "canonical right" of men, who as the guardians of orthodoxy selected some traditions that today are seen as *the* tradition. (Fischer et al., 2011, p. 22).

In a parallel genealogical move one could trace how canonical texts were engaged and drawn upon in the development of feminism as a current of thought. Thus feminism is not totally alien to the canon but has developed out of it—albeit perhaps as an unrecognized child.

An Agenda for Future Research. We propose an agenda for future research on canon and canonicity that incorporates five dimensions.

Canonical discourse. All influential canons seem to have displayed qualities considered by many to be superb, and some canons have succeeded in maintaining their supreme state over considerable time. There is, therefore, no doubt that human lives around the globe are deeply influenced by successful cultural, social, political, religious, technological, and other canons. When seen from the inside of canonical discourse, the authority of a given canon is explained as a function of superb characteristics of the canonical body: authorship, formal features, capacity for continued creative reception, and so on. These and other qualities legitimize the position of the canonical body and warrant its continued use and influence. Conversely, attempts at challenging a given canon often aim to demonstrate that the canonical collection is not so outstanding after all, that its singularity is an arbitrary historical construction, and so on. Along this axis there have been heated discussions of biblical versus extra-biblical literature, of the Western literary canon versus feminist and other literature, of European (male) philosophy versus (colloquial) feminist thinkers, and so forth (cf. earlier).

This kind of discourse is in danger of confirming the assumption that the power and legitimacy of a canon is a function of qualities inherent within the canonical collection. It draws attention away from those cultural spaces where the power of the canon is manufactured and from the groups dominating those spaces. In particular, it conceals the agency of the canonical community and of the institutions and individuals in charge of curating the canon. A truly critical analysis of any canon would, therefore, start by investigating conditions for producing canonicity: the specific mechanisms by which a canonical group ensures that its canonical body continuously retains a privileged status. To achieve such an analysis, it would be necessary to develop a deeper understanding of typical elements of canonical ecology, i.e., the interplay and interdependence of various agents, cultural products, and conditions that cooperate in producing and reproducing a given canon and its social and political discourse.

Canon as cultural capital. Like Guillory (1993) we see the dynamics of canonization through the analytical lens of Pierre Bourdieu. In this perspective, the morals, aesthetics, and other codes symbolized in the canon are those enshrined in the *habitus* of the canonical group (cf. Bourdieu, 1977, pp. 22–30, 72–87, 159–197). Individuals in this social formation understand themselves as "doing the canon" (cf. Cantwell Smith) because it is an objectification of the cognitive and motivating structures that dominate their habitus. This is one reason why the canonical body is likely to remain an instrument of power regardless of attacks on its professed qualities.

With Bourdieu (1986), we might see *the canonical body* as a case of objectified cultural capital, capable of being translated into social and monetary capital. The canonical body itself may fulfill roles in social discourse, and one could map those roles by charting what Bruno Latour (2005, pp. 44ff.) might call the agency of that canonical collection. On a more general level, a canon often becomes an icon for the values and motivations that are taken for granted in a given society, its *doxa* (Bourdieu, 1977, pp. 164–171). For this reason a canon may serve as a sort of wildcard (not semantic) argument supporting values that are taken for granted by the one playing the wildcard.

Like more traditional interpreters, feminists also have appropriated this cultural capital for their purposes. Canons have not been only obstacles to gender equality or to women as cultural agents in their own right; feminism as a current of thought emerged out of existing canons of philosophy and religion and developed in critical conversation with them. For this reason, rather than simply criticizing canons for their androcentric bias and generating alternative, gender-inclusive canons, feminist scholars should study the "mechanics of canonization" and its effect on feminist interpretations (which have their own "mechanics of canonization").

Biblical canonical ecologies. While the formally canonized biblical collection can change only within very tight constraints, the lives that people live and the habitus they continuously renegotiate may change dramatically. So the meaning of the canonical collection needs to be able to change without the collection being altered. In biblical canons the "canonical mechanics" to achieve this is the production of *authoritative commentary* (cf. Smith, 1978, pp. 26ff.). The practice of commentary seems to have followed biblical canons from their very beginning (like entries now available as redactional and other glosses in the biblical text); through the Middle Ages (for instance in the form of *glossa ordinaria*, which was regularly seen as part of *pagina sacra* and printed on the same page as the biblical text); into the Reformation era (for instance as an extensive system of introductions and other directions printed in early Lutheran Bibles). Such practice of commentary is still going on, encompassing a much wider array of commentary products than

those mentioned here. Canon and commentary have a symbiotic life: while the canon provides authority and dignity to the commentary, the commentary lends relevance and applicability back to the formal canon. In a study of a given canonical ecology these expectations would be verified and qualified with precise data. Still, it seems clear that when looking for conditions for the production of canonicity, the commentary practice of a given tradition should be one major area of research. Obviously, this applies to earlier as well as current phases in the history of a given canon. Indeed, a focus on canonical commentary practices would potentially help bridge historical and contemporary studies—for the benefit of both.

A focus on the commentary directs us even further to the institutions, groups, and individuals with the means, the know-how, and the position to produce such commentary. It also raises the issue of the media in which the canon and the commentary exist, be it oral tradition; ancient book scrolls; public reading; mass produced printed editions; performative genres such as ritual, music, or dancing; artwork in various media; digital text; and so forth. These dimensions and their myriad of variations contribute greatly to defining conditions for producing canonicity. For instance, when a biblical text migrates from the printed book and the liturgy to the theatre, its canonical ecology undergoes significant modifications. New institutions and actors are responsible for giving authoritative commentary. New constituencies take part in the canonical community and most likely they do so in different ways. Also, it seems likely that their sense of uniqueness in the canonical body as well as the quality of authority that they ascribe to the canon undergo change.

Canonization. Finally, we address the point where most discussion of the biblical canons normally begins: the issue of canonization. Traditionally, study of the history of the formation of the canons of the Hebrew Bible and the New Testament/Christian Bibles has been conducted without adequate sensitivity toward the issues of canonical ecology outlined earlier. Many historians of the canonization of the Bible disregard the variance between biblical canons, and canonization is still discussed as a function of certain qualities of the collection, usually its closure and textual stability. Hence, the history of the formation of the various Hebrew, Aramaic, Greek, Syriac, Latin, and other collections of biblical literature that were canonical at one time needs to be rewritten. Much new scholarship is needed.

Critical assessment of canons. Gender-critical as well as traditional exegetical studies run the risk of remaining under the spell of the canon—even when professing to dismantle it (as noted previously). There is a need, analytically as well as politically, to develop a truly etic (outside) view of the canonical discourse in question. Since categories of gender, as well as of religion, are socially conditioned, a thorough social theory should be among the basic tools that students of canon, canonization, and canonicity carry in their analytical repertoire. Critical inquiry into specific conditions for manufacturing canonicity in a given discourse has the promise of combining historical and contemporary studies and producing genuinely important insights.

[*See also* Authors of Biblical Books; *and* Feminism, *subentry* Second-Wave Feminism.]

BIBLIOGRAPHY

Bloom, Allan. *The Closing of the American Mind: How Higher Education Has Failed Democracy and Impoverished the Souls of Today's Students*. New York: Simon and Schuster, 1987.

Bourdieu, Pierre. *Outline of a Theory of Practice*. Cambridge, U.K.: Cambridge University Press, 1977.

Bourdieu, Pierre. "The Forms of Capital." In *Handbook of Theory and Research for the Sociology of Education*, edited by John Richardson, pp. 241–258. Westport, Conn.: Greenwood, 1986.

Bourdieu, Pierre. "The Field of Cultural Production, or: The Economic World Reversed." In *The Field of Cultural Production*, by Pierre Bourdieu, pp. 29–73. Cambridge, U.K.: Polity, 1993.

Brenner, Athalya, ed. *A Feminist Companion to Exodus to Deuteronomy*. Sheffield, U.K.: Sheffield Academic Press, 1994.

Brooten, Bernadette J. "Junia....Outstanding among the Apostles (Romans 16:7)." In *Women Priests: A Catholic Commentary on the Vatican Declaration*, edited by L. and A. Swidler, pp. 141–144. New York: Paulist Press, 1977.

Buell, Denise K. "Canons Unbound." In *Feminist Biblical Studies in the 20th Century: Scholarship and Movement*, edited by Elisabeth Schüssler Fiorenza. Vol. 10.1 of *The Bible and Women: An Encyclopedia of Exegesis and Cultural History*. Atlanta: Society of Biblical Literature (forthcoming).

Clark, Elizabeth A. *Reading Renunciation: Asceticism and Scripture in Early Christianity*. Princeton, N.J.: Princeton University Press, 1999.

Fischer, Irmtraud, Jorunn Økland, Mercedes Navarro Puerto, et al. "Women, Bible and Reception History: An International Project in Theology and Gender Studies." In *Torah*, edited by Irmtraud Fischer and Mercedes Navarro Puerto, pp. 1–30. Vol. 1.1 of *The Bible and Women: An Encyclopedia of Exegesis and Cultural History*. Atlanta: Society of Biblical Literature, 2011.

Goody, Jack. "Canonization in Oral and Literate Cultures." In *Canonization and Decanonization*, edited by Arie van der Kooij and Karel van der Toorn, pp. 3–16. Leiden, The Netherlands: Brill, 1998.

Guillory, John. *Cultural Capital: The Problem of Literary Canon Formation*. Chicago: University of Chicago Press, 1993.

Hallberg, Robert, von, ed. *Canons*. Chicago: University of Chicago Press, 1984.

Henderson, John B. *Scripture, Canon, and Commentary: A Comparison of Confucian and Western Exegesis*. Princeton, N.J.: Princeton University Press, 1991.

Horsfield, Peter. "The Ecology of Writing and the Shaping of Early Christianity." In *Religion across Media: From Early Antiquity to Late Modernity*, edited by Knut Lundby, pp. 37–53. New York: Peter Lang, 2013.

Latour, Bruno. *Reassembling the Social: An Introduction to Actor Network Theory*. Oxford: Oxford University Press, 2005.

Levering, Miriam, ed. *Rethinking Scripture: Essays from a Comparative Perspective*. Albany: State University of New York Press, 1989.

Løland, Hanne. *Silent or Salient Gender?* Tübingen, Germany: Mohr Siebeck, 2008.

Lyons, W. John. *Canon and Exegesis: Canonical Praxis and the Sodom Narrative*. Sheffield, U.K.: Sheffield Academic Press, 2002.

Owesen, Ingeborg. "Om å kanonisere det som har unndratt seg kanonisering : Feminisme og filosofihistorie." *Norsk Filosofisk Tidsskrift* 45/4 (2010): 223–236.

Pippin, Tina. *Death and Desire: The Rhetoric of Gender in the Apocalypse of John*. Louisville, Ky.: Westminster John Knox, 1992.

Reed, Kate. *New Directions in Social Theory: Race, Gender, and the Canon*. London: SAGE, 2006.

Sanders, James A. "Canon: Hebrew Bible." In *The Anchor Bible Dictionary*, edited by David Noel Freedman, Vol. 1, pp. 837–852. New York: Doubleday, 1992.

Schüssler Fiorenza, Elisabeth. *In Memory of Her: A Feminist Theological Reconstruction of Christian Origins.* London: SCM, 1983.

Schüssler Fiorenza, Elisabeth. "Introduction: Transgressing Canonical Boundaries." In *Searching the Scriptures,* Vol. 2, *A Feminist Commentary*, by Elisabeth Schüssler Fiorenza. New York: Crossroads, 1994.

Schüssler Fiorenza, Elisabeth. "Neutestamentliche Kanonbildung und die Marginalisierung von Frauen." In *Evangelien*, edited by Mercedes Navarro Puerto and Marinella Perroni, pp. 27–38. Stuttgart: Kohlhammer, 2011. Forthcoming in English as Vol. 2:1 in *The Bible and Women: An Encyclopedia of Exegesis and Cultural History* (Atlanta: Society of Biblical Literature).

Smith, Jonathan Z. "Sacred Persistence: Towards a Redescription of Canon." In *Approaches to Ancient Judaism: Theory and Practice*, edited by William Scott Green, pp. 11–28. Missoula, Mont.: Scholars Press, 1978.

Smith, W. C. *What Is Scripture? A Comparative Approach.* Minneapolis: Fortress, 1993.

Stordalen, Terje. "What Is a Canon of Scriptures?" In *Mótun menningar/Shaping Culture: Festschrift for Gunnlaugur A. Jónsson*, edited by Kristinn Ólason, Ólafur Egilsson, and Stefán Stefánsson, pp. 15–33. Reykjavik, Iceland: Hiðíslenska Bókmenntafélag, 2012.

Wollstonecraft, Mary. *The Female Reader: or Miscellaneous Pieces, in Prose and Verse; Selected from the Best Writers, and Disposed under Proper Heads; for the Improvement of Young Women, by Mr Creswick.* London: Joseph Johnson, 1789.

Jorunn Økland and Terje Stordalen

CHILDREN

This entry contains seven subentries: Ancient Near East; Hebrew Bible; Greek World; Roman World; New Testament; Early Judaism; *and* Early Church.

Ancient Near East

Childhood is a social construct, meaning that conceptions of childhood vary over time and from culture to culture. Therefore, perceptions of children and childhood in the ancient Near East most likely differed from modern Western ones, such as the idea of childhood as a special time in an individual's life. Though the study of childhood is a newly developing field of inquiry, particularly in biblical studies, ancient Near Eastern views of childhood are still not well understood (Bunge, 2008; Garroway, 2010; Koepf-Taylor, 2013). Other factors were likely involved in determining a child's social position, such as class and gender. Moreover, there is very little evidence that associates children and sexuality; thus, one must make inferences from a variety of texts. More information exists surrounding the onset of puberty and sexual maturity, which seems to mark an important point in the transition from childhood to adulthood, especially for women.

Sexual Differentiation among Children. Across the ancient Near East, children—and sons in particular—were highly desired. Distinctions according to biological sex can be seen for young children, though this differentiation occurs in various ways and at different ages. In Sumerian texts, children until age of three were called **lu.tur** "small people." The same term was used regardless of gender. After age three, the usual time of weaning, different gendered nouns were used for children, **dumu.nita** for boys and **dumu.munus** for girls (Asher-Greve, 2002, p. 15). However, already at birth, biological sex was associated with future gendered social roles. An Ur II birth incantation distinguishes between male and female babies thus:

> If it is a male, he holds in his hand a weapon and an ax, which is his strength of heroship.
>
> If it is a female, she holds in her hand a spindle and a decorated comb. (Asher-Greve, 2002, p. 13; Römer, 1982, pp. 204–207)

The son, mentioned first, is associated with physical strength and military prowess, while the daughter is linked to domestic activities and beauty (Asher-Greve, 2002, p. 14). Children were socialized by their parents into distinct gender roles, which included different attributes and occupations for men and women (Asher-Greve, p. 13; Zsolnay, 2009, pp. 108–109).

There is increasing evidence for a third, and perhaps even a fourth, category of gender in Mesopotamia (Nissinen, 1998, pp. 28–36), though these examples are primarily rendered by their association to the primary two gender categories of masculine and feminine as "not a man or a woman." Omen texts mention congenital sexual differences present at birth, such as neither penis nor vulva, neither vulva nor testicles, or both penis and vulva (Stol, 2000, pp. 104; 164 ff.). Beyond an awareness of anatomical variance, individuals who can be considered to belong to a third gender category, such as men with undescended testicles, castrates, eunuchs, or transsexuals, would not have been established at birth but later in life (Asher-Greve, 2002, p. 20).

In Egyptian tomb scenes, children of different genders appear separately, doing different sorts of activities, usually the boys with their fathers and girls with their mothers (Zinn, 2010, p. 1). Children are often depicted as naked, which could be an indicator of their sociocultural status; however, the slightly different hairdos and adornments assigned to boys and girls suggests that children had some level of sexual distinction and were not regarded as asexual beings (Landgráfová and Navrátilová, 2010, p. 66). Moreover, since Egyptian is a gendered language, it is clear in texts whether a child is male or female.

In ancient Israel, gender appears to have been marked at birth. According to Leviticus 12:1–5, the mother must observe different purification periods depending on whether she has given birth to a son or daughter—for a male child, the mother remains ceremonially unclean for seven days and blood purification is required for thirty-three days; for a female child, the period of time is exactly doubled. Regardless of whether this legal text should be understood to be normative practice, it underscores that the biological sex of the child immediately confers upon it a gendered societal role (Zsolnay, 2009, p. 109). The names children are given by their parents are also imbued with meaning. For example, a seal belonging to the daughter of a king of Judah identifies her as Ma'danâ. The root √'dn has a connection to the paradise of Eden, a place of abundance and plenty, so the name could be the parents' acknowledgment that Yahweh had provided them with an abundance of children. For a daughter, however, this name could also indicate the baby girl's potential fertility, her ability to bear future children.

Circumcision. Since circumcision affects an individual's sexual life and is usually performed during childhood, it should be given consideration. Male circumcision was practiced in ancient Egypt and Israel but not in Mesopotamia. There is very minimal evidence of female circumcision in Egypt, and no evidence in Israel or Mesopotamia (Landgráfová and Navrátilová, 2010, p. 67).

In Israel male infants were circumcised at eight days of age. Circumcision was a marker of ethnic identity in ancient Israel, specifically as a sign of the pact between Yahweh and Abraham (Gen 17:1–14). Since the identification is made on male genitalia, it is therefore gender specific, indicating that Israel's pact with Yahweh is envisioned as masculine (Zsolnay, 2009, p. 111). In Egypt, on the other hand, circumcision was performed either just before or after the onset of puberty and marked the end of childhood in males (Landgráfová and Navrátilová, 2010, p. 67). The type of circumcision also seems to have differed between Israel and Egypt as well as the age at which it was performed (Sasson, 1966, p. 474; Stager and King, 2001, p. 45).

Marriage and Virginity. The onset of menstruation was likely a factor in marking the end of childhood for girls, as they were often married shortly after beginning puberty in order to take advantage of the fertile period in woman's life (Landgráfová and Navrátilová, 2010, pp. 67–68). Though married couples could be around the same age, considerable age disparity was permitted, as in an Egyptian example where the groom was fifty-four and the bride was twelve (Zinn, 2010, p. 1). Since betrothals at times seem to have taken place before girls reached marriageable age, it appears that such betrothals would have been made during childhood (Balkan, 1986).

One biblical law provides an example of a specific type of marital arrangement made before the intended bride reached maturity. Exodus 21:7–11 addresses a man who sells his daughter as a debt-pledge, and the situation concerns her marriage into the family into which she is sold:

> When a man sells his daughter as a slave, she shall not go out as the male slaves do. If she does not please her master, who designated her for himself, then he shall let her be redeemed; he shall have no right to sell her to a foreign people, since he has dealt unfairly with her. If he designates her for his son, he shall deal with her as with a daughter. If he takes another wife

to himself, he shall not diminish the food, clothing, or marital rights of the first wife. And if he does not do these three things for her, she shall go out without debt, without payment of money.

The father is selling his daughter for sexual and reproductive purposes in the form of marriage, if perhaps a second-tier type of marriage (Westbrook, 2009, pp. 64–65). The daughter does not yet seem to be of marriageable age or else the father could just seek an advantageous marriage. Therefore, the daughter could be considered to be a child (Garroway, 2010, pp. 164–180). Though sold in the form of a future marriage arrangement to pay off her father's debt, the daughter is not a slave. If specific conditions are not met, she is released without debt.

In Mesopotamia and Israel the term usually translated "virgin" (*bĕtûlâ* in Hebrew, **ki.sikil(tur)** in Sumerian, and *batultu* and *ardatu* in Akkadian) technically indicates nubile young women of marriageable age. However, since young women at the time of their first marriage were expected to be sexually inexperienced, the terms could carry a sexual connotation in addition to being an age designation for a young woman who has reached sexual maturity (Cooper, 2002, pp. 91–93; Frymer-Kensky, 1998, pp. 79–80). Physical virginity was indicated by negative statements specifying what a woman had not done, such as the statement describing Rebekah before her marriage to Isaac "a *bĕtûlâ* who had not known a man" (Gen 24:16). The cultural assumption that young women of marriageable age are virgins is probably the cause of variability and ambiguity surrounding our understanding of these terms (Frymer-Kensky, 1998, p. 80).

Throughout Mesopotamia and Israel, female virginity was prized and even carried monetary value, as demonstrated by various laws which specify fines for illicit sex with a virgin (Exod 22:16; Deut 22:28–29; Roth, 1997, pp. 33, 106, 174–175). In ancient Egypt, however, there is no evidence of a special importance attached to virginity, though a woman's young age at the time of her first marriage probably resulted in the husband being her first sexual partner (Landgráfová and Navrátilová, 2010, p. 68).

According to Mesopotamian texts, there was no way to test virginity; its loss could only be proven by verbal admission or by being caught in the act (Cooper, 2002, pp. 94–99). However, one biblical example, Deuteronomy 22:13–20, indicates that a bride's virginity is evidenced by the presence of blood on the bed sheets. The case involves a bridegroom who accuses his bride of not being a virgin at the time of marriage. To prove their daughter's virginity, the girl's parents must produce the bed linens from the marriage night. If the bride is vindicated, the bridegroom can never divorce her, but if not, the bride is stoned by the community at the entrance to her father's house. However, such proof seems rather dubious since not all women bleed with the loss of virginity and the evidence could be easily falsified using animal blood (Frymer-Kensky, 1998, p. 95). Whether or not the law reflects actual practice, Deuteronomy 22:13–20 highlights the cultural significance of female virginity.

Though many adolescent men were probably also virgins, virginity was not emphasized for young men in the same way it was for young women. In Mesopotamia, virginity had an important ritual purpose regardless of gender (Cooper, 2002, pp. 102–103).

Illicit Sex. Incest is forbidden in Mesopotamian, Hittite, and Israelite legal codes. The law code attributed to Hammurabi of Babylon (1792–1750 B.C.E.) and the legal codes from the kingdom of Hatti (ca. 1650–1180 B.C.E.) forbid a man from sleeping with his daughter and a son sleeping with his mother. According to the biblical purity laws of Leviticus, sex with any near kinsman is prohibited (Lev 18:6–18; 20:17–21). However, in these legal texts, the age of the family members is not specified, so these laws are not expressly concerned about children. Incest is prohibited regardless of age.

Sexual relations between siblings is forbidden in the biblical purity laws; however, in narrative texts marriage between half-siblings is mentioned. Abraham and Sarah are said to be half-siblings in Genesis 20 and the idea of marriage is entertained in the story of David's son Amnon's rape of his half-sister Tamar in 2 Samuel 13. In the narrative contexts of both of these examples, however, it is clear that all parties have reached maturity. Brother–sister marriage was not excluded in ancient Egypt, although the occurrence was very rare. Within the royal family, however, consanguineous marriages had a different nature and significance, having a ritual connection with the king and queen representing the brother–sister pair Osiris and Isis as well as enhancing the power and wealth of the royal family (Landgráfová and Navrátilová, 2010, p. 69). However, examples of consanguineous marriages do not necessarily imply that the sibling couples were children at the time of marriage.

Homosexuality. There is no clear indication of age in ancient Near Eastern texts concerning homosexuality or homoeroticism. Nearly all of the meager and ambiguous documentation of homoeroticism in the ancient Near East concern male–male sexual acts whereas female–female sexual relations are not mentioned. The confessional section of the Egyptian *Book of the Dead* twice includes the statement "I have not had sexual relations with a boy," but in this case the word "boy" could be rendered "male lover" since it is same-sex relations and not age that is the focus of the statement (Nissinen, 1998, pp. 19, 144). Some Mesopotamian legal texts prohibit male-male sexual relations in which the penetrated male is the social equal of the penetrator, which probably indicates two adult males (Roth, 1997, pp. 159–160). However, other evidence from Egypt and Mesopotamia suggests a level of tolerance for same-sex interactions. The Levitical purity code of the Hebrew Bible twice forbids male-male sexual intercourse (Lev 18:22; 20:13), which would presumably apply to all males regardless of age (Olyan, 1994).

"Sex Education" in Instruction Literature. The setting of the biblical book of Proverbs is a father giving advice to his son, and this premise has similarities to Mesopotamian and Egyptian instruction literature. Among the tenets of wisdom is advice on sexual matters, particularly the avoidance of adultery. For example, the Sumerian Instructions of Šuruppak (ETCSL 5.6.1) warns "You should not play around with a married young woman: the slander could be serious. My son, you should not sit alone in a chamber with a married woman." This series of instructions also warns against having sex with a slave girl or raping another man's daughter.

The Egyptian Instruction of Any (New Kingdom) advises the "son" or student about the importance of marriage and children as well as the avoidance of unknown women:

> Take a wife while you're young,
> That she make a son for you;
> She should bear for you while you're youthful,
> It is proper to make people....
>
> Beware of a woman who is a stranger,
> One not known in her town;
> Don't stare at her when she goes by,
> Do not know her carnally.
> A deep water whose course is unknown,
> Such is a woman away from her husband.
> "I am pretty," she tells you daily,
> When she has no witnesses;
> She is ready to ensnare you,
> A great deadly crime when it is heard.
>
> (CoS 1.46:111)

In Proverbs, the "son" is particularly exhorted to avoid the "strange woman," seemingly an adulteress, and this lesson is repeated and embellished. Instead of promiscuous women, the "father" exhorts his "son" to seek Wisdom, personified as female, and to find a capable wife. Several examples can be found in Proverbs 1–7:

> My child, be attentive to my wisdom,
> 	incline your ear to my understanding;
> So that you may hold on to prudence,
> 	and your lips may guard knowledge.
> For the lips of a 'strange' woman drip honey,
> 	and her speech is smoother than oil;
> But in the end she is bitter as wormwood,
> 	sharp as a two-edged sword...
>
> Let your fountain be blessed
> 	and rejoice in the wife of your youth,
> 	a lovely deer, a graceful doe.
> May her breasts satisfy you at all times;
> 	may you be intoxicated always by her love.
> Why should you be intoxicated, my son, by another woman
> 	and embrace the bosom of an adulteress?
>
> (Prov 5:1–4; 18–20)

…For the commandment is a lamp and the teaching
   a light,
   and the reproofs of discipline are a way of life,
To preserve you from the wife of another,
   from the smooth tongue of the adulteress.
Do not desire her beauty in your heart,
   and do not let her capture you with her eyelashes;
For a prostitute's fee is only a loaf of bread,
   but the wife of another stalks a man's very life.
Can a fire be carried in the bosom
   without burning one's clothes?
   Or can one walk on hot coals
   without scorching the feet?
So is he who sleeps with his neighbor's wife;
   no one who touches her will go unpunished.

(Prov 6:23–29)

The probable social context for these texts is their use as part of scribal training. Apprentice scribes were called the "sons" of the scribal master whether or not they were the biological offspring of the teacher. Instruction literature would have been part of the education–enculturation of the young scribe and would have been copied starting fairly early in the curriculum, after the student had mastered basic signs and letters. Therefore, the student probably had yet to reach sexual or social maturity and can perhaps be considered a child. Thus, young scribal apprentices would have repeatedly copied and memorized specific principles regarding proper sexual conduct.

Love Poetry. In ancient Near Eastern love poetry, the speakers at times give indications that they could be considered minors. The female speakers in several instances mention that they live at home, and this seems to be the case for the male speakers in a couple of Egyptian love poems. The poems also focus on sensuality more than on sexual intercourse, speaking of embraces and caresses rather than intercourse (Carr, 2003; Cooper, 1997). Although the speakers of ancient Near Eastern love poems are often young and unmarried (with the exception of Sumerian royal love songs), it is not clear that they would have been regarded as children. However, the songs do present a view of romantic sexuality that seems to be associated with youth.

Narrative Literature. Ancient Near Eastern narratives provide perceptions of the transition from childhood to maturity and its connection to sexuality. In the Sumerian myth of Enki and Ninhursag, Enki deflowers and impregnates successive generations of his daughters when they come to the riverbank. Except for the final daughter who actually resists Enki, all of these goddesses are referred to by the gender neutral term **lu.tur sag.a** "beautiful child" until they become pregnant, after which point they are called **munus** "woman" (Cooper, 2002, p. 97).

In the myth of Enlil and Ninlil, the god Enlil seizes the goddess Ninlil by the riverbank, but Ninlil protests, saying:

My vagina is small and has not learned to stretch!
My lips are small and have not learned to kiss!
My mother will learn of it and slap my hand!
My father will learn of it and lay hold of me!

(Cooper, 1980, p. 185)

Ninlil's protest could indicate that she is to be considered still a child and not yet sexually mature. However, Enlil copulates with Ninlil despite her protests and impregnates her with the god Su'en, but then Enlil is banished from Ninlil's city as a sex offender. Ninlil, however, follows Enlil, and, disguised, he impregnates Ninlil three more times.

In the beginning of the Akkadian *The Epic of Gilgameš*, the citizens of Uruk complain of being oppressed by their semi-divine king Gilgameš, and the gods create Enkidu to be a rival/equal to Gilgameš. The birth goddess pinches off clay and creates Enkidu, a primitive human who has hair all over his body and lives with animals. On Gilgameš's suggestion, Enkidu becomes civilized through sexual intercourse with the prostitute Šamhat. After he sleeps with Šamhat, the animals run away from him, he can no longer run fast, but he has wisdom and understanding. Enkidu's week-long intercourse with Šamhat can be interpreted as metaphorically representative of Enkidu's childhood (Asher-Greve, 2002, p. 14). Šamhat clothes Enkidu and instructs him on eating bread and drinking beer, and persuades him to dwell in the city of Uruk, where he meets and befriends Gilgameš.

After Šamhat's "mothering" of Enkidu, providing him with basic instructions on civilized life, she brings him to Gilgameš to begin Enkidu's masculine socialization (Asher-Greve, 2002, p. 15).

In the biblical story about Jephthah's daughter (Judg 11), the leader Jephthah makes a foolish vow to sacrifice the first living thing he sees when he returns home from a victorious battle, which happens to be his daughter. Jephthah grants his daughter a two-month stay before her sacrifice so that she can wander around with other young women and "bewail [her] virginity" (Judg 11:37). Though sometimes connected to a coming-of-age ritual (Day, 1989), in the passage itself Jephthah's daughter requests time to mourn the adult life that she will not experience, which specifically includes reproductive sexuality since her virginity is emphasized. Similarly, in Mesopotamia, young men and women who die before reaching maturity were specific kinds of malevolent spirits to be warded off, and the lack of sexual experience for the female ghosts (Ardat-lilî) is particularly underscored in incantations against them (Cooper 2002, pp. 92, 103, 107–108).

The biblical story of the Garden of Eden in Genesis 2:4b–3:24 can also be interpreted as a story about the transition from childhood to maturity, and this transition is envisioned as closely connected with sexuality. The forbidden tree is associated with wisdom and understanding, and snakes are also symbolic of wisdom (Carr, 2003, pp. 45–46). Instead of death, eating the fruit brings the man and woman in the garden awareness of their sexuality through shame at their nakedness. Because of their newly acquired sexual maturity, the man and woman can no longer enjoy the simple existence in the garden but must live a life of hard work in the "real world." The story of the Garden of Eden can thus be seen as a metaphor for "growing up," envisioned as leaving behind childlike simplicity in exchange for wisdom and responsibility, with the first human couple's awareness of their sexuality representing the sexual maturation that signals the end of childhood.

[*See also* Children, *subentry* Hebrew Bible; Education, *subentries on* Ancient Near East *and* Hebrew Bible; Gender and Sexuality: Ancient Near East; Legal Status, *subentry* Ancient Near East; *and* Marriage and Divorce, *subentries on* Ancient Near East *and* Hebrew Bible.]

BIBLIOGRAPHY

Asher-Greve, Julia. "Decisive Sex, Essential Gender." In *Sex and Gender in the Ancient Near East: Proceedings of the 47th Rencontre Assyriologique Internationale, Helsinki, July 2–6, 2001*, edited by Simo Parpola and Robert M. Whiting, pp. 11–26. CRRAI 47. Helsinki: Neo-Assyrian Text Corpus Project, 2002.

Balkan, Kemal. "Betrothal of Girls During Childhood in Ancient Assyria and Anatolia." In *Kaniššuwar: A Tribute to Hans G. Güterbock on His Seventy-fifth Birthday, May 27, 1983*, by Hans Gustav Güterbock, Harry A. Hoffner, and Gary M. Beckman, pp. 1–11. Chicago: Oriental Institute, 1986.

Bunge, Marcia J., Terence E. Fretheim, and Beverly Roberts Gaventa, eds. *The Child in the Bible.* Grand Rapids, Mich.: Eerdmans, 2008.

Carr, David M. *The Erotic Word: Sexuality, Spirituality, and the Bible.* Oxford: Oxford University Press, 2003.

Cooper, Jerrold. "Critical Review of H. Behrens, *Enlil und Ninlil.*" *Journal of Cuneiform Studies* 32 (1980): 175–188.

Cooper, Jerrold. "Gendered Sexuality in Sumerian Love Poetry." In *Sumerian Gods and Their Representations*, edited by I. L. Finkel and M. J. Geller, pp. 84–97. Groningen, The Netherlands: Styx, 1997.

Cooper, Jerrold. "Virginity in Mesopotamia." In *Sex and Gender in the Ancient Near East: Proceedings of the 47th Rencontre Assyriologique Internationale, Helsinki, July 2–6, 2001.* 2 vols., edited by S. Parpola and R. M. Whiting, pp. 91–108. Helsinki: Neo-Assyrian Text Corpus Project, 2002.

Day, Peggy L. "From the Child Is Born the Woman: The Story of Jephthah's Daughter." In *Gender and Difference in Ancient Israel*, edited by Peggy L. Day, pp. 58–74. Minneapolis: Fortress, 1989.

Frymer-Kensky, Tikva. "Virginity in the Bible." In *Gender and Law in the Hebrew Bible and the Ancient Near East*, edited by Bernard M. Levinson, Victor H. Matthews, and Tikva Frymer-Kensky, pp. 79–96. Sheffield, U.K.: Sheffield Academic Press, 1998.

Garroway, Kristine Sue Hendricksen. "The Construction of 'Child' in the Ancient Near East: Towards an Understanding of the Legal and Social Status of Children in Biblical Israel and Surrounding Cultures." PhD diss., Hebrew Union College, Jewish Institute of Religion, 2010.

Hallo, William W., and K. Lawson Younger, eds. *The Context of Scripture.* 3 vols. Leiden, The Netherlands: Brill, 1997.

King, Philip J., and Lawrence E. Stager. *Life in Biblical Israel.* Louisville, Ky.: Westminster John Knox, 2001.

Knust, Jennifer Wright. *Unprotected Texts: The Bible's Surprising Contradictions about Sex and Desire.* New York: HarperOne, 2011.

Koepf-Taylor, Laurel W. *"Give Me Children or I Shall Die": Children and Communal Survival in Biblical Israel.* Philadelphia: Fortress, 2013.

Landgráfová, Renate, and Hana Navrátilová. *Sex and the Golden Goddess I: Ancient Egyptian Love Songs in Context.* Prague: Czech Institute of Egyptology, 2010.

Nissinen, Martti. *Homoeroticism in the Biblical World: A Historical Perspective.* Translated by Kirsi Stjerna. Minneapolis: Fortress, 1998.

Olyan, Saul M. "'And with a Male You Shall Not Lie the Lying down of a Woman': On the Meaning and Significance of Leviticus 18:22 and 20:13." *Journal of the History of Sexuality* 5 (1994): 179–206.

Römer, Willem H. Ph. "Geburtsbeschwörungen." In *Texte aus der Umwelt der Alten Testaments.* Vol. 2, *Religiose Texte*, edited by Rykle Borger, et al., pp. 204–207. Gütersloh, Germany: Gütersloher Verlagshaus Gerd Mohn, 1982.

Roth, Martha T. *Law Collections from Mesopotamia and Asia Minor.* 2d ed. Society of Biblical Literature Writings of the Ancient World 6. Atlanta: Scholars Press, 1997.

Sasson, Jack M. "Circumcision in the Ancient Near East." *Journal of Biblical Literature* 85 (1966): 474.

Stol, M. *Birth in Babylonia and the Bible: Its Mediterranean Setting.* Groningen, The Netherlands: Styx, 2000.

Westbrook, Raymond, and Bruce G. Wells. *Everyday Law in Biblical Israel: An Introduction.* Louisville, Ky.: Westminster John Knox, 2009.

Zinn, Katharina. "Education, Pharaonic Egypt." In *The Encyclopedia of Ancient History*, Vol. 5, edited by Roger S. Bagnall, et al. Malden, Mass.: Wiley-Blackwell, 2010.

Zsolnay, Ilona. "Do Divine Structures of Gender Mirror Mortal Structures of Gender?" In *In the Wake of Tikva Frymer-Kensky*, edited by Steven Holloway, JoAnn Scurlock, and Richard Beal, pp. 103–120. Piscataway, N.J.: Gorgias, 2009.

Erin E. Fleming

Hebrew Bible

In the Hebrew Bible, the bearing of children is both the first commandment and a great blessing (see Genesis 1:28, where the first man and woman are commanded to "be fruitful and multiply"). Having many children is both a sign of God's regard and a means of achieving immortality (see Genesis 12:2 and Genesis 15:5, where God's promises to Abraham are inextricably bound to his fathering a child). Yet, given the centrality of children to both ancient Israelite story and ideology, there is remarkably little attention paid to children qua children, and even less attention given to the sexuality of children.

The study of children in general and the sexuality of children in particular is methodologically difficult. Biologically, the human species goes through a prolonged period of immaturity and dependence (compared to other animals), then undergoes a time of sexual maturation called puberty. In some societies, sexual maturity is equivalent to adulthood; other societies define an interval between puberty and full adulthood now called adolescence. The idea of adolescence as a distinct life stage did not emerge until the nineteenth century, but there is evidence that there was some acknowledgment of this phase even before it was clearly defined. Physically, there are no definite ages for these stages, because the onset of puberty ranges depending on individual biology (genetics), and environmental influence (nutrition). In fact, almost every aspect of childhood needs to be understood as a combination of biological, environmental, and cultural effects.

The paucity of data impedes any historical study of children. Children rarely if ever provide direct recorded testimony about their lives, and adult reminiscences are not always accurate. When children do end up in written or pictorial sources, they are often the children of the elite, since these are the classes who have access to bookmaking and art. Consequently, historians have little to no access to the vast majority of children's lives and experiences. These general challenges are even more acute when the topic is sex and sexuality, since sexual attitudes and actions are often kept private (even secret) from all except those immediately concerned. Therefore, they leave no trace on the historical record.

There are aspects of Hebrew narrative that make an exploration of sex and children even more challenging. The ages of characters are rarely provided and must be inferred. Even when the age of a character is clear, chronological age is not what determines life-cycle stage in the biblical world; whether someone is a "child" or an "adult" is dictated by a combination of physiology and societal role. There are a number of words in Hebrew that refer to children: *yeled* (masculine; occurs 89 times) and *yaldāh* (feminine; 3 times), *naʿar* (masculine; 239 times) and *naʿarāh* (feminine; 62 times), and *ṭap* (collective; 42 times). However, these words cannot be used to determine age or fix classification because they are not used consistently. For example, the Levite's concubine in Judges 19 is called "girl," "concubine," and "woman" interchangeably throughout the chapter. There are no Hebrew words that are equivalent to the English "adolescent" or "teenager" with the possible exception of the rare *ʿalmāh*, which means a young nubile woman (occurs seven times). An *ʿalmāh* may or may not be already married (compare unmarried Rebekah in Genesis 24:16 and the pregnant wife in Isaiah 7:14).

Further complicating a study of the sexuality of children, the Bible is comprises materials composed by multiple hands, edited and re-edited over time. Consequently, it is difficult to separate sources and attribute them to particular historical and cultural contexts. Over the course of centuries, the definition of and expectations concerning childhood in ancient Israel and early Judaism are bound to have changed, as they have in other cultures that we can better document, but scholars cannot chart these changes with any certainty. In fact, the very idea of childhood may not have existed in the earliest texts and times. In the biblical material, the word "childhood" (*yaldût*) appears only in Ecclesiastes 11:9–10 (twice). Ecclesiastes is usually dated to the late Persian or early Hellenistic period. The appearance of the new word may indicate a new understanding of childhood as a distinct phase that can be reflected upon in the abstract. If so, it is the only change in Israelite ideology that can be documented.

Masturbation. It is much easier to chart adult attitudes toward childhood masturbation than it is to document the occurrence of childhood masturbation. Even in today's more open society, children do not generally discuss their masturbatory activi-

ties. Investigating such sexual activity in the biblical world is even more daunting. Despite the term "onanism," which currently refers to masturbation and is derived from the story of Tamar's sexual encounter with Onan (Gen 38), masturbation is completely absent from the biblical scripture (Onan is actually practicing coitus interruptus in order to prevent pregnancy). It can be assumed that the phenomenon was not unknown among Israelite children and their parents, but the biblical writers did not deem such sexual activity worthy of discussion in either law or narrative.

Sexual Activity between Children. Children have been known to engage in sexual play, although, like masturbation, such play is rarely discussed and therefore difficult to document. There is no biblical mention of sexual activity between children, with the possible exception of Genesis 21:9, where Sarah sees Ishmael "playing" with Isaac. The verb *ṣāḥaq* has a broad semantic range that includes laughing, playing, and fondling (sexually). In fact, the sexual connotations emerge just a few chapters later, in Genesis 26:8, where Abimelech sees Isaac "playing" with ("fondling" according to the NRSV) Rebekah and knows immediately that Rebekah is Isaac's wife, not his sister. The implication is clear: lovers "play," not siblings.

The boys are playing on the day that Isaac is weaned, which means that he is about two years old, but the age of Ishmael is ambiguous. Ishmael is circumcised at age thirteen (Gen 17:25), about one year before the birth of his younger brother. Ishmael should then be sixteen years old on the day of Isaac's celebration; however, a few verses later, Abraham puts Ishmael on Hagar's shoulders and sends them away (Gen 21:14). The subsequent story of their ordeal in the wilderness also seems to assume that Ishmael is a young boy. As Ishmael's age changes, so does the tenor of the story: a five-year-old and a two-year-old may be innocently curious about each other's bodies, but a young man of sixteen sexually touching a two-year-old constitutes abuse. If Sarah has seen sexual play and not just simple play, then her immediate and uncompromising reaction (ordering disinheritance and expulsion) is more understandable and justifiable.

Premarital Control of Children's Sexuality. The laws and the narratives in the Hebrew Bible indicate that, in the sexual arena, a father's control over his progeny was close to absolute. A father controlled the sexuality of his daughters and played a decisive role in finding marriage partners for both daughters and sons.

According to the legal material, girls living in their father's home were expected to be chaste, in part because their virginity was a commodity owned by the father and sold to the bridegroom. If a girl engages in sexual congress without her father's knowledge—whether she consents or not (the laws are ambiguous about whether the rape is statutory or whether the girl is a victim of violence)—the man who violated her must pay compensatory damages to her father and marry her, and the man is not permitted to divorce her (Deut 22:28–29; in Exod 22:15–16 her father has the power to refuse the marriage although he still collects the bride-price). If she is already engaged to another man, she may be guilty of adultery and stoned, depending upon the location of the rape (Deut 22:23–27). If it can be demonstrated that she was not a virgin on her wedding night, she is also subject to stoning (Deut 22:20–21).

A father could, however, offer his daughters' sexuality to other men outside of the marriage contract if he so desired. Lot resorted to this tactic in his attempt to shield his (angelic) visitors from the violence of Sodom's mob (Gen 19). His two daughters were living at home, engaged but not yet married. A similar situation is recounted at the end of Judges, and again the host offers his virgin daughter (and the concubine of his male guest) to be raped by the violent crowd outside his house (Judg 19:24). Girls were not commodities in ancient Israel (a father could only sell his daughter into slavery with the understanding that she would become the wife of either the buyer or his son [Exod 21:7–11]); but as these stories and laws reveal, their sexuality was a commodity that belonged to fathers to be sold or given away in whatever way they determined. The absolute rule of the father over his daughter's sexuality may account for a strange lacuna in the incest prohibitions in Leviticus 18. Father-daughter incest is not explicitly forbidden (although it is implicitly illegal).

Although there is no unequivocal data, there is some evidence to suggest that a girl who had begun to menstruate was eligible for marriage in ancient Israel. In the prophetic book of Ezekiel, Israel is figured as a child whom God finds as an abandoned newborn. God then cares for the child until she grows tall, develops breasts, and grows hair (presumably pubic and armpit hair). Once the breasts and hair appear, God marries his foundling (Ezek 16:7–8). Menstruation is not explicitly mentioned. Since breast formation and hair growth precede menses, it is possible that God is marrying a girl who is only on the verge of sexual maturity. Boys lack a physical change comparable to menses to mark sexual (and therefore marital) readiness. Instead, they did not marry until they were older, presumably because it was expected that they would establish themselves in some kind of economic enterprise before they started their own family.

There are no biblical laws concerning the way in which marriage arrangements are made, and the narratives contain stories where fathers find their sons a bride (Abraham arranges Isaac's marriage in Gen 24), mothers arrange marriages (Hagar finds Ishmael a wife in Gen 21), and men pick their own women (Esau in Gen 28). In some cases when a son picks his own wife, the parents are still involved in contracting the marriage (Shechem's father approaches Dinah's father in Gen 34; Samson's parents make the arrangements in Judg 14). All of these sons appear to be adults, thus demonstrating that parental control over reproductive sex (marriage being the primary arena) does not end when a boy becomes a man. There are no examples of girls initiating a marriage proposal, although certainly girls are active in forming relationships with suitors (Rachel in Gen 29) and in giving consent to arranged marriages (Rebekah in Gen 24:58).

Sex between Adults and Children. Sex with children is not prohibited in biblical law. Presuming girls married during or soon after puberty, men, then, frequently had sex with children (or at least teenagers). Concerning sex with younger, prepubescent children, biblical law and narrative is completely silent. This gap in the legal tradition does raise the possibility that adult sex with prepubescent children was condoned unless the child was already forbidden for another reason. For men, categories of forbidden children would include most relatives (Lev 18), all boys (Lev 18:22, Lev 20:13), and girls still living in their father's house (Deut 21–22). For women, forbidden categories would include most relatives as well. However, same-sex prohibitions apply exclusively to males; the concerns with virgin daughters focus on intact hymens; and there was no expectation that a boy would remain a virgin until marriage. Therefore, adult females may have had more latitude is pursuing their sexual proclivities with boys and girls. Children who were slaves would have been particularly vulnerable to sexual use by adults.

Contribution to Contemporary Concerns. Industrialized economies need a highly educated and trained workforce, both male and female; therefore, the delay of marriage and childbearing is encouraged. With the rise of financial institutions like banks and corporations, the family is no longer the center of the economic life of the community, and inheritance of wealth is no longer a family affair. To accommodate biological drives in the economies of the modern West, attitudes about premarital sexual activity, including the sexual activity of adolescent children, have changed. Parents no longer take an active role in procuring spouses for their children; fathers no longer own their daughters' sexuality, and thus a girl's virginity is no longer bought and sold.

Premarital sexual activity is broadly accepted among adults, but there are still strict prohibitions as such activities relate to children. Masturbation and some sexual play among prepubescent children is generally accepted and seen as natural and normal. The same is true for adolescent girls and boys, and older adolescents (sixteen- and seventeen-year-olds) even have intercourse without too much societal censure (as long as they do not conceive children). However, any sexual contact between people in different life stages is strictly and legally prohibited. In other words, sex between children and adults, even between pre- and postadolescent children, categories defined according to chronological age, are considered abusive and are illegal.

Such prohibition based solely on chronological age would have been incomprehensible in biblical times. Premodern societies rarely kept accurate records of age, and Israel seems to be no exception. As noted above, marital matches were frequently made between females we would consider children and males we would define as adults. Although there is no clear evidence, there is reason to suspect that sexual contact with slaves regardless of the slave's age was acceptable. As contemporary communities are rocked by sexual abuse scandals, the Bible is not an adequate resource, because it lacks explicit prohibitions against adults having sexual contact with children, and even assumes such contact is normal in certain situations. Economies have changed and with them so have societal structures, family relationships, and sexual mores. The biblical view of sexuality and children proves insufficient to ground a contemporary ethic.

[*See also* Family Structures, *subentry* Hebrew Bible; *and* Marriage and Divorce, *subentry* Hebrew Bible.]

BIBLIOGRAPHY

Ariès, Philippe. *Centuries of Childhood: A Social History of Family Life.* Translated by Robert Baldick. New York: Vintage, 1962.

Baxter, Jane Eva. *The Archaeology of Childhood: Children, Gender, and Material Culture.* Walnut Creek, Calif.: AltaMira, 2005.

Colón, A. R., and P. A. Colón. *A History of Children: A Socio-Cultural Survey across Millennia.* Westport, Conn.: Greenwood, 2001.

Eng, Milton. *The Days of Our Years: A Lexical Semantic Study of the Life Cycle in Biblical Israel.* New York: T&T Clark, 2011.

Fewell, Danna Nolan. *Children of Israel: Reading the Bible for the Sake of Our Children.* Nashville, Tenn.: Abingdon, 2003.

Frymer-Kensky, Tikva. "Law and Philosophy: The Case of Sex in the Bible." In *Women in the Hebrew Bible: A Reader,* edited by Alice Bach, pp. 293–304. New York: Routledge, 1999.

King, Philip J., and Lawrence E. Stager. *Life in Biblical Israel.* Louisville, Ky.: Westminster John Knox, 2001.

Matthews, Victor H., Bernard M. Levinson, and Tikva Frymer-Kensky, eds. *Gender and Law in the Hebrew*

Bible and the Ancient Near East. Sheffield, U.K.: Sheffield Academic Press, 1998.

Perdue, Leo G., Joseph Blenkinsopp, John J. Collins, and Carol Meyers, *Families in Ancient Israel.* Louisville, Ky.: Westminster John Knox, 1997.

Stearns, Peter N. *Childhood in World History.* 2d ed. New York: Routledge, 2011.

Jennifer L. Koosed

Greek World

While the study of children in relation to gender studies in the ancient Greek world is challenging in many respects, perhaps no other area is more challenging for modern sensibilities than the intersection of children and sexuality, on which this essay shall concentrate. For a subject rarely handled in the study of the ancient world, linking the terms "children" and "sexuality" raises several questions. It is necessary not to confuse their sexuality with ours, and it is also critical to be careful to define correctly what we understand by "children." For the Greeks' children are not our "children," and, as far as that time of their life is concerned, age represents the essential variable of development and the forms of sexuality. It is thus of major importance to know who is included in the category "children."

The linear sequencing of the ages of life that we know of in the contemporary Western world, in the form of childhood > adolescence > mature adulthood > old age, with its representations and sexual practices at every stage, did not exist in ancient Greek culture. In that context, nothing looked like this social hallway, more or less long, between childhood and grown-up maturity, which constitutes our "adolescence," itself a term and concept practically absent before the mid-nineteenth century.

To further clarify, we must distinguish boys from girls. The word most frequently used to name a male child, *pais* (plural: *paides*), is a polysemic term, the most common sense of which is "child." A Greek boy was a *pais* until a very late age, at which point he immediately became an adult. We can see this premise operative, for example, at Athens in the classical period when the time came to inscribe, at eighteen, a citizen's son among the ephebes ("youths") of the deme ("district"), the last step before reaching the age of citizenship at twenty. If the *demotes* (members of the district) noticed that a boy had not reached the required age of eighteen, they pronounced negatively, and then "he returns among the children" (*palin eis paidas*; Aristotle, *Constitution of the Athenians* 42.1). As an age group, *paides* had an institutionally visible value in education and athletic competitions. Other words were used to differentiate *paides* according to age and developmental status. *Kouros*, for instance, indicated a pubescent boy; puberty, on the social and sexual plane, marked the real separation between the two ages of the *pais*.

Girls were also called *paides*, as well as *korai* ("girls"), *thugateres* ("daughters"), and *parthenoi* ("maidens," "virgins"), but there was no word for them that evokes what we would call adolescence. Rather, an ancient Greek girl entered into sexual maturity through marriage. Thus, to locate the development of her growth and "beauty" (i.e., her entry into the field of Aphrodite), we shall use the expression *pro tou gamou*; that is, the girl *pro tou gamou* was a *parthenos* "before marriage." The average age at which a girl would marry was fourteen to fifteen years old, and she essentially passed without transition from the toys of her childhood into the bed of her husband, a reality that leads modern readers to see her as a child. Thus, there was no "adolescence" in ancient Greece; we shall speak only of children, of girls and of boys.

The second clarification concerns the living environment of children. The breeding and education within the predominantly feminine environment of the *oikos* (household) was common to both sexes until approximately seven years of age, when their courses diverged. A boy would then go out to pursue an elementary education (to which few girls had access), and then he would proceed to the palaestra ("wrestling school," often associated with the gymnasium). Even though accompanied by an adult, he thus crossed from private space into a public one.

With the exception of the opportunities offered by certain cults (where she might find the company of girls of her age), an ancient Greek girl would stay at home, where the women of the *oikos* would teach her domestic skills, especially textile work. Until marriage, she would remain confined there and closely watched. The virginity of their daughters mattered quite a bit to Greek fathers. This was not only a question of honor, of course, but also one of marital exchanges: a girl's virginity appears to have been of great value in the eyes of future sons-in-law.

Boys, who would marry much later than girls, enjoyed relative freedom, and, whether on an intellectual or physical level, they received an education, bloomed among their age group, and met adults. One consequence of this difference between male and female trajectories is fundamental to understanding the sexuality of children: with the exception of brothers and sisters, boys and girls remained largely ignorant of one another, as they had few opportunities to meet in the same space. Amorous adventures between two partners of the same age were almost impossible for these *paides*.

A Taxonomy of Polymorphous Loves. To place the sexuality of children in the framework of loving and sexual exchanges in the polis amid the rich list of possible partners for the adult citizens, an epigram of Agathias Scolaticus (*Palatine Anthology* 302) is particularly helpful, directing our focus to the modern designation "polymorphous" loves. In this way, in the ancient Greek context a distinction must be made between the sexuality related to procreation—that is, sex for the purpose of having a legitimate child, which does not concern the children under discussion in this essay—and the sexuality of recreation, which directly relates. As a kind of love, recreational sex has no other motivation than the lust of at least one of the partners. Within this taxonomy, several possible combinations of age and sex between amorous and sexual partners are possible: partners of the same sex and age (male/female homosexuality), of the same sex and different ages (pederasty), and of different sexes (heterosexuality).

For the Greeks, to prefer relations with a person of a certain sex (and of a certain age) did not exclude the possibility of attraction to other sexes, whether over the course of one's life or simultaneously, nor to other age preferences. As Plutarch notes, "Where

there is beauty, I am ambidextrous" (*Eroticus* 767a). Further, male and female homosexuals were not, ipso facto, masculinized or feminized. A male engaging in homosexual activity would only be feminized if he was an adult who preferred sodomy, playing a passive role in sexual acts with other adults; only then did the vox populi say that he took the attitudes of women and adopted a feminine *skhēma* ("form"). However, a man's preference for sex with women granted him no certificate of virility. Rather, his physical strength, his courage on the battlefield, his beard, his marriage, his children, and his authority in the household were better measures of masculinity. Thus, ancient Greek sexual and gender orientation involved far more than one's sexual partners and behaviors.

In Greek documents, a more or less tacit hierarchy for such matchings can be derived: for example, the love of women for men is less good (or beautiful) than that of men for children. This hierarchy continues: regarding homosexuality, for example, it is better to be the penetrator and not the penetrated; even better are masculine relations between an adult and a child in codified roles and positions—which is, in fact, the dominant preferred erotic model. These lines, attributed to Solon, encapsulate this point: the definition of the "lover" is "one who falls in love with a sweet young boy in his prime, desiring supple flanks and sweet mouth" (Plutarch, *Eroticus* 751c). This hierarchy of desire also carried political weight, since slaves, freedmen, and male prostitutes were forbidden to make love with free boys as male Greek citizens could.

Within this framework prostitution played an important role, primarily since, for elites, it was with prostitutes that boys exited childhood and were initiated into heterosexual relations, and also because children were among the slaves of both sexes used as prostitutes. While in later discourses there was a certain moral condemnation attached to prostitution, the Greek polis did not condemn the practice.

"The Flower of Lovely Youth": The Seduction of Boys. Having clarified terminology and sketched a taxonomy, it is possible to outline the sexual development of the son of a citizen (unfortunately, for the much more numerous noncitizens, the evidence is too scarce to draw any conclusions). He began by being courted and loved, possibly by an adult, as soon as he appeared in public space; in this relation he played a passive role. His freedom of development also allowed him erotic games with classmates of his age. But, at the same time, a neighbor's slave or attractive daughter was forbidden to him. When he reached the age where adults turned away from him, should he have the means he could frequent male or female prostitutes and courtesans. His youth was his "time of the flower," his aesthetic peak, which, as with girls, was not expressed by an arithmetical age but by a botanical image. When, then, did a boy bloom?

The Greeks divided life into *hebdomades*, periods of seven years to which they attached specific qualities: the first and the second went from birth to puberty, the time of childhood. The third began with the appearance of the first beard on the face, and was the physical age that qualified the boy as looking adult-like: his beauty, his *charis* ("grace"), and his power of seduction varied according to the evolution of his body, particularly the action of his hormones. An adult ruminating on the looks of male children expresses clearly this "erotogenic" evolution of a child's body:

> "Twelve years, a lovely age, which enchants me! But the thirteen-year-old has many more attractions! With twice seven years you have one of Love's most exquisite flowers. Still more of a charmer is the one completing his third lustrum. Sixteen years, the year of the gods! Seventeen is not for me, reserved for Zeus' hunting ground! If one falls for an older boy, it is no longer a game for children, it is 'look for your like'" (Strato of Sardis, in *Palatine Anthology*, 12.4).

The Greeks found in Homer the same sensitivity to the body of the child: "Achilles surpassed in beauty not only Patroclus but also all other heroes taken together; he still had no beard on the chin, and consequently he was the youngest, as says Homer" (Plato, *Symposium* 180a).

For adult aesthetes and lovers of the childish body, puberty (*hēbē*) was of especial importance, for in their eyes the supreme beauty of childhood lay in the juvenile passage. The age of radiant boyish beauty was one of suspended time, an intermediate period when secondary sexual characteristics are still developing, where hair blooms on the pubis and cheeks; this is "the time of their flowering." Obviously it does not last, for as soon as the pilosity spreads, as soon as the face of the *pais* passes from soft downiness into a prickly beard, and as soon as a caress on the leg collides with the "thatch," his beauty is dealt a sacred blow, as indicated in this epigram attributed to Strato: "Why are you covered down to your ankles, Menippos, you who used to tuck your tunic up to your tights! Head lowered, you hastened past me, without so much as a word; why? I know what you are hiding from me: they have come, those things I was talking about!" (*Palatine Anthology* 12.176). Without denying the beauty of other ages for both sexes, the Greeks more than other ancient cultures equated youth with beauty, which makes the youthful body's evanescence all the more appealing and sensuous. We attribute to Socrates this aphorism: beauty is "short-term tyranny" (Diogenes Laertius 5.19). The Greek *skhēma* of the body centered on this fundamental relation to pilosity: what mattered was soft, smooth, delicate skin, which the poets praise over and over again.

Pederastic Relationships. The accepted, valued form of Greek pederasty consists of a connection between a *pais*—who played the role of *eromenos* (passive form of *eraō*, to love) and who also was the beloved, the one who was requested, but who could also seduce—and an adult, the *erastes* (active form of the same verb), the lover, who pursued the *eromenos* with diligence. This privileged relationship was more or less long-lasting and visible in public places; we can speak as much about loyalty as about multiple partners. Such relationships were part of the framework of social practices, and thus obeyed rules that betray a common set of values. This framework enabled a father to be proud of seeing his son courted by adults; he prided himself on the rows of elected lovers. The strategies of seduction and their consequences for both sides are not unusual (looks, modesty, desire, jealousy, sadness, enjoyment, and so on).

When a mature man succumbed to the not-always-innocent seduction of a *pais*, sexual desire could show itself. Of course, nothing forbids us from thinking, with good reason, that chaste pederastic relations existed and lasted, but this is not the most obvious conclusion from the ancient evidence. Of the numerous extant visual representations of pederastic relationships, most of the time the lovers are depicted face-to-face, embracing; their difference in size obliges the adult to fold his knees and the child to raise his head toward him. Besides other touches and caresses, the partners practice intercrural coitus (between the thighs), the adult introducing his penis into the narrow space left free by the *pais*, who squeezes his thighs together. This form of copulation is characteristic of the difference in age of the partners. On rarer paintings representing copulation between boys of the same age, anal penetration is shown, which is also consistent with expressions used in graffiti related to male sexual behavior.

Girls and Sexuality. Regarding the sexuality of children, there are two main reasons why boys receive more attention than girls. First, there is vastly more ancient evidence regarding boys. Second, the Greeks valued male pederastic relationship as an erotic model, even to the point that it exercised an influence on the heterosexual marriage bed. Greek wives in particular seem to have been dependent on what for the most part eluded them: the love between a man and a child of the same sex.

It is extremely difficult to reconstruct the sexuality of ancient Greek girls, for no direct evidence of their voices survives. Surviving records were written by men and represent their concerns—and these sources say practically nothing. A word sometimes escapes a heroine of theatre, which enables a guess as to what she knows about adult heterosexuality: "She will need to be a prophetess to discover, unless she has learned at home how to act correctly with her bedfellow" (Euripides, *Medea* 238–240). Females would witness sexuality in their living environment: in the *oikos*, there are sisters and brothers, parents, the nursemaid, the tutor, and many sorts of slaves, all of different ages and roles; there are marriages and births following one another—many events and people with diverse sexualities. Yet we have no tangible testimony on these realities, so it is necessary to turn our attention away from the *oikos* toward other possible sources.

Studies since the late twentieth century have indicated that the sexuality of ancient girls may not be as inaccessible as was once thought. For a fraction of the Greek world, a part of the veil has been lifted due to the translation of homoerotic links contained in some ritual poetry of the archaic period. Calame's study (Calame, 1997) of a *partheneion* of the poet Alcman performed by girls' choirs in preclassical Sparta highlights its homoerotic feminine contents and restores the frame of the exchanges between the choir girls and the adult who manages them (*chorege*). In this text a choir of virgins sings of the beauty of their adult *chorege*—of her hair, voice, and skill at running. It is obvious that, in this simultaneously educational and religious environment, the girls are singing about being in love with their teacher. More still than these exceptional qualities of their choir leader, these girls sing with "the voice of an owl" (because they cannot sing as well as she sings), and for those who have not reached this "beauty," the body of the *chorege*, her maturity, and her appearance are those to which they aspire.

Here there is a parallel between the boys and girls, with key differences: while the girls love, the boys are beloved; while every boy is beautiful (*ho pais kalos*) and the others compete with him, the *chorege* concentrates the looks of all on her; it is she who is beautiful and who seduces. There are resemblances as well, particularly the educational, even initiatory, character of their relations, especially the difference in ages, so that the adult functions for the young person as a parent, or at least a guardian or teacher, implying that the relationship also plays an educational role for the child. We can conclude from this that in the absence of relationships with *paides* of their age, the adults of both sexes played an initiatory role with the children.

Marriage in Light of Children and Sexuality. We find this same initiatory aspect with marriage. Spouses can love one another, of course, but in ancient Greece, there was no marriage for love (which is, moreover, a rather recent rationale). While many men did not have much taste for marriage, there were reasons to get married: interest, ambition, to do a service, to establish a bond with another family through a wedding, and, especially, to have legitimate children, because only children produced through marriage—especially boys—were poised to inherit and to succeed the father in citizen's rights and duties.

For a man, to get married was at the same time to establish a new *oikos*, different from that of his father, autonomous and viable, as well as to acquire economic independence. These characteristics partially account for the prevailing custom about the age of the husband at marriage, which is mostly thirty years or more. At this time of his life, the one whom he marries will be far from being his contemporary, because the age gap between them can be as much as fifteen to twenty years. Such appears the confrontation that provokes marriage: between a child who has just left the toys of childhood and an accomplished man (Greek *teleios* "perfect"); between two bodies, one in the fullness of strength, sculpted by athletic exercises, and the other still immature; between two sexualities, one only evanescent and the other already polymorphic. We should not be surprised by the words of the heroines of theatre expressing the shock of this new cohabitation: "Children … the life we live in our father's home was the sweetest," says a heroine of Sophocles (*Tereus*, frag. 583). Similarly, we read of a "real" person speaking about his new wife: "When she got acquainted with me, and had been sufficiently tamed to converse … I was able to begin her education" (Xenophon, *Oeconomicus* 7.10). The child was paralyzed. How long had she remained mute?

In such a context, the golden rule of a girl's conduct was and would have to remain that of *sōphrosynē*, self-control and moderation, a virtue required also of boys, but to which were added silence and chastity. A girl kept silent and did not ask questions. The same bride who confided to her husband that everything depended on him would have been told by her mother that her "business is to be good." To be good is to live in permanent *sōphrosynē* but with the additional sudden responsibility for the internal functioning of the *oikos*.

The desire of the Greek male for this young fragile nymph, still partially a child, with a partly androgynous body, may seem strange to us. But it becomes more understandable when we consider the Greek preference for the youthful body. Her features mirror those of pederastic eroticism, linking the aesthetic and erotogenous qualities of the pubescent of either sex.

[*See also* Children, *subentries on* New Testament *and* Roman World; Family Structures, *subentry* Greek World; Marriage and Divorce, *subentry* Greek World; Same-Sex Relations, *subentry* Greek World; *and* Sexuality.]

BIBLIOGRAPHY

Boehringer, Sandra. *L'homosexualité féminine dans l'Antiquité grecque et romaine*. Paris: Les Belles Lettres, 2007.

Boehringer, Sandra. "Female Homoerotism." In *A Companion to Greek and Roman Sexualities*, edited by Thomas K. Hubbard, pp. 150–163. Blackwell Companions to the Ancient World 100. Boston: Blackwell, 2014.

Brulé, Pierre. *Women of Ancient Greece*. Translated by Antonia Nevill. Edinburgh: Edinburgh University Press, 2003.

Calame, Claude. *Choruses of Young Women in Ancient Greece: Their Morphology, Religious Role, and Social Function*. Translated by Derek Collins and Janice Orion. Lanham, Md.: Rowman & Littlefield, 1997.

Calame, Claude. *The Poetics of Eros in Ancient Greece*. Translated by Janet Lloyd. Princeton, N.J.: Princeton University Press, 1999.

Cantarella, Eva. *Bisexuality in the Ancient World*. Translated by Cormac Ó Cuilleanáin. New Haven, Conn.: Yale University Press, 1992.

Dover, K. J. *Greek Homosexuality*. London: Duckworth, 1978.

Foucault, Michel. *The History of Sexuality*. Vol. 2, *The Use of Pleasure*. Translated by Robert Hurley. New York: Random House, 1982.

Golden, Mark. *Children and Childhood in Classical Athens*. Baltimore: Johns Hopkins University Press, 1990.

Halperin, David M. *One Hundred Years of Homosexuality, and Other Essays on Greek Love*. New Ancient World. New York: Routledge, 1990.

Halperin, David M., John J. Winkler, and Froma I. Zeitlin, eds. *Before Sexuality: The Construction of the Erotic Experience in the Ancient World*. Princeton, N.J.: Princeton University Press, 1990

Pomeroy, Sarah B. *Families in Classical and Hellenistic Greece: Representations and Realities*. New York: Oxford University Press, 1997.

Sissa, Giulia. *Greek Virginity*. Translated by Arthur Gold-hammer. Cambridge, Mass.: Harvard University Press, 1986.

Winkler, John J. *The Constraints of Desire: The Anthropology of Sex and Gender in Ancient Greece*. New Ancient World. New York: Routledge, 1990.

Pierre Brulé

Roman World

When we experience people or cultures as utterly strange to us, it is most often attitudes toward the body or sexuality that cause this feeling of alienation or strangeness. Recently, scholars versed in both the ancient and the biblical tradition have pointed to the fact that in striving for self-fashioning early Christians indeed set themselves apart from their contemporaries by the rejection of same sex relations (Horn and Martens, 2009, pp. 225–232; Martens, 2009). In the Greco-Roman tradition, most of such relationships were between a somewhat older adult male and an adolescent boy. Or, to put it in another way: pagans were boy-lovers (the terms "pederasts/pedophiles" come to the mind), good Christians were not.

This article focuses on the pagan Roman world. In order to understand ancient attitudes toward children and sexuality, one must be very clear about the terms and definitions we are willing to use. Contrary to what one would like to believe, our present-day concepts of the matter are all but clear-cut. Assessing the ancient vocabulary on childhood, youth, and puberty is likewise a difficult matter, requiring methodological soundness. And in the discussion, a clear distinction needs to be made between boys and girls.

Pederasty/Pedophilia: What's in a Name? The term "pedophilia" is used quite often these days, especially in the popular media. However, the term is a psychiatric one. According to the *Diagnostic and Statistical Manual of Mental Disorders* (DSMV V, 2013), pedophilia is a form of paraphilia in which a person either has acted on intense sexual urges toward prepubescent children, or experiences recurrent sexual urges toward and fantasies about such children that cause distress or interpersonal difficulty. It is added that such urges should be felt in a period of at least six months, that the pedophile is at least sixteen years of age and five years older than the child, and that the child involved is generally age thirteen or younger (the biological aspect of prepubescence being the important marker) (Blanchard, 2010, on DSM IV). Pederasty, on the other hand, is not a psychiatric term. Anthropologists consider it an example of male age-structured homosexuality: it appears as typical of a passing stage in which the adolescent is the beloved of an older male mentor. The relationship comes to an end when the young man reaches a certain developmental threshold. As such, it is accepted as authentic in many cultures throughout the world and needs to be distinguished sharply from pedophilia (but see Montgomery, 2007, for an account on the twentieth century).

Such subtle distinctions are not made in the present-day legal discourse, which is more concerned with the issue of age of consent. In law enforcement, the term "pedophile" is used for those convicted of sexual abuse of a minor, including both prepubescent children and pubescent or postpubescent adolescents under the age of consent. In modern society a difference of only a few days may make the difference between penal sexual acts and a legally permitted relationship. In the legal systems of various countries, including those in Europe, however, there is no general agreement about this exact age of consent. Consequences of this should not be underestimated. When Cardinal Tarcisio Bertone (1934) stated that most of the child abuse cases in the Roman Catholic church were closely linked with homosexuality, he created quite a stir in the gay movement. When he referred to relationships with pubescent boys just under the legal (canonical) age of eighteen, he was indeed correct; but much of the public indignation was understandable, since people tended to confuse with the medical-psychiatric use of the term "pedophilia," not to mention yet another meaning of it (Laes, 2012, p. 104).

Indeed, there is also the popular discourse on pedophilia, which connects it to child molesting as the ultimate vice and thus evil. Thus, "the monster and the wise man," referred to in the title of Vattuone's book, are the odious figures of the modern pedophile and the great Athenian legislator Solon. Both loved boys, but no one in antiquity ever considered the wise man Solon to be a monster. The term "pedophile" developed into a label for an amalgam of persons, ranging from those favoring deeply affective relationships with adolescents to pederasts, child molesters, and even serial killers. In a way, one can state that child abuse became a prime issue only in the second half of the twentieth century. The ever increasing numbers of instances and the growing awareness of the problem in the public opinion may be partly connected with the medical attention that was brought to the fore by American pediatricians in 1961 and 1962 (Hacking, 1999, pp. 136–138).

Applying Our Concepts to Ancient Categories. Applying the somewhat confused present-day concepts to ancient categories is even more problematic.

First, the ancients did not have a concept of sexual orientation. In fact, they even lacked a proper term to denote "sexuality." What people did in bed was much more linked with preferences as food, drinking, and other bodily pleasures; it never was an essential of a person's identity (Skinner, 2005; Golden and Toohey, 2010).

Second, there was no (developmental) psychology as a separate branch of science, and third, the Roman legal definitions of adulthood were not linked that closely to the matter of age as they are today (Laes, 2011, pp. 278–280). It is safe to assume that Roman boys reached the stage of adulthood at about age fifteen, with the donning of the *toga virilis* for those belonging to the upper classes. However, this donning was not exclusively linked to age: "He [Vergil] was right to link the state of the body with the years, for in law too, we define the notion of adulthood through both aspects" (Serv. *Buc.* 8.40). It was only in the sixth century C.E., under Justinian, that the physical examination of boys came to be seen as inappropriate, and that the age of adulthood was fixed at fourteen (*Cod. Iust.* 5.6.30). Roman law provided for protection of young people, mainly in business transactions, where a tutor was needed

up to age twenty-five (*Inst. Iust.* 1.23.pr.2). Roman law then took into account a certain concept of informed consent: it distinguished between *infantes* and those young people who were near to puberty (*pubertati proximi*) and thus already responsible for their deeds (e.g., Gaius *Inst.* 3.208). None of such regulations, however, refers to informed consent in sexual relationships. Technically, boys could marry when reaching adulthood, though in practice the age of first marriage was in the mid-twenties, possibly somewhat younger for aristocrats (Scheidel, 2007). When Roman law provided for protection against sexual harassment, the social status of the boy was taken into account, not the age. For girls, the age of twelve was set as a legal marker for becoming *viripotens* or marriageable (*Dig.* 23.1.9; Ulpian and 23.2.4; Pomponius); the actual marriage age for girls was in the late teens for first marriage (Scheidel, 2007).

Fourth, the interpretation of pedophilia as a vile and monstrous deed, implying child abuse and molestation, turns up only in late ancient vocabulary. The term *paidophthoros* ("child molester") appears for the first time in *Testamentum Levi* 17:11, a text generally dated to the second century B.C.E., the Hebrew Vorlage of which is dated to the period ca. 225–175 B.C.E. Both *ktènophthoros* ("committer of bestiality") and *paidophthoros* are now interpreted as second or early third C.E. Christian interpolations in the *T. Levi*. In such cases, self-fashioning of the new religion against pagan practices was at stake, not the psychology of the victim (Martens, 2009, pp. 237–243).

The Dossier of Boys. Although some scholars have tried to prove the opposite, the evidence for boy love in the Roman Empire is massive (Laes, 2011, pp. 247–252, 262–268). The sources go from objects of art, over marriage contracts to satire/epigram, and all kinds of cursory remarks in almost any literary genre. The omnipresence of slaves in society might well have contributed to the phenomenon. One in ten families in the Roman Empire owned slaves, and possibly twice that number in towns. Horace persuades his readers rather not to burst with sexual tension but to make use of the available slave boy or girl (*Serm.* 1.2.116–119). In Artemidorus's dream book, slaves male and female play the part that masturbation plays in many cultures (*On.* 1.78). Ages are seldom mentioned, with the famous exception of charming and sexually enticing boys of age twelve in epigrams of the Anthologia Palatina (*AP* 12.4 and 12.205). Age twenty is once mentioned as an upper threshold (Ps.-Lucian, *Am.* 26): the evidence mentioned points to the moment of having the first full-grown beard as a marker for the end of pederastic relations. In the Roman Empire, the *depositio barbae*, the offering of the first beard, usually took place at around age twenty (Laes, 2011, pp. 267–268). If we believe Philo of Alexandria, young male gentiles after their fourteenth year engaged in completely shameless sexual acts with whores and other women who made a profit with their bodies (Philo, *Ios.* 43).

True, the Roman legal and moral code set quite severe boundaries, stressing the fact that every single freeborn boy with Roman citizenship was sexually off-limits (Laes, 2011, pp. 241–246). The *Sentences of Paul* explicitly mention the *puer praetextatus*, a boy up to about age fifteen, as the object of protection. The punishment envisioned by this text are severe and clearly late classical, if not postclassical: capital punishment or deportation (*PS* 5.4.1, 4 and 14). Most of the evidence suggests that whatever the law commanded, sex with freeborn boys still went on. One wonders whether the vast majority of the lower-class people ever resorted to law to resolve their cases. The law was rather used ad hoc, often in political circumstances when one tried to blame an opponent. Before the Justinian reforms, the state was never interested in nor in the possibility to prosecute "sexual offenders" (Harper, 2013, pp. 39, 221).

The Dossier of Girls. It is somewhat remarkable that most of the evidence on the issue focuses on the problem of man–boy relationships, while girls were and could undoubtedly be used for sexual purposes too. The obvious reason for girls being less mentioned is the male-oriented focus of the ancient sources. Slave girls and those belonging to the lower classes were probably subject to the same regime as boys; here we may suspect early sexual initiation as

frequent and unproblematic, that is in the eyes of the male authors of the texts that have come down to us (McKeown, 2007).

For the higher classes, virginity at the moment of marriage and gradual introduction into the world of sexuality by advice from other women were considered important (Lentano, 1996). According to Epictetus, women are considered "ladies" (*kyriai*) by men when they reach age fourteen. "Therefore, when they see that there is nothing else for them besides sharing a bed with men, they start to adorn themselves and in this they place all their hopes" (Epict. *Ench.* 40). One will notice the strongly sexual connotation of this description. The legal evidence sets age twelve as a liminal age for contracting a marriage, and the same age applied for "openly" (*palam*) having a concubine (*Dig.* 25.7.1.4; Ulpian). While there are indeed laws threatening with severe punishment "those who corrupt virgins not yet ready for sexual activity" (*nondum viripotentes virgines*) (*Dig.* 48.19.38.3; Paulus), there is also a large bulk of evidence that Roman fathers did not necessarily disapprove of marriage of girls in their early teens, even before the age of twelve. Only medical doctors seem to have cautiously objected to the practice of very early marriage, pointing to the dangers for the girl's health and the risks of early adolescent childbearing; in general they did not disapprove of sexual activity in marriage for girls after the onset of puberty (Caldwell, 2013, pp. 112–149). Roman jurists indeed discussed the problem of underage cohabitation (*Dig.* 23.1.9; Ulpian; Caldwell, 2013, p. 161), and the emperor Augustus by law prevented certain men from betrothing themselves to infant girls and thus enjoying the privileges of married men while not fulfilling the obligations (Dio Cassius 54.16.7). But to take such cases to cite most instances of marriage with early teenage girls as a kind of secured arrest, with the husband patiently awaiting the maturing of his young bride, is to dismiss the large bulk of explicit evidence on the first wedding night. To the ancients, this first night was indeed a battlefield of sex, aggression, and machismo (Caldwell, 2013, pp. 223–238).

According to Plutarch in his *Advice to the Bride and Groom*, the husband who gives up after the first disagreements that are so typical of girls is short-sighted; "unripe girls" (the fruit metaphor often occurs) who show distaste for the first experience are like people who endure the sting of the bee but allow the honeycomb to go (*Coni. Praec.* 138.2). The emphasis on coercion to sexual activity as it emerges from Ausonius's *Cento Nuptialis* is distasteful to modern sensibilities; but the author comments "for this is a story of wedding, and like it or not, the ritual does not happen any other way" (*Cent. Nupt.* 20). An epigram tells how a young bride was torn apart by watchdogs when she fled the house during her wedding night, afraid of first sexual intercourse. The poem unabashedly states that this fear is common with young girls: one should not flee from one danger to encounter another (*AP* 9.245).

Continuity or Change in Late Antiquity and the Early Middle Ages? The concepts and practices concerning children and sexuality turn out to be crucial for a better understanding of ancient society at large. This was a world where chronological age never took the major role it takes in present-day Western society—not in matters of consent to or involvement in sexual acts but also not in education or in a dossier as child labor (*Art. On.* 1.78 is a rare exception pointing at age ten as the age at which a child was perceived to be a sexual being). This was also a world that recognized the possible sexual attraction of children but never made it into an issue in its own right: while a boy age twelve was definitely still a child in Roman perception, no one would classify a twenty-year-old as such. Finally, this was a world where childhood was essentially a social rather than a psychological category. A Roman citizen twelve-year-old was protected by his medal of childhood, the *bulla*, but his age-peer slave, freed slave, or even freeborn citizen of lower status was subject to sexual advances. This dichotomy was based purely on social grounds: a future aristocratic leader should not be degraded by sexual submission in earlier stages of life.

"Where has Eros gone to?" In the sixth century C.E., the poet Agathias expresses his grief about the changed sexual mores of his time: gone were the days of adultery, gone was the love for boys (*Anthologia Graeca* 5.302). By then, the new religion of Christi-

anity had definitely changed the ancient world. To early Christians, same-sex relations (not just pederastic) and prostitution had become symbols of a culture to be fought against. In the second century, but most strongly in the fourth century, the new religion focused on free will. Jerome most saliently denounced the paradox of pagan sexual practice: they denounce *adulterium* and *stuprum* when Roman citizens are concerned, but do whatever they wish in brothels and with slave girls. In other words: pagans act as if social status and not sexual desire was the core to deciding whether something is wrong (*Ep.* 77.3). The Justinian law of 535 was "the most sweeping action yet undertaken by the Roman state" (Harper, 2013, p. 269): it radically forbade all forms of pimping, prostitution, or brothel keeping (*Nov.* 14). This was a regime performing moral crusades, using same-sex relations and pederasty to blame and prosecute political opponents, including bishops (Proc. *Anec.* 1134–36). And in the west of the Roman Empire, a Visigothic law of 533–534 prohibited masters from having sex with their slave girls; again without precedent in Roman legislation (Cass. *Var.* 9.18; *LV* 3.4.17).

The somewhat vague concept of *porneia* had become a fumigation bomb (Harper, 2013, p. 13), which was to poison the whole zone of ancient sexuality (see Rom 1:26–32 for severe condemnation of sexual offenders, including death). The result was a profoundly changed world, in which no first-century Roman would have recognized himself. The transformation was complete. And indeed, it was mostly about sex.

[*See also* Marriage and Divorce, *subentry* Roman World; Race, Class, and Ethnicity, *subentry* Roman World; *and* Same-Sex Relations, *subentry* Roman World.]

BIBLIOGRAPHY

Blanchard, R. "The DSM Diagnostic Criteria for Pedophilia." *Archives of Sexual Behavior* 39, no. 2 (2010): 304–316.

Caldwell, L. *Scripted Lives: Girls' Coming of Age in the Early Roman Empire.* Cambridge, U.K.: Cambridge University Press, forthcoming.

Golden, M., and P. Toohey, eds. *A Cultural History of Sexuality in the Classical World.* Oxford: Berg, 2010.

Hacking, I. "Kind-Making: the Case of Child Abuse." In *The Social Construction of What?*, edited by I. Hacking, pp. 125–162. Cambridge, Mass., and London: Harvard University Press, 1999.

Harper, K. *From Shame to Sin. The Christian Transformation of Sexual Morality in Late Antiquity.* Cambridge, Mass., and London: Harvard University Press, 2013.

Horn, C. B., and J. W. Martens. *"Let the Little Children Come to Me": Childhood and Children in Early Christianity.* Washington, D.C.: Catholic University of America Press, 2009.

Laes, C. "When Classicists Need to Speak Up: Antiquity and Present-Day Paedophilia–Pederasty." In *Aeternitas antiquitatis: Proceedings of the Symposium Held in Skopje, August 28 as Part of the 2009 Annual Conference of EuroClassica*, edited by Valerij Sofronievski, pp. 33–53. Skopje, Macedonia: ACPh Antika, 2010.

Laes, C. *Children in the Roman Empire: Outsiders Within.* Cambridge, U.K.: Cambridge University Press, 2011.

Laes, C. "Spiegel of Masker? De antieken en pedofilie." In *Oud maar niet out: Denken en doen met de oudheid vandaag*, edited by L. Van Hoof and P. Van Nuffelen, pp. 91–106. Leuven, Belgium: Peeters, 2012.

Lentano, M. "Noscere amoris iter": L'iniziazione alla vita sessuale nella cultura romana." *Euphrosyne* 24 (1996): 271–282.

Martens, J. W. "'Do Not Sexually Abuse Children': The Language of Early Christian Sexual Ethics." In *Children in Late Ancient Christianity*, edited by C. B. Horn and R. B. Phenix, 227–254. Tübingen, Germany: Mohr Siebeck, 2009.

McKeown, N. "Had They No Shame? Martial, Statius and Roman Sexual Attitudes towards Slave Children." In *Children, Childhood, and Society*, edited by S. Crawford and G. Shepherd, pp. 57–62. Oxford: Archaeopress, 2007.

Montgomery, H. "Child Sexual Abuse. An Anthropological Perspective." In *Children and Sexuality: From the Greeks to the Great War*, edited by G. Rousseau, pp. 319–347. Basingstoke, U.K. Palgrave Macmillan, 2007.

Scheidel, W. "Roman Funerary Commemoration and the Age of First Marriage." *Classical Philology* 102 (2007): 389–402.

Skinner, M. *Sexuality in Greek and Roman Culture.* Malden, Mass.: Blackwell, 2005.

Vattuone, R. *Il mostro e il sapiente: Studi sull'erotica greca.* Bologna, Italy: Patron Editore, 2004.

Christian Laes

New Testament

The topic of children comprises a relatively new and burgeoning area in the study of the New Testament and early Christianity (Horn and Martens, 2009). As part of the rising profile of the "history of childhood," this field is often traced back to the groundbreaking and controversial work of Philippe Ariès, *Centuries of Childhood* (1962), which is based on the notion that it was not until the modern era that most adults came to recognize childhood as a distinct phase of life. Experts in premodern eras have largely resisted this hypothesis. But many, in some way or other, have at least given a nod to Ariès by stressing the profound differences between premodern and modern conceptions of childhood. Scholars of the New Testament and early Christianity have both benefitted from and contributed to the critical engagement with the Ariès thesis, as the work of Bakke (2005), for example, indicates.

Studies on childhood have dedicated space to what ancient Christian sources disclose about the nature of children, education, work, play, and worship. Meanwhile, questions related to sexuality, such as ancient notions of puberty and sexual development, have received scant attention. An exception is the subject of sexual abuse of children. More than one treatment describes the denunciation of sexual abuse in extracanonical Christian writings of the second and third centuries C.E. If the sexual abuse of children is what comes first to mind, little wonder that the topic of children and sexuality has not attracted more interest from scholars of the New Testament, as there is hardly a topic more disquieting or more freighted with modern-day fears. The addition of the term "New Testament" may only intensify the unease of today's readers. The combination will remind many of the numerous contemporary cases of Christian clergy preying on children across North America and western Europe. Moreover, while patristic texts may join together to declare a reassuring message of disapproval of adult-child sexual activity, scholars of the New Testament will look in vain for the staunch prohibitions that surface in later Christian literature. A clear statement of outrage is absent from the New Testament, and only a handful of passages have ever been taken to imply opposition to adult–child sex.

What does the New Testament say about children and sexuality? There may be more to the question than whether or not New Testament writers take a stand against the sexual abuse of children. In what follows I will first discuss the methodological issues of approaching the topic of children and sexuality in the ancient context. The article will then turn to specific topics in the study of the New Testament. What does the New Testament say about adult-child sexual relations? Does the sexual use of slave children illuminate aspects of the New Testament? Does the New Testament imply a notion of presexual "innocence" in passages that encourage followers of Jesus to become like children? The investigation of children and sexuality in the New Testament faces serious challenges, including that of a small sample size. Yet the framework of children and sexuality may suggest new ways of thinking about the familiar texts of the New Testament.

Methodological Issues and the Ancient Context. The historical study of children has often been about "childhood" as a mental construct of adults. So it is for the study of children in antiquity. The voices of actual children are all but lost to us. There are some very rare exceptions: graffiti from schoolrooms in Pompeii and the second-century B.C.E. report of a girl's dream in the Temple of Serapis in Memphis, Egypt (*Urkunden der Ptolemäerzeit* 177, in Rowland-son, 1998, p. 102). Historians rely on sources that reflect childhood through the "mirror of adult actors," as Christian Laes (2011, p. 19) puts it. Occasionally, the mediation of adult preoccupations or filtering may strike the reader as minimal, as in Minucius Felix's poignant account of boys "skipping shells" along the seashore at Ostia (*Octavius* 3). At the other pole would be Augustine's prayerful and stylized recollection of childhood in Book 1 of the *Confessions*.

Relying exclusively on literary sources for the study of ancient childhood runs the risk of reinscribing the narrow outlook of elite authors. To broaden the view, classicists and historians have turned to the daily life of children under the Roman Empire.

The field of evidence for social history includes documentary sources such as papyri, inscriptions, and archaeological finds. Some have developed statistical models about demography and life expectancy based on ancient documentary evidence and cross-cultural comparisons. Even so, representing the experiences of actual children—slave and free, male and female—remains a matter of numerical estimates and broad contours. Moreover, as important as documentary evidence is for social historians, the perceptions of childhood as articulated in literary sources will continue to exert a strong influence over scholars who seek to comprehend the images and metaphors of childhood in the New Testament.

"Childhood" as a life stage is a meaningful notion in some ancient sources. Greek terminology that can be found scattered throughout the New Testament includes *brephos* ("baby, infant"), *paidion* ("little child"), *teknon* ("child"), and *neaniskos* ("youth"). In *On the Creation of the World* (106–107), the first-century C.E. Jewish author Philo of Alexandria outlines a set of phases in increments of seven years, a model that corresponds to similar paradigms of childhood in classical sources. Philo describes the development of the *pais* ("child") from *nēpios* ("infant"), which ends at the age of seven, to *hēbē* ("youth"), which ends at the age of fourteen. Historians warn that it is anachronistic to treat philosophical typologies as precursors to modern, psychological models about childhood development. Other sources suggest the harsh reality of adult calculations of the value of children in antiquity. The second-century C.E. physician Soranus sets out criteria for determining whether to keep or expose a newborn (*Gynecology* 2.79).

Establishing a bright line of demarcation between childhood and adulthood was no less problematic in antiquity than today. The best-known rites of passage may have affected only elite males in Rome (e.g., putting on the *toga virilis* during the festival of Liberalia). The onset of puberty in elite males, sometimes described as *meirakioumai* (or "becoming a youth"), was both celebrated and scrutinized. The second-century C.E. advice manuals of Galen and Soranus prescribe ways of diminishing the excessive wetness of children's bodies as they matured (Rousselle, 1988, pp. 58–62). The physicians instruct that the sexual appetites of young males should be regulated but not suppressed. Sperm, it was thought, achieved greatest vitality only after the age of twenty-one. The ideal age of marriage for men was the mid- to late twenties. Many females, on the other hand, may have been married prior to puberty, between the ages of twelve and fourteen.

That most readers today would view the marriage of prepubescent females as a form of child abuse indicates the gulf between ancient and modern views of gender and sexuality. The study of sexuality in the ancient world, like the study of childhood, focuses on ancient interpretations. The title of a highly influential collection of essays, *Before Sexuality* (Halperin, et al., 1990), captures such complexity. The essays suggest that the modern category of "sexuality"—which implies identity, orientation, and essence—may only distort our attempts to "listen" to what ancient sources say. Public discourse on sexuality today is propped up by forensic and scientific claims. Its prescriptive force is often concealed by the rhetoric of description. By contrast, historians of sexuality routinely note the prescriptive character of ancient "talk" about sexuality. Some of the most illuminating discussions are based on sources of the Roman era that are avowedly judgmental: the moral essays of Plutarch (e.g., *Dialogue on Love*); the invective of Roman poets such as Catullus; and the dream interpretation of Artemidorus.

Ancient sources about sex imply a scheme of penetration that supports a hierarchy in terms of status and gender. The penetrator, in the active role, was associated with power and strength; the penetrated, in the passive role, was associated with weakness and effeminacy. Both men and women, it was thought, could occupy either role, though conventional wisdom typically cast the adult male of higher status as the penetrator. Conformity to these protocols was counted as admirable; suspected deviation suffered ridicule. Idealized by Greek authors as the loving and honorable pairing of an adult male (*erastēs*) with a free youth (*erōmenos*) in his teenage years, pederasty conformed to the penetration grid. It was viewed positively in Greek sources well into the Roman era. While for many modern readers "pederasty" and "pedophilia" are synonyms, analysis of ancient literary sources and documentary evidence suggests that the admiration of pederasty was not understood to give cover to adult–child sex with male children younger than age twelve (see Dover, 1978).

Roman authors, on the author hand, largely rejected the classical Greek model of pederasty. This had little to do with the modern notion of "age of consent." Rather, it reflected anxiety about how a "passive" role might undermine the status of free male children. So too Roman scorn for Greek pederasty served to buttress the imperial claims of Rome over the Greek east. At the same time, Roman poets such as Statius express no reservations about sex with children, so long as they are *deliciae*, or "beloved slave boys."

Pedophilia and Pederasty. Is "pedophilia," the modern designation for a psychosexual pathology, a target of ancient Christian criticism? Many early Christian writings seem to employ a particular term for the sexual abuse of children: *paidophthoreō* (see, e.g., *Didache* 2:2, *Epistle of Barnabas* 19:4, and Clement of Alexandria, *Exhortation to the Greeks* 10.108.5). The term, which can also be found in *Testament of Levi* 17:10–11, may include pederasty but, according to some, was in fact designed to say something profoundly new, even "countercultural" (Martens, 2009, p. 231). Where *paiderasteō* and cognates refer to the "sexual love" of minors, *paidophthoreō* seems to suggest something else: the sexual corruption and destruction of children. Ancient Christian opposition to *paidophthoreō* may have taken its cue from Jewish sexual ethics, which rejected forms of sexual activity that were associated with pagan idolatry and not designed to lead to human reproduction.

Paidophthoreō and cognates do not occur in the New Testament. Is it nevertheless possible to see some passages in the New Testament as anticipating a "countercultural" stance against sex with children? In the Gospel of Mark, Jesus declares: "If any of you put a stumbling block [*skandalizō*] before one of these little ones [*mikros*] who believe in me, it would be better for you if a great millstone were hung around your neck and you were thrown into the sea" (9:42). Jesus goes on to urge followers to cut off hands and feet and pluck out an eye rather than be "scandalized" by these body parts and "thrown into hell" (Mark 9:43–48). A similar idea is found in the Sermon on the Mount (Matt 5:27–32). More than one scholar has noted a parallel in the Babylonian Talmud that connects the mutilation of body parts to sexual activity deemed questionable, including masturbation and sex with children (*b. Niddah 13b*). Even if one accepts what might be a dubious juxtaposition of the New Testament and the much later rabbinic literature, the warnings in the canonical Gospels about "stumbling blocks" are exasperatingly elliptical by comparison. "Little ones" in Mark 9:42 has sometimes been taken as referring to adult disciples and not children.

There is no question that ancient Jewish writings define the non-Jewish "other" as enthusiastic abusers of children. These sources typically use the vocabulary of pederasty (*paiderasteō* and cognates). The late-Antique *Sibylline Oracles* declare that Jews, unlike Phoenicians, Egyptians, Romans, and Greeks, do not practice pederasty (3.595–600; cf. 3:185–187). Philo likewise condemns pederasty (*Special Laws* 3.37–42; *Contemplative Life* 48–62).

The contrast with wider ancient society is stark. It is clear that for many Greek and Roman authors pederasty, under certain conditions, was acceptable under ancient "protocols" of penetration. The conventional nature of pederasty is illustrated by sources throughout the Roman period. The second-century C.E. Greek romance by Achilles Tatius, *Leukippe and Clitophon*, includes a lengthy debate between two male characters over the merits of female and pederastic love (2.35–38). Plutarch, in the *Dialogue of Love*, seems to sympathize with proponents of male–female sex but still allows for the vigorous defense of the alternative.

Where do the authors of the New Testament stand in this field of ancient discourse on adult–child sexual activity? Following a path struck by John Boswell's important study, *Christianity, Social Tolerance, and Homosexuality* (1980), some New Testament schol-

ars have argued that pederasty was the principal target of Paul's condemnation of sex between men (Scroggs, 1983). There are important lexical and conceptual problems with this view (see Martin, 2006, pp. 37–50). The key texts are Romans 1:25–27, 1 Corinthians 6:9, and 1 Timothy 1:10. Debate over precisely what Paul has in mind has revolved around the terms *arsenokoitēs* and *malakos*, which are employed in 1 Corinthians 6:9 and 1 Timothy 1:10. (*Arsenokoitēs* is found nowhere else in the New Testament.) Both are notoriously difficult to translate. *Arsenokoitēs* has been glossed in a rather sweeping and generic fashion, as "a man who has sex with men." But elsewhere the term occurs in lists concerned with economic transgressions such as theft (*Sybilline Oracles* 2.70–72; *Acts John* 36), leading some to wonder if Paul directs his ire at a specific kind of exploitation such as prostitution. Commentary on *malakos* (or "softness") in Pauline literature has been shaped by prejudice and stereotypes of homosexual "effeminacy." Some have pointed out that ancient authors commonly assumed that *malakos* in males was the result of excessive male-female intercourse (see, e.g., Chariton, *Charaeas and Callirhoe* 1.4).

Does either passage imply that pederasty is the problem? For the present discussion, the most striking thing about 1 Corinthians 6:9–11 and 1 Timothy 1:10–11 is that Paul does not employ the standard vocabulary of pederasty. *Paideresteō* and cognates are not present. Whatever the reasons behind Paul's seeming objection to same-sex intercourse, it is not evident that one of them was disgust at sexual relations between adults and children. Thus, a clear statement against either pederasty or what modern readers would regard now as pedophilia cannot be found in Pauline literature.

Slavery. Like pederasty, slavery is another distressing aspect of childhood in antiquity. Most modern histories of ancient childhood assume free children. We know very little about slave children. Slaves, no matter their age, were not unlike children in relation to free adult males: both were subject to corporal punishment. Many children in the slave system under the Roman Empire may have begun their lives as victims of exposure—only to be claimed by slave traders and fed into the maw of the slave economy. "House-born slaves" (*oikogeneis* or *vernae*) could be raised to perform sexually for the adult slave owners. "Beloved slave boys," or *deliciae*, were given specific hairstyles to advertise their status.

Slaves were routinely referred to using the terminology of childhood. *Pais* or "child" stands as a synonym for slave (*doulos*) in sources from the Roman period, including the writings of the New Testament. In Luke 7:7, the centurion asks Jesus for the healing of his "slave" (*pais*). Luke 7:10 concludes the pericope with the report that members of the centurion's household later found the "slave" (*doulos*) in good health (Luke 7:10; see too Luke 15:26; Matt 8:6, 8, 13). The term for "girl" (*paidiskē*) is used only in the context of slavery in the New Testament, as in the story of the fortune-telling girl in the book of Acts (16:6). The interchangeability of "child" and "slave" reflects not only the rhetoric of the "benevolent" slave owner but also the blurred lines of family life under Rome. The practice of slavery was absorbed comfortably into the institution of the family.

Pauline literature is shot through with references to slavery. Paul's letter to Philemon showcases the easy admixture of images of kinship and slavery. Some have suggested that Paul's casting of Onesimus as his *teknon* ("child," Phlm 10) disrupts Philemon's own claims as head of household and slave owner. One study has set the competing claims of Paul and Philemon to Onesimus against the backdrop of the conventional sexual use of slaves in the Roman world (Marchal, 2011). Paul's letter turns on a punning opposition between terms of usefulness and uselessness: Onesimus (which, like *chrēston*, means "useful"), who was formerly *achrēston* ("useless") to the slave owner Philemon, has become *euchrēston* ("useful") to the apostle (Phlm 11). The dialogue on love by the second-century C.E. Lucian of Samosata leaves little doubt that, within the context of slavery, sexual servitude was a primary connotation of Greek terms for "usefulness" (*Erōtes* 25, 27). Is it possible that Paul and Philemon wrangled over who had the stronger claim to the sexual use of Onesimus? The troubling implications of this interpretation are made more distressing for modern readers when we recall Paul's use of familial rhetoric, including "my child" (*teknon*), in this letter and elsewhere (e.g., Gal 4:19, 1 Thess 2:7, 11–12).

Innocence. Another area of discussion involves the identification of childhood with innocence in the scholarship of the New Testament. When Jesus instructs his followers to become like "a little child" (*paidion*; Mark 10:15; see too Matt 18:3, 19:14), what does the comparison to childhood mean? The theme of becoming like children can be found in closely related extracanonical Gospels (see, e.g., *Gos. Thom.* 22; *Gos. Eg.*, 2 Clem 12.2–6). Some have taken the comparison to childhood to refer to a presexual state (Bakke, 2005, pp. 104–105; Crossan, 1991, pp. 266–269.) A gesture to children is meant to evoke the absence of sexuality.

A caveat to this view is in order. Separating children and sexuality in the ancient context is not easily done. Adult sex with children was widely accepted in the Roman era, so long as certain conditions (e.g., slavery) were met. Greek tradition viewed pederasty as noble. Would the authors and audiences of the canonical Gospels have thought of childhood as a presexual stage of life? One should also bear in mind that Greek sources on pederasty assume both the sexual pleasure of the penetrator and the lack thereof in the penetrated (Halperin, 1990, p. 47). It may be the case that ancient Christian authors viewed children as lacking in the passions of adulthood. Such a perspective was not incongruous with the widespread expectation that at least some children would engage in sex with adults.

At least one text of the Roman era suggests that sexual activity between children was likewise part of ancient thinking. The third-century C.E. Greek romance of Longus, *Daphnis and Chloe*, is tale of exploration and discovery between two young lovers. The unfolding of the sexual "education" of the pair—which involves pain as well as pleasure—is ambiguous when it comes to the protocols of penetration. Should sex be reduced to penetrative acts of intercourse? Does the sexual experimentation of childhood call into question the order of things? Does it undermine the claims of a society based on a dichotomy of activity and passivity? *Daphnis and Chloe* suggests that some pagan authors used the nonpenetrative sexuality of children as a space to examine the tension between the authority of tradition and playful innovation. Perhaps references to becoming like children in the New Testament are doing the same.

Assessment. Before the advent of the history of childhood, a reader may have expected the topic of children and sexuality in the New Testament to refer chiefly to what New Testament writings have to say about human reproduction. Does the New Testament teach readers to procreate, or does it instead teach something else, such as sexual renunciation? Paul seems to resist a "procreationist" ideology, urging "self-control" and allowing for marital sex only if the alternative is "to be aflame with passion" (1 Cor 7:7). The Pastoral Epistles construct an ideal of womanhood that promotes sexual intercourse and childbirth (1 Tim 2:14–15).

Scholarship will likely continue to focus on the place of the New Testament in the history of adult sexuality. Yet if scholars wish to understand images and metaphors of childhood in the New Testament, they will have to reckon with the banality of adult–child sexual activity under the Roman Empire. Childhood, slavery, and sexuality were overlapping domains for authors under the Roman era. That this was also the case for the writers of the New Testament is both a plausible and sobering suggestion.

[*See also* Children, *subentries on* Early Church and Roman World; Legal Status, *subentries on* New Testament and Roman World; *and* Sexual Violence, *subentries on* New Testament and Roman World.]

BIBLIOGRAPHY

Ariès, Philippe. *Centuries of Childhood: A Social History of Family Life.* Translated by Robert Baldick. New York: Vintage, 1962.

Bakke, O. M. *When Children Became People: The Birth of Childhood in Early Christianity.* Translated by Brian McNeil. Minneapolis: Fortress, 2005.

Boswell, John. *Christianity, Social Tolerance, and Homosexuality: Gay People in Western Europe from the Beginning of the Christian Era to the Fourteenth Century.* Chicago: University of Chicago Press, 1980.

Crossan, John Dominic. *The Historical Jesus: The Life of a Mediterranean Jewish Peasant.* San Francisco: HarperSanFrancisco, 1991.

Dover, K. J. *Greek Homosexuality.* Cambridge, Mass.: Harvard University Press, 1978.

Frilingos, Chris. "'For My Child, Onesimus': Paul and Domestic Power in Philemon." *Journal of Biblical Literature* 119, no. 1 (2000): 91–104.

Halperin, David M. *One Hundred Years of Homosexuality, and Other Essays on Greek Love.* New York: Routledge, 1990.

Halperin, David M., John J. Winkler, and Froma I. Zeitlin, eds. *Before Sexuality: The Construction of Erotic Experience in the Ancient Greek World.* Princeton, N.J.: Princeton University Press, 1990.

Horn, Cornelia B., and John W. Martens. *"Let the Little Children Come to Me": Childhood and Children in Early Christianity.* Washington, D.C.: Catholic University of America Press, 2009.

Laes, Christian. *Children in the Roman Empire: Outsiders Within.* Cambridge, U.K.: Cambridge University Press, 2011.

Marchal, Joseph A. "The Usefulness of an Onesimus: The Sexual Use of Slaves and Paul's Letter to Philemon." *Journal of Biblical Literature* 130, no. 4 (2011): 749–770.

Martens, John W. "'Do Not Sexually Abuse Children': The Language of Early Christian Sexual Ethics." In *Children in Late Ancient Christianity*, edited by Cornelia B. Horn and Robert R. Phenix, pp. 227–254. Tübingen, Germany: Mohr Siebeck, 2009.

Martin, Dale B. *Sex and the Single Savior: Gender and Sexuality in Biblical Interpretation.* Louisville, Ky.: Westminster John Knox, 2006.

Rousselle, Aline. *Porneia: On Desire and the Body in Antiquity.* Translated by Felicia Pheasant. New York: Blackwell, 1988.

Rowlandson, Jane, ed. *Women and Society in Greek and Roman Egypt: A Sourcebook.* Cambridge, U.K.: Cambridge University Press, 1998.

Scroggs, Robin. *The New Testament and Homosexuality: Contextual Background for Contemporary Debate.* Philadelphia: Fortress, 1983.

Wiedemann, Thomas. *Adults and Children in the Roman Empire.* London: Routledge, 1989.

Chris Frilingos

Early Judaism

In early Judaism, as in most cultures historically, the transition from childhood to adulthood occurred around the time of puberty. Since puberty is a process that takes a variable amount of time and occurs at different ages for men and women, and also varies among individuals and populations, it is difficult to generalize about the age at which a child becomes an adult sexually. On the other hand, marriage was an event that clearly defined a person, male or female, as an adult in early Judaism. Therefore, this article will focus on discussions of sexuality prior to (first) marriage, since the bulk of the evidence in our sources relates to that transitional period now known as adolescence. Attitudes toward sexual activity involving prepubescent children will be highlighted, to the extent that the sources address it.

It is possible to make a few generalizations about children and sexuality in early Judaism, despite the very different sources available for the Second Temple period as compared with the classical rabbinic literature. First, early Jewish authors share the assumption that sexual activity within marriage is both divinely mandated for the purpose of procreation and a divinely sanctioned form of pleasure, in contrast to many early Christian authors who praised virginity more highly. Nevertheless, Jewish authors generally condemn any form of nonmarital sexual activity, although some forms (e.g., sex between males) are condemned more emphatically than others. Virginity at (first) marriage is the ideal for both sexes, but female virginity is emphasized much more. Sex between prepubescent children and adults (or adolescents) is condemned not because it corrupts the "innocence" of children (since children were seen as sexual beings) but because children are vulnerable to exploitation. These sexual mores are rooted in biblical law and narrative, but the way in which they are discussed in the early Jewish sources is influenced by the contemporaneous Mediterranean and Persian cultures.

Second Temple Judaism. The Second Temple was in existence from about 515 B.C.E. to 70 C.E., but since the Bible was still developing during the early centuries of that period, scholars of "Second Temple Judaism" tend to focus on the last two or three centuries B.C.E. and the first century C.E. Many of the texts from this period were preserved by Christians, but this article will not consider texts that were heavily redacted by Christians (such as the *Testaments of the Twelve Patriarchs*), because they may reflect Christian sexual mores rather than Jewish ones.

Age at first marriage. Although the literature of the Second Temple period lacks the specificity of later rabbinic Halacha (law) about what constitutes a "marriageable age," the existing evidence suggests an age disparity between men and women at first marriage. Thus, the period between the onset of puberty and marriage was much longer for men than for women. There was almost certainly geographical variation among the Diaspora communities, as well as variation over time, since marriage customs among Jews tended to be influenced by the surrounding cultures.

In one of the rules of the congregation found at Qumran, a young man raised and educated in the community becomes a full member at the age of twenty, before which age he is not permitted to have sexual intercourse with a woman (1QSa 1.7–11). This passage is generally understood to be prescribing a typical (or ideal) age of marriage for men in the Qumran community, since it goes on to describe other milestones in the life of a man in the congregation. A fragment of the *Damascus Document* discusses the responsibilities of a community member in giving his daughter in marriage: he must disclose to her prospective husband any blemishes she has and guarantee her virginity, having her physically examined by "trustworthy and knowledgeable women" if there is any doubt (4Q471 III, 8–15). This passage says nothing about the age of a bride, but the fact that she has no agency in the matter may suggest that she is assumed to be younger than twenty. A piece of circumstantial evidence comes from the retelling of the rape of Dinah in *Jubilees* (see below), which assumes that twelve is a marriageable age for a girl.

There is some evidence that the age discrepancy may have been greater among more Hellenized Jews. Philo (writing in the first century C.E.), in describing the stages of a man's life, puts "ripeness for marriage" between twenty-nine and thirty-five years of age (*Opif.* 103), and Josephus mentions that his first, short-lived marriage (to a virgin) took place in 70 C.E., when he would have been about thirty-two (*Vita* 414–415). Elsewhere, Josephus mentions without comment that Herod Agrippa's eldest daughter, Bernice, who was sixteen when her father died, had already been married for some time (*Ant.* 19.354; cf. 19.277).

The rape or seduction of a virgin. Philo and Josephus both comment on the biblical laws concerning the seduction or rape of an unbetrothed (Exod 22:16–17; Deut 22:28–29) or betrothed (Deut 22:23–27) virgin. Philo does not distinguish between rape and seduction, initially comparing the seduction of a virgin to adultery (*Spec.* 3.65), and later condemning it as "treating free-born women as slaves" and "doing acts of war in time of peace" (3.69, tr. Yonge). The comparison assumes that sexual exploitation of female slaves and prisoners of war is to be expected (see below), whether or not Philo himself condones it. Josephus does distinguish between the seduction and rape of a betrothed virgin, requiring the death penalty for both parties if the virgin is willing, but only for the man if she was forced, omitting the biblical distinction about whether the rape took place in the town or the country (*Ant.* 4.251–252). For the rape of an unbetrothed virgin, Josephus understands the fifty shekels that the rapist must pay her father not as "the bride price for virgins" (Exod 22:17; Deut 22:29), but rather as "the price of her mistreatment," payable only if the father chooses not to allow the rapist to marry his daughter.

The ambiguous story of the rape or seduction of Dinah (Gen 34) is retold in several Second Temple-period texts. In *Jubilees*, Dinah's innocence is emphasized by omitting the detail that Dinah "went out" (Gen 34:1) and by adding that "she was a small girl, twelve years of age" (*Jub.* 30:2). Yet the problem that *Jubilees* focuses on is not her age but the fact that her assailant was a gentile; the story introduces a lengthy polemic against intermarriage (*Jub.* 30:7–17). The book of Judith characterizes the incident as the defilement of a virgin by "strangers" (9:2) and agrees with *Jubilees* in holding the entire town of Shechem responsible for it. Josephus, while siding with Jacob's view in the story that the revenge against the town of Shechem by his sons was excessive, portrays Jacob as unwilling to give his daughter

to a "stranger" (*Ant.* 1.337–341). While all three retellings clarify that Dinah was raped rather than seduced, their main concern is to establish that because Shechem was a gentile, the law requiring a man who rapes an unbetrothed virgin to marry her (Deut 22:28–29) does not apply.

Ben Sira's comments on daughters are in keeping with his generally negative comments regarding women, but they also reveal the pressure on fathers to guard their daughters' chastity: "A daughter is a secret anxiety to her father, and worry over her robs him of sleep; when she is young, for fear she may not marry, or if married, for fear she may be disliked; while a virgin, for fear she may be seduced and become pregnant in her father's house; or having a husband, for fear she may go astray, or, though married, for fear she may be barren" (Sir 42:9–10). In another place, Ben Sira suggests that a father is responsible for regulating the sexuality of both sons and daughters: "Do you have sons? Chastise them and take for them wives in their youth. Do you have daughters? Guard their chastity [lit., body] and do not let your face shine upon them" (7:23–24, Hebrew ms A).

Sexual abuse in war. The frequency of war during the Hellenistic and early Roman periods meant that children, along with women, were vulnerable to sexual assault by victorious enemies. For example, in the book of Judith, the Israelites, under threat of invasion by Nebuchadnezzar's army, put on sackcloth and pray to God "not to give their young children [*nēpia*] as spoil [*diarpagē*] and their wives as booty" to the enemy (Jdt 4:12 lit.). In 4 Ezra, an apocalypse written after the destruction of Jerusalem by the Romans, Ezra laments, "Our children have suffered abuse … our virgins have been defiled, and our wives have been ravished" (4 Ezra 10:22). Josephus frequently assumes that women and children taken as captives of war will be sexually abused; for example, he adds captives to the list of women that a priest may not marry (*A.J.* 2.276). So when he describes the suicide pact at Masada, the likelihood that the children would be sexually abused was probably a factor in the parents' decision to kill them along with themselves (*B.J.* 7.334–36). The references to the enslavement of children and women by enemies in the third Sibylline oracle probably also envision sexual abuse (*Sib. Or.* 3.268–270, 525–530). The abuse of children in war was likewise recognized as a tragedy by non-Jewish Hellenistic historians.

Pederasty. Jewish authors of the Second Temple period harp on the issue of pederasty (sex between adult men and adolescent boys) in order to emphasize Jewish distinctiveness from the surrounding Hellenistic culture. On the one hand, they frequently allude to the biblical prohibition of sex between males (Lev 18:22), regardless of age or status. But very often, they present male homosexual encounters as the exploitation of adolescent or even preadolescent boys. For example, Pseudo-Phocylides (213) advises parents, "Guard the youthful prime of life of a comely boy [*pais*], for many [men] rage for intercourse with a male" (tr. Van der Horst). According to a eulogy of the Jewish people in the third Sibylline oracle, the Jews differ from all the surrounding cultures in that "they do not engage in impious intercourse with male children (*arsenikous paidas*)" (3.596–600, tr. Collins; cf. *Sib. Or.* 5.430–433). Similarly, Philo's apology for the Jews (*Hypothetica*, preserved in fragments by Eusebius) begins its summary of the laws of Moses with a list of sexual sins that are punishable by death: the first is pederasty, followed by adultery and the rape of a child, "for do not speak of doing so to a boy, but even to a female child" (Eusebius, *P.E.* 7.1, tr. Yonge).

Philo takes every opportunity to condemn pederasty, but his most revealing description of it is found in a passage contrasting the communal meals of the Therapeutae with banquets in his own time and with Plato's *Symposium*, both of which seem to him to be mainly about the love of boys (*Contempl.* 48–63). Significantly, the elegantly made-up and coiffed boys present at the banquets of his own day are identified as slaves (*Contempl.* 50), which adds another dimension to the exploitation that Philo assumes is inherent in pederasty. It is worth noting that in *De specialibus legibus* 2.50, Philo condemns the same men who engage in pederasty for committing adultery, and he elsewhere accuses the emperor Gaius of "lasciviousness toward boys and women" (*Legat.* 14). Thus, he does not see pederasty as an expression of same-sex attraction, but rather as a symptom of uncontrolled lust. The same can be said for most other authors of the Second Temple period: they take for granted that boys and young men arouse sexual desire in some (or most?) men, but they condemn men who act on that desire as sexual predators.

Classical Rabbinic Judaism. For the period from the second century C.E. until the rise of Islam, our main textual sources are the classical texts of rabbinic Judaism: the Mishnah, Tosefta, Palestinian and Babylonian Talmuds, and the classical Midrash. Since the late twentieth century, there has been a great deal of debate among scholars about the historical reliability of these sources and, at the same time, a growing recognition that they reflect the values and practices of only a small segment of the Jewish population during those centuries. The remainder of this article will draw on the evidence of the classical rabbinic sources without claiming that they describe historical realities or are representative of "Judaism" as a whole during this period. It will highlight differences between the Palestinian and Babylonian Talmuds on several issues related to children and sexuality.

Age at first marriage. There is a significant difference between Palestinian and Babylonian Talmuds regarding the expected or ideal age of first marriage for women and especially for men. In Palestine and in the Mediterranean Diaspora, the expectation of an age discrepancy between brides and grooms seen in Second Temple period texts continues. Women were expected to marry by their late teens, and men around the age of thirty; epigraphical evidence confirms that such a disparity in ages was in fact common in the Western Roman Empire. (The list of life stages in *m. 'Abot* 5:21 that puts marriage at age eighteen for men is a late addition to the Mishnah, since it does not appear in the Talmuds or *'Abot de Rabbi Nathan*.) In the Babylonian Talmud, by contrast, the ideal is for women to be betrothed by the age of twelve and married in their early teens, and for men to marry by the age of twenty (*b. Qidd. 29b*).

There were economic and cultural reasons for this difference. The Greco-Roman culture of the Mediterranean viewed marriage as the establishment of a new household with the goal of procreation, seen as a social good, and Palestinian Jewish sources share that ideology. The lower economic status of Jews in the Mediterranean world, which made it hard for young men to establish a household before they inherited property from their fathers, led to a later age of marriage for men in Palestine. For women, marriage in their late teens was optimal for the sake of fertility, since younger girls were both less fertile and much more likely to die in childbirth. In the Babylonian Talmud, marriage is seen as an outlet for sexual desire, so men are encouraged to marry by the time they are twenty in order to avoid sin (*b. Qidd. 29b–30a*). This ideology of marriage was shared with the surrounding Persian culture, among both Zoroastrians and Nestorian Christians. Mesopotamian newlyweds typically joined the husband's father's household, rather than immediately establishing their own household. These factors combined to encourage earlier marriage for both men and women in Mesopotamia.

Sexual maturity and virginity in girls. The Babylonian Talmud establishes clear stages of sexual maturity for girls. A girl younger than twelve years old is considered a minor (*qĕtānâ*) and is completely under her father's control; her father may sell her as a maidservant, or betroth or marry her off (*b. Ketub. 29a, 46b–47a*). A minor girl whose father has died may be married off by her mother or brothers, but she has the right to refuse her husband for as long as she remains a minor (*b. Nid. 46a*). Marriage and betrothal of a minor girl were strongly discouraged, however, both because of the risk to her life if she should become pregnant (*b. Yebam. 12b*) and because it was deemed prudent to let a girl have a voice in the choice of her husband (e.g., *b. Qidd. 41a*).

At twelve years and a day, if she has at least two pubic hairs, a girl is considered a maiden (*na'arâ*) and eligible for betrothal and marriage. She is also considered to be at the age of menstruation, whether or not she has actually begun to menstruate (*b. Nid. 5a*). Girls could be married before menarche (*b. Nid. 64b*). Once a girl becomes a maiden, her father may no longer sell her as a maidservant, but if she is raped or seduced during this period, the fine is paid to her father, since she is still under his authority (*b. Ketub. 29a–b*). Once she has been a maiden for six months, normally at twelve and a half years of age, she is considered an adult (*bôgeret*). She is now legally allowed to betroth herself, because "her father no longer has authority over her" (*m. Nid. 5:7*). She is also entitled to the proceeds of her own labor, and her father can no longer annul her vows.

In rabbinic sources, the virginity or nonvirginity of a young woman on her wedding day is assumed to be a matter of public knowledge, since there were certain wedding customs that were observed only for virgin brides (*b. B. Bat. 92b*). The amount of the *kĕtûbâ* (the settlement payable to a wife in the event of divorce or the death of her husband) was 200 *zûz* for a virgin bride, but 100 for a widow, divorcee, or other nonvirgin (*m. Ketub. 1:2*), so virginity at first marriage had monetary value as well as honor attached to it. An even more obvious distinction is that virgin brides were to be married on a Wednesday, so that if the groom had a claim against the bride's virginity, he could go to court first thing Thursday morning, when the courts convened (*m. Ketub. 1:1*). The rabbis also recognized a category of brides whose status as virgins was disputed because their hymens were not intact due to injury (*m. Ketub. 1:4*). Since the high priest must marry only a virgin, there is also a debate about whether a *bôgeret* who has not had intercourse counts as a virgin (*b. Yebam. 59a–60b*), since only a *na'arâ* can be presumed to be a "perfect virgin." Although this statement is traditionally taken to indicate that the hymen disintegrates naturally over time, the context suggests that a *bôgeret*, being no longer under her father's authority, is presumed to have had some sexual experience stopping short of intercourse, and hence is not a "perfect virgin."

Sexual maturity and legal majority in boys. From a Halachic perspective, a boy becomes a man at the age of thirteen years and a day, provided he has grown at least two pubic hairs. That is, a thirteen-year-old boy is considered a man for the purposes of forming a *minyan* (a quorum of ten for prayer), and he is bound by the commandments and by his own vows (*b. Nid. 45b–46a*). Nevertheless, he is not considered ready for marriage, because his physical and mental maturation is understood to last through his teens. In Palestinian sources, the teenage years were seen as a crucial period of character formation and thus should be devoted to Torah study to the extent possible, although Torah study was expected to continue after marriage. The Babylonian Talmud is more inclined to see a tension between the demands of Torah study and those of marriage, but at the same time the Mesopotamian sages see adolescence as a highly sexualized period, and hence favor early marriage. An often cited passage (*b. Qidd. 29b*) poses the question of whether one should study Torah first and then marry, or vice versa; the debate is presented as being resolved differently by Palestinian and Mesopotamian sages. There is little evidence that Torah study was seen as incompatible with marriage in Palestine, however; the reasons for delaying marriage were economic and cultural (see above).

Sex involving minors. The rabbis acknowledged the sexual abuse of young children, as well as the fact that children engage in sexual experimentation with one another. Before the age of majority (twelve for girls, thirteen for boys), however, children are not legally responsible for their actions; only adults who engage in sexual acts with minors are liable for punishment. Nevertheless, children are viewed as (potentially) sexual beings well before puberty. The sages determined that girls are capable of sexual intercourse from the age of three years and a day, and boys from the age of nine years and a day (*b. 'Abod. Zar. 36b–37a*). If a girl is sexually abused before the age of three, it is not legally significant, because her hymen is believed to regenerate (*m. Nid. 5:4; b. Nid. 45a*). Nine was the minimum age at which boys were believed to be capable of insemination (*m. Nid. 5:5*).

On the other hand, when the sages debate the ages at which a girl and a boy may no longer sleep naked in the same bed with their parents, the ages range from nine to twelve for girls and twelve or thirteen for boys (*b. Qidd. 81b*). That passage implies a rabbinic recognition that incest could happen between parents and children, but assumes that it is much less likely with prepubescent children. Nevertheless, there is a debate (*b. Sanh. 69b*) about whether a mother who "plays lewdly" with her son who is under nine becomes unfit to marry a priest (who must not marry a woman who has been sexually involved with a male who is forbidden to her). Most rabbinic discussions of incest deal with "forbidden unions," in the sense of marriages that are possible but not legally legitimate. The rarity of mentions of father-daughter incest in rabbinic literature (but see *m. Ketub.* 3:2) may be due to the fact that the lists of forbidden unions in Leviticus 18 and 20 do not include the union of a father with his own daughter. Although the rabbinic literature considers many situations not addressed in the written Torah, scripture remains the touchstone of rabbinic deliberations about children and sexuality.

[*See also* Children, *subentry* Greek World; Male-Female Sexuality, *subentry* Early Judaism; Marriage and Divorce, *subentry* Early Judaism; *and* Sexual Violence, *subentry* Early Judaism.]

BIBLIOGRAPHY

Boyarin, Daniel. *Carnal Israel: Reading Sex in Talmudic Culture.* Berkeley: University of California Press, 1993.

Cohen, Jeremy. *"Be Fertile and Increase, Fill the Earth and Master It": The Ancient and Medieval Career of a Biblical Text.* Ithaca, N.Y.: Cornell University Press, 1989.

Cohen, Shaye J. D., ed. *The Jewish Family in Antiquity.* Atlanta: Scholars Press, 1993.

Collins, John J. "Sibylline Oracles." In *The Old Testament Pseudepigrapha*, Vol. 1, edited by James H. Charlesworth, pp. 317–472, Garden City, N.Y.: Doubleday, 1983.

Golden, Mark. "Change or Continuity? Children and Childhood in Hellenistic Historiography." In *Inventing Ancient Culture: Historicism, Periodization and the Ancient World*, edited by Mark Golden and Peter Toohey, pp. 176–191. London: Routledge, 1997.

Hauptman, Judith. *Rereading the Rabbis: A Woman's Voice.* Boulder, Colo.: Westview, 1998.

Ilan, Tal. *Jewish Women in Greco-Roman Palestine: An Inquiry into Image and Status.* Tübingen, Germany: Mohr Siebeck, 1995.

Kraemer, David. "Images of Childhood and Adolescence in Talmudic Literature." In *The Jewish Family: Metaphor and Memory*, edited by David Kraemer, pp. 65–80. New York: Oxford University Press, 1989.

Kramer, Ross S. "Jewish Women in the Diaspora World of Late Antiquity." In *Jewish Women in Historical Per-*

spective, 2d ed., edited by Judith R. Baskin, pp. 46–72. Detroit: Wayne State University Press, 1998.

Loader, William. *Enoch, Levi and Jubilees on Sexuality: Attitudes towards Sexuality in the Early Enoch Literature, the Aramaic Levi Document, and the Book of Jubilees.* Grand Rapids, Mich.: Eerdmans, 2007.

Loader, William. *The Dead Sea Scrolls on Sexuality: Attitudes towards Sexuality in Sectarian and Related Literature at Qumran.* Grand Rapids, Mich.: Eerdmans, 2009.

Loader, William. *Philo, Josephus and the Testaments on Sexuality: Attitudes towards Sexuality in the Writings of Philo and Josephus and in the Testaments of the Twelve Patriarchs.* Grand Rapids, Mich.: Eerdmans, 2011a.

Loader, William. *The Pseudepigrapha on Sexuality: Attitudes towards Sexuality in Apocalypses, Testaments, Legends, Wisdom, and Related Literature.* Grand Rapids, Mich.: Eerdmans, 2011b.

Satlow, Michael L. *Jewish Marriage in Antiquity.* Princeton, N.J.: Princeton University Press, 2001.

Schofer, Jonathan Wyn. *The Making of a Sage: A Study in Rabbinic Ethics.* Madison: University of Wisconsin Press, 2005.

Tropper, Amram. "Children and Childhood in Light of the Demographics of the Jewish Family in Late Antiquity." *Journal for the Study of Judaism* 37.3 (2006) 299–343.

Van der Horst, P. W. "Pseudo-Phocylides." In *The Old Testament Pseudepigrapha*, Vol. 2, edited by James H. Charlesworth, pp. 317–472, Garden City, N.Y.: Doubleday, 1985.

Yonge, C. D. *The Works of Philo: New Updated Edition.* Peabody, Mass.: Hendrickson, 1993.

Karina Martin Hogan

Early Church

Early Christian communities spent little time defining the nature of childhood or the proper ages for children to engage in sexual relations, but followed the established patterns of the Greeks, Romans, and Jews. In what is said regarding children and sexuality, however, it is important always to keep in mind that the experiences of children differed pronouncedly in the early church, depending upon whether the child was a girl or boy and whether the child was free or enslaved.

Children were initiated into the sexual world in the Roman Empire with legal and cultural support at younger ages than would be acceptable today in most of the world. Puberty was typically seen as the onset for sexual relations for girls and boys in the Greco-Roman world, though there was not a strict age of consent as we see in most modern cultures. Girls in the Roman Empire were legally marriageable at age twelve, while boys in the Greco-Roman world typically married in their late twenties. Boys, however, were considered of age for pederastic relationships in the Roman Empire at the same age at which girls were considered of age for marriage.

Sexual behavior for Jewish children was only licit within marriage, and puberty was also generally the dividing line. *M. Ketubot* 3:8 and *m. Niddah* 5:7 distinguish carefully the physical development of a girl, speaking of a *bogeret* (twelve and a half years of age), a *katanah* (less than twelve years and a day) and a *na'arah* (a girl twelve years and a day). The *bogeret* was a girl who had reached physical maturity and was ready to be married. Unlike the Greeks and Romans, the age at which Jewish boys could marry was also the transition to sexual life. Some Rabbinic authorities claimed that boys should marry at the age of eighteen (*m. Avot* 5:21), while other authorities stated that a boy nine years old and a day might marry his childless sister-in-law (*m. Niddah* 5:5) in the context of levirate marriage (Deut 25:5–10). These age ranges are in line with general age and physiological considerations found among the early Christians as to readiness of children for sexual relationships (Horn and Martens, 2009, pp. 3–21).

Marriage of Children. We begin, therefore, with the marriage of girls in the early church, an area in which traditional practices transcended religion and remained intact into late antiquity. For freeborn girls, Roman, Jewish, or Christian, sexual initiation ideally occurred at marriage, and the guarding of a girl's virginity was considered the paramount duty of the father and family of the girl. There is little discussion of marriage of girls in the New Testament. Jesus's teachings on marriage deal particularly with divorce and do not discuss either the age of the participants in a marriage or sexuality within marriage (Mark 10:2–10; Matt 19:3–10). However, some have also posited that Paul's discussion in 1 Corinthians 7:36–38 is not concerned with some sort of spiritual marriage, a Christian innovation of late antiquity, but with whether a father can carry through with a marriage contract for his virgin daughter in light of Paul's teaching on the eschaton (Peters, 2002; Horn and Martens, 2009).

Ages, of course, could vary in marriage, but the early to late teens remained normative for Christian girls. The major purpose of marriage for freeborn girls also remained the same: to procreate. Procreation was at the heart of marriage in the Roman Empire, though the additional goals of social stability and inheritance were significant adjuncts to this primary purpose. These goals would be challenged by the Christian practice of celibacy. There is little or no Christian reflection on the erotic purposes of marriage for girls or boys, other than to control it strictly within the boundaries of marriage (1 Cor 7: 29). In 1 Corinthians 7, Paul breaks with social convention to highlight the responsibility of each marriage partner to meet the sexual needs of the other, with no discussion of procreation. Yet as marriage increasingly became the second best option for Christian girls, celibacy came to encompass the major sexual innovation for children in late antiquity.

Slave girls, like all slaves, could not legally be married in the Roman Empire, but their sexual life often began at a young age owing to their sexual use at the hands of their masters, which was limited only by the legal restriction that the slave be five years old (Justinian, *Digest* 38.10.10, 5). Twenty-first-century research is divided as to whether the slaves of Christians were free from sexual use at the hands of their masters, since Colossians 3:22–25, Ephesians 6:5–9, Titus 2:9–10, and 1 Peter 2:18–21 delineate the authority of masters in all things (Brooten, 2010). Others have suggested that, as treacherous as the situations were for young slaves sexually, Christian teaching might have ameliorated sexual practices within the Christian household (MacDonald, 2007). Basil of Caesarea, however, in the fourth century C.E., noted that Christian masters still forced their slave girls into unwanted sexual relations (*Letters* 199.49).

While slave girls in antiquity did engage in informal marital relationships with fellow male slaves

(Lat. *contubernium*), these had no legal standing and could be broken at a master's whim. The church, however, began to bless, or "sacramentalize," the marriages of Christian slaves (Justinian, *Digest* 48.5.6, 1; *Codex Justinianus* 9.9, 23). That such marriages took place against the wishes of their Christian masters is seen in Letter 199.18 of Basil, who lamented that slave girls were joined in "secret" marriages and brought impurity on their owner's houses by filling them with "wickedness." Basil does not describe why these secret marriages were impure, but his comments reflect longstanding ancient beliefs about the sexual immorality of slaves.

Freeborn Christian boys/young men followed the Jewish model of younger marriage around eighteen. Given that Paul thought of marriage as the only licit means to manage burning sexual passions, marriage for boys was something that late-ancient Christians thought of as essential at the youngest possible age, should they not choose the path of celibacy. John Chrysostom urged Christian boys to become engaged to a girl as young as possible; for Chrysostom, early marriage was not only a way to channel sexual energy away from improper sexual relationships (*porneia*) but also to distinguish between a slave and a freeborn boy (*On Vainglory* 71–75).

Same-Sex Relations of Girls and Boys. Same-sex relations of children with adults or between children were a part of the sexual landscape of the ancient world, but we have less data on sexual behavior between children themselves or between women and girls. Sexuality in antiquity and late antiquity was defined by men and was seen as significant insofar as it impacted men, which also led to a relative lack of writing that speaks of the sexual experience of women and girls. Same-sex relations between girls or women took place beyond the literal and figurative view of men.

The most significant passage for Christian understanding of lesbian relationships is Romans 1:26, in which Paul denounces sexual behavior between females as contrary to nature. While some scholars have argued that Paul is talking about bestiality or anal intercourse, the most convincing reading of this passage is that it speaks of sex between two females

(Brooten, 1996). On the issue of lesbian sexual relations, the Christian categorization of these acts as unnatural was in tune with the attitudes of the wider Roman Empire. The Christian response to same-sex sexual relations between women in non-canonical and proto-orthodox writings, such as the *Acts of Thomas, Apocalypse of Paul,* Tertullian, and Clement of Alexandria, is unanimously negative; in none of these cases are girls directly referenced. But in a monastic text of Shenoute of Atripe (fourth to fifth centuries C.E.), he unambiguously speaks of women who seek out girls with whom to have sexual relations and criticizes not the girls but the women for their behavior (*De vita monachorum* 26). Augustine, too, warns against "carnal relations" among married women, widows, and girls, especially since some of these girls are chaste virgins dedicated to Christ (*Epistles* 211.14).

Whereas the data on same-sex relations among girls is minimal in the writings of the early church, the texts dealing with pederasty are vast. There are two passages in the New Testament in which pederasty might be indicated. A number of scholars have proposed that the "scandal" against which Jesus warns his disciples in Mark 9:42 was the sexual abuse of children (Loader, 2012, pp. 119–135). This reading is possible, but not certain, as it reduces a general prohibition to a specific offense. 1 Corinthians 6:9–10 may give us a clearer condemnation of pederasty by use of the terms *malakoi* ("soft" or "effeminate" males) and *arsenokoitai* ("those who lie with men"). The secondary literature on these two terms is voluminous, dating back to Boswell's discussion (Boswell, 1980) and continuing unabated since then (Loader, 2012, pp. 326–332). Many scholars see the two terms together referring to male prostitution and specifically those youths who sold themselves to older men. Other scholars interpret the terms more generally, with *malakoi* referring to the "passive" partners and *arsenokoitai* denoting the "active" partners, with no particular focus on youth or prostitution. While *malakoi* does probably refer to younger males, who were often described as "soft," understanding *malakoi* as only referring to prostitutes skips over a large part of the reality of sexual

behavior and social reality in antiquity and late antiquity wherein most passive partners of men were slaves, boys, or men, who were used within households by masters. Legally, freeborn Roman boys were protected from pederastic relationships and men could face a charge of *stuprum*, a law dating from the third century C.E. that outlawed intercourse with a freeborn boy (*Digest* 47.11.1.2, 48.5.35.1, 48.5.9). There are simply too many voices, however, that indicate the constant practice of pederasty among freeborn boys to conclude that the laws had ended such practices in late antiquity.

Indeed, in late antiquity the church created new language to criticize same-sex sexual behaviors of men with boys. Christians used both the language of pederasty and a new term, *paidaphthoria*. Tatian (*Oratio ad Graecos* 28), Athenagoras (*Legatio pro Christianis* 34.1), and Clement of Alexandria (*Paedagogus* 3.3–4) criticize the treatment of the numerous slave boys used in the Greco-Roman world for sexual purposes by using the common Greek term *paiderasteō*. Yet when Christians used the noun *paidaphthoria* or the verb *paidophthoreō*, a different picture emerges. The word emerged in the late first or early second century C.E. and was used by Christians alone throughout late antiquity (Martens, 2009, pp. 252–254). The compound word is intended to convey a sense of the sexual "destruction" or "corruption" of boys, though it is possible it also reflects the sexual use of girls, and so it could be translated by our modern phrase "sexual abuse." The moral condemnations indicated by *paidaphthoria*, though, point to sexual sins within the Christian community.

Paidaphthoria was used by Christians through late antiquity in the context of expanded "Ten Commandments" lists, such as in *Didache* 2.2, *Barnabas* 19.4, Clement of Alexandria (e.g., *Paedagogus* 2.10.88, 2.10.89, 3.12.89), and Origen (e.g., *Commentarium in evangelium Matthaei* 18:15) in which Christians are enjoined not to sexually abuse children (*oude paidophthorēseis*). The same phrase continued to be used throughout the fourth and fifth centuries C.E. Apart from formulaic denunciations, though, Gregory of Nazianzus criticizes rich Christian households that featured effeminate slave boys serving at their meals, a task that often included sex (*Oratione* 14, 17). The problem was significant enough for Christians that the Council of Elvira produced canonical legislation dealing with pederasty. Canon 71 forbade "stupratoribus puerorum," which refers to pederasty, and denied Communion to those Christians, even at the end of their lives, who used boys for pederasty. It does not distinguish between slave and freeborn boys, though *stuprum* according to Roman law would only impact boys who were of freeborn status.

Monastic communities also faced the reality of pederasty. Pachomius (292–348 C.E.) writes of sexual temptation in the earliest monastic rules. In *Judicia* 7, activities of intimacy between monks and boys, such as laughing, playing, and having friendships, are strictly regulated and curtailed with threats of punishments. *Instruction* 1.35 says not to make friends with boys, for these friendships can become sexual. This prohibition is similar to that of John Cassian, wherein the monks are encouraged not to be alone with young men or hold hands with them (*De institutis* 2.15, 2). While monastic texts, such as those attributed to Ephrem Graecus, continued to warn of *paidaphthoria*, Christians enacted laws against pederasty, and same-sex behavior in general, in which both active and passive partners were condemned. In the *Codex Theodosianus* 9.7.3 and 9.7.6 those men who sexually act the part of women are to be burned. Justinian extends the punishment even to the active partner for "acts contrary to nature" (*Novellae* 77.1).

Incest. Also considered contrary to nature by most ancient legal codes was incest, though definitions varied on the degrees of consanguinity that it encompassed. The laws in the Hebrew Bible governing incest are found at Leviticus 18:6–18 and 20:11–12. The New Testament speaks of incest on a few occasions, possibly in Matthew 5:32 and 19:9, where *porneia* might refer to Levitical restrictions on degrees of consanguinity, and in the cases of John the Baptist (Mark 6:17–29; Matt 14:1–10) and Christian stepson who is purportedly living with his stepmother (1 Cor 5:1–8). All of these New Testament examples maintain Jewish restrictions on incest, but it is not clear whether children or young people were involved in any of these cases. Jewish incest

restrictions, however, would continue to be upheld by Christians in the early church.

Christians, however, do raise a potential cause of incest that aligns with their criticisms of Greco-Roman sexual behavior in general and serves to counter claims of incest made against Christians in antiquity. Ancient slave traders often found slaves among the children who were exposed by their families. These infants were often taken by pimps who raised these children to be prostitutes. Clement of Alexandria denounces the exposure of children in itself, but also suggests that men who frequent prostitutes might have sexual relations with a child whom they had previously exposed (*Paedagogus* 3.3). Justin Martyr repeats this charge, saying that most exposed children are brought up to a life of prostitution, with the boys often castrated for this purpose (*First Apology* 27–29). Tertullian speaks of an event during the time of the prefect Fuscianus (187–189 C.E.) in which a freeborn boy had been sold into slavery after wandering away from his attendants (*To the Heathen* 1.16). This boy appeared some years later at a slave market, where he was purchased by his birth father, who, unaware of who the boy was, had sexual relations with his son. When the boy was sent to work in the fields, he was recognized by his former pedagogue and nurse. When the truth came out, his parents killed themselves. These cases seem designed simply for Christian criticism of Greco-Roman sexual practices, but given the numerous exposed children who became slaves and prostitutes, such occurrences could have arisen.

Some early Christian authors even enlisted incest taboos to convince children or parents that marriage was not the best choice. In Gregory of Tours's Latin summary of the *Acts of Andrew*, one reads of a case of a planned incestuous marriage at Philippi between two sons of one family and two daughters of a second family (*Acts Andr.* 11, l. 9). The fathers of these children were brothers, so the children are first cousins (*Acts Andr.* 11, l. 1). The reason for the marriage between their children was to increase the social status of the two families and to maintain their great wealth and nobility (*Acts Andr.* 11, ll. 4–7). Prior to the marriage, though, they were asked to wait for word from the apostle Andrew, who warned them that the marriage was improper because it involved the joining together of blood relatives (*Acts Andr.* 11, ll. 9–23).

Consecrated Virginity and Asceticism. Among early Christian authors, celibacy was favored over marriage, even if incest was not involved. The preference begins with statements of Jesus that diminish the role of sexuality (Matt 19:5; Mark 12:7). Paul, in 1 Corinthians 7, continues the process of marginalizing sexuality among Christians in general. Celibacy would have its most immediate impact on children who were arriving at or who had achieved marriageable age. Christianity in late antiquity was engaged in a constant struggle with the place of sexuality, and it was the bodies of children that were caught in the middle of the fight.

The Apocryphal Acts of Apostles (second to third centuries C.E.) preserves examples of young boys and girls who had to choose between married life and virginity. In the *Acts of Thomas*, for instance, salvation can only be attained through *enkrateia*, or sexual renunciation, and it is not just *porneia* and *paidaphthoria* that must be avoided; all sexual acts are considered impure. In the *Acts of Paul* the reader meets the young girl Thecla, who is portrayed as having listened to Paul when he was preaching in Iconium. Thecla, a young *parthenos*, had been engaged to a young man, Thamyris. After hearing Paul, Thecla refused to get married to Thamyris, and no pleas from her fiancé or her mother could change her mind (*Acts Paul* 6–10, 22).

The examples gleaned from apocryphal literature do not represent marginal trends in second- and third-century Christianity. With the rise of Christian monasticism in the fourth century C.E., both boys and girls participated in the ascetic life, either chosen by their parents or by themselves. Jerome's letters provide a number of examples that assume the practice of choosing young girls for the consecrated life, including his letter to Laeta concerning her infant daughter Paula (*Letters* 107; 403 C.E.) and a letter to Gaudentius concerning his infant daughter Pacatula (*Letters* 128; 413 C.E.). Consecrated virginity had become a trend in some educated and wealthy circles of Roman Christians. Apart from detailing how to raise consecrated virgins, Jerome may have had another purpose in writing these letters. Letter 128 speaks of those living a life of supposed virginity, especially men who were supposed to be living as virgins, but whose live-in helpers were lovely young girls. Parents might have desired asceticism for their children more than the children themselves. One the other hand, some parents opposed their children's wishes to choose the life of consecrated virginity. John Chrysostom portrayed Christian parents, especially from upper classes, as resisting their children's vocation. Those parents considered the monastic life shameful and unworthy for those of noble origins. In his consolation to the monk Stagirius, Chrysostom recalled how Stagirius's father had said the monastic life made his son "shameful and unworthy" of his ancestral family (*Ad Stagirium a daemone vexatum* 2.3).

New Developments Regarding Sexuality and Children in the Early Church. Early Christianity changed the complexion of sexuality in the ancient world for children in two profound ways: one was the recategorization of pederasty as *paidaphthoria*, or sexual abuse; the second was the preference for celibacy over marriage. While the first shift ultimately reduced the sexual use of boys by men, it had the consequence of framing all same-sex relations not only as sinful but illicit. The second shift in attitude and behavior gave girls options beyond marriage, which allowed them to pursue a life of learning, for instance, as a consecrated virgin, but it also reduced sexuality in itself to something unworthy for many young Christians. This should not, however, mitigate the positive shifts which took place in the sexual lives of Christian children.

It must be noted, however, that such shifts took place in the context of general moral condemnations of sex not necessarily growing out of concern for children. No authors, for instance, consider the young age of girls marrying as a reason for avoiding marriage. Most ancient and late antique marriages, not just pederastic practice, would from a modern perspective fall under the rubric of child sexual abuse. Ancient authors, Christians included, rarely consider the topics of psychological harm or emotional trauma of children engaged in sexual relations. Notions of emotional and psychological development and the impact of sexual coercion and force upon child development were unknown to ancient thinkers (Laes, 2010). Force and coercion were hallmarks of the sexual system in general, not just for children (Harper, 2013). Considerations of social status, power differentials, gender, authority, and slavery, which defined the nature of sexual relationships in the Roman Empire, raise moral issues for modern readers, but Christian shifts in sexual practices for children were based upon moral denunciations, not concerns for the age of children. It is important to recognize that positive shifts in attitude that lessened the sexual use of children in the early church were accompanied by attitudes in which sex itself became the enemy of the Christian life.

[*See also* Children, *subentries on* Early Judaism, Greek World, New Testament, *and* Roman World; Marriage and Divorce, *subentry* Early Church; *and* Sexual Transgression, *subentry* Early Church.]

BIBLIOGRAPHY

Aubin, M. M. "More Apparent than Real? Questioning the Difference in Marital Age between Christian and Non-Christian Women of Rome during the Third and Fourth Centuries." *Ancient History Bulletin* 14 (2000): 1–13.

Boswell, John. *Christianity, Social Tolerance, and Homosexuality: Gay People in Western Europe from the Beginning of the Christian Era to the Fourteenth Century.* Chicago: University of Chicago Press, 1981.

Brooten, Bernadette J. *Love between Women: Early Christian Responses to Female Homoeroticism.* Chicago: University of Chicago Press, 1996.

Brooten, Bernadette J., ed. *Beyond Slavery: Overcoming Its Religious and Sexual Legacies.* New York: Palgrave Macmillan, 2010.

Brown, Peter. *The Body and Society: Men, Women, and Sexual Renunciation in Early Christianity.* Rev. ed. New York: Columbia University Press, 2008.

Golden, Mark. "Slavery and Homosexuality at Athens." *Phoenix* 38 (1984): 308–324.

Golden, Mark. "*Pais,* 'Child,' and 'Slave.'" *L' Antiquité Classique* 54 (1985): 91–104.

Harper, Kyle. *From Shame to Sin: The Christian Transformation of Sexual Morality in Late Antiquity.* Cambridge, Mass.: Harvard University Press, 2013.

Horn, Cornelia B., and John W. Martens. *"Let the Little Children Come to Me:" Childhood and Children in Early Christianity.* Washington, D.C.: Catholic University Press, 2009.

Hunter, David. *Marriage in the Early Church.* Minneapolis: Fortress, 1992.

Laes, Christian. "When Classicists Need to Speak Up: Antiquity and Present-Day Pedophilia–Pederasty." In *Aeternitas antiquitatis: Proceedings of the Symposium Held in Skopje, August 28 as Part of the 2009 Annual Conference of EuroClassica*, edited by Valerij Sofronievski, pp. 33–53. Skopje, Macedonia: ACPh Antika, 2010.

Loader, William. *The New Testament on Sexuality.* Grand Rapids, Mich.: Eerdmans, 2012.

MacDonald, Margaret Y. "Slavery, Sexuality and House Churches: A Reassessment of Colossians 3.18–4.1 in Light of New Research on the Roman Family." *New Testament Studies* 53.1 (2007): 94–113.

Martens, John W. "'Do Not Sexually Abuse Children': The Language of Early Christian Sexual Ethics." In *Children in Late Ancient Christianity*, edited by Cornelia B. Horn and Robert R. Phenix, pp. 227–254. Studien und Texte zu Antike und Christentum 58. Tübingen, Germany: Mohr Siebeck, 2009.

Peters, Greg. "Spiritual Marriage in Early Christianity: 1 Cor 7:25–38 in Modern Exegesis and the Earliest Church." *Trinity Journal* 23, no. 2 (2002): 211–224.

Satlow, Michael L. *Tasting the Dish: Rabbinic Rhetorics of Sexuality.* Atlanta: Scholars Press, 1995.

John W. Martens and Melvin G. Miller

CREATION

Stories about the creation of the cosmos and the physical world address existential questions about the origins of the universe and humanity. To varying degrees, all creation accounts provide visions about why the world is the way that it is. Because of this, creation stories have a particular importance for understanding perceptions about gender relations in the ancient world. Certainly, the biblical accounts of creation, especially the Garden of Eden story in Genesis 2:4b–3, have had an enormous influence on

Western civilization's views of patriarchal hierarchy and women's subordination. However, the Garden of Eden story is only one creation story among others in the Bible, and there were many other ideas of creation in the ancient Near East.

Creation accounts generally fall into two main categories: cosmologies, which are primarily concerned with the origins of the cosmos and of deities, though the creation of the physical world and human beings is often included; and primeval histories, which begin with the creation of humanity (Frymer-Kensky, 2006, p. 5). Creation accounts are categorized as literary texts, or belles-lettres, written with considerable literary skill and artistry. Modern readers do not have access to the original intent and purpose of these works, though at some level these stories must have resonated with ancient audiences. An especially important consideration for gendered perspectives on these texts is that creation stories, like all literary texts, were probably written by male scribes, an elite group of literate specialists in chiefly illiterate societies. Moreover, the intended audience for these texts was probably also men. Thus, ancient Near Eastern literature was "androcentric," meaning that it tended to focus on men; and this social context inevitably affected the perspectives on gender presented in any text, including creation stories. The discussion of ancient Near Eastern creation accounts offered in this article is merely a sampling of the main creation stories and not meant to be exhaustive.

Mesopotamia. Mesopotamian texts are recorded in two languages: Sumerian and Akkadian. In several Mesopotamian creation accounts, the god Enki (Sumerian) or Ea (Akkadian), god of fresh waters but also wisdom and craftsmanship, plays an important role. In the Sumerian myth of Enki and Ninmah (ETCSL 1.1.2), Enki devises a plan to create human beings to toil in place of the gods. Enki's mother, Namma, kneads clay, and birth goddesses pinch off pieces of the clay and bring human beings into existence with the assistance of the goddess Ninmah and several other goddesses. After the creation of humanity, the divine beings celebrate by having a feast. While drinking beer at the celebration, Ninmah brags that it is her will that determines the fate of the human beings. Enki responds by challenging Ninmah to create seven beings for which Enki cannot determine a fate. Ninmah complies and creates seven beings, each with a different defect, but Enki finds a purpose for them all. Enki then commands Ninmah to pour semen into a woman's womb and to find a purpose for the being that is born. This being is a pitiful creature that cannot do anything for itself, perhaps the first human fetus (Jacobsen, 1987, p. 156). Ninmah cannot find a purpose for the creature, and Enki is declared the victor of the contest. In this account, even though the physical act of creating human beings is brought about by goddesses, it is Enki who devises the plan and who is ultimately given credit. The contest between Enki and Ninmah highlights Enki's importance over the birth goddesses. Nevertheless, the text places the physical responsibility for creation chiefly with goddesses, which reflects women's roles in childbirth.

The Sumerian myth of Enki and Ninhursag (ETCSL 1.1.1) recounts the creation of several goddesses during the primordial time. In this text, Enki is not the mastermind behind creation but physically creates through sexual reproduction. Enki has a daughter with his wife Ninhursag but then creates several goddesses by impregnating successive generations of his daughters when they come to the riverbank. After four generations, Enki's daughter Uttu is advised by her mother not to go to the riverbank, so Enki comes to her house bringing gifts. Enki has sex with Uttu but her mother removes the semen, and though the text is fragmentary at this point, it seems that she puts Enki's semen in the ground, from which it becomes plants. Enki then eats the plants and becomes very ill. Though Ninhursag has cursed Enki, she ultimately cures him. For each part of Enki's body that is in pain, Ninhursag creates another deity and decrees a fate for it. In this text, Enki represents male sexual energy as the source of creation (Leick, 1994, p. 21), though certainly the goddesses play a role by giving birth. However, by eating the plants that grew from his semen, it is possible that Enki is pregnant (Alster, 1978, p. 19) but he cannot give birth without help from a goddess.

Like the Sumerian myth of Enki and Ninmah, the Akkadian Atrahasis story also attributes the purpose of the creation of humanity as toiling for the gods. At the beginning of the text the worker gods rebel, and Ea (the Akkadian version of Enki) suggests the creation of humankind to work in place of the gods. Ea also devises the way in which human beings will be made. Humanity is created by the midwife of the gods, who mixes clay with the blood of a slain god "who had rationality." To this mixture the gods add spit. The midwife goddess pinches off fourteen pieces of clay, seven male and seven female. The rest of the story focuses on the primeval flood that destroys all humanity except for Atrahasis. The birth goddess has an elevated role in this myth, which emphasizes and praises her efforts. However, once again the god Ea is the one with the plan. In this account, male and female humans are created simultaneously and in reproductive pairs (Asher-Greve, 2002, p. 13). More-over, the plan to curb human overpopulation at the end of the story involves creating two alternate types of females who do not bear children, an etiology for celibate priestesses and women who cannot have children (Frymer-Kensky, 2006, p. 8).

The Babylonian Epic of Creation, *Enūma eliš*, ac-counts for the creation of the cosmos, the elevation of the god Marduk, and the creation of humanity (Lambert, 2013). The gods and goddesses are created by the intermingling of salt water, the mother Tiamat, and fresh water, the father Apsu, and several successive generations of deities are born. However, all of these younger gods create noise and Apsu plots to destroy them so that he can rest. When the gods discover his plan, Ea kills Apsu. Later, Tiamat decides to destroy the gods. Marduk fights Tiamat, who is personified as a dragon, and defeats her. He splits her body into two parts and creates the heavens and the earth. Marduk is elevated to the top of the Mesopotamian pan-theon, creates humankind from the blood of the rebel god who incited Tiamat, and imposes upon human beings the toil of the gods. In this story, the primor-dial mother is demonized and killed, with her body becoming the physical world. The killer of the mother goddess is then elevated as supreme deity of the divine pantheon in a gathering of male gods. Unlike other Mesopotamian creation accounts, goddesses play no role in the creation of the physical world or even of humankind (Dalley, 1989, p. 228). Indeed, with the exception of the goddess Inana/Ishtar, goddesses generally have more limited roles and importance in Mesopotamian religion in the later second and first millennia (Frymer-Kensky, 1992).

Egypt. In ancient Egypt, creation was strongly connected to reproductive sexuality. According to ancient Egyptian literature, gender is presupposed within creation, and even when creation stems from a single source it is the result of the presence of both male and female within that source (Troy, 1997, p. 239). Nun, "the Father of the Gods," is the dark and limitless waters. Though technically a male deity, as the primordial waters he is not highly gendered as masculine and could even be seen as androgynous (Troy, p. 239).

The first Egyptian deity to create, the god Atum, is specifically gendered as male. Atum generates himself spontaneously within Nun, and he creates brother–sister/husband–wife pair Shu and Tefnut by masturbating into his own mouth and then spit-ting out the god and goddess:

> I became effective in my heart,
> I surveyed with my face.
> I made every form alone,
> Without having sneezed Shu,
> Without having spat Tefnut,
> Without another having evolved and
> acted with me.
> I surveyed in my heart by myself
> And the evolutions of evolutions became many,
> In the evolutions of children
> And in the evolutions of their children
> I am the one who acted as husband with my fist:
> I copulated with my hand,
> I let fall into my own mouth,
> I sneezed Shu and spat Tefnut.
> (Hallo and Younger, *Context of Scripture*
> 1997, 1.9: 14–15)

This creative act emphasizes male fertility, both phys-ically and also mentally, since Atum plans his crea-tion. However, feminine attributes are present in this creation since the hand of the god is interpreted as his consort and the eye of the god, gendered as female, plays an important role (Troy, 1997, p. 243). Shu and Tefnut are the first male–female gendered pair, and through sexual reproduction they bear the god Geb and the goddess Nut, earth and sky, respectively. Geb and Nut complete the creation of the physical world.

Geb and Nut have four children, the gods Osiris and Seth and the goddesses Isis and Nephthys, and this generation of gods is associated with social institutions such as kingship. Osiris and Isis demonstrate some gender ambiguity, with Isis as the active member of the pair, compensating for the passivity of her dead husband. Therefore, even specifically gendered deities could demonstrate both masculine and feminine characteristics. Osiris and Isis have a son Horus, a god specifically associated with kings. Pharaoh was thought to be his earthly manifestation. Seth and Nephthys, on the other hand, conform to specific gender roles but do not reproduce (Troy, 1997, p. 248).

Other goddesses also had important roles for the physical world. Nut, the sky goddess envisioned as a river flowing east to west, is also the mother of the sun god Re, who traveled through Nut's body every night to be reborn in the morning. The temple at Esna has preserved a late-period text in which creation comes from the goddess Neith/Mehetweret, also the mother of Re, who is the personification of the flood waters (Troy, 1997, pp. 253–257). In this text, a female deity is given a role similar to that of the male god Nun in other texts.

Israel. The Hebrew Bible contains two separate creation accounts: Genesis 1:1—2:4a, the seven-day creation of the physical world and the Sabbath, and Genesis 2:4b—3, the Garden of Eden story. For the sake of simplicity, I refer to the first text as Genesis 1 and the second as Genesis 2—3. Though these creation stories have often been conflated, scholarly consensus has long regarded them as disparate traditions, with Genesis 1 thought to be later than the Eden story of Genesis 2—3.

Genesis 1:1—2:4a. This account comprises the creation of the cosmos and the physical world from a formless void, culminating in the creation of human beings. Creation proceeds as a highly or-dered, planned event carried out by an omnipotent, if somewhat distant, deity, called 'Elohim in this text. After the creation of the physical world, the final living creatures, land animals and humans, are formed on the sixth day. The creation of human beings is recounted in Genesis 1:26–28:

> And God said, "Let us make humanity in our image, after our likeness. They shall rule the fish of the sea, the birds of the sky, the cattle, the whole earth, and all the creeping things that creep on earth." So God created humanity in His image, in the image of God He created him; male and female He created them. God blessed them and God said to them, "Be fertile and increase, fill the earth and master it; and rule the fish of the sea, the birds of the sky, and all the living things that creep on earth."

Notably, God creates men and women at the same time as the culmination of the physical world (God's final act is resting on the seventh day, resulting in the institution of the Sabbath). Male/female gender distinctions exist from the moment of humanity's creation, but both genders are made in the image of God. Moreover, both genders are given dominion over the natural world and commanded to procreate. Thus, reproductive sexuality is emphasized from the outset of humanity's existence (Stone, 2000, pp. 59–62).

By comparison to the Garden of Eden story (discussed later), Genesis 1 appears to demonstrate an equalized view of gender relations. No gender hierarchy is mentioned in this creation account—both genders are created simultaneously and share dominion over the earth as well as the responsibility of sexual reproduction. However, caution should be exercised when interpreting Genesis 1 as an emblem of gender equality. More likely, the creation account in Genesis 1 simply recognizes gender dimorphism as an essential feature of humanity. However, such recognition does not necessarily include gender equality from a social or legal standpoint (Clines, 1990, pp. 41–44; Meyers, 2012, p. 74; Shectman, 2009, pp. 130–134). In other words, Genesis 1 is concerned with biology rather than with social relationships (Bird, 1981, p. 155; Bird, 1997, p. 146).

Proverbs 8:22–31. The biblical book of Proverbs is chiefly composed of instruction literature, with the speaker as the "father" and the audience the "son" being addressed. However, one section of Proverbs describes the presence of wisdom at the creation of the cosmos. In this text, Wisdom, personified as feminine, is speaking:

> Yahweh created me at the beginning of His course
> As the first of His works of old.
> In the distant past I was fashioned,
> At the beginning, at the origin of earth
> There was still no deep when I was brought forth,
> No springs rich in water;
> Before [the foundation of] the mountains were sunk,
> Before the hills I was born.
> He had not made the earth and fields,
> Or the world's first clumps of clay.
> I was there when He set the heavens into place;
> When He fixed the horizon upon the deep;
> When he made the heavens above firm,
> And the fountains of the deep gushed forth;
> When He assigned the sea its limits,
> So that its waters never transgress His command;
> When He fixed the foundations of the earth,
> I was with Him as a confidant,
> A source of delight every day,
> Rejoicing before Him at all times,
> Rejoicing in His inhabited world,
> Finding delight with humankind.

In the Hebrew Bible, Yahweh is characteristically a male deity, though occasionally he is given feminine characteristics, such as being both father and mother (Deut 32:18; Isa 42:14, 46:3-4). In this text, wisdom, personified as female, is envisioned as present before the creation of the cosmos and as a companion to Yahweh. The text elevates a concept associated with the feminine as the first creation, a suitable feminine pairing with a masculine deity. However, Wisdom does not participate in the act of creation itself.

Genesis 2:4b—3. Perhaps more than any other biblical text, the creation account in Genesis 2—3 has impacted views of gender relations. Interpretations of the Garden of Eden story have often been highly detrimental for women, and this text has been used to support arguments for women's inferiority, weakness, and subordination to men as well as views of women as deceptive temptresses who lead righteous men astray. The main arguments about gender relations tend to coalesce around three passages: the creation of the woman (Gen 2:18-24), the blame attributed to the woman in eating the fruit from the forbidden tree (Gen 3:1-7), and God's pronouncement to the woman (Gen 3:16).

Rather than a creation of the cosmos, Genesis 2—3 focuses on the creation of humanity and their lineage and is an etiological folk tale, an explanation of how things came to be (Frymer-Kensky, 2006, p. 5; Meyers, 2012, p. 67). Indeed, when the story begins, God (here called Yahweh 'Elohim) has already created heaven and earth. The first action of the story is the creation of a human being, *hā'ādām* in Hebrew, from the dust of the earth and the breath of the deity (Gen 2:7). Though the characters in this tale are often referred to as Adam and Eve, they are not actually given these proper names until the end of the story for Eve (Gen 3:20) and even later for Adam (Gen 4:25). With the term *hā'ādām* used to designate the human being, the story engages in word play with the Hebrew word for "earth," *hā'ādāmâ*, the raw material used to make the human. An English rendering of this pun would be earthling/earth or human/humus (Meyers, 2012, p. 71; Trible, 1978, p. 77). As Hebrew is a gendered language, it is apparent that *hā'ādām* is a masculine noun. However, it has been suggested that the gender of the noun does not necessarily correlate to male gender and that the original "earthling" in Genesis 2 should be understood as androgynous since there is as yet no sexually differentiated human being (Bal, 1987, 113–114; Knust, 2011, pp. 51–53; Meyers, p. 72; Trible, p. 80;). Although this is certainly logical, against such an interpretation it has been pointed out that the original *hā'ādām* remains associated with the man after the woman is created, culminating in the name of the man as "Adam" (Clines, 1990; Gardner, 1990; Jobling, 1978; Lanser, 1988; Milne, 1989).

A key issue in the creation of woman is her designated purpose. Yahweh 'Elohim decides, "It is not good for the earthling to be by itself [i.e., the only one of its kind]. I will make a suitable partner for it" (Gen 2:18). On the basis of traditional translations "helper" or "helpmate," it has long been argued that women were created to be assistants to men. However, this view of "helper" has been criticized by feminist scholars, who particularly note the Hebrew term's association with Yahweh (Bal, 1987, p. 115; Meyers, 2012, p. 73; Trible, 1978, p. 90). Although this argument is a helpful corrective against misogynist interpretations, the verse likely refers to Yahweh creating a corresponding pair and does not relate to gender equality in social or legal terms (Meyers, 2012, p. 73).

After Yahweh 'Elohim forms the woman, he brings her to the earthling, now clearly the man. The man exclaims, "This one at last is bone of my bones and flesh of my flesh! This one shall be called 'Woman,' for from Man was she taken." The man names the woman, just as he also names the animals. In the word for "woman," there is another example of world play between a created object and its raw material. In this case "wo-man" (Hebrew *'iššâ)* is formed from man (Hebrew *'iš*). After the man names the woman, the text inserts what is possibly an etiological saying, "Hence a man leaves his father and mother and clings to his wife, so that they become one flesh." This statement reflects the opposite situation of Israelite marriage, where typically the woman left her household at marriage and lived with her husband's family. However, the passage understands (hetero-)sexual unions as representing the original unity of men and women at creation and sexual companionship as more important than biological family ties. Genesis 2 ends by noting that the man and woman were naked in the garden but felt no shame. Though sexually differentiated, humans do not yet possess awareness of sexuality.

This situation changes when the man and the woman, convinced by the "crafty" serpent, eat fruit from the Tree of the Knowledge of Good and Evil. The serpent does not represent Satan in Genesis, but this association emerges among later interpreters. In the ancient Near East snakes could symbolize wisdom but also immortality since they shed their skin (Carr, 2003, pp. 45–46). The serpent engages the woman in dialogue and gives assurance that eating the tree's fruit will not cause death.

When the woman saw that the tree was good for eating and a delight to the eyes, and that the tree was desirable as a source of wisdom, she took of its fruit and ate. She also gave some to her husband with her, and he ate. Then the eyes of both of them were opened and they perceived that they were naked; and they sewed together fig leaves and made loincloths for themselves. (Gen 3:6–7)

As the Hebrew makes clear, the man is with the woman for the entire discussion with the snake. Therefore, the woman is not deceptive, nor is she a temptress. It is not clear why the woman talks to the snake instead of talking to the man. It has been used as a traditional argument for woman's weakness or even inclination for evil, but there is no indication of this in the biblical text. In fact, the woman appears intelligent and perceptive (Fewell and Gunn, 1993, p. 30–31; Niditch, 2012, p. 31; Trible, 1978, p. 110). Perhaps the reason could be that wisdom was envisioned as feminine, and the forbidden tree is connected to wisdom and understanding (Meyers, 1988, p. 91). Whatever the case, the man and woman do not die—the serpent is right about this—but instead become cognizant of their nakedness (Carr, 2003, p. 46; Niditch, 2012 p. 31). What the man and woman gain from eating of the tree is awareness of their sexuality (Simkins, 1998, pp. 47–48).

When Yahweh discovers that the humans have eaten from the forbidden tree, he makes pronouncements against the serpent, the woman, and the man. The man and the serpent are both explicitly cursed, but the woman is not. Moreover, Yahweh's pronouncement against the woman is considerably shorter than the others. However, it is perhaps the most troubling verse for gender relations in the entire Hebrew Bible (Meyers, 1988, p. 95):

> I will make great your toil and many
> your pregnancies;
> With hardship shall you bear children.
> Yet, you shall desire your man
> And he shall overrule you.
>
> (Gen 3:16)

The man's curse is that the ground he must till will be hard and cause him much toil until he finally returns to the earth when he dies. Both punishments return to the original creation puns—the man was created from earth and his punishment connects to the earth; woman was created from man, and her punishment affects her relationship with the man, especially her role in sexual reproduction. Carol Meyers has argued that Yahweh's pronouncement upon the woman reflects the dangers that were associated with pregnancy and childbirth in ancient Israel (and other premodern societies) and that the man's "rule" over the woman refers to overcoming female reluctance to sexual reproduction (Meyers, 1988, pp. 99–121; Meyers, 2012). However, the story also represents an idealized image of gender relations in the garden, demonstrating recognition, however implicit, that gender relations in ancient Israel were not what they were originally meant to be.

Adam and Eve in later traditions. The story of the first man and woman in the Garden of Eden and their expulsion from paradise after eating the forbidden fruit has inspired various opinions and retellings for millennia (Meyers, 2012, pp. 60–65; Stewart, 2012). However, the rest of the Hebrew Bible makes no allusion to the story of the Garden of Eden. References to Adam and Eve begin to appear only in the third century B.C.E. and later, when Genesis 2–3 was part of the canon of Hebrew scriptures. These interpretations often tell us more about contemporary perspectives than the meaning of the biblical text itself.

Several references to Adam and Eve appear in Apocryphal texts. The earliest is the third century B.C.E. book Tobit, which refers to Adam and Eve in a marriage prayer: "You made Adam, and for him you made his wife Eve as a helper and support" (Tob 8:6). The early second-century B.C.E. book of Sirach (also known as Ben Sira or Ecclesiasticus) makes possibly the earliest connection between women, sin, and death (Kvam et al., 1999, p. 49): "From a woman sin had its beginning, and because of her we all die" (Sir 25:24). The first-century C.E. texts 2 Esdras 3:20–26 and 2 Baruch 48:42–47 both focus primarily on Adam's responsibility in the expulsion from Eden.

The New Testament also alludes to the Garden of Eden story, particularly among the Pauline and deutero-Pauline letters. In 1 Corinthians 15:21–22 and Romans 5:12 Paul compares sin and death coming into the world through Adam to the reconciliation and life through Christ, with no mention of Eve in these texts. Paul briefly mentions the serpent deceiving Eve by his cunning in 2 Corinthians 11:3. However, several references to Genesis 2–3 are used to support arguments for the subordination of women. In 1 Corinthians 11:7–12 Paul instructs women to veil themselves but asserts that a man should not have his head veiled "since he is the image and reflection of God; but woman is the reflection of man. Neither was man created for the sake of woman, but woman for the sake of man." The deutero-Pauline letters contain examples of similar perspectives. The first letter to Timothy relates women's subordination to men's authority to the Garden of Eden story in Genesis 2–3, stating, "For Adam was formed first, then Eve; and Adam was not deceived, but the woman was deceived and became a transgressor. Yet she will be saved through childbearing, provided they continue in faith and love and holiness, with modesty" (1 Tim 2:12–15). Ephesians 5:21–6:9 quotes Genesis 2:24 about a man leaving his father and mother and joining his wife in one flesh and applies it to women's subordination to their husbands.

One example in the synoptic gospels could also be an indirect reference to Eden. In the Gospel of Mark, Jesus is questioned by the Sadducees regarding the bonds of marriage after the resurrection. The Sadducees intend to outwit Jesus by giving an example of a woman who had married seven brothers through the custom of levirate marriage and asking Jesus whose wife she would be in the resurrection. "Jesus said to them, 'Is not this the reason you are wrong, that you know neither the scriptures nor the power of God? For when they rise from the dead, they neither marry nor are given in marriage, but are like angels in heaven'" (Mark 12:24–25). Early Christianity's vision of the kingdom of God is a return to an Eden-like state, but with the divine qualities of such an existence enhanced. With the end of marriage, the key institution of post-Eden reality, there comes also the potential end of gender hierarchy, as evidenced by the important roles held by women in the early church (Niditch, 1985, p. 95).

Although early Jewish and Christian texts demonstrate some variety of interpretations regarding Eve's status and blame for expulsion from the Garden, the view of Eve becomes increasingly negative. One popular work circulating in the first centuries C.E. was the pseudepigraphical Life of Adam and Eve, also called the Apocalypse of Moses. This retelling depicts an Eve ridden with guilt who claims that "all sin has come about through me" (*Apoc. Mos.* 32:3), though in the Apocalypse of Moses Eve also gives her own account of what happened in Eden and this section gives a more sympathetic view toward her (Arbel, 2012; Kvam et al., 1999, pp. 42–43; Levison, 1978, p. 150). Early church fathers such as Tertullian and Augustine viewed Eve as inferior and responsible for introducing sin into the world. Christian tradition in particular focused on the idea of "original sin" and the notion of a "fall," and theologians became especially fixated on the figure of Eve. With the serpent playing an increasingly satanic and phallic role, Eve became the antithesis of the Virgin Mary (Stewart, 2012). One of the most influential interpretations of Genesis 2–3 in the English-speaking world has been John Milton's epic poem *Paradise Lost*, which treats Eve as clearly inferior to Adam (e.g., *Paradise Lost* 10:150–151). As the result of this interpretative history, Eve came to represent all women's inferiority and weakness, on the one hand, and danger and deception on the other, especially regarding female sexuality. Though not monolithic, arguments for women's subordination based on Genesis 2—3 have persisted for over two millennia.

Genesis 2—3 has also been important for modern biblical scholarship, especially with the rise of feminism. Almost since its inception, feminist thinking has made use of the Bible. Since the Bible is seen by many as a sacred text, it therefore provides support for patriarchy and authorization for women's oppression, and this is especially the case with Genesis 2—3. First-wave feminists encountered arguments of women's inferiority based on Genesis 2—3 as an obstacle in getting the vote. During the second wave of feminism in the 1960s and 1970s, some feminists advocated rejecting Genesis 2—3 as harmful to women. However, biblical scholar Phyllis Trible and literary critic Mieke Bal argued that the original text was not as misogynistic as traditional interpretations of it but was instead a positive text for women and gender equality (Bal, 1987; Trible, 1978). Trible's work especially has been influential within biblical scholarship, though many of her arguments have been critiqued and her view of Genesis 2—3 as a proto-feminist text is regarded as positivistic, even by scholars with sympathetic aims (Clines, 1990; Gardner, 1990; Jobling, 1978; Lanser, 1988; Milne, 1989). Another major figure in recent interpretations of Genesis 2—3 is Carol Meyers, who has provided a historical interpretation of Genesis 2—3 based on archaeology and socio-anthropology of women's lives in Iron Age Israel (1988; 2012). Other recent scholarship has interpreted Genesis 2—3 as a wisdom text or a coming-of-age tale (Carr, 2003, pp. 45–46). Moreover, the binary division of gender as well as the presentation of heterosexuality as normative in Genesis 2—3 has also been discussed (Stone, 2000, pp. 62–68).

Looking to an ancient text such as Genesis 2—3 for answers to modern ethical debates surrounding gender equality is bound to yield an inadequate return. Living thousands of years ago, the writers of these stories were unaware of these issues. However, scholars can continue to utilize varieties of interpretive tools to understand better conceptions of gender in the Bible and the ancient Near Eastern world.

[*See also* Deity, *subentries on* Ancient Near East *and* Hebrew Bible; Education, *subentries on* Ancient Near East *and* Hebrew Bible; Imagery, Gendered, *subentry* Wisdom Literature; *and* Marriage and Divorce, *subentry* Hebrew Bible.]

BIBLIOGRAPHY

Alster, Bendt. "Enki and Ninhursag: The Creation of the First Woman." *Ugarit Forschungen* 10 (1978): 15–27.

Arbel, Vita Daphna. *Forming Femininity in Antiquity: Eve, Gender, and Ideologies in the Greek Life of Adam and Eve.* New York: Oxford University Press, 2012.

Asher-Greve, Julia. "Decisive Sex, Essential Gender." In *Sex and Gender in the Ancient Near East: Proceedings of the 47th Rencontre Assyriologique Internationale, Helsinki, July 2–6, 2001,* edited by Simo Parpola and Robert

M. Whiting, pp. 11–26. CRRAI 47. Helsinki: Neo-Assyrian Text Corpus Project, 2002.

Bal, Mieke. *Lethal Love: Feminist Literary Readings of Biblical Love Stories.* Bloomington: Indiana University Press, 1987.

Bird, Phyllis A. *Missing Persons and Mistaken Identities: Women and Gender in Ancient Israel.* Minneapolis: Fortress, 1997.

Bird, Phyllis A. "'Male and Female He Created Them': Genesis 1:27b in the Context of the Priestly Account of Creation." *Harvard Theological Review* 74 (1981): 129–159.

Carr, David M. *The Erotic Word: Sexuality, Spirituality, and the Bible.* Oxford: Oxford University Press, 2003.

Clines, David J. A. *What Does Eve Do to Help? And Other Readerly Questions to the Old Testament.* Sheffield, U.K.: JSOT, 1990.

Dalley, Stephanie. *Myths from Mesopotamia.* Rev. ed. Oxford: Oxford University Press, 2000; orig. 1989.

The Electronic Text Corpus of Sumerian Literature (ETCSL). http://etcsl.orinst.ox.ac.uk.

Fewell, Danna Nolan, and David M. Gunn. *Gender, Power, and Promise: The Subject of the Bible's First Story.* Nashville, Tenn.: Abingdon, 1993.

Frymer-Kensky, Tikva. *In the Wake of the Goddesses: Women, Culture, and the Biblical Transformation of Pagan Myth.* New York: Free Press, 1992.

Frymer-Kensky, Tikva. *Studies in Bible and Feminist Criticism.* Philadelphia: Jewish Publication Society, 2006.

Gardner, Anne. "Genesis 2:4b-3: A Mythological Paradigm of Sexual Equality or the Religious History of Pre-exilic Israel?" *Scottish Journal of Theology* 43 (1990): 1–18.

Hallo, William W., and K. Lawson Younger, eds. *The Context of Scripture.* 3 vols. Leiden, The Netherlands: Brill, 1997.

Jacobsen, Thorkild. *The Harps That Once...: Sumerian Poetry in Translation.* New Haven, Conn.: Yale University Press, 1987.

Jobling, David. *The Sense of Biblical Narrative.* Vol. 2. Sheffield, U.K.: JSOT Press, 1978.

Knust, Jennifer Wright. *Unprotected Texts: The Bible's Surprising Contradictions about Sex and Desire.* New York: HarperOne, 2011.

Kvam, Kristen E., Linda S. Schearing, and Valarie H. Ziegler, eds. *Eve & Adam: Jewish, Christian, and Muslim Readings on Genesis and Gender.* Bloomington: Indiana University Press, 1999.

Lambert, W. G. *Babylonian Creation Myths.* Winona Lake, Ind.: Eisenbrauns, 2013.

Lanser, Susan S. "(Feminist) Criticism in the Garden: Inferring Genesis 2-3." *Semeia* 41 (1988): 67–84.

Leick, Gwendolyn. *Sex and Eroticism in Mesopotamian Literature.* London: Routledge, 1994.

Levison, John R. "The Exoneration of Eve in the Apocalypse of Moses 15-30." *Journal for the Study of Judaism in the Persian, Hellenistic and Roman Period* 20 (1978): 135–150.

Meyers, Carol. *Discovering Eve: Ancient Israelite Women in Context.* Oxford: Oxford University Press, 1988.

Meyers, Carol. *Rediscovering Eve: Ancient Israelite Women in Context.* Oxford: Oxford University Press, 2012.

Milne, Pamela J. "The Patriarchal Stamp of Scripture: The Implications of Structuralist Analyses for Feminist Hermeneutics." *Journal of Feminist Studies in Religion* 5 (1989): 17–34.

Niditch, Susan. *Chaos to Cosmos: Studies in Biblical Patterns of Creation.* Studies in the Humanities 6. Chico, Calif.: Scholars Press, 1985.

Niditch, Susan. "Genesis." In *Women's Bible Commentary,* 3d ed., edited by Carol A. Newsom, Sharon H. Ringe, and Jacqueline E. Lapsley, pp. 27–45 Louisville, Ky.: Westminster John Knox, 2012.

Shectman, Sara. *Women in the Pentateuch: A Feminist and Source-Critical Analysis.* Sheffield, U.K.: Sheffield Phoenix, 2009.

Simkins, Ronald A. "Gender Construction in the Yahwist Creation Myth." In *Genesis: A Feminist Companion to the Bible.* 2d Series, edited by Athalya Brenner, pp. 32–52. Sheffield, U.K.: Sheffield Academic Press, 1998.

Stewart, Anne W. "Eve and Her Interpreters." In *Women's Bible Commentary,* 3d ed., edited by Carol A. Newsom, Sharon H. Ringe, and Jacqueline E. Lapsley, pp. 45–50 Louisville, Ky.: Westminster John Knox, 2012.

Stone, Ken. "The Garden of Eden and the Heterosexual Contract." In *Take Back the Word: A Queer Reading of the Bible,* edited by Robert E. Goss and Mona West, pp. 57–70. Cleveland, Ohio: Pilgrim, 2000.

Stone, Ken. *Practicing Safer Texts: Food, Sex, and Bible in Queer Perspective.* London: T&T Clark, 2004.

Trible, Phyllis. *God and the Rhetoric of Sexuality.* Philadelphia: Fortress, 1978.

Troy, Lana. "Engendering Creation in Ancient Egypt: Still and Flowing Waters." In *A Feminist Companion to Reading the Bible: Approaches, Methods, and Strategies,* edited by Athalya Brenner and Carole Fontaine, pp. 238–268. Sheffield, U.K.: Sheffield Academic Press, 1997.

Erin E. Fleming

D

DEITY

This entry contains six subentries: Ancient Near East; Hebrew Bible; Greek World; Roman World; New Testament; *and* Early Church.

Ancient Near East

This article presents a general overview of gender constructs that may or may not be revealed in the actions and characteristics attributed to various Mesopotamian deities in the cuneiform record. Sources that inform this overview are predominantly literary: myths, legends, hymns, and royal inscriptions. These texts provide the most description. Unfortunately, due to the vagaries of discovery, scribal curriculum, and political and religious interests, it must be accepted at the outset that this knowledge base is inherently limited and biased. While we have dated royal and dedicatory inscriptions that contain references to gods, our Sumerian literary texts—hymns and prayers—date predominantly to the Old Babylonian period (some containing modified versions of older texts) and primarily come from two southern sites: Nippur and Ur. Akkadian texts date to later periods, but even the majority of these are known to us only from late copies discovered in the Neo-Assyrian library of Aššurbanipal. Royal inscriptions, hymns, and prayers are rife with imperialist goals. The texts from Nippur and Ur are undoubtedly colored by the cults of Nippur and Ur. With this said, much can be gleaned from these accounts. In what follows, when a god is first mentioned, the name is followed by an f (for female) or m (for male) in parentheses to alert readers to that god's sex, e.g., Enlil(m) or Ninlil(f). In many cases it is unknown what, if any, sex a god was given.

Early Scholarship and Reality. When the ancient Near East was stumbled upon (sometimes quite literally) by curious Westerners in the latter half of the second millennium C.E., these early travelers, soon to be scholars, began to find evidence of a rich polytheistic society. Seeking to make sense of this seemingly very foreign world, they explained the new discoveries in terms of what they already knew. In addition to multiple other ideas, they theorized in an astral pantheon, an agricultural one, and a "primitive" religion at whose heart was a great single deity (a mother goddess). Because these early scholars continued to seek a blueprint for the ancient world in one already known to them, female gods were assumed to be mere shades of their male active counterparts (except for this early "mother goddess"): every family needed a patriarch and every patriarch needed a loving if nondescript female partner. Mesopotamian religion does and does not fit these models. Mesopotamian gods were at times, and in different regions, grouped into families and there was a great goddess who was motherly in that she ushered in all life; there was also, however, a great god who was the essence of all fertility. The gods were, somewhat late in the cuneiform record, associated with or viewed as planets and stars; yet they were also rulers over cities and lands, multiple aspects of human society, flora, fauna, and meteorological phenomena. Gods rarely jockeyed for power among themselves, and the sex and gender of a god, in the main, seems to have had little correlation with the manner by which mortal sex and gender was assigned and/or performed.

Language. On a certain level, it must be assumed that Sumerians, at least, were not overly concerned with the sex and gender of deities. The Sumerian language has grammatical gender but it is assigned according to sentient versus nonsentient and not feminine versus masculine. The Sumerian word for god, **diĝir**, is unisex. This means that unless there are additional indicators (e.g., the god is said to be a father or mother), it cannot be known what sex the deity is. This makes it impossible to parse out the gender of deities listed in the earliest god lists, unless they rose to such importance as to have made their way into later more descriptive texts. The Akkadian language does differentiate masculine and feminine, although not consistently (third-person verbal forms are unisex in Old Babylonian and can lead to ambiguity of subject). Moreover, many religious literary texts are not written in Akkadian; only during the latter half of the second millennium did such texts begin to be written predominantly in this Semitic language. It is also during this time that the vast plethora of gods begins to be syncretized to such an extent that relatively few deities remain active by the later periods in Mesopotamian history.

Descriptions. Dissimilar from the mortal world, the sex of a god is not assigned based on his or her genitalia, nor is the gender of a god assigned based on the god's sex. Rather, the visual presentation or textual description of a god occurs after the sex has been agreed on by a culture, if any sex has been decided at all. How these designations are assigned is obscure and eludes any simple rationale. Visually, gender differentiation can be obvious and accords with visual gender differ-

entiation of mortals, such as the presence or absence of a beard. Hairstyles and dress might also provide marking, as do half- or seminude depictions. Dress is not a consistent marker, however, since martial Ištar dons masculine clothing and stance but sometimes lifts her skirt to show her sex. This alerts the viewer that she performs a construct of divine femininity that is more closely aligned with divine masculinity. All gods, regardless of sex, when described anthropomorphically are good looking, sexy, and awesome to behold. Female and male gods, when not depicted anthropomorphically, take various forms. They are amorphous, such as Nammu/Tiāmat(f), who seems to be essentially an enormous womb filled with amniotic fluid. Apsû(m), too, is fluid waters, taking even less shape as the underground "sweet waters" = semen. When Tiāmat fights she becomes a great flying dragon creature; when she is eviscerated by Marduk(m), her body becomes the earth on which humans live and the sky in which birds fly. Enlil is a great mountain, and Inana(f) and Ninurta(m) are the size of mountains when they each destroy Ebih (a mountain) and Asag (a mountain creature with a rock army). Marduk is so large that as a child the four winds are his playthings. On Middle Babylonian *kudurru* (large commemorative stones), gods are symbolized. Except for Gula(f), who is given the shape of a mortal woman, gods are represented by a turtle, spade, lightning, snake, and goat, among other images. In texts, gods are frequently described as giant bovines, serpents, or celestial in nature. An(m) is the heavens. Appearing as planets and stars, Nana/Sîn(m) is the moon god and father of the Utu/Šamaš(m), the Sun, and his twin sister Inana/Ištar, Venus. Even though he is their father, Nana is smaller than his son but larger than his daughter (as seen by the naked eye). Nergal(m) is the red planet, Mars, and Ninurta(m) is Sirius, the brightest star in the sky.

Functions of Gods. In the Mesopotamian evidence, the gods function within both biological/societal roles and the administration of justice.

Biological/societal. It might be assumed that the sex and gender of gods mirrors the mortal world with regard to function and actions. Certainly this is true when the gods are grouped together in families. In domestic scenes, gods can be described as acting as would mortals. When Ninisin(f) is promised as wife to Ninĝirsu(m) and comes to reside in the house of her father-in-law Enlil, she is said to be the **egia** (Akk. *kallatu*) "bride in residence." When Dumuzi(m) woos Inana in the many love songs devoted to the couple, Dumuzi acts as would be expected of any mortal suitor. He brings gifts to the family and dances about like a young lad in love.

The sex of gods who preside over procreation also aligns with the sex roles of mortals. The gods of the womb and birth are female: Nammu/Tiāmat, Ninmaḫ/Bēlet-ilī, and Ninimma; however, the god of gestation, Nana, is male. The male moon god may have presided over gestation because of his role in the determination of a month. Fertility itself was presided over by the water god Enki/Ea(m) and the rain god Iškur/Adad(m). Water was the equivalent of semen, considered the source of all life. In addition, the societally gendered roles of weaving—governed by Uttu(f)—and ploughing—governed by Ninazu/Ninĝirsu/Ninurta(m)—mirror mortal practice (although men did weave). Thus, when describing procreative and domestic roles, the sex and gender of a god could follow mortal constructs; however, more abstract realms over which gods presided cannot be so easily explained.

Justice, societal order, and destiny. Many gods had two vital roles: to function as patron deity over a city(ies) or land(s) and to function as the ruler of a realm such as medicine, irrigation, or animal husbandry. Some more minor gods did not function as patrons and instead served in the entourage of the greater gods in the roles of ministers, heralds, or butlers. Various major deities, or consortiums of deities, also controlled mortal justice, societal order, and the destinies of gods and peoples.

Justice and the execution of justice were carried out by a variety of deities. Utu/Šamaš was god of justice par excellence and continued in this capacity throughout the long cuneiform record. The martial gods carried out justice (periodically with the help of mortals), and hence they occasionally are referred to as guardians of right and wrongdoing. Because there is no evidence that mortal women wielded weapons in any Mesopotamian society during any

period (and in fact there is ample evidence that supports martial activity as a facet of a construct of masculinity), we might expect that goddesses were not martial. Yet, although many deities of war were considered male (e.g., Ninĝirsu, Ninurta, Nergal, Adad, and Zababa), there were multiple martial goddesses (e.g., Ištar/Inana, Annunītum, Ulmašitum, Ninsi'anna, and Ninisin).

One might argue that all male martial deities are in some way versions of each other, since all female martial deities seem to be forms of Ištar; however, when acting in a battle setting all male and female war gods are described similarly. Martial gods are heroes who delight in battle. If there is rebellion on the horizon, they are quick to act. They execute mountains, as do Inana in *Inana and Ebih* and Ninurta in *Lugal-e*; they lead kings to war, as do Nergal, Ninurta, and Ištar in the Assyrian royal inscriptions; and they carry out destruction and murder at the behest of Enlil, as does Ninisin when she declares that "after I had destroyed [the city] like water, drowned it like the harvest, after I had grabbed [the rebel] as a threshing sledge grabs barley, after I had set him ablaze like esparto grass, I struck him with the mace and killed him" (ETCSL 4.22.1: 118–120). War gods desire power in addition to blood, as does Ninurta in *Ninurta and the Turtle* when he attempts to acquire the Tablet of Destinies. Nergal/Erra also seeks power when he wishes to wrest control from Marduk in the *Erra Epic*, as does Inana/Ištar when she travels to the Netherworld to usurp Ereškigal(f) in the bilingual *Ištar's Descent to the Netherworld*. All gods, martial or otherwise, are described as sullen, spoiled, impetuous, and disruptive when enraged. For a god to be calmed, be it Enlil when he chooses to destroy a city or land or Ereškigal when she flays Ištar, his or her heart must be cooled and his or her ego soothed.

As patron, a deity was the protector of a city (or land) and her people. According to the *Sumerian Temple Hymns*, the function of protector of a city was neither particularly masculine nor feminine, at least during the Old Babylonian period. This text, which praises the temples of various cities, lists patron gods that are 40 percent female. A patron deity proclaims a good fate for the king and city and acts as a lobbyist before the council of gods, so that they too may proclaim a good fate for the king and city. A propitious reign was filled with agricultural abundance, lack of plague, good market prices, and safe highways. To keep a patron deity content, the king of the city or ruler of several cities needed to tend to the basic needs of the gods, e.g., feeding, clothing, and entertaining them, and to ensure that the god(s) was(were) properly worshiped through various religious rites. If a king failed in his duties, the god or council of gods could remove his or their protection and "hand over" the city (or land) to another ruler. During this change of power the city (or land) would become the victim of war, drought, starvation, rape, pillaging, inflation, and various other atrocities.

Whereas in the north various gods had the power to revoke kingship (e.g., Adad and Ištar), in southern Sumer the fate of a city was more likely at the mercy of four great gods: An of the heavens, Enlil of the air/lands, Enki of the waters, and Ninmaḫ/Ninḫursaĝ/Aruru of the foothills or netherworld. These gods are not only the patrons of their own cities but as the rulers of the four regions (sky, land, water, netherworld) they could sit in counsel together and decree more universal fates. Of the four, Enlil is most often described as the instigator of the destruction of a city or region. Destruction could be ordered because of divine displeasure with offerings, as in the case of Ur-Nammu in the *Death of Ur-Nammu*. Or, as in several tales, the gods merely become irritated by the noise made by the multitude of people populating their cities. Sometimes, as recorded in the *Sumerian King List*, the reason for a change of rule is unknown even to the gods themselves.

Since patron gods could be of either sex, the indifference to these horrors expressed by the god and the compassion needed to alleviate the suffering was neither a masculine nor feminine trait. Somewhat gendered is a god's described reaction to the destruction of his or her own city. In the *Lament for Sumer and Ur*, all male gods are said to "take an unfamiliar path," while all female goddesses lament bitterly: "Alas, the destroyed city, my destroyed house."

However, lest it be thought that only female deities are prone to lamenting, in the *Lament for Uruk* all of the Anuna gods cry and in the *Lament for Eridu* Enki weeps bitter tears, wails, fasts, and becomes despondent. Damgalnuna, his wife, claws at her breast, eyes, and hair while wailing. To calm their deep sadness, the lament is recited to soothe the heart of the chief patron, Enki, so that the gods may return to his city. Enlil acts similarly in the *Cursing of Akkade*. After Enlil decrees the destruction of Akkade, each deity removes his or her gift from the city: Ninurta, the royal insignia; Utu, speech; Enki, wisdom; and Inana, weapons. Akkade then descends on the Ekur, temple of Enlil. Enlil's response to the ransacking of the Ekur is to become severely depressed, lie down, and fast. Finally, when Ur is destroyed, in the *Lament for Ur*, Nana goes before his father Enlil to beg for an end to the travesties. He wears the garment of mourning. Ultimately, An, Enlil, Enki, and Ninmaḫ allow for peace and rejuvenation to return to the land just as they also decree the restitution of all of Sumer and Akkade in the *Lament for Nippur*. In this lament, Enlil destroys his own city because he is angry. He makes the great **me**, the organizing principles of the universe, fly away, thus causing chaos.

The exact connection between the **me** and the Tablet of Destinies is unclear. The Tablet, worn around the neck of Aššur in the Neo-Assyrian period, originally had been kept and inscribed by Nisaba(f). According to the *Temple Hymns*, fates were decreed at the temples of Ninḫursaĝ at Ereš and Adab, since Ninḫursaĝ is the midwife who ordains destinies. According to the myth *Enlil and Sud*, once they are married Sud/Ninlil (daughter of Nisaba/Ninḫursaĝ) will sit with Enlil in the Ekur and determine the fates. Perhaps the Tablet comes to be in Enlil's possession when the two houses of Nisaba/Ninḫursaĝ and Enlil join, since it is from Enlil that the Anzû bird steals the Tablet in order to rule in the *Epic of Anzû*. Ninurta, son of Enlil, must battle Anzû to return the Tablet to his father.

In *Ninurta and the Turtle*, Anzû also tries to steal the Tablet of Destinies, here equated with the **me**. The powers fall into the Abzu, dwelling of Enki. Multiple myths record Enki as keeper of the **me** and organizer of the universe. In *Enki and the World Order*, the god assigns functions to the deities; in *Inana and Enki*, it is from Enki that Inana receives the **me**, which she then brings to her city Uruk. Several of Inana's temples (including her temple at Aššur) are referred to as the residences of the **me**. But this is true for Ninurta as well. Both Inana and Ninurta are said to decree destinies—Ninurta with this father Enlil, and Inana with the three great gods: An, Enlil, and Enki. Eventually, when Marduk rises in power, his son Nabû, who is essentially syncretized with Nisaba, resides in the temple called the house which gathers the seven **me** of heaven and earth.

Power Shifts. Throughout the length of Mesopotamian history, certain functions normally associated with one deity might transfer or be absorbed by another deity. For example, Ninĝirsu, a god of the ancient Sumerian city Lagaš, was both a hero and an agricultural god who came to be syncretized with Ninurta, the son of Enlil. After this merging it becomes almost impossible to separate one god from the other. Similarly, when Babylon rises in prestige, its minor god, Marduk, acquires the great *mušhuššu* dragon from the god Ninazu(m) after the city of Ninazu, Ešnunna, is conquered. Because Nabû(m), god of Borsippa, is the son of Marduk, he acquires the function of patron of the scribes from Nisaba, the mother-in-law of Enlil. In this exchange, Nabû also gains the designation Sovereign of Sexual Attraction from Nisaba.

This kind of transfer/syncretization can also be from male god to female god. In the Sumerian tale *Inana and Enki*, Inana travels to Eridu to acquire the **me** from Enki. This tale is thought to explain the rise of Uruk, city of Inana. Perhaps the most obvious absorption of powers is recorded in the *Enūma Eliš*. At the end of this Akkadian myth, Marduk receives fifty names, each representing a power normally held by a different god. Even the number fifty is indicative of a transfer of power, first being associated with Ninĝirsu, then with Ninurta, then with Enlil, and finally with Marduk. It should also be noted that when Marduk choses to battle the mighty Tiāmat, he declares that a woman's strength is not as great as a man's. It is difficult to decide if this should be

read more than as a mere highly provocative taunt, for certainly Ištar of Arbela continued to strike fear into the hearts of men as war god of the Assyrians as long as the text was in major circulation.

The transfer of power between deities is often seen as reflecting a shift from a more matriarchal or "woman friendly" society to a patriarchal one. This is one explanation for the account in which both Enlil and his son Ninurta rename Nisaba and Sud. After marrying Sud, daughter of Nisaba/ Ninḫursaĝ, Enlil renames her Ninlil and acquires the prestige of her family line. In the bilingual myth *Lugal-e*, Ninurta, son of Enlil, gives Enlil's sister the great Ninmaḫ the new name Ninḫursaĝ and places her in charge of the stones that he has just conquered. This act not only solidifies his power to name his own aunt but explains the superiority of Nippur over Ereš, city of Ninḫursaĝ. However, the very opposite transfer is recorded in *Inana and An*. In this Sumerian tale, Inana takes over the heavens and is said to be "more powerful than An." It is thought that this myth records the preeminence of Inana in the Eana of Uruk, the temple complex she shares with An.

The preeminence of Inana/Ištar during various points in Mesopotamian history, therefore, is not the result of a great matriarchy. Rather, empires such as the Old Akkadian Sargonic and the Neo-Assyrian Sargonid had Inana/Ištar as their most powerful deity. As a city, land, or empire rises in prestige so too do its primary gods.

Other. This survey has by necessity been brief and general. It has left out certain major deities, such as Gula/Ninisin, the great healer, and her medical assistant son, Ninazu. It also does not discuss gods connected to illness, such as Erra, who may bring plague; Šamaš, who may cause leprosy; and Gula, who seems to be able to curse a person with dropsy. Nor does it consider the many malevolent divine beings, such as the daughters of An, the Sebetti, or various demons, all of whom are rarely sexed. It does not provide discussion of minor deities, such as the vizier Ninšubar, who is female when ministering to Inana and male when aiding An. Ninšubar is further equated with the sister of Dumuzi, Geštinana in some texts, and with Pabilsaĝ, the husband of Gula, in others. Finally, it must be noted that even within different regions, gods may have different sexes. Dumuzi-abzu, a god of incantations, is female at Lagaš and male in Eridu. In the most cited example of this phenomenon, the Sun is male in Mesopotamia proper and female in Anatolia (modern Turkey). In both regions, the Sun is a grand judge who presides over justice.

In short, gender, sex, and deity are as complex as the religion(s) of Mesopotamia itself. Each function, description, and transfer of power must be contextualized according to authorial intent, audience, purpose, setting, and period, for it is difficult to know the ways of the gods.

[*See also* Gender and Sexuality: Ancient Near East.]

BIBLIOGRAPHY

Asher-Greve, J. "Decisive Sex, Essential Gender." In *Sex and Gender in the Ancient Near East: Proceedings of the 47th Rencontre Assyriologique Internationale, Helsinki, July 2–6, 2001*, edited by S. Parpola and R. M. Whiting, pp. 11–26. CRRAI 47. Helsinki: Neo-Assyrian Text Corpus Project, 2002.

Asher-Greve, J. "The Gaze of Goddesses: On Divinity, Gender, and Frontality in the Late Early Dynastic, Akkadian, and Neo-Sumerian Periods." *NIN* 4 (2003): 1–59.

Asher-Greve, J., and J. G. Westenholz. *Goddesses in Context: On Divine Powers, Roles, Relationships and Gender in Mesopotamian Textual and Visual Sources*. Bristol, Conn.: Vandenhoeck & Ruprecht, 2013.

Cooper, J. S. *An-gim dím-ma: The Return of Ninurta to Nippur*. Rome: Pontificium Institutum Biblicum, 1978.

The Electronic Text Corpus of Sumerian Literature. http://etcsl.orinst.ox.ac.uk

Groneberg, B. "The Role and Function of Goddesses in Mesopotamia." In *The Babylonian World*, edited by B. Groneberg, pp. 319–331 New York: Routledge.

Michalowski, P. *The Lamentation over the Destruction of Sumer and Ur*. Winona Lake, Ind.: Eisenbrauns, 1989.

Parpola, S., and R. M. Whiting. *Sex and Gender in the Ancient Near East: Proceedings of the 47th Rencontre Assyriologique Internationale, Helsinki, July 2–6, 2001*. Helsinki: Neo-Assyrian Text Corpus Project, 2002.

Westenholz, J. G. "Towards a New Conceptualization of the Female Role in Mesopotamian Society." *Journal of the American Oriental Society* 110 (1990): 510–521.

Westenholz, J. G. "Goddesses of the Ancient Near East 3000–1000 B.C." In *Ancient Goddesses: The Myths and the Evidence*, edited by L. Goodison and C. Morris, pp. 63–82. Madison: University of Wisconsin Press, 1998.

Zsolnay, I. "Do Divine Structures of Gender Mirror Mortal Structures of Gender?" In *In the Wake of Tikva Frymer-Kensky*, edited by Steven Holloway, JoAnn Scurlock, and Richard Beal, pp. 103–120. Piscataway, N.J.: Gorgias.

Ilona Zsolnay

Hebrew Bible

Many of the world's religions consider one or more female deities to be powerful forces and legitimate objects of veneration. In mainstream Judeo-Christian tradition and practice, however, female deities are noticeably absent. In the latter third of the twentieth century, as feminists within Judeo-Christian tradition began to articulate notions such as patriarchy, androcentricity, and gender equality, this lack of female divinity was rendered problematic. Interpreting Genesis 1:27 to mean that the image of God comprises both male and female, one stream of theologically oriented scholarship focused on demonstrating that certain texts attribute female characteristics and roles to Yahweh, and thereby asserted that this deity should not be envisaged simply as male. A second approach has been to reassess what the Hebrew Bible, and Hebrew Bible scholars, have had to say about female deities and their worship.

A God Both (and Neither) Male and Female. The initial terms of reference and conceptual frame for attributing female characteristics and social roles to Yahweh were laid out in the 1970s by Phyllis Trible in response to the Women's Liberation Movement's denigration of the Bible and its God. Her starting point was the conviction that biblical faith does not support either the creation or perpetuation of patriarchy, and that the interpretational challenge lay in translating biblical faith without sexism (Trible, 1973, pp. 30–31). She proceeded without evident reflection on the essentialist implications of what she accepted as indicative of female, or feminine, roles and attitudes, and did not employ a concept of gender. This conceptual naïveté persisted in much subsequent literature on the topic. The project of affirming women's equality by arguing that Yahweh is both (and neither) male and female was eclipsed to a certain extent by the second approach noted earlier.

Female images of Yahweh. Although acknowledging the overwhelming predominance of "masculine" language and imagery used to describe Yahweh in the Hebrew Bible, Trible and others argued that numerous texts draw upon female anatomy and social roles to portray this deity. Prominent examples include those that, ostensibly, depict Yahweh in labor (Isa 42:14; cf. 66:9), speak of Yahweh giving birth (Num 11:12; Deut 32:18), acting maternally (Isa 49:15, 66:13) or in the role of a midwife (Ps 22:9–10), or performing typically female tasks such as providing food and drink (Exod 16:4–36; 17:1–7; Hos 11:4; Neh 9:15) and clothing (Gen 3:21; Neh 9:21). That the Hebrew Bible clearly and consistently uses masculine pronouns in reference to Yahweh has been explained by noting that Hebrew has grammatically masculine and feminine genders but no neuter and, since all names and epithets of Yahweh are grammatically masculine, God is referred to, both in Hebrew and in English translation, with masculine pronouns such as "he." Thus, grammatical gender has made a powerful contribution toward (mis)conceptualizing Yahweh as male (Meyers, 1990, p. 526). For example, regarding Psalm 22:9's "yet it was you [Yahweh] who took me from the womb; you kept me safe on my mother's breast," the fact that this "you" in the Hebrew is masculine singular does not preclude Trible (1973, p. 33; 1978, p. 22) from describing Yahweh in this verse as a female midwife.

Several of the texts routinely cited as presenting female images of God have been interpreted differently. Take, for example, Isaiah 49:15:

Can a woman forget her nursing child,
or show no compassion for the child of her womb?
Even these may forget,
yet I [Yahweh] will not forget you.

While this verse clearly compares Yahweh's bond (with Jerusalem) with a mother's attachment to her infant, there is nothing that compels the reader to envisage Yahweh as maternal/female as a consequence of the comparison. Numbers 11:12 provides another example. In this verse, an exasperated Moses says to God:

Did I conceive all this people? Did I give birth to them, that you should say to me, "Carry them in your bosom, as a nurse carries a suckling child, to the land that you promised on oath to their ancestors"?

That Moses's rhetorical questions are intended to be answered in the negative is not in dispute. What is in contention is whether Moses's speech necessarily implies that Yahweh gave birth to and suckled Israel, thereby suggesting that God is female.

Gynomorphism, deity, and simile. In numerous texts in the Hebrew Bible Yahweh is portrayed anthropomorphically, that is, in human form. Examples include Yahweh breathing into the nostrils of the first human the breath of life (Gen 2:7), walking in Eden at the time of the evening breeze (Gen 3:8), feeling regret (Gen 6:6), and enjoying the aroma of roasting flesh (Gen 8:21). Given that the term "anthropomorphic" can be construed as nonspecific about gender, "gynomorphic" was coined to mean in human female form and contrasted with "andromorphic." However, when "gynomorphic" is used in the literature that interprets certain texts as illustrating that Yahweh is not always envisaged as male, "gynomorphic" is qualified by terms such as "speech," "language," and "imagery." These qualifications in effect subtly enlarge the range of texts that can be described as gynomorphic such that "gynomorphic" is no longer being employed strictly as a gender-specific subcategory of "anthropomorphic." To illustrate, consider Isaiah 42:14b: "now I [Yahweh] will cry out like a woman in labor, I will gasp and pant." Yahweh in this text is not portrayed as human in the same way as the deity is portrayed anthropomorphically in the examples from Genesis. Rather, in Isaiah 42, the deity is said to scream and gasp and pant *like* a woman does when she is in labor (Darr, 1987). Isaiah 66:13 provides another example of so-called gynomorphic imagery being applied to God: "As a mother comforts her child, so

I [Yahweh] will comfort you." While the imagery of a mother comforting her child is clearly maternal/gynomorphic, Yahweh is not thereby envisaged by the author as being a comforting mother. In other words, unlike the standard examples of anthromorphism of the type drawn from Genesis, both Isaiah texts employ the literary trope known as simile, and neither simile entails gendering Yahweh female.

The compassionate Womb? In the Hebrew Bible, Yahweh is frequently described as a compassionate deity. In Hebrew, the noun *raḥămîm* ("compassion"), the verb *riḥam* ("have compassion"), and the adjective *raḥûm* ("compassionate") share both the clearly related meanings as well as the three consonants *rḥm* and thus can be described, inaccurately but pragmatically, as sharing the same root. The Hebrew word for "womb," *reḥem*, includes the same three consonants, and on this basis it has been argued that "womb" and "compassion" are meaningfully related, the latter being an abstract, metaphorical extension of the meaning of the concrete noun "womb." Thus compassion, including Yahweh's compassion, is imbued with meaning that derives from a uniquely female body part and so is deemed an essentially female emotion (Trible, 1978, pp. 31–59).

From an etymological point of view it is possible that the word for "womb" derives from a root distinct from that of "compassion." This is because Hebrew *ḥ* represents the merger of two consonants that were distinct in proto-Semitic, and so the fact that "womb" and "compassion" share the consonants in rḥm is not incontrovertible evidence that they share the same etymology. In any event, shared etymology does not entail shared meaning in the mind of the speaker of a language, nor does lack of a shared etymology preclude a semantic relationship in the speaker's mind. Furthermore, even if we grant that "womb" and "compassion" are somehow related, it does not logically follow that their relationship to one another is that of an abstract tenor and concrete vehicle of a metaphor, nor does a speaker's or writer's use of the word "compassion" necessarily evoke uterine imagery for the hearer or reader.

Gender, sexuality, and monotheism. That the Hebrew Bible does not ever depict or allude to Yahweh having sex with a female deity has been cited as further evidence that Yahweh was not envisaged strictly as male. Whereas various deities of the surrounding cultures were often presented in their respective texts as sexually active, Yahweh's asexuality set this deity radically apart from other gods. Additionally, that Yahweh exhibits female traits and characteristics has been construed as evidence that in Yahwistic monotheism, the God of Israel absorbed the roles and powers associated elsewhere with female as well as male deities.

No Hebrew Bible text depicts or alludes to Yahweh having intercourse with a female deity, but several passages (see especially Jeremiah 2, 3, and 13; Ezekiel 16 and 23; Hosea 2) employ metaphor to portray Yahweh as the sexually betrayed and vengeful husband of a promiscuous wife. A subset of the passages (e.g., Ezek 16:20–21 and 23:37) speaks of children of this union, and Ezekiel 16:8 (cf. Ruth 3:3–9) arguably alludes to Yahweh's consummation of the marriage. Figurative language aside, the Hebrew Bible, when speaking of the deity anthropomorphically, generally avoids discussing or depicting the divine groin. Howard Eilberg-Schwartz has argued that the overall reticence to imagine the deity as explicitly, sexually male in Jewish monotheism serves to deflect the "homoerotic dilemma" (1994, p. 130) that Yahweh's sex posed for male adherents.

Female Deities in the Hebrew Bible. For much of the twentieth century, there was a scholarly consensus concerning the fundamentals involved in the worship of female deities in the ancient Near East. This consensus included the tenets that any goddess named in the Hebrew Bible was, by definition, non-Israelite, and any veneration of a goddess in Israelite religion was both illicit and entailed participation in cultic intercourse. This consensus began to be challenged in the 1980s by a generation of scholars who were better attuned to reflecting critically on the rhetorical and ideological positions presented by various biblical texts, conversant with formulating gender-nuanced questions, and more comfortable crossing disciplinary boundaries. The challenge was aided by the discovery, at Kuntillet Ajrud in the northeastern Sinai Peninsula and at Khirbet el-Qom in the foothills of Judah, of ninth/eighth century B.C.E. inscriptions plausibly interpreted to pair Yahweh either with a goddess named Asherah or the cult object that symbolized her.

The twentieth-century consensus. Prior to the 1980s, biblical scholars typically distinguished sharply between ancient Israelite religion and the religions of other ancient Near Eastern societies. These scholars were especially concerned with distinguishing ancient Israelite religion from its closest and most dangerous competitor, so-called Canaanite nature/fertility religion. This type of religion was thought to be primitive and characterized by a focus on the promotion of human, animal, and agricultural fecundity, and aided, according to some scholars, by *hieros gamos*, the sacred sexual union of a god and goddess (and perhaps enacted by their royal and/or priestly human representatives). Fertility cult worship was also imagined to entail so-called sacred (or cultic, or temple) prostitution. Precise reconstructions differed, but basically women were thought to have ritual premarital or extramarital sex with a man or men as a form of homage and/or to stimulate, by imitative magic, the fertility of crops and herds. In sharp contrast, proper (and decidedly superior) Israelite religion was understood to be grounded in history, ethically based and antithetical to Canaanite religion, including the Canaanite worship of female "fertility goddesses," and the immoral and degrading sexual practices that this worship was imagined to require. Thus, by definition, Israelite religion was supposed to preclude the veneration of goddesses and the concomitant, sexually oriented fertility cult that, allegedly, various Hebrew Bible texts alluded to and condemned.

Challenges to the standard paradigm. Several lines of argumentation have contributed to the disassembling of the aforementioned consensus position. All are built to some degree upon a fundamental appreciation of viewing Canaanite and Israelite religion as developing out of a shared cultural past and of acknowledging the vested interests of the various biblical authors and their modern interpreters alike. Initially, it has been observed that consensus position scholarship was rooted in a late nineteenth- and early twentieth-century social evolutionary model, which was, additionally, ethnocentrically skewed toward Western, Christian, androcentric values. This model viewed goddess worship as originating during a supposed primitive, matriarchal phase in the development of human societies during which humans lived in harmony with nature, and women were equal or superior to men and, immorally, had multiple sexual partners. The type of goddess worshipped during this period was imagined to be a great mother/fertility goddess who, like mortal women of the era, mated with various partners. This rudimentary stage was superseded by patriarchal societies characterized by political states, ethical systems, monogamous marriage, and kinship traced through the father. So-called sacred prostitution, in which women had promiscuous sex in honor of the goddess, was understood to be a survival of the prior, inferior phase of human development.

The consensus position has also been critiqued on other grounds. First, consensus position scholarship perpetuated the Hebrew Bible's hostile stance toward Canaanite religion, without taking adequate account of the polemical nature of the biblical texts. Second, the nature/history dichotomy does not stand up to scrutiny but is instead a modern, Western construct that has been retrojected onto the relevant biblical and nonbiblical texts. Third, it has been demonstrated that not all female deities in the literature of other ancient, androcentric cultures figure as sexually active and reproductive "fertility" goddesses, and so the mere presence of goddesses in Canaanite religion does not necessarily entail that each and every one functioned in a sexual capacity. Indeed, reappraisal of the mythological texts concerning the "Canaanite" goddess Anat has led to the conclusion that the texts do not portray her as sexually active. Finally, it has been observed that Canaanite societies were no less stringent than Israelite societies when it came to controlling female sexuality, as they too placed a crucial emphasis on paternity. Thus it is implausible that Canaanites would have been any more likely than Israelites to tolerate a practice that involved premarital or extramarital sexual activity of their wives and daughters.

Yahweh and Asherah? The Hebrew Bible makes numerous references to a wooden cult object called an *'ăšērâ*, or asherah, which the NRSV most often translates as "sacred pole" (e.g., Deut 16:21; Judg 6:25–30; 1 Kgs 16:33; 2 Kgs 13:6). Though not all scholars agree, most maintain that this object symbolized Asherah, a goddess of the same name. The vast majority of references to Asherah or her cult symbol occur in a section of the Hebrew Bible that scholars call the Deuteronomistic History (hereafter DH) and portions of the books of Chronicles that have DH as their source. The compilers of DH had a vested interest in supporting the Davidic royal house, and they advocated the exclusive worship of Yahweh in his temple in Jerusalem, the seat of the Davidic dynasty. They branded all Israelite worship of deities other than Yahweh as apostasy, and all worship of Yahweh anywhere other than the Jerusalem temple as illicit. In accordance with these biases, DH uniformly condemned the worship of Asherah and her cult symbol.

In spite of DH's censure, it seems clear from the testimony of DH itself that Asherah was venerated, even in the Jerusalem Temple, during the reigns of some Davidic monarchs. Indeed, DH praises the Davidic kings whom it credits with ridding Jerusalem of Asherah worship (1 Kgs 15:9–13; 2 Kgs 18:1–5; cf. 2 Kgs 23:4–7, 25) and castigates one ruler in particular, Manasseh, for reinstating Asherah worship in the Jerusalem temple (2 Kgs 21:1–9). Seen in light of the inscriptional evidence from Kuntillet Ajrud and Khirbet el-Qom, Saul Olyan (1988) has proposed that outside of Deuteronomistic circles and/or prior to Deuteronomistic influence, Asherah was venerated, unproblematically, in conjunction with Yahweh and perhaps as his divine spouse, even by members of the Davidic dynasty in the Jerusalem temple. Susan Ackerman (2003, pp. 459–461) has further argued for linking the worship of Asherah with the Davidic queen mother and dynastic succession.

Astarte. The Hebrew Bible mentions a goddess named Astarte three times (1 Kgs 11:5 and 1 Kgs 11:33; 2 Kgs 23:13) and pluralizes her name with reference to deity several times; all occurrences are in DH. The three singular references explicitly associate Astarte with the Canaanite (or, more correctly, Phoenician) city-state of Sidon, and attribute the introduction of her worship, considered illegitimate, into the Davidic kingdom to Solomon's marriages to Sidonian princesses (1 Kgs 11:1–8). That Solomon, in the tenth century B.C.E., was responsible for introducing Astarte's worship into the environs of Jerusalem is not verifiable by extant, nonbiblical evidence. However, that Astarte was in fact a deity of importance to a royal dynasty in Sidon is corroborated, for example, by the sarcophagus inscriptions of two kings of the sixth/fifth centuries B.C.E., Tabnit and his son and successor, Eshmunazor. Taken together, these inscriptions state that three consecutive rulers (counting the co-regent Ummiashtart) of this dynasty served Astarte and no other deity as priests, and Tabnit invokes her and no other deity to protect his remains against grave robbers. Perhaps Astarte was this dynasty's patron deity.

With the exception of one problematic reference (1 Sam 31:10), DH uses the plural form of Astarte's name with reference to deity (NRSV "the Astartes") in its depictions of the pre-monarchic Israelites' routing by their enemies when they worshipped foreign deities, as opposed to their success in battle when they worshipped Yahweh alone (Judg 2:11–15; 10:6–9; 1 Sam 7:3–4; 12:9–11). These depictions conform to the compilers of DH's stereotypical attribution of conquest to the abandonment of the exclusive worship of Yahweh. It is unclear what the compilers of DH intended to convey through the pluralized form of Astarte's name. One option is that it means "goddesses," generically. Another is that it conveys the notion of multiple, local manifestations of a single goddess. There is no consensus on this point.

The Queen of Heaven. Jeremiah 7:18 and 44:17–19, 25 make reference to a deity called "the Queen of Heaven," a title mentioned nowhere else in the Hebrew Bible. It is unclear whether this title is an epithet of Asherah, of Astarte, or of another deity. Jeremiah 7:17–18 depicts this deity's cult as family-based and widespread in sixth century B.C.E. Judah and Jerusalem. Jeremiah 44 is addressed to the refugees from Judah in Egypt, where they had fled to escape the Babylonian subjugation of Judah and Jerusalem in the early sixth century B.C.E. Jeremiah blames the Egyptian communities' plight on their and their ancestors' worship of gods other than Yahweh. The people assembled in Pathros respond (vv. 15–18) that when they and their ancestors and rulers regularly propitiated the Queen of Heaven, times were good and they had plenty to eat. It was only when they ceased giving cult to the Queen of Heaven that they began to die from hunger (*rāʾāb*) and the sword. This link in the text between starvation and enemy invasion (cf. 44:13) bespeaks a reality of war: starvation as a consequence of the invading army's plundering of crops and herds (Jer 5:17) and the siege conditions endured by those trapped inside Jerusalem (Jer 21:7 and 9; see also 2 Kgs 25:1–3). That the people attribute having plenty of food to their giving cult to the Queen of Heaven and their lack of food to ceasing this propitiation should not be viewed in isolation from the historical circumstances of the Babylonian invasion and thereby dubbed an example of the practice of nature/fertility religion.

Sacred prostitution. That normative Canaanite and illicit Israelite worship of female deities entailed the practice of so-called sacred prostitution has also been called into question. Remarkably, all of the nonbiblical, ancient Near Eastern and classical sources previously cited as primary evidence for the practice have been discredited, on a variety of grounds. In light of this negative reevaluation of the nonbiblical sources upon which the biblical practice has been reconstructed, and in conjunction with the objections to the twentieth-century consensus noted earlier, it is no longer acceptable to translate Hebrew *qādēš* as "[male] temple prostitute" and *qĕdēšâ* as "[female] temple prostitute," as the NRSV does (e.g., Gen 38:21; Deut 23:18 [English v. 17]; plurals 1 Kgs 15:12; Hos 4:14). Furthermore, the frequent use in biblical texts of the language of female sexual promiscuity to denote apostasy, such as the use of the verb *zānâ*, "to whore, prostitute," in the sense of accusing the people of whoring after other gods (e.g., Exod 34:15; Lev 17:7; Deut 31:16; Judg 2:17), or to speak of personified Jerusalem as Yahweh's insatiably adulterous wife (e.g., Ezek 16), must be divested of any allusions to sacred prostitution

or cultic sex. Unlike the interpretation of scholars of the consensus position, this sexual language must be understood metaphorically and not as derived from and indicative of sexual fertility rites that typified foreign/Canaanite cults. The effectiveness of the language of specifically female sexual infidelity derives from its power to persuade a (male) audience to accept the purveyor of the metaphor's point of view (Shrofel, 1999, 141–166).

[*See also* Deity, *subentry* Ancient Near East; Feminism, *subentry* Second-Wave Feminism; Imagery, Gendered, *subentry* Prophetic Literature; *and* Religious Participation, *subentry* Sacred Prostitution.]

BIBLIOGRAPHY

Ackerman, Susan. "At Home with the Goddess." In *Symbiosis, Symbolism, and the Power of the Past: Canaan, Ancient Israel, and Their Neighbors from the Late Bronze Age through Roman Palaestina*, edited by William Dever and Seymour Gitin, pp. 455–468. Winona Lake, Ind.: Eisenbrauns, 2003.

Bird, Phyllis A. "'Male and Female He Created Them': Genesis 1:27b in the Context of the Priestly Account of Creation." *Harvard Theological Review* 74 (1981): 129–159.

Budin, Stephanie L. *The Myth of Sacred Prostitution in Antiquity*. Cambridge, U.K.: Cambridge University Press, 2008.

Darr, Katheryn Pfisterer. "Like Warrior, Like Woman: Destruction and Deliverance in Isaiah 42:10–17." *Catholic Biblical Quarterly* 49 (1987): 560–571.

Day, Peggy L. "Yahweh's Broken Marriages as Metaphoric Vehicle in the Hebrew Bible Prophets." In *Sacred Marriages: The Divine-Human Sexual Metaphor from Sumer to Early Christianity*, edited by Martti Nissinen and Risto Uro, pp. 219–241. Winona Lake, Ind.: Eisenbrauns, 2008.

Day, Peggy L. "Hebrew Bible Goddesses and Modern Feminist Scholarship." *Religion Compass* 6, no. 6 (2012): 298–308.

Eilberg-Schwartz, Howard. *God's Phallus and Other Problems for Men and Monotheism*. Boston: Beacon, 1994.

McCarter, P. Kyle. "Kuntillet ʿAjrud," "Khirbet el-Qom," "The Sarcophagus Inscription of Tabnit, King of Sidon," and "The Sarcophagus Inscription of ʾEshmunʿazor, King of Sidon." In *The Context of Scripture*, Vol. 2, *Monumental Inscriptions from the Biblical World*, edited by William W. Hallo and K. Lawson Younger Jr., pp. 171–173, 179, 181–183. Leiden, The Netherlands: Brill, 2003.

Meyers, Carol. "Female Images of God in the Hebrew Bible." In *Women in Scripture: A Dictionary of Named and Unnamed Women in the Hebrew Bible, the Apocryphal/Deuterocanonical Books, and the New Testament*, edited by Carol Meyers, pp. 525–528. Grand Rapids, Mich.: Eerdmans, 2000.

Miller, Patrick D., Jr. "The Absence of the Goddess in Israelite Religion." *Hebrew Annual Review* 10 (1986): 239–248.

Olyan, Saul M. *Asherah and the Cult of Yahweh in Israel*. Atlanta: Scholars Press, 1988.

Shrofel, Karin R. "No Prostitute Has Been Here: A Reevaluation of Hosea 4:13–14." M.A. thesis, University of Winnipeg, 1999.

Trible, Phyllis. "Depatriarchalizing in Biblical Interpretation." *Journal of the American Academy of Religion* 41, no. 1 (1973): 30–48.

Trible, Phyllis. *God and the Rhetoric of Sexuality*. Philadelphia: Fortress, 1978.

Peggy L. Day

Greek World

The Greeks envisioned their deities in highly anthropomorphic terms, and so it is not surprising that gender was a prominent aspect of all Greek gods. The Greek pantheon included both male and female deities whose identities encompassed a wide spectrum of social and sexual roles. Greek deities could be youthful or mature. They participated in a full range of family relationships, including husband or wife, mother or father, brother or sister, and daughter or son. All Greek male deities were sexually active; many female deities were also sexually active, although at least three Greek female deities remained aloof from sexual entanglements. Greek male deities took part in a cross-section of activities similar to those of human males. Female deities were engaged in an even broader range of activities, both those considered stereotypically feminine and also those usually associated with men, such as hunting and warfare.

The gender of a deity is expressed in several ways: through language using grammatical gender, through literary descriptions of appearance and activities, and through visual representations depicting the deity's anatomy and costume. Language offers one of the clearest indicators of gender. The Greek language, like most Indo-European languages, uses one of three genders, masculine, feminine, and neuter, for all nouns and adjectives. Thus a male deity is regularly described with masculine grammatical forms, and a female deity with feminine forms. This feature carries over into substantive adjectives, for example, the powerful one, the swift one, the deity who shoots from afar; the same adjective can be applied to either a male or a female deity, and the sex of the deity is evident from the grammatical gender. Zeus, a male deity, is *potnios*, powerful, and Athena, a female deity, is *potnia*, powerful. When substantive adjectives appear on inscribed votive offerings (gifts to the gods), the grammatical gender expresses the gender of the deity receiving the gift. As examples, a bronze statuette of a male figure from Thebes was dedicated *toi Hekaboloi*, to the (male) god who shoots from afar (i.e., Apollo), while a stone statue of a female figure from Naxos was dedicated *tei Hekebolei*, to the (female) deity who shoots from afar (i.e., Artemis). Both Apollo and Artemis were archers and so the same adjective is used to describe both gods, but the grammatically gendered language makes clear the gender and thus the identity of the deity for which the dedication was intended.

Literary and Visual Images of Deities. Most of our information on the gendered aspects of a deity's appearance, actions, and areas of divine power comes from literary texts and visual images. Among masculine deities, the leading Greek deities are Zeus, the sky god and dominant male; Poseidon, god of the sea; and Hades, god of the Underworld, also known as Ploutos. Numerous descriptions comment on their power, strength, and masculine appearance. In visual representations all three are regularly depicted as mature figures with heavily muscled bodies and full beards; often they are shown nude with clear depiction of male genitalia. All play the social role of an older male, since each was married and Zeus and Poseidon had children born from the marriage. Zeus, and to a lesser extent Poseidon, were also perpetual philanderers, credited with frequent extramarital affairs with women and boys.

Such liaisons could produce a younger generation of gods, including Apollo and Artemis, Hermes, and Dionysos. Extramarital affairs with human women also produced illegitimate children, some of whom grew up to become major heroes, such as Herakles and Perseus.

The younger male deities are similarly presented as thoroughly masculine figures. This group includes Apollo, Dionysos, Hermes, Ares, and Hephaistos. Of this group Apollo is especially prominent; he is an archer and a warrior in addition to his identity as the god of light, truth, and prophecy. He is consistently described as a young man who was sexually active and fathered several children with mortal women, although he himself was not thought to be married. Always handsome and frequently shown nude, the figure of Apollo formed an archetype for the high-status young Greek male, whose strength and power enabled him to play a dominant role and engage in unrestricted sexual behavior with impunity. The other male deities were less strongly defined characters, and their powers were more limited. Hermes was the messenger of the gods and the patron of travelers; he also conducted the souls of the dead to the afterlife. In visual representations Hermes, like Apollo, was a handsome young man, best known through a famous statue of the nude god holding the infant Dionysos. Dionysos, the god of wine and the son of Zeus and a mortal woman, is usually presented as an older bearded man. He appears regularly with two sets of companions, a group of women called maenads, known for wild dancing and unrestrained emotional expression, and satyrs, half-men, half-goat creatures notorious for their intense sexual appetites. These followers of Dionysos engaged in activities, which challenged the conventional norms of appropriate gendered behavior that expected modesty from women and sexual restraint from both genders, although the god himself did not take part in these actions. Ares, son of Zeus and Hera, was the god of war. Despite the prevalence of warfare in Greek society, he was an unattractive figure, known for his violent nature and his adulterous affair with the goddess Aphrodite; in both actions Ares represents the unpleasant side of un-

controlled masculine behavior. Hephaistos, the god of industry and crafts, also appears in literature and in visual representations as a masculine figure whose physical labor as a skilled craftsman is appropriate for his gender. Hephaistos was exceptional among the Greek gods in one key aspect: he lacked physical beauty but instead was considered ugly and physically disabled.

Prominent female deities in the Greek pantheon include Hera, Demeter, Hestia, Artemis, Athena, and Aphrodite. They comprised a wide range of ages, appearances, social roles, and divine functions. Some female deities were thought to be married and/or sexually active, although three, Hestia, Artemis, and Athena, did not engage in sexual activity and carefully guarded their virginity. As in the case of the male deities, a deity's feminine gender is made clear through the use of grammatically gendered language, through written descriptions of appearance and activities, and through representations of the deity in the visual arts.

Hera, Demeter, and Hestia were considered to be part of the older generation of gods, mature figures whose social role approximated that of a matron of a household. Of the three, Hestia is a colorless character; she was the goddess of the household hearth (her name simply means "hearth" in Greek), and while she received acknowledgement in household religious practices, she was never the subject of any literary narrative nor is she portrayed in the visual arts. Hera and Demeter, in contrast, were both extremely prominent figures who are featured regularly in literature, art, and cult practices.

The dominant female divinity in the Greek pantheon was Hera, guardian of women, marriage, and the home. She was the wife of Zeus and mother of several divine children, including the major gods Hephaistos and Ares and a minor goddess Hebe, cupbearer of the gods and personification of youth. In literature the picture of Hera is mixed or negative; she can appear beautiful and alluring, as in the *Iliad* 14.292–351, where she seduces Zeus to distract him from the Trojan War, but more often she was portrayed as a shrew and a nag, constantly berating her husband for his many extramarital affairs and in some cases persecuting the children that resulted from these affairs. In cult practice, however, Hera was an important and powerful deity in her own right, the sole deity celebrated at several important sanctuaries including those at Argos and Samos; here she was revered for her power and her ability to protect the people of her cities. The disparity between Hera's negative image in literature and her positive presence in religious cult practice may reflect the different audience of these two institutions. Greek literature, especially the epics, was primarily directed to an audience of male elites, and to this group Hera symbolized the stereotype of a domineering and controlling wife, one whose presence created an unwelcome restraint on her husband's behavior, especially his sexual behavior. In cult practice, in contrast, the deity was a figure of power and respect, valued by all her worshippers, female and male, for her protection of the home and the community.

Demeter, goddess of agriculture, especially cereal crops, was another important figure. Her role in promoting and protecting the fertility of the soil was an extension of her feminine gender, since the fertility of the earth was likened not only to the ability to bear children but also to sexual intercourse, which was often compared to plowing a fertile field. Apart from her divine protection of agriculture, Demeter was best known as a mother, whose close relationship with her daughter Persephone was celebrated in both literature and cult practice. Persephone's divine father was Zeus, but Demeter's personal relationship with Zeus is rarely mentioned. Rather, the bond between mother and daughter is regularly emphasized and forms the basis of joint worship of the two goddesses. The *Homeric Hymn to Demeter* celebrates this bond, as it relates how Persephone was snatched forcibly from her mother to be the bride of Hades in the Underworld, the land of the dead. The emphasis of the hymn is on the mother's grief when she loses her daughter to a marriage arranged for the convenience of the bride's father and husband, the mother's response to the trauma of separation from her daughter, and the continuation of the close ties between mother and daughter even after

the daughter's marriage. The divine relationship between Demeter and Persephone may have helped Greek women adjust to similar circumstances in their own lives, since Greek women lived in a patrilocal society of arranged marriages between young brides and older husbands. Demeter's power over agriculture and fertility was especially evident in her most famous cult ritual, the Eleusinian Mysteries. The participants in this ritual were sworn to secrecy, and many details of the rites remain unknown to us, but the Mysteries seem to have celebrated Persephone's separation from her mother in the Underworld, her return, and their reunion. The sorrow of separation and death gave way to the renewed fertility of the soil and the symbolic rebirth of the soul. Thus in both myth and cult practice, Demeter's feminine gender and her status as a mother were key to her divine power.

Two other major female deities, Athena and Artemis, were thought to belong to a younger generation of deities and so youthfulness was an element of their identities. Both were active, self-reliant figures whose areas of influence overlapped with traditional male activities. Both were also perpetual virgins, and their refusal to marry or bear children formed part of their independent character. Athena, a warrior goddess, was one of the most powerful and widely worshipped divinities in the Greek world. She is clearly female; she is always described in the feminine grammatical gender, and in the visual arts she is clearly portrayed with the body and clothing of a woman. Yet she regularly appears with the equipment of a warrior, a helmet, shield, and spear, wearing her *aegis*, a distinctive breastplate with the head of the Gorgon in the center. Her militaristic attributes and active nature endowed her with an identity that seems more masculine than feminine. The goddess had sprung, fully grown and fully armed, out of the head of Zeus, and in several texts, notably Aeschylus's tragedy *Eumenides*, her asexual birth formed the source of her strength and her lack of identification with a traditional female role. She was often the protector of heroes such as Herakles, Perseus, and Odysseus, and shared in their inclination for swift action and great deeds. In addition to her persona as a warrior goddess, Athena was highly intelligent and regarded as the goddess of wisdom. She was also an important protector of cities; her shrines were often located in the heart of a city, especially Athens, her namesake city, and many cities in Asia Minor.

Artemis was another figure whose identity skirted the boundaries of traditional gender stereotypes. She was identified as a daughter and sister, the sister of Apollo; their birth on the island of Delos was well known. A passage in the *Odyssey* (6.102–109) celebrates her relationship with her mother, Leto, and the mother's pride in her daughter. In visual representations Artemis regularly appears as a beautiful young woman who is active and athletic. Yet Artemis, like Athena, never married nor had any sexual contact with men, and Greek legend recounted several tales of tragic deaths for mortal men such as Actaeon and Orion who were attracted to her. She was a hunter, regularly portrayed in hunting costume while carrying a bow and arrow; she was frequently found in the mountains and often associated with wild animals. Apart from the sanctuary on Delos, Artemis was usually venerated separately from her brother Apollo. She was a deity of great power, a tamer of animals who controlled the unknown and the wilderness. Her areas of concern, especially hunting, the mountains, and the wilderness outside settled urban territory, and her active and independent personality were all qualities traditionally associated with masculine behavior and activities. Yet despite her independent nature and unmarried status, Artemis was a deity of great importance to women: she presided over the major transitions of women's lives, including puberty, marriage, and childbirth.

The other major female deity in the Greek pantheon, Aphrodite, was unabashedly feminine in her appearance and activities. Aphrodite was the goddess of sexuality and desire. Her physical charms were regularly emphasized: Homer speaks of the goddess's "neck of surpassing beauty, her desirable breasts, her brilliant eyes" (*Iliad* 3.397–398). No one, human or divine, could withstand her powers of seduction. In the visual arts, too, Aphrodite was the personification of female beauty and desirability; not surprisingly, the deity was the first female figure to be represented nude in a major work of sculpture, by the sculptor Praxiteles in the mid-fourth century B.C.E. Although the work is only known to us through later reproductions, the statue conveys through its body type and coy pose (the goddess partially covers her genitals with one hand, thereby drawing attention to them) the Greek view of the desirable female form, one that was widely imitated in later images. Nude images of Aphrodite form a striking contrast to the frequent depiction of male nudes, divine and human. The nude male body can signify masculinity, strength, power, and—especially in the fifth century B.C.E. and later—Greek identity (since nude Greek males often appear in sharp contrast to clothed foreigners) but rarely open sexuality. Female figures, in contrast, are shown nude for only one reason: to enhance their sexual allure. Aphrodite's sexuality was also the source of her considerable power, since she was able to compel both men and women to give in to the pull of sexual desire, often against their will. Of all the Greek deities, Aphrodite is the clearest example of a deity in a heavily gendered role. She represented human need for sexuality and fear of the loss of control that submission to erotic emotions can bring.

In addition to the major Olympian gods, there were numerous minor deities in the Greek pantheon, each with a gendered identity. Among these were personifications of abstract qualities, such as Victory (Nike), Divine Justice (Themis), and Divine Retribution (Nemesis). Such personifications were always female and were depicted in the visual arts as beautiful young women. Their gendered appearance may be an extension of the language, since in Greek, abstract nouns normally have feminine gender. Other divinities that represented abstract concepts appear as groups of women, such as the Nymphs, Graces, and Fates. Although each member of the group lacks an individual personality, the group as a unit had a form and identity that alludes to the characteristic described. Thus the Nymphs (spirits of woodland and water) and the Graces were shown as beautiful young women, while the Fates, personifying the inevitable portion of life's sorrows, were ugly older women. Other immortal figures include frightening bogeys that symbolized objects of fear, such as the Sphinx, bringer of death, and the Gorgons, who could turn people into stone; these were composites of human and animal features, but the human half was clearly female. Such figures probably reflect a fear of death and the ritual pollution associated with death, a pollution that transferred to human women.

Human Rulers as Gods. In addition to eternally immortal figures, some human beings, especially rulers, could gain immortality. Beginning in the later fourth century B.C.E., several hereditary monarchs in the Greek world were worshipped as divinities, either during their lifetime or after their death. The concept of a divine ruler became prominent in the Greek world with the conquests of Alexander of Macedon, whose personal charisma and unrivaled military successes made him an object of admiration and adoration. He was thought to be the son of Zeus, and after his death he received divine honors in several Greek cities, especially the city where he was buried, Alexandria in Egypt. Subsequent rulers received divine honors for exceptional activities, for example military conquest or protection of a city, although the ruler cult was not a universal expectation for every monarch but was normally granted only to a particularly strong or beneficial ruler. These rulers were normally men, although some ruling queens in Hellenistic Egypt, such as Cleopatra VII, were also divinized. The royal wife, the queen consort, could also be the object of divine cult. A queen consort might receive divine honors for generous donations to a religious sanctuary or acts of charity; for instance, Laodike III of Macedon endowed dowries for poor girls in the city of Iasos. These were actions traditionally associated with wealthy women.

Modern Debates Regarding the Categories of Divine Gender. The key role of gender in the personalities and actions of Greek deities is in part an extension of their anthropomorphic qualities. All Greek deities have gender, just as they have other human characteristics such as age and eye color, personality and sexual appetites, with the exception that deities were immortal. Because of this, many have assumed that Greek deities represent projections of human imagination and human desire: Greek gods are larger than life figures with unlimited power who enjoy the benefits of human existence with few of its problems. To an extent, the actions and personalities of many Greek deities support this assumption. Greek male deities such as Zeus, Poseidon, and Apollo have the qualities of human males, but they are stronger, more successful, and not subject to the constraints of human social mores. Some Greek female deities typify the traditional roles of human women, such as Hera, guardian of the household; Demeter, protector of fertility; and Aphrodite, emblematic of female sexual appeal.

Yet this is an overly simplistic viewpoint. For one, many of the deities that we meet in Greek literature and art of the first millennium B.C.E. were descendants of much older deities whose gender was already fixed and remained constant, even as their identity and personality were absorbed into the Greek pantheon. Zeus was related to an older Indo-European sky and weather god; Athena was the descendant of a Bronze Age female warrior deity; and the identity of Artemis owed much to earlier Anatolian divine figures, which were tamers of wild animals. Gender is a powerful element of the Greek pantheon, but it did not originate there.

Furthermore, the assumption that Greek deities reflect the social behavior of human beings is only partially correct. While many aspects of male deities—their strength, their warlike tendencies, their protection of craftsmen and travelers, and their active sexuality—mirror the qualities that human males have or would like to have, the same explanation cannot be applied to female deities. Female deities can be wives and mothers, seducers and protectors of the household, but they can also be warriors, hunters, and craftsmen who act independently of a male guardian, activities denied to Greek human women whose lives in a patriarchal community were highly restricted. This is the aspect of divine gender that seems to cause the greatest difficulty to contemporary observers. In our society the term "goddess" (avoided elsewhere in this article) normally carries the connotation of female sexuality (e.g., Marilyn Monroe, a modern sex goddess). Yet the application of this concept to ancient Greece misses the wide variety of functions and attributes found in Greek female deities, many of them unrelated to sexuality and childbearing. Nor are Greek female divinities less important than males: for example, Athena the warrior is strong, independent, and much revered, while Ares, also a warrior, is a bully and a coward, the least honored of the gods. Clearly more is going on than the magnification of human actions.

In sum, gender and anthropomorphic behavior were key components of Greek divinities. In some cases these concepts follow the expectations of human social norms and in others they deliberately transgress standard patterns of human gendered behavior. In this as in other aspects of the Greek response to the divine, the Greek religious experience resists easy categorization.

[*See also* Masculinity and Femininity, *subentry* Greek World; *and* Religious Participation, *subentry* Greek World.]

BIBLIOGRAPHY

Arafat, Karim W. *Classical Zeus: A Study in Art and Literature.* Oxford and New York: Oxford University Press, 1990.

Beaumont, Lesley. "Born Old or Never Young? Femininity, Childhood and the Goddesses of Ancient Greece." In *The Sacred and the Feminine in Ancient Greece*, edited by S. Blundell and M. Williamson, pp. 71–95. London and New York: Routledge, 1998.

Bremmer, Jan N., and Andrew Erskine, eds. *The Gods of Ancient Greece: Identities and Transformations.* Edinburgh Leventis Studies 5. Edinburgh: Edinburgh University Press, 2010.

Burkert, Walter. *Greek Religion: Archaic and Classical.* Translated by John Raffan. Oxford: Blackwell, 1985.

Clark, Isabelle. "The Gamos of Hera: Myth and Ritual." In *The Sacred and the Feminine in Ancient Greece*, edited by S. Blundell and M. Williamson, pp. 13–26. London and New York: Routledge, 1998.

Clay, Jenny Strauss. *The Politics of Olympus: Form and Meaning in the Major Homeric Hymns.* Princeton, N.J.: Princeton University Press, 1989.

Cole, Susan Guettel. "Domesticating Artemis." In *The Sacred and the Feminine in Ancient Greece*, edited by S. Blundell and M. Williamson, pp. 27–43. London and New York: Routledge, 1998.

Foley, Helene, ed. *The Homeric Hymn to Demeter: Translation, Commentary, and Interpretive Essays.* Princeton, N.J.: Princeton University Press, 1994.

King, Helen. "Bound to Bleed: Artemis and Greek Women." In *Images of Women in Antiquity*, edited by A. Cameron and A. Kuhrt, pp. 109–127. Detroit: Wayne State Press, 1983.

Lloyd, Alan B., ed. *What Is a God? Studies in the Nature of Greek Divinity.* London: Duckworth, 1997.

Mikalson, Jon D. *Ancient Greek Religion.* Malden, Mass.: Blackwell, 2005.

Parker, Robert. *On Greek Religion.* Ithaca, N.Y.: Cornell University Press, 2011.

Sissa, Giulia, and Marcel Detienne. *The Daily Life of the Greek Gods.* Translated by Janet Lloyd. Stanford, Calif.: Stanford University Press, 2000.

Stroud, Joanne H., ed. *The Olympians: Ancient Deities as Archetypes.* New York: Continuum, 1996.

Lynn E. Roller

Roman World

Ancient Romans recognized a virtually unlimited number of divine powers that preserved their world, and each divinity had a narrow sphere of interest. Roman religion was therefore primarily cultic; that is, worship was performed in the context of various discrete cults dedicated to individual deities according to traditions that were believed to conform to the deity's own wishes.

Roman Religion in the Regal and Republican Periods (Eighth Century B.C.E.–ca. 31 B.C.E.). The cultic nature of Roman religion makes generalization difficult, since each cult developed with relative independence and had its own traditions. Nevertheless, there are some general trends in Roman religion that emerge concerning gender.

Basics of Roman religion. What is often called the Roman "civic religion" was an aggregate of individual cults managed by four official priestly colleges on behalf of the Roman people (*populus Romanus*). Funds for these cults were provided in turn by the kings (until ca. 509 B.C.E., during what historians call the "regal" period of Roman history), by the senate (from ca. 509 B.C.E.–ca. 31 B.C.E., during the "republican" period of Roman history), and by the emperors (from 31 B.C.E. to 380 C.E., during the "imperial" period of Roman history, until the Christian emperors began to persecute the old cults).

The Romans provided public funds to cults because they considered these cults essential to maintaining a condition of divine favor that they called the "peace of the gods" (*pax deorum*). Rituals that maintained the "peace of the gods" were said to be performed "on behalf of the state" (*pro populo*).

Gods with Greek equivalents. It is common knowledge that at some point in early Roman history many Roman deities came to be identified with individual Greek gods and goddesses. By the late republic (first century B.C.E.), such identifications had obscured the original Roman character of the deity. For example, the Roman goddess Minerva assumed all the attributes of the Greek Athena (e.g., armor); the Roman god Jupiter assumed all the attributes of the Greek god Zeus (e.g., thunder). Ceres assumed all the attributes of the Greek goddess Demeter (e.g., a cornucopia representing agricultural abundance). Roman gods with Greek equivalents had fully anthropomorphic iconography, and always had a defined gender, either male or female. In the case of Ceres, though, it is not altogether certain that the Romans always considered her a goddess: Ceres's gender may originally have been ambiguous or fluid (see below), but the association between Ceres and the Greek goddess Demeter gave to Ceres all of Demeter's attributes, including her female gender.

The worship of abstractions. Most religious communication in ancient Rome was conducted in the Latin language, and in Latin, all nouns by convention fall into a gender, whether masculine, feminine, or neuter. A few ceremonies were performed in Greek, but the same is true of that language. Despite the fact that nouns had fixed gender, the ancient Roman scholar Marcus Terentius Varro (first century B.C.E.), in his *Antiquitates rerum divinarum* (Antiquarian Studies of Divine Subjects) saw Roman civic religion as the creation of idealized ancestors who originally instituted the worship of philosophical and abstract gods that lacked anthropomorphic qualities like gender. For Varro, contact with the Greeks and their elaborate mythology and an-

thropomorphic cult images caused Roman worship to "go astray" (*errorem addidisse*, fr. 18) to the point that Roman gods looked human.

Modern archaeology provides us with ample evidence that anthropomorphic deities were worshipped in Italy long before Varro supposes, but Varro's theory of Roman gods as pure abstractions had some truth, since the Romans did develop a tradition of worshipping abstract principles. One of the most important examples is *Fides* ("faithfulness"), who represented the trustworthiness that underlay the legitimacy of the Roman social order. *Concordia* ("harmony") protected the "concord of the orders," or the harmony among the social classes that was supposedly established after a generation of social upheaval in the early days of the republic. These deities are not genderless, but rather have gender that is assigned to them by the conventions of the Latin language. Both Fides and Concordia, like most abstract nouns in the Latin language, are grammatically feminine, and so the Romans conceived of these particular recipients of their worship as goddesses with the forms of human women.

Gods with ambiguous or fluid gender. It may seem from casual observation that all Roman gods had defined gender. This was certainly true in the case of gods with Greek counterparts and of the abstractions, as well as goddesses like Bona Dea (more on whom below) and Flora, a fertility goddess. It is also the case with many gods, like the masculine Dius Fidius, who ensured the sanctity of oaths. It was not the case, however, that all Roman gods had clearly defined gender. Sometimes Roman gods lacked a stable, defined gender. This aspect of Roman religion desperately needs more scholarly attention: why some gods had ambiguous or fluid gender—and what it means—we cannot hope to understand until scholarship takes the gender ambiguity of some Roman gods more seriously.

The best attested example of a Roman god with ambiguous or fluid gender is Pales, on whose festival, the Parilia (April 21), Romulus supposedly founded the city of Rome. In our sources, the name Pales can be either masculine or feminine, and, to add further confusion to the matter, the name can also be either singular or plural. Another example of a deity with ambiguous or fluid gender is Robigo/Robigus. On the festival of the Robigalia, a dog was sacrificed in order to alleviate wheat rust (in Latin, *robigo, robiginis* f.) from the crops. The deity placated by this ritual is often called by the grammatically feminine name Robigo, but in other sources the name is converted to a masculine form, Robigus.

Gendered pairs of gods. There are intriguing traces of an obscure opposite-gender counterpart to several well-known Roman goddesses and gods. For example, the goddess Ceres had an obscure male counterpart named Cerus. The well-known god Faunus had a female counterpart named Fauna, and the well-known god Liber had a female counterpart named Libera. Ancient commentators sometimes identified these counterparts as consorts, parents, children, or siblings. However, it is possible that these gendered pairs were originally doubles of the same deity.

The pairing may go back to a well-attested Roman tradition whereby, if the Romans were unclear about the exact qualities of a deity whom they wished to address, they would address the deity as "whether a god or a goddess" (*sive deus sive dea*). The Romans may have devised feminine and masculine forms of divine names when they were not sure whether a particular deity wished to be addressed as a god or a goddess; and even when one name came to predominate over time, the vestigial opposite-gender name could have remained in the tradition. Since gods like Pales could have an unfixed gender, we should entertain the possibility that Liber and his sister Libera were originally different names for the same ambiguously gendered deity or divine concept. The issue of gendered pairs of gods may not really be separate from the issue of gods with ambiguous or fluid gender.

Priestesses and goddesses. In the Greek tradition, it was generally (though not universally) customary for the worship of a god to be officiated by a priest and the worship of a goddess to be officiated by a priestess. In the Roman tradition, this was certainly the case in the worship of the goddess Vesta, whose sacred hearth was tended by the seven vestal virgins; it was also true of Ceres in the classical period. The worship of Roman goddesses, nevertheless, was very often in the hands of a priest and not a priestess. The *flamen Floralis* (priest of the goddess Flora) provides one example. The scholarly view often repeated in the twentieth century that women had no formal role in maintaining the "peace of the gods" has, however, rightly been abandoned. Our sources leave no doubt that women actively participated in Roman religion. One Roman priesthood about whose function we are particularly well-informed was the *flamen Dialis* (the priest of the god Jupiter), and the wife of the priest also had priestly duties and received the feminine form of the word "flamen" as a title: she was called the *flaminica Dialis* (the priestess of Jupiter). The *flaminica* was indispensable, and the *flamen Dialis* had to resign his post at the death of his priestess wife.

Periodically the noble women of Rome would gather to worship some of their goddesses in cults that were barred to all men and probably to nonaristocratic women as well. The secrecy of these rites was well maintained, and even the identities of the goddesses worshiped were obscured by vague titles like Bona Dea (the "Good Goddess") and Mater Matuta (variously interpreted as "Good Mother" or "Mother Dawn"). In the case of Bona Dea, the women gathered in the house of one of the highest magistrates every year, and the ceremony was officiated by the magistrate's wife together with the vestal virgins. In the case of Mater Matuta, we are told that the women would gather at Mater Matuta's temple, beat a slave woman, and drive her out of the sanctuary; the significance of this cruel ritual, however, was clear only to the participants.

Goddesses whose worship was in the hands of women sometimes seem to have presided over spheres of life that the Romans considered feminine. For example, worshipers of Mater Matuta prayed for their nieces and nephews first, and then for their own children, and so reaffirmed the extended ties of family; women prayed to Ceres for fertility and to Juno Lucina for easy childbirth. This gendered division in Roman worship, however, does not necessarily create a gulf in Roman concepts of gendered worship. Roman women were definitely responsible for placating the gods and protecting the state and populace. Far from dismissing Bona Dea as a marginal figure, the Roman statesman Cicero (*De haruspicum responsis* 37) states specifically that the women sacrificed "on behalf of the state" (*pro populo*). Within their own spheres of activity, Roman women collaborated with Roman men to preserve the "peace of the gods," and by extension to preserve the Roman state and its citizenry—just as Roman goddesses collaborated with Roman gods.

Imperial Cult (31 B.C.E.–380 C.E.). Roman religion was a network of cultic traditions that were practiced in the city-state of Rome in Italy and focused upon its well-being. It is impossible to speak of Roman religion in a fully meaningful sense outside of the vicinity of Rome itself. Nevertheless, the city-state of Rome grew to be the administrative center of a world empire, and religious traditions in conquered provincial territories adapted to acknowledge this reality.

The Roman Empire was vast, stretching from Spain to Iraq and from England to Egypt at its height, and it was culturally diverse. All subject peoples, whether Celts, Greeks, Persians, Egyptians, or any others, maintained their own unique ancestral traditions with little or no interference from Rome. Still, throughout the empire most subject peoples participated in a new institution that scholars today call the "imperial" cult. In its most basic form, the imperial cult was the granting of divine honors (sacrifices, prayers, vows, and festivals) by local people to a Roman emperor, and in every region of the empire the imperial cult remained one cult among many. This cult was the only religious institution outside of Rome that we can, at least in a qualified sense, consider "Roman."

The focus of the imperial cult was not necessarily limited to the person of the emperor, but often included worship of members of the emperor's family, especially women (wives, daughters, mothers, and sisters). Gender ambiguity did not appear in the imperial cult. For the purposes of worship, imperial men and women acquired divine identities consistent with their own human gender.

Imperial cult at Rome. There were three distinct regions of the empire that treated the imperial cult somewhat differently. The first region was the city of Rome itself, and the other two regions were the western and eastern halves of the empire. The official civic religion of the city-state of Rome never recognized the divinity of an emperor or any member of his family until after that person's death. Upon an imperial person's death, the senate could and often did vote to proclaim him or her a *divus* ("god") or a *diva* ("goddess"). The first emperor proclaimed a *divus*, in 14 C.E., was Augustus; his wife Livia died in the year 29 C.E., and was belatedly declared a *diva* in the year 41 C.E. Subsequent emperors received their legitimacy in part from their connection to a deified imperial ancestor or ancestors, just as Augustus during his lifetime claimed to be the "son of a god" (*divi filius*) because of his (adoptive) father, the deified Julius Caesar.

In the first generations of the empire, imperial women were made priestesses of the cults of the *divi*; Livia, for example, was the priestess (*sacerdos*) of the deified Augustus after his death. For several years, this was the highest honor that an imperial woman could expect in Rome. The first imperial woman to be recognized as a *diva* was Drusilla, the sister of the emperor Caligula (r. 37–41 C.E.), but this deification after her death in 38 C.E. was controversial even in antiquity. Roman historians (like Suetonius in *Life of Caligula* 24) were very hostile to Caligula. They claimed that he had an illicit sexual interest in his sister, and implied that the deification was a sign of Caligula's supposed mental instability. It is uncertain to what extent we should accept these accounts, since our sources on Caligula (especially Suetonius and Cassius Dio) were senators and reflect senatorial, anti-imperial bias.

Susan Wood (1995) has attempted to explain the deification of Drusilla in more rational, dynastic terms. After internal strife had reduced the Julio-Claudian dynasty to a handful of family members, Caligula may have been eager to exalt all three of his sisters publicly as carriers of the imperial blood and potential mothers of a legitimate heir. When Drusilla predeceased Caligula, he asked the senate to give her the title *diva* (the senate was not in the habit of refusing Caligula's "requests," and so the young emperor could count on the unorthodox deification becoming a reality). Drusilla's immense value lay not in any illicit sexual interest that Caligula took in her but in the fact that she possessed the dwindling blood of Augustus Caesar. Her deification would have recognized this fact.

Augustus's wife Livia was deified three years after Drusilla, in the year 41 C.E., during the reign of the emperor Claudius. Claudius (r. 41–54 C.E.) was the son of Livia's son (Augustus's stepson) Drusus, and when he asked the senate to make his grandmother a *diva*, it was at least in part to legitimize his own rule, since Claudius was descendent of Augustus neither by blood nor by adoption. Livia provided a more widely accepted precedent than Drusilla, and the deification of imperial women at Rome became common practice thereafter.

In theory, at least, the emperor was only the foremost citizen of Rome and its guardian. He could claim a privileged position by a familial connection to divinities, but he did not disrupt the civic cult of Rome to the point of demanding worship within Rome itself. The *divi* and *divae*, on the other hand, became a standard feature of Roman religion, and were frequently invoked in prayers, even in prayers to other gods—as the inscriptions of a priesthood called the Arval Brethren make clear in prayers to the goddess Dea Dia. The cults of the *divi* and *divae* helped to maintain the stability of the state and the peace of the gods, which were still treated as inseparable.

Romans continued the practice of worshipping abstractions, but they placed these abstractions in a specifically imperial context. So, the goddess Peace (Pax) came to be worshipped as the Peace of the Emperor (Pax Augusta) and was the recipient of a costly sculpted altar in Rome, the Ara Pacis Augustae (Altar of the Peace of the Emperor). Harmony (Concordia) was worshipped as the Harmony of the Emperor (Concordia Augusta), and so on. These abstractions are grammatically feminine, and were depicted with female form in their iconography; the major exception is Honos ("honor"), which is grammatically masculine, and therefore depicted as a male figure.

The fact that the words for the rest of these abstractions were grammatically feminine enabled them to be identified with imperial women. Sometimes, feminine abstractions at least bore the likeness the imperial wife—especially on imperial coinage. Examples include Salus ("safety"), Pax ("peace"), Fortuna ("luck"), and Securitas ("security"). For example, a coin in Rome, dating to 22–23 C.E. (during the reign of Livia's son, the emperor Tiberius) depicts Livia as Pietas ("piety"). This was during her tenure as Augustus's priestess. Tiberius denied Livia official divine honors, both when she was alive and after she died, but her image paired with Pietas did not count as worship. Rather, it only suggested divinity for Livia and by implication all imperial persons.

Imperial cult in the Latin west. Even before the imperial administration officially recognized the fact, the Roman Empire was always divided roughly in half. The western half of the empire was ethnically and linguistically diverse, but the common language of communication was Latin. The imperial cult in the Latin west was largely an extension of traditional Roman practice, with one major innovation: the living emperor and his wife received worship as divinities, even in colonies of Roman citizens. The priest of the living emperor was given the Roman title *flamen*, while the priestess to the emperor's wife was given the title *flaminica*. In the western imperial cults, the *flaminica* was often, but did not have to be, the wife of the *flamen*.

In the west, imperial women could also be identified with Roman goddesses. Ceres (the goddess of fertility) was by far the most popular. For example, a temple near the theater in Leptis Magna in what is now Libya contained a statue of "Ceres Augusta," whose statue bore the likeness of Livia. Cults to imperial abstractions were common.

Imperial cult in the Greek east. Worship of the emperor and his family in the Greek-speaking east had its roots in earlier Hellenistic ruler cults, particularly the cults of the Ptolemies of Egypt. For centuries before the rise of the Roman Empire, Greeks had worshipped kings and queens, often in the guise of traditional gods and goddesses. A continuation of this practice for Roman emperors and their families was natural and inevitable. There were cults to imperial abstractions, as in the Latin west, but it was more common in the east to identify the emperor or the emperor's wife with Greek goddesses. Images of imperial women as goddesses and inscriptions to imperial women with divine epithets, such as "Livia Demeter" in Cyzicus and "Drusilla the New Aphrodite" in Ephesus, proliferated.

Gender, divinity, and imperial power. There is a general consensus that the imperial cult was in some way a religious response by the emperor's subjects to his immense, almost limitless power. The emperor was always a man; why imperial women were granted divine honors and what this signifies is debated. Some argue that deified imperial women by their fertility represent the continuity of the imperial family and the future stability of the empire. This is an interpretation that is persuasive in the case of several imperial women who are identified with Cybele, the Great Mother; but it is less so in the case of Athens, where an inscription identifies Livia with the goddess Athena Polias, who was a local goddess—a virgin goddess—and so should have had a local interest.

Some have noted that power, especially martial power, is traditionally a masculine trait (see Fischler, 1998, p. 165). This may be true in the human world of Greek and Roman cultures, but both traditions also recognized warrior goddesses. For example, Juno was worshiped in Rome under the epithet "Regina" ("queen") and was depicted as a warrior and protector of the city. The Greek goddess Athena was usually depicted as clad in armor. When imperial women are portrayed as or identified with such goddesses, there is no choice but to assume that they are similarly invested with power.

Our understanding of power—or rather, our understanding of the ancients' understanding of power—may have to be broadened. Of course, imperial women were dependent upon the emperor for their power and prestige: imperial women were always under the control of the emperor, as was the rest of the empire. Imperial women were nonetheless immensely wealthy, influential, and famous people, and their depiction as goddesses hardly diminishes them. In a polytheistic system, there was no need to assume that power had one single face. Though the emperor was supreme, it would have been perfectly natural for people to worship other members of the imperial family, just as countless Roman gods and goddesses were honored and worshiped in addition to Jupiter, their king.

[*See also* Deity, *subentries on* Greek World *and* New Testament; Political Leadership, *subentry* Roman World; Religious Leaders, *subentries on* New Testament *and* Roman World; *and* Religious Participation, *subentry* Roman World.]

BIBLIOGRAPHY

Beard, Mary, John North, and Simon Price. *Religions of Rome.* 2 vols. Cambridge, U.K.: Cambridge University Press, 1998.

Colantoni, Elizabeth. "Male/Female in the Roman World." In *Thesaurus cultus et rituum antiquorum.* Vol. 8, *Private Space and Public Space; Polarities in Religious Life; Religious Interrelation between the Classical World and Neighbouring Civilizations; and Addendum to Vol. 6*, pp. 270–282. Los Angeles: J. Paul Getty Museum, 2012.

Edlund-Berry, Ingrid E. M. "Whether Goddess, Priestess, or Worshipper: Considerations of Female Deities and Cults in Roman Religion." In *Opus Mixtum: Essays in Ancient Art and Society*, edited by Brita Alroth, pp. 25–33. Acta Instituti Romani Regni Seuciae 21. Stockholm: Åströms Förlag, 1994.

Fischler, Susan. "Imperial Cult: Engendering the Cosmos." In *When Men Were Men: Masculinity, Power, and Identity in Classical Antiquity*, edited by Lin Foxhall and John Salmon, pp. 165–183. London: Routledge, 1998.

Fishwick, Duncan. *The Imperial Cult in the Latin West: Studies in the Ruler Cult of the Western Provinces of the Roman Empire.* 3 vols. Leiden, The Netherlands: Brill, 1987–2005.

Flory, Marleen B. "The Deification of Roman Women." *Ancient History Bulletin* 9, nos. 3–4 (1995): 127–134.

Lipka, Michael. *Roman Gods: A Conceptual Approach.* Religions in the Graeco-Roman World 167. Leiden, The Netherlands: Brill, 2009.

Mikocki, Tomasz. *Sub specie deae: Les impératrices et princesses romaines assimilées à des déeses—Étude iconologique.* Rome: Bretschneider, 1995.

Pomeroy, Sarah B. *Goddesses, Whores, Wives, and Slaves: Women in Classical Antiquity.* New York: Schocken, 1975.

Price, S. R. F. *Rituals and Power: The Roman Imperial Cult in Asia Minor.* Cambridge, U.K.: Cambridge University Press, 1984.

Schultz, Celia E. *Women's Religious Activity in the Roman Republic.* Chapel Hill: University of North Carolina Press, 2006.

Spaeth, Barbette Stanley. *The Roman Goddess Ceres.* Austin: University of Texas Press, 1996.

Wood, Susan. "Diva Drusilla Panthea and the Sisters of Caligula." *American Journal of Archaeology* 99, no. 3 (July 1995): 457–482.

Zanker, Paul. *The Power of Images in the Age of Augustus.* Translated by Alan Shapiro. Ann Arbor: University of Michigan Press, 1988. English translation of *Augustus und die Macht der Bilder,* first published in 1987.

Joshua L. Langseth

New Testament

Although it is true that people in the ancient world thought about categories of female and male and the nature of sexual difference, scholarly interest in using gender as an analytical category applicable to all aspects of life, including those concerning the divine, is modern. Following the publication of Simone de Beauvoir's *The Second Sex* (1949) in the 1960s, particularly in Europe and North America, gender came to be understood as malleable, unstable, and an effect of culture: one is not born but rather made into a girl or boy. Feminist analysis of gender next explored the effects of cultures of oppression on the development of male and female roles and ways that both sexes might be freed from the restrictions of gender norms. Applying the analytical category of gender to antiquity, scholars developed new research topics such as the construction of sexual difference and sexuality and ideals of masculinity. It is arguable that Greek philosophy from Plato and Aristotle begins with the idea of a male rational principle reflecting cosmic social order that, in turn, identifies an inferior female

principle as materiality, body, and emotions. Even if the account in the Hebrew Bible of the creation of humanity in the divine image includes both male and female (Gen 1:26), the privileging of masculine images for God in biblical and Christian tradition scarcely balances the notion that all language about God is metaphorical and analogical.

New Testament Language: *Proskuneō, Proskynēsis.* The verb *proskuneō,* to prostrate before someone (usually male) or something more powerful, transcendent or holy, or to do obeisance in the presence of a deified ruler, connotes respect, honor, worship, and submission. Slaves and inferiors venerate and obey (their) masters (Gen 33:6; Matt 18:26). In Persian culture it is normative before divinized rulers like Cyrus (ca. 580–530 B.C.E.), as Xenophon (*Cyropaedia* 5.3.18) describes in his fourth-century B.C.E. biography of Cyrus the Great. In the Hebrew Bible Abraham venerates guests (Gen 18:2) and angels (Gen 19:1). To Joseph as Pharaoh's delegate in Egypt his brothers "came and bowed themselves before him with their faces to the ground" (Gen 42:6). Angels, Jews (including Jesus), Samaritans, Jewish proselytes, and Jesus followers (later Christians) all worship God (Heb 1:6; Exod 34:14: John 4:20; Luke 4:8; Acts 8:27; Rev 7:11). Israel also worships other gods or idols (Num 25:2; Judg 2:12) and is warned away from them by prophets, judges, and also God (Deut 4:19; 5:9).

The term *theos,* god, for the object of veneration, is predicated of Hellenistic rulers and Roman emperors. Roman emperors, however, did not use *theos* of themselves when communicating in Greek to subjects. Assimilating emperor to god, whether to Zeus, Helios, or Dionysus, or empress to Hera, Aphrodite, and Demeter, is not about incarnation but is rather a predicate of divine power. Gods often appeared in human form (*theos epiphanēs*), and immortality (*athanatos*) could be predicated of the emperor's benefaction and reign. Imperial cults are to express *eusebeia* (piety) toward the emperor/empress and to the gods.

Consider Alexander the Great and *proskynēsis.* After Alexander defeated the Persian king Darius and became the king of Asia, he seems to have wanted to create personal power based on collaboration between trusted Macedonians/Greeks and Persians. In 331 B.C.E. Egyptian priests welcomed Alexander as son of Zeus in temples in Egypt at Siwa and Bahariya. In 328 B.C.E., he proposed the introduction of *proskynēsis* as a demonstration of his status as king through an essential part of Persian court ceremonial. Historians of Alexander point out that certain Greeks and Macedonians refused to comply. After the death of Alexander in the ensuing struggles of the successors (Diadochi), Diodorus Siculus reports that Eumenes in 318 B.C.E. set up Alexander's throne in a royal tent, together with the diadem and other tokens of royalty, to secure his status and facilitate transition to a new order by enjoining "common obeisance to Alexander as to a god" (*Biblioteca historica* 18.60.4–61.2).

What of Jesus? It is too simplistic to say of Jesus in Matthew's Gospel that he "is rendered homage as messianic king and helper" (Danker, 2000, p. 882b), since the first to venerate him as a child in Matthew's Gospel are outsiders, namely, Magi from the east (Matt 2:2, 11). Others, especially outsiders—a leper, a centurion, and a Canaanite woman—venerate Matthew's Jesus as a person of power (8:2; 9:18; 15:25; 20:20), while Jesus advocates worship of God (Matt 4:10). Only once do disciples collectively recognize Jesus's power and venerate him as the Son of God (NRSV Matt 14:33: "worshiped him" [*proskuneo*]). With the case of Alexander in mind, we can imagine that for Greek readers Jesus was on one occasion given divine honors by followers as a human Son of God. After resurrection, the same male and female disciples venerate Jesus, although some doubt (Matt 28:9, 17; cf. Luke 24:52). First-century veneration of Jesus is a contested issue. The meaning of *proskynēsis* varies in different contexts. It is therefore not helpful to read fourth-century Christianity and confessional notions back into first-century texts.

In Mark's Gospel, Jesus is designated "Son of God" at baptism. Read through a Roman lens, adoption involved a person's designation as successor to the emperor, which in the first century C.E. (when dynastic adoption was particularly frequent) would have meant highest honor. Thus references to Jesus's designation by God as "Son of God," "Christ," and "Lord," in Romans 1:3–4; Acts 2:36; Philippians 2:9–11; and Mark 1:11, indicate assigning to Jesus great honor associated with imperial adoption (see Peppard, 2011).

God as Father (Aramaic: *Abba*). Jesus has only one father in Matthew's Gospel: the heavenly Father, object of the disciples' prayer in the Lord's Prayer. Disciples are siblings, that is, children of the heavenly Father. Furthermore, this affiliation is exclusive: Jesus admonishes his followers: "Call no one father on earth, for you have one Father, the one in heaven" (23:9). Throughout the Gospel, Matthew also shows Jesus responding to the challenge of incorporating non-Jewish believers into Matthew's Jewish community. While there were provisions for converting to Judaism, at heart being Jewish was about being descended from the ancestral fathers Abraham, Isaac, and Jacob. The "house of Israel" is not a metaphor; Israel was the other name of Jacob, and the house of Israel means the descendants of Jacob. The extent to which family controls participation in the Jewish community becomes apparent when one looks at inheritance law: strictly speaking, there was no possibility of making a will under Jewish law, because the Torah determined succession absolutely. The observant Jew could not will his estate to someone outside the family, nor could he or she inherit from someone who was not a Jew. This made converting to Judaism problematic for very practical reasons, since the convert became ineligible to inherit from anyone. Because inclusion in the Jewish community is so much a family matter, part of Matthew's task is to reframe family so that descent from Jacob or from Abraham is not required for full participation in the Matthean Jewish community. Matthew reserves the authority of "the fathers" for "the Father in heaven" alone. Only in the Gospel of Matthew does Jesus command his disciples, "Call no man father." Since God is the only Father Jesus recognizes, an absolute and uncompromising rejection of the role or authority of the human, biological father distinguishes the composition of this family.

In spite of the fact that modern scholars have made it clear that Abba isn't "Daddy," preachers and theologians continue to assert that Jesus's address to God (e.g., in Gethsemane) reflects a unique relationship, central to Jesus's teaching and distinct from Judaism. But "Abba" is not a unique way to address God.

In Mark's account of Gethsemane Jesus prays to be delivered from arrest, torture, and the crucifixion. "Abba, Father, for you all things are possible; remove this cup from me; yet, not what I want, but what you want" (Mark 14:36). Only Mark's Gospel preserves Jesus's address to God as "Abba," and only in Gethsemane. No other Gospel indicates that Jesus prays to God in this way. And Mark's Gospel has no version of the Lord's Prayer.

Most scholars agree that only Mark conveys Jesus's use of Aramaic. When Jesus uses Aramaic, the words are translated into Greek presumably for the sake of Mark's listeners who were not familiar with Aramaic. The fact that Mark *glosses* Jesus's Aramaic speech is worth noting. Is it likely that Jesus uttered a bilingual prayer in Gethsemane using both Aramaic and Greek in the opening petition? Probably not. But Mark renders the scene by keeping the strangeness of the Aramaic while translating the foreign word into Greek. So Mark moves hearers from the unknown language of Aramaic to the more universally known one, Greek, by rendering "Abba" as "Father!"

Jesus's petitionary language is the same as that of other Jews of his time (e.g., Sir 23:1, 4; Wis 14:3). In the Dead Sea Scrolls 4Q372 1:16, the "Joseph prayer," Joseph calls God "my Father" and pleads that God save him from the hands of the Gentiles. So to argue that no contemporary Jewish prayer contains this form of address for God is to ignore the evidence. Jesus is a devout Jew whose prayer language fits with his time and place.

Further, to argue that Jesus's use of "Abba" is unique is simply wrong. On two occasions in his letters, Romans 8:15 and Galatians 4:6, Paul describes "Abba, Father!" as the cry of believers calling on a relationship to God they can now claim as their own. Paul's letters predate the Gospels. The cry "Abba, Father!" recorded by Paul expresses the ecstatic speech of those newly adopted into the faith from a Gentile background in Asia Minor or elsewhere. It is better to say that Jesus's address of God as "Abba" is distinctive rather than unique.

Son of (M)man/Human One. Some years ago, and not without controversy, Geza Vermes indicated that when Jesus uses the term "son of man" self-referentially, it is not only fully consonant with his first-century Jewish milieu but is also a way of speaking about human identity (Vermes, 1973). The titular usage employing capital letters, "the Son of Man," occurring in the NRSV, seems to refer to a specific figure, perhaps the one in Daniel 7:13. In both cases, the Greek word *anthrōpos* can be rendered inclusively as "the son of Humanity" or, with the Common English Bible, as "the Human One."

Logos. As far as identification of the deity with a specific gender, the history of translation of key terms matters a great deal for modern interpretation. For example, the Greek term "Logos" in John 1:1 is invariably rendered "Word" but, as we see from William Tyndale's rendition of John 1 in his 1526 New Testament, is not invariably masculine.

Tyndale renders Logos in John 1:3 thus: "All things were made by it, and without it was made nothing that made was.... In it was lyfe." If the pronoun *autos* replaces and derives meaning from the antecedent noun, the appearance of *autou* in v. 3 refers to Logos, and since Logos is personified and inanimate, the translation of *autos* is "it." This is what Tyndale does. Now this rendition continues in the Geneva Bible of 1560 and the Bishops' Bible of 1568. Compare these three translations with the 1611 Authorized Version (KJV), which consistently renders Logos and the consequent pronoun *autos* as "he"—as in, "All things were made by him." Thus the translators of the KJV are proposing that Logos (the antecedent for *autos*) is equivalent to Jesus. This is hardly a fair rendition, however. If John had seen Logos as Jesus, John would have used Jesus instead of Logos. But John didn't do this. So Tyndale, and after him the Bishops' Bible and the Geneva Bible attest a rendition of John 1 in English that better represents the Greek.

The rendition of Tyndale continues into v. 14: "And that word was made flesh and dwelt among us, and we saw the glory of it, as the glory of the only begotten son of the father, which word was full of grace and verite," and is similarly rendered by the Bishops' Bible and the Geneva Bible. But this is not the case with the KJV, whose legacy passes into the RSV and the NRSV.

Sophia (Wisdom). Scribes of the wisdom tradition in the Second Temple period composed the wisdom Psalms (Pss 1 and 119, thanking God for the Torah; Ps 19 praising God the Creator), the laments and arguments of Job, the hymns of Ben Sirach to creation and the Torah, and the poems about Wisdom inserted into the collections of Proverbs (such as 8:22–31) and the (Greek) Wisdom of Solomon.

Changes to the scribal profession occurred in the Hellenistic period. Sirach continues the traditional notions of conservative wisdom offering study in a school. When Greek became the common language, Greek ideas of the individual emerged in Qohelet (Ecclesiastes) and the Wisdom of Solomon. But Qohelet uses skeptical wisdom to argue against the justice of God and the developing idea of an afterlife. Other wisdom traditions include the idea of afterlife (for the righteous faithful, according to the Wisdom of Solomon) and the idea that hidden wisdom is mediated through revelation.

In the poem of Sirach 24, Wisdom's role in creation and Israel's history is described. Whereas Job 28 described a search for Wisdom to which only God knows the way, Wisdom herself speaks here describing her origins: "I came forth from the mouth of the Most High and covered the earth like a mist." Hellenistic goddesses like Isis spoke of themselves in this way. Wisdom traverses the earth seeking a resting place among all the nations. At the Creator's command, Wisdom takes up residence in Jerusalem, "taking root in an honored people," where she flourishes like "a cedar in Lebanon." Giving forth perfume and incense as part of temple worship, she next invites all who desire "to eat your fill of my fruits." Sirach then identifies Wisdom as Torah, "the law that Moses commanded us."

Sirach proposes that Wisdom is the creation and gift of Yahweh to humans. Torah cannot be attained by human effort. The idea that Wisdom as Torah descends from God presents an accessible Wisdom to a postexilic audience in response to the destruction of Jerusalem and the temple. Now Wisdom is present in creation, dwelling with humans as Torah, and accessible to all through teaching that takes root and in teaching that is poured out like overflowing water. Sirach may have been the first to show Wisdom as Torah residing on earth. Gender analysis asserts that Wisdom is a creation of male authorship, but the longevity of Wisdom traditions in the East and West invites reassessment.

Traditions of embodied wisdom continue in the New Testament, though are configured differently than what is contained in Proverbs. Jesus speaks as Wisdom herself in Matthew's Gospel and in the Gospel of Thomas inviting all to "learn of me for I am meek and humble of heart" (Matt 11:28–30, cf. *Gos. Thom.* 90). Matthew's Jesus teaches higher righteousness through fulfillment of the Law. However Jesus's teaching reflects the shift of traditional wisdom teachings from the family to the individual, incorporating a new context of the afterlife. Jesus's traditional teaching on marriage prohibits divorce except on grounds of adultery. In the same passage, Jesus also commends a distinct group of disciples who make themselves eunuchs for the sake of the kingdom. Now, married and single persons are included as Jesus's disciples.

Jesus Sophia traditions are additionally discernible in early Christian and Byzantine history. According to Tertullian and Epiphanius, so-called church fathers who wrote in the third and fourth centuries, respectively, in the Montanist churches of Asia, Phrygia, and North Africa, spiritual gifts such as prophecies and visions abound. These churches were founded by Montanus, with the female prophets Maximilla and Prisca, and even Epiphanius's hostile reports attest charismatic speech. Maximilla, for example, reports a vision of the resurrected Christ. "In the form of a woman, clothed in a shining robe, Christ came to me and put wisdom in me and revealed to me that this place is sacred and that it is here that Jerusalem will descend from heaven" (Epiphanius, *Panarion* 49.1). Maximilla connects the appearance of Christ in a female form with wisdom granted to a woman.

From the sixth century C.E. onward, Byzantine icons and frescoes feature prominently in places of worship as intersections between the faithful and holy figures both in private devotion and public worship, and serve as an important aspect of how New Testament representations of the gendered deity were appropriated in later historical circumstances. Heirs to the Roman tradition of portrait painting and illustrated biblical and liturgical manuscripts, the images in these traditions appear to be circumscribed in their range. For example, in many examples of Jesus Christ Pantocrator icons, Jesus displays Matthew 11:28, a passage connected with Wisdom, discussed earlier. But a different image of Jesus Sophia exists in the fourteenth-century frescoes of the Church of Santo Stefano in Soleto in the region of Salento, southern Italy. Byzantine hegemony in southern Italy (880–1071 C.E.) establishes the context of both Greek inscriptions and artistic expression of the Salento fresco artists into the subsequent Norman period. But Byzantine art historians tend to ignore southern Italy, possibly because

Jesus Sophia. Detail, frescoes at the Church of Santo Stefano, Soleto, Italy (14th century C.E.). Photo by Deirdre Good.

the frescoes and art of Salento are on the edges of the Byzantine world. Perhaps one could say that the fresco inscribed "Sophia the Logos of God" in the east wall of the church is not an anomaly but "a Byzantine regional type with unusual iconographic features" (Safran, 2012, pp. 503–504).

Paraclete (Greek: *paraklētos*). When Jesus speaks of the Spirit (*pneuma*) as a masculine *paraklētos* in John 14, 15, and 16, he is speaking metaphorically. The first two appearances of the term *paraklētos* occur after Jesus has directed the disciples to follow his commandments (John 14:15, 23) in order to attain eternal life. The *paraklētos* functions in the context of judgment, because that one will speak before God the judge on humankind's behalf as one of more elevated status than a legal patron (Latin: *advocatus*). In John 14:1–7, it is the Spirit of truth who will teach and remind everyone of what Jesus said (John 14:26), be a witness for Jesus and the disciples (John 15:26–27), and prove the world wrong about sin, righteousness, and judgment (John 16:8–11). This is similar to Paul's statement in Romans 8:26, that "the Spirit itself intercedes in our unutterable groans."

At John 16:7–8 Jesus declares, "I tell you the truth, it is to your advantage that I go away; for if I do not go away, the *paraklētos* will not come to you; but if I go, I will send Him [Greek: *auton*] to you." The subject is spoken of as a masculine personal pronoun "he" in agreement with the masculine *paraklētos* but what the Gospel writer wrote simply accords with the requirements of Greek grammar by matching the gender of the pronoun with the gender of the noun it refers to. The text continues, "And He, when He [Greek lit. "when that one"] comes, will convict the world concerning sin and righteousness and judgment." Similarly, all the masculine pronouns in John 16: 13–14 are correct but correspond to the grammatically masculine *paraklētos* and thus do not address the question whether the Spirit of truth is personified.

Conclusion. If John's Logos Christology, for example, is analyzed from a gender-critical perspective, perhaps as dialogue with the Word, the Gospel exhibits both emancipatory and constricting engagements between Jesus and individuals. Mary, as one whom Jesus loved, hosted the second-to-last supper, wherein she is represented as playing the role of Jesus, kneeling, wiping, and pouring out substance of inestimable value. As community leader, Mary is the host, the one who knows what is to come, the one who anticipates Jesus's example of foot washing and symbolically washes him. On the other hand, Jesus disaffiliates from his mother (John 2:4), separates husbands from wives (John 4:17–18), and affiliates a new son to his mother from the cross (John 19:25–26). This mixed evidence is not unlike the problem of anti-Judaism in the Fourth Gospel, which reaches to the core of the message and is intrinsically oppressive rather than revelatory. One cannot excise anti-Jewish elements to save the healthy core of the message. A hermeneutical solution might be that scriptures themselves are not the only place or the end of divine revelation. The author of John was a fallible human being. Yet the Gospel cannot be reduced to its anti-Jewish elements. It projects an alternative world of all-inclusive love and life that transcends its anti-Judaism (and gender discrimination) and this world of the text rather than the world of the author is a witness to divine revelation.

[*See also* Deity, *subentry* Early Church; Imagery, Gendered, *subentries on* Gospels *and* Wisdom Literature; Jesus; Patriarchy/Kyriarchy; *and* Rhetorical-Hermeneutical Criticism.]

BIBLIOGRAPHY

Berger, Michel, and André Jacob. *La chiesa di S. Stefano a Soleto: Tradizioni byzantine e cultura tardogotica.* Lecce, Italy: Argo, 2007.

Bieringer, Reimund, Didier Pollefeyt, and Frederique Vandecasteele Vanneuville, eds. *Anti-Judaism and the Fourth Gospel.* Louisville, Ky.: Westminster John Knox, 2001.

Danker, Frederick Wilhelm, ed. *A Greek-English Lexicon of the New Testament and Other Early Christian Literature.* 3d ed. Chicago: University of Chicago Press, 2000.

Holmes, Brooke. *Gender: Antiquity and Its Legacy.* New York: Oxford University Press, 2012.

Lopez, Davina C. *Apostle to the Conquered: Reimagining Paul's Mission.* Paul in Critical Contexts. Minneapolis: Fortress, 2008.

Peppard, Michael. *The Son of God in the Roman World: Divine Sonship in Its Social and Political Context.* New York: Oxford University Press, 2011.

Price, S. R. F. "Gods and Emperors: The Greek Language of the Roman Imperial Cult." *Journal of Hellenic Studies* 104 (1984): 79–95.

Safran, Linda. "'Byzantine' Art in Post-Byzantine South Italy? Notes on a Fuzzy Concept." *Common Knowledge* 18, no. 3 (2012): 487–504.

Vermes, Geza. *Jesus the Jew: A Historian's Reading of the Gospels.* London: Collins, 1973.

Deirdre Good

Early Judaism

See Deity, *subentry* Hebrew Bible.

Early Church

God, says Jerome (fourth–fifth century C.E.), has no gender. This is evident to him in the various grammatical identifications of the Holy Spirit: feminine in Hebrew, neuter in Greek, and masculine in Latin. Yet this denial of gender identity for the deity belies the images and metaphors by which God is known in the early Christian tradition, building as they do on language and depictions of the Hebrew deity. The question of the deity's gender has implications not only regarding conceptualization of God but also for understanding the human person (made in the "image of God" [Gen 1:27]), as well as practical implications for God-language in prayer and worship.

Hebrew Tradition. Gendered deities are commonplace in many religious traditions but monotheistic religions insist on a divine simplicity. At the same time, the language and imagery used for God in monotheistic traditions reveal a complex understanding of the divine. Monotheistic religions generally refer to the deity ("god") in the masculine gender; this is true of the God of Israel, who is often described with masculine language. One metaphor for the relationship between God (Yahweh) and the people of Israel is that of a faithful husband and an adulterous wife (who is often shamed by her husband; see Jeremiah 2, 3, 13; Ezekiel 16, 23; the metaphor is most fully developed in the book of Hosea). Although cultic and political faithfulness is expected of the nations of Israel and

Judah, God, understood as husband, can have more than one partner (at least if they are the "twin sisters" of Ezek 23), thus reflecting the culture's different gender expectations. Gender-based violence is revealed in imagery of God punishing the nation (the unfaithful wife) or the city, the "daughter" who is stripped or threatened with rape (Lam 1:8–10). God also appears as a warrior, an enthroned ruler, and a judge, among other images.

Although the feminine divine is often suppressed in the Hebrew tradition, a key element in the Hebrew scriptures is the idea of God as one who liberates, overturning systems of oppression. This life-giving principle lends itself to being imagined in female terms. Given the predominance of male, including violent, images for God in the Hebrew tradition, it is even more striking when grammatically feminine language or images of women are used to depict God. One metaphor for the God of Israel is that of a pregnant woman (Isa 46:3–4) or a woman in labor (Isa 42:14; see also Deut 32:18), or even a mother bear (Hos 13:8). The language used to describe divine compassion employs the Hebrew word for "womb" (*reḥem*). But female metaphors for God also go beyond maternal images.

The most developed treatment of a feminine aspect of the divine in the Hebrew tradition can be found in Wisdom literature, in which the feminine Wisdom is the consort of God (Proverbs, Sirach, Wisdom of Solomon). The image may originate as an expression of divine marriage (with Wisdom as Yahweh's bride), but it is more developed than a simple pairing of male and female deities. First, the personification of *ḥokhmah* (*sophia* in Greek) as a woman stems from the grammatical gender of the Hebrew term. In addition, in this literature that generally conceives of only two roles for women (either model wives or beguiling temptresses of men), Wisdom becomes a seducer of human men, enticing them and calling them to learn from her. But she appears primarily as a way of speaking of the divine quality of wise thought and action and, as such, takes on a creative as well as educative role. She is present at and a participant in the creation of the world (Prov 8:22–31). It is this last characteristic of Wisdom that will be especially developed in the Christian tradition.

New Testament. Many of the claims made about Wisdom in the Hebrew tradition, including dwelling with God and participating in creation, are applied to the divine Logos in the prologue to the Gospel of John. One claim made in John 1:14 for the Logos had not been applied to divine Wisdom: that the Logos "became flesh and lived among us." Although the concept of the Logos as the presence of God in the world had been developed in Jewish philosophical writings of the Second Temple period, it is here explicitly associated with the person of Jesus. That characteristics of the feminine Wisdom are now applied to the masculine Logos could be seen as natural and appropriate, given the maleness of Jesus. Because of the grammatical gender of each term, it is unsurprising that the concepts would be personified as gendered beings. But Jesus of Nazareth is not simply the personification of a concept but an actual male person, a reality that has contributed to claims that men are more appropriately representative of the divine or that women are unfit to serve in ministerial roles. Although these claims have been challenged as misappropriations of divine metaphor and allusion and as inadequate in light of Jesus's own ministry, the reality remains that Christianity identifies a male person as the visible manifestation of God (Col 1:15). Yet Christian theological reflection has often maintained that Jesus's maleness, far from suggesting divine maleness, is not significant for Christological or soteriological claims. Indeed, various Christologies in the New Testament often develop different aspects of the Hebrew tradition, especially the identification of Jesus with Wisdom (see not only John 1:1–18 but also, among many examples, 1 Cor 1:30, or in the background of the hymns found in Phil 2:6–11 and Col 1:15–20).

A common way of speaking of the divine in the New Testament is to use images of men, in particular "father" (see, e.g., John 4:23 or Gal 4:6). But there are also images of women's activities that are illustrative of divine activity or the promises associated with God's reign. A woman's act of kneading dough (Matt 13:33; Luke 13:20–21) is compared with the expansiveness of the reign of God; heavenly rejoicing over a repentant sinner is similar to a woman's joy in finding a lost coin (Luke 15:8–10). The gospels record Jesus using the image of a mother hen to speak of himself (Matt 23:27; Luke 13:34). And it is the language of "rebirth" (John 3:1–7) that is used to describe the life provided by the divine spirit.

Although Paul addresses God as Father, he also hints at a more complex understanding by alluding to the declaration in Genesis 1:26–27 that humans are made in the image of God as "male and female." For Paul, Christian baptism reverses any divisions among humans, and there is, in particular, "no longer male and female" (Gal 3:28), a direct allusion to the Genesis passage. Although Paul never reveals an idea of a hermaphrodite deity or an androgynous first creature, some early, especially gnostic, Christian sources reveal the notion of a restored human, a reunified male and female, as the goal and reward of human life.

Early Christianity. The early centuries of Christianity saw various developments of these themes as well as new ideas. While committed to monotheism, many Christians also began to express belief in Jesus's divinity and in the working of the Holy Spirit, and the most common way to articulate the idea of relationships within the Godhead was through the terms Father, Son, and Holy Spirit. Gregory of Nazianzus (fourth century C.E.) emphasized that the terms "Father" and "Son" are used as metaphors to describe relations within the Trinity and should not be misunderstood to indicate divine maleness. Indeed, a favorite way to reflect on this emerging Trinitarian thought was through the image of Wisdom (*sophia*), which corresponded in some ways with rabbinic reflection on *shekinah* as the presence of God. Whether due to a desire to recognize a feminine divine or simply due to the use of languages that utilize grammatical gender and therefore naturally lend themselves to representations of God in gendered terms and images, Christianity has always produced fruitful imaginings of the divine that employ female as well as male embodiments.

Gnostic traditions. Early Christian gnostic movements made ample use of categories of gender—with both positive and negative ramifications—when reflecting on divine reality. Because gnostic Christianity was far from monolithic, the importance of gender in gnostic texts cannot be oversimplified. Sometimes gender appears to be an important aspect of a text's themes; at other times it seems incidental. What is certain is that there is greater attention given to gender in general and feminine images in particular in these texts. This reality does not necessarily suggest greater attention to or appreciation for real women or their roles in society, although that may indeed have been the case at times. At other times there is, in ascetic gnostic texts, clear denigration of the role of women as, for example, bearers of children. In general, gnostic texts demonstrate a decided proclivity toward gendered images, both male and female.

Gnostic Christians preserved texts with important female figures in them, such as Norea, a gnostic savior figure, or Barbelo, a divine (often) feminine principle and emanation of the Father, the originating divine principle. The divine emanations in gnostic thought appear in gendered pairs of one male and one female element, which complement one another in an ideal state of fullness. An element acting alone apart from a consort, as in the case of Sophia in some myths, allows evil to be introduced in the world, causing a state of chaos and separation. Sometimes Christ and the Holy Spirit are paired, and in one version of the myth Christ is sent to bring the fallen Sophia back into a state of unity and fullness; he appears on earth as Jesus, who teaches humans about their origin in the spiritual world. In the Christian gnostic sacramental system of the Gospel of Philip, it is the decidedly female Holy Spirit who is at work in the world, especially in ritual actions, including the highest ceremony of the bridal chamber, reflective of the spiritual bridal chamber, the world of light and fullness.

Valentinian gnostic texts also affirm a feminine Spirit, which is identified with the bosom of the Father (*Gos. Truth* 24:9–14) and is the one who reveals the Son, hidden in the Father. Elsewhere, it is denied that Mary conceived by the Holy Spirit, for "When did a woman ever conceive by a woman?"

(*Gos. Phil.* 55:26). Irenaeus (second century C.E.) and Epiphanius (fourth century C.E.) both knew of gnostic groups that speak of a "Mother on high" whom Irenaeus says is also called Holy Spirit.

Alexandrian and Antiochene schools. Other Christian writers develop an understanding of divine activity in the world in part in response to gnostic thought. Many follow the practice, begun in the Gospel of John, of using similar language of the Logos as had been used of Wisdom in the Hebrew tradition. Justin Martyr (second century C.E.) reflects on the personified Wisdom in Proverbs in speaking of the Logos. Athenagoras the Athenian (second century C.E.) speaks of God creating the universe through the Logos (the Son), which is best expressed as the eternal mind of the Father, an idea that will be furthered by Christians of the Alexandrian school, developing Platonic ideas in thinking of God as Mind. Athenagoras quotes Proverbs 8:22 on Wisdom to speak of the Son and declares that the Son is the intelligence, reason, and wisdom of the Father. The Spirit is described as an emanation or effluence, in language reminiscent of Wisdom of Solomon 7:25 with respect to Wisdom.

Representatives of the Antiochene school of early Christian thought reflect similar fluidity of expression, sometimes using language of Wisdom to speak of the Logos, sometimes to speak of the Spirit. Theophilus of Antioch can identify the Logos with Wisdom but at other times speaks of them differently. God created the world "by the Logos and Wisdom," but the Logos is elsewhere the same as the Spirit and Wisdom and that which inspired the prophets.

By the time of the Trinitarian controversy in the fourth century, Greek-speaking Christians were largely in agreement that Proverbs 8:22 and following could be applied to the second person of the Trinity. It was one of the hallmarks of the teaching of Arius on the Son, the reality of which moved the council members at Nicea to turn to Greek philosophical terminology to reflect their understanding of relations in the Godhead.

Syriac Christianity. Although Greek and Latin Christian writers, with their varying emphases, influenced much of the reflection on God in western Christianity, fertile ground for poetic reflection could be found in eastern, especially Semitic, Christianity, with its appreciation for and development of the language and metaphors of the Hebrew tradition. Principal among these was the idea of the femininity of the Spirit and her role as mother of Jesus.

In early writings in Syriac, including biblical translations, the Spirit is always treated as grammatically feminine. By the fifth century C.E., the Spirit is sometimes treated as feminine in Syriac biblical texts and sometimes as masculine. The trend of treating the Spirit as masculine, surely due to influence from the Latin West, continues, so that masculine verbs and adjectives gradually come to replace feminine ones when paired with the feminine noun *ruḥa*. This is true of both biblical and nonbiblical writings, so that by the sixth and seventh centuries, the feminine Spirit is treated as if grammatically masculine. At the same time, authors continue to use mother imagery in reference to the Spirit.

Such shyness with feminine language for Spirit is unknown in the early centuries of Christianity in Syria. Use of the feminine term *ruaḥ* (breath, wind, spirit) in Hebrew texts, together with the image of the divine spirit hovering like a mother bird (Gen 1:2), contributes to the idea of the Holy Spirit (or "Spirit of holiness" in early Syriac biblical texts) as a Mother. The Spirit can be understood as feminine apart from the mother image; some authors identify the biblical Rebecca or Eve as the Holy Spirit, while Synesios of Cyrene speaks of the Holy Spirit as the mother, the sister, the daughter. But Christians in the early centuries who spoke a Semitic language (namely Syriac) were fond of the idea of the Spirit as Mother. There are links here with gnostic thought, some of which flourished in Semitic regions, but it would be incorrect to identify these texts as themselves gnostic. The *Odes of Solomon*, surviving in Greek and Syriac, preserves graphic imagery for the Spirit. Grammatically feminine in Syriac, she is the air that produces music from stringed instruments and leads in praise of God. She rests on and transports the odist to heavenly heights and provides protection. In two places in the *Odes*, she appears as a bird, flying and cooing over the Messiah (apparently referring to the presence of the Spirit at the baptism of Jesus) and also serving as a messenger. In Ode 28, the "wings of the Spirit" are those of a mother dove, who provides protection, comfort, and warmth to young nestlings. The hovering dove of Genesis has become a mother dove, caring for her offspring.

The feminine imagery for God used in Ode 19 defies attempts to apply consistent gendered imagery to God. The Father has breasts that produce sweet milk that is offered to the odist; the Son is the cup from which the milk is drunk. The feminine Spirit is the one who milks the Father's breasts and subsequently opens her bosom (or that of the Father?) to mix the milk from the Father's breasts. The ode goes on to describe the birth of the child, perhaps to a human mother, but also perhaps to the Spirit as Mother.

The idea of the Spirit as the Mother is developed most fully in the *Acts of Thomas*, often in liturgical prayers. The *Acts of Thomas* was most likely written in Syriac and survives in both Syriac and Greek, but the Greek seems to be closer to the original and contains the most colorful and primitive language. In a prayer over the bread of the Eucharist, there may be an identification of the name of the Mother and the name of Jesus: "We pronounce over you the name of the Mother, of an ineffable mystery, and of hidden authorities and powers. We pronounce over you your name, Jesus." Elsewhere, most notably in two corresponding initiatory prayers, it becomes clear that the Spirit is the Mother. Both prayers invoke an addressee with an appeal to "come," followed by feminine participles that describe the figure's activity, and both call for the presence of the "Mother." In the prayer over the oil of an initiatory anointing (*Acts Thom.* 27; author's translations), an appeal is made to "come, compassionate Mother," and later, "come, Mother of the seven houses, so that your rest might be in the eighth house." This prayer explicitly identifies the addressee as the "Holy Spirit," who is described as "perfect compassion" and "revealer of hidden mysteries." Mention of the seven houses recalls the seven pillars of the house built by Wisdom in Proverbs 9:1; in Sirach 24:4–8, Wisdom seeks a

resting place on earth. There is thus a striking resemblance between the Mother in this prayer and the figure of Wisdom from the Hebrew tradition. The second initiatory prayer, in a eucharistic setting, again calls the feminine addressee "perfect compassion"; she is one who reveals secrets and "makes visible what is hidden." She is also the "holy dove which bears twin nestlings" and "hidden Mother." Although not explicitly identified as the Holy Spirit in this prayer, the similarity with the first initiatory prayer and the use of images, such as dove, that are elsewhere associated with the Spirit, suggest that this is the intended meaning here as well. The Spirit is here a revealer, and in particular reveals the presence of the Anointed One.

An early identification of a mother figure, probably understood as the Spirit, as well as allusion to the dove with twins, comes from a thinker of the same general region of northern Mesopotamia that produced the *Acts of Thomas*, but from a slightly earlier period. Bardaiṣan, a Christian court philosopher in Edessa, speaks of the Spirit bearing two daughters, and also uses explicit language of Father and Mother. Although Bardaiṣan claims to be monotheistic, he is criticized by Ephrem (fourth century C.E.) for holding to the idea of a divine pair of Mother and Father, who unite sexually to produce a son. Ephrem may be reflecting the thoughtworld of later Bardeṣanites or ascribing to Bardaiṣan ideas of a Father–Mother–Son triad known in the region both outside of Christianity and in Marcioniate thought.

Ephrem himself does not use mother language for the Spirit but regularly identifies the Spirit as feminine and uses other feminine imagery for the divine as well. He is perhaps the first to use nursing imagery to describe how Christ gives life ("he is the living breast," *Hymns on the Nativity* 4.150) and often uses the image of the womb of God. The womb that hides Jesus's human nature is the "great womb of divinity" (*Hymns on the Nativity* 13.7).

The Persian sage Aphrahat (fourth century C.E.), a younger contemporary of Ephrem, does not hesitate to employ mother language for the divine spirit. Reflecting on Genesis 2:24, which declares that a man leaves his father and mother for his wife, Aphrahat suggests that the meaning pertains to the unmarried man who "loves and reveres God his father and the Holy Spirit his mother, and he has no other love" (*Demonstrations* 18.10). Aphrahat also speaks of the Spirit hovering like a mother bird. From a similar time and region, the Macarian homilies refer to the Spirit as Mother. And the seventh-century Syrian Martyrius speaks of the Spirit as a mother who hovers over the community, while Moshe bar Kepha (ninth century C.E.) says that the Holy Spirit hovered over John the Baptist and acted as his mother.

Syriac-speaking Christianity, followed by those authors who inherit its images, clearly has the most vibrant and most developed understanding of a feminine Spirit, but the idea was known in other regions as well. The aforementioned Jerome, who declares that God has no gender, was led to this conclusion after quoting from the now lost *Gospel of the Hebrews*. The fullest form of the quotation, placed on the lips of Jesus, is found in Origen (third century C.E.): "Even so did my mother, the Holy Spirit, take me by one of my hairs and carry me away on to the great mountain Tabor" (*Commentary on John* II.12). And Clement of Alexandria (second–third century C.E.) uses feminine imagery for God, by declaring that the Father became feminine and indeed, in loving humans, has become a mother.

Assessment. Early Christian language for God, building on that used in the Hebrew tradition, most often employs male images and terminology for the Godhead. But this is balanced by denials that God is gendered, coupled with a variety of female metaphors, resulting in rich and varied patterns of God language.

[*See also* Deity, *subentries on* Greek World, Hebrew Bible, New Testament, *and* Roman World; Imagery, Gendered, *subentries on* Gospels, Pauline Literature, Prophetic Literature, *and* Wisdom Literature; *and* Jesus.]

BIBLIOGRAPHY
Ahearne-Kroll, Stephen P., Paul A. Holloway, and James A. Kelhoffer, eds. *Women and Gender in Ancient Religions: Interdisciplinary Approaches*. Wissenschaftliche Untersuchungen zum Neuen Testament 263. Tübingen, Germany: Mohr Siebeck, 2010.

Børresen, Kari Elisabeth, ed. *The Image of God: Gender Models in Judaeo-Christian Tradition*. Minneapolis: Fortress, 1995.

Brock, Sebastian. "The Holy Spirit as Feminine in Early Syriac Literature." In *After Eve*, edited by Janet Martin Soskice, pp. 73–87. Women and Religion Series. London: Marshall Pickering, 1990.

Harvey, Susan Ashbrook. "Feminine Imagery for the Divine: The Holy Spirit, the Odes of Solomon, and Early Syriac Tradition." *St. Vladimir's Theological Quarterly* 37 (1993): 111–39.

Jones, Simon. "Womb of the Spirit." Ph.D. diss., University of Cambridge, 1999.

King, Karen L., ed. *Images of the Feminine in Gnosticism*. Studies in Antiquity and Christianity. Philadelphia: Fortress, 1988.

Lattke, Michael. *Odes of Solomon*. Hermeneia. Minneapolis: Fortress, 2009.

McFague, Sallie. *Models of God: Theology for an Ecological, Nuclear Age*. Philadelphia: Fortress, 1987.

Myers, Susan E. *Spirit Epicleses in the* Acts of Thomas. Wissenschaftliche Untersuchungen zum Neuen Testament 2.281. Tübingen, Germany: Mohr Siebeck, 2010.

Nissinen, Martti, and Risto Uro, eds. *Sacred Marriages: The Divine-Human Sexual Metaphor from Sumer to Early Christianity*. Winona Lake, Ind.: Eisenbrauns, 2008.

Ruether, Rosemary Radford. *To Change the World: Christology and Cultural Criticism*. New York: Crossroad, 1981.

Schüssler Fiorenza, Elisabeth. *In Memory of Her: A Feminist Theological Reconstruction of Christian Origins*. New York: Crossroad, 1983.

Soskice, Janet Martin. *The Kindness of God: Metaphor, Gender, and Religious Language*. Oxford: University Press, 2007.

Susan E. Myers

DISABILITY STUDIES

Disability studies are an interdisciplinary approach to the experiences, portrayals, and social treatment of persons with disabilities. "Disability" as a phenomenon is a social, cultural, and political construction and experience, rather than solely a medical or diagnostic issue to be fixed or treated. Impairment as an occurrence of physical or cognitive traits considered nonnormative from a biological/medical viewpoint becomes "disability" when social or structural discrimination against persons with impairments is experienced.

There is no single method for studying disability within the field of biblical interpretation. Understandings of impairment and conceptualizations of "disability" vary widely across contexts and are adaptable to various methodologies employed within biblical studies. The perspectives and theories provided by disability studies are a valuable analytical tool for investigations into social constructions of bodily differences and their meanings in ancient religious, political, cultural, and social contexts.

Theory and Models of Disability Studies in Biblical Interpretation. Disability studies and theories present a flexible mode of critical inquiry. Hence there is no specific "disability methodology," but rather a disability studies lens or interest that may be taken up by scholars of various disciplines and used within a discipline's jargon and styles of inquiry. Disability scholars have identified various models through which disability has been regarded or analyzed.

Medical model. The medical model of understanding disability charts deviations from a presumed ideal "normal" body, and lists impairments (such as deafness, blindness) or diagnosis (multiple sclerosis, autism) when referring to "disability." Before disability studies emerged on the academic scene in the 1980s, historical critical biblical scholarship employed this model to medically diagnose biblical characters, presuming it is possible to identify conditions described in ancient texts with modern medical categories. This kind of inquiry tends to ignore the different and changing cultural values attached to certain conditions. Biblical and related ancient literatures rarely make a distinction between medical and religious practices, but rather subsume medicine—like politics, economics, and education—under religious practices. Generally, medical conditions are not the concern of biblical texts in terms of diagnosis, but rather are presented within theological frameworks.

Moral/religious model of disability. The moral or religious model is perhaps the most pertinent within studies of biblical or other ancient literatures. Through this lens, disability or other physical differences are read as divine punishment or reward, curse or blessing, connected to the demonic or the divine, caused by sin and/or remedied by divine intervention. Physical or mental impairments are aligned with moral value and thus may lead to disablement. This critical lens highlights how disability is rarely, if ever, perceived and engaged as a neutral category or in an impartial manner. Biblical representations of impairment/disability are complex. Hebrew biblical texts most commonly (though not always) connect impairment/disability to sin, and New Testament representations continue such textual associations. In most cases impairment/disability is presented more negatively than positively, including descriptions of disability as punishment for sin or an opportunity to test one's faith, to inspire others, or to demonstrate God's healing power or mysterious action.

Social and cultural models of disability. Informed by critical theories of race, gender, and sexuality, the social model of disability focuses on the constructed dimensions and culturally shaped perceptions of variations in mental and physical embodiment. It posits the distinction between impairment as physical or cognitive traits considered to be medically or biologically nonnormative and disability as the social and structural discrimination against persons with impairments. The issues to be analyzed and addressed are not located in the individual but in the social, political, and cultural spaces, processes, and attitudes that take a "normal" body as the ideal for architecture, environment, social interaction, and access and that stigmatize what is perceived as deviation from normal embodiment. Closely related is the cultural model, which does not strictly divide between disability and impairment and focuses on larger sociocultural structures. This model, which largely underpins North American biblical scholarship on disability, serves as an analytical tool for investigating how embodied differences are used to organize, explain, narrate, and interpret within a cultural world. Descriptions of impairment/disability are analyzed for their role in creating, shaping, and maintaining culture and its hierarchies, processes, values, etc., especially in regard to establishing the (arbitrary and changing) "normal."

Minority and limits model. The minority model of disability focuses on people with disabilities as an excluded or oppressed group, experiencing discrimination and prejudice based on conceptions of "normal." As such, ableism functions similarly to sexism or racism, and it directs the focus of inquiry toward social barriers and biases. Analyses from this perspective focus on addressing prevailing prejudices and biases regarding "disability." The limits model does not posit disability in opposition to normalcy but frames it as a normal part of human existence. Insisting that all human existence is at most temporarily able-bodied, this model highlights that all human experience includes interdependence, and "disability" (while not ignoring the real, concrete range of embodied experiences) remains an unstable category. These models, along with the social and cultural models, underpin theological work influenced by disability studies, insisting that theological constructions need to reject hierarchical and binary divisions based on "normal" (e.g., Betcher, 2007; Creamer, 2009).

Disability Perspectives as Methodology in Biblical Interpretation. The categorical and methodological nuances of disability studies have sparked a renewed interested in the study of disabilities in biblical studies, noting historical diversity in thought structure, value system, narrative aim, and linguistic options and devices. Biblical literatures rarely depict actual lived experiences of impairment/disability. Ideologically charged disability imagery and terminology are representations with sociopolitical function in audiences past and present, shaping patterns of thought and interpretation. The study of textual representations of impairment/disability aids in understanding respective ancient worlds, their cultural and linguistic productions, and the creation and shaping of social categories and differentiation via disability as a narrative trope. Normative identities are constructed via creations of the "problem" of disability. "Normal," "healthy," and "pure" emerge by defining, naming, classifying, and mapping out

variation and by constructing it as different/deviant (Davis, 2002).

Biblical scholarship engaging disability studies considers depictions of illness or embodied difference in particular biblical texts within historical, ideological, and theological contexts of identity construction. What are the values and expectations of a society communicated within a text? How do depictions of physical and mental conditions communicate or impact these expectations? How do representations of impairment/disability function as a stock feature of characterization and as an opportunistic metaphorical device, as "narrative prosthesis" of a story? In other words, how does disability serve as a means to distinguish a character from the norm while at the same time performing a metaphorical function to connect the narrative to a more abstract concept (Mitchell and Snyder, 2000)?

Disability Studies and Intersections with Gender Studies in the Hebrew Bible. Biblical Hebrew has no single term that groups physical, cognitive, emotional, and social impairments the way modern English terms do. Notions of disability were in operation in Hebrew and ancient Near Eastern texts, and conceptual groupings of terms demonstrate that "disability" functioned socially and abstractly, albeit structured by different subcategories than we find in modern understandings. Hebrew Bible texts posit ethical obligations to treat persons with disabilities fairly, though the persons addressed are the assumed able-bodied who are to be charitable, with little agency understood in those to be pitied. Textual presentations of physical and mental conditions show nuanced variations and changing groupings and associations, and meanings and ideological significances associated with conceptual categories need to be extracted. For example, cultic demand for bodily wholeness and social regulation of access for defective/mutilated bodies may negatively depict impairments (e.g., blindness as a curse, Deut 28:28–29). Some physical differences are categorized as defects, while others are socially and ritually enabling.

Representations of impairment/disability may occur in pairings such as whole/defective, clean/unclean, holy/common, honored/shamed, blessed/

cursed, loved/hated, and beautiful/ugly, establishing inclusion or exclusion, value or stigma, and classifying persons into unequal social groupings in the evaluative discursive context at hand. Impairment/disability as identifying marker may be associated with the poor, the widow, and the alien, or with the weak, the ignorant, the corrupt, or those experiencing divine rejection and contempt (Exod 23, Deut 16, Isa 56).

Groupings of impairment/disability tend to follow distinctions of mental or physical conditions, appearance, bodily vulnerability, and the occurrence of disease. The types of impairment/disability may be distinguished by class and gender, animality and humanity, visibility and invisibility, and permanence. The social, economic, and religious consequences of categories of difference might, but do not have to, lead to exclusion, depending on representation and narrated power relations. It is denigrating when comparative mechanisms are deployed, associating certain differences with negative value, affirming the weakness or vulnerability of certain conditions, or connecting idols with disability language and therefore with the persons associated with the condition (Abrams, 1998; Olyan, 2008).

Defect/blemish and impurity. The Hebrew *mûm* (blemish or defect) and *tumah* (impurity) are terms covering conditions that modern readers might associate with impairment and disability, dividing up skin anomalies, body leaks, and things cut/uncut into differently valued types. What exactly qualified as a blemish differs in various texts and depends on the specific sociocultural location. Among animals, a determination of defect as visual deviation from normal works well. For human bodies, most (though not all) defects are visible to the eye, long-lasting or permanent, distinguished by physical dysfunction, and often come embodied as asymmetry. Word associations, for example with divine curse and punishment or with the poor, the afflicted, the dependent, and the sufferers, may group words indicating defective body parts, such as humpbacked, deaf, blind, lame, or mute (Deut 28:28–29; Ps 146; Zeph 1:17; Job 29:12–16).

While deafness, muteness, certain skin blemishes, genital flows, or menstruation are not blemishes,

they could be paired with conditions that were classified as such (Lev 19:14; Isa 29:18, 35:5, 43:8). Asymmetry might characterize a defect (e.g., a limp, an improperly set broken leg, loss of an eye or tooth) but is also a feature of nondefective skin disease (Lev 12:12–17; Num 12:12). Blemishes may interact with categories of beauty and perfection, but without perfect overlap. Mobility, speed, height, clear skin, and strength qualify a man's beauty (1 Sam 10:23–24, 17:42; Song 2:9–9, 2:17, 8:14). Women's beauty is constructed similarly, though with the addition of features like symmetrical teeth and breasts (Gen 39:6; Song 4:1–5, 6:6). For both genders, beauty is often associated with lack of defects (Dan 1:4; Song 4:7, 6:9). A person with blemishes might be described as ugly, yet while perfection is required to be beautiful, not all free from blemish are beautiful; for instance, a person might be sighted but not beautiful (Gen 29:17). Many if not most blemishes have somatic dysfunctional qualities, though there are some impairments/disabilities, such as deafness and muteness, which are nondefective (Olyan, 2008).

Priestly regulations. Levitical holiness codes for the male priestly cast do not associate blemishes or illness with punishment for sin as non-Priestly narratives tend to do (e.g., in the case of *zaraʿat*, "skin disease," Num 12; 2 Sam 3:2; 2 Chr 26:16–21). Rather, priestly laws in Leviticus 12–15 represent certain conditions as naturally occurring impurities, originating with the LORD and imbued with cultic and ritual implications, but not connected to moral guilt. Disability in this context then may refer to specific physical differences that would lead to stigmatization via exclusion from specific priestly tasks, but not necessarily to social marginalization.

Priestly and Deuteronomic texts present an ideal "normal" body for the context of ritual service. This sanctifiable "pure" body is defined via the "abnormal" that is imagined as separate and displaced from the former (Deut 7:15, 24:8; Num 5:1–5, 12:14–15; 2 Chron 26:21). Defects on a priestly body would disqualify, and thus (temporarily) exclude, the afflicted priest from carrying out duties. Priests were only fit to officiate in the liminal space of the sanctuary, within the symmetry of heaven and earth, if they were unblemished, of pure lineage, and ritually pure (untouched by the taint of death or dysfunction), for fear that a priestly defect would profane the sanctuary. Regular Israelites who were blind and/or lame were excluded from the temple (possibly because of an association with pollution) and thus socially disabled (2 Sam 5:8). Priests with such impairments, excluded from performing (Lev 21:16–23) the highest priestly functions, still maintained their status if ritually pure (e.g., they could still eat ritual offerings).

The exact construction of bodily wholeness as "normal" versus blemish as disqualifying is unclear, though appearance and visible markers are major considerations in Leviticus. Visual and spatial dimensions may be significant considerations in priestly regulations, with priests serving as visual representatives of the unseen perfect body of God in sacred spaces and thus requiring symmetrical and orderly bodies. Deafness, mental disability, or inability to speak does not disqualify. Visible blemishes such as eczema or leaking sores could be a defect yet pure; other scaly, dry skin diseases were not a blemish but impure. Those blemishes covered by clothing or not visible to the eye (certain skin blemishes or deafness) do not disqualify or disable. For example, while blind persons cannot serve as priests, they can eat the sacred donations. Priests who are deaf can serve and eat, but priests with scale disease may do neither (Lev 21:21–23).

The meaning of blemish and associated disability shifts with changing religious ideologies and practices. For example, after the destruction of the Second Temple in 70 C.E., rabbinic laws and practices emerge as oral culture, turning from concerns regarding visible blemishes to stigmatization of impaired ability to discern, understand, and transmit, such as deafness, speech impairment, and intellectual disabilities (Abrams, 1998, 2007; Baden and Moss, 2011; Olyan, 2008; Raphael, 2008; Stewart, 2011; Watts Belser, 2011).

Genital flows and parturition. Genital flow of reproductive fluids and parturition causes ritual impurity. These conditions are connected to fertility for both genders and are not necessarily disabling. As temporary conditions they might be stigmatizing

and lead to limitations in social and cultic life, but they are cast in terms of pollution rather than defect. Priestly laws align genital discharge and childbirth with unavoidable human activity rendering a person ritually impure. In these texts, neither menstruation nor parturition are associated with divine curses, with marginal groups (the poor) or marginalized characteristics (weakness, dependence, ignorance), or with defectiveness (deafness, muteness, other impure genital flows). Yet while women with menstrual flows or in childbirth are associated with pollution and therefore restricted in their contact with others, males as regular emitters of semen are not subject to such stigmatization, being only associated with minor impurities (Lev 15:16–18) (Baden and Moss, 2011; Olyan, 2008; Stewart, 2011).

Male genital damage. The average and normative Israelite is constructed as able-bodied male (e.g., in terms of call for warfare; 1 Sam 11:1–11), and men with defects or blemishes may be feminized through association with women or groups cast as vulnerable and dependent (Job 29, Ps 146). Impairment/disability can establish and maintain gendered categories and hierarchies of inclusion and exclusion. Men with genital damage are prohibited from entering the temple sphere in Deuteronomy 23:2, an exclusion presented within a larger context of denying entrance to males descending from Ammonite and Moabite immigrants. This prohibition may be connected to ideological concerns regarding reproduction (Isa 56:3), stigmatizing men due to fertility concerns (rather than the concern with profanation in 2 Sam 5:8).

Some representations use gendered impairment/ disability to prophetically reorder social structures. Isaiah 56 proclaims that devout eunuchs, though infertile and stigmatized via associations of weakness, immobility, and dependency (Jer 31:7–9; Isa 33:17–24), may take up a central place in the LORD's temple and thus be fully included in the cultic community because of the LORD's intervention. In the utopian future of Isaiah 56, men with damaged testicles may hold positions of authority, in some ways becoming superior to unblemished, fertile men. While the narrative use of eunuch imagery might stigmatize, historical evidence supports eunuch employment in Israelite monarchies, hinting at complex multiple identity negotiations—social, ritual, political, and gendered—in their respective contexts (Olyan, 2008; Lemos, 2011).

Circumcision, as intentionally caused bodily alteration, is not considered a blemish warranting exclusion from the community as cutting off other naturally occurring skin and exposing body parts underneath (e.g., lip or eyelid) could be. Rather, the presence of the foreskin itself is the defect; circumcision is the very sign of inclusion in the ritual and sociopolitical community, an act of physical alteration that renders the male body complete. It may be interpreted as the ritualized removal of a gendered defect, a sign constructing gendered social inclusion and gendered lived experience via male (social and physical) ability (Gen 34:14; Exod 12:48; Jos 5:9). Circumcision as enabling impairment is such a significant social ability that it may metaphorically extend to other body parts and by implication to women. For example, dysfunctional ears and lips, those that do not hear/listen/speak pleasingly to the LORD, are referred to as uncircumcised (Jer 6:10), and obedience to the LORD is effected through circumcision of the heart (Deut 10:16; Jer 4:4; 9:25). Biblical texts also report circumcision as a tactic of revenge for Dinah's rape, and David took 200 Philistine foreskins to satisfy a bride price (Gen 34; 1 Sam 18:25–27) (Olyan, 2008).

Female fertility and barrenness. Gender and gendered bodily abilities signify power relations and construct social norms and hierarchies. Divine commands and social anxieties around reproduction as well as ritual purity construct "woman" in terms of childbearing, mothering, and menstruating. Menstruation and parturition may effect and symbolize marginalization of women, but biblical texts need to be examined for textual distinctions in regard to devaluing physical and mental conditions. Most narratives conceptualize female infertility as a narrative device, presenting it as a disabling condition, associated with divine punishment or disfavor, and social exclusion or decline in status. The barren or miscarrying woman as motif represents child-lessness from all causes as disability, stigmatized through mockery, depression, and condemnation (Num 5:11–31; Exod 23:26; Judg 13:2–3; 1 Sam 1:11; Isa 54:1). There is a spectrum of representation evident in biblical texts, referring to barrenness as a divine curse or natural affliction, describing individuals or communities. The central commonality of barrenness is its rhetorical employment for theological ends to demonstrate the LORD's power, though with varying rhetorical means (Baden, 2011).

In Jeremiah, body images and rhetoric promote a particular view of proper religious observance, with disabled bodies representing condemned forms of religiosity. Gendered impairment may signal a misfit between a given body and an expected social performance. Because female infertility excluded infertile women from the expected and valued roles for women in a patriarchal society (also notable in the mostly female associated usage of the key term *'akar* "barren"), infertility was a gendered disabling experience in ancient Israel. In Jeremiah 3–4, unapproved female sexuality is represented as a cause of female disability, and as a complex metaphor connecting sexual infidelity with barrenness and childlessness, linking religious infidelity with unnaturalness and inappropriate human religious performance. Yet most of the disability tropes in Jeremiah are attributed to male figures, with hearing/deafness as a sorting mechanism for the implied abled (obedient) or disabled (disobedient) audience. Vision and mobility impairment occur together, signifying religious fidelity and proper/failed moral-intellectual insight (Raphael, 2008; 2011).

Disability as narrative trope in identity constructions. As literary and cultural device, disability tropes may connect to moral or ethical conditions of person or group. Impairments per se are not good or bad, and as staples of prophetic rhetoric are employed with variations and nuances. Literal or metaphorical, representational uses of disability include its valuation in a representational economy, often used by, about, and addressed to an implied able-bodied audience and with able-bodied narrative trajectories. Disability tropes need to be contextualized, as status hierarchies and status oppositions other than e.g., whole/blemished may mitigate or exacerbate the impact of the latter, depending on social context or narrative use.

Not always effecting stigmatization and exclusion, representations of impairment/disability in some narratives serve to underscore special interest and divine care for those marginalized, or emphasize divine agency through a main character. In the Isaac story, Isaac was blind and yet a powerful patriarch. It is blindness that leads to Isaac falling for a trick, but his blindness is part of the character driving the divine drama in the story of the patriarchs. Divine power is also made known in Sarai, Rachel, and Rebekah, whose transformed infertility is the site for divine promise and intervention. As they are the wives of patriarchs, these women's bodies become the site of fertility and nation building, but through demonstrated divine intervention only. Samson's blinding puts a narrative focus on his weakness and ineffectuality, and his blindness serves as narrative support to underscore divine power and agency.

Disability and masculinity. Leprosy as disability is the narrative hinge upon which religious identity and male power depend in the story of Naaman, as he is healed and converted and therefore normalized as one who serves and worships the LORD. The Deuteronomy narrative is driven by the struggle against idolatry, centralization of the cult, monotheism, and the observance of the law in allegiance to the covenant. The removal of Naaman's leprosy/disability constructs his masculinity, albeit still inferior in a hierarchy of male power, as he appears now with the skin of a "little boy" (2 Kings 5:3, 14). Other male characters (Gehazi and the king of Aram), though able-bodied, but greedy and not loyal to the LORD, are struck with or depicted with disability (leprosy or death) to signal the lowest position within the male hierarchy in this story (Strimple and Creangă, 2010).

Complex identity constructions of kingship, masculinity, and disability are at work in the Mephibosheth narrative (2 Sam 16; 1 Kgs 2). Here, the physical impairment/disability remains a permanent trait of Mephibosheth, and the clusters of meaning emerging through the disability motif within the narrative are connected to complex constructions

of national identity (e.g., in differentiating Saul and David) and shifting dynamics of belonging inside/outside of Israel (Schipper, 2006).

Sin and disability in the suffering servant. Isaiah's suffering servant (Isa 52:13–53:5) links disabilities, sin, suffering, and atonement. The metaphorical blindness and deafness of people who should see and hear is judged and punished, yet the prophet's disabling conditions (being wounded and cut off from the group) are precisely what enable him to perceive and follow through on the prophetic mission. Disability here serves as the device to describe and narrate the relation between parties in communication, and the value ascribed depends on the various and shifting associations of the impairment with other factors (the characters in the plot, the intentional or involuntary mode of acquisition of the impairment, acceptable or inacceptable use of it, or the metaphorical use referring to an inner or outer condition). Like the disloyalty in Deuteronomy 28 that brings about physical and mental illness, Israel's metaphorical characterization as a person with disability serves to link physical disability to moral disability. Israel's immorality is symbolized by physical disabilities, willfully brought upon by Israel itself (Isa 42:18–20). The vision of the messiah of the Talmudic sages is associated with a disabled person, physically blemished, ritually impure, excluded from society, yet the one bringing about redemption (Abrams, 2007; Raphael, 2008).

Disability Studies and Intersections with Gender Studies in New Testament Scholarship. Few New Testament scholars have explicitly taken up disability studies, though in the twenty-first century much attention has been paid to "the body" in topics such as healing, medicine, miracles, or concepts of femininity/masculinity or health. While some intersectional work connecting these interests with disability studies is beginning to emerge, disability and its representations in New Testament texts has been explored more within theological scholarship, with Nancy L. Eiesland's *The Disabled God* (1994) marking the emergence of disability theologies. Eiesland reconstructs the divine/Christ as a broken, disabled body, repositioning the disabled person at the center of theological knowledge. From here, disability theologies developed a variety of ways to deconstruct disabilities in biblical texts, and reconstruct, where possible embracing disability through theological imaginations—for example, the Interdependent God (Black, 1996), the Accessible God (Block, 2002), the Deaf God (Lewis, 2007; Morris, 2008), or biblical-theological anthropologies engaging experiences of disability, e.g., autism (Gillibrand, 2010; Reynolds, 2008), Down syndrome (Yong, 2007), or profound intellectual disability (Haslam, 2012; Reinders, 2008).

Representations of disability in New Testament literature most commonly center on interests of embodiment and healing. Similar to Jewish cultures, Greeks or Romans had no linguistic equivalent to "disability." Though they had descriptive and diagnostic vocabulary for curable diseases, terminology for permanent conditions were more generic and meaningful in context only (e.g., "ugly," "maimed," "weak"). Discourses in antiquity regarding bodily functioning were pervasively dualistic, relegating those believed to perform bodily functions improperly to the margins of social life along dualisms of sick/healthy, abnormal/normal, unnatural/natural, weak/strong, imbalanced/balanced, porous/impermeable. The Hippocratic corpus posits abnormal bodies versus wise bodies; the writings of Galen present weak bodies versus functioning bodies; the Asclepius cult of the Greco-Roman world demonstrates a distinction between unnatural states of bodily dysfunction and divinely offered health/bodily function. Depending on the worldview framing concepts of the body and bodily conditions, disease could be an effect of an uncontrolled, imbalanced body or of one that was porous and permeable (Moss, 2010).

Sin and healing. Sin and retribution/redemption are conceptual dynamics found in New Testament narratives in which impairments occur, connected to sin-illness causalities found in Hebrew scriptures. The healing accounts of New Testament Gospels and Acts display narrative dualistic mechanisms of exclusion and return to community through messianic intervention, for example the ostracized bodies of

the blind, lame, and leprous; the bedridden and paralyzed; the mute and those deformed by demons/spirits (Mark 2:1–12, 3:1–6 par., 7:31–37, 8:22–26, 10:46–52 par.; Matt 9:27–31, 20:29–34; Luke 7:1–10, 14:1–6; John 5:1–13, 9:1–41; Acts 3:1–10, 8:7, 9:32–43, 14:8–19). The narrative trope of healing the blemished and disabled serves to support the messianic storyline of Jesus fulfilling Jewish prophecies, mandating his authority, and bearing good news to the poor.

Sometimes healing narratives dismantle the causality between sin and illness, challenging the views of purity and impurity in Jesus's time by physically including the disabled and sick, especially on the Sabbath (e.g., Luke 5:12–26, 6:6–11). Sometimes authors associate impairments/disabilities with sin (Mark 2:10); other authors refute this connection and assert it as willed by God to promote God's works (John 9:1–4); others point to ethical/moral failings that effect disablement or cause the body to give into weakness and illness (Luke 1:20,64; 1 Cor 11:29–30). Metaphorically, disabilities such as blindness and deafness (failure to understand) serve to underscore healing acts as salvific (Mark 4:12; Matt 15:14; Luke 6:39; John 9:39–41; Acts 28:26), connecting healing of the body with healing of the soul, and implying a certain restorative trajectory toward able-bodied-ness.

Disability, gender, and healing. Parallel to concepts of healthy and sick bodies in the ancient world are gender constructions, with the masculine body characterized as strong, balanced, hard, impermeable, and the female body as weak, uncontrolled, soft, and porous. In narratives such as the healing of the woman with the flow of blood, the woman's body is doubly effeminate: weak and leaky, and unnaturally so. In Mark's account of healing the woman with the flow of blood (Mark 5:25–34), her body comes to resemble the healthy masculine ideal, hardened and dry. Jesus, on the other hand, as the source of healing, is described in feminine terms also, with the healing power leaking out of his body, drawn out by the woman and uncontrolled by Jesus. While this subverts conceptualizations of masculinity and purity, it is also a narrative layer of identity construction, porosity not necessarily being negative, but possibly suggesting divinity via an epiphany motif (divine leaking through the boundaries of the human form concealing the deity) (Moss, 2010).

Disability, gender, and divine presence. Similar to the use of images of the Suffering Servant in Isaiah, Paul reenvisions the ideal of unblemished masculinity, divine presence, and divine action with suffering and disability in/through broken-bodied-ness. Paul represents divinity and divine reign through Jesus's stigmatized body (Gal 4:13–15, 5:6). The crucified body as symbol of ultimate stigmatization, emasculated (crucifixion as penalty for slaves or other-lower status persons) and victimized, stands in to signify divine wisdom and power (1 Cor 1:23–24). Satan, as God's agent, is described as the cause of Paul's impairment to keep him humble (2 Cor 12:5). The precise nature of Paul's condition remains unclear, though it signals some sort of functional impairment and experiences of disability. The alternative discursive practices in Paul's letters parallel the centrality of Jesus's suffering and bodily weakness that becomes the site of positive/liberatory identity formation (Albl, 2007; Henning, 2011).

Disability and resurrection. Understandings of disability and the body as identity markers come into play in early Christian conceptualizations of the resurrection. Jesus became disabled in death, and the signs of his bodily impairment and suffering did not disappear after resurrection, nor did they disqualify him from leadership (his place in the masculine hierarchy was preserved, and even glorified to an extent). The bodily wounds are the primary identity marker by which Jesus is recognized (Luke 24; John 20). While Jesus is the archetype for the resurrection of the dead, impairment/disability do not necessarily continue after death in early Christian concepts. When Christian identity is worked out through conceptions of the resurrection, it is not the disabled divine Christ that serves as prototype of identity. Rather, the rhetoric of restoration and healing in resurrection continue attitudes toward disability and construct bodily continuity after death in conjunction with eschatological healing. Concepts of completed salvation and restoration with God require the transformation of disabled bodies into "normal" bodies in order to signal one's identity as part of the Christian community. In the emerging doctrine of resurrection, scarred martyrs will retain their bodily marks as part of their honored identity, yet their bodies will be proportionate and intact. Augustine for example posits that gendered bodily functions or aesthetics will be restored, such as signs of fertility, beards, or seeing eyes (Moss, 2011).

Outlook. As the work of intersecting disability studies with scholarship in religious studies continues to gain greater acceptance and academic traction, more biblical scholarship is expected to emerge out of publications such as the *Journal of Religion, Disability, and Health*, and from groups like the Healthcare and Disability in the Ancient World program unit of the Society of Biblical Literatures, including explorations of new angles on gender and sexuality, disability and imperial power, and other complex sociopolitical identity negotiations (e.g., Moss and Schipper, 2011). In order to counter habitually deployed oppressive ableist interpretations today, disability tropes in biblical narratives warrant careful consideration. Contextual identity constructions may be unpacked without replicating ableist biases in religious discourses, preventing oversimplified tracing of discrimination against people with impairment to monolithically and anachronistically read texts.

[*See also* Imagery, Gendered, *subentries on* Deuteronomistic History *and* Priestly Material; Intersectional Studies; *and* Masculinity and Femininity, *subentry* Hebrew Bible.]

BIBLIOGRAPHY

Abrams, Judith Z. *Judaism and Disability: Portrayals in Ancient Texts from the Tanach through the Bavli.* Washington, D.C.: Gallaudet University Press, 1998.

Abrams, Judith Z. "Misconceptions about Disabilities in the Hebrew Bible." *Journal of Religion, Disability, and Health* 10, no. 3–4 (2007): 73–84.

Albl, Martin. "'For Whenever I Am Weak, Then I Am Strong': Disability in Paul's Epistles." In *This Abled Body: Rethinking Disabilities and Biblical Studies*, edited by Hector Avalos, Sarah J. Melcher, and Jeremy Schipper, pp. 145–158. Atlanta: Society of Biblical Studies, 2007.

Avalos, Hector. *Illness and Health Care in the Ancient Near East: The Role of the Temple in Greece, Mesopotamia, and Israel*. Atlanta: Scholars Press, 1995.

Avalos, Hector. *Health Care and the Rise of Christianity*. Peabody, Mass.: Hendrickson, 1999.

Avalos, Hector, Sarah J. Melcher, and Jeremy Schipper, eds. *This Abled Body: Rethinking Disabilities and Biblical Studies*. Atlanta: Society of Biblical Studies, 2007.

Baden, Joel S. "The Nature of Barrenness in the Hebrew Bible." In *Disability Studies and Biblical Literature*, edited by Candida R. Moss and Jeremy Schipper, pp. 13–27. New York: Palgrave Macmillan, 2011.

Baden, Joel S., and Candida R. Moss. "The Origin and Interpretation of ṣāraʿat in Leviticus 13–14." *Journal of Biblical Literature* 130, no. 4 (2011): 643–662.

Betcher, Sharon V. *Spirit and the Politics of Disablement*. Minneapolis: Fortress, 2007.

Black, Kathy. *A Healing Homiletic: Preaching and Disability*. Nashville, Tenn.: Abingdon, 1996.

Block, Jennie Weiss. *Copious Hosting: A Theology of Access for People with Disabilities*. New York: Continuum, 2002.

Brock, Brian, and John Swinton, eds. *Disability in the Christian Tradition: A Reader*. Grand Rapids, Mich.: Eerdmans, 2012.

Collins, Adela Yarbro. "Paul's Disability: The Thorn in His Flesh." In *Disability Studies and Biblical Literature*, edited by Candida R. Moss and Jeremy Schipper, pp. 165–184. New York: Palgrave Macmillan, 2011.

Creamer, Deborah Beth. *Disability and Christian Theology: Embodied Limits and Constructive Possibilities*. Oxford: Oxford University Press, 2009.

Davis, Lennard J. *Enforcing Normalcy: Disability, Deafness, and the Body*. London: Verso, 1995.

Davis, Lennard J. *Bending Over Backwards: Disability, Dismodernism, and Other Difficult Positions*. New York: New York University Press, 2002.

Davis, Lennard J., ed. *The Disability Studies Reader*. 4th ed. New York: Routledge, 2013.

Dorman, Johanna. "The Blemished Body: Deformity and Disability in the Qumran Scrolls." Ph.D. diss., Rijksuniversiteit Groningen, 2007.

Eiesland, Nancy L. *The Disabled God: Toward a Liberatory Theology of Disability*. Nashville, Tenn.: Abingdon, 1994.

Garland, Robert. *The Eye of the Beholder: Deformity and Disability in the Graeco-Roman World*. Rev. ed. London: Bristol Classical, 2010.

Garland Thomson, Rosemarie. *Extraordinary Bodies: Figuring Physical Disability in American Culture and Literature*. New York: Columbia University Press, 1997.

Gillibrand, John. *Disabled Church—Disabled Society: The Implications of Autism for Philosophy, Theology, and Politics*. Philadelphia: Jessica Kingsley, 2010.

Haslam, Molly C. *A Constructive Theology of Intellectual Disability: Human Being as Mutuality and Response*. New York: Fordham University Press, 2012.

Henning, Meghan. "In Sickness and in Health: Ancient 'Rituals of Truth' in the Greco-Roman World and 1 Peter." In *Disability Studies and Biblical Literature*, edited by Candida R. Moss and Jeremy Schipper, pp. 185–204. New York: Palgrave Macmillan, 2011.

Hentrich, Thomas. "Masculinity and Disability in the Bible." In *This Abled Body: Rethinking Disabilities and Biblical Studies*, edited by Hector Avalos, Sarah J. Melcher, and Jeremy Schipper, pp. 73–87. Atlanta: Society of Biblical Studies, 2007.

Lemos, T. M. "'Like the Eunuch Who Does Not Beget': Gender, Mutilation, and Negotiated Status in the Ancient Near East." In *Disability Studies and Biblical Literature*, edited by Candida R. Moss and Jeremy Schipper, pp. 47–66. New York: Palgrave Macmillan, 2011.

Lewis, Hannah. *Deaf Liberation Theology*. Aldershot, U.K.: Ashgate, 2007.

Mitchell, David T., and Sharon L. Snyder. *Narrative Prosthesis: Disability and the Dependencies of Discourse*. Ann Arbor: University of Michigan Press, 2000.

Morris, Wayne. *Theology without Words: Theology in the Deaf Community*. Aldershot, U.K.: Ashgate, 2008.

Moss, Candida R. "The Man with the Flow of Power: Porous Bodies in Mark 5:25–34." *Journal of Biblical Literature* 129, no. 3 (2010): 507–519.

Moss, Candida R. "Heavenly Healing: Eschatological Cleansing and the Resurrection of the Dead in the Early Church." *Journal of the American Academy of Religion* 79, no. 4 (2011): 991–1017.

Moss, Candida R., and Jeremy Schipper, eds. *Disability Studies and Biblical Literature*. New York: Palgrave Macmillan: 2011.

Olyan, Saul M. *Disability in the Hebrew Bible: Interpreting Mental and Physical Differences*. New York: Cambridge University Press, 2008.

Raphael, Rebecca. *Biblical Corpora: Representations of Disability in Hebrew Biblical Literature*. London: T&T Clark, 2008.

Raphael, Rebecca. "Whoring after Cripples: On the Intersection of Gender and Disability Imagery in Jeremiah." In *Disability Studies and Biblical Literature*, edited by Candida R. Moss and Jeremy Schipper, pp. 103–116. New York: Palgrave Macmillan, 2011.

Reinders, Hans S. *Receiving the Gift of Friendship: Profound Disability, Theological Anthropology, and Ethics.* Grand Rapids, Mich.: Eerdmans, 2008.

Reynolds, Thomas E. *Vulnerable Communion: A Theology of Disability and Hospitality.* Grand Rapids, Mich.: Brazos, 2008.

Schipper, Jeremy. *Disability Studies and the Hebrew Bible: Figuring Mephibosheth in the David Story.* New York: T&T Clark, 2006.

Schipper, Jeremy. "Deuteronomy 24:5 and King Asa's Foot Disease in 1 Kings 15:23b." *Journal of Biblical Literature* 128, no. 4 (2009): 643–648.

Schumm, Darla, and Michael Stoltzfus, eds. *Disability in Judaism, Christianity, and Islam: Sacred Texts, Historical Traditions, and Social Analysis.* New York: Palgrave Macmillan, 2011.

Stewart, David Tabb. "Sexual Disabilities in the Hebrew Bible." In *Disability Studies and Biblical Literature*, edited by Candida R. Moss and Jeremy Schipper, pp. 67–88. New York: Palgrave Macmillan, 2011.

Strimple, Cheryl, and Ovidiu Creangă. "'And His Skin Returned Like a Skin of a Little Boy': Masculinity, Disability and the Healing of Naaman." In *Men and Masculinity in the Hebrew Bible and Beyond*, edited by Ovidiu Creangă, pp. 110–126. Sheffield, U.K.: Sheffield Phoenix, 2010.

van der Toorn, K. *Sin and Sanction in Israel and Mesopotamia: A Comparative Study.* Assen, The Netherlands: Van Gorcum, 1985.

Watts Belser, Julia. "Reading Talmudic Bodies: Disability, Narrative, and the Gaze in Rabbinic Judaism." In *Disability in Judaism, Christianity, and Islam: Sacred Texts, Historical Traditions, and Social Analysis*, edited by Darla Schumm and Michael Stoltzfus, pp. 5–27. New York: Palgrave Macmillan, 2011.

Yong, Amos. *Theology and Down Syndrome: Reimagining Disability in Late Modernity.* Waco, Tex.: Baylor University Press, 2007.

Heike Peckruhn

ECONOMICS

This entry contains seven subentries: Ancient Near East; Hebrew Bible; Greek World; Roman World; New Testament; Early Judaism; *and* Early Church.

Ancient Near East

This article is organized into four sections: cuneiform evidence for ancient Near Eastern economic activities; issues in reconstructing Mesopotamian economies; gendered dimensions of ancient Near Eastern economies; and a final assessment.

The Economic Archives Written on Cuneiform Tablets. Because cuneiform writing was first created to track the economic activities of large temple households and because its medium was mostly indestructible clay, the written evidence from Mesopotamia is huge: vast records document the economic proceedings of temples, palaces, and private households. The administration of the temple complexes of Uruk in southern Babylonia, for example, covers about three thousand years, spanning the complete Mesopotamian civilization from the origins of cuneiform writing around 3100 B.C.E. until its last upsurge under the Seleucid rulers, albeit with a few interruptions.

Temple and palace archives. Temple and palace archives from other cities cover a much shorter period, usually within a single millennium. These institutional files track the management of temple and palace assets, such as agricultural land, natural resources, traded and manufactured commodities, and labor. The bureaucrats attached to these households developed an intricate system of lists enumerating such details as laborers, deliveries, and expenditures; balanced accounts; labels attached to containers; and sealed tablets recording transfers of commodities with individuals outside of the household. From the second millennium onward, these dealings with outsiders sometimes take the form of bilateral contracts transacted with entrepreneurs who executed a part of the institution's activities—such as tax farming or retail sale of surpluses—in return for silver. Besides the management of household assets, also recorded are the economic aspects of cultic and political obligations, such as the expenditures on the occasion of a religious festival or an official visit of the king.

Private archives. Private economic activities are recorded on a significant scale only from the beginning of the second millennium B.C.E. onward. Around 1900 B.C.E., urban residents discovered the advantages of a written archive. These archives consist mainly of bilateral contracts; administrative accounts occur only in the largest private archives, when the size of the business activities exceeded the capacities of a single manager. Two types of contracts occur in these files: title deeds and obligations. The title deeds establish the ownership of family properties such as real estate, slaves, prebends, and occasionally furniture and silver. They take the form not only of purchase contracts, exchange documents, bequests, and inheritances but also of marriage and adoption contracts in which the person entering a new household brought his or her own possessions in the form of a dowry or a legacy. Title deeds were transferred together with the property to which they pertain, and the resulting "chains of transmission" may have been kept in the family archive over several generations. These title deeds allow an estimation of the economic resources of a family.

On the other hand, obligations—such as loans, rentals, and leases, which were kept by the party to whom the commodity was due—were destroyed as soon as they were fulfilled. This part of the archive reflects the current affairs of the archive holder and the manner in which he exploited his assets. In times of economic hardship, archives accumulate obligations that cannot be repaid. When obligation default occurs on a large scale, Mesopotamian kings occasionally intervened by cancelling all debts of a noncommercial nature and all the transactions resulting from such debts (such as sales of real estate or family members as a compensation of the commodity owed) to restore economic stability.

Unfortunately, legal and administrative documents are extremely concise and their interpretation requires significant background knowledge about the participants and the context of the transaction. Only those aspects of a transaction that were legally vital (the identification of the participants, the description of the object transferred or owed along with its value, and the future obligations attached to the transfer) or exceptional (such as an unusual interest clause or bigamy in marriage contracts) are described in a comprehensive way. The reasons for the conclusion of a contract and the exact relation between the different parties can only rarely be reconstructed on the basis of contextual evidence.

Occasionally, the archives contain letters between business partners, and these may provide more elaborate descriptions of the proceedings. The archives

of merchant families organizing the trade between Aššur and Anatolia during the nineteenth century B.C.E., found in Karum Kaneš, consist mainly of business correspondence of that type. During the first millennium B.C.E., these practices culminate in large archives documenting the activities of family firms such as the Murašûs and the Egibis. The introduction of "family names" besides the patronymic to identify participants in the contracts reinforces the economic power of the leading urban families.

In contrast to the abundant hands-on documentation, the Mesopotamian civilization has left us no theoretical or contemplative economic treatises. The price settings in codices and astronomical diaries and the prospects of the growth of cattle herds bring us as close as we can get to the abstraction of the ancient Mesopotamian economic reality. Moreover, the sources are not spread evenly over time, space and, more importantly, social environment. They originate mainly from cities, towns, or administrative centers. Small villages and rural settlements are investigated only rarely because they are difficult to locate in the alluvial plain and do not yield much written documentation since their smaller-scale context does not require a comprehensive administration. In a parallel manner, lower classes are documented only from the perspective of the institutional households and the upper layers of the society as dependents—i.e., workforce or debtors. Women as well are particularly underrepresented in the written documentation, as discussed in the text that follows. Thus, the archives provide us with only peepholes into some of the households that constitute the complex and constantly changing urban society of Mesopotamia.

The Reconstruction of the Near Eastern Economy. Prior to discussion of the role of gender, the next paragraphs provide an overview of the major characteristics of the Mesopotamian economy.

An economy of "households." The extremely detailed but fragmentary source material has hampered the mapping of a comprehensive picture of the society and the economy of Mesopotamia. For a long time, the archives of institutional households and of wealthy town dwellers have distorted our view at the expense of the less documented parts of the economy. As a result of this bias, the third millennium has long been characterized as a society in which all the economic means of production were in the hands of the temple or the palace. The private archives that appear at the beginning of the second millennium B.C.E. have been considered as a sudden and complete change. A closer look at the cuneiform documentary sources, however, shows that the changes do not have to be situated in the society and its economy but instead may reflect innovations in record keeping, in which different types of households are increasingly integrated within different political constellations.

At the end of the third millennium B.C.E., the so-called Ur III dynasty (2100–2004 B.C.E.) kept an extremely detailed administration of households and tried to exercise direct authority over the temple and other households. During the subsequent Old Babylonian period (2004–1595 B.C.E.), administration was left to the individual households of the temples and the local governmental institutions, and the central authorities appropriated part of the revenues of the local households through middlemen. This latter policy proved to be more effective and became the more common way of incorporating the local households into the state administration during the first millennium. Also, the administration of these second and first millennium institutional households was less extensive than that of the Ur III state and does not display an exhaustive documentary coverage.

An integrated picture. In the course of its three millennia of existence, Mesopotamian society witnessed increasingly successful attempts toward political unification, but the cities along with their attendant temples remained the pulse of the country. In Babylonia, the alluvial plain can sustain sizable urban populations through irrigation agriculture and through livestock breeding, whereas in the more arid regions of Assyria cities must rely on trade (and on alternatives like levying taxes and undertaking military campaigns) to provide for their populations. The resulting political configurations in Babylonia and Assyria did not significantly alter the organization of the family households and the temple households, the two cornerstones of the Mesopotamian cities. With varying success, the political structures attempted to incorporate the households into their state structures to access their resources (such as labor, land, silver, and authority over groups of the population). A key tactic for doing so was an increasing integration of the different segments of the society. Several members of established families were involved in the cults in their respective cities through (fractions of) prebendary offices. Although these offices could be alienated and divided in fractions expressed in terms of a year (in the first millennium B.C.E. they could comprise only a fraction of a day per year), they preferably were sold or transferred to members of the same family. Only during the Neo-Babylonian period were parties in a contract identified with their family name alongside their patronymic. For the earlier periods, identifications depend on the family lineages, which can be reconstructed from archival documentation but that remain fragmentary.

Through an elaborate system of middlemen, many of these families were also involved in the management of palace assets. Over time, these activities become part of their family estate, together with their landed property and other assets. The members of the urban middle class may thus have been engaged in managing their own landed properties (fields, gardens, built property), investing their surpluses by issuing credit, and engaging in trade, while also participating in operations involving palace assets and executing temple duties in return for a share in the offerings, a salary, the yields of the fields attached to the temple office, and the social privileges associated with the system (Waerzeggers, 2010, pp. 301–326).

The family estate was transferred to the next generation through a system of male partitive inheritance. Daughters received smaller shares of the movables as a dowry when they married. Pieces of the family estate could be sold, exchanged, or bequeathed. The number of preserved title deeds gives the impression of intensive speculation in the real estate and prebend market, but many of these transactions took place between members of the same family, for example, to reorganize one's share after the division of the paternal estate. In many periods or regions of Mesopotamian history, a hesitation toward and (partial) restriction of the alienation of real estate or temple offices can be observed.

The processes of integration of the local households by temples and rulers can be observed in the cuneiform record by reconstructing the careers and responsibilities of household managers. Especially in the Neo-Babylonian period, the political interference in the temples and their hierarchy becomes apparent (e.g., Waerzeggers, 2010, pp. 53–54, 327–353). Loans were a useful tool to regulate the interaction between the different households.

In these early urban societies, labor was one of the most valuable assets. Institutional households could obtain a labor force through a system of corvee workers, via dependents who would receive rations—a system that is well attested during the third millennium B.C.E.—and via laborers who were hired during peak periods such as harvest time (Jursa, 2010, pp. 660–728). Deportations in the context of military campaigns, through which large groups of people were resettled far away, also constitute a factor in the state of affairs. Slaves were not employed on a large scale (as in the Roman world) but were one of the assets in the family holdings (cf. Jursa, 2010, pp. 232–240). People could be turned into slaves when they or their parents were unable to repay their debts or when they were captured as prisoners of war. Well-to-do families often owned at least one or two chattel slaves, as can be seen when the family estate is inventoried on the occasion of a division of an inheritance or the bequest of a dowry. Occasionally, slave women could be employed outside the house as tavern keepers. In Mesopotamian literature as well, a female tavern keeper plays a role in the character of Siduri in the Epic of Gilgamesh.

The problem of the theoretical framework. The source material is not the only hurdle to be cleared when discussing the Mesopotamian economy. The theoretical framework that—often unconsciously—underlies the analysis also needs to be clarified. Different approaches, inspired by Marxism, substantivism (introduced in the study of the ancient Near East by Polanyi), and modernism identify very different principles underlying the activities—for example, price setting through market mechanisms and profit seeking versus redistribution and reciprocity. Today, it is generally accepted that the Mesopotamian economy was fundamentally different from the present-day system, both in scale and in principles, and that ancient as well as modern systems are embedded in their own social and economic contexts; moreover, terminology used to describe ancient economies is borrowed from modern economic theory and therefore may unintentionally impute more capitalistic features than intended by the ancient author. The economy of any society contains elements of all the different "ideal types" discussed by economic historians: reciprocity and redistribution as well as market mechanisms and maximization of profit are present in ancient economies as well as in modern ones, but their relative importance differs significantly and cannot be assessed for the ancient societies.

The Respective Positions of Men and Women in Different Levels of the Economy. In the complex economic reality of the ancient world, men and women played very different roles. As can be expected, men are much more prominent in the documentation. Only in the case of slaves, who appear as the objects of title deeds rather than as active participants, is gender more in balance. This bias reflects the traditional roles of the different sexes in the Mesopotamian patrilinear society: men generally occupied the position of heads of the households, inherited the productive components of the family estate, and performed most of the outdoor activities, whereas women fulfilled tasks within the constraints of the house(hold). These latter, "female," activities are rarely put in writing. This is the case in private as well as in institutional households, as illustrated in the following paragraphs. Since 2012, some case studies on the economic activities of women in Mesopotamia are presented on the website http://refema .hypotheses.org, coordinated by Francis Joannès, Fumi Karahashi, Bertrand Lafont, and Yoko Wataï.

Moreover, the archival documents not only mostly concern men but are also mostly written by men.

Only a small number of documents, all dating to the Old Babylonian period (ca. 1900–1600 B.C.E.), are explicitly written by female scribes: namely, some of the legal documents belonging to the archives of the *nadītum* priestesses from Sippar and four school exercises (cf. Lion, 2011). Apart from these attestations, female scribes occur in lists of personnel from the palaces of Mari, Nineveh, and Kalhu. Apparently, female scribes could exercise their profession in a nearly exclusively female environment, although the largest part of the archives of the *nadītum* priestesses, queens, and princesses were still written by male scribes.

The royal family. All Mesopotamian kingdoms were headed by a male ruler, who was succeeded by his son or his brother or thrown off his throne by a male usurper. In the economic sphere, these kings acted as heads of their royal households, with the help of a hierarchy of administrators. The rulers or their delegates received portions in the redistribution system of local (temple) households, and they occasionally regulated the economics of their country by proclaiming a debt cancellation.

When, rarely, the king's mother or wife was able to acquire an influential position, like Sammu-ramat, mother of Adad-narari III of Assyria (823–811 B.C.E.), she was not able to establish a permanent economic role. However, some female members of the royal family were the heads of temple households. The best-documented example is the administrative archive of the household of the goddess Bau, governed by the queen of Lagaš. From the second half of the third millennium onward, female members of the royal family were often installed as high priestesses of esteemed temples located in religious centers outside the royal capital. The extent of the queen's or princess's actual clout in the economic management, however, remains unknown. These households may well have been "female" in name only, since the other priests and officials of these temples were all men.

Administrative offices. On the other hand, the lists of personnel of the women's quarters in the palaces (Mari, ca. 1800 B.C.E., and Nineveh and Kalhu, seventh century B.C.E.) include several female scribes besides a majority of male administrators. Thus, only the female segments of the institutional households have female personnel on all the levels of management. When women occur in lists of redistributional expenditures in the institutional archives, they apparently represent households of a female disposition.

The clergy. Besides the—often royal—high priestesses of some important temples whose economic independence cannot be assessed, the important and economically relevant temple offices were held by male priests. When a woman did acquire a prebendary office by virtue of being a widow or sole heir, she was required to secure a male to execute the office by adopting a person or transferring the office to her sons. During the largest part of the first millennium B.C.E., women could own prebendary offices but could not buy them; they could acquire prebends only when they were a sole heir or a widow without children. This practice changes toward the Seleucid period, when women are allowed to buy prebends (Waerzeggers, 2010, pp. 49–51, 92–97).

A large amount of archival records has survived from the beginning of the first half of the second millennium B.C.E. documenting the activities of *nadītum* priestesses, women who vowed their lives to a god and lived celibate (or chaste married) lives. On their ordination, these women received a bequest including landed properties instead of the traditional dowry, which included only movables. This endowment theoretically allowed them to provide for themselves. Still, it remains difficult to estimate the actual independence of these women, since the *nadītum's* brothers seem to be responsible for the actual management of their assets and give their *nadītum* sister a yearly allowance.

The families in the cities in the urban families. Social constraints, crystallized in marriage and inheritance traditions, determined the options for men and women in the management of the family estate. Whereas women received a share of the movable properties (including slaves) as a dowry when they left their paternal house on marriage, all the sons of a family inherited an equal share in the estate, landed properties, and prebends as well as movables. With these productive assets, men could establish themselves as heads of their own nuclear households. Besides the contracts from the family archives, the Code of Hammurabi provides invaluable information concerning the position of and the relation between the two sexes in the family households and more specifically about the ownership of the different parts of the family estate.

In the Neo-Babylonian period women occasionally invested parts of their dowry by lending small sums of silver (Jursa, 2010, pp. 244–245). Most contracts in which women play an active role do not specify the circumstances in which these women operated. When a woman owned or received real estate, we can assume that she was a widow or that she had a cultic status. Even then, the actual management of the assets may have remained in the hands of her brother or husband. In Nuzi, a mid-second millennium B.C.E. kingdom in modern-day Syria, some contracts illustrate that daughters were "adopted" as sons when they were the sole heir—a tactic for maintaining the patrilinear transmission of productive assets.

The "working classes." The laborers referred to in the labor administration of temples and palaces had to perform activities on a large scale, such as agricultural tasks, building activities, military campaigns, crafts, and industries. Only in the textile industry, as weavers, did female laborers hold a majority. In other crafts and in agricultural work, women were employed less systematically than men. Female workers were allotted lower rations than their male adult counterparts.

The slaves. Only for slaves do the sources depict both sexes more or less equally. Most often, slaves are mentioned in contracts documenting the ownership of the assets of a private household. The tasks of these slaves most often lie within the limits of the family abode, although the details of their economic activities are not recorded. This situation suggests that the economic value of female workers mainly functioned within the constraints of the house.

Babylonia was not the best of worlds for women. Occasionally, a woman played a prominent role in the economic arena, but such examples are rare and occur only in the absence of a man, when a woman was widowed or ordained as a priestess. In normal circumstances, her economic activities were located close to the fireside.

[*See also* Family Structures, *subentry* Ancient Near East; Legal Status, *subentry* Ancient Near East; Marriage and Divorce, *subentry* Ancient Near East; *and* Religious Leaders, *subentry* Ancient Near East.]

BIBLIOGRAPHY

Briquel-Chatonnet, Françoise, Saba Farès, Brigitte Lion and Cécile Michel, eds. *Femmes, cultures et sociétés dans les civilisations méditerranéennes et proche-orientales de l'Antiquité.* Topoi Supplément 10. Lyon, France: De Boccard, 2009.

Carnet de REFEMA. http://refema.hypotheses.org.

Garfinkle, Steven J. *Entrepreneurs and Enterprise in Early Mesopotamia: A Study of Three Archives from the Third Dynasty of Ur (2112–2004 B.C.).* Cornell University Studies in Assyriology and Sumerology. Bethesda, Md.: CDL, 2012.

Hudson, Michael, Baruch A. Levine, Marc Van de Mieroop, and Cornelia Wunsch, eds. *International Scholars Conference on Ancient Near Eastern Economies.* 4 vols. Cambridge, Mass.: Harvard University; Bethesda, Md.: CDL, 1996–2004.

Jursa, Michael. *Aspects of the Economic History of Babylonia in the First Millennium B.C.: Economic Geography, Economic Mentalities, Agriculture, the Use of Money and the Problem of Economic Growth.* Alter Orient und Altes Testament 377; Veröffentlichunen zur Wirtschaftsgeschichte Babyloniens im 1. Jahrtausend v. Chr. 4. Münster, Germany: Ugarit-Verlag, 2010.

Lion, Brigitte. "Literacy and Gender." In *The Oxford Handbook of Cuneiform Culture,* edited by Karen Radner and Eleanor Robson, pp. 90–112. Oxford: Oxford University Press, 2011.

Lion, Brigitte "Sexe et genre: Des filles devenant fils dans les contrats de Nuzi et d'Emar." In *Femmes, cultures et sociétés dans les civilisations méditerranéennes et proche-orientales de l'Antiquité,* edited by Françoise Briquel Chatonnet, Saba Fares Drappeau, Brigitte Lion and Cécile Michel. Topoi, Supplément 10. Lyon, France: De Boccard, 2009.

Postgate, J. N. "System and Style in Three Near Eastern Bureaucracies." In *Economy and Politics in the Mycenaean Palace States,* edited by Sofia Voutsaki and John Tyrell Killen, Suppl. Vol. 27, pp. 181–194. Cambridge, U.K.: Cambridge Philological Society, 2001.

Radner, Karin. "Assyrische Handelspolitik: Die Symbiose mit unabhängigen Handelszentren und ihre Kontrolle durch Assyrien." In *Commerce and Monetary Systems in the Ancient World: Means of Transmission and Cultural Interaction,* edited by Robert Rollinger and Christoph Ulf, pp. 152–169. Stuttgart: Franz Steiner Verlag, 2004.

Steinkeller, Piotr. "Archival Practices at Babylonia in the Third Millennium." In *Ancient Archives and Archival Traditions: Concepts of Record-Keeping in the Ancient World,* edited by Maria Brosius, pp. 37–58. Oxford Studies in Ancient Documents. Oxford: Oxford University Press, 2003.

Stol, Marten. *Vrouwen van Babylon: Prinsessen, priesteressen, prostituees in de bakermat van de cultuur.* Utrecht, The Netherlands: Kok, 2012.

Van de Mieroop, Marc. *Cuneiform Texts and the Writing of History.* London: Routledge, 1999.

Waerzeggers, Caroline. *The Ezida Temple of Borsippa: Priesthood, Cult, Archives.* Achaemenid History 15. Leiden, The Netherlands: Nederlands Instituut voor het Nabije Oosten, 2010.

Anne Goddeeris

Hebrew Bible

To better understand the life of the average Israelite, one must examine the stage on which daily life occurred—the home. Daily life centered on what could be described as "household economics."

Economic Production Modes in Ancient Israel. The Israelite household economy evolved from a simple subsistence level in the early Iron I Age (ca. 1200–1000 B.C.E.) to a more complicated system under the monarchy in the Iron II period (1000–586 B.C.E.). During the early Iron Age, Israel was predominantly a community-based society with a household-dominant mode of production. Early Israel was agrarian/pastoral and was mostly free of the extraction of surplus goods by a dominating class. With the growth of the monarchy, Israel grew into a native tributary mode, which extracted surplus from households by (1) state taxation and corvée, (2) interest on debt and rental fees by elites, and (3) tribute and indemnity in the form of higher taxes ultimately imposed on the monarchy by foreign powers. Native rulers, foreign rulers, and domestic landholders and merchants exploited households. With the destruction of Israel (ca. 721 B.C.E.) and Judah (ca. 586 B.C.E.), "Israel" developed into a foreign tributary mode, where foreign rulers imposed tribute on households. This continued through the Hellenistic (ca. 333–63 B.C.E.) and Roman periods (ca. 63 B.C.E.–330 C.E.). However, when Judah was restored in the Persian Period (ca. 539–333 B.C.E.), elites were permitted to maintain some level of control providing they remained loyal, preserved domestic stability, and delivered tribute to the imperial power. Notwithstanding modes of production, there was usually a dominant tribute-imposing class that consisted of the political elite. This elite class extracted (or attempted to extract) surplus from the dominated tribute-bearing class, which consisted of agrarian and pastoral producers, as well as other occupational groups. Regardless of changes that the institution of monarchy initiated, the household and its economy were common denominators throughout Israel's history.

The Israelite Household. The household economy during Israel's Iron Age can be described as "pioneer." Most Israelites lived in rural settlements, such as villages, hamlets, or farms, and were preoccupied with living and surviving off of the often inhospitable land. Those who lived in urban settlements, such as fortified, administrative, and capital cities, were likewise concerned with living off the land, but not to the extent of their rural cousins. Rural or urban, Israel consisted of agrarian communities where the household was the nucleus of daily life.

The Israelite household entailed social, material, and behavioral aspects, all of which were significant to its economy. The social aspect consisted of household demographics, including the number of people who lived or worked within the household and their relationship to each other. Possible members of a household included family members who lived and worked together, unrelated members who lived within the dwelling (such as slaves), and those related/nonrelated members who worked at the household but did not live in the dwelling (such as hired workers). The material aspect consisted of the actual dwelling or house, accompanying buildings and land, activity areas, and possessions. The final aspect is the behavioral aspect, made up of activities household members performed.

The ancient Israelite household is often referred to in the Hebrew Bible as the *bet ʾav* ("house of the father") and more rarely as *bêt ʾēm* ("house of the mother"). The physical dwelling of the *bet ʾav* has long been the subject of scholarly discussion and is often referred to as "the Israelite house," "the pillared house," "the four-room house," and "the Iron Age house." Excavated Iron Age dwellings in Israel have a similar plan and common features: a back broad room with one to three (typically three) rooms or chambers running perpendicular to the broad room, frequently divided by pillars. The social aspect of the *bet ʾav* consisted primarily of related family members: the father (or patriarch), the mother (or matriarch), possibly secondary wives, unmarried children and paternal sisters, and married sons and their families, as well as nonrelated members such as slaves, hired workers, foreigners, and guests. Israelite families were predominantly patrilineal, where group membership and inheritance is traced through the father's line, and patrilocal, where newlyweds live within the household of the husband's family. The extended family of the *bet ʾav* was the *mišpaḥah*, or clan, which could occupy most of a village or nearby settlements. Several clans made up a *šebet*, or tribe, which typically lived within the same geographical region and allied together against common enemies, famine, and other catastrophes. It was uncommon for Israelites to think of themselves as individuals. Rather, they saw themselves as members of a group or community: family, clan, and tribe (Shafer-Elliott, 2013, p. 14; Meyers, 1988, p. 38; Matthews and Benjamin, 1993, p. 9; Stager and King, 2002, pp. 28–35).

The behavioral aspect consisted of activities household members performed. Household activities predominantly had to do with surviving off the land. They can be placed into the following categories: production, distribution, transmission, food preparation and consumption, reproduction, and ritual. Production involves tasks of agriculture and animal husbandry, such as planting, harvesting, and breeding. Distribution includes gifts and reciprocal exchange, as well as the act of distribution itself including storage and transport. Transmission is considered part of distribution, but is concerned with transferring rights, roles, land, and property between generations. The preparation of foodstuffs into products and meals, and the consumption of them, makes up the preparation and consumption category. Reproduction consists of the rearing and socialization of children, while the ritualistic category deals specifically with informal and formal worship within the household (Wilk and Rathje, 1982, pp. 618, 622, 624, 627, 630; Goody, 1982, pp. 44–49).

The daily life of the Israelite household centered on activities that were agrarian and pastoral in nature. The task-oriented existence had daily, seasonal, and annual activities, not to mention unpredictable and sporadic ones. Daily chores consisted of intense labor utilizing all available daylight hours, often working around environmental and ecological limitations such as limited water supplies, drought, poor soil quality, and erosion. Activities included, but were not limited to: shepherding and maintenance of herds; planting and harvesting produce such as cereals, legumes, grapes, and summer fruit, including olives; processing foodstuffs into products that could be consumed, stored, and exchanged; producing textiles and garments, tools and implements; and producing and maintaining the dwellings, agricultural buildings, and terraces (Meyers, 1997, p. 23).

Gender Archaeology. The question of who participated in these activities is complicated. Gender archaeology attempts to answer this question and "considers people in the past, especially the relationships of women and men to the social, economic, political, and ideological structures of particular societies" (Nelson, 1997, p. 5). Gender archaeology attempts to clarify the relationship of material remains to actual activities, participants in such activities, and behaviors behind those activities. As useful as gender archaeology is, gender cannot be directly observed through material remains. For instance, when a cooking pot is excavated, the pot itself is not male or female; rather, the person who used it was. Gender archaeology helps infer who was active behind the artifacts and the behaviors and ideology associated with those tasks by utilizing several resources: ethnography, ethnoarchaeology, iconography, and textual resources. Ethnography is "the study of contemporary cultures through direct observation," while ethnoarchaeology is "the study of contemporary cultures in order to understand the behaviors and relationships that underlie the production and use of the material culture of a past society." Observing and studying the remains, activities, and behavior of a present-day traditional culture in various areas of daily life provides insight into, and possible reconstruction of, the daily chores of ancient counterparts. Iconography, or representational art, and textual resources reflect actual and/or idealized aspects of a society. This interdisciplinary approach allows us to better understand the daily activities of the ancient Israelite household (Nelson, 1997, p. 17; Shafer-Elliott, 2013, pp. 19–20, 30, 117–118; Meyers, 2003).

Biblical Research. Few biblical scholars have written as extensively on the Israelite household as Carol Meyers. Her work on the household, its activities, and the various roles of women within households has contributed greatly to our understanding of gender in ancient Israel. Meyers proposes that the survival of any group is dependent upon three factors: procreation (reproduction), production (subsistence), and protection (defense). She suggests that the irregularity of gender roles occurred when an uneven amount of energy was given to one of these three categories. For instance, the procreation factor was largely a female responsibility. Biological factors such as menstruation, pregnancy, birth, lactation, and weaning played a role in the female's division of labor. The female's reproductive role dictated that the majority of her daily chores occurred within or near the physical dwelling. Likewise, the protection factor was dominated by males, who were involved in defensive/offensive engagements. This leaves the production factor, which encompasses animal husbandry, farming, and the chores that stem from them like food preparation and storage. The production factor crossed the so-called gender line in that all members of the household were required to participate. However, certain elements within the production factor, such as chores that require more strength like plowing, indicate that it can be seen as predominantly under the male domain. Under certain repetitive conditions, like planting/harvest or war, females were required to bear more production responsibilities. Meyers cites social scientific research stating that the average ratio of female to male household contribution in subsistence households is 2:3, with women supplying 40 percent of the labor. Societies that maintain this ratio value both male and female contributions and correlate with greater prestige for women. Consequently, an increase in female production responsibilities increased female authority and status. Each member was expected to participate in the survival of the household, regardless of sex, age, or other differentials. The division of production labor solely by gender was a luxury that few agrarian households could afford. Authority and power were in the hands of the older generations, both male and female, rather than one gender (Meyers, 1983, pp. 574–576; Meyers, 2008, p. 780; Frymer-Kensky, 1998, p. 96).

Gender and Domestic Chores. Biological factors such as reproduction and physical strength were determining factors in who did what. Men, women, and children carried out daily activities, with certain times of the year, like planting and harvest, requiring contributions from everyone. Beyond those seasonal times, women's reproductive roles required them to contribute closer to the dwelling. Chores typically done within or near the dwelling include food preparation and weaving. In the archaeological record, material culture such as cooking pots, ovens, grinding stones and slabs, pestles and mortars, and loom weights and whorls are often found within the dwelling or its outdoor courtyard. Cereals used for bread and porridge were essential to the Israelite diet, so much so that the Hebrew word for bread, *leḥem*, is synonymous with food. Processing grain into an edible form involved a complex chain of activities: soaking, milling, and grinding grain into flour that would be made into dough. Processing grain would occupy at least two hours per day, usually within the dwelling or its courtyard. The location of ovens and food preparation objects indicates that cooking and baking took place in centralized locations, either inside the dwelling or in an adjacent courtyard. The central location of ovens permitted women to conduct other household tasks while preparing food. Centralized ovens also allowed for the sharing of ovens (and fuel) with other women, facilitating social relationships and cohesion among the group (Lev 26:26) (Baadsgaard, 2008, p. 42; Ebeling, 2010, pp. 32–33; Meyers, 2003, p. 436; Meyers, 1997, p. 25).

Ethnography, ethnoarchaeology, and iconography typically show women in charge of production activities that were carried out at or near the dwelling. Consequently, women dominated certain domestic activities that required the development of technological skills, which men may not have had to the same extent. The household matriarch was in a sense the household manager and directed the manufacture of household goods like soap, pottery, baskets, cloth, and tools. As manager of the household, the matriarch had authority over major aspects of production: the preparation, storage, distribution, and consumption of food. What and how much produce was to be prepared as a meal or stored as other foodstuffs like beer, wine, oil, parched grain, and dried fruits and vegetables, and who was going to perform these activities, were not only matters of household economics but also survival in a subsistence household. The matriarch as household manager would need significant skill, expertise, and diplomacy, resulting in household power and prestige (Matthews and Benjamin, 1993, p. 25; Meyers, 1988, p. 147).

Gender and the Hebrew Bible. Textual resources for understanding daily life in ancient Israel are primarily found within the Bible. However, the Hebrew Bible is not concerned with illustrating the daily lives of average Israelites. Rather, it reflects the concerns of elite, urban men. It ignores not only women, but also the average man, woman, and child unless they have a role in the purpose of the text. On the other hand, some biblical passages provide a glimpse into what daily life was like. One such passage is found in Leviticus 27, which is seen as an appendix dealing with vows and dedications. A vow was viewed as a conditional promise made to God, to be satisfied if the requested conditions came about. More specifically Leviticus 27 addresses: (1) how an Israelite made a vow or dedication at a local sanctuary; (2) how the value of that vow and dedication was determined; and (3) whether or not the vow and dedication had an acceptable monetary substitute. The

priesthood restricted whose vows were binding, what could be promised, where the vow was fulfilled, whether a monetary substitute was acceptable, and where payment could be made. Vows made by women who were under the economic and social protection of their fathers or husbands were binding unless said males annulled them. Vows made by women who were divorced or widowed were binding since they were seen as independent (Num 30). The centralization of worship to Jerusalem limited the ability to fulfill vows and dedications, leading to monetary substitution. Leviticus 27 provides a list of monetary equivalents for vows or dedications to the sanctuary divided into categories based on age and gender (Lipka, 2008, pp. 773–775).

Age	Male	Female
1 month–5 years old	5 shekels of silver	3 shekels of silver
5–20 years old	20	10
20–60 years old	50	30
60+	15	10

Source: Meyers, 1983, p. 585 (modified).

Here, females in each age category have a lower value than males. The highest value given for both males and females is listed in the 20–60 age category. Traditionally this list has been viewed as communicating worth, indicating that men were seen as more valuable than women in ancient Israel. More recently, scholars reevaluating this list through the lens of social scientific approaches argue that the monetary value listed in Leviticus 27 denotes the worth of the production capacity of the individual in terms of service to the sanctuary, not the intrinsic worth of the actual person. In early Israel, vows dedicating oneself or one's child for lifelong service to the sanctuary were made (see Hannah's vow in 1 Sam 1). When this type of dedication was not feasible, vows of service or the monetary worth of service were made instead. The monetary value represents the amount the service would be worth, not the individual. Dedicating silver or other goods worth the value of the service provided resources that maintained the sanctuary and the priests who supervised its activities (Lipka, 2008, pp. 773–775; Meyers, 2008, p. 780; Meyers, 1983, pp. 582–586).

The monetary scale in Leviticus 27 reflects the economic productivity potential of males and females at various stages of life. The youngest age category is one month to five years old (Lev 27:6). This value takes into consideration the high infant mortality rate within the Israelite household and suggests that a child could not be dedicated before it was one month old. Most agrarian households expected children to participate in simple daily tasks. The second age group, 5–20 years old, has a low economic value for women (Lev 27:5). This low economic value reflects women's preoccupation during this age period with reproduction, not production. Marriages were arranged for daughters when they reached puberty and were able to conceive. As part of their husband's *bet ʾav*, women were expected to contribute just like everyone else, but reproduction was their main occupation. Consequently, women in this age group were unable to contribute as much to the household economy. Thus, their production value was at its lowest. A secondary factor could also be the high rate of death during childbirth. The third age group is 20–60 years old (Lev 27:3–4). In this age group, the productive worth of males is at its highest. Twenty years seems to be a significant age for men, since at this age they were able to serve in the tabernacle and be recruited for military activities (Num 1:3; Num 4:3, 23). The monetary value ascribed to males in this group reflects their high production capacity. The females' production capacity increases as their reproductive role diminishes. The final age category, 60 years old and older, reflects a sharper decrease in men's economic value than in women's (Lev 27:7). Women were able to maintain their contribution to the household economy with only minimal decrease, whereas men's contribution decreased, possibly because of warfare and the high physical demand upon them at the 20–60 year old range. A final stipulation for the poor found in Leviticus 27:8 states that priests assessed the monetary value of the vow based on what can be afforded (Lipka, 2008, pp. 773–775; Meyers, 2008, p. 780; Meyers, 1983, pp. 582–586).

Other incidents involving economic compensation include marriage. When a young woman reached marriageable age (most likely soon after puberty), her parents arranged a marriage for her, typically within their *mišpaḥah* or *šebet*. Betrothal gifts were exchanged to solidify the alliance between two families. A *mohar* was a betrothal gift in the form of money, goods, land, or service from the groom and his *bet ʾav* to the bride's (see Gen 34:8–17; Exod 22:16). The loss of a household member, even through marriage, put the household at a productive disadvantage, since there was one less person to contribute to the household economy. The *mohar* was intended to ease the loss to the household economy of the bride's *bet ʾav*. The bride's household also gave a betrothal gift or dowry to the groom's household in the form of money, goods, or transferable land (see 1 Kings 9:16). However, the dowry was seen as a way to provide security for the bride, who, in theory, maintained possession of it. Likewise, if a woman of marriageable age lost her virginity to a man outside of an arranged marriage, then the man must pay her father and mother the amount of the *mohar* given for virgin brides, which was more than that for widows or divorced women (Exod 22:16–17; Deut 22:28–29). The sexuality of female members of the household was more of an economic concern than an ethical one (Goodfriend, 2008, p. 437; O'Donnell-Setel, 1992, p. 34; Frymer-Kensky, 1998, p. 80).

Economic compensation covered other members of the household, even ones not yet born (Exod 21:22–25). If a pregnant woman was injured during a fight and miscarries, the assailant was required to compensate the household monetarily according to what her husband demands. The fetus was a prospective member of the household; thus, a potential contributor to the household economy is lost. The ordinance also states that if any other injury to the pregnant woman occurs, including death, exact retaliation is expected. *Lex talionis*, or law of retaliation, was not an excuse for violence; rather, it limited revenge by controlling the type of injury that could be given. Any severe injury to or loss of the woman would affect the household's survival by diminishing its membership and her contribution to the *bet 'av* (Goodfriend, 2008, pp. 433–434; O'Donnell-Setel, 1992, p. 34).

Lack of descendants also greatly affected the household. In Numbers 27, the unmarried daughters of Zelophehad petitioned their case to Moses. Since Israel was a patrilineal society, and Zelophehad died leaving only daughters, their father's inheritance would be lost. The daughters proposed a new law that would enable women to inherit land in certain circumstances. The daughters were unmarried and no longer had a father to protect them; as a result, they represented less fortunate members of society. The daughters utilized language that emphasized the *bet 'av* and their desire to see it and their father's name continue. The Lord granted their petition unconditionally and added that it be given to them as their own inheritance, which they could bestow themselves. Consequently, when there was no son to inherit the *bet 'av*, daughters had priority over others in the household, clan, or tribe. Later, in Numbers 36, the elders of the tribe to which the daughters of Zelophehad belong (Manasseh) propose that they marry only within the clan or tribe so that the land would not be lost permanently. This condition should not be viewed as an objection to women owning land; rather, it should be seen as preserving tribal land (Goodfriend, 2008, pp. 970–974, 1025–1027; Doob-Sakenfeld, 1992, p. 50; Pressler, 1998, p. 166).

Conclusion. The study of gender and economics centers on everyday activities and behaviors within the household. The survival of the household dictated who did what activity and when. All physically able members of the household regardless of sex, age, or other differentials participated in the survival of the household. Authority and power within the household was primarily based on generations, rather than gender. Young men and women within the household were under the protection of their matriarch and patriarch.

[*See also* Family Structures, *subentry* Hebrew Bible; Legal Status, *subentry* Hebrew Bible; *and* Marriage and Divorce, *subentry* Hebrew Bible.]

BIBLIOGRAPHY

Baadsgaard, Aubrey. "A Taste of Women's Sociality: Cooking as Cooperative Labor in Iron Age Syro-Palestine." In *The World of Women in the Ancient and Classical Near East*, edited by Beth Alpert Nakhai, pp. 13–44. Newcastle upon Tyne, U.K.: Cambridge Scholars, 2008.

Childs, Brevard S. *The Book of Exodus: A Critical, Theological Commentary.* Old Testament Library. Philadelphia: Westminster, 1974.

Doob-Sakenfeld, Katharine. "Numbers." In *The Women's Bible Commentary*, edited by Carol A. Newsom and Sharon H. Ringe, pp. 45–51. Louisville, Ky.: Westminster John Knox, 1992.

Ebeling, Jennie R. *Women's Lives in Biblical Times.* London: T&T Clark, 2010.

"Experimental Archaeology," in Tell el-Far'ah Dictionary/Pictionary. http://farahsouth.cgu.edu/dictionary/#E.

Frymer-Kensky, Tikva. "Virginity in the Bible." In *Gender and Law in the Hebrew Bible and the Ancient Near East*, edited by Victor H. Matthews, Bernard M. Levinson, and Tikva Frymer-Kensky, pp. 79–96. Journal for the Study of the Old Testament Supplement Series 262. Sheffield, U.K.: Sheffield Academic Press, 1998.

Goodfriend, Elaine. "Mishpatim: Rules for Life in a Covenant Community." In *The Torah: A Women's Commentary*, edited by Tamara Cohn Eskenazi, pp. 427–443. New York: URJ, 2008.

Goody, Jack. *Cooking, Cuisine, and Class: A Study in Comparative Sociology.* Cambridge, U.K.: Cambridge University Press, 1982.

Gottwald, Norman K. "Social Class as an Analytic and Hermeneutical Category in Biblical Studies." *Journal of Biblical Literature* 112, no. 1 (1993): 3–22.

Lipka, Hilary. "B'chukotai." In *The Torah: A Women's Commentary*, edited by Tamara Cohn Eskenazi, pp. 765–779. New York: URJ, 2008.

Matthews, Victor H., and Don C. Benjamin. *Social World of Ancient Israel, 1250–587 B.C.E.* Peabody, Mass.: Hendrickson, 1993.

Meyers, Carol. "Procreation, Production, and Protection: Male-Female Balance in Early Israel." *Journal of the American Academy of Religion* 51, no. 4 (December 1983): 569–593.

Meyers, Carol. *Discovering Eve: Ancient Israelite Women in Context.* Oxford: Oxford University Press, 1988.

Meyers, Carol. "The Family in Early Israel." In *Families in Ancient Israel*, edited by Leo G. Perdue, Joseph Blenkinsopp, John J. Collins, and Carol Meyers, pp. 1–47. Family, Religion, and Culture. Louisville, Ky.: Westminster John Knox, 1997.

Meyers, Carol. "Women and the Domestic Economy of Early Israel." In *Women in the Hebrew Bible: A Reader*, edited by Alice Bach, pp. 33–43. New York: Routledge, 1999.

Meyers, Carol. "Engendering Syro-Palestinian Archaeology: Reasons and Resources." *Near Eastern Archaeology* 66, no. 4 (2003): 185–197.

Meyers, Carol. "Another View of B'chukotai." In *The Torah: A Women's Commentary*, edited by Tamara Cohn Eskenazi, p. 780. New York: URJ, 2008.

Nelson, Sarah Milledge. *Gender in Archaeology: Analyzing Power and Prestige*. Walnut Creek, Calif.: AltaMira, 1997.

Noth, Martin. *Numbers: A Commentary*. Translated by James D. Martin. Old Testament Library. Philadelphia: Westminster, 1968.

O'Donnell-Setel, Drorah. "Exodus." In *The Women's Bible Commentary*, edited by Carol A. Newsom and Sharon H. Ringe, pp. 26–35. Louisville, Ky.: Westminster John Knox, 1992.

Pressler, Carolyn. "Wives and Daughters, Bond and Free: Views of Women in the Slave Laws of Exodus 21: 2–11." In *Gender and Law in the Hebrew Bible and the Ancient Near East*, edited by Victor H. Matthews, Bernard M. Levinson, and Tikva Frymer-Kensky, pp. 147–172. Journal for the Study of the Old Testament Supplement Series 262. Sheffield, U.K.: Sheffield Academic Press, 1998.

Shafer-Elliott, Cynthia. *Food in Ancient Judah: Domestic Cooking in the Time of the Hebrew Bible*. Sheffield, U.K.: Acumen, 2013.

Stager, Lawrence E., and Philip J. King. *Life in Biblical Israel*. Louisville, Ky.: Westminster John Knox, 2002.

Wilk, Richard R., and William L. Rathje. "Household Archaeology." *American Behavioral Scientist* 25 (1982): 617–639.

Von Rad, Gerhard. *Deuteronomy: A Commentary*. Translated by Dorothea Barton. Old Testament Library. Philadelphia: Westminster, 1966.

Yasur-Landau, Assaf, Jennie R. Ebeling, and Laura B. Mazow, eds. *Household Archaeology in Ancient Israel and Beyond*. Culture and History of the Ancient Near East 50. Leiden, The Netherlands: Brill, 2011.

Yee, Gale. "Gender, Class, and the Social-Scientific Study of Genesis 2–3." *Semeia* 87 (1999): 177–192.

Cynthia Shafer-Elliott

Greek World

Scholarship on the ancient Greek economy has not always taken into account the work done by women. That *oikonomikos* (literally "household management," from whence the English "economics" is derived) was part of the vocabulary of the educated elite, however, "indicates that estate management had become a science" by the early fourth century B.C.E., the time of Xenophon's writing of the *Oikonomikos*, a dialogue perhaps best known for the reported conversation between Socrates and the gentleman farmer Ischomachus on "wifely didactics" (Pomeroy, 1994, p. 47; Too, 2001).With agriculture central to all production, and the *polis* a community made up of individual households, *oikonomia* was not merely a private matter. *Oikonomia* was the science of managing an estate (*oikos*) so as to yield a profit—*oikous auxein* (6.4), in Xenophon's words. What was produced would have to be sold, or exchanged, while expenses included paying for sacrifices, public banquets, hospitality (*xenia*), horse maintenance, liturgies, and dowries for the daughters of the family. Increasing the household wealth were the wife's dowry, agricultural produce, the sale of horses, slaves, and sheep.

Although most women in ancient Greece did not participate in the labor market, they were involved in the domestic economy where, in typical patriarchal fashion, the fruits of their labor were appropriated by their head-of-household husbands. Xenophon, nevertheless, was the first Greek author to give "full recognition to the use-value of women's work, and to understand that domestic labour has economic value even if it lacks exchange value" (Pomeroy, 1994, p. 59). Yet the skills women were perfecting in the domestic sphere might also be turned into exchange value profits. Brock's study of women's participation in "the world of exchange and paid labor" (1994, p. 338) turns up a huge range of work with which citizen women were occupied. Educated in wool-working and textiles production (Xenophon, *Oikonomikos* 7.6), aristocratic women were turning to these skills for extra income during times of economic hardship, especially during the Peloponnesian War (Xenophon, *Memorabilia*, 2.7: Aristarchus's female relatives set up their own domestic textile "factory"). In addition to their central role in textile production women are attested as bread makers; vegetable sellers; and ribbon, garland, and net weavers. There were female innkeepers, bathers, and washerwomen. Participation of women in the crafts market is also attested: two cobblers, a gilder (cursed with her husband the helmet maker), and perhaps even a potter (Brock, 1994, p. 342). Socrates's mother, Phainarete, was reputedly a midwife, and there is evidence that by the fourth century B.C.E. women were practicing obstetrics as well.

Not all of these occupations were equally well respected. Female bakers and bread sellers in Athens (Aristophanes, *Frogs* 857–858; *Lysistrata* 458; *Wasps* 238) are represented in comedy as loud-mouthed abusive types, which, as Brock suggests, "might be simply popular prejudice, but a low class status elsewhere is suggested in the linking of bread sellers with prostitutes by Anacreon PMG 388.4–5" (1994, p. 339). Many of the aforementioned occupations rely, unsurprisingly, on skills women would have developed in the domestic sphere, such as washing, baking, cooking, weaving, child care, and so on. Least well understood is women's contribution to Athenian agriculture. Here the interference of ideology (i.e., the cultural expectation of female seclusion) makes it especially difficult to gauge the reality. In Demosthenes 57, for example, Euxitheos is forced to defend his claim to citizenship against allegations that his mother, because she has done menial wage labor, was not of citizen status. The Greek cultural bias against working women makes the evidence of the archaeological record—on women's tombstones, nursing is the best-attested female occupation—especially valuable.

That citizen wives lived out their lives in the domestic quarters, secluded and unseen except by other women and family members, is challenged by the widespread references in literary sources (especially Old Comedy) to working women whose jobs would have taken them into different neighborhoods of the city and maybe also into the fields on a daily basis (see the market scenes at *Wasps* 493–499 and *Lysistrata* 555–564). The ideology of female seclusion prominent in Greek textual sources thus requires qualification, and we may conclude that the notion that women spent only minimal time outdoors, as indexed by their pale complexions in Greek

iconography, is best taken as a societal ideal rather than as a norm.

Xenophon's *Oikonomikos* and the Good Wife. Aristotle frames marriage as a hierarchical relationship, one that subordinates the wife to her husband (*Politics* 1252a: 24b–27). Xenophon's account, by contrast, describes the wife as a partner in marriage, her management of domestic affairs complementing her husband's management of agricultural matters. Socrates suggests to his interlocutor Critoboulos that the wife who is a good partner (*koinonon agathēn*) contributes as much to the good of the household as her husband (*Oikonomikos* 3.15–16), and it is to substantiate this claim that he recounts at some length his earlier conversation with Ischomachus on precisely this subject.

Set in Athens, the first half of the *Oikonomikos* is devoted to the theory and the second half to the practice of running an estate. The conversation between Ischomachus and his wife is "mediated by a process of triple quotation" (Murnaghan, 1988, p. 10), a literary framing device that places the content of what on the surface appears to be a fairly straightforward, pedestrian discussion of home economics between scare quotes, as it were. The effect is to defamiliarize what might appear almost too "natural" to require exposition. The household was generally aligned in the popular imagination with private wealth. But as Murnaghan has argued, the main objective of the *Oeconomicus* is to eliminate "the distinction between public and private interests" (1988, p. 10). If Xenophon can depict farming as an egalitarian pursuit that requires little specialized education or knowledge, then the running of the farm and household would take on the appearance of advancing the public (collective) good rather than merely increasing the wealth of estate owners.

As a member of the landowning class, Xenophon was writing for a community concerned with the ever-widening gap between public and private interests. By, for example, likening well-ordered kitchen utensils to a dithyrambic chorus, Xenophon's dialogue may be trying to suggest a harmonious balance between the public and private spheres: the orderly household is presented as a counterpart to the well-governed state. Although its apparent focus is on training the wife to become an autonomous and productive manager of the domestic quarters, Xenophon's "dialogue is not really concerned with her as a distinct individual"; the wife, rather, comes to symbolize her husband's "mastery of the feminine potential for disorder and self-indulgence in his own personality" (Murnaghan, 1988, pp. 13–14). This accounts for the curiosity that it is a *man* teaching his young wife skills that ordinarily would have been passed down by mothers to their daughters. Like its framing, the content of the dialogue is markedly fictional—some would even say "utopian."

Men and women, according to Ischomachus, are suited by nature to their social roles (7.23–24), men naturally gravitating to the outdoors, where their bodies are better equipped for "enduring cold and heat, journeys and campaigns," while women, less capable of such endurance, have had meted out to them "a larger portion of affection for newborns" (trans. Xenophon IV, 2013). She enjoys a share of "memory" (*mnēmē*) and attention (*epimeleia*) equal to her husband's as well as the capacity to practice self-control (7.26), yet the apparent symmetry between husband and wife in Ischomachus's household nevertheless conceals a deeper disparity: the highest compliment a woman can be made is that she has a "masculine mind," as Socrates's pronounces of Ischomachus's spouse (10.1). In the world of Xenophon's dialogue, the sexes perform complementary roles, but they are not social equals. Still, the *Oikonomikos* offers overall a more positive representation of women as economic players than is found in the archaic poetic tradition represented by Hesiod and Semonides. For Hesiod, women are the descendants of Pandora, whose acceptance by Prometheus augurs in an era of scarcity and toil (before woman, men were living a Golden Age existence); Semonides compares women to various unflattering forms of animal life, reserving his singular praise for the bee-wife.

With Persephone's descent to Hades providing the mythical model, marriage signaled the "death" of girlhood for the bride, who was often only half the age of her prospective husband (fifteen years old, on average, to his thirty years), and who followed the groom to his new home, leaving behind her entire known world. Marriage inaugurated a new phase of life whose main purpose was to bear children who would carry on their father's name and, among the land-owning classes, inherit their father's estate (*oikos*). Our literary sources rarely record the experience of marriage from a female point of view: the textual tradition was almost entirely male-authored and transmitted. But Greek drama does give imaginative glimpses of what it may have been like for those wives whose status in their own marriage was undermined by an inability to procreate. In Euripides's *Andromache*, for example, the childless Hermione feels her wifely position threatened by the presence of noble concubine Andromache, who has borne a son for Hermione's husband, Neoptolemus. Hermione turns to her father for help. As the legitimate wife plots to kill the concubine and her son while being simultaneously courted by Orestes, her husband's eventual murderer, the entire household and its domestic world hang precariously in the balance. Andromache's estimation in the eyes of her "husband" stems from her having performed the essential role of the ideal wife—she is the mother of Neoptolemus's only son.

Conversely, the fact that Hermione can hold the entire household hostage to her malign schemes shows what power a wife might derive from her (well-to-do) natal family, the material expression of which was to be found in her dowry. The dowry—(moveable) wealth that a wife brought with her into her marriage—served as capital for the estate of her husband but at the same time remained a permanent link between the woman and her natal family; unless she needed to call in favors to negotiate her status within her husband's household (à la Hermione), the wife's dowry primarily served the needs of the husband. But it may have functioned as a psychological deterrent, keeping the husband's transgressive behaviors in check. For in the event of a divorce, he would be legally obligated to repay to his father-in-law the entire value of the dowry his wife had brought with her into their marriage.

Moreover, the category of moveable property known to us from the forensic sources as *himatia kai chrysia* ("garments and gold jewelry") suggests that women may have contributed to their own dowries with the weaving they did in their fathers' homes. Schaps describes this collocation as "a technical term for the personal accoutrements brought along by the bride into the husband's house" (1979, p. 10). We still do not know whether these personal items were included in the calculation of the monetary value of a woman's dowry; counting them as part of the dowry would have created an intimate tie between a woman's social agency and her economic wherewithal. The connection is one that tragedy exploits to great effect, particularly in its examination of wives who avenge themselves on wayward husbands through the medium of poisoned, or otherwise dangerous, fabrics—a topic explored in the next section. Hermione's particular plight, then, is the stuff of myth, but the social and economic situation in which she finds herself was real enough.

"Bad" Wives: The *Oikos* Turned Inside Out. An important source of economic, and hence of social, agency for women can be found in the production of textiles, themselves a form of "liquid wealth" (Pomeroy, 1994, p. 62). Women from all social strata (slaves, noblewomen, goddesses) are shown working at the loom in Homeric epic. But as Lyons (2012) has recently argued, whereas gifts of cloth are for the most part harmless in epic, in tragedy, textiles form the centerpiece of dangerous exchanges. In epic, the good wife weaves and cloaks her husband in the works of her loom (think: Penelope). The wives in Aeschylus's *Agamemnon* and Sophocles's *Trachiniae*, by contrast, turn textiles into husband-killing weapons. Clytemnestra is never directly associated with weaving, but Deianeira inadvertently murders her husband, Herakles, with a robe she has woven with her own hands. Lyons reads Deianeira as a "kind of latter-day Pandora," a wife who also stores her poisons in an urn, this one made out of bronze (2013, p. 82). Tragedy offers ample evidence that in the cultural imaginary of the ancient Greeks, "marriage becomes the site of greatest anxiety about women and exchange" (Lyons, 2012, p. 90).

In *Agamemnon*, when Clytemnestra asks the Herald to convey to her husband, newly returned from Troy,

that she has been faithful during his long absence, she says that he will find her in his house, a trusty guard-dog "just as he left her." She exploits the imagery of the seal to strengthen her rhetoric. Tell my husband, she says, "that I have not broken his seal in all the length of time" he has been away (pp. 609–610). Clytemnestra clearly intends to highlight her housewifely preservation of the goods that are safely sealed in jars in the storerooms. But in an interlinear gloss, an ancient commentator on the play noted that *sēmantērion* suggests "chastity seal." The subtext of Clytemnestra's metaphor is that the wife's body is itself a vessel to which the husband alone has authorized access. In leaving for war, Agamemnon would have expected his wife to remain "sealed" until his return. But even the oblique assertion that she has been faithful to her husband rings slightly false, and what she says in the next two lines easily converts suspicion into alarm.

Clytemnestra concludes her speech with the striking assertion that she knows "no more of the pleasure nor of the rumor of another man than she has knowledge of the *dyeing* (or tempering) *of bronze.*" The phrase *chalkou baphas* (p. 612) refers to the process of "tempering" metal. But *baphē* is the technical term for dyeing fabric as well. The phrase thus alludes proleptically to the manner in which her murder of Agamemnon will combine the crafts of metallurgy and cloth-making. She of course knows a great deal about the "tempering" of bronze. But in emphasizing her ignorance in this regard, she anticipates for her audience how her murder of her husband will take the form of a perverted act of wifely virtue, an act ironically fitting for this woman of "man-counseling heart" (*androboulon...kear,* 11). The "tempering of bronze" will in fact become a dyeing of fabric.

Clytemnestra, then, "weaves," but only in the sense of turning her own husband into the *ergon* (the "work") of her right hand, as she boasts triumphantly over his corpse:

Test me as if I were a senseless woman, but I speak to those who know with untrembling heart. As for you, it is the same (to me) whether you praise me or blame me: This man is Agamemnon, my husband, and a corpse, the work (*ergon*) of this right hand—a just craftsman. This is how it is. (*Agamemnon*, 1401–1406)

Here Clytemnestra plies craft metaphors, calling herself a *tektōn* and the murder itself, or, rather, her husband's body, an *ergon*. It is telling that she frames the murder as a matter of woven works (*erga*), considering that any reference to their crafting was precisely what was missing from her description of the garments in the Carpet Scene, where she had lured her husband to tread expensively dyed, money-bought, purple fabrics (e.g., 949 *argurōnētous t'huphas*: "silver-bought weavings"). There, Clytemnestra avoided saying by whose hands the *heimata* were made; she represented them as artifacts mysteriously generated by the house, their origins ascribed to the sea (958–965). Here, by calling Agamemnon's corpse the "work of her right hand" Clytemnestra takes credit for the first time for an artisanal product. But her blended metaphor—based on *baphas*—effectively collapses the boundaries between the feminine sphere of cloth and the masculine world of war from which Agamemnon has recently returned.

Clytemnestra as the disgraced wife is traditionally contrasted with Penelope, Odysseus's faithful wife, who waited patiently for her husband and kept to womanly tasks and roles (see in particular Agamemnon's praise of Penelope at *Odyssey* 24.192–202). But Penelope used the womanly craft of weaving to exert a typically female devious agency, keeping the suitors at bay for three years (*Odyssey* 24.139–145). Though "tempering" the sword and dyeing fabric in her husband's blood, Clytemnestra did not weave when she would have been expected to—to preserve and increase her husband's wealth. Instead she has saved her one act of "weaving" for his homecoming and death. By specifying, however, that she has performed the deed (*ergon*) with her *right* hand, Clytemnestra privileges the masculine sense of *baphē*, since the right hand is the weapon-wielding one. When not engaged in combat, men used the right hand customarily for sealing oaths with a handshake. Weaving proper, by contrast, was either the work of a hand (right versus left remaining unspecified) or of hands, plural. Her mixed metaphor perfectly captures the

perverted kind of "weaving" Clytemnestra has done; hers is a murder that takes aim simultaneously at her husband as target and the normative practice of women's work.

Clytemnestra's "weaving" in this way commemorates Agamemnon's death rather than the hands of the weaver. It does not proclaim his fame (*kleos*) to the world, as Penelope's weaving did for Odysseus in the *Odyssey*, or as Helen's will do for herself. What Clytemnestra has woven is not the *robe* of death—she has "woven" her husband dead. When she stands boastfully over her kill, she takes credit for the dead bodies, robe-wrapped, that lie before her, spread out for all to see. To return to the other wife, the inadvertently murderous Deianeira of Sophocles's tragedy, if Herakles at first takes the robe as evidence that his wife has plotted a Clytemnestra-style homecoming for him, he later changes his mind when he hears from his son of the centaur's role in persuading Deianeira (Sophocles, *Trachiniae* 1141–1142). Hyllus has only to mention the name "Nessus" (1141) and Herakles is reminded of an ancient prophecy told to him by his father. Nessus, Herakles realizes, is the key to decoding this prophecy that foretold his death at some unspecified time in the future, at the hands of "one who does not breathe" (1160). Herakles, however, would not have been taken in by Nessus's trick, were it not for his wife's "sealing" of the box containing the poisoned robe with her distinctive signature-ring, the *sphragis* that Clytemnestra also mentioned, metaphorically, as a guarantor of her sexual fidelity.

Deianeira explains to the herald Lichas, who will deliver her robe to Herakles, that the mark of her seal ring is a sign (*sēma*, 614) that her husband will easily recognize (614–615). What the seal of her *sphragis* guarantees is not a discursive truth, but rather the gift's origin: the *sēma* functions as a surrogate for the act of physically handing over the robe in person. Because it marks the origin of the container, moreover, it effectively labels the object as an extension of the domestic interior. In recognizing his wife's *sphragis*, Herakles handles the box confidently as a familiar entity; it is a reified fragment of the *oikos* itself.

Wooden chests containing textiles are especially evocative of danger in tragedy. In *Trachiniae* and probably *Medea* as well poisoned fabrics are transported in these sealed boxes. Lissarague suggests that the representation of boxes, chests, and baskets on vases and other vessels delineates the feminine space of the Greek household, where women engaged in wool-working and oversaw the domestic economy. Of the representation of containers on a terracotta plaque from Lokri (British Museum, inv. no. TC 1226), Lissarague writes: "The gathering of containers of all types clearly defines an indoor space where things are put away and stored" (1995, p. 95). On the tragic stage as well, chests and containers act as symbols of the deepest and darkest recesses of the royal palace. Containing things that are normally kept hidden from view, they offer the spectator a tantalizing glimpse into the domestic interior, whose furnishings and invisible trappings only occasionally spill out into the visible realm of the city's public spaces. A combustible mixture of textiles smeared with deadly *pharmaka* are contained in these innocent-looking vessels, whose contents are presented as gifts—their potency unknowable before the deadly drugs kick into action under the catalyzing force of daylight and the warmth of human flesh. The victims of these textiles' carnivorous force realize their predicament only when it is already too late. Herakles hardly suspects that the box containing a robe from Deianeira will turn out to be his final and deadliest labor yet, for the robe is reassuringly packaged in a box sealed with Deianeira's personal *sphragis* (acting here as her signature), its exterior designed to instill trust. Such was the inherent doubleness of *oikonomia* for the ancient Greeks.

[*See also* Children, *subentry* Greek World; Economics, *subentries on* New Testament *and* Roman World; Family Structures, *subentry* Greek World; Marriage and Divorce, *subentry* Greek World; *and* Social Interaction, *subentry* Greek and Roman Worlds.]

BIBLIOGRAPHY

Brock, Roger. "The Labour of Women in Classical Athens." *Classical Quarterly* 44 (1994): 336–346.

Cox, Cheryl A. *Household Interests: Property, Marriage Strategies and Family Dynamics in Ancient Athens.* Princeton, N.J.: Princeton University Press, 1998.

Foley, Helene Peet. *Female Acts in Greek Tragedy.* Princeton, N.J.: Princeton University Press, 2001.

Foxhall, Lin. "Household, Gender, and Property in Classical Athens." *Classical Quarterly* 39 (1984): 22–44.

Foxhall, Lin. *Studying Gender in Classical Antiquity.* Cambridge, U.K.: Cambridge University Press, 2013.

Just, Roger. *Women in Athenian Law and Life.* New York: Routledge, 1991.

Lissarague, François. "Women, Boxes, and Containers: Some Signs and Metaphors." In *Pandora: Women in Classical Greece*, edited by Ellen Reeder, pp. 91–101. Baltimore: Trustees of the Walters Art Gallery; Princeton, N.J.: Princeton University Press, 1995.

Lyons, Deborah. *Dangerous Gifts: Gender and Exchange in Ancient Greece.* Austin: University of Texas Press, 2012.

Murnaghan, Sheila. "How a Woman Can Be More Like a Man: The Dialogue between Ischomachus and His Wife in Xenophon's *Oeconomicus.*" *Helios* 15 (1988): 9–22.

Pomeroy, Sarah B. *Xenophon, Oeconomicus: A Social and Historical Commentary.* New York: Oxford University Press, 1994.

Reeder, Ellen D., ed. *Pandora: Women in Classical Greece.* Baltimore: Trustees of the Walters Art Gallery; Princeton, N.J.: Princeton University Press, 1995.

Saller, Richard P. "Household and Gender." In *The Cambridge Economic History of the Greco-Roman World*, edited by Walter Scheidel, Ian Morris, and Richard Saller, pp. 87–112. Cambridge, U.K.: Cambridge University Press, 2007.

Schaps, David. *Economic Rights of Women in Ancient Greece.* Edinburgh: Edinburgh University Press, 1979.

Too, Yun Lee. "The Economies of Pedagogy: Xenophon's Wifely Didactics." *Proceedings of the Cambridge Philological Society* 47 (2001): 65–80.

Xenophon. *Memorabilia, Oeconomicus, Symposium, Apology.* Translated by E. C. Marchant and O. J. Todd. Revised by J. Henderson. Cambridge, Mass.: Harvard University Press, 2013. First published 1923.

Zeitlin, Froma I. "The Economics of Hesiod's Pandora." In *Pandora: Women in Classical Greece*, edited by Ellen Reeder, pp. 49–56. Baltimore: Trustees of the Walters Art Gallery; Princeton, N.J.: Princeton University Press, 1995.

Melissa Mueller

Roman World

The Roman economy was a typical premodern system in that agriculture was the primary component and production was located predominantly within households. It expanded steadily with the growth of the empire, but began to wither in the fifth century C.E.

Family and *Familia*. Any investigation of economics and gender must begin with the family, which functioned as the basic social and economic unit in the Roman world. Production and commerce were centered on the family, which was also the primary mechanism for transferring wealth and property across generations. This idea of family encompassed two interconnected issues: The first was a legal definition of "family" that was based upon the concept of the *paterfamilias* and its relationship to property rights. *Paterfamilias* is best translated as "head of household" and described the eldest male in a direct agnatic lineage; the *familia* consisted of all the descendants of the *paterfamilias* (children, grandchildren, great-grandchildren) following a male descent line. The second was an understanding of "family" as the unit formed by parents and their children; authors frequently used the term *domus* (house) to refer to the household or nuclear family.

Under Roman law, a male *paterfamilias* possessed complete financial and legal power (*patria potestas*) over his descendants (the *familia*). This meant that a *paterfamilias* alone possessed legal ownership over the property held by members of his *familia*. Children, grandchildren, and possibly the wife of the *paterfamilias* could own nothing, and anything acquired by these individuals became the legal property of the *paterfamilias*. When a *paterfamilias* died, each of his sons (and quite possibly his daughters) became a *paterfamilias* in his or her own right. Social custom dictated that all children—including daughters—should inherit on an equal (or near-equal) basis.

The Roman economy swelled during the military expansion of the Republican Era (sixth to first centuries B.C.E.), and the increasing amount of wealth and complexity of commercial transactions made this system of property ownership increasingly cumbersome and inefficient. Accordingly, Roman law developed the *peculium* as a means to mitigate the situation. The *peculium* was a fund granted by the *paterfamilias* to someone in his *potestas* (a daughter, grandson, slave, etc.) to manage as his or her own money in order to pay for life expenses. The individual treated this money as his or her own, but it remained the legal property of the *paterfamilias* and it was revocable at any time.

In a landmark study on life expectancy, Richard Saller added a new wrinkle to our understanding of the *paterfamilias* and the economic landscape of ancient Rome (1994, pp. 9–69). Combining data from funerary monuments, comparative demographic information, and a very sophisticated computer modeling program, he determined that the relatively short life expectancy in the Roman world meant that most adults would not have been in the power of a *paterfamilias*. Using the most optimistic assumptions, his model shows that more than 25 percent of all Roman children would have lost their father by the age of fifteen, nearly 50 percent would have lost their father by twenty-five, and 80 percent would have lost their father by the age of forty. These percentages are based on the most generous assumptions about life expectancy; the actual percentages of Romans without a living father were almost certainly even higher.

Rights of Women. Roman women possessed greater property rights and economic agency than women in nearly any other premodern society; they could own land and possessions, form contracts, and conduct financial transactions. Roman law protected the assets of married women, requiring that they be held independently from those of their husbands. This was especially important because the social expectations regarding equal distribution of patrimonies meant that women had a realistic opportunity to acquire wealth. Upon the death of her father (or her husband if she was under his *potestas*), a woman would become independent (*sui iuris*) and a *paterfamilias* in her own right. Finally, Roman women possessed the right to make wills and control the distribution of their assets after their death.

There were some constraints placed upon the property rights of women, most notably that they needed a guardian (*tutor*) to approve major financial transactions for their entire lives. This condition was more restrictive than that for men, who needed a *tutor* only until the age of fourteen and then were under a limited financial guardianship (*cura*) until the age of twenty-five. A *paterfamilias* might name a *tutor* for a dependent in his will, or, in cases where he died intestate, a magistrate would appoint an individual (until the first century C.E., usually the closest male agnate). Women were generally not eligible to serve as guardians themselves, although in the Imperial Era exceptions were sometimes made in cases involving a mother and child.

The primary duties of the guardians of adult women were to approve large commercial transactions and the creation of a will. By the end of the Republican Era, the institution had begun to weaken; a woman gained some legal recourse to compel a *tutor* to grant his approval and the capability to apply for a new guardian if she believed that hers was not acting in her best interest. In the first century C.E., the emperor Augustus introduced a law that allowed women who gave birth to three children to be wholly exempted from needing guardianship.

Roman women possessed no direct political rights, meaning that they could not vote in elections, hold political office, or serve on juries. Women were allowed to make public speeches in a law court, but only if they were personally involved in a case. Nonetheless, the ability to own property gave women the means to influence affairs or enact civic change. There are many examples of women exercising de facto political power through men (often their male relatives) and using their own resources to enact civic change. The exercise of this political influence became more common and wide reaching after the advent of the empire, when government came to be located in the imperial family. As the wives, daughters, and sisters of emperors (and emperors-to-be), women such as Livia and Agrippina the Younger became immensely powerful political figures. Women controlled a substantial amount of wealth in the Roman world; they frequently had their own clients (both men and women) and acted as civic patrons, providing funds for the construction of buildings and monuments throughout the Mediterranean region.

Marriage and Divorce. The foundation of the Roman household was the nuclear family, and newlyweds usually established their own residence (made possible by the grant of a *peculium* if they remained in the *potestas* of a *paterfamilias*). The average age of first marriage seems to have been the late teens for women and the late twenties for men (although the average ages for members of the senatorial order were about four to five years younger for both men and women). This meant that on average the age difference between husband and wife was about ten years, although it was not unusual to see even larger age gaps for later marriages. For example, Pliny the Younger married his third wife, Calpurnia, when he was in his forties and she was in her teens. Marriage was frequently used to cement political and/or economic alliances between families, which explains the earlier ages of marriage for Roman elites.

By the late republic, both individuals needed to give their consent in order to be married (in the early republic, a *paterfamilias* may have been able to force his children to marry against their will, but the evidence is unclear). Individuals under the *potestas* of a *paterfamilias* also needed to gain his consent to get married (regardless of their age). However, early in the Imperial Era, daughters gained the power to legally compel their *paterfamilias* to issue his consent.

A Roman wedding was a public celebration, the focal point of which was a "rite of passage" procession from the bride's current house to the new house that she would share with her husband. Before departing, the bride made a sacrifice of her childhood toys to her old household gods. Her family then escorted her to new house and symbolically handed her over to the groom, effectively transforming her from a girl to a *matrona*—a Roman woman.

There were two forms of marriage (or marriage statuses), and each had important economic repercussions for the families involved. A marriage *cum manu* (with authority/control) transferred a woman from the *potestas* of her father to that of her husband, who then became her *paterfamilias*. A marriage *sine manu* (without authority/control) meant that the woman remained under the *potestas* of her father. Both forms existed during the republic, but *sine manu* marriages became much more common than *cum manu* marriages by the late republic/early empire. The most likely reason for this shift was the growing wealth of Rome, which meant that more was at stake financially. Marriages *sine manu* allowed families greater control over their resources, since a woman's dowry and/or share of the inheritance would remain under the control of her birth family after her death (rather than passing to her husband).

According to Roman tradition, the bride's family was supposed to provide her husband with a dowry, ostensibly for her expenses in an amount relative to their socioeconomic standing. The husband was to manage these resources for his wife, but he could keep any profit earned. His access to the dowry itself was limited by law, since in cases of divorce, a husband was required to repay the dowry to the *paterfamilias* of his former wife.

A primary goal of marriage was the production of children and the extension of the family line. All children came under the *potestas* of the father, which meant that a woman might be a *paterfamilias* herself, but would never have any individuals under her authority (other than slaves, whom the law classified as owned property).

Unsurprisingly, with marriage being an instrument of political alliance, divorce in the Roman world was common and easily accomplished. Both women and men had the right to initiate divorce, which gave wealthy women a degree of leverage; with the advent of marriage *sine manu*, women or their family members retained ownership of their property, and divorce would remove these resources from the former husband. Up until the mid-second century C.E., a *paterfamilias* could dissolve a dependent's marriage, even against his or her will. In cases of divorce, it was customary for any children to remain with their father (who was their *paterfamilias*). Accordingly, mothers had very little legal authority over their children.

Social Expectations. Gendered norms and idealized virtues helped to define individuals' places in the Roman world, which in turn had significant ramifications for their socioeconomic participation. Our understanding of gender and social expectations is dominated by elite male voices, given the nature of the surviving sources. However, the fact that most of these ideals appear in the funerary inscriptions of more middling citizens suggests that they were well diffused throughout Roman society.

Men were supposed to engage in "public" affairs such as politics, warfare, and commerce in accordance with their socioeconomic status. Concepts of masculinity centered on qualities and virtues such as physical strength, emotional self-control, honorable conduct, and loyalty/service to the Roman state. The last of these was tempered by a sense of freedom and bodily integrity that came with the possession of citizenship.

One critical offshoot of this vision of masculinity was a denigration of both wage labor and commerce in general. The inherent obligations of wage labor and the fact that the work was being done for the benefit of another individual encouraged an association with servitude. Similarly, commerce was deemed to be a low and disreputable endeavor, and thus not suitable for elite men. As the supposed moral core of Rome, they would ideally earn their income from their land, and Roman law technically restricted members of the senatorial order from engaging in business enterprises (although most found ways to circumvent these regulations). Despite this negative association, participation in commerce came to be seen as the hallmark of the equestrian order. An individual's occupation was commonly cited and celebrated in funerary epitaphs, and Sandra Joshel has persuasively demonstrated that many people in the Roman world—and especially slaves and freed slaves—embraced their profession as an integral aspect of their identity (Joshel, 1992).

Roman women led a much less secluded life than many other women in the ancient world; they commonly attended large dinner parties and public events, including spectacles, shows, religious events, and even political gatherings. Upper-class women generally received a rudimentary education, which involved instruction in reading, writing, basic mathematics, literature, arts, and music. The social role expected of most Roman women was that of wife and mother;

a wedding was supposed to be the seminal moment in a woman's life. While women performed a variety of household tasks, spinning wool was imbued with particular moral significance and was treated as the activity par excellence for the virtuous Roman woman.

The single most important determinant of a woman's virtue and honor was her sexuality. For a respectable woman, any sexual activity outside of marriage was potentially shameful and detrimental to her social status. Moreover, illicit sexual acts, such as engaging in adultery and prostitution, could diminish a Roman woman's legal rights. Concerns about association with (or accusation of) dishonorable conduct might deter or influence a woman's participation in public life.

Labor and the Economy. In every respect, ancient Rome was a slave society; slaves were ubiquitous at all levels of society and in every component of the economy. While there has been significant debate among modern scholars about the exact number of slaves, all agree that slaves were a very significant part of the Roman labor force. Roman law classified slaves as property owned by a *paterfamilias* and, as such, they were also considered to be part of the *familia*.

The division of labor in Roman society was rooted in the male/outdoor, female/indoor model prevalent in most premodern agricultural communities. In this model, men performed the outdoor/public labor that generated tangible sustenance, whereas women were responsible for the maintenance and support of the household (although for upper-class men and women this meant overseeing the servants and slaves rather than doing the work themselves). One important contributing factor to this model was the perceived bodily weakness of women, which encompassed both a physical and an intellectual deficiency. Accordingly, the type of labor classified as "male" acquired more prestige than "female" work. Other important factors were a sense of propriety and a desire to embody the idealized virtues and satisfy social expectations prevalent in Roman society. While it would have been uncomplicated for slave owners to ignore these conventions, given the marginalized status of the laborers, the surviving sources indicate an overwhelming adherence to these gendered norms. One major exception was the use of male slaves to perform lesser "female" tasks as a form of extravagant conspicuous consumption.

Agricultural labor. Agriculture was the primary component of the Roman economy, and most labor was dedicated to food production. Duties would have included the planting and harvesting of crops, animal husbandry, and the construction and maintenance of the necessary supplies and infrastructure. The majority of the people in the Roman world worked smaller household farms with subsistence-level production. Families maintained their own plots, with men focusing on the agricultural tasks and women on household upkeep and ancillary support work. Family labor might be supplemented by a few slaves and/or hired wage laborers. Alternatively, male householders might hire themselves out as temporary wage laborers as situations demanded.

The influx of wealth and prisoners of war that occurred with military expansion during the Republican Era led to the creation of giant agricultural estates (*latifundiae*) staffed by slaves. Our information on the agricultural work performed by men and women predominantly comes from the agronomic writings of Cato, Varro, and Columella, who offered instructions and advice for ideal estate operation. In addition to the cultivation of crops, key agricultural industries included the production of wine and olive oil.

The bulk of the agricultural work was assigned to men—specifically male slaves; very little is said about the work of women. Perhaps most telling about Roman attitudes toward agricultural labor are the estate parameters formulated by Cato, in which the author outlined the precise types of equipment and personnel necessary to ensure the ideal operation of a farm. Here Cato specified the exact number of slaves needed to staff an estate, but only mentioned one woman on his lists: the *vilica* (*De agri cultura* 10–11).

The *vilica* was the household manager, who was commonly the wife/partner (*contubernalis*) of the *vilicus*, the slave or freedman placed in charge of an agricultural property. A *vilica* need not necessarily have been a slave, but slaves frequently fulfilled this role. According to the agronomists, the primary responsibility of the *vilica* was to assist her partner in the oversight of the villa, which included supervising the household stores, the production of wool, and the preparation of food. The *vilica* was not solely responsible for performing all of these duties, only for managing, instructing, and assisting other household slaves engaged in these tasks. The most probable duties for these women would have been textile production, food service, and household cleaning. Furthermore, Columella implied that it was not unusual for female slaves to be working outside of the villa in some capacity. He advised that the *vilica* have wool work available for days when a woman could not perform tasks outdoors because of inclement weather (*De re rustica* 12.3.6). It is likely then that female slaves would have participated principally in ancillary support work, such as cooking, cleaning, and the tending of small animals, rather than the primary agricultural production of the estate.

Despite trivializing women's labor, Roman authors recognized that the presence of female slaves was a useful, and perhaps necessary, component of a stable household. While the agronomists largely ignored female slaves as a source of labor, they did mention these women as a potential reward and support network for male slaves. Varro argued that allowing estate overseers (*praefecti*) to have fellow slaves as conjugal partners made them "stronger and more attached to the farm," and it was on account of these relationships that slave families from Epirus were both very reputable and valued (*Rerum rusticarum de agri cultura* 1.17.5). Female slaves were also highly valued for their reproductive capacity, which was necessary to replenish the labor force; children of slaves were born as slaves themselves.

Urban labor. There is evidence for a diversity of skilled artisanal work and large-scale manufacturing taking place in urban locations. The best sources for the range of tasks and services being completed is the collection of funerary inscriptions in the *Corpus Inscriptionum Latinarum*. Free people and slaves labored in the same occupations, often working side by side with one another.

The scope of tasks broadened, yet women still remained centered on the household and personal service, and men on income and material production. Roman cities were financial and industrial hubs at the center of wide-ranging trade routes that spanned the Mediterranean world. Men engaged in a wide variety of commercial and artisanal activities, ideally in accord with their socioeconomic standing. Sons generally learned a trade from their father, although some artisans (especially those without male children) might take on an apprentice. Women worked primarily in service jobs, especially food preparation, hospitality, personal care, and prostitution; storefront commerce; and the manufacture of textiles, clothing, jewelry, and perfume. There is some evidence of women holding more prominent professional positions, but they seem to be the exception rather than the norm in the Roman economy. Female slaves appear as personal attendants and secretaries for women, weavers, seamstresses, midwives, wet nurses, and caregivers for young children. Moreover, as in the case of rural households, women would often work alongside their husbands in a support capacity (especially in less wealthy families), essentially creating family-owned and -operated businesses.

It was common for artisans to organize themselves into associations (*collegia*) by craft. *Collegia* functioned as community support organizations; members and their families came together to fund burials, celebrate religious rituals and holidays, exercise political influence, and provide sustenance and care to associates in need. There is also evidence to suggest that some *collegia* made use of communal workspaces in order to boost production and profits. Modern scholars have debated the extent to which *collegia* actually worked as business collectives or guilds, but generally all agree that there were economic and social advantages gained through participation.

[*See also* Education, *subentry* Roman World; Family Structures, *subentry* Roman World; Legal Status, *subentry* Roman World; Marriage and Divorce, *subentry* Roman World; Masculinity and Femininity, *subentry*

Roman World; *and* Social Interaction, *subentry* Greek and Roman Worlds.]

BIBLIOGRAPHY

Dixon, Suzanne. *The Roman Family*. Baltimore: Johns Hopkins University Press, 1992.

Gardner, Jane F. *Women in Roman Law and Society*. Bloomington: Indiana University Press, 1986.

Gardner, Jane F. *Family and* Familia *in Roman Law and Life*. Oxford: Clarendon, 1998.

Hasegawa, Kinuko. *The* Familia Urbana *during the Early Empire: A Study of Columbaria Inscriptions*. BAR International Series 1440. Oxford: Archaeopress, 2005.

Joshel, Sandra. *Work, Identity, and Legal Status at Rome: A Study of the Occupational Inscriptions*. Norman: University of Oklahoma Press, 1992.

Kampen, Natalie. *Image and Status: Roman Working Women in Ostia*. Berlin: Mann, 1981.

McGinn, Thomas A. J. *The Economy of Prostitution in the Roman World: A Study of Social History and the Brothel*. Ann Arbor: University of Michigan Press, 2004.

Milnor, Kristina. *Gender, Domesticity, and the Age of Augustus: Inventing Private Life*. Oxford: Oxford University Press, 2005.

Roth, Ulrike. "Inscribed Meaning: The *Vilica* and the Villa Economy." *Papers of the British School at Rome* 72 (2004): 101–124.

Saller, Richard P. *Patriarchy, Property and Death in the Roman Family*. Cambridge, U.K.: Cambridge University Press, 1994.

Saller, Richard P. "*Pater Familias, Mater Familias*, and the Gendered Semantics of the Roman Household." *Classical Philology* 94 (1999): 182–197.

Scheidel, Walter, ed. *The Cambridge Companion to the Roman Economy*. Cambridge, U.K.: Cambridge University Press, 2012.

Scheidel, Walter, Ian Morris, and Richard Saller, eds. *The Cambridge Economic History of the Greco-Roman World*. Cambridge, U.K.: Cambridge University Press, 2007.

Treggiari, Susan. "Jobs for Women." *American Journal of Ancient History* 1 (1976): 76–104.

Treggiari, Susan. *Roman Marriage: Iusti Coniuges from the Time of Cicero to the Time of Ulpian*. Oxford: Oxford University Press, 1991.

Matthew J. Perry

New Testament

Several difficulties complicate the effort to understand the interaction of gender and economic realities in the New Testament world. Historians of the Roman economy have tended, until recently, to treat economic patterns and questions of mode of production without particular regard to gender. Similarly, historians of Roman law, which was predominantly concerned with property, have discussed women primarily as they appear in the ancient sources: that is, as their behavior as wives, mothers, or daughters affected the property and honor of Roman men. Gender roles, on the other hand, have been more often scrutinized from the perspective of cultural anthropology than of economics. Given the androcentric nature of the New Testament texts and of the cultural matrix in which they were written (and in which they tend still to be interpreted), simply putting gender at the center of analysis and taking women's roles seriously (a modest definition of feminist scholarship) requires diligent and imaginative effort.

Through the end of the twentieth century, much mainstream scholarship on the social world of the New Testament was less interested in economic realities than in broad generalizations regarding "honor and shame" cultures and social status. Some scholars could imagine first-century poverty as resulting from "some unfortunate turn of events or some untoward circumstances," being normally neither enduring, nor pervasive, nor related to fundamental socioeconomic patterns such as class (Malina, 2001, pp. 99–101). Other scholars announced a "new consensus," according to which the early Christian assemblies constituted a cross-section of Roman society, including a preponderance of individuals from broadly defined middle and lower classes, meeting by necessity in the more spacious homes of a few wealthier and higher-status members. This conclusion was drawn, in part, from Paul's statement that the Corinthian church had from the beginning included "not many" wise, powerful, or nobly born members—which implied that it did include a few well-to-do members (1 Cor 1:26–27). Whatever differences in socioeconomic status existed in these early assemblies, they were mitigated by the convergence of other factors (gender, ethnicity, family pedigree, education, individual achievement) to produce an indeterminate flux of "ambiguous status" (see Meeks 1983, pp. 51–73). The attraction of the new movement lay not in any promise to bring about significant change in material conditions but, to the contrary, in its practice of a "love patriarchalism" that "allows social inequities to continue but transfuses them with a spirit of concern, of respect, and of personal solicitude" (Theissen, 1978, p. 139).

Since the turn of the twenty-first century, however, some New Testament scholars have pushed back against this alleged consensus. They have used more sophisticated methods to bear out older observations from classical historians regarding the "steep social pyramid" of ancient Rome, topped by a tiny but powerful and wealthy aristocracy and, at the bottom, a much greater mass of the totally indigent—a reality to which modern language of a middle class "simply does not fit" (MacMullen, 1974, pp. 88–120). Against the tendency to regard poverty as a relative matter of social perception, these scholars insist that poverty was materially an absolute condition for those living "at or near subsistence level, whose prime concern it [was] to obtain the minimum food, shelter, and clothing necessary to sustain life, whose lives [were] dominated by the struggle for physical survival" (Meggitt, 1998, p. 5). The Pauline congregations, no less than the apostle himself, probably "shared in this general experience of deprivation and subsistence" (Meggitt, 1998, p. 75).

The Economy of the Principate. At the beginning of the common era, tremendous wealth flowed into Rome, extracted from the natural resources of conquered lands and from the labor of the ever increasing numbers of the empire's subjects. To some, the fabulous luxury of Rome was an outrage crying to heaven for redress (Rev 18). But to others, probably the majority of the surviving literary sources, it was evidence of Rome's superiority and a matter of pride to loyal subjects (witness Aelius Aristides's *Panegyric on Rome*, mid-second century C.E.).

The Principate (beginning with Augustus, the *princeps* or "first man" in Rome, 27 B.C.E.–14 C.E.) marked a dramatic consolidation of the power of the Roman upper classes to extract wealth from the Italian lower classes and, increasingly, from the lands and peoples within the empire's expanding reach. The Roman Republic had long exemplified what Karl Marx called the "Asiatic" mode of production, and what Gerhard Lenski termed an agrarian tributary empire: a system in which surplus agricultural production (that is, production beyond the subsistence needs of the producers) was effectively reallocated to the metropolitan center. The regular means of redistribution were taxes, tributes, and tithes, revenues normally sacralized by a temple system and represented ideologically as the reciprocity owed to human and divine lords for their beneficence. The facts were more brutal: in its provinces, Rome tended to contract tax collection to locals, free to profit as they might, breeding corruption and considerable cruelty, as Philo (*De spec. leg.* 2.92–94; 3.158–62) and a wealth of papyri from Roman Egypt attest.

With the Principate, agricultural economies became increasingly capitalized. Rome incorporated conquered lands into the imperial economy, ensuring the cooperation of local aristocracies by guaranteeing their enrichment. Substantial numbers of people from the lower classes were enslaved and resettled on agricultural plantations in Italy as well as in the provinces. With market prices undermined by slave labor, independent small landholders were further stressed by taxation. Increasingly, their lands were confiscated through foreclosure, and they were reduced to tenancy (sharecropping), or replaced with slaves. Josephus (*Ant.*) and the Gospels speak to what on some estimates was the conversion of 60 to 70 percent of arable lands in Galilee and Judea to export-oriented agriculture. The elements of this new economy fill Jesus's parables: newly purchased fields, with newly installed fences and presses; idled men seeking daily hire to work fields at demeaning wages, managed by contemptuous and brutal overseers; produce appropriated by agents, stockpiled in newly constructed barns, until sold (and exported) to enrich owners in distant lands. The influx of slave populations into the economy did not so much alter the agricultural mode of production as alienate it from its traditional moorings in family, clan, and village, and thus reorient it to the generation of profits for strangers.

New and more exploitative relationships were normalized through the ideology and practice of patronage and clientelism, at least for those above the level of subsistence. (So successful was this ideological project that Roman patronage continues to appear to some contemporary historians both ubiquitous and inevitable, despite the equally abundant evidence of countervailing collective effort and strategies of mutuality among the poor.) Similar persuasive effects were achieved through civic ceremony, panegyric, and iconography, which represented Augustus as the most pious and beneficent of lords and the most solicitous and just of "fathers," not only as *pater patrias* ("father of the fatherland") but also as head of a "household" that included the civil service in Rome.

The Symbolic Domestication of the Feminine. The gender-coded Roman order was expressed in a gendercoded ideology of masculine supremacy and aggression, and feminine docility and weakness. Visual representations of conquered peoples, in monumental sculpture throughout the empire, included vanquished women and children: notoriously, the image on a Roman coin of a defeated Jewish woman seated beneath a palm tree with the legend "Iudaea Capta," "defeated Judaea." But such images of defeated women also represented conquered nations in the repertoire of Roman imperial iconography, a blurring of meanings that normalizes both imperial conquest and the patriarchal subordination of women, including their control through physical and sexual violence.

At the same time, Roman cities, and most spectacularly Rome "herself," were represented symbolically as idealized, royal, and divinized women, often seated on thrones or wearing crowns (resembling the city's walls) or other emblems of deity. The cults of Livia, Augustus's wife, and of the goddess Roma were popular in Greece and Asia Minor. Virtues and ideologically construed aspects of Roman supremacy (peace, victory, fecundity) were likewise represented as idealized, divine feminine figures. The image of the proper Roman matron—tranquil, still, controlled—was ubiquitous. Through such schedules of iconic representation, actual women of the ruling and lower classes alike were schooled in the values of the Roman order. They were invited to suspend their own social experience of the privileges or, more often, the burdens of imperial rule and to identify rather with the projection of one or another heavily *symbolic* femininity, either representing the Roman order as holy and life-giving or representing subject peoples as destined to submission or degradation. The symbolization of Rome as the "great whore" in Revelation 17 is clearly an aggressive reversal of this encoded imperial strategy, as is the projection into heaven of the sanctified community as an idealized woman, "clothed with the sun" (Rev 12). Notably, the wickedness of the imperial city is manifest in its economic exploitation and devaluation of the whole earth; but no countervailing practices of a just or life-giving economy are named. Rather, the apocalyptic resolution of earthly injustice has become thoroughly transcendent, deferred to the arrival of the heavenly Jerusalem.

Women in the Rural Economy. Women's prospects were closely circumscribed within agricultural communities like those in Galilee. Strong gender norms prevented their direct involvement in fieldwork or fishing, thus limiting the general productivity of their communities, and confined them to "domestic" work, largely invisible in our sources. Despite their considerable labor in that sphere and its indirect contribution to clan and village alike, their welfare remained dependent on male relations—fathers, then husbands, then sons—by custom and by law. (We learn that a number of women accompanied Jesus and his male disciples to Jerusalem only because they are mentioned performing the genderspecific work of "serving" the men [*diakonein*: Matt 27:55, Mark 15:41]. Otherwise, their identities are lost to us—were they wives, daughters, sisters of the male disciples, or independent women acting on their own? Their presence in other Gospel scenes is quite invisible.) The situation of rural women was inevitably worsened when their villages lost control over their production to bankers and tax "farmers." When women are mentioned in the Gospel accounts, they often appear in desperate situations: awaiting food in hungry throngs (Matt 14:21; 15:38), mourning the loss of a last male relative (Luke 7:11–12), being beaten by a wicked fellow slave (Luke 12:45), ransacking the house in search of a single coin (Luke 15:8), imploring justice from an indifferent judge (Luke 18:2–6), contributing the last fragments of livelihood to the upkeep of the Temple (Mark 12:42–43; Luke 21:2–3). Widows were especially vulnerable; social legislation in the Torah made them dependent on the brothers of the deceased husband or, failing these, on the community's aid, but their stereotyped mention as objects of pity suggests that these mechanisms were inadequate to make up the loss of a husband.

If, as some have argued, Jesus's intentions included a revitalization of traditional village economic life and resistance to the inroads of financial capitalization, women would inevitably have benefited, albeit indirectly. But women's economic status is not itself described as an explicit concern in his interactions with them, which tend instead to align with the norms of patriarchal honor. Thus, Jesus is described as defending a woman accused of adultery from the prescribed death penalty (John 8:3–11), but he does not address the selective prosecution of the woman alone (see Lev 20:10). Neither his rejection of divorce (Matt 19:3–8; Mark 10:2–12) nor his answer to the Sadducees' question regarding a woman married in succession to seven brothers (Mark 12:18–27; Luke 20:27–38) mentions the wife's welfare as a concern. His refusal of aid to a woman's sick child (Matt 15:22–28; Mark 7:25–30) is couched in an ethnic insult ("dogs"), and it is overcome by the woman's persistence (her "faith"), not by an awakened solicitousness on Jesus's part for her or her child's welfare.

Even the large-scale infusion of slave labor into agricultural plantations did not markedly improve food production in the empire; it simply made agriculture more profitable for the landowners. Peasants, sharecroppers, and slaves probably never provided more than enough surplus to feed a tenth of the empire's population (those living in cities). Cooperative efforts among the urban poor toward mutual survival inevitably fell short of the capacity for self-sufficiency that was imaginable in rural areas; thus, the early communities of Jesus's followers in Jerusalem and Judea were unable to sustain egalitarian

ideals for long. Luke describes the "apostolic communism" practiced in Jerusalem in ideal terms (Acts 2:44–45; 4:32–37), but then reports that this amazing meeting of everyone's needs depended on a daily distribution of food that proved unreliable or unsustainable, leaving out some widows (Acts 6:1–2). Luke never reports the problem's resolution, proceeding instead to narrate the spread of apostolic preaching. (The long-lived hypothesis that communities of Jesus's followers remained vital in Galilee after his death is an extrapolation from prophecies in Matt 26:32; 28:7, 10; Mark 14:28; 16:7; alas, these are no substitute for hints at socioeconomic realities.)

Women in Urban Households. In urban households as well as rural, women's labor was chiefly confined to the domestic sphere: nursing, child care, preparing food, and providing clothing for the family, all labor-intensive activities but generally invisible in our sources. Female slaves were similarly more occupied with domestic tasks than with manufacture, where male slaves predominated. Female and male slaves alike were subject to the indignity of sexual use by their masters and their masters' guests, but in the domestic sphere, female slaves were more common and thus perhaps more commonly abused.

We know, especially from funerary inscriptions, of women active in crafts and trade, but they are a minority and generally appear in gender-specific roles (food preparation, clothing manufacture, hospitality, prostitution). Probably necessity dictated that many women worked alongside their husbands (e.g., Priscilla and Aquila, Acts 18:2–3), and probably far more often than appears in our sources. To speak of such craftworkers as "middle class" would, again, be anachronistic.

Luke's naming of Lydia, a woman of some means and apparent independence (Acts 16:14–15), was probably meant to encourage other such women of means to emulate her hospitality, but we cannot say how many such women there were. Augustus's marriage legislation in 17 B.C.E. and 9 C.E. has often been hailed as "liberalizing," allowing women more economic independence. This understanding of the legislation has spawned speculation regarding the creation of a subclass of "new" women available as leaders and patrons to the nascent Christian assemblies (and as a source of vexation to the apostle Paul, who considered their expressions of freedom from more conventional mores personally shocking and disruptive to the assembly). That legislation, however, probably affected a small number of elite women in Rome and the provinces. It had the effect, and probably the purpose, of allowing a growing aristocracy to accumulate and retain more wealth, thus fixing the gulf of economic disparity, even as it presented to the lower classes a picture of a more stable, and more virtuous, ruling class.

But what of the role of women as benefactors of the early church? The picture of an assembly gathered in the spacious dining room of a wealthy patron, drawn from excavations of grand estates in well-heeled neighborhoods of Athens and Rome, still predominates in scholarly imagination, but it is giving way to a very different picture of "tenement churches" gathered in the courtyards and common areas of the close-packed apartment buildings and *insulae* (islands) that covered most of the residential areas of Roman cities. On the second view, women's leadership would have been more congruent with their management of "domestic" space. Here, patronage (as traditionally understood) would have been less important than practices of economic mutuality as the social interstitial tissue of the early movement.

But the rhetoric of patronage, of gratitude for benefits received, could be adapted to promote and encourage mutually advantageous actions in communities where gross inequalities of status and wealth, that is, the asymmetry usually taken to define patronage, were the exception. Note that Paul readily identified a number of women associates, ostensibly as apostolic peers and even superiors and benefactors: for example, Phoebe, "deacon" and "benefactor" (*prostatis*) of Paul and many others (Rom 16:1–2); Prisca, a co-worker, who with her husband risked her life for Paul (Rom 16:3); Junia, who with Andronicus (her husband?) was "prominent among the apostles" and "in Christ before" him (Rom 16:7).

Women's Patronage and Women's Mutuality. Nowhere have these issues been more closely examined—and contested—than in Corinth. Paul's letters (as we have them, fragmentarily, in 1 and 2 Corinthians) give us our most detailed information about social realities in that assembly. Gerd Theissen's landmark work (1978) saw economic stratification in the congregation as the primary factor in the range of controversies that occupy those letters. An explosion of subsequent studies have sought to relate archaeological and inscriptional data, models of social and economic relationships, and Paul's rhetoric, though often on the assumption (albeit often implicit) that Paul's "opponents" were high-status Corinthian men. Antoinette Clark Wire's "reconstruction" of the Corinthian "women prophets" proceeds instead on the assumption that since women were clearly present and the community's questions about marriage occupied Paul's attention, women in Corinth were a significant target of Paul's rhetoric in 1 Corinthians. Observing that women are directly in view at several points in the letter (7:1–39; 11:2–16; 14:34–35), Wire further argues that they are the primary target of the whole of the letter. Wealthy and powerful males may have been present, but what drives Paul's letter, Wire argues, is the discrepancy between his own social experience of having lost privilege and status, a loss he identifies with coming to "know Christ" (see Phil 3:7–11), and the experience of lower-status women who have found new freedom and opportunities as they gather in Christ's name and in the power of the Spirit.

One of the contributions of Wire's work is to articulate a plausible interaction between gender and economic status in Corinth. The measure of autonomy experienced by some Corinthian women as sanctified members of a community of equals implies their freedom from the constraint of patriarchal marriage. Wire considers Augustus's "liberalizing" legislation a possible factor, but also infers from 1 Corinthians 7 that women have taken the initiative to withdraw from betrothals and to withdraw sexually from their marriages (if not actually to divorce). Subsequently other scholars have suggested that higher-status women, enjoying new privileges under the Augustan "reform" legislation, began to appear in public in ways that obscured or removed the cultural signals of their "belonging" to their husbands.

Wire's argument goes in a different direction, suggesting that the material condition enabling the autonomous practices of *lower*-status holy women in Corinth is the mutual support they have found in the Spirit-filled gatherings of the assembly, separate from the conventionally patriarchal lines of marriage and patronage. Another contribution of the work is Wire's framing of Paul's rhetorical response less as a matter of strategic calculation, his desire to safeguard "his" church, than as expressing the social perception of a higher-status male who regards his own experience of status loss as normative for the assemblies.

We know from the late second- or early third-century *Acts of Paul* that at least in some Christian communities, the "gospel" Paul proclaimed was remembered as including the autonomy of women free from the constraints of marriage. Thecla, who responds to Paul's "gospel of virginity," breaks off her engagement to a Roman aristocrat. Her own subsequent evangelization in cities of Asia Minor draws other women away from high-status husbands and fiancés, eliciting anger from the offended men and civil efforts to punish the offending women. Missing from the story, however, is any reference to such practices among these women as might sustain them materially as a community. One possible inference is that at least for the intended audience of the text, the practice of Pauline "virginity" is an option primarily for women of independent means. The text proved quite popular nevertheless, surviving in numerous copies, including early Greek Bibles.

Meanwhile, the pseudo-Pauline writings that proved far more successful (Ephesians, Colossians 1, 2 Timothy, Titus) adopted an unambiguous program of subordination of slaves and wives alike. These texts do not simply identify proper attitudes within the life of a worshipping congregation; they also powerfully reinforce the embedment of economic power and control in the patriarchal household, rather than the potentially more egalitarian assembly.

[*See also* Economics, *subentries on* Early Church *and* Roman World; Historical-Critical Approaches; Jesus; *and* Social Interaction, *subentry* New Testament.]

BIBLIOGRAPHY

Friesen, Steven J. "Poverty in Pauline Studies: Beyond the So-Called New Consensus." *Journal for the Study of the New Testament* 26, no. 3 (March 2004): 323–361.

Gardner, Jane F. *Women in Roman Law and Society.* Bloomington: Indiana University Press, 1986.

Garnsey, Peter, and Richard Saller. *The Roman Empire: Economy, Society, and Culture.* Berkeley: University of California Press, 1987.

Hopkins, Keith. *Conquerors and Slaves.* Cambridge, U.K.: Cambridge University Press.

Lopez, Davina. *Apostle to the Conquered: Re-imagining Paul's Mission.* Paul in Critical Contexts. Minneapolis: Fortress, 2008.

MacMullen, Ramsay. *Roman Social Relations 50 B.C. to A.D. 284.* New Haven, Conn.: Yale University Press. 1974.

Malina, Bruce J. *The New Testament World: Insights from Cultural Anthropology,* 3d ed. Louisville, Ky.: Westminster John Knox, 2001.

Meeks, Wayne A. *The First Urban Christians.* New Haven, Conn.: Yale University Press, 1983.

Meggitt, Justin J. *Paul, Poverty, and Survival.* Edinburgh: T&T Clark, 1998.

Osiek, Carolyn, and Margaret Y. MacDonald, with Janet H. Tulloch. *A Woman's Place: House Churches in Earliest Christianity.* Minneapolis: Fortress, 2006.

Saller, Richard. "Women, Slaves, and the Economy of the Roman Household." In *Early Christian Families in Context: An Interdisciplinary Dialogue,* edited by David L. Balch and Carolyn Osiek, pp. 185–204. Grand Rapids, Mich.: Eerdmans, 2003.

Ste. Croix, G. E. M. de. *The Class Struggle in the Ancient Greek World.* Ithaca, N.Y.: Cornell University Press, 1981.

Theissen, Gerd. *The Social Setting of Pauline Christianity: Essays on Corinth.* Translated by John Schütz. Philadelphia: Fortress, 1978.

Wire, Antoinette Clark. *The Corinthian Women Prophets: A Reconstruction through Paul's Rhetoric.* Minneapolis: Fortress, 1990.

Neil Elliott

Early Judaism

The study of gender and economics in early Judaism is beset by the same difficulties as any investigation that seeks to move beyond the androcentric gaze. In ancient sources all people are men unless otherwise specified. Social and economic differentiation based on sex and consequently constructed gender roles are discussed only insomuch as they intrude, for good or for ill, upon an otherwise exclusively male reality. Women (like children and those of low social status) appear only occasionally in ancient sources. On such occasions, information about them can rarely be taken at face value.

Literary and documentary sources comprise the two broad categories of evidence pertaining to gender and economics in early Judaism. Literary sources speak of "women" as an abstract category, prescribing how they should behave or where they ought to be without reference to individual women or the realities of everyday life. Authors also invoke women as rhetorical stereotypes, emblematic of either good or evil. Documentary evidence, on the other hand, offers specific information about individual women but without indicating the degree to which their circumstances should be taken as representative of most or all women. Hence, literary sources are unhelpfully general and stereotypic, while documentary data are frustratingly particular and specific.

Despite the problematic nature of these sources, their evidence permits the broad conclusion that women made significant contributions to the economic and social structures of their communities, however much those contributions went unacknowledged or contravened idealized visions of Jewish society. Women worked, inherited, owned, and sold property; lent and donated money; initiated legal proceedings to assert their rights; and received public recognition for contributions to their communities.

Literary Sources. In many respects, postbiblical literature takes its attitudes toward women from biblical precedents. The sign of Abraham's covenant was marked upon men only, by means of circumcision. God's commandments were given to and incumbent upon Israel's male members at Sinai. Proverbs' wisdom addressed "my son" specifically, not "my child" as some inclusive-language English translations would have it. The prophetic books metaphorically position Israel as a harlot who, after chastisement, could regain her status as a virtuous wife. While the biblical text does allow for greater ambiguity in the characters of some individual women,

women in the abstract have little middle ground between the extremes of virtue and vice.

In other ways, however, the opportunities available to virtuous women—at least in the literary rhetoric of male authors—decline in the postbiblical period. Whereas the capable wife of Proverbs 31 is actively and publically engaged in commerce and receives praise for her economic and social contributions to the household, many early Jewish authors appear to adopt the Hellenistic ideal that modest women are properly secluded. This ideal is prescriptive rather than reflective of an actual change in economic and social possibilities open to women, perhaps indicating the adoption/adaption of Greek gender values by Jewish authors.

Postbiblical literary sources tend to place women in one of two categories: paragons of virtue or epitomes of vice. By implication, all women fit into one or the other of these categories. Any knowledge of women's social and economic opportunities in early Judaism is filtered through an author's idea of how those opportunities might classify a woman as virtuous or unrighteous. The remarks that the following postbiblical literary sources make on the economic and social realms open to Jewish women in the Hellenistic and Roman periods must be read in light of the aforementioned tendencies of the writers to speak generally, prescriptively, and categorically about women and their activities. Nonetheless, they provide occasional comments about social and economic factors pertaining to women that transcend generalizations and offer small glimpses into issues such as employment possibilities, legal standing and guardianship, inheritance, and property ownership.

Philo of Alexandria. Philo epitomizes the practice of dividing women into two groups: pious wives who modestly remain in seclusion and harlots who do not. In *Special Laws* 3.169 he lists various occupations suitable for Jewish men before noting that women are best suited to staying behind closed doors. Philo's experience of women appears to have occurred among the upper classes of cosmopolitan Alexandria, among whom the practice of seclusion was more feasible.

More usefully, Philo reveals that, at least in Alexandria, some Jewish women followed the Roman practice of *tutela* and were represented by a guardian for legal and financial purposes (*Special Laws* 3.67). His brief comment does not reveal whether this practice was universal or mandatory among the Jewish communities of Hellenistic Egypt.

Flavius Josephus. Josephus discusses the prominent women of Jewish history from biblical characters to Hasmonean and Herodian royalty but spends little time discussing the role of women in Jewish society more generally. He concurs with the Torah prohibition on women as witnesses, noting that their boldness and levity make them unsuitable (*Jewish Antiquities* 4.219), so it appears that this stricture was still in place in the first century C.E. Josephus also notes, critically, that the Herodian princess Salome presented her husband with a note of divorce (*Antiquities* 15.259). Jewish law (Deut 24:1–4) gives that right only to husbands, but Salome may have taken advantage of Roman legal precedent.

Third Maccabees. The inaccurately named 3 Maccabees shares Philo's expectation that modest women remain secluded. When, according to the story, Ptolemy IV attempts to enter the Jerusalem Temple, the population of Jerusalem is thrown into disarray and mourning, to the extent that mothers and nurses abandon infants and young women their secluded chambers (3 Macc 1:18–20). While the author's comment clearly comes as part of a hyperbolic description of the lengths to which the Jerusalem community went to protect the sanctity of the Temple, it illustrates the expectation that young women remain secluded.

Judith. Judith, a postbiblical novella, takes numerous liberties with historical fact to establish its fictional character. With that practice in mind, a reader cannot be sure how seriously to take the comment that Judith inherited and maintained the estate of her husband, Manasseh, including money, slaves, livestock, and land (Jdt 8:7b). Heroines of novellas were necessarily beautiful and pious; they were usually wealthy as well, and it is possible that the inheritance mentioned is simply part of a plot device to portray Judith with the requisite endowments. On the other hand, inheritance by daughters was a continually contested issue in both biblical and postbiblical periods.

Testament of Job. In light of Judith's inheritance, the pseudepigraphic *Testament of Job*'s disinheriting of Job's daughters is of particular interest. The biblical book of Job mentions that his daughters were given an inheritance along with their brothers (Job 42:15b). The *Testament of Job* changes the story to say that they were given protective amulets or girdles, which, when they put them on, transformed the women into angels singing hymns to the mysteries of heaven (*T. Job* 46–50). While the author of the *Testament* might have considered his change a positive one for the daughters, this revision alters one of the few biblical stories of daughterly inheritance (cf. Num 27 on the daughters of Zelophehad).

The Damascus Document. The sectarian literature of the Qumran community—an at least intermittently celibate group of male would-be priests—is an unexpected source for information on Jewish women's social and economic roles. Contrary to expectation, the *Damascus Document* includes women within its vision of the community. Moreover, women's legal circumstances are improved upon in comparison with biblical law in several ways.

First, witnesses must testify to a women's immodest behavior and a hearing must be held where the accused may defend herself before she can be made to undergo the test for adultery (cf. Num 5). Similarly, if a prospective husband has suspicions about his fiancée, she must be examined before the wedding rather than after, thus risking only shame rather than the execution demanded by Deuteronomy 22:20–21. Women also benefit economically from the community's prohibition of polygyny.

The sectarian community's authoritarian structure and emphasis on purity also meant that, in many cases, men's actions and bodies are regulated with a stringency elsewhere required only of women. While women of the community were still as strictly regulated in terms of purity and sexual behaviors as elsewhere in Jewish society, men lost some of their normative freedoms and privilege through submission to the authority of the community.

Finally, the *Damascus Document* describes a community that appears to welcome women's participation in its institutions. Girls and boys both received an education. Contrary to biblical law, women's oaths were honored and women were able to take the oath of covenant and become full members of the community. As full members, they could participate in restricted community meetings. A group of elder women, "the Mothers," might have had lesser status than the corresponding "Fathers," but were still recognized as an authoritative body.

The New Testament. Ordinarily a useful source for some elements of early Judaism, the New Testament has more to say about the economic and social circumstances of Paul's female gentile converts, such as Lydia, the purple-cloth dealer of Acts 16:14–15, than about Jesus's Jewish female followers. Like his male followers, they were presumably peasants who had no means or standing. Luke 8:3 briefly mentions a group of women who provided for Jesus and his disciples out of their own resources. The New Testament includes no socially or economically prominent Jewish women comparable to Nicodemus (John 3) or the rich young man (Mark 10:17–22).

Rabbinic texts. Rabbinic attitudes toward women are as varied as the texts themselves and cannot easily be summarized. Exceptional women appear occasionally in the pages of the Mishnah, Tosefta, and Talmuds. One of the best known is Beruriah, whose expertise in Torah was acknowledged as equal to that of male scholars. Generally, however, the rabbis adhere to the idealized vision of pious women as separated and secluded, even while their stories and discussions belie that prescriptive ideal. Women in rabbinic texts attend synagogue, buy and sell goods at the market, and participate in the social events of their communities. While it is clear that not all rabbinic voices approve of the many activities in which Jewish women were engaged, it is also evident that their disapprobation was not universal.

Documentary Sources. Literary sources are supplemented in the postbiblical period with two types of documentary evidence:

(1) archives, receipts, and other personal social and economic records, and

(2) inscriptions documenting women's social prominence and economic wherewithal in the form of donations.

These types of data are invaluable for countering literature's prescriptive notions of how early Jewish women should participate in economic and social activities.

As significant as these finds are, they represent only the tiniest fraction of Jewish women in the post-biblical period. To say anything substantive about women generally based on these documentary data requires extrapolation from a very small number of examples.

The women represented in the following papyrological and epigraphic sources are primarily property owners and financial patrons. Their social and economic circumstances should not be taken as normative or representative of those of all Jewish women.

An additional difficulty with documentary data, particularly inscriptions, is their deceptively straightforward nature, which has contributed to a false notion that such data do not require interpretation. In reality, inscriptions and other documentary data are as affected by social conditions as literary texts, albeit in different ways. The ongoing disagreement over whether titles such as "head of the synagogue" and others are primarily religious or socioeconomic in their implication exemplifies the challenge of interpreting laconic epigraphic statements. Despite their difficulties, documentary data are an excellent complement to literary sources for determining how gender shaped social and economic conditions in early Judaism, in some places confirming and in others expanding upon the possibilities open to women in social and economic spheres.

The Nahal Hever archives. Used as a hiding place during the Bar Kochba revolt, the so-called Cave of Letters yielded some of the best-preserved documentary evidence for Jewish lives in the second-century C.E. Roman province of Arabia. Notable among these documents are the collections of legal documents belonging to two Jewish women, Babatha and Salome Komaise, from the village of Maoza on the southeastern shore of the Dead Sea. Their archives offer concrete examples of how issues of property, inheritance, and guardianship, discussed generally and rhetorically in literature, played out in the real lives of Jewish women.

Analysis of the legal documents in the Babatha and Salome Komaise archives suggests that Jewish women could and did receive, own, sell, and gift property but could not inherit property from either their husbands or their fathers. In contrast to the biblical succession in Numbers 27:8, which says that daughters would inherit after sons but before brothers of a deceased man, the archives indicate that the brother and nephews of a deceased man took precedence over daughters. To circumvent these inheritance practices, property was transferred to wives and daughters in the form of gifts. Thus Babatha's father gifted property to both his wife and his daughter; Babatha's second husband gifted property to the daughter of his first marriage; and Salome Komaise received a gift of property from her mother, Salome Grapte. Inheritance customs might have disenfranchised women, but strategies existed to protect their financial interests.

When given property, the women in the Nahal Hever archive appear to have retained control over it regardless of their marital status. Although her stepfather witnessed the gift made to Salome Komaise by her mother, this new husband was not otherwise involved in the legal disposition of his wife's property. Babatha's claim to ownership of four date groves is in her own name without reference to her second husband, Yehudah. Another contract documents a loan of 300 denarii made by Babatha to Yehudah, further attesting to her control of her own financial resources.

Evidence in the archives also demonstrates that women could sell or gift their property to others. As mentioned, Salome Komaise's mother makes a gift of property to her daughter, perhaps on the occasion of the latter's marriage. Babatha's father purchased a date grove from a Nabataean woman, 'Abi'adan.

Philo's comment that guardians represented women in legal and financial matters is at least partially supported by the documents in the Nahal Hever archives. Husbands most commonly served as guardians of their wives in the archive documents, except in cases where the document consists of a contract between husband and wife, in which case another man, often a family member, served as guardian. Despite their presence, there is little indication in the Nahal Hever archives that male administrators exercised any real control over the financial dealings of the women over whom they had guardianship.

Although the issue of guardianship does not seem to have inhibited women's control of their own financial matters, guardianship did create a problem for Babatha because she could not act as a guardian for her son from her first marriage. Instead two guardians were appointed by the town council. Babatha had several legal interactions to ensure that these guardians acted in the best interest of her son. Jewish tradition considered children of deceased fathers to be orphans, and Babatha refers to her son in this manner in documents pertaining to him.

Evidence from the Nahal Hever archives suggests that while inheritance laws disenfranchised women, in practice Jewish families had alternative means to protect the financial interests of women. Once property was legally in female hands, no restrictions were apparently imposed upon its use, sale, or disposition. Women were in some cases represented by male guardians in their legal and financial transactions, but were not apparently constrained by their representation. In Babatha's case, however, the rules of guardianship did affect her insomuch as her son was considered an orphan and taken from her control after the death of her first husband.

Egyptian papyri. Papyrus documents preserved by the dry Egyptian climate and published in the *Corpus Papyrorum Judaicarum* (*CPJ*) offer small snapshots into the social and economic circumstances of Jewish women in the postbiblical period. While no multidocument archives comparable to those of Babatha or Salome Komaise have been found to date, individual documents supplement our knowledge of possibilities open to Jewish women in Roman Egypt.

Little is known about jobs or professions available to women outside the home. Household tasks of both wives and female slaves or servants are known from various sources. The picture of women's employment opportunities is augmented by contracts for the engagement of Jewish women as wetnurses (*CPJ* 146 and 147). These contracts document one of the only known extramural, income-earning jobs available to a group almost exclusively unrepresented in any source: Jewish freed- or free women of lower economic status.

Philo's comment on the practice of guardianship is substantiated in the Egyptian papyri, although, as at Nahal Hever, Jewish women do not seem impeded by their guardians in the transaction of business. Guardianship aside, the Egyptian papyri likewise demonstrate Jewish women's capacity to control and administer property independently. *Corpus Papyrorum Judaicarum* 453 attests to a female property owner leasing her land to a tenant. In *Corpus Papyrorum Judaicarum* 26, a woman stands as the guarantor of a loan between two men.

In the matter of inheritance, Jewish women in Egypt appear to have been able to inherit directly, in contrast to the situation described by the Nahal Hever documents. *Corpus Papyrorum Judaicarum* 143 documents the receipt of half a total inheritance of 200 silver drachmae and terms for distribution of the balance to a Jewish woman. In *Corpus Papyrorum Judaicarum* 455, a Jewish woman complains of theft from a threshing floor that she had inherited from her husband. The capacity to inherit could also be a mixed blessing. *Corpus Papyrorum Judaicarum* 148 attests to a Jewish freedwoman inheriting the debt of her patron.

The Egyptian papyri support the general picture of Jewish women's social and economic circumstances evident in contemporaneous literary sources and documentary evidence. At the same time, however, differences in details such as inheritance practices caution against drawing overly universal or broad conclusions. Local customs likely dictated the particular opportunities available to women in a given time and area.

Epigraphic evidence. Inscriptions in both Palestine and the Mediterranean Diaspora attest to Jewish women donating money to their communities' synagogues as well as to other civic projects. Financial patronage of both civic and private institutions is well attested in the Hellenistic and Roman periods. Some Jewish communities apparently emulated this practice, albeit with various adaptations.

A woman named Theopempte, referred to as a head of the synagogue, and her son Eusebios donated a chancel screen to a synagogue in Caria. Jael, a *prostates* (patron), together with her son Josua, heads a list of financial patrons in the city of Aphrodisias. Nine women are credited with financing various lengths of mosaic floor at the synagogue in Apamea, each "in fulfillment of a vow," for the salvation of herself and her family. These inscriptions are just a few of the many testifying to various forms of women's financial contributions to Jewish community institutions.

A singularly unusual inscription is that of Rufina from Smyrna, which documents that she, a Jew and head of the synagogue, constructed a tomb for the exclusive use of her and her husband's freedpersons and slaves. Rufina is given sole credit for the construction of the tomb without mention of whether the aforementioned husband is deceased or living.

The question of whether women's financial support of synagogues constituted "leadership" and was sometimes rewarded in Greco-Roman fashion with titles of honor has yet to be definitively resolved. In some cases, like those of Theopempte and Jael, titles and donations are linked, while elsewhere, as at Apamea, no such designations are given. This ambiguity leaves open the question of how to understand titles in nondonative contexts, such as the numerous funerary inscriptions that commemorate titled women.

The discussion of titles and women usually falls under the rubric of women's religious role in early Judaism rather than their socioeconomic roles. In this situation, however, the two categories cannot easily be distinguished. Whether or not women were named head of the synagogue, mother of the synagogue, elder, etc. because they gave money, it does seem likely that once named, monetary support was part and parcel of their role. Regardless of whether these titles are seen as having primarily religious or economic import, their inclusion in funerary inscriptions attests to such titles' concomitant social significance for those who held them.

Summation. In contrast to earlier periods, the study of how gender affected social and economic conditions in early Jewish communities benefits from a greater variety of complementary source material. The prescriptive, generic view of women provided by literary sources' elite male gaze is nuanced by highly individualized documentary data on particular, but perhaps unrepresentative, women. Taken together, sources indicate that a variety of social and economic opportunities were available to Jewish women in the postbiblical period. These opportunities, however, were as heterogeneous and variable as other aspects of Jewish communities at the time and preclude generalizations about economics, society, and gender in early Judaism.

[*See also* Legal Status, *subentry* Early Judaism; Political Leadership, *subentry* Early Church; *and* Religious Leaders, *subentry* Early Judaism.]

BIBLIOGRAPHY

Primary Sources

Corpus Inscriptionum Iudaeae/Palaestinae. 3 vols. Berlin: De Gruyter, 2010–2012.

The Documents from the Bar Kokhba Period in the Cave of Letters. 2 vols. Jerusalem: Israel Exploration Society, 1989–2002.

Horbury, William, and David Noy, eds. *Jewish Inscriptions of Graeco-Roman Egypt.* Cambridge, U.K.: Cambridge University Press, 1992.

Inscriptiones Judaicae Orientis. 3 vols. Tübingen, Germany: Mohr Siebeck, 2004.

Noy, David, ed. *Jewish Inscriptions of Western Europe.* 2 vols. Cambridge, U.K.: Cambridge University Press, 1993–1995.

Tcherikover, Victor A., ed. *Corpus Papyrorum Judaicarum.* 3 vols. Cambridge, Mass.: Harvard University Press, 1957–1964.

Secondary Sources

Baker, Cynthia M. *Rebuilding the House of Israel: Architectures of Gender in Jewish Antiquity.* Stanford, Calif.: Stanford University Press, 2002.

Brooten, Bernadette. *Women Leaders in the Ancient Synagogue: Inscriptional Evidence and Background Issues.* Chico, Calif.: Scholars Press, 1982.

Greenfield, Jonas. "The Texts from Naḥal Ṣe'elim (Wadi Seiyal)." In *The Madrid Qumran Congress: Proceedings of the International Congress on the Dead Sea Scrolls, Madrid 18–21 March, 1991,* edited by Julio Trebolle Barrera and Luis Vegas Montaner, pp. 661–665. Leiden, The Netherlands: Brill, 1992.

Ilan, Tal. *Integrating Women into Second Temple History.* Peabody, Mass.: Hendrickson, 2001.

Kriger, Diane. *Sex Rewarded, Sex Punished: A Study of the Status "Female Slave" in Early Jewish Law.* Boston: Academic Studies Press, 2011.

Meyers, Carol, ed. *Women in Scripture: A Dictionary of Named and Unnamed Women in the Hebrew Bible, the Apocryphal/Deuterocanonical Books, and the New Testament.* Boston: Houghton Mifflin, 2000.

Oudshoorn, Jacobine G. *The Relationship between Roman and Local Law in the Babatha and Salome Komaise Archives: General Analysis and Three Case Studies on Law of Succession, Guardianship, and Marriage.* Leiden, The Netherlands: Brill, 2007.

Wassen, Cecilia. *Women in the Damascus Document.* Atlanta: Society of Biblical Literature, 2005.

Carrie Elaine Duncan

Early Church

A study of economics and gender in the early church reveals both Greek and Roman influence, as well as points of divergence from those influences. As with the Greeks and Romans, early Christians understood space as either private or public, with women belonging in private space and men in public space. That the early church accepted this may be seen in the deutero-Pauline household codes and in the *Didascalia*'s opposing depictions of the "good" widow who "remains at home" and the "bad" widow who is a "gadabout." Indeed, in exhorting women to keep to their homes, the *Didascalia* likens good women to the altar of God, stating, "For the altar of God never strays or runs about anywhere, but is fixed in one place" (15.3.6). As a result of this gendered division of space, a gendered division of labor developed. However, this ideal representation did not necessarily reflect the reality of the lives of Greek, Roman, or Christian women.

Sources. Literary, epigraphic, and documentary evidence are the main sources of information about the roles of women in the ancient economy. It is undisputed that certain biases and constraints accompany each body of evidence: literary evidence presents the perspectives of elite, literate men; epigraphic evidence, particularly funerary inscriptions, likely reveals more about ancient ideals than ancient reality; and documentary evidence is overwhelmingly geographically limited to those regions in Egypt where conditions lent themselves to the preservation of papyri. Taken together and interpreted according to its genre and context, however, our evidence does illuminate our understanding of economics and gender in the early church.

Labor in the Private Domain. The labor involved in ensuring the smooth functioning of the household economy was almost certainly entirely undertaken by women. Throughout history, housework performed by elite and nonelite women included childcare, textile production (spinning, weaving, sewing, and mending of clothes), food preparation, and water carrying (Pomeroy, 1995; Treggiari, 1979). Christian women engaged in similar work.

Childcare. Literary evidence of different genres, including household codes, letters, and apocryphal texts, consistently emphasizes the role of women in bearing and caring for children. A number of Christian examples of reliefs of women bathing infants have also been found in Roman Ostia (Kampen, 1981). Women might also work in the home of another woman as a wet nurse or a nurse.

The ongoing nature of childcare is attested in P. Benaki 4 (fourth century C.E.), a letter from a mother to her son informing him that she had sent him "a basket of parsley roots, a basket of shoots (?) and a basket of some small raisins." He was then given these instructions: "Wash them and put them outside in the sun, wherever possible. Then put them into a funnel and two Knidian jars, and, when you have them ground into flour, let me know by letter" (Bagnall and Cribiore, 2006, p. 326). Clearly, this Christian mother continued to care for her son, who was evidently grown and independent. Even women in monastic communities engaged in childcare, as attested by a letter from Maria, a nun, to Apa Kyriakos, her anchorite, in which she reported that she had taken an orphan into her home (O. Brit. Mus. Copt. add. 23, sixth to eighth centuries C.E.).

Textile production. Christian women were encouraged to engage in textile production, as attested in Jerome's advice on how to raise a daughter: "Let her learn too how to spin wool, to hold the distaff, to put the basket in her lap, to turn the spinning wheel and to shape the yarn with her thumb" (*Letter* 107.10; translation in Kraemer, 2004, p. 174). Textile production freed the mind for prayer (Jerome, *Letter* 130.15), and the clothes produced, which were to be warm and modest, could be worn, sold (with the proceeds being given to the poor), or given to the poor directly (Clark, 1993). Evidence that Christian women did engage in weaving may be found in P.Oxy. 31.2599 (third to fourth century C.E.). In this letter, the woman Tayris wrote to her father, Apitheon, to request that weaving equipment, specifically, two weaver's combs, be sent to her. She also mentioned that Didyme should continue to make "double thick material" (translation in Rowlandson, 1998, pp. 269–70; see also Bagnall and Cribiore, 2006, pp. 400–401).

Food preparation. In his description of the housewife, Jerome acknowledges the work performed in the private domain by women and then places a further burden on her shoulders, namely, the practice of hospitality:

> Over there the babies are prattling, the children hang on her for kisses, the accounts are being added up, and the money got ready for payment. Here a posse of cooks, girded for action, is pounding meat, and a crowd of weaving-women chattering. Then a message comes that her husband has brought his friends home. She circles the rooms like a swallow: is the couch smooth? Have they swept the floor? Are the cups properly set out? Is dinner ready? (*Against Helvidius* 20; translation in Clark, 1993, p. 99)

In this text, the wife oversees not only childcare, financial transactions (on which, see below), and textile production but also food preparation for the members of the household and her husband's friends.

In ascetic communities, women continued to bear this responsibility. Thus, according to Gregory of Nyssa, Macrina baked bread with her own hands, while Paula and her daughter prepared vegetables together (*Life of Macrina* 11). Food preparation and other kitchen work was thought to develop humility. Thus, Palladius told the story of a member of the Pachomian convent at Tabennisi who "showed her humility by insisting on staying in the kitchen doing menial tasks, even when it was not her turn" (*Lausiac Hist.* 34; Clark, 1993, p. 103).

Labor in the Public Domain. While the Greek and Roman ideal was one in which labor undertaken in the public sphere was the responsibility of men, other bodies of evidence reveal that women could and did labor in the public domain as well.

Preparing women for work. Most girls would have learned the skills necessary to manage a household from her parents. It was also possible for girls to learn a trade through an apprenticeship, as attested by three apprenticeship contracts for freeborn females. In P.Heid. 4.326 (98 C.E.), "a man and a woman entrust their daughter to another man and another woman" (van Minnen, 1998, p. 201) and P.Heid. 4.327 (99 C.E.) refers to this earlier document, identifying it as an apprenticeship contract for the daughter. In a second apprenticeship contract (SB 18.13305, 271 C.E.), a man entrusted a girl to a craftswoman named Aurelia Libouke, and in a third apprenticeship contract (KSB I 045, eighth century C.E.), a woman entrusted her daughter to a craftswoman named Maria (van Minnen, 1998).

That Christian girls should be educated is clear from Origen's practice of teaching both men and women (Eusebius, *Hist. eccl.* 6.8.2). It is also suggested by the circulation of Coptic versions of the *Acts of Paul and Thecla* in Christian Egypt, in which Thecla was depicted as being able to write to her son from prison (Rowlandson, 1998). The belief that Christian girls should be educated is most prominently seen in the importance that Jerome placed on literacy for girls. Thus, his letter to Eustochium included the following advice on the rearing of her daughter:

> Get for her a set of letters made of boxwood or of ivory and called each by its proper name. Let her play with these, so that even her play may teach her something. And not only make her grasp the right order of the let-

ters and see that she forms their names into a rhyme, but constantly disarrange their order and put the last letters in the middle and the middle ones at the beginning that she may know them all by sight as well as by sound. Moreover, so soon as she begins to use the style upon the wax, and her hand is still faltering, either guide her soft fingers by laying your hand upon hers, or else have simple copies cut upon a tablet; so that her efforts confined within these limits may keep to the lines traced out for her and not stray outside of these. Offer prizes for good spelling and draw her onwards with little gifts such as children of her age delight in. (Jerome, *Letter* 107.4; translation in Kraemer, 2004, p. 170)

As she progressed in the skills of reading and writing, she should also learn Greek and Latin (Jerome, *Letter* 107.9). The ultimate goal of this education was to enable her to read the scriptures.

Women as scribes. Literate women were sometimes employed as scribes (Gk. *grammateusasa* and/or *kalligraphia*, Lat. *libraria*), as attested in both Greek and Latin inscriptions (e.g., CIL 6.3979, 7373, 8882, 9301, 9525, 9541, 9542, 33892, 37802), as well as in "an early second-century marble relief from Rome that preserves an illustration of a female record keeper or clerk" (Haines-Eitzen, 2000, pp. 44–47). According to Eusebius, Origen, while still in Alexandria in 232 C.E., worked with female scribes: "As [Origen] dictated there were ready at hand more than seven shorthand-writers, who relieved each other at fixed times, and as many copyists, as well as girls trained for beautiful writing" (Eusebius, *Hist. eccl.* 6.23; translation in Haines-Eitzen, 2000, p. 42). This is consistent with the later accounts of Melania the Younger (ca. 383–439 C.E.), who "copied them [the Old and New Testaments] herself and furnished copies to the saints by her own hands" (Gerontius, *Life* 26; translation in Haines-Eitzen, 2000, p. 48) and the monastic women at the convent of Caesaria the Younger in Arles who "beautifully copy out the holy books" (*Vita Caesarius* 1.58; translation in Haines-Eitzen, 2000, p. 49).

Women in sales and services. In her study of inscriptions, Treggiari noted that a woman's name was frequently paired with a man's, suggesting that many women worked alongside their husbands in public spaces. Thus, she concludes, "it would seem reasonable that the wife specialised in selling, while her husband produced the goods in the back shop" (Treggiari, 1979, p. 76). Indeed, some women did work as dealers of such items as perfume, incense, or purple, and one Christian woman is known to have been a bottle seller (*lagunaria*). A woman might also work in the public domain at tasks associated with the private domain if the work was organized at a commercial scale, as was the case for some women weavers.

Women might also offer services as an innkeeper, a cookshop owner, or a brothel keeper; women who worked in inns or cookshops were also expected to offer the services of a prostitute (Treggiari, 1979). Certainly, the early church frowned on this practice.

Women and financial transactions. A woman might engage in financial transactions by administering the family estate following the death of her husband. She might also do so following a divorce, for if the marriage had been arranged without *manus* (authority) and her father was deceased, then the dowry would be returned to the divorced woman, who would then have control over its management. It is unclear whether the practice of the early church involved marriages with or without *manus*. It is clear, however, that divorce was not encouraged in the early church. Rather, marriage was conceived as a lifelong arrangement (Clark, 1993). Thus, examples involving Christian women engaged in financial transactions likely have widows in view.

There is evidence attesting that Christian women managed their family's finances. In P.Mich. 3.221 (296 C.E.), Ploutogenia wrote to her mother concerning financial transactions: "The bronze vessels that you have by you, give them to Atas and then get them back from the same Atas full. And write to me how much money you received from Koupineris and do not be neglectful" (Bagnall and Cribiore, 2006, p. 294). In SB 14.11588 (late fourth century C.E.), Aria wrote to her son to chastise him for neglecting her and to inform him that she was in need of money. In

doing so, she offered a clear account of her financial transactions:

> And I wish you to know that of the 1,000 myriads (of denarii) I did not get anything from…nianos except the 500 myriads, would you get them and send them? You know where I got them. And I went to the bleacher for the 3½ pounds. And as you said, "Go to my sister Maria and she will give them to you," I went and she gave me nothing. So, what does go right for me? So know this too, know that the orphan child is in my house and I also need to spend for myself. And about the two and a half pounds—2½—I owe nothing except the pay for the bleacher. But if I owe something, I pay with this stuff of mine. And in fact I have sold the same linen stuff at 10 myriads per pound. (Bagnall and Cribiore, 2006, p. 302)

Whether Aria was experiencing numerous mishaps or simply enjoyed complaining, she demonstrated her ability to handle her family's finances, providing for herself as well as an orphan, and paying various debts.

In their financial transactions, women provided for their families, as in the cases of Aurelia Julia, a Christian woman, who used her wealth to establish a family tomb (Gibson, 1978, no. 32, 296/7 C.E.), and Melania the Elder (ca. 340–410 C.E.), who provided for her son. They also provided for the church, as in the cases of Paulinus of Nola (ca. 354–431 C.E.), Macrina (327–379 C.E.), and Paula (347–404 C.E.), who all established monasteries out of their own funds.

There is also evidence of women in monastic communities engaging in economic activities. A pair of letters from the fourth century C.E. are thought to have been written by nuns because of their references to "the sisters." In the first letter (P.Oxy. 14.1774), Didyme and the sisters wrote to "my lady sister Atienatia" as follows: "Let us know if you received your orders. There is a balance with us from the money of your orders, I believe of 1,300 denarii. Canopic cakes received for you from them will be dispatched" (Bagnall and Cribiore, 2006, p. 194). In the second letter (SB 8.9746 = SB 3.7243), we learn that Didyme and the sisters received "7 double knidia [containers of wine] and a coarse sack of sour grapes." They also inquired about the supplies that they had sent:

> I wish you to know about the cloth that you sent to Loukilos that I sent you 2 pairs of sandals of the same value, which were bought directly from the weavers for 4 talents (?) but that you did not mention to me in writing, and through the sailor Sipharos son of Plou… (?) for the bride of Pansophios (? or daughter-in-law of Pansophion) a large ostrich egg and a small basket containing Syrian palm dates, but you did not write about them. (Bagnall and Cribiore, 2006, p. 196)

That these women were receiving orders for goods, making disbursements, expecting acknowledgements, and keeping financial accounts suggests to Elm that they were "running a small business, which specialized in the distribution of goods" (Elm, 1994, pp. 242–243).

Women and property. Christian women also managed property. Demetrias, a fatherless heiress, "was given the property which would have been her dowry, and used it to fund church-building in Rome after the Gothic sack of 411" (Clark, 1993, p. 54). In her letter to her brother Eudaimon and sister-in-law Apia (P. Neph. 18, mid-fourth century C.E.), Taouk wrote about an *aroura* of land and six *artabas* of wheat:

> I am writing this for the second time to you about the one aroura. For as you see me in such a state, and this…because you have right now 6 artabas from my supply, even though you know the price of the wheat, (and) that I am a woman, I cannot buy (it). Nor on the other hand did you write, "We don't want the aroura."…take it myself or give it to Erisia (?), and what I gave through you, you ought to send me by yourself, the six artabas, or whatever…If you rob me, let me know and you will see before God. (Bagnall and Cribiore, 2006, p. 207)

Apparently, Taouk felt that Eudaimon and Apia should have delivered to her the wheat that she claimed they owed her.

Women and the agricultural economy. In addition to the "indoor housework," women might also have contributed labor to the agricultural economy. Scheidel (1995; 1996) accepts that Roman sources stress that women should remain indoors and engage in textile production; however, he argues that in order to survive, women, particularly those who were non-elite, could not have been exclusively engaged in domestic work, but would have participated in agricultural work as well. While women likely did not engage in plowing, there is evidence that they harvested, gleaned, and threshed grain. They also participated in grape and olive harvesting, as well as wine and olive oil production. Women even participated, in limited ways, in animal husbandry. A number of texts refer to women milking sheep or cattle, and to women tending sheep or goats (Philostratus, *Lives of the Sophists* 2.554; Horace, *Epodes* 2.39–46; Dio Chrysostom 1.53ff.). That Christian women also contributed to the agricultural economy is attested in P.Mich. 3.221 (ca. 296 C.E.), for Ploutogenia exhorts her mother, "Take care of the irrigation machine and of your cattle" (Bagnall and Cribiore, 2006, p. 294).

Assessment. By examining the work performed by women in the early church, a picture emerges that reveals their not insignificant contributions in both the private and the public domain to a broad variety of sectors within the ancient economy. Whether the women were elite or nonelite, or whether they lived in the city or the countryside, it is clear that their labor was considerable.

[*See also* Economics, *subentries on* Greek World, New Testament, *and* Roman World; Family Structures, *subentry* Early Church; Legal Status, *subentry* Early Church; *and* Marriage and Divorce, *subentry* Early Church.]

BIBLIOGRAPHY

Bagnall, Roger S., and Raffaella Cribiore. *Women's Letters from Ancient Egypt, 300 BC–AD 800.* Ann Arbor: University of Michigan Press, 2006.

Clark, Gillian. *Women in Late Antiquity: Pagan and Christian Lifestyles.* Oxford: Clarendon, 1993.

Elm, Susanna. *Virgins of God: The Making of Asceticism in Late Antiquity.* Oxford Classical Monographs. Oxford: Oxford University Press, 1994.

Gibson, Elsa. *The "Christians for Christians" Inscriptions of Phrygia: Greek Texts, Translation, and Commentary.*

Harvard Theological Studies 32. Missoula, Mont.: Scholars Press, 1978.

Haines-Eitzen, Kim. *Guardians of Letters: Literacy, Power, and the Transmitters of Early Christian Literature.* Oxford: Oxford University Press, 2000.

Kampen, Natalie. *Image and Status: Roman Working Women in Ostia.* Berlin: Mann, 1981.

Kramer, Ross Shepard, ed. *Women's Religions in the Greco-Roman World: A Sourcebook.* Oxford: Oxford University Press, 2004.

Pomeroy, Sarah B. *Goddesses, Whores, Wives, and Slaves: Women in Classical Antiquity.* New York: Schocken, 1995.

Rowlandson, Jane, ed. *Women and Society in Greek and Roman Egypt: A Sourcebook.* Cambridge, U.K.: Cambridge University Press, 1998.

Scheidel, Walter. "The Most Silent Women of Greece and Rome: Rural Labour and Women's Life in the Ancient World (I)." *Greece and Rome*, 2d ser., 42 (1995): 202–217.

Scheidel, Walter. "The Most Silent Women of Greece and Rome: Rural Labour and Women's Life in the Ancient World (II)." *Greece and Rome*, 2d ser., 43 (1996): 1–10.

Treggiari, Susan. "Lower Class Women in the Roman Economy." *Florilegium* 1 (1979): 65–86.

Van Minnen, Peter. "Did Ancient Women Learn a Trade Outside the Home? A Note on SB XVIII 13305." *Zeitschrift für Papyrologie und Epigraphik* 123 (1998): 201–203.

Agnes Choi

EDUCATION

This entry contains seven subentries: Ancient Near East; Hebrew Bible; Greek World; Roman World; New Testament; Early Judaism; *and* Early Church.

Ancient Near East

This article discusses formal, standardized education. Other types of education, such as guidance that might have been informally passed down from parent to child, have left little if any information behind in the historical or material records. Formal education is typically associated with the rise of civilization and the formation of political entities, for it is these entities that most require the administrative services of a trained scribal class. It must be stated from the outset, however, that though professional scribes constituted an artisanal class, there were people outside this category, such as religious officials, merchants, and members of the royal elite, who also learned to read and write. Although written materials provide our primary insight into educational practices, it is important to remember that the cultures of the ancient Near East were predominantly oral, and education generally focused on memorization and the ability to repeat information verbally (Carr, 2005; Delnero, 2012). Throughout the ancient Near East, formal education was primarily a male prerogative, but the evidence, though limited, of female professional scribes and of literate women in various periods and locations suggests that women were not entirely precluded from receiving standardized training.

Mesopotamia. The majority of data regarding formal, standardized education derive from Mesopotamia, whose major writing medium was clay tablets. Once dried, writing on clay is more easily preserved; therefore, more material exists for Mesopotamian scribal activity and training than for cultures who wrote on perishable materials such as papyrus or leather. Information regarding scribal education in Mesopotamia is found primarily in the archaeological remains, though some information may also be gleaned from the literary texts copied by the scribal students themselves. These texts must be used with caution, however, as they portray scribal training and the scribal profession in an idealized or even humorous light and were used to enculturate and indoctrinate future scribes (Carr, 2005, pp. 31–34; Kramer, 1990, p. 37; Michalowski, 1987, p. 63).

Sumerian schools were called "tablet houses" (**edubba'a**), where the "master" (**ummia**) was surrounded by his "sons" (**dumu**), whom he taught the basics of the scribal profession. Typically, the structure of schools resembled that of apprenticeships—small-scale operations, usually in private homes, with scribal masters teaching their biological sons as well as a few additional students (Charpin, 2010, pp. 26–32).

Fourth and third millennia B.C.E. At the end of the fourth millennium, the cuneiform script was developed in the city-state of Uruk, primarily for purposes of accounting and increasingly as a means of recording the Sumerian language. Lexical lists, the earliest known materials associated with scribal education, were uncovered there. Lexical lists include thematic lists of nouns, such as professions, fish, cattle, vessels, and wood, and appear to have been somewhat standardized, with little deviation among the known copies recovered from various Sumerian city-states. By the third millennium, Mesopotamia was an increasingly bilingual society, with Sumerian likely spoken side by side with Akkadian. Scribes were educated in both languages, and a column of items in Akkadian was eventually added to some lexical lists.

At the end of the third millennium, a basic corpus of lexical lists continued to be employed, regarded as sources of esteemed knowledge from high antiquity. During this period, it is likely that the government founded some schools. Indeed, King Šulgi of Ur (2094–2047 B.C.E.) claims that he established at least two schools, one in Nippur, the other in Ur; though it is not clear whether this is merely a boast or reflects historical reality (Veldhuis, 1997).

The Old Babylonian period. The Old Babylonian (OB) period (ca. 1792–1525 B.C.E.) provides the most information for scribal education, and it is in this period that the material remains of schools have most arguably been found. The material culture not only suggests the physical location of OB scribal training was in small private houses, such as those found at Nippur and Ur; it also contains a variety of tablet types that seem to be associated with particular levels of scribal training. For example, one square type of exercise tablet has a master's model in the left-hand column and a student's copy on the right. The right sides of these exercise tablets are often thinner because of student erasure and recopying. Also, there are lentil- or bun-shaped tablets with a line of text that is a teacher's model followed by student copies.

Moreover, the curriculum present within these tablets suggests that education was carried out in two phases. In Phase I, cuneiform sign lists, lexical lists, and mathematical exercises were initially practiced, followed by model contracts and proverbs, which allowed students to learn Sumerian grammar and syntax and prepared them for the literary compositions learned in Phase II. Phase II seems to have entailed learning the sequence of ten texts known as the Decad (Delnero, 2006; Robson, 1999; Tinney, 1998; Veldhuis, 1997). By the OB period, Sumerian was no longer spoken widely, but education continued to be focused on learning to write Sumerian, the primary language of scholarship.

Later second and first millennia B.C.E. In the later Mesopotamian textual record, fewer numbers of advanced scribal exercises appear, but this is probably due to students writing more frequently on perishable materials such as wooden writing boards, papyrus, and parchment rather than to a lack of scribal tradition (Civil, 1992, p. 305). The greatest evidence for education during the second half of the second millennium is a variety of exercise tablets dated via their archaeological contexts. The major innovation of this period was the introduction of Akkadian literature into the educational corpus (Charpin, 2010, p. 46; Veldhuis, 2000). It is also at this time that Sumero-Akkadian textual traditions began to spread far outside of their traditional geographic region, as Akkadian became the lingua franca of the Late Bronze Age (Charpin, 2010, p. 46).

Though many texts from the first millennium are extremely fragmentary and written in handwriting that is quite difficult to read, education seems once again to have been divided into two phases. Elementary exercises containing sign, syllable, and vocabulary lists are found on large, multicolumn tablets. Exercises from the second phase of education are found on smaller one- or two-column tablets. These latter tablets typically contain literary texts, bilingual or Akkadian, along with lexical excerpts. Literary texts known from this period include literary prayers, narratives, omens, and royal inscriptions. Also, during the first millennium, there was an increased focus on magic and divination, and advanced scribes, especially those associated with the temple, would specialize beyond the general educational corpus and master specific divinatory corpora, such as omen and spell lists (Gesche, 2001, pp. 212–220).

Women in Mesopotamian education. Though the vast majority of educated persons seem to have been male, there is evidence that some women in Mesopotamia were educated. The latter can be identified in the textual record from the end of third millennium to the mid-first millennium B.C.E. From nineteenth- and eighteenth-century Sippar, private archives attest to the use of female scribes by *nadītum* priestesses, elite women consecrated to the god Šamaš (Lion, 2001; 2009; 2011). The eighteenth-century Mari archives also attest the use of female scribes in the royal palace (Ziegler, 1999). Moreover, in the colophon of four OB school exercises, the writer indicates that she is female (Lion, 2011, p. 100). From the Neo-Assyrian period (934–609 B.C.E.), two female scribes are included in a list of nearly 200 women found at the palace at Nineveh, and another female scribe of the queen's household is mentioned in a group of loan documents (Radner, 1997, pp. 83–88, 100).

A number of women outside the scribal profession also seem to have been able to read and write and to have had access to education of some sort. For example, regarding royal women, a letter from the Neo-Assyrian king Assurbanipal's sister to his wife exhorts her to practice her tablets (Luukko and Van Buylaere, 2002, no. 28). Also, in the corpus of Old Assyrian letters (ca. 1910–1830 B.C.E.), correspondence from the merchants' wives seem to have been written by the women themselves (Michel, 2001, pp. 419–511; 2009). Enheduana (2285–2250 B.C.E.), daughter of Sargon of Akkad and *en*-priestess to the god Nana of Ur, is credited with a number of literary compositions. Though debate surrounds Enheduana's authorship of these texts, her association with this literature "supposes a conception of written culture and poetry that, at the level of the most powerful elite, did not exclude women" (Lion, 2011, p. 97).

Ugarit and Hatti. In Late Bronze Ugarit (ca. 1450–1200 B.C.E.), scribal practices resembled those found in Mesopotamia. There, however, education seems to have occurred in the realm of the temple. The library of the high priest appears to have been a center for training scribes and for preserving literary texts. Many of the tablets found there appear to have been copy exercises and practice tablets. Often students would add their names and that of their teacher to their exercises, identifying themselves with the word for "student," *kabzuzu*. Scribal education at Ugarit was multilingual. Many grammatical lists contain columns of words and phrases written in Sumerian, Akkadian, Hurrian, and sometimes Hittite and Ugaritic. Akkadian literary texts from Ugarit were often copies of "classic" Mesopotamian literature. Finally, as in Mesopotamia several texts contain mention of fathers and sons who both held the office of scribe (Rainey, 1969, pp. 126–147). Even less is known about scribal education practices in the Anatolian kingdom of Hatti (ca. 1600–1180 B.C.E.); however, they too seem to have been greatly influenced by Mesopotamian scribal practices (McMahon, 1989, pp. 62–77; van den Hout, 2012).

Egypt. Information regarding scribal education in ancient Egypt is derived mostly from texts, and as the Egyptians typically wrote on perishable materials such as papyrus and wood, even this textual evidence is limited. What remains is found in tomb inscriptions and on statuary; in student exercises, found especially on ostraca (pottery shards reused as writing surfaces); and in literary texts. Though it is unlikely that Egyptian educational practices remained static over the course of centuries, many of the literary texts that were part of the curricula of earlier periods were copied and continued to be used in the scribal training of later periods. With regard to precise information about the nature of scribal training in Egypt, however, these literary texts, like those from Mesopotamia, should be used with caution.

It should be noted that scribal education was a prerequisite for Egyptians holding high-ranking offices (Zinn, 2012, p. 1). Moreover, as those from any social class could be educated, scribal training served as a way to overcome social barriers (Szpakowska, 2008, p. 104). Though scribes would often educate their biological sons, there is also evidence for education extending beyond the family unit (Janssen and Janssen, 1990; Williams, 1972).

The location of schools. There is some evidence for "schools" in ancient Egypt, frequently associated with temples, but, as in Mesopotamia, education was probably conducted on a small-scale apprenticeship model. The earliest occurrence of the Egyptian word for "school" (*ansēbe*) comes from the First Intermediate period (ca. 2181–2055 B.C.E.) and was found on a Tenth Dynasty (ca. 2160–2025 B.C.E.) tomb inscription. Several schools are also mentioned on New Kingdom (sixteenth–eleventh centuries B.C.E.) private statuary and stelae, such as the statue of Bekenkhons, High Priest of Amun, which references one in the temple of Mut; and a stele in the British Museum (BM 1131) that references one in the temple of Amun (Williams, 1972).

Two terms often associated with education appear in the texts: the "House of Education" and the "House of Life." These institutions are sometimes conflated but seem to have served different functions. The "House of Education" seems to have been a place where young apprentice children learned several disciplines, whereas the "House of Life," though possibly training advanced scribal students, was more of a scriptorium or repository of knowledge used by professional scribes. It is not impossible that these two institutions were located in the same or in nearby areas (Gardiner, 1938).

Several New Kingdom architectural structures have either been associated with education or identified as schools. The most famous is the "school" of the Ramesseum, a temple built during the reign of Ramses II, ca. 1800 B.C.E., on the western bank of Luxor. This school was found in the economic and administrative complex of the temple. In this area, many ostraca were recovered written in a remedial hieratic hand, possibly belonging to students. An esplanade or terrace east of the area suggests that education might have been conducted outdoors, with small nearby rooms serving as offices for instructors (Le Blanc, 2004).

Scribal curriculum. Based on *Papyrus Anastasi I*, a satirical literary piece from the New Kingdom Dynasties 19–20 (1292–1069 B.C.E.) apparently used in the training of scribes, it seems that eventually students wrote from dictation and memory. It is possible that during the elementary levels of education in some periods, children recited their lessons in a

singsong fashion, as the *Instructions for Merikare*, a Middle Kingdom (2050–1800 B.C.E.) text, admonishes its readers not to "kill a man whose efficiency you know, with whom you once sang the writings." The surviving texts also reveal that written material would often first be inscribed by a teacher and then copied by a student.

Various texts exemplifying grammatical instruction have also been found. The earliest examples date to the Middle Kingdom and the latest to the period of the Ptolemies (305–30 B.C.E.). Comprehensive lists, such as onomastica, served as pedagogical aids. These lists cataloged animals, plants, minerals, meteorological and geographical terms, names of professions, titles of officials, and so on. Two hieratic ostraca convey lists of verbal paradigms. Several demotic texts contain lists of nouns formed with certain prefixes. Students also learned mathematics (Szpakowska, 2008, p. 107).

The advanced literature used within schools was called sb_3yt, "teaching." Such literature, attributed to teachers and authority figures, is among the earliest and best-attested examples of scribal curriculum, spanning the Old, Middle, and New Kingdoms. Within many of these literary texts, pupils were referred to as "sons" or "children." Using these texts, students were intended to not only hone their reading and writing skills but also were admonished in the proper ways of correct speech, court etiquette, and ethical conduct. During the Middle Kingdom, a consistent core group of writings was developed that was used for centuries. Some famous examples include the Instructions of Dua-Khety for his son Pepy, also known as The Satire of the Trades, in which the scribal trade is lauded as the highest of all professions. Another important curricular text was called Kemyt, meaning "completion," a collection of idioms and formulae compiled during the Eleventh Dynasty (ca. 2134–1991 B.C.E.) that was used for a millennium.

The New Kingdom village of Deir el-Medina is noteworthy. It was inhabited by an atypical number of highly literate and/or skilled artisans (along with their families) brought together for the construction of Pharaonic tombs and thus provides a rare window into Egyptian education. Onomastica and literary texts were found there, as well as numerous ostraca containing student exercises. Many school exercises were signed by their student copyists, who listed their title as "assistant" or "apprentice." These signatures or colophons also reveal that some students were taught by their fathers or grandfathers. One student was sent by his literate father for advanced instruction by someone of higher rank (McDowell, 1996; 2000).

Women in Egyptian education. As in Mesopotamia, formal, standardized education was predominantly received by men, and in Egyptian texts regarding education, female students are not generally referenced. One exception to this is a late Ramesside letter from Deir el-Medina (P. Leiden I 370) that mentions a daughter in the context of encouraging the recipients to work hard in their studies and also mentions the same daughter writing a letter (Toivari-Viitala, 2001, p. 189). Furthermore, professional female scribes were among the entourage of a queen of the Thirteenth Dynasty. Beyond the scribal profession, there is some evidence for female literacy. A statue of Queen Hatshepsut's daughter Nefrure depicts her alongside her tutor Senenmut and the records of Queens Tiy and Nefertiti reflect their education (Brunner, 1957, p. 46; Williams, 1972, p. 220). Moreover, five New Kingdom Theban tombs covering a span of 300 years give evidence of literacy among non-royal women (Bryan, 1984).

Southern Canaan, Israel, and Judah. Early Canaanite language texts written in both cuneiform and linear alphabetic scripts have been recovered from the Late Bronze–early Iron Ages, and linear alphabetic script became the dominant writing tradition in Canaan during this time. Linear alphabetic was typically incised in stone or clay or painted on clay or papyrus. One of the earliest student exercises probably included writing the alphabet in a fixed sequence, and such texts are called abecedaries. One of earliest examples of an abecedary from southern Canaan comes from Izbet Ṣarṭah and dates to the twelfth century.

Around the end of the eleventh to the beginning of the tenth century B.C.E., the form of the linear alphabetic script became standardized, a development probably influenced by northern Canaanites, the Phoenicians. After this period, this script that was in use both in Phoenicia proper and in southern Canaan is often referred to as Phoenician. Another abecedary, this one written in Phoenician script, has been recovered from southern Canaan from around this period, the tenth-century Tel Zayit abecedary. A second potential student exercise, possibly exhibiting a next level of scribal training, also dates to the tenth century and is written in the Phoenician script and Canaanite language—the Gezer calendar. This "calendar" is a list of agricultural seasons, and the small tablet on which it occurs is a palimpsest, with evidence of much erasure and reuse, possibly associated with writing practice. These tenth-century texts are of particular importance with regard to discussions of literacy and education during the time that the kingdoms of Israel and Judah began to emerge in southern Canaan.

By the ninth century B.C.E., a Hebrew script that was distinct from the Phoenician emerged, and it is also from this period that the earliest inscriptions written definitively in the Hebrew language derive.

Debate regarding "schools" in Iron Age (ca. 1200–586 B.C.E.) Israel/Judah. There is significant debate regarding the precise locus of and impetus behind scribal training in ancient Israel and Judah, especially concerning at what point in the history of these polities such training would have occurred (Crenshaw, 1998; Davies, 1995; Jamieson-Drake, 1991; Lemaire, 1981; Puech, 1988; Rollston, 2008; 2010; Schniedewind, 2004; Weeks, 1994; Whybray, 1974). No architectural remains of schools have been found in southern Canaan. The Hebrew Bible refers to the activities of scribes (e.g., 1 Kgs 11:41, 14:19, 29; 2 Kgs 12:11, 25:19; Jer 36:12, 37:15, 20, 36:32, 52:25; 2 Chr 24:11); however, it does not discuss scribal training specifically. The presence of a formal, standardized education system within Israel/Judah from at least the ninth century, if not before, is suggested by the following: the earliest Hebrew epigraphs, which derive from the ninth century, though limited in number, demonstrate standardization and consistency of script and spelling. Furthermore, the more numerous Hebrew epigraphic examples from the eighth century and later employ a complex hieratic numeral system; are largely administrative in nature, with letters and documents exhibiting systematized formulae and writing conventions; and the occurrence of errors is rare (Carr, 2005; Puech, 1988; Rollston, 2010).

Scribal curriculum. In addition to abecedaries, early exercises probably included the repeated writing of words, such as examples found at Kuntillet 'Ajrud (late ninth–early eighth century B.C.E.) and at Kadesh Barnea (seventh century B.C.E.). Also, in this respect, the sequences of hieratic Egyptian numerals found in the ostraca from Kadesh Barnea and the consistent use of epistolary formulae in the ostraca from Arad and Lachish (seventh–sixth centuries B.C.E.) should be mentioned. The best potential example of scribal training comes from Jerusalem. This two-line inscription, arguably a teacher's model copied by a student, is dated to the seventh century B.C.E. The first line of text is written in a competent, trained hand; the second is a copy of the first, written in a remedial hand (Rollston, 2010, pp. 111, 121).

For more advanced training, we are forced to rely on potential examples from the Hebrew Bible, as no advanced curricular texts are available from the epigraphic record. Possible examples include alphabetic acrostic poems such as Psalms 9, 10, 25, 34, 119, 145; Proverbs 31:10–31; and Lamentations 1—4. In these poetic texts, each line begins with the corresponding letter of the Hebrew alphabet, and such texts would have served as aids to memorization. Another set of biblical texts that is considered a major candidate for scribal education is the instructional literature or sayings attributed to a sage found in Proverbs, Job, and Qohelet. As in Mesopotamian and Egyptian education, such texts would serve the dual purpose of increasing competency in reading and writing as well as socializing a young student (Carr, 2005, pp. 111–173). The instruction texts from the book of Proverbs also use the familial language, "father"/"son" (Prov 1:8, 4:3, 6:20), attested in Mesopotamian and Egyptian educational systems.

Women in ancient Israelite/Judahite education. The only potential example of women's involvement in education within ancient Israel/Judah is found in Proverbs 31:1—the sayings of an otherwise unknown King Lemuel attributed to his mother. In this instructional text, the advice is given from mother to son instead of from father to son. On analogy with Mesopotamia and Egypt, we may speculate that women of certain classes, such as the royal elite or those in scribal families, received education, but there is no material or biblical evidence regarding the precise nature of women's education in ancient Israel or Judah.

[*See also* Education, *subentry* Hebrew Bible; *and* Religious Leaders, *subentry* Ancient Near East.]

BIBLIOGRAPHY

Brunner, Helmut. *Altägyptische Erziehung.* Wiesbaden, Germany: Harrassowitz, 1957.

Bryan, Betsy. "Evidence for Female Literacy from Theban Tombs of the New Kingdom." *Bulletin of the Egyptological Seminar* 6 (1984): 17–32.

Carr, David M. *Writing on the Tablet of the Heart: Origins of Scripture and Literature.* Oxford: Oxford University Press, 2005.

Charpin, Dominique. *Reading and Writing in Babylon.* Translated by Jane Marie Todd. Cambridge, Mass.: Harvard University Press, 2010.

Civil, M. "Education (Mesopotamia)." In *The Anchor Bible Dictionary*, edited by D. N. Freedman, Vol. 2, pp. 201–205. New York: Doubleday, 1992.

Crenshaw, James L. *Education in Ancient Israel: Across the Deadening Silence.* New York: Doubleday, 1998.

Davies, Graham I. "Were There Schools in Ancient Israel?" In *Wisdom in Ancient Israel: Essays in Honor of J. A. Emerton*, edited by John Day, Robert P. Gordon, and H. G. M. Williamson, pp. 199–211. Cambridge, U.K.: Cambridge University Press, 1995.

Delnero, Paul. "Variation in Sumerian Literary Compositions: A Case Study Based on the Decad." Ph.D. diss., University of Pennsylvania, 2006.

Delnero, Paul "Memorization and the Transmission of Sumerian Literary Compositions." *Journal of Near Eastern Studies* 71 (2012): 189–208.

Gardiner, Alan. "The House of Life." *Journal of Egyptian Archaeology* 42 (1938): 157–179.

Gesche, Petra D. *Schulunterricht in Babylonien im ersten Jahrtausend v. Chr.* Edited by M. Dietrich and O. Loretz. Alter Orient und Altes Testament 275. Münster, Germany: Ugarit-Verlag, 2001.

Jamieson-Drake, David W. *Scribes and Schools in Monarchic Judah: A Socio-archaeological Approach.* Journal for the Study of the Old Testament Supplement Series 109. Sheffield, U.K.: Sheffield Academic Press, 1991.

Janssen, Rosalind M., and Jac. J. Janssen. *Growing Up in Ancient Egypt*. London: Rubicon, 1990.

Kramer, Samuel N. "The Sage in Sumerian Literature: A Composite Portrait." In *The Sage in the Ancient Near East*, edited by John G. Gammie and Leo G. Perdue, pp. 31–44. Winona Lake, Ind.: Eisenbrauns, 1990.

Leblanc, Christian. "L'école des scribes de Ramsès II." *La Recherche, l'actualité des sciences* 379 (2004): 70–74 and illustrations.

Lemaire, André. *Les écoles et la formation de la bible dans l'ancien Israël*. Orbis Biblicus et Orientalis 39. Göttingen, Germany: Vandenhoeck & Ruprecht, 1981.

Lion, Brigitte. "Dame Inanna-ama-mu, scribe à Sippar." *Revue d'Assyriologie* 95 (2001): 7–32.

Lion, Brigitte. "Les femmes scribes de Sippar." *Topoï Supplément* 10 (2009): 289–303.

Lion, Brigitte. "Literacy and Gender." In *The Oxford Handbook of Cuneiform Culture*, edited by Karen Radner and Eleanor Robson, pp. 90–112. Oxford: Oxford University Press, 2011.

Luukko, Mikko, and Greta Van Buylaere. *The Political Correspondence of Esarhaddon*. Helsinki: Helsinki University Press, 2002.

McDowell, Andrea G. "Student Exercises from Deir el-Medina: The Dates." In *Studies in Honor of William Kelly Simpson*, edited by P. D. Manuelian, pp. 601–608. Boston: Museum of Fine Arts, 1996.

McDowell, Andrea G. "Teachers and Students at Deir el-Medina." In *Deir el-Medina in the Third Millennium A.D. A Tribute to Jac. J. Janssen*, edited by R. J. Demarée and A. Egberts, pp. 217–233. Leiden, The Netherlands: Nederlands Instituut voor het Nabije Oosten, 2000.

McMahon, Gregory. "The History of the Hittites." *Biblical Archaeologist* 52, nos. 2–3 (1989): 62–77.

Michalowski, Piotr. "Charisma and Control: On Continuity and Change in Early Mesopotamian Bureaucratic Systems." In *The Organization of Power: Aspects of Bureaucracy in the Ancient Near East*, edited by M. Gibson and R. D. Biggs, pp. 47–57. Chicago: Oriental Institute, 1987.

Michel, Cécile. *Correspondance des marchands de Kaniš au début du IIe millénaire avant J.-C.* Paris: Cerf, 2001.

Michel, Cécile. "Les femmes et l'écrit dans les archives paléo-assyriennes." *Topoï Supplément* 10 (2009): 253–272.

Millard, Alan. "An Assessment of the Evidence for Writing in Ancient Israel." In *Biblical Archaeology Today: Proceedings of the International Congress on Biblical Archaeology, Jerusalem, April 1984*, pp. 301–312. Jerusalem: Israel Exploration Society, 1985.

Puech, Émile. "Les écoles dans l'Israël préexilique: Données épigraphiques." In *Congress Volume: Jerusalem 1986*, edited by J. A. Emerton, pp. 189–203. Supple-ments to Vetus Testamentum 40. Leiden, The Netherlands: Brill, 1988.

Radner, Karen. *Die neuassyrischen Privatrechtsurkunden als Quelle für Mensch und Umwelt*. State Archives of Assyria Studies 6. Helsinki: Neo-Assyrian Text Corpus Project, 1997.

Rainey, Anson F. "The Scribe at Ugarit: His Position and Influence." In *Proceedings of the Israel Academy of Sciences and Humanities*, Vol. 3, pp. 126–147. Jerusalem: Israel Academy of Sciences and Humanities, 1969.

Robson, Eleanor. *Mesopotamian Mathematics, 2100–1600 B.C.: Technical Constants in Bureaucracy and Education*. Oxford Editions of Cuneiform Texts 14. Oxford: Clarendon, 1999.

Rollston, Christopher A. "The Phoenician Script of the Tel Zayit Abecedary and Putative Evidence for Israelite Literacy." In *Literate Culture and Tenth-Century Canaan: The Tel Zayit Abecedary in Context*, edited by Ron E. Tappy and P. Kyle McCarter Jr., pp. 61–96. Winona Lake, Ind.: Eisenbrauns, 2008.

Rollston, Christopher A. *Writing and Literacy in the World of Ancient Israel: Epigraphic Evidence from the Iron Age*. Atlanta: Society of Biblical Literature, 2010.

Schniedewind, W. M. *How the Bible Became a Book*. Cambridge, U.K.: Cambridge University Press, 2004.

Szpakowska, Kasia. *Daily Life in Ancient Egypt: Recreating Lahun*. Malden, Mass.: Blackwell, 2008.

Tinney, Steven. "Texts, Tablets, and Teaching: Scribal Education in Nippur and Ur." *Expedition* 40.2 (1998): 40–50.

Toivari-Viitala, Jaana. *Women at Deir el-Medina: A Study of the Status and Roles of the Female Inhabitants in the Workmen's Community during the Ramesside Period*. Leiden, The Netherlands: Nederlands Instituut Voor Het Nabije Oosten, 2001.

van den Hout, Theo. "Administration and Writing in Hittite Society." In *Archivi, depositi, magazzini presso gli ittiti: Nuovi materiali e nuove ricerche/Archives, Depots and Storehouses in the Hittite World: New Evidence and New Research*, edited by M. E. Balza, M. Giorgieri, and C. Mora, pp. 41–58. Genoa: Italian University Press, 2012.

Veldhuis, Niek. "Elementary Education at Nippur: The Lists of Trees and Wooden Objects." Ph.D. diss., University of Groningen, 1997.

Veldhuis, Nick. "Sumerian Proverbs in Their Curricular Context." *Journal of the American Oriental Society* 120 (2000): 383–399.

Weeks, Stuart. *Early Israelite Wisdom*. Oxford: Oxford University Press, 1994.

Whybray, R. N. *The Intellectual Tradition in the Old Testament*. Beihefte zur Zeitschrift für die Alttestamentliche Wissenschaft 135. Berlin: de Gruyter, 1974.

Williams, Ronald J. "Scribal Training in Ancient Egypt." *American Oriental Series* 92 (1972): 214–231.

Ziegler, N. *La population féminine des palais d'après les archives royales de Mari: Le Harem de Zimrî-Lim.* Florilegium Marianum 4. Paris: Société pour l'Étude du Proche-Orient Ancien, 1999.

Zinn, Katharina. "Education, Pharaonic Egypt." In *The Encyclopedia of Ancient History*, edited by Roger S. Bagnall, Kai Brodersen, Craige B. Champion, Andrew Erskine, and Sabine R. Huebner, Vol. 5, pp. 1–5. Malden, Mass.: Wiley-Blackwell, 2013.

Heather D. D. Parker and Erin E. Fleming

Hebrew Bible

In ancient Israel, education involved distinct social actors (parents, elders, teachers) in different social contexts and took different forms at different times and places. Scholarly discussions of education in the Hebrew Bible, however, have often centered on the education of scribal elites.

The Question of Education. In the past scholars often assumed, on analogy with Egypt and Mesopotamia, that in ancient Israel, elite scribes were educated in "schools" associated with the Temple or court. Gerhard von Rad, for instance, described a "Solomonic enlightenment" in the tenth century B.C.E., when the Israelites came into contact with, and imitated, the cultural traditions of civilizations like Egypt.

However, no direct evidence for formal scribal schools in ancient Israel or Judah exists. The notion of a Solomonic enlightenment has been discredited by archaeological evidence that Solomon's reign was not as extensive or extravagant as biblical literature suggests. Moreover, extrabiblical evidence for education in ancient Israel—mostly epigraphical—is ambiguous and not extensive. It has been interpreted both to support the existence of an extensive scribal educational system (Lemaire, 1981; Davies, 1995) and to deny the existence of such "schools" (Weeks, 1994). The biblical texts offer even fewer clues regarding educational institutions such as scribal "schools" prior to the early second century B.C.E. and Ben Sirach's allusion to a "house of instruction" (Sir 51:23), which many scholars understand as a reference to some sort of formal school in Jerusalem in the Hellenistic epoch.

Although epigraphic evidence from the Levant does suggest that some education in basic literacy took place in ancient Israel and Judah, it does not make clear the social or institutional context of this education. In fact, scholars seem to imagine different things by "school," with some describing a highly developed formal institution and others using the term in a more modest sense. Basic moral education of children (cf. Deut 6:1–9) likely took place in the extended family, and would have been offered by mothers, fathers, and others. Proverbs 1:8, for example, speaks of the educational work of both fathers and mothers: "Hear, my child, your father's instruction, and do not reject your mother's teaching" (cf. Prov 4:3; 6:20; 10:1; 15:20; 23:22; 28:7, 24; 29:3, 15, 17; 30:17; 31:1). It is possible that for some children, basic literacy was introduced in this familial context as well. For the bulk of the populace, however, learning agriculture or handcrafts, not letters, would have been a primary concern.

Yet the mere existence of a sophisticated ancient literature in Hebrew—the Bible—suggests that some sort of formal educational institutions existed alongside household-based teachings. Scholars question whether there were sophisticated scribal "schools" associated with the royal court or the Temple, as analogies with Egypt and Mesopotamia might suggest. More likely, something like scribal guilds— perhaps associated with scribal families—educated scribes for service in the central institutions and bureaucracies of Israel and Judah. These guilds would have produced some scribal scholars—"master scribes" or "sages"—who were able to produce, preserve, learn, and teach sophisticated texts like those found in the Hebrew Bible. Despite the Bible's legendary account of Solomon's kingdom (1 Kgs 1—11) in the tenth century B.C.E., archaeological evidence suggests that it was not before the eighth century B.C.E. that Israel and Judah were large or sophisticated enough to demand or support a significant scribal class (Jamieson-Drake, 1991).

Intellectually Elite Scribes. It is likely that biblical texts are ultimately the product of intellectually or educationally elite scribes or sages. These scribes would have been overwhelmingly male and most often socially well placed. However, contrary to what is sometimes assumed, the ideological interests and values of the sages who produced this literature would not have been identical to the interests of the 1–2 percent of the population that constituted the economic and political elite. Scribal perspectives and values should thus not be uncritically collapsed into the perspectives of that elite, just as they should not be viewed as identical to the concerns and interests of the 80–90 percent of the population that made up the peasant agricultural population.

Though the scribal "class" would have been socially distinct, marked by education and elevated literacy, it was likely also quite diverse. The Bible records that some scribes held high positions in the political institutions of ancient Israel. These individuals, if they were not a part of the political and economic elite, likely did identify closely with those elites (2 Sam 8:17, 20:25; 1 Kgs 4:3). Yet some scribes would have been occupied with mundane tasks—for example, the penning of marriage contracts and economic records—making strong identification with rulers and aristocrats less likely. Still others would have held more ambiguous positions in different levels of the administration of the institutions of court and Temple. These scribes likely understood their work and social station as qualitatively distinct from other social actors, whether peasant agriculturalists, artisans, or political-economic elites (cf. Sir 38:24—39:11). This difference was largely constructed through scribal education. As Ben Sirach put it, scribes were not occupied with, and had little time for, agriculture or handcrafts. They were, rather, "concerned with prophecies" and preserving "the sayings of the famous" and "seeking out meanings of proverbs" and parables (Sir 39:1–3; cf. Prov 1:2–6).

Besides managing religious, political, and economic institutions, largely on behalf of the political and economic elite, some master scribes or sages also produced, read, and taught sophisticated texts like those preserved in the Tanakh. They were, in other words, the guardians (and in part the creators and authors) of ancient Israel's literary, ethical-theological, and historical traditions. This is important since these traditions articulated key scribal values and virtues—diligence, loyalty, patience, honesty—as well as biblical notions of social justice, or "justice and righteousness." As David M. Carr has explained, scribes were not trained merely to serve as bureaucrats and copyists. A scribe's education was not simply about acquiring literacy—learning to read and write, or to record financial records. Rather, scribal education in ancient Israel and Judah also likely involved moral-ethical instruction and centered on the study of culturally significant texts, some of which would come to make up the Tanakh. Scribes learned these texts not simply by copying them but by hearing them dictated, by memorizing them, and sometimes by orally reciting or "performing" them. When instructing younger scribes, master scribes who possessed a deep familiarity with culturally significant texts would have been able to reproduce such texts orally, or creatively construct "new" texts from material they had learned. These culturally significant texts would have formed something like an educational curriculum for scribes. By becoming intimately familiar with such works, scribes internalized the virtues, values, and perspectives of the literature they learned. The traditions a scribe mastered and wrote down on skin or shard thus also came to be written "on the tablet of the [scribe's] heart" (Prov 3:3, 7:3; cf. Deut 6:5, 11:18; Carr, 2005).

Education in justice. One set of values that scribal education would have inculcated was the "justice and righteousness" that obligated the ruling political and economic elite to ensure the most vulnerable were cared for. Indeed, if the prophets—whose texts scribes also preserved and redacted—protested social-economic injustice, then Israel's scribes and sages promoted, at least in part, a positive vision for social justice. Proverbs, for example, likely a key text in the scribal curriculum, seeks to instill social virtue—"justice, righteousness, and equity"—in its hearers (Prov 1:3) and praises the rule of monarchs who ensure justice in their realms (e.g., Prov 16:10, 13; 20:26, 28; 29:4, 14). It also insists on fair economic practices (Prov 11:1; 16:11; 20:10, 23) and demands justice in the legal sphere for the poor and marginalized (e.g., Prov 22:22–23). Job claims to have protected the poor, widow, orphan, and traveler (e.g., 29:12–17), while the royal figure in Ecclesiastes laments the absence of justice (Eccl 3:16—4:3). Psalm 72, explicitly related to the wise king Solomon, likewise recounts the role of the ideal king who was to "judge [his] people with righteousness and [his] poor with justice" (Ps 72:2). Much of the scribal impulse toward social justice can also be mapped in other literature of the Hebrew Bible, most obviously the Exodus and legal traditions. The concern with social justice is also a significant part of other ancient Near Eastern traditions with which Israelite, Judahite, and later Judean scribes would have been familiar.

Of course, the Bible's educational ethos of social justice is, in general, paternalistic and patriarchal. As elsewhere in the ancient Near East, in the Bible the king and other social-political elites were to act as "father" to the community and care for those in their charge. Those at the pinnacle of the patriarchal order were ultimately responsible for ensuring that those lower on the chain of socioeconomic being— the poor and needy—were cared for. Special concern was directed toward those with liminal social status due to their not being associated with a patriarchal household—widows, the fatherless, and foreigners. The economically and socially vulnerable were to be assisted and protected. Their status, however, was not necessarily transformed. Even the eighth-century prophets of Israel and Judah do not offer a vision of economic revolution. What was intolerable to them was not the mere existence of the needy (and certainly not a system of patriarchal privilege) but the gross oppression of the poor by those who were responsible for caring for them.

Though rhetorically distinct from prophetic discourse and emerging from an educational and literary context that was likely not as morally urgent as that which motivated the prophet's demands for social justice, the Bible's scribal voice of justice is nonetheless also a form of rhetorical and ideological "social control" over the political and economic elite. Scribal values evident in the classic texts that

formed the ancient scribal educational curriculum would have also been transmitted or communicated to the political and economic elite. These elites, like the peasant agriculturalists and the artisans, would have been broadly familiar with Israel's social justice traditions. However, some members of the economic and political elite would have gained awareness of these texts through informal or formal instruction mediated to them by scribes. Such familiarity was vital, since the powerful social positions inhabited by the political and economic elite made them morally vulnerable, liable to oppressing the poor and taking advantage of the marginalized. Scribes addressed this reality not through prophetic oracles or visions but through education that transmitted and promoted a scribal social justice ideology that acknowledged the legitimacy of political and economic elites only insofar as they were agents of social justice.

The paternalistic and patriarchal perspective of scribal education is evident not only in the Hebrew Bible's notions of social-economic justice but also in the representation and construction of women and women's roles in social life, including education. Although a mother's voice and teaching are alluded to on many occasions in Proverbs, the wisdom discourse of this key educational text primarily reflects the teaching of fathers directed to a male audience, as its warnings against contentious wives and adulterous relationships with the strange or foreign woman make clear (see Prov 19:13; 21:19; 27:15 and 2:16–19; 5:3–14, 19–20; 6:24–35; 7:1–27). Although Woman Wisdom in Proverbs takes on divine attributes (8:22–31) and is a rich resource for considering feminine aspects of the divine, she is also one half of a patriarchal binary conception of "woman." Woman Wisdom—a symbol of the values and virtues of scribes—is cast as a legitimate object of male desire, but only in relation to the dangerous attractions of the strange or foreign woman, who is symbolically linked to Woman Folly (9:13–18). Indeed, the social justice presented in the Bible is one that understands women's sexuality and social status only in relationship to men. Normally, unmarried women would belong to their father's household, and married women's status would be derived through their husband's household. At least one wisdom text even seems able to envision a man's punishment for failure to embody a patriarchal sexual ethic in the form of rape and humiliation of his wife (Job 31:9–10, although the verses may be interpreted otherwise).

The education of the body. Certain biblical passages, especially in Proverbs, suggest that it was not only the student's mind that was instructed during the education of scribes. The body of the young scribe was also disciplined. "Spare the rod, spoil the child" remains a popular proverb that derives from Proverbs 13:24. But other texts from the Bible and ancient Near Eastern literature testify to the physical discipline associated with scribal education. Carr suggests that scribal education was at least in part ideologically conceived as the "humanizing" of the young scribe (Carr, 2005). The physical disciplining of youthful scribes can be conceived as part of this humanizing. Just as the Egyptian *Instruction of Any* (Anii) knew that the wild natures of brutish animals could be tamed through physical discipline, so too Proverbs draws similar analogies: "A whip for the horse, a bridle for the donkey, and a rod for the back of fools" (26:3).

Given the patriarchal and paternalistic tendency of the education envisioned in the Hebrew Bible, the humanizing of male youths through scribal moral education and physical discipline can also be conceived as the masculinizing of these youths—the production of scribal men in the ancient patriarchal hierarchy. Carol A. Newsom has recognized that the young male addressees of Proverbs 1—9 are encouraged to forgo the immediate but transitory benefits of aligning themselves with their male peers (cf. 1:10–19). They should, rather, patiently identify with the instructional voice of the father, who stands at the pinnacle of the social hierarchy and whose place the "son" can expect to inherit (Newsom, 1989). Similarly, in Proverbs 4:1–3, although a mother's teaching is mentioned, it is the instructing voice of the father that speaks. He identifies with the son, or student, to encourage the son to identify with the father and his teaching, rather than with the mother. The father recalls that, like the addressee, he was once

a young son, who was "tender" and the "favorite" of his "mother." But just as the son must now do, he also subjected himself to his own father's teaching. The teaching of the father's father, now directed to the text's addressee, was to "hold fast" to patriarchal instruction. Immediately, however, the young male addressee is exhorted to "acquire wisdom" (4:5). Although some scholars understand Wisdom here to be portrayed as a matron figure, it is likely that she is described in a symbolic language of erotic desire associated with patriarchal marriage (cf. the rhetoric of Boaz's acquiring of Ruth as wife [Ruth 4:10]). Proverbs 4:6 exhorts: "Do not forsake her [Wisdom], and she will keep you; love her and she will guard you" (cf. 2:17). The second half of verse 2:7 deploys images that are in Song of Solomon associated with patriarchal marriage practices: "She [Wisdom] will honor you if you embrace her. She will place on your head a fair garland; she will bestow on you a beautiful crown" (cf. Song 3:6–11). The youth who would become a wise "man" must thus abandon identification with his mother and, like a man, acquire a wife, who is Wisdom.

Proverbs' instruction to the addressee to avoid adultery with another man's wife and enjoy marriage (cf. Prov 5:15–20) is also an effort to move the youth to adopt and value the patriarchal order, to which he will be a beneficiary—if he accepts the father's teaching. What's more, a number of passages compare the wise and wisdom to images that are perhaps more sharply and clearly masculine images. In Proverbs 16:32, for example, the person who possesses the key wisdom virtue of patience—"one who is slow to anger" and "whose temper is controlled"— is "better than" the "mighty" and "one who captures a city." Similarly, Proverbs 24:3–4 links wisdom with the fundamental patriarchal act of building a house-(hold). Subsequently, verse 5 (although difficult to render) associates wisdom with manly strength, while verse 6 returns to martial imagery to describe a wise man's worth: "A wise man [*geber chakam*] is mighty, and a man of knowledge [*'ish da'at*] increases strength, for by wise guidance you can make your war, and salvation is with an abundance of counselors." Ecclesiastes 7:19 and 9:17–18 are rhetorically similar: "Wisdom gives strength to the wise more than ten rulers that are in a city"; "The quiet words of the wise are more to be heeded than the shouting of a ruler among fools. Wisdom is better than weapons of war."

Education beyond the scribes. Other social actors attested in the Hebrew Bible—e.g., priests and prophets—were also involved in education, broadly conceived, in ancient Israel. Alongside other duties, priests also learned and taught Torah, especially as this related to questions of cleanness and uncleanness. Leviticus 10:10–11 instructs Aaron in the duties of the priests: "You are to distinguish between the holy and the common, and between the unclean and the clean; and you are to teach the people of Israel all the statutes that the LORD has spoken to them through Moses." Prophets too taught the people the divine's expectations for the ordering of their life together. Although the Psalms do not regularly employ an instructional rhetoric, they are in a broad sense—like much biblical literature—also concerned with teaching the people.

Thus one largely encounters a patriarchal and paternalistic scribal vision of education in the Hebrew Bible. Leadership in the highest status positions in ancient Israel (e.g., priest, prophet, scribe) with which education was associated was dominated by males, and the figures traditionally associated with Torah, wisdom literature, and the Psalms are men—Moses, Solomon, and David. The literary and ideological "fingerprints" of sages and other elite males are therefore most visible on biblical literature. However, this fact should not be overstated. With some methodological and hermeneutical effort one can also discover traces of the voices of others in the texts that possibly formed part of the educational curriculum of scribal elites.

The methodological challenges involved in recovering female and nonelite voices in the Bible are considerable. Nevertheless, the male scribes ultimately responsible for biblical literature did not live in a social and ideological vacuum. Nor did the literary tradition over which they were guardians develop in a social and ideological vacuum. Hence we can expect that the voices of women and nonelite others have not been completely erased in scribal discourses.

As noted above, forms of elementary moral education were likely offered by parents and clan elders, including mothers, rather than scribes. It is probable too that many of the Psalms, which do not reveal an explicit instructional rhetoric, but nonetheless indirectly teach worshipers about worship, ritual, and the divine, were not the pure invention of a cultic or scribal intelligentsia. Rather, such texts likely were formed out of responses to the real-life situations of the entire worshipping community. Likewise the prophetic voice in the Bible is not exclusively male. The explicit mention of at least five female prophets in the Hebrew scriptures (Miriam, Deborah, Huldah, Noadiah, and the prophet in Isaiah 8:3) may suggest that women played a larger role in prophetic instruction than is often thought.

Biblical wisdom literature also attests to a significant role for women in education. For example, Proverbs records the instruction of a queen mother to her son Lemuel (Prov 31:1–9). Comparative studies of instructional texts have revealed that her voice belongs to a chorus of other socially and economically well-placed women throughout the ancient Near East who attained scribal training (Fontaine, 2002). It is also likely that the sages or scribes who produced Proverbs incorporated the wisdom of the broader agricultural, folk population into this key text (e.g., Prov 10—29). Especially the first half of many of the lines in Proverbs 25—29 (and elsewhere) might be derived from folk sayings, to which women and other nonelites contributed.

The Hebrew Bible's visions of education are thus not merely those of elite male figures. Rather, they include, in submerged and dialogical fashion, the voices of the entire community of Israel and Judah (and later Judea). Yet the ability to hear nondominant voices in the Bible is not merely a question of finding the right method to excavate those voices. It is also related to hermeneutics and the role of interpreters in understanding biblical texts. The social contexts and experiences—or subjectivity—of some contemporary readers provide them with a different lens through which to read biblical texts, or differently attuned ears with which to hear submerged biblical voices. For example, readers from cultures where folk proverbs remain common may be better situated to hear the oral wisdom of the agricultural peasant population of ancient Israel in the midst of written scribal texts. So too poor and marginalized readers bring a knowledge of the brutal realities of social and economic oppression that can "thicken"— and sometimes problematize—understandings of the Bible's paternalistic concern with the needy. Likewise, some women readers or queer commentators may more aptly ask about, identify, and describe female voices in biblical books or more deftly uncover the patriarchal and normative assumptions about gender and sexuality in those texts and the interpretive tradition.

[*See also* Authors of Biblical Books; Canon/Canonicity/Canonization; Economics, *subentry* Hebrew Bible *and* Imagery, Gendered, *subentry* Wisdom Literature.]

BIBLIOGRAPHY

Carr, David M. *Writing on the Tablet of the Heart: Origins of Scripture and Literature.* Oxford: Oxford University Press, 2005.

Davies, Graham I. "Were There Schools in Ancient Israel?" In *Wisdom in Ancient Israel: Essays in Honour of J. A. Emerton,* edited by John Day, Robert P. Gordon, and H. G. M. Williamson, pp. 199–211. Cambridge, U.K.: Cambridge University Press, 1995.

Fontaine, Carole. *Smooth Words: Women, Proverbs, and Performance in Biblical Wisdom.* London: Sheffield Academic Press, 2002.

Jamieson-Drake, David W. *Scribes and Schools in Monarchic Judah: A Socio-Archeological Approach.* Sheffield, U.K.: Almond, 1991.

Lemaire, André. *Les écoles et la formation de la Bible dans l'ancien Israël.* Fribourg, Switzerland: Editions Universitaires, 1981.

Newsom, Carol A. "Woman and the Discourse of Patriarchal Wisdom: A Study of Proverbs 1–9." In *Gender and Difference in Ancient Israel,* edited by Peggy L. Day, pp. 142–160. Minneapolis: Fortress, 1989.

Weeks, Stuart. *Early Israelite Wisdom.* New York: Oxford University Press, 1994.

Timothy J. Sandoval

Greek World

In spite of scholarly attempts to offer a holistic view of Greek education in antiquity, literary and material evidence suggests that schools in the Greek-speaking world were not organized in a rigid system but offered a variety of educational solutions. *Paideia*, the Greek term for education, describes the action of rearing a child (Gr. *pais*), but it would be a mistake to confine *paideia* to the realms of childhood and schooling. Greek *paideia* embodied the complex set of ancient lore, traditions, and customs that constituted the foundation of the shared identity of Greek elites. Rather than describing a set of notions to be learned before adulthood, *paideia* expressed the idea of life as a form of continuing education. Education was not limited to the school years. Aiming at ensuring the development of young individuals into loyal citizens, the educational experience of younger generations would continue outside school in a variety of social, religious, and military capacities. The Greek city itself, with its political life, would ideally constitute a place of unceasing opportunities for learning.

Schooling in the Ancient Greek World. Greek schools were called *didaskaleia* ("teaching places") or *grammatodidaskaleia* ("places for teaching letters") in the case of institutions of primary education (Cribiore, 2001, p. 18). Later papyrological evidence from Hellenistic and Roman times shows that places where young people received their education could also be called *scholai* (Cribiore, 2001, pp. 20–21). Originally, however, *scholē* meant "leisure" as opposed to "business" or "occupation" (Gr. *ascholia*). The Greek notion of school therefore conveys the elitist idea of a commitment to learning away from the mundane concerns of work and trade.

The traditional staples of ancient Greek education were literacy (Gr. *ta grammata*), music (Gr. *mousikē*), and athletics. Music comprised a wide range of artistic and social activities besides the ability to play a musical instrument. School would normally begin around the age of seven. Sources, however, vary on this point. Plato (ca. 427–347 B.C.E.) sets the time necessary to learn how to read and write at three years starting from the tenth year of age (*Laws* 809e–810a). It is unclear how much schooling children would receive at home from their parents or from slaves and professional tutors hired for the purpose. In his *Politics,* Aristotle (ca. 384–322 B.C.E.) says that children should not receive any schooling before the age of five, and should be taught at home between the ages of five and seven (1336a–b).

Historians of education have classified Greek schools according to modern models, identifying a primary level as well as secondary education and institutions of higher education, wherein rhetoric was taught (Marrou, 1956). This classification, however, can be misleading if taken as an indication of a systematic distinction between institutions of different levels (Clarke, 1971). The distinction between lower and higher levels of education pertained to the curriculum and not to the institution attended. Consistency was guaranteed by what was taught rather than by how, where, and by whom. It was not uncommon for Greek students of different skills and levels of education to attend the same school, where they were taught different parts of the curriculum, sometimes by the same teacher (Cribiore, 2001, pp. 37–38). Experienced teachers were expected to be able to teach at more than one level so that a clear distinction was not always possible.

Teachers of different levels, however, represented slightly different professional categories. The primary school teacher was called *didaskalos* or *grammatodidaskalos* or *grammatistēs* and was in charge of teaching the basics of the Greek language. Secondary teachers introduced children of fourteen and older to grammar and literature and were called grammarians (Gr. *grammatikoi*), although at times sources are confusing and describe them simply as *didaskaloi*. Rhetoric was the responsibility of *rhētores* and *sophistai* who would introduce their pupils to the theory and practice of the composition of public speeches. Most of the teaching at any level could be entrusted to *kathēgētai*, itinerant private tutors whom families would hire for the education of their children. Crucial in the Greek schooling system was the role of the pedagogue (Gr. *paidagōgos*), a house slave who was in charge of all the practicalities of the educational process, from homework to corporal punishment. Teachers were generally male; evidence of women teachers is scant and comes mostly from papyri from Hellenistic and Roman times.

Social class, wealth, and gender, rather than age and intellectual ability, seem to have been crucial factors in predicting whether a student would have the possibility of attending prestigious schools and being taught by highly qualified teachers. Marrou (1956, p. 381) points out that Aristotle was aware of the existence of schools for slaves (*Politics* 1255b) and had advised masters on the necessity of giving an education to slaves who were requested to perform activities typical of freeborn people (*Oeconomicus* 1344a). Greek education, however, seems to have been aimed mostly at the freeborn and the wealthy. In comparison with the public school system endorsed in most contemporary societies, Greek schools were private. Parents had to pay teachers for the education of their children (Cole, 1981, p. 226; Griffith, 2001, p. 24). Plato (*Protagoras* 326c) observes that only the wealthiest could afford a better education for their children and keep them at school for a longer time. Although the majority of freeborn citizens would probably have some schooling at a point in their life, the number of those who could stay at school for any significant period of time must have been relatively small (Harris, 1989).

Greek Education and the "Love of Boys." Regarding gender roles in Greek education, attention must be paid to the educational function of that emotional and most frequently sexual relationship which sources call "love of boys," or pederastic love. The term "pederasty," adopted in scholarship to describe the love of an older man for a young boy (Foucault, 1990; Marrou, 1956; Percy, 1996), comes from the Greek *paiderastia*. The Greek word, however, is rare in the classical period (Xenophon, *Anabasis* 7.4.7; Plato, *Symposium* 181c, 184c, and 192b). It is used more frequently in ancient Jewish and Christian sources in a derogatory and polemical sense (Philo, *De vita Contemplativa* 52, 61; Tatian, *Oration* 10, 19; Clement of Alexandria, *Paedagogos* 2.52). Characteristic of classical Greek pedagogy, these relationships would tie an older youth or man, the lover or admirer (Gr. *erastēs*), to a young boy in his formative years, the beloved (Gr. *erōmenos* or *erastos*). The Greeks attributed a critical educational function to the typical asymmetry of pederastic love (Foucault, 1990,

p. 195). Difference of age was a central feature of these relationships to such an extent that institutionalized pederasty in ancient Greece may mark the survival in Greek society of ancestral rituals of initiation of young males into sexual and social maturity (Lear and Cantarella, 2008, pp. 8–9).

Through a gendered lens, the behavior expected of the *erastēs* and the *eromenos* represented a fundamental stage in the construction of Greek masculinity. While the adult admirer would take an active role in the relationship, displaying dominance and persistence but also unselfish dedication and temperance (Gr. *sōphrosunē*), the beloved is initially confined to a passive role and characterized as selfish and capricious (Dover, 1978, p. 169; Lear and Cantarella, 2008, p. 105). In Greek idealizations of pederasty, as, for example, in Plato's *Symposium* (ca. 385–380 B.C.E.), a key factor in the development of the relationship was the willingness of the beloved to emulate the virtues and education of the *erastēs* (Dover, 1978, p. 202). Thus in the loving relationship with an older and more experienced male, boys were supposed to find an apt introduction to the social, moral, and cultural values they were expected to adopt in adult society. In educational settings, teacher-student and, less frequently, student-student relationships were thus tolerated, even encouraged, as an ideal form of mentoring. The hypothesis that similar asymmetrical relationships existed between young female and adult women has been investigated by Marrou (1956, pp. 33–35), in particular in relation to homophilic love in the works of Sappho. The extent to which the relationships described by Sappho served an educational and societal purpose, however, cannot be demonstrated.

Apart from the idealizations of elite groups, the educational purposes of this kind of relationship represented only part of a more complex social and sexual phenomenon. Courtship of boys by adult males in classical and Hellenistic times, however, remained a widespread and socially codified way of favoring the transmission of traditional lore from older to younger generations of males in most Greek societies (Foucault, 1990, p. 196; Percy, 1996).

Ancient Debates about the Education of Women.
Generally, how young women were educated reflects the same rigid socially imposed gender roles that are detectable elsewhere in ancient Greek societies. In the Socratic dialogue *Oeconomicus*, Xenophon (ca. 430–350 B.C.E.) gives voice to the typical expectations of Greek society that a young woman should be instructed in domestic matters at home by her family and husband. In the society depicted by Xenophon, women live in seclusion, subjected to the authority of their parents first and then of their spouses. As shepherds and riders are held responsible for the bad behavior of their sheep and horses, says Socrates in Xenophon's dialogue, so husbands are accountable for the bad behavior of their wives (3.11–12). The wife of one of the characters of the dialogue, Ischomachus, was not even fifteen when she married (7.5). Husbands, says Xenophon, should take responsibility for the instruction of their young and inexperienced wives before entrusting them with important domestic affairs (3.14). The problem exposed by Xenophon constituted a common issue in the education of women. Social seclusion and early marriage could frequently jeopardize a girl's chances to proceed to more advanced levels of education. Blundell (1995, p. 140), however, highlights how Xenophon's attitude attributing great relevance to women's domestic duties represents the views of an educated elite, whereas uneducated Athenians would probably pay little attention to the domestic activities of their wives and to their education.

Plato and Aristotle seem to envisage access to education for boys and girls alike (Cole, 1981, 227). However, they present their views as contradicting common practice, suggesting that in their time the access of women to traditional education was still perceived as a less frequent, if not exceptional, event. Plato's discourse on the necessity of educating women is expounded in the fifth book of the *Republic* (ca. 380 B.C.E.) and in the seventh book of the *Laws*. Plato is among the first ancient thinkers to advocate universal education. However, the kind of education for women envisaged therein is very different from the views endorsed by Xenophon and challenges the rigid differentiation of gender roles of traditional Greek societies. In Plato's view, young women should receive the same education as young men, following the same curriculum. He argues that women should carry out the same social, military, and civic duties of men, by analogy with the natural order of animal societies where there is no distinction between the social role of male and female individuals (*Republic* 451d). Since women have the same duties as men, says Plato, it necessarily follows that women should receive the same education given to men (*Republic* 451e). In the *Republic*, the education of women is still limited to the guardians (Gr. *phylakes*), the ruling class of Plato's utopian state. In the *Laws*, however, Plato lays out a detailed plan of public education, where the responsibility of educating the young passes from the parents directly under the control of the state, extending compulsory state education equally to all freeborn, irrespective of gender and social class (*Laws* 804d).

Aristotle expounds his views on the education of women in the *Politics*. His position on the education of women tries to accommodate Plato's utopia within a more traditional system, close to the views expressed in Xenophon's *Oeconomicus*. As far as relationships between genders, social classes, and age groups are concerned, Aristotle advocates the preservation of a model of dominance where men rule over women, freeborn over slaves, and adults over children (*Politics* 1259a). Like Plato, Aristotle argues that education should be the responsibility of the state rather than be entrusted to private initiative (*Politics* 1337a). Since education is vital for the survival of the state, it should be treated as a matter of public interest. Unlike Plato, however, Aristotle does not suggest that women should receive the same education imparted to men. Rather, they should have access to education insofar as a better education allows them to be more efficient in their traditional duties within their household (*Politics* 1260b). As the state is an aggregate of households, says Aristotle, the improvement in domestic administration offered by the education of women would necessarily have positive consequences for the life of the state. Though dependent on Plato's views, Aristotle's position on the education of women does not challenge the subordinate role attributed to women in the traditional social constructs of ancient Greece (Blundell, 1995, p. 186).

Women in Greek Schools. Evidence for the education of Greek women in schools is poor and refers mostly to primary education. As women would marry at a young age, often in their mid-teens, their chances to proceed to secondary education were exceedingly low. Owing to social restrictions, the education of the majority of girls and young women took place for the most part in the home in the form of private tutoring. Since the advancement to the highest level of the curriculum, the rhetorical level, would often entail the need to relocate to attend lectures of more qualified teachers, it was unlikely that women would reach the third level of education (Cribiore, 2001, p. 104). Educated women in ancient Greece were thus more likely to belong to upper class households that could afford to educate their female offspring at home, having first paid for the schooling of their male children.

The issue of home schooling for young women should be seen within the general question regarding the existence of places for the education of boys and girls in ancient Greece. Archaeological evidence of constructions built for the exclusive purpose of schooling is very scant, particularly for earlier times. As mentioned, teachers were responsible for finding suitable accommodation for their classes and it was not uncommon for classes of different levels to be held in the same open space. It all depended on the availability of suitable space, ranging from shared public spaces such as temples and colonnades in city markets, to rented rooms in private houses. In the countryside and wherever the climate would allow, extemporaneous classes could also be held in the open air. In Hellenistic and Christian Egypt, monastery cells and even ancient tombs are known to have been used as classrooms (Cribiore, 2001, p. 23). The fact that women studied at home under private tutors does not imply that their education was of an inferior quality. The discriminatory factor was a different curriculum. Since rhetoric and literature were aimed at equipping men with tools for political and social roles unavailable to women, the presence of women in higher education was mostly perceived as unnecessary and socially impractical.

Material evidence for the education of women comes from papyri, inscriptions, and pottery and can offer some insight into the involvement of women in Greek educational institutions (Cole, 1981; Cribiore, 2001). A particular case is that of the presence of women in the *gymnasia*, spaces designed for athletics and some artistic activities such as music and dance. *Gymnasia* were not primarily schools but multifunctional centers for sport, culture, and socializing (Cribiore 2001, p. 35; Harris, 1989, pp. 134–135). As places where athletes contested naked in demanding displays of physical strength, however, *gymnasia* were perceived as an eminently male space, resulting in another factor of exclusion of women from the traditional curriculum. Although Spartan education already prescribed that girls would take part in athletic contests (Plato, *Laws* 806a; cf. Kennell, 1995, p. 46), Plato in the *Republic* considered the idea of women exercising in the *gymnasion* as an obstacle to his proposal to extend traditional education to women (*Republic* 452b). Evidence from papyri and inscriptions from Egypt and Asia Minor, however, provides a few instances of girls applying for membership in *gymnasia* and of a woman taking part in the administration of *gymnasia* as *gymnasiarchis* or female superintendents of athletic training (Cribiore, 2001, p. 36). Although the exact nature of the involvement of female students and superintendents in *gymnasia* remains difficult to assess, these examples prove the presence of women in educational settings that scholarship had so far considered restricted to the exclusive use of male individuals.

In Greek painted pottery, representations of women being educated or using writing tools are less frequent than the same scenes featuring boys and men. Although this does not prove that women did not receive any form of education, it may suggest that Greek artists did not ascribe social or artistic relevance to women's education (Lewis, 2002).

Papyrological sources display a few instances in which women are described as "lady teachers," using the expression *deskalē* or *hē didaskalos* with a feminine article (Cribiore, 2001, p. 51). In a mummy portrait discovered in 1911 by Petrie in the Fayyum cemetery of Hawara in Egypt (first century C.E.), a woman called Hermione is described as *grammatikē*, suggesting her high level of education and perhaps hinting at her involvement in school teaching (Cribiore, 2001, p. 79; Morgan, 1998, p. 155).

Legacy: Educated Women in the Greek World. The major point of contention in contemporary debates on Greek education and gender pertains to a correct assessment of evidence of women's literacy. Contemporary scholarship has criticized historians of education for having replicated their ancient sources paying little attention to gender issues (Harris, 1989, pp. 22–23). As mentioned, the material evidence studied by Cole (1981) and Cribiore (2001) shows that women's literacy may have been less exceptional than suggested by ancient Greek authors. Regarding women's literacy, private correspondence from the papyri found in the Upper Egyptian town of Oxyrhynchus has proven particularly relevant. As some of these letters appear to have been written by women, they compel scholars to reconsider the evidence in support of women's literacy in Greco-Roman Egypt. The interpretation of these sources is made difficult by the fact that letters signed by women could have been dictated to male scribes. Palaeographical considerations, however, suggest that at least in some instances these papyri are autographs written in the handwriting of the female subscriber (Cribiore, 2001, p. 101). Another problem raised by the use of papyrological evidence from Egypt is that these documents reflect local customs and may be inadequate to describe the situation in other parts of the Greek-speaking world (Harris, 1989, p. 10). Private letters of women from other parts of the Roman Empire (Roman Britain and Palestine), however, seem to confirm the evidence from Egypt (Cribiore, 2001, p. 101).

Greek literature also contains a few examples of highly educated women. The poet Sappho (seventh century B.C.E.) is an exceptional example of a literate woman from archaic Greece. In some Greek sources, women styled as courtesans (Gr. *hetairai*) are often described as educated women. Lucian (ca. 125–180 C.E.) portrays *hetairai* in the act of reading and writing letters (*Dialogues of the Courtesans* 10.2–4). Plutarch (ca. 46–120 C.E.) depicts Aspasia (fifth century B.C.E.), the mistress of Pericles (ca. 495–429 B.C.E.), as an educated and influential courtesan (*Pericles* 24). In *Menexenus* 326b–c, Plato portrays Aspasia as a skilled rhetorician. Plato's testimony on Aspasia's skills in rhetoric, however, does not provide much information about her literacy and the amount of schooling she received (Cole, 1981, p. 225). Some philosophical circles, in particular the Pythagoreans, seem to have included women philosophers who most probably had had access to some forms of higher education (Cole, 1981, p. 229; Marrou, 1956, p. 206; cf. Iamblichus, *Life of Pythagoras* 267). Literate women from educated elite groups, however, are hardly representative of the quality of women's education in the Greek world at large. The percentage of women who had access to education remained in any case smaller than that of men of similar social class and geographical provenance (Cole, 1981, p. 226; Harris, 1989, p. 48).

Although important to reassess women's literacy in antiquity, the presence of educated women in the ancient Greek world does not necessarily imply a radical change in the perception of their gender role. The Neoplatonic philosopher Porphyry (ca. 233–306 C.E.), for example, was familiar with the existence of women philosophers in Pythagorean circles and had married an educated woman, Marcella, of whom he praises the disposition to philosophy (*Letter to His Wife Marcella* 3). Porphyry, however, observes that he has ceased to regard his educated wife as a woman and exhorts her to consider her own soul as the soul of a man if she really wants to excel in virtue (33). Porphyry's example shows that traditional preconceptions about gender survived also among the highly educated in philosophical circles open to women. Thus the mere multiplication of examples and material evidence of literate women in the Greek world cannot change the fact that Greek education remained "essentially masculine" (Morgan, 1998, p. 48) in its premises even when women were granted access to it.

[*See also* Children, *subentries on* Greek World, New Testament, *and* Roman World; Education, *subentries on* Ancient Near East, Early Judaism, New Testament, *and* Roman World; *and* Same-Sex Relations, *subentry* Greek World.]

BIBLIOGRAPHY

Blundell, Sue. *Women in Ancient Greece*. London: British Museum Press, 1995.

Clarke, Martin L. *Higher Education in the Ancient World*. London: Routledge & Kegan Paul, 1971.

Cole, Susan Guettel. "Could Greek Women Read and Write?" In *Reflections of Women in Antiquity*, edited by Helene P. Foley, pp. 219–245. New York and London: Gordon and Breach, 1981.

Cribiore, Raffaella. *Gymnastics of the Mind: Greek Education in Hellenistic and Roman Egypt*. Princeton, N.J.: Princeton University Press, 2001.

Dover, Kenneth J. *Greek Homosexuality*. London: Duckworth, 1978.

Foucault, Michel. *The History of Sexuality*, Vol. 2: *The Use of Pleasure*. Translated by Robert Hurley. New York: Vintage, 1990.

Griffith, Mark. "Public and Private in Early Greek Institutions of Education." In *Education in Greek and Roman Antiquity*, edited by Yun Lee Too, pp. 23–84. Leiden, The Netherlands: Brill, 2001.

Harris, William V. *Ancient Literacy*. Cambridge, Mass.: Harvard University Press, 1989.

Kennell, Nigel M. *The Gymnasium of Virtue: Education and Culture in Ancient Sparta*. Chapel Hill: University of North Carolina Press, 1995.

Lear, Andrew, and Eva Cantarella. *Images of Ancient Greek Pederasty: Boys Were Their Gods*. London: Routledge, 2008.

Lewis, Sian. *The Athenian Woman: An Iconographic Handbook*. London: Routledge, 2002.

Marrou, Henri I. *A History of Education in Antiquity*. London: Sheed and Ward, 1956. English translation of *L'histoire de l'éducation dans l'Antiquité* (1948).

Morgan, Teresa. *Literate Education in the Hellenistic and Roman World*. Cambridge, U.K.: Cambridge University Press, 1998.

Percy, William A. *Pederasty and Pedagogy in Archaic Greece*. Urbana: University of Illinois Press, 1996.

Daniele Pevarello

Roman World

The roots of ancient Roman education reach into its soil. Not only was the citizen-farmer a much idealized civic actor to whose performance young men were encouraged to aspire, but also theorists and teachers of rhetoric compared young students to land or plants needing care and cultivation (e.g., Quintilian, *Institutio oratoria* 2.4.10ff). The Latin word "cultus" (cultured), applicable to the development and refinement of gentle hills or of gentlemen, captures that latter correspondence in a word. No exemplum of the citizen-farmer was more valorized in civic education than that of Cincinnatus, whose deeds the historian Livy records in his account of the political unrest that marked periods of the fifth century B.C.E. (*Ab urbe condita* 3.26–29). Materials from the third century and not the fifth, however, provide a richer source of evidence for what one could cautiously call "native" Roman education; that is, education before, to alter the famous phrase of Augustan-age poet Horace (65–8 B.C.E.), the pedagogical arts of captive Greece fully captured comparably uncultivated Rome (*Epistles* 2.1.156–157).

Among the extant writings of Cato the Elder (234–149 B.C.E.) are a complete treatise on farming and fragments from both his speeches and a collection of maxims addressed to his son. In his biography of Cato the Elder, the Greek moralist Plutarch (ca. 46–120 C.E.) recounts Cato's hands-on approach to his son's education. Cato himself taught his son how to read, even though he had a house slave who was an adept schoolmaster, and also tutored him in law and trained him in athletics (*Cato the Elder* 20.4). He even wrote his *History of Rome* in large letters so that his young son could read of Rome's traditions. Cato seems to have been representative of his time and of later ones, in that the education of one's children fell to the *paterfamilias* to execute; his dedication to the task, however, surely exceeded the norm. Cato had set himself to "moulding and fashioning his son to virtue," or *aretē* in Greek (20.6). As Stanley F. Bonner explains, the Latin word *educatio* originally "referred not to schooling and intellectual progress but to the physical rearing of the child and his or her training in behavior" (1977, p. xi). This manner of education would have cultivated a respect for and habits in keeping with traditional Roman values, such as *pietas* (piety), *fides* (fidelity), and *dignitas* (character, clout). Though Cato thought it unseemly

that his son should feel indebted to a slave for something so precious as education, house slaves often tutored the sons and daughters of their masters.

Cato the Elder merits mention above all due to the centrality of his definition of an orator as a "vir bonus dicendi peritus" (good man skilled in speaking) in Quintilian's 12-volume treatment of oratorical education, written in the late first century C.E. (*Institutio oratoria* 12.1.1). During Cato's lifetime, though, the arrival of Greek rhetoricians in Rome ostensibly threatened the order of things. For that reason, the senate issued a decree in 161 that expelled from Rome (ostensibly Greek) philosophers and rhetoricians. Later, in 92, a censorial edict forbade "Latini rhetores" from teaching, but evidence suggests unsuccessfully (Suetonius, *On Teachers of Grammar and Rhetoric* 25.2–4). No doubt throughout the second and first centuries Greek *grammatikoi* (grammarians, teachers of letters) were entering Rome in ever-greater numbers as well. It was with such teachers, Greek or Roman, that elite children began their formal educations, either in the home with expensive private tutors or at a school with public instructors. Evidence suggests that upper-class boys *and* girls received grammatical instruction, though only boys went on to study rhetoric and philosophy, but for rare exceptions (see below).

The Educative Role of Grammatical Training. As its Greek etymology suggests, grammar was the study of "letters." In her study of ancient literate education, Teresa Morgan dispels the ancient and contemporary assumption that the teaching of grammar was lowly, basic, and ever enforced by mindless drills. Given that "teachers and grammarians were and are highly educated individuals, and boys, and girls, learning to read and write Latin and Greek have always belonged to a tiny elite," she writes, we ought to recognize that "grammar was an elitist activity, however elementary it looked to aristocrats and intellectuals" (1998, p. 163). The emperor Vespasian (9–79 C.E.) even granted grammarians and rhetoricians tax-free status in recognition of their public importance and contributions.

Training in grammar involved a series of activities and practices that can somewhat safely be classified into language instruction and textual criticism. Language instruction included learning letters, syllables, parts of speech, declensions, conjugations, syntax, and vocabulary. It also included recitation exercises during which students would have worked on their pronunciation, enunciation, pacing, and rhythm, and learned to listen to the texture of words. In some cases, students would have received instruction in and about both Latin and Greek. Textual criticism involved the careful reading of writers—poets, historians, published orators—who were considered canonical. Students were trained to render a judgment (the Greek *krisis*, whence "criticism") of some property of the text. They also engaged in imitation (*mimēsis*, *imitatio*) of exempla, modeling sentence length and syntactical difficulty, for example. It was not only grammatical structure that students were asked to notice and imitate, however, but also the character and choices of the great men who wrote them or who were written about.

Some plays of the comedic playwright Plautus (ca. 254–184 B.C.E.) give hints of what early schooling was like, as does the odd papyrus scrap containing student scratchings of grammatical exercises, but the works of Dionysius of Halicarnassus (ca. 60–ca. 7 B.C.E.) and Quintilian (ca. 35–ca. 100 C.E.) contain the most extensive appraisals of the teaching of grammar during the first hundred years of imperial Rome. Likely because both Dionysius and Quintilian treat grammar as either the precursor to or part of an orator's development, neither mentions female students.

Dionysius toggles "between grammar and rhetoric" (de Jonge, 2008); his treatise *Peri suntheseōs onomatōn* (On the Putting Together of Words) in particular evidences that quality. That treatise presents a dynamic fusion of the approaches of philosophical schools to matters of grammar and rhetoric, from the syntax theory of the Stoics to the style theory of the Peripatetics, and of poetic and musical theory besides. Perhaps the most significant development is Dionysius's attention to and extension of the exercise known as metathesis, or rewriting the masters by reordering their sentence parts, and tinkering with the individual words themselves.

Practicing drills and developing skills of adaptability equipped a student to think of the components of his own compositions as capable of being otherwise, as requiring shaping to fit certain audiences and situations. In that way, grammatical training prepared students to think rhetorically.

In the preface to his magisterial *Institutio oratoria* (The Education of an Orator), Quintilian explains that his study begins with an incipient orator's earliest days, unlike others that focus solely on putting the finishing touches on an already highly trained orator or on the figment of the imagination that is the perfect orator (though it does not take him long to begin speaking to this ideal—1 pref. 9; 1.10.4). The first book opens with the birth of a son whose father has the highest of hopes for his child and so seeks out the best teachers at every stage of his son's education. Quintilian goes on to lay out, in great detail, the nature of grammatical study. In those early books, Quintilian mentions women of two types: nursemaids or wet-nurses and mothers. In finding the former, a father must be scrupulous, as small children are the most impressionable. Ideally, he should find a woman philosopher, but if he cannot, a woman of upstanding character who speaks correctly will suffice (1.1.4–5). Mothers should be as highly educated as possible, and those who are not ought to double their efforts to ensure their children receive every educational advantage (1.1.6–7).

Though the study of poetics and the composition of verses may not have been a standard part of the grammatical curriculum, it became increasingly popular as elite families began to take leisure activities more seriously. Horace's *Ars poetica* (13 B.C.E.), explicitly addressed to the aristocratic Piso boys, guides young men in the creation of verses that are *utile* and *dulci* (sweet and useful; line 343) and advises them not to be hasty in making public creations that could use further maturation. In the second century C.E., Plutarch instructs young people on the most useful ways of listening to and thinking about poetry in his *De audiendis poetis* (On Listening to Poetry), suggesting poetry's established place in pedagogy.

The Educative Role of Rhetorical Training. Roman rhetorical education arose in response to a demand for instruction on practical methods of public persuasion that might have been frenzied but for the tempering effect of the taint of Greekness coursing through rhetorical theory. To ask to what extent one can discern uniquely Roman contributions to the teaching of rhetoric is to ask the wrong question; as Jeffrey Walker has noted and traced, ancient rhetorical education retained certain basic patterns of instruction across teachers, governments, cultures, and centuries. He credits its stability to its effectiveness: it "met the needs and aspirations of its student clientele, and performed important social functions. In short, it worked" (2011, pp. 4–5).

Roman rhetorical treatises, like Greek ones, often engage questions of what a young person requires—in terms of temperament and talents—to practice an ethical kind of rhetoric. Others focus nearly exclusively on techniques and technicalities. Cicero's two-book treatise *De inventione* (On Invention), likely written in the mid-90s B.C.E., centers on the first canon of rhetoric: the discovery and developments of arguments. He opens by wondering whether eloquence has served humanity well or ill, and by championing the union of *eloquentia* and *sapientia* as a check on the occasional wayward tendencies of the former and inward tendencies of the latter (1.1–5). In the prologue to Book 2, he acknowledges that he has pieced together the most useful and fruitful parts of a range of materials on invention, likening himself to the painter Zeuxis, who constructed an image of Helen by combining the most beautiful parts of the most beautiful women (2.1). This imitative, combinational approach befits his having written the work as a teenager, unifying what he was learning about invention from his tutors and their book rolls.

The unknown *auctor* (author) of *Rhetorica ad Herennium* (Rhetorical Treatise for Herennius), long wrongly attributed to Cicero, organized his rhetorical treatise according to the five canons of rhetoric: invention, arrangement, style, memory, and delivery, although he inverts memory and delivery and saves style for last. This work, typically dated to the late first or early second decade of the first century B.C.E., is the most complete surviving technical treatise from the ancient Roman rhetorical tradition. The *auctor* translates many Greek rhetorical terms, and his treatment of memory is the most detailed surviving account of ancient mnemonic techniques.

Cicero's mature work *De oratore* (On the Orator, 55 B.C.E.) is a sophisticated treatment of the figure of the orator. Framed as a multiday conversation among the morally and skillfully best orators of the 90s, the dialogue centers on the issue of whether talent or art, study, and exercise most make the oratorical man. The two young students who are privy to the discussion are especially keen to learn just what magical quotient yields rhetorical power and perfection. In his *Brutus* (46 B.C.E.), a history of Roman rhetoric's development, Cicero tells of his own education and his affection for his at-home tutors, especially the Stoic Diodotus (§305–316). Cicero also recounts his travels throughout Asia Minor, taken in his twenties at the prompting of friends and doctors who worried about the strain he put on himself while speaking in public, and explains that he sought out teachers known for their corrective rigor who would rid him of his harmful habits (§316).

Being the most extensive treatment of ancient education to weather the ages, Quintilian's *Institutio oratoria* ranges widely, from the construction of arguments, to the application of *pathos* (an emotional appeal), to the use of the rhetorical figure *zeugma*. As mentioned above, Quintilian borrowed his famous definition of the orator as a "vir bonus dicendi peritus" from Cato the Elder. Training in rhetoric was, above all, training in virility (being a *vir*). Quintilian's advisements in the books about rhetorical style and delivery, especially, warn against the effeminate, from diction that is too made up—colored with rouge and kinked with curling irons—to gestures and gaits that seem limp or swishy. In this way, he followed the lead of masculinity-gripped discussants in Cicero's rhetorical works (Connolly, 2010).

Likely during the same decade in which Quintilian wrote the *Institutio*, the orator and historian Tacitus (ca. 56–117 C.E.) contributed to the discussion about oratorical education in his *Dialogus de oratoribus* (Dialogue of the Orators). Set in the mid-60s, the dialogue purports to put poetry on trial after one of the discussants opts to leave the squabble of the forum for the quiet of Mount Helicon. In an effort to defend the oratorical life, his friends begin to wonder about its merit, especially as compared to earlier times. The last third of their debate (§28–41) turns to finger-pointing about why oratory no longer reaches the heights, and one interlocutor even blames the damaging influence of glib Greek nursemaids (§29).

The satirists Petronius (27–66 C.E.) and Lucian (ca. 125–ca. 180 C.E.) both address professors of rhetoric who are catering to the nouveau riche and encouraging affectations of learnedness. Petronius's narrator, Encolpius, begins the *Satyricon* with a swipe at rhetoricians who feed their students sickly sweet compositions and encourage them to create the same, and he argues for a return to the old, rigorous, gradual method of training in eloquence (1–4). Similarly, Lucian envisions two competing educational approaches to rhetoric, the one arduous and its pupils reserved, the other easy and its pupils flamboyant (*Rhetorum praeceptor*).

One ancient educational debate occurring anew concerns rhetoric's decline narrative, begun in the writings of Cicero during the disintegration of the republic and continued in various texts written throughout the series of emperors that followed. According to that narrative, the "death" of the republic marked the end of public eloquence able to steer events. Since the late twentieth century, however, scholars have argued that post-Republican orators could and did, in fact, put their talents and efforts toward civic purposes, especially bureaucratic and epideictic (ceremonial) ones (see, e.g., Walker, 2000, *Rhetoric and Poetics*). Kathleen Lamp (2013) has explored the rhetorical interactions between Augustus (63 B.C.E.–14 C.E.) and the Roman people, pointing out that the study and practice of rhetoric during the *res publica* was a decidedly elite and often antipopulist affair that we ought not to romanticize as the democratic antithesis to the autocratic.

After training with a *grammaticus*, a *rhetoricus*, and perhaps also with a philosopher or two, elite Roman men would begin an apprenticeship (*tirocinium*) through which they would receive training in their occupation. Before that, however, wealthy young men of highly cultured families often traveled to Greece or Asia Minor to complete their formal educations. For many, that entailed the extensive study of logic, dialectic, ethics, and other traditional provinces of philosophy. Such travel, akin to the current-day *peregrinatio academica*, was formative for some and utterly transformative for others. In his *De finibus bonorum et malorum* (On the Ends of Goods and Evils), Cicero recalls the academic trek to Athens he and friends undertook upon the completion of their at-home learning with tutors. The young men marvel breathlessly as they move from the site of Plato's Academy to the wave-clanging bay of Piraeus where Demosthenes built up his vocal power. Piso exclaims that the pleasure of hearing about one's intellectual idols and reading their works pales in comparison to the thrill of stepping through their haunts (5.1). As a father, Cicero wrote his hugely historically influential, Stoic-oriented *De officiis* (On Duties; 44 B.C.E.) for his son, who was supposed to be studying philosophy in Athens but was misbehaving, not unlike some students today when they leave home for college.

The pedagogical practicalities of rhetorical instruction. The process of becoming habituated into a rhetorical way of thinking, speaking, and being required a student to possess inborn talent (*ingenium*), study exemplary orators and treatises (*imitatio, ars*), and flex his oratorical muscles (*exertatio*). The most well-known set of preparatory exercises are the *progymnasmata*, a term clearly borrowed from athletics. They are usually counted as fourteen, ranging from vivid description (*ekphrasis*) to invective (*psogos*), and all prepared an aspiring orator to address facets of real rhetorical situations he might face. *Progymnasmata* also socialized elite young men to think of themselves as culturally entitled to speak in public and to speak up for others who were not permitted to speak. Through the *progymnasma* of character making (*ēthopoeia*), they learned to craft language that sounded like those who could not speak in a particular public setting (a mother) or at all (a murdered person) (see Bloomer, 1997, "Schooling in Persona"; Fleming, 2003).

Training in *declamatio* (declamation) became a staple of the school curriculum in the first century

B.C.E. and was distinguished by two types of practice speeches: *controversiae* (mock judicial speeches) and *suasoriae* (mock deliberative speeches). One ancient source for declamatory practices is Seneca the Elder (54 B.C.E.–39 C.E.), who reflects on the sorts of topics upon which he and his fellow students declaimed (*Controversiae* and *Suasoriae*). A debate related to the decline narrative of rhetoric debate concerns the role of declamation. Did it encourage useless, directionless chatter about far-fetched and fanciful topics? Or was declamation a kind of preparatory play that encouraged the kind of inventiveness that makes for nimble orators? Both Tacitus (§35) and Petronius (1–4) scoffed at the utility of declamation, but Erik Gunderson has countered that "in their declamation we…see Romans coming to be, and not a dying rhetoric passing away" (2003, p. 25).

Women's Places in Ancient Roman Education. Women found their educational opportunities shaped by their familial relationships. The families into which they were born and to which they in turn gave birth after marriage closed or opened portals of educational engagement. Sometimes even, the tightest family bonds could be liberating: daughters of certain elite men likely received additional instruction and encouragement from their fathers beyond what they received from in-home tutors, even gaining the confidence to participate in public life.

Cornelia (ca. 191–100 B.C.E.), the daughter of the general Scipio Africanus, wife of Tiberius Sempronius Gracchus, and mother of Tiberius and Gaius Gracchus, received a first-rate education and took great care over that of her sons. She receives the highest of praise from several orators, especially for the eloquence of the advisory letters she wrote to her sons, which evidently circulated beyond them to wider readerships (e.g., Cicero, *Brutus* §104, §211; Quintilian 1.1.6–7). Though few, if any, of their own words survive, the daughters of several illustrious republican consuls are worth mentioning because of the historical afterlives their family names afforded them: Hortensia, daughter of Hortensius; Porcia, daughter of Cato the Younger and wife of Brutus; and Tullia, daughter of Cicero. Of the three, only Hortensia took her learning into the public sphere.

Famously, and not without scandal, she spoke publicly in front of the Second Triumvirate when they levied upon women of her class a sizeable tax in 43 B.C.E. Quintilian adds that her speech was still read in his time—that is, more than 100 years postdelivery—"and not merely as a compliment to her sex" (1.1.6). She was successful in getting the tax reduced, and a version of her speech is preserved in the *Civil Wars* of Appian (ca. 95–ca. 165 C.E.).

Poetic and philosophical texts, too, feature traces of educated women. The *docta puella* (learned girl) was a fixture of elegiac poetry that seems unlikely to have been a fiction, given the status of women in the same social circles as the poets who invoke the figure (James, 2003). The learned girl was educated enough to appreciate the highly allusive poetry she ostensibly inspired. The most famous *doctae puellae* are Catullus's Lesbia, Ovid's Corinna, Propertius's Cynthia, and Tibellus's Delia, all pseudonyms. Enjoying a lofty position in the poetic tradition is the sixth-century B.C.E. lyric poet Sappho. For instance, the author of *Peri hupsous* (On Heights), usually referred to as Longinus, esteemed her verses as a model of *hupsos*, ranking her alongside Plato, Demosthenes, and even the writer of Genesis. The Stoic school of philosophy seems to have accommodated women more readily than some others on the basis of women sharing in virtue.

The wives of emperors are a category unto themselves. The most renowned for her own learnedness and contributions to culture, and philosophical culture in particular, was the Syrian-raised Julia Domna (170–217 C.E.), wife of the Emperor Septimius Severus. Among her circle was the sophist Philostratus (170–247 C.E.), who wrote, inter alia, a biography of Apollonius of Tyana, a wandering wise man of the first century C.E. whom early Christians likened to Jesus.

[*See also* Children, *subentry* Roman World; Education, *subentries on* Early Church, Greek World, *and* New Testament; Family Structures, *subentry* Roman World; *and* Legal Status, *subentry* Roman World.]

BIBLIOGRAPHY

Bloomer, W. Martin. "Schooling in Persona: Imagination and Subordination in Roman Education." *Classical Antiquity* 16, no. 1 (1997): 57–78.

Bloomer, W. Martin. *The School of Rome: Latin Studies and the Origins of Liberal Education.* Berkeley: University of California Press, 2011.

Bonner, Stanley F. *Education in Ancient Rome: From the Elder Cato to the Younger Pliny.* Berkeley: University of California Press, 1977.

Connolly, Joy. "Virile Tongues: Rhetoric and Masculinity." In *A Companion to Roman Rhetoric*, edited by William Dominik and Jon Hall, pp. 83–97. Malden, Mass.: Blackwell, 2007.

de Jonge, Casper C. *Between Grammar and Rhetoric: Dionysius of Halicarnassus on Language, Linguistics and Literature.* Leiden, The Netherlands: Brill, 2008.

Fleming, J. David. "The Very Idea of a *Progymnasmata*." *Rhetoric Review* 22, no. 2 (2003): 105–120.

Gunderson, Erik. *Declamation, Paternity, and Roman Identity: Authority and the Rhetorical Self.* New York: Cambridge University Press, 2003.

James, Sharon L. *Learned Girls and Male Persuasion: Gender and Reading in Roman Love Elegy.* Berkeley: University of California Press, 2003.

Joyal, Mark, Iain McDougall, and J. C. Yardley. *Greek and Roman Education: A Sourcebook.* New York: Routledge, 2009.

Lamp, Kathleen S. *A City of Marble: The Rhetoric of Augustan Rome.* Columbia: University of South Carolina, 2013.

Marrou, H. I. *A History of Education in Antiquity.* Translated by George Lamb. New York: Sheed & Ward, 1956.

Morgan, Teresa. *Literate Education in the Hellenistic and Roman Worlds.* New York: Cambridge University Press, 1998.

Walker, Jeffrey. *The Genuine Teachers of This Art: Rhetorical Education in Antiquity.* Columbia: University of South Carolina, 2011.

Walker, Jeffrey. *Rhetoric and Poetics in Antiquity.* New York: Oxford University Press, 2000.

Michele Kennerly

New Testament

Like other first- and second-century texts, the New Testament does not have much to say about education directly. The apostles' lack of an elite education in rhetoric (*agrammatos,* "illiterate," and *idiōtēs,* "plebian" or "unskilled") makes Peter's boldness astonishing to the Sanhedrin (Acts 4:13). Like most children who will follow their parents as farmers, fishermen, or craftspersons, young boys may have acquired rudimentary ability to write, read, or use numbers at home. Unlike the wealthy elite who could advance from rudimentary instruction in letters to sustained study with a teacher (*bêt midraš,* "house of instruction," Sir 51:23) and then even leave home for advanced instruction in rhetoric, philosophy, or Torah (Acts 22:3), boys would begin working at nine or ten. Girls were expected to master the domestic skills expected of wives. Papyri remains indicate that while more women than men lacked the ability to put their name on documents, some women had enough Greek to sign their names and even draft their own letters. Elite women took pride in a more fluent literacy and are sometimes depicted with a book roll (Rowlandson, 1998, pp. 299–303).

Some mothers may have provided the initial training in writing letters and words for young children. At the other end of the educational spectrum, few of the elite completed the five- or six-year training of an accomplished orator. Doing so was a sign of wealth or political ambition (Cribiore, 2001, p. 224). Paul's claim to have advanced beyond others his age "in Judaism" because he was extraordinarily "zealous for my ancestral traditions" (Gal 1:14) suggests a comparable ambition within a Jewish educational setting. Rhetorically, Paul invokes the status attributed to those who completed such advanced training to undermine the authority of opposing teachers in Galatia in a way that would be familiar to his gentile audience. Whether or not he actually completed it remains unclear, since the comparable appeal to impeccable Jewish credentials in Philippians 3:4b–6 does not employ the educational motif in asserting Paul's former zeal.

Training Young Jews in Torah. Jewish sources understand the parental obligation to discipline sons (Sir 7:23) as providing an education in Torah. And 4 Maccabees 18:10–19 depicts this paternal instruction in "the law and the prophets" spanning the whole sweep of the canonical story from Abel, Isaac, and Joseph to Ezekiel's vision of dried bones restored to life. The story concludes with Moses's teaching, "I [= God] kill and I make alive," (Deut 32:39; cf. 30:20). Nor is instruction limited to males and a few elite women as would have been the case for literature or philosophy. The entire populace is invested in Torah observance (Neh 8:2–3); 2 Timothy 3:14–17 attributes the learning of Paul's trusted younger associate Timothy (Phil 2:22) to his mother and grandmother. Their teaching involves Jewish scriptures, "the sacred letters" as well as Christian faith (2 Tim 3:15). Greek-speaking Jews would have agreed with the value of providing such an education (*paideia*) from a young age, "all scripture is God-inspired and useful for instruction, for conviction [of the sinner], for correction, for education in righteousness (v. 16; Marshall, 1999, pp. 787–795).

Jewish apologists depict the sabbath assemblies as the occasion for spreading knowledge of virtue throughout the entire populace (Josephus, *Ag. Ap.* 1.60; 2.170–178, 204; Philo, *De spec. leg.* 2.62). Unlike most peoples who require experts to deal with their laws, any Jew can repeat their laws readily: "we have them as if engraved on our souls" (Josephus, *Ag. Ap.* 2.178). The male head of a Jewish household is responsible for transmitting knowledge of Torah to his wife, children, and slaves (Philo, *Hypothetica* in Eusebius, *Praep. Ev.* 8.7.14). A similar obligation for education in scripture and the virtues that derive from imitating ancestral examples is implicit in Christian "household code" material. Bishops must be capable managers of their own households, keeping children disciplined with all serious conduct (*semnotēs*, 1 Tim 3:4). Debates over whether the respectable or serious conduct is a trait of the father or the children is somewhat beside the point, since the intent is for parents and teachers to provide the model imitated by the young (Marshall, p. 480). Ephesians 6:4 uses more explicitly educational terminology, "raise them in the discipline (*paideia*) and instruction (*nouthesia*) of the Lord." Since "Lord" clearly refers to Jesus in Ephesians, the author has a form of Christian training or character formation in view rather than the "law and the prophets" of the Jewish examples.

Torah Study, Reading, and Writing. To describe the sabbath gatherings as schools of virtue (Philo, *De spec. leg.* 2,62) does not indicate whether or not Jews had a higher rate of literacy than that of the larger population. Individuals might learn Torah through hearing it read and expounded. For example, in the messianic rule of the Qumran covenanters the gathering includes women and children as well as males, "they shall assemble… including children and women, and they shall read into [their] ears all the precepts of the covenant, and shall instruct them in all their regulations, so that they do not stray in [their errors]," (1 QSa i, 4–5; Martínez and Tigchelaar, trans.). The inscription from a Jerusalem synagogue says that it was built by the priest Theodotus Vettinus, "for reading the Law and teaching the commandments," (Snyder, 2000, p. 178). Depictions of the diaspora synagogues in Acts also presume that instruction involved oral commentary on the Law (Moses) and the prophets (Acts 13:15; 15:21). Since Paul encounters prominent female "God-fearer" Lydia at the place of prayer in Philippi (Acts 16:11–15), it would appear that women and perhaps children were routinely present in the sabbath assembly.

Although these examples only require a few individuals able to read the written texts, other pieces of evidence associate literacy with Torah commentary. A child's education began as copying individual letters, letter combinations, and eventually brief passages. Writing preceded reading in elementary pedagogy (Cribiore). *Jubilees* 12.25–27 has Abram instructed in Hebrew, the language spoken by all humanity prior to the fall. He must copy ancestral books in Hebrew before beginning to study them. Not all texts used in some form of public instruction were copied out by individuals who were able to write fluidly. The commentary on Habakkuk from Qumran was apparently copied out letter by letter. Inability to process words and phrases in copying suggests that the individual writer was not very literate (Snyder, 2000, p. 145). Hermas, the Christian visionary in early second century C.E. Rome, has similar difficulty copying out the small book transmitted by Lady Church: "I took it to a certain place in the field and copied it all letter by letter because I was having trouble separating the syllables. When I had completed the little book it was suddenly snatched out of my hand" (*Shepherd of*

Hermas, 2.1.4; Osiek, trans., 1999). Hermas is told to disseminate the written revelation for instruction in the community. Inclusion of a woman, Grapte, among the recipients, suggests that her role in admonishing (*nouthetein*) women is correlated with an ability to read (Osiek, 1999, p. 14). Similarly, Luke's depiction of Jesus teaching during a sabbath assembly (Luke 4:16–30) assumes that he has first read from an Isaiah scroll. Luke may be presuming a model typical of the more advanced teaching in schools generally rather than the specific practices of first-century Galilean synagogues (Snyder, 2000, p. 179). Even in the *Shepherd of Hermas,* most of the subsequent instruction relies on oral teaching and memory rather than reading the revealed text (Osiek, 1999, p. 15).

Therefore, while sects within Judaism like the Qumran covenanters that advocate continuous, sustained study of "the book of Moses and the prophets and the writings of David" (4 QMMT [= 4Q 397] 14,21) may have possessed a high degree of literacy among members, it does not follow that Jews generally differed from the larger population. Most would not have been educated beyond the rudiments of scratching out one's name, recognizing some words, and figuring taught at home. Examples of such low-level literacy include tomb inscriptions, graffiti scratched on stone, lists of goods, public notices, and the numbers used to guide builders (Millard, 2000, pp. 88–123). Facility with reading and writing demanded a level of education available only to the elite (ibid., pp. 154–158). Such a class distinction is particularly evident in the case of literate women. Since girls were married by their mid-teens, they did not have the later teens to go away to study with a famous teacher that their brothers did. Consequently, those women who were literate enough to read scrolls—not merely sign their names or scratch out a few words—must have belonged to wealthy families (Taylor, 2003, pp. 94–96).

Who Were the Scribes? Scribes are referred to in the Gospels frequently in phrases that suggest they were a distinct group with some legal expertise and teaching authority (Mark 11:18; Luke 6:7; Matt 5:20). Trying to determine the level of education possessed by scribes proves more difficult. Other sources do not support the assumption that "the scribes" formed a well-defined class (Schams, 1998, pp. 100–104). It is difficult to discern what distinguished sage, scholar, and scribe in Sirach 38:32—39:11, for example. Each one combines elements of skill, knowledge, and piety. Josephus refers to scribes at various levels of society. Some are government officials in various capacities (*J.W.* i, p. 529; cf. Sir 39:4); others associated with the Jerusalem Temple (*J.W.* v, p. 532), and still others at a lower village level perform functions that required literacy (*J.W.,* i, p. 479). The sort of commercial literacy necessary for government or even record keeping in the Temple did not mean that such scribes could read or compose a text in classical Hebrew. Thus there is a difference between scribes in first-century C.E. society and the older image of a scribe as the master of the ancient textual tradition in Nehemiah 8, for example.

Given the number of scrolls containing texts employed by members of the new covenant community, one might expect some reference to scribes in the Dead Sea Scrolls. But the only examples are references to highly esteemed ancient figures such as Enoch ("scribe of righteousness," *1 Enoch* 12:4; 15:1; 92:1) and David (11 Q Ps^a 27.2, in a list extolling his wisdom, piety, and literary work). This association of scribes and revered figures from the past surfaces in Matthew 23:34, "I send you prophets, sages, and scribes." Matthew 13:52 suggests that there may have been Christian scribes, including the evangelist, who provided leadership in some early Christian communities. Thus the older sense of the scribe as one able to instruct others in the religious tradition sits alongside the more routine bureaucratic official, the purveyor of day-to-day literate skills, and the narrative characterization in the Gospels, a member of a group opposed to Jesus.

Scribes within the narrative world of the Gospels and the Jewish scriptures are all males as are those mentioned in Josephus. The story of Jesus and the woman taken in adultery incorporated into the Fourth Gospel at John 7:53—8:11 confirms Jesus's position as "learned" in the written tradition despite the lack of such education possessed by persons of his social class (John 7:14–17). Teaching the people in the Temple area sets Jesus up for this challenge by the scribes and Pharisees. By twice writing on the ground (John 8:6, 8), Jesus silently demonstrates possession of the scribal literacy that would permit him to determine a case raised by the Torah of Moses.

Although the New Testament does not contain any women functioning as "scribes" in a religious, administrative, or village capacity, scholars have found some evidence for female scribes (Haines-Eitzen, 2000). Eusebius comments that Origen's patron provided shorthand writers (*tachugraphoi*), copyists (*bibliographoi*), and girls trained for beautiful writing (*korais epi to kalligraphein 'ēskēmenais*; Eusebius, *Hist. eccl.* 6.23). At least eleven women are identified as "scribes" in epigraphic evidence from Rome, some serving as clerk-secretaries or copyists. Girls competed in contests for "fine writing" in Pergamum. An early second-century C.E. marble relief depicts a woman record keeper in a butcher's shop. Though it may have been more typical to find female scribes associated with literate elite women as was the case with the amanuensis for Egnatia Maximilla, who went into exile with her husband under Nero (Tacitus, *Ann.* 15.71), both Origen's "fine writers" and the butcher's record keeper show that they also worked for males (Haines-Eitzen, 2000, pp. 5–47). None of our earliest New Testament papyri were copied by scribes trained in the book-hand that "fine writing" requires. Like others of the record-keeping, document-producing class who occasionally copied literary works, these Christian scribes write more legibly than in documents or private letters but lack the techniques of educated literary copyists (ibid., pp. 63–68). Therefore, it is possible that a very inexperienced hand, using irregular letter forms and spacing between letters, such as the scribe responsible for P[72] (1–2 Pet, Jude, third century C.E.) was female. Even if women were not the authors of any New Testament books, women could have served as the scribes who copied them.

Schooling in Christian House Churches. The presence of children in Christian households (1 Cor 7:14b) as well as the assumption that non-Jewish believers will know and apply exempla from the Torah to their own experience (e.g., 1 Cor 10:1–13; 2 Cor 3:7–18) suggest that some form of education occurred in house churches. Scholars have tended to look to the philosophical school as a model for exhortation in the Pauline churches, but little attention has been paid to the education of children and slaves at home. In the second century C.E. Celsus accused Christians of encouraging children who rebelled against the legitimate authority of fathers and schoolmasters (Origen, *Against Celsus* 3.55). Perhaps the training children received in the house churches fueled such suspicions as well as the emphasis on obedience to paternal authority in the household codes (e.g., Eph 6:4; MacDonald, 2011, pp. 88–89).

To what extent did women educate other members of house churches, adults as well as children? The New Testament does not provide a direct answer. Those women who were patrons, hosting a church community, are more likely to be literate and/or have slaves with that skill than lower-class members of the group (Taylor, pp. 94–96). Some passages in the Dead Sea Scrolls appear to refer to female elders (4Q 502) or "trustworthy women" (4Q 159), indicating that some women were at least distinguished for their knowledge of sectarian Torah observance. They may have played a role in educating children and other less learned members of the sect. Several passages in the New Testament suggest controversy over women teaching, and Paul in 1 Timothy 2:12 prohibits a woman from either teaching or having authority over a man. The first-person-present tense verb, "I am not permitting" suggests a newly imposed regulation. Since the noun *didaskalia* ("teaching") is used for the received, apostolic teachings in the Pastoral Epistles, the cognate verb *didaskein* must refer to instructing the congregation, not some private conversation about the faith (Marshall, p. 455).

The Pastoral Epistles adopt a rhetorical tactic of portraying women as particularly susceptible to false teachers who invade households with the intent of capturing "silly women," leading them into all sorts of sin (2 Tim 3:6–7). Instruction in the scriptures should be the remedy for such gullibility much as some recommended that women study philosophy rather than engage in the thoughtless behavior typical of females (e.g., Seneca, *Moral Essays* 2.14, 1). Timothy had received such instruction since childhood, first from his mother and grandmother, later from Paul himself (2 Tim 5; 2:2; 3:14–15; Marshall, pp. 787–789). Elsewhere in the Pastoral Epistles, revered older women charged with teaching younger women how to properly manage a household are referred to as "good teachers" (*kalodidaskaloi;* Titus 2:3). It remains unclear whether these female elders (*presbutidas*) provide instruction in the scriptures or merely serve to inculcate by example culturally admired virtues of piety, self-control, and devotion to one's family. Emphasis on the latter is generally correlated with the suggestion that conversion of subordinate members of the household (women, children, slaves) left the churches open to criticism and pressure from outsiders (Marshall, pp. 243–250).

It is difficult to say whether denying women the authority to teach men and describing older women teaching younger ones proper deportment and household management have been introduced as new restrictions. Are women being pushed aside from roles as teachers in the house churches? But there is no question about the prominence of a female prophet teaching in Thyatira (Rev 2:20–23). John excoriates her as a new "Jezebel" for leading the faithful astray into sexual immorality and eating idol-meat, stock accusations that provide no information about her actual teaching. His oracle threatens her and her followers ("children") with death, "and all the churches will know that I [= God] am the one who searches minds and hearts and will repay each of you as your works deserve" (v. 23b). The author demands that believers in Thyatira, "who do not hold this teaching" (v. 24), drop any association with "Jezebel" or her followers. How plausible such a dissociation would have been depends upon the size and demographics of house churches in that city.

Since early Christian communities depended upon the reading and interpretation of texts from the Greek translation of the Jewish scriptures, letters from the apostles, and by the second-century "memoirs of the apostles," possession of texts and ability to read them was essential. If the "Jezebel" of Thyatira was not engaged in the inspired oral prophecy associated with women elsewhere in the New Testament (e.g., 1 Cor 11:3–16; Acts 21:9) but had a school in

her house, then believers may have been less willing to cut her off as a teacher than Revelation would suggest. The possibility that the Christian visionary of Revelation finds himself pitted against other teachers with access to the written scriptures adds another dimension to the heavenly scrolls associated with the Apocalypse (Rev 5:1; 10:9–10).

Scrolls are the medium in which literary works are disseminated. Funerary depictions of women holding scrolls claim that the deceased belonged to the wealthy elite able to educate its daughters. When opened by the Lamb, the scroll with seven seals unleashes the first series of plagues (Rev 5:1—6:1). But it possesses a peculiar feature, writing on both sides (Rev 5:1), not the format of a usable scroll text. Scholars recognize the allusion to Ezekiel 2:9–10 and a similar scroll with writing on the outside pictured at Dura Europus. However artistic representations of readers show the scroll open across their laps with writing on one side only. Codex pages are inscribed on both sides. Perhaps the seer of Revelation is not himself literate at the elite level. He eats the little scroll received from the hand of an angel in Revelation 10, a collage of allusions to Ezekiel and other passages from the scriptures (Ezek 2:9–10; 3:1–3; Ps 119:103). By associating his visionary prophecy with heavenly scrolls, just as he had co-opted the authority of apostolic letters by opening with seven letters from the Son of Man to the angels of seven churches (Rev 2:1—3:22), the seer trumps human claims to authority based on reading and interpreting written texts.

[*See also* Education, *subentries on* Early Church, Early Judaism, *and* Roman World; Family Structures, *subentry* Roman World; *and* Religious Leaders, *subentry* New Testament.]

BIBLIOGRAPHY

Bowman, A. K., and G. Woolf, eds. *Literacy and Power in the Ancient World.* Cambridge, U.K.: Cambridge University Press, 1994.

Carr, D. M. *Writing on the Tablet of the Heart: The Origin of Scripture and Literature.* New York: Oxford University Press, 2005.

Cribiore, R. *Gymnastics of the Mind: Greek Education in Hellenistic and Roman Egypt.* Princeton, N.J.: Princeton University Press, 2001.

Haines-Eitzen, K. *Guardians of Letters: Literacy, Power, and the Transmitters of Early Christian Literature*. New York: Oxford University Press, 2000.

Harris, W. V. *Ancient Literacy*. Cambridge, Mass.: Harvard University Press, 1989.

Johnson, W. A., and H. N. Parker, eds. *The Culture of Reading in Greece and Rome*. Oxford: Oxford University Press, 2009.

MacDonald, M. Y. "Beyond Identification of the Topos of Household Management: Reading the Household Codes in Light of Recent Methodologies and Theoretical Perspectives in the Study of the New Testament." *New Testament Studies* 57 (2011): 65–90.

Marshall, I. H. *The Pastoral Epistles*. Edinburgh: T&T Clark, 1999.

Millard, A. *Reading and Writing in the Time of Jesus*. Sheffield, U.K.: Sheffield Academic Press, 2000.

Morgan, T. *Literate Education in the Hellenistic and Roman Worlds*. Cambridge, U.K.: Cambridge University Press, 1998.

Osiek, C. *The Shepherd of Hermas: A Commentary*. Hermeneia. Minneapolis: Fortress, 1999.

Rowlandson, J., ed. *Women and Society in Greek and Roman Egypt*. Cambridge, U.K.: Cambridge University Press, 1998.

Schams, C. *Jewish Scribes in the Second Temple Period*. Sheffield, U.K.: Sheffield Academic Press, 1998.

Smith, C. S. *Pauline Communities as "Scholastic Communities": A Study of the Vocabulary of "Teaching" in 1 Corinthians, 1 & 2 Timothy and Titus*. Tübingen, Germany: Mohr Siebeck, 2012.

Snyder, H. G. *Teachers and Texts in the Ancient World: Philosophers, Jews, and Christians*. London: Routledge, 2000.

Taylor, J. E. *Jewish Women Philosophers of First Century Alexandria: Philo's "Therapeutae" Reconsidered*. Oxford: Oxford University Press, 2003.

Pheme Perkins

Early Judaism

Literary sources suggest that education for children and adults was an important component of social and intellectual life for ancient Jews, especially boys and men, and centered primarily on the study of Torah. Our knowledge of the social reality of ancient Jewish education, however, is limited both by the nature of the extant sources, which are typically more prescriptive and idealizing than descriptive, and by the fact that the authors of these sources were, by definition, of the literate, educated elite, i.e., those who most valued education. Ancient Jewish educational ideals and institutions may also be viewed within a broader cultural landscape that included Greek *paideia*, Roman epigraphical habits and legal codification, Christian *askesis*, and East Syrian scholasticism (Becker, 2010; Hezser, 2001; Najman, 2010; Satlow, 2003).

The Value of Torah Study. In biblical passages, God commands the people of Israel to devote their time to meditating on and learning God's commandments (Deut 4:9, 6:7, 6:20–25, 11:19, 31:9–13, 31:22, 32:7; Exod 13:14) and such practice was portrayed as worship of God (Pss 119:54; 135). Building on earlier Wisdom traditions (Job 28; Prov 8), Ben Sira identifies God's companion Wisdom (*hokhmah*), who was present at the world's creation, with the Torah of Moses (Sir 24). Going further, the rabbinic midrash Genesis Rabbah opens with a portrayal of the Torah aiding God in creation and serving as the blueprint of the world (*Gen. Rab.* 1:1; *m. Avot* 3:14, 3 *Enoch* 41). Pursuit of the Torah through study and interpretation, then, is part of comprehending the fabric of the created world as Second Temple and rabbinic Jews envisioned it. It was not only an intellectual endeavor and a religious practice, but also a way of accessing the divine (*m. Avot* 3:2; *Sifre Deut* 49).

At Qumran, a significant portion of each day and night was devoted to the study of Torah (1QS 6:6–7). Philo values study as the exercising of the soul on the sabbath as well as on regular days, and as the pursuit of ordinary people and those who devote the entirety of their lives to philosophical endeavors (Philo, *Spec.* II.15.60–64; *Hyp.* 7:12–14; *Contempl.*). Josephus similarly boasts about the education the entire community—men, women, children—received during public gatherings, and highlights the command to teach children in particular (*C. Ap.* 2:175–178, 2:204).

In rabbinic sources, teaching and studying Torah is regarded as a most important and sacred practice (e.g., *m. Pe'ah* 1:1; cf. *t. Pe'ah* 4:19). For the rabbis, Torah study included the written law (scripture) and the oral law (rabbinic traditions), which together constituted "Torah" writ large (*Sifra Behukotai* 2; *Sifre Deut.* 351; *Lev. Rab.* 22; *y. Ber.* 1.7, 3b; *b. Hag.* 6b; *b. Shabb.* 31a;

Seder Eliyahu Zuta 2; *Tanhuma Ki Tisa* 34) and formed the curricular backbone. One midrash contrasts the merits of "study" and "deeds" and concludes that "study" is preeminent because it leads to good "deeds" (*Sifre Deut* 41; cf. *b. Sotah* 21a), though the logic of the narrative somewhat undermines this hierarchy by suggesting that the ultimate goal of study is righteous action (Hirshman, 2006). In another midrash, Torah study is regarded as so powerful that it protected a person from the evil inclination (*Sifre Deut* 45).

In the Babylonian Talmud, Rabbi Akiva's greatness as a teacher is stressed through his numerous—24,000—students (*b. Yeb.* 62b). Rabbi Shimon bar Yohai did not cease his study even to recite the Shema (*y. Ber.* 1:3, 3c; *Sifrei Deut* 42). It is a great misfortune to withhold teachings from others or to waste one's time in matters unrelated to learning (*Song. Rab.* 2:5; *b. Sanh.* 91b; *b. Sanh.* 99a), and someone who teaches his son Torah is rewarded as though he "taught him, his son and his son's son until the end of all time!" (*b. Qidd.* 30a). Not least, God is described as spending three hours each day teaching schoolchildren in heaven (*b. Avod. Zar.* 3a–b), and the world continues to exist because of the purity of schoolchildren (*b. Shabb.* 119b).

Literacy and Elementary Education. Education during the Second Temple period was centered in priestly and scribal circles, although basic primary education likely took place in the home (Sir 7:23). Sources describe Aaron and Levi—representatives of the priestly caste—as teachers of God's laws (Sir 45:17; *Jub.* 31:15–17; 45:15; *T. Levi* 13:2–3). But the Torah was also regarded as belonging to the entire nation, available for study by everyone. After the destruction of the Temple it was no longer priests who were charged with educational tasks (Baumgarten, 2001; 2 Macc 2:13–15; *m. Avot* 1:1).

In Tannaitic times (70–220 C.E.), it was still seen as a parental responsibility to teach children, though by the amoraic period (220–450 C.E.) that work was often delegated to professional teachers (*m. Qidd.* 4:14; *t. Hag.* 1:2; *y. Ket.* 8:11, 32c; *Gen. Rab.* 63; *b. Sukkah* 42a; *b. Qidd.* 29a–30b; *b. Ketub.* 50a; *b. B. Bat.* 21a). The Babylonian Talmud specifies that a father must teach his *son* Torah and a craft, and another opinion

adds that he must also teach his son to swim (*b. Qidd.* 29a). Elementary education in the rabbinic period was devoted to teaching male children how to read and interpret scripture (*torah*) and law (*mishnah*), and was eventually regarded as an essential institution in all cities and villages (*m. Shabb.* 1:3; *t. Meg.* 3:38; *Sifre Deut.* 19; *y. Hag.* 1, 76c; *y. Meg.* 4, 73d; *y. Ta'an.* 4, 69a–b; *B. Bat.* 21a; *b. Sanh.* 17b; *b. Shavu.* 5a). Schools were sometimes connected with synagogues (*y. Ketub.* 13:1, 35c; *y. Meg.* 3:1, 74a). Sources insist that each child was to be included, regardless of social and financial background, and such opportunity was highly valued (*b. Shavu.* 5a; *Abot R. Nat.* 3; Hirshman, 2006). Even Jerome muses about the Jews, "In childhood they acquire the complete vocabulary of their language and learn to recite all the generations from Adam to Zerubbabel with such accuracy and facility as if they were simply giving their names" (Jerome, *Letter to Titus* 3:9, cf. Jerome's commentary to Isa. 58:2, CCSL 73:660; Hirshman, 2006). The Babylonian Talmud, in a saying attributed to Rabbi Judah the Patriarch, states, "One does not suspend the studies of the school children even for the building of the Temple" (*b. Shabb.* 119b), a hyperbolic statement that highlights the importance of elementary education. The category of *Am Haaretz* ("people of the land") derogatively refers, in rabbinic sources (e.g., *b. Ber.* 47b), to those whom the rabbis considered to be uneducated in Torah and its practices (Safrai, 1968).

Presumably, relatively few families had the interest in cultivating such skills and piety or could afford to send their sons to school and forgo their sons' income. Our knowledge of literacy in this period supports this assumption: in the first few centuries C.E. literacy was not common among those beyond the political, administrative, and cultural elites, while by the third century literacy seems to have become more widespread, as indicated by material evidence including burial and synagogue inscriptions and documentary and epigraphical sources (Hezser, 2001). Those children who did attend schools began to study between the ages of five and seven and concluded their studies between the ages of twelve or thirteen (*m. Avot* 5:22; *b. B. Bat.* 21a;

b. Ketub. 50a). Should a boy be inclined and sufficiently talented, he would continue to study with a rabbinic sage thereafter, but few seem to have advanced so far (*Lev. Rab.* 2:1).

Girls and women seem to have been excluded from formal educational institutions. Even so, rabbinic sources mention the possibility of women being called publicly to read from the Torah (*t. Meg.* 3:11–12; *b. Meg.* 23a) and teaching (*m. Qidd.* 4:13; *y. Qidd.* 4:11, 66c). Despite a lack of formal educational opportunities, we can also assume that women were informed about laws pertaining to food preparation, menstrual and other forms of impurity, family matters, and rabbinic teachings, and that they acquired this knowledge from their homes and other informal and noninstitutionalized means of education (Beer, 2005; Hauptman, 2010; cf. *t. Kel. B. Bat.* 1.6; *t. Kel. B. Qam.* 4.17; *t. Nid.* 6:8; *y. Shabb.* 4.1, 6d; *y. Shabb.* 1:3, 3b; *y. Hallah* 1:5, 57d; *y. Bets.* 2:1, 61b; *y. Bets.* 4.5, 62c; *b. Bets.* 32b; *b. Ketub.* 63a; *b. Shabb.* 134a; *b. Eruv.* 53b; *b. Nid.* 24b; *b. Nid.* 48b; *Lam. Rab.* 1.19).

The education of gentiles in matters of biblical interpretation and Jewish law was also a point of contention, some rabbinic sources arguing that study ought to remain within Jewish rabbinic circles and others permitting and even encouraging outreach to gentiles (*Sifre Deut* 33:4; *Sifra* on Lev 18:5; *Sifre Num* 1:20; Hirshman, 2006).

Construction of Gender through Rabbinic Study.
Ancient Jewish "maleness" was constructed through diligent Torah study, and in turn Torah study was gendered as a male practice. Rabbinic sources suggest that only men generally cultivated the necessary self-control required for study (Satlow, 1996; *m. Avot* 4:1; *b. Sanh.* 75a; *b. Qidd.* 80b; *Sifre Deut* 33; *b. Avod. Zar.* 19a; *Gen. Rab.* 22.4). Moreover, the object of study—the Torah, Wisdom—is presented in feminized and eroticized terms (Prov 8; Sir 24; Bar 3:9—4:4; Wis 8:2, 3:10–14), implying that, within a heterosexual paradigm, desire for sexual encounter is (or should be) replaced by the thrill of study and the pursuit of the Torah (Boyarin, 1993; *b. Eruv.* 64a; *b. Sotah* 4b; *Sifre Deut* Piska 402).

Part of the process of defining rabbinic male identity through Torah study was forcefully excluding women from the obligation to study Torah. In its interpretation of Deuteronomy 11:19 ("Teach them to your children [lit. sons]…"), *Sifre Deut* 46 definitively reads women out of the commandment: "'Teach them to your sons'—'your sons' and not your daughters…." The all-encompassing "children" in the biblical passage is reinterpreted in literalist terms by the rabbinic midrash, implying that the obligation refers only to sons, to the exclusion of daughters (cf. *b. Qidd.* 30a, on Deut 6:7). Other rabbinic sources characterize women's study as a waste of time (e.g., *m. Sotah* 3:4, "Rabbi Eliezer says: anyone who teaches his daughter Torah, teaches her nonsense," cf. *b. Sotah* 21b) or even as a dangerous enterprise (e.g., *y. Sotah* 3.4, 19a, which suggests that a woman may use her Torah knowledge to seduce men). This very *mishnah* is actually a response to a comment by Ben Azzai, who requires that a man teach Torah to his daughters (*m. Sotah* 3:4, though *torah* in this passage may simply refer to the laws of adultery). The Tosefta even permits menstruants, postnatal women, and others with bodily impurities to "read Torah, the Prophets, the Writings, the Mishnah, the Midrash, the *halakhot* and *aggadot*" (*t. Ber.* 2:12), implying that regular reading of scripture by women was not unusual. There are in addition narratives about women attending rabbinic sermons in the synagogue (Ilan, 2005; *Lev. Rab.* 9:9) and transmitting rabbinic traditions (Hauptman, 2010: *y. Shabb.* 13:6, 14b; *y. Ter.* 11; 10, 48b; *b. Men.* 68b; *b. Ber.* 39b; *b. Hul.* 44b). In a dialogue with Matrona, Rabbi Leazer declares that "the words of Torah should be burned rather than transmitted to a woman" (*y. Sotah* 3.4, 19a; *Num. Rab.* 9.48; *b. Yoma* 66b).

The polemical tone of many of these statements and the contradictions between them makes it virtually impossible to determine women's actual level of scholastic opportunity and achievement during the long rabbinic period. What seems clearer is that, with time, rabbinic stringencies against women's formal study of Torah developed and did eventually limit women's education, though women continued to learn through informal channels in a variety of contexts.

Rabbinic Institutions. We generally rely on the rabbinic literary corpus itself for information on the nature and venues of rabbinic study as well as curricular matters, however fraught relying on such sources can be. The current scholarly consensus has been articulated by Jeffrey Rubenstein (2007). In the Tannaitic period, rabbinic study was oral and took place primarily in "disciple circles," in which disciples studied with their masters in private dwellings, without proper school buildings, hierarchies, bureaucracies, and curricula (*t. Ber.* 2:13, 4:18; *m. Avot* 1:4). Disciples memorized and interpreted texts and served as personal and judicial apprentices until they were ready to educate their own disciples. Not much is known about the rabbinic "study house" (*bet midrash*) of this early period other than the fact that it seems to have been located in a private home or gatehouse (*t. Shabb.* 2:5, 5:13; *t. Sotah* 13:3). The "House of Hillel" (*bet hillel*) and the "House of Shammai" (*bet shammai*) were likely early disciple circles that met in houses (*m. Shabb.* 1:4), while a somewhat larger school is associated with the family of the Patriarch Rabban Gamaliel (*t. Pesah.* 3:11). Rabbinic and nonrabbinic teaching also took place in other venues, including the marketplace and courtyard (Rubenstein, 2007).

Study houses remained the primary venue of rabbinic teaching also during the amoraic period in Palestine, even as rabbis relocated to larger towns and cities (*y. Ta'an.* 1:2, 64a; *y. Meg.* 4:12, 75c). An inscription found on a lintel of a home in the Golan reads "this is the study house [*bet midrash*] of R. Eliezer HaKappar." Two other terms are also employed in amoraic sources in reference to venues of rabbinic gathering, instruction, and deliberation: "assembly house" (*bet va'ad, be va'ada*; *y. Bik.* 1:8, 64d; *y. Ber.* 4:1, 7d; *y. Shabb.* 10:5, 12c), and "hall" or "great hall" (*sdar, sdara' rabba*; *y. Shabb.* 4:2, 7a; *y. Ta'an* 2:2, 65c; *y. Shabb.* 6:2, 8a). By the end of the amoraic period, a small "academy" (*yeshivah*) had probably been established in the Galilee, and it is perhaps in this setting that the Palestinian Talmud was compiled and edited. Among all five generations of amoraim, the number of rabbis did not exceed 300, plus additional students and sages not mentioned in the sources, suggesting that the level of institutionalization even in this later period was fairly limited (Rubenstein, 2007).

In Babylonia, rabbinic study began after the students of Rabbi Yehudah Ha-Nasi brought the Mishnah to Babylonia around 220 C.E. As in Palestine during the amoraic period, individual rabbinic masters in Babylonia taught independent disciple circles in a "master's house" (*be rav*), and disciples could transfer to another master teacher at will or upon the death of their mentor (*b. Nid. 47a*; *b. Men.* 7a; *b. Ta'an.* 23b–24a; *b. Ta'an.* 9a–b). A shift in institutionalization of education can be detected in the later layers of the Babylonian Talmud, dating from the sixth and seventh centuries C.E.: a permanent rabbinic "academy" (*yeshiva, metivta*) with a highly hierarchical and organized structure was established. The academy catered to anywhere between 50 to 100 full-time students as well as others at any given time. Within the academy, the strongest students sat in the first rows and the weakest were seated in the back, and students were promoted or demoted based on their performance in dialectical discussions. The academy was led by a "head of the academy" (*rosh yeshivah, resh metivta*), who sat in an elevated position in the front (*b. B. Qam.* 117a, b; Goodblatt, 1975; Rubenstein, 2007). The organization of rabbinic academies at this time had striking affinities with contemporaneous East Syrian schools and might indicate a shared scholastic culture in the Mesopotamian region, if not in the content of study then in institutional structure (Becker, 2010).

Curriculum. What did the rabbinic curriculum of study include and entail? In the earliest generations, it was the Hebrew Bible, the "written Torah," and nonwritten rabbinic traditions, the so-called oral Torah, that stood at the center of the rabbinic curriculum. To the extent that we can make any generalizations about the variety of paths of potential study, sources suggest that one began with scripture and moved progressively to more difficult rabbinic traditions. Age was sometimes but not always a factor in determining how to advance in the curriculum (*m. Kin.* 3:6; *m. Avot* 4:20, 5:21; *y. Avod. Zar.* 2:7, 41d; *b. Shabb.* 63a; *b. Ber.* 28a). It has been suggested that instruction in scriptural interpretation began with the book of Leviticus and its priestly laws, as the rabbinic commentary on Leviticus (*Sifra*) contains within it hints of its use early in the educational process. Some rabbis specialized in certain areas, such as nonlegal material (*aggadah*), scriptural interpretation, or liturgy (*Gen. Rab.* 12:10; *b. Avod. Zar.* 4a; *Lev. Rab.* 23:4, 30:1). A late rabbinic midrash describes the curriculum as starting with learning to read and write from a wooden tablet and later a parchment scroll, then advancing to Genesis, the rest of scripture, Mishnah, Sifra (commentary on Leviticus), Mekhilta (commentary on Exodus), Tosefta, Talmud, and last *aggadah* (*Tanhuma*, cf. *t. Sotah* 7:20; *Lev. Rab.* 2:1; *b. Sukkah* 28a; *b. Qidd.* 30a; Origen, *Song of Songs* 23; Hirshman, 2006).

Tension between Marriage and Learning. Marriage and Torah study are often presented as obligations at odds with one another in rabbinic culture (precedents in earlier Jewish literature include: Philo, *Cont.* 68–69; *Hypoth.* 11.1–12; Josephus, *Bell.* 2.120–61; Sir 9:1–9, 19:2–3, 25:16–26, 36:21–25, 42:9–14). Several rabbinic sources offer advice about navigating between the two: one source legislates the length of time a student may leave home without returning to his wife (*b. Ketub.* 61b ff.), and another debates whether men should marry or study first, the implication being that the two responsibilities could not be fulfilled simultaneously (*b. Qidd.* 29b: "Our Rabbis taught: If one has to study Torah and to marry a wife, he should first study and then marry, but if he cannot [live] without a wife, he should first marry and then study. Rav Judah said in Samuel's name: The *halakhah* is, [a man] first marries and then studies. Rabbi Yohanan said: [With] a millstone around the neck, shall one study Torah! Yet they do not differ: the one refers to ourselves [Babylonians], the other to them [Palestinians]").

In the Babylonian Talmud's presentation of Rabbi Akiva's education, the rabbi's decision to leave his wife in order to attend a House of Study becomes a central theme (*b. Ned.* 50a). When the rabbi returns home after twelve long years of study, he overhears his wife tell a detractor that she would encourage her husband to devote his life to study for yet another twelve years, which prompts him to continue his studies for a total of twenty-four years. Rabbi Akiva's wife's piety—that she encouraged her husband

to pursue a life of learning—is her defining characteristic and facilitates the emergence of the greatest of scholars, though the practice of leaving one's wife to study is regarded more ambivalently in other texts (e.g., *b. Ketub.* 61b ff.; Boyarin, 1993).

Exceptional Women. Despite the exclusion of women from the obligation of Torah study and the absence of women in rabbinic study houses and academies, exceptions do appear in rabbinic sources. The most playful example of a well-read woman is Beruriah, daughter of Rabbi Hananiah ben Teradion and wife of Rabbi Meir. In the Babylonian Talmud, Beruriah is portrayed as a wise and witty woman who knows the intricacies of both Torah and Mishnah. She reprimands Rabbi Yosi for not adhering to a mishnaic principle (*b. Eruv.* 53b), scolds a student for improperly reciting traditions (*b. Eruv.* 53b–54a), and bests her husband (*b. Ber.* 10a). In all three narratives, Beruriah uses her exacting reading of biblical and rabbinic passages to point out the flaws in her (male) counterparts' words and actions, implying that she was at least as educated in such texts as her interlocutors. In another passage, Beruriah is evoked as an example of someone with an impressive ability to learn hundreds of halakhic matters from many teachers in a single day (*b. Pesah.* 62b); this same text refers to her study of the "Book of Genealogies" over the course of three years. The Tosefta also mentions a woman named Beruriah, who appears in the study house and exhibits a deep knowledge of the laws of ritual purity (*t. Kel. B. Mesi'a.* 1.6; cf. *m. Kel.* 11:4, which edits Beruriah out). None of these sources necessarily comments on a single historical figure or on the state of women's education; the figure of Beruriah is used in these narratives as a stock character. Yet the fact that rabbinic texts employ this learned female figure should not be altogether explained away without entertaining the possibility that some women did excel in learning despite prohibitions and cultural pressure that made such an education far less common among ancient Jewish women. Another potentially well-educated rabbinic woman is the daughter of Rav Hisda, mentioned in the Babylonian Talmud in the context of *halakhic* discussions (*b. B. Bat.* 12b; *b. Ketub.* 85a).

Tal Ilan (2005) has suggested that nonrabbinic women also had access to avenues of learning based on her analysis of sources such as an Aramaic letter on papyrus clumsily written by an ordinary woman named Harqan to her brother in Egypt (MS. Oxford Bodleian Library, *Pap. Heb. E. 120*), and a quotation preserved in the Byzantine lexicon *Suda* that mentions "a woman of Hebrew descent, Moso, who composed (a book) 'the Law of the Jews.'" Although the sources are problematic, they might indicate the presence of women with sufficient educational background to compose letters and perhaps even books. Indeed, in the first century Philo describes Torah-seeking and philosophy-seeking women among the Therapeutae (Philo, *Contempl.*), and there is definitive evidence that women served in positions of leadership and teaching in ancient synagogues, including in the role of *archisynagogissa* (Brooten, 1982), which suggests that some women did attain higher degrees of learning, if not primarily in rabbinic circles then in other venues of Jewish communal life.

Education beyond Torah Study. As early as the Mishnah, men were discouraged from teaching their sons Greek because they should be devoting their time to the study of Torah. This was of course not the case with a scholar such as Philo. An exception was made for those from the house of the Patriarch Rabban Gamaliel because of their dealings with the local government. The Babylonian Talmud preserves a debate about whether Greek language and Greek wisdom (science, philosophy) are both prohibited. In contrast, even the earliest rabbinic sources permit and even encourage women, who are exempt from Torah study, to engage in such educational endeavors (Vidas, 2013; *m. Sotah* 9:15, 15:8; *t. Avod. Zar.* 1:20; *y. Sotah* 9:15, 24c; *y. Peah* 1:1; 15c; *b. Ber.* 22a). The Yerushalmi goes so far as to state that "a man is permitted to teach his daughter Greek, because it is like a jewel for her" (*y. Sotah* 9:15, 24c). Beyond rabbinic circles, women played a role in magical practices, medicine, and other spheres of life that presupposed educations in scripture and other realms.

[*See also* Education, *subentries on* Hebrew Bible, *and* New Testament; Family Structures, *subentry* Early Judaism; Imagery, Gendered, *subentry* Wisdom Literature; *and* Religious Leaders, *subentry* Early Judaism.]

BIBLIOGRAPHY

Baumgarten, Albert. "Literacy and the Polemics Surrounding Biblical Interpretation in the Second Temple Period." In *Studies in Ancient Midrash*, edited by James L. Kugel, pp. 27–41. Cambridge, Mass.: Harvard University Center for Jewish Studies, 2001.

Becker, Adam H. "The Comparative Study of 'Scholasticism' in Late Antique Mesopotamia: Rabbis and East Syrians." *Association for Jewish Studies Review* 34.1 (2010): 91–113.

Beer, Ilana. "Women's Education and Study of Torah in the Teaching of the Sages of the Mishnah." In *Feasts and Fasts: A Festschrift in Honour of Alan David Crown*, edited by Marianne Dacy, Jennifer Dowling, and Suzanne Faigan, pp. 141–154. Sydney: Mandelbaum, 2005.

Boyarin, Daniel. *Carnal Israel: Reading Sex in Talmudic Culture*. Berkeley: University of California Press, 1993.

Brooten, Bernadette. *Women Leaders in the Ancient Synagogue: Inscriptional Evidence and Background Issues*. Providence, R.I.: Brown Judaic Series, 1982.

Carr, David. *Writing on the Tablet of the Heart: Origins of Scripture and Literature*. New York: Oxford University Press, 2008.

Goodblatt, David M. *Rabbinic Instruction in Sasanian Babylonia*. Leiden, The Netherlands: Brill, 1975.

Hauptman, Judith. "A New View of Women and Torah Study in the Talmudic Period." *Jewish Studies: An Internet Journal* (2010): 249–292.

Hezser, Catherine. *Jewish Literacy in Roman Palestine*. Tübingen, Germany: Mohr Siebeck, 2001.

Hezser, Catherine. "Private and Public Education." In *The Oxford Handbook of Jewish Daily Life in Roman Palestine*, edited by Catherine Hezser, pp. 465–481. New York: Oxford University Press, 2010.

Hirshman, Marc. "Torah in Rabbinic Thought: The Theology of Learning." In *The Cambridge History of Judaism*, Vol. 4: *The Late Roman-Rabbinic Periods*, edited by Steven T. Katz, pp. 899–924. Cambridge, U.K.: Cambridge University Press, 2006.

Hirshman, Marc. *The Stabilization of Rabbinic Culture, 100 C.E.–350 C.E.: Texts on Education and Their Late Antique Context*. New York: Oxford University Press, 2009.

Ilan, Tal. "Learned Jewish Women in Antiquity." In *Religiöses Lernen in der biblischen, frühjüdischen und frühchristlichen Überlieferung*, edited by Beate Ego and Helmut Merkel, pp. 175–190. Tübingen, Germany: Mohr Siebeck, 2005.

Lapin, Hayim. "Jewish and Christian Academies in Roman Palestine." In *Caesarea Maritima: A Retrospective after Two Millennia*, edited by K. G. Holum and A. Raban, pp. 496–512. Leiden, The Netherlands: Brill, 1996.

Najman, Hindy. "Test and Figure in Ancient Jewish 'paideia.'" In *Authoritative Scriptures in Ancient Judaism*, edited by Mladen Popović, pp. 253–265. Leiden, The Netherlands: Brill, 2010.

Rubenstein, Jeffrey. "Social and Institutional Settings of Rabbinic Literature." In *The Cambridge Companion to the Talmud and Rabbinic Literature*, edited by C. E. Fonrobert and M. S. Jaffee, pp. 58–74. Cambridge, U.K.: Cambridge University Press, 2007.

Safrai, Shmuel. "Elementary Education: Its Religious and Social Significance in the Talmudic Period." *Cahiers d'Histoire Mondiale* 11 (1968): 148–169.

Satlow, Michael. "'Try to Be a Man': The Rabbinic Construction of Masculinity." *Harvard Theological Review* 89 (1996): 19–40.

Satlow, Michael. "'And on the Earth You Shall Sleep': 'Talmud Torah' and Rabbinic Asceticism." *Journal of Religion* 83.2 (2003): 204–225.

Vidas, Moulie. "Greek Wisdom in Babylonia." In *Envisioning Judaism: Studies in Honor of Peter Schäfer on the Occasion of his Seventieth Birthday*, edited by Ra'anan Boustan, Klaus Hermann, Reimund Leicht, Annette Yoshiko Reed, and Giuseppe Veltri, with Alex Ramos, pp. 287–305. Tübingen, Germany: Mohr Siebeck, 2013.

Sarit Kattan Gribetz

Early Church

How one assesses the intersection between gender and education in early Christianity is a function of the particular texts and perspectives one chooses to privilege. In some respects, the work is akin to putting together a large puzzle. Reassembling the various segments to configure a whole picture is not only practically challenging but also fraught with disparate ideological renderings of ancient sources. The questions presented by a paucity of secure evidence are myriad. Because the few explicit descriptions of women's education are preserved solely in texts written by men, the interpretive task has historically been one of reading around the edges and between the lines. Since the same evidence can be used to support different conclusions, inferences are at best tentative, and not infrequently contradictory. While adopting and maintaining a flexibly nuanced, critical hermeneutic is essential, it is only by placing emergent Christian source material in conversation with established models and examining development across a broad chronological trajectory that even the most impressionistic sketches can be drawn.

Established Models. Within an ancient frame, it is clear that who received an education, where, and to what extent was largely a function of class and gender. For both men and women, the privileges that derived from being socially and economically well situated were determinative. Financial wherewithal and elite connections allowed not only greater access but also the availability and affordability of materials for reading and writing, as well as a "felt need" for those cultural assets and opportunities that literacy could provide (Harris, 1989).

Simultaneously, by every measure, the gendered character of literate investment is irrefutable (cf. Cribiore, 2001, pp. 74–101; Haines-Eitzen, 2012, pp. 19–21). Overall estimates of ancient literacy range from 5 to 15 percent. For women these numbers would have been much lower. Even within society's upper strata, access was uneven. Because the goal was shaping future citizens, the normative model was male. In papyrological sources, women's hands are more likely to evidence the painstaking characteristics of slow writers. As women were more often recipients than senders of letters, their correspondence is significantly less common than men's. While commemorative inscriptions suggest that a limited number of women worked as teachers of grammar or fulfilled scribal duties, when women surface in pedagogical sources it is generally in one of two roles: either as providers of education to their children or as recipients of primary and grammatical instruction in a private or semiprivate setting.

Such statistics challenge "progressive" pedagogical visions, articulated across generations of ancient elite civic discourse. Writing in the fourth century B.C.E., Plato envisions the model society as one in which the young "are children of the [*polis*] even more than children of their parents" (*Laws* 7.804d [Bury]). Enjoining "the female sex...[to] share with the male, to the greatest extent possible, both in education and in all else," he recommends that girls participate in gymnastics and music, and "women abstain from wool-work, [in order to] weave for themselves...a life that is not trivial...nor useless" (*Laws* 7.805d–806a [Bury]). Aristotle premises that because women compose half of the free population, they should be accorded commensurate educational opportunity (*Politics* 1260b). Four centuries later, Musonius Rufus, nicknamed the "Roman Socrates," promotes the study of philosophy for women as well as men (*Epistle* 3.4.13a). His contemporary Quintilian extols a household structure in which both parents, "not...only the fathers," are "as highly educated as possible" (*Institutes* 1.1.6 [Butler]).

Less optimistic readings of the same source material emphasize the degree to which these gender-neutral ideals are tied to better execution of highly gendered, domestic tasks. Plato suggests that an elementary education will help young girls advance on "the path of domestic tendance and management and child-nurture" (*Laws* 7.806a [Bury]). Premising that "only if the household is good can the state be good," Aristotle links women's education to better preparing their elite male offspring to "grow up to be...partners in the government of the state" (*Politics* 1260b [Rackham]). Musonius Rufus commends the study of philosophy as an aid to better execution of domestic duties (*Epistle* 3.4.13a). Quintilian acclaims women's education as the most effective means of providing future citizens and statesmen with exemplary models in speech and character from birth (*Institutes* 1.1.6).

Outside the domestic sphere, refractions of women's investments in literate pursuits become less sanguine. Included among collections of extant school *sententiae* is the injunction that teaching a woman "letters" is like "giving poison to a deadly asp" (Menander, *Synkrisis* 1.209–210 [Jaekel]). Similarly repurposed, a sentence elsewhere attributed to Diogenes the Cynic likens a woman being taught "letters" to "a sword being sharpened" (P. Bouriant 1.141–168 [Collart]).

References to "educated women" likewise surface in literary descriptions of public or private leisure settings. As stock figures of dubious character, these women are pictured as adept at witty wordplay deployed in the service of entertaining male clients with clever sexual innuendo and verbal repartee. Socrates names "delightful speech" one of the courtesan's seductive tools (Xenophon, *Memorabilia* 3.11.10 [Marchant]). Athenaeus credits the courtesan's facility with "quick rejoinders" to investment in "getting an education and devoting...time to learning" (Athenaeus, *Deipnosophists* 13.583 [Gulick]). Juvenal satirizes the woman who "[recites] from Palaemon's *Grammar*, always observes the laws and rules of speech, [who is] learned in antiquities, [and] knows lines from the ancients" as transgressing gendered norms. "If she must appear so excessively learned and eloquent, she may as well be a man" (*Satire* 6.434–456 [Braund]).

The extent to which such depictions accurately reflect investments of real women is difficult to determine. As a tool for casting aspersion, however, recurrent assignation affords a glimpse of the contested landscapes encountered by women who engaged in intellectual pursuits beyond domestically defined parameters. Evidence that derives from emergent Jewish-Christian circles registers similar tensions.

Emergent Christianity. Primary layers of Christian source material place the center of emergent praxis within household settings. The same texts picture both women and men in teaching roles. Whether the authority accorded these individuals suggests commensurate investment in literate education remains a question. However, sustained arguments have premised the plausibility that "many, if not all, of the women" depicted in various synagogue and/or house church leadership roles "would have possessed sufficient formal education to carry out [their] responsibilities" (Kraemer, 1991, p. 230). Some suggest that women named in the earliest layers of tradition may have had greater access to education than their male counterparts.

The letters attributed to Paul have proved key to these debates. In assessing literacy and social status, the so-called Corinthian women prophets play a central role in early discussion. Equal attention has been accorded Paul's commendations of the deacon and emissary Phoebe (Rom 16:1), repeated salutations to the house-church leaders Priscilla and Aquila (1 Cor 16:19; Rom 16:3), and passing affirmation of "Chloe's people" (1 Cor 1:11). Read in conversation with women's letters that survive on papyri, the details transmitted in Paul's greetings show striking affinity with the relative degree of self-determination communicated in missives composed by women of some financial independence (Bagnall and Cribiore, 2006). As self-represented in letters preserved on papyri, these women traveled to address business interests, maintain family and communal relationships, and attend to trade and financial matters of some consequence. Extant archives affirm that neither did this small subset of the literate population shrink from directly addressing male relatives and dependents on matters pertinent to their interests (Cribiore, 2001, pp. 88–101).

Such a frame lends suggestive context to proscriptions encountered in the deutero-Pauline letters, which are later. As these missives register the sharpening tone of gendered debates, they arguably likewise refract the emergence of a communal hierarchy that extends beyond the household sphere (1 Tim 2:11–15; 1 Cor 14:33b–36). Ensuing leadership disputes are perhaps most stridently articulated in the sexualized images that attend John of Patmos's likening the female head of a sister synagogue to the caricatured Jezebel encountered in Hebrew scripture (Rev 2.20–23). In gendered hyperbole that surpasses the negative personifications of educated women encountered in the comic poets, these graphic depictions render patent the real social consequences of transgressing bounded norms.

Authorship. Beyond the undisputed letters of Paul, the writers of the earliest layers of Jewish-Christian source material remain anonymous. While no secure record of female authorship survives, gender has proved a perennial element in debates addressing the production of extant texts (Kraemer, 1991). Assessment of literacy and access to education is implicit. Like the record of literate investments encountered in women's letters preserved on papyri, references to Jewish-Christian women reading and writing are dispersed, but suggestive.

Philo's *De vita contemplativa* arguably portrays both men and women engaged in study and hymnographic composition (3.29–30). The *Testament of Job* presents the protagonist's three daughters as his "prophetic" heirs. As each woman exercises her respective gift, the two remaining sisters are depicted "not[ing] things down for the other," while their uncle Nereos also "wrote out a book of notations for… [their] hymns as a safeguard" (*Testament of Job* 46–52 [Kraft and Timbie]). As reported, these compositions, no longer extant, were preserved as "The Hymns of Amaltheias-Keras" and "The Hymns of Cassia" (*Testament of Job* 49–50 [Kraft and Timbie]). A discussion, framed as a debate between "a Montanist" and "an Orthodox," concerns the teachings of Maximilla and Priscilla, two female prophets. At issue are books that have been disseminated by the women, "in their own names" (*Debate between a Montanist and an Orthodox* [Heine]). The *Acts of Thecla* introduces Thecla first as a student of the Apostle Paul (2.1–4), then as a teacher in her own right (10.4–15). Assessments of Thecla's level of formal education remain intimately linked to debates about class and social status in emergent Christian communities. However, Thecla's importance as a model and namesake to literate women of subsequent eras is well established (Davis, 2001).

Literacy. While tradition premises early Christian constituencies composed predominantly of technical literates, the parameters of praxis remain a locus of ongoing investigation and debate (Haines-Eitzen, 2000; 2012). As ancient breakdowns between the highly literate and the "unlettered" fell largely along class lines, those most able to read and write were simultaneously the least likely to do so. In turn, whether individuals who acquired and retained the *teknika* associated with scribal literacy were understood as "literate" is a matter of perspective.

In Acts, Paul is attributed didactic authority by virtue of having received an elite Jewish education at the feet of Gamaliel (22:3). Simultaneously, the greetings that introduce and conclude the seven letters that most securely derive from his hand indicate that scribes were employed in transcribing and/or composing this earliest extant corpus of "Christian" documents. Each secretary/amanuensis is identified as male. However, in gauging demographics of gender, social status, and levels of education in emergent Christian communities, whether one conceives these individuals as servants, slaves, or Paul's artisan colleagues is significant.

Professionally, scribes straddled and blurred the boundaries between literate elites and the unlettered. As slaves, freedpersons, and/or artisans who made a living by the written word, they performed the functions of reading and, more importantly, writing for others in society. The most highly trained scribes learned and practiced their trade as slaves in elite households. However, scribes were also publicly available for hire by illiterate and/or semiliterate individuals. Scribes assisted in filling out routine paperwork, writing letters, and preparing other forms of official documentation. Since even fully literate citizens (like Paul) called upon others' services for most written composition and communication, scribes were also employed in preparing literary documents for dissemination through bookshops, libraries, or personal networks (cf. Haines-Eitzen, 2000).

The preface to the extracanonical *Shepherd of Hermas* introduces its male protagonist as the slave of one Rhoda of Rome. In a dreamlike state, Hermas is instructed by a female figure to take the book that she is reading and copy it. In contrast to the apparent literacy of the woman commissioning the work, Hermas seems to be less than fully literate, taking the book and "cop[ying] it all letter by letter, [because he] could not distinguish the syllables" (*Shepherd of Hermas* 2.1.4 [Lake]). Later in the narrative, the same female figure adds additional words to the book, then instructs Hermas to "write two little books and send one to Clement and one to Grapte" (*Shepherd of Hermas* 2.4.3 [Lake]). Grapte is in turn commissioned to share the book with the orphans and widows in her care.

Narrative sources routinely frame scribal literacy as solely technical. However, the parameters that defined literacy were social as well as practical. Relative to one's geographic and economic location, being cast as illiterate could mean anything from not knowing basic letters to not being fully educated in high culture. Even elite literacy in nondominant tongues (e.g., Aramaic, Coptic, Syriac) was measured differently from linguistic facility with Greek and/or Latin. Within this frame, extant textual remains affirm a spectrum of education and expertise. The higher wages assigned individuals capable of both transcribing and composing texts likewise attest that some subset of the scribal class was more than technically literate (cf. Haines-Eitzen, 2000; Cribiore, 2001).

Female scribes most often appear in the employ of female householders, undertaking correspondence and administrative affairs on their behalf. However, given a greater density of male scribes overall, Hermas's service to Rhoda could hardly have been unusual. Eusebius's fourth-century depiction of Origen's prolific textual production includes scribal assistants of both genders. As reported, this extensive stenographic staff was engaged by the wealthy male householder Ambrose and included "more than seven short hand writers…as many copyists, as well as girls trained in [calligraphy]" (*Ecclesiastical History* 6.23 [Oulton]).

The forms that emerge from this range of relatively early source material are hazy. Contours grow more definitive, however, as emergent Christian practice absorbs the privileges implicit to its developing imperial persona. If the teaching and literary output of figures like Origen have sometimes been linked to ostensible reimagination of gendered parameters, in broader purview they serve rather to confirm the enduring character of established norms.

Developing Christianity. The most explicit articulation of a "Christian" educational curriculum can be securely dated to the fourth century. It is preserved in correspondence originating from an ascetic community in Bethlehem. Founded and administered by

Paula, a wealthy Roman aristocrat turned Palestinian ascetic, the community was also home to Jerome, Paula's arguably less elite male compatriot. Included in a letter directed to Laeta, the elite Paula's daughter, this early pedagogical program is tailored to address the needs of Laeta's young daughter, also named Paula.

Christian curriculum. Jerome's missive both affirms elite practice and registers Christian adaptation of dominant pedagogical forms. As an aid to learning the alphabet, Jerome suggests that Laeta have "a set of letters made…of boxwood or of ivory," so that young Paula may learn to call each by its proper name. In order to recognize letters by sight as well as by sound, he recommends that the child "not only [be made to] grasp the right order of the letters and remember their names in a simple song, but also frequently upset their order and mix the last letters with the middle ones, the middle with the first" (*Epistle* 107 [Wright]).

Moving from letters to syllables to words, Jerome advises that the very names used in forming sentences not be assigned haphazardly, but "chosen and arranged on purpose" (*Epistle* 107 [Wright]; cf. Quintilian, *Institutes* 1.1.24–37). With the aim of training both tongue and memory, he suggests that these wordlists include "the names of the prophets and the apostles, and the whole list of patriarchs from Adam downward, as [given by] Matthew and Luke." As biblical content replaces material drawn from classical mythology, instead of lines from Homer, Paula's "tongue…[should] be imbued with the sweet music of the Psalms." Maxims and short sentences excerpted from classical tragedy, comedy, and philosophy should be replaced with "rules of life [from] the proverbs of Solomon." Rather than "silks or gems," Paula's treasures ought to be "manuscripts of the holy scriptures." In these, she should "think less of gilding…Babylonian parchment, and arabesque patterns, than of correctness and accurate [punctuation]" (*Epistle* 107 [Wright]).

Emphasizing the difficulties implicit in Laeta's tackling such instructional goals amid the busy duties of running a Roman household, Jerome likewise advocates a geographical shift. Removing the locus of instruction from its urban household setting,

he urges Laeta to send young Paula to Bethlehem, to be educated in her grandmother's monastery. Here, in an establishment organized and administered by two aristocratic women (the elder Paula and her sister, Eustochium), Jerome offers his services as tutor. As Paula's ideal instructor, a man of "approved years, life, and learning," he likens his proposed role to that of Aristotle teaching Alexander "his first letters" (*Epistle* 107 [Wright]; cf. Quintilian, *Institutes* 1.1.23–24).

Christian classrooms. While the adjustments that characterize Jerome's proposed curriculum appear significant, extant material evidence suggests that early meldings of Christian content were hardly uniform or unilateral (Larsen, 2013). Elsewhere, Jerome is critiqued for not limiting the sources of his instruction to biblical texts, and also for introducing "the comedians and lyrical and historical writers" to a group of young boys who, like Paula, "had been entrusted to him" for instruction (Rufinus, *Apology* 2.8 [*NPNF*[2]]).

Even among a developing class of Christian elites, whether Paula's educational access should be deemed exceptional is not immediately clear. As suggested, when Jerome is depicted in a more formal teaching role, it is not as Paula's tutor but as an instructor in a classroom composed of young boys. In an alternate geographical locus, when John Chrysostom presses Christian parents to send their children to be educated in monasteries, his target population is also male. Employing explicitly gendered language, Chrysostom recommends that instruction begin once boys have reached the age of ten and continue for at least ten years (*Against Opponents of the Monastic Life* 3).

A broader range of sources, also derivative of Christian ascetic settings, lends added texture to these accounts. Again registering structures aimed at the education of children in Christian communal settings, the *Asketikon* of Basil, named by some the earliest monastic rule, revives the Platonic ideal that the young "should be trained…as common children of the [community]" (Basil, *Longer Rule* 15 [Wagner]; cf. Plato, *Laws* 7.804d–e). The *Precepts* of Pachomius, a relatively contemporaneous document of Egyptian provenance, mandates lessons in reading and memorization of scripture for anyone who "enters the monastery uninstructed" (*Precepts* 139–140 [Vielleux]).

The *Life of Macrina*, a tribute to Basil's sister and mentor, frames its elite protagonist's pedagogical formation in terms reminiscent of the course of study recommended for young Paula (962a–d). It presents the elite Macrina absorbing into her household structure local orphans—a class of individuals that would have been disproportionately female (Gregory of Nyssa, *Life of Macrina* 988a–b; cf. Elm, 1994, pp. 92–93). Whether Macrina's elite education extended to the young women in her care is never explicitly stated. However, a broader array of source material is again suggestive.

An informal body of instructions originating in Egypt appears to presume at least a measure of technical literacy on the part of its audience. Arguably, directed to a community of female ascetics in Palestine, the fourth of fifty-six "exhortations to virgins" enjoins its recipients to greet the morning "with book in hand" (Evagrius, *Exhortations to Virgins* 4 [Sinkewicz]). An attendant letter commends its recipient's "love of learning" (Evagrius, *Epistle* 20 [Bunge]). Borrowing language from the early *Precepts* of Pachomius, a sixth-century "rule" directed to a female community in Gaul mandates that "no nun [shall] be allowed to enter who does not learn letters." In a related vita, the community's elite abbess, Caesaria, is depicted assuming responsibility for scribal instruction of the women under her direction (*Life of Caesarius* 1.58 [Klingshirn]).

Observations. Literary and material evidence, stretching from the classical to the Christian era, reflects pedagogical landscapes that remain relatively static across a broad chronological and geographical trajectory (Morgan, 1998; Cribiore, 2001). Thus contextualized, the impressionistic sketches encountered in emergent layers of Christian education find provocative complement both in Greco-Roman pedagogical sources and in their fourth- and fifth-century Christian reframings. As classical ideals that place female literacy in the service of managing estates arguably serve to legitimate female oversight of Christian ascetic communities, gendered norms remain firmly ensconced within an expanded household model.

How early such rearticulation of "domestic tendance" begins remains a question dependent on the source material one chooses to privilege. Some judge the households referenced in the writings of Paul and depicted in the *Acts of Thecla* to already contain the pedagogical seeds of literate investment that appear to take root in later establishments (Davies, 1980). Even here, however, the record remains uneven.

The intellectual accomplishments of elite female ascetics are well documented (Elm, 1994 and elsewhere). They can, as such, easily distract from familiar echoes of established practice (Elm, 1994). When John Chrysostom addresses his upwardly mobile, urban parishioners, he encourages them to send young boys, not girls, to be educated in monastic classroom settings. In turn, when cataloguing the sacrifices made by his widowed mother, Chrysostom measures the "great sums of money invested" in his own elite education against the "lesser anxiety" of raising a daughter (*Concerning the Priesthood* 1.5.44 [*NPNF*[1]]). As young Paula's education is removed from Roman villa to Palestinian monastery, it remains within the private household sphere.

If alternate domestic configurations extended educational opportunities to a broader cross-section of women, the shape and scope of attendant pedagogical aims is more difficult to ascertain. What is patent, however, is the degree to which the conventions of Christian education develop in conversation with established forms. Albeit arguably reframed, the enduring normativity of elite prerogative and gendered subjectivity remains securely stable.

[*See also* Authors of Biblical Books; Education, *subentries on* Early Judaism, Greek World, New Testament, *and* Roman World; Family Structures, *subentry* Early Church; Legal Status, *subentry* Early Church; *and* Religious Leaders, *subentry* Early Church.]

BIBLIOGRAPHY

Primary Sources

Acts of Thecla. Translated by J. K. Elliott. *Apocryphal New Testament.* New York: Oxford University Press, 1993. In *Women's Religions in the Greco-Roman World: A*

Sourcebook, edited by Ross Shepard Kraemer, pp. 297–308. New York: Oxford University Press, 2004.

Aristotle. *Politics*. Translated by H. Rackham. Loeb Classical Library. Cambridge, Mass.: Harvard University Press, 1959.

Athenaeus. *Deipnosophists*. Translated by C. B. Gulick. 7 volumes. Loeb Classical Library. Cambridge, Mass.: Harvard University Press, 1967–1971.

Basil. *Longer Rule*. In *Saint Basil: Ascetical Works*. Translated by M. Monica Wagner. New York: Fathers of the Church, 1950.

Caesarius. *Life of Caesarius of Arles*. In *Caesarius of Arles: Life, Testament, Letters*. Translated by William E. Klingshirn. Liverpool, U.K.: Liverpool University Press, 1994.

John Chrysostom. *Against the Opponents of the Monastic Life*. In *A Comparison between a King and a Monk/Against the Opponents of the Monastic Life*. Translated by David G. Hunter. Lewiston, N.Y.: Edwin Mellen, 1989.

John Chrysostom. *On the Priesthood*, edited by Philip Schaff. Select Library of the Nicene and Post-Nicene Fathers of the Christian Church, 1st ser., Vol. 9. Repr. Peabody, Mass.: Hendrickson, 1994.

The Debate between a Montanist and an Orthodox. Translated by Ronald Heine. In *Women's Religions in the Greco-Roman World: A Sourcebook*, edited by Ross Shepard Kraemer, pp. 93–94. New York: Oxford University Press, 2004.

Eusebius. *Ecclesiastical History*. Translated by J. E. L. Oulton. 2 vols. Loeb Classical Library 153, 265. Cambridge, U.K.: Harvard University Press, 2000.

Evagrius. *Epistle 20*. In *Briefe aus der Wüste: Evagrios Pontikos*, edited and translated by Gabriel Bunge. Trier, Germany: Paulinus-Verlag, 1986.

Evagrius. *Exhortation to Virgins*. In *Evagrius of Pontus: The Greek Ascetic Corpus*. Translated by Robert E. Sinkewicz. Oxford: Oxford University Press, 2003.

Gregory of Nyssa. *The Life of Macrina*. In *Saint Gregory of Nyssa: Ascetical Works*. Translated by V. W. Callahan. Washington, D. C.: Fathers of the Church, 1967.

Jerome. *Select Letters*. Translated by E. A. Wright. Loeb Classical Library 262. Cambridge, Mass.: Harvard University Press, 1933.

Juvenal. *Satires*. Edited and translated by Susanna Morton Braund. Loeb Classical Library 91. Cambridge, Mass.: Harvard University Press, 2004.

Menander. *Synkrisis Menandrou kai Philistionos*. In *Menandri Sententiae*. Edited by Siegfried Jaekel. Leipzig: Teubner, 1964.

Musonius Rufus. *Epistulae*. In *Musonius Rufus, "The Roman Socrates."* Edited by Cora E. Lutz. New Haven, Conn.: Yale University Press, 1947.

Pachomius. *Pachomian Koininia*. Vol. 2: *Precepts*. Translated by Armand Veilleux. Kalamazoo, Mich.: Cistercian Publications, 1981.

Philo. *On the Contemplative Life*. In *Philo*, Vol 9. Translated by F. H. Colson. Loeb Classical Library 363. Cambridge, Mass.: Harvard University Press, 1954.

Plato. *Laws*. Translated by R. G. Bury. 2 vols. Loeb Classical Library 187, 192. Cambridge, Mass.: Harvard University Press, 1984.

Quintilian. *The Institutio oratoria of Quintilian*. Translated by H. E. Butler. 4 vols. Loeb Classical Library 124–127. Cambridge, Mass.: Harvard University Press, 1953–1959.

Rufinus. *Apology against Jerome*. Edited by Philip Schaff and Henry Wace. Select Library of the Nicene and Post-Nicene Fathers of the Christian Church, 2d ser., Vol. 3. Repr. Peabody, Mass.: Hendrickson, 1994.

Shepherd of Hermas. In Vol. 2 of *The Apostolic Fathers*. Translated by Kirsopp Lake. 2 vols. Loeb Classical Library 25. Cambridge, Mass.: Harvard University Press, 1913.

Testament of Job. Translated by Robert A. Kraft and Janet Timbie. In *Women's Religions in the Greco-Roman World: A Sourcebook*, edited by Ross Shepard Kraemer, pp. 340–343. New York: Oxford University Press, 2004.

Xenophon. *Memorabilia*. Translated by E. C. Marchant. Loeb Classical Library 168. Cambridge, Mass.: Harvard University Press, 2013.

Secondary Sources

Bagnall, Roger S., and Raffaella Cribiore. *Women's Letters from Ancient Egypt, 300 B.C.–A.D. 800*. Ann Arbor: University of Michigan Press, 2006.

Collart, Paul, ed. *Les Papyrus Bouriant*. Paris: Édouard Champion, 1926.

Cribiore, Raffaella. *Writing, Teachers, and Students in Graeco-Roman Egypt*. American Studies in Papyrology 36. Atlanta: Scholars Press, 1996.

Cribiore, Raffaella. *Gymnastics of the Mind: Greek Education in Hellenistic and Roman Egypt*. Princeton, N.J.: Princeton University Press, 2001.

Davies, Stevan L. *The Revolt of the Widows: The Social World of the Apocryphal Acts*. Carbondale: Southern Illinois University Press, 1980.

Davis, Stephen J. *The Cult of Thecla: A Tradition of Women's Piety in Late Antiquity*. Oxford Early Christian Studies. New York: Oxford University Press, 2001.

Elm, Susanna. *Virgins of God: The Making of Asceticism in Late Antiquity*. Oxford Classical Monographs. Oxford: Clarendon, 1994.

Haines-Eitzen, Kim. *Guardians of Letters: Literacy, Power, and the Transmitters of Early Christian Literature.* New York: Oxford University Press, 2000.

Haines-Eitzen, Kim. *The Gendered Palimpsest: Women, Writing, and Representation in Early Christianity.* New York: Oxford University Press, 2012.

Harris, William V. *Ancient Literacy.* Cambridge, Mass.: Harvard University Press, 1989.

Kraemer, Ross Shepard. "Women's Authorship of Jewish and Christian Literature in the Greco-Roman Period." In *"Women Like This": New Perspectives on Jewish Women in the Greco-Roman World*, edited by Amy-Jill Levine, pp. 221–242. Atlanta: Scholars Press, 1991.

Kraemer, Ross Shepard, ed. *Women's Religions in the Greco-Roman World: A Sourcebook.* New York: Oxford University Press, 2004.

Kraemer, Ross Shepard, and Mary Rose D'Angelo, eds. *Women and Christian Origins.* New York: Oxford University Press, 1999.

Larsen, Lillian I. "On Learning a New Alphabet: The Sayings of the Desert Fathers and the Monostichs of Menander." *Studia Patristica* 55, no. 3 (2013): 59–78.

Morgan, Teresa. *Literate Education in the Hellenistic and Roman Worlds.* Cambridge, U.K.: Cambridge University Press, 1998.

Lillian I. Larsen

FAMILY STRUCTURES

This entry contains seven subentries: Ancient Near East; Hebrew Bible; Greek World; Roman World; New Testament; Early Judaism; *and* Early Church.

Ancient Near East

The absence of depictions of families in the visual record of the ancient Near East in the late periods (Neo-Assyrian, Neo-Babylonian/Achaemenid) forces any description of family structures to depend heavily on the textual record. The enormity of that documentation—one could easily count upward of 50,000 Neo-Assyrian and Neo-Babylonian texts in museums, libraries, and collections worldwide—means that this overview of a complex and fascinating topic survey needs be selective in its approach. Thus, an unfortunate omission here must be contributions from the emerging field of household archaeology (Foster and Parker, 2012; Herrmann, 2011), which not only considers the material evidence of individuals and their aggregations into families and households but also seeks to explain human processes that reflect the activities that related or closely associated individuals perform in the spaces they inhabit and in which they conduct the business of their lives. It is nonetheless hoped that the broad outlines drawn from the documentary record reflect the scope of family structures in the first millennium B.C.E.

Literary documents from the Neo-Assyrian library of Ashurbanipal and the library at Neo-Babylonian Sippar contain no extensive descriptions of family life. However, they do sport insightful and sometimes compassionate sketches of divine households, filled with the same indiscretions and joys that beset their human counterparts. Episodes in the Creation Epic (*Enuma eliš*) detail both the roiling anger of an exhausted mother, Tiamat, at the noisy (divine) children who deprive her of much-needed sleep and Anu's grandfatherly pride in Marduk's prowess, which, coupled with devotion, leads him to fashion celestial toys that amuse Marduk, demonstrate his potency, and confirm him as the ultimate vanquisher of Tiamat and her vengeful plan.

Like the literary texts, the corpora of legal and administrative texts do not explicitly concern themselves with portrayals of family structure or process. Yet, in preserving details of the activities across all socioeconomic levels and of named individuals and family members marked with kinship terminology, they offer an entrée into understanding first-millennium B.C.E. family and household structures, in primarily the human, but also in the divine, realm. Brief notices hinting at the composition of divine families appear in economic and administrative sources recording the intersection and interdependency of royal (palace) and divine (temple) households. Research exploring these interconnections (e.g., Waerzeggers, 2010) continues to deepen the understanding of the social organization of both institutions.

Sources. While the terms "Neo-Assyrian" and "Neo-Babylonian," founded in temporal and geographical criteria, impose constraints on some research agendas, here they serve well enough as rubrics by which the documentation may be defined. The bias that inheres in the Neo-Assyrian and Neo-Babylonian sources stems from their origins in the documentation of imperial and cultic administrative practices, thus privileging study of upper-class families and family structures. Nonetheless, concerns with proper administration of society's economic foundations mean that those documents do not preclude glimpses of the composition and conditions of lower-class families. A comprehensive study of nearly 450 Neo-Assyrian texts (Galil, 2007)—legal transactions, administrative records, court decisions, letters, and ration and census lists originating from six cities, including three imperial capitals (Nineveh, Aššur, and Calah)—shows that socially and economically constrained families were organized along the patrilineal family lines that characterize all ancient Near Eastern families. The fifteen Harran census texts tally households, taking account of land and animals in addition to inventorying people. While the exact purpose of the census texts remains unknown, these administrative records make explicit the makeup of 101 families, first noting male, then female, adults, followed by the number, sex, and age groups of children in each household. Neo-Assyrian slave sale records indicate that families could range in size, from a two-person childless couple to a family of ten persons. Ages of children can be approximated when, for example, children are termed "suckling" (*ša šizbi/zizibi*) or "weaned" (*pirsu*). No documentation confirms the age at which this transition from a state of dependence on the mother occurred, yet the lack of additional descriptors associated with young children suggests that, once weaned, they were reckoned among the productive members of a household. Another indirect indicator of a child's young age is a notation concerning his or her height: those said to measure 3–5 "spans" (*rūṭu*),

equivalent to approximately 21–47 inches, must have been infants or toddlers.

While the administrative documentation concerned with lower-class families offers insights into the statistical composition of the Neo-Assyrian family, the extensive epistolary record originating from the Assyrian court (State Archives of Assyria—SAA) offers more intimate glimpses of aspects of royal family life. From a correspondence focused primarily on matters of succession, political engagement, and other affairs of state, a number of tender scenes emerge. Anxiety about royal infants' elevated fevers (SAA 10 213) and sleeplessness (SAA 10 214), documented in letters between the king and royal doctors, would be familiar to modern-day parents. Another letter (SAA 10 188) reports that Ashurbanipal's dead mother, Ešarra-hammat, returned as a ghost to ensure her son's claim to the throne—a dramatic, if fictional, expression of maternal devotion growing out of tensions that beset the royal family following the elevation of Ashurbanipal to crown prince over his older brother, the rightful heir.

Similarly, tens of thousands of Neo-Babylonian legal and administrative documents focus on the upper-class urban elite and their interactions with palace and temple. Although abundant details of the day-to-day functioning of civic and cultic enterprises are not intended to document families and family structures, the preservation of personal names in standardized naming conventions enables the creation of onomastica (lists of names) and prosopographical notices (family and social connections) from each city and throughout the long sixth century (a construct that reflects the continuity of social and economic trends from the late seventh to the early fifth centuries B.C.E.; see Jursa, 2010). Together, these support an increasingly comprehensive understanding of family structure in the Neo-Babylonian period.

Terminology. Attested in sources throughout the first millennium, the vocabulary of family relationships identifies members of the nuclear family as well as individuals incorporated into households through sanguineous (blood) and affinal (legal, typically marriage or adoption) ties. In Akkadian, father, mother, son, daughter, brother, sister, and wife are designated *abu, ummu, māru, mārtu, aḫu, aḫatu, aššatu*, respectively. Names of grandfathers and great-grandfathers followed *mārmaru*, "son of the son," and *liblibbu*, "descendant," the penultimate term in sequences such as "personal name (PN), son of PN2, *mārmāri* PN3" or "PN, son of PN2, grandson of PN3, *liblibbi* PN4." Akkadian possesses a limited vocabulary of terms for affinal relatives: father-in-law, *emu*; son-in-law, *ḫatanu*; daughter-in-law, *kallatu*, are those most frequently attested. Other relationships, including brother-in-law and sister-in-law, are expressed through periphrastic expressions, e.g., "daughter of the father-in-law." Daughters-in-law are identified by both blood and marital lines: "PN, daughter of PN2 (and) wife of PN3, son of PN4" establishes PN as the daughter-in-law of PN4.

Terms for kin groups in historical inscriptions, as well as in legal and administrative texts, include *kimtu, nisūtu, qinnu,* and *salātu*. Each of these can embrace a broad range of meanings; for example, *qinnu* designates animal lairs, human families of low social status, urban elites, and foreign royalty, as well as groups of individuals linked by social or professional rather than biological ties. In addition to these terms that identify specific family members and familial connections, a variety of naming practices provide insight into the organization of families and their place in a variety of social contexts.

Sociology of the Family. The notion of "family" encompasses networks extending across sanguineous and affinal lines and longitudinally through time, beyond the nuclear family and the generations that immediately precede it. Neo-Babylonian onomastics permit identification of members of families and provide markers for discovering individual agency and native conceptions of family organization. In legal and administrative texts, transaction participants' names appeared in two- or three-tiered filiation statements that also included the name of the participant's father (or ancestor, in the two-tiered genealogy) and ancestor (Nielsen, 2011). This standardized naming pattern makes it possible to identify progenitors who, unless they were themselves principals in transactions, would otherwise

disappear from the documentary record. In the Hellenistic period, expansion of filiation statements to four or five generations, combined with the practice of papponymy—the naming a child for a male ancestor (typically a grandfather)—makes possible recovery of family trees to a depth of as many as eight generations and provides both evidence and a framework for exploring the impact of cultural hybridity on family structures in Hellenistic Babylonia (Langin-Hooper and Pearce, 2013).

In those dense genealogies, some men and women bore "double names," a secondary appellation in Akkadian, Aramaic, or Greek. Akkadian names paired with Aramaic or Greek reflect the multicultural composition of some families. The agency of women is proven by the documentation of women acting as principals in legal or economic transactions, representing their own economic interests or those of their husbands. Naming a female child for a grandmother known to have participated in economic and legal transactions validated the significant roles women played in the community's social and economic life, even as they served, through marriage, to link important branches of urban families.

Naming practices recorded in the genealogical lines of these women show them to have been transmitters of familial and cultural identity as well. Documented cases of maternal-line papponymy (a child named for a male ancestor on the maternal line) indicate that children born in marriages between women of Greek background (as determined by their fathers' Greek names) and men whose Babylonian names point to Babylonian identity were nearly as likely to bear Greek names as they were to have Babylonian names. To the extent that the linguistic origin of a personal name is an indicator of cultural identification (a point still much discussed), maternal-line papponymy attests that in some culturally hybrid families, the cultural heritage of the mother was as valid as that of the father.

Urbanites' claims of descent from putative or known ancestors offer another resource for recovering family structure within Neo-Babylonian society. The overwhelming preponderance of masculine clan names—fewer than a half-dozen female family names are preserved (Wunsch, 2006)—underscores the patrilineal organization of kinship lines in the inventory of clan names. Clan names may be derived from professions: Nappaḫu and Gallābu are Akkadian counterparts to "Smith" and "Barber," well-known surnames in the English-speaking world. Prebendary offices lent their names to families holding these hereditary temple posts that provided income from the performance of ritual duties such as butchering, baking, or even ox herding. Certain names had strong association with particular cities; thus, a member of the Ibnaya family likely hailed from Borsippa, while a descendant of Kuri probably came from Uruk.

The patrimonial organization of ancient Near Eastern society is further evident in the institution of the *bīt abi*, "paternal estate." Already documented in the second-millennium Levant (Schloen, 2001), the expression *bīt abi* may reflect attachment to physical structures connected to a family's historic past. Neo-Assyrian royal inscriptions and Neo-Babylonian archival and administrative documents confirm it as an agnatic (paternal line) institution that served primarily socioeconomic functions, including redeeming from strangers its members' alienated property and, above all, maintenance of its economic contents.

Continuity of family and family lines depends on the addition of family members, with growth achieved through marriage and its expectation of offspring. When biological issue from a marriage was lacking, adoption brought children into the family. The primary motivation for the adoption of boys was the acquisition of heirs to maintain the patrimony. This applied equally in the urban sector and in Neo-Babylonian temple institutions, in which childless priests adopted sons and consecrated them into the hereditary office, thus preserving tradition and guaranteeing transmission of prebendary income to yet another generation. Although the format and content of Neo-Assyrian adoption records differ according to the gender of the adoptee, they all confirm the economic function of the institution in the preservation of the patrilineal organization and focus of ancient Near Eastern society (Radner, 1997). Clauses that confirm adoptive boys as their fathers' heirs do not appear in texts recording girls' adoptions, which appear to have taken place for

other economic, as well as humanitarian, reasons: a transfer of assets accompanied girls' adoptions, and the girl might provide domestic service in the household of her adoptive parents.

In spite of the limitations the documentation imposes, many features of family structures are evident in the textual record of the late first millennium B.C.E. In combination with studies of marriage and divorce, a picture of these active households, engaged participants, and enduring social institutions endures to this day.

[*See also* Economics, *subentry* Ancient Near East; Legal Status, *subentry* Ancient Near East; *and* Marriage and Divorce, *subentry* Ancient Near East.]

BIBLIOGRAPHY

Allison, Penelope M., ed. *The Archaeology of Household Activities*. London: Routledge, 1999.

Baker, Heather D. "The Social Dimensions of Babylonian Domestic Architecture in the Neo-Babylonian and Achaemenid Periods." In *The World of Achaemenid Persia: History, Art, and Society in Iran and the Ancient Near East*, edited by John Curtis and St. John Simpson, pp. 179–194. London: I. B. Tauris, 2010.

Galil, Gershon. *The Lower Stratum Families in the Neo-Assyrian Period*. Culture and History of the Ancient Near East 27. Leiden, The Netherlands: Brill, 2007.

Herrmann, Virginia Rimmer. "The Empire in the House, The House in the Empire: Toward a Household Archaeology Perspective on the Assyrian Empire in the Levant." In *Household Archaeology in Ancient Israel and Beyond*, edited by Assaf Yasur-Landau, Jennie R. Ebeling, and Laura B. Mazow, pp. 303–320. Culture and History of the Ancient Near East 50. Leiden, The Netherlands: Brill, 2011.

Jursa, Michael. *Neo-Babylonian Legal and Administrative Documents: Typology, Contents, and Archives*. Guides to the Mesopotamian Textual Record 1. Münster, Germany: Ugarit-Verlag, 2005.

Jursa, Michael. *Aspects of the Economic History of Babylonia in the First Millennium B.C.: Economic Geography, Economic Mentalities, Agriculture, the Use of Money, and the Problem of Economic Growth*. Alter Orient und Altes Testament 377. Münster, Germany: Ugarit-Verlag, 2010.

Langin-Hooper, S. M., and L. E. Pearce. "Mammonymy, Maternal-Line Names and Cultural Identification: Clues from the Onomasticon of Hellenistic Uruk." *Journal of the American Oriental Society* 133 (2013).

Nielsen, John P. *Sons and Descendants: A Social History of Kin Groups and Family Names in the Early Neo-Babylonian Period, 747–626 B.C.* Culture and History of the Ancient Near East 43. Leiden, The Netherlands: Brill, 2011.

Parker, Bradley J., and Catherine P. Foster, eds. *New Perspectives on Household Archaeology.* Winona Lake, Ind.: Eisenbrauns, 2012.

Radner, Karen. *Die neuassyrischen Privatrechtsurkunden als Quelle für Mensch und Umwelt.* State Archives of Assyria Studies 6. Helsinki: Neo-Assyrian Text Corpus Project, 1997. See esp. pp. 137–143, 200–202.

Radner, Karen. "The Royal Family: Queen, Crown Prince, Eunuchs, and Others." *Knowledge and Power.* Higher Education Academy, 2012. Available online at http://oracc.museum.upenn.edu/saao/knpp/essentials/royalfamily/.

Schloen, J. David. *The House of the Father as Fact and Symbol: Patrimonialism in Ugarit and the Ancient Near East.* Studies in the Archaeology and History of the Levant 2. Winona Lake, Ind.: Eisenbrauns, 2001.

State Archives of Assyria Online: http://oracc.museum.upenn.edu/saao.

Waerzeggers, Caroline. *The Ezida Temple of Borsippa: Priesthood, Cult, Archives.* Leiden, The Netherlands: Nederlands Instituut voor het Nabije Oosten, 2010.

Wunsch, Cornelia. "Babylonische Familienamen." In *Babylonien und seine Nachbarn in neu- und spätbabylonischer Zeit: Wissenschaftliches Kolloquium aus Anlass des 75. Geburtstages von Prof. Dr. Joachim Oelsner, 2. und 3. März 2007,* edited by Manfred Krebernik and Hans Neumann. Münster, Germany: Ugarit-Verlag, forthcoming. Preprint version at http://www.academia.edu/1220404/Babylonische_Familiennamen_preprint_version_.

Wunsch, Cornelia. "Findelkinder und Adoption nach neubabylonischen Quellen." *Archiv für Orientforschung* 50 (2003–2004): 174–244.

Wunsch, C. "Metronymika in Babylonien: Frauen als Anherin der Familie." *Šapal tibnim mû illakū: Studies Presented to Joaquín Sanmartín on the Occasion of His 65th Birthday,* edited by Gregorio del Olmo Lete, Lluís Feliu, and Adelina Millet Albà, pp. 459–469. Aula Orientalis Supplementa 22. Barcelona: Editorial AUSA, 2006.

Laurie E. Pearce

Hebrew Bible

The Hebrew Bible reflects the reality of the importance of family throughout all of its texts. Within ancient Israel, family provided one of the key institutions undergirding the social life of the people. In many ways, the family served as a linchpin, connecting the wider social and economic structures to the micro-sociological actions of individuals and small groups. Thus, family is important not only as an institution of its own but also because it formed the matrix in which individuals expressed and manifested much of their sexuality and gender roles. Similarly, both ancient and modern societies view sexual and gender performance in relationship to family roles.

Any study of the family in history faces the challenge of anachronism, by which we make assumptions about the ancient family because of our experiences of or rhetoric about contemporary families. This is a particular danger because terms such as "the family," "to be a family," and "family values" are so charged in modern discourse, infused with emotional meaning and political significance. Israelite families are strikingly different from families in the modern period in their structure, boundaries, self-understanding, values, and social function.

Although scholars operate with many definitions of "family" in ancient Israel, perhaps a consensus definition would integrate two factors: a sense of lasting relationship (whether genetic, covenantal/contractual/legal, or affinitive) that results in long-term actions of intimacy and loyalty. Such a definition has the advantage of uniting both feeling and action, as well as recognizing that the connections that form family may come from a variety of sources and may find expression in a variety of structures. For sociological purposes, however, it is beneficial to focus on observable social formations. For this reason, we use the term "household" alongside "family." Many families are households, and many households are families, but there can be differences between the two. Two sisters, for instance, may understand themselves as family (i.e., a genetic connection with long-term loyalty and intimacy) yet may not live with each other as part of the same household. At the same time, a household may include family members (those who share genetic relationships and those who are related by legal convention such as marriage or adoption) as well as nonfamily members (such as servants and slaves). Archaeology gives us much more evidence about household than about family. The distinction between family and household is very helpful for analytic purposes, although the original source material of the Hebrew Bible often provides information that does not adhere strictly to such contemporary categories.

Ancient Israelite families and households probably evidenced significant variation in structure and composition in different geographical areas as a result of local customs, and the patterns of family and household probably changed significantly over time. However, modern scholarship cannot easily determine local or chronological variation. Archaeological evidence shows a number of specific examples of households, but it remains difficult to establish a clear pattern. Likewise, the Hebrew Bible portrays many families as well as households, but the texts do not give the reader clear indication of how much these families would be representative of most Israelite families. Since many of the families depicted in the Hebrew Bible are particularly wealthy or powerful families, they may not be very representative. We also do not know how to determine the accuracy of these portrayals. As a result, modern scholarship cannot construct a clear argument for the ways in which the Israelite family varied by region or class, or changed over time, with few exceptions.

Terminology for Family and Household. One of the most distinctive terms in the Hebrew Bible that corresponds to family or household is the *bet 'av*, literally, the "house of the father." This term is used at times in a sense that seems technical, to represent a subdivision of the population, perhaps a clan or part of a tribe. It is used both for a collection of several actual households and also a for a unit of family connection larger than a household. For instance, Abraham desires to find a wife for his son Isaac, but he specifies that the wife must come from Abraham's "father's house" (Gen 24:38, 40), which lies at some distance. This does not refer to the physical house where Terah (Abraham's father) resided; instead, the term must mean something similar to "kindred." This father's house is at a geographical distance and it refers to more than any single household. In the genealogies and population statistics of Numbers 3, the term appears frequently, and the New Revised Standard Version often translates it as "ancestral house," i.e., all of the descendants of a

great-grandfather or some other deceased ancestor. Not all members of this *bet 'av* would know each other or gather regularly, but it would serve as an organizational unit within society. In other places, *bet 'av* seems to refer to smaller units, possibly as small as a nuclear family in a single household (2 Sam 19:28, for instance). Probably many uses of the word *bayit* "house" should be understood as household, in the context not so much of the physical structure but of the social unit and its ongoing function.

The analogous term *bet 'im* ("mother's house") is also used in the Hebrew Bible, although only a few times. In Genesis 24:28, a servant woman shared news with her mother's house. This seems to be a household, although some would argue that it refers only to the female members of the household. Likewise, Ruth 1:8 refers to a mother's house in a way likely to mean a single household, as do Song of Songs 3:4 and 8:2.

Another term, *mishpahah*, is at times synonymous with *bet 'av* (Gen 24:38, 40), but at other times means something more generic (Gen 8:19, where birds and other animals leave the ark in their own *mishpahah*, which seems to indicate "species"). The word also appears in the phrase "all the *mishpahot* of the earth" (Gen 12:3, 28:14). In Exodus 6, *mishpahah* seems to be a population unit greater than a *bet 'av*, suggesting to some that *bet 'av* might be "clan" whereas *mishpahah* would indicate a "tribe," or a grouping of clans. At times (especially in Joshua), *mishpahah* functions as a military unit, from which a certain number of troops would be sent. A larger unit of "tribe" would be the *shevet* or *mateh*, terms that also refer to a rod or a staff that may well be a symbol of authority over such a large tribe (for example, see 1 Sam 9:21). The twelve tribes of Israel are referred to with these terms.

Social Function of the Larger Family. The *mishpahah* or the *bet 'av* (within the larger meanings of the term) functioned as extended family, i.e., groups larger than a household and often ranging over a significant geographical area. These families were not in frequent contact with each other; they might or might not have recognized each other by sight. These larger families might have functioned as administrative units, by which a more centralized government could assess what the families owed in terms of money or people for service. At times, such as in Abraham's consideration for Isaac, there was a desire to marry within the *mishpahah* or *bet 'av* but yet from well outside of the individual's household or region. Thus, these larger families might have represented an endogamous grouping, a group of affinity within which people could marry but outside the close family with whom intermarriage or sexual relations was illegal (Lev 20:10–14, 17–21). Larger family units functioned as recourse for households and other smaller family units in times of crisis such as famine, war, or oppression; people turned to their more distant relatives for help in such times.

Social Roles of the Household. Within the household, social roles were paramount in performing daily life and in establishing relationships with other members of the household. A household would consist of those people inhabiting a single physical dwelling place (whether a permanent structure or a tent). Although we do not know the average size of a household, it may well have consisted of as few as three or four individuals and as many as fifteen to twenty people. Each *bet 'av* had one person designated as the "head" of the *bet 'av* (e.g., Num 1:4). Similarly, each household was ruled by one head of the household, who was the decisive voice in internal matters as well as in relations with other households. Usually, the household consisted of a number of people who shared genetic relationships, as well as others with whom the connections were legal. Households were usually multigenerational.

For example, a household might have included an adult woman and an adult man in a long-term sexual relationship, as well as the children produced by that sexual relationship. Because marriage or sexual relationships in ancient Israel were polygynous, the household might have included additional adult women in long-term sexual relationships with that adult man, as well as the children of those unions. The adult man functioned as head of household, and likely was the oldest male of the household. The adult women all had a legal connection to the head of the household, and the children all had a genetic relationship to the head. To this group of people, the family may well have added other persons. For instance, the household may have purchased slaves or employed servants who lived within the household. These persons were probably not considered permanent members of the household, but their membership in the household was contingent on a length of time of service (possibly negotiated as part of the purchase price). Such service could have been lengthy, and slaves or servants might have been born in the household (Gen 14:14). Persons also could have been added to the family on the basis of genetic connection, if those persons were not part of another household. This could have been the result of individual death or warfare; for example, the death of a head of household (by natural causes, or by death in battle) could have caused a household to dissolve, and the members of the household might have joined the household headed by a brother, son, or other relative of the deceased. In that case, the newly added members might have been the nephews, nieces, aunts, or sisters-in-law of the new head of household. Merging households in this way after the death of a head would have depended on family loyalty to continue the benefits of household membership, necessary for survival.

The head of the household may have been thought of as "father" for the household and would have been a genetic father to many members. The head would have also been considered as the ruler and owner of all the persons in the household, as well as the owner of household property and goods. This rule by the head may have been despotic or generous, but in either case the members of the household would have had little recourse against the decisions and actions of the head. It is likely that the head's rule of the household would have included sexual access to any member of the household, except for those members in particular relationships to the head for which sexual activity was prohibited by law and custom. For instance, sex between a male head of household and his daughter-in-law was prohibited (Lev 20:12), as was sex between that man and his full or half sister (Lev 20:17), his wife's mother (Lev 18:17, 20:14), his uncle's wife or his brother's wife (Lev 20:20–21), or his granddaughters (Lev 18:10); those regulations are presented as pertinent whether or not these relatives are within the same household. However, the male head of household would have had sexual access to the other women of the household, including slaves and servants, as illustrated by a number of Hebrew Bible narratives.

For the adults within a household, parenting would have been an important social role. Men and women alike would have been expected to teach and train children. In ancient Israel, it is likely that children would have been expected to contribute to family life through their own labors at earlier ages than in modern society, but children would still have received instruction, guidance, and discipline from their parents and other adults of the household. This education would have included moral, religious, and cultural aspects alongside practical and occupational instruction. Older children and youth (including siblings) may well have shared some parts of child-rearing and child-care responsibilities, along with older adults such as grandparents or aunts and uncles.

Continuation of Family. Family and household are not merely static realities; they continue over time. Within households, the multigenerational nature of the inhabitants allows for births to balance deaths, at least in many cases. Over time, households may grow or shrink, but many of them endure at about the same size for subsequent generations. This continuation of the household and the family is not automatic, however.

Israelite families were patrilineal. In other words, membership in the household and the family came from fathers, and their offspring lived together in one household and were members of the same larger family, attached also to the father's father's family. Women moved between households, and their descendants were considered part of the child's father's family rather than the mother's family. By contrast, Jewish society in more recent centuries has been predominantly matrilineal, measuring membership in the community and society by whether or not the mother is Jewish, not the father. Thus, genealogies of the Hebrew Bible typically list fathers and sons in subsequent generations; women are absent or mentioned infrequently.

Women moved from one household to another through marriage, usually going from their father's household to their husband's. This arrangement may have involved the purchase of the woman, negotiated between the two male heads of households. Such a price, as well as the dowry, is mentioned in some Hebrew Bible texts and presumed to be a frequent practice, despite the rarity of direct references. Perhaps the practice of dowries was limited to wealthy families, especially among the royal court. It may also be true that formal marriages and weddings occurred only within the upper classes. Whether this was the case or not, it is likely that most couples were from closely related social classes; marriage was not a frequent means of social mobility. Also, many couplings were within the extended family of the clan or tribe, although it is not possible to know how frequently or consistently this was practiced.

Inheritance law allowed property to be passed from a father (i.e., a head of household) to sons, thus allowing the land and goods to stay as an economic basis for the household to continue into another generation. Usually, inheritance went to the oldest son, without the property being divided among younger sons. This kept the wealth of the household relatively intact from one generation to another.

Ancient Israel also practiced adoption, so that a head of household could designate a man other than his son as the household heir. Perhaps the best known case is that Abraham, before he had sons, named Eliezer of Damascus as his heir (Gen 15:2–4). Whether adoption was widespread is not known. If there were no surviving sons, daughters could inherit the household property (Num 26:33), although this seems to be infrequent.

Endangered Families. Families and households faced many challenges in ancient Israel. Famine, plague, pestilence, and warfare could reduce the population of an area in a very short period of time. In such situations, an individual household could experience a collapse in its economic viability, if even a few of its members were killed or injured. Much of the warfare consisted of skirmishes between villages with the intent of stealing food or other goods; this could greatly diminish the viability of a small number of targeted households. Ancient Israel likely experienced higher mortality rates than modern society, at almost every age.

When a male head of household died, the entire household was placed at risk. Perhaps a new head of household emerged, such as the oldest son and heir of the deceased head. With a new head of household, the household may have again become economically viable and may have been able to survive. In other cases, the household dissolved, and the members scattered. Without the protection of the household and its social stability, women and children became widows and orphans. Other households perhaps added these unattached persons to their own numbers, and this may have been a common practice for neighbors or for non-household family members who belonged to the larger family such as the *bet 'av* or *mishpahah*. Individuals needed to be members of households to be economically viable and in order to be economically productive; the society could not afford many unattached individuals. Thus, the care for widows and orphans is an oft-repeated norm and value within ancient Israelite society, expressed in many Hebrew Bible and subsequent texts (for instance, Exod 22:22; Deut 10:18, 14:29, 26:12–13, 27:19; Pss 68:5, 146:9; Isa 1:17; Mal 3:5; Tob 1:8; Jas 1:27). Although families and neighbors were the predominant source of care for those without households, the society considered such care as a responsibility to be shared by all people and in many ways the foundation of all social justice.

At times, warfare and skirmishes resulted in the kidnapping of survivors, usually women, to be added to the households of the victors. Judges 21 tells one of these stories, where the tribe of Benjamin was left without women to be part of viable households. To counter this situation, Israelites raided the city of Jabesh-Gilead to capture women and advised the Benjaminites to kidnap women during the festival at the city of Shiloh, to repopulate the female portions of Benjaminite households. Such a large scale abduction is an atrocity, but the ancient Israelites probably knew of other occasions when such kidnappings occurred in smaller numbers. As Judges 21 illustrates, these kidnappings could instigate chains of violence that only served to disrupt other households. Throughout Israel's history, such violence was one of the greatest risks to the household, whether the violence was organized or random. As a result, households would have needed to protect all of its members at all times.

Productivity. Households are sites for emotional life and for education, as well as for daily life and culture, but there was also an economic aspect to the ancient Israelite household. In modern societies, especially industrialized societies, the individual is presumed to be the basic economic unit. Individuals learn skills, engage in occupations, produce goods, earn wages, buy commodities, and own property. These individuals may or may not share their goods with others, whether family members or members of the same household. By contrast, the household was the basic economic unit in ancient Israel. Although the head of household was considered the legal owner of the persons and property in the household, the lived reality may have been much more communal (although not egalitarian). The household worked together, whether in farming, raising livestock, or manufacturing goods. The household was the recipient of the foodstuffs that they produced, and shared among themselves. The goal of such distribution was to enable the household as a whole to survive and to produce more in the future, so that survival could continue. Labor was often done by the household, or by teams selected from within the household. Together, the household made a contribution to the village or city in which the members lived. In most cases, the household produced all of the food for the household, as well as most of the goods for the household (textiles, pottery, simple tools, buildings, and furniture), although some would be traded between households. The largest part of the economy was the production and consumption of goods within the household.

As Israel experienced some degree of urbanization, the economy likely became more specialized, with trades emerging, such as merchants, weavers, toolmakers, scribes, and so forth. Even in this economic diversification, the trade may well have existed within a household. Such a household would still produce many of its own basic goods but would concentrate on a special trade and produce excess to trade to other households or even other villages or cities. The bulk of goods may still have been produced and consumed within the household. Furthermore, the household (or a significant group within the household) may have practiced the trade or craft together, producing the goods as a household for sale or barter to other households. Certainly, the education for specialized trades was likely to occur within the household, with one generation passing the skill to the next generation within the household through mentoring and apprenticeship models. In this way, the household remained the principal economic unit even as economic diversification took place in ancient Israel.

Cultural Change and Adaptation. Because the household was such a foundational reality within Israelite life, it was the primary mode of transmitting culture from one generation to another. When cultural contact affected Israel through interaction with neighboring societies, the household and the family were the key institutions through which the society processed cultural change and adaptation. Over time, this resulted in changes in family values and meanings, as well as roles and structures, but it was a very slow process for ancient Israel.

Although we cannot develop a full history of the Israelite family, we do know that certain changes transpired between the days of the Israelite monarchy and the times of imperial colonialism during the postexilic period, when Israel experienced the influence of Persian and Hellenistic (and later Roman) Empires. These large cultural powers, supported by military might and economic strength, had a significant impact on Israelite life, especially in matters such as gender roles. Some Hebrew Bible texts explain certain customs to the reader, presumably because those customs had changed between the setting of the story and time of reading. We read within the Hebrew Bible the differences between women who are unable to own property and those who can (Prov 31). This probably reflects cultural change over time. Other neighboring cultures may well have been the source or instigation for such change. If so, we would expect that change would be filtered through the

family and household, with changing expectations about gender roles, age roles, and sexual performance to appear within the household as well as outside in the wider culture. Cultural contact may disturb and disrupt the household, but the household adapts and changes itself over time. Individuals who take new roles within the family and household may then enact those new roles in the rest of society, too, and may do so with the backing of the economic and emotional unit of the household, giving individuals leverage to take new roles in society and create wider cultural change. The household becomes the first realm of contact between Israel and other cultures, as well as the institution through which change occurs. Thus, the family and household, in both its structure and its roles, are vital for our understanding of the entirety of ancient Israelite society.

[*See also* Economics, *subentry* Hebrew Bible; Education, *subentry* Hebrew Bible; Family Structures, *subentry* Early Judaism; Legal Status, *subentry* Hebrew Bible; *and* Marriage and Divorce, *subentry* Hebrew Bible.]

BIBLIOGRAPHY

Archer, Leonie J., Susan Fischler, and Maria Wyke, eds. *Women in Ancient Societies: "An Illusion of the Night."* New York: Routledge, 1994.

Bendor, S. *The Social Structure of Ancient Israel: The Institution of the Family (Beit 'ab) from the Settlement to the End of the Monarchy.* Jerusalem: Simor, 1996.

Berquist, Jon L. *Controlling Corporeality: The Body and the Household in Ancient Israel.* New Brunswick, N.J.: Rutgers University Press, 2002.

Bunge, Marcia J., Terence E. Fretheim, and Beverly Roberts Gaventa, eds. *The Child in the Bible.* Grand Rapids, Mich.: Eerdmans, 2008.

Campbell, Ken, ed. *Marriage and Family in the Biblical World.* Westmont, Ill.: IVP Academic Press, 2003.

Cohen, Shaye J. D., ed. *The Jewish Family in Antiquity.* Brown Judaic Studies 289. Atlanta: Scholars Press, 1993.

Dutcher-Walls, Patricia, ed. *Family in Life and in Death: The Family in Ancient Israel, Sociological and Archaeological Perspectives.* Library of Hebrew Bible/Old Testament Studies. New York: T&T Clark, 2009.

Hess, Richard S., and M. Daniel Carroll R., eds. *Family in the Bible: Exploring Customs, Culture, and Context.* Grand Rapids, Mich.: Baker Academic, 2003.

Knight, Douglas A. *Law, Power, and Justice in Ancient Israel*. Library of Ancient Israel. Louisville, Ky.: Westminster John Knox, 2011.

Koepf-Taylor, Laurel W. *Give Me Children or I Shall Die: Children and Communal Survival in Biblical Literature*. Minneapolis: Fortress, 2013.

Meyers, Carol. *Rediscovering Eve: Ancient Israelite Women in Context*. New York: Oxford University Press, 2012.

Perdue, Leo G., Joseph Blenkinsopp, John J. Collins, and Carol Meyers. *Families in Ancient Israel*. Family, Religion, and Culture. Louisville, Ky.: Westminster John Knox, 1997.

Stager, Lawrence E. "The Archaeology of the Family in Ancient Israel." *Bulletin of the American Schools of Oriental Research* 260 (Autumn 1985): 1–35.

Steinberg, Naomi. *The World of the Child in the Hebrew Bible*. Sheffield, U.K.: Sheffield Phoenix, 2013.

Stone, Ken. *Sex, Honor and Power in the Deuteronomistic History*. Journal for the Study of the Old Testament Supplements 234. Sheffield, U.K.: Sheffield Academic Press, 1997.

Washington, Harold C. *Wealth and Poverty in the Instruction of Amenemope and the Hebrew Proverbs*. Society of Biblical Literature Dissertation Series 142. Atlanta: Society of Biblical Literature, 1994.

Jon L. Berquist

Greek World

In his discussion of the ideal city, the Greek philosopher Aristotle describes the family as the smallest but most vital constituent of a city-state (Gk *polis*), comprising four elements: the male, the female, the servant, and children (*Politics* 1.1.3–6, 1252A–B). For poorer families the servant might be a beast of burden, for others a male and/or female slave, whose children were in turn the property of the master of the household.

Terminology. The most common Greek word used to refer to what we would think of as "family" was *oikos* (plural *oikoi*), "household," as opposed to *oikia*, which was the physical structure of the house. Other key terms are *pater* (father), *mētēr* (mother), *huios* (son), *thugatēr* (daughter), *adelphos* (brother), and *adelphē* (sister). A very young baby might be called a *brephos* and a young child a *teknon*, which as neuter nouns might indicate subconsciously that young children were thought of as essentially asexual, or *pais*, which could be qualified with a masculine or feminine definite article or adjective to indicate sex. This word could also be used to mean "young slave." A parent might be a *goneus* (plural *goneis*), which might also refer to grandparents or great-grandparents (Isaeus 1.39, 8.32). Ancestors further back were termed *progonoi* (literally "born before").

The genos. Each household was also a member of other, wider key social groups. The first of these was the *genos* (plural *genē*), linked linguistically with *goneus* and *progonoi* above, and best translated as "family line." The *genos* was the family unit that stretched backward through time to ancestors, in particular from several *oikoi* to one shared ancestor, and forward to descendants. As in many other ancient cultures, deceased ancestors, and indeed the living elderly, were usually treated with great respect (see Women, Children, and the Elderly below). Ancestors were honored within a private family cult, which bound the unit together on a deeper, religious level. Continuance of the *genos* into future generations was therefore not simply a family affair, but also had important, wider social significance. All ancient Greek families had a morbid fear of their *genos* dying out, so marriage and the procreation of legitimate children (and heirs) were of paramount and constant concern.

It therefore follows that Greek marriages appear not to have been based on romantic sentiment, but rather on a practical need to perpetuate the *genos*. This is evidenced, for example, by the classical Athenian marriage formula, which united the couple "for the ploughing of legitimate children." This near paranoia about the importance of succession helps to explain many of the elaborate provisions that functioned in many different Greek communities to ensure, firstly, the purity of the bride; secondly, her fertility; and, thirdly, her role as a mother of legally legitimate, free children. This concern for the *genos*, which overrides personal preferences, lies behind what may seem to us as callous actions by Greek men, such as Jason in Euripides's tragedy *Medea*

(431 B.C.E.). Medea had helped Jason to escape from his enemies, deserting her family and homeland and following him to the strange Greek city of Corinth. She had provided Jason with sons, but in the play Jason decides that he will abandon Medea in order to marry the daughter of the Corinthian king, Creon. He states that his reason is his concern for his *genos* (l.564): marriage to the princess will secure his children's future. In this context, Medea is dispensable.

The *genos* comprised more than one *oikos*, so members of the same *genos* might not necessarily be kinspeople. Indeed, within each *genos* there appears to have operated a hierarchy of family units, with the land-owning, aristocratic families often playing a leading role, for example in ritual activity through hereditary priesthoods.

The phratry. Each *oikos* also belonged to another social group, the phratry. The origin of these is obscure, but some suggest that they may have originated as military defense units. The ancient Greek word *phratēr* originally meant a brother by blood, and in classical Athenian law the members of the phratry were expected to act in cases of violence against members of an *oikos*, if the members of that *oikos* did not. The phratries were also connected in Athenian society with the villages, or demes, which held lists of citizens.

The kurios. The Greek *oikos* was always headed officially by a man, which reflected the wider, often starkly patriarchal nature of ancient Greek culture. Although the treatment of women varied greatly from city to city throughout the archaic and classical periods, they were always thought to be in need of the supervision of a male, usually because of their alleged weakness of mind. The most common Greek word for the head of the household was *kurios* (plural *kurioi*), his control being called *kurieia*. These words have connotations of power and control, and thus differ significantly in nuance of meaning from the similar role of "guardian" in ancient Roman society, the *tutor*, which is based on *tutus*, meaning "safe," or the "father of the family" (Lat *paterfamilias*).

In certain cases a woman of the *oikos* might hold temporary control over it. We have the example of

Penelope in the *Odyssey*, as well as the wife of an Athenian naval official who left her in control of his estate while he was away (Demosthenes 47). Similarly, a widow might temporarily act to safeguard family property until her children reached the legal age of majority. However, in these cases it is important to note that the woman merely protects existing property; she does not have the power to dispose of it herself as she wishes. We only hear of women disposing of such property in the frequently atypical Greek community of archaic and classical Sparta, where daughters could also inherit their father's property and the right to dispose of it, provided that they also passed this on to their children.

The Household and Land. Along with perpetuating the *genos*, one of the main concerns of the Greek *oikos* was the preservation of its property, especially its land. The Greek word often used for this is *klēros* (plural *klēroi*), meaning "allotment." Most ancient Greek communities were principally agrarian, and so they fiercely protected their land, on which the financial security of the *oikos* relied, often engaging in generation-long violent conflicts with neighbors over ownership. The land that an *oikos* owned was therefore jealously guarded, and was considered important for the well-being and survival of the city-state as a whole. In several cities (e.g., Athens, Corinth, and Thebes) laws prevented such land from falling into the hands of those not of the *oikos*. As such the *kurios* can be thought of as a caretaker of land, which has been lovingly protected and transmitted across the generations.

The wider social importance of the land owned by an *oikos* is shown by the fact that ownership of land which was part of the city was one of the exclusive rights of the (male) citizen. Only in exceptional cases was such land given to people who were not citizens. One such example, which highlights the value of this right, was the granting "to own land" (Gk *gēs enktēsis*) within a city-state to specially selected individuals as a reward for civic service, especially in another city or overseas (e.g., *proxenoi*, "ambassadors").

Women, Children, and the Elderly. The *kurios* of an *oikos* had legal control over its property, and also over the people contained within it. Foremost among these were the women of the household and the children, who would usually not have any active legal identity of their own. Let us consider first his control of his wife. This would come from the day of their marriage and might last her whole life, if he outlived her and did not divorce her. The *kurios* would act as the public legal representative of the household in all matters, even those that concerned his wife. Women in most ancient Greek societies of the archaic and classical periods did not control large amounts of money or property. Any property that came with them as brides, in the form of a dowry, would be at the disposal of the bridegroom. The *kurios* could decide to divorce his wife whenever he wished. This may often have been on the grounds of possible infertility (few Greek scientists entertained the view that infertility could be a male affliction). In such cases the divorced woman might return to a *kurios* in her original, natal family.

While the *kurios* legally represented his wife in most cases, the exception was in public and private religious activity. Women could hold public priesthoods and were responsible for domestic cult, particularly worship of Hestia, goddess of the hearth fire, which symbolized the household. The ideality of Euripides's self-sacrificing tragic heroine Alcestis is illustrated by her farewells to her hearth fire, her marriage bed, children, and servants.

The *kurios* was also in control of his daughters from their birth to their marriage. The men of the bride's and groom's families would usually make the match. We have very little evidence for even elite women being consulted about marriage in any archaic or classical Greek society. The *kurios* of the bride might bestow a dowry to the bridegroom. He would then surrender his daughter to the bridegroom, who then became her *kurios*. Some matches, of course, were between families of unequal wealth. Hence we find traces in some Greek literature, especially comic drama and satire, of the image of the wealthy, dowered bride and the poorer husband, who might complain of being nagged by his wife (e.g., Aristophanes's *Clouds*). In later classical and Hellenistic times we have evidence that some wealthy fathers might retain

some kind of informal influence over their married daughters, even perhaps encouraging a divorce, if a father feared for his property or for his daughter's well-being.

Legitimate and free sons would remain under the care of their *kurios* until they reached the age of majority, usually around sixteen years of age. They would then join the citizen body, which comprised only men and entitled them to serve on juries, hold political office, and participate in the citizen army. From the Hellenistic period this last duty may have begun to lapse, with the advent of professional soldiers.

A further group of women under the control of the *kurios* were elderly women. The old woman was termed a *graus* in Greek, which effectively meant "a woman past childbearing age." A son might be the *kurios* for his elderly widowed mother, as he inherited his mother's dowry on his father's death. Indeed, Greek culture universally valued the elderly, perhaps because their survival was a sign of the goodwill of the gods. To care for the elderly (Gk *gēroboskein*) was an important social duty within the family. In classical Athenian law mistreatment of parents was a serious offense ("Aristotle," *Constitution of Athens* 56.6); conversely, a defendant in court might list as a virtue his care of his parents, and anyone standing for public office was explicitly asked whether they treated their parents well ("Aristotle," *Constitution of Athens* 55.3). Elderly women were especially valued for their luck in surviving the life-threatening dangers of pregnancy and childbirth, and so would have been important and valued members of Greek households.

The Household and the Law. The relationships within a kinship group had to be clearly defined by law. In classical Athens the close kinship group was called the *anchisteia*, which extended to the children of first cousins. This definition is sometimes manipulated by speakers in fourth-century B.C.E. forensic oratory, but may have come into being in the early sixth century B.C.E., when the Athenian lawgiver Solon was conducting his far-reaching social and legal reforms. Members of this group had the obligation to avenge any violent death within the group, to bury the dead, and to seek religious purification, along with the right to inherit estates left vacant after the death of group members.

The central role of the family in the Greek state is illustrated by its treatment in law. In classical Athens family disputes were considered so important to the state that they were classed not as private but public suits. This meant that any male, not simply the alleged victim, could bring court action against an alleged offender.

Legitimacy and Inheritance. Children not born in a legitimate marital relationship were termed bastards (Gk *nothos*, plural *nothoi*). Often the children of slaves or concubines, such male children could not automatically inherit property from their natural father. However, a father, or, after his death, his kinsmen, might officially recognize a bastard as heir, if there was no living male heir.

As ancient Greek communities were patriarchal, inheritance usually passed through the male line. However, issues arose when a father died with no immediate male heir but with a surviving daughter. We have evidence for very similar provision for such scenarios in the laws of classical Athens and the inscriptional law code for Gortyn, on Crete. In classical Athenian law a daughter of such a father, on his death, would become an *epiklēros*. This is often translated as "heiress," but the ancient concept is significantly different: the *epiklēros* did not have the right to dispose of her father's property. Her kinsmen would then arrange for her to marry her nearest agnatic relative, such as a father's brother. Scholars believe that this system may have been established by the Athenian lawgiver Solon during the sixth century B.C.E. He also apparently required the husband of an *epiklēros* to have intercourse with her at least three times a month, and, if that did not produce an heir, to allow his wife to have intercourse with her husband's nearest kinsman (Plutarch, *Solon* 20.2–3). In such cases it is clear that personal considerations came second to the needs of the *oikos*.

Similarly, male orphans who had come into an inheritance could be adopted by relatives to keep the property within the family. In classical Athens the chief magistrate, the *archōn*, was responsible for looking after orphans and their property, as well as ensuring that *kurioi* looked after *epiklēroi* and widows.

Alternative Households. Although it was not strictly part of a man's *oikos*, he might develop a "family" relationship parallel to that with his wife with a concubine (Gk *pallakē*), who may in some cases have been a former prostitute (as happened, for example, in Menander's comic drama *The Samian Woman*). The legal status of the concubine and her children was decidedly open to interpretation. While the Athenian lawgiver Solon, for example, passed laws to protect concubines from physical assault if they were "kept for breeding free children" (Plutarch, *Solon* 23.1), they might also need specific protection after the death of their male protector. In his will the philosopher Aristotle makes detailed provisions for the maintenance and support by his heirs of his concubine, Herpyllis, who survived him. However it is also significant that Aristotle also asks to be buried with his wife, who had predeceased him (Diogenes Laertius, *Lives of the Eminent Philosophers* 5.11–16).

While the family unit of "father, mother, legitimate natural children" was common to most Greek states, two exceptions deserve mention. The elite families of Sparta (*Spartiatai*) required bachelors to marry, but allegedly placed less importance on linear legitimacy, in an effort to maintain their numbers. The same motive explains their practice of marrying girls at the age of eighteen, rather than younger, so that their bodies were strong enough to bear many children successfully. Spartan practice may also have influenced the ideal state imagined in Plato's *Republic*, where children were held in common by the ruling class.

Affection within the Household. One Greek term that is often used to refer to the family is *philoi*, literally "loved ones." This can also refer to friends, but is related to *philein*, one of the Greek verbs for "to love," which is frequently used to refer to affection between family members. Also used for intrafamily affection is the verb *stergein*. The verb *pothein* is used of the emotional longing for something that one once had, such as the love felt for the deceased.

While the importance of legitimate marriage to provide heirs for the *oikos* and *genos* is unquestioned, and in cultures where marriages for most sections of society were arranged by men, it is important to consider whether or not affection ever grew out of such arranged relationships. It is striking from a modern perspective that affection or companionship as a reason for or result of marriage is rarely mentioned before the Hellenistic period. The relationship between what would often be a much older man and young woman is usually not discussed in those terms. More often the husband is the guardian or, indeed, "teacher" of the wife. The most celebrated text for this aspect of family life is Xenophon's *On Household Management* (Gk *Oikonomikos*). This work is presented as a dialogue featuring the philosopher Socrates in discussion with a young male friend, Ischomachus, on the duties of the head of the household. Among other practical responsibilities, the husband is advised to educate his young wife in household affairs. There is no mention of them having any kind of sentimental relationship. Xenophon's work is clearly idealizing: young girls had little formal education during the archaic and classical periods, and what they did receive would have been precisely regarding how to run a household successfully, often passed on from their mother or other older women. However, another work by Xenophon, also a dialogue featuring Socrates, *Symposium*, presents a male-only dinner party, where the guests are entertained by, among others, enticing young male and female dancers. After witnessing their re-creation of an erotic dance, Xenophon ends the work by noting that the guests rushed off back to their own wives. The implication is that the men were fired by lust, rather than affection. This sexual dimension of the marital relationship is also confirmed by the behavior of the husbands and wives in Aristophanes's comedy *Lysistrata* (411 B.C.E.). The women of Greece decide to force their warring husbands to broker peace by abstaining from sex. This ploy is presented as succeeding when political means have failed. Its success as a plotline requires the audience to acknowledge marriage as a sexually desirable relationship. However, with often large age gaps between partners, marital love only really seems to get discussed from the Hellenistic period, especially with the influence of Stoicism.

Affection between parents and children, and between brothers and sisters, is much more widely attested in Greek literature. Classical Athenian tragedies abound in plots that depend on close ties of love between fathers, mothers, sons, and daughters. The myth behind Aeschylus's *Oresteian Trilogy* starts with a father, Agamemnon, being required, reluctantly, to sacrifice his daughter Iphigeneia to the goddess Artemis, so he can sail to the war on Troy. His wife, Clytemnestra, then plots revenge for this outrage, eventually killing her husband (and his concubine). Their son, Orestes, and daughter Electra then in turn exact revenge by killing their own mother and her lover.

Fathers in Athenian drama are usually depicted as taking care of their daughters, as would be expected of an Athenian *kurios*. Agamemnon is presented as reluctant to kill his daughter in both Aeschylus's *Agamemnon* and, especially, in Euripides's *Iphigeneia at Aulis*, where dramatic power derives from the strong bonds of affection between father and daughter. Fathers also look after daughters in comedies (e.g., Aristophanes's *Acharnians*; Menander's *Duskolos/Bad-Tempered Man*, *Perikeiromene/The Girl with Her Hair Cut Short*, and *Misoumenos/The Hated Man*).

The special affectionate bond between mothers and sons is noteworthy in Greek literature. The archaic epic poem *The Iliad* presents several such moving relationships. The Greek hero Achilles has a constant and loving protectress in his divine mother, Thetis; the Trojan hero Hector is the dearest son of his mother, Hecuba. Similarly *The Odyssey* presents the love of the heroine Penelope for her maturing son by Odysseus, Telemachus, and Odysseus's own tender relationship with his mother, Anticleia. In one of the most touching scenes in the poem, where Odysseus meets and talks with her ghost, we learn that she died of grief at her separation from her son. He tries in vain to embrace her three times, and three times she flits away like a dream (*Odyssey* 11.84–89, 152–224, esp. 206–208).

Family relationships between female members are not always tender and positive, however. Classical Athenian tragedy also presents several examples of mothers and daughters or sisters in conflict.

In Sophocles's *Antigone* (discussed further below) Sophocles creates a new mythical character for the traditional storyline in her sister Chrysothemis (meaning "Golden Justice"). When Antigone is determined to disobey the legal prohibition to bury their brother, Chrysothemis is used to voice the other side of the dilemma, that women are weak and should obey the laws of the state. Chrysothemis is depicted as loving her sister and worrying for her safety, while Antigone treats her dismissively. In Euripides's tragedy *Electra* we see the bitter feelings that the daughter Electra has for her mother, Clytemnestra, vividly presented in a climactic scene, where the daughter exultantly lures her mother into an ambush to murder her. Her mother had come to help her daughter after she had been informed (deceitfully) that her daughter had just given birth. Clytemnestra's sympathy and desire to help her daughter are rewarded with death.

Brother-sister love is clearly presented in several surviving Greek tragedies. The most notable example is the relationship between Orestes and his sister Electra in the various versions of the Oresteian myth (Aeschylus's *Oresteia*, especially *The Libation Bearers*; Sophocles's *Electra*; Euripides's *Electra*; Euripides's *Orestes*). As the male, Orestes is the prime mover of revenge against their mother in Aeschylus and Sophocles, whereas the Electra of Euripides's *Electra* is much more proactive and murders her mother, while Orestes murders his mother's lover. In Euripides's *Orestes*, Electra cares tenderly for her brother, as he suffers the madness inflicted upon him by the Furies, who exact revenge on him for matricide. Equally influential on later Western literary tradition is the plot of Sophocles's tragedy *Antigone*, which rests upon the deep love of a sister, Antigone, for her deceased brother Polyneices, whom she dares to bury although the king of her city has forbidden it. Her love for her brother is strengthened by her profound belief that all the dead, whatever their crimes, deserve burial rites in the eyes of the gods. Sophocles is thus able to place an examination of the tension between duties to the state and to the gods within the frame of family ties. The classical Athenian context of the writing and production of these plays helps partly to explain the focus on this particular relationship, as a brother might often have

acted as *kurios* to his sister, so their close family relationship also had a legal dimension. This theme is also developed in later comedy of the fourth century B.C.E., where several plays by the Athenian Menander depict the care and protection of a sister by a brother (e.g., *Heros/Guardian Spirit*, *Perikeiromene/The Girl with Her Hair Cut Short*, *Sikuonios/The Sicyonian*).

Sources and Reconstruction. The range of sources available for the Greek family is wide: fictional, philosophical, historiographical, and medical works; inscriptions (epitaphs); and material evidence (tomb excavations and reliefs, temple reliefs, vase painting, statuary). However, certain key factors should be addressed when interpreting this evidence, factors that emphasize how selective the evidence can be. Firstly, most of what survives was produced by and for the male elite. Secondly, our evidence for some sites, especially classical Athens and Hellenistic Alexandria, heavily dominates the picture. Thirdly, although much remained the same regarding the family over centuries in the Greek world, change did occur, especially in the Hellenistic period, when women in particular developed greater financial freedom. The Roman Empire spread Greco-Roman family ideologies even farther afield. However, despite these developments, the family unit remained the fundamental building block of civilized society.

[*See also* Family Structures, *subentries on* Early Church, New Testament, *and* Roman World; Legal Status, *subentry* New Testament; *and* Marriage and Divorce, *subentries on* Greek World *and* New Testament.]

BIBLIOGRAPHY

Cantarella, Eva. *Pandora's Daughters: The Role and Status of Women in Greek and Roman Antiquity*. Translated by Maureen B. Fant. Baltimore: Johns Hopkins University Press, 1987.

Cohen, David. *Law, Sexuality, and Society: The Enforcement of Morals in Classical Athens*. Cambridge, U.K.: Cambridge University Press, 1991.

Harrison, A. R. W. *The Law of Athens*. Oxford: Clarendon, 1968–1971.

Just, Roger. *Women in Athenian Law and Life*. London: Routledge, 1989.

Lacey, W. K. *The Family in Classical Greece*. London: Thames & Hudson, 1968.

Lefkowitz, Mary R., and Maureen B. Fant, eds. *Women's Life in Greece and Rome: A Source Book in Translation.* 3d ed. London: Duckworth, 2005.

MacDowell, Douglas M. *The Law in Classical Athens.* London: Thames & Hudson, 1978.

Neils, Jennifer, and John H. Oakley, eds. *Coming of Age in Ancient Greece: Images of Childhood from the Classical Past.* New Haven, Conn.: Yale University Press, 2003.

Patterson, Cynthia B. *The Family in Greek History.* Cambridge, Mass.: Harvard University Press, 1998.

Pomeroy, Sarah B. *Goddesses, Whores, Wives, and Slaves: Women in Classical Antiquity.* New York: Schocken, 1975.

Pomeroy, Sarah B. *Families in Classical and Hellenistic Greece: Representations and Realities.* Oxford: Oxford University Press, 1997.

Reeder, Ellen D., ed. *Pandora: Women in Classical Greece.* Princeton, N.J.: Princeton University Press, 1995.

Sealey, Raphael. *Women and Law in Classical Greece.* Chapel Hill: University of North Carolina Press, 1990.

Richard Hawley

Roman World

Discussions of the elite Roman family frequently adopt a multigenerational and diachronic perspective. In describing Roman society of the classical period, which extended from the early second century B.C.E. to the early second century C.E., studies ordinarily focus on how it functioned as a gerontocratic and aristocratic patriarchy. Thus they characteristically foreground the legal right of *patria potestas*, "paternal power of life and death," possessed by male heads of households, *patres familiae*, for as long as they lived, over family members—legitimate offspring and often spouses, as well as slaves. Such studies also tend to emphasize the importance of agnatic relationships, kinship ties traced through male relatives on the paternal side of the family: in part because the Roman system of naming foregrounded agnatic blood bonds, in part because the ancient Roman political system itself placed a high premium on the political achievements of earlier, similarly named male ancestors.

As a result of these Roman naming practices and political values, our extant evidence on the elite Roman family from and about this historical period itself encourages such a perspective. It, too, invites attention to the similarly named agnatic kin of the individual elite Romans, from other and particularly earlier generations, female as well as male relatives, featured in its pages. This testimony is limited, both in quantity and in scope. Most of these witnesses to and chroniclers of Roman society are themselves elite Roman males involved in the workings of its political system.

Yet our most important sources on the ancient Roman family dynamics of the second and first centuries B.C.E. include the biographies of several politically eminent Roman men from this era, written long after their actual lifetimes by a Greek author, Plutarch, during the early second century C.E. When supplying memorable anecdotes that illustrate the distinctive moral qualities of his subjects, Plutarch frequently spotlights the interactions of these men with family members from their own as well as older and younger generations. To be sure, there are other ancient authors who offer valuable evidence about some of these same "noble Romans." Some even include the very same, or at least similar, information. But even though his reliability may be debatable, Plutarch often serves as our only source for a particular incident in the lives of various, mid-to-late Republican Roman males. Although it is important to examine evidence from other ancient classical authors, it is not always possible.

Nevertheless, Plutarch's particular interest in the familial relationships of his subjects leads him to furnish much information of consequence to studies of the structure and function of elite Roman families, including attention to issues as challenging as the interrelationships between half siblings. For example, at chapter 24.2–5 in his life of the elder Cato (234–149 B.C.E.), Plutarch reports that Cato's grown son, informed of his aged father's decision to remarry, inquired if his own conduct was to blame. Cato, Plutarch continues, assured his son that he found him blameless, but merely wished to leave "more individuals like him as sons to himself and citizens to the state." Plutarch emphasizes the low social standing of Cato's bride, his second wife Salonia, contrasting it implicitly to the aristocratic origins of her predecessor, Cato's first wife Licinia. Like the second century C.E. antiquarian Aulus Gellius, who also furnishes details on Cato's two marriages at *Attic Nights* 13.20.16, Plutarch observes that Cato's son by this late second marriage even bore a name identifying him as the descendant of his maternal grandfather Salonius, so as to differentiate himself from his elder half brother. Yet Plutarch represents Cato himself as making no distinction between the offspring of his first and of his subsequent marriages, although his two sons were decades apart in age, and of very different maternal lineages.

What Plutarch relates about the elder Cato warrants notice for various reasons. The legal authority possessed by Roman fathers over all of their legitimate children may help explain Cato's purported refusal to distinguish between his offspring by two different wives. Because, however, Roman mothers did not possess legal authority over any of their children, one might expect to find sharp distinctions made between the offspring that Roman women bore to different husbands, with children from a woman's different marriages residing in different homes and having limited if any contact with one another. But both Plutarch and other ancient sources report several instances of close, mutually supportive ties between children of the same mother by different fathers. Chief among these ties, to be examined below, are the strong bonds enjoyed by the elder Cato's own descendants more than a half-century after he sired his second legitimate son by his second wife: those of Cato the Younger, the elder Cato's great-grandson, with his own half brother Quintus Servilius Caepio and half sisters, both named Servilia.

Plutarch's Testimony and the Mediterranean Family Model. Anecdotes of the kind furnished by Plutarch may tempt scholars to schematize the workings of the elite Roman family by subsuming it under a model propounded by the social scientist Peter Laslett. The characteristics of this "Mediterranean family pattern" include patri-virilocal residence for young married couples along with early and near-universal marriage for women and a considerable age gap between husband and wife. Plutarch reports that Cato's son married his wife Aemilia, a daughter of the great Roman general Lucius Aemilius Paullus

by his first wife Papiria, after Paullus's victory at the battle of Pydna in 168 B.C.E. (*Cato Major* 20.8). Information that Plutarch supplies in his life of Paullus about the dates of Paullus's marriages suggests that Aemilia would have been in her mid-to-late teens; what Plutarch relates in his life of the elder Cato suggests that her husband was several years her senior.

A few chapters later, Plutarch tells us that the widowed elder Cato made plans to take a second wife only after this son evinced his displeasure with the secret visits to his father's bedroom by a slave girl who provided the septuagenarian with sexual services (*Cato Major* 24.2). Plutarch underscores that the son and his new wife occupied the same dwelling as Cato, noting, "in a small house with a young bride in it Cato's carryings on were perceived." So, too, Plutarch's life of Lucius Aemilius Paullus relates that another of Paullus's daughters resided with her husband, Lucius Aelius Tubero, and sixteen of his kin in straitened financial circumstances (5.3–5). The first-century C.E. moralist Valerius Maximus makes the same claim about these Aelii Tuberones (*Memorable Deeds and Sayings* 4.4.9).

Evidence for such practices seems at first glance to fit elite Roman families to Laslett's Mediterranean pattern. Yet it is important to contextualize the information that Plutarch provides, in passing, about the residential arrangements of Cato's son and daughter-in-law and that Valerius Maximus as well as Plutarch furnish about her sister who wed Lucius Aelius Tubero. Since Valerius Maximus and Plutarch do not say how typical these arrangements were, we cannot determine if they are to be interpreted as constituting a pattern. It is altogether possible that Plutarch and Valerius Maximus cite these living arrangements only because they were unusual among members of the Roman elite at that time. Elsewhere in his life of the elder Cato, Plutarch does make it clear that Cato possessed a great deal of wealth, including property. He thereby raises the possibility that Cato chose to live with his adult married son in a small house to advertise his austere and frugal way of existence, thereby promoting his well-polished political image as a simple-living, indulgence-hating traditional-minded Roman.

To be sure, many ancient sources, Plutarch among them, attest that early and virtually universal marriage for elite women, before the age of twenty, to men several years their senior was a common phenomenon among the mid-to-late Republican Roman elite. To judge from our sources, too, some daughters of the most prominent families married for the first time when barely into their teens. But although early marriage for women is also part of Laslett's Mediterranean family pattern, we should observe that frequent remarriage, resulting from both spousal death and divorce, was a fact of elite Roman life in this period as well. Not surprisingly, since all marriages were arranged by the male kin of the nuptial couple, we also encounter instances of forced divorce, with elder family members ending what appear to have been successful and mutually satisfactory unions to relocate male and female children in new, more politically and economically advantageous ones.

Patria potestas allowed a Roman father to dissolve a child's marriage. But some cases of forced divorce, described by Suetonius as well as Plutarch, involved parties other than fathers exerting pressure on married couples to terminate their current marriages and enter new unions. For example, in his life of the younger Cato, Plutarch reports that the distinguished orator Quintus Hortensius Hortalus asked this Cato to end his daughter Porcia's marriage (25.2–5). This entreaty eventuated in Cato's ending, albeit temporarily, his own marriage instead and giving his own wife Marcia in marriage to Hortensius. It is difficult to see how this particular Roman elite brand of "traffic in women" fits into Laslett's Mediterranean family pattern, since religious traditions in preindustrial Mediterranean countries, many of them Catholic, frowned on divorce. Therefore, although Laslett's Mediterranean family pattern has proven "good to think with" in trying to draw conclusions from our evidence—and about our evidence—from Plutarch as well as others on the elite Roman family, what emerges from this evidence about the elite family in mid-to-late Republican society seems too complex to fit into this, or any, pattern.

Half Sibling Ties among Roman Elite Families. A close examination of what Plutarch, often supported by other sources, relates about half siblings among the Roman elite attests to the social complexities of family structure and function while at the same time underscoring some distinctive features of the elite Roman family. Again, we cannot extract much information from our limited evidence. For example, neither Plutarch, nor any other ancient source, happens to describe the personal interactions between the elder Cato's two sons by his two different marriages. Such interactions, of course, were unlikely to have involved socially consequential displays of emotional, political, or financial support. According to Aulus Gellius (13.20.9), Cato's older son died when he was a grown man about to assume the praetorship, when his half brother was still a small child. These sources likewise fail to mention interactions between the children of Lucius Aemilius Paullus by his first wife Papiria—who include not only the daughters married to Cato's son and Lucius Aelius Tubero but also the illustrious political leader Scipio Aemilianus—with the two sons of Paullus's second union: this may be because both of these sons died at early ages, twelve and fourteen respectively, before they were in a position to benefit from publicly supportive conduct from their half siblings.

Plutarch's life of the younger Cato is more informative on this score. It begins by stating that the death of both his parents left this Cato an orphan, together with his "brother Caepio" and "sister Porcia." Yet Plutarch adds, with the Greek adjective *homometrios*, that Cato also had "a sister of the same mother, Servilia." Although Plutarch thereby indicates that Servilia and Cato did not share both parents, he refers to Caepio merely as Cato's *adelphos* (brother) without acknowledging—through the use of Caepio's full name, Quintus Servilius Caepio, or this same adjective—that Cato and Servilia were full siblings and Cato and Caepio half siblings.

By testifying to the extraordinarily close ties between Cato and Caepio and consistently identifying Caepio as Cato's *adelphos*, the first eleven chapters of Plutarch's life may explain why Plutarch does not initially indicate that the two were half rather than full brothers. Plutarch relates that their mother's brother Livius Drusus reared all of this sister's children after their mother's death (*Cato Minor* 1:1). He then observes that one of Drusus's friends faulted Cato as a child for refusing to lobby his uncle on behalf of Roman citizenships for Rome's Italian allies, comparing Cato's conduct unfavorably to that of "your brother" Caepio (2:1–3). Valerius Maximus relates a slightly different version of this same story (*Memorable Deeds and Sayings* 3:1.2).

Plutarch goes on to report that as a small boy Cato was asked whom he loved best, and he repeatedly said "my brother" (3:5). Plutarch then remarks that Cato's affections for his brother intensified as he matured and that when Cato was twenty years old he would not dine, travel, or go out into the forum without Caepio (3.5–6). Plutarch claims, too, that Cato volunteered to fight in the war against Spartacus for the sake of his brother, since Caepio was a military tribune (3.8.1). Finally, Plutarch describes Cato's unsuccessful struggles to reach Caepio's deathbed in Thrace, Cato's abundant show of grief at Caepio's passing and lavish expenditures on his funeral, and Cato's insistence on not seeking reimbursement from Caepio's estate, which he and Caepio's young daughter jointly inherited (3.11).

Later in his life of the younger Cato, Plutarch accords substantial attention to Cato's supportive conduct toward his surviving female half siblings. He reports that although Cato prosecuted Lucius Murena for having secured election to the consulship with Decimus Junius Silanus by bribery, he exempted Silanus from prosecution because he was the second husband of, in Plutarch's words, "Cato's sister Servilia" (*Cato Minor* 21.3). A few chapters later, Plutarch describes how, during a Roman senate meeting, Cato suffered embarrassment over the torrid erotic content of a note sent to this half sister, Servilia, by her lover and Cato's foe, Julius Caesar (24.1–2). Nevertheless, after Cato demanded to read its message, he threw the note back to Caesar with a dismissive remark and resumed the speech he was in the process of delivering.

Plutarch further relates that Cato opposed attempts by Gaius Memmius to deny Lucius Licinius Lucullus a triumph when Lucullus returned from the east in 66 B.C.E. because Lucullus was married to "the other"

Servilia, a half sister whom Plutarch similarly identifies only as a "sister" (*Cato Minor* 29.3). Plutarch actually introduces this other half sister named Servilia earlier in his life of the younger Cato, at 24.3, where he states that Lucullus drove her from his house because of her sexual misbehavior. Yet Plutarch later relates that after Lucullus's death Cato took this half sister and her young child by Lucullus with him to Asia, remarking that she put an end to much of the criticism leveled against her moral failings by submitting to Cato's guardianship and willingly sharing his wanderings and modes of living (54.1).

Plutarch, moreover, represents Cato's helpful and generous behavior toward his two half sisters and their husbands as no different from his conduct toward his full sister Porcia and her husband Lucius Domitius Ahenobarbus. He observes that Cato evinced strong political support for Domitius by persuading him to stand for the consulship against Pompey and Crassus in 56 B.C.E. (*Cato Minor* 41.2–3). Cato, Plutarch states, even protected Domitius physically when Pompey's partisans ambushed him, suffering an arm wound in the process.

It warrants emphasis, too, that Cato favored his half sister Servilia, notwithstanding her long liaison with his enemy Caesar, over his full sister Porcia in a crucial way: by showing a special interest in Marcus Junius Brutus, Servilia's son by her first husband. To be sure, Cato's beloved half brother—and Servilia's full brother—Quintus Servilius Caepio accorded Brutus special treatment as well by adopting him in his will. But Plutarch reports that Brutus was invited, as a very young man, to accompany his "half uncle" Cato on a trip to Cyprus, where Brutus won Cato's praise by taking capable charge of King Ptolemy's treasures (*Brutus* 3). Brutus, Plutarch says, "had a higher esteem for Cato than for any other Roman" (2.1); Cato, of course, eventually became Brutus's father-in-law as well as his uncle, since Brutus later took Cato's widowed daughter Porcia as wife. Besides strengthening his ties with his own half sister Servilia through his union between her son and his daughter, Cato appears to have strengthened ties between his own offspring by his two wives, Atilia and Marcia, with Hortensia, the widow of his half brother (and Brutus's adopted father) Caepio, through a controversial marriage, mentioned previously, that made this half sister-in-law the half sister to Marcia's own offspring.

Plutarch further relates that Hortensia's father Quintus Hortensius Hortalus was eager to share a bond of kinship with Cato: he thus tried to persuade Cato to dissolve his daughter Porcia's marriage to her first husband Lucius Calpurnius Bibulus, by whom she had two sons, and give her to him as "noble soil for producing children" (*Cato Minor* 25.205). When Cato denied Hortensius's request, Hortensius then asked to wed Cato's own wife Marcia, since she was still of child-bearing age and Cato had enough heirs. Although Marcia was pregnant at the time, Cato consented to this arrangement. First, he sought and received the approval of Marcia's father, Lucius Marcius Philippus, later the stepfather of the man who became the emperor Augustus, and agreed to join Philippus in giving the bride away.

Marcia's marriage to the much older Hortensius proved fruitful, producing a half sibling for both Marcia's children by Cato as well as for Hortensius's daughter. Furthermore, when Hortensius died and left Marcia a very rich widow, Cato married her again, prompting Julius Caesar to accuse Cato of both greed and "trafficking in marriage" (*Cato Minor* 52.3–5). Plutarch defends Cato, asserting that to charge Cato with a sordid love of gain is like reproaching Heracles with cowardice. And Cato himself, Plutarch tells us, justified his remarriage on the grounds that his household and daughters, presumably by both Atilia and Marcia, needed someone to take care of them. Such a practice seems consonant with the traditions of Cato's family, which sought to keep children from their parents' different marriages together, in this case with either their own father, their own mother, or both. As Plutarch remarks at *Brutus* 7, Cato's half sister Servilia followed similar practices in strengthening ties between her children by her two unions: one of the Juniae, daughters of Servilia's second marriage to Decimus Junius Silanus, was married to Gaius Cassius Longinus, conspiratorial ally of her own half brother Brutus.

Contingent Kinship: The Challenges of Our Evidence. Again, the exigent and problematic nature of our evidence for elite half sibling relationships during the mid-to-late Republic limit the inferences we can draw from it, whether about Roman society as a whole or even about the elite Roman family at that particular time. In discussing the family of the elder and younger Cato, I have tried to adduce testimony about interactions within families for which Plutarch is an important but not the sole surviving source and for which we have evidence earlier than that provided by Plutarch. But it is not always possible to find evidence of this kind. Furthermore, some sources on elite families that postdate Plutarch, such as Aulus Gellius's disquisition on the descendants of the elder Cato, are extremely valuable in spite of their later date.

So, too, even the evidence of earlier sources supporting Plutarch's contentions tends to be anecdotal and, with a few notable exceptions such as that written by the second century B.C.E. Greek historian Polybius, written long after the familial interactions it claims to document. Solely on the basis of what Plutarch reports in his life of the younger Cato, scholars have concluded that Plutarch's testimony to genealogical material is vague, inconsistent, and unreliable, since Plutarch's primary concern is moral: to illustrate the ethos desirable in the statesman. Yet however frustrating we find Plutarch's anecdotal, vague, and inconsistent mode of exposition and the anecdotes supplied by other ancient sources, it is nearly impossible to trace relationships between elite Roman children who shared a mother but not a father, because children of different fathers had different names.

It merits emphasis as well that the evidence we have examined on half sibling ties in Roman families only illuminates the practices of the Republican political elite, who had vested interests in marrying their daughters as early as possible (and, some would add in jest, recalling the adage about Chicago, as often as possible) for the sake of forging political alliances and producing heirs. But even if they were not representative of all Roman households, elite families of this period were important in their own right as powerful political institutions and as models for less affluent and advantaged Romans in their family lives. And it is worth reminding ourselves that our slim, anecdotal, selective evidence on elite Roman half siblings, from sources often written much later than the events they describe, have special value for attempting to document feelings and behavior and for problematizing the efforts made by some prosopographical studies to extrapolate political allegiances solely on the basis of agnatic ties.

Indeed, in a society such as that of elite Rome in the mid- and late Republican period—with its arranged marriages; frequent and even forced divorces; and a high likelihood that one or more parents would die from disease, war, or childbirth—the valuation of half siblings by Roman elite families is not difficult to understand. Endeavors by family members of an earlier generation and by half siblings themselves to strengthen emotional and familial ties among offspring who shared only one parent functioned as an important survival strategy for both the families themselves and for their individual members. As we have seen, the significance accorded to promoting and sustaining bonds among half siblings also may account for such ostensibly anomalous behavior as the younger Cato's cohabitation with his former wife Marcia after she was widowed by the illustrious orator Quintus Hortensius, along with their children from their various marriages.

Finally, the accounts we have examined and the conduct and feelings of elite Romans themselves that they describe help substantiate Butler's contention about the socially contingent nature of kinship as strategic, shifting, and contingent (2000). Scholars such as Butler and Rubin (1996), however, argue that kinship systems sustain social structures primarily through promoting exchanges of women by their male kin, so as to effectuate marital arrangements linking men and women of approximately the same generation. Yet efforts by elite Roman Republican families to privilege and strengthen sibling ties do not involve exchanges of marriageable women by men for reproductive purposes, although often half siblings themselves, such as the younger Cato and his half sister Servilia, seem to have strengthened their ties to one another through marriages between their own offspring. In fact, the adoption of men by other families entailed the exchange of younger males by older males. An examination of half siblinghood in elite Roman society points us the significance that Romans accorded to blood relationships to and through both men and women, to the extent that ties of blood might at times be of greater consequence than paternal rights of control over offspring.

[*See also* Family Structures, *subentries on* Greek World *and* New Testament; Legal Status, *subentry* Roman World; *and* Marriage and Divorce, *subentries on* Greek World, New Testament, *and* Roman World.]

BIBLIOGRAPHY

Astin, Alan E. *Scipio Aemilianus.* New York: Oxford University Press, 1967.

Astin, Alan E. *Cato the Censor.* New York: Oxford University Press, 1978.

Butler, Judith. *Antigone's Claim: Kinship between Life and Death.* New York: Columbia University Press, 2000.

D'Arms, John. *Romans on the Bay of Naples: A Social and Cultural Study of the Villas and their Owners from 150 B.C. to 400 A.D.* Cambridge, Mass.: Harvard University Press, 1970.

Dixon, Suzanne. "The Circulation of Children in Roman Society." In *Adoption et Fosterage*, edited by Mireille Corbier, pp. 217–230. De l'Archéologie à l'Histoire. Paris: De Boccard, 1999.

Dixon, Suzanne. *Cornelia, Mother of the Gracchi.* Oxford and New York: Routledge, 2007.

Gordon, H. L. "The Eternal Triangle, First Century B.C." *Classical Journal* 28, no. 10 (1933): 574–578.

Hallett, Judith P. *Fathers and Daughters in Roman Society: Women and the Elite Family.* Princeton, N.J.: Princeton University Press, 1984.

Hallett, Judith. "Queens, *Princeps* and Women of the Augustan Elite: Propertius' Cornelia-Elegy and the *Res Gestae Divi Augusti.*" In *The Age of Augustus*, edited by Rolf Winkes, pp. 73–88. Publications d'Histoire de l'Art et d'Archéologie de l'Université Catholique de Louvain 44; Archaeologia Transatlantica 5. Providence, R.I.: Center for Old World Archaeology and Art, Brown University; Louvain-la-Neuve Belgium: Institut Supérieur d'Archéologie et d'Histoire de l'Art, Collège Érasme, 1985.

Hallett, Judith. "Fulvia, Mother of Iullus Antonius: New Approaches to the Sources for Julia's Adultery at Rome." *Helios* 33, no. 2 (2006): 149–164.

Hallett, Judith. "Recovering Sulpicia: The Value and Limitations of Prosopography and Intertextuality." In

Receptions of Antiquity, edited by Jan Nelis, pp. 297–331. Ghent, Belgium: Academia Press, 2011.

Harders, Ann-Cathrin. "An Imperial Family Man: Augustus as Surrogate Father to Marcus Antonius' Children." In *Growing Up Fatherless in Antiquity*, edited by Sabine Huebner and David Ratzan, pp. 217–240. New York: Cambridge University Press, 2008.

Harich, Henriette. "Catonis Marcia: Stoisches Kolorit eines Frauenportraits bei Lucan (II 326-350)." *Gymnasium* 97 (1990): 212–223.

Laslett, Peter. "Family and Household as Work Group and Kin Group: Areas of Traditional Europe Compared." In *Family Forms in Historic Europe*, edited by Richard Wall, Jean Robin, and Peter Laslett, pp. 513–563. New York: Cambridge University Press, 1983.

Rubin, Gayle. "The Traffic in Women: Notes on the Political Economy of Sex." In *Feminism and History*, edited by Joan W. Scott, pp. 105–151. New York: Oxford University Press, 1996.

Severy, Beth. *Augustus and the Family at the Birth of the Roman Empire*. New York: Routledge, 2003.

Treggiari, Susan. *Roman Marriage. Iusti Coniuges from the Time of Cicero to the Time of Ulpian*. New York: Oxford University Press, 1991.

Judith P. Hallett

New Testament

Familial language in New Testament texts appears most frequently in the Pauline and deutero-Pauline letters in which matters of everyday practice appear. In the Gospels, familial language is often mentioned in passing, with the exception of Jesus's warning that his mission destroys familial relationships, pitting sons against fathers, daughters against mothers, and daughters-in-law against mothers-in-law (Matt 10:35–39; see also Luke 14:26). In these pairings, it is those with the least power who rise against the powerful. While each pairing is unisex, the power differentials make them useful for talking about gender as a social construct in antiquity. Those with the most power to make decisions for others who were connected to them through familial ties are often understood in masculine terms. Those who are subordinate are often feminized. Tracing gender through power networks reveals a fuller picture of how family life unfolds in the New Testament.

Given this idea of power networks, our assumptions about gender roles in ancient families should be interrogated. Prohibitions in New Testament texts against women participating in leadership often signal the historical reality of their leadership. Likewise, arguments for or portraits of women in subordinate positions are not necessarily evidence of actual subordination. For example, traditionally Jesus's disciples were understood as exclusively male without families. Yet Jesus heals Peter's mother-in-law along with many others to whom hospitality is extended (Matt 8:14–17). While the mother-in-law plays a servant role in Matthew's version of the story, the fact of her inclusion illustrates first of all that families were vitally important to Jesus's and the disciples' work. Secondly, this story suggests that Peter's mother-in-law was not an incidental person or even mere support staff in the life of the disciples. Rather she was a leader in the movement, bringing together many kinds of people under her household for the purpose of healing. To conclude that she and other members of the disciples' familial structures were only ancillary to Jesus's ministry assumes that textual marginalization reflects historical marginalization.

Terminology. Greek does not have a word whose semantic range approximates "family" in English. There are words that describe relationships: *mētros* (mother), *pater* (father), *thugatēr* (daughter), *uios* (son), *adelphē/adelphos* (sister/brother), *despotēs* (master), *klēronomos* (heir), *doulos* (slave). These relationships are situated in particular power networks constituted by the relationship described. The word *genos* is sometimes translated as family, although it denotes a tribe, a familial lineage, and is often closely associated with *ethnos* or the larger ethnic/cultural/racial group to which a person belongs. This lack of clear vocabulary suggests that nuclear families were not the primary social units in New Testament texts. Indeed, texts that are often considered determinative for "family values" discuss relationships within a different social system.

Households and Household Codes. The word *oikos* is sometimes translated as family, although it more often refers to the physical space of a house or the conceptual understanding of a household. As a concept a household signals more than a nuclear family or even an extended family tree. Rather, it signals the collective group of persons whose livelihood, religious orientation, dwelling place, and/or social status are connected to a single person or a couple who are considered the head of a household. For example, a wealthy landowner who also had a house in a city (Luke 20:9–19; Matt 21:33–46; Mark 12:1–12) may have counted myriad slaves, clients (people who work for him/her), children, adopted children, a spouse, and perhaps adult siblings or parents as part of her or his *oikos* (household). The household was the fundamental unit of society and with the rise of the Roman Empire became the fundamental political unit as well. All inhabitants of the empire were considered members of the emperor's household. This shift in social structure did not dissolve existing households, but rather put each one under the patronage of the emperor. Such a move claims the power of the *paterfamilias* over all households, including those in the New Testament. Ephesians 2:19 claims this power instead for God, suggesting that those in Christ are no longer alienated from the household of God but rather are members.

In Acts and Paul's letters, several examples of households emerge. Peter seeks refuge at the house of Mary, the mother of John-Mark, after his stay in prison in Jerusalem. Rhoda, an enslaved member of the household, meets Peter at the gate (Acts 12:12–17). Lydia and her household (presumably enslaved persons, employees, and perhaps children or parents) were baptized after hearing Paul in Philippi (Acts 16:14–15), and she sheltered Paul and Silas after their release from prison there (Acts 16:40). Prisca and Aquila worked with Paul, risking their lives for him, and were known in the Roman community to which he writes (Rom 16:4–5). They also sponsored a gathering in their household in Asia (1 Cor 16:19). Nympha hosted an assembly in her household, perhaps in Laodicea (Col 4:15). In Philemon, Paul greeted Philemon, Apphia, Archippos, and a gathering in a household using the second person singular, but it is unclear which of the three named addressees was considered the household head (Phlm 2). In this list most, if not all, of the households are named for the women at their head. Lydia, Mary, and Nympha

seem to be heads of households. Prisca is always mentioned with Aquila. Apphia, whether or not she is married to Archippos or Philemon, could be a household head. While we are tempted to conclude that Christ-following households were more egalitarian, evidence exists in antiquity for women as heads of household across the Mediterranean.

Given these identifications of households with women, we should be careful to note that households or even physical house structures did not play the same role of dividing public and private space as they do today. First, the physical house structure was not synonymous with the concept of household, as the example of the imperial household shows. The most lavish houses, especially in the cities of Asia Minor and Greece, would have contained public spaces that were sites for economic, religious, and political transactions. Even more so, housing for tradespersons, skilled laborers, small-scale merchants, tavern operators, and other less wealthy persons would have been connected with workshops, warehouses, or shop spaces. Less lavish housing would also have provided fewer boundaries between dwellings. In addition, households were not necessarily contained in a single physical house. A wealthy head of household could maintain multiple houses in different cities or across urban and rural landscapes. Thus, households were not private domestic entities to which women were confined as opposed to public political space outside the house in which only men functioned. Instead households were the basic unit of the social and civic world in the first century C.E. The fact that the New Testament remembers women participating in economic, civic, social, and religious life as leaders of households should not be surprising.

The term *oikonomia* refers to the management of this collective group at the hands of the head of a household (Lat *paterfamilias*). Most ancient literature discussing household management in an ideal sense assumes that men are heads of households—an ideal that stands in tension with historical actualities. In these ideal portraits, householders' wives assist in management tasks. Yet these texts betray an ideal that was possible only for the wealthiest ranks of society. In the New Testament, we find three separate lists, instructing different members of households about their proper relationship to the head (Col 3:18—4:1; Eph 5:21—6:9; 1 Pet 2:18—3:7; see also 1 Tim passim; Tit 2:3–10). Called household codes, or *Haustafeln*, these texts argue for a kind of household management that draws on Aristotle's *Politics* and Arrius Didymus's application of it to imperial ideologies. The New Testament household codes draw on ancient rhetoric that creates a clear patriarchal structure for household relationships. For example, Colossians 3:18—4:1 addresses three reciprocal pairs of household relationships: husbands and wives, fathers and children, masters and slaves. Interpreting Paul's instructions in 1 Corinthians 7 about the relationship of husbands to wives, the writer of Colossians suggests that those of whom subordination (*hupotassō*) and obedience (*akouō*) to husbands, fathers, and masters is required should understand that obedience and subordination as directed toward God (Col 3:23–25). As a result, relations of subordination and obedience are divinely sanctioned. Yet we have already seen that historical practices may not have borne out the gender divisions that patriarchy implies. Some women were heads of households (Lydia, Acts 16:14–15); others owned slaves (Mary, Acts 12:12). Some slaves wielded power over others, including free persons (see Matt 21:23–35). Thus, we must consider the intersectional nature of power structures when analyzing gender, ethnicity, economic status, and social status in New Testament communities.

The household codes essentialize persons and roles, suggesting that households in the Christ community should model themselves after imperial household ideologies. Women qua women are only mentioned in husband-wife relationships, even though enslaved persons in antiquity were feminized because of their subordination and availability to their masters for sexual use (see below). These lists also implore children to obey parents. Yet for enslaved children, such obedience is ambiguous at best, as they would frequently need to decide between obedience to master and obedience to parent. Reading these lists with an understanding that identities are intersectional shows the ways in which the codes reflect an attempt to impose elite household social relationships on a community for whom such structures are much more complicated in their everyday interactions.

Inheritance. The lack of vocabulary for nuclear families, and particularly vocabulary denoting the same kind of emotional ties as in modern families, highlights the main reason for invoking familial language: it often describes inheritance lines for passing on property. As such, familial language is often gendered, prioritizing fathers, sons, and powerful male figures. While technically under Roman law daughters/women could not inherit or own property without a male guardian, women found ways to circumvent these legal restrictions. While some enslaved persons or freed persons found opportunity and had the resources to pass wealth to their progeny, the Roman imperial inheritance system was only available to very few. Even for households with little wealth to inherit, a person's legal status determined the transmission lines according to gender. Scholars have noted that patrilineage (inheritance through the father's lineage; see Matt 1:1–16 and Luke 3:23–38) was a privilege of elites, while matrilineal inheritance (inheritance through a mother's lineage) often connoted enslaved status. Jesus's genealogy in Matthew uses both male and female characters to trace his family lineage, including women whose ethnic heritage and sexual history do not fall into traditionally respectable categories (e.g., Rahab, Ruth, Tamar, Mary). In both Matthew and Luke, the authors make the case that Jesus's inheritance comes from a particular kind of genealogical relationship to God, either through Abraham (Matt 1:2) or through Adam (Luke 2:38).

Children and Adoption. Children in antiquity were an investment rather than an object of emotional attachment. As such, children of the head of the household and those who were enslaved were often perceived similarly. Once a child (including an adopted child) reached the legal age of inheritance, his or her status changed within the household. Sons (including adopted sons) became heirs. Daughters became marriageable, often with the aim of increasing familial wealth. Slaves remained under their owner's complete control. Large numbers of children from a married head-of-household couple were not the norm; thus disputes over distribution were uncommon. Not only was infant mortality (and mortality in childbirth) very high in the ancient world, but the practice of exposure was also prevalent. Children with birth defects or who were unwanted were often abandoned. Most of these exposed children died; others were picked up by slave traders. While little is known about them, some children were adopted into households as enslaved foster children (*threptoi*).

Ancient biography often included a birth narrative of the person and stories of the adult-like wisdom and comportment of that child. Luke's Gospel, in particular, follows this convention with Jesus teaching in the temple at the young age of twelve (Luke 2:41–52). The temple officials recognize and marvel at his wisdom even as his parents reprimand him for staying behind when his kin group starts the journey home. Jesus the child, then, is remarkable for his adult-like qualities. Matthew's Jesus teaches using a child (Matt 18:1–5) and suggests that his adult followers should become like children. This teaching suggests a reversal in values rather than a celebration of childhood innocence. Adult-like wisdom is not what will earn reward in the kingdom of heaven.

Adoption (*huiothesia*) was prevalent, particularly among ruling elite families as a means of passing on wealth and titles. Augustus, for example was the adopted son of Julius Caesar. Hadrian adopted Lucius Verus and Marcus Aurelius, who had already adopted Antoninus Pius, creating the Antonine dynasty in the second century. The goal of adoption was not to obtain children or even to care for children in need of parents; rather, adoption was a means to ensure succession of wealth and power. An adopted son was considered the legitimate heir to his new father's estate regardless of the existence of biological children. Single men could adopt sons without necessarily marrying. In fact, Seneca suggests that the decision process for considering a wife is similar to that for considering an adopted son. Women, however, were rarely adopted as heirs. The exception may be Livia, whom Augustus adopted (his own wife!) in order to ensure Tiberius's inheritance, since Tiberius was a minor at Augustus's death. There is

no evidence of women adopting heirs themselves. Thus adoption is primarily a means of continuing male lines of authority.

Paul's letters to the Galatians and Romans use adoption metaphors to describe the relationship between God and those in Christ who will inherit the promises God made to Abraham (Gal 3:29—4:6). Through adoption (*huiothesia*) believers in Christ become heirs. Paul's argument, drawing on adoption as a legal means for inheritance, first reminds readers that slaves and children not yet of age possess the same social status within households: they live under the authority of the head of the household (Gal 4:3). Paul suggests that both those who are descendants of Abraham (Jews) and those who are not (gentiles) must be adopted in order to inherit the promise (Gal 4:5). The alternative is to remain a slave to the spirits of the world. In Romans 8:12–17, Paul uses this adoption metaphor again in connection with slavery and urges readers to live according to the Spirit of God, as if they were adopted children that is children who will inherit all that belongs to God. Once again, the alternative is to be enslaved. This juxtaposition of heir and slave draws on gendered hierarchies within the ancient world: heirs are by definition male children with power, wealth, and social prestige, while slavery feminizes persons, male or female. Paul continues, however, arguing that his readers are joint heirs with Christ, sharing both in Christ's suffering (which would indicate enslavement and feminine lack of power) and eventual glory (which vindicates both enslavement and feminine weakness).

Enslaved Persons. Enslaved persons were considered part of a household and thus were included in families. Evidence suggests that even very small households in antiquity would have owned a slave or two. In Luke 17:7–10 Jesus draws on this assumed reality when he suggests that the disciples should understand themselves as slaves to God, constantly obedient and attentive to the needs of God's household. In the parable, the master has only one slave who works in the field and comes in for more service at the end of the day. This parable values obedience to the male householder, and by metaphorical extension to God. Some interpreters see the replacement of the male householder with God as a subversive reversal of power dynamics. Others notice that the gendered power structures remain in place with the metaphor substituting one male power figure for another (albeit a more benign one). Regardless of how one interprets power relationships in the parable, the underlying relationship between master and slave is one fundamental to representations of familial relationships in the New Testament.

While some enslaved persons whose masters were wealthy and socially well placed had access to some of that wealth, social influence, and political power, most were owned en masse with little or no power. Many belonged to households with midrange to lower-level economic, social, and political status. These households depended on their slaves for their economic health. For example, in Acts 16:16–19, Paul and Silas encounter an enslaved girl in Philippi whose powers of divination bring her owners significant income. When Paul and Silas become annoyed with her heralding of them as slaves of the Most High God, they exorcise her divining power. Luke says that her owners are so upset that they report Paul and Silas to the Roman officials. While it is possible to understand this enslaved girl as liberated from her exploitation, Luke never mentions her manumission, but rather assumes she remained with her original household. Even if she had been manumitted, freed persons remained members of their former masters' households as clients under the patronage system. In other words, familial ties that were drawn through enslavement remained even when legal status changed.

In addition to the enslaved girl in Acts, the New Testament names several other persons who are slaves, such as Rhoda, the slave who greets Peter at the gate of Mary's house (Acts 12:12). Onesimus, about whom Paul writes his letter to Philemon, Apphia, and Archippos, is another (Phlm 10). While scholars dispute the nature of Paul's request regarding Onesimus, nevertheless his relationship with the household in which the Christ-following community meets is the main subject of the letter. Other characters in Paul's letters bear names consistent with current or former

enslavement: Tertius the scribe (Rom 16:22) and Epaphroditos, a coworker of Paul's in Philippi (Phil 2:25–29). The power dynamics present between enslaved members of households and those who were free, particularly masters, feminized enslaved persons.

As a result, enslaved persons were understood as sexually available to their masters. Indeed, this availability was part of the *macula servus*, or stain of slavery, that accompanied anyone who had been enslaved at any point in his or her life. Although 1 Corinthians in particular discusses sexual morality between men and women who have choices about their sexual partners, the case can be made that sexual relations between master and slave do not count as sexual immorality (*porneia*) or sexual behavior prohibited in Paul's rhetoric for its pollution of the body of Christ (1 Cor 6:15–20). Sexual relationships between masters and slaves remained unquestioned in New Testament texts.

Enslaved family ties often extended across several households. This fact complicates the idea that households were the basic familial units in antiquity. Enslaved persons with familial relationships could belong to different households. Thus a mother might have one owner while her children and their father each have different owners. While Acts does relate that whole households (including slaves) were baptized at once (Lydia's household, Acts 16:14–15), some enslaved persons were members of early Christian communities but not members of a Christian household (1 Tim 6:1–2). In addition, the household codes in Colossians 3:18—4:1 and Ephesians 5:22—6:5 as well as the discussions in 1 Corinthians 7:21–24, 1 Peter 2:18–25, and 1 Timothy 6:1–2 address enslaved persons directly, in the vocative case. Such direct address to enslaved persons is highly unusual in ancient literature. These passages by and large instruct enslaved persons to remain subordinate and obedient to their masters, hinting that in reality they functioned more as equal partners in the Christian community. In contrast to the instructions that attempt to solidify discrete household structures according to gendered power rules, the actual practices of early Christian communities often flowed across household and familial boundaries. Other groups in antiquity, such as the Therapeutae and Cynics, also reconfigure family without reference to the basic structures of household order (i.e., slavery, marriage/inheritance, etc.).

Celibacy. Enslaved persons had no means to practice celibacy or even monogamy; their role in the familial structure precludes such discipline. For others, New Testament texts are mixed about whether celibacy allows for greater concentration on Jesus's mission or poses threats in leaving women's sexuality uncontrolled. Paul writes in 1 Corinthians 7:7–8 that widows should remain unmarried like Paul himself unless they cannot practice self-control. This self-control is gendered as a male value; thus widows who exhibit male qualities of control are acceptable. The assumption that women were sexually available and unable to engage in appropriate control leads later interpreters of Paul to oppose celibacy (1 Tim 4:3–5, 5:14). First Timothy discusses widows and celibacy in the same vein, but instead of advising self-control, the text suggests that young women have little or no control (1 Tim 5:11–13). We see a significant shift between 1 Corinthian's instructions on marriage and celibacy (1 Cor 7:7–9) and the writer of 1 Timothy. First Corinthians allows for celibate/unmarried women while 1 Timothy portrays them as silly or even dangerous. Such shifts in the portrait of women's sexuality may reflect attempts to curtail women's leadership in some early Christian communities.

[*See also* Children, *subentries on* New Testament *and* Roman World; Family Structures, *subentries on* Early Church *and* Roman World; Legal Status, *subentries on* New Testament *and* Roman World; *and* Race, Class, and Ethnicity, *subentry* New Testament.]

BIBLIOGRAPHY

Ahearne-Kroll, Stephen P. "'Who Are My Mother and My Brothers?' Family Relations and Family Language in the Gospel of Mark." *Journal of Religion* 81 (2001): 1–25.

Balch, David L., and Carolyn Osiek, eds. *Early Christian Families in Context: An Interdisciplinary Dialogue.* Grand Rapids, Mich.: Eerdmans, 2003.

Glancy, Jennifer A. "Obstacles to Slaves' Participation in the Corinthian Church." *Journal of Biblical Literature* 117 (1998): 481–501.

Hodge, Caroline E. Johnson. *If Sons, Then Heirs: A Study of Kinship and Ethnicity in the Letters of Paul.* New York: Oxford University Press, 2007.

Hodge, Caroline Johnson. "Married to an Unbeliever: Households, Hierarchies, and Holiness in 1 Corinthians 7:12–16." *Harvard Theological Review* 103 (2010): 1–25.

MacDonald, Margaret Y. *The Pauline Churches: A Sociohistorical Study of Institutionalization in the Pauline and Deutero-Pauline Writings.* Society for New Testament Studies Monographs 60. New York: Cambridge University Press, 1988.

Moxnes, Halvor, ed. *Constructing Early Christian Families: Family as Social Reality and Metaphor.* London: Routledge, 1997.

Osiek, Carolyn, and David L. Balch. *Families in the New Testament World: Households and House Churches.* Louisville, Ky.: Westminster John Knox, 1997.

Peppard, Michael. *The Son of God in the Roman World: Divine Sonship in its Social and Political Context.* New York: Oxford University Press, 2011.

Saller, Richard P. "*Pater Familias, Mater Familias,* and the Gendered Semantics of the Roman Household." *Classical Philology* 94 (1999): 182–197.

Schüssler Fiorenza, Elisabeth. *In Memory of Her: A Feminist Theological Reconstruction of Christian Origins.* New York: Crossroad, 1983.

Katherine A. Shaner

Early Judaism

The early concept of the family, whose roots we find in the Bible, was patrilineal. The family unit was headed by a male—the father, and the sons were those who were connected to him by ties of consanguinity. During the Mishnaic period (second century B.C.E.–second century C.E.), a conceptual transformation took place as part of the new consciousness that had developed, perhaps under the influence of Roman society, regarding the significance and purpose of creating marriage ties and regarding the structure of the family. Instead of the extended family that included all of the father's relatives, the concept of the nuclear family, consisting of the married couple and their offspring, began to take hold in Jewish society. Within the nuclear family the status of the wife–mother rose, and she was regarded as no less an essential element than the father, although his superior status was preserved, as can be understood from the Mishnah in tractate *Keritot:*

> The father comes before the mother in all places. You might think that it is because the honour due to the father exceeds the honour due to the mother, therefore Scripture stated (Lev. 19:3) ye shall fear every man his mother and his father, to teach that both are equal. But the sages have said: The father comes before the mother in all places, because both a man and his mother are bound to honour the father. (*m. Ker.* 6, 9)

The Purposes of the Family. From rabbinic literature, i.e., the Mishnah, Tosefta (Eretz Israel 100 B.C.E.–200 C.E.), Talmud (Eretz Israel and Babylon 300–600 C.E.), and Midrash (Eretz Israel, parallel to Talmudic period) it may be understood that the family is grounded in three domains: existential, economic, and cultural-national.

Existential. At the existential level, two purposes may be noted: one is the maintenance of the individual's bodily health and happiness, and the other maintaining the order that allows for life in civilized society. The individual's health and happiness are achieved by (1) regulating sexual activity, as the sage R. Huna said: "He who is twenty years of age and is not married spends all his days in sin"; the Talmud took this to mean "spends all his days in sinful thoughts" (*b. Qidd. 29b*); and also (2) by alleviating loneliness and arousing a feeling of joy that is the result of marital life for, "Any man who has no wife lives without joy" (*b. Yebam. 62b*). However, the individual achieves happiness primarily because it is only through a conjugal relationship that physical and spiritual completeness can be achieved, in the words of R. Eleazar: "Any man who has no wife is not a proper man [human being]" (*b. Yebam. 63a*). The sense of wholeness is also associated with the ability to create continuity, that is, to produce offspring and to be certain of their affiliation for, "A man who is childless is accounted as dead" (*b. Ned. 64b*).

The other purpose—creating the possibility of civilized life within human society—is achieved by regulating what is permitted and what is forbidden in the field of sexual relationships. The permissiveness that is accepted in modern society was impossible in ancient society, where sexual relations were directly related to siring offspring. Numerous Talmudic sources express reservations about unbridled sexual relationships because they may produce *mamzerim* (progeny produced from an illicit sexual relationship).

Since producing progeny was a matter of prime importance for ancient Jewish society, it was very strict in all matters relating to illicit sexual relationships, such as sexual relations between a man and woman who were forbidden to be together, either because of a blood relationship or because the woman was betrothed or married. Engaging in illicit sexual relations is one of the three gravest transgressions under Jewish law, which a person is required to avoid committing even at the cost of his life.

This strict observance of the laws regulating sexual behavior, rooted in the Bible, was not practiced by the gentile nations among whom the Jews lived and therefore it may not be attributed to environmental influence. Some theorize that its basis was the desire to ensure genealogical purity, as may have been true during the Second Temple Period when the priestly class (*kohanim*) enjoyed a superior status in society. However, Jewish society during most of the Mishnaic and Talmudic periods was a society of sages, and their status was not determined by family pedigree. Therefore, it is not likely that the desire to preserve the family lineage was the reason for the strict laws governing sexual behavior. It would, then, seem that the norm of having sexual relations within a family framework was related to the desire to avoid siring compromised children or unidentified, hence unprotected, children.

Economic. At the economic level, the family was intended to be a kind of work group or partnership for the purpose of producing, acquiring, and organizing the food, clothing, and housing essential for survival and managing property and money. The division of labor between the married couple was quite clear: the man worked as breadwinner, usually outside the home, as a farmer, artisan, or merchant while the woman was occupied with domestic tasks. An essential characterization of this division of labor is provided by the Talmud, which attributes it to

Elijah the prophet. Elijah answers the question of how a woman helps a man: "If a man brings wheat, does he chew the wheat? If flax, does he put on the flax? Does she not, then, bring light to his eyes and put him on his feet!" (*b. Yebam. 63a*). Talmudic literature has few references to women engaged in crafts or commerce, and these few might have been divorced or widowed women. However, there are several accounts of women who helped their husbands with agricultural work or in storekeeping.

Jewish law laid down the division of financial responsibilities and rights in the family so that the man owned and managed his wife's property and money. At the same time, he was responsible for her support and welfare, for feeding his young sons and daughters, and for bequeathing his property to his sons. The wife was responsible for the household and all of the work associated with its maintenance. The man's financial obligations toward his wife, according to the Torah, include: "her food, her clothing, and her marriage duty" (Mekhilta de-Rabbi Ishmael *Mishpatim, Masekhta de-Nezikin* par. 3). In addition, according to the Mishnah, he owes her the value of her *ketuba* (marriage contract) in the event that he divorces her or dies (a minimum of 200 *zuzim* if she was married as a virgin and 100 *zuzim* if as a widow or divorcee), medical expenses, ransom from captivity, and burial expenses. He further pledges that after his death, she will continue to receive food and housing, as will her daughters until they are betrothed. In addition, if he marries another woman and sires children with her, the sons of each wife will inherit their mother's *ketuba* separately from the rest of the inheritance (*m. Ketub.* 4: 6–11).

Her obligations toward him include her handiwork (from which we may infer that women engaged in cottage industries that supplemented the family income), anything she finds, assets that came to her as a gift or by inheritance, and the "seven kinds of work that a woman performs for her husband, grinding [grain], baking bread, washing clothes, cooking, nursing her child, making ready his bed, and working in wool" (*m. Ketub.* 5:5).

Cultural-national. At the cultural-national level, many rabbinic sources express the view that the marital relationship upon which the family is built is directed by God and is an actualization of the original act of creation. Placing the family so high on the scale of religious values is derived from the fact that it helps maintain and develop society and the nation. The first objective of the rabbis in creating the family framework was to create cells where the content, values, and religious rituals upon which the national and religious culture of the Jewish people is based could be preserved and developed. During most of the Second Temple Period and the entire period of the Mishnah and Talmud, the Jewish nation was under foreign occupation and had no political center, or even one spiritual-religious center. The family, then, was the place where religious rituals and practices were preserved and cultivated through the celebration of festivals such as Passover and Sukkot and the weekly Sabbath rituals.

Family Structure. In ancient Jewish society, as in other societies in the Middle East, there was a tendency to marry within an endogamous cohort group. There is fairly extensive documentation, in Second Temple literature as well as in rabbinic literature, of the preference for this type of marriage, which was not obligatory. It is possible that the tendency to endogamous marriages initially stemmed from the desire to preserve assets, particularly land, within the tribe. However, the fact that this tendency continued after the destruction of the Second Temple and the forced separation from the land that followed it shows that what began as a tribal tendency developed into a general aspiration to preserve the purity of the lineage.

In the Jewish juristic literature there are no sources that prohibit marrying more than one wife. On the contrary: there are sources from the Mishnaic period that deal with the problems that arose in families where two or more wives live alongside each other. Is this discussion theoretical or does it reflect the reality in Eretz Israel? It seems that early Jewish society in Eretz Israel was primarily monogamous, for there are few Eretz Israel sources that document concrete examples of polygamous families. However, the phenomenon of polygamy in Eretz Israel, albeit negligible, cannot be taken lightly because for the rulers of the land (i.e., the Romans) marriage to more than one woman was considered a serious crime. The instances of a proliferation of women in Jewish Eretz Israel society may be explained as a consequence of the destruction of the Temple and the Bar Kokhba Revolt, which caused a shortage of young men on the one hand and the proliferation of both young widows who needed levirate marriages and needy women who needed financial support on the other. It is possible that in such circumstances a man who was financially well established may have married more than one woman to redeem a woman who was widowed with no children, or undertook the support of a poor woman or even several poor women.

Babylonian Jewry lived among the polygamous Persians. Based on a number of adages spoken by the rabbis, it seems that they were influenced by their environment and did not object in principle to the system of polygamy. The Babylonian sage Rava said: "A man may marry wives in addition to his first wife, provided only that he possesses the means to maintain them" (*b. Yebam. 65a*). On the practical level there is only one example of a concrete case of marriage to two women simultaneously (*b. Ketub. 70b*). However, more than a few commentaries and sayings of the Babylonian sages attest that they knew families that had at least two wives (*b. Ned. 20b*; *Yebam. 11a, 12a*, and more). It would therefore seem that Jewish society in Babylon did not object to polygamous marriages, even though there is not enough evidence that this pattern of marriage was prevalent there.

Relationships between family members. As noted, the Jewish family in the period of the Mishnah and Talmud was a patriarchal family with a definite hierarchy between the man and the woman, and the woman's total economic and functional dependence on her husband. In view of this, it is interesting to realize from a series of laws, adages, and cases brought in the rabbinic literature that there was a heightened awareness of the importance of feelings and romance in relations within the couple. The men were called upon to moderate their control over their wives and to treat them respectfully and sensitively. The requirement to limit their control is re-

flected in several laws in the Mishnah that threaten exercising the sanction of divorce with full payment of the *ketuba* against husbands who tyrannize their wives by depriving them of benefits (*m. Ketub. 7:1-5*). Likewise, it is seen in the laws that allow a woman to divorce her husband and receive the money of her *ketuba* if she cannot endure bodily defects, diseases, or odors that appeared in him [after they were married] (*m. Ketub. 7:10*). The expectation that men will treat their wives with dignity and consideration is reflected in the words of the sages of both Eretz Israel and Babylon. The early Eretz Israel sage R. Hiyya called upon men to pamper their wives with clothing and jewelry and to cultivate their beauty (*b. Ketub. 59b*), and the Talmud relates that despite the fact that his wife mistreated him, he always would bring her gifts (*b. Yebam. 63a*). The Babylonian sage Rav described the ideal relations between a husband and wife as friendship: "for Rav Judah said in the name of Rav: A man may not betroth a woman before he sees her, lest he [subsequently] see something repulsive in her, and she become loathsome to him, whereas the All-Merciful said (Lev 19:18), but thou shalt love thy neighbour as thyself" (*b. Qidd. 41a*).Thus he recommended that "one should always be heedful of wronging his wife, for since her tears are frequent she is quickly hurt" (*b. Meṣiʿa 59a*). From a source dated to the Mishnah period (*baraitha*) cited in the Babylonian Talmud, one may learn of the expectation of romantic love for it promises a good life to "the man who loves his wife as himself, who honours her more than himself" (*b. Yebam. 62b*).

Women were expected not to anger their husbands with spiteful, contrary behavior and to demonstrate affection and intimacy. The Babylonian sages Abaye and Rava described a wicked woman as one who serves her husband but speaks to him rudely or turns her back on him and does not listen when he speaks (*b. Yebam. 63b*). From these descriptions one sees the expectation that there be verbal communication between the couple and criticism of women who may have fulfilled their duties toward their husbands but did not communicate with them or whose relationships were warped. From the response attributed to Babylonian sage R. Huna in the

Mishnah in *Ketubbot* 5:5, which states that a woman who brought four servants with her to the marriage can exempt herself from housework, we can see that women were expected to demonstrate affection and intimacy to their husbands. R. Huna is quoted as responding to the law in the Mishnah "If four servants," with these words: "she may lounge in an easy chair. Although it has been said, she may lounge in an easy chair, she should nevertheless fill for him his cup, make ready his bed and wash his face, hands and feet" (*b. Ketub. 61a*).

The sources quoted indicate that although in Jewish society in the Mishnaic and Talmudic period marriage was not based on romantic love, and despite the hierarchy of relationships between the man and the woman in the family, there was an expectation of an emotional tie and harmony within the couple.

In Jewish society, fertility was raised to a supreme level of importance religiously and morally, and was regarded as the raison d'etre of the world and of the human being. The institution of the family was the proper framework to produce offspring with clear affiliation and identity. Although the woman gives birth, the father was given authority and trust to determine who his children are and thus even to disinherit. During the Mishnaic and Talmudic period, there was a trend to limit the father's authority and to circumscribe it with fixed, delineated legal formulas. The children ceased to be the property of the father, and the concepts of ownership and property were replaced by the concept of responsibilities and rights. The father's responsibilities toward his son are "to circumcise him, to redeem him [from the Kohen], to teach him Torah and a craft, and to marry him off, and some say, also to teach him to swim" (*t. Qidd.* 1:11). In addition to these responsibilities, the father is required to pay for educating his children to religious observance (*b. Sukkah 42b*), and for the nursing of his children in the event that the mother does not nurse them. In exchange for fulfilling these obligations to his offspring, the father is given several rights that pertain mainly to his daughters. He is entitled to annul their vows and to receive their betrothal fee and the profits that have accrued through their handiwork. In addition to the father's

special rights regarding his daughters, both parents are entitled to receive honor and care even when this involves monetary expenditures from both sons and daughters (*y. Qidd.* 61:3 and *Pe'ah* 15:3; *b. Qidd. 30b–31a*).

Since the family identity is determined by the father, those considered siblings are sons and/or daughters who were born from one father and one mother, or from one father. The only differences in responsibilities and rights between the siblings are between the eldest brother and the other brothers, and between the brothers and the sisters. There is a difference between the responsibility of the eldest son and his brothers: it is incumbent upon the father to redeem the firstborn son of the mother from the *kohen* (*m. Bek.* 8:1). If the father did not fulfill his responsibility, the son is obligated to redeem himself when he grows up (*b. Qidd. 29b*). Another difference, and this time as a privilege, relates to the inheritance from his father. The first son of the father receives double what the other brothers received in his father's estate (*m. Bek.* 8:1). In all other matters, the brothers from one father are equal. The main difference between brothers and sisters is the inheritance. The Mishnah relied on the biblical verse: "If a man die and have no sons, then you shall cause his inheritance to pass to his daughter" (Num 27:8) and ruled that a son has precedence over a daughter and all of his issue have precedence over a daughter (*m. B. Bat.* 8:2). It seems that in the Second Temple period, there were those who tried to change the ruling that a daughter does not inherit, and it was the subject of a fierce debate between the Pharisees and the Sadducees (*b. B. Bat. 115b*). Later the Jews and Christians also debated it (*b. Šabb. 116b*).

In any event, the Babylonian sage R. Huna quoted his teacher Rav's harsh reaction to the attempt to institute the practice of passing the inheritance to a daughter: "R. Huna said in the name of Rav: Anyone, even a prince in Israel, who says that a daughter is to inherit with the daughter of the son, must not be obeyed; for such [a ruling] is only the practice of the Sadducees" (*b. B. Bat. 115b*).

Since daughters did not inherit, they were given the possibility of enjoying benefits from the inheritance their brothers received from the father. The Mishnah (*m. Ketub.* 4:11) determined that the husband pledges to his wife (though he did not explicitly write it out) "the female children that will be born from our marriage shall dwell in my house and be maintained out of my estate until they shall be taken in marriage." He is liable because [this clause] is a condition laid down by the court of law and is not left to his discretion.

It is written in the Babylonian Talmud: "If anyone brings up an orphan boy or girl in his house, the scripture accounts it as if he had begotten him" (*b. Meg. 13a*; *Sanh. 19b*). Similar ideas appear in an Eretz Israel Midrash. "The one who raises him is called the father rather than his biological father" (*Exod. Rab.* 46 lit.). However, despite the positive view of adoption reflected in these texts, the law does not determine the legal status of the adopted child. The adoptive father, legally, is not the father of the adopted child, and therefore the restrictions against marrying blood relatives does not pertain. The adoptee does not receive the inheritance unless the father, before his death, specifically bequeathed his property or part of it to him.

Widows and orphans represent a weak, vulnerable population. Therefore, Talmudic literature (in line with the biblical injunctions that preceded it) contains many warnings about harming them, physically or emotionally. A widow, as long as she has not remarried and has not demanded the payment owed to her from her marriage by the heirs in a court of law, must be allowed by the heirs to continue living in the house where she lived when her husband was still alive, or they need to rent her another place to live that is not inferior to where she had lived with her husband. In addition, the heirs must supply her maintenance, including medical expenses and clothing, at the standard that she enjoyed in her husband's lifetime. It appears that the practice both in Eretz Israel and in Babylon was that in return for the benefits granted to the widow by the heirs, she gave them the profits of her handiwork and whatever she found (*b. Ketub. 96a*). Widows were allowed to leave the state of widowhood and become betrothed to anyone except the High Priest, beginning ninety days after the death of their husband. This was the period required to determine if she was pregnant from her first husband to identify if the offspring belonged to her first or second husband. A widow who was pregnant or nursing a child had to wait until the child was twenty-four months old so that the infant would not be deprived if his mother became pregnant from her new husband and subsequently her milk supply was adversely affected (*b. Yebam. 42a*).

Orphans who were orphaned in childhood are the most weakened group in the population; therefore caring for them is considered charity. The Eretz Israel sage R. Samuel b. Nahmani interpreted the verse in Psalms 106:3: "Happy are they who maintain justice and do righteousness at all times" by saying "This refers to a man who brings up an orphan boy or orphan girl in his house and enables them to marry" (*b. Ketub. 50a*). Along with the theoretical ruling it seems that the rabbinical courts also took care of orphans. The Talmud recounts that "Rabban Gamliel and his court were the fathers (i.e., protectors) of the orphans" (*b. B. Qam. 37a*). From several sources of the Mishnaic period, it emerges that Jewish law was more solicitous of orphan girls than of orphan boys because they were more vulnerable. It was further ruled in the Mishnah that orphan girls who have no property at all are maintained from the public funds: "If an orphan is given in marriage she must be given not less than fifty *zuz*. If [charity] funds are available, she is to be fitted out in accordance with the dignity of her position" (*m. Ketub.* 6:5). All orphans are exempt from various taxes that the public is required to pay.

[*See also* Family Structures, *subentry* Hebrew Bible; *and* Marriage and Divorce, *subentry* Early Judaism.]

BIBLIOGRAPHY

Albeck, Shalom. *The Principles of Marriage and Family Law in the Talmud.* Ramat-Gan, Israel: Bar-Ilan University Press, 2010 (Hebrew).

Baron, Salo W. "The World of the Talmud." In *Social and Religious History of Israel*, pp. 73–88. Ramat-Gan: Massada, 1968 (Hebrew).

Hauptman, Judith. "Marriage." In *Rereading the Rabbis: A Woman's Voice*, pp. 60–76. Boulder, Colo.: Westview, 1998.

Peskowitz, Miriam. "Family Ties in Antiquity: Evidence from Tannaitic Literature and Roman Galilean Architecture." In *The Jewish Family in Antiquity*, edited by Shaye J. D. Cohen, pp. 9–33. Atlanta: Scholars Press, 1993.

Rabello, A. Mordecai. "Patria Potestas in Roman and Jewish Law." In *Dinei Israel: Annual of Jewish Law and Israeli Family Law*, pp. 85–153. Tel Aviv: Faculty of Law, Tel Aviv University, 1974.

Yarbrough, Larry. "Parents and Children in Jewish Family of Antiquity." In *The Jewish Family in Antiquity*, edited by Shaye J. D. Cohen, pp. 39–59. Atlanta: Scholars Press, 1993.

Shulamit Valler

Early Church

Knowledge of family structures in the early church comes to us only indirectly, since there is no explicit early Christian data on the subject, especially compared to the numerous patristic texts on virginity, asceticism, and marriage. It is further complicated by the fact that whatever picture we can gather on early Christian families from the often fragmentary literary sources emerges from and reveals the perspectives of the male, educated, wealthy upper order, mediated by the theological and moral lenses of the church fathers. Material culture can supplement literary sources, but those artifacts are scanty and require much scholarly inference. It is instructive to remember that early Christians were part of the Roman world and largely operated within its social structures, despite the church fathers' antifamilial and ascetic claims. Hence, drawing on Roman sources sometimes fills in the gap. However, modern readers must bear in mind inherent biases and limits of the extant sources, as well as the interpretive standpoints of modern scholarship.

The basic structure of early Christian families followed that of the contemporary Roman *familia*, which legally included all persons and properties under the power of the *paterfamilias* (*patria potestas*), including his legitimate children, his son's children, and his children by adoption. The mother (*materfamilias*), while important as the father's lawful wife and bearer of his children, was extraneous to this legal understanding as *manus* marriage, whereby the wife came under the legal control (*manus*) of her husband, had been in decline by the late republic. The Roman family was also based on the understanding of *domus*, the household, including *familia*, slaves, and the broad kinship group including *materfamilias*, patrilineal and matrilineal kin, ancestors and descendants, freedpersons, clients, and other boarders and residents of the household. While both *familia* and *domus* encompassed extended kin beyond the nuclear family (father-mother-children triad), for which the Romans had no vocabulary, the common structure featured in the patristic sources is the "nucleated" *domus*, that is, the household centered on parents and children with slaves, and with some variations of other extended family members (Martin, 1996, p. 58). The "Christians for Christians" funerary epitaphs from Anatolia (ca. 250–350 C.E.) show dedications made to deceased family members by surviving relatives as a group, frequently three generations based on the "nucleated *domus*," with a combination of a brother, grandparent(s), grandchildren, or a sister/brother-in-law (Johnson, 1995). Augustine's disclosure of his own family and those of his congregants in his writings confirms a similar pattern: the nucleated *domus*, with grandparents, (male) cousins, nephews, nurses, and family property, including slaves, as well as Augustine's concubine and son.

Social Roles of Mothers and Fathers. Early Christians generally adopted the Stoic idea of the household as part of the natural social order, stemming from the joining (*coniugium, copulatio*) of man and woman and resulting in children, and thus as the "seedbed" of the state (Cicero, *De officio* 1.17.54; Augustine, *De civitate Dei* 15.16.3). They also regarded the household as a mini-church whose members should lead lives of redemption, virtue, and holiness worthy of its head, the Christ (John Chrysostom, *Homiliae in epistulam ad Ephesios*). As the oldest living male and formal head of the family, the *paterfamilias* was also the *dominus*, master of the household, whose legal power and authority over his descendants and householders was virtually absolute and lasted until his death. The *paterfamilias* functioned as a mediator of the household, church, and larger society; his chief role was to protect his household, ensure its peace and harmony, and keep it in the right order with his *potestas* and Christian principles as a miniature state and church

(Chrysostom, *Homiliae in epistulam ad Ephesios*). The patriarchal structure of Christian family is shown in this pivotal role and significance of the *paterfamilias*. As already reflected in the deutero-Pauline writings (Eph 5:22—6.9; Col 3:18—4.1; 1 Tim 3:4—5, 12), Augustine emphasizes that domestic peace leads to civic peace, that is, maintaining household harmony and order contributes to that of the state; therefore, the father should adopt the rules of the state in governing his household in such a way that his house fits in with civic peace, including discipline and corporal punishment for the disobedient (*De civitate Dei* 19.16). This kind of paternal authority will not be necessary in the heavenly household in the eschatological state, but until then the father is obliged to use his power to ensure domestic peace while he should also be concerned for the household's spiritual welfare, namely, worship and service of God, and should treat all in his household, particularly his children and slaves, with equal affection and prayers for their salvation (*De civitate Dei* 19.16). Thus the coercive paternal authority in controlling and disciplining all of his householders is counterbalanced by charity and love (Shaw, 1987, p. 18; cf. *Sermones* 349.2), especially as he is to love, care, educate, and provide for his wife and children as a husband, father, and master (John Chrysostom, *Homiliae in epistulam ad Ephesios*; cf. Tertullian, *Adversus Marcionem* 2.13).

The duty of the *materfamilias* was to govern daily household affairs, support her husband's career and interests, bear and rear his children, and keep family honor with her pietas, chastity, modesty, and Christian moral guidance. By the (late) fourth century C.E., in the absence of *paterfamilias, materfamilias* stood as a mediator between domestic and civic contexts, receiving the same honors and dignities as her husband, exercising power over the *domus* and interacting with the larger social, religious, and political community and leaders; daughters, even as adults, remained silent in the public arena behind their mothers' maternal authority. For example, Emmelia, who bore nine children, including Macrina (the Younger), Basil the Great, and Gregory of Nyssa and outlived her husband by about thirty years, raised her children (with the help of wet nurses and Macrina), ensured their education and establishment in life, and shaped religious life and devotion at home. Her matriarchal role further included administering the family's considerable possessions as she paid taxes in three different provinces, distributing them among her numerous children, and finally blessing each of her children at her deathbed (Gregory of Nyssa, *Vita Macrinae*). Emmelia's household reflected the local Cappadocian elites' vision for civic order and harmony by ensuring her family honor and order through the virtues of her sons (Basil's holiness) and daughters (Macrina's chastity) and her public activities.

Roles of Parents and Children. The exercise of the *patria potestas* in love reflects traditional *pietas*, which implied strong family loyalty, duty, and affection that in turn was expected from one's spouse, siblings, parents, and children. Children unquestionably owed respect, duty, and compliance (*obsequium*) to their parents. The Christian household code emphasized the reciprocal nature of this *pieta* between parents and children. Parents, once the father decided his newborn child would live as his own (even as the church and Christian imperial law strongly discouraged, if not condemned, exposure), had an *obligatio* of raising their children—providing food, clothing, shelter, and *paideia* (education); establishing them in careers; arranging their marriages; and leaving them their fair share of inheritance. Both fathers and mothers were responsible for carefully monitoring their children's progress and behavior, raising them to be good citizens and Christians (Nathan, 2000, p. 143). Wealthy Christian parents, especially in the post-Constantinian era, were concerned for their children's advancement and success in the elite careers and in their corresponding reputations and honors through classical *paideia*, marriage arrangement, and inheritance/wealth, as church fathers expressed frustrations and warnings in their letters and treatises to their "worldly" congregants (e.g., Chrysostom, *Homiliae in epistulam ad Ephesios; De inani gloria*).

Both Christian and non-Christian sources emphasize that children were to honor their parents, as their obedience was a necessary element of family life. Children's proper conduct was critical to the virtue and honor of the family, and the rebellious son or the naughty daughter was thought to have transgressed family boundaries, thus bringing shame on the entire family (Horn and Martens, 2009, p. 86). In Christian households, however, children's obedience to parents was to be qualified "in the Lord" as the church fathers advised them not to obey "unbelieving" or "heretical" fathers (Chrysostom, *Homiliae in epistulam ad Ephesios*). Adult children's filial piety mandated supporting and caring for their aging parents before any obligation to their friends or other relatives (Augustine, *Ep.* 243.12; *Sermones* 276.1–2). With increasing ascendancy of ascetic movements in the fourth century and on, the duty both to obey parents and to look after them became more complicated when some children chose virginity and religious life at a young age even against the wishes of Christian parents (e.g., Macrina, at twelve, insisted on widowhood when her fiancé died). In such cases, church fathers often supported the children's choice against the physical fathers/parents who wanted obedience and grandchildren (Ambrose, *De virginibus* 1.65–66; Jerome, *Ep.* 24), while the fourth-century Council of Gangra condemned both parents and children who neglected their respective duties under the pretense of ascetic piety (Canon 15–16). In some cases, ascetic daughters persuaded their widowed mothers to follow similar pursuits and looked after them in a transformed relationship as sisters in ascetic communities.

Christian *Paideia*. Christian parents were responsible for nurturing and disciplining their children in Christian *paideia* in addition to, or in place of, traditional *paideia*. Its fundamental element was inculcating in the child a proper sense of the fear of the Lord with the Word of God, captured in the exhortation of Polycarp of Smyrna in the mid-second century: "Train up their children in the knowledge and fear of God" (*Letter to the Philippians* 4; cf. *Didache* 4.9; *Epistle of Barnabas* 19.5). Fear and knowledge of God, which is wisdom (Prov 1:7), is the virtue of all virtues, and as such spurns "desires, wealth, worldly reputation, and power" (Chrysostom, *De inani gloria* 86, 87). Fear of God should also govern the training of their children in trades so that they would be diligent and understand labor as part of Christian *paideia*

(*Didascalia* 22). Parents are likened to artists fashioning, restoring, and refining the image of God in their children by modeling a godly pattern of life and exercising "tough love" (Chrysostom, *Homiliae in epistulam ad Ephesios; De inani gloria* 96). As such, their neglect of this responsibility, including neglecting the dedication or baptism of their children, is repeatedly threatened with divine punishment; parents are responsible to God for their children's sins and eternal destiny (*Didascalia* 22; *Apostolic Constitutions* 4.11; Jerome, *Ep.* 107.6).

Fathers. Fathers have specific obligations corresponding to their sex in Christian *paideia*. John Chrysostom in *De inani gloria* provides a picture of a father's role in Christian *paideia* for an elite household in Antioch (ca. fourth century C.E.). Fathers must train their sons to be "athletes of Christ" and "soldiers of God" with strict discipline and moral rules. Fathers should train their boys first in controlling the tongue with "the words of God," which should be on their lips without ceasing (28–30). In particular, fathers should strictly enforce boys' fair treatment of slaves not just in speaking but also in demeanor and behaviors (31, 69), so that they will abstain from ill-treating those of freeborn, and of their own elite, status. Moreover, boys should hear "nothing harmful from servants or tutor or nurses" (37), including their "frivolous and old wives' tales" (38). Instead, parents are to tell them the biblical stories, carefully chosen for their age-appropriate moral and didactic values (39), and take their sons to church to hear those stories (41). Starting from the story of Cain and Abel and proceeding to that of Jacob and Esau, the flood, and to the stories of hell and grace in the New Testament at a later age, Chrysostom intends these biblical stories to offset the negative influence of slaves (39–53).

A father should especially guard the boy's eyes (55), as seeing naked women in the theater might arouse desire and increase the danger of him losing his virginity; the key to keeping him from such "corruption" (*lumē*) is limiting the boy's access to women until after the age fifteen when his "natural desire" arises (56–60). The father should remind the boy that spectacles involving naked women are for slaves and thus unseemly for his status, and parents should never send their sons to the theater (79). In fact, the boy is to "see no woman" and speak only to his mother (62) even in the household, and the father should instill into him a "resolute spirit against womankind" (62). Chrysostom is especially concerned about not letting the boy have sexual relations with a slave girl or woman (62). Rather, the boy should keep hearing the story of the patriarch Joseph for the reward of living a sober life (61); it is the father's duty to promise and procure for him a virtuous girl of similar socioeconomic status for marriage, while they are both virgins, before the boy takes up public duty (81). And the hope of meeting this beautiful and virtuous betrothed should safeguard his virtue and "ward off every evil," as he should care about his reputation, as well as about being reported to his betrothed (81–82).

If sexual restraint (*sōphrosynē*) and purity were a significant way to distinguish an elite Christian boy from a slave, his father must also ensure his social and moral superiority to and difference from his slaves at all times (79). In controlling spirit (*thumos*) and passions (*kratein toū pathou*) (68), the boy, from earliest childhood, should first receive training in patience with respect to suffering wrongs, and also in courage with regard to executing justice on behalf of others (66). Again, the household is a fitting context for the boy to exercise those virtues, especially as he deals with spiteful or disobedient slaves. The boy should neither be indulgent nor harsh with slaves; when provoked by his slaves or friends, he is to show poise and learn equability "on all occasions" to the extent that if he were to strike his slave, his father would punish him (68–69). As he willingly relinquishes the "rights" of a free man, he will become "strong and simple and courteous" toward the servile (70). The boy should continually exhibit gentleness in treating slaves like brothers and forgiveness in not getting angry or abusive if a slave breaks his writing instruments (72–73); if he could control his anger from his loss, he has already displayed "all the marks of a philosophic mind" (*megistēs philosophias*; 73). Chrysostom knows too well that anger was a mark of weakness and effeminacy (Marcus Aurelius, *Meditations* 11.18). The father makes sure that the

boy's training in these virtues heightens his "natural difference" from slaves, for he will become the master of those slaves "not by doing as they do, but by [his] habits, so that being a free man, [he is] never a slave of his slaves" (71). Chrysostom's vision for Christian *paideia* is intended to groom a male heir to succeed his father, continuing his physical household and reinforcing existing social hierarchies.

Although Chrysostom's rhetoric is idealistic, and although he was childless, he reveals contemporary knowledge of children at different ages. The father's disciplinary technique corresponded to the Roman understanding of children as irrational, wild, "dumb beasts" that required significant energy to socialize, indoctrinate, and discipline into human society (Augustine, *Enarrationes in Psalmos* 31.2.23). Children exhibit "natural" traits devoid of reason, restraint, and virtue such as greed, ignorance, anger, insolence, and attachment. Drawing on Proverbs, early Christian writings encourage fathers to use rebukes, threats, and corporal punishment for children's disobedience and transgression and for correcting their behaviors, especially the sons (Theophilus of Antioch, *Ad Autolycum* 2.25; *Shepherd of Hermas, Mand.* 1.2.2; *Didascalia* 22; *Apostolic Constitutions* 4.11). Chrysostom discourages fathers from using beating but encourages an effective use of its threat, stern looks, and reproaches as ways to instill fear, thus bringing boys to proper fear of the Lord (*De inani gloria* 30).

Mothers. Although boys came under the purview of their fathers, the mother's role in Christian *paideia* regarding sons was just as significant. Gregory of Nazianzus received his first teaching in the faith from his mother, Nonna, who was influential in the conversion and ministry of her husband, Gregory the Elder (Gregory of Nazianzus, *Oratio* 2.103, 18.11). Emmelia led her children to the cult of the Forty Martyrs and guided their religious instruction, including Melania's training in scripture (Basil, Ep. 223.2; Gregory of Nyssa, *Vita Macrinae* 2). Monica's dedication to Christian *paideia* for her children is well known; she not only supported Augustine's classical *paideia* but also was largely responsible for his eventual conversion. She raised Augustine as a Christian against her husband's wishes; initiated him into the catechumenate; admonished him against committing adultery, deception, and cruelty; followed him to Rome to monitor his soul; and modeled for him faith, courage, piety, and prayerfulness (*Confessions* 1.11.17, 2.3.6–7, 9.9.22, 9.13.36). When Augustine finally converted, Monica was ecstatic and witnessed his baptism by Ambrose; she then engaged in philosophical and theological discussions with him almost until her last days (e.g., *Confessions* 9.10).

Still, the primary role of mothers was bringing up daughters. They should train their daughters to "repress" their "natural" tendencies of flightiness, love of finery, personal adornment, and extravagance (Chrysostom, *De inani gloria* 90). Elite girls could avoid female vanities and become athletes for Christ presumably by following at least some of Chrysostom's precepts for boys, such as controlling (sexual) desires and angers and treating their slaves fairly. Acquiring such virtues would help them to be virtuous wives fitting for virtuous men. Indeed, it was a mother's responsibility to prepare, preserve, and present her daughters suitably for marriage, and to be watchful after marriage for her daughter's well-being, even as the father saw to the proper marriage of a daughter and was responsible for drawing up marriage contracts (Gregory of Nyssa, *Vita Macrinae*).

With the popularity of asceticism and monasticism, "manly" virtues like self-control were also available to elite Christian girls, especially from the fourth century onward. In two letters on the parental education of young girls dedicated to virginity (*Ep.* 107 and 128), Jerome advises strict enforcement of habits of restraint in diet and behavior in those girls as early as possible, along with regular rewards for their efforts (*Ep.* 107.8, 128.1). As a mother's relationship to her daughter is likened to that of Hannah to Samuel or Elizabeth to John the Baptist (*Ep.* 107.3; cf. Chrysostom, *Homiliae in epistulam ad Ephesios*), her role is even more crucial as a parent and teacher (*Ep.* 128.3a). She is to accompany the girl at all times, including on visits to night vigils, martyrs' shrines, and churches, and should be a stern disciplinarian in her *paideia*, which involves learning letters and writing, reading, and advanced study of the Bible at the age of seven (when the girl develops moral understanding and capacity), as well as spinning (*Ep.* 107.11–12, 128.3a). The

mother should raise the girl in seclusion, having her associate only with girls, protecting her from worldly influences and slaves' vices, and, similar to Chrysostom's advice, depriving her of any external adornment, cosmetics, or fine clothing (*Ep.* 107.5, 9; 128.4). Most importantly, the mother should model virtue for the consecrated girl just as the father should for the boy (*Ep.* 107.9; Chrysostom, *De inani gloria*). Such gendered advice reflects a heavy influence of Quintilian adapted to an emerging Christian elite culture.

Endogamy/Exogamy. Roman law prohibited any close-kin marriage within the direct line of descent but still allowed a certain degree of endogamy, which had been practiced among the *honestiores*, including the imperial families, for political and economic alliances and protection of family inheritances. In Egypt, cross-cousin and uncle-niece marriages took place more liberally across the social spectrum well into the Byzantine period. As Shaw's study (1987) shows, it seems that kin endogamy was generally not noticeable or significant among the Christian plebs in Augustine's North African community. Grubbs demonstrates that late ancient (Christian) elites, like Roman elites of the earlier period, often engaged in kin endogamy despite the injunctions of church and state, such as Melania the Younger, who married one of her relatives in obedience to her parents, and Petronius Probus and his wife, Anicia Faltonia Proba (1995, p. 153).

Christian sources typically encouraged religious or community endogamy within Christian communities despite a pervasive reality of exogamy, or "mixed" marriages between Christians and non-Christians. Tertullian's ostensible warnings against such marriages in his treatise *Ad uxorem* belies the complex social situation and dilemma of elite Christian women in North Africa in the early third century, given the power of their fathers to contract their marriages and the prospect of submitting to authority of their non-Christian husbands when there were no suitable Christian men of their rank in prospect. The Roman bishop Callistus's "countercultural" policy to recognize the concubinage of an elite Christian woman with a man of inferior status (most likely her freedman) was a way to negotiate such realities in the West ("Hippolytus," *Refutatio omnium haeresium* 9.12). Michele Salzman's epigraphic study (1989) of aristocratic women's marriage patterns shows that a majority of them practiced religious endogamy in the fourth century, suggesting a possible overall trend in the broader Christian population. At the same time, that Christian parents, whether by choice or necessity, still continued to contract the marriages of their sons or daughters with pagan partners is evident in repeated prohibitions in the canons of local, regional, and ecumenical councils (e.g., Council of Elvira, ca. 306 C.E., Canon 15). Notably, although Monica was born and raised in a Catholic family at Thagaste, she was entrusted to a pagan, Patricius, whom she served as her *dominus* (*Confessions* 9.8.17m 9.9.19). Gregory of Nazianzus's mother, Nonna, a Christian, was given to Gregory the Elder, who was a member of a syncretistic cult in Nazianzus at the time of his marriage. Monica and Nonna could serve as prominent examples of Jerome's triumphant rhetorical statement about Christian women converting their polytheistic husbands (*Ep.* 107.1).

Adoption. Adoption was widely practiced in Roman society. The most significant cases concerned the adoption (*adrogatio*) of relatives or adults (*sui iuris*, "in his own power"), for reasons of inheritances, political loyalty, succession, or personal affection. While most Christian references to adoption indicate a figurative and spiritual nature, formal adoptions must have been common among Christian households of all statuses. Augustine reports that "many men" who have no natural children (sons) adopt a son in their mature age to have an heir and therefore to transmit inheritance (*In epistulam Johannis ad Parthos tractatus* 2.1.13). "Informal" adoption included raising abandoned children or exposed infants as demanded by Christian texts (e.g., *Apostolic Constitutions* 4.1) or bringing up martyrs' children such as Felicitas's daughter (*Passio Santarum Perpetuae et Felicitatis* 15.7); these children generally belonged to the informal category of *alumnus* (Gk *threptos*): the abandoned child who was brought up in someone else's home.

Inheritance. Since the family was not only the fundamental social unit but also the core economic unit, securing inheritance was critical. One of the essential responsibilities of the *paterfamilias* was to keep family patrimony and transmit it to his descendants as a *bonus*. Fathers could use inheritance as a means to control and discipline sons (and daughters), warning and domesticating wayward, rowdy, and recalcitrant sons (Chrysostom, *De inani gloria* 71; Augustine, *Enarrationes in Psalmos* 91.3), disinheriting some and favoring others (Ambrose, *Hexameron* 18.58). Cyprian reveals Carthaginian Christians' concern with expanding and protecting their patrimony (*De lapsis* 5, 11), which eventually led to their apostasy during the Decian persecution. Thus his impassioned call for them to give their inheritance away as alms as a sure remedy for their apostasy would have been even more poignant (*De opere et eleemosynis*). Cyprian himself dispensed his property for the relief of the poor upon his conversion to Christianity and throughout his episcopacy (*Vita Cypriani* 2, 3, 15). Augustine donated his share of family inheritance to the church at Thagaste when he became bishop in 395–396 C.E. From late antiquity onward, the church became a significant competitor for family inheritances and legacies of the elite, as shown by some prominent widows who inherited magnificent family patrimonies and turned them into charities, legacies, and endowments for churches and monasteries.

[*See also* Children, *subentries on* Early Church, New Testament, *and* Roman World; Education, *subentry* Early Church; *and* Marriage and Divorce, *subentries on* Early Church *and* Roman World.]

BIBLIOGRAPHY

Clark, Gillian. "The Fathers and the Children." In *The Church and Childhood*, edited by Diana Wood, pp. 1–27. Oxford: Blackwell, 1994.

Giardina, Andrea. "The Family in the Late Roman World." In *The Cambridge Ancient History*. Vol. 14: *Late Antiquity: Empire and Successors A.D. 425–600*, edited by Averil Cameron, Bryan Ward-Perkins, and Michael Whitby, pp. 392–415. Cambridge, U.K.: Cambridge University Press, 2000.

Grubbs, Judith Evans. *Law and Family in Late Antiquity: The Emperor Constantine's Marriage Legislation.* Oxford: Clarendon, 1995.

Guroian, Vigen. "The Ecclesial Family: John Chrysostom on Parenthood and Children." In *The Child in Christian*

Thought, edited by Marcia J. Bunge, pp. 61–77. Grand Rapids, Mich.: Eerdmans, 2001.

Harrison, Carol. "The Silent Majority: The Family in Patristic Thought." In *The Family in Theological Perspective*, edited by Stephen C. Barton, pp. 87–105. Edinburgh: T&T Clark, 1996.

Horn, Cornelia B., and John W. Martens. *"Let the Little Children Come to Me": Childhood and Children in Early Christianity*. Washington, D.C.: Catholic University of America Press, 2009.

Jacobs, Andrew S., and Rebecca Krawiec. "Fathers Know Best? Christian Families in the Age of Asceticism." *Journal of Early Christian Studies* 11, no. 3 (2003): 257–263.

Johnson, Gary J. *Early-Christian Epitaphs from Anatolia*. Atlanta: Scholars Press, 1995.

Leyerle, Blake. "Appealing to Children." *Journal of Early Christian Studies* 5, no. 2 (1997): 243–270.

Martin, Dale B. "Construction of the Ancient Family: Methodological Considerations." *Journal of Roman Studies* 86 (1996): 40–60.

Nathan, Geoffrey S. *The Family in Late Antiquity: The Rise of Christianity and the Endurance of Tradition*. London: Routledge, 2000.

Rawson, Beryl, ed. *Marriage, Divorce, and Children in Ancient Rome*. Oxford: Clarendon, 1991.

Saller, Richard P. "*Familia, Domus*, and the Roman Conception of the Family." *Phoenix* 38 (1984): 336–355.

Salzman, Michele Renee. "Aristocratic Women: Conductors of Christianity in the Fourth Century." *Helios* 16 (1989): 207–220.

Shaw, Brent D. "The Family in Late Antiquity: The Experience of Augustine." *Past and Present* 115 (1987): 3–51.

Helen Rhee

FEMINISM

This entry contains three subentries: First-Wave Feminism; Second-Wave Feminism; *and* Third-Wave Feminism.

First-Wave Feminism

First-wave feminists used a variety of arguments to make their case for greater rights for women. Reflecting the many intellectual and social changes of their century, they argued from natural law, human rights, the idea of social progress, and God's plan of creation. The Bible itself evoked a mixed response.

Some feminists indicted it as a major tool in the centuries-long subordination of women, while others argued that its true message preached women's equality. Some others thought the biblical text, like religion itself, was irrelevant to the struggle for women's suffrage and the reform of society.

First-wave feminism in the United States is typically defined as the period from the Women's Rights Convention in Seneca Falls, New York, in 1848 to the establishment of women's voting rights in 1920. Women's rights, however, arose within a broad international network of relationships that accelerated in the nineteenth century, aided by increased travel, wider distribution of books and magazines, the establishment of telegraph links, reform movements like abolitionism that spanned the Atlantic, and Catholic and Protestant missionary and revival movements. Lucretia Mott (1793–1880) and Elizabeth Cady Stanton (1815–1902) conceived of the Seneca Falls convention while in London at the World Anti-Slavery Convention in 1840. A Finnish feminist spoke at an international women's meeting in Washington in 1888 of the "golden cables of sympathy" that united women in the Atlantic community (McFadden, p. 2).

The Enlightenment thinkers of the late seventeenth and eighteenth centuries developed ideas of the rights of the individual and the supremacy of reason over revelation, setting the stage for thinkers like Mary Wollstonecraft and John Stuart Mill to extend its reasoning to women's rights. They also provided the support for science and empirical method as an alternative to revealed religion in the search for truth. Virtually all first-wave feminists appeal to natural law and empirical evidence to counter religious arguments against equality.

Darwin's work *On the Origin of Species* (1859) received widespread attention and acceptance. His theory of natural selection undermined literalist readings of Genesis, encouraging more varied understandings of the text. Applying scientific method to the study of the Bible itself gave rise to newer methods of analysis, or criticism, starting in the late eighteenth century but blossoming in the nineteenth. "Lower criticism" considered many manuscript variants and tried to establish the best versions of the text, while "higher criticism" considered the historical milieu of the Bible's composition, its differing authors, and the deliberate editing of the texts. These methods coming out of Europe, especially Germany, assumed the strong influence of human beings on the composition of the Bible, thus undermining the notion of its divine authorship or absolute textual unity. These ideas were discussed in the popular press, so were accessible to feminist interpreters.

Social Change. Activists in England began to press for reform of laws unfair to women. The Caroline Norton case in 1836 eventually led to reform of divorce laws, custody laws, and women's right to inherit property. Josephine Butler campaigned successfully against the Contagious Diseases Acts in the 1860s, which targeted women for forced gynecological examinations and possible imprisonment. *The English Woman's Journal* was founded in the mid-nineteenth century to deal with women's issues in the workforce, including harassment and unequal pay.

Industrialization and urbanization in the nineteenth century changed the lives of middle-class women. De Groot and Taylor argue that the new reality of husbands supporting the family by working outside the home for long periods helped the Victorian idea of the "two spheres" of home versus public life take shape. The "cult of true womanhood" implied that women were too virtuous and dignified to act outside the home, and should shun the rough-and-tumble of commerce, industry, and politics. Yet the authors maintain that the two-spheres idea laid the groundwork for feminism by isolating women by gender and handing over to women the responsibility for educating the children and training them in morals (de Groot and Taylor, 2007, pp. 3–7). Women had to learn as much as possible about scripture and related matters. Moreover, movements to reform society, especially temperance, required women to gather in solidarity, extending the idea of home. The slogan of the Women's Christian Temperance Union was "Home Protection." Female seminaries were founded, including Troy Female Seminary by Emma Willard in 1821 and Hartford Female Seminary by Catherine Beecher in 1823, with the goal of educating women in the same areas as men, including theology and languages.

Suffrage was one of multiple reform movements in the nineteenth century, including abolitionism and temperance, and many of the same people were active in more than one cause. Slavery in particular had forced a confrontation with the Bible and a veering away from literalism. A plain reading of both the Hebrew Bible and the New Testament, especially letters attributed to Paul, would seem to give divine sanction to slavery. Abolitionists could not afford to be literalists, and derived more subtle and complex interpretations of difficult passages to argue against slavery. Some women's rights advocates engaged in a similar process to promote the Bible as an instrument of women's equality.

The Second Great Awakening, a revival movement in American Protestantism in the early 1800s, promoted individual experience of the Spirit as authentic for females and males alike, and also provided women opportunities to join communal gatherings and act as public leaders. Phoebe Palmer (1807–1874), one of the founders of the Holiness movement within the Methodist church, preached publicly, wrote and published, and founded a mission in the Five Points district of New York City. Methodist women like Helenor Alter Davisson were circuit riders, traveling preachers who held camp meetings and preached throughout the Midwest. Jarena Lee and other women in the African Methodist Episcopal Church commonly preached and held meetings. The main Methodist hierarchy later clamped down on women's preaching, but as Willard and others point out, it was much too late to entertain Paul's prohibitions against women speaking in church or teaching. Women were already doing both.

On a different part of the religious spectrum, the growth in the Northeast of Unitarianism and its offshoot, Transcendentalism, also stressed the value of the individual, and the latter the importance of personal intuition. Cady Stanton was friendly with the Boston Unitarians and Transcendentalists, and says that she was particularly imbued with the ideas of Boston abolitionist and minister Theodore Parker (1810–1860). Like the evangelicals, these groups stressed individual religious experience, thus legitimating women as spiritual beings.

The Bible as Egalitarian. The first extended analysis of the Bible from a perspective of women's rights in America came from the hand of Sarah Grimké (1792–1873), a convert to the Religious Society of

Friends (Quakers) from Charlestown, South Carolina. Growing up on a plantation, from childhood Grimké chafed against the slaveholding of her own family and the limitations on women's education and possibilities. She joined her sister Angelina and brother-in-law Theodore Dwight Weld in battling slavery, touring the country and shocking some hearers by speaking to "promiscuous assemblies," mixed audiences of men and women. Sarah Grimké wrote her *Letters on the Equality of the Sexes* (1837) to Mary Parker, the president of the Boston Female Anti-Slavery Society, and it was first published as a series in abolitionist newspapers. This same year also saw her brother-in-law's publication of *The Bible Against Slavery*. Since Grimké and the Welds shared a household, one can imagine the rich discussions of the Bible and the development of similar methods of interpretation around slavery and women's rights.

Grimké's overarching position was that the Bible reflects God's design of absolute equality and complementarity of the sexes, but that the text had been infected with patriarchy by faulty translation and the imprint of culture. A combination of the creation stories in Genesis 1–2 and Galatians 3:28 show the Creator's design for men and women to share as equals in improving the world. Throughout her letters and other essays she cites Genesis 1:26–27, the locus classicus asserting human dignity, where male and female are created at the same time, both in the image of God. Even Genesis 2, the creation of the woman from Adam's rib, indicates equality. The following passage is typical of her combination of the creation stories in Genesis and Paul's programmatic statement in Galatians to assert her conviction of the Bible's essential egalitarianism:

> Surely no one who contemplates, with the eye of a philosopher, the design of God in the creation of woman, can believe that she is now fulfilling that design. The literal translation of the word "help-meet" [KJV] is a helper like unto himself;…It will be impossible for woman to fill the station assigned to her by God, until her brethren mingle with her as an equal, as a moral being; and lose, in the dignity of her immortal nature, and in fact of her bearing like himself the image

and superscription of her God, the idea of her being female. The apostle beautifully remarks, "As many of you as have been baptized into Christ, have put on Christ. There is neither Jew nor Greek, there is neither bond nor free, there is neither *male* nor *female*; for ye are all one in Christ Jesus." (Grimké, 1838, pp. 23–24)

Women's equality comes directly from God, not human invention, and inequality is both unscriptural and blasphemous (Grimké, 1988, pp. 125, 160–161). Jesus, in spite of his failure to address the issue of women's subordination at all, presents an ethic in the Sermon on the Mount that applies to women and men alike (Grimké, 1838, p. 16). Along with many later feminist interpreters, she cites antiwomen statements from Paul as the source of women's troubles in Christianity, and attributes them to his Jewishness.

To undermine statements that suggested women's subordination, Grimké employed what today's scholars would call "cultural criticism." Deliberately or not, she says, translators of the Bible have injected a false idea of women's inferiority into a purely egalitarian text because they lived in a culture that saw women as slaves or empty-headed dolls (Grimké, 1838, pp. 12, 102). The original biblical text is inspired, but the translations, especially the King James, are corrupt. For example, the so-called curse on Eve in Genesis 3:16, "Your desire will be for your husband, and he shall rule over you," is not a command from God, but a regretful prediction of one of the ills that will afflict society (ibid., p. 7). Grimké also looks to individual women as models, the prophets Miriam and Deborah in the Hebrew Bible and the preachers and deacons Phoebe, Priscilla, and Philip's daughters in the Pauline corpus.

Lucretia Mott delivered her *Discourse on Woman* in 1849 and continued to argue for women's rights using the Bible as only one of her sources. As a Quaker, she did not see the Bible as the sole source of truth but subject to "the inner light" possessed by each individual. Many of her arguments echo Grimké's—the fundamental equality and complementarity of men and women, the holding up of biblical women as models of authority and identifying the misuse of the Bible to limit women's possibilities under the influence of contemporary culture. Both the laws of Moses and Jesus's teaching apply to men and women alike. It is theological and church authorities who have twisted it to their own purposes. In a speech at a women's rights conference in Cleveland in 1853, she is blunt, saying, "The pulpit has been prostituted, the Bible has been ill-used.... The practice has been, to turn over its pages to find example and authority for the wrong, for the existing abuses of society.... We have been so long pinning our faith on other peoples' sleeves that we ought to begin examining these things daily, ourselves, to see whether they *are* so; and we should find on comparing text with text, that a very different construction might be put upon them"(quoted in Greene, 1981, p. 151).

The most complex and witty defense of women's rights using the Bible came from Frances Willard (1839–1898), a reformer on multiple fronts, who is best known as the longtime president of the Women's Christian Temperance Union (WCTU). Raised a devout Methodist, her childhood home in Oberlin, Ohio, was a stop on the Underground Railroad. As president of the WCTU, Willard promoted a "do-everything" policy to reform society that included prison reform, free kindergarten, labor reform, and women's rights.

In *Woman in the Pulpit* (1888), her extended argument for ordination of women as ministers in her own tradition, Willard shares many convictions with Grimké and Mott, but goes beyond them in her methods. She explicitly rejects literalism, analyzes material in ways that mirror the historical-critical methods developing at the time, and is not afraid to needle preachers and laypeople who misappropriate the Bible. She loved the Bible but rejected literalism early in life, calling it a straitjacket and a dangerous tool. If men wish to keep women in subjection by citing Eve's punishment for the sin in the garden, she suggests, then they had better be equally certain to fulfill Adam's curse, to daily "eat his bread in the sweat of his face." Such wooden literalism, she says, is "a two-edged sword, and cuts both ways" (Willard, 1987, p. 33).

Not only does Willard identify the influence of her own culture on translations in her time, she suggests that tampering with manuscripts may have distorted the text from the very beginning. In this she echoes "lower criticism," which recognizes deliberate or unconscious alteration of different manuscripts. She notes how a Christian missionary of her own time deliberately removed a reference to women fellow preachers of Paul to avoid offending the sensibilities of his Chinese hearers. "Who can tell what weight a similar motive may have had with transcribers of the New Testament in the uncultivated ages of the early church?" (Willard, 1987, p. 32).

Willard also was aware of forms of "higher criticism," as it was called, the attempt to reconstruct the history of the text (Willard, 1995, pp. 388–389). She lines up contradictory biblical statements about women to show that more than one voice exists within the text. Paul's statements adjuring women's silence in the churches are defeated by the many numerous verses that show women praying and prophesying in Judges, Joel, and Luke (Willard, 1987, pp. 27–28). Identifying different strains of thought undermines any idea of the Bible as a unified, direct revelation, which was the objection of some traditionalists against the Documentary Hypothesis, the identification of sources within the Pentateuch. While Willard is loosely doing the same thing, she is not overly reverential toward "scientific criticism," as she calls it, saying it is "the most misleading of all arts," which she expects to improve as humanity develops (p. 230). References to new European methods of historical criticism were common in the popular press, and its value was debated in *The Independent*, a publication she read and wrote for. While she imitated some of its ideas, they did not interfere with her appreciation of the Bible. The biblical text was for Willard not immutable, but part of a larger plan of "progressive revelation," the gradual evolution of humanity to higher forms of spiritual attainment. Men and women interpret best in a "stereoscopic," complementary way, with women expected to inject "a pinch of common sense" (Willard, 1987, p. 26). Complementarity of the sexes is the ideal situation from which humanity can go forth to reform the world. God, Jesus, and human beings are both male and female, she believes. She speaks of the motherhood of God (p. 76), and says, "Christ is as much the typical woman as the typical man of the race" (p. 90).

African American women faced double discrimination because of their gender and race, including from the suffrage movement itself. The Bible was a crucial voice of truth for them in asserting the essential dignity of all humanity. Sojourner Truth employed two biblical examples in her famous 1851 "Ain't I A Woman" address for women's equality, suggesting that if Eve's sin upset the world, she should have a chance to set it right again, and that Jesus came into the world through God and a woman, without any man's help. Virginia Broughton (1858–1934) was a Baptist writer and missionary who gathered biblical material supporting women's authority to preach in her work with Bible Bands, groups of women who studied the Bible daily. Anna Julia Cooper (1858–1964), a historian with a doctorate from the University of Paris-Sorbonne, also learned biblical languages when a student at Oberlin College. Her *A Voice from the South* (1892) argues for the education and increased rights of black women. She does not engage in close exegesis, but harmonizes biblical ideas with women's equality. The Bible and Christianity for her represent allies in women's search for justice. We do not see African-American women critiquing the Bible on cultural or other grounds, but understanding it as a fundamentally liberationist text.

The Bible as a Source of Women's Subordination. Other women's rights leaders saw the Bible as deeply implicated in women's subordination. Matilda Joslyn Gage (1826–1898) was one of the commentators in Elizabeth Cady Stanton's commentary *The Woman's Bible* and also one of the editors of the first three volumes of *History of Woman Suffrage*. In *Woman, Church, and State* (Gage, 1893), Gage indicts the Bible as the source of patriarchy and denial of women's rights because it promotes polygamy, the idea of wives and daughters as property, and the idea of a male supreme God who desires war, discord, and child sacrifice (p. 43). The cardinal teaching of the fall of Adam through marriage to Eve resulted in "the union of the state with the church in the enforcement of man's 'curse' upon women" (p. 463). She contrasts biblically based society with other cultures, like those of ancient Egypt, the Iroquois, and the Hindus, cultures where, she maintains, women enjoyed more

power and status. While in her view the Bible cannot really be saved as a moral document, she does show it is sometimes misread, and sees God as separate from the biblical text, as a "spirit or vivifying intelligence," able to be rendered male, female, or neutral. The feminine element shows itself in the gender of the Greek words for "spirit" (*pneuma*) and "wisdom" (*sophia*) and the Hebrew word for "understanding" (*bina*), one of God's attributes in the kabbalists' schema (pp. 43–46).

Gage ferrets out examples of powerful women of the Bible whose influence has not been properly credited by the text itself or Christian tradition: Solomon's mother, Bathsheba, aided his ascent to power (Gage, 1893, pp. 61–63); the Queen of Sheba was a matriarch of her people (pp. 66–70); and the woman clothed with the sun in Revelation possesses spiritual and occult powers misappropriated by the church (pp. 176, 181).

In her entries in *The Woman's Bible* Gage sharpens her diatribe against the Bible, its core ideas, and its use by church, state, and society:

> From "Thou shalt not make a graven image, or any likeness of anything in heaven above, the earth beneath, or the waters under the earth," down to "A woman shall not speak in church, but shall ask her husband at home," the tendency of the Bible has been to crush out aspiration, to deaden human faculties, and to humiliate mankind. From Adam's plaint, 'The woman gave me and I did eat,' down to Christ's 'Woman, what have I to do with thee?' the tendency of the Bible has been degradation of the divinest half of humanity—woman….But our present quest is not what the mystic or the spiritual character of the Bible may be; we are investigating its influence upon woman under Judaism and Christianity, and pronounce it evil. (Stanton, 2002, vol. 2, pp. 208–209)

The Woman's Bible. Elizabeth Cady Stanton, one of the most influential and far-sighted founders of the American movement for women's rights, gathered a committee of women to write a commentary on the Old and New Testaments. Raised a Presbyterian in upstate New York in an abolitionist family, Cady Stanton became acquainted with virtually every major figure in both the abolitionist and suffragist movements. She was close to the New England Unitarians and Transcendentalists, enjoying the friendship of Theodore Parker, William Ellery Channing, and Ralph Waldo Emerson during her years in Boston.

Her committee included some Europeans, but most entries were written by American women of Protestant background, but minus any biblical scholars or evangelicals. The commentary picked out sections of the Bible where women appear or are glaringly absent, and made brief comments. The comments are far from uniform, and many reflect nineteenth-century attitudes: the identification of God with Nature, the uncoupling of "pure religion" from its institutional manifestations, Orientalism, anti-Judaism, interest in mysticism and the occult, knowledge of emerging methods of historical criticism, belief in science and progress, and progressive revelation. The work is not easily classified. While it harbors much critique, it also appreciates the unique emotional place of the Bible for individuals and the culture. To some colleagues who wanted to dismiss the Bible altogether as a worn-out relic of a barbarous past, Cady Stanton replied, "The sentimental feelings we all have for those things we were educated to believe sacred, do not readily yield to pure reason." For women who still held the Bible to be divinely inspired, Cady Stanton encouraged them to submit their exegesis, but also to accept the new methods of biblical criticism (Stanton, 2002, vol. 1, pp. 11–12).

Like the Transcendentalists, Cady Stanton identified God with Nature, and viewed an abstract, permanent force, "the Spirit of All Good," as a purer notion than an anthropomorphic God. The historically limited and contingent narratives of the Hebrew Bible she considered more primitive and suspect. The story of the expulsion of Hagar and Ishmael in Genesis 21:1–21 evokes disdain: "Does anyone seriously believe that the great spirit of all good talked with these Jews, and really said the extraordinary things they report? It was, however, a very cunning way for the Patriarchs to enforce their own authority, to do whatever they desired, and say the Lord commanded them to do and say thus and so" (Stanton, 2002, vol. 1, p. 40). The "God of the Jews," that is, of the Hebrew Bible, the commentary characterizes as "the Jewish Lord, guiding and directing that people in all their devious ways, and sanctioning their petty immoralities," quite unlike "our ideal of the great first cause, a God of justice, wisdom and truth" (vol. 1, p. 47).

Predictably, the Hebrew Bible comes under attack from the commentators for its treatment of women, for cruelty, and for deficient morality. Often "the Jews," as the first section of the commentary calls the biblical writers, are the source of it. The Noah story shows the "low ideal the Jews had of the great first cause" (Stanton, 2002, vol. 1, p. 35), while the courtship of Isaac and Rebekah, despite its sweetness, shows the Jewish Lord "guiding the people in all their devious ways, and sanctioning their petty immoralities" (vol. 1, p. 47). Sarah's cruelty to Hagar is partially excused as reflecting the moral standards of the time (vol. 1, p. 141). Exodus 1:5, counting Jacob's descendants as seventy souls, raises speculation that the Bible may not have counted women as souls (vol. 1, p. 69).

Some contributors are more generous. Clara Bewick Colby argues that some revelations remain true, but the text has been misused to shore up preexisting prejudices, and that the translators were not divinely inspired. The call for a wife "to obey" her husband is better understood as "to defer to." She echoes Sarah Grimké when she maintains that the curse against Eve was not meant as a command from God, but as a sorry prediction (Stanton, 2002, vol. 1, p. 37).

The Woman's Bible does not fall into the trap of assigning all negative morality and antiwoman prejudices to the "Jewish" past in the Hebrew Bible or to Judaism of their own time. Colby sees the narrative of Isaac and Rebekah's meeting as evidence of Rebekah's "personal freedom and dignity," showing that Jewish women enjoyed better treatment than those of neighboring peoples (Stanton, 2002, vol. 1, pp. 48–49). Christians have missed the significance of Deborah from Judges 4 and 5, Clara B. Neyman asserts: "How could Christianity teach that women should be silent in the church when already among the Jews equal honor was shown to women?" (vol. 2, p. 21). Cady Stanton resists the idea that the New Testament was an improvement over the Old when it comes to women. "While there are grand types of women presented under both religions [Judaism and Christianity], there is no difference in the general estimate of the sex. In fact, her inferior position is more clearly and emphatically set forth by the Apostles than by the Prophets and the Patriarchs" (vol. 2, p. 113).

The commentary notes some women exemplars in the biblical text, but misses others. It makes nothing of Hagar and little of baby Moses's rescuers, the midwives Shiphrah and Puah and Pharaoh's daughter. Miriam is cited briefly, while much is made of the prophet and judge Deborah (Stanton, 2002, vol. 2, pp. 85–92). Ruth, Huldah, and Esther are lauded, and Vashti, the queen who refuses to come at her husband's call in the book of Esther, comes in for special admiration. Showing courage and self-respect, "she is true to the Divine aspirations of her nature" (vol. 2, p. 88).

The New Testament receives much less attention than the Old. The commentary praises the Canaanite woman who convinces Jesus to heal her daughter (Matt 15:1–28), Elizabeth and Anna from Luke's gospel, and Jesus's mother. Jesus's mother has not been fully appreciated, says Cady Stanton, and "the best thing about the Catholic Church is the deification of Mary" (Stanton, 2002, vol. 2, pp. 143–144). Mary's example evokes a meditation on motherhood itself from Cady Stanton. The notion of the church as a womanly institution, "Mother Church," brings Lucinda Chandler to declare that without a recognition of the feminine element in God and complete equality of men and women in the church, the church cannot be thoroughly Christian (vol. 2, 173). Matilda Joslyn Gage composed comments on Revelation, arguing for its mystical and astrological interpretation, pointing to the great cosmic battle for women's elevation. Cady Stanton is considerably less taken with the work, because of its violence and negative depiction of woman (vol. 2, pp. 176–184).

Some women leaders mentioned by Paul in Romans, such as Phoebe, Priscilla, and Junia, are identified in the commentary. Oddly enough, no one picks out the women followers of Jesus, evident especially in Mark's gospel. Even Mary of Bethany's stance as a disciple who sits at Jesus's feet (Luke 10:38–42) is ignored. No one notes the significance of Mary Magdalene as the first to find the empty tomb and report the event that signaled the resurrection, nor of her honor as the first to meet the risen Jesus in John's gospel.

Jesus and Paul. The teachings of Jesus and Paul present special problems for anyone looking for the biblical sources of women's rights. Jesus never said anything explicit about women, and Paul said rather too much. The nineteenth century saw the first quest to uncover the historical Jesus by D. F. Strauss and Albert Schweitzer. Feminist interpreters shared with these questers the assumption that the "real" Jesus could be discovered through critical methods, a Jesus distinct from his Jewish environment, the writings of the gospel authors, and institutional Christianity. This pure and abstract Jesus is always visualized as a champion of women's equality, and a paradigmatic male and female.

The interpreters rely on arguments from silence, ignoring occasional statements he seems to make to men alone, and noting Jesus's example in his relationships with women. Grimké, for example, maintains that the kernel of Jesus's teaching, the Sermon on the Mount in Matthew 5—7 is addressed to men and women together. Willard calls Jesus an "emancipator" and "deliverer" of women (Willard, 1987, pp. 23, 51), who treated women as disciples. In the second chapter of *Woman in the Pulpit* she cites the commissioning of the Samaritan woman to preach (John 4) and Mary Magdalene to declare the resurrection, Martha's declaration of Jesus's messiahship (John 11:27), and women's reception of the Spirit at Pentecost (Acts 1:13–14) as proof that the women around Jesus were disciples, even if they were not "called" like the men. *The Woman's Bible* deals less with Jesus than with the characters of the Hebrew Bible. Nor does it always assume that Christianity was an automatic boon for women. Nevertheless, Jesus enjoys immunity from any charge of patriarchy or antiwoman prejudice (Stanton, 2002, vol. 2, pp. 114, 164–165).

Paul is forced by some interpreters to shoulder the blame for much of the teaching of subordination of women that underlies much Christian teaching. For Grimké and some commentators in *The Woman's Bible*, the prejudice is attributed to Paul's Jewishness. Grimké cites the commentary by Adam Clarke that explains the command for women to keep silent in the churches (1 Cor 14:34) as "a Jewish ordinance. Women were not permitted to teach in the assemblies or even to ask questions" (Grimké, 1838, pp. 111–112). According to her, the enthusiasm the women showed in the church was also the fault of Judaism. Repressed under Judaism, when they were set free by Christianity, they temporarily got carried away (p. 111). The same reasoning applies to 1 Timothy 2:11–12 and the command that women may not teach or have authority over men (p. 114).

The Woman's Bible is not uniform in its treatment of Paul, and we have seen that Cady Stanton herself does not usually favor Christianity over Judaism, but a few cases of anti-Judaism appear. Lucinda Chandler says Paul's commands for women's silence were not inspired but holdovers: "He carried the spirit of the Talmud, 'aggravated and reinforced' into Christianity." Jesus himself made no claims for dominion of any sex over the other (Stanton, 2002, vol. 2, p. 165). Louisa Southworth similarly suggests these rules are anachronisms based on some "absurd old myth" that Paul probably heard from his teacher Gamaliel (vol. 2, pp. 158–159). Willard, although she shares the distrust of translations and accepts the imprint of cultural biases on biblical interpretation, seems free of anti-Jewish prejudice. She ultimately sees the text as liberating, and so perhaps is less inclined to assign blame.

The Bible as Irrelevant. For many women the Bible itself was not a particular focus, except to the extent that it bolstered the power of churches and clergy to hold women back. Lucy Stone (1818–1893), who with Cady Stanton and Anthony was a driving force in women's suffrage and feminism, responded to a heckler at a women's rights convention in Cincinnati in 1917 who called the movement a group of "disappointed women." Turning the jibe around, she said, "In education, in marriage, in religion, disappointment is the lot of women. It shall be the business of my life to deepen this disappointment in every

woman's heart until she bows down to it no longer." Arguing against the idea of two separate spheres, she said God equipped women for greater things: "I have confidence in the Father to believe that when He gives us the capacity to do anything He does not make a blunder" (Stanton et al., 1881–1922, vol. 1, pp. 165–167).

Ernestine Rose also considered biblical and religious teaching to be beside the point. A Polish Jew and daughter of a rabbi, she became an atheist, but defended Judaism and battled anti-Semitism in a set of published exchanges with newspaper editor Horace Seaver. Nevertheless, when the Reverend Antoinette Brown, the first woman ordained as a minister in the United States, offered a resolution at a women's rights convention in Syracuse in 1852, stating that the Bible recognizes the equality and rights of women, Rose successfully blocked it. She said,

> I cannot object to anyone interpreting the Bible as he or she thinks best; but I do object that such interpretation go forth as the doctrine of this convention, because it is a mere interpretation and not even the authority of the Book; it is the view of Miss Brown only, which is as good as that of any other minister, but that is all. For my part I reject both interpretations. Here we claim human rights and freedom based upon the laws of humanity and we require no written authority from Moses or Paul, because those laws and our claim are prior even to these two great men. (Harper, 1899, p. 65)

[*See also* Feminism, *subentries on* Second-Wave Feminism *and* Third-Wave Feminism.]

BIBLIOGRAPHY

Durso, Pamela. *The Power of Woman: The Life and Writings of Sarah Moore Grimké.* Macon, Ga.: Mercer University Press, 2003.

Gage, Matilda Joslyn. *Woman, Church, and State: A Historical Account of the Status of Woman through the Christian Ages: With Reminiscences of the Matriarchate.* Chicago: C. H. Kerr, 1893. Available online at https://archive.org/details/womanchurchstateoogagerich.

de Groot, Christiana, and Marion Ann Taylor, eds. *Recovering Nineteenth-Century Women Interpreters of the Bible.* Atlanta: Society of Biblical Literature, 2007.

Greene, Dana. "Quaker Feminism: The Case of Lucretia Mott." *Pennsylvania History* 48 (1981): 143–154.

Grimké, Sarah Moore. *Letters on the Equality of the Sexes and the Condition of Woman.* Boston: Isaac Knapp, 1838. Available online at http://www.archive.org/stream/lettersonequalitoogrimrich#.

Grimké, Sarah Moore. *Letters on the Equality of the Sexes and Other Essays.* Edited by Elizabeth Ann Bartlett. New Haven, Conn.: Yale University Press, 1988.

Harper, Ida Husted. *The Life and Work of Susan B. Anthony,* Vol. 1. Indianapolis, Ind.: Bowen-Merrill, 1899. Available online at https://archive.org/details/lifeandworksusaoounkngoog.

McFadden, Margaret H. *Golden Cables of Sympathy: The Transatlantic Sources of Nineteenth-Century Feminism.* Lexington: University of Kentucky Press, 1999.

Mott, Lucretia. "Discourse on Woman." Available online at http://gos.sbc.edu/m/mott.html.

Setzer, Claudia. "Slavery, Women's Rights, and the Beginnings of Feminist Biblical Interpretation in the Nineteenth Century." *Postscripts: The Journal of Sacred Texts and Contemporary Worlds* 5.2 (2009): 145–169.

Setzer, Claudia. "A Jewish Reading of *The Woman's Bible.*" *Journal of Feminist Studies in Religion* 27.2 (2011): 71–84.

Setzer, Claudia. "Frances Willard, the Undermining of Literalism, and the Reform of Society." In *Finding Themselves: Women and the Bible in the 19th Century,* edited by Angela Berlis and Christiana de Groot. Leiden, The Netherlands: Brill, forthcoming.

Stanton, Elizabeth Cady. *Eighty Years and More: Reminiscences, 1815–1897.* New York: Schocken, 1971. First edition available online at http://digital.library.upenn.edu/women/stanton/years/years.html.

Stanton, Elizabeth Cady. *The Woman's Bible: A Classic Feminist Perspective.* Mineola, N.Y.: Dover, 2002. First edition available online at http://www.gutenberg.org/catalog/world/readfile?fk_files=2267536.

Stanton, Elizabeth Cady, Susan B. Anthony, and Matilda Joslyn Gage. *History of Woman Suffrage.* 6 vols. Rochester, N.Y.: Susan B. Anthony and Charles Mann Press, 1881–1922.

Willard, Frances E. "Woman in the Pulpit." In *The Defense of Women's Rights to Ordination in the Methodist Episcopal Church,* edited by Carolyn DeSwarte Gifford. New York: Garland, 1987.

Willard, Frances E. *Writing Out My Heart: Selections from the Journal of Frances E. Willard, 1855–96.* Edited by Carolyn De Swarte Gifford. Urbana: University of Illinois, 1995.

Claudia Setzer

Second-Wave Feminism

Unlike first-wave feminism of the nineteenth-century United States, second-wave feminism emerged as an entirely secular movement, in which religious groups, activists, and scholars of theology and religion played only a marginal role. This is also true for feminist Bible scholars who have not significantly participated in setting the agenda for the feminist movement as it developed during the late 1960s and early 1970s in Western societies (Scholz and Matthews, 2013; Scholz, 2007, 2014). In fact, some pioneering feminist thinkers, such as Mary Daly, characterized the Bible as the antithesis of feminist principles owing to its androcentric and sexist nature. In a much translated and widely distributed essay, Daly observes that "in the documents of scripture, church fathers, popes, and theologians throughout the centuries we find an astonishing contrast between, on the one hand, the teachings concerning the value and dignity of the human person and, on the other hand, an all-pervasive misogynism and downgrading of women as persons" (Daly, 1970, p. 138).

Since 1970, therefore, the feminist value of the Bible has been questioned again and again. Some, such as Alison Jasper, advise "to give the whole thing up as a bad job, a dead horse which it is pointless to flog any further" (Jasper, 2001, p. 110). Others, such as Shulamith Firestone, who grew up in a highly religious family, came to feminism to escape their experiences of severe patriarchal domination and wanted to have little to do with religion. They maintained that feminists should not waste their energies on religious institutions and practices, powerful sources for the subordination and oppression of women. In their view, religions would only change once women enjoyed equal educational, professional, and political opportunities and positions with men. Since a major goal of second-wave feminism was freedom from traditions, conventions, and laws oppressive to women for millennia, secular feminists gave feminist theologians and Bible scholars curious glances at best, as they saw little merit in a systematic engagement with religious sources and traditions. To them, religions were in opposition to the liberation of women from patriarchy.

Endorsing Women, Faith, Queer Sexualities, or Economic Neoliberalism? Feminist suspicion toward religion has not deterred those feminists who hold on to their religious faith traditions or have become academics in theological and religious studies. Interestingly, when the second-wave feminist movement came into being in North America, a considerable number of women scholars had recently earned or were in the process of earning their doctoral degrees in biblical studies. Among them have been women scholars in Hebrew Bible and New Testament, such as Alice Bach, Phyllis Bird, Athalya Brenner, Sheila Briggs, Bernadette J. Brooten, Claudia V. Camp, Adela Yarbro Collins, J. Cheryl Exum, Elisabeth Schüssler Fiorenza, Esther Fuchs, Tikva Frymer-Kensky, Carol Meyers, Carol A. Newsom, Letty Russell, Jane Schaberg, Luise Schottroff, and Phyllis Trible (see also Scholz, 2012b; Lopez and Penner, 2012). They turned to the emerging feminist discourse to inform their burgeoning scholarship. However, much of feminist biblical studies developed in relative isolation from feminist theories and the field of women's studies and what later expanded into gender studies (Trible, 1982a; Hackett, 1987, Coggins, 1988; Day, 1991; Frymer-Kensky, 1994). Pamela Milne explains that the disconnect between feminist biblical studies and women's and gender studies is related to the fact that feminist Bible scholars have felt primarily accountable to the academic discipline in which they had earned their doctoral degrees and in which they were hired to teach at institutions of higher learning (Milne, 1997, p. 44). Often, they developed their work without considering the general feminist agenda, as articulated by the feminist movement and secular feminist theorists, despite some calls to do so since the early stages of feminist biblical exegesis (Wire, 1986). To Milne, mainstream feminist discourse thus mainly ignored feminist biblical scholarship.

There is yet another reason for the disconnection. According to Milne, feminist biblical scholars have not usually articulated the relationship between their feminist and theological convictions and, in fact, often defended the Bible as a women-friendly authority for women (Trible, 1982a, 1982b; Schüssler Fiorenza, 1982; Tolbert, 1983). Sometimes, they have reinforced the androcentric status quo, advanced neoliberal feminist recuperations of the Bible, ignored or dismissed feminist theories, and reauthorized the "fathers" of the field. Esther Fuchs eloquently articulates this problem (Fuchs, 2008). In her view, a neoliberal trend has emerged in feminist biblical studies since the 1990s. It has enabled feminist Bible scholars to conceptualize their work by merely adding "women" to the existing field of biblical studies. This add-on approach advances a reformist and gradualist agenda, adheres to the notion of inevitable progress in social change and advancement, and does not question existing epistemologies and binary dualisms. Fuchs explains that this neoliberal compliance relies on an essentialist view of gender, as if fixed and unchanging traits shape women's identities formed by women's experiences that are self-evident and universally valid for women anywhere and at any time.

In addition, such feminist biblical work, which Fuchs identifies in such books as Ilana Pardes's *Countertraditions in the Bible* (1992), Susan Ackerman's *Warrior, Dancer, Seductress, Queen: Women in Judges and Biblical Israel* (1998), and Tikva Frymer-Kensky's *The Bible and Women's Studies* (2006), rarely refers to feminist genealogies of knowledge, rarely acknowledges its indebtedness to feminist mothers, and rarely mentions methodological or theoretical departure from feminist predecessors. Fuchs states: "Contemporary neoliberal theories seek to introduce a commonsense, natural, and straightforward reading of the Bible, where women appear as real individuals, as universal typologies, or as sources of antipatriarchal thinking. This approach is positivist and essentialist" (2008, p. 63). It ignores what Fuchs characterizes as the "foundational proposition in feminist theory": "that 'woman' is a construct, much as the definitions of gender and sex are culturally determined, [and] that all three are implicated in historical processes and transformations" (2008, p. 65). In short, according to Fuchs, key feminist Bible scholars are more loyal to male-dominated conventional approaches than to feminist theories, and so they reinscribe "conventional hegemonic methodologies" (2008, p. 65), the disciplinary status quo of biblical studies.

Other scholars highlight other factors as contributing to the ambiguity, hesitation, and even rejection of feminist goals in feminist biblical exegesis. Pamela Milne observes an increasing professionalization and depoliticization of feminist Bible work since the 1970s (1997, p. 53). Feminist interpreters, trained by professional biblical scholars in seminaries and universities and aiming for recognition and acceptance in academic institutions of higher learning and in professional biblical scholarly organizations such as the Society of Biblical Literature (SBL), have been coopted into supporting the status quo. For them to be offered academic positions, their work has to comply with the standards of the field. They have to get reference letters for employment, tenure, and promotion, as well as collegial support for their publications. Hence, Milne argues, feminist scholars usually rely on "traditional methods of analysis to investigate non-traditional questions (i.e., questions of relevance and interest to women and about women) from feminist perspectives" to change "the way individuals interpreted biblical texts about women" (1997, p. 53) Such work is highly technical and, as dominantly practiced in biblical studies, focuses on biblical texts as the primary resource for reconstructing ancient Israelite history and women's roles in biblical stories and poems. Carol Meyers wrote a classic feminist-historical book on the Hebrew Bible (1988, *Discovering Eve*); Elisabeth Schüssler Fiorenza published a classic feminist-historical treatise on the Second Testament (1983, *In Memory of Her*); and Phyllis Trible produced a classic feminist-literary interpretation on the Hebrew Bible (1978, *God and the Rhetoric of Sexuality*).

Yet, Milne notes, feminist biblical scholars do not usually study women readers and their attitudes to the Bible. As employment opportunities have sharply decreased since the early 1990s, a wide acceptance of the professional and depoliticized standards in academia in general and biblical studies in particular dominates (Scholz, 2012a). This is how Milne articulates the conundrum for feminist scholars:

> At a time when few teaching positions are available, and when departments of religion and religious studies

are being "down-sized" or eliminated in favour of more "essential" disciplines, women—who have entered the discipline in record numbers over the last decade—find themselves shut out by economic factors that compound the problem of sexist bias that has traditionally been a systemic barrier to women in this field. Personally, I do not think the economic argument is unrelated to the problem of sexist bias. The devaluing of the field that we can now observe at many institutions may well be linked to the fact that what was once a virtually all-male discipline is now no longer so. (Milne, 1997, p. 43)

Milne thus worries about the long-term viability of feminist scholarship in biblical studies, primarily owing to the gradual disappearance of teaching positions.

Teresa J. Hornsby offers an even more disconcerting view of the status of biblical scholarship engaged with feminist, gender, and sexuality issues. She argues that the development from a women-centric focus to a more broadly conceptualized gender and queer agenda is not indicative of a subversive positioning of feminist biblical studies, as for instance suggested by Deryn Guest (2012). Rather, according to Hornsby, both women-centric and queer approaches in biblical studies need to be understood as accommodating the forces in the economic-capitalist globalized world in which we live, since "sexuality and gender are constructed in collusion with capitalistic power" (2011, p. 137). Therefore, Hornsby claims, as capitalism changes and shifts, sexual and gender norms do too. She bases her analysis on three assumptions, namely, that "power produces sexual normatives," "the dominant form that this power takes in Western Euro cultures is neoliberal capitalism," and "Christianity (indeed, organized religion) is an arm of power that aids in this production" (p. 137). Accordingly, calls for changes in feminist, gender, and queer biblical scholarship, as well as in other areas of culture and society, are linked to the shift from a "closed, centrally powerful, and industrial" economic system to one that is "open, globally diverse, and electronically based" (p. 137). Consequently, to Hornsby, theoretical inclusions of nonheteronormative and queer sexualities in culture, theology, and biblical interpretation are not deconstructive moves for overcoming worldwide oppression but "capitalism's use of Christian theology to construct the types of sexual/economic subjects it needs" (pp. 141–142). And what is needed are bodies willing to submit and to enjoy masochistic positions in the societal-economic interplay of power, and, Hornsby explains, feminist, gender, and queer biblical exegesis assists in this process even if this help is provided unintentionally; such is the power of the neoliberal capitalist system over every body and thing.

Hornsby illustrates these dynamics in cultural and exegetical feminist and nonfeminist approaches to the passion narratives of Christ and to Pauline theology, arguing that "the end product is an extraordinarily submissive body—a body that connects suffering with hope and humiliation with empowerment" (Hornsby, 2011, p. 149). Since the dynamics in capitalism produce, reproduce, and sustain this kind of masochistic positioning for all people—no longer only for those performing as women as the position of the victim is increasingly masculinized, heteronormative expectations lessen and sociocultural space for queer desire increases. In other words, to Hornsby, queering the Bible does not challenge neoliberalism, because "queer sexualities are manufactured and serve power just as much as a sanctioned sexuality" (p. 153). Since capitalism needs people with "more open, fluid, ambivalent sexual identities," willing to suffer for this elastic and promised space, calls for feminist, gender, and queer readings of the Bible (and culture) accommodate this need. In Hornsby's assessment of feminist, gender, and queer biblical interpretation, then, resistance to neoliberalism is an illusion because the feminist agenda is always already part of economic neoliberalism.

Hornsby's dystopian explanation takes on almost totalitarian proportions without any alternative options. Borrowing from Foucault without explicitly saying so, her discussion is a cautionary note about the difficulties of resisting the cultural, sociopolitical, economic, and religious dynamics of one's time (see, e.g., Heller, 1996; see also Justaert, 2010). The jury is still out on whether feminist biblical scholarship can be reduced to helping those performing as women become fully integrated into a societal-economic system dependent on a large and continuous supply of willing consumers who buy and comply. Milne's suggestion that feminist biblical scholars connect their work directly to the social, political, legal, and economic goals of the feminist movement seems harmless (Milne, 1997, p. 59). Nevertheless, her proposal to relate biblical exegesis to feminist theories and practices may be a better option than falling into resigned inaction because, according to Hornsby, resistance is futile.

On a Future of Feminist Biblical Studies. It should thus not be a surprise that feminist Bible scholars wonder about the next step. After almost every biblical woman character has been identified, every scholarly method applied, and practically every biblical text analyzed for its gender ideology (Meyers et al., 2000), the question is what remains to be done if we do not want to merely give in to the neoliberal status quo. Perhaps this is one of the reasons why feminist biblical scholars are currently in the process of surveying and assessing the field. For instance, Athalya Brenner poses the following questions when she reflects on the future of the field:

> *Quo vadis*, feminist biblical scholarship?…What is beckoning? Where do you want to go? Is the Master's House still the house you long to possess, only that you would like to become its legitimate(d) masters and mistresses instead of marginal(ized) lodgers? Would you like to move it (houses can be moved now from one location to another)?…Will an act of exchanging places within the accepted power paradigms be the object of desire? Are new structures of dominance, a shift in majority/minority balances, being implemented? Are you, we, aspiring to conquistador positions in the names of the proverbial "oppressed"? Should we not simply demolish the house instead of merely deconstructing it and its inhabitants, in order to build a completely new one instead? And if so, who will get right of occupation in the new house, and on what terms?…The contenders are many and the audiences are dwindling, as we are becoming more and more radicalized. Whose scholarship will matter, say, twenty-five years hence? (Brenner, 2005, p. 338)

Brenner wonders about the existing power hierarchies, as feminist Bible scholars adapt to the status quo or even change it. It is a reflection on the in-house situation of feminist Bible studies at the dawn of the twenty-first century.

Yet Brenner's concerns do not address the larger intellectual and societal developments, in contrast to Milne, who considers the political and social implications of biblical exegesis for women in the past and the present. But even Milne's analysis is text-centered, as if the identification of textual meaning and its gender ideology were already present in the text (Milne, 1997, p. 11). Others, such as Deryn Guest, recommend that feminist biblical scholarship "tool up and become even more expansively theory-rich, able to bring the critical studies of masculinities, queer studies, trans studies, intersex studies, and lesbian and gay studies into negotiation with feminist theory without necessarily privileging what have been, to date, stalwart feminist positions" (2012, p. 150). Still others observe that feminist biblical exegetes need to be committed to intersectional hermeneutics and take seriously connections between sexism, racism, classism, homophobia, and geopolitics. Already in 1982, Katherine Doob Sakenfeld acknowledged "the cultural and functional inseparability of racism, sexism, and classism" (1982, p. 19). She saw these issues addressed "on the theological front" but not in biblical studies where "the literature dealing with these three 'isms' remains on three separate tracks" (p. 19). She recognized that "we Bible specialists have more work to do in this area" (p. 19).

Womanist theologians pressed the concern for an intersectional analysis. In 1987, Toinette M. Eugene, an ethicist and womanist scholar, called for a womanist biblical hermeneutics. She noted that owing to women of color's "doubly and triply oppressed" status in patriarchal society, it does not suffice to identify patriarchal oppression with androcentrism alone. Sexism must be understood as part of other oppressive ideologies, such as racism, militarism, or imperialism, because "the structures of oppression are all intrinsically linked" (Eugene, 1987, p. 20; see also Williams, 1986). She advised that feminist bib-lical hermeneutics "articulate an alternative liberating vision and praxis for all oppressed people by utilizing the paradigm of women's experiences of survival and salvation in the struggle against patriarchal oppression and degradation" (Eugene, 1987, p. 25). In her view, a feminist biblical hermeneutics is "the litmus test for invoking scripture as the Word of God" (p. 24), and the question is "whether or not biblical texts and traditions seek to end all relations based on oppressive domination and exploitation" (p. 24).

Eugene's demand for the inclusion of other forms of social analysis did not, however, find full articulation in the 1980s. During this phase most feminist biblical scholars focused on gender and androcentrism alone, as Nyasha Junior observes:

A brief survey of key works in that field [feminist biblical studies] attests to the lack of substantive impact that womanist approaches have had on the discipline of biblical studies. The volume edited by Adela Yarbro Collins, *Feminist Perspectives on Biblical Scholarship* (1985), does not include an article on black feminist or womanist thought. In Letty Russell's edited volume, *Feminist Interpretation of the Bible* (1985), Cannon, an ethicist, contributes an article on black feminist consciousness. In addition, Cannon writes "Womanist Interpretation and Preaching in the Black Church," in Elisabeth Schüssler Fiorenza's *Searching the Scriptures* (1993). In the seventeen volumes of the Feminist Companion to the Bible series, edited by Athalya Brenner, only one article has an explicitly womanist approach. Brenner's overview volume, *A Feminist Companion to Reading the Bible* (1997), does not include an article on womanist biblical interpretation. In the nine volumes of the Feminist Companion to the New Testament and Early Christian Writings series, edited by Amy-Jill Levine, there are no articles from a womanist perspective. Moreover, to date there is no full-length monograph on womanist biblical interpretation or edited volume utilizing womanizing approaches. (Junior, 2006, p. 44)

The omission of race, class, and geopolitical dynamics as analytical categories in much of the pioneering work in feminist biblical studies is obvious, and so feminist biblical scholars from around the world have embraced intersectional, postcolonial, and dialogical hermeneutics (e.g., Dube, 2000; Kwok, 2006; Mbuwayesango and Scholz, 2009; Kim, 2010).

Yet again and again, some feminist scholars charge that second-wave feminist aims of equality and women's rights have been coopted by the status quo. They are thus less optimistic about the future of feminism in general and feminist biblical studies in particular (Exum, 2010). In their view, feminist calls to action often become secondary, and the impetus toward sociopolitical, economic, and cultural transformation has been neglected. Loyalty to conventionally defined hermeneutical and methodological principles overshadows feminist biblical works. Perhaps unsurprisingly, then, twenty-first-century feminist biblical research often engages in depoliticized and technical projects that comply with dominant standards, norms, and expectations. As Caroline Vander Stichele and Todd Penner state, the guild of biblical studies "maintains a strong line of male-identified scholarly assessment and production" (2009, p. 169), and "the difference that is tolerated does not challenge the phallocentric and colonial structures of the guild" but rather contributes to "solidify its hold" (p. 170; see also Fuchs, 2003). Feminist biblical scholarship, like other marginalized discourses by the "excluded other," functions as a "fetish" and "is granted access to the formal structure as a beneficent gesture" (p. 169; see also Scholz, 2005). In other words, feminist biblical scholars are relatively far from restructuring the master's house, although they often contribute to making it stronger and last longer.

"The Unfinished Business of the Twenty-First Century": The Case of Gender and Sexual Violence against Women and Girls in Feminist Biblical Studies. There is, however, hope. Since the early years of the second-wave feminist movement, violence against women and girls has been on the top of the agenda. Susan Brownmiller's book on rape brought the topic out of the shadows and engendered debates about origins, mechanisms, and consequences of gender and sexual violence against women and girls (Brownmiller, 1975; see also Scholz, 2000a, 2000b). In fact, feminists have

developed the idea of a global "rape culture" to capture the extent of violence against women and girls. In an important anthology, Emilie Buchwald, Pamela R. Fletcher, and Martha Roth define rape culture as "a complex of beliefs that encourages male sexual aggression and supports violence against women … a society where violence is seen as sexy and sexuality as violent" (Buchwald et al., 1993, p. v). A widely distributed book by New York Times writers Nicholas D. Kristof and Sheryl WuDunn (2009) illustrates the extent of worldwide gender and sexual violence against women and girls, and recent revelations about sexual violence in the U.S. military (Nelson, 2002; Benedict, 2010) have reminded people that gender and sexual violence against women and girls, even when defined as a "linguistic fact" (Marcus, 1992), shapes the lives and opportunities of millions and millions of women and girls in cruel, limiting, and profoundly damaging ways.

Feminist scholars in biblical studies have taken the topic very seriously. In 1984, Phyllis Trible examined four biblical narratives on sexual violence against and murder of women and girls from a feminist perspective (Trible, 1984). Her bold and by now classic study inspired other feminist interpreters to investigate biblical prose and poetry on the topic and relate it to the Bible's interpretation histories and the manifold rape-prone and misogynist assumptions in society and culture (Setel, 1985; Bal, 1987; Weems, 1995; Dijk-Hemmes, 1993; Brenner 1993; Exum, 1993, 1996; Selvidge, 1996; Scholz, 2000b; Hens-Piazza, 2003; Baumann, 2003; Anderson, 2004; Parry, 2004; Bader, 2006; Schroeder, 2007; Yamada, 2008; Scholz, 2010a; O'Brien and Franke, 2010; Rapoport, 2011). What remains to be done is placing this work into the sociological contexts of the hermeneutical debate (Scholz, 2010b, 2013) and comprehensively integrating feminist work into standard commentaries and introductions to the Bible (e.g., Niditch, 2008). Churches and synagogues also need to foster serious conversations and education processes about the Bible and its connections to gender and sexual violence. To read the many biblical stories of women, girls, and some men who are depicted as enduring gender and sexual violence, among them Dinah, Tamar, Abishag the Shunammite,

Susannah, Hagar, Bilhah, Zilpah, Sarah, Rebecca, Ms. Gomer, Ms. Potiphar, Delilah, Lot's daughters, the women of Jabesh-gilead and Shiloh, Joseph, Samson, and Ehud, ought to demonstrate that "in naming it [sexual violence], we reclaim the truth which we know, that the way things are is not the way they have to be" (Fortune, 2005, p. 237). Although sometimes feminist interpreters get confused about the methodological, hermeneutical, and linguistic legitimacy of analyzing biblical texts on gender and sexual violence according to this principle (e.g., Fewell and Gunn, 1991; Gravett, 2004; Lipka, 2006), explorations of the phallocentric ideology in biblical literature and its manifestation in commentaries, sermons, and culture demonstrate the ongoing need for wrestling with this tradition (O'Brien, 2001). However, the existence of so many texts on gender and sexual violence in the Hebrew Bible does not mean that only the Hebrew Bible mentions such acts. For instance, the New Testament feminist scholar Jane Schaberg identifies sexual violence in the story of Mary, the mother of Jesus, in the Gospel stories (Schaberg, 1987). Rather, the mention indicates that the recognition of gender and sexual violence in biblical literature confronts a major injustice in today's world. It demonstrates that feminist Bible scholars need to resist, dismantle, and oppose rape-prone assumptions, conventions, and conduct wherever they appear, including in the Bible. The aim is not to single out the Bible but to develop an understanding of religious texts and traditions as contributing factors to gender and sexual violence in the world today (Scholz, 2004).

Toward the Nurturing of Alliances: Concluding Comments. Schüssler Fiorenza proposes that feminist biblical scholarship "must be informed by a hunger and thirst for justice" so that feminist interpretations resemble "a critical quilting of meaning" and articulate a "wholistic biblical vision of well-being for all" (2006). It seems obvious in the age of global corporate economic domination, especially in the United States, that the nurturing of alliances beyond the narrow confines of one's immediate affiliation is essential to making this proposal a reality. Feminist Bible scholars will need to resist, perhaps more than ever, the lure and rewards of what postcolonial theorists call the empire. At the same time they will need to articulate and build theoretical and practical alternatives so that the next generation is able to continue the work. The establishment of institutions that foster such emancipatory alternatives in biblical studies and in the world remains foremost on the agenda of feminist biblical studies in the twenty-first century. Such institutions, broadly conceived, are much needed so that the field of feminist biblical interpretation will continue producing innovative and important scholarship that contributes to eliminating structures of domination and to nurturing religious, societal, political, and economic forces of justice and peace.

[*See also* Gender; Heteronormativity/Heterosexism; Postcolonial Approaches; Queer Readings; Sexual Violence, *subentry* Hebrew Bible; *and* Womanist Criticism.]

BIBLIOGRAPHY

Anderson, Cheryl B. *Women, Ideology, and Violence: Critical Theory and the Construction of Gender in the Book of Covenant and the Deuteronomic Law.* New York: T&T Clark International, 2004.

Bach, Alice, ed. *Women in the Hebrew Bible: A Reader.* New York: Routledge, 1999.

Bader, Mary Anna. *Sexual Violation in the Hebrew Bible: A Multi-Methodological Study of Genesis 34 and 2 Samuel 13.* New York: Peter Lang, 2006.

Bal, Mieke. *Lethal Love: Feminist Literary Readings of Biblical Love Stories.* Bloomington: Indiana University Press, 1987.

Baumann, Gerlinde. *Love and Violence: Marriage as Metaphor for the Relationship between YHWH and Israel in the Prophetic Books.* Translated by Linda M. Maloney. Collegeville, Minn.: Liturgical Press, 2003.

Benedict, Helen. *The Lonely Soldier: The Private War of Women Serving in Iraq.* New York: Beacon, 2010.

Brenner, Athalya. "On 'Jeremiah' and the Poetics of (Prophetic) Pornography." In *On Gendering Texts: Female and Male Voices in the Hebrew Bible*, edited by Athalya Brenner and Fokkelien van Dijk-Hemmes, pp. 177–193. Leiden, The Netherlands: Brill, 1993.

Brenner, Athalya. "Epilogue: Babies and Bathwater on the Road." In *Her Master's Tools? Feminist and Postcolonial Engagements of Historical-Critical Discourse*, edited by Caroline Vander Stichele and Todd Penner, pp. 333–338. Atlanta: Society of Biblical Literature, 2005.

Brenner, Athalya, ed. Feminist Companion to the Bible Series. 24 vols. Sheffield, U.K.: Sheffield Academic Press, 1993–2002.

Brooten, Bernadette J. *Love Between Women: Early Christian Responses to Female Homoeroticism*. Chicago: University of Chicago Press, 1996.

Brownmiller, Susan. *Against Our Will: Men, Women, and Rape*. New York: Simon & Schuster, 1975.

Buchwald, Emilie, Pamela R. Fletcher, and Martha Roth, eds. *Transforming a Rape Culture*. Minneapolis: Milkweed, 1993.

Coggins, Richard. "The Contribution of Women's Studies to Old Testament Studies: A Male Reaction." *Theology* 91, no. 739 (January 1988): 5–16.

Daly, Mary. "Women and the Catholic Church." In *Sisterhood Is Powerful: An Anthology of Writings from the Women's Liberation Movement*, edited by Robin Morgan, pp. 137–153. New York: Vintage, 1970.

Day, Peggy L. "Biblical Studies and Women's Studies." In *Religious Studies: Issues, Prospects, Proposals*, edited by Klaus K. Klostermaier and Larry W. Hurtado, pp. 197–209. Atlanta: Scholars Press, 1991.

Van Dijk-Hemmes, Fokkelien. "The Metaphorization of Woman in Prophetic Speech: An Analysis of Ezekiel 23." In *On Gendering Texts: Female and Male Voices in the Hebrew Bible*, edited by Athalya Brenner and Fokkelien van Dijk-Hemmes, pp. 167–176. Leiden, The Netherlands: Brill, 1993.

Dube, Musa W. *Postcolonial Feminist Interpretation of the Bible*. Saint Louis, Mo.: Chalice, 2000.

Eskenazi, Tamara Cohn. *The Torah: A Women's Commentary*. New York: URJ Press, 2008.

Eugene, Toinette M. "A Hermeneutical Challenge For Womanists: The Interrelation between the Text and Our Experience." In *Perspectives on Feminist Hermeneutics*, edited by Gayle Gerber Koontz and Willard Swartley, pp. 20–28. Elkhart, Ind.: Institute for Mennonite Studies, 1987.

Exum, J. Cheryl. "Raped by the Pen." In *Fragmented Women: Feminist (Sub)versions of Biblical Narratives*, pp. 170–201. Valley Forge, Pa.: Trinity Press International, 1993.

Exum, J. Cheryl. "Prophetic Pornography." In *Plotted, Shot, and Painted: Cultural Representations of Biblical Women*, pp. 101–128. Sheffield, U.K.: Sheffield Academic Press, 1996.

Exum, J. Cheryl. "Where Have All the Feminists Gone? Reflections on the Impact of Feminist Biblical Exegesis on the Scholarly Community and Women's Lives." *lectio difficilior: European Electronic Journal for Feminist Exegesis* 2 (2010). http://www.lectio.unibe.ch/10_2/exum_feminists.html.

Fewell, Danna Nolan, and David M. Gunn. "Tipping the Balance: Sternberg's Reader and the Rape of Dinah." *Journal of Biblical Literature* 110, no. 2 (Summer 1991): 193–211.

Fortune, Marie M. *Sexual Violence: The Sin Revisited*. Cleveland, Ohio: Pilgrim, 2005.

Frymer-Kensky, Tikva. "The Bible and Women's Studies." In *Feminist Perspectives on Jewish Studies*, edited by Lynn Davidman and Shelly Tenenbaum, pp. 16–39. New Haven, Conn.: Yale University Press, 1994.

Frymer-Kensky, Tikva. *Studies in Bible and Feminist Criticism*. Philadelphia: Jewish Publication Society, 2006.

Fuchs, Esther. "Men in Biblical Feminist Scholarship." *Journal of Feminist Studies in Religion* 19, no. 2 (Fall 2003): 93–114.

Fuchs, Esther. "Reclaiming the Hebrew Bible for Women: The Neoliberal Turn in Contemporary Feminist Scholarship." *Journal of Feminist Studies in Religion* 24, no. 2 (2008): 45–65.

Gravett, Sandie. "Reading 'Rape' in the Hebrew Bible: A Consideration of Language." *Journal for the Study of the Old Testament* 28, no. 3 (March 2004): 279–299.

Guest, Deryn. *Beyond Feminist Biblical Studies*. Sheffield, U.K.: Sheffield Phoenix, 2012.

Hackett, Jo Ann. "Women's Studies and the Hebrew Bible." In *The Future of Biblical Studies: The Hebrew Scriptures*, edited by Richard Elliott Friedman and H. G. M. Williamson, pp. 141–164. Atlanta: Scholars Press, 1987.

Heller, Kevin Jon. "Power, Subjectification, and Resistance in Foucault." *SubStance* 25 no. 1 (1996): 78–110.

Hens-Piazza, Gina. "Terrorization, Sexualization, Maternalization: Women's Bodies on Trial." In *Pregnant Passion: Gender, Sex, and Violence in the Bible*, edited by Cheryl A. Kirk-Duggan, pp. 163–177. Atlanta: Society of Biblical Literature, 2003.

Hornsby, Teresa J. "Capitalism, Masochism, and Biblical Interpretations." In *Bible Trouble: Queer Reading at the Boundaries of Biblical Scholarship*, edited by Teresa J. Hornsby and Ken Stone, pp. 137–155. Atlanta: Society of Biblical Literature, 2011.

Jasper, Alison. "Raising the Dead? Reflections of Feminist Biblical Criticism in the Light of Pamela Sue Anderson's Book *A Feminist Philosophy of Religion*, 1988." *Feminist Theology* 9, no. 26 (January 2001): 110–120.

Junior, Nyasha. "Womanist Biblical Interpretation." In *Engaging the Bible in a Gendered World: An Introduction to Feminist Biblical Interpretation in Honor of Katharine Doob Sakenfeld*, edited by Linda Day and Carolyn Pressler, pp. 37–46. Louisville, Ky.: Westminster John Knox, 2006.

Justaert, Kristien. "Liberation Theology: Deleuze and Althaus-Reid." *SubStance* 39, no. 1 (2010): 154–164.

Kim, Seong Hee. *Mark, Women and Empire: A Korean Postcolonial Perspective.* Sheffield, U.K.: Sheffield Phoenix, 2010.

Kristof, Nicholas D., and Sheryl WuDunn. *Half the Sky: Turning Oppression into Opportunity for Women Worldwide.* New York: Knopf, 2009.

Kroeger, Catherine Clark, and Mary J. Evans, eds. *The IVP Women's Bible Commentary.* Downers Grove, Ill.: InterVarsity, 2002.

Kwok, Pui-lan. "Making the Connections: Postcolonial Studies and Feminist Biblical Interpretation." In *The Postcolonial Biblical Reader,* edited by R. S. Sugirtharajah, pp. 45–63. Malden, Mass.: Blackwell, 2006.

Levine, Amy-Jill, ed. Feminist Companion to the New Testament and Early Christian Writings Series. London: Continuum, 2001–.

Lipka, Hilary B. *Sexual Transgression in the Hebrew Bible.* Sheffield, U.K.: Sheffield Phoenix, 2006.

Lopez, Davina C., and Todd Penner. "Feminist Scholarship on the New Testament." *Oxford Bibliographies* 2012. http://www.oxfordbibliographies.com.

Marcus, Sharon. "Fighting Bodies, Fighting Words: A Theory and Politics of Rape Prevention." In *Feminists Theorize the Political,* edited by Judith Butler and Joan W. Scott, pp. 385–403. New York: Routledge, 1992.

Mbuwayesango, Dora R., and Susanne Scholz. "Dialogical Beginnings: A Conversation on the Future of Feminist Biblical Studies." *Journal of Feminist Studies in Religion* 25, no. 2 (Fall 2009): 93–103. See also the ensuing nine responses on pp. 103–143.

McKinlay, Judith E. *Reframing Her: Biblical Women in Postcolonial Focus.* Sheffield, U.K.: Sheffield Academic Press, 2004.

Meyers, Carol. *Discovering Eve: Ancient Israelite Women in Context.* New York: Oxford University Press, 1988.

Meyers, Carol, Toni Craven, and Ross S. Kramer, eds. *Women in Scripture: A Dictionary of Named and Unnamed Women in the Hebrew Bible, the Apocryphal/Deuterocanonical Books, and the New Testament.* Boston: Houghton Mifflin, 2000.

Milne, Pamela J. "Toward Feminist Companionship: The Future of Feminist Biblical Studies and Feminism." In *A Feminist Companion to Reading the Bible: Approaches, Methods, and Strategies,* edited by Athalya Brenner and Carole Fontaine, pp. 39–60. Sheffield, U.K.: Sheffield Academic Press, 1997.

Nelson, T. S. *For Love of Country: Confronting Rape and Sexual Harassment in the U.S. Military.* New York: Haworth Maltreatment and Trauma Press, 2002.

Newsom, Carol A., Sharon H. Ringe, and Jacqueline E. Lapsley, eds. *Women's Bible Commentary.* 3d ed. Louisville, Ky.: Westminster John Knox, 2012.

Niditch, Susan. *Judges: A Commentary.* Louisville, Ky.: Westminster John Knox, 2008.

O'Brien, Julia M. "In Retrospect…Self-Response to 'On Saying No' to a Prophet." In *Prophets and Daniel,* edited by Athalya Brenner, pp. 206–219. Feminist Companion to the Bible, 2d Ser., 8. London: Sheffield Academic Press, 2001.

O'Brien, Julia M., and Chris Franke, eds. *The Aesthetics of Violence in the Prophets.* New York: T&T Clark, 2010.

Parry, Robin Allinson. *Old Testament Story and Christian Ethics: The Rape of Dinah as a Case Study.* Bletchley, U.K.: Paternoster, 2004.

Rapoport, Sandra E. *Biblical Seductions: Six Stories Retold Based on Talmud and Midrash.* Jersey City, N.J.: Ktav, 2011.

Russell, Letty M., ed. *Feminist Interpretation of the Bible.* Oxford: Blackwell, 1985.

Sakenfeld, Katharine Doob. "Old Testament Perspectives: Methodological Issues." *Journal for the Study of the Old Testament* 22 (1982): 13–20.

Schaberg, Jane. *The Illegitimacy of Jesus: A Feminist Theological Interpretation of the Infancy Narratives.* San Francisco: Harper & Row, 1987.

Scholz, Susanne. "Defining Rape: Feminist Scholarship on Rape since the 1970s." In *Rape Plots: A Cultural Feminist Study of Genesis 34,* pp. 19–44. New York: Peter Lang, 2000a.

Scholz, Susanne. *Rape Plots: A Feminist Cultural Study of Genesis 34.* New York: Peter Lang, 2000b.

Scholz, Susanne. "Religion." In *The Encyclopedia of Rape,* edited by Merril D. Smith, pp. 206–209. Westport, Conn.: Greenwood, 2004.

Scholz, Susanne. "The Christian Right's Discourse on Gender and the Bible." *Journal of Feminist Studies in Religion* 21, no. 1 (2005): 81–100.

Scholz, Susanne. "From the 'Woman's Bible' to the 'Women's Bible': The History of Feminist Approaches to the Hebrew Bible." In *Introducing the Women's Hebrew Bible,* pp. 12–32. New York: T&T Clark, 2007.

Scholz, Susanne. *Sacred Witness: Rape in the Hebrew Bible.* Minneapolis: Fortress, 2010a.

Scholz, Susanne. "A Third-Kind of Feminist Reading: Toward a Feminist Sociology of Biblical Hermeneutics." *Currents in Biblical Research* 9, no. 4 (October 2010b): 1–22.

Scholz, Susanne. "Occupy Academic Bible Teaching: The Architecture of Educational Power and the Biblical Studies Curriculum." In *Teaching the Bible in the Liberal Arts Classroom,* edited by Jane S. Webster and Glenn S. Holland, pp. 28–43. Sheffield, U.K.: Sheffield Phoenix, 2012a.

Scholz, Susanne. "The Old Testament, Feminist Scholarship." *Oxford Bibliographies,* 2012b. http://www.oxfordbibliographies.com.

Scholz, Susanne. "Convert, Prostitute, or Traitor? Rahab as the Anti-Matriarch in Biblical Interpretations." In *In the Arms of Biblical Women*, edited by John T. Greene and Mishael M. Caspi, pp. 153–186. Piscataway, N.J.: Gorgias, 2013.

Scholz, Susanne. "'Stirring Up Vital Energies': Feminist Biblical Studies in North America." In *The Bible and Women: An Encyclopaedia of Exegesis and Cultural History*. Vol. 10, *The Twentieth Century*, edited by Elisabeth Schüssler Fiorenza. Atlanta: Society of Biblical Literature, 2014.

Scholz, Susanne, and Shelly Matthews. "Feminist Biblical Interpretation." In *The Oxford Encyclopedia of Biblical Interpretation*, edited by Steven L. McKenzie. New York: Oxford University Press, 2013.

Schottroff, Luise, Silvia Schroer, and Marie-Theres Wacker. *Feminist Interpretation: The Bible in Women's Perspective*. Translated by Martin Rumscheidt and Barbara Rumscheidt. Minneapolis: Fortress, 1998.

Schottroff, Luise, and Marie-Theres Wacker, eds. *Feminist Biblical Interpretation: A Compendium of Critical Commentary on the Books of the Bible and Related Literature*. Translated by Martin Rumscheidt et al. Grand Rapids, Mich.: Eerdmans, 2012.

Schroeder, Joy A. *Dinah's Lament: The Biblical Legacy of Sexual Violence in Christian Interpretation*. Minneapolis: Fortress, 2007.

Schüssler Fiorenza, Elisabeth. "Feminist Theology and New Testament Interpretation." *Journal for the Study of the Old Testament* 22 (1982): 32–46.

Schüssler Fiorenza, Elisabeth. *In Memory of Her: A Feminist Theological Reconstruction of Christian Origins*. New York: Crossroad, 1983.

Schüssler Fiorenza, Elisabeth. *Wisdom Ways: Introducing Feminist Biblical Interpretation*. Maryknoll, N.Y.: Orbis, 2001.

Schüssler Fiorenza, Elisabeth. "Reaffirming Feminist/Womanist Biblical Scholarship." *Encounter* 6, no. 4 (Autumn 2006): 361–373.

Selvidge, Marla J. "Reflections on Violence and Pornography: Misogyny in the Apocalypse and Ancient Hebrew Prophecy." In *A Feminist Companion to the Hebrew Bible in the New Testament*, edited by Athalya Brenner, pp. 274–285. Sheffield, U.K.: Sheffield Academic Press, 1996.

Setel, T. Drorah. "Prophets and Pornography: Female Sexual Imagery in Hosea." In *Feminist Interpretation of the Bible*, edited by Letty M. Russell, pp. 86–95. Oxford: Blackwell, 1985.

Tolbert, Mary Ann. "Defining the Problem: The Bible and Feminist Hermeneutics." *Semeia* 28 (1983): 113–126.

Trible, Phyllis. *God and the Rhetoric of Sexuality*. Philadelphia: Fortress, 1978.

Trible, Phyllis, ed. "Effects of Women's Studies on Biblical Studies." Special issue, *Journal for the Study of the Old Testament* 7, no. 22 (February 1982a).

Trible, Phyllis. "Feminist Hermeneutics and Biblical Studies." *Christian Century*, 3–10 February 1982b, pp. 116–118.

Trible, Phyllis. *Texts of Terror: Literary-Feminist Readings of Biblical Narratives*. Philadelphia: Fortress, 1984.

Trible, Phyllis, and Letty M. Russell, eds. *Hagar, Sarah, and Their Children: Jewish, Christian, and Muslim Perspectives*. Louisville, Ky.: Westminster John Knox, 2006.

Vander Stichele, Caroline, and Todd Penner. *Contextualizing Gender in Early Christian Discourse: Thinking beyond Thecla*. London: T&T Clark, 2009.

Washington, Harold C., Susan Lochrie Graham, and Pamela Thimmes, eds. *Escaping Eden: New Feminist Perspectives on the Bible*. Sheffield, U.K.: Sheffield Academic Press, 1998.

Weems, Renita J. *Battered Love: Marriage, Sex, and Violence in the Hebrew Prophets*. Minneapolis: Fortress, 1995.

Williams, Delores S. "The Color of Feminism, or Speaking the Black Woman's Tongue." *Journal of Religious Thought* 43, no. 1 (Spring/Summer 1986): 42–58.

Wire, Antoinette Clark. "Theological and Biblical Perspective: Liberation for Women Calls for a Liberated World." *Church and Society* 76, no. 3 (January–February 1986): 7–17.

Yamada, Frank M. *Configurations of Rape in the Hebrew Bible: A Literary Analysis of Three Rape Narratives*. New York: Peter Lang, 2008.

Yee, Gale A., ed. *Judges and Method: New Approaches in Biblical Studies*. 2d ed. Minneapolis: Fortress, 2007.

Susanne Scholz

Third-Wave Feminism

Feminism as a movement has broadly manifested itself in three phases that are classified as first-, second-, and third-wave feminism. First-wave feminism began in the West in the nineteenth and twentieth centuries and advocated for basic female rights and dignity. However, given that as a people's movement feminism is inherently dynamic in nature, new needs and challenges gave rise to second-wave feminism in 1970s.

Second-wave feminism continues into the twenty-first century, concurrent with though distinct from third-wave feminism. Because third-wave feminism is essentially inclusive and intersecting, seeking not to undermine the experiences of any women, it does not dismiss second-wave feminists who spoke from their authentic experiences. Nonetheless, third-wave feminism critiques second-wave feminism for assuming that women's experiences are universal, and it questions essentialism of any sort. Considering each experience of each woman to be unique and authentic, third-wave feminism affirms multivocalism and seeks to liberate subjects from frameworks prescribed or defined by others. Rejecting all frameworks, third-wave feminism is by its nature dynamic and always in the process of becoming. Consequently, third-wave feminism becomes absolutely situational, individualistic, and decentralized by abstaining from deontological aims and goals, unlike the second-wave feminists, who work toward a universal goal for all women.

Third-Wave Feminism: A Brief Discussion. Rebecca Walker can be credited with launching the new movement in 1992 when she declared that she was the Third Wave (Heywood, 2006, vol. 1, p. 5), arguing that her feminist articulations were distinct and different from what was being defined as feminism. Walker's book *To Be Real* gives analytical explanation of this new intergenerational movement. In it, she explains that those in the third wave do not consider male and female as a binary as do those in the second wave. While some in the third wave disassociate themselves from second-wave feminists, Leslie L. Heywood claims that third wavers do not reject second-wave feminism as such but instead correct its essentialist assumptions (Heywood, 2006, vol. 1, p. 139).

While there are numerous points of divergence between third- and second-wave feminism, a few are worth special attention.

Third-wave feminism is postmodernist in orientation, focusing on the self rather than group, context, community, religion, or society at large. If self-centered perspectives incidentally benefit a larger group, such benefits are welcomed, but the primary purpose of third-wave feminism is not social change. Third-wave feminism is individualistic, not contextual, in its essence (Strauss, 2000) and thus cannot be defined or standardized. With each personal story, feminism gets defined differently.

While third-wave feminism is individualistic, it also claims to be inclusive, accepting every experience as authentic and every discussion as important. Thus third-wave feminism rejects stereotypes and all forms of essentialism and universalization. It does not seek to qualify itself to fit into any standards or framework, and thus does not operate according to rules, expectations, norms, and standards.

Third-wave feminism affirms femininity or "girl power" loudly and clearly. Third-wave feminists celebrate femininity as powerful rather than shameful (Wolf, 2005, pp. 14–15). They critique second-wave feminists for entering the male world of masculinity and mimicking male role models in order to project power. According to third-wave feminists, second-wave feminism is counterproductive, causing females to disown femininity and thus submit to genderism with its inherent discrimination against women.

Third-wave feminism drew strong initial attention as a movement addressing and intersecting with several areas and issues, but it has not yet influenced the field of religion as much as other fields. Some of the compelling works of third-wave feminism, while addressing other justice issues, have not approached religion as a resource or even something to critique. Whether the absence of religion in third-wave feminism is incidental, intentional, or the result of indifference is unclear. Is third-wave feminism a postreligious/nonreligious movement?

Third-Wave Feminism and Its Relevance. Younger third-wave feminists have been critical of first- and second-wave feminists for paying less attention to a feminine lifestyle, and for foregoing the fun of carrying femininity for the sake of power (Baumgardner and Richards, 2006, pp. 302–303). Affirming inclusivism as opposed to exclusivism, they see no point in a sex or gender war. They often distance themselves from the hate that is often associated with the label "feminist" in society.

In these critiques, third-wave feminists have sometimes underestimated the major struggles of first- and second-wave feminists, who had to break through patriarchal systems with an aggressive attitude when a merely assertive attitude was not enough. They took on the roles needed because of their passion for women's justice and left comfort zones in order to enter into the masculine world, where they were not welcomed and had to fight for every achievement. Third-wave feminists have stereotyped all the second-wave feminists as angry, boring, asexual beings, without appreciating their sacrifice, namely having to let go of their femininity, and the fun associated with being dolls. The sacrifice of first- and second-wave feminists both epistemologically and practically secured the enjoyments that young women today take for granted. It is easier to be a "girly girl" and enjoy femininity than to sacrifice the comfort zone of being dressed up and wearing makeup, and sitting on a comfortable couch in a room cooled by air conditioning.

Third-Wave Feminism and the Bible. In the West, second-wave feminism has challenged other fields with corrective epistemological theories and has itself been challenged. Similarly, its theories and articulations have been received, adopted, expanded— and challenged—by people all over the world.

Some non-Western readers have received feminism with open arms to alter and appropriate in their specific contexts (such as Asia). Others have resisted the nuances connected with the term "feminism" and introduced distinct terms for their own women's movements, attempting to address the ways in which the complex realities of injustice define their "women's issues" differently than second-wave feminists did. While second-wave Western feminism categorized humans into male and female and challenged male domination, other prominent biblical readers and theologians have sought to assert female subjectivity while also attempting to understand the multilayered and complex issue of women's subjectivity.

Alternative women's movements critique and challenge second-wave feminism for positing Western women's experience as the standard and norm for feminist theories and thus universalizing women's oppression as seen and experienced by Western women. Such universalizing tendencies have ignored other layers of oppression that women experience:

racism, regionalism, classism, casteism, colorism, colonialism, ageism, religion, and so on. In critical response to the second-wave feminism of the West, alternative women's movements stress the contextuality, multilayered oppression, and distinctive experiences of women. Examples of alternative women's movements include womanist, mujerista, Asian and Asian American, and Latino. Pioneers of these different movements include Delores Williams, Ada María Isasi-Díaz, Kwok Pui-lan, María Pilar Aquino, and Musa Dube. In addition, postmodern feminism, postcolonial feminism, and Indian feminism suggest the contextualization of feminism.

Some of these movements have understood the label "feminist" as exclusive for white, Western feminism, whereas others have received it as open to contextualization and qualification. Yet, despite the labels, all movements agree on justice for women. For instance, not all Hispanic women speaking for women's justice necessarily claim to be using a mujerista perspective, nor can any mujerista stake a claim over all Hispanic women while remaining sensitive to women's freedom and justice. Similarly, not all black and other women of color of African descent who are part of the women's movement are essentially womanist nor claim to be womanist. For instance, Monica A. Coleman asks, "Must I be a womanist?" suggesting ambiguity around the claims, definitions, and essentialization of people and labels. While she feels at home with womanist articulations, she is not as uneasy and distant as others in responding to the word "feminism." Womanists and feminists are personally important to Coleman, and she calls her predecessors of the movement "godmothers" (Coleman, 2006, p. 86). This is a clear example of third-wave feminist claims to appreciate ambiguity and individual preference without needing to find a home in a feminist village.

Developments in women's movements have been both chronological and contextual. Third-wave feminism emerges both from an intergenerational paradigm shift and from the resistance, division, rejection, and mutual learning emerging from the critical dialogue between contextualized women's movements and Western feminism.

Although first- and second-wave feminism differ in goals, aims, and means of advancement, the distinction between them becomes less clear when discerning their intersection with biblical studies. Differences between second- and third-wave feminist approaches to biblical studies are also not sharply drawn, particularly in comparison to the situation in secular feminism. While secular third-wave feminists often sharply debate secular second-wave feminists, these tensions are less evident in the field of biblical studies, where there is loyalty, sympathy, and mutual learning among the second- and third-wave feminist scholars of the Bible. Most of the feminists of the younger generations find second-wave feminism both helpful and useful, and members of the older generations are open to new perspectives and appreciate the critical conversations, especially when some of the questions once posed by second-wave feminists are no longer relevant in today's contexts, especially in Western societies. Compared to secular feminism, second- and third-wave feminist scholars of the Bible engage more in dialogue than debate.

Therefore it is difficult to place the feminist scholars of the Bible under a single umbrella of either second or third-wave feminisms, as there is no critical border that divides them in feminist biblical hermeneutics. Even though a postmodern feminist biblical scholar defines oneself as a third-wave feminist, broadly speaking, one also seems to affirm first- and second-wave feminist theories and interpretations of the Bible as pillars for third-wave feminism and consider that third-wave feminism is an upgraded version of feminism that fits the age and cultures of the postmodern era. Similarly, third-wave feminism is not in contrast or necessarily in disagreement with first- and second-wave feminisms; it engages in a critical yet affirming dialogue that is informative and educational in both directions in biblical studies, since both second- and third-wave feminism coexist as concurrent. Most contemporary feminist works are a compilation of essays that suggests the importance of diversity and inclusiveness. Contrary to some interpretations, second-wave feminists are no longer exclusivists, nor are they blind to diversity and multiple perspectives. Second-wave feminists in the twenty-first century are open, committed to diversity, and passionate about being inclusive in their approach, and they do not necessarily engage in sex and gender wars. Thus it is hard to discern sharp differences between second- and third-wave feminism related to biblical interpretation: they overlap in extendedness and openness, while focusing on a specific context. Third- and second-wave feminism have many points of convergence and common goals rather than divergence and division.

Third-wave feminism has much to offer in dealing with the challenges inherent to third-wave feminist hermeneutics of the Bible. It offers the tools for eliminating the distinctions between central and marginal, dominant and subordinate, and upper and lower binary poles, as it that affirms every experience and every category is authentic by rejecting essentialism and thus theoretically offering liberation to all people.

[*See also* Asian/Asian American Interpretation; Feminism, *subentries on* First-Wave Feminism *and* Second-Wave Feminism; Intersectional Studies; Mujerista Criticism; *and* Womanist Criticism.]

BIBLIOGRAPHY

Aquino, María Pilar, Daisy L. Machado, and Jeanette Rodríguez. *A Reader in Latina Feminist Theology: Religion and Justice.* Austin: University of Texas Press, 2002.

Baumgardner, Jennifer, and Amy Richards. "Manifesta: Young Women, Feminism, and the Future." In *The Women's Movement Today: An Encyclopedia of Third-Wave Feminism*, vol. 2, *Primary Documents*, edited by Leslie L. Heywood, pp. 297–310. Westport, Conn.: Greenwood, 2006.

Choi, Hee An, and Katheryn Pfisterer Darr, eds. *Engaging the Bible: Critical Readings from Contemporary Women.* Minneapolis: Augsburg Fortress, 2006.

Coleman, Monica A. "Must I Be a Womanist?" *Journal of Feminist Studies in Religion* 22, no. 1 (2006): 85–96.

Dube, Musa W. *Postcolonial Feminist Interpretation of the Bible.* Saint Louis, Mo.: Chalice, 2000.

Grant, Jacquelyn, ed. *Perspectives on Womanist Theology.* Atlanta: ITC, 1995.

Heywood, Leslie L., ed. *The Women's Movement Today: An Encyclopedia of Third-Wave Feminism.* 2 vols. Westport, Conn.: Greenwood, 2006.

Heywood, Leslie, and Jennifer Drake, eds. *Third Wave Agenda: Being Feminist, Doing Feminism.* Minneapolis: University of Minnesota Press, 1997.

Hunt, Mary E., and Diann L. Neu, eds. *New Feminist Christianity: Many Voices, Many Views.* Woodstock, Vt.: SkyLight Paths, 2010.

Isasi-Díaz, Ada María. "Mujeristas: A Name of Our Own." In *The Future of Liberation Theology: Essays in Honor of Gustavo Gutiérrez*, edited by Marc H. Ellis and Otto Maduro, pp. 410–419. Maryknoll, N.Y.: Orbis, 1989.

Kitzberger, Ingrid Rosa, ed. *The Personal Voice in Biblical Interpretation.* London: Routledge, 1999.

Kwok, Pui-lan. *Introducing Asian Feminist Theology.* Cleveland, Ohio: Pilgrim, 2000.

Kwok, Pui-lan. *Postcolonial Imagination and Feminist Theology.* Louisville, Ky.: Westminster John Knox, 2005.

Kwok, Pui-lan, ed. *Women and Christianity.* London: Routledge, 2010.

Schüssler Fiorenza, Elisabeth. *Sharing Her Word: Feminist Biblical Interpretation in Context.* Boston: Beacon, 1998.

Schüssler Fiorenza, Elisabeth. *Wisdom Ways: Introducing Feminist Biblical Interpretation.* Maryknoll, N.Y.: Orbis, 2001.

Straus, Tamara. "A Manifesto for Third Wave Feminism." AlterNet, 24 October 2000. http://www.alternet.org/story/9986/a_manifesto_for_third_wave_feminism.

Streufert, Mary J., ed. *Transformative Lutheran Theologies: Feminist, Womanist, and Mujerista Perspectives.* Minneapolis: Fortress, 2010.

Walker, Rebecca, ed. *To Be Real: Telling the Truth and Changing the Face of Feminism.* New York: Anchor, 1995.

Williams, Delores S. *Sisters in the Wilderness: The Challenge of Womanist God-Talk.* Maryknoll, N.Y.: Orbis, 1993.

Wolf, Naomi. "'Two Traditions,' from *Fire with Fire.*" In *The Women's Movement Today: An Encyclopedia of Third-Wave Feminism*, edited by Leslie Heywood, vol. 2, pp. 13–19. Westport, Conn.: Greenwood, 2005.

Surekha Nelavala

G

GAY LIBERATION

Gay liberation perspectives on the Bible have their antecedent roots in the post-World War II homophile movement, before the Stonewall Rebellion in New York, which is usually associated with the rise of gay liberation. In this era, the homophile movement confronted the exclusions of homosexuals from all denominational Christian churches. This led to the founding of an independent Catholic church by George Augustine Hyde to minister to homosexuals excluded from churches. Various pastoral attempts to deal with the growing, increasingly visible homophile movement led to the creation of the Moral Welfare Council in the Church of England, in the United Kingdom, and the later ecumenical Council of Religion in San Francisco. The publication of Derrick Sherwin Bailey's *Homosexuality and the Western Christian Tradition* (1955) and Robert Wood's *Christ and the Homosexual* (1960) marked significant theological milestones for the development of gay Christian scholars. Bailey's monograph would have significant impact on later gay interpretations of the biblical texts that churches applied or misapplied to homosexuals. In October 1968, Reverend Troy Perry founded the Metropolitan Community Church (MCC) in Los Angeles for homosexuals who were excluded from their churches. Within the founding MCC, the first Jewish gay/lesbian synagogue in America, Beth Chayim Chadashim, was formed. The formation of gay/lesbian communities of faith and later denominational gay/lesbian groups provided sites for resistant apologetics to contest interpretations that misapplied texts to homosexuals. This entry will summarize several decades of gay liberationists and allies engaging in (1) apologetics over a handful of scriptural texts and (2) hermeneutical readings of the scripture from the contextual grid of their erotic experiences and lives.

"A (Holy) Pissing Contest." This section heading originates with Tim Koch (2001), who describes as a "pissing contest" the apologetic debates between those who cite scriptural texts or so-called texts of terror to condemn modern homosexuality and those gay scholars and others who challenge such readings. In the 1970s, there were three classic gay attempts to wrestle with the biblical texts commonly applied to homosexuality. John McNeill's *The Church and the Homosexual* was published with an imprimatur in 1976. McNeill writes in his autobiography that a colleague at Union Theological Seminary shared with him an anonymous manuscript on homosexuality and the New Testament. He incorporated some of the argumentation in his book, and only later came to know that the manuscript was a draft of John Boswell's *Christianity, Social Tolerance, and Homosexuality* (McNeill, 1998, *Both Feet Firmly Planted*). The second book, released in 1978, was Tom Horner's *Jonathan Loved David*. Finally, Boswell's book was published in 1980, winning an American Book Award for history. These classics empowered gay/lesbian Christians to reconcile their sexual orientation with their Christian practices in denominational resistance groups and the MCC. McNeill's and Boswell's books were translated into several foreign languages for Catholic and Protestant Christians struggling with gay/lesbian issues. One result was the silencing of the Jesuit McNeill by Cardinal Joseph Ratzinger. Boswell's history launched a scholarly cultural battle over the texts of terror. There has subsequently been a taking back of the interpretation of the texts by gay scholars as well as allied heterosexual scholars from mainline Protestant denominations, such as Victor Furnish, Robin Scroggs, George Edwards, Martti Nissinen, Walter Wink, and Dan Via.

Traditional and contemporary Jewish interpretations of the destruction of Sodom and Gomorrah are seldom used as condemnations of homosexuality, for Jewish discussions of homosexuality focus instead on Leviticus. Genesis 19 is traditionally used instead in rabbinic and orthodox traditions to condemn violence and inhospitality (Greenberg, 2004). Bailey follows a similar line of interpretative reasoning in his exegesis of the destruction of Sodom and Gomorrah. This emphasis on inhospitality has been popular among a certain group of gay authors (McNeill, Boswell, Helminiak). Another interpretation has focused primarily on the attempted rape and phallic violence against God's two messengers (Goss, 2002; Long, 2006). Judges 19 is often used to underscore the rape and violence theme. Michael Carden (2004) has traced the development of the biblical myth of Sodom from early interpretations to a modern myth of divine extermination of homosexuals. Mark Jordan (1997) has reconstructed the invention of the theological notion of sodomy from Peter Damien and its trajectory within Roman Catholic moral theology.

The two verses in Leviticus (18:22 and 20:13) are employed in condemnations of homosexuality within the orthodox traditions of Judaism (Greenberg) as well as Christianity. Bailey, McNeill, Horner, and Boswell read these verses as condemning male temple prostitution; but later scholarship by Saul Olyan (1996), Daniel Boyarin (1995), and David Stewart (2006) has dismissed the cultic male prostitution thesis, reading these verses within the context of the Holiness Code. The condemned acts are now often seen as violations of male gender privilege when a male is penetrated by another male (Goss, 2002). The earlier published work of Jacob Milgrom (1991) suggests that, since semen is not involved in women's relationships, there is no symbolic loss of life, and so women's homosexuality is not mentioned. Milgrom also suggests that condemnation is confined to anal intercourse among Jews in the land of Israel. Olyan construes the Hebrew "the lying down of a woman" (*miskebe issa*) as a euphemism for a man functioning like a woman in male passive anal intercourse, a violation of gender roles. He concludes that sexual acts between women were not included in the Leviticus condemnation because, unlike the mixture of semen and excrement in male to male intercourse, they do not violate the purity codes. Stewart has made the claim that these verses about male anal intercourse condemn male to male incest (2006).

With his discussion of 1 Corinthians 6:9, Boswell initiated a frenzy of articles on the varying translations of *malakoi* and *arsenokoitēs* (also in 1 Tim 1:10) in numerous Bibles. He claims that there is no connection between the two words and passive and active homosexual acts, as some have argued. Boswell notes that until the twentieth century *malakoi* was understood to refer to masturbation, while *arsenokoitēs* meant "male prostitute." Dale Martin (2006) has offered the most conclusive evidence on what Paul was referring to with these two words. Martin argues that *malakoi* refers to a range of activities considered "effeminate." Martin notes the rarity of the term *arsenokoitēs*, but also that it appears in a list of sexual sins in *Sibylline Oracle* 2, denoting sins of economic injustice. Biblical mistranslations of these words as "homosexual perverts," "catamites," "sodomites," and the like have been used to justify prejudice and religious violence against homosexuals, and so have been resisted by gay liberationists.

Gay interpretations also focus on Romans 1, where Paul presents his notion of sin among the gentiles and the consequences of idolatry. The consequence of gentile idolatry is the impurity of exchanging natural for unnatural relations, usually understood as homoeroticism. This is the only place in the Bible where female homoeroticism is mentioned. Boswell strangely argues that the passage refers to heterosexually oriented people engaged in homosexual sex, and that homosexual acts are not unnatural except for heterosexually inclined individuals. McNeill echoes a similar perspective in his interpretation of exchanging natural for unnatural relations (1976). This interpretation appears to be driven by Catholic moral theological arguments on natural law. James Miller (1995) understands these verses to refer to unnatural heterosexual anal intercourse by men and women. Thomas Hanks (2006) follows a similar line of interpretation, arguing that Paul refers to male/female anal intercourse used to avoid procreation. L. William Countryman (1988) and Daniel Helminiak (1994) understand Paul's condemnation of homoeroticism as a reaction to violation of the purity codes. Bernadette Brooten (1996) brings gender analysis to these verses, understanding female homoeroticism within the larger context of Judaism and the Greco-Roman culture. Robert Goss reads Paul as referring to transgressions of ancient gender codes by homoerotically inclined men and women.

Robert Williams (1992) makes a distinction between biblical truth and biblical trash when reading scripture, citing Elisabeth Schüssler Fiorenza's principle of identifying the word of God by whether or not it seeks to end relations of domination or exploitation. Peter Gomes (1996) states that homophobic prejudice rather than historical and contextual interpretation most often shapes the reading of all these texts.

Homoerotic Readings of the Scripture. In addition to rereading texts used to condemn homosexuality, gay interpreters have challenged presumptive heteronormative readings of the First and Second Testaments by finding hints there of homoeroticism. Gay homoerotic readings have focused on three principal texts: David and Jonathan, the Q tradition of the centurion and his boy/slave (Matt 8:5–13, Luke 7:1–10), and Jesus and the beloved disciple. A few readers also note the youth in Mark 14:51–52, Secret Mark, and John, and Ruth and Naomi.

Horner (1978) points out how some biblical scholars fail to acknowledge the intimate relationship between the heroic warrior-king David and Jonathan. He traces homoerotic readings of the narrative tradition surrounding Jonathan and David through the ages by men attracted to men. Likewise, Boswell (1994) notes that Jonathan and David have functioned as models of same-sex fidelity for men attracted to men in some of the "prayers for making brothers" or same-sex blessings. Ward Houser (1990) points out that in previous centuries the story was a coded reference to homoerotic relations when such relations were socially unacceptable. Houser provides a historical thematic survey of representations of the homoerotic relationship between David and Jonathan in literature from the Renaissance to the present. A nineteenth-century Jewish artist, Simeon Solomon, understood the biblical relationship of Jonathan and David as biblically sanctioning same-sex relationships (Seymour, 1997). Both the growing reclamation of Jonathan and David as lovers within Jewish and Christian LGBT faith communities and these earlier traditions of homoerotic reading of David and Jonathan's relationship provided impetus for further gay liberation readings (Johansson, 1990; Williams, 1992; Comstock, 1993; Jennings, 2001, 2005).

Horner seems to be the first author to suggest a homoerotic reading of the Q story of the centurion and his boy/slave (Matt 8:5–13, Luke 7:1–10), noting that the centurion displayed more than ordinary concern for the health of his boy (*pais* in Matthew, a word that sometimes has erotic connotations) or slave (*doulos* in Luke). He observes that if Jesus was disturbed by the homoerotic relationship of the centurion with boy, he would have noted the situation. Instead, Jesus praises the centurion for "no greater faith." This initial homoerotic reading of the Q story has been developed further by a number of gay interpreters (Williams, 1992; McNeill, 1995, 2008; Hanks, 2000; Jennings, 2003; Bohache, 2006; Goss, 2006; Long, 2006). Nissinen points out that in the Greco-Roman world, it was common for master and slave to enter a sexual relationship. While mainline scholarship has rarely discussed possible homoerotic connotations of the Q story, the biblical scholar Gerd Theissen, in his narrative quest for the historical Jesus, also sees a homoerotic relationship in the centurion and his boy/slave (1987). McNeill observes how Catholics on Sunday receive Communion, paraphrasing the words of the centurion in a homoerotic relationship with a younger male: "Lord, I am not worthy to receive you under my roof. Just say the word, and my soul will be healed." This reading has empowered LGBT Catholics and ex-Catholics.

Horner was not the only modern author to suggest a homoerotic reading of Jesus and the beloved disciple. Boswell (1980), Goss (2002), and Jennings (2003) have traced trajectories in Christian history in which the story of Jesus and the beloved disciple played on the erotic spiritualities and literary imaginations of men attracted to men. Three writings from the late 1960 and the early 1970s that sparked the religious imaginations of gay Christians are covered by Horner as background for his discussion of Jesus and the beloved disciple (1978). The first was a paper delivered at a conference at Oxford in 1967 by the Anglican canon Hugh Montefiore, who raised the possibility that Jesus may have had homosexual tendencies. The second was the published analysis of the fragment of Secret Mark by the biblical scholar Morton Smith. There was a public outcry because the fragment speaks about the youth Jesus raised from the dead spending the night with him naked in a baptismal initiation. Many religious leaders and biblical scholars discredited Smith's work as a fraud and forgery. Others attacked Smith as attempting to justify his own homosexuality. The third work was William Phipps's book *Was Jesus Married?* (1970), which precipitated debates about the sexuality of Jesus. After his examination of the evidence, Horner concludes that nothing can be proved from such assertions, and he preserves a construction of Jesus as man for all.

These earlier works provided a background for gay Christian interpreters to revisit the taboo subject of Jesus's sexuality and reclaim Jesus and the beloved disciple. Many gay Christians have reimagined Jesus and the beloved disciple as a homoerotic grace. Robert Williams relies upon Montefiore, earlier conversations on the sexuality of Jesus, and Morton's publications on Secret Mark to affirm that Jesus is gay. He dwells on the strange incident of the nude youth (Mark 14:50–52) and Jesus in the Garden of Gethsemane. This incident has a long history in the erotic imaginations of Christian men who were attracted to men. Williams suggests that Jesus had an explicitly sexual encounter with the youth, whom he identifies as Lazarus. He wrote a fictional work on Jesus, describing in detail Jesus having homosexual sex. The manuscript was sent by Williams's executor to HarperSanFrancisco, but the press declined to publish the manuscript because of the explicit erotic scenes.

Ted Jennings (2003) suggests that Lazarus is the beloved disciple and argues that the material in John's Gospel makes it clear Jesus had a homoerotic relationship with the beloved disciple. He acknowledges that the sources do not give us an idea of how Jesus's love for the beloved disciple was sexually expressed. Jennings is quick to make the case that whatever relationship Jesus had with Lazarus did not impede his love for others. Jennings maintains that this reading is a dangerous memory for an emerging orthodox church whose primary values are ascetical, misogynistic, erotophobic, and antipederastic. In a similar fashion, Goss (2000) reads Jesus and the beloved disciple in a time of AIDS. Goss noticed frequently that, at the bedside of a dying gay man, both his lover and mother were present. The dying man was concerned for his lover and mother. Thus the scene at the cross in John 19:26–27 was reenacted many times during the AIDS pandemic. Goss reads the story as bereavement narrative intertextually with the loss of his lover to AIDS. Jesus on the cross attempts to create a family of choice between beloved and mother during the time of death.

The Episcopal priest and poet Malcolm Boyd (1990, 1994) explores the question of whether Jesus was "gay." He claims that Jesus exhibits qualities that form a gay archetype: vulnerability, sensitivity, shunning power for service, being gentle and strong, and breaking boundaries for love. Terrence McNally wrote *Corpus Christi*, a gay retelling of the life and passion of Joshua/Jesus, struggling against cultural and religious homophobia. A touring production has taken the play, along with a documentary, *Playing with Redemption*, as part of an "I Am Love Campaign" to numerous U.S. cities. Finally, there is the gay countercultural parody of San Francisco's Sisters of Perpetual Indulgence, who celebrate the Hunky Jesus contest on Easter Sunday. Jesus is eroticized by gay men in this iconoclastic celebration in Dolores Park. These homoerotic readings counter ascetical, misogynistic, and erotophobic constructions of Jesus and Christological formulations that subvert his incarnational fleshiness.

The gay biblical scholar Dale Martin (2006) acknowledges the gay imagination interpreting Jesus's sexuality in John's Gospel, one of the most homoerotic, sensual gospels. Martin notes, however, that, as with all imaginative readings of Jesus, how people imagine the sexuality of Jesus reveals more about how they feel about sexuality than about the historical Jesus. While I agree with his conclusion, I would add that homoerotic readings of Jesus's sexuality have provided moments of self-accepting grace throughout history for men who were attracted to men.

Lesbian Contributions and the Critique of Gay Androcentrism. In *Love Between Women*, biblical scholar Bernadette Brooten (1996) acknowledges that Boswell's work made a lasting contribution to the study of same-sex love and sexuality and Christianity. It suffered, however, from a lack of gender analysis and unbalanced discussion of male homoeroticism over female homoeroticism in the ancient world. Brooten suggests that paucity of material on female homoeroticism was due to male authors attempting to fit it into a male framework. Mary Rose D'Angelo (1997) applies Adrienne Rich's notion of lesbian continuum to pairs of women missionaries and explores female same-sex intimacy in early Christianity without ever discussing female homoeroticism. "Lesbian continuum" denotes an emotional bonding between women or women-identified experiences without focused attention on whether there were homoerotic desires or practices. The Jewish lesbian scholar Rebecca Alpert, on the other hand, observes that Jewish lesbians have occupied the narrative silences of the Hebrew scriptures by writing lesbian Midrash to surface their erased presence from the text (1997). Where gay men have focused on David and Jonathan or Jesus and the beloved disciple, Alpert offers a lesbian reading of Ruth and Naomi. Thus women ancestors are given voice beyond their erasures.

In *When Deborah Met Jael*, Deryn Guest maintains that same-sex activities have been observed widely across cultures and historical periods of time. She explores why male perspectives have failed to uncover female homoerotic relations in past historical cultures, in particular, the storyworld of ancient Near Eastern cultures and the Greco-Roman world. She argues that it is not unreasonable to hypothesize that female homoeroticism has been suppressed in the Hebrew Bible, not because it was a matter of little cultural importance but because its "thinkability" as a cultural category would be disruptive to the Hebrew sex/gender system (2005, p. 128). Gender complementarity has been used to justify a heteronormative mantra, "Adam and Eve, Not Adam and Steve." Guest builds upon the earlier work of Brooten, D'Angelo, and Alpert and criticizes gay liberation strategies of reading the scriptures for their androcentric focus. Lesbian-identified interpretations elevate lesbian experience as a fundamental hermeneutic criterion. For Guest there are four interweaving hermeneutical strategies for reading Scriptural texts: (1) a commitment to engage the text with hetero-suspicion; (2) a commitment to disrupt gender binaries; (3) strategies of appropriation or reclamation; and (4) and a commitment to make a difference. These strategies disrupt heterocentric and androcentric interpretative traditions that have absented or ignored female homoerotic relations. Guest looks at gay efforts to wrestle with and exonerate the scriptures or at times to reject the authority of scripture. Ultimately, she argues for an "ethically lesbian-identified hermeneutic," but suggests that, if such a lesbian hermeneutics is to make a difference, interpreters may pay a price.

Queer Critiques and Opportunities. In addition to lesbian critiques, gay men of color have added criticisms of the shortcomings of white gay male interpreters writing from privileged social positions. In his reading of Galatians, Patrick Cheng (2006) reads queerly from his social location as an Asian American gay man against heterosexist as well as dominant white gay male culture. He criticizes the dominant gay male culture for imposing its cultural values and norms on ethnic gay minorities. He compares gay Asian American voices to the gentiles in Galatians who search in vain for affirmation of their uncircumcised penises in a world of white gay males and their racist norms of male beauty. Similar criticism is offered from a nongay perspective by Tat-siong Benny Liew (2001), who notes that many queer readings neglect race, ethnicity, and class and shortchange possible readings of the text from often ignored hybrid gay-identified voices. Such criticisms are justified, for the primary gay voice of color on biblical interpretation from the 1990s is Peter Gomes. Building upon earlier scholarship on the texts of terror, the African American pastoral theologian Horace Griffin (2006) points out that the black church fails to extend its rich history of using the Bible to oppose oppression to homophobic readings of scripture. Because of its quest for respectability and internalization of white racist portrayals of black sexuality, the African American church has adopted conservative gender and sexuality mores that influence scriptural interpretations. Griffin argues that it is anachronistic to address twenty-first-century homosexuality with ancient understandings of sexuality and gender. Finally, Manuel Villalobos (2011) has produced a transgressive borderland reading of the baptism of the Ethiopian eunuch by Phillip.

Goss, Stone, Williams, and gay-affirming scholars such as Jennings and Nissinen have built their approaches on feminist biblical hermeneutics and historical reconstruction of gender/sex codes in the ancient world. They have attempted to move beyond the negative apologetics in interpretative battles over the texts of terror applied to same-sex sexuality. Stone (2002) has been critical of some apologetic biblical interpretations driven by theological concerns, noting the value of critical and historically contextual reconstructions of homoeroticism in the wider networks of cultural gender/sex codes. This approach demands a hermeneutical comprehension of current gender/sex ideologies in the interpretative enterprise of reconstructing and comprehending the sex/gender codes from the ancient Near East and the Greco-Roman world.

[*See also* Queer Readings; Queer Theory; *and* Same-Sex Relations, *subentries on* Hebrew Bible *and* New Testament.]

BIBLIOGRAPHY

Alpert, Rebecca T. *Like Bread on the Seder Plate: Jewish Lesbians and the Transformation of Tradition.* New York: Columbia University Press, 1997.

Bailey, Derrick Sherwin. *Homosexuality and the Western Christian Tradition.* London: Longmans, Green, 1955.

Bohache, Thomas. "Matthew." In *The Queer Bible Commentary*, edited by Deryn Guest et al., pp. 487–516. London: SCM, 2006.

Boswell, John. *Christianity, Social Tolerance, and Homosexuality: Gay People in Western Europe from the Beginning of the Christian Era to the Fourteenth Century.* Chicago: University of Chicago Press, 1980.

Boswell, John. *Same-Sex Unions in Premodern Europe.* New York: Villard, 1994.

Boyarin, Daniel. "Are There Any Jews in 'the History of Sexuality'?" *Journal of the History of Sexuality* 5, no. 3 (January 1995): 333–355.

Boyd, Malcolm. "Was Jesus Gay?" *The Advocate* 565 (4 December 1990): 90.

Boyd, Malcolm. "Survival with Grace." In *Gay Soul: Finding the Heart of Gay Spirit and Nature*, edited by Mark Thompson, pp. 229–248. San Francsco: HarperSanFranciso, 1994.

Brooten, Bernadette J. *Love Between Women: Early Christian Responses to Female Homoeroticism.* Chicago: University of Chicago Press, 1996.

Carden, Michael. *Sodomy: A History of a Christian Biblical Myth.* London: Equinox, 2004.

Cheng, Patrick S. "Galatians." In *The Queer Bible Commentary*, edited by Deryn Guest et al., pp. 624–629. London: SCM, 2006.

Comstock, Gary David. *Gay Theology without Apology.* Cleveland, Ohio: Pilgrim, 1993.

Countryman, Louis William. *Dirt, Greed, and Sex: Sexual Ethics in the New Testament and Their Implications for Today.* Philadelphia: Fortress, 1988.

D'Angelo, Mary Rose. "Women Partners in the New Testament." In *Que(e)rying Religion: A Critical Anthology,* edited by Gary David Comstock and Susan E. Henking, pp. 441–455. New York: Continuum, 1997.

Gomes, Peter J. *The Good Book: Reading the Bible with Mind and Heart.* New York: William Morrow, 1996.

Goss, Robert. *Jesus ACTED UP: A Gay and Lesbian Manifesto.* San Francisco: HarperSanFrancisco, 1993.

Goss, Robert. "The Beloved Disciple: A Queer Bereavement Narrative in a Time of AIDS." In *Take Back the Word: A Queer Reading of the Bible,* edited by Robert Goss and Mona West, pp. 206–218. Cleveland, Ohio: Pilgrim, 2000a.

Goss, Robert E. "Jonathan and David." In *Reader's Guide to Lesbian and Gay Studies,* edited by Timothy F. Murphy. Chicago: Fitzroy Dearborn, 2000b.

Goss, Robert. *Queering Christ: Beyond Jesus ACTED UP.* Cleveland, Ohio: Pilgrim, 2002.

Goss, Robert E. "John." In *The Queer Bible Commentary,* edited by Deryn Guest et al., pp. 548–565. London: SCM, 2006.

Greenberg, Steven. *Wrestling with God and Men: Homosexuality in the Jewish Tradition.* Madison: University of Wisconsin Press, 2004.

Griffin, Horace L. *Their Own Receive Them Not: African American Lesbians and Gays in Black Churches.* Cleveland, Ohio: Pilgrim, 2006.

Guest, Deryn. *When Deborah Met Jael: Lesbian Biblical Hermeneutics.* London: SCM, 2005.

Guest, Deryn, Robert E. Goss, Mona White, and Thomas Bohache, eds. *The Queer Bible Commentary.* London: SCM, 2006.

Hanks, Thomas D. *The Subversive Gospel: A New Testament Commentary of Liberation.* Translated by John P. Doner. Cleveland, Ohio: Pilgrim, 2000.

Hanks, Thomas. "Romans." In *The Queer Bible Commentary,* edited by Deryn Guest et al., pp. 582–605. London: SCM, 2006.

Helminiak, Daniel A. *What the Bible Really Says about Homosexuality.* San Francisco: Alamo Square, 1994.

Horner, Tom. *Jonathan Loved David: Homosexuality in Biblical Times.* Philadelphia: Westminster, 1978.

Houser, Ward, and Warren Johansson. "David and Jonathan." In *The Encyclopedia of Homosexuality,* edited by Wayne R. Dynes et al., pp. 296–299. New York: Garland, 1990.

Jennings, Theodore W., Jr. "YHWH as Erastes." In *Queer Commentary and the Hebrew Bible,* edited by Ken Stone, pp. 36–74. London: Sheffield Academic Press, 2001.

Jennings, Theodore W., Jr. *The Man Jesus Loved: Homoerotic Narratives from the New Testament.* Cleveland, Ohio: Pilgrim, 2003.

Jennings, Theodore W., Jr. *Jacob's Wound: Homoerotic Narrative in the Literature of Ancient Israel.* New York: Continuum, 2005.

Jordan, Mark D. *The Invention of Sodomy in Christian Theology.* Chicago: University of Chicago Press, 1997.

Koch, Timothy R. "Cruising as Methodology: Homoeroticism and the Scriptures." In *Queer Commentary and the Hebrew Bible,* edited by Ken Stone, pp. 169–180. London: Sheffield Academic Press, 2001.

Liew, Tat-siong Benny. "(Cor)Responding: A Letter to the Editor." In *Queer Commentary and the Hebrew Bible,* edited by Ken Stone, pp. 182–192. London: Sheffield Academic Press, 2001.

Long, Ronald E. "Disarming Biblically Based Gay-Bashing." In *The Queer Bible Commentary,* edited by Deryn Guest et al., pp. 1–18. London: SCM, 2006.

Martin, Dale B. *Sex and the Single Savior: Gender and Sexuality in Biblical Interpretation.* Louisville, Ky.: Westminster John Knox, 2006.

McNeill, John J. *The Church and the Homosexual.* Kansas City, Kans.: Sheed Andrews & McMeel, 1976.

McNeill, John J. *Freedom, Glorious Freedom: The Spiritual Journey to the Fullness of Life for Gays, Lesbians, and Everybody Else.* Boston: Beacon, 1995.

McNeill, John J. *Both Feet Firmly Planted in Midair: My Spiritual Journey.* Louisville, Ky.: Westminster John Knox, 1998.

McNeill, John J., and Mark D. Jordan. *Sex as God Intended: A Reflection on Human Sexuality as Play.* Maple Shade, N.J.: Lethe, 2008.

Milgrom, Jacob. *Leviticus 1–16: A New Translation with Introduction and Commentary.* New Haven, Conn.: Yale University Press, 1991.

Miller, James E. "The Practices of Romans 1:26: Homosexual or Heterosexual?" *Novum Testamentum* 37 (1995): 1–11.

Nissinen, Martti. *Homoeroticism in the Biblical World: A Historical Perspective.* Translated by Kirsi Stjerna. Minneapolis: Fortress, 1998.

Olyan, Saul M. "'And with a Male You Shall Not Lie the Lying Down of a Woman': On the Meaning and Significance of Leviticus 18:22 and 20:13." *Journal of the History of Sexuality* 5 (1994–1995): 179–206.

Phipps, William E. *Was Jesus Married?: The Distortion of Sexuality in the Christian Tradition.* New York: Harper & Row, 1970.

Seymour, Gayle M. "Simeon Solomon and the Biblical Construction of Marginal Identity in Victorian England." In *Reclaiming the Sacred: The Bible in Gay and Lesbian Culture,* edited by Raymond-Jean Frontain, pp. 97–119. New York: Haworth, 1997.

Stone, Ken. "Homosexuality and the Bible or Queer Reading? A Response to Martti Nissinen." *Theology and Sexuality* 14 (2001a): 107–118.

Stone, Ken, ed. *Queer Commentary and the Hebrew Bible*. London: Sheffield Academic Press, 2001b.

Stone, Ken. "What Happens When 'Gays Read the Bible'?" In *The Many Voices of the Bible*, edited by Seán Freyne and Ellen van Wolde, pp. 77–85. London: SCM, 2002.

Stewart, David Tabb. "Leviticus." In *The Queer Bible Commentary*, edited by Deryn Guest et al., pp. 77–104. London: SCM, 2006.

Theissen, Gerd. *The Shadow of the Galilean: The Quest of the Historical Jesus in Narrative Form*. Philadelphia: Fortess Press, 1987.

Villalobos, Manuel. "Bodies *Del Otro Lado* Finding Life and Hope in the Borderland: Gloria Anzaldúa, the Ethiopian Eunuch of Acts 8:26–40, y Yo." In *Bible Trouble: Queer Reading at the Boundaries of Biblical Scholarship*, edited by Teresa J. Hornsby and Ken Stone, pp. 191–222. Atlanta: Society of Biblical Literature Atlanta, 2011.

Williams, Robert. *Just As I Am: A Practical Guide to Being Out, Proud, and Christian*. New York: Crown, 1992.

Wood, Robert Watson. *Christ and the Homosexual: Some Observations*. New York: Vantage, 1960.

Robert E. Shore-Goss

GENDER

Gender theory is an interdisciplinary area of study that explores the nature of gender/sex identity. Since Simone de Beauvoir made the famous statement "One is not born, but rather becomes, a woman" in the mid-twentieth century, the concept of "woman" as a social construct has been explored and dissected by theoreticians in a variety of academic disciplines. In making this landmark observation, Beauvoir did not necessarily mean that the biological category of "woman" did not exist, but that the behavioral characteristics and expectations inscribed on female identity were culturally constructed to be the "other" to the first sex—to male identity.

Beauvoir's statement encapsulates the gender debate: whether how we develop as individuals—as men and women—is controlled by our biological nature or by our environment. The distinction between sex and gender, so clearly articulated by second-wave feminism, is that the former refers to the physical characteristics inscribed on the body to identify it as male or female, while the latter refers to distinctive roles ascribed to the two sexes by the societies they live in and the identities they assume within those roles as men and women. From ancient times biological sex and gender were inextricably bound together, the former constructing the identity and life expectations of the latter. Aristotle (384–322 B.C.E.) was the most influential figure among the classical philosophers in enshrining essentialism into Western and colonial culture. In Aristotelian understanding the biology of the individual formed the essence of that individual in terms of identity and was irreducible, unchanging, and inescapable.

The renaissance of Aristotelian ideas within the Roman world ensured his influence extended into emerging Christianity and continued on as that belief system developed into the religion of the empire. Aristotle's ideas on natural order (men are rulers by nature, women subject to that rule) are evident in writings ascribed to the foundation figures in the evolution of Christianity, including Paul of Tarsus and Augustine, and on into the scholastic period and beyond through the work and legacy of Thomas Aquinas. Contemporary teaching within the Roman Catholic tradition continues to draw on Aristotelian essentialism to explain why, for example, because of her nature, a woman cannot perform the role of priest just as a man cannot give birth to be a mother.

Contemporary gender theory includes those who would wish not only to question the impact of Aristotelian essentialism on the lives of men and women as social beings but also to destabilize the very notion of biological essential difference. By exploring the question of essence, feminist deconstruction has exposed the arbitrary nature of biological assignment—of naming a newborn "male" or "female." Discussing the subject of ambiguous biological sexual identity in the form of the hermaphrodite, Judith Butler explores how a human being whose biological make up falls "outside" of the male/female binary divulges the very instability of that binary. She/he uncovers how that sexual binary is a construction and opens up the possibility that it might be constructed differently.

This position within the gender theory debate, shared by Monique Wittig, would inquire whether it is not only the ways we behave as "men" and "women" that are socially constructed, but also the ways we are classified biologically at birth. Thus our biological identity within the categories of male and female rests on a subjective decision at our birth, and how we live out those identities is "performative" rather than essential to our nature, and as such they are opened up to be performed in alternative ways. Other theorists, including Luce Irigaray, Julia Kristeva, and Hélène Cixous, work within recognizable categories of male and female, revealing and critiquing the evolution of "woman" as the passive subject of the male gaze, then reconstructing her in her own image, by exploring ways of women becoming authentic subjects with agency.

Evolution of Gender Theory. The antecedents to gender theory are diverse and complex; in general terms it can be said to have existed ever since humanity intellectually began to perceive and reflect on the differences between men and women, but the rise of feminism at the end of the nineteenth century, the "first wave," provided a focal point from which to initiate the questions that would lead to the work of gender theorists a century later.

The political and social agenda for first-wave feminists was mirrored by second-wave feminists. The campaigns of the secular women's liberation movement in the 1960s and 1970s led to the introduction of legislation prohibiting explicit sexual discrimination in the workplace. By placing first-wave feminism, and its rebirth in the second wave during the second half of the twentieth century, in a wider context they can both be identified as clear illustrations of "high modernity," with the ascendancy of man at the heart of the modernity project naturally evolving into the ascendancy of woman—with both agendas universal in character. The work of the philosopher Mary Daly is a clear example of feminism in this context. Her critical maxim, "When God is male, the male is God," cuts through to the core of Western and postcolonial civilization, identifying patriarchy to be the fundamental, overarching, and universal problem with women as its victims, and providing the answer in the form of lesbian separatism.

The unease felt about this tendency to universalize women's experience, together with the obvious privileged position of white, Western women activists, became articulated in critiques levelled at feminists by other women. By foregrounding the multiplicity of women's experiences in place of a universal shared experience as women inevitably led to fragmentation and the impossibility of a singular women's movement in political or social terms. In this context the phenomenon of womanism arose as a rallying point for women of difference, rebutting the universal diagnosis and "cure-all" approach found among certain second-wave feminists. Womanism became a collective for voices from diverse contexts and with diverse agendas, divulging the irony that the original exclusion suffered by women who had been at the vanguard of second-wave feminism was inadvertently being dealt out by those women to women of difference.

This focus on difference is highly significant for gender theory, since the rejection of "woman's experience" in place of "women's experiences" weakens the notion of any essential, unifying commonality among women. This widening and deepening of the critical lens marks the shift from second- to third-wave feminism. The three waves remain connected, however, through the common legacy of modernist critiques of patriarchy formulated by first- and second-wave feminists across the academic disciplines, which continue to provide the critical stance for gender theorists.

The intellectual environment of postmodernity that gradually emerged from the radical ideas fermented in the 1960s gave the impetus to contemporary gender theory, marking a shift in feminist thinking from the context of "high modernity." The postmodern iconoclastic world of ideas offered fertile ground for gender theorists to begin to assimilate the profound questions necessary to uncover how gender had been constructed down the centuries by societies and cultures dominated by a patriarchal worldview. The term "postmodern" is a contentious one, creating a category, which, in itself, is a concept to be resisted by those who would be contained by it. If, however, "postmodern" is understood not as a confining category, but rather as a descriptive term for an impulse, or a wave, running through the world of ideas, taking on divergent shapes and forms across academic disciplines, permeating throughout wider culture, then, in this fluidity, it allows for multiple and diverse manifestations.

The "postmodern turn" heralded the challenge to universal truths, or metanarratives, that characterized the age of modernity, that is, the general theories that explained—and held together—the status quo within culture and society, and which had gone largely unquestioned in the past. By opening up these metanarratives to critique, postmodern thinkers allow alternative and marginalized narratives to be foregrounded. In doing so, those traditional metanarratives become displaced and their limitations exposed, among them the normative understanding of gender identity. The tools for dismantling these metanarratives were provided by poststructuralism and deconstruction, with two of the foremost figures in these movements, Michel Foucault and Jacques Derrida, respectively, having significant influence on gender theorists across Europe, the United States, and postcolonial contexts.

Feminist critiques across academic disciplines challenging the supposed neutrality and objectivity of traditional scholarship converged with the "postmodern turn," questioning the universal claims embedded in modernity. Feminists, along with other radical thinkers, identified academic claims of objectivity to be in actuality subjective positioning by men of a particular culture, class, and race. "Bias," rather than being a derogatory label used to dismiss an argument, became the means of authenticating one. Subjectivity became the accepted stance in place of elusive, or nonexistent, objectivism. However, the notion of subjectivity for women is particularly problematic, since the female subject, or self, within a universe constructed by men, is a male construct. Gender theory reflects on this problematic and suggests means of enabling, or creating, the female subject(s).

While the encounter between feminism and the postmodern often seems to elude the material world, hovering instead in the abstract world of ideas, there is one point in history that is pivotal for understanding subsequent developments and debates in gender theory, and that is the events that occurred in Paris in May 1968. Inspired by leftist politics, large numbers of students, workers, and professionals came out together onto the streets of Paris in a series of spontaneous protests, shunning the conventional channels for change in society. Disorder was advocated instead of order; all social and political structures were interrogated and found wanting. While the physical upheaval eventually subsided, the intellectual world exploded with questions and challenges that would last for decades, and through those events a new French feminism was born.

This movement rejected liberal modernity's political ideal of equal participation, whereby women would be accommodated into the existing sociopolitical structures on a par with their male counterparts. Instead the new critique focused on those structures themselves, calling for their radical transformation rather than their superficial reform. The profundity of these new sexual politics dug away at the foundations of the familiar edifices of civilization, removing its many layers to reach down to the core questions of human identity. Psych et Po (Psychanalyse et Politique) was the name adopted by the new movement, chosen because political feminism without psychoanalysis could only remain a superficial enterprise achieving mere cosmetic change. Psychoanalysis was unique in its discourse on sexuality and the distinction between the sexes. If psychoanalysis could be politicized with a feminist agenda, then the political could be psychoanalyzed. Major figures in the Psych et Po group included Hélène Cixous, Catherine Clément, Luce Irigaray, and Julia Kristeva. They envisaged the emergence of a feminine identity formed on its own terms and not in relation to masculine identity. Tensions grew between Psyche and Po and liberal reformist feminists, whose rhetoric the former considered androcentric and even prompted some to discard the term "feminist" in protest, leading to the separation of Psyche and Po from the rest of the women's groups. This rift reached beyond the borders of France, manifesting itself globally in the repeated clash between the Psyche and Po group and their adherents on one side and egalitarian feminists and lesbian separatist groups on the other.

The spirit and momentum of Paris in 1968 united the theorists of Psyche and Po, and while over time each evolved their ideas as individual thinkers, they shared another foundational influence: the psychoanalysis of Jacques Lacan. Feminist theorists in France and beyond have a relationship with Lacan's ideas that is invariably ambivalent. They are indebted to his work on gender construction and the formation of the subject, which provides a conceptual framework that opens the way for them to develop a concept of the feminine subject. For Lacan the subject is socially constructed by language, and gender and sexuality are not biological givens but emerge within the sociolinguistic construction of subjectivity.

While Lacan is the significant psychoanalytical influence for French feminist theorists, Jacques Derrida's deconstruction project provided a vital philosophical and literary frame. Derrida's method of reading texts by placing the focus on the exception rather than the rule and thereby undermining the dominant narrative is akin to feminist hermeneutics of reading "against the grain"; for example, a proscription forbidding women from teaching men signifies that there was a context where women *were* teaching men. Such a strategy, switching the focus on destabilizing factors—the chaotic—to expose the fragility of the edifices of modernity's sociopolitical structures when applied to gender construction enables a profound critique of patriarchy beginning with the very basis of language itself. Moreover, Derrida's critique of Western reality that is arranged according to hierarchical binaries (culture/nature, good/evil, and so on), where one part is privileged to the detriment of the other, with the male/female binary being the paradigmatic illustration, serves to support a feminist critique of gender hierarchy. The Hegelian resolution of these binary oppositions, in brief, was for the difference between them to be negated or subsumed. Male and female become synthesized into "humanity." Thus binary opposition could be overcome, but hierarchy remained. Instead, Derrida's concept of *différance* puts emphasis on the presumed negative part of the binary, and unlike Hegel he does not allow that negative part to be subsumed into the "positive," arguing that negativity must be sustained without resolution. Derrida's *différance* allows for the feminine to coexist alongside the male without becoming negated by it or simply being the "other" in relation to the male subject.

Alongside Derrida, Michel Foucault's critical work on power and knowledge provided rich terrain in which gender theory could germinate and develop. Foucault's influence on contemporary gender theory is extensive, particularly in contributing to Judith Butler's "performativity." Foucault's process of genealogy, evolving from the work of Nietzsche, presents a way of understanding history that, instead of using it as a means of affirming values and structures of the present, seeks to uncover the arbitrary nature of the past, that is, the discourses created to explain and control the world we live in, including how we have inherited perceptions of the body.

"New" Essentialism. Gender theorists have wrestled with the concept of essentialism from the beginnings of feminism as a political movement. Traditional essentialism, inherited from classical philosophy and theology that intertwines sex and gender so that the life expectations of men and women are bound by their biological sex, might be rejected, but the existence of a commonality among women that extends beyond biology and into shared experience was a vital factor within gender theory among second-wave feminists. Without some commonality, not only would a political women's movement lack any meaningful cohesion; without properties essential to women, then "women" as a category would not exist. While Aristotelian ideas on sexual hierarchy could have no place in a feminist agenda, the idea of a feminine shared essence could not be rejected without losing the ideal of a universal women's experience.

Essence as debated in second-wave feminism was based on social construction, where shared invariant social characteristics became the basis for feminist universalism. Identifying these invariant characteristics remained elusive and virtually impossible without straying into the territory of biological determinism. For example, relational behavior within domestic and work environments was arguably a feminine trait, as suggested by Carol Gilligan. Second-wave feminists have not been static theoreticians, and as socially constructed essentialism was subjected to intense critique, it became as questionable as its biological counterpart.

The tension of choosing between a biologically driven essentialism on the one hand and fragmentation of any form of women's movement on the other could be overcome by opting for the concept of a nominal essence such as that posited by John Locke (1632–1704). Locke differentiated between natural essence and nominal essence, the latter being a linguistic contingence used to group or name commonalities without attaching permanence to them. Nominal essence allows experience to be the basis of commonality among women, but the fluidity of nominal essence allows the basis to change depending on context. While this does not allow for a universalist feminism, it allows feminism, or feminist politics, to be a site for a shared nominal essence—which identifies with women's experiences at particular moments in history. This can be termed strategic essentialism, which can be relative, adapting and modifying depending on context.

Irigaray. Luce Irigaray's work is an illustration of how some contemporary theorists have remained essentialists, but have articulated a means of evolving female subjectivity that is complete in itself, rather than existing always as the "other" in relation to the male subject. Irigaray is a key figure among French feminists; born in Belgium, she moved to Paris in 1960. From the 1960s she worked at the Centre Nationale de la Recherche Scientifique. Although regarded as a central figure among "new" essentialists, her work defies any attempt at a static categorization, since her thought is constantly fluid and in process. Her writings span a range of subjects that include linguistics, literature, philosophy, psychoanalysis, and religion; she holds doctorates in linguistics and philosophy, and she trained as a Lacanian analyst. The key and constant issue Irigaray wrestles with across these subjects is sexual difference. Her critics argue that this focus blinds her to other crucial differences, such as class or color or sexual orientation.

In contrast to theorists who reject essentialism based on nature, she embraces the concept of "woman," deliberately using biological terminology to explore ways of redefining "woman," but in such a way that is not based on notions of "the other." This "new" essentialism deconstructs the phenomenon "woman" as the constructed "other" within the patriarchal gaze and in its stead presents possibilities for reconstructing woman subjectively. For Irigaray woman can become woman through and of herself, without reference to male identity.

The application of "mimesis" (*mimétisme*) in Irigaray's work takes the constructed notion of "woman" and parodies it, or mimics it into becoming authentic female subjectivity. This strategy resembles what Derrida has termed "paleonymy," that is, maintaining an old name in order to introduce a new concept, and thus summoning up a memory of the old only for it to be confronted by the new. Having deconstructed the patriarchal construct of woman as "other" to man, from its dissolution and by means of her application of the concept of mimesis, she presents the birth of authentic woman, emerging from within that difference, to be "herself" for the first time. Irigaray's use of mimesis ("imitation")—her parody of the constructed notion of woman—allows for the appropriation of femininity with the female as subject.

As she was baptized a Catholic and educated in a Christian context, religion is an explicit theme in Irigaray's work, and this background is clearly evident in her use of imagery and language. She engages directly with feminist biblical exegesis in "Equal to Whom?," ostensibly a review of Elisabeth Schüssler Fiorenza's book *In Memory of Her*, but more like an essay extending and developing themes she had explored in another essay, "Divine Women," identifying the lack of a feminine divine as a central issue for understanding women's lack of subjectivity. In her essay "La Mystérique" she engages with the phenomenon of mysticism within religious traditions, discovering elements that have a particular resonance with women. Her creation of this neologistic term, *la mystérique*, illustrates the richness of Irigaray's use of language. Within it are incorporated and compacted the concepts of hysteria, mysticism, mystery, and the feminine. In mysticism she recognizes a female domain, which challenges traditional revelation based on reason with a more embodied discourse. Mysticism bypasses the male ecclesial hierarchy, allowing women a means of communing with the divine. The accounts of female mystics, where they become one with their divine companion, synchronize with Irigaray's idea of the "divine within" in her reconstruction of the female subject.

Irigaray's contention that female subjectivity has been hampered by an absence of the feminine divine is introduced in her essay "Divine Women," and here the influence of Ludwig Feuerbach's *Essence of Christianity* is clearly evident. Irigaray discusses how a god imagined as male has enabled men to become subjects and to develop an authentic sense of self, thus developing Feuerbach's notion of God as the expression or extension of man's ideal. Without that vital link between gender and the divine, or that divine genealogy, women become the "other" not only to men but to the notion of divinity itself. This lack of a feminine divine has both debilitated women from developing themselves as subjects and distorted the mother-daughter relationship, a relationship that is rejected in favor of submissiveness to the God/father/husband.

Like Julia Kristeva, Irigaray wants to "heal" the mother/daughter relationship from its diagnosis in traditional psychoanalytical writings, and move away from the Oedipal script that sets daughter against mother. Also, like Kristeva, Irigaray calls for the affirmation of the significance of maternity. She suggests an alternative order where God would be incarnate within each woman, and in the female sex, ensuring a divine element for daughter-woman-mother. This lack of the feminine divine, created by theologians, is affirmed and intensified through psychologists and psychoanalysts. If this absence is not addressed, women are destined to remain constituted from outside, by society that ascribes them with relative identities as daughters of fathers, wives of husbands, mothers of children. With the feminine divine women can be affirmed and fulfilled as individuals and as members of society.

Thus, rather than rejecting the concept of God as an impossible male construct, Irigaray believes it is necessary to reconstruct God as a feminine concept. In her essay "The Redemption of Women," Irigaray takes the Christian concept of the virgin mother and transforms it into a metaphor for women's becoming. Rather than merely translating the icon of virgin mother represented in the person of Mary, Irigaray transforms it into an autonomous mode of being as a woman, but still in relation to, though not subject to, the other. Irigaray uncovers the possibility of reshaping the concept of incarnation by focusing on Mary, the virgin mother who mediates between the divine and the material.

Irigaray works with the notion of difference, and proposes a new essentialism that is both individual and independent of the masculine "other." In the biblical world, maleness and masculinity can be understood to be constructed as the "other" to God. The implications of Irigaray's analysis of gender can offer wider implications for biblical studies, suggesting new ways of reading biblical texts that impact on both male and female images.

Cixous. The archetypes portrayed in the biblical creation story provide rich terrain for gender theorists working from an essentialist position. The characters, the setting, and the events played out in this narrative have been a constant identity reference for Western, colonial, and postcolonial cultural consciousness—and unconsciousness. This is neatly summed up by Hélène Cixous's comment in "The Author in Truth": "Every entrance to life finds itself *before the apple*" (1991, p. 150). As in the case of Irigaray, Cixous's religious background is evident in her use of language and imagery. Born in French Colonial Algeria to a Sephardic Jewish family, Cixous arrived in France in 1956 to study at the University of Bordeaux. Her Jewish and foreign identity together with her femaleness intensified her feeling of alienation, or "otherness." Cixous resists the categories of academic disciplines, which historically allowed no place for the "other," and instead produced writings that cross over the boundaries between philosophy, psychoanalysis, literature, and gender theory. The majority of her writings are in the form of novels, manifesting her concept of *écriture feminine*, in which she explores possibilities for authentic relationships between the masculine subject and the feminine "other." From the late 1970s Cixous's work has been marked increasingly by the use of religious imagery, and by making explicit reference to her relationship with God. This relationship she puts into a prophetic context, transforming her writing into a form of divine revelation.

In her essay "The Author in Truth," Cixous presents a feminist interpretation of the story of the Garden of Eden. This engagement with the Eden story mirrors the primary position afforded to it in the essentialist thinking of ancient and traditional religious writing. By resorting to this foundation myth, contemporary feminist theory opens up the narrative once more to shift it away from the patriarchal, or phallocentric, interpretation that had become almost an intrinsic part, fused to the narrative itself. In her reading of this scene from Genesis, she makes a sharp contrast between the "apple," which signifies a means to female subjectivity, and the prohibition against eating it made by God, which signifies its denial. Cixous plays with the homophony that exists in French between the nouns *scène* (scene) and *cène* (meal). The focus is placed on Eve's consumption of the fruit, on her pleasure in opening up to the "other" that is represented by the fruit. In recognizing that knowledge and taste go together Cixous allows Eve an element of subjectivity that goes beyond the mere senses of sight and taste. The first woman understands that the "apple" holds the secret of empowerment.

Essentialist positioning among feminist gender theorists engages intellectual tools of the academic disciplines, in particular philosophy, psychoanalysis, linguistics, and literary theory, to deconstruct the phallocentric creation of subjectivity that had left women in the role of the "other" to the masculine subject. It allows the construction of alternative visions that enable not only female subjectivity in and of itself but a vision of utopian, or prelapsarian, complementarity between the sexes. Such essentialist ideals are criticized for maintaining heterosexuality as the central paradigm. Sexual hierarchy might be dealt with, but sexual difference based on material difference remains in place. Maintaining material essentialism, but with the possibility of female agency, allows for the continuance of a site for feminist politics.

Antiessentialists/Strict Constructionists. The tension within feminism on the question of essentialism, whether material or strategic, can be seen as the dividing line between second- and third-wave feminists, with the latter rejecting essentialism in any form and in its stead opting for radical constructionism.

Wittig. Monique Wittig, however, is a theorist whose context places her among new-essentialist French theorists, but whose ideas belong with the constructionists. The problematic over essentialism is foregrounded in her work, which rejects unequivocally the ideas of those who theorize sexual difference based on biology, as well as the categories of masculine and feminine. Gender itself was constructed by men, she argues, for those they classed as women, and thus gender exists only to define what is in oppression. Her political ideas were nurtured against the backdrop of the Paris riots in 1968, but her feminist stance set her in opposition to the Psych et Po French feminist movement that arose in the aftermath of that political and social unrest. In asserting that there is no such thing as "feminine essence," Wittig's feminism echoes Derrida's deconstruction project of encouraging suspicion of any search for "essence" that limits ontology.

Her essay "One Is Not Born a Woman" borrows its title from Simone de Beauvoir's famous dictum and proceeds to develop the embryonic theory of gender production implicit in Beauvoir's words. Wittig's critique of a masculinized culture is profound, positing that heterosexuality orders all human relations and controls how we conceptualize the world. The ultimate means of political resistance is the establishment of a lesbian culture. A lesbian is not a woman, Wittig argues, whether economically, or politically, or ideologically. A woman exists only in a specific social relation to a man, and that relationship, according to Wittig, is one of servitude. Only a lesbian can be a female subject with agency, set apart from male definition.

In order to reconceive the world from this perspective, Wittig rewrites the religious past, but instead of recourse to Mother Earth imagery, she elevates the powerful warrior goddesses. The foundation story for Judaism and Christianity receives a radical exegesis that eradicates the figure of Adam. Eve stands alone in the Garden, taking and eating the fruit for the benefit of womankind. Wittig's call for the establishment of a lesbian culture is cast as a utopian vision, offering a female subjectivity that, at best, only exists on the cultural margins.

Butler. The North American critical philosopher Judith Butler, like Wittig, opens up the question of the stability of sexual difference itself. Also like Wittig, Butler is critical of the theoretical stances occupied by the Psych et Po French feminist movement. Her criticism of Irigaray centers on the issue of essentialism. After an expansive exegesis of Irigaray's critique of the absence of the feminine in Platonic metaphysics, underlining her focus on sexual difference, it remains for Butler "radically unclear" whether the materiality of bodies can be the axis of feminist theory. This critique illustrates the contrast in gender theory between the various shades of essentialism and strict constructionism. Butler has published widely in the fields of Continental philosophy, literary theory, feminist and queer theory, and cultural politics. *Gender Trouble*, published in 1990, is arguably the work that has had the greatest impact within gender theory debates.

In *Gender Trouble* Butler takes Foucault's process of genealogy much further into the arena of gender theory, presenting an antiessentialist critique of identity categories. This Butler describes in terms of a critical genealogy of gender ontologies. Following Foucault, Butler reveals gender categories as political formulations rather than essential markers of identity. Rather than search for the origin of male and female gender, Butler sees the pragmatic project to be more one that destabilizes the dominant discourse of gender itself, since it is a construction and regulation of identity. Utilizing genealogy Butler demonstrates how identity categories have been regarded as primordial truths preceding history but are in fact human constructions within history,

constantly being reaffirmed by reenactment. They are the creations of institutions and practices. A fixed matrix of oppositional heterosexuality has been constructed that links and binds sex, gender, and desire together. This matrix, Butler argues, is unstable and arbitrary, not simply because it fuses gendered behavior within biological boundaries but because the process of binary sexual designation is essentially random. Butler illustrates her theory with the story of the nineteenth-century hermaphrodite Herculine Barbin. Barbin's journals had earlier been published by Foucault, who drew attention to this phenomenon, which disrupts the binary discourse of sexual difference. Building on and critiquing Foucault's comments, Butler examines the case of Barbin and demonstrates that gender, as it is constructed in the dominant discourse, is fragile; it is something that is "performed" by individuals. Gender constitutes the given identity, and in the case of Barbin, that identity, named arbitrarily, is acted out in his/her body. Butler contends that there is no such thing as gender identity, only the actions that performatively constitute it.

Instead of understanding identity categories ontologically—with the foundational binary of masculine and feminine gender, underpinned by compulsory heterosexuality—which inform and formulate particular sociopolitical contexts, they are in actuality the products of those contexts. Clearly, the Bible, in both religious and cultural terms, can be understood as such a discourse par excellence, which has constructed and confirmed those identity categories. But as Butler points out, the institutions, practices and discourses that construct identity are themselves multiple and diffuse with their own histories. She contends that subversion of given gender roles is consistently evident within dominant cultural discourse, and she takes these exceptions within discourse to demonstrate the fragility of constructed gender. Butler suggests that the reality of plurality can be recognized, encouraging a proliferation of cultural configurations of sex and gender existing within the established discourses, divulging the flimsy construct of the male and female, masculine and feminine binaries.

However, there is a lack of reality to existence "outside" constructed identity. Any space has to be negotiated within existing sociopolitical realities, and by the very act of negotiating, an engagement occurs, and one identity becomes subsumed by another. Butler's concept of performative gender expressed in *Gender Trouble* was criticized for not taking into account the realities of enforced identity through race—and the accompanying dominant white liberal humanist discourse—as well as gender. In *Bodies That Matter* (1993), Butler addresses the materiality of the body more closely, and suggests that criticism on this issue is a misreading of her ideas, which, she argues, do offer a way forward for identities to shift, and not necessarily at the cost of the negation of others. The option of performative identity remains an unreality for the majority, who cannot envision the possibility of life beyond their constructed reality. In 2004 Butler published *Undoing Gender*, which reconsiders her concept of performativity and presents a more "grounded" excursus situating her ideas within a framework where human beings have to negotiate to survive.

However, this criticism is suspended when the scene of the performance is something beyond human controlled space. The fragility of given gendered behavior patterns is clearly apparent in biblical narrative, whatever the theological purpose it serves may be. The biblical law codes reflect an uncompromising construction of prescribed gendered behavior, but set beside them are narratives that subvert them. Applying Butler's model of deconstruction, we might understand, for example, the figure of Judith as an individual figure who performs gender across a spectrum of possibilities, defying clear identification within any given constructed role. Whatever the author of the book of Judith's theological intention might have been, the elusive figure of the main character offers us a subversive, even anarchic, paradigm of gender play evident within the theocratic metanarrative of biblical tradition.

By uncovering the discourse of gendered identity and revealing its constructed constituents, not only do theorists open up potential means of understanding human agency in contemporary times, but their work provides a useful hermeneutical lens for reading biblical literature, arguably the foundational narrative for Western and colonial culture. Not least, gender theory reveals that the premodern understandings of the human subject might have more in common with the postmodern than they ever had with modernity.

[*See also* Creation; Feminism, *subentries on* First-Wave Feminism *and* Second-Wave Feminism; Heteronormativity/Heterosexism; *and* Womanist Criticism.]

BIBLIOGRAPHY

Beauvoir, Simone de. *The Second Sex*. Translated and edited by H. M. Parshley. New York: Knopf, 1971.

Butler, Judith. *Gender Trouble: Feminism and the Subversion of Identity*. New York: Routledge, 1990.

Butler, Judith. *Bodies That Matter: On the Discursive Limits of "Sex."* New York: Routledge, 1993.

Butler, Judith. *The Judith Butler Reader*. Edited by Sarah Salih. Malden, Mass.: Blackwell, 2004a.

Butler, Judith. *Undoing Gender*. New York: Routledge, 2004b.

Cixous, Hélène. "The Author in Truth." In *Coming to Writing, and Other Essays*, edited by Deborah Jenson, pp. 136–181. Cambridge, Mass.: Harvard University Press, 1991.

Daly, Mary. *Beyond God the Father: Toward a Philosophy of Women's Liberation*. Boston: Beacon, 1973.

Derrida, Jacques. "Plato's Pharmacy." In *Dissemination*, pp. 67–186. Translated by Barbara Johnson. London: Athlone, 1981a.

Derrida, Jacques. *Positions*. Translated by Alan Bass. Chicago: University of Chicago Press, 1981b.

Foucault, Michel. *The History of Sexuality*. Vol. 1, *An Introduction*. Translated by Robert Hurley. Harmondsworth, U.K.: Penguin, 1984a.

Foucault, Michel. *The History of Sexuality*. Vol. 2, *The Use of Pleasure*. Translated by Robert Hurley. Harmondsworth, U.K.: Penguin, 1984b.

Foucault, Michel. *The History of Sexuality*. Vol. 3, *The Care of the Self*. London: Penguin, 1988.

Gillis, Stacy, Gillian Howie, and Rebecca Munford, eds. *Third Wave Feminism: A Critical Exploration*. 2d ed. New York: Palgrave Macmillan, 2007.

Irigaray, Luce. "*La Mystérique*." In *Speculum of the Other Woman*, pp. 191–202. Translated by Gillian C. Gill. Ithaca, N.Y.: Cornell University Press, 1985a.

Irigaray, Luce. *This Sex Which Is Not One*. Translated by Catharine Porter. Ithaca, N.Y.: Cornell University Press, 1985b.

Irigaray, Luce. "When the Gods Are Born." In *Marine Lover of Friedrich Nietzsche*, pp. 121–190. Translated by Gillian C. Gill. New York: Columbia University Press, 1991.

Irigaray, Luce. "Divine Women." In *Sexes and Genealogies*, pp. 55–72. Translated by Gillian C. Gill. New York: Columbia University Press, 1993.

Irigaray, Luce. "Equal to Whom?" Translated by Robert Mazzola. In *The Essential Difference*, edited by Naomi Schor and Elizabeth Weed, pp. 63–81. Bloomington: Indiana University Press, 1994.

Irigaray, Luce. "The Redemption of Women." In *Luce Irigaray: Key Writings*, edited by Luce Irigaray, pp. 150–164. London: Continuum, 2004.

Joy, Morny, Kathleen O'Grady, and Judith L. Poxon, eds. *French Feminists on Religion: A Reader*. London: Routledge, 2002.

Piskorowski, Anna. "In Search of Her Father: A Lacanian Approach to Genesis 2–3." In *A Walk in the Garden: Biblical, Iconographical, and Literary Images of Eden*, edited by Paul Morris and Deborah Sawyer, pp. 310–318. Sheffield, U.K.: JSOT Press, 1992.

Sawyer, Deborah F. *God, Gender, and the Bible*. London: Routledge, 2002.

Sawyer, Deborah F. "Gender Criticism: A New Discipline in Biblical Studies or Feminism in Disguise?" In *A Question of Sex? Gender and Difference in the Hebrew Bible and Beyond*, edited by Deborah W. Rooke, pp. 2–17. Sheffield, U.K.: Sheffield Phoenix, 2007.

Schor, Naomi, and Elizabeth Weed, eds. *The Essential Difference*. Bloomington: Indiana University Press, 1994.

Schüssler Fiorenza, Elisabeth. *In Memory of Her: A Feminist Theological Reconstruction of Christian Origins*. 2d ed. London: SCM, 1995.

Deborah F. Sawyer

GENDER AND SEXUALITY: ANCIENT NEAR EAST

Ancient Near Eastern societies were organized hierarchically, with gods at their apexes. Because these were also hegemonies, massive and diminutive socially supported mechanisms were in place to institutionalize this social ordering. Ancient Near Eastern societies were also patriarchal. Gods of both sexes might rule over various confederacies of people, but kings and fathers presided over nations and families. Within the family, the hierarchical arrangements were somewhat nuanced in that age could trump gender. As advised in the *Instructions of Šuruppak*, a Sumerian wisdom text that was copied down well into the later periods of Mesopotamian history:

> The elder brother is indeed like a father; the elder sister is indeed like a mother. Listen therefore to your elder brother, and you should be obedient to your elder sister as if she were your mother. (ETCSL 5.6.1: 172–174)

> You should not speak arrogantly to your mother; that causes hatred for you. You should not question the words of your mother and your personal god. The mother, like Utu, gives birth to the man; the father, like a god, makes him bright(?). The father is like a god: his words are reliable. The instructions of the father should be complied with. (ETCSL 5.6.1: 255–260)

Although some publications investigate the various expectations for and actions of kings and the jobs performed by average men, women, and children in these societies, examination into ancient Near Eastern gender constructs and the role of sexuality in these paradigms is still in its infancy. Furthermore, the ancient Near East was not a monolithic entity. It encompassed a vast region, comprised multiple peoples, and changed both dramatically and subtly over several millennia. These realities, combined with the vagaries of archaeological discovery, make any comprehensive summary not only injudicious but also impossible at this time. Fortunately, we have discovered hundreds of thousands of cuneiform tablets, thousands of which are inscribed with proverbial statements and mythological accounts. What is then possible, and what is provided here, are some of the most obvious and literal definitions for constructs of gender and sexuality that might be culled from the cuneiform record.

Origin of the Sexes. Multiple cuneiform texts allude to, briefly mention, or plainly detail the creation of mortals. Two Sumerian texts, the *Song of the Hoe* and *Enki Goes to Nippur*, simply state that people essentially grew out of the earth like plants. A third Sumerian text, the *Flood Story*, credits the creation of mortals to the four chief deities: An, Enlil, Enki, and Ninḫursaĝ.

Akkadian texts and the Sumerian tale *Enki and Ninmah* provide a different account. These texts attribute the manufacture of humans to three deities: the matriarch goddess alternatively named Ninmah/Nintur/Ninhursag̃ (Sum.) or Bēlet-ilī/Mami/Aruru (Akk.); the male god of fecundity Enki (Sum.) or Ea (Akk.); and a womb goddess who is sometimes primeval, Nammu or Tiāmat.

In *Enki and Ninmah*, after the goddess Nammu creates the "senior" gods and these gods give birth to lesser gods, the lesser gods begin to complain that they have been given a heavy workload. At this time, Enki instructs Nammu:

> My mother, the creature you planned will really come into existence. Impose on him the work of carrying baskets. You should knead clay from the top of the **abzu**; the birth-goddesses(?) will nip off the clay and you shall bring the form into existence. Let Ninmah act as your assistant; and let Ninimma, Šu-zi-ana, Ninmada, Ninbarag, Ninmug....and Ninguna stand by as you give birth. My mother, after you have decreed his fate, let Ninmah impose on him the work of carrying baskets. (ETCSL 1.1.2: 30–37)

Thus, it is Nammu's original idea to create humans, but it is Enki who advises her as to how and which materials to use. Mortals must be made from the clay of the **abzu**, the subterranean waters. Multiple womb goddesses are then necessary for their gestation, and Ninmah must establish the destiny of these unsexed ungendered new beings.

Further along in the story, Ninmah boasts, "A person's body can be either good or bad and whether I make a fate good or bad depends on my will" (54–55). Enki then challenges Ninmah and declares that he will counterbalance her. In order to test Enki's assertion, Ninmah creates a variety of disabled mortals (e.g., one with broken feet). For each of these Enki is able to assign a place in society. Enki then takes it upon himself to design a creature to test Ninmah's skill at allocating destinies. With the help of a womb goddess, Enki creates Umul, a creature so weak, feeble, deaf, and dumb that he or she cannot function. Ninmah decrees that the creature

is neither alive nor dead and therefore belongs to no known realm and cannot be a part of any society. It is difficult to understand how Enki wins this contest because the text is quite broken, but all are told at the conclusion of the account to praise the penis of Enki.

Similar motives for the creation of humans are recorded in the Akkadian texts *Atrahasīs* and *Enūma Eliš*, and the bilingual *Creation of Humanity*. In each account, as in *Enki and Ninmah*, mortals are devised for the express purpose of laboring for the gods. *Atrahasīs* and *Enūma Eliš* both record that mortals were created after rebellions. In *Atrahasīs*, rebellion occurs because of the workload placed upon the Igigi gods by the Anunnaki. To squash the mutiny, the Anunnaki decide to create laborers. Bēlet-ilī is summoned, but, before she can begin her work, she declares that Ea must aid her. Ea then commands that one of the rebelling gods must be slaughtered so that Bēlet-ilī can mix his flesh and blood with purified clay. This she does and then nips off fourteen pieces of earth. Seven pieces she puts to the right and seven to the left. With the help of the womb goddesses, Bēlet-ilī creates seven males and seven females. The text is careful to state that the new beings are created in sets.

In *Enūma Eliš*, a great coup occurs with the young god Marduk remaining the victor. After creating the world out of his vanquished nemesis the goddess Tiāmat, Marduk promptly declares that he will create humans to relieve the work of the gods. He then slaughters the "god who makes war," Qingu, for it is Qingu's punishment to be exsanguinated for the project. Marduk performs the creation with the help of Ea. No further details are given. No matriarch deity is involved in the creation, nor are any womb goddesses mentioned. In the bilingual *Creation of Humanity*, the Anuna gods decide to slaughter an Alla-god from Uzuma. It is presumed that he too is a rebel of some sort, as he is mentioned in the company of other vanquished foes elsewhere. Although no further details are provided, the purpose for the creation of humanity is once again to toil for the gods.

Other Akkadian (and bilingual texts) tend to credit only the matriarch goddess and do not mention

Ea or a womb goddess. In *Ludlul Bēl Nēmeqi* and *Nisaba and Wheat*, it is Aruru alone who is said to have created mortals out of clay with her fingers. In the late Akkadian dialogue *The Babylonian Theodicy*, one speaker attributes the creation of humans to Aruru, but his companion attributes it to three gods: "Narru, the king of the gods, who created humans the majestic Zulummar, who dug out the clay/And mistress Mami, the queen who formed them" (BWL, p. 89: 276–278). Narru is here an alternative name for Anu-Enlil and Zulummar for Ea.

These myths not only describe feminine and masculine roles in procreation but also demonstrate that neither mortal sex, female nor male, was "naturally" privileged over the other. The sexes were not ranked at the outset, with one sex created as primary and the other as secondary. In each of these tales, the sex of the original human is either not mentioned or humans are created in pairs. It should be noted, however, that the right side is frequently the masculine side, the side of fortune, and the left side is feminine, the side of ill omen. Some suggest that when, in *Atrahasīs*, Bēlet-ilī sets seven pieces of clay to the left and seven to the right, this differentiation indicates that men were considered inherently superior. Perhaps, but the placement is more likely a portent: women are not created inherently inferior but are recognized to have received an ill-fated assignment in society.

That neither male nor female children were automatically prized is reflected in two directives in the *Instructions of Šuruppak*: "You should not abuse a ewe; otherwise you will give birth to a daughter. You should not throw a lump of earth into a money chest(?); otherwise you will give birth to a son" (ETCSL 5.6.1: 246–247). In theory at least, parents could avoid producing either a daughter or son. This proverb's suggestion that male children could also be undesirable may surprise the modern reader.

Mesopotamians were well aware that sexual intercourse between females and males of various species could lead to pregnancy. There is evidence that males were believed to be responsible for engendering the child while females were responsible for the gestation and delivery only; thus, mortal women are the equivalent of the womb goddess. This view is also exhibited in the above quoted proverb: "The mother, like Utu, gives birth to the man; the father, like a god, makes him bright(?)." Fecundity was a masculine responsibility. In the Sumerian myth *Enki and Ninhursaĝ*, Ninmaḫ, a divine being, is referred to as *bānītu* ("creatrix"); and yet the Akkadian term *bānû* "creator, begetter" is not used of mortal women but only fathers and grandfathers. The gods of abundance (Sum. **hegal**; Akk. *hegallu*) were Enki/Ea and the weather god Adad.

The myths discussed in the preceding also reveal another gendered role in procreation: the bestowal of a mortal's fate. Although in *Enki and Ninmaḫ* Enki's cunning is said to trump Ninmaḫ's ability to dictate fate, such a view is challenged by the *Instructions of Šuruppak*, which claims: "The wet-nurses in the women's quarters determine the fate of their lord" (ETCSL 5.6.1: 254); similarly, a birth incantation invokes Gula, the goddess of medicine and midwifery, to "determine [the child's] fate when cutting the umbilical cord" (Stol, 2000, p. 61).

Gender Terms. Sumerian has multiple abstract terms for age categories. One such example is **nambanda** ("childhood"), which can be used adverbially "childish/childlike." Most of these age categories are unisex and unigender. Four are not:

1. **namkisikil** "youthful femininity, maidenly"
2. **namguruš** "youthful masculinity, youthfully (m)" (**namšul**)
3. **namumma** "senior femininity, elderly (f)"
4. **namabba** "senior masculinity, elderly (m)"

None of these four terms occurs frequently, but the Sumerian debate poem the *Heron and the Turtle* (ETCSL 5.9.2) demonstrates that each was considered a separate performance with differing characteristics:

The small **enbar** reed tightens her headdress: it is good as a young maiden (**namkisikil**).

The **ubzal** reed goes about the city: it is good as a young man (**namĝuruš**).

The **gašam** reed digs in the ground: it is good as an old man (**namabba**).

The **zi** reed…on its own: it is good as an old woman (**namumma**).

It is difficult for the modern reader to grasp firmly the differing qualities of the various reeds, but their specified actions are informative. From this list it may be ascertained that youthful femininity is associated with appearance, youthful masculinity with public action, elder masculinity with a stubborn nature, and perhaps elder femininity with some form of independence.

Two additional abstract gendered categories, **nammunus** and **namnitah,** refer to femininity and masculinity more generally but their attestation is exceedingly rare. Akkadian also has age-based categories, but it does not have age-based gender categories. It has only "general femininity" (*sinnišūtu*) and "general masculinity" (*eṭlūtu* or *zikrūtu*). An alternative method of referring to a gendered performance is to say that someone is behaving "like a woman" or "like a man." This is rare.

That gender roles were conferred at birth according to sex is revealed by an exceptionally early Sumerian ritual that prescribes: "If it is female, let her bring out of it the spindle and a pin; / If it is a male, let her bring out of it the throwing stick and the weapon" (Stol, 2000, p. 60). Similar to the modern Western practice of dressing female babies in pink and male babies in blue, these objects symbolically assign an expected gender performance for each originally unmarked child. The deity associated with ordaining gender roles and their characteristics is the goddess Inana. It is unclear if this power is merely a result of her having received the great **me** (the organizing principles of society) or if the ability is specific to her.

There is much debate over whether a third and possibly fourth gender was recognized in any ancient Near Eastern culture during any period. This article does not address this issue, in part because there is no incontrovertible evidence for such a conception, but also because several articles in this volume discuss the arguments for and against this possibility.

Išme-Dagan K records that Inana was entrusted by the divine couple Enlil and Ninlil:

…to turn a man into a woman and a woman into a man, to change one into the other, to make young women dress in order to be masculine (**namguruš**) on their right side, to make young men dress in order to be feminine (**namkisikil**) on the left side. (ETCSL 2.5.4.11: 21–23)

This sentiment is repeated in the great bilingual hymn to Inana *Ininšagura*. To perform this gender reassignment, Inana reverses the expected procedure stated in the birth incantation. She places spindles into the hands of men and gives weapons to women. Although Inana does not give a comb to the men in this text, a royal dedication by Ur-Namma to the Netherworld goddess Ḫušbisaĝ confirms its symbolic nature. The Sumerian king gives her "a silver hair clasp adorned with lapis-lazuli, and a comb of [general] femininity" (**nammunus**). Inana is also said to have the ability to alter a man's masculinity (*zikrūtu*) in the Akkadian *Erra Epic*, a text dated to the Middle Babylonian period (or possibly later). That masculinity continued to not be an assumed quality is confirmed when the Neo-Assyrian kings refer to masculinity as a divine gift granted to them by the gods Nergal, Ninurta, and Sîn. That youthful masculinity was not considered eternal is demonstrated by the proverb: "My youthful masculinity (**namguruš**) has left my loins, like a runaway donkey" (ETCSL 6.1.9: 8).

Definitions of Masculinity and Femininity. The Sumerian term for general masculinity, **namnitah,** is attested only once and in reference to the female deity Inana. In the Sumerian legend *Gilgameš and the Bull of Heaven*, the young goddess is said to grasp the tether of the bull of heaven in a "masculine" fashion. Here a masculine performance is characterized by confidence, strength, and power.

The "place of masculinity" (**ki.namnitah**) is an alternative name for the battlefield (also known as the "playground of Inana"). In the Sumerian tale *Gilgameš, Enkidu, and the Netherworld*, the youthful Enkidu does not die in battle (i.e., on the field of masculinity) as expected but instead travels to the Netherworld of his own accord, a remarkable feat. Throughout Mesopotamian history, war was seen as a festival to perform masculinity. This is confirmed by its attestation in the Akkadian text the *Erra Epic* and in the bilingual myth the *Exploits of Ninurta*, a text copied into the Neo-Assyrian period. In this latter text, the god Ninurta is implored, "Do not lift your arm to the smiting of weapons, to the festival of youthful masculinity (Sum. **ezen namĝuruš.a(k)**; Akk. *isinni eṭlūti*), to Inana's dance! Lord, do not go to such a great battle as this!"

Kings, mortal and divine, are frequently extolled for their youthful masculinity, which is characterized by military acumen and prowess. The Ur III king Šulgi, designated as the "god of youthful masculinity" (**namĝuruš**), declares "[I am] the foremost of the troops. When I stretch the bowstring on the bow, when I fit a perfect arrow to it, I shoot the bow's arrow with the full strength of my arms" (ETCSL 2.4.2: 81–83). In a hymn to Inana (*Inana E*), her paramour Dumuzi is lauded as "complete in his youthful masculinity" (**namĝuruš**), for he rejoices in battle as at a festival. Dumuzi is the "mighty hero, [who] kills everyone with his shining (**šita**) mace" (ETCSL 4.7.5: 31–33). The Old Babylonian king Samsu-iluna calls himself the great dagger of youthful masculinity (**ĝiri gal namĝuruš.a[k]**). Ištar is also said to receive masculinity (*eṭlūtu*), greatness, and strength from Enki in the Old Babylonian Akkadian myth *Aguašaya*; she is also said to perform a whirl-dance, which demonstrates her masculinity (*zikrūssa*). The purpose of the text is to both praise and consider her fiercely martial nature. That strength is a characteristic of youthful masculinity is further confirmed when the legendary hero Gilgameš is extolled for being beautiful in his masculinity, possessed of power. Finally, the Neo-Assyrian king Šalmaneser III attributes his ability to subjugate lands to his masculinity (*zikrūssu*).

Although in the preceding examples the masculinity of mortal kings, male divine beings, and the goddess Inana/Ištar is extolled and construed primarily as a martial performance, cuneiform texts also counsel a very different construct of masculinity for a young man to perform. The Sumerian text the *Song of the Hoe* praises the agricultural implement, the hoe, as the strength of youthful masculinity (**namĝuruš**).

This would seem to indicate that an ability to perform difficult manual field work was considered part of the ideal masculine construct. General prescriptions for normative gender performances may be discerned from proverbial and wisdom texts. In the *Instructions of Šuruppak* (ETCSL 5.6.1), a noble son, Ziusudra, is advised to be a prudent and reserved man. Multiple directives advise that he not be "quarrelsome" and stay far away from arguments, lest he become entangled in them and disgrace himself. He is further advised to remain sexually sensible and modest: "You should not have sex with your slave girl: she will chew(?) you up" (49); "You should not commit rape on someone's daughter; the courtyard will learn it" (62); and, "You should not play around with a married young woman: the slander could be serious. My son, you should not sit alone in a chamber with a married woman" (33–34). Ziusudra is told to be restrained in his revelry: "You should not pass judgment when you drink beer" (126); he also is advised to be married, for "A married man is well equipped; the unmarried man makes his bed in a haystack" (185–186). Seemingly contrary to the praise of a man who wars, Ziusudra is counseled to "know submission," not murder people, and be restrained.

Sumerian and Akkadian proverbial sayings, which reflect and perpetuate cultural values and were copied in scribal classrooms almost verbatim for millennia, corroborate the performance of the nonviolent nonaggressive construct of masculinity advised in the *Instructions of Šuruppak*. According to these maxims, the respected man is mentally and emotionally disciplined, married, and dependable. Responsibility for and to others is extolled by the proverb: "The early working shepherd, the early working farmer, the young man who got married while he was young— who compares to them?" (ETCSL 6.1.19: g7). Failure to provide for one's family is condemned by the proverb: "He who does not support a wife, he who does not support a child, has no cause for celebration" (ETCSL 6.1.1:153). Promiscuity is never extolled as a masculine virtue or as a naturalized expectation. Instead, it is written that, "A dishonest man chases after women's genitals; an unreliable man has two sickles" (ETCSL 6.23: 9).

Promiscuity of the mouth was also denigrated. To perform ideal masculinity, a man must be of considered mind and speech, so that he may proudly say: "My mouth makes me comparable with men. My mouth gets me reckoned among men" (BWL, p. 238: 5–8).

Although the audience for both wisdom and proverbial texts ostensibly may have been both sexes, the phraseology of the proverbs suggests that men were the ultimate targets. Men are advised proper wife selection: "The wife of a man who cannot talk well is a female slave" (BWL, p. 238: 3–4); "A man [installs] a good woman as a fertile field"; "By marrying a spendthrift wife, by begetting a spendthrift son (I got solace for my unhappy heart and confirmed it). A spendthrift wife in the house is worse than all devils" (BWL, p. 267: 4–7); and "A thriftless wife living in a house is worse than all diseases" (ETCSL 6.1.1:154). Proverbs such as these also encourage husbands to police the behavior of their wives and passively advise them in societally condoned behavior.

As signified by the spindle, the symbol of femininity in the birth incantation, the manufacture of textiles was typically a women's profession. In the myth *Enki and the World Order*, Enki is said to improve the feminine (**nammunus**) task of weaving by creating the loom. The ideal role for a woman in Mesopotamian societies was first and foremost to support her mother and father, and, once she left home, her husband and his family. In the Sumerian legend *Sargon and Ur-Zababa*, the good wife of Lugal-zage-si is said to be a shelter for either her husband or son. Proverbial sayings reinforce such constructs of femininity: "A man's wife is his supervisor(?). A man's son is his protective shade. A man's daughter is his eager servant. A man's daughter-in-law is his policeman" (ETCSL 6.1.19: C7). These are folk sayings, however: while they may reveal societal tenets, reality could be quite different, as displayed by a letter in which a daughter pleads for her father to take her advice, "even if [she is] a woman" (ARM 10 31 r. 7).

The proverbs suggest various expectations for girls and women. They should be dependent: "A woman with her own property ruins the house"

(ETCSL 5.6.1: 220). They should consider themselves fortunate to be married: "A plant sweet as a husband does not grow in the steppe" (ETCSL 6.1.1:126). They should be demure, while boys should be vocal: "A chattering girl is silenced by her mother. A chattering boy is not silenced by his mother" (ETCSL 6.1.1:185). If a husband is reserved and does not establish verbal submission over his wife, his authority is questioned: "He whose speech is humble, his wife is a slave girl."

Alternative constructs of femininity are also evident during certain periods. Proper young women were instructed not to emulate a slave girl. Although married female slaves might interact with their husbands as freewomen did, proverbial descriptions suggest that a servant or slave girl's interactions with her male (and likely female) owners were not always decorous. Proverbial sayings describe these girls and women as outspoken, willful, and occasionally cantankerous. Proverbial sayings and wisdom texts repeatedly mock men who let their female servants/slaves control them. Senior femininity (**nammumma**) may have been associated with prestige: "The goat spoke in the manner of a wise old woman but acted in the manner of an unclean woman" (ETCSL 6.1.3:153). Although generally assumed to refer to a prostitute, the proverbial statement, "My vagina is fine; (yet) according to my people (its use) for me is ended" (BWL, p. 248: 14–16) likely concerns an (older) woman who could no longer bear children. She seems to suggest that although she may not be able to attract a man through her procreative abilities, she can still provide sexual pleasure and is therefore of some use to society.

Sexuality. To maintain hierarchically ordered gender systems, a society must sanction particular sexual activities and their gendered performances. Cuneiform law codes and administrative texts regulate who is responsible for transgressions of proper sexuality—for example, if a young woman's "pure" status is "taken" by a sexual encounter or if a highborn man's status is "taken" through rape. Love Lyrics and love poetry celebrate particular feminine and masculine erotic characteristics and particular sexual performances: in both, vaginal penetration is persistently highlighted. Another genre, omens, reveals that certain sexual actions were thought to herald future outcomes: for example, male sexual penetration of a highborn man portends a rise in status. Although the law codes state that a man who commits a same-sex act is to be gang raped, the omen suggests that it is beneficial for a man to sexually penetrate a highborn man.

This section of this article investigates Sumerian and Akkadian texts that present sexual scenarios and activities and sexually objectified body parts that are celebrated. First, however, a disclaimer is in order. Most of the cuneiform texts that explicitly mention sexual acts have deities as their protagonists rather than humans. While recognizing that norms for divine and human agents may have differed, the discussion that follows does treat the actions of deities as reflective of expected human sexual performances.

Sexuality was considered one of the great **me**, the building blocks of society. These "blocks" ranged from various skills (e.g., metallurgy) to abstract concepts such as strife and harmony. When in the Sumerian myth *Inana and Enki* Inana travels to visit Enki to procure the **me**, among the many items she receives from him are "the standard, the quiver, sexual intercourse, (and) kissing" (ETCSL 1.3.1: F29). Because kissing traditionally follows sexual intercourse in Sumerian texts, this list should likely be understood as progressive: penis, vagina, sexual intercourse, kissing.

In the myth *Enki and the World Order*, Enki is said to assign sexuality to Ezina, "Barley":

> Enki placed in charge of all this her whose head and body are dappled, whose face is covered in syrup, the mistress who causes sexual intercourse, the power of the Land, the life of the black-headed—Ezina, the good bread of the whole world. (ETCSL 1.1.13: 330–334)

Later in the same text, Inana is referred to as the one "of the great **me** who allows sexual intercourse in the open squares of Kulaba (an ancient Sumerian city)."

So important was sex that persons who died before experiencing it were lamented as not having lived a full life. Two of the Mesopotamian demons were those who died too young to have had sexual intercourse, the female Ardat-lilî and the male Eṭel-lilî. Owing to jealousy, Ardat-lilî could cause problems with pregnancies, nervous behaviors, and elicit seizures, while Eṭel-lilî could cause medical problems for children.

Texts in which deities or kings are the lovers are referred to by modern scholars as Love Lyrics. These were written in Sumerian and date to the early Old Babylonian period, but they reflect Ur III (and possibly earlier) traditions. The designation that appears on many of these texts is either **bal.bal.e** (possibly meaning "dialogue or duet") or a term that suggests accompaniment by a musical instrument. Most of the Love Lyrics revolve around the divine pair Inana and Dumuzi, but there are several texts in which the lovers are the Ur III king Šu-Sîn and his wife Kūbatum. The texts are filled with both suggestive and frank statements of desire and sexual arousal. Lovers meet at dusk in gardens, streets, squares, and in homes. Lovemaking tends to take place indoors on syrup-laden beds with the lingering scent of cedar. Frequently, agricultural metaphors are employed to great effect, highlighting the ardor of the protagonists, who are compared to rising apple trees, burgeoning lettuce, date syrup, and beer. In allusions to sexual intercourse, the woman is a well-watered furrow. The man is entreated to plough the field, dig the ditch, or churn the butter.

A genre of texts in which deities and/or, possibly, mortals, are the protagonists are simply referred to by modern scholars as love poetry. These texts were written in either Sumerian or Akkadian and likely date to the Old Babylonian period and later. We know of them primarily from several very broken compositions but also from two Middle Babylonian catalogs that list "titles" for hundreds of poems. Many of these are classified as *zamāru* ("song") or **bal.bal.e**. The titles and the few full exemplars of the genre suggest that these compositions were not as explicit as the Love Lyrics, although the subject matter seems to be similar. The settings are gardens and streets at dusk, and the main speakers seem to be women. The dialogue format is common. Many of the texts do not focus on descriptions of sexual arousal but appear to have been marriage rituals between gods. These *hadāšu/hadaššūtu* texts continue to be attested into the Neo-Assyrian and Neo-Babylonian periods. The main couples were Nanaya and Muāti; Nabû, Tašmētu, and Nanaya; Šamaš and Aya (Sippar); Marduk and Sarpanītu (Babylon); Anu and Antu (Uruk); and perhaps Bānītu and Ninurta.

Gods and kings are also depicted as lovers in myths and certain hymns outside of the "love" corpus. Divine couplings are the subject of the Sumerian myths *Enlil and Ninlil*, *Enlil and Sud*, *Enki and Ninḫursaĝ*, *Marriage of Martu*, and the Akkadian myth *Nergal and Ereškigal*. Certain vignettes in *The Epic of Gilgameš* also fall into this category.

Incantations for the acquisition of a love interest, known as *râmu* ("love charms"), span almost the length of the written record. The earliest date to the Old Akkadian period and were written in Akkadian. The protagonists are generally described as having a burning passion; they declare that they are no longer able to function properly in life without said interest and implore the gods to intervene. Many of the tropes are similar to those found in the Love Lyrics and love poetry. Alternatively, incantations to expel a love adversary were called *zêru* ("hate charms"). Exemplars of this type of "sinister magic" are few and demonstrate an extreme jealousy on the part of the protagonist.

The largest collection of incantations that address sexual matters are erectile dysfunction prescriptions known as *šazigas*. Written in Akkadian, these texts never specify whether the purpose of the alleviation of the dysfunction is pleasure or procreation. A Middle Assyrian MA catalog of *šazigas* discovered in the Assyrian city of Aššur lists prescriptions with such titles as:

> Incantation: Wild Ass! Wild Ass! Wild bull! Wild Bull!
> Incantation: Ram who has an erection for mating.
> Incantation: Let the wind blow! Let the grove quake!
> [Incantation]:Flow river of potency! (Biggs, 1967, pp. 12–13)

As the titles make apparent, the tone, settings, and metaphors are quite different from those of the Love Lyrics and love poetry. These texts do not describe lush agricultural locations with rich aromas, hazy breezes, and sweet substances. Instead, in the *šazigas* male sufferers are commanded to perform as wild animals or as weapons. The setting is the bedroom, but an incantation priest or even livestock might be present. Several different deities are invoked to aid the patient, such as the trio Ištar, Nanaya (designated as the *bēlet kuzbi*, "Sovereign of Sex Appeal"), and/or Išhara (who is referred to as the *bēlet ramê*, "Sovereign of Love"). Occasionally the goddesses Gazbaba and Kanišurra are also called upon. A second set of invoked gods is Ištar (referred to as *telītu*, "the able one"), Ea, Šamaš, and Asalluḫi. A very few call upon Ištar and Marduk. In these instances, Ištar is called *bēlet ramê*, likely because she is syncretized with Išhara. Erectile dysfunction is described as a man's potency being blocked or bound: potency must be released. In only one instance is a witch mentioned as the culprit. In one text, the problem is attributed to the "Hand of Ištar"; in another, to the "Hand of Marduk and Ištar." Actual sexual diseases are described as "The Hand of Šamaš," which is upon a man when his penis drips blood; and "The Hand of Sîn," which may be the diagnosis for a penis covered in sores.

Terminology. As in any culture, Mesopotamian texts describe body parts, sexual actions, love, and lust in multiple euphemistic ways. The following list gives some of the more general, frequently attested, and provocative expressions for the body; not intended to be exhaustive, this list does not, in the main, include legal terms, which tend to be imprecise and reserved.

Body parts/fluids.

body: Sum. **su, su.bar**; Akk. *zumru*
breasts: Sum. **ubur**; Akk. *tulû*
   nipple: Sum. **akan**; Akk. *ṣertu*
buttocks: Sum. **dur, gudu**; Akk. *šuburru*
   anus: Sum. **ki.bid**; Akk. *qinnatu*
eyes: Sum. **igi**; Akk. *īnu*
face: Sum. **muš**; Akk. *zīmu, maḫrum, pānû*
   forehead **saĝ.ki**; Akk. *pūtu*
genitalia/crotch: Sum. **ur**; Akk. *ūru, sūnu*
   lap/knees: (occasional euphemism for crotch) Sum. **murub**; Akk. *birku*

heart/core: Sum. **šag**; Akk. *libbu, karšu, qablu*

lip(s) (also labia): Sum. **nundum, tun**; Akk. *šaptu*, pl. *šapātu*

mouth (also vagina): Sum. **ka**; Akk. *pû*

penis: Sum. **ĝeš**; Akk. *išaru/ušaru/mušaru*

more euphemistic: Sum. **dim** "pillar"; Akk. *emūqu* "strength," *qaštu* "bow"

semen (water): Sum. **a**; Akk. *riḫītu*

more euphemistic: **a** "strength, sexual potency"; Akk. *idu*

to be impotent is to have no strength *idi la išû*

testicles: Sum. **šir**; Akk. *išku*

thigh: Sum. **haš**; Akk. *ḫallu, emšu, šapru, pēmu*

vagina: Sum. **gala, guruš-garaš**; Akk. *ḫurdatu, bissūru* (labia see lips above)

more euphemistic: mouth (see above), lip(s) (see above)

vaginal secretion (urine): Sum. **kaš**; Akk. *šīnātu*; also, *ru'tu* (spittle)

Verbs used to indicate sexual activities.

to desire: Sum. **al dug**; Akk. *erēšu*

to embrace: Sum. **gu la**; Akk. *edēru*

to ejaculate/inseminate: Sum. **dub nir**; Akk. *reḫû*

to engage in coitus: Sum. **ĝeš dug, ĝeš du** "to do the penis" or **haš dug** "to do the thigh" or **ene sud dug** "to do far-away play"; Akk. *salālu* "to sleep," *niālu/nâlu* "lie down," or *reḫû*, "to pour out," and, occasionally, *erēšu* "to sow" or *petû* "to open." More derogatory (used primarily of animals): *rakābu* "to mount or ride."

to have an erection: Sum. **ĝeš zig, šag zig**; Akk. *nīš libbi*

to kiss: Sum. **ne sub**; Akk. *nasāku*

to masturbate (masculine): Sum. **ĝeš zig** "to stimulate the penis"

to (make) love: Sum. **ki aĝ**; Akk. *ramû*

to touch: Sum. **šu dug, šu tag**; Akk. *lapātu*

Additional.

to be naked: adj. Akk. *erû*

to (be) strip: Sum. **sug, zil**

Sex Appeal. The Sumerian term for charm/seductiveness is **hili**, Akk. *kuzbu*. The Sumerian term for

lust is **la-la**, Akk. *lalû* or *dādu*. All of these terms may be used of either sex and at times do not seem to take on different attributes when used of a particular sex. The essential meaning of all of these terms is a sexy lushness, a luxuriant sensuality.

Many of the Mesopotamian gods are referred to as having **hili** or **la-la**. In the bilingual myth *Lugal-e*, the god Ninurta is said to have inexhaustible **hili** (*kuzbu*), while the goddess Nanše's **hili** is praised when her priest Ur-Ningirsu says that "he created [an] (object of) feminine **hili** (**hili nammunus.ak**) for her" (RIME 3/2.01.02.2030). In *Rim-Sîn H*, Nintur is said to have created Inana daughter of An as the goddess who speaks with femininity (**nammunus**), who is filled with seductiveness (**namhili**). Sumerian kings are frequently said to have been chosen to rule because of their **hili** or **la-la**. The goddess Bau selects the Lagašite king Gudea for this reason, as Inana does the Ur III king Šulgi, and Nanaya does Išbi-Erra, king of Isin. It is not only female deities who select for this reason. Nana, the male moon god, who is said to be full of both **hili** and **la-la**, chooses the Ur III king Ur-Namma in part because of his **hili**. Although we have no texts that truly extol the average person's level of sex appeal, it must be presumed to have been of significant import since there was a very real fear of it being taken, as is revealed in the great anti-witchcraft text Maqlu:

[The witch] robs the handsome young man of his strength. She takes the pretty girl's fruit.
With her glance she takes her sex-appeal (*kuzubša*).
She glimpses the young man; she robs him of his strength. She glimpses the girl; she takes her fruit.
(Meier, 1937, p. 22 III: 8–12)

In *Enki and the World Order* (ETCSL 1.1.13), Enki is the god whose word "fills the young man's heart with vigour…[and] bestows loveliness (**hili**) on the young woman's head, so that the people in their settled cities gaze at her in wonder" (32–37). According to the hymn *Inana C*, "desirability (**la-la**) and arousal (erection),…are yours, Inana" (120–121); thus, this goddess too was in charge of sex appeal. As mentioned previously, in *šaziga* invocations several goddesses are said to be in charge of sexuality: Išhara (occasionally Ištar) is called the *bēlet ramê* ("Sovereign of Love") and Nanaya is the *bēlet kuzbi*. In other cuneiform texts, the sun god Šamaš is said to be the *kuzbu* of the land, and in others the grain goddess Nisaba is the *kuzbu* of the gods. In one ritual, Nisaba is said to be the one who places *kuzbu* on people. When the god Nabû takes over Nisaba's role as divine scribe during the late Middle Babylonian period, he also seems to take over this function, for he comes to be called the *kuzbu* of the gods. In a prayer to the moon god Sîn, Tašmētum, the consort of Nabû, is said to be the goddess of *kuzbu* and *dādu*.

What Is Attractive/Sexy. As much of the information presented here will suggest, sexual activity was meant to be enjoyed for its own sake and not necessarily only for procreative purposes. Although offspring were a desired product of a marital union, there is evidence for methods to avoid pregnancy and birth. Certain stones and plants bear names such as the "not giving birth stone" and the "not getting pregnant plant." There are also laws that proscribe abortion (indicating that if practiced it was illicitly done); however, these may have more to do with violations of paternal rights than concern with children themselves.

Descriptions detailing the physical beauty, attractive nature, or magnificent actions of gods and kings can be found in a variety of genres from hymns to prayers to royal inscriptions. Because of this, the descriptions discussed in the following section are restricted to those that occur in texts of an obviously sexual nature.

Nubility. The age of socially accepted sexual maturation for girls seems to have been when they were pubescent (Sum. **ki.sikil**; Akk. *ardatu*, *batultu*), that is to say, when they exhibited pubic hair and when they developed protruding breasts. In *Dumuzi and Inana* (*DI*) *C*, Inana declares exuberantly:

> See now, my breasts stand out; see now, hair (**siki**) has grown on my vagina (**gala**), signifying (?) my progress to the embrace of a man. Let us be very glad! Dance, dance! O Bau, let us be very glad about my vagina

(**gala**)! Dance, dance! Later on it will delight him, it will delight him! (ETCSL 4.8.3: 42–48)

In legal situations, the terms for pubescent and prepubescent girl (Sum. **ki.sikil.tur**; Akk. *batūltu*) come to also mean "a virgin girl." In the myth *Ninlil and Enlil*, the young (**ki.sikil**) goddess Ninlil, in describing her physical state, cries to the young Enlil: "My vagina is small, it does not know pregnancy. My lips are young, they do not know kissing." Unlike Inana, who delights in her sexual readiness (and her future partner's enjoyment of it), Ninlil either plays coy in the myth or seeks to dissuade Enlil's advances with these statements.

The Akkadian term for a virgin boy is *batūlu*. It is rarely attested; it appears only in parallelism with *batūltu*. The term for a pubescent boy is Sum. **ĝuruš**; Akk. *eṭlu*. The term for prepubescent boy is Sum. **ĝuruš.tur**; Akk. *batūlu*. Depending on the interpretation of the metaphors present, *DI E* might contain a scene in which Inana rejoices in the sexual maturation of Dumuzi. The text begins with Inana declaring:

> He has sprouted (**ba.lam**), he has burgeoned (**ba.lam. lam**), he is well-watered lettuce, my shaded garden of the desert, richly flourishing, my grain lovely in beauty (**hili**) in its furrows he is well-watered lettuce; my first-class fruitful apple tree, he is well-watered lettuce. (ETCSL 4.8.5: 1–4)

"Sprouted" (**ba.lam ba.lam.lam**) has the further connotations of "to flourish; to make grow luxuriantly." Lettuce is generally understood by modern scholars to symbolize pubic hair; thus, it may be that Inana delights in Dumuzi having grown luxuriant pubic hair signifying sexual maturity. This supposition is supported by her further praise of him as a fruitful apple tree. If the tree is understood to be Dumuzi's penis and the apples testicles, the fact that the testicles are "fruitful" suggests Dumuzi has reached gonadarche, puberty. The reason for Dumuzi's "burgeoning" may be because Inana's "grain [is] lovely in (**hili**) in its furrows," but then we might expect a description of the tree growing from a sapling to a sturdy tree.

Descriptions. When they wished to appear attractive to a love interest, both men and women used similar preparations. In *DI C*, when getting ready for her "date" with her paramour, Inana says:

> I have put lots of kohl on my eyes, I have arranged…the nape of my neck.
>
> I have washed my dangling hair, I have tested my weapons that make his reign propitious. I have straightened my tousled head of hair, I have tightened my loosened hairgrips, and let my hair fall down the back of my neck. I have put a golden bracelet on my wrist. I have put little lapis-lazuli beads round my neck, and arranged their buttons over my neck muscles. (ETCSL 4.8.3: 9–18)

And when Gilgameš is said to be particularly sexually appealing to Ištar it is because:

> He washed his hair, he cleaned his bow, he shook his locks down over his back. He cast aside his dirty things, he clothed himself with his clean things, he wrapped himself in cloaks, tied with a sash. Gilgameš put on his crown. (George, 2003, p. 619: vi 1–5)

Both Inana and Gilgameš are concerned with their appearances. The text accentuates their long flowing hair, weapons (euphemism?), and ornamentation (which likely signify their social statuses).

The term for the hair that Gilgameš shakes down his back is *qimmatu* (Akk.), **suhur** (Sum.). The more common term for locks is *šārtu*; *šipātu* (Akk.), **siki** (Sum.). The term **suhur**/*qimmatu* refers to the top of a plant, perhaps a palm tree, where there is the most foliage. It also can indicate a lush crown or mane whose tresses, like those of a horse, go down the back. A curious proverb equates the sex appeal of **suhur** with that of a penis: "A shepherd's sex appeal (**hili**) is his penis; a gardener's sex appeal is his hair (**suhur**)" (ETCSL 6.1.16B: 8–9). *DI Y* suggests that this type of hair is particularly sexy (ETCSL 4.8.25). Inana repeatedly refers to her paramour as, "My one distinguished by a shock of hair (**suhur**), my one distinguished by a shock of hair!" (**suhur**) (34–35). She further exclaims, "Rub it against our breast, my sweet!" (41). Similarly, in *Šu-Sîn A*, the queen Kūbatum declares

that, in addition to his other sexually appealing attributes, her husband Šu-Sîn is well suited for the mane (**suhur**) that he wears.

Sparkling or beautiful eyes seem to be a specifically masculine sexual asset. In *Ninĝišzida C*, the **hili** of youthful masculinity (**namĝuruš**) is equated with having sparkling eyes and in *DI B* and *D* Inana extols the magnificence of Dumuzi's beautiful eyes.

Dumuzi's **hili** is also compared to a lush garden that arouses Inana's interest. In *DI B*, Inana declares: "My desirable one, my desirable one, your charms (**hili**) are lovely, my desirable apple garden, your charms (**hili**) are lovely" (ETCSL 4.8.2: 27–28).

Syrup or honey (Sum. *lal*; Akk. *dišpu*) can also describe the nature of a person's sex appeal. In this same text (*DI B*), Inana is referred to as being a sappy vine and syrup mouthed. Vaginas can also be referred to as sweet. In *DI Y*, Dumuzi declares: "Come(?), my beloved sister! I will…mouth. Her genitals are as sweet as her mouth. Her mouth is as sweet as her genitals" (ETCSL 4.8.25: 48–50).

A further example is *Šu-Sîn A*: "Like her beer her genitals are sweet, her beer is sweet. Like her mouth her genitals are sweet, her beer is sweet." And, in a love charm meant to attract a man, a woman wishes: "May my lips be honey, may my hands be sex appeal (*kuzbu*). May the lip of my pot be a lip of honey" (*ZA* 32 48–50). This association of a woman's sex appeal with her genitalia (pot of honey) is also established in the *Epic of Gilgameš* where Šamhat is commanded to "open her crotch (*ūru*)" so that Enkidu may partake of her *kuzbu*. But being sweet and syrupy is not a feminine attribute alone. In *Šu-Sîn B*, the king's incredible **hili** is referred to as being as sweet as syrup, and in *DI D*, Dumuzi's bed is "dripping with syrup."

Derrières, penises, and bosoms are far less the subject of erotic verse than vaginas. It may be that Inana refers to Dumuzi's penis in *DI Y* when she declares: "My ivory figurine, my golden figure! My object fashioned by a skilled carpenter! My one worked on by a skilled metal worker!" (ETCSL 4.8.25: 46–47). And in *DI B*: "My holy statuette, my holy statuette, your charms (**hili**) are lovely. My alabaster statuette adorned with a lapis-lazuli jewel, your charms (**hili**) are lovely" (ETCSL 4.8.2: 31–32). It is possible that in each of these excerpts the fashioned figurine/holy statuette may refer to an actual statue of Dumuzi, or it may be a double entendre. In *Nanaya H*, the quality of the Nanaya's vagina and buttocks might be celebrated, but the text is too broken to be sure. In cuneiform texts, mention of breasts tends to be reserved for dealing with medical/lactating issues and, in the case of buttocks/anus, medical issues or to explicate humorous proverbial advice.

Explicit Desire for Sex. Cuneiform texts demonstrate a candor that can make the modern reader blush. Although both sexes are described as desirous of sexual intercourse, male protagonists are most often depicted as demanding and aggressive and female protagonists as yearning, even imploring. This is particularly true of the Love Lyrics, love poetry, and love charms (in the latter, both sexes tend to be pitiful). In myths and potency incantations, the situation is very different. In these texts, goddesses and women demand sex and command their men to perform sexually.

The god Enki's desire for sex is direct and blunt when he says to Ninḫursaĝ: "Lie down for me in the marsh, lie down for me in the marsh" in *Enki and Ninḫursaĝ* (ETCSL 1.1.1: 70). Following their coupling, Enki essentially becomes an incestual rapist. He has sex not only with a very unwilling Ninḫursaĝ but also with their three subsequent daughters. Perhaps remembering her experience with Enki, in *Enlil and Ninlil* (ETCSL 1.2.1) Ninḫursaĝ warns her daughter Ninlil to be modest and not go down to the riverbed lest Enlil see her. If this happens, Ninḫursaĝ warns: "Straight away he will want to have intercourse, he will want to kiss! He will be happy to pour lusty semen into the womb, and then he will leave you to it!" (20–21). Ninlil does go down to the riverbed, and Enlil is as aggressively direct as Enki when he says to the goddess: "I want to have sex with you, I want to kiss you" (28–29). Ultimately, Enlil impregnates Ninlil, and scholars debate whether this is one of the first literary records of rape.

A very different tone is apparent in *DI D1*, which describes a goddess's desire for sexual intercourse with her husband:

She desires it, she desires it, she desires the couch.
She desires the couch of heart's joy, she desires the couch.
She desires the couch of the sweet embrace, she desires the couch.
She desires the kingly couch, she desires the couch.
She desires the queenly couch, she desires the couch.
(ETCSL 4.8.30: 18–22)

In these lines, the bed that she desires is the equivalent of the heart's joy, which in turn is equivalent to the sweet embrace, literally the couch of "the good lap/groin." In *Inana H* and *DI P*, the goddesses Nanaya and Inana, speaking in the first person, are both explicit and direct. Nanaya declares to a possible lover: "Do not dig a canal, let me be your canal. Do not plough a field, let me be your field. Farmer, do not search for a wet place, my precious sweet, let this be your wet place..., let this be your furrow..., let this be your desire!" (ETCSL 4.7.8: A 21–29). And in *DI P*, Inana inquires: "My own genitals, the maiden's, a well-watered opened-up mound—who will be their ploughman? My genitals, the lady's, the moist and well-watered ground—who will put an ox there?" (ETCSL 4.8.16: B 26–28).

In none of these examples does the speaker demand sex. Instead, the audience is informed that she "wants it." Both goddesses entice their paramours by indicating that they are sexually aroused and desire penile penetration. Inana's call in *DI P* is answered by Dumuzi, who gallantly declares he will come to his lady's aid: "Lady, the king shall plough them for you; Dumuzi the king shall plough them for you" (ETCSL 4.8.16: B 29–30). Nanaya's petition also seems to be answered, but the text is not as explicit.

Sexual intercourse also seems to be the primary goal of Kūbatum in *Šu-Sîn B*; however, her approach is not to describe her own arousal but rather her ability to please her husband:

Man let me do the sweetest things to you. My precious sweet, let me bring you honey. In the bedchamber dripping with honey let us enjoy over and over your allure, the sweet thing. (ETCSL 2.4.4.2: 9–10)

I know where to give physical pleasure to your body…I know how to bring heart's delight to your heart…Since you have fallen in love with me, lad, if only you would do your sweet thing to me…if only you would handle your sweet place, if only grasp your place that is sweet as honey. (ETCSL 2.4.4.2: 18–23)

It is debated by modern scholars whether this text was written because Kūbatum had genuine affection for Šu-Sîn or if the text was in fact commissioned by the king to make it appear as if he was incredibly desired.

Vegetative metaphor was not the only type of imagery utilized. In two texts, Dumuzi the dairy farmer seems also to be quite capable of pleasing Inana sexually. In a *balbale to Inana* we read:

Lady, you who wander among sweet-voiced cows and gentle-voiced calves in the cattle-pen; young woman, no sooner will you arrive there, Inana, than the churn should sound! May the churn of your spouse sound, Inana, may the churn of Dumuzi sound! May the churn sound, may the churn of Dumuzi sound! (ETCSL 4.8a: 1–8)

And in *DI P*:

Make the milk yellow for me, my bridegroom, make the milk yellow for me, and I will drink the milk with you, my bridegroom! Wild bull Dumuzi, make the milk yellow for me, and I will drink the milk with you, my bridegroom!…the goat's milk…the fold; lord (?) of all things, fill my holy churns. (ETCSL 4.8.16: C18–23)

The confident sexual nature of female deities is also apparent in Akkadian literature. In *The Epic of Gilgameš*, Ištar demands of Gilgameš, "you be the bridegroom!…grant me your fruits." In one of Gilgameš's several retorts to this mandate, he recalls that the goddess commanded a former lover, Išullānu: "put out your hand and stroke our vagina" (*hurdatu*). It is possible that this latter statement is the same as a curious set of instructions found in *DI B*. The woman says:

You are to place your right hand on my genitals while your left hand rests on my head, bringing your mouth close to my mouth, and taking my lips in your mouth: thus you shall take an oath for me. This is the oath of women, my brother of the beautiful eyes. (ETCSL 4.8.2: 21–26)

The text in *The Epic of Gilgameš* could simply refer to clitoral stimulation as it seems to in an OB Bawdy Ballad in which several young men (and women?) petition Ištar the *telītum* ("able one") for the honor of stroking her vagina/clitoris (*hurdatu*). In the text, Ištar seems to agree, for what follows this is an incredible orgy in which the inexhaustible Ištar has sexual intercourse with 120 young men.

In the Middle Babylonian version of the Akkadian myth *Nergal and Ereškigal*, Nergal is commanded to travel to the Netherworld, for its queen, Ereškigal, wishes to kill him. When he arrives, Nergal is too fast for the goddess and is able to throw her off of her throne. He grabs her by the hair, but just as he is going to execute her she offers him her kingdom. He acquiesces, seizes her (marries?), and kisses her. He then wipes away her tears. The writing also contains an Akkadian pun: Ereškigal wished for his *mūtu* ("death") but gets him as a *mutu* ("husband").

In the Neo-Assyrian version of this myth, Ereškigal attempts to seduce Erra (Nergal), but when he sees her body the god does not "get aroused as a man for a woman." Something then transpires (the text is broken) and her attempts at seduction work the second time. The gods embrace and have sexual intercourse for seven days. Erra finally departs, even though Ereškigal pleads for him to stay:

Erra, my voluptuous lover!
I had not had my fill of his charms, but he left me!
   Erra, my voluptuous lover!
I had not had my fill of his charms, but he left me!
(Foster, 1996, p. 519: iv 54–57)

Eventually, Erra returns to the Netherworld, and the text reads similarly to the Middle Babylonian version with a twist. While Erra is once again said to throw Ereškigal off of her throne and grab her by her hair, they proceed to make mad passionate love again for seven days. In the end, Ereshkigal gets her man.

A Different Tone: *Šazigas*. In the *šazigas*, erectile potency incantations that date to the Middle Babylonian and later periods, emphasis continues to be placed on vaginal intercourse; however, instead of rather graphic agricultural metaphors (ploughing) in which female genitalia (furrows) take pride of description, these texts focus almost entirely on describing the patient's erection and his penetrative performance. Rarely are female genitalia mentioned.

To "cure" the patient, a medical professional/incantation priest (*āšipu*) or a female participant is instructed to cry out statements such as, "Violent Stallion whose sexual excitement is a devastating flood!" (Biggs, 1967, p. 17, 1:13), or orders such as, "Get excited like a stag! Get an erection like a wild bull!" (p. 22 6:2), or, simply, "Get excited! Get excited! Get an erection! Get an erection!," "Make love to me!," "Let your strength (*emūqān*) rise for you! Let your tired knees (*birku*) rise (*tebû*) for you!" (p. 31, 13:48–49).

Unlike in the Sumerian "love songs," in these texts penises (*išaru*) are mentioned by name and the suffering man's penis is commanded to be like a stick of *martû*-wood, extended like a *mašgašu*-weapon, or taut as a harp string. In one of the few instances in which female genitalia are mentioned, the woman states: "My vagina (*ūru*) is the vagina (*ūru*) of a bitch! His penis is the penis (*ušaru*) of a dog! As the vagina (*ūru*) of a bitch holds fast the penis (*ušaru*) of a dog, (so may my vagina [*ūru*] hold fast his penis [*ušaru*])!" (Biggs, 1967, p. 33, 14: 9–10). Gone is the imagery of a sexually aroused woman (moist furrows): it is replaced by images of clamps and quivers. Battle imagery and duty is no more apparent than in this example: "May the quiver not become empty; May the bow not become slack! Let the batt[le of] my lovemaking be waged!" (Biggs, 1967, p. 37, 18: 3′–4′). Here the quiver (= vagina) is not to be empty (referring either to its need for a "stiff arrow" or possibly to semen, that which generally fills the "quiver"). The bow is used as metaphor rather than the arrow: like a bow that has not been stretched taught, a penis is flaccid before prepared for use.

Unlike the seemingly terrifying imagery and quite possibly intimidating commands barked at the suf-fering man, the actions the participants are advised to take are rather practical: rubbing oil on and/or stroking genitalia. Less practical, it seems, are the sympathetic magic techniques of tying rams and sheep to beds and carving up various birds.

[*See also* Deity, *subentry* Ancient Near East; Political Leadership, *subentry* Ancient Near East; Popular Religion and Magic, *subentry* Ancient Near East; *and* Religious Leaders, *subentry* Ancient Near East.]

BIBLIOGRAPHY

Alster, B. "Sumerian Love Songs." *Revue d'Assyriologie et d'Archéologie Orientale* 79 (1985): 127–159.

Alster, B. "Marriage and Love in the Sumerian Love Songs, with Some Notes on the Manchester Tammuz." In *The Tablet and the Scroll: Near Eastern Studies in Honour of William W. Hallo*, edited by Mark E. Cohen, Daniel C. Snell, and David B. Weisberg, pp. 15–27. Bethesda, Md.: CDL Press, 1993.

Alster, B. *Proverbs of Ancient Sumer: The World's Earliest Proverb Collections.* 2 vols. Bethesda, Md.: CDL Press, 1997.

Alster, B. *Wisdom of Ancient Sumer.* Bethesda, Md.: CDL Press, 2005.

Asher-Greve, J. "Decisive Sex, Essential Gender." In *Sex and Gender in the Ancient Near East: Proceedings of the 47th Rencontre Assyriologique Internationale, Helsinki, July 2–6, 2001*, edited by Simo Parpola and Robert M. Whiting, pp. 11–26. CRRAI 47. Helsinki: Neo-Assyrian Text Corpus Project, 2002.

Bahrani, Z. *Women of Babylon: Gender and Representation in Mesopotamia.* London: Routledge, 2001.

Biggs, R. D. *Ša.zi.ga, Ancient Mesopotamian Potency Incantations.* Texts from the Cuneiform Sources 2. Locust Valley, N.Y.: Augustin, 1967.

Biggs, R. D. "Conception, Contraception, and Abortion in Ancient Mesopotamian." In *Wisdom, Gods and Literature: Studies in Assyriology in Honour of W. G. Lambert*, edited by A. R. George and I. L. Finkel, pp. 1–14. Winona Lake, Ind.: Eisenbrauns, 2000.

Black, J. A. "Babylonian Ballads: A New Genre." *Journal of the American Oriental Society* 103 (1983): 25–34.

Cooper, J. S. "Enki's Member: Eros and the Irrigation in Sumerian Literature." In *DUMU-E₂-DUB-BA-A: Studies in Honor of Åke W. Sjöberg*, edited by Hermann Behrens, Darlene T. Loding, and Martha T. Roth, pp. 87–89. Occasional Publications of the Samuel Noah Kramer Fund 11. Philadelphia: University Museum, 1989.

Cooper, J. S. "Gendered Sexuality in Sumerian Love Poetry." In *Sumerian Gods and Their Representations*, edited by I. L. Finkel and M. J. Geller, pp. 84–97. Groningen, The Netherlands: Styx, 1997.

Cooper, J. S. "Virginity in Ancient Mesopotamia." In *Sex and Gender in the Ancient Near East: Proceedings of the 47th Rencontre Assyriologique Internationale, Helsinki, July 2–6, 2001*, edited by Simo Parpola and Robert M. Whiting, pp. 91–112. CRRAI 47. Helsinki: Neo-Assyrian Text Corpus Project, 2002.

The Electronic Text Corpus of Sumerian Literature. http://etcsl.orinst.ox.ac.uk

Foster, B. *Before the Muses*. Ann Arbor, Mich.: CDL Press, 1996.

Gadotti, A. "Why It Was Rape: The Conceptualization of Rape in Sumerian Literature." *Journal of the American Oriental Society* 129 (2009): 73–82.

George, A. R. *The Babylonian "Gilgamesh" Epic: Introduction, Critical Edition and Cuneiform Texts*. Oxford: Oxford University Press, 2003.

Groneberg, B. "Searching for Akkadian Lyrics: From Old Babylonian to the 'Liederkatalog' KAR 158." *Journal of Cuneiform Studies* 55 (2003): 55–74.

Guinan, A. K. "Left/Right Symbolism in Mesopotamian Divination." *State Archives of Assyria Bulletin* 10 (1996): 5–10.

Hoffner, H. A., Jr. "Symbols for Masculinity and Femininity and Their Use in Second Millennium Magic Ritual." *Journal of Biblical Literature* 85 (1996): 326–334.

Hurowitz, V. "An *Old Babylonian Bawdy Ballad*." In *Solving Riddles and Untying Knots: Biblical, Epigraphic, and Semitic Studies in Honor of Jonas C. Greenfield*, edited by Ziony Zevit, Seymour Gitin, and Michael Sokoloff, pp. 543–558. Winona Lake, Ind.: Eisenbrauns, 1995.

Lambert, W. G., and A. R. Millard. *Atra-[H]asis: the Babylonian Story of the Flood*. Oxford: Clarendon, 1969.

Lieck, Gwendolyn. *Sex and Eroticism in Mesopotamian Literature*. London: Routledge, 1994.

Livingstone, A. *Court Poetry and Literary Miscellanea*. State Archives of Assyria 3. Helsinki: Helsinki University Press, 1989.

Meier, G. *Die Assyrische Beschwoerungssammlung Maqlu*. AfO Beiheft 2. Berlin: Weidner, 1937.

Nissenen, M. *Homoeroticism in the Biblical World: A Historical Perspective*. Translated by Kirsi Stjerna. Minneapolis: Fortress, 1998.

Nissinen, M. "Akkadian Rituals and Poetry of Divine Love." In *Mythology and Mythologies: Methodological Approaches to Intercultural Influences*, edited by R. M. Whiting, pp. 93–136. Melammu Symposia 2. Helsinki: Neo-Assyrian Text Corpus Project, 2001.

Parpola, S., and R. M. Whiting, eds. *Sex and Gender in the Ancient Near East: Proceedings of the 47th Rencontre As-*

syriologique Internationale, Helsinki, July 2–6, 2001, Part I. Helsinki: Neo-Assyrian Text Corpus Project, 2002.

Sefati, Y. *Love Songs in Sumerian Literature: Critical Edition of the Dumuzi-Inanna Songs*. Bar-Ilan Studies in Near Eastern Languages and Culture. Publications of the Samuel N. Kramer Institute of Assyriology. Ramat-Gan, Israel: Bar-Ilan University Press, 1998.

Stol, M. *Birth in Babylonia and the Bible: Its Mediterranean Setting*. Cuneiform Monographs 14. Groningen, The Netherlands: Styx, 2000.

Westenholz, A., and J. Westenholz. "Help for Rejected Suitors—The Old Akkadian Love Incantation MAD V 8." *Orientalia* 46 (1977): 198–219.

Westenholz, J. G. "Love Lyrics from the Ancient Near East." In *Civilizations of the Ancient Near East*, Vol. 2, edited by J. Sasson, pp. 2471–2484. Peabody, Mass.: Hendrickson, 2000.

Wiggermann, F. A. M. "Sexualität. A." *Reallexicon der Assyriologie und vorderasiatischen Archaologie* 9 (2010): 410–426.

Zsolnay, I. "Do Divine Structures of Gender Mirror Mortal Structures of Gender?" In *In the Wake of Tikva Frymer-Kensky*, edited by Steven Holloway, JoAnn Scurlock, and Richard Beal, pp. 103–120. Piscataway, N.J.: Gorgias.

Ilona Zsolnay

GENDER TRANSGRESSION

This entry contains six subentries: Hebrew Bible; Greek World; Roman World; New Testament; Early Judaism; *and* Early Church.

Ancient Near East

See Gender and Sexuality: Ancient Near East.

Hebrew Bible

The Hebrew Bible is not readily associated with gender transgression. On the contrary, its opening chapters, relating the creation of man and woman, appear to supply a foundational template for the binary pairing of man and woman. The gendered norms for these two sexes become quickly apparent: prescriptively in the law codes of the Pentateuch, and implicitly through the representations of masculinity and femininity that permeate biblical narrative. The creation stories do not so much reflect a divinely ordained sex/gender system as construct it, while law codes provide prescriptions for a society where transgressions are evidently anticipated. As speech acts, law codes perform and enact, constructing rather than reflecting realities. As for biblical narratives saturated with representations of masculinity and femininity, these certainly reify gender norms, but they also provide subversive cracks that, once opened, cannot readily be closed and forgotten. Thus Ken Stone (2007) observes that the gender polemic used against Abimelech is a risky strategy, because by focusing on instabilities in the performance of "doing man," the narrator simultaneously draws attention to the flimsiness of apparent norms. Some methodological approaches are particularly adept at investigating these fissures, such as feminist criticism, queer criticism, and the critical study of masculinities.

Key Texts and Vocabulary. The key texts discussed are organized broadly into three categories: those that attempt to restrict or contain the potential for gender transgression; those that play with gender norms in a subversive, entertaining manner; and the gender-bending at the heart of the relationship between the Lord and Israel.

Texts restricting or containing gender transgression. Prominent among texts in this first category is the ban on cross-dressing (Deut 22:5). Grammatically, this verse reveals anxiety for the borders of the masculine: there will be no item pertaining to a male (*keĺi-geber*) upon a woman, and vice versa. Accoutrements of gender are envisaged within the scope of this text since the reach of *keĺi* goes beyond clothing. Distaff and spindle are, for example, typically associated with women (Prov 31:19, 2 Sam 3:29) while weaponry, especially the bow, is reserved for men (2 Sam 22:35). Athalya Brenner (1997) rightly suspects that, in safeguarding the right to male-only dress and equipment, Deuteronomy 22:5 attempts to safeguard male autonomy and social supremacy.

Regardless of how insulting it is to women, biblical narrators know that associating a man with the trademark items of a woman or with womanly behavior is an easy way to cause affront. In 2 Samuel 3:29, David's curse on Joab's house includes reference to there being a male (the participle is masculine) grasping a *pelek*. Those convinced by the link with the Phoenician *plkm* suppose crutches, but others accept the Masoretic Text and translate "holds a spindle." The implication is that Joab's descendants will include one associated with the female gender. Wilhelm Nowack (1902) thus suggested that Joab's house will be afflicted by an "effeminate stay-at-home." Such translations are no doubt accurate, but critical distance from the text is necessary so that ideologies about gender are not unthinkingly endorsed and passed on. The negative value judgments about effeminacy are caught up within the ancient cultural milieu where codes of honor and shame are foundational. In this system, maintenance of masculine norms sustains honor, but association with femininity is a thing of shame. It is unlikely that 2 Samuel 3:29 carries any broader reference to cultic rituals that provoked gender change, but Harry Hoffner (1966) noted how symbols of masculinity and femininity featured in ancient Near Eastern loyalty oaths when warriors are threatened with being turned into women should they not uphold their promises.

Further key texts attempting to contain gender transgression include Leviticus 18:22 and 20:31, which stipulate that a man should not "lie the lying down of a woman" (*miškĕbê ʾiššâ*) with another man. Often assumed to be texts about sexuality, these are centrally texts about gender. As Saul Olyan (1994) has persuasively argued, the act envisaged is anal penetration and the confusion that results when a male is penetrated—for a man who puts himself, or another man, in the receptive position of a woman betrays gender norms. The law declares (constructs) such an act *tôʿēbâ*, a word often translated as "abomination" but which connotes more generally a sense of boundary-crossing or the reversal of convention. Olyan argues that it is the potential for mixing semen and excrement that prompts the prohibition and believes that the law originally addressed the penetrating man. Jerome Walsh (2001) contrarily contends that grammatically to "lie the lying down of a woman" is akin to standard Hebrew idioms such as "to dream a dream." These texts thus relate to a subject's action, and to lie the lying down of a woman is therefore better translated "to lie with a male as a woman would" (2001, p. 205). The prohibition relates to the fact that gender roles and boundaries have been troubled: its rationale is to contain such transgression. The death penalty indicates how serious a matter this was considered to be.

Texts subverting gender norms. Although the texts above strongly proscribe gender transgression, narrative texts use gender transgression to create humorous tales of the unexpected, or to satirize, or to shock. In fact, biblical narrators were particularly adept at manipulating gender norms to suit certain ideological purposes. Deliberate feminization of the foreign male, for example, shows how gender norms can be subverted for the purposes of satire. The figurative rapes of Eglon and Sisera in Judges 3–5 provide good illustration. And when the prophets envisage the day of the LORD, they picture enemy soldiers crying like women in labor, or experiencing womanly fear and trembling, with their "hands" going limp (Isa 13:7–8, 19:16–25; 21:3–4; Jer 48:41; 49:22; Nah 3:13). Musing on such images, Jeremiah 30:5–6 provocatively has the LORD wondering whether men can actually give birth! When it comes to womanizing the enemy, gender transgression is evidently a phenomenon that can be played with entertainingly in the Hebrew Bible.

Arguably, laws that relate to the inappropriate grasping of a man's genitals (Deut 25:11–12), the status of the man with crushed testicles (Lev 21:20), or the eunuch (Deut 23:1; cf. Isa 56:3) concern gender. But since these texts deal primarily with bodily wholeness and sex norms they are not discussed further here. Of greater relevance are texts that refer to the deliberate castration or bodily abuse of enemy soldiers. In 1 Samuel 18:25 Saul demands one hundred Philistine foreskins from David in return for his daughter. This is not just an act of castration, it is an affront to gender, calling into question Philistine manly honor. The rape of enemy soldiers on the battlefield, a documented ancient practice, is similarly a gendered act that womanizes the defeated.

Rape may be envisaged in Dagan's full frontal submission to the LORD in 1 Samuel 5:3 and in the "affliction" of the men of Ashdod by the "hand" of the LORD ("hand" can be used euphemistically to refer to genitals). Jennings notes how such an interpretation has coherence with other texts where the threat or actuality of phallic violence upon the foreigner is present (Gen 19, Judg 19).

Masculinizing women is also an option when the narrator wants to criticize members of the Israelite community who do not measure up. In these cases, gender norms are transgressed in order to vilify and mock. Jezebel's dominant agency exposes Ahab's weakness while stories of Israelite woman warriors shame their male counterparts. Thus, in Judges 4, Deborah's proactive battle-ready stance mocks Barak's trepidation. Esther's and Judith's actions similarly play with the gendered expectations of the intended audience. When it suits the ideological purpose, female masculinity is a thing positively extolled.

Jael, however, is in a category of her own: in this case, a liminal figure has been created whose gender is thoroughly disrupted. Note, for instance, that her name is grammatically in the form of a third person masculine singular, and that in Judges 4:20 Sisera instructs Jael to stand at the entrance to the tent by using a second person masculine imperative. Commentators immediately begin to emend, assuming an error; but these appear to be recuperative strategies, intending to contain the strange she/he liminal figure that is emerging from the page. Yet more is to come: this masculinized Jael subsequently engages in a figurative phallic rape of a passive Sisera whose death throes are unmistakably sexualized. All this before the narrator has her extolled as most blessed of women (5:24). Jael's quick recuperation is understandable: when a society is founded on a rigid binary system, there is no room for such gender ambiguity. Therefore, when women are no longer women, but cannot be said to be properly men either, such a society comes face to face with the specter of chaos—a real threat to the system that has to be contained. A queer reading is adept at teasing out the unsettling phenomenon that the narrator has conjured: a character whose performativity offers the reader an unintelligible gender that gives the lie to ideas of sex as abiding substance.

Deborah Sawyer (2002) convincingly demonstrates how a full range of characters slide across gender spectrums when it suits the narrator, most notably when the narrator wants to advocate for theocratic power. Female characters do quite well out of this maneuver. They step outside the constraints of the home and ownership by father, brother, or husband, and take up activities, sometimes warlike, to demonstrate that sometimes God's best men are women. Male characters fare less well because in order to preserve alpha maleness for the deity, their own male prerogatives such as impregnation of women, or their values such as honor, are lost. For feminists with Christian or Jewish allegiances, these examples of female strength, initiative, and agency are liberatory. For others, such as Sawyer, it is the deity (read male narrator) who wins. The gender "transgressions" of Deborah or Judith are celebrated, but only because they serve a larger patriarchal agenda. From this perspective, the best that can be said is that their stories blunt the otherwise restrictive prescriptions and norms that limit their activities, and are a welcome respite from stories of women as victims of men (such as those of Jephthah's daughter and the Levite's concubine in Judges 11 and 19). The reader is thus advised to pay attention to the narrator who casts the characters in order to put forward a politics under the guise of divine speech and action.

Texts that reconfigure gender norms in the Yahweh-Israel relationship. Perhaps less well noted, but permeating much of the Hebrew Bible, are the gender shifts at the heart of the Israel-Yahweh relationship. Within the covenantal relationship, which is founded upon a heterosexual framework, Israel is repeatedly feminized as the wife of Yahweh. This is seen most starkly in those texts where Israel is described as the adulterous wife; bold and brazen, she cuckolds the deity with her foreign paramours (Hos 1–3, Isa 47, Jer 2–5, Ezek 16, 23). A certain queerness arises from placing the *male* Israelite audience in the position of subservient wife (the homoerotic connotations have been addressed by Eilberg-

Schwartz, 1994). Less provocatively, but with a similar feminizing effect, other prophetic texts put Israel in a wifely position. Julia O'Brien (1996) notes the gender shifts in Malachi 2:11, where wayward Judah is "she" who has acted treacherously. Resisting the tendency for commentators to emend, ignore, or deflect the gender switches in Malachi 2, O'Brien commendably lets them stand, noting how Judah is thus rendered liminal: both male and female, wife and son. In a different vein, but commenting on how male members of the Israelite community are feminized, Deborah Rooke (2009) addresses Exodus 28:42–43 and Leviticus 16:4, where priests are instructed to wear breeches. Musing on the rationale for such laws, she concludes that it is necessary for priests to neutralize the material sign of their maleness in a submissive acknowledgment of the deity's masculine power and authority. Overall, such observations cohere with Sawyer's thesis that a theme of "demasculinization" runs through the Hebrew Bible, which advocates a model of maleness that is subservient to the deity.

Passing. There are several narratives where characters disguise themselves in order to pass as someone else (Gen 38, 1 Sam 28, 1 Kgs 20, 22), but in these cases the characters remain in their assigned gender. Arguably there is a case of excessive gender performativity when Tamar ratchets up her performance in order to lay a false trail for Judah, her father-in-law. The closest we come to gender passing, however, is in the language S. Tamar Kamionkowski (2003) uses for her analysis of Ezekiel 16. In this chapter, the community of Israelite males is imaged as Woman/Jerusalem who does not stay within the boundaries allotted to her sex. Rather, she acts in an aggressive and independent manner, which Kamionkowski (2003, p. 7) describes as "attempting to pass for a male." In fact there is a double passing going on, for Ezekiel's metaphor has a Judean/exilic male community imaged in terms of personified city (Jerusalem) whose aggressive behavior and agency marks her as male. Her transgression is thus also double: not only one of unfaithfulness to her divine husband but one of subverting the defined roles for women. Ezekiel's response to this specter is to reimpose gender norms in a brutal way by having Woman/Jerusalem publically humiliated, stoned, and abused. This enables two simultaneous things to happen: the deity reclaims a position of power and superiority, and Ezekiel/his community is able to express and recover from the cultural trauma of an exile experience that had left them shamed and emasculated. Kamionkowski persuasively argues that Ezekiel's metaphor has its roots in the way he and his male compatriots were traumatized by the events surrounding the Babylonian exile, not least recognizing and surviving the humiliation meted out to defeated men on the battleground. However, the reader is left with the image of a male audience addressed as female whore. While the male audience might have been able to align itself with the deity and so reflect the shame onto the metaphorical woman, this is a sleight of hand/mind that does not entirely displace the odd gender shifts that have been summoned.

Issues of Performance. Gender norms are often thought to be pinned to the prior given of biological sex. The complex series of gendered rules about what one can wear, where one can go, and how one performs the given sex satisfactorily, thus emerge from the two-sex binary. In this view, gendered performances become a way of distinguishing and enforcing the male/female boundaries so that sex itself remains stable as the prior biological "given." However, biblical texts such as Deuteronomy 22:5 demonstrate that it is the *gendered performances* that have priority. This text forbids women to adopt the items associated with men and thereby to perform an identity commonly thought to be the prerogative of men. "*Doing* man" is thus vital to the biblical notion of "being man." Male self-esteem, sense of self, purpose, and dignity seem to stem from having behaviors and items of masculinity carefully restricted. The man/woman binary depends not so much on biological appendages, or lack of, but on the gendered behaviors associated with each sex. Thus, it is gender performativity that is vital when it comes to maintaining the kind of society envisaged by Genesis 1—3. However, although biblical legal prescriptions uphold a rigid two-gender system, the narratives contain characters who can assume the gendered behavior and appearance of their gender opposite; and the prophetic corpus contains unexpected, radical gender shifts in the feminization of Israel and Judah.

It could be argued that the revelry in gender transgression only serves to uphold the gender binary. Al Wolters (1998), for example, builds a strong case for demonstrating how the sex/gender binary remains intact despite the fluidity of gendered imagery applied to both women and men. To some extent he is right. The male-female binary has a resilience that despite the flirtations with unexpected gendered activities or names proves seemingly resistant to any undoing of that binary. Even queer theory, which arguably has the best tools to unhinge the sexed binary, has a difficult task. The glimpses readers are given of unexpected and odd genderings in the Hebrew Bible might do some subversive work insofar as those glimpses offer the reader a vision of an alternative way of understanding sex/gender, but this would be dependent on the resistant reader.

However, Wolters's claim that grammatical gender designators (pronouns, verbs, pronominal suffixes) consistently identify the residual natural gender of the person, even when they are otherwise imaged, has an exception in Jael. Wolters might look to the surrounding female grammatical designations, but the two masculine designations, at minimum, bring gender trouble to the story. Here is a case where the narrator creates something that, once out of the bag, is not easy to recapture.

If our understanding of both sex and gender is always shaped by language and the discourses of our cultural context, then the part played by scriptural texts in that cultural knowledge has to be noted. In Wolters's article, the grammatical designations that he carefully identifies are assumed to point to a given reality. Although the grammar *appears* to be endorsing sex distinctions, this is due only to a prior ideological commitment to the supposed realities of those distinctions. The grammar, rather, is constructing sexed differences, creating the distinction with boundary-words such as "male" and "female." It takes effort to make visible how this happens because language is so easily taken as a given. Wolters is right that the language of the Hebrew Bible affirms the "given" sex of characters while the metaphor or simile portrays them in cross-gender ways. But what Wolters does not address is that language thus iterates a perception of male/female categories, reifying the cultural consensus that certain reproductive parts of the body render one male or female. If this is seen instead as an ideological maneuver, then the significance of the Hebrew Bible as an ancient but hugely influential cultural discourse becomes evident. Moreover, the task of interpretation can then be recognized as the ideologically driven work it actually is.

Gender Transgression and Ethical Exegetical Responsibility. Biblical interpretation can no longer be an act of investigating the meaning of a text for its author and ancient audience, then repeating that meaning to a modern audience. Biblical texts continue to be cited in political debate, wielded authoritatively to lobby for various ideological positions. They are "live" texts that remain influential for our understanding of gender. This means that biblical interpretation does not happen in a neutral, objective bubble; it takes place in the heat of controversy and debate. This is particularly so when it comes to gender transgression and current political and religious discourses pertaining to homosexuality, transsexuality, and transgender. Accordingly, for queer and gender critics, the commodification of information into an encyclopedia entry does not go far enough if the social and political effects of these texts are not addressed. Readers are thus encouraged to consider how ideologically led hermeneutical strategies are always at work in citations of texts such as Deuteronomy 22:5 or Leviticus 18:22 in contemporary discourses.

The emphasis, in conservative discourses, is on the prescriptive key texts that attempt to contain gender transgression. Far from being a bastion of gender normativity, though, the Hebrew Bible provides repeated flashes of subversive gender-play that to some extent expose the ultimate artifice of gender performativity and fragility of the idea that there is any ontological grounding for gender stability. Acknowledgment of these texts makes room for a broader view and a deeper, more nuanced understanding of how gender is constructed, manipulated, and subverted in ways that might surprise the general public.

[*See also* Creation; Family Structures, *subentry* Hebrew Bible; *and* Imagery, Gendered, *subentries on* Deuteronomistic History *and* Prophetic Literature.]

BIBLIOGRAPHY

Brenner, Athalya. *The Intercourse of Knowledge: On Gendering Desire and "Sexuality" in the Hebrew Bible.* Biblical Interpretation Series 26. Leiden, The Netherlands: Brill, 1997.

Butler, Judith. *Gender Trouble. Feminism and the Subversion of Identity.* London: Routledge, 1990.

Eilberg-Schwartz, Howard. *God's Phallus and Other Problems for Men and Monotheism.* Boston: Beacon, 1994.

Guest, Deryn. "Judges." In *The Queer Bible Commentary*, edited by Deryn Guest, Robert E. Goss, Mona West, and Thomas Bohache, pp. 167–189. London: SCM, 2006.

Guest, Deryn. "From Gender Reversal to Genderfuck: Reading Jael through a Lesbian Lens." In *Bible Trouble: Queer Reading at the Boundaries of Biblical Scholarship*, edited by Teresa J. Hornsby and Ken Stone, pp. 9–43. Semeia Studies 67. Atlanta: Society of Biblical Literature, 2011.

Hoffner, Harry A., Jr. "Symbols for Masculinity and Femininity: Their Use in Ancient Near Eastern Sympathetic Magic Rituals." *Journal of Biblical Literature* 85 (1966): 326–334.

Jennings, Theodore W., Jr. "YHWH as Erastes." In *Queer Commentary on the Hebrew Bible*, edited by Ken Stone, pp. 36–74. London and New York: Sheffield Academic Press, 2001.

Kamionkowski, S. Tamar. *Gender Reversal and Cosmic Chaos: A Study in the Book of Ezekiel.* London: Sheffield Academic Press, 2003.

Nowack, Wilhelm. *Richter, Ruth, und bücher Samuelis.* Göttingen, Germany: Vandenhoeck & Ruprecht, 1902.

O'Brien, Julia M. "Judah as Wife and Husband: Deconstructing Gender in Malachi." *Journal of Biblical Literature* 115, no. 2 (1996): 241–250.

Olyan, Saul. "'And with a Male You Shall Not Lie the Lying Down of a Woman': On the Meaning and Significance of Leviticus 18:22 and 20:13." *Journal of the History of Sexuality* 5, no. 2 (1994): 179–206.

Rooke, Deborah W. "Breeches of the Covenant: Gender, Garments, and the Priesthood." In *Embroidered Garments: Priests and Gender in Biblical Israel*, edited by

Deborah W. Rooke, pp. 19–37. Hebrew Bible Monographs 25, King's College London; Studies in the Bible and Gender 2, Sheffield, U.K.: Sheffield Phoenix, 2009.

Sawyer, Deborah F. *God, Gender, and the Bible.* London and New York: Routledge, 2002.

Stone, Ken. "Gender Criticism: The Un-manning of Abimelech." In *Judges and Method: New Approaches in Biblical Studies,* 2d ed., edited by Gale A. Yee, pp. 183–201. Minneapolis: Fortress, 2007.

Walsh, Jerome T. "Leviticus 18:22 and 20:13: Who Is Doing What to Whom?" *Journal of Biblical Literature* 120, no. 2 (2001): 201–209.

Wolters, Al. "Cross-Gender Imagery in the Bible." *Bulletin for Biblical Research* 8 (1998): 217–228.

Deryn Guest

Greek World

Like other societies, the ancient Greeks subscribed to highly polarized notions of gender. Men were associated with the public sphere and the military while women were prescribed roles almost exclusively within the private, domestic sphere. Much of what we know about ancient Greece derives from Athens, however, and the roles of women may have varied somewhat in other Greek city-states. We are told by Plutarch (*Life of Lycurgus* 14) that Spartan women were taught to use weapons and had more of a public presence than at Athens. In contrast, the definition of a good woman, according to the Athenian statesman Pericles, was that she had no reputation among men, either for ill-repute or good deeds (Thucydides 2.46).

The relationship of gender variance to sexuality was different in ancient Greece than it is today. Whereas the modern gay male is often assumed to be effeminate and lesbians correspondingly masculine, in ancient Greek there was no word that can be translated as homosexual. Plato (*Symposium* 191e–192b) does describe men whose primary attraction was to other men, however, even though men were expected to marry. In direct contrast to modern thought, however, Plato (*Symposium* 192a) calls these men the "most masculine." Plato (*Symposium* 191e) also briefly mentions the *hetairistria*, a woman whose primary attraction was to other women. The only other occurrence of this term is found centuries later in Lucian's *Dialogues of the Courtesans* (5), but here it is assumed that the *hetairistria* is masculine. A woman named Megilla is described as a *hetairistria*, and calls herself by the masculine name Megillos in the bedroom. Megilla/Megillos takes an active role in sex with other women and is called a Lesbian, which may simply mean that s/he is from the island of Lesbos. That said, the Roman Horace (*Epistles* 1.19.28) called Sappho "masculine," and some association between female homoeroticism and masculinity clearly existed among the Romans and possibly even the Roman-era Greeks such as Lucian.

The most important factor in gauging masculinity in classical Greece was *andreia*, the virtue of bravery. A man who did not live up to Greek expectations of warlikeness was called a *tresas*, or coward, by the Spartans (Herodotus 7.231), and a *kinaidos* by the Athenians. Likewise, a woman who was bold or courageous, or for that matter even outspoken, could be called masculine.

The Greek *Kinaidos*. In a comic play by Aristophanes, *The Clouds* (353), the *kinaidos* is described as a shield-thrower, one who in retreating from the enemy throws down his heavy shield in order to run rather than stand his ground to fight and potentially die for his country. In this play, a man named Cleonymus is labeled effeminate because he is a cowardly "shield-thrower" (*rhipsaspis*; 353). Socrates, the main character of *The Clouds*, teaches his pupil Strepsiades to feminize the ending of Cleonymus's name, calling him Cleonymē (*Clouds* 680). We cannot determine if Cleonymus was a real person, although we know that Socrates was, and Aristophanes tends to lampoon historical personages. If indeed Cleonymus had been a real person, he must have been made fun of not only on the stage but by passers-by on the streets as well. His behavior (cowardice) was viewed as gender transgression, and he was made the laughingstock of Athens for it. Similarly, a fragmentary play by Eupolis, the *Astreteutoi* (men who have not been on military service), was alternatively titled *Androgunoi* (effeminate men). Athenian comedy mirrored the ideology of masculinity that we find in legal and other sources. For example, an Athenian male could be stripped of all legal rights for deserting his comrades on the battlefield (Andocides 1.74).

Hence, the most effeminate behavior in men was cowardice. The *kinaidos* was also effeminate by Greek standards, and the epithet could be hurled as abuse in courts of law. Demosthenes, for example, was called a *kinaidos* by his enemy Aeschines. Aeschines (2.151) implies that Demosthenes was both a coward and effeminate when comparing him to a warrior named Philon: "Which of the two would you expect they will pray for, ten thousand hoplites who are like Philon, so well-conditioned with respect to his body and so chaste with respect to his soul, or sixty thousand *kinaidoi* just like you?" The term *kinaidos* is possibly derived from the verb *kinein*, which means to shake or move. The word *kinaidos* seems to have originally connoted a dancer who, by shaking his buttocks, elicited anal sex (*Corpus Inscriptionum Graecarum* 4926; Pliny, *Natural History* 32.146, 37.153). Calling an adult male a *kinaidos* implied that he engaged in passive homosexuality and/or prostitution. In the fourth century B.C.E., the Athenian Timarchus was accused of addressing the assembly after prostituting himself and "debauching his body," and hence, by implication, was a *kinaidos* (Aeschines 1). He was tried, found guilty, and was given the legal status of *atimia* (dishonor). He would not have been allowed to speak in the assembly or exercise the other prerogatives of a citizen because he had allegedly prostituted himself (Aeschines 1.28–29).

The term *kinaidos* seems to have pointed more toward deviation from Greek masculinity than to a specific sexual orientation, however. In other words, a lack of sexual chastity (e.g., taking the passive role in sex with other men as an adult or prostituting oneself) was only one aspect of deviance from the norm of masculinity. The *kinaidos* was a cowardly, failed man. Plato's *Timaeus* (90e) goes so far as to argue that cowardly males would be reincarnated as women. Hence, the *kinaidos* could be marginalized as an outcast. The effeminacy of the *kinaidos* could lower him from male citizen status to the political status of a woman or noncitizen.

The Physiognomy of the *Kinaidos*. The ancient Greeks seem to have believed that a *kinaidos* could be spotted from afar by his body gestures and movements, or, in more scholarly terms, his physiognomy. The earliest surviving text to describe this dates to the fourth century B.C.E., and is found in the collected works of Aristotle (*Physiognomy* 808a7–11). Here the *kinaidos* is described as limp-wristed, knock-kneed, holding his head to the right, and swaggering his hips or tightly controlling them.

Later Greek texts, stemming from the Roman era, elaborate upon this theme. A second-century C.E. text by Polemo, *Physiognomy*, provides the best example. Polemo (2.1.192F) asserts that sex and gender are not the same thing. He argues that something of the masculine and something of the feminine can be found in each person, but one of these will prevail. Masculine women will tend to bear male children, and feminine men will sire female children. The orderly man, according to Polemo, has a deep voice, and his eyes hold a courageous gleam (58.1.262F). He walks like a lion, and, if ever he bends his neck, it is only slightly (50.1.262F). In contrast, the *androgunos*, the effeminate man, has a shrill voice, always tilts his head to the side, never holds his loins still, and has a provocative look in his eyes.

The term *kinaidos* was borrowed by the Romans, and transliterated into Latin as *cinaedus*. The Roman *cinaedus* exhibited similar variations from expected norms of masculinity as the Greek *kinaidos*, but there were some differences in the cultural context. First and foremost, the Romans saw any kind of passive participation in anal intercourse as completely violating the norms of masculinity. For the Athenian Plato (*Symposium* 184b–e), a Greek youth might "gratify" his lover's sexual needs if he were receiving some educational benefit from the relationship (although this was not acceptable behavior for an older, fully adult Athenian male). Among the Romans, taking the passive role at any age could mean forgoing one's masculinity altogether—a man was meant to be active in sex in the Roman mind-set. The Romans further described the *cinaedus* as being sexually insatiable (e.g., Catullus 33). Once the *cinaedus* had passed over into the realm of passive unmanliness, it was as if a disease of lust had taken over his body. The Romans did not entirely frown upon what we today would call homosexual relations, but they expected that male citizens would only take an active, penetrating role with others. Male slaves could be the target of such sexual acts, as could wives, prostitutes, or other noncitizens. *Cinaedi* are described as lingering at the public baths looking for sex (e.g., Martial 1.96.9–14), wearing jewelry (Petronius, *Satyricon* 23.3), shaving their bodies smooth, and wearing womanish see-through clothing (Juvenal, *Satire* 2). The Romans saw these acts as physically taking on the characteristics of a woman.

The Spartan *Tresas*. The Spartans, like their Athenian counterparts, had very narrow definitions of masculinity. A Spartan male who was perceived as a coward in battle was even more marginalized than the Athenian *kinaidos*. He was forced to shave half of his beard, signifying that he was only half of a man (Plutarch, *Life of Agesilaus* 30.3). Other Spartans would mock the *tresas* verbally, and refuse to share fire with him, give him a seat at an event, or give way to him if they crossed his path (Xenophon, *Spartan Society* 9; Plutarch, *Life of Lycurgus* 21). As the Spartans practiced eugenics, neither the disgraced man nor his sisters would be allowed to procreate. Plutarch (*Sayings of Spartans–Moralia* 241A) preserves stories of mothers who killed their male children for cowardice, and he referred to them using a neuter pronoun. The Spartan coward was not called a woman, and this seems to indicate the higher status of women in Sparta than at Athens. A Spartan woman might show more bravery than a coward.

The *Galli*. The most obvious case of gender variance in an ancient Mediterranean context was the *gallus*, or priest of the Mother Goddess. The *galli* were either intersexed at birth or were males who castrated themselves, wore either women's or androgynous clothing, and took on a passive sexual role with men. The cult of the Mother Goddess was imported from Anatolia to Rome in the second century B.C.E. (Livy 29.10, 14), and became important there. The fourth century C.E. text of Firmicus Maternus (4.2)

alleges that the *galli* wore makeup and "disgraced" themselves as men by wearing women's clothing. Maternus further tells us that they nursed their "tresses," gave performances in temples, and paraded their "unchaste bodies" in processions. They also told fortunes. The *galli* served a role in ancient Mediterranean religions that was similar to that played by the Indian *hijra* to this day. In South Asia, the *hijras* are considered neither male nor female, although they tend to wear women's clothing.

The presence of *galli* in Roman-era Greece is documented by Apuleius (*Metamorphoses* 8.24–30). Apuleius's main character, Lucius Apuleius, is turned into a donkey and is sold to a traveling band of *galli*. The *galli* are depicted as sexually passive. In the story, they wear heavy rouge and eye makeup, bright colored clothing, and even girdles. They have long hair and cut their arms to make themselves bleed. They act as though they are in ecstatic possession by the god. Crowds gather to watch them and drop money into the pockets of their robes. Though they are described very negatively, the crowds must have thought that they held some power with the gods (or at least the mother goddess Cybele), and further found them entertaining. Their shows were perhaps not unlike modern drag performances. At one point in the story, they pick up a "young laborer" at the baths and bring him back to their quarters for dinner and to use him sexually. Apuleius indicates that, as priests, they were meant to be chaste, but their sexual exploits are discovered and they have to leave town.

The Medicalization of Gender Variance in the Hippocratic Treatise *On Regimen*. Differing causes of gender variation are found within Greek texts. The Hippocratic treatise *On Regimen* views gender, regardless of biological sex, as varying due to several factors, the first of which is the mixing of seed at conception. Unlike Aeschylus (*Eumenides* 658–660) and Aristotle (*On the Generation of Animals* 727a–b), who saw only the father contributing reproductive matter when "sowing" the mother's womb, the Hippocratics believed that both parents contributed seed (*On Regimen* 1.27). Furthermore, they described both the male and female as emitting two kinds of seed, also male or female. The gender expression of the conceived was a result of what kind of seed the mother and father each contributed, and how their reproductive matter mixed together.

There were six different potential outcomes of this reproductive process (*On Regimen* 1.28–29). In cases where both parents emitted male seed, the sex of the child would be male. Additionally, that child would become the most manly of men, and the most brilliant (the Greeks unflinchingly saw intelligence as a male attribute). In situations where both parents emitted female seed, the offspring was thought to become female. She would be the most feminine and "shapely" of women, as well as the most soft-spoken.

In cases where each parent emitted a different sexed seed (e.g., the father's was female and the mother's male) a battle was thought to ensue in the womb, and the sex and gender makeup of the child would ultimately be the result of this battle. If the father emitted male seed and the mother emitted female seed and the father's seed won the battle of the womb, then the child would be biologically male but less manly than the child conceived from male seed contributed by both parents. In the case where the father emitted female seed, the mother emitted male seed, and the mother's seed proved prevalent in the womb, the child would be an *androgunos*, which literally means "man-woman," but refers to the child who would become the most effeminate of males, and the most cowardly. In the case where the father emitted male seed, the mother emitted female seed, and the mother's seed won the battle of the womb, the child would be bolder than the most feminine of women yet still feminine to a degree. In the case where the father emitted female seed and the mother male seed and the father's seed won the battle, the offspring would then be the most masculine of women, and she is described as bolder than other women.

While there is an idea of gender fluidity in the Hippocratic text *On Regimen* (as mentioned above), the author asserts that, through diet and proper exercise, a man and woman might control the kind of seed they produce. The optimal outcomes were, of course, the most masculine of men and the most feminine of women, even though the text clearly acknowledges variation from these ideals. These same ideals are presented in other Greek literature as well. For example, in Aeschylus's trilogy *The Oresteia*, Clytemnestra is presented as a bold, courageous, manly and hence monstrous woman who takes male prerogative by killing her husband, Agamemnon, to avenge his sacrifice of their daughter to the god Poseidon. Likewise, her lover Aegisthus is presented as effeminate, failing to act like a man by allowing Clytaemnestra to do so. Although the Greeks clearly recognized gender variance, they frowned upon it.

Gender Variance in Astrological Texts. In Greek astrology, the cause of gender variance was explained by the alignment of the planets and stars on the day a person was born. In contrast to earlier Athenian texts, which emphasize courage as defining masculinity and fearfulness as defining femininity or effeminacy (regardless of the sex of a person), these astrological texts place much more emphasis on sexuality and performing proper sexual roles, where men take an active, penetrating role and women a passive, receptive one. Deviance from these norms is explained in the texts as both being caused by the heavens yet simultaneously being an illness.

Male effeminacy, according to the first-century C.E. astrologer Dorotheos of Sidon (*Carmen Astrologicum* 2.7.9), was caused by a particular configuration of Venus and Saturn. The man born under these auspices would take the passive role in sex with other men, which is viewed as a role reversal by Dorotheos, because he is taking the role of a woman. Likewise, when Saturn or Mars is in Capricorn, Aquarius, Aries, Taurus, or Pisces, a woman will take an active role in sex, meaning that she will penetrate other women, in contrast to males who "will not do to women as they ought to" (2.7.12). Despite the fact that such gender variance is directly caused by the alignment of the heavens on the day of birth, Dorotheos still sees such proclivities as illnesses.

Manetho (*Apotelesmatika* 4.358), an astrologer who also lived approximately in the first century C.E., describes women called *tribades* who perform the sexual functions normally thought of as male. The birth of the *tribas* is explained by the alignment of Venus and Saturn, as Dorotheos also described. A number of other Greek and Latin astrological texts make similar claims.

Cross-Dressing: The Anakreontic Vases. We know much less about gender variance in terms of dress and other personal habits. Cross-dressing is rarely described in ancient Greek literature, but vase painting does provide us with some evidence. Men may have dressed as women for religious or other reasons, as shown in the Attic Anakreontic vases, produced between 510 and 460 B.C.E. They depict individuals who have beards but wear female clothing and earrings and have other attributes associated with women. Perhaps the men here were imitating the god Dionysus, who is himself represented as rather androgynous. Scholars have argued that these individuals are portrayed in a *komos* procession, a parade in honor of the god Dionysus. While the exact meaning of these images is lost to us, they seem to portray some religious activities in which individuals express themselves in an androgynous way.

Girls going through puberty seem to have performed "Amazon dances" in which they were armed, and, in contrast to the *komasts* of Dionysus, dressed in male clothing. And, of course, the Greeks were fascinated by the Amazons, the ultimate representation of female masculinity in Greek thought. According to the orator Lysias (2.4), the Amazons were the first to make iron weapons, and were superior to men in the making of war, at least until they met their match in the Athenians and were defeated. Lysias writes that the Amazons of Themiscyra "were esteemed more as men on account of their courage than as women on account of their nature [*phusis*]. They were thought to excel men more in spirit than they were thought to be inferior due to their bodies."

Asceticism, Opting Out of Prescribed Gender Roles, and Cross-Dressing. With the advent of Christianity, both men and women could opt out of marriage and the expectations of gender by becoming ascetics. In some cases, ascetics wore clothing of the opposite sex, and might be considered "transgendered" in our modern terminology. In the ancient Greek world, one of the most interesting examples of an ascetic who might fit this epithet is Saint Eugenia (Aelfric, *Life of Eugenia*).

Eugenia was born in Alexandria, Egypt, during the Roman era, and was martyred on 25 December 258 C.E. Her father was alleged to be Philip, the Roman governor of Egypt at the time. Eugenia's flirtation with gender ambiguity actually began before her conversion to Christianity. Perhaps to opt out of gender expectations, Eugenia fled her father's house wearing men's clothing (or perhaps simply because it was easier to travel and live alone as a man rather than as a woman). Eugenia was baptized by the bishop of Heliopolis, Helenus. She was able to "pass" as a man, and eventually became an abbot. Eugenia's reasons for dressing like a man may have been due to necessity, if not simply her own choice. Whatever the case may have been, a woman made sexual advances to Eugenia, or so the story goes. When Eugenia refused her suitor, the woman accused the abbot of adultery. She stood trial, but her father turned out to be the judge. Her identity was then revealed, and she was acquitted. Philip himself converted to Christianity at this point, became the bishop of Alexandria, but was executed by order of the Roman emperor for his conversion. Saint Eugenia fled to Rome, where she proselytized but was eventually martyred herself, on none other than what we now recognize as Christmas Day. While the facts of this story have been questioned, the context at least suggests that ascetics might opt out of traditional gender roles, even if they had to do so in disguise.

[*See also* Gender; Gender Transgression, *subentries on* Early Church, New Testament, *and* Roman World; Male-Female Sexuality, *subentry* Greek World; Religious Leaders, *subentry* Ancient Near East; *and* Sexual Transgression, *subentry* Greek World.]

BIBLIOGRAPHY
Anson, J. "The Female Transvestite in Early Monasticism: The Origin and Development of a Motif." *Viator* 5 (1974): 1–32.
Brooten, Bernadette J. *Love between Women: Early Christian Responses to Female Homoeroticism.* Chicago: University of Chicago Press, 1996.

Frontisi-Ducroux, Françoise, and François Lissarrague. "From Ambiguity to Ambivalence: A Dionysiac Excursion through the 'Anakreontic' Vases." In *Before Sexuality: The Construction of Erotic Experience in the Ancient Greek World*, edited by David M. Halperin, John J. Winkler, and Froma I. Zeitlin, pp. 211–256. Princeton, N.J.: Princeton University Press, 1990.

Gleason, Maud W. "The Semiotics of Gender: Physiognomy and Self-Fashioning in the Second Century C.E." In *Before Sexuality: The Construction of Erotic Experience in the Ancient Greek World*, edited by David M. Halperin, John J. Winkler, and Froma I. Zeitlin, pp. 389–415. Princeton, N.J.: Princeton University Press, 1990.

Nanda, Serena. *Neither Man nor Woman: The Hijras of India*. Belmont, Calif.: Wadsworth, 1990.

Penrose, Walter. "Bold with the Bow and Arrow: Amazons and the Ethnic Gendering of Martial Prowess in Ancient Greek and Asian Cultures." Ph.D. diss., City University of New York Graduate Center, 2006.

Pomeroy, Sarah B. *Spartan Women*. New York: Oxford University Press, 2002.

Roscoe, Will. "Priests of the Goddess: Gender Transgression in Ancient Religion." *History of Religions* 35, no. 3 (1996): 195–230.

Taylor, Rabun. "Two Pathic Subcultures in Ancient Rome." *Journal of the History of Sexuality* 7, no. 3 (1997): 319–371.

Williams, Craig A. *Roman Homosexuality*. 2d ed. Oxford: Oxford University Press, 2010.

Winkler, John J. "Laying Down the Law: The Oversight of Men's Sexual Behavior in Classical Athens." In *Before Sexuality: The Construction of Erotic Experience in the Ancient Greek World*, edited by David M. Halperin, John J. Winkler, and Froma I. Zeitlin, pp. 171–210. Princeton, N.J.: Princeton University Press, 1990.

Walter D. Penrose Jr.

Roman World

On reflecting on advances in knowledge made during his lifetime, the first-century philosopher Seneca marvels at discoveries that surely await future generations (*Natural Questions* 7.30.5–6). Yet his excitement is brief, dimmed by a sense that his generation's intellectual progress is not matched by a corresponding moral improvement. "We have not yet completed the one task to which we apply our whole minds," he notes, "becoming as immoral as possible." The evidence that "vice is still in progress" is that men no longer act like *men*. Instead they develop "sleek, glossy bodies," wear "female beauty treatments" and "prostitutes' colors," and "tiptoe along with delicate mincing steps." Where "one man cuts off his genitals, another escapes to the obscene section of the gladiator's school," and each man devises "ways of damaging our masculinity, so that it may suffer degradation since it cannot be discarded" (*Natural Questions* 7.31.2–3, trans. Hine).

Seneca was not the only Roman writer to worry about morals and manliness. Indeed, few subjects excited the male elite authorial imagination more than gender transgression, which herein means deliberate or unwitting crossing of boundaries between the normative self and the abject other as defined by the differences ascribed to males and females. "Gender transgression" denotes the importance of gender norms that were broadly imposed, on men in this case, in the Roman world. Normative gender ideals were inextricably linked to elite notions of morality and respectability. These notions in turn reflect values and behaviors comprising the elite's self-understanding, which justified their superior social standing within the broader imperial order.

Of *Malakoi* and Men. Perhaps the trait most commonly associated with "unmen" is *mollitia* or *malakia*, terms generally meaning "softness" in both Latin and Greek, and rendered as "effeminacy" in discourses on male bodies and behaviors. Used routinely to insult or accuse, "effeminacy" functioned as a metaphor for moral degeneracy, one freighted with long-held assumptions about the physical and moral deficiencies of women. To call a man *malakos* was the ancient equivalent of telling a boy he "throws like a girl." The discourse of *malakia* as "effeminacy" targets any perceived nonconformity for public humiliation and is ultimately predicated on male fear of being identified with anything "feminine."

Even if associated with transgressive sexual practice, the catalog of *malakia* extends beyond sex and gender, intersecting with other social markers such as legal status, class, ethnicity, age, and ableness. Discourses of effeminacy ultimately reflect elite male efforts to ensure that the behaviors and bodies of their peers conformed to ruling class ideals. Self-appointed guardians of moral order first looked to the (male) body for signs of conduct unbecoming a *vir bonus*.

To assess and decode a man's appearance or actions, Roman moralists drew on the fundamental axiom of physiognomy, the ancient practice of reading the body wherein a person's physical aspect corresponded with, and thus expressed, his or her moral character (Vander Stichele and Penner, 2009, pp. 45–49, 63–67). What physiognomy also provided, even in less precise and more popular forms, was a means of classifying manhood and morals, enabling ready identification of transgression. When a Roman-era writer commented on the effeminacy of a rival, a people, or an entire generation, he thus noted, in detail, how a man walked (Polemo, *Physiognomica* 1.260), talked (Lucian, *Demonax* 12), dressed (Juvenal 2.65–81), groomed (Pliny, *Natural History* 13.18–25), and gestured (Plutarch, *Julius Caesar* 4.4).

Standard stereotypes depicted young boys, slaves, uneducated workers/speakers, prostitutes, actors, bandits, and tyrants, among others, as particularly deficient males owing to their vulnerable social status or excessive, indulgent habits (Edwards, 1993, pp. 63–97, 98–136, 190–195; Williams, 1999, pp. 15–60, 125–159). The "ultimate scare figure," though, was the eunuch, whose physical condition was a constant reminder that the seemingly stable foundation of masculinity, the male body, might easily crumble, and with it the illusion of natural superiority (Lucan, 10.133–4; Brown, 1988, p. 10; Williams, 1999, pp. 128–129). What Paul of Tarsus, who apparently disdained "soft" men (1 Cor 6:9), might say about the Matthean Jesus and his willingness to see eunuchs as positive ego-ideals for males (Matt 19:12), would be interesting to know (Conway, 2008, pp. 123–124).

Accusations of effeminacy typically said more about the accuser's concerns than the accused's behavior. The ubiquity of the discourse in the ancient record arguably reflects the difficulty many elite males had defining "what it meant to be a man" in the multicultural context of Roman imperial order. Again, protocols for male behavior were bound up with notions of respectability that reflected how elites saw themselves. These values provided ideological justification for the elites' social standing, not least by mystifying their dependency on the labor of women and slaves and by rationalizing political subordination to the emperor as his "co-workers" in managing the empire (Martin, 2006, p. 76; Cassius Dio, *Roman History* 52.19.2–3). To some Roman-era moralists, though, the privileged position of such men exposed them to "alien" cultural refinements that seemed to undermine traditional notions of *Romanitas* and manliness (Edwards, 1993, p. 95); to other writers, leading men in Rome and in Greek-speaking eastern cities were also tempted/threatened from "within" by ambition and competiveness (Dio Chrysostom, *Orations* 32).

Conduct Unbecoming. Above all else, the *malakos* male demonstrated a lack of self-mastery (*enkrateia*), the rule of one's body and passions (Edwards, 1993, p. 12; Williams, 1999, p. 127),which resulted in "incontinence" (*akrasia/incontinentia*) just as a lack of moderation (*sophrosynē*) resulted in "immoderation" (*aklosasia/intemperentia*; Foucault, 1985, pp. 63–65). Lack of self-mastery was a stereotypical character flaw of women and slaves (Arius Didymus; Achilles Tatius 7.10; Petronius, *Satyrica* 26; Pliny, *Letters* 3.14; *Digest* 21.1; Seneca, *Letters* 16 and 17; Dionysius of Halicarnassus 4.24; Columella, *On Agriculture*, 1.7.6, 1.8.2). To indulge excessively in one's "desires" (*epithymia*) and "pleasures" (*hedonē*), especially those of gluttony and lust, was to behave in servile, womanish, and hence unmanly ways, based on such popular assumptions about the inability of women or slaves to control their appetites and emotions (Slavish: Aulus Gellius 19.2; Plutarch, *Moralia* 5B–D; 76B–D; 78E–79; 83 A–E; 686C; Cicero, *Philippics* 2.58, 201; Dio Chrysostom *Orations* 1.65; 4.103; 8.8; 7.5.133–135; 32.60, 67, 51, 69, 70–72; 33.52; Seneca, *Letters* 47.16–17; Epictetus 4.1.15–18; Womanish: Plutarch, *Moralia* 145a–c; Musonius Rufus 3.15; Juvenal 6; Cicero, *Republic* 1.67; Horace, *Odes* 3.6.24; Ps.-Aristotle, *Physiognomica* 812a; Dionysius of Halicarnassus 2.24–26; Livy 34.2–4). Recycling these tropes, Paul claims that the unmanly "old self" has been crucified, via baptism, and so one is "no longer enslaved to sin" and its "passions," so that the new self might be a "slave to righteousness" instead (Rom 6:6, 12, 18; Kunst, 2004, pp. 171–173).

Elite writers widely agreed that "soft" men constituted a lamentable effect of Rome's success in the late republic and early principate. Imperial expansion, they observed, increasingly brought decadent foreign cultures into Rome, along with vast sums of wealth too often spent pursuing all-consuming pleasures, new and old (Livy, *Preface* 11; Polybius 31.25.4–5; Sallust, *Catiline* 10; Seneca, *To Helvia* 10.3; Juvenal 11.77–119; cf. Edwards, 1993, pp. 173–206). "Those things bring most pleasure," Juvenal observed, "whose price is highest" (11.16). Luxurious living threatened to undermine the self-mastery of elite Roman men, and with it the ideological justification of elite rule (Edwards, 1993, pp. 175, 195–198).

The personal failings of leading men as "men" were often associated with larger political threats and public crises (Edwards, 1993, pp. 176–178). Marc Antony, for example, embodied the dangers of wealth and wanton living to the stability of the Roman state—at least, according to his detractors. Antony's inability to control his desires was evident in his inability to control his body, which, it was said, was used sexually by both women (Cicero, *Philippics* 13.24; Horace, *Epodes* 9.12–14) and men (Cicero, *Philippics* 2.44–45; 2.77), consumed inhuman amounts of food and wine (Macrobius, *Saturnalia* 3.17.15), relieved itself in a golden toilet (Pliny, *Natural History* 33.14), and publicly erupted in drunken vomiting (Cicero, *Philippics* 2.63).

Had he known about such stories, they might have provided interesting object lessons for the Markan Jesus, who at one point decries vice, listing those representing failure of self-mastery, such as "fornication," "adultery," "avarice," and "licentiousness," on the grounds that "it is what comes out of a person that defiles" (Mark 7:20–23). In any case, according to Matthew's gospel, Jesus himself was accused of being a "glutton and a drunkard, a friend of tax collectors and sinners," invectives best understood as gendered attacks on his self-mastery and

reputation as a public figure (Mark 11:19). Using rhetorical strategies that would be familiar to Cicero or Juvenal, some early Christian writers took aim at the masculinity of rival teachers or hostile outsiders as a means of warding off threats to their authority.

Young Roman men who indulged excessively were chided for ruining their families' wealth and reputations. They were warned that pursuing expensive pleasures was a form of madness that could disqualify them for public office and lead to debt, prostitution, or the gladiatorial arena. In the Greek-speaking cities of the east, dissolute aristocrats were denounced for corrupting future civic leaders, rendering them unfit to govern; decadence tarnished an entire city's reputation and invited the parental figure of Rome to come rule those who could not rule themselves as free men. Similarly, some early Christians warned of unmanly "false prophets" and "false teachers" who "have hearts trained in greed," "indulge their flesh in depraved lust," "revel in pleasure in the day time," and "have eyes full of adultery;" they are "like irrational animals" and "slaves of corruption," but could still lead "many" to follow "their licentious ways" (2 Pet 2:1–19; cf. 2 Tim 3:1–9; Knust, 2004, p. 119).

In discourses on specific passions, surrendering to pain (*ponos*), fear (*phobos*), or grief (*lypē*) was obviously unmanly. "Thus everything comes down to this," explained Cicero, "that you rule yourself [and] see to the same thing especially in pain: not to do anything in a base, timid, ignoble, slavelike, or womanish way" (*Tusculan Disputations* 2.53, 55; Epictetus 3.24.20). What constituted "surrendering," however, was sometimes unclear. Though Jesus did not weep before or during his crucifixion, for example, he did fall down "deeply grieved" (*perilypos*) and die with a "loud shout" (*phonē megalē*; Mark 14:33, 15:37; Matt 26:38; 27:50). Whether that behavior would have been seen as consistent with a "noble death" or as a loss of self-mastery is a disputed matter among interpreters, ancient and modern (Thurman, 2003). Where Jerome or Origen saw courage and self-control on Jesus's part, observations from Celsus or Porphyry describe a man broken by grief and fear (Origen, *Against Celsus* 2.24–25, 7.55; Jerome, *Commentary on Matthew* 4.26.8).

Moral reflections on two other passions—anger and sexual desire—reveal competing imperatives at work in discourses of manly self-mastery. Regarding anger, the problem is whether it "should be regarded as a loss of control and therefore effeminizing, or as an active display of one's convictions—a manly act" (Conway, 2008, p. 26). To be moved by desire to rectify an injustice or affront was to many elites a sign of "activity," "boldness," "force of character," firmness of resolution, and "hatred of evil"; it was thus an appropriate response for men who were challenged by others (Plutarch, *On Controlling Anger* 456F; Conway, 2008, p. 28). As an inherently irrational passion, anger (*thymos*), and especially rage (*orgē*), could lead a man to act violently without forethought or justification, which to other elite writers signaled a lack of self-mastery more characteristic of women.

Indeed, the second-century physician Galen described violent anger as a hyperaggressive, but still womanish, passion by contrasting the example of his calm, restrained father with that of his explosive mother (*Passions of the Soul* 1.4; 1.7). The discourse on anger thus brought two axioms of elite masculinity, active behavior and rational self-control, into tension with one another. This is evident in early Christian discourse as well, as many of the same texts that warn of the dangers of uncontained rage and instruct Christian males to cultivate more peaceful virtues also valorize actions of Jesus or God that are presented, explicitly or implicitly, as expressions of anger or wrath (Matt 5:21–22; 21:12–13), an ideological contradiction with implications for gender studies that awaits more scholarly discussion.

Sex and the City. No sphere of gender transgression in the Roman world has received as much scholarly attention as sexual desire and behavior. Sexual desire (*epithymia*) and the problem it posed to one's self-mastery was a recurring preoccupation in key discourses such as medicine, literature, and philosophy (Foucault, 1985, 1986; Martin, 2006, pp. 51–76; Vander Stichele and Penner, 2009, pp. 50–62). These discourses primarily reveal a tension between two competing imperatives with respect to male

sexuality. Males were expected to follow the "prime directive of masculine sexual behavior" (Williams, 1999, p. 18). That is, they were expected always and only to play the "active" sexual role by penetrating a partner (of either sex), thus symbolically subjugating him or her as a social inferior. Elite males were also expected to extend their dominant social position into the future by marrying and begetting the next generation of leading men. However, doctors and philosophers counseled these same, civic-minded males to maintain strict discipline over their sexual appetites and to regulate and limit their sexual activity, even in marriage (Brown, 1988, pp. 5–32).

Such "emphasis on self-control complicates the ideology of masculinity, insofar as it seems to push against the idea of generativity and reproduction," and even the association of masculinity with domination of others (Conway, 2008, p. 26). Learning self-mastery had as its goal sexual continence or moderation but not prolonged renunciation or permanent bachelorhood; the uncommon individual who deliberately forsook all pleasure, perhaps for life as a philosopher (Philostratus, *Apollonius of Tyana* 1.13.3), faced penalties under Augustan law and might be chided to marry or mocked for his pretensions (Lucian, *Demonax* 55; Achilles Tatius, *Leucippe and Cleitophon* 8.5.7). More alarming to many social critics was an incontinent (*akolasias*) male who pursued sex the way a glutton (*phagos*) sought ever more food and wine. Like the glutton, the adulterer could be called *malakos* because of his obsession with ephemeral pleasure and the debilitating effect it had on his constitution and character (Edwards, 1993, pp. 34–62; Martin, 2006, pp. 44–47).

Ancient medical writers might have regarded sex as natural, but they nevertheless cautioned against frequent or vigorous intercourse because of the vital heat spent in the form of semen with each act—a loss that, it was believed, could decrease fertility, increase the chances of illness, and generally make the male body cooler, weaker, and more woman-like (Brown, 1988, pp. 17–25). "Men who remain chaste," counseled the physician Soranus, "are stronger and better than others and pass their lives in better health" (*Gynaecia* 17.30.2). In contrast to modern equations of hypersexuality with hypermasculinity, ancient males overly preoccupied with sexual pleasure were seen as unmanly slaves to desire, at least by their censorious peers (Musonius Rufus 12.10–45; Aulus Gellius 19.2; Edwards, 1993, pp. 195–198). As a counterbalance to such stern attitudes, the authors of Latin love elegies and Greek novels explored, in different ways, the unstable state of a male ego captivated by desire for a seductive, and often elusive, woman, putting a sympathetic spin on the experience of *eros* (Konstan, 1994; Skinner, 1997).

Yet to a renowned orator and statesman like Dio Chrysostom there was nothing sympathetic about a male who let his unchecked desire wreak moral havoc among the urban aristocracy. Lamenting the corrupt ways of city life in the Greek east, he singles out for reproach the "man whose appetite is insatiate" (*apalastos ton toiouton epithymion*) to easy seductions and "a woman's love," who thus turns "his assault to the male quarters, eager to befoul the youth who will very soon be magistrates and judges and generals" because he believes "that in them he will find a kind of pleasure difficult and hard to procure." Like a drunkard grown bored of his usual fare (*Orations* 7.152), such a man is driven to look for new sources of pleasure, young city-dwelling males in this case, even if he ruins the reputations of future public officials in the process (Martin, 2006, p. 57).

What most alarmed Dio and other Roman moralists was that unrestrained sexual appetite easily led to transgressive sexual behavior, acts "contrary to nature" (*para physin/contra naturam*). In philosophical and popular discourses, such acts included penetrating or fellating one's self, intercourse with a god or goddess, a corpse, or an animal, as well as sex between two women or two free men (Artemidoros, *Interpretation of Dreams* 1.80; Moore, 2001, pp. 141–145). Moralists generally accepted that freeborn men made sexual use of male slaves or youths (Musonius Rufus 86.10; Williams, 1999, pp. 234–244).

When reading ancient descriptions of "unnatural" behavior, it is important to remember the difference from modern meanings of "natural." This becomes apparent when considering a broader range of acts deemed *kata physin* or *para physin* in ancient discourse (Williams, 1999, pp. 231–244). Contemporary men's and women's hairstyles are not thought to reflect "natural" differences between the sexes (cf. 1 Cor 11:2–16; Seneca, *Controversiae* 1.8–9; Lucian, *Dialogues of the Courtesans* 5.3); nor might we say that someone being carried in a litter (Seneca, *Letters* 55.1) or walking backward displays a "hatred of nature" (Cicero, *On the Ends of Good and Evil* 5.35). When reading ancient discourses on sex or gender it is also important to bear in mind that appeals to "nature" serve the ideological function of positioning ruling class values as self-evident.

What Dio tries to protect in his critique of unnatural sex, then, is not only the state of young male bodies, but the collective aristocratic body, reflecting that class and gender were mutually defining categories in Greco-Roman culture (Moore, 2001, p. 140). These relationships only become more complicated in ancient discourses on sex. In virtually all of our extant elite male-authored texts, sex was imagined as a zero-sum competition between "active" penetrators and "passive" receptors, whose position symbolized his or her inferior role in the act and, by implication, in society at large (Moore, 2001, pp. 134–146; Foucault, 1986, p. 30). To penetrate was to "play the man" and to be penetrated was to "play the woman." Accordingly, sex between males was "unnatural" because it required one male to transgress "natural" gender boundaries in order to assume a position for which he was ill-equipped. Plutarch is blunt on this point: "but to consort with males (whether without consent, in which case it involves violence and brigandage; or if with consent, there is still weakness and effeminacy [*malakia kai thlytati*] on the part of those who, contrary to nature [*para physin*], allow themselves in Plato's words 'to be covered and mounted like cattle')—this is a completely ill-favored favor, indecent, an unlovely affront to Aphrodite" (*Moralia* 751; cf. Plato, *Laws* 636a–c).

To moralists like Plutarch and Paul, it seems that (male or female) same-sex sex threatened the idea of male superiority. While a female who penetrated others assumed a symbolically male role, a male who submitted to (oral or anal) penetration became symbolically female, even subhuman. In each case, hierarchical differences between males and females were undermined and boundaries of masculinity blurred, much to the dismay of those invested in such differences (Martin, 2006, pp. 58–60; Moore, 2001, pp. 148–154). Hence the tendency of elite male writers to deploy invective toward *tribades,* females whose acts with others, especially females, are routinely described as "monstrous" (Ovid, *Metamorphoses* 9.666–727; Martial 1.90, 7.67, 7.70; Seneca, *Epistles* 95.20; Seneca, *Controversiae* 1.2.23; Lucian, *Dialogue of the Courtesans* 5.4; Brooten, 1996, pp. 42–56). Hence, too, the persistent *cinaedus/kinaidos* stereotype, the "ideological scare figure for Roman men," as a "diseased" gender-deviant whose addiction to being anally penetrated epitomizes a life dedicated to singing, dancing, and other "soft" pursuits (Williams, 1999, pp. 172–181). Next to the *cinaedus* stood the *pathicus, fellator,* and *cunnilingus* as stock examples of failed men all too willing to surrender themselves to satisfy the sexual desires of others, male or female. Juvenal held such men in as much contempt as Paul, an alignment of interests reflecting the hegemonic hold of ancient discourses on manliness (Juvenal 2.1–22, 36–50, 65–98, 115–132, 137–148, 162–170).

Assessment. It is apparent that discourses concerning Roman gender transgression are animated in part by desires to shore up group identities, not only by reinforcing class boundaries but also by demarcating ethnic or cultural boundaries under imperial rule. When Paul links same-sex sex with idolatry (Rom 1:18–32), he is recycling Jewish stereotypes of morally depraved gentiles. According to some recent interpretations, he may have done so as a way of challenging presumptions that elite Romans and Greeks had a monopoly on self-mastery (Knust, 2004). Likewise, Josephus defended his Jewish *ethnos* from moral slander by denigrating the heritage of his Egyptian critics as one of slavery and softness (*Against Apion* 2.125–134; *Jewish Antiquities* 2.201–202). Elsewhere, he more subtly implied that the rigors of Jewish practice produced men who surpassed the legendary Spartans in courage and endurance (*Against Apion* 2.225, 228–231, 273, 292–294), perhaps an implicit retort to Roman rep-

resentations of Jews as a defeated, feminized people, exemplified by "Judaea Capta" coins issued after the Jewish war of 66–74 C.E. (cf. *Jewish War* 6.33–53).

Both Paul and Josephus thus appropriated familiar rhetorical strategies of self-definition from Jewish, Greek, and Roman traditions. While many Latin writers regularly derided Greek cultural products and practices, especially those from the cities of Asia, as soft (Edwards, 1993, pp. 92–97; 177–178), a Greek-speaking Syrian satirist, Lucian of Samosata, could accuse the imperial capital itself of harboring unmanly decadence (*Nigrinus* 15–16; Kunst, 2004, 167). In a similar rhetorical vein, Greek novelists could expose the violence of imperial rule without ever mentioning Rome by name, in part by depicting the struggle of noble Greek youths against the sexual assaults of barbarian princes and rapacious bandits as an allegory for the position of Greek elites in a world bound together by powers that were a rule unto themselves.

In a striking first-century monument to Roman conquest, the Sebasteion in Aphrodisias, gendered and sexual tropes are critical to visual articulations of Roman, Greek, and barbarian identities. A particularly arresting relief depicts the Roman conquest of Britannia as the subjugation of a half-naked barbarian woman by a heroically nude Claudius. Pinning her down with one knee, he pulls her hair with one hand and is poised to strike her prone body with the other, while she raises one arm to appeal for mercy or ward off the blow. That the image conflates military conquest with sexual violence and thus masculinity with domination and femininity with submission is apparent (Lopez, 2008, pp. 42–45). That such an image was commissioned by Greek elites of a "free" Roman city, perhaps as a way of eliding their own submission to imperial rule via visual alignment of Greeks and Romans against the rest of the barbarian nations, is a small testimony to the use of gender stereotypes to guard against various possible transgressions in the Roman world.

[*See also* Gender Transgression, *subentries on* Early Church *and* New Testament; Masculinity and Femininity, *subentry* Roman World; Same-Sex Relations, *subentry* Roman World; *and* Sexual Transgression, *subentries on* New Testament *and* Roman World.]

BIBLIOGRAPHY

Brooten, Bernadette. *Love Between Women: Early Christian Reponses to Female Homoeroticism.* Chicago: University of Chicago Press, 1996.

Brown, Peter. *The Body and Society: Men, Women, and Sexual Renunciation in Early Christianity.* Lectures on the History of Religions 13. New York: Columbia University Press, 1988.

Conway, Colleen. *Behold the Man: Jesus and Greco-Roman Masculinity.* New York: Oxford University Press, 2008.

Edwards, Catharine. *The Politics of Immorality in Ancient Rome.* New York: Cambridge University Press, 1993.

Foucault, Michel. *The History of Sexuality,* Vol. 2: *The Use of Pleasure.* Translated by Robert Hurley. New York: Vintage, 1985.

Foucault, Michel. *The History of Sexuality,* Vol. 3: *The Care of the Self.* Translated by Robert Hurley. New York: Vintage, 1986.

Knust, Jennifer. "Paul and the Politics of Virtue and Vice." In *Paul and the Roman Imperial Order,* edited by Richard Horsley, pp. 155–174. Harrisburg, Pa.: Trinity Press International, 2004.

Konstan, David. *Sexual Symmetry: Love in the Ancient Novel and Related Genres.* Princeton, N.J.: Princeton University Press, 1994.

Lopez, Davina C. *Apostle to the Conquered: Reimagining Paul's Mission.* Paul in Critical Contexts. Minneapolis: Fortress, 2008.

Martin, Dale B. *Sex and the Single Savior: Gender and Sexuality in Biblical Interpretation.* Louisville, Ky.: Westminster John Knox, 2006.

Moore, Stephen D. *God's Beauty Parlor: And Other Queer Spaces In and Around the Bible.* Contraversions. Stanford, Calif.: Stanford University Press, 2001.

Skinner, Marilyn. "*Ego mulier*: The Construction of Male Sexuality in Catullus." In *Roman Sexualities,* edited by Judith P. Hallett and Marilyn Skinner, pp. 129–150. Princeton, N.J.: Princeton University Press, 1997.

Skinner, Marilyn. *Sexuality in Greek and Roman Culture.* Malden, Mass.: Blackwell, 2005.

Thurman, Eric. "Looking for a Few Good Men: Mark and Masculinity." In *New Testament Masculinities,* edited by Stephen D. Moore and Janice Capel Anderson, pp. 137–162. Semeia Studies 45. Leiden, The Netherlands: Brill, 2003.

Vander Stichele, Caroline, and Todd Penner. *Contextualizing Gender in Early Christian Discourse: Thinking Beyond Thecla.* New York: Continuum, 2009.

William, Craig. *Roman Homosexuality: Ideologies of Masculinity in Classical Antiquity.* New York: Oxford University Press, 1999.

Eric Thurman

New Testament

Many contemporary theorists argue that gender (and, some would add, sex) is a social construction produced by a multiplicity of discourses in any given time and place. A particular culture enforces sex/gender norms that must be performed, and it is the compulsive repetition of such performances that creates the illusion that sex and gender are permanent, stable essences. The very need for repetition, however, opens up space for performing a culture's sex/gender norms transgressively, thereby demonstrating that sex and gender are actually unstable and contingent social constructions. The study of gender transgression in the New Testament has focused on a number of interrelated performances of sex/gender that confuse, trouble, and/or cross boundaries, thereby destabilizing and denaturalizing binary constructions of sex/gender.

Mixing Masculinity and Femininity. Binary sex/gender systems construct certain activities and attributes as masculine and others as feminine. One form of gender transgression, then, is mixing masculine and feminine activities and/or attributes. In the Gospel of John, women perform activities that their culture gendered feminine, such as serving meals to men (12:1–2) and ritually preparing the bodies of the dead (12:3–8), but they also perform activities gendered masculine, such as taking the initiative in theological debate with Jesus (4:19–24) and testifying to his resurrection (20:16–18). Likewise, Jesus defends his (figurative) household against a hostile world (17:12–15), an activity gendered masculine, but he also literally (6:5–13) and figuratively (6:48–51) serves meals. While scholars disagree as to whether the Gospel of John as a whole reinforces or resists its culture's sex/gender norms, this gender mixing does open up space for questioning these norms.

There is a general consensus among scholars that the characterization of the Logos/Jesus in the Gospel of John has been influenced by the characterization of female-personified Wisdom in texts such as Proverbs and Sirach. Both figures are presented as the first being created and as a participant in the work of creation (Prov 8:22–31; Sir 24:9; John 1:2–3, 10). Both pitched their tents and lived among humans (Sir 24:8, 10–12; John 1:14). Both provide long life (Prov 3:16; John 10:27–28) and invite others to eat and drink of them (Sir 24:19–21; John 6:50–51). Some scholars have concluded that the result of the interfigurality of Logos/Jesus and Wisdom is the cooptation and supersession of a female figure by a male figure. Other scholars argue, however, that this interfigurality produces a Jesus who transcends the boundaries of binary sex/gender. Reading through the lens of cross-dressing, Tat-siong Benny Liew (2009) suggests that John's Wisdom/Jesus puts on gender both to conceal and to reveal, thereby demonstrating that gender itself is an effect of bodily performances rather than an expression of an immutable essence at a person's core.

Some scholars have defined this combination of masculine and feminine attributes as androgyny. In 1 Corinthians 11:2–16, in the context of a debate about how one should be dressed while prophesying, Paul redeploys material from the creation stories in Genesis to construct a gendered hierarchy in which Christ is the head of man, and man is the head of woman. Most scholars define the rhetorical situation as one in which Paul is trying to dissuade some Corinthian women who have stopped wearing veils while prophesying. Paul does not make this rhetorical situation explicit, however, and the text does not prevent a reader from imagining a rhetorical situation in which Paul is also trying to dissuade some Corinthian men from wearing veils while prophesying. There are numerous examples of ritualized cross-dressing in human history. Perhaps, then, women and men in Corinth were performing a religious androgyny in opposition to Paul's proposed sex/gender hierarchy.

Androgyny and Transgenderism. Androgyny is a contested concept in the study of gender transgression in the New Testament. On the one hand, various myths circulating in Greco-Roman antiquity, including certain interpretations of the creation stories of Genesis, posited androgyny as the idealized origin and/or destiny of humankind. Some scholars argue, therefore, that androgyny undermines the binary sex/gender system, thus opening up space for new and multiple yet-to-be-imagined expressions of sex/gender. On the other hand, Greco-Roman philosophical/medical discourses posited a "one-sex model," in which male and female genitals were mirror images of each other. In this model, the exterior genitals of males defined the perfect human form, while the interior genitals of females were the result of some imperfection. Some scholars argue, therefore, that in the Greco-Roman context androgyny would not have been understood as a combination of equally valued sexes/genders, but instead as the movement of a body from the imperfect female end of the sex/gender continuum to the perfect male end.

Another word that has been used to describe the practices of the prophesying women of Corinth is transgendered. "Transsexual" is a label that has typically been applied to those who seek, or are required to seek, surgery in order to make their bodies appear more like the bodies of those defined as the opposite sex. "Transgendered" has been used to refer to a broader range of practices that embody, distort, invent, mix, and challenge a variety of gender expressions, often without surgery. Transsexuals have been subjected to a medical rhetoric that demands that their bodies suffer the physical trauma of surgery in order to move from one normative sex/gender category to the other, thus preserving the binary sex/gender system. Many of those who construct themselves as transgendered have resisted this rhetoric, insisting that one can already perform gender transgressively without normalizing surgery, thus undermining the binary sex/gender system. Joseph A. Marchal (2010) has argued that in 1 Corinthians 1–4, Paul is attempting rhetorically to reform the community's identity through a narrative of status earned by suffering, like the medical narrative of transsexuality. Using Paul's rhetoric to reconstruct the situation of the audience, he argues that the prophesying women of Corinth were instead performing a narrative of an identity that already is, without the need for normalizing suffering, like the transgendered narrative.

"Lesbian Men," Effeminacy, and Emasculation. The French feminist theorist Monique Wittig famously argued that one is not born a woman, but rather one becomes a woman through one's social relationships with men. Seeking the disappearance of women as a social-political-economic class, Wittig focused on a figure she defined not as androgynous or transgendered, but rather as "lesbian." She argued that because the lesbian is not defined by social relationships with men, she is not a woman; rather, she exceeds binary categories of sex/gender. Gillian Townsley has applied Wittig's concept to the cross-dressing men of Corinth, describing them as "lesbian men" who are thus not men, as they exceed binary sex/gender. Wittig's theory still provokes debate, and Townsley argues that it has often been misunderstood, particularly in the United States. Some scholars will question whether Townsley's application of lesbian to the Corinthian men undermines the specificity of lesbian identities, while others will find in it an effective attempt to rethink "lesbian" in performative rather than essentialist terms.

In 1 Corinthians 6:9–10, Paul lists categories of persons who will not inherit the kingdom of God, including *malakoi*. The New Revised Standard Version and the New International Version translate this word as "male prostitutes," while the Revised Standard Version and Today's English Version translate the combination of this Greek word and the one that follows as "sexual perverts" and "homosexual perverts," respectively. All these translations focus on sexuality. The translation in the King James Version, however, is "effeminate." Male gender transgression, effeminacy, could be referred to by a constellation of Greek and Latin terms including *malakos* and *mollis*, which signify softness. While sexual receptivity to other males could define one as effeminate, so could a high-pitched voice, the use of cosmetics, or depilation (in addition to or apart from sexual

receptivity). The decision, then, to translate *malakoi* in terms of sexuality rather than gender reflects contemporary ideologies and concerns.

That Paul shared the dominant Greco-Roman culture's aversion to gender-transgressive males is reinforced by Romans 1:18–32. Here Paul constructs an analogy between idolatry as a violation of the cosmic hierarchy and male-male sexual activity as a violation of the sex/gender hierarchy. In light of this analogy, the disease of effemination threatened not only the social but the cosmic order. On the one hand, an accusation of effeminacy could therefore function as a weapon in the public competition for social recognition as a man, and some scholars argue that Paul is here taking up this weapon against those in his audience who judge others (2:1). On the other hand, feminizing a sexually receptive male is an attempt to maintain a construction of heterosexuality that depends on a rigidly binary sex/gender system by conforming one male to the sexual role of a woman. Stephen D. Moore (2001) argues that this attempt fails in Romans, however, because there are no females at the heart of Paul's theology. All the roles are played by males—God, Jesus, and Paul—none of whom Paul is ultimately willing to feminize, and thus Romans 1:18–32 ends up creating a crisis for the binary sex/gender system itself.

In 1 Corinthians 6:12–20, Paul addresses another group of Corinthian men, those who are having sex with prostitutes. As long as the men were playing the penetrative role, this behavior would not have been constructed as gender transgression in the dominant Greco-Roman culture. Paul, however, does not approve of such activity. In his attempt to dissuade the Corinthian men, he could have made use of a Greco-Roman rhetoric of *askesis* (asceticism) that reinforced the dominant Greco-Roman construction of gender by constructing self-control as a means of self-mastery, and thus a demonstration of a man's ability not only to dominate others but also to dominate his own passions. Instead, Paul argues that a man does not possess exclusive control over his own body. If he joins Christ, he becomes a member of Christ; if he has sex with a prostitute, he becomes a member of a prostitute. This understanding of Paul's rhetoric is reinforced by 1 Corinthians 7:4: "For the wife does not have authority over her own body, but the husband does; likewise the husband does not have authority over his own body, but the wife does." Paul's rhetoric thus emasculates these Corinthian men by refusing them control over their own bodies.

Emasculation is also an issue in Galatians. Most scholars who have analyzed this letter in terms of gender highlight its central focus on circumcision, which privileges the male's penis as the bearer of sacred identity. Marchal (2010) has suggested reading the letter from the perspective of the intersexed, although his conclusions differ from those here. "Intersexed" is a contemporary term for human bodies that at birth do not conform to either of the anatomical patterns normatively defined as male and female, but such bodies were also known in antiquity and were constructed as "hermaphrodites." In order to preserve the binary sex/gender system, American medical protocols typically require that such bodies be altered surgically as soon as possible to make them more closely conform to one of the two normative patterns. Medical professionals employ gendered criteria in deciding which pattern to impose. Generally, an intersexed infant is only constructed as a boy if the penis size indicates the future ability to penetrate a vagina. The key factor in constructing an intersexed infant as girls, however, is the maintenance of reproductive capacity. Intersexed activists have contested these protocols, arguing that intersexed individuals should have the right to make their own decisions about surgery when they are old enough. On the one hand, like contemporary American medical professionals, Paul puts the penis at the center of determining identity. On the other hand, like contemporary intersexed activists, he opposes compulsory "surgery" (circumcision). In the dominant Greco-Roman culture, circumcision and castration were both constructed as genital mutilation, and Paul's awareness of this may be reflected in Galatians 5.12: "I wish those who unsettle you would castrate themselves!" Paul's rhetoric could be read as a defense of gender transgression in its opposition to normalizing surgery, but it could also be read as a defense against gender transgression in its opposition to the decision of some Galatian men to be circumcised.

Eunuchs. The mention of castration points to a final figure that has generated a good deal of scholarship on gender transgression in the New Testament—the eunuch. The practice of castrating animals to make them tractable dates back to at least 2300 B.C.E., and the practice of castrating human males likely did not take long to develop after that. At first castration may have served as a means of humiliating enemies and punishing criminals, but in the institutional context of the ancient Near Eastern harem, it became a means of producing males that could police the sexuality of the ruler's women without impregnating them. This is the origin of the ancient institution of court eunuchs. Such eunuchs served in royal households as doorkeepers, cupbearers, messengers, tutors, bodyguards, and harem guards, and as rulers sought ways to counterbalance the power of nobility, they even came to serve as royal administrators and officials.

In addition to the Roman Empire, eunuchs were employed in the royal courts of Persia, China, and India, and they were probably employed in the royal courts of Assyria, Israel, and Judah as well. Those living in the Roman Empire would also have been familiar with a second group of eunuchs associated with the cult of the goddess Cybele. This cult had its origins in Anatolia in the seventh century B.C.E., from which it spread to Greece and later to Rome, where a temple was built for Cybele in the early second century B.C.E. Each year on the Day of Blood, some of Cybele's devotees would castrate themselves and receive women's clothing to wear. Called *galli*, these self-castrated slaves of the goddess played a role in the annual Roman festival of Cybele, and Greco-Roman works of fiction suggest that they could also be found traveling through the provinces as mendicants.

Two texts have provided the focal points for the study of eunuchs in the New Testament: Matthew 19:12 and Acts 8:26–40. In the first, Matthew's Jesus refers to three different groups of eunuchs: those who have been eunuchs from birth, those who have been made eunuchs by others, and those who have made themselves eunuchs for the sake of the kingdom of heaven. The first group would have included those the ancients called hermaphrodites, as well as others who were born sterile. Some scholars have employed the contemporary notion of sexual orientation, which posits that each person has a stable, lifelong sexual attraction to the opposite and/or the same sex/gender, to argue that this category could also have included males who had sex with other males exclusively, who would thus not have been able to reproduce. The second group would have included court eunuchs. There are also examples in Greco-Roman texts of young men being castrated in order to preserve the youthful beauty that some older men found sexually attractive. Some scholars have suggested, therefore, that this second group could also have included males who had been castrated to serve as prostitutes or as the beloveds of powerful men.

The area of greatest debate, regarding Matthew 19:12, is the identification of the third group of eunuchs. Some scholars have affirmed the traditional Christian reading as a metaphorical reference to those who choose celibacy. There is certainly support for this reading in the literary context, as the saying is part of a wider discourse about marriage and divorce. In Matthew 19:3–9, Jesus is asked by some Pharisees whether it is lawful to divorce one's wife for any cause, and his response restricts divorce to cases of unchastity. In 19:10–11, his disciples declare that if this is the case, then it is better not to marry, and Jesus responds that this teaching can only be accepted by those to whom it is given. There are also other passages in the Gospel that reinforce the idea that Jesus endorsed celibacy. He himself is referred to as a bridegroom in 9:15, but notably absent in the rest of the Gospel is a bride. Also, in a discussion about resurrection, which could be read as an ideal state to which Matthew's community should aspire, Jesus says that in the resurrection men do not marry and women are not given in marriage (22:30).

The description of the third group as those who have made themselves eunuchs, however, seems to suggest the self-castration of the *galli*. This would mean that it is given to some of Jesus's male disciples to castrate themselves in some sense. The fact that there are stories that claim that the early Christian theologian Origen castrated himself, whether or not they are true, demonstrates that early Christians could imagine taking the last part of Matthew 19:12 literally. Most readers, however, have taken it metaphorically. While the dominant Greco-Roman construction of binary sex/gender certainly depended on a distinction between male and female bodies, it also depended on a distinction between men and "unmen." To earn the status of man, a male had to be a free adult citizen who was always publicly perceived to be hard, active, and impenetrable. All others—male and female— were unmen. The fact that castration could move a male body from the category of man to the category of unman highlighted the frightening reality that masculinity could be lost. For male disciples, to castrate themselves metaphorically by renouncing marriage would have meant renouncing the traditional role of men as householders. As is suggested in the discussion of the qualifications of bishops in 1 Timothy 3:4, it was in his role as householder that a man proved his ability to dominate others—wife, children, and slaves. There is support for this reading in the literary context. Immediately following the saying about eunuchs, Jesus announces that it is little children to whom the kingdom of heaven belongs (9:13–14). In other places in the Gospel, including 24:45–51, Jesus asks his disciples to identify with slaves. In asking his disciples to identify with eunuchs, children, and slaves, then, he was asking them to become unmen.

To explain the consequences of such a renunciation of masculinity, Rick Talbott (2006) has utilized Elisabeth Schüssler Fiorenza's concept of kyriarchy, a social-political-economic system designed to secure the control of emperor/master/father/husband over all others. The symbolic castration of Jesus's male disciples was one way of castrating the system itself, thus opening the way for equality between men and women, or men and unmen, in the Matthean community. This symbolic castration can also be read in terms of the concept of compulsory heterosexuality, a social-political-economic system in which the imperative to reproduce is secured by a rigidly binary construction of sex/gender. The refusal to marry and establish a household, then, represented resistance to a masculinity defined by heterosexuality and reproduction.

As the distinction between men and unmen suggests, the dominant Greco-Roman construction of masculinity depended on more than a binary opposition of sex/gender (male/female). It also depended on binary oppositions of class (free/slave), race (citizen/foreigner), and sexuality (penetrator/penetrated). Eunuchs were not simply unmen; rather, they were figures who blurred the boundaries and troubled all the distinctions upon which masculinity depended. They were bodies moved by castration from the category of male to female/both/none. Although some would have been the freeborn children of citizens, their castration typically marked them as slaves, and the prohibition of castration within the bounds of the Roman Empire resulted in their identification as foreigners. In terms of sexuality, eunuchs could certainly be seen as unmen who allowed themselves to be penetrated by others, even including women in the case of cunnilingus (the Romans understood oral sex as the penetration of a mouth), but Roman men also feared them as hypermasculine men who could penetrate their wives without leaving any evidence in the form of pregnancy.

Acts 8:26–40 narrates the story of the baptism of a character identified as "an Ethiopian eunuch, a court official of the Candace, queen of the Ethiopians, in charge of her entire treasury" (8:27). Manuel Villalobos (2011) reads the Ethiopian eunuch through the lens of Gloria Anzaldúa's concept of the *mestiza*, a hybrid figure who dwells in the borderlands and celebrates the ambiguity and ambivalence that reign there. The initiation of the Ethiopian eunuch into the community of believers through baptism is an invitation to the community to embrace the *mestiza* and the borderlands.

Most queer theorists argue that all binary oppositions between "the normal" and "the abnormal" depend on the naturalization of social constructions of identity. Queering involves the utilization of multiple strategies to deconstruct and to denaturalize these social constructions. Drawing on the work of Judith Butler, I have described the goal of queering as opening up space for bodies previously labeled nonhuman or less than human to be recognized and embraced as fully human (Burke, 2013). Eunuchs as figures in texts have the potential to queer the discourses of gender, class, race, and sexuality upon which the dominant Greco-Roman construction of masculinity depended. The baptism of the Ethiopian eunuch, then, inscribes into early Christian discourse the deconstruction and denaturalization of binary oppositions between "the normal" and "the abnormal" for the sake of the inclusion of all bodies in the community of believers.

[*See also* Gender; Gender Transgression, *subentry* Roman World; Homosexual/Queer; Masculinity and Femininity, *subentry* New Testament; Patriarchy/Kyriarchy; Queer Readings; *and* Queer Theory.]

BIBLIOGRAPHY

Anderson, Janice Capel, and Stephen D. Moore. "Matthew and Masculinity." In *New Testament Masculinities*, edited by Stephen D. Moore and Janice Capel Anderson, pp. 67–91. Semeia Studies 45. Atlanta: Society of Biblical Literature, 2003.

Burke, Sean D. *Queering the Ethiopian Eunuch: Strategies of Ambiguity in Acts*. Emerging Scholars. Minneapolis: Fortress, 2013.

Hester, J. David. "Eunuchs and the Postgender Jesus: Matthew 19.12 and Transgressive Sexualities." *Journal for the Study of the New Testament* 28, no. 1 (2005): 13–40.

Hornsby, Teresa J., and Ken Stone, eds. *Bible Trouble: Queer Reading at the Boundaries of Biblical Scholarship*. Semeia Studies 67. Atlanta: Society of Biblical Literature, 2011.

Kitzberger, Ingrid Rosa. "Transcending Gender Boundaries in John." In *A Feminist Companion to John*, edited by Amy-Jill Levine and Marianne Blickenstaff, vol. 1, pp. 173–207. Sheffield, U.K.: Sheffield Academic Press, 2003.

Liew, Tat-siong Benny. "Queering Closets and Perverting Desires: Cross-Examining John's Engendering and Transgendering Word across Different Worlds." In *They Were All Together in One Place? Toward Minority Biblical Criticism*, edited by Randall C. Bailey,

Tat-siong Benny Liew, and Fernando F. Segovia, pp. 251–288. Semeia Studies 57. Atlanta: Society of Biblical Literature, 2009.

Marchal, Joseph A. "Bodies Bound for Circumcision and Baptism: An Intersex Critique and the Interpretation of Galatians." *Theology and Sexuality* 16, no. 2 (2010): 163–182.

Marchal, Joseph A. "The Corinthian Women Prophets and Trans Activism: Rethinking Canonical Gender Claims." In *Bible Trouble: Queer Reading at the Boundaries of Biblical Scholarship*, edited by Teresa J. Hornsby and Ken Stone, pp. 223–246. Semeia Studies 67. Atlanta: Society of Biblical Literature, 2011.

Martin, Dale B. *Sex and the Single Savior: Gender and Sexuality in Biblical Interpretation.* Louisville, Ky.: Westminster John Knox, 2006.

Moore, Stephen D. *God's Beauty Parlor, and Other Queer Spaces In and Around the Bible.* Stanford, Calif.: Stanford University Press, 2001.

Moxnes, Halvor. "Asceticism and Christian Identity in Antiquity: A Dialogue with Foucault and Paul." *Journal for the Study of the New Testament* 26, no. 1 (2003): 3–29.

Moxnes, Halvor. "Jesus in Gender Trouble." *CrossCurrents* 54, no. 3 (2004): 31–46.

Swancutt, Diana M. "'The Disease of Effemination': The Charge of Effeminacy and the Verdict of God (Romans 1:18–2:16)." In *New Testament Masculinities*, edited by Stephen D. Moore and Janice Capel Anderson, pp. 193–233. Semeia Studies 45. Atlanta: Society of Biblical Literature, 2003.

Talbott, Rick. "Imagining the Matthean Eunuch Community: Kyriarchy on the Chopping Block." *Journal of Feminist Studies in Religion* 22, no. 1 (2006): 21–43.

Villalobos, Manuel. "Bodies *Del Otro Lado* Finding Life and Hope in the Borderland: Gloria Anzaldúa, the Ethiopian Eunuch of Acts 8:26–40, *y Yo.*" In *Bible Trouble: Queer Reading at the Boundaries of Biblical Scholarship*, edited by Teresa J. Hornsby and Ken Stone, pp. 191–222. Semeia Studies 67. Atlanta: Society of Biblical Literature, 2011.

Vorster, Johannes N. "Androgyny and Early Christianity." *Religion and Theology* 15, nos. 1–2 (2008): 97–132.

Sean D. Burke

Early Judaism

The primary sources this article explores are materials dating from the destruction of the Temple through the sixth century (the Mishnah and Tosefta, the Babylonian and Palestinian versions of the Talmud, and various works of Midrashic literature). In none of these sources does gender transgression appear as an explicit expression of identity or even as an explicit act. Nowhere are there examples of transsexual or transgendered individuals per se, either real or fictional. That is not to say that the sages of the rabbinic period do not wrestle with some forms of gender transgression, both in law and in narrative. This article addresses three ways in which that wrestling appears: through transgressive categories, through laws against transgressive behavior, and through transgressive personalities.

Rabbinic literature operates within a paradigm of the gender binary that manifests in several ways. Within the realm of the theoretical, in which gender is constructed and replicated, the binary nature of the rabbinic gender system becomes clear through discussions about those who do not fit into the categories "male" and "female." Within the realm of law, gender is primarily constructed by distinct divisions between those commandments that obligate women and those that obligate men. Following a series of laws beginning with how a woman is "acquired," *m. Qiddushin* 1:7 addresses some of these category divisions directly. Although these commandments are portrayed as faithful to their biblical sources, they often reimagine, embellish, or create laws *ex nihilo* in the absence of existing ones. For example, the laws concerning marriage and divorce are based on extensive interpretations of four short biblical verses (Deut 24:1-4). In other cases, such as laws concerning women and study, the rabbis address issues that the biblical text does not.

Gender Transgressive Categories in Rabbinic Literature. The primary way in which rabbinic literature disrupts the binary sex/gender system is through the creation of entirely new categories of sex/gender. I do not differentiate here between sex and gender, since one of the goals of the rabbinic texts is to build a system of daily behavior (in the form of law) that conforms with a person's biological sex. Thus, a transgression of one is necessarily a transgression of the other. These categories are in some cases loosely modeled after Greek and Roman ones, and in others constructed independent of either the biblical text or the Greek and Roman world.

The category of *saris*, or eunuch, derives its title from a term already used in biblical texts. Although in the biblical context there is some debate about whether the term merely refers to palace guards, it is understood to have sometimes referred to castrated or genitally dysfunctional males employed by royalty to guard their harems (Tadmor, 1995). In rabbinic texts, this term is subdivided into two new categories, the congenital eunuch (*seris chammah*) and the "man made" eunuch (*seris adam*). Greek and Roman texts use the Greek *eunoukhos* and the Latin *spado* as overarching descriptors for both a castrated male and a "natural" eunuch (Matt 19:12; Ulpian, Dig., 50.16.128) and often portray them both as gender crossers. The term *aylonit* (along with its referent, the congenitally infertile woman) seems to have been invented as a category by the sages themselves. Its "etymology" is explained in the Talmud as deriving from the Hebrew word *ayil*, or ram, making her a "ram-like" or "male-like" woman (*b. Ketub.* 11a).

As *legal* categories, these are the creations of the tannaitic sages. Because of the many laws that pertained to reproduction, and because of a fascination with that which defies their constructed categories, the sages explored these particular categories in order to ask the question: What do we do when a person is not physically able to carry out the commandment to procreate? In levirate marriage, for example, a man must marry the widow of his deceased brother in order to carry on the line of the brother. But do we allow levirate marriage if the widow is not physically able to carry on this line? What if the brother is physically unable? Although the rabbis employed these categories to explore particular questions, unlike the Greek and Roman materials, rabbinic law did not consider them gender crossovers, nor is the question of which sex/gender category to place them in ever raised. The laws that pertain to the *seris adam*, the *seris chammah* and the *aylonit* treat them entirely as male and female, respectively.

The two categories that the rabbinic sages employ to explore the issue of the sex/gender binary and its limitations are the *androgynus* and the *tumtum*. The *androgynus* (a term borrowed from the Greek) is one who has both male and female genitalia. The *tumtum*, a term derived from the Hebrew root *tmtm*, to confuse, is one who has a membrane covering the genitals, so that s/he is *either* definitely male or definitely female (unlike the *androgynus*), but her/his sex is undiscoverable.

The rabbinic corpus engages on multiple levels with the question "what do we do with that which transgresses known categories?" The sages use the *androgynus* and *tumtum* to explore precisely these questions in the realm of sex/gender. Thus, the *tumtum* opens up the question: What do we do if a commandment is incumbent upon a certain sex, but we do not (and cannot) know a certain person's sex? According to what sex/gender do we treat this person? By the same token, the *androgynus* explores the question: What do we do if a person's sex/gender is unclear? Do we consider that person to belong to a specific sex/gender? Or do we treat her/him as an entirely new category of sex, a "third sex"?

The most extensive answer to the question of how to regard the *androgynus* appears in *t. Bikkurim* 2:3–7. The text explains that the *androgynus* is in some ways (legally) equivalent to a man, in some ways to a woman, in some ways to both, and in some to neither. The text then offers examples of each of these cases: the *androgynous* may marry (a woman) but may not be married (by a man), becomes impure by both seminal emissions (as a man) and menstrual blood (as a woman) and may not be alone with either a man or a woman. The text enumerates laws having to do with inheritance, appearance, purity, access to holy food, civil law, and more.

R. Yose (rather than the anonymous voice of the majority) makes the final pronouncement in this section of Tosefta: "An *androgynus* is a creation *sui generis*, and the sages could not determine whether s/he is a man or a woman." On the one hand, R. Yose seems to open the possibility that gender is not binary and that perhaps a third gender category exists in the rabbinic paradigm. On the other hand, given that the rabbinic world is governed by gender specific laws about every aspect of a person's daily life, R. Yose's statement leaves open the question: What does the *androgynus do*? How must s/he conduct him/herself on a daily basis? Without expounding on the principle, R. Yose's statement holds no sway.

R. Yose continues: "But this is not the case regarding a *tumtum*, rather, s/he is either a doubtful man or a doubtful woman." In most cases, the *tumtum* and the *androgynus* share the same restrictions, but from time to time the fact that the *tumtum's* sex/gender lies within the binary system (although it is unknown) has its own implications. For example, whereas an *androgynus* may perform a commandment on behalf of another *androgynus* (since they may be considered a category of their own), a *tumtum* may not perform a commandment for anyone else at all, since s/he may, in fact, be a female.

The sages' treatment of these categories is an opening into a more varied gender spectrum that is unabashedly discussed in rabbinic sources. What one finds, however, when carefully examining the issues, is that the texts treat the *androgynus* and *tumtum* not as people free to define their own gender, but rather, as a gender class relegated to the lowest rung of the ladder. The rabbinic allowance for sex/gender fluidity, therefore, is complicated by the social or legal status of the sex/gender transgressor.

Laws against Gender Transgressive Behavior. Aside from the many laws assigning certain behaviors to men and others to women, which certainly aim to preserve and protect the gender binary, the primary biblical law explicitly forbidding *crossing* gender lines appears in Deuteronomy 22:5: "A woman shall not put on the apparel of a man (*k'li gever*), and a man shall not wear the clothing of a woman (*simlat isha*), for any person that does these is an abomination to the LORD your God." This biblical verse quite clearly prohibits cross dressing of any sort.

A Midrash in Sifre Deuteronomy (Ki Tetze, 226), however, takes the plain meaning of the text in a different direction. The Midrash asks rhetorically, "could this verse possibly come to tell us merely that a woman should not wear white clothes and a man should not wear coloured clothes?" The interpretation following this question focuses on the word "abomination," which for the rabbis, refers very specifically to a sexually transgressive act. Since merely cross-dressing would not constitute such an act, this verse cannot refer to cross-dressing itself. It must then refer to cross-dressing in order to pass, so that one can engage in adulterous or licentious behavior. The rabbis thus remove the prohibition two steps from its original. Whereas the biblical prohibition is against cross-dressing, the rabbinic prohibition is against passing, and not merely passing but passing for the sake of deception and licentious (heterosexual) behavior. The Sifre then offers a second interpretation of this verse, associating the prohibition on women cross-dressing with donning weapons and going to war, although it understands the biblical prohibition on male cross-dressing quite literally rather than reinterpreting it. Yet another interpretation of the verse is found in Midrash Tannaim, a compilation of early rabbinic sources. Here the association with licentious behavior is explicit, although the fear is not only of the behavior itself but also of being suspected of that behavior.

In all of these sources, it is not cross dressing per se that is censured by the rabbis, but the possible intentions behind or ramifications of that cross dressing. In addition, in all but one of these sources, even those ramifications are understood in the context of deception for the purpose of engaging in heterosexual liaisons rather than as gender transgressive. Only once, in *b. Berakhot 43b*, does R. Yochanan limit the proscription on men wearing perfume in the market to places in which there is a suspicion of sexual encounters between men. It seems, both by the extreme paucity of discussion regarding transvestism, as well as by the focus of the concerns that are expressed, that the issue is of little concern to the rabbis of the rabbinic period.

Gender Transgressive Figures. When it comes to discussing figures who do not fit the binary gender paradigm, the question of transgression becomes somewhat more difficult, requiring us to identify the parameters of gender conformity in the rabbinic period in order to define what transgresses those norms. We therefore keep to a few cases in which there is some clear reference or hint in the text itself to sex/gender confusion or transgression or in which it is clear that gender roles have been reversed.

Although figures who explicitly transgress gender roles are hard to come by in rabbinic literature, there are hints of gender transgression that occur in several contexts. Once in a while, for example, the rabbis understand (or transform) biblical figures into gender transgressors. In other cases, one of the rabbis himself (or his wife or daughter) is alluded to in these terms through physical descriptions that evoke femininity, association with verses that refer to women, or (more typically for women) participation in activities that are the exclusive realm of the other sex/gender. Finally, the male God *himself* is periodically referred to in feminine terms.

Biblical figures. While certain biblical figures are not portrayed as gender crossers in the Bible itself, Midrashic stories position them as such, attributing to them bodies that do not fit the sex/gender "norm." To resolve the pronominal contradiction in Genesis 1:26: "...and God created the *ADAM* in His image, in the image of Elohim He created *him, male and female* He created *them,*" Genesis Rabbah 8:1 posits that the first human was an *androgynus,* *both* male and female. In addition, two *Midrashim* in *b. Yevamot 64a* refer to Abraham and Sara as *tumtumin* and to Sara as an *aylonit.* Both cases, however, are concerned with the couple's childlessness, rather than with the potentially gender transgressive qualities of these two categories. Although the categories of *tumtum* and *androgynus* described above appear only twice in rabbinic literature to describe a particular biblical figure's transgressive body, other cases of transgression are also present.

Genesis Rabbah 30:8 posits that Mordechai, having unsuccessfully searched for a nursemaid for his cousin Esther, nursed her from his own breast milk. The text records that those who heard this laughed aloud, whereupon R. Berekhiah chastised them by invoking a *mishnah* that states "the milk of a male is pure" (*m. Mak.* 6:7), proving that men can

produce milk as women can. Gwynn Kessler (2005) notes that although the text is subversive in its suggestion that gender is not fixed, it immediately corrects that subversion by naturalizing a man's capacity for nursing, returning Mordechai to the realm of "normal" masculinity, even while his body produces breast milk.

Although the above Midrashim seem value neutral, gender crossing is also presented pejoratively. Sexual penetration, for example, was considered in Roman culture (and, it seems, by early rabbis) as a power relationship of ("male") penetrator and ("female") penetrated. Though rabbinic culture is largely homosocial, sex between two males is censured.

Transgressive rabbis. In addition to transfiguring biblical figures into gender transgressors, rabbinic sources sometimes understand the rabbis themselves as gender transgressors. In the case of Elisha ben Abbuyah (also called *Acher,* or "other"), the Midrash deploys biblical verses that have no direct connection with the rabbi himself to associate him with gender crossing. Acher is the paradigmatic heretic—a great sage who forsakes *halakhah* (Rabbinic law). Although the Palestinian Talmud does not explicitly paint him as a gender transgressor, it draws on verses from the book of Ruth in order to overlay Ruth's story onto his (*p. Ḥag.* 2:1, *77b–c*). After Acher's death, Rabbi Meir, his student, spread his cloak upon Acher's burning grave while citing verses from Ruth 3:13. The verses equate R. Meir with the redeemer Boaz speaking to the decidedly female Ruth, the position now held by Acher. Moreover, the initial act in which R. Meir spreads the cloak over the grave strongly evokes the scene in the book of Ruth in which Ruth begs Boaz: "spread your wings over your maidservant for you are my redeemer" (Ruth 3:9). The text twice positions the already transgressive Acher as the vulnerable Ruth, while Meir plays the virile Boaz.

Transgressive wives and daughters. Although rabbis' wives (or for that matter, any women) are rarely mentioned in the rabbinic corpus, a few stories portray women as transgressing gender, usually in the form of a role reversal. In these stories, a woman is so versed in rabbinic law that she tricks a rabbi into ruling in her favor or teaches (or reprimands) a male of the rabbinic academy.

The main woman known for this type of exchange is Beruriah, the wife of R. Meir. In one of the Beruriah tales she meets up with Rabbi Yose the Galilean who asks her: "By which road do we go to Lod?" She reprimands him, saying: "Stupid Galilean! Do the sages not say 'Do not engage in too much talk with a woman?!' You should have said 'by which to Lod?'" (*b. ʿErub. 53b*). In another tale, Beruriah uses the exposition of biblical texts in order to teach her husband, a well known sage, a lesson in mercy (*b. Ber.* 10a). By engaging in rabbinic discourse and turning that discourse back on the rabbis themselves, Beruriah plants herself firmly in the realm of men. Rachel Adler (1988) explicitly refers to Beruriah's "gender crossing" when she claims that the Beruriah traditions are meant to explore the question, "What if there were a woman who was just like us?"

In similar tales, Yalta (traditionally known as the wife of R. Nachman) also challenges the legal system of the rabbis. In one case, on receiving a verdict from one rabbi that a sample of menstrual blood that she has shown him renders her impure, she seeks a second contradicting opinion. The text asks how the second sage could have ruled against the first, given that a sage may not reverse an earlier ruling and answers that Yalta explained to the second sage that the first had "a pain in his eye" (*b. Ned. 20b*). In her analysis, Charlotte Fonrobert considers Yalta "not as circumventing the authority of the self-fashioned experts, but as competing with it" (Fonrobert, 2007, p. 120).

In her article "Desireable but Dangerous," Dvora Weisberg (2004) argues that daughters hold a liminal role in biblical, pre-rabbinic, and rabbinic literature. Daughters of rabbis are often portrayed as experts in matters of law, and at the same time, untrustworthy because of their agility with the exegesis of biblical text—traditionally the realm of the rabbis.

Transgressive God. Although the depiction of God as male could ultimately be said to be metaphoric, it nevertheless pervades the biblical and rabbinic sources. Thus, when the rabbis apply feminine imagery to God, that choice is itself transgressive. When God's manna is compared to breast milk, for example, it confers upon God the role of nursing mother to an entire nation (*b. Yoma 75a*; Pesikta d'Rav Kahannah 12:25; *Sifre Num* 89).

Similarly, a Midrash describes the Israelite women in Egypt birthing their children in the fields to avoid Pharoah's edict to kill the Hebrew male babies (*b. Soṭah 11b*). In this Midrash, God sends an angel to care for the newborns as a midwife would do. Using Ezekiel 16 as a prooftext, the Midrash hints that God himself is the midwife (stated explicitly in Exod Rabbah 1:12, a much later compilation). God then collects two round objects, one of oil and one of honey, and "nurses" the infants. The (albeit rare) image of God as nursing mother or nursemaid, defies the otherwise overwhelming image in rabbinic (and biblical) texts of God as male.

[*See also* Legal Status, *subentry* Early Judaism; *and* Male-Female Sexuality, *subentry* Early Judaism.]

BIBLIOGRAPHY

Adler, Rachel. "The Virgin in the Brothel and Other Anomalies: Character and Context in the Legend of Beruriah." *Tikkun* 3, no. 6 (1988): 28–32; 102–105.

Alexander, Elizabeth Shanks. *Gender and Timebound Commandments in Judaism.* Cambridge, U.K.: Cambridge University Press, 2013.

Boyarin, Daniel. *Carnal Israel: Reading Sex in Talmudic Culture.* The New Historicism 25. Berkeley and Los Angeles: University of California Press, 1993.

Boyarin, Daniel. "Why Is Rabbi Yoḥanan a Woman? Or a Queer Marriage Gone Bad: 'Platonic Love' in the Talmud." In *Authorizing Marriage?: Canon, Tradition, and Critique in the Blessing of Same-Sex Unions*, edited by Mark Jordan, pp. 52–67. Princeton, N.J.: Princeton University Press, 2006.

Brower, Gary Robert. "Ambivalent Bodies: Making Christian Eunuchs." Ph.D. diss., Duke University, 1996.

Fonrobert, Charlotte Elisheva. "Regulating the Human Body: Rabbinic Legal Discourse and the Making of Jewish Gender." In *The Cambridge Companion to the Talmud and Rabbinic Literature*, edited by Charlotte Elisheva Fonrobert and Martin S. Jaffee, pp. 270–294. Cambridge Companions to Religion. Cambridge, U.K., and New York: Cambridge University Press, 2007.

Gleason, Maud W. *Making Men: Sophists and Self-Presentation in Ancient Rome*. Princeton, N.J.: Princeton University Press, 1995.

Halperin, David M. *One Hundred Years of Homosexuality and Other Essays on Greek Love*. The New Ancient World. New York and London: Routledge, 1990.

Ilan, Tal. *Mine and Yours Are Hers: Retrieving Women's History from Rabbinic Literature*. Arbeiten zur Geschichte des antiken Judentums und des Urchristentums 41. Leiden, The Netherlands, and New York: Brill, 1997.

Kessler, Gwynn. "Let's Cross That Body When We Get to It: Gender and Ethnicity in Rabbinic Literature." *Journal of the American Academy of Religion* 73, no. 2 (June 2005): 329–359.

Kuefler, Mathew. *The Manly Eunuch: Masculinity, Gender Ambiguity, and Christian Ideology in Late Antiquity*. Chicago Series on Sexuality, History, and Society. Chicago: University of Chicago Press, 2001.

Lev, Sarra. "How the 'Aylonit Got Her Sex." *Association of Jewish Studies Review* 31, no. 2 (November 2007): 297–316.

Lev, Sarra. "'And He Despised the Birthright': Esav as Transgendered." In *Torah Queeries: Reading the Bible through a Bent Lens*, edited by Joshua Lesser, Gregg Drinkwater, and David Schneer, pp. 38–42. New York: New York University Press, 2009.

Love, Karen. *Lies Before Our Eyes: The Denial of Gender from the Bible to Shakespeare and Beyond*. New York: Peter Lang, 2005.

Niditch, Susan. *My Brother Esau Is a Hairy Man: Hair and Identity in Ancient Israel*. New York: Oxford University Press, 2008.

Satlow, Michael L. "'They Abused Him Like a Woman': Homoeroticism, Gender Blurring, and the Rabbis in Late Antiquity." *Journal of the History of Sexuality* 5, no. 1 (1994): 1–25.

Tadmor, Hayim. "Was the Biblical Sārîs a Eunuch?" In *Solving Riddles and Untying Knots*, edited by Ziony Zevit, Seymous Gitin, and Michael Sokoloff, pp. 317–326. Winona Lake, Ind.: Eisenbrauns, 1995.

Weisberg, Dvora. "Desireable but Dangerous: Rabbis' Daughters in the Bavli." *Hebrew Union College Annual* 75 (2004): 121–159.

Sarra Lev

Early Church

Unlike the modern notion of two separate and stable categories of male and female, gender in antiquity was regarded as layered and fluid, and gender transgressions were commonplace. This configuration of gender certainly had an impact on early Christian discourses and practices. This entry discusses the tropes of gender transgression most commonly mobilized by early Christians and queries the social and religious agenda such transgressions were made to serve. It also highlights gender transgressions that troubled early Christians and investigates why, in a system replete with boundary crossing, these were particularly disconcerting.

Generally speaking, gender in antiquity was understood to inhere in the body, yet individuals were classified as "male" or "female" less according to genitalia than to physiology and bodily function. Specifically, male bodies were considered to be dry, tight, and hard, while women's bodies were wet, loose, and soft. Moreover, what individuals did with their bodies was constitutive of their gender: whereas men penetrated and implanted seed, women menstruated, were penetrated, provided the womb in which a fetus grew, birthed children, and nurtured the young with breast milk. Beyond the body, gender was also assigned to stereotypical features of character, behavior, and appearance. Men were thought to be rational, self-possessed, and moderate, while women were passionate, irrational, and immoderate. Finally, more abstractly, all things honored, valorized, and praised were regarded as "masculine," while anything that deviated from these ideals was marked "feminine." Because gender could be read from different registers—from the body, behavior, or ideals—it was possible for an individual to be deemed "manly" one day and "womanish" the next or to be regarded as "virile" in some ways and "effeminate" in others. Consequently, we find many attributions of polygendered identities: she-men (*gunnis*), half-men (*semivir*), virile women (*gunē andreia*; *mulier virilis*), and everything in between.

Gender in Early Christianity. Whereas "pagans" relied on medical literature and mythic stories to corroborate gender categories, Christians used their own history and scriptures to explain gender difference and to encourage some types of gender transgression. Some early Christian thinkers maintained that gender difference resulted from the

Fall. Prior to the first sin, they argued, Adam and Eve were not "gendered" because they were not sexually active (which would have distinguished the penetrator from the penetrated) nor did they bear children (which would have distinguished the one who implants the seed from the one who bears the child). Once they committed the first sin, though, they were punished with death and thus needed to procreate to perpetuate the species. Consequently, gendered differences—presumably lying dormant to that point—became operative. The goal of the Christian, some argued, was to return to the prelapsarian, nongendered paradisiacal condition in which humans were most truly in the "image of God" (Gen 1:26–27).

Other Christian thinkers looked not backward but forward, arguing that gender categories would cease to exist in the heavenly realm. Extrapolating Jesus's teaching that resurrected Christians would be "like the angels" who "neither marry nor are given in marriage" (Luke 20:35–36), they concluded that there would be no sexual activity and thus no basis for gender difference in heaven. Whether Christians aspired to return to their paradisiacal genderlessness or to attain their eschatological genderlessness, they agreed that gendered difference was an inferior (albeit perhaps necessary) condition of the present realm, a condition that perfected Christians would eventually overcome.

They found additional support for idealized genderlessness in Jesus's praise for those who excise corporeal markers of their gender ("eunuchs who have made themselves eunuchs for the sake of the kingdom of heaven," Matt 19:10–12), in Paul's claim that "in Christ" gender differences have been dissolved ("There is no longer male and female; for all of you are one in Christ Jesus," Gal 3:28), and in deutero-Paul's call for a "unity of faith" that breaks down all divisions in the Christian community (Eph 4:13).

Despite this genderless ideal, early Christians preserved a preference for masculinity. The genderless nature to which they aspired was nevertheless coded "masculine" to designate its superiority to the condition left behind. Conflating the genderless angelic state with a manly state, Gerontius reports that "in truth, [Melania] surpassed the limits of her

female nature and acquired a disposition that was manly, or rather that was angelic" (*vita Mel.* 39).

Moreover, because manliness to Christians, as to Greeks and Romans, was constituted first and foremost by virtue—the terms for "virtue" (*virtus, andreia*) derive from terms for "man" (*vir, andros*)—in order for Christian women to be considered virtuous, they needed to assimilate manliness. The parity and unity that would be accomplished once the gender of all Christians was dissolved would be accomplished by elevating women to manliness. Clement of Alexandria, for example, asserts that a "woman is translated into a man when she becomes unfeminine, manly, and perfect" (*strom.* 6.12). The Christian philosopher Porphyry urged his wife: "Do not consider yourself a woman…flee all that is effeminate in the soul as if you had taken a man's body (*ep.* 33).

Finally, salvation was coded a masculinizing process, as we see in the Nag Hammadi tractate *Zostrianos*, wherein the protagonist exhorts his audience to "flee from the madness and the bondage of femaleness and choose for yourselves the salvation of maleness" (131.5–8), as well as in the Gospel of Thomas, where Jesus himself promises to help women transition: "I myself shall lead her in order to make her male, so that she too may become a living spirit resembling you males. For every woman who will make herself male will enter the kingdom of heaven" (*log.* 114). While femaleness was considered a hindrance to Christian perfection, the achievement of full masculinity was the basis of idealized genderlessness, true Christian unity, and salvation itself.

Virile Women: Christian Martyrs and Ascetics. Given this foundational reasoning, a Christian woman was praised for becoming a "female man of God" (*hē anthropos tou theou*), a moniker most frequently earned by female martyrs and ascetics. In each case, their spiritual progress was measured by their ability to divest themselves of their feminine qualities and to adopt instead Christian masculinity.

A typical feature of female martyr accounts is their gradual weaning from womanly attachments and obligations. In the *Martyrdom of Perpetua and Felicitas*, for instance, the two female protagonists prepare for their trial in the arena by shedding their role as mothers. Perpetua prays that her infant will no longer need her breast milk. When God grants her wish, she is able to give her child over to the care of relatives. Felicitas, her pregnant companion, cannot be martyred alongside her companions unless she gives birth, so she prays for an early delivery. After God answers her plea, she rejoices and joins the others in the arena, with seemingly no regard for the newborn she abandons.

Once female martyrs disentangled themselves from their obligations as mothers, disavowing the conventionally approved uses of their female bodies (i.e., childbirth and childrearing), they adopted new roles as martyrs and found new manly uses for their bodies. In the arena, they are stylized as hypermasculine athletes and gladiators who possess manly courage, rationality, and self-control. The martyr Blandina, for instance, endures such an extraordinary degree of torture that she is likened to a "noble athlete," and those abusing her admit to being "defeated" since they could find no torture that would break her (Eus. *hist. eccl.* 5.1.18–19). Other female martyrs demonstrate the character traits of noble gladiators: fighting with full conviction, having no fear of death, and, in defeat, holding out their necks to receive the death blow (Sen. *ep.* 30.8; Cic. *tusc.* 2.17.41). Perpetua, for instance, stayed "the trembling hand of the young gladiator [assigned to execute her] and guided [the sword] to her throat. It was as though so great a woman," the author concludes, "could not be dispatched unless she herself was willing" (*pass. Perp.* 21). The courage and volition exhibited by female martyrs led witnesses to consider their designation as "women" no longer appropriate. In his homage to the martyr Julitta, for example, Basil of Caesarea wonders: "Is it indeed fitting to call 'woman' one whose great soul overshadowed the weakness of [her] female nature?" (*hom. in mart. Jul.*).

The authors of the martyr acts further punctuate the gender transformation of female martyrs through descriptions of their bodies. Blandina, for instance, was nailed to a stake in order to be devoured by animals, but to the spectators, "she appeared as if hanging on a cross," leading them to conflate her with "him who was crucified for them, though in the form of their sister" (Eus. *hist. eccl.* 5.1.41). Additionally, in a dream that directly precedes her martyrdom, Per-

petua sees herself engaged in a fight with an Egyptian (a stand-in for the Devil). As she is stripped of her clothes in order to receive the customary rub down before a contest, she glimpses her naked body and declares, "I am a man" (*sum masculus*; *pass. Perp.* 10).

Female Christian ascetics were also regarded as virile. Taking their cue from Paul, who argued that the unmarried were not distracted by the affairs of the world and thus "may be holy in body and spirit" (1 Cor 7:32–35), these Christians renounced their worldly possessions and attachments, including money, marriage, sex, and children, in order to life a live wholly devoted to God. Because they abandoned the defining roles of wife and mother, Christian writers such as Jerome no longer identified them as women: "As long as a woman is devoted to birth and children, she is different from a man, as the body is different from the soul. But if she wishes to serve Christ more than the world, then she will cease to be a 'woman' and will be called a 'man'" (*Ephes.* 3.5; cf. Jer., *Helv.* 22).

Some Christians regarded these female ascetics as having returned to their created, pregendered state or as having accomplished already the genderless condition of the heavenly realm (e.g., Gr. Nyss. *virg.* 13); others claimed they had achieved a sort of "third sex" (Tert. *virg.* 11); while still others called them "manly" and "virile." Attributions of masculinity were appropriate given that the lifestyles of female ascetics more closely resembled those of men than other women: they traveled, engaged in theological study (and possibly public debate), and were accorded more public visibility and honor. Moreover, given their extreme regimes of fasting and bodily discipline, the distinctively feminine features and processes of female ascetics' bodies abated—most notably, their breasts disappeared and they stopped menstruating—until eventually their bodily appearance became largely indistinguishable from that of their male counterparts (e.g., *vit. Hil.*; *vit. Apoll.* 216–217; Latin *vit. Pelag.* 14; Syriac *vit. Pelag.* 45; *vit. Mar.* 5; *vit. Dan.* 8).

The virtue and wisdom of female ascetics further bolstered their claims to manliness and virility. John of Ephesus, for instance, describes Mary the anchorite as "a woman who by nature bore only the form of females, but…bore the character and soul and will not only of ordinary men, but of mighty and valiant men" (*vit.* 28). Similarly, Paulinus of Nola extols Melania the Elder as "a perfect woman in Christ…[possessing] the courage of a manly spirit…[and] a virile soul" (*ep.* 45.2–3). Amma Sarah, an ascetic who for sixty years endured battles against demon opponents in the Egyptian desert, asserts about herself: "According to nature I am a woman, but not according to my thoughts" (*apoph. pat. Sarah* 4).

In an attempt to exhibit outwardly the masculinity they believed they possessed in their soul, virtue, and behavior, many female ascetics neglected their appearance, dressing in shabby clothes, refusing to bathe, and neither styling their hair nor applying makeup. As such, they diminished their sexual allure and distanced themselves from the seductive impulses thought to inhere in all women. Some female ascetics went even further: they cut their hair short, donned male clothing, and adopted men's names (e.g., *ATh* 25, 40; Syria *vit. Pelag.* 36; *vit. Euphr.*; *vit. Dan.* 8). For Basil of Ancyra, this corporeal transformation was a decisive part of the spiritual process of perfection: "Although clothed in a female body, [women] have by means of asceticism beaten off the form [of the body] for the sake of the soul and have made themselves, through virtue, appear like men, just as their souls have been created equal. And just as men, through asceticism, pass from men to the rank of angels, so also these women, through asceticism, pass from women to the dignified status of men" (*virg.* 51).

Although certain Christian women were pronounced "virile" in light of their extraordinary feats of courage, virtue, and wisdom or to mark their holiness, femininity itself was not redeemed from its inferior place on the gender spectrum. Christian women were not regarded as pious and holy *as women*, but only as they transcended elements of their vile femininity and assimilated masculinity. Thus, the stereotypical features of "female" and "male," as well as the hierarchical relation between these categories, remained firmly intact even as exemplary Christian women were elevated beyond the boundaries of femininity.

Virile Women as Sources of Pride and Shame. Discussions of Christian women's virility served not only to honor the individual martyrs or ascetics featured in early Christian literature but also to assert the supremacy of Christianity vis-à-vis her adversaries. The manliness of female Christian protagonists was regularly cast against the effeminacy—weakness, degeneracy, and irrationality—of Christian opponents. From the perspective of Christian martyrdom accounts, for example, the balance of power and virtue—always coded masculine—shifts from the persecutors to the persecuted, challenging the conventional estimation of both. One example is Febronia's martyrdom account, wherein the judge orders her to be stripped naked in the arena and then chides her by claiming that she finds pleasure in being ogled. To this, Febronia retorts that it is not her nakedness that causes offense and shame, but rather the judge's base mind. He sees only a whore, betraying his own simple perception and ignoble character. Rather, she avers, she is better perceived as a (male) athlete, one who will eventually conquer him (*Febr.* 24). Here the judge is rendered shamefully womanish in comparison to Febronia. In addition to demonstrating Febronia's personal manliness, the story elevates Christianity by demonstrating that extraordinary virtue could be obtained even by Christianity's weakest members—women.

The manliness of ascetic women was similarly deployed to goad Christian men to greater piety. Mere women, some exclaimed, should not outstrip their male counterparts in Christian discipline given that they are naturally less capable of manliness. John Chrysostom, for example, incites the Christian men in his congregation, saying: "Women eclipse us! How contemptible! What shame this is! We hold the place of the head, yet are surpassed by the body!" (*hom. in Eph.* 13; cf. Aug. *serm.* 9.9.12; *apoph. pat. Sarah* 9).

Feminizing Virile Christian Women. As seen above, attributions of manliness functioned to honor individual Christian women, to provide evidence of the superiority of Christianity over against her pagan neighbors, and to prod Christian men to greater virtue and piety. Given this range of social and rhetorical agendas this trope was made to serve, it is not surprising that we find so many references to manly women in early Christian sources. Yet many male Christian leaders opposed Christian women who claimed too much virility or who affected too masculine an appearance. Arguing that Christian women could, in the present age, achieve manliness only to a point, they wished not to collapse entirely the gender binary. They took this stand in order to preserve hierarchal ranks and relations configured along gendered lines. Simply put, men did not want to disrupt the subordination of women to men in the social sphere. Of particular concern were questions about whether virile women possessed the authority to teach and baptize. The answer among leading Christian men was a resounding no, and they justified this position by arguing that virile women were still to be classified as "women" even if they had exceeded the boundaries of their natural gender (e.g., Tert. *bapt.* 17; Tert., *praescr.* 41).

To preserve gendered roles and hierarchies, prominent Christian leaders imputed aspects of femininity to the very women they elsewhere extolled as manly. Specifically, they stressed that, no matter how virile their soul, spirit, or behavior was, their body ultimately fixed them firmly within the category of woman. Palladius, for example, when eulogizing Olympias, imposes a bodily limit on her full gender transformation, deeming her "not a woman, but a manly creature: a man *in everything but body*" (*vit. Chrys.* 56, emphasis added), and Gregory of Nazianzus commends his mother for "displaying, *in female form*, the spirit of a man" (*de rebus suis* 120, emphasis added). Although at times a pious woman's body is used as a device to signal her masculine spiritual progress and virtue, here we see her body is cited as evidence of gender difference, ensuring that attributions of virility do not go so far as to erase hierarchies based in gender difference. At times both moves coexist in the same narrative. For example, in Perpetua's martyr narrative, her body is cast as a man when stripped naked in her vision, but when she and Felicitas appear in the arena, attention is drawn to Perpetua's "delicate" female form and to Felicitas's breasts, which are still dripping with milk (*pass. Perp.* 20). Similarly, even though ascetic women's bodies, mortified through ascetic practice, largely conformed to the look of men's bodies, their *vitae* persistently point to the fact that they cannot completely manifest masculine corporeality given their soft, high voices and their inability to grow beards (e.g., *vit. Mar.*

5; *vit. Hil.*). Moreover, even those ascetics who pass their whole lives as men and eunuchs in male monasteries are, after their deaths, remembered as "women" (e.g., *vit. Mar.* 18; Syriac *vit. Pelag.* 50; Latin *vit. Pelag.* 15). Regardless of a woman's manly use of her body, her bodily form was identified as the definitive feature of her gender identity and served as a limit to her complete gender transformation.

Additionally, virile Christian women continued to be cast in roles and inscribed with qualities typically associated with femininity. Because Perpetua was so devoted and loyal to Christ, she was called his "bride" (*pass. Perp.* 18), and when Blandina encouraged her fellow martyrs she was deemed their "noble mother" (Eus. *hist. eccl.* 5.1.55). Female ascetics are similarly figured as wedded to God and as mothers of spiritual children (Jer. *ep.* 22.20; Ambr. *virg.* 1.6.30; cf. Or. *hom. in Num.* 20.2.2). Moreover, sometimes women's acts—even acts deemed inherently manly—were cast in highly sexualized terms, as in the depiction of the martyr Agnes in the arena:

> When Agnes saw the grim figure standing there with his naked sword her gladness increased and she said: "I rejoice that there comes a man like this, a savage, cruel, wild man-at-arms, rather than a listless, soft, womanish youth bathed in perfume, coming to destroy me with chastity's death. This is my lover, I confess, a man who pleases me at last. I shall rush to meet his steps halfway so I don't put off his hot desires. I shall welcome his blade's full length; within my breast I shall draw the force of the sword to my bosom's depths." (Prudent. *peristeph.* 14.69–80)

Thus, even though many of these women rejected marriage, childbirth, and good looks, they could not wrest themselves from feminine roles and associations that haunted them.

Womanish Christian Men. Although Christian women were to strive to adopt masculine qualities, behaviors, and states of mind, Christian men were to preserve and perfect their inherent manliness. When they did transgress their gender, they were labeled unmanly (*anandros*) or effeminate (*mollis*, *malakos*), shameful monikers meant to persuade them to adopt the behaviors sanctioned by the church. For example, as Polycarp of Smyrna readies himself for martyrdom in the stadium, he hears a voice from heaven urging him: "Be strong, Polycarp, and act like a man" (*pass. Polycarp* 9). Similarly, in the process of learning how to properly govern his Christian community, a heavenly messenger charges Hermas to "be a man" (*Herm.* vision 1.4.3).

Yet when Christian men are put in situations that threaten their ability to remain manly, they find creative readings of scripture to nonetheless preserve their reputation. In the *Martyrdom of Sergius and Bacchus*, when the two protagonists refuse to sacrifice to Zeus, the emperor orders that they be stripped of their military garb and dressed in women's clothing (to mark their religious perversity through gender perversity). In response, the men chant Isaiah 61:10: "We rejoice in you, Lord, because you have clothed us with the garment of salvation…as brides you have decked us with women's gowns and joined us to you" (*pass. Serg. et Bac.* 7). They accomplish the seemingly impossible task of aligning holiness with femininity by appealing to the biblical trope of the soul or the church as the "bride of Christ" (e.g., Isa 49:18, 61:10; Mark 2:19; Matt 9:15; Luke 5:35; Rev 19:7, 21:2; *2 Clem* 14.2; cf. Orig. *hom. 1 in Gen.* 15). More remarkable are occurrences of crossing—what would be broadly perceived as gender demotion—voluntarily assumed by Christian men who were under no social pressure or constraints. Origen's infamous self-castration was a drastic elision of his corporeal masculinity (Eus. *hist. eccl.* 6.8.1), yet one that he justified with scripture (Matt 19:12). Men who undermined their masculinity were more troubling than women's transgressions into virility because they unsettled the presumed superiority of masculinity, rendering it, through their disavowal, no longer the ideal.

[*See also* Gender; Gender Transgression, *subentry* New Testament; Male-Female Sexuality, *subentry* Early Church; *and* Masculinity and Femininity, *subentry* Early Church.]

BIBLIOGRAPHY

Aspegren, Kerstin. *The Male Woman: A Feminine Ideal in the Early Church.* Edited by René Kieffer. Uppsala, Sweden: Academia Ubsaliensis, 1990.

Brown, Peter. *The Body and Society: Men, Women, and Sexual Renunciation in Early Christianity.* New York: Columbia University Press, 1988.

Burrus, Virginia. "Mapping as Metamorphosis: Initial Reflections on Gender and Ancient Religious Discourses." In *Mapping Gender in Ancient Religious Discourses*, edited by Todd Penner and Caroline Vander Stichele, pp. 1–10. Leiden, The Netherlands: Brill, 2007.

Castelli, Elizabeth. "'I Will Make Mary Male': Pieties of the Body and Gender Transformation of Christian Women in Late Antiquity." In *Body Guards: The Cultural Politics of Gender Ambiguity*, edited by Julia Epstein and Kristina Straub, pp. 29–49. New York: Routledge, 1991.

Clark, Elizabeth A. "Sex, Shame, and Rhetoric: En-gendering Early Christian Ethics." *Journal of the American Academy of Religion* 59, no. 2 (1991): 221–245.

Clark, Gillian. "Women and Asceticism in Late Antiquity: The Refusal of Status and Gender." In *Asceticism*, edited by Vincent L. Wimbush and Richard Valantasis, pp. 33–48. New York: Oxford University Press, 1995.

Cloke, Gillian. *This Female Man of God: Women and Spiritual Power in the Patristic Age, A.D. 350–450.* New York: Routledge, 1995.

Cobb, L. Stephanie. *Dying to Be Men: Gender and Language in Early Christian Martyr Texts.* New York: Columbia University Press, 2008.

Cooper, Kate. *The Virgin and the Bride: Idealized Womanhood in Late Antiquity.* Cambridge, Mass.: Harvard University Press, 1996.

Kuefler, Mathew. *The Manly Eunuch: Masculinity, Gender Ambiguity, and Christian Ideology in Late Antiquity.* Chicago: University of Chicago Press, 2001.

Miles, Margaret. *Carnal Knowing: Female Nakedness and Religious Meaning in the Christian West.* Boston: Beacon, 1989.

Shaw, Teresa M. *The Burden of the Flesh: Fasting and Sexuality in Early Christianity.* Minneapolis: Fortress, 1998.

Upson-Saia, Kristi. *Early Christian Dress: Gender, Virtue, and Authority.* New York: Routledge, 2011.

Vorster, Johannes N. "Androgyny and Early Christianity." *Religion and Theology* 15 (2008): 97–132.

Kristi Upson-Saia

H

Heteronormativity/Heterosexism

Heteronormativity is the dominant belief system concerning sexuality that relies on fixed and binary genders, and the certainty that heterosexuality is the norm that occurs naturally, that is, apart from cultural influences. All other sexual relationships are deemed culturally produced (unnatural) and are regulated and defined in relation to heterosexuality, and are thus devalued. In this system, females and males are assumed to be the only appropriate sexual partners. Heterosexism, then, is a systematic social bias, which stems from heteronormativity, in which society rewards heterosexuals (in the form of economic benefits and civil rights) and punishes all other sexualities.

Rich's "Compulsory Heterosexuality and Lesbian Existence." The first work that specifically addressed a systemic heteronormative bias was Adrienne Rich's groundbreaking 1980 essay, "Compulsory Heterosexuality and Lesbian Existence." In this work, Rich critiques four prominent books, the theses of which do not seem to suspect that heterosexuality is imposed on women and, thus, women are not free to choose their sexuality. Although each of the works Rich critiques are feminist and positively received as such, Rich asserts that none seems to recognize that women do not *freely* choose heterosexuality. Rich asks this question of each text: Would women nec-

essarily *choose* heterosexuality? Instead, she argues, heterosexuality is compulsory for women—it is not a freely given choice; it is sometimes forcibly, always subliminally imposed through institutionally grounded propaganda. For example, Rich notes that in many works from the field of psychological development, women's first primary relationships are with women. Some theorists posit that in "normal" development, women turn away from these initial female relationships toward a heterosexual relationship. This turning away is unquestionably presented as a natural life-cycle development with no suspicion of, or investigation into, the cultural machinations that work to produce such a shift. Rich asks why: Why would women "naturally" turn away from positive, nurturing, and supportive relationships?

Departing from the discourse of psychological development, Rich also shows how heteronormativity is an integral component of economic theory. In an analysis of Catherine A. MacKinnon's study, *Sexual Harassment of Working Women: A Case of Sex Discrimination*, Rich emphasizes the connections between heterosexuality and capitalism. In order to receive economic sustenance, women must adhere to a heterosexual matrix. In other words, being a sexually available heterosexual woman is the primary qualification for employment for women. The economic system (Fordist capitalism usually) works to exclude any woman who does not at least pretend to be heterosexual. The theme of "woman as commodity" is one that becomes central in later articles involving the idea of heteronormativity, particularly those by Gayle Rubin, discussed in the following section.

Rich concludes that as long as heterosexuality in women is presumed to be innate, thus natural, lesbian relationships (or any situation in which women reject the social requirements of heterosexuality) are seen as deviant or pathological, or at least considered irrelevant and banal. What is at stake, according to Rich, is the strength and independence that come as a result of women realizing that they have the power to choose their relationships. Indeed, when women cannot choose their own relationships without being demonized, stigmatized, or rendered pathologically deviant, they are deprived of a collective (political and psychic) power and remain dependent, fragmented, or invisible.

Rubin's "Thinking Sex." In her highly influential 1984 article, "Thinking Sex: Notes for a Radical Theory of the Politics of Sexuality," Gayle Rubin reveals what has been in plain sight all along: that in Western cultures, sex is (1) valued negatively and is (2) punished on an unbalanced scale as an "especially heinous sin" with the harshest of punishments. Rubin shows that (3) sexuality and sexual acts are hierarchical—married, reproductive heterosexuals are at the top of the pyramid. In this system, heteronormative is good, natural, and blessed. Rubin also observes that (4) there is a false belief of a "domino theory of sexual peril"—if any nonheterosexual, monogamous sexuality is permitted, then anything goes—a slippery slope from nonmonogamous, casual sex to bestiality or necrophilia, for example. Finally, Rubin perceives and illustrates that (5) alternative sexualities are perceived to be destructive to the social fabric.

Rubin offers an analysis of a sexual matrix, which is culturally produced through social, political, and economic institutions, and works to keep heteronormativity in place. Rubin reiterates what Michel Foucault argued a decade earlier, that sexuality has a history. In other words, it is not a naturally occurring force that exists prior to, or apart from, social determinations; new sexualities are constantly pro-

duced. What Rubin adds to this conversation is that not only are sexualities produced, but that attitudes about sex (specifically, "sex negativity") are culturally produced so that heterosexuality sits inside the charmed circle as the only normal and natural sexuality. And although Western cultures tend to see all sexuality as "dangerous" and often view all sex with suspicion, there is one erotic behavior that becomes acceptable: heterosexuality that is monogamous. As both Rich and Rubin observe, sexuality is culturally constructed and is political. It is organized into "systems of power," according to Rubin, which reward certain sexualities (monogamous heterosexuals) while punishing all others. Again, heterosexism is protected by the all-encompassing conviction that it occurs naturally, apart from cultural construction, is normal (while all else is deviant) and is prescribed and thus blessed by God.

Butler's *Gender Trouble*. Judith Butler's 1990 publication of *Gender Trouble* has remained the definitive work to which most gender theorists have responded in one way or another. Butler's particular addition to the preliminary works on heteronormativity is that gender and sex are not connected in anything but cultural terms, and neither preexists (or exists apart from) history; there is no understanding of sex apart from its cultural creations. Sex does not create gender; gender creates sex. Bodies merely perform masculinity and femininity, which poses as "natural" through bodily markers. This illusory two-sex system (heteronormativity) requires desire to be exchanged only between the binary male/female. Yet, the illusion of binary sexes seems to fix gender (though sex, like gender, exists as a grid); and upon this illusion of two and opposing genders rests heteronormativity, or what Butler refers to as "the heterosexual matrix." Butler writes, "The institution of compulsory and naturalized heterosexuality requires and regulates gender as a binary relation in which the masculine term is differentiated from a feminine term, and this differentiation is accomplished through the practices of heterosexual desire" (Butler, 1990, pp. 22–23). All power rests upon this construct: as the designations "male" or "female" become intelligible, no space is left for any other expression of sex; and as these two are deemed as the only two proper expressions of desire, there is only a place for heterosexuality. All other sexualities, then, are aberrant, thus abhorrent.

Warner's *Fear of a Queer Planet*. Also published in 1990 was Michael Warner's introduction to his edited work *Fear of a Queer Planet*. It is in this essay that the term "heteronormativity" first appears. Warner articulates (or reiterates) those points that Rich, Rubin, and Butler laid out: "themes of homophobia and heterosexism may be read in almost any document of our culture [which] means that we are only beginning to have an idea of how widespread those institutions and accounts are" (Warner, 1990, p. 6). Following the challenge of Eve Kosofsky Sedgwick (in *Epistemology of the Closet*, 1990) to require a critical analysis of modern homo/heterosexual definition in any effort to study Western culture, the essays in Warner's book pragmatically illustrate just how heterosexism permeates and is inculcated into every micro or macro aspect of culture. For example, citing the issue of geriatric care, Warner notes that in heteronormativity, care of the elderly tends to go to offspring and spouses, which leaves many elderly gays and lesbians with a "disproportionately high likelihood of neglect" (p. 8). Throughout the book, the writers expose heterosexism in all corners: a homophobic bias in child raising; a tension between "a reproductivist conception of the social," and homosociality within Marxist theory; and how "heterosexuality" is judicially constructed.

In addition to concretizing the term "heteronormativity," Warner defends the use of the word "queer" to talk about all that is in opposition to that heteronormativity. He argues that it is in its very inspecificity (ambiguity) that the term "queer" works. Because "normal sexuality and the machinery of enforcing it do not bear down equally on everyone" (p. 16), "queer" works because it defines opposition broadly, across social, political, sexual, and violent terrains. "Queer" exposes those vast processes of "normalization" as the systemic origins of phobia and queer bashing, as opposed to believing that queer bashing is a result of periodic intolerance and random acts of violence.

Ingraham's *Thinking Straight*. One of the most recent essays that specifically address heteronormative and heterosexism is Chrys Ingraham's 2005 introduction to her book *Thinking Straight*. This introduction summarizes those things about a heteronormative culture that have been said already: that heterosexuality is posed as good, natural, and normal and homosexuality is its opposite; that sex (as well as gender) is socially constructed; that the heterosexual norm is institutionally upheld and promoted and all other sexualities are devalued on a descending grid.

Ingraham adds to this discussion by observing that there is something else at work here other than merely a heterosexual will to power; it is yet to be seen what is gained or lost in the recent Western social acceptance of gay marriages (which shows that "sex" really is not the issue—the integral part seems to be that there are [only] two individuals, and these two divide work by a pseudo-gendered system). Ingraham makes it clear that by looking strictly at heterosexuality (and other sexualities) primarily through a sexual lens, all other factors of human relationships (intimate, platonic, or formal) are rendered secondary. She writes, "In other words, as we socially and culturally create sexual behavior identities as organizing categories, we elevate relations of the body above all other terms for human interaction—mind, heart, soul, values, and so on" (Ingraham, 2005, pp. 2–3). The newfound acceptance of same-sex, monogamous couples (what Lisa Duggan terms "homonormativity") indicates that sex really is not the true determinate of "right" or "wrong" sexuality, but rather the pay-offs tend to be economically grounded. The mainstream presence of the "good" gay, according to Ingraham, is an indication that the economic system has discovered the gay marketplace (p. 6). Once, but no longer, an economic necessity for women, the institution of marriage (and the $35 billion a year wedding industry) turns toward the "marketing of romance" (p. 6). Heterosexuality becomes less compulsory; Ingraham claims that "the gradual codification of gay and lesbian rights and the growing awareness that benefits and rewards distributed on the basis of heterosexual marriage are inherently undemocratic has led to an erosion of heterosexual supremacist beliefs and practices" (p. 7). In response to this recent loosening of the heterosexual grip, major institutions (such as state and religion) are re-securing what has historically been their power base, as evidenced by a heightened amount of activity on their parts. Because of these "dramatic changes occurring in institutionalized heterosexuality" (p. 10), Ingraham calls for a critical study of heterosexuality.

Ingraham's observations are right in line with Foucault's: that power sustains itself by creating, policing, and controlling (rather, *attempting* to control) sexualities through the social institutions of religion, medicine, psychology, judiciary, and economics. Within this most recent shift that Ingraham describes, it is unclear what is being produced: Is it a reimagining of heterosexuality that allows the inclusion of same sex couples? Or is it a reimagining of homosexuality that allows it to be viewed as stable, natural, and normal, and defines it over and against the trans other? It appears to be both. What this shift reveals is that "sex" is not the hinge pin; it is gender. Nonetheless, homosexuality's "moving to center" is problematic, according to Judith Halberstam, Lisa Duggan, and Susan Stryker, among others.

Homonormativity. The construction of the term "homosexuality" in relation to the dominant term "heterosexuality" renders the two inextricable; their interdependent relationship until more recent times has been one of opposites. Yet, as the two become coalesced under a new "homonormativity," there opens a space for new others.

The first use of "homonormativity" is usually attributed to Lisa Duggan in "The New Homonormativity: The Sexual Politics of Neoliberalism." Duggan defines it as "a politics that does not contest dominant heteronormative assumptions and institutions, but upholds and sustains them, while promising the possibility of a semi-mobilized gay constituency and a privatized, depoliticized gay culture anchored in domesticity and consumption" (Duggan, 2002, p. 50). However, in the introduction *Female Masculinity*, Judith Halberstam declares that, "female masculinity is generally received by hetero- and homo-normative cultures as a pathological sign of misidentification

and maladjustment" (Halberstan, 1998, p. 9). Halberstam's understanding of, and her focus on, homonormativity are subtly different from Duggan's. For Duggan, homonormativity is a neoliberalist strategy by which gays and lesbians seek inclusion into the status quo. By accepting heteronormative constructions of male and female, and mimicking normal lifestyles (marriage, parenting, home ownership), gays and lesbians move toward the center of Rubin's "charmed circle" (Duggan, 2002, p. 153).

Halberstam, on the other hand, recognizes that any expression of a gender that does not match the physical body is disparaged equally within both heteronormative and homonormative contexts. The move to the center by some gays and lesbians creates an even greater chasm between gender normativity and the queer community—particularly the "gender queers," those who choose to perform a gender that appears to be at odds with their bodies—or as Susan Stryker's descriptive "those individuals who lived in one social gender but had a bodily sex conventionally associated with the other" (Stryker, 2008, p. 146).

Both Duggan and Halberstam see homonormativity as a doomed strategy; it affords civil rights to some, yet this strategy is a superficial and temporary fix. Homonormativity results in reiterating the gender roles that anchor heteronormativity to power (even though the connections to bodies may seem to be more lax) and regularly punishes "those who fail to do their gender right" (Butler, 1990, p. 140) The sociopolitical fallout is an even greater degree of marginalization for trans communities. Julia Serano, a trans activist, sees this move to the center by gays and lesbians (and the subsequent disassociation with the trans communities) as a calculated political strategy; by excluding the "most deviant" from the public face of the gay liberation movement, gays and lesbians could make the case that apart from sexual orientation, "we are just like everyone else" (Serano, 2007, p. 355). This is homonormativity, and it was/is a highly successful strategy in terms of securing civil rights, gaining positive public visibility in mass media, and a reduction in (though not an eradication of) gay bashing, among other things.

Susan Stryker (2008) elucidates Serano and Halberstam's critique of homonormativity in her article "Transgender History, Homonormativity, and Disciplinarity." She notes that even in the early 1990s, she and other transgender activists realized that non-transgendered gays and lesbians, who base their identity politics on heteronormative gender roles, "often had more in common with the straight world" than they did with gender queers (p. 146). The problem is, according to her, homosexuality is a category of sexual orientation based upon heteronormative notions of gender; in fact, all of the sexualities (hetero, homo, bi) depend upon this dominant gender binary of man and woman, which trans folks then problematize by queering the relationship of "sexed body and gendered subject" (p. 147). In other words, the trans person could claim an identity of male or female, or resist this binary altogether. In addition to misconstruing transgender as a type of gender, homonormative persons, claims Stryker, tend to misconstrue transgender as a sexual orientation that takes the form of a desire or a fetish. Rather, she thinks that "trans" is more a modality than a category—one that would be better aligned with concepts such as race, or class—groupings that can intersect at any point, any type of sexual orientation or gender.

Homonormative gay and lesbian strategies "queerify" the transsexual to set up their own boundaries of normality. Riki Anne Wilchins says it clearly: the gay movement lost its soul when it went from "we are queer, we are worthy of human rights," to "being gay is just as good as being straight" (Wilchins, 1997, p. 69). She asks, that for an identity, such as gay, or straight, or transgender, "to be visible and distinct, how many other complex and unnamed identities have to be silenced and erased?" (p. 61). Homonormativity, as does heteronormativity, must take on an "other" for its own survival, since it has now been taken into service of heteronormativity. The "other," the opposing part of the binary, becomes the gender queer, or transgendered/transsexual person.

Heterosexism and Cissexism. Closely related to heteronormativity, heterosexism would be the way that a heteronormative worldview is manifested within social contexts. If it is assumed that heterosexuality is the norm, that it occurs naturally, or is divinely blessed or sanctioned, then it is also assumed that those persons who identify as heterosexual would receive more benefits, rights, rewards, and be looked upon favorably, in general. Everyone, then, who does not claim to be heterosexual is perceived as and treated as a second-class citizen, and is discriminated against in every level of social encounters (legal, medical, religious, etc.).

At the institutional level, heterosexism is evident in the fact that in most cities, same-sex couples cannot legally marry one another; they cannot adopt children together or have equal custodial rights as heterosexuals; they do not have hospital spousal rights (if hospitals give power of attorney or decision-making power to closest relatives, the same-sex partner can be [legally] excluded from visitation or critical health care decisions); they do not have rights of survivorship to shared property.

Like sexism, racism, or classism, heterosexism depends upon the assumption that there is a "normal," thus superior, way of being. And those who view themselves to be in the better of any of the previously mentioned binaries do not see the privilege society grants them: there may be an assumption that those in the lesser binary do not deserve the same rights and privileges (this seems to be most evident in racism and in heterosexism) or they are ignorant (or in denial of) their own privilege.

Cissexism, a more recent term, which is becoming more pervasive in studies of gender and sexuality, is defined by Serano as: "The belief that transsexuals' identified genders are inferior to, or less authentic than, those of cissexuals (i.e., people who are not transsexual and who have only ever experienced their subconscious and physical sexes as being aligned)" (Serano, 2007, p. 12). As with heterosexism (and racism, classism, and sexism), privilege is invisible to the dominant group, and basic privileges are denied to the "lesser" group, in this case, non-cissexuals (transsexual/transgender persons). Since Western social arrangements depend upon heteronormativity (there being two, and only two, sexes that occur naturally), cissexuals' privilege tends to occur on a more personal level (in addition to institutional biases). For example, to some this may seem to be a trivial matter, but transgendered persons are often denied equal access to public restrooms or department store fitting rooms. However, this ostensibly slight discrimination is critical: all of Western culture stands upon a two-sex system. The one way this system is concretized (made "real") is through the separation of the physical, naked body in public space (restrooms and dressing rooms). If there is any intrusion into the fantasy of a "two sexes and two genders" system, the center cannot hold. It is no coincidence, then, that violence against trans persons is extraordinarily high, which appears to be connected to the very high occasion of suicide attempts: One in twelve of all trans persons will be physically assaulted—one in eight if you are a trans person of color (Dunbar, 2006, p. 323–337) According to the National Coalition of Anti-Violence Programs' 2012 report (NCAVP), this rate is one and a half times larger than non-trans LGB persons. In addition to the constant threat of physical violence, the attacks on transsexual persons are, predictably, economic. According to key findings of the 2009 report of the National Center for Transgender Equality and the National Gay and Lesbian Task Force, transgendered people have double the rate of unemployment than the population as a whole; 97 percent of the 6,450 respondents reported harassment on their jobs; 15 percent exist below the poverty level at an income of less than $10,000 annual income. These statistics attest to all the ways that a culture, whose existence depends upon heteronormativity, will punish those who fail to do their gender right.

The intense amounts of violence and economic punishment are "logical" extensions of a belief that the trans person's gender is "fake" because it does not occur "naturally" and is not connected to the sex that the trans person was born with (Serano, 2007, p. 13). Thus, according to a dominant heterosexist/cissexist ideology, transsexuality is unnatural, deviant, and against God's order, which, therefore, removes divine blessing and sanctions violence against it. Serano points out that this belief that a gender is inauthentic if it cannot be connected to one's sex is naïve. She writes, "We make assumptions every day about other people's genders without ever seeing their birth certificates, their chromosomes, their genitals, their reproductive systems, their childhood socialization, or their legal sex. There is no such thing as a 'real' gender—there is only the gender we experience ourselves as and the gender we perceive others to be" (p. 13).

Heteronormativity and Biblical Studies. If the power of heteronormativity resides in its unquestioned status of "normal," and its unchallenged place at the foundation of a sexuality that is "good" and "blessed," the buttress of the whole façade is Bible translation and interpretation. Only in the last few decades have scholars initiated a critique of the heterosexism that permeates all Bible reception since the nineteenth century. The burgeoning field of Queer Biblical Studies has produced compelling scholarship, which seeks to show the heteronormative biases that punctuate biblical interpretation. For example, as one reads Genesis, apart from the example of Rebecca and Isaac, where does one actually find one man married to one woman? Apart from the purity codes of Leviticus, where does one find a clear condemnation of homoeroticism in the Hebrew Bible? How should one understand the place of Ebed-Melech (Jer 38:7), an Ethiopian eunuch (intersexed perhaps) who rescues Jeremiah and is blessed by God? Indeed, a prominent (and dominant) reading of the relationship of God to Israel (and later, Jesus to the church) is one of husband and wife, the groom and the bride. Yet, ironically, as queer readers point out, the "people" of Israel, and the "church" are also presented in masculine terms (as are God and Jesus). Thus, if one holds on to that metaphor of marriage, both examples are *same-sex* marriages. As postmodern readers of the Bible suggest, the reader makes meaning. Heteronormativity is not in the text, waiting to be discovered; the interpreter, or reader, brings the assumption of heteronormativity to the text, and uses the text to justify heteronormativity.

Summary. Like the air we breathe, heteronormativity and heterosexism are pervasive yet invisible;

it is an assumed and unquestioned notion that there are only two naturally occurring and opposite sexes, and each is, naturally, attracted to the other. This heterosexual desire is created and blessed by a deity. These assumptions then dictate that there are, indeed, only two genders. Hence, any and every expression of gender that does not "match" one's assigned physical sex is rendered deviant; any sexual desire not directed to one's opposite sex is aberrant. This aberrance is interpreted as sin or as unnatural, which justifies punishment and violence against sexual and gender "queers."

Heteronormativity is a culturally produced ideology, justified and maintained institutionally through religious beliefs, economic and political systems, medical classifications, psychiatric diagnoses, and judicial processes. The dominant premise of heteronormativity permeates every detail of someone's life: love, marriage, aging, death, reproduction, property ownership, leisure time, and so forth. Only in recent times has the "natural" occurrence of heteronormativity been challenged, and with this recognition has come a chipping away of the mighty fortresses of heterosexism. Through academic studies of heterosexuality and through the visibility and increased activism of sexual and gender queers, more and more are questioning the presumed natural, divinely blessed, and normal status of heterosexuality.

[*See also* Gender; Sexuality; Sexual Transgression; *and* Transgender/Third Gender/Transsexualism.]

BIBLIOGRAPHY

Butler, Judith. *Gender Trouble.* New York: Routledge, 1990.

Duggan, Lisa. "The New Homonormativity: The Sexual Politics of Neoliberalism." In *Materializing Democracy: Toward a Revitalized Cultural Politics,* edited by Russ Castronovo and Dana, D. Nelson, pp. 175–194. Durham, N.C.: Duke University Press, 2002.

Dunbar, Edward. "Race, Gender, and Sexual Orientation in Hate Crime Victimization: Identity Politics or Identity Risk?" *Violence and Victims* 21, no. 3 (2006): 323–337.

Foucault, Michel. *A History of Sexuality.* Vol. 1. Translated by Robert Hurley. New York: Vintage, 1986.

Halberstam, Judith. *Female Masculinity.* Durham, N.C.: Duke University Press, 1998.

Ingraham, Chrys. "Introduction: Thinking Straight." In *Thinking Straight: The Power, the Promise, and the Paradox of Heterosexuality,* edited by C. Ingraham, pp. 1–11. New York: Routledge, 2005.

National Center for Transgender Equality and the National Lesbian and Gay Taskforce. *National Transgender Discrimination Survey,* November 2009. http://transequality.org/Resources/Trans_Discrim_Survey.pdf (accessed 17 June 2013).

Rich, Adrienne. "Compulsory Heterosexuality and Lesbian Existence." *Signs: Journal of Women in Culture and Society* 5, no. 4 (1980): 631–660.

Rubin, Gayle. "Thinking Sex: Notes for a Radical Theory of the Politics of Sexuality." In *Pleasure and Danger,* edited by Carol Vance, pp. 143–178. New York: Routledge and Kegan, Paul, 1984.

Rubin, Gayle. "The Traffic in Women: Notes on the 'Political Economy' of Sex." In *Literary Theory: An Anthology,* 2d ed., edited by Julie Rivkin and Michael Ryan, pp. 770–794. Malden, Mass.: Blackwell, 2004.

Sedgwick, Eve Kosofsky. *Epistemology of the Closet.* Berkeley: University of California Press, 1990.

Serano, Julia. *Whipping Girl: A Transsexual Woman on Sexism and the Scapegoating of Femininity.* Berkeley, Calif.: Seal Press, 2007.

Simoni, J. M., and K. L. Walters. "Heterosexual Identity and Heterosexism: Recognizing Privilege to Reduce Prejudice." *Journal of Homosexuality* 1, no. 1 (2001): 157–173.

Stryker, Susan. "Transgender History, Homonormativity, and Disciplinarity." *Radical History Review* 100 (2008): 145–157.

Warner, Michael. "Introduction." In *Fear of a Queer Planet: Queer Politics and Social Theory,* edited by Michael Warner, pp. 3–17. Minneapolis: University of Minnesota Press, 1993.

Wilchins, Riki Anne. *Read My Lips: Sexual Subversion and the End of Gender.* Ithaca, N.Y.: Firebrand, 1997.

Teresa J. Hornsby

HISTORICAL-CRITICAL APPROACHES

Modern feminist and gender-critical biblical interpretation is intricately bound up with various approaches to biblical interpretation falling under an umbrella called "historical criticism." Often considered the "traditional" paradigm over against which the "innovation" of feminist and/or gender-critical studies of biblical literature are positioned, a more nuanced view reveals an interdependence of "tradition" and "innovation," or at least adaptations of tradition toward innovative ends. One might say that historical criticism, as a paradigm for conducting biblical scholarship, along with approaches associated with linguistic and cultural turns, critical theory, and liberationist movements, has provided an important means by which various forms of feminist and gender-critical biblical interpretation have proliferated and flourished. Thus, understanding the contours and legacies of historical-critical approaches to biblical literature enhances an understanding of the contemporary methodological landscape of the field.

Historical Criticism: Origins, Meanings, and Legacies. Historical criticism is, in essence, the basic method used by most contemporary scholars of the ancient world. In its broadest connotation, it designates studying historical texts, traditions, and/or communities within their particular historical milieu, examining either or both synchronic and diachronic contexts for understanding historical phenomena *historically*. In some sense, the phrase "historical criticism" in the field of biblical and cognate studies would seem somewhat redundant to historians in other disciplines, since most historically inclined scholarly fields deploy the basics of historical criticism as *the single* methodology, even as individual historians might have particular accents and predilections regarding their topics and sources. To make sense of the term "historical criticism" as a paradigm in biblical and cognate studies, one must understand something of the unique and peculiar history of the discipline itself—especially the relationship between the burgeoning field of historical studies in the study of ancient Hebrew and Christian traditions and the religious authority of ecclesial institutions, which were invested in negotiating the types of approaches used and conclusions reached in relation to scripturally authoritative texts.

The Bible, as a sacred text in the West, obviously has long held a special position in terms of social, cultural, and political configurations. Religious authority in the West, while itself having varied fortunes in different regions and time periods, nevertheless has maintained a particularly potent influence over the broader matrices of existence—particularly in terms of power relationships. One cannot discount the reality that people's deep, confessional religious sensibilities are linked to particular understandings of the Bible as a sacred text, as "scripture"—nor is it profitable to take a cynical position regarding such matters. Thus, unlike other ancient texts that do not enjoy the same scriptural status, historical understandings of the Bible—its texts, contexts, and afterlives—have posed, and continue to present, an enduring set of problems for interpreters.

Regardless of the particular and prevalent personal and/or political motivations of religious authorities, already before the Enlightenment and the development of modern "scientific" ways of knowing, there were various proponents of critical engagement of the Bible. During the Protestant Reformation, for example, Martin Luther (1483–1546) and John Calvin (1509–1564) made critical observations regarding some minor points of historical details that seemed to be exaggerated in biblical texts. The case of Galileo Galilei (1564–1642) and his famous "Letter to the Grand Duchess Christina" on biblical interpretation (1615)—and his subsequent heresy trial and famous conflict with Cardinal Bellarmine—also signals that critical engagement of biblical texts is not simply the result of nineteenth-century German scholarly innovation. The Dutch philosopher Baruch Spinoza (1632–1677) was (in)famous for questioning the unity and cohesion of the Pentateuch, one of the hallmarks of later historical-critical approaches that would also contribute to conflict between Christian scholars of the Bible and ecclesial authorities. Richard Simon (1638–1712), a French contemporary of Spinoza and a Catholic priest, is often considered the "father" of source criticism of the Pentateuch. These developments happened before Johann Gottfried Herder (1744–1803) and others, some fifty years later, developed the philological method that was to become key to modern historical study of the Bible. Further, these critics had precedent in fourteenth-century scholars—and, to be sure, one cannot discount the major contributions made in the twelfth century by Rabbi Abraham Ben Meir Ibn Ezra (1089–ca. 1164), who already had noted that Moses could not have written most of the material in the Pentateuch.

Already in the fifteenth and sixteenth centuries early biblical critics came into conflict with church hierarchies. Spinoza's contemporary Simon first thought his source-critical perspective on the Pentateuch would be met with acceptance by the Catholic church hierarchy, but while it did receive some initial support it was eventually denounced. Herein, then, lies the specific dilemma posed by historical-critical approaches to the Bible. It is within this matrix that one must understand how it is that biblical scholars, even now, refer to "historical criticism" as a distinct form of historical study. It is precisely because historical criticism became a method that was deployed over against *religiously authoritative readings* of biblical texts that it makes sense to refer to it as a distinctive category in biblical and cognate studies.

Although there is not one single, linear trajectory by which historical criticism developed, the German tradition of critical biblical scholarship expended significant energy rethinking the biblical theological paradigms that tightly wed the religious nature of the text to church authority. With respect to the historical study of Jesus, for instance, Martin Kähler (1835–1912) argued for a distinction between a "Jesus of history" and the "historic, biblical Christ" (1896). German theologians and scholars in the late eighteenth and early nineteenth centuries attempted to negotiate relationships between the constrictions of the church and the freedom of the historical-critical interpreter.

On the American scene, perhaps no proponent of historical criticism was as famous—or as controversial—as Charles Augustus Briggs (1841–1913), a Presbyterian minister and professor of Semitic and Cognate Languages at Union Theological Seminary in New York. Like many of his contemporaries, Briggs had studied in Germany and brought aspects of the historical-critical spirit back to the United States, even if in reconfigured form. In his inaugural address, "The Authority of Holy Scripture" (1881),

Briggs sought to create a sharp distinction between the freedom of biblical critics and the power of the church to determine practice and meaning in interpretation. Among other suggestions, his address admonished readers not to act as "infants" regarding biblical texts, allowing ministers, teachers, and other authorities to serve as "parents." Briggs's unapologetic stance toward critical historical study of biblical literature—that it represented a means for Bible-reading people to "grow up" and think independently—resulted in a heresy trial in the Presbyterian church, whereby he was stripped of ministerial status. The principles for which he stood his ground, however, were to become standard scholarly historical practice and led, in many ways, to delineations of "historical criticism" as a separate form of biblical investigation that stood over against ecclesial hierarchical interpretation. Many scholars joined the company of Briggs in being charged with heresy or otherwise having their employment threatened because of their allegiance with historical-critical approaches to biblical literature, marking historical criticism as not simply an innocent exercise but as a dangerous intellectual practice that could threaten one's professional livelihood.

Historical criticism today is indebted to the complex legacy briefly outlined above. In the twentieth century, once historical study became acceptable in its own right, both inside and outside church communities, the method as such expanded into a broadly conceived array of scholarly strategies comparable to critical historical study in other disciplines. Because of the long-standing scriptural and religious status of biblical texts, scholars deploy historical criticism on both sides of the so-called divide between academy and church: some critique religious authority and claim to be more radical in their research, and others utilize the same methods either in service to the church or in ways that do not undermine religious sentiments of believers. It is perhaps one of the ironies of the development of historical criticism that it has come to mean something quite general with respect to its application. For that reason, the unique designation "historical criticism" or "historical-critical approaches" makes the most sense when viewed in relationship to its interactions and antagonisms with ecclesial hierarchies. In contemporary usage, "historical criticism" tends to signify historical study as opposed to other kinds of study, such as theological or reader-response criticisms.

At the same time, and importantly for understanding the relationship of feminist and gender-critical involvements and entanglements with historical-critical approaches to biblical literature, "historical criticism" has also come to stand for a particular historicist approach to biblical texts that focuses on positivistic investigations and objectivist, nonbiased conclusions, both of which are assumed to be apolitical in nature (Collins, 2005; Schüssler Fiorenza, 1999). Thus, biblical critics who are inclined toward ideological-critical approaches often distinguish their work from "historical criticism," which they cast as a conservative, antiquarian orientation to historical study that does not appreciate the role of modern contexts or interpreters in the determination of meaning. Even in classical, nonbiblical forms of historical scholarship, New Historicism and the Linguistic Turn had raised these same issues for the study of history. Among its critics in biblical and cognate studies, then, "historical criticism" has become a cipher for controlling, determined, authoritative readings of the biblical text that parallels, somewhat ironically, the earlier authoritative position of ecclesial structures that historical criticism challenged. Now it is not necessarily religious authority but the authority of historical critics that is considered oppressive of individual and minority voices that themselves seek to counteract long-standing religious oppression.

Historical Criticism in Gendered Perspective. Historical critics of the nineteenth and early twentieth centuries have been critiqued for their singular focus on male figures and major institutional structures rather than on marginalized peoples and perspectives. However, in contextualizing historical criticism it is important to identify the foundations underlying the assumptions of those earlier biblical critics. Clearly most of the earliest historical critics were (white) males, but other factors also shaped

their thinking about the ancient world and the questions that drove their investigative enterprise. In what follows, we highlight a few of the trajectories that help better contextualize historical criticism. In addition to the interaction with ecclesial authorities there are numerous other points of connection to broader trends in historical study—which itself is intricately connected to a variety of developments in nineteenth-century society (Penner, 2008).

Philology—the study of language—is perhaps one of the quintessential points from which to trace a historical-critical lineage during this early era. By the time of the Renaissance and Reformation period, humanists had begun to engage the fundamental function of language in terms of translation and meaning. By the time of Herder, however, we witness a broad investment in the philological enterprise. Herder's emphasis on the connection between the "essence" of a particular people or "folk" and their language—that the "soul" and "blood" of a people, from their intellectual and cultural ideas to their religious and social experiences, was embodied in their language—was formative for scholars studying the ancient world. It was assumed, for example, that those who were Hebrew speaking had a different conception of the world than those who were Greek speaking. Whatever one thinks about earlier philological theory, it is apparent that it profoundly influenced the shaping of historical criticism in biblical and cognate studies. The study of language lies at the center of much of the conversation that would follow, and formative developments in studying ancient social, political, and religious life began with philological investigation. The *Theological Dictionary of the New Testament* (TDNT; 1933–1979) is probably the most important example of the interconnection between philology and "folkish" sociocultural issues; while a later work, the majority of the views in this German intellectual project have their root in earlier historical-critical investigations. One cannot thus fully appreciate earlier incarnations of historical criticism without an understanding of the systemic and dramatic impact of philology on the discipline.

Such associations of language with sociocultural and religious assumptions and values were thoroughly manifested in the history-of-religions (*Religionsgeschichtliche Schule*) approach to biblical literature. Whether exploring Hebrew Bible or early Christian backgrounds, in this approach the scholar presupposed the presence of genealogical relationships between the "proximate other" cultures of antiquity and biblical traditions. One notable trajectory of scholarship focused on tracing the filiations between biblical literature and "pagan" traditions, seeking to locate from whence and how biblical concepts and ideas arose. Given that historical criticism was committed to studying biblical traditions *in context*, its practitioners sought contextual backgrounds and literary parallels; the biblical materials were assumed not to have been created *ex nihilo*. How might ancient Mediterranean mythology have influenced the Genesis narrative? How might Persian religion have contributed to the rise of Jewish apocalyptic? What role did Greek and Roman mystery cults play in the development of early Christian rituals? Were Paul's views on Jewish law informed by Hellenistic Jews like Philo? Ultimately, scholars believed that most biblical concepts, while unique to the biblical tradition in some respect, were influenced by contemporaneous cultures. This particular investigative commitment was paramount for the early period of historical criticism.

Alongside philology and comparison, perhaps the larger framework that guided interpretation was the focus on *institutions*. This particular aspect of intellectual history cannot be overemphasized, as it is the hallmark of the cultural matrix in which modern historical criticism was forged. The rise of the independent nation-state in European countries; the increasing focus on citizenship identity and rights; the emergence of secular institutions of law, education, and government; the development of the university as a site of national interest and support; and the proliferation of colonial endeavors are just a few of the elements that shaped interpretive interest in institutions. The Prussian empire is the example par excellence of this type of environment. Hegel's (1770–1831) philosophy of history accented the growing

presence of the "spirit" in history as manifested in the development of institutional structures. Leopold Von Ranke (1795–1886), often considered one of the "founding fathers" of modern historical study, focused almost solely on institutional history. It should not be assumed that these scholars were ignorant of alternative or people's histories. However, in the environment in which European social, cultural, and intellectual traditions held prominence in value over colonized peoples, it fell to anthropologists and museums to collect data on those peoples not considered part of European institutional history. Ultimately, historians needed a structure that was readily definable and stable over lengthy periods of time to assess more fully the development and betterment of human culture.

It is easy to judge early historical critics as androcentric and oblivious to marginalized peoples in history. However, the phenomena must be understood within the larger paradigm of their scholarship. Modern historians take for granted the myriad of studies that inform our work and provide opportunities to do microhistory, but such was not available to scholars 200 years ago. Moreover, the emphasis on the male "great figures" of history, including those in the biblical traditions, may have been influenced by historical criticism's institutional focus: one could argue that the focus on institutions brought male subjects into view rather than male subjects being the major concern in the first place. Only once a language and perspective was developed to talk about noninstitutional history could scholars talk about those who were disconnected from and oppressed by institutional structures. From the standpoint of institutional history, the issue of "marginalization" could not enter the conversation.

To be sure, significant critiques can be made of early historical-critical biblical scholarship, some of which have implications for gender studies. Obviously, the "problem" of Judaism and Jews in Europe, especially following widespread Jewish emancipation throughout the nineteenth century, informed historical-critical approaches to both Hebrew and early Christian texts and traditions. Moreover, the continued and at times hostile interactions between

Catholic and Protestant traditions are evident particularly in Protestant interpretations of both Judaism (sometimes used as a signifier for Catholicism) and later institutionalized forms of early Christian social and religious structures.

More to the point, however, these engagements can be viewed through a gendered lens, wherein certain traditions were effeminized in relationship to idealized forms of biblical texts and traditions. Prophetic materials, for example, were valorized over priestly traditions. The apostle Paul was viewed more highly than Peter, who was associated with the origins of Catholicism. Early Hellenistic Judaism was often utilized as a buffer zone for early Christian materials, becoming a conduit through which the "pagan" material was transmitted to early Christianity but itself immune to "impurity." When considering earlier incarnations of biblical studies through a gender-critical lens, then, one might take numerous directions in analyzing the ideological frameworks of early historical critics. Such interventions, however, would be significantly different from the type we find in later feminist and gender-critical biblical scholarship.

Gendered Intersections with Historical-Critical Approaches. Several key components of historical-critical approaches have proven fruitful to feminist and gender-critical investigation of biblical texts and traditions. These include the stance that all texts are human productions, located in time and space, and are therefore reflections of the concerns and cultures of those times and places; the understanding that the communities and cultures in which biblical texts were originally produced, assembled, read, and interpreted are necessarily different than our own; and the hope that historical criticism helps modern readers not only to understand the ancient contexts better but also to recognize the hermeneutical distance between "us" in the present and "them" in the past. Similarly, proponents of historical-critical approaches have emphasized that texts can mean differently across time and cultures rather than having a singular, static, and fixed meaning for all times, places, and peoples.

Importantly for studies that foreground concerns about gender and status, historical-critical approaches have tended to maintain that the freedom to ask critical questions of biblical texts—without automatic adherence or capitulation to predetermined, dogmatically and ecclesiastically circumscribed answers—is central to biblical scholarship. One of the complex legacies of historical criticism is its insistence that historical study, coupled with power analysis, allows interpreters to challenge and move beyond conveniently reified claims to authority based on "what the Bible says" on any number of theological, political, and/or social issues. Such assumptions and methodological commitments have proven useful to feminist and gender-critical biblical scholars, who have sought to (re-read) biblical literature from the perspective of women and to take gender seriously as a category of analysis.

Different moments in feminist and gender-critical biblical interpretation have exhibited alignment with different aspects of historical-critical approaches. Four major methodological issues can be noted. First, although historical-critical approaches might appear to be predominantly concerned with the distant past, it is also the case that all biblical interpretation takes place in the present, which decisively shapes interpretive methods, questions, and practices. Thus, feminist and gender-critical biblical scholarship may have historical interests, but it is ultimately conducted in response to present-day concerns—specifically, but not limited to, the oppression of women and other historically underrepresented peoples. Second, gender-sensitive interpreters maintain that it is safe to assume that biblical texts, as human artifacts, are also products of elite, literate cultures—which, for better or for worse, are most likely male-centered, or androcentric, in nature. Such an assumption renders those texts—and, indeed, most texts and contexts, across time and cultures—androcentric in nature, which in turn affects how biblical texts have been deployed and interpreted. Third, the genre and provenance of sources consulted will greatly affect the questions posed of those materials. Using court and other state documents, philosophical treatises, and similar sources as parallels for biblical texts in historical reconstructive efforts and exegesis will yield different results than

than using material culture, hymns to goddesses, and other sources more reflective of non-elites. And fourth, feminist and gender-critical interpreters have stressed that an interpreter's social identity—not only gender but also sexual orientation, race, class, age, and so on—makes as much of a difference in conducting readings of biblical texts as do contexts and histories of interpretation. Therefore, in the eyes of feminist and gender-critical interpreters of the Bible, there can be no "innocent" or "objective" historical investigation. One contribution of feminist and other cultural-studies approaches to historical criticism is the revelation that writing history is a means of writing ourselves, even when it might appear (or an author might insist) otherwise (Tolbert, 2013).

Feminist and Gender-Critical Appropriations of Historical-Critical Approaches. Encounters between feminist and gender-critical scholars and historical-critical approaches have not taken place in a vacuum but in concert with broader epistemological trends concerning gender, sex, and sexuality in the humanities, social sciences, and natural sciences, along with social movements at large. Within biblical scholarship, of special interest is the appropriation of historical-critical approaches toward feminist and gender-critical ends, as well as the amplification of aspects of historical-critical methodologies through their incorporation into broader analysis that attends to the dynamics of power, status, and ideology.

For those sensitive to women's and gender concerns in readings of biblical literature, the appropriation of historical-critical approaches has been of key importance. Historical-critical methods have been used to refute biblical justifications for women's subservience and oppression in the present. For example, in the struggles for abolition and women's rights during feminism's "first wave" in the late nineteenth-century United States, historical criticism was employed in the service of women. For example, Briggs's daughter, Emilie Grace, was the first woman to graduate from Union Theological Seminary (1897), was herself trained in biblical studies, and wrote a historical-critical dissertation on the role of the deaconess in biblical and early Christian literature. Perhaps most notably, the composition of *The Woman's Bible* (1895–1898) by Elizabeth Cady Stanton and 26 other women had as its explicit goal the refutation of ecclesiastical authorities that maintained that women ought to be subject to men, including those who had just published the Revised Version of the Bible (1881–1894). By providing a different version of the scriptures that took seriously the concerns of women, coupled with a critical historical understanding of the ancient texts, Stanton and her committee sought to prove that women's oppression was not "in," or demanded by, the scriptures per se—but was to be more properly located in the reading of scriptures by humans who were invested in the continued domination of women, even as women desired otherwise for themselves. Thus, *The Woman's Bible* was to provide a radical and liberating perspective for the women of Stanton's time, using then-contemporary developments in historical understandings of biblical literature to do so.

The Woman's Bible was controversial upon its publication, endured challenges from the mainstream religious establishment as well as from feminist colleagues, and was certainly not the only attempt to apply feminist consciousness to the "new" historical criticism of the Bible (Calvert-Koyzis and Weir, 2010). However, its legacy for feminist and gender-critical appropriations of historical-critical approaches to biblical interpretation endures. Subsequent uses, particularly since the 1970s, have aimed to provide alternatives to dominant, patriarchal, and androcentric readings and deployments of biblical literature. As far as published scholarship is concerned, seminal contributions have taken the form of anthologies (e.g., Collins, 1985; Russell, 1985), commentaries (e.g., Newsom and Ringe, 1992; Schüssler Fiorenza, 1993 [which was dedicated to the 100-year anniversary of *The Woman's Bible*]; Schottroff and Wacker, 1998), compendia series of essays on canonical biblical books and extra-canonical literature (e.g., Brenner, 1993–2002; Levine et al., 2003–2009), studies that emphasize feminist and gender criticism in historical reconstruction efforts and biblical theology (e.g., Schüssler Fiorenza, 1983), and historical and contextual literary readings of "troubling" biblical texts (e.g., Trible, 1984).

For the most part, much feminist and gender-critical biblical scholarship has made broad and conscious use of historical-critical approaches. Such scholars explain that their goal is to counter the pervasive idea that biblical literature offers nothing "positive" for women, as well as to recover an ancient past that is usable and defensible by women and other dominated peoples. In turn, these studies are often conducted in concert with movements for women's inclusion in religious hierarchies, leadership roles, and communities at large. Although scholarly analyses may vary, the overarching theme and contribution of this work is to depatriarchalize biblical narratives, biblical scholarship, the study of religion, and perhaps even the world as a whole (Trible, 1973). The "revolutionary" potential of feminist and gender-critical biblical scholarship, in its myriad forms, lies in an insistence that "the personal may be political, the marginal can and at times should be centered, that the objective is a fallacy and the subjective may be an asset rather than a hindrance, that new topics can be brought into the discussion…" (Brenner, 2013). Hence, despite their androcentric and patriarchal origins, historical-critical approaches have proven to be an ally in feminist and gender-critical biblical scholarship, both in nurturing and expanding the presence of female (and nondominant male) scholars in the guild as well as "changing the subject" of biblical interpretation through attending to the areas of investigation and inquiry raised by such interpreters.

In recent years, "changing the subject" in biblical scholarship has perhaps allowed historically informed feminist and gender-critical analysis to realize its greatest potential. Using the same methods espoused in what is considered "traditional" biblical studies, feminist scholars have asked different questions about gender, status, and identity in biblical texts and ancient contexts. Reading primary materials alongside sources usually marginalized in historical reconstructive work, such interpreters have been able to use ancient evidence to write women and other non-elites back into ancient religious and biblical history. Following similar developments in classics and women's social history, exemplary studies such as Brooten 1982, Schüssler Fiorenza 1983, Kraemer 1988, Meyers 1988, and Schottroff 1995 have made the case that women were far from absent in the ancient contexts associated with social and religious activity. Such scholarship also has reiterated the prevalence of feminine qualities and personifications in conceptions of the divine. Documenting women's presence, and even leadership, in ancient religions has made it nearly impossible for contemporary scholars to conceive of an ancient biblical world without women (and other non-elites), or to imagine that such perspectives are not worth engaging in considerations of biblical texts, contexts, and histories of interpretation.

Feminist and gender-critical engagements with historical-critical approaches, along with reader-response criticism and methodological contributions associated with the Linguistic Turn, have in addition underscored the key role of the identity of the interpreter in the interpretation of texts. While historical criticism has often been described as concerned solely with the ancient past, feminist and gender-critical engagements (along with related approaches associated with racial-ethnic minority scholarship, postcolonial and disability studies, and queer theory) have suggested that who readers are in the present will drive the character of their interest in the past. Every encounter with biblical literature is ultimately reflective of the time and place in which it is conducted; such encounters say more about the interpreter(s) than the texts being interpreted. In this way, a key tenet of historical-critical approaches—that meaning changes over time and according to whom is doing the meaning-making—is not challenged but both affirmed and amplified through feminist and gender-critical explorations and contributions (Vander Stichele and Penner, 2005).

Assessment. Historical-critical approaches have engendered a complex, at times controversial, and by no means univocal legacy in biblical scholarship. While historical criticism has come to be linked to that which is "traditional" and "patriarchal" in biblical studies, it also has been quite useful to those who seek different ways of engaging biblical texts as far as gender, sex, and sexuality are concerned. Feminist and gender-critical scholarship that makes use of historical-critical approaches has brought attention to gender as a means of organizing human hierarchies and institutions, across time and cultures. It has also provided occasion to revisit the question of how, and why, the Bible has been used in trenchant justifications of women's inferiority and/or subservience, asking where alternative, "positive" readings of ancient biblical texts can be located, and what difference the findings can make in the present. Further, historically inclined feminist and gender-critical scholarship has underscored the need for sustained attention to power relationships, both in the biblical texts themselves and also in their deployments (Schüssler Fiorenza, 2009). Finally, scholarly engagements afforded by the intersection of historical-critical approaches and gender issues have reiterated the need to ask basic questions about the task, process, and outcomes of writing history—who participates, on what terms, and to what ends.

[*See also* Feminism, *subentries on* First-Wave Feminism *and* Second-Wave Feminism; Intersectional Studies; Linguistic Turn Approaches; *and* Rhetorical-Hermeneutical Criticism.]

BIBLIOGRAPHY

Brenner, Athalya, ed. Feminist Companion to the Bible Series. 24 vols. Sheffield, U.K.: Sheffield Academic Press, 1993–2002.

Brenner, Athalya, ed. "Quo Vadis Domina? Reflections on What We Have Become and Want to Be." *Lectio Difficilior* 1 (2013). http://www.lectio.unibe.ch/13_1/brenner_athalya_quo_vadis_domina.html

Brooten, Bernadette. *Women Leaders in the Ancient Synagogue: Inscriptional Evidence and Background Issues.* Brown Judaic Studies 36. Chico, Calif.: Scholars Press, 1982.

Calvert-Koyzis, Nancy, and Heather Weir, eds. *Breaking Boundaries: Female Biblical Interpreters Who Challenged the Status Quo.* Library of Hebrew Bible/Old Testament Studies 524. New York: T&T Clark, 2010.

Collins, Adela Yarbro, ed. *Feminist Perspectives on Biblical Scholarship.* Biblical Scholarship in North America 10. Chico, Calif.: Scholars Press, 1985.

Collins, John. *The Bible after Babel: Historical Criticism in a Postmodern Age.* Grand Rapids, Mich.: Eerdmans, 2005.

Kraemer, Ross Shepard, ed. *Maenads, Martyrs, Matrons, Monastics: A Sourcebook on Women's Religions in the Greco-Roman World.* Minneapolis: Fortress, 1988.

Kraemer, Ross Shepard, ed. *Unreliable Witnesses: Religion, Gender, and History in the Greco-Roman Mediterranean.* New York: Oxford University Press, 2011.

Levine, Amy-Jill, with M. M. Robbins, eds. Feminist Companion to the New Testament and Early Christian Writings Series. 13 vols. Sheffield, U.K.: Sheffield University Press, Cleveland, Ohio: Pilgrim; New York: T&T Clark, 2003–2009.

Meyers, Carol. *Discovering Eve: Ancient Israelite Women in Context.* New York: Oxford University Press, 1988.

Newsom, Carol A., and Sharon H. Ringe, eds. *The Women's Bible Commentary.* Louisville, Ky.: Westminster/John Knox, 1992.

Penner, Todd. "*Die Judenfrage* and the Construction of Ancient Judaism: Toward a Foregrounding of the Backgrounds Approach to Early Christianity." In *Scripture and Traditions: Essays on Early Judaism and Christianity [in Honour of Carl Holladay],* edited by Patrick Gray and Gail O'Day, pp. 429–455. Novum Testamentum Supplement Series 129. Leiden, The Netherlands: Brill, 2008.

Russell, Letty, ed. *Feminist Interpretation of the Bible.* Louisville, Ky.: Westminster/John Knox, 1985.

Schottroff, Luise. *Lydia's Impatient Sisters: A Feminist Social History of Early Christianity.* Trans. Martin and Barbara Rumscheidt. Louisville, Ky.: Westminster/John Knox, 1995.

Schottroff, Luise, and Marie-Therese Wacker, eds. *Kompendium Feministische Bibelauslegung.* Gütersloh, Germany: Chr. Kaiser, Gütersloher Verlagshaus, 1998.

Schüssler Fiorenza, Elisabeth. *In Memory of Her: A Feminist Theological Reconstruction of Christian Origins.* New York: Crossroad, 1983.

Schüssler Fiorenza, Elisabeth. *Rhetoric and Ethic: The Politics of Biblical Studies.* Minneapolis: Fortress, 1999.

Schüssler Fiorenza, Elisabeth. *Democratizing Biblical Studies: Toward an Emancipatory Educational Space.* Louisville, Ky.: Westminster/John Knox, 2009.

Schüssler Fiorenza, Elisabeth, ed. *Searching the Scriptures.* 2 vols. New York: Crossroad/Herder, 1993.

Stanton, Elizabeth Cady. *The Woman's Bible.* 2 vols. New York: European Pub. Co., 1895–1898.

Tolbert, Mary Ann. "Writing History, Writing Culture, Writing Ourselves." In *Soundings in Cultural Criticism:*

Perspectives on Culture, Power, and Identity in the New Testament, edited by Francisco Lozada Jr., and Greg Carey, pp. 17–30. Soundings Series. Minneapolis: Fortress, 2013.

Trible, Phyllis. "Depatriarchalizing in Biblical Interpretation." *Journal of the American Academy of Religion* 41 (1973): 30–48.

Trible, Phyllis. *Texts of Terror: Literary-Feminist Readings of Biblical Narratives*. Overtures to Biblical Theology 13. Philadelphia: Fortress, 1984.

Vander Stichele, Caroline, and Todd Penner, eds. *Her Master's Tools? Feminist and Postcolonial Engagements with Historical-Critical Discourse*. Global Perspectives on Biblical Scholarship 9. Atlanta: Society of Biblical Literature, 2005.

Davina C. Lopez and Todd Penner

HOMOSEXUAL/QUEER

What is the difference between "homosexual" and "queer"? Is this difference significant? Does this difference matter for the interpretation of biblical images, ideas, or arguments? Does this difference connect to ancient ideas about sexual (or erotic) practices and ideas? If so, what impact (if any) should it have on biblical hermeneutics? This entry aims to address such questions, even as it problematizes what such questions can lead to, within and beyond biblical studies.

"Homosexual" and "Queer" Difference? "What is the difference between "homosexual" and "queer"?"

Queer. The term "queer" is used in a couple of ways in contemporary English. Often "queer" is used as a noun or adjective for an attribute, a kind of person, or a term of identification or description. In such contexts one can meaningfully say: "I am queer," or "We're here, we're queer, get used to it." In practice, this use of queer has often functioned as a replacement for a series of cumbersome abbreviations like LG, LGB, LGBT, or even LGBTIQA, for lesbian, gay, bisexual, trans, intersex, queer or questioning, and ally (though asexual also appears in some contexts). "Queer" can be a convenient umbrella term, then, a way of including a range of people who could be seen as departing from heterosexist and cisgendered expectations, experiences, or worldviews. ("Cisgender"

refers to alignment between gender identities, sexed bodies, and gender assignments made at birth.)

This umbrella use for "queer" can be found in a few different contexts in biblical interpretation. For instance, *The Queer Bible Commentary* introduces its contents by stressing that it will address lesbian, gay, bisexual, and/or transgender issues (Guest et al., 2006, p. xiii). In the eyes of its editors, this quartet is what can make a commentary queer. This "big tent" approach is also reflected in earlier proposals for a queer biblical hermeneutics. Robert Goss insists elsewhere:

> The strength of a queer interpretive model is precisely that it is not exclusively gay identified or exclusively lesbian identified. It includes critical feminist hermeneutics and practice. Both feminist and queer interpretive models arise from an interlocking discourse and practice of resistance, conflict, and struggle for liberation. (Goss, 1993, p. 80)

In both of these instances, homosexuals appear under the sign of queer. In fact, in Goss's earlier formulation "queer" does conceptual work similar to "homosexual," since both terms can be applied to homosexual females (lesbians) and males (gay males). Still, though "queer" is a point of identification, it does not belong exactly to any one group. In these instances, it was used to identify and foster forms of solidarity across groups. Many of the earliest users of the term "queer" in biblical hermeneutics emphasize analogies and alliances between and among those who might fit with LGBT identities, as well as feminist and other liberation-oriented groups. Is this, then, what makes an approach or a community queer? Does the inclusion of both male and female homosexuals make the difference? Or is the key a distinctly political aim, akin and indebted to feminist actions? Or perhaps bisexual and/or trans folk are the necessary supplement to homosexual (where LG meets the BT) to make something queer?

It is not completely accurate to describe queer as an uncomplicated story of convenience and coalition. The selection of this particular word is purposeful, given the pejorative or derogatory uses of "queer". It is a term that can evoke bad feelings. As a term that aims to pathologize or marginalize its targets, "queer" means "odd," "abnormal," or "perverse." It has been used both as slang for homosexuals and as a homophobic term aimed at those who do not adequately fit with dominant points of view. Therefore, its use for a different purpose indicates a spirit of reclamation and even defiance in the face of insult and injury. The force and often the excitement of this term comes from the resignifying, even the reversal, in its evaluation. Those groups and scholars who have reclaimed this word do not dispute that it connotes abnormality or nonconformity; rather, they dispute that such a contrary relation to "the normal" and "the natural" is negative. "Queer," then, can indicate a challenge to regimes of the normal, a desire to resist and contest such a worldview. In this second sense, queer is less an identity and more a disposition, a mode of examining the processes that cast certain people and practices into categories of normal and abnormal and then of interrogating the effects of such processes. "Queer" can also work more like a verb or adverb, an action or a particular way of acting, now qualified, altered, and resituated. In this sense one can "queer" an arrangement of power and privilege, or interpret queerly by attending to certain dynamics.

This latter sense is mostly how I use the term (Marchal, 2011), since this is its more frequent connotation in queer studies. One can trace the origins of the latter meaning not only through political groups like ACT UP or Queer Nation but also through important strains within the academic subdisciplines of both women's studies and lesbian and gay studies in the 1980s. In the decade that followed, queer studies began to congeal, as the work of scholars like Judith Butler, Michel Foucault, and Eve Kosofsky Sedgwick (among others) found wider audiences. Their work called a certain kind of critical attention to ideas and practices that seemed normal or natural, particularly within heteronormative contexts. Foucault's work helped to formulate the key idea of *normalization* for queer studies. Foucault describes normalization as those exercises in power that perform and combine five particular operations:

(1) comparing activities, (2) differentiating between them, (3) arranging them into a hierarchy of value, (4) imposing a homogenized category to which one should conform (within this hierarchy), and (5) excluding those who differ and are, thus, abnormal (Foucault, 1979, pp. 182–184).

Thus, while queer studies could be described as the study about, or from the perspective of, LGBTIQ people (corresponding to the first sense of queer described above), it just as often involves study about these processes called "normalization," which have often been used against LGBTIQ people (corresponding more to the second sense described). Ken Stone similarly differentiates between two kinds of queer biblical commentary, the first "a reading produced by a reader who is 'queer,' where 'queer' is understood to communicate lesbian, gay, or bisexual identities, experiences, or social locations" (Stone, 2001, p. 19), and the second those that that "take as their point of departure a critical interrogation and active contestation of the many ways in which the Bible is and has been read to support heteronormative and normalizing configurations of sexual practices and sexual identities" (p. 33).

Could one classify the first sense of queer, then, as belonging to the label "homosexual" (and their allies) and the second sense as somehow *more* queer, or more fitting some label "queer?" The difficulty with this solution is that many proponents of queer studies and politics would interrogate this labeling process for its potential disciplinary effects. Thus, Butler insists:

If the term "queer" is to be a site of collective contestation, the point of departure for a set of historical reflections and futural imaginings, it will have to remain that which is, in the present, never fully owned, but always only redeployed, twisted, queered from a prior usage and in the direction of urgent and expanding political purposes. (Butler, 1993, p. 228)

Though this formulation repeats the contrast between the attributive, nominal use and the more verbal sense of "queer" (with a certain emphasis on the latter), it also destabilizes how "queer" can behave in either sense. Elsewhere, Butler argues that queer theories should have no "proper object" (1994). Though it has historical and topical ties to lesbian and gay studies, queer studies is not confined to the study of sexual minorities or sexuality. In fact, one origin story often told for queer theory begins with a key essay by Teresa de Lauretis (1991), in which she calls for greater critical attention to differences within and between sexual minority communities in light of dynamics of gender, race, class, and geography (a not uncommon refrain in women's studies of this era, indicating the close ties between these subdisciplines). De Lauretis addresses some queers—homosexuals and allies in lesbian and gay studies—by queerly interrogating what (else) she, they, or even "we" could be doing. Thus, queer studies does not belong to any one group, and it aims not to divide its labors between the study of various categories and dynamics of normalization. To do so would inhibit any attempt to interrogate how certain norms are created and enforced, particularly given how people socially construct the meaning of something like "sexuality" differently through gender, race, ethnicity, class, religion, age, ability, and national or colonial factors.

The resistance that many queer theorists show toward limiting their tasks to one set of questions and concerns stresses the mobility of a term like "queer." Butler highlights the counterintuitive efficacy of this emphasis:

> The political deconstruction of "queer" ought not to paralyze the use of such terms, but, ideally, to extend its range, to make us consider at what expense and for what purposes the terms are being used, and through what relations of power such categories have been wrought. (Butler, 1993, p. 229)

Instead of being a source of frustration, this quality of queer theories allows them to adapt to new contours and critically reflect on their own practices. Since the queer is arrayed in a contesting relation with and against the normal, there is an underlying suspicion about imposing only one meaning or insisting that there is only one task for queer thought and activism. Thus, no definition or description of "queer" within queer theories can be exhaustive; in fact, any claim to give the final, definitive version of what queer is or does would itself be *un*-queer.

Homosexual. So there are troubles defining exactly what "queer" is; or, put another way, queering troubles the practice of defining terms, particularly (though not only) when such practice works toward normalizing or naturalizing ends. Perhaps, then, one will have greater luck defining and describing "homosexual." After all, homosexual at times appears as a point of contrast in many discussions of queer. Homosexual seems to connote an identity, whereas queer interrogates processes of identification. One can be a homosexual; queer appears to be more ambiguous.

Indeed, thus far, this entry has proceeded as if people already know what homosexual means, expending greater energy on that which seems more elusive, perhaps because it is of more recent vintage. It might therefore surprise some how modern the concept of homosexuality is. David Halperin makes this point from the beginning of his essay (and the book it opens) by titling it "One Hundred Years of Homosexuality" (1990). Here, Halperin highlights the point that the term "homosexual(ity)" does not appear in English until 1892, an adaptation of the German term first coined in 1869 by Karl-Maria Kertbeny. The term catches on as a sexological classification in the medical literature of the late nineteenth and early twentieth centuries, as it helped to specify this kind of deviation within a range of other deviations also viewed as perversions. Homosexuality was a medicalized pathology that focused attention upon the gender of a person's sexual object choice. Such a classification coincided with the medical emphasis on sex as dimorphic and bipolar. The emphasis on sexed categories aided a number of political and cultural purposes at the time, countering, for instance, the era's movements for women's rights. It also provided a (seemingly) stable basis for the application of homosexual as a classification, since it involved identifying who was attracted to the "same" (*homo-*) sex (males attracted to males, females to females).

Thus, both "queer" and "homosexual" have origins in efforts to pathologize and marginalize. Neither term is ancient. In fact, "homosexual" is a compound that outrages scholars of Greek and Latin, combining as it does the Greek *homo-* with the Latin *sex/sexualis*. Yet, in the modern diagnostic setting of its origin, "homosexual" enjoys the veneer of antiquity and, thus, authority for the professional who deploys it. This perhaps is what distinguishes these terms from each other: "homosexual" is clinical, while "queer" is more colloquial. Though the coining of the former makes it possible for those so diagnosed to identify each other and organize to counter their treatment, queer's mundane origin implies a more direct and confrontational mode. Homosexual liberation, for instance, aimed at removing homosexuality from the *Diagnostic and Statistical Manual of Mental Disorders* as a psychiatric pathology, staking a claim to variation, but also some normalcy in this variation. Queer, on the other hand, affirms claims about abnormality and strangeness, but reverses claims that such abnormality is problematic. Still, both kinds of action interrogate the authority of classifying disciplines. It may just be that homosexual and queer connote different settings and thus different modes for such challenges.

Impressions can therefore be mistaken when it comes to these terms. The attempt to make "homosexual" universalizable in its medicalized application belies the particular modern context for its earliest uses. Further, the impression that homosexuals are somehow departures or derivations from something or, more pointedly, those someones who precede them—heterosexuals—is upended by the historical priority of the concept homosexuality. Heterosexuality as a concept depends upon homosexuality. Further, "heterosexuality" originated as a pathological term, not as reference to the unmarked, default, seemingly natural or normal kind of sexuality (Halperin, 1990, pp. 158–159). Indeed, recalling original descriptions of heterosexuality as types of perversion could be a productive, if provocative way of resituating heteronormativity's investment in one particular way of sorting only certain desires, practices, and identifications as acceptable, normal, and good. This sort of fixation is described in other settings as fetish.

There is much within the relatively short histories of homosexuality and heterosexuality that is strange, unexpected, even disruptive to normative claims about genders, bodies, and sexualities. The act of historicizing the terms of sexuality and gender, then, can be rather queer. Indeed, queer theorists have highlighted how dependent heterosexuality is on homosexuality. Heterosexuality demands to be recognized as natural, normal, and therefore good sexuality, the only possible outcome. Yet its definition requires the existence of homosexuality as a contrasting term, disrupting its totalizing claims. Homosexuality affirms this definitional difference, but undermines the qualities that heterosexuality claims for itself. Heterosexuality is revealed as inherently unstable, needing constant explanation and reiteration to produce itself, and its accompanying concepts of gender, as natural (Butler, 1991). These must be repeated, requiring copies of copies of what they are producing as "natural." This indicates the distinctive cultural work it takes to produce heterosexuality as normative, how incessantly it has to claim its timelessness. The time it takes to continuously shore up the position it anxiously claims for itself indicates how precarious and troubled heterosexuality is.

Historical Differences? Many scholars insist, with justification, that there were no "homosexuals" in the ancient world. One cardinal moment for those making such declarations of discontinuity between concepts of "sex," past and present, is found in Foucault's landmark *History of Sexuality*:

> Sodomy was a category of forbidden acts; their perpetrator was nothing more than the juridical subject of them. The nineteenth-century homosexual became a personage, a past, a case history, and a childhood, in addition to being a type of life, a life form, and a morphology.... The sodomite had been a temporary aberration; the homosexual was now a species. (Foucault, 1990, p. 43)

Foucault's aim in this instance was to contrast the homosexual, as the bearer of a kind of *identity*, with perverse sexual practices (like sodomy), as *acts*.

Indeed, this contrast between being and doing may linger in various attempts to differentiate homosexual and queer.

The modern use of "homosexual," then, is a product of the sort of break Foucault is taken to be describing. Homosexual is a kind of sexual orientation, reflecting a person's individual identity and inner life. One does not have to do certain sexual practices to be a person with this orientation. One need only desire sexual contact with someone of the same sex. "Sameness" is limited to this one factor, obscuring other bases for sorting sexual practices, like certain acts, sensations, timing, or positions, among others. This way of categorizing people on the basis of attraction to one sex or the other, as an expression of inner being, marks the modern homosexual as different from those who had similar kinds of sexual contact before sexual orientation developed as an explanatory schema. Thus, it is with some justification one can also insist there were no heterosexuals in the ancient world, since sorting under the rubric "orientation" also defines heterosexuality.

Yet the reclamation of a usable past has been a persistent project for lesbian and gay studies. If one learns to look at the archive from the right angle, or ask the right sort of questions, one can see all the gays and lesbians who were "hidden from history" (Duberman et al., 1989). These figures are not isolated in the margins, but can be found at the heart of the literary, historical, and social canon (particularly, but not only, in the West). Thus, Sedgwick responds:

> Not only have there been a gay Socrates, Shakespeare, and Proust but...their names are Socrates, Shakespeare, and Proust; and beyond that, legion—dozens or hundreds of the most centrally canonic figures in what the monoculturalists are pleased to consider "our" culture. (Sedgwick, 1990, p. 52)

The affirmative possibilities of such lesbian and gay visibility impact both political and historical horizons. Here, Sedgwick departs from the narratives of historical alterity in the arguments made by Foucault and Halperin. Rather than imagining a great paradigm shift, complete break, or eclipsing succession from one view of sexual relations to another, Sedgwick traces the possibilities of models coexisting. While Halperin and, in some ways, Foucault have denaturalized assumptions about the past, Sedgwick seeks to denaturalize assumptions about the present, especially regarding "homosexuality as we know it today" (1990, pp. 44–48). This is one reason Sedgwick's work is taken up in queer studies: Sedgwick can be enlisted to critique the way in which some lesbian and gay history stabilizes both the past and the present, potentially reinforcing disciplinary forces of normalization.

Still, there is some use to narrating the different ideas about sexual practices, ancient and more recent. Denaturalizing assumptions about the past, a site often cited in modern debates about who or what is normal, can be an important strategy in contesting the terms of these debates. The different way ancient sources describe and prescribe sexual activities has even led some scholars to replace the term "homosexual" with "homoerotic" when discussing peoples around the ancient Mediterranean. Ostensibly, this helps to dissociate ancient practices from modern identities shaped by sexual orientation. Yet the replacement is still shaped by the doubled narrowing of focus to sexual-object choice and the classification of humans as "same" (or not) on the basis of sex/gender (retaining the homo-), in keeping with assumptions about sexual orientation.

As indicated above, Halperin makes a strong distinction between ancient and contemporary ideas about sexuality. Discussing the ancient way of categorizing practices, he recommends "not to speak of it as a sexuality at all but to describe it, rather, as a more generalized ethos of penetration and domination" (Halperin, 1990, pp. 34–35). In this ethos sex acts are not mutual activities. They are not done with someone, but they are done to, on, or upon someone, reflecting an asymmetrical hierarchy between participants. Sex acts, in this view, should indicate and correspond to the relative status of the participants: the dominant party, typically imagined as an elite, free adult male, will be the insertive participant, while the receptive "participant" should be socially and politically subordinate to the insertive. In this arrangement there is a remarkable indifference to the sex of the receiving body: females, younger males, and slaves and foreigners (of both sexes) are appropriate and interchangeable receptacles. However, gendered ideas are not absent from these scenarios; they are just differently arranged. The main division is not between male and female but between insertive imagined as "active" and receptive imagined as "passive," which, in turn, mostly corresponds to ancient ideas about masculinity and femininity. If an elite, free adult male is going to maintain his masculinity, he must act in all ways (including sexually) according to his higher status, dominant, active, and thus insertive. As long as the higher-status male behaves as an impenetrable penetrator, the sex act could be classified as natural.

The proper and thus natural role of a social subordinate in this ancient ethos was to be passive and receptive, and any departure from this grid would be imagined as unnatural. This explains why the ancient Greek word used for "sexual" acts within this grid is *chrēsis*, or "use," since a superior *makes use* of another, inferior body as a receptacle of their penetration. Grappling with this ancient context, of course, impacts the interpretation of biblical texts, including those that ostensibly tell people what "the Bible says" about homosexuality (like Rom 1 or 1 Cor 6), even as it conditions many more besides (within the Pauline corpus, for instance, review 1 Thessalonians, Philemon, and even Philippians in this light). Biblical texts repeat these terminologies of nature and use in troubling ways. The acts reflected in these kinds of texts inevitably reflect the status of those involved, as all proper and natural acts reflect and reinforce the difference between a social superior and inferior.

This sexual-social protocol for sorting acts also clearly demonstrates how status is gendered. This indicates the utility of terms like wo/men and kyriarchy, introduced by the feminist biblical scholar Elisabeth Schüssler Fiorenza (2001, pp. 57–59, 107–109, and 216). Within this system the terms of womanliness or femininity have been applied to both females and non-elite males, who might have been historically classified as somehow "like women." In this ancient ethos, a feminine or effeminized status is reflected by one's susceptibility to penetration and is by no means limited to the kinds of people that one *might* think of as "women" now. This protocol is a prime instance of how gendered terms are also used to define non-elite or subaltern males as women, or wo/men (see Schüssler Fiorenza, 2001, p. 58). Some scholars in Classics recognize this gendered differential within socio-sexual status, offering terms like "unmen." Jonathan Walters (1991) introduces this helpful label for a series of people because most of our Greek and Roman sources insist that not all adult males were seen as "real men" (*viri*) in the ancient world. *Viri* is not a term that can be applied to all adult males. It excludes non-elite working groups, slaves, or any conquered or disreputable person, all of whom were available for penetrative use by their social superiors. Gender, ethnic, imperial, and economic categories intertwine in this system; in searching for sexuality, one instead finds a system of gender and much more.

In these ancient contexts, sexuality may not be an identity, exactly; but acts that one might call sexual are tied to claims about the status of a person (or nonperson, as the case may be). Sexuality or eroticism involved differentiations of gender. Gender, in turn, was a marker of status tied to dynamics of ethnicity, economy, and empire (among others). The intertwining and interlocking of these dynamics reflects Schüssler Fiorenza's analysis of kyriarchy. As a replacement for patriarchy and its more simplified, dualistic analysis of power in gendered terms alone, kyriarchy highlights how multiple and mutually influential structures of domination and subordination function together in pyramidal relations determined not only by sexism but also by racism, classism, ethnocentrism, heterosexism, colonialism, nationalism, and militarism (among others) (Schüssler Fiorenza 2001, pp. 118–124, 211). Kyriarchy is a system where only certain kinds of males are "men"—elite, educated, freeborn, propertied, imperial, and typically from particular racial/ethnic groups—who rule all who might be wo/men—females but also non-elite, uneducated, enslaved, subaltern, and/or often racially or ethnically dominated groups of males.

This sort of analysis explains how elite groups in the ancient context could and would differentiate between "real" men and unmen (alongside "other" women), as Walters and others have highlighted.

Erotic contact, then, is not just some "private" matter, nor is it a thing that people do with one part of their bodies. Rather, it is a reflection of the way embodied entities are placed in relation to each other, as an expression of their social status, likely best explained in terms of one's placement within pyramidal structures of relation like kyriarchy. In narrating the difference that marks ancient worldviews about erotic acts, though, I have come back around to the utility of analytic terms that can be used for a variety of places and times (like kyriarchy). Insisting upon a whole new set of terminologies when discussing the ancient setting of texts, like the biblical ones, might not always be the most helpful strategy. Indeed, in contemporary queer studies, scholars have reflected upon the possibilities within failed masculinities or alternative masculinities (Halberstam, 1998), in ways not so distanced from how ancient elites worried over maintaining their impenetrable penetrator status or puzzled over how to compliment a good elite adult woman as *vir*-tuous. These anxieties reflect the sort of instability Butler notes for more recent gender and sexual norms (described above). Further, the sorts of characterization, condescension, and condemnation the ancient Romans directed toward their imperial-erotic subordinates as monstrous Others resonates not with modern concepts of the homosexual but with the continued targeting of some racialized groups (the terrorist/Muslim) as perversely motivated, queerly situated, monstrous fags (see Puar and Rai, 2002). There might still be some virtue in considering the strange, even queer continuities or recurrence within sites that cross an (apparent) ancient/modern impasse.

Such continuities and discontinuities, resonances and differences can be traced by reconsidering another gendered and sexual term: lesbian. Some scholars, like Valerie Traub, insist that the historical contingency and epistemological inadequacy of this term should somehow be marked whenever it is used (which is why she italicizes *lesbian* in Traub, 2002). This is a compelling suggestion, connected to points made above about distinctions across the centuries and false totalizations within inherently unstable identity markers. On the one hand, the modern origin of "lesbian" as a specifically sexological term shares a common medicalized root with the homosexual as cases of gendered inversion. On the other, this gendered nonconformity as a "masculine" female corresponds to many ancient treatments of females who were characterized as improperly "active" (or insertive) because they had erotic contact with other females. While not ignoring the discontinuities, such potential continuities are among the reasons Bernadette Brooten presents her work as a part of lesbian history. By way of analogy, Brooten notes:

> The historical discontinuities are, however, no greater than with such other terms as "slavery," "marriage," or "family," and yet we have no qualms about applying these terms to historical and cross-cultural phenomena, even though, for example, a "family" can include slaves or not, multiple wives or not, or the legal power of a man to kill family members or not. (Brooten, 1996, p. 18)

In such instances, using (rather than evading) a term that seems obvious or always already understood cannot be dismissed as evidence of an essentialist position if it helps to trace historical or cultural differences.

"Lesbian" as a term can matter and materialize in rather different ways than one might expect, especially when trying to draw hard and fast lines between queer, homosexual, and homoerotic. Even from within her deconstructive critique of certain rhetorical and organizational practices, Butler cannot completely dissociate from the word: "This is not to say that I will not appear at political occasions under the sign of lesbian, but that I would like to have it permanently unclear what that sign signifies" (1991, p. 14). Lesbian here sounds as mobile, even labile, as queer elsewhere. Lesbian, then, matters and materializes in different ways within at least some biblical scholarship. Deryn Guest, for instance, presents a consciously and critically lesbian-identified biblical hermeneutic, often by way of stark contrasts to queer theory or hermeneutics. She carefully historicizes the various meanings of "lesbian," even while maintaining that lesbians have a unique vantage point for interpretation (Guest, 2005, pp. 9–58). Yet the kind of difference this difference makes is in the way lesbians prefer "reading straight texts aslant" (p. 18; cf. 114). This sort of reading practice sounds remarkably, even ironically like the one described at length about (American, upper-to-middle-class, mostly white) gay males in Halperin's *How to Be Gay* (2012).

Certain lesbian and gay practices can appear to be more alike than different, bringing us back around to one formulation of "queer" as referring to gays and lesbians under one banner. Of course, the twist in both of these works is that these identities are less matters of being than of doing, echoing queer theorists. These works symptomize a slippage between lesbian and queer, or gay and queer, and then perhaps, in combination, homosexual and queer. Guest, Halperin, and many others describe reading a certain way, approaching a structure, or interpreting a phenomenon (whether it be Judy Garland, *Mansfield Park*, or the Bible), by attending to certain dynamics. This sounds a great deal like learning to interpret queerly.

Confusion and ambiguities will persist if one seeks to create or maintain strict lines between points of reference like homosexual and queer, ancient and modern, homosexual and heterosexual, gendered and sexual, homoerotic and gay, lesbian and straight. Indeed, after a while one might want to interrogate why and how such borders or lines or zones need to be policed. No doubt, from certain vantage points described here, one could justifiably try to retitle Halperin's book as *How to Do Things Queerly*, or crankily submit that Guest, Goss, West, and Bohache's massive commentary is really a *(Mostly) Homosexual Commentary*. Yet, from another vantage point, such line drawing and label guarding is ultimately counter to the ethos of queer. In the end questions about the impact of these (and many other) acts present an im-portant trajectory for rethinking and resisting the conditions that construct and constrain still other strange ways of doing and being.

[*See also* Heterosexism/Heteronormativity; Queer Readings; Queer Theory; *and* Sexuality.]

BIBLIOGRAPHY

Brooten, Bernadette J. *Love Between Women: Early Christian Responses to Female Homoeroticism*. Chicago: University of Chicago Press, 1996.

Butler, Judith. "Imitation and Gender Insubordination." In *Inside/Out: Lesbian Theories, Gay Theories*, edited by Diana Fuss, pp. 13–31. New York: Routledge, 1991.

Butler, Judith. *Bodies That Matter: On the Discursive Limits of "Sex."* New York: Routledge, 1993.

Butler, Judith. "Against Proper Objects." *differences* 6, no. 2–3 (1994): 1–26.

de Lauretis, Teresa. "Queer Theory, Lesbian and Gay Studies: An Introduction." *differences* 3, no. 2 (1991): iii–xviii.

Duberman, Martin, Martha Vicinius, and George Chauncey Jr., eds. *Hidden from History: Reclaiming the Gay and Lesbian Past*. New York: NAL, 1989.

Foucault, Michel. *Discipline and Punish: The Birth of the Prison*. Translated by Alan Sheridan. New York: Vintage, 1979.

Foucault, Michel. *The History of Sexuality*. Vol. 1, *An Introduction*. Translated by Robert Hurley. New York: Vintage, 1990.

Goss, Robert E. *Jesus ACTED Up: A Gay and Lesbian Manifesto*. San Francisco: HarperSanFrancisco, 1993.

Guest, Deryn. *When Deborah Met Jael: Lesbian Biblical Hermeneutics*. London: SCM, 2005.

Guest, Deryn, Robert E. Goss, Mona West, and Thomas Bohache, eds. *The Queer Bible Commentary*. London: SCM, 2006.

Halberstam, Judith. *Female Masculinity*. Durham, N.C.: Duke University Press, 1998.

Halperin, David M. *One Hundred Years of Homosexuality: And Other Essays on Greek Love*. New York: Routledge, 1990.

Halperin, David M. *How to Be Gay*. Cambridge, Mass.: Belknap, 2012.

Marchal, Joseph A. "'Making History' Queerly: Touches across Time through a Biblical Behind." *Biblical Interpretation* 19 (2011): 373–395.

Puar, Jasbir K., and Amit S. Rai. "Monster, Terrorist, Fag: The War on Terrorism and the Production of Docile Patriots." *Social Text* 20, no. 3 (Fall 2002): 117–148.

Schüssler Fiorenza, Elisabeth. *Wisdom Ways: Introducing Feminist Biblical Interpretation.* Maryknoll, N.Y.: Orbis, 2001.

Sedgwick, Eve Kosofsky. *Epistemology of the Closet.* Berkeley: University of California Press, 1990.

Stone, Ken. "Queer Theory and Biblical Interpretation: An Introduction." In *Queer Commentary and the Hebrew Bible*, edited by Ken Stone, pp. 11–34. Cleveland, Ohio: Pilgrim, 2001.

Traub, Valerie. *The Renaissance of Lesbianism in Early Modern England.* Cambridge, U.K.: Cambridge University Press, 2002.

Walters, Jonathan. "'No More Than a Boy': The Shifting Construction of Masculinity from Ancient Greece to the Middle Ages." *Gender and History* 5 (1993): 20–33.

Joseph A. Marchal

1

Imagery, Gendered

This entry contains seven subentries: Priestly Material; Deuteronomistic History; Prophetic Literature; Wisdom Literature; Apocalyptic Literature; Gospels; *and* Pauline Literature.

Priestly Material

When approaching the intersection of gender and priestly writing, a number of central questions emerge. (1) What actually constitutes a priestly text? (2) What pieces of the Hebrew Bible do we examine for gender-related content? (3) What is the gender identity of the author or authors of priestly writing? (4) What is the approach of the author(s) to gender-related issues such as hierarchy, power, and exclusivity?

Identifying Priestly, priestly, and Holiness Material. Identification of the authors of biblical writing inevitably incites strong scholarly responses, ranging from denial that it can be done to the promulgation of a reliable methodological approach. When used as a tool for greater understanding rather than as end in itself, source criticism (identifying sources/authorship in the Pentateuch) provides a helpful point from which to begin a set of inquiries. Priestly writing can be divided into two or more subsections. For this article, the lower case "p" as "priestly" indicates

writing either by the Priestly (P) writer (primarily the narratives in Genesis, Exodus and Numbers, and Leviticus 1—16) or the Holiness (H) writer (Lev 17—26). Although dates for priestly writing vary substantially among scholars, linguistically focused studies place P in the preexilic period (1000–587 B.C.E.), followed by H in the late preexilic period (650–587 B.C.E.). Numerous scholars follow Wellhausen (1957, pp. 127–145) and others, however, in placing P and H in the exilic (587–538 B.C.E.) or postexilic periods (538–400 B.C.E.). Some scholars separate priestly narratives in Genesis, Exodus, and Numbers from the corpus of priestly laws in Leviticus and in sections of Numbers. I do not see a convincing reason to do so.

Gender Identity of the Author. Although most consider the question of whether a man or woman wrote sections of the Hebrew Bible irrelevant (since we have no definite proof and since it is unlikely that a woman was trained to read and write in this age), it may be worth considering why the question arises. Understanding the biographical details of a writer's life is always illuminating to us as readers. If someone purports to be an expert on mysticism, we wonder if that person has had any real engagement with mystical experience. It changes the way we read a text if we think someone has an inside perspective about what she or he is writing. Friedman (1987, p. 86) wonders if the author of J (Jawist)

Source could have been female, and students regularly ask whether it is possible that the book of Ruth was written by a woman. These questions arise because these stories read as if the person writing understands the life of women.

If one writes about women, we naturally wonder if the writer is an insider. Although some men can write as insiders as Wally Lamb does in *She's Come Undone* or even Alexander McCall Smith in the *No. 1 Ladies' Detective Agency* novels, it is difficult to think of men writing these books. In the case of priestly writing, nothing suggests that the writer is a woman, but there are some theological principles that do suggest the writer knows something about female anatomy and has some appreciation for women as divinely ordained counterparts for men. Because the worldview of the priestly writers is hierarchical, it is doubtful that someone on a lower rung of the hierarchy would have been selected either to copy or create sacred literature.

Power, Hierarchy, and Exclusivity. The priestly worldview is hierarchical and follows a descending order as follows:

1. High priest and his family, including women (Lev 1)
2. Priest and his family, including women (Lev 1)
3. Levite man (Num 16:8; 1:47–53; 8:20–22)
4. Israelite man and woman (Lev 16:16)
5. Wife and daughter of a priest (Lev 22:12–13)
6. Non-Israelite resident alien (Lev 17:8, 10; 22:17–18; 19:33)
7. Israelite male slave/servant (Lev 25:35–43)
8. Israelite female slave/servant (implied by above?)
9. Foreign slave to the priest (25:44)
10. Foreign (nonresident) man (Lev 22:10)
11. Foreign woman (based on metaphor and narrative such as Num 25:6–19)

No list such as this appears in one place in the Hebrew Bible, but this hypothesized one may be helpful. This ladder stipulates who can get closest to the Holy of Holies and who can partake of sacred food. Saul Olyan's (2000, p. 31) work on hierarchy in the biblical representation of the cult breaks down each of these categories and finds helpful nuances: for example slaves of foreign origin who live in the homes of priests are treated differently than foreigners in general.

Thus far we have acknowledged that priestly writing imagines a Deity concerned with categorical distinctions and their prioritization. Though partaking of special food (Lev 22:10) and securing a cohesive connection to the clan by encouraging endogamous marriages (Lev 22:12) constitutes exclusivity, other areas that seemingly lend themselves to exclusion or gender hierarchy do not. We find this both with regard to the purity laws and in priestly narratives, where priestly writing constructs male and female identity in relationship to one another and to the Deity.

Purity. Because of the ways in which the Priestly writer constructs hierarchy, the assumption has been made that the priestly conception of bodily impurity is also hierarchical with men closer to the "pure" and women closer to the "impure." However, though no one doubts that taboos about menstrual blood were present in Israelite society (the word for menstruating woman, *ndh*, carries with it a linguistic relationship with "throwing away" or discarding), the Priestly writer, through a carefully constructed chiastic (a chiasm is a literary structure, showing parallel words or themes in, typically, an ABCC1B1A1 schema), goes out of his way to demonstrate that both men and women have the potential to become impure and both have remedies for their impurities.

This chiastic structure is located in Leviticus 15 and has been identified in two separate ways. Some prefer reading verse 18 as the chiastic midpoint (Meachem, 1999; Milgrom, 1991; Whitekettle, 1991). This verse posits that pollution results from heterosexual (for the Hebrew Bible—"normative") intercourse. Others argue, to my mind more convincingly, that verse 18 is not the midpoint of the chiasm (Ellens, 2003; Philip, 2006; Wenham, 1979); rather, the center of the chiasm is found in two sets of verses. The first set outlines the pollution of healthy/normative male discharge (vv. 16–18) and the impurity that results for a female partner during intercourse.

The second outlines the pollution of healthy female discharge (i.e., menstrual blood; vv. 19–24) and the resulting pollution for the male sexual partner.

The way in which we interpret the intention of the biblical writer has implications for how we understand the construction of gender in priestly writing. One could argue that in both schemas there is an attempt to demonstrate parity when disclosing the potential impurities of men and women. This is an essential point. It dispels the myth that somehow women are at the bottom of the priestly hierarchy because their impurity is more contaminating than that of their male counterparts (Ruane, 2007; Wegner, 2003). Normal female impurity is more contaminating than normal male impurity, but the text never indicates that their impurity is the reason that they may not function as priests.

The implications of the second schema are important to understand as well. If the chiasm is understood according the second division, it is not intercourse that is highlighted but rather the dual direction of the impurity from male to female and then from female to male. Although it is widely assumed that the chapter focuses on the general notion that bodies convey impurity rather than on the act of intercourse per se, the second schema suggests that men have the ability to pollute all things and people, and specifically women with whom they come into sexual contact. Complementarily, women have the ability to pollute all things and people, and specifically men with whom they come into sexual contact.

The Priestly writer goes out of his way to build this literary structure, even while he understands that menstrual blood pollutes for a longer time than does semen. Both fluids, however, are categorized under normal or expected impurities, in contradistinction to the abnormal emissions that can be present in both men and women. The Priestly writer could have easily created a set of laws distinctive for women and relegated female bodily impurities to women's space. He could have done this by placing the laws of menstruation and abnormal female emissions in Leviticus 12, alongside the impurities connected with childbirth. The writer even adds the comparative statement that lochial (blood connected to childbirth) blood is like menstrual blood (Lev 12:2), suggesting an even more logical decision to place the laws together. But the Priestly writer does not organize the laws in this way. As Milgrom (1991, p. 905) has intuited, the organization moves from the longest period of pollution, the woman who has given birth (Lev 12), to the one who has scale–disease (*tsara'at*; Lev 13—14), to the lesser bodily impurities described above (Lev 15). If anyone fails to adhere to the correct purification processes, and/or fails to adhere to other ethical commandments, the following rites of the Day of Atonement (Lev 16) serve to purify the whole house of Israel and those who live among them.

Some have argued against the parity of gender expressed in the chiasm. Wegner (2003, p. 457) and Ruane (2007, p. 74) have rightly noted that in Leviticus 15 the woman, unlike the man, does not come "before Yahweh" to offer the sacrifice. When she brings an offering to mark the end of her period of impurity, the woman must access the priest to complete her final step toward purification. Milgrom (1991, p. 934) also noted the lack of parity in the wording but felt that the woman's participation in the cult is implied by the literary structure. Ruane (2007, p. 74) noticed the lack of parallel language in the description of washing as a means of purification before the sacrificial offering. Ruane (2007, p. 77) argues that this lacunae suggests that the author of the text simply did not include this information because, building on Wegner, the woman never got close enough to offer the sacrifice. Furthermore, Ruane (2007, p. 78) argues that the woman is disqualified from the offering because she menstruates, an impurity that has more potential to pollute than does semen.

Both objections to the clear parallels in the chiastic structure are valid but the conclusions drawn may be overstated. Although Milgrom may dismiss the issue as a wording problem, women may not have come as close to the offering as men did. Ruane's suggestion that the woman is disqualified from these rites because she menstruates, however, is overstated. There is not enough evidence in the text to suggest this conclusion. Furthermore, I would submit that women of priestly descent were not disqualified from service in the sacred precinct because of their proclivity to menstruate: the text never states this nor does it imply this.

Yahweh is constructed as male in the text, and even though it is the Priestly writer who says "in the image of Elohim he created it/him; male and female he created them" (Gen 1:27), there is a profound sense of maleness that infuses the Priestly conception of the Deity. Like Leviticus 15, however, Genesis 1:27 also demonstrates that the Priestly writer attempts to portray a parity of the sexes in the creation of the human being. Although we cannot know the true extent to which women were involved in the offering of animal sacrifice, we can say that the Priestly writer attempted, to the best of his ability, to present a picture in which both men and women are the potential bearers of bodily impurities. Both men and women have normal and abnormal emissions and both have the potential to purify themselves from these ritual impurities. Although men serve as priests, we must distinguish between those who operated within that hierarchy and the writer/theologian who carefully constructed a redeeming paradigm of gender relationships in both Genesis 1 and Leviticus 15. The writer may benefit from priestly privilege, but he strives to situate that privilege in the context of the totality of human experience.

Narrative. The other way in which the Priestly writer creates a complicated picture of gender relations is in the narrative sections of the Pentateuch. We have shown that Genesis 1:1—2:4a suggests that the original birth of the human being is a spontaneous and simultaneous creation of male and female. In the Priestly conception of the primeval world, the time before time (Gen 1—11), there is no gender hierarchy. However, the writer lives in a divided world where men lord over women, the Deity has power over human beings and animals, and the Israelites are at war with their neighbors. Although the Priestly writer will go to great lengths to redeem Israelite women, such as in the chiastic construction in Leviticus 15, foreign women are on the lowest rung of the hierarchy.

Before exploring the Priestly writer's perspective on foreign women, we look more closely at another narrative concerning Israelite women. It has been demonstrated that the Priestly writer is in a dialogue of sorts with the combined Jahwist and Elohist (JE) narratives. Genesis 1 is a priestly response to J's (the Jawhist source) Genesis 2—3. An entirely different creation story is put forth by P in which the Deity speaks an ordered universe into existence, in contradistinction to J's Deity who shapes the human being from the clay of the earth and breathes life into it. J's deity walks in the garden and rebukes the first creatures for disobedience. Friedman (1987, pp. 54–60), and more recently Wright (2011), has shown that the Priestly flood narrative is crafted in direct response to J's flood story. Goldstein (2009; 2010) has shown that in the Priestly version of the announcement of the birth of Isaac, the matriarch Sarah is redeemed from J's depiction of her as doubting. In J (Gen 18:12), Sarah laughs at the news that she will bear a child in her old age, while in P Sarah is identified as "she from who kings will come" (Gen 17:16); it is Abraham who scoffs at God's messenger. Goldstein (2010, p. 45) describes the Priestly writer as a benevolent patriarch in his depiction of Israelite women. In P's view, furthermore, it is the women who give freely of their jewelry to construct the Tabernacle (Exodus 35:22, 26), in contrast to the jewelry given by men (but likely from their wives) in Exodus 32, the E source.

In contrast to the benevolence shown to Israelite women, the Priestly writer has nothing good to say about foreign women. In the narratives about foreign women, we see a xenophobic misogyny creeping into the gendered images in Priestly writing. The most difficult episodes are found in the book of Numbers in the heresy and its aftermath at Baal Peor. In Numbers 25, Israelite men "whore" (Hebrew, *znh*) after Moabite women, evoking retributive plague. In the same episode (seemingly spliced together, as vv. 1–5 appear to be J), priestly material adds that a Midianite woman and an Israelite man are discovered in a sexual encounter at the entrance of the Tent of Meeting. Phineas drives a spear through the offensive couple and the plague ceases (Num 25:11–13).

The act of zealotry is rewarded and contextualized as both reparative and salvific for the people. Almost more disturbing is Numbers 31:14–15, in which Moses rebukes his army for sparing the women in the battle against Moab, casting blame upon them for leading his people astray. Certainly there are some geopolitical issues in the case of both Moab and Midian, and as such, the Bible is often ambiguous in both its hatred and love of the foreigner (such as the book of Ruth's generous portrayal of Moab and the shining portrayal of Jethro, Moses's Midianite father-in-law). But these episodes involving foreign women are definitively Priestly in nature and cast a dark shadow over the some of the more redemptive aspects of Priestly writing that have been highlighted above.

[*See also* Authors of Biblical Books; Creation; Imagery, Gendered, *subentries on* Deuteronomistic History *and* Prophetic Literature; Legal Status, *subentry* Hebrew Bible; *and* Male-Female Sexuality, *subentry* Hebrew Bible.]

BIBLIOGRAPHY

Ellens, Deborah. "Menstrual Impurity and Innovation in Leviticus 15." In *Wholly Woman, Holy Blood: A Feminist Critique of Purity and Impurity*, edited by Kristin de Troyer, J. A. Herbert, J. A. Johnson, and A. M. Korte, pp. 29–43. Harrisburg, Pa.: Trinity Press International, 2003.

Friedman, Richard Elliot. *Who Wrote the Bible?* New York: Summit, 1987. Repr. San Francisco: HarperCollins, 1997.

Goldstein, Elizabeth. "Genealogy, Gynecology, and Gender: The Priestly Writer's Portrait of a Woman." In *Embroidered Garments: Priests and Gender in Biblical Israel*, edited by Deborah W. Rooke, pp. 74–86. Sheffield, U.K.: Sheffield Phoenix, 2009.

Goldstein, Elizabeth. "Impurity and Gender in the Hebrew Bible: Ideological Intersections in the Books of Leviticus, Ezekiel and Ezra." Ph.D. Diss., University of California, San Diego, 2010.

Meachem, Tirzah "An Abbreviated History of the Development of the Jewish Menstrual Laws." In *Women and Water: Menstruation in Jewish Life and Law*, edited by R. R. Wasserfall, pp. 23–37. Hanover, N.H.: Brandeis University Press, 1999.

Milgrom, Jacob, *Leviticus 1–16*. Anchor Bible. New York: Doubleday, 1991.

Olyan, Saul M. *Rites and Rank: Hierarchy in Biblical Representations of Cult*. Princeton, N.J.: Princeton University Press, 2000.

Philip, Tarja. *Menstruation and Childbirth in the Hebrew Bible: Fertility and Impurity*. New York: Peter Lang, 2006.

Ruane, Nicole, "Bathing, Status and Gender in Priestly Ritual." In *A Question of Sex: Gender and Difference in the Hebrew Bible and Beyond*, edited by Deborah Rooke, pp. 66–81. Sheffield, U.K.: Sheffield Phoenix, 2007.

Wegner, Judith Romney. "'Coming before the Lord': The Exclusion of Women from the Public Domain of the Israelite Priestly Cult." In *The Book of Leviticus*, edited by R. Rendtorff and R. A. Kugler, pp. 451–465. Leiden, The Netherlands: Brill, 2003.

Wenham, G. J. *The Book of Leviticus*. New International Commentary on the Old Testament. Grand Rapids, Mich.: Eerdmans, 1979.

Wellhausen, Julius. *Prolegomena to the History of Ancient Israel: The Classic and Original Statement of the Theory of "Higher Criticism" of the Old Testament*. New York: Meridian, 1957.

Whitekettle, Richard. "Leviticus 15:18 Reconsidered: Chiasm, Spatial Structure and the Body." *Journal for the Study of the Old Testament* 49 (1991): 31–45.

Wright, David. "Profane versus Sacrificial Slaughter: The Priestly Recasting of the Yahwist Flood Story." International Meeting of the Society of Biblical Literature, London, England, 2011. Section 5–16, 5 July 2011.

Elizabeth W. Goldstein

Deuteronomistic History

The phrase "Deuteronomistic History," hereafter DH, is used by scholars to refer to the books of Deuteronomy, Joshua, Judges, 1 and 2 Samuel, and 1 and 2 Kings. The phrase is associated with the German scholar Martin Noth, who argued in the 1940s that these books comprised a single literary document created during the Babylonian Exile, which is the context in which the history concludes in 2 Kings 25. While this literary work incorporated older sources and traditions, Noth believed that a single author/editor, referred to as the "Deuteronomist," was responsible for putting it together in something close to its present form. The resulting theological-historical narrative suggests to its audience that the Babylonian Exile and other disasters took place because the Israelites failed to live up to the stipulations of the covenant God made with them, which are laid out in the book of Deuteronomy.

Since the time of Noth, numerous scholars have proposed variations on his theory. These variations recognize that DH contains within it multiple layers and traditions. While some scholars work to reconstruct those layers, others argue that this heterogeneity is significant enough that it is no longer useful to refer to the books together as a single "Deuteronomistic History." In spite of such disagreement, it remains clear that recurring theological themes and literary-linguistic features appear across the books. Thus, even scholars who dispute or take no position on Noth's original theory sometimes retain the phrase "Deuteronomistic History" as a way of acknowledging such continuities.

Gender: Audience and Perspective. Although the book of Deuteronomy opens with an address to "all Israel" (Deut 1:1), a close analysis of DH indicates that much of it assumes a male audience and patriarchal perspectives. The second person masculine pronoun, "you," which appears frequently in both plural and singular forms beginning already in Deuteronomy 1:6, may in some cases be inclusive of women, but in other cases it is clear that males specifically are being addressed. In Deuteronomy 3:19, for example, where three tribes are addressed as "you" in the masculine plural, Moses explicitly tells them to leave "your women, your children, and your livestock" while fighting alongside the other tribes. In Deuteronomy 5:21, God uses a second person masculine singular pronoun to tell the Israelites, "You will not desire the wife of your neighbor. You will not desire the house of your neighbor, or his field, or his male slave, or his female slave, or his ox, or his donkey, or anything that is your neighbor's." These and comparable passages indicate that, while legal texts are meant to direct the conduct of women as well as men, their literary form and content assume a male audience and a society structured around male heads of households, to whom women are subordinate (Fewell and Gunn, 1993; Pressler, 1993; Anderson, 2004).

The narratives of DH also reflect a patriarchal society. Women appear much less frequently than men in the narratives; when they do appear, they often are subordinate to their fathers and husbands. Fathers give their daughters away in marriage through negotiations with other men (Josh 15:16–17 [=Judg

1:12–13]; Judg 15:2; 1 Sam 18:17–27; 2 Sam 13:13) and otherwise control their fates (Judg 11:34–40; 19:24). The word usually translated "husband" may be used interchangeably with words for "master" (e.g., Judg 19:3, 27). Although polygyny is evident from multiple narratives, women may have only one husband at a time. The subordination of the *pilegesh*, sometimes translated as "concubine" or "secondary wife," to her husband or "master" may make her more vulnerable to sexual violence (Judg 19:25; 2 Sam 16:20–22).

Yet there are also women who play powerful and/or crucial roles in DH. Although some of these women are represented negatively, such as Delilah (Judg 16:4–21), Jezebel (1 Kgs 18:4, 19:1–2, 21:5–26; 2 Kgs 9:30–37), and Athaliah (2 Kgs 11), others are represented positively, including Rahab (2:1–21, 6:22–25), Deborah the prophet and judge (Judg 4:4–16, 5:7), Jael (Judg 4:17–22, 5:24–27), and Huldah the prophet (2 Kgs 22:11–20). Even women in subordinate social roles may act assertively without negative consequences as does Achsah (Josh 15:18–19 [= Judg 1:14–15]).

Thus, it is unhelpful to assume that gender symbolism in DH can be explained solely on the basis of a simple distinction between powerful men and subordinate women, though gender subordination obviously exists. More complicated dynamics are also at work, and need to be teased out.

Characterization and Gender Role: Between Conformity and Nonconformity. Because much of DH consists of narrative literature, the most common use of gendered imagery involves characterization. Narrative texts often represent characters in roles or behaviors that are assumed by the texts' writers to be appropriate to the characters' identities as male or female. For example, many male characters in DH, including some of the most significant characters such as Joshua, Saul, and David, are frequently represented in situations of military conflict. By contrast, very few female characters are represented as being directly involved in military situations. Apart from women who may be specified as objects of mass slaughter along with other inhabitants of their towns (e.g., Josh 6:21, 8:25; Judg 21:11; 1 Sam 15:3, etc.), the female characters who play roles in military situations, such as Deborah and Jael, do so in situations that are described in ways that allow us to understand them as exceptional. Otherwise, women are usually represented playing nonmilitary roles in military stories, such as waiting for returning soldiers (Judg 5:28; 2 Sam 6:16) or singing and dancing in celebration of returning soldiers (Judg 11:34; 1 Sam 18:6–7). Similarly, many male characters in the books of Samuel and Kings are represented as kings, while only two female characters—the Queen of Sheba (1 Kgs 10:1–13) and Athaliah (2 Kgs 11:1–20)—are represented as monarchs rather than kings' wives.

As these examples illustrate, gender expectations frequently link literary characters to specific social roles in DH (Brenner, 1984). Although in many cases such expectations remain in the background, in other cases the representation of characters acting in conformity with gender expectations plays a role in moving the narrative forward. For example, the assumption that a woman will be unhappy unless she bears children and grateful when she does structures the story of Hannah and makes possible the story of Samuel (1 Sam 1). The assumption that a brother will feel compelled to respond in a forceful way to the man who sexually dishonors his sister and, through her, the honor of her family structures the story of Amnon, Tamar, and Absalom and makes possible the story of conflict between Absalom and David (2 Sam 13:20–33). In these and other cases, behavior that conforms to gender expectations does not simply contribute to characterization; it also drives plot development.

Narrative effects of characterization and plot are not only achieved in DH when characters act in conformity with gender norms. They are also achieved when characters act in ways that do not conform to gender norms. This use of gender imagery recognizes that, while societal expectations for proper gendered behavior exist, individuals embody such expectations to varying degrees. The speech of biblical characters themselves occasionally acknowledges that this is the case. When the Philistines in 1 Samuel 4:9 use the exhortation "Be strong and act like men" to encourage one another to fight, or when David in 1 Samuel 26:15 taunts Abner by asking, "Are

you not a man?" their rhetoric indicates an awareness that it is possible to act in more manly and less manly ways. The context of warfare in these passages is significant. If masculinity was "measured" in the ancient Near East by the demonstration of military fortitude, as biblical scholars have long recognized (Hoffner, 1966, p. 327; cf. Chapman, 2004), then a male who is unsuccessful in battle is in danger of losing his manhood. Thus, in DH as in other parts of the Hebrew Bible, men who lose wars are in danger of "becoming women," as Jeremiah 51:30 indicates has happened with the Babylonians. Female characters, too, may conform to expectations for women's behavior to greater or lesser degrees. The representation of mothers eating their own children during a military siege (2 Kgs 6:24–31; cf. Deut 28:53–57) shocks Israel's king, and by extension the reader, precisely because it transgresses expectations for maternal behavior.

DH makes use of this gender variability for narrative effect. Because gender norms are often implicit rather than explicit, and because ancient assumptions about gender may be different than contemporary norms, the interpretation of passages that utilize this narrative device can be challenging. Nevertheless, a reading that takes into account images of gender nonconformity may shed light on connotations that particular passages had for an ancient audience.

Political Leadership, Gender, and Power. In DH, some of Israel's political and military leaders are represented more positively and others more negatively, with several leaders represented both positively and negatively at different points in their story. Evaluations of these leaders are more explicit in some cases than others. In particular, DH evaluates leaders according to their willingness or ability to suppress religious practices that DH considers to be in violation of God's covenant with Israel, promote religious practices that DH considers to follow that covenant, and deliver Israel from its enemies.

On a more implicit level, however, gender dynamics also play a role in DH's representation of Israel's leaders, their reputations, and their contests for precedence. As noted above, most of Israel's monarchs and judges are male. Their struggles for power and prestige are sometimes narrated in ways that suggest that men who aspired to political leadership had to demonstrate that they were more "manly" than their rivals. Leaders and aspiring leaders apparently felt threatened at times by rivals who were perceived as being more "manly" by others. In 1 Samuel 18:7–9, for example, Saul becomes angry when the women of Israel greet the returning Israelite army by singing, "Saul has killed his thousands, and David his ten thousands." Saul is suspicious that David's superior reputation as a warrior indicates that he will acquire, or wants to acquire, Saul's kingdom (18:8).

The gendered imagery that structures the narration of David's rise to power goes beyond military skills, however. Two Samuel 3:1 notes that, during a war that followed the death of Saul, "David was becoming stronger and stronger while the house of Saul was growing weaker and weaker." This statement is followed immediately by a list of six sons who are born to David by six different women (2 Sam 3:2–5). Although Deuteronomy 17:17 warns that kings who gather too many wives or too much silver or gold—or, in Deuteronomy 17:16, too many horses—may turn away from God's path (as Solomon eventually does in 1 Kings), God is represented in 2 Samuel 12:8 as making a connection between David's acquisition of multiple women and David's acquisition of "the house of Israel and Judah," that is, the throne. This link between women and kingship may seem odd until we recognize, in Jo Ann Hackett's words, "that a man's public display of masculinity is one key to his ability to rule" in DH (Hackett, 2012, p. 158). David is able not only to gather multiple women (including some wives of former rivals, e.g., Abigail and possibly Ahinoam [Levenson and Halpern, 1980]) but also to sire children, another signifier of manhood in the ancient Near East (Hoffner, 1966, p. 327). Thus the list of David's sons and their mothers is not neutral genealogical information, but a demonstration of David's "potency" in both senses of the word: he is a powerful man, demonstrating military skills and an ability to gather women, and he is able to generate offspring. The symbolism works in reverse when David becomes an old man: in 1 Kings 1:1–4, both David's age

and the impending end of his rule are symbolized by his impotence with Abishag, the beautiful young woman he sleeps with to keep warm.

Whereas David's rise to power is symbolized in part by his manliness, the legitimacy of the house of Saul may be undermined in part through gender symbolism. Although Jonathan's love for David works to David's benefit, the narration of it calls into question Jonathan's manhood. Jonathan's narrative functions parallel to those of such women characters as Abigail and his sister Michal, who also assist and/or love David (Jobling, 1998, p. 162). The implication of homoeroticism in Jonathan's love for David, though attractive for queer readings of the Bible, may have been understood in the ancient world as denigration of his manhood and hence his ability to rule (Ackerman, 2005). Aspersion on the manhood of the house of Saul continues after the deaths of Saul and Jonathan. When Saul's surviving son, Ishbaal (or Ish-boshet), confronts Abner about his sexual relations with Saul's concubine Rizpah, Abner angrily puts him in his place and asserts that he will help David gain the throne. Ishbaal's unmanly fear (2 Sam 3:11) may confirm Abner's recognition that Ishbaal is not kingly material.

Although David's performance of manhood demonstrates his ability to rule, David's rivals can also attack David's manhood to call into question his legitimacy as a leader. The clearest example of such an attack occurs in the story of Absalom, who revolts against the rule of his father. After David flees from Jerusalem before the arrival of Absalom's army, Absalom rapes ten of David's "concubines" on the roof of the palace "before the eyes of all Israel" (2 Sam 16:22). By usurping his father's place sexually as well as militarily, Absalom attempts to strengthen claims he has already made that he can fulfill kingly duties more effectively than his father (15:1–6). His sexual actions also build on other signifiers of masculinity, such as vengeance of his sister's rape (13:20–33), good looks (14:25), exceptionally long hair (14:26), and the ability to sire children (14:27). By publicly taking his father's women, he attempts to assert symbolically that his own manhood is superior to that of his father. Although Absalom's revolt is ultimately unsuccessful (perhaps because he dishonors his own father), his actions fit into a series of stories in which male characters jockey for power and prestige by manipulating relations with women and symbols of gender and sexuality (Stone, 1996).

Symbolic Emasculation. Absalom's attempt to show that his manhood is superior to that of his father might be seen as a symbolic emasculation of his father. The use of symbolic emasculation in situations of conflict is clear at other points in DH.

Sometimes symbolic emasculation is accomplished through the rhetorical speech of characters. In 2 Samuel 3:29, for example, David angrily exclaims, "May the house of Joab never lack someone with a discharge, and someone who is leprous, and someone who takes hold of a spindle, and someone who falls by the sword, and someone who lacks food." Work with a spindle is associated with women and so is shameful for men. David in effect is cursing Joab by declaring that the men of his house will be effeminate (Hoffner, 1966, p. 332).

Symbolic emasculation can also be accomplished through actions rather than speech. Saul's request for Philistine foreskins (1 Sam 18:25), though intended as a trap for David (18:21), may contribute to DH's representation of the Philistines as "womanish" (Jobling, 1998, p. 216). When an Ammonite king cuts the beards and skirts of David's messengers, he performs a kind of symbolic castration on them and insults David, who has sent them (2 Sam 10:4). The men are ashamed and remain away from court until their beards have regrown (10:5). The cutting of Samson's hair can also be interpreted as a kind of symbolic castration (Judg 16:19). Significantly, it takes place near the conclusion of a story in which Samson has been continually represented in terms of such symbols of manhood as strength, the ability to fight and kill enemies, and a sexual desire for women.

Symbolic emasculation also takes place in DH through descriptions of death. In Judges 4:21, Jael kills Sisera by driving a tent peg through his head. Scholars have long noted connections between death and eroticism in this scene (e.g., Niditch, 1989; Fewell and Gunn, 1993). Conventional gender positions are reversed when the active female killer penetrates the body of a male object. Thus Gale Yee argues that

Jael's tent peg functions as a "ravaging phallus" in the "unmanning" of Sisera (Yee, 1993, p. 116). Similar dynamics are at work when a woman drops a millstone from a tower and crushes the head of Abimelech in Judges 9:53 (Stone, 2007; 2009). In both stories, a woman kills a man by causing a deadly, phallic weapon to penetrate him from above. The structural positions of the characters—with the woman on top and the man below—contribute to the symbolism of unmanning. Abimelech himself calls attention to the shame that accrues to a soldier who is killed by a woman (Judg 9:54). A somewhat different conjunction of death and symbolic emasculation appears in Judges 3, where Ehud the Israelite slaughters Eglon, the Moabite king. A number of biblical scholars have noted that the narration of this killing scene involves what Deryn Guest calls "sexual innuendo" (Guest, 2006, p. 171). Through the use of multiple words and images that elsewhere have sexual connotations (for example, "hand," which can be a euphemism for the penis; "belly," which can also mean "womb"; "he came into," which can also refer to intercourse, etc.), the killing of Eglon is represented as a symbolic rape, and hence emasculation, of a Moabite king by a phallic Israelite hero.

The Dangerous Foreign Woman. Several of the stories that rely on symbolic unmanning also utilize another recurring gender-related image: the dangerous foreign woman. DH's suspicion of foreign women is apparent already in Deuteronomy 7:3–4, which warns that intermarriage with non-Israelites may lead Israelite men to worship other gods. Judges 3:5 states that intermarriage had exactly this consequence after the Israelites settled in Canaan. Although Samson's desire for foreign women is partly caused by God (Judg 14:4), it also leads to multiple conflicts. Solomon is criticized not because of the extraordinary number of his wives and concubines (which symbolizes the extent of his power) but rather because foreign wives and concubines cause him to worship foreign gods (1 Kgs 11:1–8).

The chief example of a female character in DH who embodies the dangerous foreign woman is Jezebel. Like Solomon's women, Jezebel, a Phoenician, is blamed for causing her Israelite husband,

Ahab, to do evil (1 Kgs 21:25). Her wicked deeds go far beyond that, however. She also kills prophets of Yahweh (18:4, 13), supports prophets of Baal and Asherah (18:9), and threatens to kill Elijah (19:2). In 1 Kings 21, where her husband appears weak and passive, and hence unmanly, after Naboth refuses to sell him a vineyard (21:4), Jezebel takes the initiative to have Naboth killed on false charges, allowing Ahab to acquire the vineyard. The contrast between Ahab and Jezebel reverses gender expectations, casting aspersion on both characters simultaneously. Due to her wickedness, DH describes her as dying under gruesome and shameful circumstances: after she is thrown from a window and trampled by horses, dogs eat most of her body (2 Kgs 9:30–37). Although 2 Kings 9:22 refers to Jezebel's "whoredoms" and "sorceries," the sexual language is likely to be an example of the symbolic use of sexual promiscuity as a metaphor for religious infidelity, discussed further below. Jezebel's sexual reputation is largely a consequence of later tradition rather than the Hebrew Bible itself. Nevertheless, DH's use of sexual metaphors for Jezebel's wickedness may be one source of the later popular association between her name and sexuality.

In spite of the characterization of Jezebel and some other women (e.g., Athaliah in 2 Kings 11) as wicked, DH does not uniformly represent dangerous foreign women as evil. It also characterizes some foreign women as dangerous to Israel's enemies and helpful to Israel. Examples include Rahab and Jael, referred to above.

Sexual Symbolism and Religious Infidelity. In Deuteronomy 31:16, God warns Moses that the Israelites will "whore" (*zanah*) after other gods and break their covenant. Though DH does not make significant use of this metaphorical representation of religious infidelity as female sexual promiscuity, God's warning is fulfilled in Judges 2:17. There, in the course of describing the cycle of religious infidelity, punishment, repentance, and deliverance that characterized the period of the judges, the narrator states that the Israelites "whored [*zanu*] after other gods and bowed down to them." Similar language can be found in the story of Gideon (Judg 8:27, 33). Such passages, together with the reference to Jezebel's

"whoredoms," indicate that the writers and editors responsible for DH were aware of this tradition of using sexual imagery for religious transgression, which is found more extensively in other parts of the Hebrew Bible, especially the Latter Prophets.

[*See also* Imagery, Gendered, *subentry* Prophetic Literature; Masculinity and Femininity, *subentry* Hebrew Bible; *and* Political Leadership, *subentry* Hebrew Bible.]

BIBLIOGRAPHY

Ackerman, Susan. *When Heroes Love: The Ambiguity of Eros in the Stories of Gilgamesh and David.* New York: Columbia University Press, 2005.

Anderson, Cheryl. *Women, Ideology, and Violence: Critical Theory and the Construction of Gender in the Book of the Covenant and the Deuteronomic Law.* London: T&T Clark, 2004.

Brenner, Athalya. *The Israelite Woman: Social Role and Literary Type in Biblical Narrative.* Sheffield, U.K.: Sheffield Academic Press, 1984.

Chapman, Cynthia R. *The Gendered Language of Warfare in the Israelite-Assyrian Encounter.* Winona Lake, Ind.: Eisenbrauns, 2004.

Fewell, Danna Nolan, and David Gunn. *Gender, Power, and Promise: The Subject of the Bible's First Story.* Nashville, Tenn.: Abingdon, 1993.

Guest, Deryn. "Judges." In *The Queer Bible Commentary*, edited by Deryn Guest, Robert E. Goss, Mona White, and Thomas Bohache, pp. 167–189. London: SCM, 2006.

Hackett, Jo Ann. "1 and 2 Samuel." In *Women's Bible Commentary: Revised and Updated Third Edition*, edited by Carol A. Newsom, Sharon H. Ringe, and Jacqueline E. Lapsley, pp. 150–163. Louisville, Ky.: Westminster John Knox, 2012.

Hoffner, Harry A., Jr. "Symbols for Masculinity and Femininity: Their Use in Ancient Near Eastern Sympathetic Magic Rituals." *Journal of Biblical Literature* 85 (1966): 326–334.

Jobling, David. *1 Samuel.* Collegeville, Minn.: Liturgical Press, 1998.

Levenson, Jon D., and Baruch Halpern. "The Political Import of David's Marriages." *Journal of Biblical Literature* 99 (1980): 507–518.

Niditch, Susan. "Eroticism and Death in the Tale of Jael." In *Gender and Difference in Ancient Israel*, edited by Peggy L. Day, pp. 43–57. Minneapolis: Fortress, 1989.

Pressler, Carolyn. *The View of Women Found in the Deuteronomic Family Laws.* Berlin: Walter de Gruyter, 1993.

Stone, Ken. *Sex, Honor and Power in the Deuteronomistic History*. Sheffield, U.K.: Sheffield Academic Press, 1996.

Stone, Ken. "Gender Criticism: The Un-Manning of Abimelech." In *Judges and Method: New Approaches in Biblical Studies*, 2d ed., edited by Gale A. Yee, pp. 183–201. Minneapolis: Fortress, 2007.

Stone, Ken. "How a Woman Unmans a King: Gender Reversal and the Woman of Thebez in Judges 9." In *From the Margins 1: Women of the Hebrew Bible and Their Afterlives*, edited by Peter S. Hawkins and Lesleigh Cushing Stahlberg, pp. 71–85. Sheffield, U.K.: Sheffield Academic Press, 2009.

Yee, Gale A. "By the Hand of a Woman: The Metaphor of the Woman Warrior in Judges 4." In *Special issue: Women, War, and Metaphor: Language and Society in the Study of the Hebrew Bible*, edited by Claudia V. Camp and Carole R. Fontaine. *Semeia* 61 (1993): 99–132.

Ken Stone

Prophetic Literature

The books of Isaiah through Malachi, designated as the Latter Prophets in the Jewish canon and Prophets in the Christian canon, employ a wide range of literary devices. In short prose sections and especially in extended poetic passages, prophetic literature reframes reality through alliteration, assonance, paronomasia, hyperbole, and irony.

Perhaps the most distinctive and ideologically fraught characteristic of prophetic language is its propensity toward comparison. Episodic similes and extended metaphors transport one set of characteristics or relationships into the conceptual domain of another. In the Prophets, the divine-human encounter becomes a warrior's rape of a woman captured in war, a father's anguished yet justified beating of a disobedient son, a husband's jealous battering of his whoring wife, a mother's compassion for her helpless infant, or a farmer's care for and exasperation over his fickle crops.

Drawing heavily from the conceptual domain of human relationships, prophetic metaphor reflects the patriarchal/heteronormative character of ancient Israelite society and the patriarchal patterning of the ancient Israelite family. Yahweh's power is depicted through masculine images—Warrior, Father, Husband, and King—while divine anguish is depicted as a woman's cry in childbirth or a mother's care for an infant. The dependency and infidelity of Israel (and other nations) are typified in feminine terms—Daughter, Wife, and Whore—while chosenness is compared to the favor given a first-born Son. When Son Israel is punished, he is beaten; when Daughter Zion is punished, she is sexually violated. In metaphor as well as in culture, gender matters.

Second-wave feminist biblical criticism (beginning in the 1970s and continuing into the present) has insisted that gendered prophetic metaphor is misogynistic not only in origin but also in effect. Offering scenes of women's sexual violation for the reader's instruction/pleasure and normalizing the male right to control female sexuality, prophetic literature has been deemed pornographic and dangerous to women's well-being. Third-wave feminism and queer studies, on the contrary, have found gender unstable in the Prophets. Underscoring the grammatical ambiguities of prophetic language and the essentialist assumptions of many feminists, more recent gender critique has suggested the ways in which the Prophets not only reflect but also subvert ancient and modern constructions of gender.

The Conceptual Domains of Prophetic Metaphor. The linguist George Lakoff describes metaphor as "cross-domain mapping," the construal of one set of relationships within the conceptual realm of another (1993). In this mental operation, the rules of the "source domain" to which the comparison is drawn (also called the "frame") govern the "target domain" under consideration. According to Lakoff, metaphors are not simply rhetorical devices but structures in which we think. They thus serve ideological functions, perpetuating the power dynamics inherent in the source domain and limiting perceptions of the target domain. Seen in this light, the imputation of heteronormative gender to other categories of human existence serves to normalize and naturalize heteronormativity itself.

Prophetic literature crafts myriad individual comparisons (at least eleven in Hosea 13 alone), but three heavily gendered conceptual domains dominate prophetic metaphor: family, warfare, and "nature." Of these, the family domain is the most significant, not only due to its greatest frequency but also due to its reach into the other two realms. Indeed, family is the "home" to which prophetic metaphor repeatedly returns.

The family domain. Prophetic literature frames various relationships as "family." When insisting that two parties are equal in origin, interests, and/or faults, the Prophets dub them siblings: in Malachi and Obadiah the nations of Edom and Judah become brothers bound by birth and loyalty, and in Ezekiel 16 and 23 the cities of Jerusalem and Samaria appear as unequally depraved sisters. As discussed below, Jerusalem is Daughter when vulnerable, and Yahweh is Mother when nurturing. Most often, however, prophetic literature most often depicts Yahweh's interactions with Israel and Judah as (1) that of a father with his son and (2) that of a husband with his wife (commonly called the marriage metaphor). These metaphors pervade Hosea, Isaiah, and Jeremiah, though they also appear in almost all of the prophetic books.

Many interpreters laud these metaphors for depicting God's care for humans in intimate and emotionally poignant terms. Walter Brueggemann, for example, has repeatedly stressed the pathos imputed to Yahweh in the book of Hosea by means of metaphor: in Hosea 2:14–23, Yahweh is a "resilient and determined lover" (2008, p. 14) who will not give up Wife Israel even though his honor has been violated and an anguished father who, in an irrational display of love, cannot abandon the son that he once loved and taught to walk. According to Brueggemann, the parent-child and husband-wife metaphors provide readers hope that "YHWH's commitment goes beyond formal obligation to the irrationality of emotional attachment" (2008, pp. 15–16).

To the contrary, second-wave feminists have forcefully insisted that the pathos of these metaphors constitutes their greatest danger. By sympathetically characterizing the deity's feelings, prophetic metaphor justifies not only divine brutality but also patriarchy and its promotion of violence against women and children. Indeed, the family reflected and constructed by prophetic metaphor is consistently patriarchal. Human fathers are lords and masters over their children (Jer 3:14), with the implied right to disown them (Hos 2), adopt them (Ezek 16), name them (Hos 1—2), and physically punish them for disobedience (Isa 1, 3; Mal 3:17). While both parents deserve honor (Ezek 22:7; Mic 7:6), fathers alone are owed obedience (Isa 1; Jer 3; Mal 1:6, 3:17). In Hosea's marriage metaphor, only the husband's "irrational emotion" can disrupt his "rational" right to control the sexuality of his wife: he can threaten, strip, withhold food and clothing, and "slay her with thirst" (Hos 2:5 [Eng 2:3]).

Modern English translations often obscure the degree to which familial relations in the Prophets are dictated by gender. The New Revised Standard Version (NRSV), for example, consistently translates the Hebrew term *bēn/bānîm* ("son/sons") as "child/children," a translation that could be justified on the grounds that Hebrew has no gender-inclusive plural forms but nonetheless ignores Israel's gender-differentiated rules for sons and daughters. While fathers in ancient Israel "owned" both sons and daughters, sons (at least oldest sons) alone inherited their fathers' property and authority; contra the NRSV, Jeremiah 3:19–22 likely refers to the intention of Yahweh God to give land to *sons* rather to *children*. Moreover, the term "marriage metaphor" is misleading, since the relationship imagined by the Prophets is not the romantically sparked partnership of equals celebrated by many in the modern West. Since biblical Hebrew has no word for "marriage," all references to "marriage" or "marry" in the Hebrew Bible have been added by a translator; in the text, a man "takes" (*lqḥ*; Hos 1:2) or "rules over" (*b'l*; Isa 62:5) a woman. Translators often offer "wife" for Hebrew *'iššâ* ("woman"; Hos 1:2) and "husband" for Hebrew *'iš* ("man"; Hos 2:16) and *b'l*, ("master"; Jer 31:32).

The prophetic characterization of Israel as Whore (Hebrew *znh*) also reflects highly differentiated gender norms. As Phyllis Bird's classic study (1989) has shown, while literally *znh* signifies a professional prostitute, the term is widely used as slur against all women whose sexuality remains beyond patriarchal control, including those within the family. Adultery (*n'p*) is equated with harlotry (*znh*) in Isaiah 57:3, Jeremiah

3.8, Hosea 2: 3 (Eng 2:1), and Hosea 4.13–14. In Ezekiel 16 and 23 both charges are made against Samaria and Jerusalem, the unfaithful daughters-turned-wives of Yahweh: they play with dildos (Ezek 16:17), pay multiple partners for sex (Ezek 16:32–34), and dote on males whose "members are like those of donkeys, whose emissions are like those of stallions" (Ezek 23:20). When Israelite males are called *znh*, they are denigrated by use of a feminine-specific slur.

Such language, contend second-wave feminists, is not only patriarchal but also misogynistic, justifying and taking pleasure in the debasement of women. The anger-abuse-romance cycle of Hosea 1—2 has been linked to classic patterns of domestic violence (Weems, 1995; O'Brien, 2008; Scholz 2010), and Drorah Setel (1985) has deemed passages such as Hosea 1—3 and Ezekekiel 16 and 23 as pornographic, prompting Athalya Brenner (1993) to coin the term "pornoprophetics" for ways in which the Prophets revel in sexual violence against women. As elsewhere in the Hebrew Bible, men are assumed to desire and penetrate women, while women desire and are penetrated by men.

The military domain. Prophetic metaphor also draws heavily from the conceptual domain of military conflict, frequently depicting Yahweh as a warrior who marches either to punish or save Israel. Thorough studies of the Divine Warrior motif have traced its likely roots to ancient Near Eastern cosmological combat myths and explored its development through the Hebrew Bible and New Testament. Of greatest interest to gender critics, however, have been the constructions of masculinity and femininity reflected in this metaphor.

As demonstrated by Cynthia Chapman, biblical texts join Assyrian art and literature in linking masculine identity with military performance (2004, p. 7). Just as Assyrian reliefs depict victorious kings lifting massive clubs of war in muscled arms and portray vanquished soldiers as sexually submissive, so too prophetic literature depicts Yahweh wielding nations as clubs of war (Isa 10:5; Jer 51:20–23; Zech 9:13) in his powerful arm (Isa 30:30, 40:10, 52:10; Jer 21:5, 32:21) and tauntingly calls defeated foes "women" (Nah 3:13). In the Prophets, "unrivaled, royal mascu-

linity was reserved for their god Yahweh" (Chapman, 2004, p. 60).

Weakness, in turn, is marked as feminine. In this metaphor, Judah and other nations most often become women whose fates rest in the warrior's strong hand. Bracing for the Warrior's march against them, Egyptians tremble like women (Isa 19:16); anticipating the Warrior's rescue, Daughter Zion shouts in joy (Zeph 3:14–20).

Throughout the Prophets, vulnerable cities and countries are characterized as Daughter, sometimes Virgin Daughter. While clearly drawn from the conceptual domain of the family, this metaphor does not operate relationally, as those discussed above do. The City-as-Daughter is invoked in relation not to Yahweh as Father but to Yahweh as Warrior. As Chapman explains, every occurrence of the "Daughter Zion" metaphor appears in a military context: "Daughter Zion is always the pawn or prize in a military battle between men and Yahweh" (Chapman, 2004, p. 93). Just as in an ancient Israelite family, daughters are powerless to control their marriages, safety, vows, and bodies, so too, the Prophets claim, nations are powerless in the face of Yahweh the virile Warrior (O'Brien, 2008).

Second-wave feminists have drawn attention to the ways in which the Warrior's vengeance on metaphorical daughters, like the Husband's vengeance on this metaphorical Wife, is graphically described as sexual violation. In both domains, vocabulary for such assault includes "lifting up the skirt" (Nah 3:5; Jer 13:22–27); the revealing of one's "shame" (Jer 13:26; Isa 47:2–3); the opening of "gates" (Isa 3:26; Gordon and Washington, 1995); and violence done to the "hind parts" (Jer 13:22). Females in both conceptual domains are called *znh*, taunted, and raped; in both conceptual domains, Yahweh perpetrates these acts and invites other men to watch (Jer 13:25–27; Nah 3:6; Hos 2:12 [Eng 2:10]).

The domain of "nature." In addition to these and other human relationships, prophetic metaphor also draws from the conceptual domain of the non-human world. In Hosea alone, the deity is likened to a lion, leopard, maggot, bear, cypress, and showers; Israel becomes a heifer, unturned cake, dove, wild ass, grapes, figs, palm, luxuriant vine, dew, mist, chaff, smoke, lily, and forest. Micah depicts Israel as a heifer who treads grain and sheep gathered in a pen. An extended metaphor in Isaiah 5 portrays Yahweh as a vinedresser whose work proves futile when his vineyard produces wild grapes rather than good fruit.

These and other comparisons allow the Prophets to underscore characteristics conceptually identified with various aspects of the world: the ferocity of bears and lions, the perdurance of the evergreen, the repulsive destruction of maggots. Many interpreters value these nonhuman images as liberating alternatives to sexist imagery—"natural" rather than "social" or "political." In these metaphors as in human society generally, however, gender constructs not only shape perceptions of the world but also grow in power when they become the unquestioned template for all of reality.

The prophetic proclivity to imbue the world with gender deserves a fuller discussion, but several aspects are noted here:

1. *The imposition of patriarchal family roles onto the behavior of animals.* Nahum 2 imagines patriarchally defined gender roles as operating in a lion's den: the (male) lion hunts prey and provides for his "family." This metaphor shames the king of Assyria (the lion) as unable to fulfill his masculine duty to protect Nineveh (his lioness) and the inhabitants of his land (the cubs)—one of the many ways that the book of Nahum seeks to insult the king of Assyria by maligning his manhood (O'Brien, 2008).

2. *The imposition of gendered characteristics onto land.* In Isaiah 5, Yahweh the vinedresser digs, clears, plants, builds, and hews his vineyard, but it fails to produce and thus deserves to be destroyed. The underlying assumption of an active agent who inserts seed into a passive agent reflects not only ancient views of agriculture but also, as Carol Delaney (1998) has shown, patriarchally shaped ideologies of procreation. In the Hebrew Bible, both land

and women are implanted with seed and prove either fertile or barren; neither male infertility nor farmers' failures are considered. The fusing of land with the feminine is evident not only in Isaiah 5, in which a love-song is sung for the vineyard, but also strikingly in Hosea 2, in which Israel-the-whoring-wife becomes indistinguishable from Israel-the-land: Yahweh controls not only his wife's access to food but also the production of the land itself.

3. *The combination of conceptual domains.* Prophetic literature often pairs nonhuman imagery with gendered human imagery in ways that underscore gender assignments. Depictions of Yahweh as lion interweave with depictions of Yahweh as a Warrior (Isa 31:3–9; Jer 4:6–7, 25:8), both underscoring Yahweh's masculine might. In Micah 4:13, Daughter Zion becomes a threshing heifer, strong yet subservient: Yahweh's beast of burden. Isaiah 1:2–4 claims that sons naturally obey fathers just as oxen and donkeys naturally obey masters.

Responses to Gender in the Prophets. Most second-wave feminists, as noted above, have strongly critiqued the gender ideology of the prophetic books, especially the book of Hosea and its "marriage metaphor" (see multiple essays in Brenner, 1993). Contending that depictions of God the Raping Warrior, God the Beating Father, and God the Abusive Husband are detrimental to women, Cheryl Exum (1995), Gerlinde Baumann (2003), Judith Sanderson (1992), and a host of feminist interpreters have called readers to recognize and resist these appalling misogynist claims about people and about the divine. Many, like Yvonne Sherwood (1996), excoriate interpreters who ignore, explain, or mirror the patriarchal assumptions of these texts. Second-wave feminists have explored other misogynistic imagery in the Prophets as well, including the depiction of evil itself as a woman in Zechariah 5:5 (Barker, 1978) and the repulsion toward the female body in Ezekiel 24 (Galambush, 1992).

A countermovement within second-wave feminism has undertaken the task of retrieval, attempting to discern positive aspects of prophetic imagery. Julianna Claassens (2012), for example, reclaims the positive feminine imagery for Yahweh neglected in feminist discourse: God as Mourner or Wailing Woman (Jer 8:22—9:1) and God as Mother (Isa 42:13–15; 49:15). Sophia Bietenhard praises Micah's imagery for Daughter Jerusalem, "a kind of imagery that begins with women's experiences of life, integrates them into its theological reflection, and eventually becomes the creative, formative energy that enables one to manage the present and hope for the future" (Bietenhard, 2012, p. 425). Christl Maier takes a middle ground, suggesting that the feminine personification of Zion as daughter, wife, whore, mother, and queen is so multivalent that its value can only be judged by individual readers (2008, p. 217). While recognizing the marriage metaphor as abusive, Renita Weems (1995) also praises its insistence on human responsibility and the possibilities of love; she calls not for resistance to Hosea's imagery but for great readers who can both appreciate and talk back to this emotionally powerful text.

Within and alongside second-wave feminism, some interpreters have highlighted the textual and ideological instability of gender in prophetic imagery. In numerous performances of the marriage metaphor, feminine and masculine pronouns unexpectedly shift (O'Brien, 1996), leading Erin Runions to claim that binary gender is assumed not by the text but by the reader (2001). Sherwood's classic study of Hosea (1996) traces the inconsistencies in its comparisons (Gomer was unfaithful prior to being "taken," while Israel was once a pure bride). For second-wave feminists, deconstructionist readings the Prophets reveal just how untenable patriarchy's claims about women really are.

To the contrary, twenty-first-century queer criticism of the Prophets attributes gender shifting in prophetic imagery not to accidental slippages but to the inherent fluidity of gender and sexual desire. In such discussions, Jeremiah has taken center stage. Stuart Macwilliam explores the homoerotic resonances of Jeremiah 20:7 which portrays Yahweh as a "demanding and ineluctable [male] seducer" (Mac-

william, 2002, p. 402) of the unmarried male prophet and criticizes second-wave feminists for essentializing gender, failing to notice the way in which Woman Israel is not only lambasted Whore but also the positive model for the community's future. Ken Stone (2007) deems the prophet's repulsion-attraction response to the violent Yahweh in Jeremiah 20:7 as sadomasochistic. Reading from a "translesbigay" perspective, Angela Bauer-Levesque (2006) contends that Jeremiah "embraces gender-fluid images and traditional sexualized power dynamics with pornography dimensions, all mixed together" (p. 388).

Conclusion and Trajectories for Exploration. Second-wave feminists and queer critics generally agree that prophetic imagery reflects the patriarchal structures of its various source domains. Just as the "everyday" realities of ancient Israel—family, warfare, and the "natural" world—are saturated with power dynamics, so too are the metaphors that rely on those domains. Scholars disagree, however, on the degree to which this imagery necessarily reinforces patriarchy. If readers reject binary definitions of gender and the assumption of heteronormative desire, must they also reject prophetic texts? Might they instead find in the Prophets a kindred queer spirit?

Focused primarily on power dynamics within the source domain of prophetic metaphor, biblical scholars have explored less fully the significance of particular metaphors for the Prophets' theological/ideological target domain. Comparing Yahweh to Father and Husband within a patriarchally structured family allows the Prophets to promote a theological worldview in which divine power is normal, justified, and beneficent: just as a caring patriarch "must" control the disobedient sons whom he loves, so too the compassionate divine "must" inflict suffering on errant humans. These familial metaphors offer a single explanation of the fall of Israel and Judah: national defeat is divine punishment for human transgression of known commandments. Obscured from view are other causes for Israel's fate: superior strength of opposing armies, failure of national leadership, divine absence, or divine caprice.

[*See also* Family Structures, *subentry* Hebrew Bible; Feminism, *subentry* Second-Wave Feminism; *and* Marriage and Divorce, *subentry* Hebrew Bible.]

BIBLIOGRAPHY

Barker, Margaret. "The Evil in Zechariah." *Heythrop Journal* 19 (1978): 12–27.

Bauer-Levesque, Angela. "Jeremiah." In *Queer Bible Commentary*, edited by Deryn Guest, Robert E. Goss, Mona West, and Thomas Bohache, pp. 386–393. London: SCM, 2006.

Baumann, Gerlinde. *Love and Violence: Marriage as Metaphor for the Relationship between YHWH and Israel in the Prophetic Books.* Translated by Linda M. Maloney. Collegeville, Minn.: Liturgical Press, 2003.

Bietenhard, Sophia. "Micah: Call for Justice—Hope for All." In *Feminist Biblical Interpretation: A Compendium of Critical Commentary on the Books of the Bible and Related Literature*, edited by Luise Schottroff and Marie-Therese Wacker, pp. 421–432. Grand Rapids, Mich.: Eerdmans, 2012.

Bird, Phyllis. "'To Play the Harlot': An Inquiry into an Old Testament Metaphor." In *Gender and Difference in Ancient Israel*, edited by Peggy L. Day, pp. 75–94. Minneapolis: Fortress, 1989.

Brenner, Athalya. "On 'Jeremiah' and the Poetics of (Prophetic?) Pornography." In *On Gendering Texts: Female and Male Voices in the Hebrew Bible*, edited by Athalya Brenner and Fokkelien van Dijk-Hemmes, pp. 178–193. Leiden, The Netherlands: Brill, 1993.

Brueggemann, Walter. "The Recovering God of Hosea." *Horizons in Biblical Theology* 30 (2008): 5–20.

Chapman, Cynthia R. *The Gendered Language of Warfare in the Israelite-Assyrian Encounter.* Winona, Ind.: Eisenbrauns, 2004.

Claassens, L. Juliana M. *Mourner, Mother, Midwife: Reimagining God's Delivering Presence in the Old Testament.* Louisville, Ky.: Westminster John Knox, 2012.

Delaney, Carol. *Abraham on Trial: The Social Legacy of Biblical Myth.* Princeton, N.J.: Princeton University Press, 1998.

Exum, Cheryl. "The Ethics of Biblical Violence against Women." In *The Bible in Ethics: The Second Sheffield Colloquium*, edited by John Rogerson, Margaret Davies, and M. Daniel Carroll R., pp. 252–271. Sheffield, U.K.: Sheffield Academic Press, 1995.

Galambush, Julie. *Jerusalem in the Book of Ezekiel: The City as Yahweh's Wife.* Atlanta: Scholars Press, 1992.

Gordon, Pamela, and Harold C. Washington. "Rape as a Military Metaphor in the Hebrew Bible." In *A Feminist Companion to the Latter Prophets*, edited by Athalya Brenner, pp. 308–325. Sheffield, U.K.: Sheffield Academic Press, 1995.

Lakoff, George. "The Contemporary Theory of Metaphor." In *Metaphor and Thought*, 2d ed., edited by Andrew Ortony, pp. 202–251. Cambridge, U.K.: Cambridge University Press, 1993.

Macwilliam, Stuart. "Queering Jeremiah." *Biblical Interpretation* 10 (2002): 384–404.

Maier, Christl M. *Daughter Zion, Mother Zion: Gender, Space, and the Sacred in Ancient Israel.* Minneapolis: Fortress, 2008.

O'Brien, Julia M. "Judah as Wife and Husband: Deconstructing Gender in Malachi." *Journal of Biblical Literature* 115 (1996): 241–250.

O'Brien, Julia M. *Challenging Prophetic Metaphor: Theology and Ideology in the Prophets.* Louisville, Ky.: Westminster John Knox, 2008.

Runions, Erin. *Changing Subjects: Gender, Nation, and Future in Micah.* London: Sheffield Academic Press, 2001.

Sanderson, Judith. "Nahum." In *The Women's Bible Commentary*, edited by Carol A. Newsom and Sharon H. Ringe, pp. 217–221. London: SPCK, 1992.

Scholz, Susanne. *Sacred Witness: Rape in the Hebrew Bible.* Minneapolis: Fortress, 2010.

Setel, T. Drorah. "Prophets and Pornography: Female Sexual Imagery in Hosea." In *Feminist Interpretation of the Bible*, edited by Letty M. Russell, pp. 86–95. Philadelphia: Westminster, 1985.

Sherwood, Yvonne. *The Prostitute and the Prophet: Hosea's Marriage in Literary-Theoretical Perspective.* Sheffield, U.K.: Sheffield Academic Press, 1996.

Stone, Ken. "'You Seduced Me, You Overpowered Me, and You Prevailed': Religious Experience and Homoerotic Sadomasochism in Jeremiah." In *Patriarchs, Prophets, and Other Villains*, edited by Lisa Isherwood, pp. 101–109. London: Equinox, 2007.

Weems, Renita J. *Battered Love: Marriage, Sex, and Violence in the Hebrew Prophets.* Minneapolis: Fortress, 1995.

Julia M. O'Brien

Wisdom Literature

The canonical wisdom books (Proverbs, Job, Ecclesiastes/Qoheleth, and the Song of Solomon) span the entire length of ancient Israel's history. Their content, ascriptions of authorship, and editing range from the period of settlement (1200–1000 B.C.E.) through the monarchies (1000–587 B.C.E.) to the Second Temple period of postcolonial rule (539–63 B.C.E.). Deuterocanonical and other late wisdom books (Wisdom of Jesus Ben Sira [Sirach], Wisdom of Solomon, Qumran, New Testament, and Talmud) range from the Greco-Roman periods into late antiquity and beyond (second century B.C.E. to seventh century C.E.).

Gender in the World of the Sages. Through these varying social contexts, the views of the sages on gender fluctuate over time. The authors' primary goal of promulgating practices and points of view for a secure Jewish future that would be both rooted in an ancient past and flexible enough to weather changing historical conditions accounts for many strange manifestations of gender ideology in these monotheistic, patriarchal texts, such as scribal goddesses and a female Wisdom participant in God's work of creation. In every case, the wisdom traditions of the Jewish sages drew from a robust international milieu of bureaucratic, diplomatic literature found throughout the ancient Near East and used in the education of elite males. Sages readily drew from those worlds and their views of women but refined and tweaked those legacies based on the Israelite experiences of the Iron Age through the Roman period. Their gender ideology is uniform in viewing women through the lens of male expectations, experience, and needs, both positive and negative.

Proverbs. Proverbs, the earliest of the wisdom books, provides the basic matrix for thoughts about gender in Israelite and later Jewish society. The book is a composite, probably edited in the Persian or Ptolemaic period but containing materials that might have originated orally among highland tribes (Prov 10—15); clear collections produced under the monarchies (Prov 16—30); adaptation of Egyptian wisdom texts (Prov 22—24); and a final postexilic coda (Prov 31) that is entirely devoted to the trope of positive women. This thematic ending on women, their place in society, and their teachings forms a clear parallel to the Second Temple "theological" introduction of Proverbs 1—9, with its emphasis on a cosmic, female Wisdom and her contrast, the Negative Female.

Scholars disagree about the genesis of these female pairings: Did the goddess-like Woman Wisdom and Woman Stranger shape views of real women of biblical times, or did the experience of real women

give contours to the cosmic female figures? Clearly, both arenas interact continuously to shape the sages' teachings and reflect a single ideology of gender. Though the views on the Female Other shift as a reflection of the different life settings of the sections of Proverbs, especially as the elite, city society begins to predominate over portraits of village life, it is fair to say that no other book within the Law or Prophets gives cosmic or everyday females such a starring role in both structure and content of the text itself.

Wife and mother. The wife and her role in village and town life during the monarchies is featured in Proverbs 10—30, showing many shared affinities with female characterization found in the rest of the Bible. Some of the characterizations are positive: the sages knew fully well that without the significant participation of women in the economic life of the family, no man or male organization could expect to succeed (Prov 18:22, 19:14; cf. 11:16, 22; 12:4; 14:1). Village economies were based on subsistence agriculture, where women's work in the "maintenance" activities of production (food, fabrication of textiles, and progeny) and consumption (food preparation and delivery, allotment of clothing, socialization of children) were essential to all aspects of social and material life (Meyers, 2009). Women of the agricultural household often worked in groups of mutual aid based on kinship or contiguity, directed by the senior wife of the unit. Their activities produced informal networks of information and assistance, extending well beyond the nuclear or extended family household. As such, women had vital information about community well-being necessary to the political and leadership activities of their menfolk. Female networks provided many opportunities for the display of daily wisdom in management, settlement of disputes, and training of young children. The use of the "house" motif (that is, the family unit and the spaces it occupies) makes clear that wives have paramount roles in this sphere (Prov 11:19; 12:7; 14:1; 14:11; 15:6; 15:25; 15:27). Their wisdom or folly was rooted in their performance as "lady of the house."

Other characterizations are negative. A bad wife is a disaster for husband and household. She is compared to dripping leaks in the roof (Prov 19:13; 21:9); it is better to live on the corner of a rooftop than share a domicile with her, and a deserted island is a better option as a dwelling place than her home (Prov 27:15–16). Of course, the sages never question *why* a woman nags or scolds, but behind every shrew is a husband who has failed in some duty: a sluggard, a lazy or inept worker, a violent or hasty male who troubles his household and disrupts a woman's smooth running of domestic tasks or, perhaps worst of all, a man who fails to father the precious boy who establishes a wife's full status and personhood.

The most important form of female "production" was that of creating the next generation, both in terms of biological fertility and subsequent socialization of the young. Any disruption in fertility was disastrous all around. In child rearing, the mother was the earliest teacher for both genders and continued in that role for her daughters as they grew, while men took over the training of sons. Daughters worked inside the household, and though they are never mentioned in Proverbs, the terms for "female servant" probably refer to them. The "mother's teaching" (literally, "the Torah of the mother") was binding on children, and valued equally with the father's (Prov 1:8; 4:3; 6:20; 31:1–9, 26).

The Woman of Substance (Prov 31:11–22). Proverbs begins with a female Cosmic Wisdom in Proverbs 1—9 (see below); it ends with her earthly incarnation: the exemplary "Strong Woman," or "Woman of Worth/Substance," "Strong Woman," "Good Wife." This praise poem extols the wife of an elite household of the Persian or Hellenistic period. She is the source of all of the material goods that Woman Wisdom extended to her male followers in Proverbs 1—9: increased wealth, an orderly, productive household, income from her entrepreneurial work in textiles—all of which bring honor to her husband (Yoder, 2001, pp. 75–93). Like Woman Wisdom, the elite city wife engages very little in the tedious, labor-intensive maintenance activities of her earlier, agricultural, village sister (maidservants/daughters take care of that aspect of production). Rather, she is shown more as household manager, teacher, and highest exemplar of women's wisdom. Her role as re-

ligious teacher and leader is exemplified in her use of language: she teaches a "Torah of *ḥesed*," a fleshed-out example of the mother's Torah of earlier chapters (Prov 31:26). Her special outreach to the poor (that is, a community beyond her household) is especially featured as a subset of her "motherly" knowledge and action. This gendered Torah is elaborated as a different—perhaps even uniquely female—kind of teaching: Motherly Torah is a "Torah of compassion" or "loving kindness." The Hebrew word for "compassion" is *ḥesed*, the same word used for "covenant love," which is God's special gift to those in Israel's covenant. This association elevates her teaching and action theologically to a level that far surpasses the image of a meek, kindly, self-effacing, helpful homebody. This connection is usually overlooked by interpreters: clearly, it is easier or more comfortable for some to emphasize the negative characterizations of women that feed a gender ideology of female inferiority and contingencies.

Negative females. Several different groups of women inversely related to the positive ideology of wives and mothers appear: loose women (usually rendered as "adulteresses"), foolish women, prostitutes, and "strangers" (either due to ethnicity or because they are the wife of another man and thus "strange" and forbidden). In the cosmic treatment of the Negative Female, we will see that this category as a whole aligns with the actions of the forbidden goddesses of surrounding cultures.

The adulteress. Worse than a simple fornicator, the adulteress earns her horrific portrayal from the fact that she is someone else's property. A crime of theft and not interpersonal betrayal, adultery persistently poses the potential for male shame. Few things are more heinous to the sages than male inability to control a woman's sexual activity or secure progeny whose parentage is absolutely beyond reproach. Whether in the tribal life of the village, in the elite life at court, or out of postcolonial concerns over keeping inheritance pure and within the ethnic group, the adulteress evokes patriarchal fears, leading to a transfer of negative goddess characteristics to her and the threat of death to any man who sleeps with her. Worse than a prostitute (*zonah*;

whom one need only "buy" for a day's bread), this *nokriyah*, literally "foreign," is the sum of all male fears.

Prostitute. Far less worrisome to the sages is the simple prostitute (Heb. *zonah*). Clearly not belonging to any one man, she represents only the opportunity for fornication (not adultery) and can simply be bought for a small sum (Prov 6:26) and then discarded. Across the ancient international spectrum, young men were advised against such fascinations or sexual outlets: Mesopotamian proverbs consider prostitutes a danger because they do not show loyalty to any one man and possess a ready source of income that makes them independent. Such indulgences lessen a man's status with other men, and only the legitimate wife can provide a bulwark against her charms.

Like other writers from antiquity, the sages do not consider the dire circumstances that force women into prostitution. The prostitute may be a true "foreigner" with no relative to defend her honor; indeed, it is the lack of a male protector that condemns the prostitute to low status. Her unreliability is showcased in the case of Rahab in Joshua 2, who is portrayed as without loyalty to her own people.

Woman Wisdom and Woman Stranger. Woman Wisdom appears in the materials of the Second Temple period, as does her Wicked Twin, the composite Woman Stranger. Hebrew language lacks a neuter gender, so abstract concepts (Torah, wisdom, knowledge, insight, etc.) are rendered by the feminine gender, and yet the shocking portrayal of intellectual knowledge as an active, exalted personified female is not simply a matter of grammatical convention.

Woman Wisdom in Proverbs 1—9 has been seen as an Israelite shadow of scribal goddesses Ma'at in Egypt, whom kings must possess or fail as kings, or Nisaba in ancient Sumer, who rewards the sages with all kinds of benefits (Lang, 1975; Clifford, 1999). She carries the traits of other goddesses as well: the flexible Hathor of Egypt, goddess of love, war, and acrobats, may be the origin of the Darling Girl frolicking before the biblical God at creation (Prov 8:21 ff.; Lang, 1975); Isis, the foundation of the Pharaoh's

throne, may give the mothering aspect to personified Wisdom of the Jesus Movement (Meyers et al., 2000). The Goddess-Bride of the sacred marriage rites between kings and goddesses (represented by elite priestesses) may underlie the sages' urgings to make Wisdom one's mate ("say to Wisdom, 'My Sister,'" Prov 7:4). For other interpreters, Woman Wisdom is the Jewish answer to the wisdom goddesses of the Greco-Roman philosophy with which Israel came into contact during the Second Temple period (Fox, 2000). Along with the goddesses found lurking behind her skirts, Wisdom is also imaged in ways that relate directly to biblical traditions of wife and mother, teacher and manager, elite wife, and loving partner (see above). She also shares traits with Israelite prophets in her angry, public denunciation of those who stray from her teachings.

The negative repository of all the sages' fear is Wisdom's twin, Woman Stranger/Woman Folly. Imaged as vindictive goddess, adulteress, forbidden wife of another, outsider to the insider ethnic group, or just an overwhelming compilation of all negative gendered traits, she too displays strong mythological influences. She brings death to innocent (or just plain stupid) males who fall for her allure (Prov 2:16–19; 6:26; 7:22–27; 9:18), like the scorned goddess of epic traditions (Clifford, 1999). Emphasis on female speech is a trope: her words are "smooth" and oily—that is, pleasing and seductive, thus dangerous to men. Only the blessings and rewards of sweet-talking cosmic Woman Wisdom (Prov 2:16–19; 5:1–23; 6:20–35) or the charms of one's own wife (Prov 5:18–20) are proof against the charms and tricks of the Negative Female.

The Book of Job. Job's story is set in the patriarchal ancestor period but was in all likelihood composed in the Second Temple period. Although Job is a foreigner, all of his values reflect the biblical ideals, and gendered concepts continue the basic themes found in Proverbs. Job's wife encourages him to end his suffering by cursing God, prompting a quick death by retributive punishment. While this may be quite sensible, it prompts Job to compare her speech to that of "foolish women" (Job 2:9–10), implying that "wise women" exist as well. By the end of Job's tribulations, he has reconsidered the meaning of female kin: his daughters are cited by name in Job 42:13–15 (his new sons are not), and Job defies custom by giving them an inheritance along with their brothers (Fontaine, 1982; Follis, 1987). The "Wisdom" that is the topic in Job 28's Wisdom Hymn is usually interpreted as an abstraction, but ecotheologians have questioned whether it might well be Woman Wisdom appearing here, witnessed to by all of Earth's creatures and entities, even the Pit (Habel, 2003)

Ecclesiastes. The latest canonical book, Ecclesiastes, displays an elite ennui and disgust with life that has been correlated with male shame induced by colonial rule (Seow, 1997). Such shame causes the author to view all others as instruments (concubines, slaves, entertainers or as allegorical tropes for the body in old age), not as persons related to him in a meaningful way; he has no use for women's procreative capacities. While his summary teaching suggests "seizing the day" by rejoicing with one's own wife, he spends more time warning about the woman who traps men in her snares (Eccl 7:26–28). "Woman as threat" is a familiar motif from Proverbs and other regional wisdom traditions.

Gendered Wisdom in the Apocrypha. Jewish wisdom literature (Sirach Wisdom of Solomon, Baruch, and Esdras) continues the tropes begun in Proverbs: Woman Wisdom is Mother, Bride, Teacher, and Torah. She gains significant enhancement from her association with the hallmark of Jewish identity, the revealed Torah, but also absorbs many of the features and activities of the Hellenistic Isis (Kloppenborg, 1982; Reese, 1970). In her composite form, which links goddesses in a positive way to the traditions of an exemplary Torah given to the Jews, she is more than a match for the Greek Athena and Roman Minerva, or the various ideologies of Philosophy as superior to Jewish traditions.

The Dead Sea Scrolls. Female Wisdom appears in the sectarian instructions of 4Q185 and 4Q525, where she is decisively equated with the Torah. This move continues Proverbs' celebration of Woman Wisdom, a source of instruction for godly and pure living (Harrington, 1996). Even more interesting is the treatment of Woman Folly/Strange Woman in

4Q184 where she has become the complete amalgam of death-dealing goddesses, lurking to lure men into the pit. This epitome of wickedness has been thoroughly demonized, with her "filth" (that is, menstrual blood) in her skirts almost more abhorrent to the authors than the death that it symbolizes. In the heightened purity fixations of the Qumran communities, female blood—a positive source of pure heritage that secures the election of the chosen community—has utterly morphed into the defiling symbol of embodiment and become equivalent to the rotting grave.

Wisdom in the New Testament. The New Testament fully appropriates the Cosmic Wisdom of the Hebrew Bible. Jesus interprets himself as a sage-child who vindicates Mother Wisdom in Luke 7:35. Woman Wisdom's deeds vindicate her in Matthew 11:19, and she sends prophets and apostles in Luke 11:49 (all three passages are derived from the Sayings Source, Q). In 1 Corinthians 1:24, the identity of Jesus is handled differently with respect to female personification: Paul symbolically transforms Jesus's gender, calling him the *sophia* (Gk."wisdom") of God, thus removing the Mother Wisdom of the Gospels from the equation. Many of these ideas are developed more fully in noncanonical Christian literature of the period: the Sayings Source Q, the *Gospel of Thomas*, the *Apocryphon of John* (Gilhus, 2008), the *Sophia of Jesus Christ*, and various Gnostic texts of wisdom mythology. The Christological hymns in John and Colossians clearly draw on Jewish wisdom mythology derived from Proverbs 8, Wisdom 7:25–28, and Sirach 24:3–22, positing Christ as preexistent, like Wisdom in Proverbs 8.

The Song of Solomon. Viewed by most as a collection of love lyrics thematically organized around seeking and finding, the Song of Solomon links earlier ideas to later, lush love poems, mostly in the female voice. Usually dated to sometime in the Hellenistic period, it has much earlier antecedents in Mesopotamian ritual texts (the Sacred Marriage Rite; Nissinen and Uro, 2008, pp. 173–218) and Egyptian love poetry from the New Kingdom (Songs of the Harper; Fox, 1985). Some have postulated their use as an *epithalmion*, a praise poem recited as part of wedding feasts (Murphy,

1990). However, the poems are drenched in the local territory and key vocabulary of the Promised Land that invite a more materialist interpretation. The explicit language and astonishing portrait of female speech and agency outside of (or preceding) a marital relationship scandalized both Jewish and Christian authorities, prompting deliberate mistranslation of some pronouns to gender the sexual advances made as male. The overall allegorizing of the characters, locations, and motifs transforms the Song into a story of love between God and Israel (both land and inhabitants) or Christ and the church/soul. Interpretations resulting from such allegorizing have been far-fetched, but unsuccessful in dampening the plain sense of the text: love is as strong as death.

Gender-bending characterization. The love story between a rural girl and her shepherd love, or a young woman at court, betrothed to King Solomon and denigrated by the city women of Jerusalem, is told in images and scenes that drip with honey. They conjure up visions of luscious and dangerous love that drives the partners to daring acts of pursuit. Neither character is directly named. "Solomon" appears in the "king fiction," a technique often used to render atypical texts acceptable to conservative editors (so, too, with the cynical and agnostic Ecclesiastes's linkage to Solomon). The male lover is sometimes shepherd, sometimes elite king of the Jerusalem court; he is imaged as an apple (?) tree, grand sculpture, and gazelle; and he also shyly peeps through the lattices of the girl's home. The female protagonist, "Beloved," is similarly difficult to identify. She is sometimes a village guardian of vineyards familiar with the hills where her shepherd love finds pasture; at other times, she is associated with the royal court, seen coming up from the desert in a luxurious (wedding?) procession, and sometimes also saddled with officious brothers seeking to marry her off advantageously. She is mistaken for a prostitute and portrayed as a bride dancing between two (hostile?) kin groups at her marriage celebration. She initiates intimate encounters, seeking her love in the nighttime streets or by the daytime watering holes of his flock. She imagines him in her dreams, in her mother's bedroom, in gardens with pure springs and wells, in fields bursting into bloom, beneath the apple tree where her mother enjoyed intimacies, and at private meals in a banqueting house or his chambers, where his lovemaking is the sweetest food of all. She talks about her love openly to the all-female group of onlookers, the Daughters of Jerusalem, who interact like background singers to the lead vocal diva.

Both lovers are likened to elements of the natural world that "cross-gender" ancient expectations: each partner is both mobile and stationary. The common gender ideology is evident: she is fixed and civilized, busily providing fruits to be consumed, while he is mobile and wild, doing as he pleases according to his animal nature. While the image of the male lover as a gazelle suggests unrestricted movement, he also is portrayed as standing still, a nonthreatening tree or sculpted work of art reminiscent of columns of the Temple. Likewise, images for Beloved are dual: some emphasize her "rooted" and fertile nature to which access is restricted (a locked garden, a dove in a rock cleft, a dweller inside garden walls), but others show her remarkable mobility (searching night and day, a flock of goats or ewes, flowing waters). Striking military imagery is applied to her; delicate animal beauty is attributed to him. The two find parity when they move toward each other or find stillness in each other's company.

Reversing the curse. Genesis 3:16b has long been interpreted as enforcing gender hierarchy on the basis of a supposed "curse" in response to an "original sin" of a sexual nature. While essential to patriarchal control of women, such an interpretation cannot be supported textually (Meyers, 1989; Trible, 1978). Beloved's words in Song of Solomon 7:10 correct perverse readings of Genesis 3 and foreground the equality of sexes both made in the Divine Image (Gen 1:26–28): "I am my Beloved's; his desire is for me!" Desire between the cross-gendered partners—both moving, both fixed—is underscored for its equalizing effect: she desires him, he desires her, and it leads not to death but to new life. If the Song was indeed collected, edited, and promoted by the Sages, it embodies a cosmic wisdom most essential to the children of Earth.

[*See also* Deity, *subentries on* Ancient Near East *and* New Testament; Jesus; Imagery, Gendered, *subentry* Gospels; *and* Religious Participation, *subentry* Sacred Prostitution.]

BIBLIOGRAPHY

Clifford, Richard. *Proverbs: A Commentary*. Louisville, Ky.: Westminster John Knox, 1999.

Follis, Elaine R., ed. *Directions in Biblical Hebrew Poetry*. Journal for the Study of the Old Testament Supplement Series 40. Sheffield, U.K.: Sheffield Academic Press, 1987.

Fontaine, Carole R. *Traditional Sayings in the Old Testament: A Contextual Study*. Bible and Literature 5. Sheffield, U.K.: Almond, 1982.

Fontaine, Carole R. *Smooth Words: Women, Proverbs, and Performance in Biblical Wisdom*. Sheffield, U.K.: Sheffield Academic Press, 2002.

Fox, Michael V. *The Song of Songs and the Ancient Egyptian Love Songs*. Madison: University of Wisconsin Press, 1985.

Fox, Michael V. *Proverbs 1–9: A New Translation with Introduction and Commentary*. New York: Doubleday, 2000.

Gilhus, Ingvild Sælid. "Sacred Marriage and Spiritual Knowledge: Relations between Carnality and Salvation in the Apocryphon of John." In *Sacred Marriages: The Divine-Human Sexual Metaphor from Sumer to Early Christianity*, edited by Martti Nissinen and Risto Uro, pp. 487–510. Winona Lake, Ind.: Eisenbrauns, 2008.

Habel, Norman C. "The Implications of God Discovering Wisdom in Earth." In *Job 28: Cognition in Context*, edited by Ellen vanWolde, pp. 281–297. Leiden, The Netherlands: Brill, 2003.

Habel, Norman C., and Shirley Wurst. *The Earth Story in Wisdom Traditions*. Earth Bible 3. Sheffield, U.K.: Sheffield Academic Press, 2001.

Harrington, Daniel J. *Wisdom Texts from Qumran*. London: Routledge, 1996.

Kloppenborg, John S. "Isis and Sophia in the Book of Wisdom." *Harvard Theological Review* 75 (1982): 57–84.

Lang, Bernhard. *Frau Weisheit: Deutung einer biblischen Gestalt*. Düsseldorf, Germany: Patmos, 1975.

Meyers, Carol. *Discovering Eve: Ancient Israelite Women in Context*. New York: Oxford University Press, 1988.

Meyers, Carol. "In the Household and Beyond: The Social World of Israelite Women." *Studia Theologica* 63 (2009): 19–41.

Meyers, Carol, ed. *Women in Scripture: A Dictionary of Named and Unnamed Women in the Hebrew Bible, the Apocryphal/Deuterocanonical Books, and the New Testament*. Boston: Houghton Mifflin, 2000.

Murphy, Roland E. *The Song of Songs: A Commentary on the Book of Canticles or the Song of Songs*. Edited by S. Dean McBride Jr. Hermeneia. Minneapolis: Fortress, 1990.

Nissinen, Martti, and Risto Uro, eds. *Sacred Marriages: The Divine-Human Sexual Metaphor from Sumer to Early Christianity*. Winona Lake, Ind.: Eisenbrauns, 2008.

Reese, James M. *Hellenistic Influence on the Book of Wisdom and Its Consequences*. Analecta Biblica 41. Rome: Biblical Institute Press, 1970.

Seow, C. L. *Ecclesiastes: A New Translation with Introduction and Commentary*. Anchor Bible Commentaries 18, pt. 3. New York: Doubleday, 1997.

Trible, Phyllis. *God and the Rhetoric of Sexuality*. Philadelphia: Fortress, 1978.

Yoder, Christine Roy. *Wisdom as a Woman of Substance:a Socioeconomic Reading of Proverbs 1–9 and 31:10–31*. Berlin: Walter de Gruyter, 2001.

Carole R. Fontaine

Apocalyptic Literature

Readers of the great literary apocalypses may quickly discern that they have entered a man's world. The most influential apocalypses all feature male narrators: Enoch, Daniel, Ezra, Baruch, Abraham, John, Hermas, Peter, and Isaiah. Apocalyptic visions often depict the world in terms of men (or male beings) and their struggles: the Watchers of Enoch, the Son of Man of Enoch and Daniel, the wise of Daniel, and the 144,000 of Revelation are all male. Commentators still grapple with assessing Revelation, which defines its feminine symbols primarily in terms of sexual status—whore, mother, and bride—while its "men" experience a fuller range of activities, including the use of women. However, when we attend to the texts in more detail, and when we apply gender analysis to male as well as female imagery, things grow more complicated—and more interesting.

Apocalyptic Visionaries. With notable exceptions, Jewish and Christian literary apocalypses feature pseudonymous male narrators, who describe the experience of their visions. For example, when the book of Daniel turns from the section of court legends (chs. 1—6) to its visionary section, the narrative voice moves from third person to first person, from a description of the adventures of Daniel and his colleagues to an extended recitation of Daniel's own visionary experiences (7:2; see 10:1–2). The rest of the book continues as first person reportage (though see 10:1–2). The notable exceptions include Revelation and *Hermas*, which do not rely on pseudonymity, along with the Sibylline Oracles and the two apocalypses of Mary, which feature women as visionaries. Although the Sibylline Oracles do reveal the future, as some apocalypses do, they do not technically constitute literary apocalypses.

The apocalyptic visionaries function as characters within their own first-person narratives. Their pseudonymity provides several clues for gender-sensitive approaches to their characterization. For one, all of the pseudonymous visionaries bring authority to their apocalypses. Enoch, Abraham, Moses, Isaiah, Ezra, Baruch, Peter, and Paul all represent important figures in these sacred stories. Daniel's history remains murkier, though the attachment of his visionary reports to legends concerning his wisdom and ability to interpret dreams suggests that ancient audiences may have been more familiar with him. Moreover, the visionaries all carry mystical associations: some traditions credit Enoch, Moses, and Baruch with having escaped death, while Moses and Isaiah have directly seen God.

In addition to their authority and mystical credentials, apocalyptic visionaries inherit an array of conventional behaviors from the biblical tradition, including encounters with sacred beings. Visionaries therefore deport themselves according to the same patterns that apply to Abraham, Jacob, Moses, and other biblical characters who encounter angels and experience theophanies. Such encounters place heroic men in a complicated social space: though they are great masculine heroes who lead households and peoples, display remarkable courage, and exercise great authority, they find themselves facing beings of higher status. In apocalypses they fall prostrate, plead ignorance, act as suppliants, undergo (sometimes severe) correction, and lose control of their own bodies. The apocalypses go to great lengths to demonstrate not their masculine self-control but their human vulnerability.

Daniel provides a fairly typical case. Daniel 1—6 locates Daniel among those high-status young men who were "without physical defect and handsome, versed in every branch of wisdom, endowed with knowledge and insight, and competent to serve in the king's palace" (1:4, NRSV). Daniel and three colleagues demonstrate their religious fidelity by abstaining from the king's luxurious diet, yet after ten days they look more impressive ("better and fatter") than their peers (1:15). In addition to his trust in God, Daniel's skills include facility regarding visions and dreams (1:17). Daniel and his friends demonstrate "ten times" the competence of the king's resident magicians (1:20). In the king's service Daniel achieves success and status, serving as patron for his friends (2:49). He even shows generosity toward the Babylonian wise men competing with him for status (2:24). Daniel remains faithful to God despite potentially deadly tests. Parts of the story go so far as to contrast Daniel's masculine resolve with the debasement, confusion, and inconstancy shown by the great kings (see 4:32–33; 5:1–10; 6:14–18).

In contrast, the book's visionary section features a different Daniel. First-person verbs figure prominently, inviting readers to align their perspective with Daniel's. "I watched" and "as I was watching" recur in chapters 7 and 8. Heavenly beings address Daniel directly (7:16; 8:16–17; 9:21–23; 10:10–21) and affirm Daniel's favor in the sight of God (9:23; 10:11, 19; 12:13). Daniel shows a great deal of initiative in this visionary section. He fasts, prays, and seeks clarification from his heavenly guides. But Daniel also records his moments of weakness, confusion, and fear (7:15, 28; 8:15–17, 27; 10:8–9, 15–17). The section even suggests that Daniel's visions make him ill (7:28; 8:27; 10:8). Daniel, like all the apocalyptic visionaries, embodies a combination of virtue, strength, and vulnerability that complicates stereotypical presentations of ancient Mediterranean masculinity.

Characters and Symbols. Given the nature of apocalyptic discourse, interpreters may struggle to distinguish between an apocalypse's straightforward characters and its symbols. For example, Revelation 2 characterizes a woman prophet as "Jezebel." The name is symbolic, as it invites readers to imagine connections between this prophet and the biblical Jezebel, but the text seems to connote an actual individual known to the audience. By contrast, we interpret Revelation's Whore as a symbol. Though most commentators agree that the Whore has something to do with Roman imperialism, she does not indicate a single individual or institutional reality but evokes a larger set of associations. The distinction is challenging for gender-critical interpretation.

First Enoch and *Jubilees* relate a common tradition concerning a group of angels called the Watchers. (Though *Jubilees* is not a literary apocalypse, it participates heavily in apocalyptic motifs.) Both texts provide interpretations of the bizarre passage in Genesis 6:1–4, in which the "sons of God" see that mortal women are beautiful and take (*lqḥ*) women for themselves, producing a race of Nephilim, or giants. The Genesis account immediately precedes the story of the great flood. *Enoch* and *Jubilees* link the two stories by identifying the Watchers as rebellious angels who cause great corruption and violence, thereby provoking God to send the flood. In both *1 Enoch* and *Jubilees* God judges these angels, consigning them to a realm of punishment.

The first section of *1 Enoch*, the Book of the Watchers (chs. 1—36), devotes more attention to these angels than does *Jubilees*. It even provides their names (6:7–8). The account says little about the Watchers. They are male, and they are motivated by desire. They know in advance that their deed is sinful. The account does not reflect any interest in the women's responses: they give birth to the Watchers' monstrous offspring, and the Watchers provide the women with forbidden knowledge. The combination of gigantic offspring and forbidden knowledge leads to the violence that provokes divine judgment. From the point of *1 Enoch* and *Jubilees*, that the Watchers find the women attractive provides sufficient explanation for their motives. The two traditions show no interest in the responses or experiences of the women: not only are they passive sexual objects, they are also passive recipients of forbidden knowledge.

Some apocalypses devote a great deal of attention to male angels and their place in the heavenly realm. *First Enoch* opens with references to God's mighty army and thousands of holy ones, an appearance that terrifies the Watchers (1:4–9). This scenario implies a militant host of male heavenly beings, some aligned with God and others in opposition. The Book of the Watchers offers conflicting traditions regarding the names of the angels and their rankings. Shemihazah leads the wicked Watchers with the support of a hierarchically ranked set of other named angels (6:3–7). Each possesses specialized knowledge (8:1–3). Meanwhile, God commissions four archangels—Michael, Sariel, Raphael, and Gabriel—with distinctive assignments (chs. 9—10): *1 Enoch* 87:2 assigns their appearance as that of "white men." However, *1 Enoch* 20:1–7 names seven (not four; see 90:71) archangels and their jurisdictions. All of these beings receive masculine names. The Book of the Luminaries, another of *1 Enoch*'s constituent parts (chs. 72—82), begins with the motions of the sun and the moon but goes on to elaborate the jurisdictions of various angels who regulate the heavenly bodies (see esp. 82:9–20).

Every literary apocalypse includes an interpreting angel, a male being who instructs the visionary and interprets the vision. These beings, who sometimes but not always receive names, routinely inspire fear through their very appearance. On occasion, however, visionaries "talk back" to these angelic mediators. Though Uriel admonishes Ezra that his "understanding has utterly failed" (4:2), Enoch abandons neither his questions nor his complaint.

The enigmatic Son of Man figure emerges in apocalyptic literature. Some interpreters translate the term as "Human One," reflecting ordinary use. Ezekiel, for example, employs the phrase 93 times (Collins and Collins, 2008, p. 75; the NRSV renders the Hebrew term, *ben adam*, as "mortal" in Ezekiel). Ezekiel shares some characteristics with the literary apocalypses: the prophet experiences miraculous transportation and receives visions of the divine throne and the ideal Jerusalem; his visions include a climactic battle; and the vision of the dry bones sounds very much like a resurrection. Indeed, Ezekiel heavily influences the great literary apocalypses. However, in Daniel, the Similitudes of Enoch (*1 En.* 37—71), 4

Ezra, and Revelation, "Son of Man" clearly indicates more than an ordinary mortal.

Daniel describes "one like a Son of Man" riding the clouds of heaven (7:13). The imagery recalls Yahweh, who rides upon the clouds (see Pss. 68:4; 104:3), though this one like a Son of Man is presented before the Ancient of Days. Among other things, the one like a Son of Man receives dominion while all peoples serve him. The Similitudes of Enoch adapts the scene from Daniel, including its description of the Ancient of Days (46:1; see Dan 7:9), but now the Son of Man is a definite figure: an eschatological judge and messiah who attains divine status. Revelation draws upon this same imagery, though with differences: the risen Jesus himself takes on the characteristics of the Ancient of Days (1:13–15). *Fourth Ezra*, a Jewish apocalypse written very close to the composition of Revelation, likewise blends messianic aspirations with the Son of Man as a heavenly being: he flies with the clouds, vanquishes his enemies, and forms a peaceable people (13:1–13). The apocalypses present somewhat diverse images of the Son of Man, but they all involve an eschatological figure who restores order. The Similitudes, Revelation, and *4 Ezra* attach messianic associations to the figure, as does Revelation. With respect to gender, this male eschatological actor embodies ferocity and executes justice.

Animals figure prominently in apocalyptic imagery. In almost every case the animals are male, but we encounter some exceptions. All of the menacing beasts are male, though their masculinity is more assumed than emphasized. Daniel's fourth beast is "terrifying and dreadful and exceedingly strong" (7:7), while the ram with two horns is also characterized by his strength (8:4). Revelation's enormous dragon, identified as Satan, fights against Michael and the angels and chases the woman clothed with the sun. Frustrated in his pursuit, the dragon demonstrates anger and makes war on the saints (Rev 12:1–18). The beast of Revelation 13 reflects features from Daniel 7, notably arrogance and hostility. The *Shepherd of Hermas* 23—24 likewise features a beast, though this beast represents persecution rather than a particular political reality.

The "Animal Apocalypse" (*1 En.* 85—90) lays out human history through a succession of animals.

Adam appears as a bull, Eve as a cow, and their descendants as a race of bulls and cows. When one of their children, a red calf, disappears, the Eve-cow searches for it and laments until the Adam-bull comes to quiet her (85:6–7). The Animal Apocalypse treats wicked characters as black bulls or as predatory species—all male—and the elect as calves, bulls, sheep, and other domesticated animals. Beyond Eve and the women who are impregnated by the Watchers (who take the guise of black bulls with prominent penises), the account includes women among the cattle but does not dwell upon them in any specific way. The actors are all male, including rams and shepherds, who receive authority over the sheep from time to time.

Revelatory Women. Both *4 Ezra* and the *Shepherd of Hermas* feature women whose presence provides a primary vehicle for revelation.

Fourth Ezra consists of a series of seven visions, and many interpreters regard the fourth vision as not only the center of the series but also its turning point. In visions 1–3 the seer continues to pose challenges to his heavenly interlocutor, but in visions 5–7 he is compliant. Vision 4 (9:38—10:59) offers the most dramatic moment in the overall apocalypse, characterized through a grieving mother. After Ezra has spoken his mind, he turns and sees a woman who is clearly in a state of grief. Her only son, born after thirty years of barrenness, has died upon entering his wedding chamber. She intends to mourn and fast until she dies. Ezra, preoccupied with his own grief over Jerusalem's destruction, offers poor consolation. Having called her "most foolish of women" (10:6), he compares her devastation to Zion's, offers her hope of meeting her son in the resurrection, and tells her to return to her husband. Ezra attempts to counsel the woman a second time, but then the woman is transformed. Her face flashes like lightning, and she cries aloud, shaking the earth with the volume of her voice. Terrified, Ezra averts his gaze. When he looks up, the woman has disappeared and in her place stands a great city. Uriel comes and explains to Ezra that the woman "is" Zion. The vision has allowed Ezra to see Zion's true glory.

Many contemporary readers will find themselves taken aback by the gendered dynamics of Ezra's encounter with the woman. The story affirms that Ezra receives the vision of her glory because he truly tried to comfort her (10:49–50). Few would find his behavior particularly comforting. On the other hand, the seer finds himself overwhelmed by the intensity of the woman's transformed appearance and her loud cry (10:25–26).

Fourth Ezra's woman Zion provides an interesting contrast with *Hermas*'s woman church. Both images provide interpretations of a collective reality, the glory of God's people (Humphrey, 1995). However, the woman who appears in *Hermas* plays an even more critical role in the development of that apocalypse. *Hermas* begins with a series of five visions, four of which feature the woman. In the first the former slave encounters his owner, Rhoda, whom he had once desired. Rhoda scolds him for this sin and calls him to pray for mercy. Later Hermas encounters a different woman, elderly and radiant in appearance. She too admonishes Hermas for his conduct and exhorts him to manliness. Hermas's second vision again features the elderly woman, who hands over a book she had read to Hermas in the first vision. Hermas wrongly guesses that the woman is the Sibyl, only to learn that she instead embodies the church. Her age reflects how the world was created for the church's sake. The elderly woman again appears in Hermas's third vision, encouraging him to pray for righteousness. The woman now reveals a tower: "The tower that you see being built, it is I, the church" (11.3, author's translation). Throughout *Hermas* the tower constitutes the prevailing symbol for the church: good stones fit in, and poor stones do not. (At this point the apocalypse also introduces seven women who embody the virtues necessary for inclusion in the tower: faith, self-control, simplicity, knowledge, innocence, dignity, and love.) Vision 3 concludes with a revelation concerning the three forms in which the woman has revealed herself: elderly and seated, elderly but standing and with a more youthful face, and finally young and beautiful. These three forms reflect diverse states of spiritual strength. A young woman, dressed as if coming from her bridal chamber, guides Hermas through vision 4.

Hermas's reference to the Sibyl reflects ancient women's frequent participation in oracular activity. In Greco-Roman tradition the Sibyls are aged women who deliver their oracles in a state of fierce frenzy. Often based at revered sites, the Sibyls uttered veiled prophecies concerning public events. Roman officials routinely consulted the Sibyl at Cumae. Jews and Christians alike developed books of Sibylline Oracles, which often addressed their own historical and cultural concerns.

Assessing Revelation. Revelation poses a classic case for gender-sensitive interpretation of apocalyptic literature. Its dramatic symbols include four women: "Jezebel" (a pseudonym for an actual woman), the woman clothed with the sun, Babylon the prostitute, and the New Jerusalem, adorned as a bride for her husband. Aligned with the lamb are the woman clothed with the sun and the New Jerusalem, the lamb curses Jezebel, while Babylon is aligned with the beast and consigned to destruction. All four figures are defined primarily in terms of their sexual status: the wicked women are identified with sexual sin (*porneia*), the woman clothed with the sun gives birth, and the New Jerusalem dresses as a bride.

We may also assess the roles of Revelation's male characters. Male protagonists fight to establish their power (Moore, 1999) and relate to these women in sexualized ways: the lamb throws Jezebel on a bed, the dragon (Satan, 12:9) pursues the woman clothed with the sun and seeks to devour her child, Babylon rides the beast, and the lamb marries the New Jerusalem. If we may assume Revelation's saints to be male, they receive instructions to "come out" from Babylon (18:4) and an invitation to "come" to the bride and enter the city (22:17; Pippin, 1992, p. 82). Meanwhile, both Jezebel and Babylon participate in *porneia* with the lamb's enemies and later suffer sexualized degradation (2:21–23; 17:16; 18:3, 9). Most remarkable is the depiction of the lamb's 144,000 followers, who "have not defiled themselves with women, for they are virgins" (14:4).

Clothing imagery attends three of the four women. The woman of Revelation 12 is clothed with the sun and wears a crown (12:1); Babylon wears purple and scarlet and is "adorned with gold and jewels and pearls" (17:4); and the bride wears white linen (19:8)—though the New Jerusalem herself is also adorned with precious stones, gold, and pearls. Clothing provides a less significant marker for the male counterparts of these women, though tattoos do play a role for both male and female symbols (13:1; 17:5; 19:12, 16): the lamb's robe is dipped in blood (19:13; see 1:13); the lamb, dragon, and beast alike wear crowns or diadems (12:3; 13:1; 19:12).

With respect to gender, ethical and theological appraisals tend to cluster around the sexualized ways in which Revelation presents "Jezebel," the woman clothed with the sun, Babylon, and the bride. Some interpreters regard this pattern as irredeemably misogynistic: positively or negatively, Revelation values women only in terms of their sexual status (Pippin, 1992). Others emphasize that Revelation appropriates stock images from biblical prophecy and Greco-Roman iconography: the images may indeed carry misogyny, but they aim to destabilize Roman kyriarchy (Rossing, 1999; Schüssler Fiorenza, 1991). Still others acknowledge Revelation's problematic symbolism but also point out the power and influence assigned to Revelation's female symbols (Collins, 2009). And still others observe that while Revelation participates in ancient misogynistic imagery, it undermines that system in significant ways (Huber, 2007).

Fewer interpreters have addressed masculinity in Revelation. Stephen Moore (2009) reads Revelation as striving toward masculinity through dominance, a "hypermasculinity" that betrays its own vulnerability and ultimately undermines itself. Tina Pippin (1992) perceives in Revelation not merely the subordination of women but a deep aversion toward them: the New Jerusalem includes only men.

Sexuality and Asceticism. Ancient apocalyptic literature reflects an emphasis on sexual asceticism and sexual sin. The Book of the Watchers and *Jubilees* share a common concern regarding interspecies sex between the Watchers and mortal women. The Essenes, John the Baptist, Jesus, and Paul apparently all practiced celibacy (see also Rev 14:4).

In his dispute with the Sadducees Jesus imagines a postresurrection state in which marriage is obsolete (Matt 22:30; Luke 20:34–36): the Essenes apparently believed they lived among angels, while Jesus imagined an angelic postresurrection state, a tradition reflected in *Hermas* (101.24; 102.2; Bucur, 2006). *Hermas* begins with the visionary being scolded for looking upon Rhoda with desire (1.1–9), though sexuality constitutes a relatively minor interest for that apocalypse (though see *Hermas* 29—32). Quite striking are the punishments for sexual sin set forth in the *Apocalypse of Peter* and the (later and derivative) *Apocalypse of Paul*. These sins receive no more attention than others, but the *Apocalypse of Peter* does reflect ancient assumptions about gender roles and sexuality: women who adorn themselves to attract men hang by their hair, while adulterous men hang by their genitals.

Conclusion. Ancient Jewish and Christian apocalyptic literature features male visionaries, male heavenly beings, and for the most part male actors. On the other hand, this literature also includes women and men as vehicles of revelation, occasionally imagines women in powerful albeit symbolic roles, and sometimes undermines conventional gender expectations.

[*See also* Gender; Gender Transgression, *subentry* New Testament; Male-Female Sexuality, *subentry* New Testament; Masculinity and Femininity, *subentries on* New Testament *and* Roman World; *and* Sexual Transgression, *subentry* Roman World.]

BIBLIOGRAPHY

Bucur, Bogdan. "Observations on the Ascetic Doctrine of the *Shepherd of Hermas*." *Studia Monastica* 48 (2006): 7–23.

Collins, Adela Yarbro. "Feminine Symbolism in the Book of Revelation." In *A Feminist Companion to the Apocalypse of John*, edited by Amy-Jill Levine, pp. 121–130. Feminist Companion to the New Testament and Early Christian Writings 13. London: T&T Clark, 2009.

Collins, Adela Yarbro, and John J. Collins. *King and Messiah as Son of God: Divine, Human, and Angelic Messianic Figures in Biblical and Related Literature.* Grand Rapids, Mich.: Eerdmans, 2008.

Huber, Lynn R. *Like a Bride Adorned: Reading Metaphor in John's Apocalypse.* Emory Studies in Early Christianity 12. New York: T&T Clark, 2007.

Humphrey, Edith McEwan. *The Ladies and the Cities: Transformation and Apocalyptic Identity in Joseph and Aseneth, 4 Ezra, the Apocalypse and the Shepherd of Hermas.* Journal for the Study of the Pseudepigrapha Supplement Series 17. Sheffield, U.K.: Sheffield Academic Press, 1995.

Levine, Amy-Jill, ed. *A Feminist Companion to the Apocalypse of John.* Feminist Companion to the New Testament and Early Christian Writings 13. London: T&T Clark, 2009.

Moore, Stephen D. "War Making Men Making War: The Performance of Masculinity in the Revelation to John." In *The Apocalyptic Imagination: Aesthetics and Ethics at the End of the World*, edited by S. Brent Plate, pp. 84–94. Glasgow, U.K.: Trinity St. Mungo, 1999.

Moore, Stephen D. "Hypermasculinity and Divinity." In *A Feminist Companion to the Apocalypse of John*, edited by Amy-Jill Levine, pp. 180–204. Feminist Companion to the New Testament and Early Christian Writings 13. London: T&T Clark, 2009.

Pippin, Tina. *Death and Desire: The Rhetoric of Gender in the Apocalypse of John.* Literary Currents in Biblical Interpretation. Louisville, Ky.: Westminster John Knox, 1992.

Rossing, Barbara R. *The Choice between Two Cities: Whore, Bride, and Empire in the Apocalypse.* Harrisburg, Pa.: Trinity Press International, 1999.

Schüssler Fiorenza, Elisabeth. *Revelation: Vision of a Just World.* Proclamation Commentaries. Minneapolis: Fortress, 1991.

Greg Carey

Gospels

Both "imagery" and "gender" are highly contested categories in New Testament scholarship; thus, some definitions and caveats are in order. For this entry, "imagery" refers to mentions of concrete objects, actions, or scenes that evoke sense impressions for the audience. Imagery functions on multiple levels, drawing upon the conceptual domain(s) invoked by concrete references to suggest deeper significance. In literary-critical terms, "imagery" includes such figures of speech as metaphor, simile, personification, metonymy, synecdoche, archetypes, and symbolism. Interpreting literary imagery is com-plicated because such images carry different connotations for readers across temporal, geographic, and linguistic divides. Furthermore, with the exception of "parables," the Gospels rarely explicitly label literary images as such. (The only place where "image" [*eikon*] is mentioned explicitly in the Gospels is when Jesus points to Caesar's image on a coin in Matthew 22:20//Mark 12:16//Luke 20:24.)

Furthermore, contemporary gender theory underscores that "gender" is a socially constructed category that does certain kinds of ideological work. Categories like "female," "male," "femininity," and "masculinity" are necessarily context-contingent; gendered behavior is subtly acculturated, performed, upheld, and contested across different cultures. Thus, "gender" should not be simplistically equated with so-called natural, biological gender, or fixed "sex." Queer studies helpfully challenges the monolithic heterosexual male/female binary, understanding gender and sexuality as open to constant variation.

Recognizing that gender is socially shaped illuminates the essentialist discourses about gender found in many ancient sources. As Colleen Conway and others demonstrate, ancient views of gender were constructed on a sliding scale, with ideal "manhood" or "womanhood" dependent upon social status, im/moral character, and specific roles and behaviors (2008, pp. 164–167). Most extant ancient literature, crafted by elite males, reflects a dualistic understanding of "maleness" and "femaleness," often using this reductionistic view as a metaphorical means of organizing society. Ancient elite male authors typically further their own patriarchal interests; traditionally, modern scholars have reinscribed these assumptions in their readings of biblical texts. Contemporary feminists rightly deconstruct such tendencies, pointing out that gender constructions have *always* been contested, subverted, and destabilized; the Gospels exhibit deep ambivalences over "appropriate" gender roles and spaces. Although masculine imagery is ubiquitous, this androcentrism reflects males' hegemony at the time, not their inherent moral or spiritual superiority. Gender is not tied to goodness or badness per se in the Gospels; men and women provide positive and negative examples. The Gospels also lack explicit references to standard Greco-Roman tropes regarding gender, such as the view that male bodies were hot, dry, dense, and strong, whereas female bodies were cold, wet, porous, and weak. Biblical scholars have begun identifying potentially transgender, gender-neutral, and/or cross-gender Gospel imagery in order to broaden the conversations around gender and biblical interpretation.

An additional complicating factor is that Greek and English indicate gender differently. Translation is always inexact due to semantic asymmetry (when the source language lacks lexical equivalents in the target language). For instance, Greek indicates gender using inflected nouns, adverbs, and adjectives, whereas English restricts gender designators to pronouns like "she" and "he." Some Greek words are lexically gendered (e.g., *sophia*, which is feminine), but the referent itself is not gender-specific. Writers also describe male figures engaged in biologically female activities like childbirth (e.g., Septuagint [LXX] of Deuteronomy 32:13). Thus, identifying "gendered" images invites further reflection on if/how gender is relevant in any given context.

In light of the foregoing, this entry describes the multiple, sometimes contradictory ways that Gospel imagery constructs, utilizes, and represents gender. The discussion is organized into categories of conceptually gendered referents.

Gendered Imagery for the Godhead. Language projects gendered imagery, drawn from human experience, onto God, who transcends gender. Although the preponderance of male God imagery and grammatically masculine God references leads many to think God is ontologically male, the Gospels include feminine images for the Godhead as well.

Gendered imagery for God. Perhaps the most familiar biblical archetype for God is that of "God as Father." Jesus calls God "Father" (or the more intimate Aramaic term "Abba," Mark 14:36) throughout the Gospels (e.g., Matt 5:16, 45; 6:8, 14–15, 32; 10:20, 29, 32–33; 11:27; 16:17, 27; 18:10, 14, 19, 35; 20:23; 24:36; 26:29, 39, 42, 53; 28:19; Luke 10:21//Matt 11:25–26; 26:39, 42//Luke 22:42; 23:46; John 5:18). He teaches his disciples to pray to "our Father" (Matt 6:9//Luke 11:2), exhorts them to be perfect like their heavenly Father (Matt 5:48; cf. Luke 6:36), and reassures them that their heavenly Father will give them good gifts (Matt 6:6, 18; 16:27; 7:7–11//Luke 11:11–13; Luke 12:32). Jesus even instructs his disciples to "call no one your 'father' on earth, for you have one Father, who is in heaven" (Matt 23:9). Contemporary scholars disagree about whether this metaphor legitimates or undermines what Elisabeth Schüssler Fiorenza calls kyriarchal structures—unequal "stratifications of gender, race, class, religion, heterosexualism, and age" resulting in domination and submission (Nasrallah and Schüssler Fiorenza, 2009, p. 9).

Several related images stem from the metaphor of God as Father. In ancient Rome, the ideal father was the *paterfamilias* ("father of the family"), the head of the household, who alone owned property and passed it on to the oldest legitimate male heir. Though the New Testament includes exceptions (e.g., Lydia in Acts 16), the Gospels only portray males atop the household hierarchy as "lord" (*kurios*) and "master of the house" (*oikodespotes*, *oikonomos*). Through both simile and metaphor, Jesus's parables depict God as the *oikodespotes* (Matt 20:1–16; 21:33–44; Luke 14:15–24), *kurios* (Matt 18:23–35; 20:1–16; 21:28–31, 33–44; Luke 16:1–13), or *oikonomos* (Luke 16:1–13).

The *paterfamilias* was responsible for sowing procreative seed. Using offspring imagery metaphorically, the Gospels pick up on the well-established belief in antiquity that procreation resulted from male desire and action; women were vessels for the man's seed. In John 1:12–13, Jesus's followers "become children of God . . . born, not of blood or of the will of the flesh or of the will of man, but of God" (cf. Matt 3:9). Peacemakers will be called "sons of God" (Matt 5:9) and will "inherit" the kingdom (Matt 25:34). More implicitly, agricultural imagery points toward God's initiative as the "Lord of the harvest" (Luke 10:2) who sows spiritual seeds and begets spiritual offspring (Matt 15:13). Throughout the Gospels, especially in the parables, God is portrayed as the ultimate authoritative property-owning, procreative male (Matt 21:33–43//Luke 20:14//Mark 12:7; Luke 15:11–32).

The Matthean parables depict God in the exclusively male role of king (Matt 18:23–35; 22:2–14). The theme of divine kingship, woven throughout the Hebrew Bible (e.g., Exod 15:3, 18; Pss 10:16; 47; 66:7; 93; 96—99; 145; Jer 10:10), also extends into the Gospels implicitly through references to the "kingdom of God" and "kingdom of heaven."

The Lucan parables portray God as a woman working leaven into bread, a stereotypically "female" activity (Luke 13:21). Some of the parables describing God fit the Lucan pattern of so-called gender pairs—pairings of a story about a male character with a similar story about a female character. In Luke 15, for example, God is pictured as a woman seeking a lost coin (15:8–10), and then as a father rejoicing over his son's return (15:11–32).

Gendered imagery for Jesus. Inextricably connected to the imagery of God as Father is the prevailing Gospel metaphor of Jesus as Son. God explicitly calls Jesus his "beloved son," the "chosen" one (Mark 1:11; 9:7//Matt 3:17; 17:5//Luke 3:22; 9:35). Despite later Trinitarian formulations, the Gospels emphasize the Son's submission to the Father (Mark 14:36//Luke 22:42; John 5:19, 20, 30; 6:38; 7:16; 12:49; 14:31; 15:10). Some scholars have argued that this obedience feminizes Jesus, while others insist that this strictly refers to his position vis-à-vis God while fulfilling his earthly mission. Jesus's sonship is further developed through a thinly veiled allusion in the parable of the wicked tenants, where the tenants kill the heir (Jesus), whom the vineyard owner (God) sends to collect his share of the crops (Matt 21:33–43//Mark 12:1–12//Luke 20:9–19).

In addition to relational metaphors, the Gospels also apply imagery used for God directly to Jesus. Like God the Father, Jesus is depicted as a master (John 15:15–20) over members of his household (*oikodespotes* in Matt 10:24–25; 13:24–30, 36–43; Luke 12:39, 13:25–27; *kurios* in Matt 10:24–25; 24:45–51; 25:14–30; Luke 12:35–48; John 13:16). Jesus appears as the sower of seed, where the good seed are "children of the kingdom" (Matt 13:24–30, 36–43). Jesus also refers to himself metaphorically in stereotypically male roles and vocations: at times he is a bridegroom, whose presence alludes to messianic times

(Matt 9:15; implied in 25:1–13; Mark 2:19–20; Luke 5:34–35; John 3:29). Elsewhere, he is a king (Matt 25:34–46) or a shepherd (Matt 25:32; Luke 15:1–7; John 10:11, 14). In Luke 19:11–27, a nobleman leaves home to claim royal power; many have taken this as an allusion to Jesus's own impending departure.

Still, Jesus is not only associated with masculine imagery. Jesus himself uses maternal imagery, lamenting over Jerusalem, "O Jerusalem, Jerusalem! How often would I have gathered your children together as a hen gathers her brood under her wings, and you would not" (Matt 23:37//Luke 13:34). Elsewhere, a woman blesses Jesus by blessing his mother—a common Greek circumlocution. Using a gendered metonymy, she cries, "Blessed is the womb that bore you and the breasts at which you nursed!" (Luke 11:27).

John's particularly rich repository of imagery has been interpreted variously with respect to gender. John's Jesus is called the "Logos," a particularly complex Greco-Roman philosophical concept. Typically translated "the Word," Logos signifies reason/thought/idea/wisdom (1:1–3, 14) and has generative power (1:3, 10), though note that the latter references use the general term *ginomai* ("to come from/originate from"), not the specific term for conception and birth (*gennaō*). Many scholars argue that John's depiction of the masculine Logos becoming flesh in a male Jesus eclipses the feminine Sophia (Wisdom) tradition found in Matthew and Luke (Matt 11:19; Luke 7:35, 11:49). Others, however, discern similarities between the Johannine Jesus and images of Sophia elsewhere in contemporaneous literature.

Barbara Reid asserts that John's symbolic imagery transgresses conventional gender expectations "throughout the whole gospel" (2011, p. 191). For instance, John uses birthing language (*gennaō*) to describe God begetting spiritual children (1:13; 3:3–8; cf. 16:21). When a soldier pierces the crucified Jesus, blood and water flow from his side—the two fluids integral to the birth experience (19:34); theologically, Jesus's death "births" new life for Christians. In John 7:38, Jesus refers to the source of living water as *koilia*, a term usually translated "belly," but used elsewhere to indicate a mother's womb (e.g., Matt 19:12; Luke 1:41, 42, 44; 2:21; 11:27;

23:29; John 3:4). For some, the ambiguity suggests that, as the source of the Holy Spirit who nourishes believers, Jesus is like the mother who nourishes her child. Another image often connected with (feminine) nourishment is Jesus's reference to himself as the "bread of life" (John 6:35, 48, 51).

Queer readings focus on Gospel passages with homoerotic undertones (e.g., John 13:23, where the Beloved Disciple reclines on Jesus's bosom, or John 19:26–27, where Jesus establishes a new "family of choice," just as homosexual couples do today). Some propose that Mark's "naked young man" was Jesus's lover (Mark 14:50–52). Queer theology reads Jesus's resurrection as God's "coming out"; whereas closeted bodies are dead, coming out engenders freedom, truth, and new life.

Gendered imagery for the Holy Spirit. The Holy Spirit has long been considered feminine. Although in Greek "Holy Spirit" is neuter, some ancient church traditions (like the Syriac church) used feminine pronouns, probably because in Hebrew, "Holy Spirit" is feminine. As Jesus teaches Nicodemus, the Spirit metaphorically gives birth to new believers (John 3:3–13; cf. 1:13); this creative, life-giving force often is understood as maternal. Portraying physical birth as a metaphor for spiritual rebirth, Jesus's evocative teachings in John 3 are deepened by the double meaning of the terms "spirit" (*pneuma*), also translated "wind," and "born again" (*gennaō anōthen*), also translated "born from above" (John 3:3, 7).

In each Gospel, the Holy Spirit descends "like a dove" at Jesus's baptism (Matt 3:16–17//Mark 1:10//Luke 3:22//John 1:32–33). Though "dove" is not explicitly gendered in the Gospels, for ancient Mediterranean readers, the image may have evoked the well-known iconographic uses of the dove as a symbol of feminine fertility generally and of the goddess Asherah specifically.

Gendered Imagery for the Christian Community. Historically, the Christian community has been conceived in feminine terms, partly because the Greek word for church, *ekklēsia* ("civic assembly," Matt 16:18; 18:17; Acts 5:11; Rom 16:5; 1 Cor 1:2; Eph 1:22; 3:10; Heb 12:23), is grammatically feminine. Still, kaleidoscopic clusters of gendered images for the Christian community emerge in the Gospels, and while several of these are gendered, inconsistencies abound. Broadly, we find familial, pastoral, and national images, as well as gendered social categories and characters that represent the church symbolically.

Familial images. Many components of the Gospels' depictions of the Christian community coalesce under the rubric of familial imagery. For instance, when Jesus is called the "bridegroom," by implication, the church becomes the "bride of Christ" (Matt 9:15; 25:1–13; Mark 2:19–20; Luke 5:34–35; John 3:29), an image also applied to God's people in the Hebrew Bible (Isa 62:5; Jer 2:2; Hos 2:16–20).

Jesus often discounts biological families to emphasize spiritual kinship (Matt 10:21, 35, 37; 12:46–50; 19:29; 23:8; Mark 3:31–35; 10:29–30; 13:12; Luke 8:19–21; 14:26; 18:29; 21:16). Additionally, while God is consistently depicted as the father, his people concomitantly are cast as "sons of God" (Matt 5:9), "sons of the resurrection" (Luke 20:36), and heirs of eternal life (Matt 19:29). Though daughters were not primary heirs in a patriarchal culture, their honor was valued as a reflection of the father's honor. Jesus uses "daughter of Abraham" as a term of endearment (Luke 13:16), and employs a similar Hebrew idiom for the inhabitants of Jerusalem: "the daughter of Zion" (Matt 21:5). Several times, Jesus refers to the people of God using gender-inclusive terms for "child/ren" (Matt 2:18; 3:9; 7:11; 9:2; 10:21; 11:25; 15:26; 18:3–5; 19:14, 29; 21:16; 23:37; Mark 7:27–28; 9:37; 10:14–15, 24, 29; 13:12; Luke 3:8; 6:41–42; 7:35; 9:47–48; 10:21; 13:34; 14:26; 15:32; 17:3; 18:16–17, 29; 19:44; 22:32; John 1:12; 8:39; 11:52). Jesus also uses fraternal imagery (though note that in Greek, "brothers" often was gender-inclusive, "brothers and sisters") to describe spiritual unity within the family of God (Matt 5:22–24; 7:3–5; 18:15, 21, 35; 20:17; 21:23; 25:40; 28:10). This Matthean metaphor depicts an entire spiritual family: "For whoever does the will of my Father in heaven is my brother and sister and mother" (Matt 12:50).

Pastoral images. The Gospels commonly draw ecclesiological imagery from the natural world; scholars debate the gendered dimensions of such references. For example, when Jesus is the good shepherd, God's people are the flock (Matt 7:15; 9:36; 10:6, 16;

12:11; 15:24; 18:12; 25:32–33; 26:31; Mark 6:34, 14:27; Luke 12:32, 15:4–6; John 10:2–27, 21:15–17). Behind this image may be the common ancient identification of sheep (men's animals) with masculinity (honor, strength, superiority) and goats (women's animals) with femininity (shame, weakness, inferiority); such thought patterns would render passages like Jesus's allegory of the final judgment thoroughly gendered (Matt 25:31–46).

Jesus's juxtaposition of the "lilies/flowers," who "do not spin" (Matt 6:28//Luke 12:27), with the "ravens/birds," who "do not reap" (Matt 6:26//Luke 12:24), has been read as gendered imagery: the lilies are associated with the "female" task of sewing clothes, while the birds are associated with the "male" task of reaping the harvest. Another possibly gender-related agricultural image is Jesus's extended metaphor in John 15:1–6, where he insists that only "branches" (believers) that abide in the "vine" (Jesus) will "bear fruit" (live abundantly). Although scholars typically agree that this passage draws upon the common Hebrew Bible idiom that the people of God are a vine or vineyard (e.g., Isa 5:1–7), they disagree over whether this image should be read as celebrating female sexuality (Song 1:6), dehumanizing women as commodities valued for fertility (Ps 128:3), or gender-neutral.

National-religious images. Ancient Israelites commonly spoke of "Zion" in feminine terms, while "Israel" was typically masculine. The early church adopted the name "Israel" for itself (Matt 15:24; Luke 2:32, 34; Mark 12:29), along with synonyms closely related to the male gender (e.g., "circumcision," "the patriarchs," "Abraham and his posterity," "the twelve tribes," Matt 3:9; 8:11–12; Luke 1:55; 3:8; 13:28–29; John 7:22). Twice in the Gospels, we find the idiomatic phrase "daughter of Zion" referring to God's people (Matt 21:5; John 12:15). Congruous with national-religious language is the implication that God rules over the heavenly kingdom (e.g., Matt 18:1–35; 22:1–10; 25:1–13).

Gendered categories used symbolically. Complex historical ambiguities notwithstanding, the Gospels portray gendered social categories as representatives of certain groups, or of particular virtues or vices. For example, widows emblematically represent society's poor, vulnerable, and marginalized

insofar as they depended upon patriarchal social systems (Matt 22:24; Mark 12:19, 40; Luke 4:25; 7:12; 20:28, 47). At the same time, widows embody virtues such as selflessness, generosity, and persistence in prayer (Mark 12:41–44//Luke 21:1–4; Luke 2:36–37, 18:1–8; 21:1–3).

Jesus utilizes another gendered social category in the parable of the wise and foolish virgins (Matt 25:1–13), which is likely grounded in the Hebrew Bible picture of the Jewish people waiting dutifully for God, their bridegroom. Note that a similar contrast between wisdom and folly can be found, though differently gendered, in the simile of the wise man who builds his house on rock and the fool who builds his house on sand (Matt 7:24–26//Luke 6:48–49).

Jesus describes discipleship using a mix of gendered images. In John 16:20–22, Jesus likens the disciples' suffering at the crucifixion to a woman in labor: both experiences entail suffering but end in joy. Elsewhere, Jesus teaches his followers to reveal the truth and wait expectantly for his return by comparing them to the master of a house (Matt 13:52; 24:43//Luke 12:39). To illustrate the cost of discipleship, Jesus employs the images of a tower builder planning his work and a king preparing for battle—both stereotypically male domains (Luke 14:28–32).

Using the gender-ambiguous category of the eunuch, Jesus commends those who "become eunuchs" (usually interpreted as embracing celibacy and self-control) for the gospel (Matt 19:12). This saying has been read as a direct challenge to Roman cultural notions of masculine privilege (Kuefler, 2001) and/or as Jesus "queering" normative heterosexual conceptions of the family. Others consider Jesus's affirmation of eunuchs to represent acceptance for all who have (what some consider) physical abnormalities.

Specific characters who function symbolically. Many Gospel characters have been interpreted as paradigms for virtue or vice. Jesus himself uses a female character this way when he refers to Lot's wife (alluding to Genesis 19:26) as a negative example (Luke 17:32). Still, whether the people populating the Gospels' pages conform to or transgress gender expectations remains the subject of much scholarly debate.

Jesus's virgin mother, Mary, epitomizes godly obedience; when Jesus commits her to the Beloved Disciple's care in John 19:26–27, some scholars see her as symbolizing the (feminine) Johannine community, entrusted to the leadership of the (male) Beloved Disciple (Malina and Rohrbaugh, 1998, pp. 272–273). Martha's sister Mary has been read as the church, learning silently at Jesus's feet (Luke 10:38–42) and waiting dutifully for her messiah/bridegroom to call her (John 11:20, 28–29).

The disciples on the Emmaus road have been read as "queer" representatives of the church: outside the male Jerusalem leadership circle, they recognize Jesus in the breaking of the bread (the brokenness of their experience), and, as Goss writes, they have a "natural gift of queer hospitality" (Guest et al., 1996, p. 545).

In contrast to the people of God as a wise, faithful virgin, the Hebrew Bible depicts foolishness as an adulterous temptress (e.g., Dame Folly versus Lady Wisdom in Proverbs 9). The Gospels implicitly connect a temptress with folly when Herodias convinces Herod to behead John the Baptist (Mark 6:14–29; Matt 14:1–12). On the other hand, the Gospels challenge such associations by including women known for their sexual indiscretions in Jesus's genealogy (Matt 1:1–17; Luke 3:23–28), through Jesus's commendation of the "sinner in the city" who anoints his feet (Luke 7:36–50), and through Jesus's forgiveness of an adulteress (John 8:1–11; though note that the earliest and best Greek manuscripts do not contain this pericope).

Gendered Imagery for the End Times. Jesus uses gendered imagery to describe the eschaton: the end times will be like "birth pains" (Mark 13:8//Matt 24:8) and will be especially hard for pregnant or nursing women (Matt 24:19). To underscore the horror of coming calamities, Jesus reverses typical associations of barrenness with judgment, declaring that barren women will be grateful for their childlessness (Luke 23:29).

In addition to childbirth imagery, Jesus describes the Son of Man's sudden return this way: "There will be two women grinding grain together; one will be taken and the other left" (Luke 17:35//Matt 24:41). If this is paired with the saying about the men in the field (Luke 17:36//Matt 24:40; though the earliest and best Lucan manuscripts do not contain this saying), this could indicate that gender will be unimportant at the end of the age; in the meantime, gender roles are upheld (Luke 17:20–37//Matt 24:29–44).

[*See also* Deity, *subentry* New Testament; Gender; Jesus; Masculinity and Femininity, *subentry* New Testament; Queer Readings; *and* Queer Theory.]

BIBLIOGRAPHY

Conway, Colleen M. *Behold the Man: Jesus and Greco-Roman Masculinity.* New York: Oxford University Press, 2008.

Foxhall, Lin. *Studying Gender in Classical Antiquity.* Cambridge, U.K.: Cambridge University Press, 2013.

Guest, Deryn, Robert E. Goss, Mona West, and Thomas Bohache, eds. *The Queer Bible Commentary.* London: SCM, 2006.

Kuefler, Mathew. *The Manly Eunuch: Masculinity, Gender Ambiguity, and Christian Ideology in Late Antiquity.* Chicago: University of Chicago Press, 2001.

Lee, Dorothy A. *Flesh and Glory: Symbolism, Gender and Theology in the Gospel of John.* New York: Crossroad, 2002.

Malina, Bruce J., and Richard L. Rohrbaugh. *Social-Science Commentary on the Gospel of John.* Minneapolis: Fortress, 1998.

Minear, Paul S. *Images of the Church in the New Testament.* Philadelphia: Westminster, 1960.

Nasrallah, Laura, and Elisabeth Schüssler Fiorenza. *Prejudice and Christian Beginnings: Investigating Race, Gender, and Ethnicity in Early Christianity.* Minneapolis: Fortress, 2009.

Neyrey, Jerome. "Jesus, Gender, and the Gospel of Matthew." In *New Testament Masculinities*, edited by Stephen D. Moore and Janice Capel Anderson, pp. 43–66. Semeia Studies 45. Atlanta: Society of Biblical Literature, 2003.

Patella, Michael F. *The Gospel According to Luke.* New Collegeville Bible Commentary, New Testament 3. Collegeville: Liturgical Press, 2005.

Reid, Barbara. "Birthed from the Side of Jesus (John 19:34)." In *Finding a Woman's Place: Essays in Honor of Carolyn Osiek*, edited by David L. Balch and Jason T. Lamoreaux, pp. 191–214. Eugene, Ore.: Pickwick, 2011.

Ryken, Leland, James C. Wilhoit, and Tremper Longman III. *The Dictionary of Biblical Imagery.* Downers Grove, Ill.: InterVarsity, 1998.

Seim, Turid Karlsen. *The Double Message: Patterns of Gender in Luke-Acts.* Edinburgh: T&T Clark, 1994.

Van der Watt, Jan G. *Family of the King: Dynamics of Metaphor in the Gospel According to John.* Leiden, The Netherlands: Brill, 2000.

Michal Beth Dinkler

Pauline Literature

Paul makes abundant use of bodily and familial imagery and social tropes, all of which are gendered in complex ways. These may be broken down into familial and household metaphors, military and athletic metaphors, and body language. Such gendered imagery is not to be confused with Paul's practices and teaching in regard to women and men, but it does introduce the question of its effects in the early churches and the subsequent reception history of the Pauline literature.

Family Metaphors. Paul uses both paternal and maternal metaphors to talk about God and about himself, as well as sibling language to address the members of his churches. The references to God as father are ubiquitous, while Paul's references to himself as father are relatively rare. Conversely, maternal references to God are rare, occurring primarily through echoes of prophetic texts, while maternal imagery for Paul's own ministry occurs with roughly the same frequency as his paternal self-references.

Paternal imagery. Paul occasionally refers to himself as the father of his congregations. This imagery is more complex than may be immediately evident, however. Thus, for example, he uses the masculine sense of the verb "to beget" (*gennaō*) to denote the event of conversion, whether through his own preaching or that of others (Phlm 10; 1 Cor 4:14–15; Gal 4:23, 29); insofar as this denotes a punctiliar event more than an ongoing relationship, it is not precise to translate the verb as "I became your father" (Phlm 10; 1 Cor 4:15b). Paul does, however, call himself "father" in relationship to the churches he founded, albeit rarely. In 1 Corinthians 4:15a he invokes his paternal authority to issue a call to imitation, in line with the widespread Greco-Roman view that the father is to be a role model for his children.

Hence in 1 Thessalonians 2:11–12 Paul says that he and his coworkers Sylvanus and Timothy dealt with the Thessalonians "like a father with his children" by encouraging them to lead a life worthy of God. So also in Philippians 2:22 the metaphor of father-son relationship denotes intimacy in service of the Gospel. Similarly, in the deutero-Pauline 1 Timothy 5:1, speaking to someone as to a father is contrasted with harsh treatment.

In accordance with Jewish tradition, Paul also refers to Abraham as "father"; Abraham is the father of Israel. In Paul's interpretation of the Abrahamic traditions, however, Abraham is the father of all who believe in Christ, whether circumcised or uncircumcised (Rom 4:11–12, 16–18; Gal 3:29).

By far the most frequent use of "father" in Paul's letters denotes God (twenty-two times in the undisputed letters, and seventeen times in the deutero-Pauline letters, including Colossians). The source of this paternal language for God is debated. There are precedents in Judaism, although relatively few. For example, using the language of royal adoption, God promises to be a father to the house of David (2 Sam 7:14; cf. Pss 2:7; 89:26–27) and is addressed as the father of Israel (Isa 63.16; 64:8; Jer 31:9 [38:9 Septuagint (LXX)]). In Hosea 11:1 God says, "Out of Egypt have I called my son." The term implies a relationship between God and God's chosen people, and thereby denotes a history characterized by protection, deliverance, covenant, judgment, mercy, and promise. Paul evokes this history explicitly when he says of his fellow Jews, "To them belong the adoptive sonship [*huiothesia*], the glory, the covenants, the giving of the law, the worship, and the promises" (Rom 9:4, lit.). The question is how much this history is invoked every time Paul calls God "father." Insofar as in Paul's usage elsewhere the language of adoption includes gentiles, as well as Jews, as God's adopted children through baptism into Christ (Gal 4:5–6; Rom 8:15–17), Paul refigures the meaning of God's identity as "father" Christologically. This does not leave behind Israel's history, but rather includes gentile Christians in that history, even as Christ is in Israel's story. Hence Paul can say to the gentile Corinthians, "*Our* fathers were all under the cloud, and all passed through the sea....For they drank from the spiritual rock which followed them, and the Rock was Christ" (1 Cor 10:1–4; emphasis added).

Whether Paul's frequent designation of God as father derives from traditions about Jesus's own practice is difficult to say. Insofar as Paul's letters predate the writing of the Gospels, they are our first written evidence that early Christians called God "father." At the same time, it is intriguing to note that the phrase "Abba father" occurs only in Galatians 4:6 and Romans 8:15, each time attributed to the active presence of the Holy Spirit in human hearts, and in Jesus's prayer in Gethsemane in Mark 14:36. Did the author of Mark know Paul's letters, or do these texts jointly attest to an earlier Jesus tradition? Furthermore, insofar as Paul refers to God as "the father of our Lord Jesus Christ" (Rom 15:6; 2 Cor 1:3, 11:31; cf. Col 1:30; Eph 1:3), he links the designation either to the usage of Jesus, a statement about Jesus's identity in relationship to God, or both. Furthermore, at times Paul claims that those who are baptized into Christ share in Christ's sonship and thereby call God "father." "In Christ Jesus you are all sons of God through faith" (Gal 3:26); through receiving adoption as children (*huiothesia*) believers receive the Spirit of God's son in their hearts, crying "Abba father" (Gal 4:5–6; Rom 8:15). Whether or not the terminology comes from earliest Christian practice dating back to Jesus, it seems clear that Paul linked the naming of God as father to union with Christ.

Maternal imagery. Paul refers to his own ministry with explicitly maternal imagery in three places: One Thessalonians 2:7, linked to his first use of the term "apostle"; 1 Corinthians 3:1–3; and Galatians 4:19. He also uses maternal metaphors to denote the labor of creation (Rom 8:22), and the labor-free childbearing of "Jerusalem above" who is "our mother" (Gal 4:26–27). The imagery is diverse and richly allusive, with echoes of prophetic texts from Israel's scripture on the one hand and appeals to the daily experience of life in the Roman Empire on the other.

Infants and nurses. One Thessalonians 2:7 contains a variant in the earliest manuscripts. Some manuscripts read, "We became gentle among you, like a nurse caring for her children." Others read, "We

became infants among you, like a nurse caring for her children." The difference in Greek between "gentle (*ēpioi*)" and "infants (*nēpioi*)" is one letter, suggesting the ease with which a scribal error could be made. External textual evidence points to the priority of "infants" as Paul's intent, although the struggle to make meaning of the text has led scholars and translators to adopt "gentle" (NRS, RSV, NAB, NASB, NEB). Giving weight to the external evidence, however, suggests that Paul employs a mixed, highly gendered, and countercultural metaphor to amplify the meaning of his first use of the term "apostle" in reference to himself and his coworkers (Gaventa, 2007). If so, then the term "infants" contrasts the apostles' guilelessness with the characteristics of charlatans: greed, flattery, and praise mongering (1 Thess 2:6–7a; cf. 1 Cor 14:20). The term "nurse" evokes the widespread presence of nurses in the empire and their reputation as nurturing, intimate caretakers of young children. The combination of two such contrasting images in one mixed metaphor suggests not only the fluidity of Paul's appropriation of familial metaphors—especially since a few verses later he will refer to himself as a father to the Thessalonians (1 Thess 2:11)—but also the new relational dynamics present in the metaphorical family grouping of those who belong to Christ. Here family metaphors serve not to reify existing social structures but to destabilize them.

Mother's milk. In 1 Corinthians 3:1–3 Paul employs mother and child metaphors somewhat differently. Here the image of children (*nēpioi*) denotes immaturity rather than innocence: the Corinthians are still children who need milk rather than solid food. Paul, however, is again like a nurse, in that he is the one who provides milk. Whereas the metaphor of milk versus solid food is frequent in both Jewish and pagan writing (Philo, *That Every Good Person Is Free*, 160; *On the Preliminary Studies*, 19; Epictetus, *Discourses*, 2.16.49), the designation of oneself as a nursing mother is not, perhaps because it would subvert one's identity as a "real man" (*sklēros anēr*; cf. Aristotle, *Physiognomonics* 807a–b). Paul, however, seems willing to appropriate such a countercultural self-description in line with the more radically countercultural message he proclaims—the reign of a crucified lord (Gaventa, 2007). Thus his maternal self-description expresses the lowly status he exhibits as a spectacle to the world, foolish, weak, disreputable, poor, and hungry (1 Cor 4:9–14).

As in 1 Thessalonians 2, this lowly imagery paradoxically leads directly into Paul's self-designation as a "father" to his converts. Paul writes "to admonish you as my beloved children" (*hōs tekna mou agapēta*) and immediately adds, "For though you may have ten thousand pedagogues, you do not have many fathers. But in Christ Jesus I begot you through the Gospel" (1 Cor 4:14–15, lit.). And while the image of a nursing mother evokes the experience of intimate care and provision, the image of the father leads to two culturally familiar exhortations: a call to imitate the father rather than, by implication, other purported leaders (1 Cor 4:16–17), and a threat of corporal punishment when Paul visits the recalcitrant Corinthians (1 Cor 4:21; cf. 2 Cor 11:2). Yet the preferred mode of Paul's appearance is not "with a rod" but with the feminine quality of "a spirit of gentleness." And his "ways in Christ" to be imitated are his downward social mobility for the sake of the Gospel.

It thus appears that Paul utilizes gendered cultural tropes in paradoxical ways as he presents and defends his apostolic authority in the service of a fleshly, crucified Lord. He willingly assumes the lower status and vulnerability of women, slaves, and children, yet he also asserts his authority in masculine terms. On balance, however, the traditional marks of male power are reframed through the message Paul preaches, his own physical and mental sufferings, and his valorization of weakness. The Paul who threatens the Corinthians with a rod is also the Paul who himself has been beaten with rods, as well as flogged, stoned, made homeless, exposed to the elements, and afflicted with anxiety, and who in the midst of all this chooses to "boast of my weakness" (2 Cor 11:24–30).

Labor pains. In Romans 8:22, the metaphor of labor pains signifies the groaning and distress of the created order as it awaits deliverance from futility and death (cf. also 1 Thess 5:3). The metaphor dates back at least to Homer's depiction of battle (*Iliad* 11.268–272), and is frequent in the prophetic texts. It denotes the intense terror and agony of those who suffer the depredations of war, whether as soldiers, as the citizens of the mother city, or indeed as the mingled lament of the prophet and the LORD (Jer 8:21). Notably, in Isaiah 42:13–14 the LORD both "goes forth like a soldier" and says, "I will cry out like a woman in labor, I will gasp and pant. I will lay waste mountains and hills." The imagery thus combines both masculine and feminine characteristics in one intense metaphor. Isaiah 45:10 even more explicitly combines paternal and maternal imagery by addressing God as both a father who begets and a mother who labors. Such combined imagery for God also occurs in the Dead Sea Scrolls (1QHᵃ 17:35–36; Eastman, 2007).

Paul himself also suffers maternal "labor" with the Galatians, whom he calls "my children" (*tekna mou*; Gal 4:19). Here the metaphor draws on prophetic images both of Jerusalem the mother city and of God as the one who miraculously brings the people of God to birth, even in the face of barrenness and human futility. Possibly Paul is echoing Isaiah 45:9–11, noted above. Shortly thereafter in Galatians 4:27, Paul quotes Isaiah 54:1 to depict the heavenly Jerusalem as a mother city who miraculously bears children without experiencing labor pains, and in fact, without a man. This miraculous childbirth signifies the birth of the Galatian churches through God's faithfulness to the promise to Abraham, rather than through merely human—indeed masculine—agency. In the context of Galatians, Paul is refiguring the story of Sarah and Hagar from Genesis 16: Hagar was a slave woman who bore Abraham a son, Ishmael; Sarah was Abraham's barren wife who subsequently bore Isaac. Both Hagar and Sarah signify mother cities, one in slavery and the other free; one with children/inhabitants through merely human, indeed masculine, means and the other only by divine power and faithfulness. The gendered imagery is complex and susceptible to a variety of interpretations, but at the very least it valorizes the miraculous power of God over merely human agency, and it uses the ancient trope of a barren mother to do so.

Language of the household. Paul's use of parental language serves a polemical purpose insofar as it militates against divisions in his communities, particularly between Jewish and gentile believers. It is as "sons of God" through baptism into Christ that believers are also Abraham's offspring and therefore heirs of God's promises to Abraham (Gal 3:26; 3:29, cf. Rom 8:15–17). The language of sonship here confers the status of heirs; that it does not exclude women is clear from the intervening claim that in Christ there is "not male and female" (Gal 3:28 lit.). Indeed, when Paul quotes 2 Samuel 7:14 in 2 Corinthians 6:16 he not only changes the singular "you" to a plural, but also adds the phrase "and daughters" to the promise, thereby reading "I will be a father to you, and you will be sons and daughters to me" (lit.).

Paul also frequently uses the neuter plural term "children" (*tekna*) to address believers, both as God's children and as his own children (cf. Rom 8:16–21; 1 Cor 4:14–17; 2 Cor 6:14; Gal 4:19). Overwhelmingly, however, Paul uses the term "brothers" (*adelphoi*) to address his fellow believers. As part and parcel of the familial metaphors throughout Paul's letters, this terminology locates Paul's addressees in a fictive kinship group that provides a new relational matrix for both gentile and Jewish Christ-believers. This new place of belonging entails both a support system and obligations, as indicated by the metaphor of brotherly relationship. It is a matter of scholarly debate whether the masculine metaphor included women as individuals with their own gifts and standing or whether women were simply viewed as adjuncts to the male members of the congregation. Given, however, that women clearly had distinctive leadership roles in Paul's churches, and that he addressed some of them by name, the former seems more likely (cf. Rom 16:1–15; 1 Cor 1:11; Phil 4:2). The question remains, however, how the imagery functioned. That it did not foster simple equality between Paul and his converts is evident from the fact that he never refers to himself as a brother (Aasgaard, 2004). Rather, the language appears to warrant his calls to mutual acceptance within the fellowship (Rom 14:10–21); it binds the new believers into a primary social group that surpasses other bonds.

"Masculine" Metaphors. In addition to the familial imagery throughout his letters, Paul employs two cultural tropes associated with "real men": the soldier at war and the athlete.

Soldier. Paul calls on his converts to be "soldiers" in the service of Christ when he exhorts them to present their bodily members to God as "weapons (*hopla*) of righteousness" (Rom 6:13). He uses the same imagery in 2 Corinthians 6:7, where "the weapons of righteousness for the right hand and for the left" are elements in a lengthy description of his ministry as a "servant of God" (2 Cor 6:4). The exhortation combines both high-status and low-status descriptors: "in honor and dishonor, in ill repute and good repute" (2 Cor 6:8). This military imagery belongs to Paul's conviction that "the end of the ages has come" (1 Cor 10:11), and that therefore those who are in Christ are enrolled in God's apocalyptic war against the powers of sin and death (1 Thess 5:8; Rom 13:11–12; cf. Eph 5:11). Both women as well as men are enrolled in this war, thereby attributing culturally "masculine" characteristics to women.

In 2 Corinthians 10:3–6, however, Paul writes.

"For though we walk in the flesh we do not wage war according to the flesh. For our weapons [*hopla*] are not fleshly, but have power through God to destroy fortresses. We destroy arguments [*logismoi*] and every proud obstacle raised up against the knowledge of God. We take every thought [*noēma*] captive to the obedience of Christ. We are ready to punish every disobedience when your obedience is complete" (author's translation).

This is heavily gendered language. Paul attributes to himself the role of a soldier, using a common philosophical topos for the virtuous man who erects a fortress of reason within himself against the passions that wage war on the soul (Malherbe, 1989). But Paul reverses the imagery from a defensive posture to an offensive one, in which arguments (*logismoi*) are not the means of defense against passions but the target of Paul's attack. Furthermore, his weapons are not fleshly, but powerful through God. In the larger context of the passage, Paul also defends his "unmanly" appearance, which is "humble" (*tapeinos*—2 Cor 10:1), while his bodily presence is "weak" (*asthenēs*) and his speech (*logos*) is "contemptible" (*exouthenēmenos*—2 Cor 10:12). He brags about beatings that mark his body as "whippable" and therefore of low status (2 Cor 11:23–25; Glancy, 2010). Paul is differentiating his ministry from that of culturally acceptable "manly" preachers, the "super-apostles" (2 Cor 11:5). By implication, the impressive appearance and rhetoric of the "super-apostles" belongs in the category of "fleshly weapons." The warrant for this judgment is none other than Christ himself, whose "gentleness and kindness" are the basis of Paul's appeal to the Corinthians (1 Cor 10:1).

Athlete. Paul also uses the agonistic imagery of the Isthmian Games, which took place near Corinth, to depict the struggles of Christian existence:

> Do you not know that in a race [*en stadiō*] the runners all compete, but only one receives the prize? Run in such a way that you may win it. Every athlete [*agōnizomenos*] exercises self-control [*enkrateuetai*] in all things; they do it to receive a perishable wreath, but we an imperishable one. So I do not run aimlessly, nor do I box as though beating the air; but I punish my body and enslave it, so that after proclaiming to others I myself should not be disqualified. (1 Cor 9:24–27, lit.)

Again, this is heavily gendered imagery, drawing on a widespread philosophical trope of the virtuous man as one who has mastery of himself and his body. In the context of the passage, the imagery supports Paul's call for his converts to exercise self-control and restraint on behalf of their siblings "for whom Christ died" (1 Cor 8:11; cf. Thiselton, 2000). Here true "masculinity" (for both women and men) consists in self-mastery in service to others.

Body Language. For Paul, the disposition of individual physical bodies cannot be separated from their partnership in the larger, metaphorical social "body" of all who have been baptized into Christ. Thus he follows his exhortation to "present your bodies as a living sacrifice to God" with the proclamation, "We, who are many, are one body in Christ, and individually we are members one of another" (Rom 12:15). The imagery is familiar in Hellenistic speeches designed to facilitate social order and harmony (Martin, 1995). For the purposes of gender analysis, of note is Paul's

implicit destabilizing of the social hierarchy, in which women's or effeminate men's bodies were lower than manly men's and were associated with shameful parts of the body. Paul does not explicitly refer to matters of gender. He does, however, insist that "the members of the body that seem to be weaker are indispensable, and those members of the body that we think less honorable we clothe with greater honor, and our less respectable members are treated with greater respect" (1 Cor 12:22–23). He does not do away with differences nor indeed with hierarchy, but he does potentially subvert their effects within relationships in the fellowship.

"Not Male and Female" (Galatians 3:28). It is apparent that Paul combines "masculine" and "feminine" traits, as understood in Greco-Roman culture, in paradoxical ways. This is particularly evident in his self-descriptions: he is weak yet deploys divinely powerful weapons to destroy fortresses; he is infant, nurse, and father; he opposes the "reasonings" of the typical virtuous wise man, yet also exercises the self-control that characterizes such a wise man. He labors like a woman in childbirth; he bears the rod as an authoritative father while also suffering under the rod. He is weak and thereby strong. For Paul these gendered paradoxes derive directly from the identity of Christ, who was "crucified in weakness, but lives by the power of God" (2 Cor 13:4).

[*See also* Family Structures, *subentries on* New Testament *and* Roman World; Masculinity and Femininity, *subentries on* New Testament *and* Roman World; *and* Paul.]

BIBLIOGRAPHY

Aasgaard, Reider. *My Beloved Brothers and Sisters: Christian Siblingship in Paul.* London: T&T Clark, 2004.

Eastman, Susan. *Recovering Paul's Mother Tongue: Language and Theology in Galatians.* Grand Rapids, Mich.: Eerdmans, 2007.

Gaventa, Beverly Roberts. *Our Mother Saint Paul.* Louisville, Ky.: Westminster John Knox, 2007.

Glancy, Jennifer A. *Corporal Knowledge: Early Christian Bodies.* New York: Oxford University Press, 2010.

Harrill, J. Albert. "Invective against Paul (2 Cor 10.10), the Physiognomies of the Ancient Slave Body, and the Greco-Roman Rhetoric of Manhood." In *Antiquity and Humanity: Essays on Ancient Religion and Philosophy Presented to Hans Dieter Betz on His 70th Birthday*, edited by Adela Yarbro Collins and Margaret M. Mitchell, pp. 189–213. Tübingen, Germany: Mohr Siebeck, 2001.

Larson, Jennifer. "Paul's Masculinity." *Journal of Biblical Literature* 123, no. 1 (Spring 2004): 85–97.

Malherbe, Abraham J. *Paul and the Popular Philosophers.* Minneapolis: Fortress, 1989.

Martin, Dale B. *The Corinthian Body.* New Haven, Conn.: Yale University Press, 1995.

Moxnes, Halvor, ed. *Constructing Early Christian Families: Family as Social Reality and Metaphor.* London: Routledge, 1997.

Osiek, Carolyn, and David L. Balch. *Families in the New Testament World: Households and House Churches.* Louisville, Ky.: Westminster John Knox, 1997.

Penner, Todd, and Caroline Vander Stichele, eds. *Mapping Gender in Ancient Religious Discourses.* Leiden, The Netherlands: Brill, 2007.

Thiselton, Anthony. *The First Epistle to the Corinthians: A Commentary on the Greek Text.* Grand Rapids, Mich.: Eerdmans, 2000.

Susan Grove Eastman

INTERSECTIONAL STUDIES

In 1989 Kimberlé Crenshaw introduced and coined a new concept to the study of feminism, women, and gender: Intersectionality. By emphasizing the problematic aspects of feminism's lack of interest in how gender, race, and sex are interlocked and construct each other, intersectionality has become the primary analytic tool that feminist and antiracist scholars deploy for theorizing identity and oppression (Nash, 2008). Some scholars even talk about "the intersectional turn" (Mattsson, 2010, p. 7). Intersectionality has only recently been employed in biblical interpretation, and Elisabeth Schüssler Fiorenza finds it "more than surprising" that scholarship of early Christianity has not embraced the "rich body of critical feminist work on intersectionality" (Schüssler Fiorenza, 2009, pp. 4–5). Although the theory itself is rather new to the field, the concerns of it—that oppression parameters are connected and identities are constructed by complex intersections

of social categories—has been vibrant in feminist biblical interpretation for several decades, as for example articulated by the Hebrew Bible scholar Sarojini Nadar: "racism is sexism is classism is homophobia" (Nadar, 2009, p. 226).

What Is Intersectionality? Within recent interdisciplinary research the concept of intersectionality has gained increasing currency. When white Western feminists in the 1960s and 1970s started to criticize male-centrism, their insights about oppression "as a woman" tended to conflate the experiences of one particular group of women with those of all women. In the early 1980s African American scholar-activists in particular started to question the hegemony of white women within the feminist movement. They argued that the experiences of African-American women are not shaped only by race but also by gender, social class, and sexuality. Awareness of how different social divisions cannot be understood in isolation, but are mutually modifying and reinforcing each other, is central to intersectional studies.

Instead of examining gender, sexuality, race, ethnicity, class, disability, and age as separate categories of oppression, intersectionality explores how these categories overlap and mutually modify and reinforce each other. Every person belongs to more than one category, and faced with discrimination it might be difficult to articulate which correlative system of oppression is at work. Various oppressive mechanisms can work together and create new hierarchies and systems of discrimination.

One important issue to discuss is whether intersectionality, although aiming at highlighting complexity, as an implicit side-effect nevertheless functions to uphold the given categories. Are the categories such as gender, class, and race stable and already given? While it is argued that so-called third-wave feminism has responded to the collapse of the category "women," intersectionality needs the categories as a premise when highlighting overlapping categories. One way out of this dilemma is to use intersectionality to nuance identities and challenge the stability of any group identity. Rather than using impulses from poststructural thinking to argue that categories do not exist, intersectionality can destabilize ancient and modern power structures and ways of organizing identity that employ gender, class, race, and so on. This combination of reading strategies seems to follow recent trends in which interpreters embrace multilayered approaches and prefer to draw on a diversity of theoretical thoughts within the humanities as well as the social sciences.

Intersectionality originates from discourses in which it functioned as a tool to understand discrimination and the subordinated, but it may be employed in order to understand difference in general and how identities are negotiated. To move beyond uniformity and simplification is useful to understand identities, regardless of where a person is located in the hierarchies.

Asking the Other Question. How the concept or theory of intersectionality can contribute to a methodology has been suggested by Mari Matsuda and her way of "asking the other question":

> The way I try to understand the interconnection of all forms of subordination is through a method I call "ask the other question." When I see something that looks racist, I ask, "Where is the patriarchy in this?" When I see something that looks sexist, I ask, "Where is the heterosexism in this?" When I see something that looks homophobic, I ask, "Where are the class interests in this?" (Matsuda, 1990, p. 1189)

Her insights may help us look for what is not necessarily visible at the surface. When readers are enthusiastic about the women at the empty tomb and their role in the oral transmission, for example, Matsuda may challenges us to ask about female slaves or children and those who did not know the language. In addition, intersectionality offers tools to decode complex identity, regardless of where in the hierarchy the character to be discussed can be located. In fact, one of the benefits of intersectionality is that it emphasizes the relational nature of identity and highlights interaction between the categories as a separate object for analysis (Saga, 2011, p. 236–237).

Intersectionality also challenges interpreters to be critical of their own production of knowledge. My scholarly work as a feminist concerns how gender hierarchies work to exclude women, in past and present; however, intersectionality helps one realize that although it is important to be sensitive to issues of marginality, one must also be aware of certain hierarchies. It is not only gender systems that construct dominant discourses, silencing the voices from the margins: sexism, today and in history, overlaps with other systems of discrimination. If interpreters pay attention only to elite women, we risk reproducing and legitimating the oppression of marginalized women and men. Although ancient sources are most interested in the elite, intersectionality can help fill in the gaps by providing tools to unpack the rhetoric of the given text and suggest different ways of reading.

Intersectional Tendencies in Biblical Scholarship. Several interpreters interested in gender mechanisms, working on biblical literature or other ancient texts, have noticed that gender cannot be studied in isolation, although they have not explicitly drawn on the theory of intersectionality. They have indeed asked the other question, to ancient texts as well as to contemporary practices, and challenged biblical scholars who have focused on gender to include more complex perspectives.

Delores Williams (1993) was one of the pioneers in her groundbreaking work on the foreign slave woman Hagar in Genesis, discussing how various power aspects were connected, in past and present, such as color, motherhood, slavery, and gender. Elisabeth Schüssler Fiorenza has contributed significantly to the discussion by highlighting and remembering non-elite women. She talks about kyriarchal/kyriocentric (from the Greek term for lord) in order to "underscore that domination is not simply a matter of patriarchal, gender-based dualism but of more comprehensive, interlocking, hierarchically ordered structures of domination, evident in a variety of oppressions, such as racism, poverty, heterosexism, and colonialism" (Schüssler Fiorenza, 1999, pp. 1–23). Bernadette Brooten's (2010) work on female homoeroticism and slavery, as well as her research project on feminist sexual ethics, represent important contributions in which social categories such as gender, sexuality, class, ethnicity, and religion are connected in mutual ways.

Many biblical characters have complex identities in which several identity categories intersect. A complex web of identity markers construct a cultural complex social environment in which concrete persons with concrete bodies were located. Cross-cutting ties, multiple loyalties, and diverse combination of identities are relevant for describing the environment that biblical interpreters work with. Several identity categories were subject to constant renegotiation, and identity construction often seems to be a work in progress. Even the most prominent person could change status and position during his or her lifespan, due to a variety of reasons. People could move or travel, forced or voluntarily, or could be sick or injured. Jews could be enslaved. A person who was not born a slave could become a slave, but there were also possibilities to be freed from enslavement; the thin line between slave and free was at once an object for fear and hope.

Categories did not operate in isolation but were interconnected and influenced each other. A brief look at the Ethiopian eunuch (Acts 8:26–40) will immediately illustrate these points. What kind of person was this character? As a black, castrated Jewish man on his way home from worship in Jerusalem, he seems to collapse several parameters of gender, ethnicity, and status, and intersectional theory can help us see how the various categories are interlocked and mutually construct each other.

Applying Intersectional Theory in Biblical Interpretation. Intersectionality aims at theorizing intersecting social categories in identity and oppression. What can intersectionality do with biblical studies? Who have tried to apply it in their interpretations?

In the huge amount of reference literature with gender perspectives that have been produced since the mid-1990s, we find several titles such as *Women in the Bible, Biblical Women,* and *Named and Unnamed Women in the Old and New Testament.* Intersectional awareness would examine such overviews and ask the other question: Are slave women counted as women? Can we read between the lines and find invisible non-elite women? How much attention is given to named or privileged women, and how much attention is given to foreign, disabled or enslaved women or girls?

One strong test case is how the two women in Acts 16 are represented. The purple-cloth trader Lydia in Philippi, who prayed together with other women and converted with her whole household (Acts 16:13, 40), is one of the most prominent women in the New Testament. She is always mentioned among New Testament or early Christian women, as an argument for female leadership. But Paul and Silas also meet another woman in Philippi: we read about an ambiguous encounter with an annoying demon-possessed slave girl who is a fortune-teller. Although she cries out loud the truth about Paul and his fellows, Paul heals her, silences her, and her owners get angry (Acts 16:16–18). This rather strange story, among the few in the Luke-Acts tradition in which a woman is reported as a talking agent, has not been given so much attention from feminists as has Lydia's story, probably because she is unnamed, enslaved, and seems to belong to an opposing spiritual tradition than Paul. Intersectional critique would challenge the tendency to highlight Lydia and not the truth-talking slave girl as women of the New Testament (Kartzow, 2012, p. 129–132).

Since 2006 intersectionality has been mentioned occasionally at various sessions at the Society of Biblical Literature, most frequently in papers dealing with stories about Hagar in the Hebrew Bible or in early Christian literature or the Ethiopian eunuch in Acts. Many conversations with neighboring theories, such as queer theory and postcolonial studies, have often taken place.

With the anthology *Prejudice and Christian Beginnings: Investigating Race, Gender, and Ethnicity in Early Christian Studies,* intersectionality as a theoretical concept was given a welcome introduction to the field of biblical studies. The book seeks to continue the conversation started at Harvard Divinity School at a conference titled "Race, Gender, and Ethnicity." In the introduction, the interdisciplinary concept on intersectionality is connected to replacement of the category of "hierarchy" with the neologism *Kyriarchy* (Schüssler Fiorenza, 2009).

In the Scandinavian countries biblical interpreters were influenced by the theoretical work of gender scholars and colleagues who had embraced intersectionality since the early 2000s (De los Reyes and Mulinari, 2005). The interdisciplinary Norwegian research project "Jesus in Cultural Complexity" (2008–2011) wanted to use intersectionality in the study of early Christian texts, and in publications and conferences invited international scholars to participate (Cultural Complexity, 2010).

In the 2013 publication in English and German titled *Doing Gender—Doing Religion: Fallstudien zur Intersektionalität im frühen Judentum, Christentum und Islam*, interdisciplinary and interreligious perspectives are presented, and the connection of intersectionality and the interpretation of religious writings has become a transatlantic dialogue.

Challenging Intersectionality. Although intersectionality obviously has its weak points and pitfalls, it can help interpreters solve essential challenges of complexity when dealing with ancient texts.

One important task—when theories of intersectionality are traveling from studies of oppression and power to interpretation of ancient texts—is to find relevant categories. What categories to include is an ongoing discussion for intersectional thinkers, often marked by adding "etc." to the suggested list of categories. The standard gender, sexuality, class, race, age, and health are not necessarily the most important categories for conceptualizing the ancient society. The relevance of the social categories of gender, race, and class are also contested in interdisciplinary discussions; in postwar and postcommunist context especially the latter two terms may seem problematic. If we use class to theorize the difference between slave and free in antiquity, it has some rather different connotation than in Marxist ideology. The differences or similarities between race and ethnicity, as well as the meaning of these terms vis-à-vis nationality or religion in an ancient context, are indeed complex and need to be discussed when intersectionality is used to interpret biblical texts.

For example, if we want to understand the role of Hagar in the Hebrew Bible, Sarah's slave girl from Egypt who was brought to Abraham because Sarah did not have any children, the category of motherhood would be essential with all its various intersections with slavery, race, and sexuality. Bible interpreters will need to relate stories of her to those of other slave women who gave birth on behalf of their owners, in order to decode how various power structures constructed the vulnerability and destabilizing potential of female slave's reproductive bodies.

Intersectionality offers a language to talk about cultural complexity and our role in the production of knowledge. Jennifer Glancy has pointed out that "intersectional identities are expressed and negotiated through corporal encounters. Through bodies and embodied exchange, cultural complexity *takes place*" (Glancy, 2010, p. 362; Eriksen, 2009).

Applying Intersectionality to Biblical Studies: Two Case Studies. The technique of asking the other question could be used in the interpretation of any given text. When working on Hebrew Bible texts on Joseph in Pharaoh's household in Egypt, for example, intersectionality will help us see that he is a privileged man, although being a Jew and a former slave. In what ways are gender, class, and ethnicity intersecting in the various stories of Joseph?

The following two texts are rich on interlocked categories and intersectionality enable us to theorize identity and oppression.

The parable of the watchful slaves in Luke 12:35–48. In this synoptic parable the master leaves the house and leaves one of his male slaves in charge of the household. This wicked slave calculates that it may take a while before the master returns, and he begins to beat the other slaves and eat and get drunk. The social scenario and household hierarchy represented in the parable generates a whole set of intersectional questions, dealing with social class, gender, generation, and violence.

Both Luke and Matthew (Matt 24:42–51) have this parable, but with different terms for slaves (Matt: *doulos*, Luke: *pais*). Only Luke divides the beaten slaves into male and female (Luke 12:45). Both Evangelists put this parable in the mouth of Jesus, and none of them challenges or condemns the slavery institution and gender divided violence on slave bodies.

If intersectionality is used to theorize how social categories intersect in order to understand identity and oppression, we see that slaves represented the margins of the ancient household. For Luke it also makes sense to divide these marginal characters into male and female, but why does he do this? Does the wicked slave beat female slaves in another way than male? Does this gender divide among slaves aim at describing sexualized violence? Or were also male slaves, whose bodies could be penetrated, equally targets of sexualized violence?

By help of intersectionality there are more challenges to this parable. Lukan terminology opens up for a variety of scenarios: either the trusted slave strikes his fellow slaves, as the synoptic parallel in Matthew says (Matt 24:49), or the trusted slave strikes the children. The phrase in Luke 12:45 can be translated as either "male slaves and female slaves" or as "boys and girls" whom the slave manager starts beating. Such physical punishment was probably common in ancient households, where slave bodies were part of their owner's property, and children had to obey they parents and their caretakers, who could also be slaves.

Overviews or reference books of women or girls in the Bible must include these female slaves, in the same way as the demon-possessed slave girl in Acts 16 should be mentioned alongside Lydia. Female slaves should be made visible as women, who although they were enslaved were also human beings, with reproductive bodies, passion, and pain, with brains, thoughts, ideas, feelings, and dreams. As owned female bodies they had some very specific restrictions and life conditions, and translations should not hide this fact by calling them servants, as if they had a paid work they could choose.

In the parable, Luke constructs ideology and meaning by use of violence and abuse according to power structures in which class, gender, and age intersect. Slavery in antiquity was needed to help free families live proper family lives.

In our age of globalization, class, race, age, and gender also intersect to construct certain power relations, within or outside of families, that which look much like slavery. In addition, the way the Bible can be used in current discussions of family values is of relevance when intersectionality is applied to biblical texts. The conservative nuclear family ideology based on biblical texts faces some major challenges when confronted with early Christian slave bodies, and intersecting structures involving children and women, such as in the Lukan parable. Intersectionality challenges biblical interpreters to ask the other question and theorize the gaps in the ancient sources, in order to engage in structures that uphold hierarchies.

Intersecting categories in Galatians 3:28. The "baptism formula" in Galatians 3:28 ("There is no longer Jew or Greek, there is no longer slave or free, there is no longer male and female; for all of you are one in Christ Jesus") has been called the Credo for feminist theology. By help of intersectionality, and the technique of asking the other question, this verse can be interpreted in specific ways.

This statement in Galatians, within scholarly discussions of equality and hierarchy, is often pitted against the household codes in other letters using a model of pure origins and decline: the household codes represented a reaction against earlier freedom and innovation. The argument goes: Although second- and third-generation Christians took over contemporary patterns of power and dominance, the more authentic Pauline statement (Gal 3:28) functions to reduce or eliminate the hierarchical structure of the household codes.

In the interpretative tradition of Galatians 3:28, nationality/ethnicity, class, and gender are often seen as three separate contrasting categories. The focus is on the binarity or polarity within the three relationship pairs. Intersectionality emphasizes that we cannot add gender to class to ethnicity as representing parallel realities, but we must take into account how the categories mutually influence and construct each other. The statement does not give us three separate contrasts only; we need to couple and combine all of them and then we get eight possible categories:

1. Jewish slave male
2. Jewish slave female

3. Jewish free male
4. Jewish free female
5. Greek slave male
6. Greek slave female
7. Greek free male
8. Greek free female

In theory we can combine these categories, but could they have been combined in practice in Paul's and the Galatians' social environment? We now need to ask the other question(s):

- Taking into account the strong focus on circumcision in the Letter to the Galatians, are the terms "Jew or Greek" here to be understood for males only? Are they meant to be ethnic categories or religious or racial or national?

- If enslavement, at least legally, severed ties to an *ethnos* and *genos*, did it make sense to consider a slave either Jewish or Greek?

- Could slaves be included in the gender relationship pair? Female slaves were categorized as slaves, and not as women, at least in ideal discourses.

- Free is above slave as male is above female in the ancient Mediterranean world, but it is not given who holds privilege and who is subordinated in the relation of Jew and Greek. Does Paul create his own hierarchy here?

- Slave/free and male/female are mutually exclusive, but there were several Greek-speaking Jews in the ancient world.

The point here is that intersectionality may help us see the complexity and lead us to new questions to ask. The verse from Galatians 3:28 is first decoded and theorized by help of intersectionality, and then the new theoretical pattern of eight categories has to be challenged by the other question, up and against what we think we know about the social environment of antiquity. By theorizing identity and oppression in this key verse of the New Testament, intersectionality may give interpreters ideas where to look for new insights.

An Intersectional Turn in Biblical Studies? Intersectionality offers some useful tools when interpreters of the Bible are interested in theorizing oppression and identity. Insisting that categories such as gender, ethnicity, or class cannot be understood in isolation since they are interlocked and construct each other mutually, interpreters are challenged to take into account the extremely complex social environment of the ancient world. The characters we read of in biblical literature, and the way theology, ideology, or history is constructed, are influenced by complex webs of intersecting structures. An "intersectional turn" within the field would represent that some of the complexity and multiplicity of the ancient texts—and their interpreters—would come to the surface as relevant for the production of knowledge for biblical studies.

[*See also* Gender; Patriarchy/Kyriarchy; Race, Class, and Ethnicity *subentry* New Testament; Rhetorical-Hermeneutical Criticism; Sexuality; *and* Womanist Criticism.]

BIBLIOGRAPHY

Brooten, Bernadette J., with Jacqueline L. Hazelton, eds. *Beyond Slavery: Overcoming Its Religious and Sexual Legacies*. New York: Palgrave Macmillan, 2010.

Crenshaw, Kimberlé. "Demarginalizing the Intersection of Race and Sex: A Black Feminist Critique of Antidiscrimination Doctrine, Feminist Theory, and Antiracist Politics." *University of Chicago Legal Forum* 139 (1989): 139–167.

Cultural Complexity and Intersectionality in the Study of the Jesus Movement. Theme issue with contributions from Denise Buell, Jennifer Glancy, Marianne Bjelland Kartzow, and Halvcor Moxnes. *Biblical Interpretation* 18, no. 4–5: (2010).

De los Reyes, Paulina, and Diana Mulinari. *Intersektionalitet: Kritiska reflektioner över (o)jämlikhetens landskap*. Stockholm: Liber, 2005.

Eisen, Ute E., Christine Gerber, and Angela Standhartinger, eds. *Doing Gender—Doing Religion: Fallstudien Zur Intersektionalität im Frühen Judentum, Christentum und Islam*. Tubingen, Mohr Siebeck, forthcoming.

Eriksen, Thomas Hylland. "What Is Cultural Complexity?" In *Jesus Beyond Nationalism: Constructing the Historical Jesus in a Period of Cultural Complexity*, edited by Halvor Moxnes, Ward Blanton, and James G. Crossley, pp. 9–24. London: Equinox, 2009.

Glancy, Jennifer A. "Jesus, the Syrophoenician Woman, and Other First Century Bodies." *Biblical Interpretation* 18, nos. 4–5 (2010): 342–363.

Gressgård, Randi. "Mind the Gap: Intersectionality, Complexity and 'the Event.'" *Theory and Science* 10, no. 1 (2008): 1–15.

Kartzow, Marianne Bjelland. "'Asking the Other Question': An Intersectional Approach to Galatians 3:28 and the Colossian Household Codes." *Biblical Interpretation* 18, nos. 4–5 (2010): 364–389.

Kartzow, Marianne Bjelland. *Destabilizing the Margins: An Intersectional Approach to Early Christian Memory.* Eugene, Ore.: Pickwick; 2012.

Maseno, Loreen Iminza, and Marianne Bjelland Kartzow. "Widows, Intersectionality and the Parable in Luke 18." *International Journal for Sociology and Anthroplogy* 2, no. 7 (2010): 140–148.

Matsuda, Mari J. "Beside My Sister, Facing the Enemy: Legal Theory out of Coalition." *Stanford Law Review* 43 (1990): 1183–1192.

Mattsson, Katarina. "Genua och vithet i den intersekstionella vändingen." *Tidsskrift för genusvetenskap* 1–2 (2010): 7–22.

Moxnes, Halvor, and Marianne Bjelland Kartzow. "Complex Identities: Ethnicity, Gender and Religion in the Story of the Ethiopian Eunuch (Acts 8:26–40)." *Religion and Theology* 17, nos. 3–4 (2010): 184–204.

Nadar, Sarojini. "The Bible in and for Mission: A Case Study of the Council of World Mission." *Missionalia* 37, no. 2 (2009): 210–228.

Nash, Jennifer C. "Re-tinking Intersectionality." *Feminist Review* 89 (2008): 1–15.

Saga, Stine Kiil. "Teologi for hundene?" *Kirke og kultur: Religion og Samfunn* 3 (2011): 229–240.

Schüssler Fiorenza, Elisabeth. *Rhetoric and Ethic: The Politics of Biblical Studies.* Minneapolis: Fortress, 1999.

Schüssler Fiorenza, Elisabeth. "Introduction: Exploring the Intersections of Race, Gender, Status, and Ethnicity in Early Christian Studies." In *Prejudice and Christian Beginnings: Investigating Race, Gender, and Ethnicity in Early Christian Studies*, edited by Laura Nasrallah and Elisabeth Schüssler Fiorenza, pp. 1–23. Minneapolis: Fortress, 2009.

Sengupta, Shuddhabrata. "I/Me/Mine—Intersectional Identities as Negotiated Minefields." *Signs: Journal of Women in Culture and Society* 31, no. 3 (2006): 629–639.

Vander Stichele, Caroline, and Todd Penner. *Contextualizing Gender in Early Christian Discourse: Thinking Beyond Thecla.* London: T&T Clark, 2009.

Verloo, Mieke. "Multiple Inequalities, Intersectionality and the European Union." *European Journal of Women's Studies* 13, no. 3 (2006): 211–228.

Williams, Delores S. *Sisters in the Wilderness: The Challenge of Womanist God-Talk.* Maryknoll, N.Y.: Orbis, 1993.

Yuval-Davis, Nira. "Intersectionality and Feminist Politics." *European Journal of Women's Studies* 13, no. 3 (2006): 193–209.

Marianne Bjelland Kartzow

J

JESUS

Certain scholars explain the presence of women followers in Jesus's retinue on the basis of Jesus's teaching of the Kingdom of God: Jesus's message would have been clearly understood as an explicit challenge to the patriarchal bias of his culture. Schüssler Fiorenza calls this aspect of his message a "critical feminist impulse that came to the fore in the vision and ministry of Jesus" (Schüssler Fiorenza, 1983, p. 107). Some see Jesus's message of the Kingdom similarly and cite his "radical egalitarianism" in the midst of a culture that devalued both women and the poor peasant underclass. Yet, little in the sayings generally considered authentic merits such elaborate claims insofar as women are concerned. Although his teaching demonstrates a clear awareness of poverty and a critique of class inequity in ancient Palestine, it does not show an equivalent of a critique of patriarchy, nor a similar interest in gender concerns. Thus, Jesus's teaching on social issues and the Kingdom of God does not extend to the concerns of women nor was it aimed at a clear social program geared toward major social change for women. As such, it should not be labeled "egalitarian." In fact, Jesus's parables have little interest in "gender" at all, focusing rather on the issues of class. Both women and men in the parables are portrayed as incompetent, but their actions do not challenge gender roles. An overview of Jesus's most famous parables will suffice to make this point.

Women in the Parables of Jesus. The parables of Jesus have long vexed New Testament scholars. Only recently freed from centuries of misleading allegorical interpretations, the parables continue to attract the attention of many serious commentators, and books on the subject have become legion. Most scholars now agree that the parables were not intended to be complex allegories containing several points of reference, but are stories that create their own narrative world. The allegorization of Jesus's parables began early in Christian tradition, a tendency that can be seen in Mark's version of the parable of the Sower (Mark 4:3–20) or Matthew's version of the parable of the Banquet (Matt 22:1–14). Other parables went through a process of alteration either in oral retelling or in written redaction. In spite of this, the parables remain the bedrock of historical information concerning Jesus, as well as the defining center of his proclamation of the Kingdom of God.

Since the parables use images drawn from everyday Palestinian life, women and women's activities occasionally figure as the point of comparison to the Kingdom of God. This leads certain scholars to posit an anti-patriarchal or egalitarian ethic for Jesus's teachings overall. On closer analysis, however, the images and roles of women in Jesus's parables are unexceptional. Stories involving women simply reflect the presence of women in Jesus's social environment; they are told to make points about the Kingdom of God, not about the status of women. Activities such as kneading bread, carrying grain jars, sweeping floors, and grinding meal not only reflect traditional roles of women in ancient society but also their juxtaposition in the gospels over against typical male roles such as planting seeds, shepherding sheep, parenting sons, and reclining on couches for meals reinforces gender roles rather than challenging them (Levine, 1994, pp. 23–24). This arrangement of parables in gendered pairs is arguably secondary to the tradition and reflects either the legal interests of a document like Q or simply the tendency in that social environment toward a gendered division of labor among peasants and the lower classes. Such images reflect everyday situations from ancient Palestine and force the hearer to active thought concerning either the Kingdom of God or the situation described in the story itself.

Recent feminist analysis has drawn attention to the feminine imagery of Jesus's parables, which can be viewed in either a positive or negative light (Durber, 1992, pp. 59–78; Levine, 1994, pp. 25–26; Schottroff, 1995, pp. 79–118; Waller, 1979, pp. 99–109). However, in spite of the tendency among certain feminist scholars to characterize Jesus's overall teaching as anti-patriarchal, the evidence of the parables reveals that Jesus was part of the patriarchal society in which he lived and that he evinced similar patriarchal biases. For example, as Nicola Slee (1984) has pointed out, of the 104 parables and sayings of Jesus in Matthew, 47 involve human actors, with 85 characters in all. Of the 85, 73 are men and 12 are women—5 of whom are foolish maidens. In the 94 parables and sayings in Luke, 51 concern human actors, with 108 characters. Of those 108, 99 are men and 9 are women. Slee is right to caution that the predominance of male characters in Jesus's parables and sayings alone suggests that Jesus, like other speakers and writers of his day, was by nature predisposed to reimagine in his narratives a world dominated by men and their concerns and shows little interest for women and women's concerns (1984, pp. 20–31; Durber, 1992,

p. 69). There are in fact only five parables now arguably considered authentic that utilize images of women: the Leaven (Matt 13:3/Luke 13:20–21/*Gos. Thom.* 96), the Lost Coin (Luke 15:8–9), the Empty Jar (*Gos. Thom.* 97), the Unjust Judge (Luke 18:2–8), and the Prodigal Son (Luke 15:11–32). And of these only four focus on actions of women, since in the last case women are mentioned only briefly as the prostitutes (*pornai*) upon whom the Prodigal Son squanders his money (Luke 15:20). Indeed, the Empty Jar from the *Gospel of Thomas* has only recently been considered in these discussions—a fact that reflects the increasing tendency to include evidence for Jesus's teachings from *Thomas* as equally significant for reconstructions of the historical Jesus.

In spite of the presence of images of women in these parables, it is difficult to argue that the first three demonstrate any subversion of gender roles. Rather, the parables of the Leaven, the Lost Coin, and the Empty Jar underscore common gendered roles from antiquity by creating images of women engaged in everyday activities. Further, the feminine activities described in these parables are not themselves referents for the Kingdom of God.

The Leaven. The parable of the Leaven is assuredly an authentic parable of Jesus. Since *Thomas* has introduced a contrast of the small amount of the leaven with the large size of the leavened loaves (*Gos. Thom.* 96; Funk et al., 1988, p. 29; contra Waller, 1979, p. 10), the version found in Luke 13:20–21/Matt 13:33 (Q) is arguably the earliest. The original parable thus compares the Kingdom of God (or Heaven) to leaven (*zyme*), which a woman (*gynē*) takes and hides (*egkryptō*) in a very large amount of flour until the leaven spreads throughout. The use of "to hide" is surprising in combination with leaven. The verb *phyraō* ("to knead") is more to be expected (cf. Hos 7:4, Septuagint). Scholars have suggested various interpretations of the parable by emphasizing the smallness of the beginnings of the Kingdom in contrast to its later size (Jeremias, 1972, p. 146; Perrin, 1967, pp. 157–158), the mysterious nature of the Kingdom's growth (Jeremias, 1972, p. 146; Perrin, 1967, pp. 157–158), the reversal of expectations of the nature of God's reign (Scott, 1989, pp. 321–329; Funk et al., 1988, p. 29), the culmination of the Kingdom of God in Jesus's ministry (Dodd, 1961, pp. 154–155), or the domestic work of women as an example of the activity of God (Schottroff, 1995, pp. 79–90; Waller, 1979, p. 107).

The most current proponent of the popular pro-female interpretation is Barbara Reid, who in several articles and books has concluded that this parable gives us the "female face of God" (2002, p. 284; 1996, pp. 169–178). This reading of the parable leads to obvious feminist conclusions as God is not only thought of as a man: "Jesus' teaching and praxis contradicts such a notion and invites believers to envision God in such a way that women and men are both seen to reflect God's image equally" (Reid, 1996, p. 176). Further, Reid argues that the woman's working in the leaven is "a metaphor for women exercising roles and ministry that have been traditionally closed to them, especially leadership and decision making" (1996, p. 176). Thus, the corruption of the yeast represents what some will consider a corruptive influence in the church. However, this common reading of the parable is most certainly wrong. Decades ago Amos Wilder pointed out the essentially secular nature of Jesus's parables. The persons, scenes and images are not necessarily "religious" in character (1964, p. 81). Thus, the woman in the parable of the leaven should not be considered an image of God as Reid and others have contended, but simply an ordinary woman, doing an ordinary, everyday activity. The power of the image is its realism.

In any case, however, the parable clearly highlights the images of the leaven and the meal—rather than the woman herself—as the point of comparison for the reign of God. Thus, even though the image is one of women's domestic work, the focus is still the leavening, not the woman. Since leaven was regarded in Judaism as a symbol of corruption (Exod 12:15; Mark 8:15; 1 Cor 5:7), Jesus's comparison of leaven to God's Kingdom is very provocative (Funk et al., 1988, p. 29). Indeed he quite reverses the expectations of his hearers. What appears to be the activity of corruption—the overproduction of leavened bread (Levine, 1994, p. 25, contra Schottroff, 1995, pp. 79–90; Waller, 1979, p. 107)—is essential and characteristic of the reign of God. Thus, the parable turns not on the fact that

this is a woman's activity, or on the unexpected comparison of leaven to divine activity, but to the makeup of the kingdom itself, which includes lower classes and outcasts in Jesus's close circle of followers (Scott, 1989, pp. 321–329). Reid too sees this connotation of the parable, seeing in it an allusion to the kingdom's inclusion of "sinners" and the unclean (Reid, 1996, p. 173; 2002, p. 286). The parable thus highlights Jesus's inclusion of those rejected by the wider society within his group, coming close to the significance of the Feast parable, which also emphasizes the inclusion of outcasts in the kingdom.

The Lost Coin. The Lost Coin (Luke 15:8–10) contains what may be a similar story of domestic incompetence followed by the surprising joy of rediscovery. A woman loses (*apollymi*) one drachma of the ten she has, searches for it, and upon its rediscovery rejoices with her women neighbors. This parable is coupled in Luke with the parable of the Lost Sheep and followed by the parable of the Prodigal Son. In Luke the parable concerns the joy in heaven over human repentance, an interpretation that is widely considered secondary (Crossan, 1992, p. 38). The image is again unexpected. A woman searches diligently for something that on the face of it is of limited intrinsic value. A drachma was a Greek silver coin equal in worth to a denarius, which was a day's pay for a male fieldhand (Schottroff, 1995, p. 92; Scott, 1989, p. 311). Of course the drachma may be worth considerably more to her, since women workers made barely half as much as men for the same amount of manual labor. The single drachma is thus enough for roughly two days of subsistence level support for one person (Schottroff, 1995, p. 94). Some interpreters have proposed that the money was part of the woman's dowry, but nothing in the text suggests this (popularized by Jeremias, 1972, p. 134; rejected by Schottroff, 1995, pp. 95–96; Scott, 1989, p. 311).

Given Luke's context and interpretation, it is difficult to consider the woman a feminine image for God or Jesus. As John Dominic Crossan has said, there is no tradition comparable to John 10:11, "I am the good shepherd," declaring "I am the good housewife" (1992, p. 38). Still, such a reading remains popular, essentially following the Lukan interpretation in which the shepherd, the woman, and the father all represent images of insistent divine activity (Durber, 1992, p. 71; LaHurd, 2002, pp. 66–67, 72; Schottroff, 1995, p. 100). Reid has gone so far as to call the woman "Sophia Incarnate" (Reid, 2002, p. 287; 1996, pp. 179–189). However, it is interesting that even rural women in Yemen showed little interest in the use of the image of the woman as an image for God. Rather they were interested in the act of searching and "reasons for the intensity of the search" (LaHurd, 2002, pp. 66–67). Thus, again, it is best not to assume the woman's activity represents God's activity. The power of the story is its realism, not its religious connotations. This parable rather further associates the reign of God with the unexpected. What appears to be of little value is highly prized, and the kingdom is again associated with the poor, and one might add, the incompetent, but probably not with the unclean (contra Scott, 1989, p. 313; cf. Crossan, 1992, p. 72).

The Empty Jar. The parable of the Empty Jar contains yet another image of womanly inattention or incompetence (*Gos. Thom.* 97): the Kingdom of "the Father" is compared to a woman carrying a full jar of meal. In the *Gospel of Thomas* the Empty Jar is set between the parables of the Leaven (96) and the Assassin (98). The image of the woman is also one of domesticity and failure. Although hardly a clear image of uncleanness simply due to her femaleness, the woman does not notice when her jar is broken and thus loses all of her grain, the basic means of subsistence for the poor in antiquity (Levine, 1994, p. 25). The tension inherent in this story is underscored by a well-known parallel in the Hebrew Bible, the story of the widow of Zarephath (1 Kgs 17:8–16; Waller, 1979, p. 103). In a time of famine Elijah is told to go to the widow of Zarephath who has been commanded to feed him. When Elijah finds her, she tells him that she has nothing prepared and only a small amount of meal and oil. Miraculously, the grain in her jar does not run out and she, her child, and Elijah subsist on cakes baked from her supplies for many days. The Empty Jar parable reverses the story of Elijah and the widow Zarephath: no prophet comes to the woman's aid; her jar remains empty. Once

again, expectations for the reign of God are reversed (Scott, 1989, p. 79). The images of women in these three parables are hardly complimentary. One loses a coin worth two days' sustenance, another spills her grain without noticing it, another overproduces bread; the point of each parable is made at a woman's expense.

The Unjust Judge. The final authentic parable that employs the image of a woman is usually called the Unjust Judge (Luke 18:2–8). Although occasionally named after the widow in the story, the main character in the story is the man (Schottroff titles this parable the Stubborn Widow; 1995, p. 101). In this story, a woman receives justice at court, not because her cause is just nor because the judge she approaches is just but because she is persistent to the point of threatening the judge with a black eye ("she will wear me out," literally "give me a black eye" or "bruise" [*hypopiazō*]). The image is striking to the point of being humorous. The contrast between the social and economic circumstances of the two characters in the story is stark: the judge would be a member of the urban elite, the woman of the urban poor (Scott, 1989, pp. 180–181). In a long history of Jewish tradition, widows belonged to a category of persons who needed special protection from God: "widows, orphans, and foreigners." Israelites were commanded to protect these classes. Just as God protected the Israelites while they were in bondage in Egypt, so he is the patron of the most needy of the Israelite community (Ps 68:5; 146:9; Deut 10:18).

Indeed, the treatment of widows, orphans and foreigners amounted to a gauge for determining the faithfulness of the Jewish people (Deut 24:17–18; Exod 22:21–24; Ezek 22:7; cf. Zech 7:10; Ps 94:6; Isa 1:23; 10:1–2; Jer 5:28).

Many commentators see the parable in terms of the analogy between the judge and God: If a widow can get justice from an unjust judge, how much more likely will God respond to persistent prayer? Luke's appended interpretation encourages this reading (18:6–8; Jeremias, 1972, p. 156) but is probably secondary (Jeremias, 1972, p. 156). Reid also rejects this interpretation, as the judge does not have the right characteristics to represent God, as he is unjust and dishonest (1996, p. 192; 2000, p. 31; 2002, p. 291). Still, she assumes that one of the characters must represent God, and so she decides the figure of God in the story is the woman (Reid, 1996, p. 192; 2000, pp. 31–32; 2002, pp. 292–293). Thus, God as a woman is relentlessly pursuing justice. However, such a pushing of the story in such a theological direction weakens the force of the image, which has its power in its realism and ordinariness. The parable tells us something about the kingdom, not God.

Read without this interpretation, the parable takes on a quite different meaning. The emphasis falls on the woman's unflagging insistence for vindication, not on the action of the judge whose motive is self-interest. The parable portrays a disadvantaged widow gaining justice by her own means, without reliance upon God (Scott, 1989, pp. 186–187). It might fittingly be likened to Luke's parable of the Unjust Steward (16:1–8), in that the overwhelmingly aggressive and even insubordinate behavior of the widow achieves her intended result. Jesus's description of this woman, although hardly complimentary, is in marked contrast to the images of domestic failure in the parables of the Leaven, the Lost Coin, and the Empty Jar. Such a story surely reinforces shrewd, calculated, and resistant behavior on the part of the oppressed and is not merely a metaphor for the continuation of the kingdom (Scott, 1989, pp. 186–187). Still, since the internal monologue is that of the judge, the story reflects not the woman's perspective but the man's.

Men in the Parables of Jesus. The bulk of Jesus's parables focus on male characters. However, little in the representation of men in the parables deviates from ordinary, expected male roles, with the exception, perhaps, of the father in the parable of the Lost Son. The parables with men are similar to the parables with women in that the men are not portrayed in complimentary ways but are often fools. Although the parables using male characters do not necessarily subvert gender roles, there is a balance between the male characters and female characters in that all fail in some way and therefore surprise the audience with their actions.

The Lost Sheep. The parable of the Lost Sheep reflects images common in the heritage of the Hebrew Bible. In the scriptures, the image of the Shepherd is a positive one and occasionally represents the loving care of God, who is likened to a shepherd (Ps 23:1). Shepherds and sheep were no doubt common in a nomadic and agricultural society. However, during the first century, shepherds were marginalized in the culture and to be a shepherd was to be one of the outcasts of society (Bailey, 1983, p. 147; Scott, 1989, p. 405). Thus, in rabbinic literature shepherds are among the forbidden occupations and equated with robbers, as they allow sheep to graze on others' land and essentially steal from them (*m. Qidd.* 4:14; Scott, 1989, p. 413). The image of the Shepherd would thus have not aroused sympathy on the part of Jesus's hearers. No doubt they would have objected to being likened to one.

The parable is found in three versions: Matthew 18:12, Luke 15:4–6, and *Gospel of Thomas* 107. In Matthew, the Shepherd is likened to the leaders of the church, who are not to allow the "little ones" (probably those excommunicated from the congregation; Scott, 1989, p. 406) to perish. This context is so connected to the concerns of the early church that Matthew's version is unlikely to be the most original (Bailey, 1983, pp. 151–153; Scott, 1989, p. 406; contra Linnemann 1982, pp. 65–66). In Luke, the Shepherd represents Jesus, or God, who seeks after the "sinners," especially the "tax collectors and sinners" with whom Jesus seeks to eat. In Luke, the parable is paired with the parable of the Lost Coin, and both parables are told to encourage the Pharisees to join Jesus in his table fellowship with "tax collectors and sinners" (Scott, 1989, p. 407). Luke's context is so convincing that many interpreters have assumed that it reflects the situation of Jesus. Here interpreters follow Dodd, who sees that the setting is Lukan but thinks Luke has hit upon the right context from the life of Jesus (Dodd, 1961, p. 92; Jeremias, 1972, p. 40; Linnemann, 1982, p. 69). The *Thomas* version is slightly different and contrasts the size of the lost sheep to the other smaller 99. The lost sheep is therefore loved because it is bigger (*Gos. Thom.* 107). This version is certainly secondary and foreign to the interests of Jesus (Funk et al., 1988, p. 38; Scott, 1989, pp. 408–410). The Lukan version, although in a redactional context that is no doubt secondary, is therefore probably the earlier version.

In the Lukan version, a shepherd leaves 99 sheep and goes in search of one that he has lost. In the other versions the sheep goes astray on its own, but in the Lukan version it is the shepherd who has lost the sheep. He is therefore at fault (Bailey, 1983, p. 149; Scott, 1989, pp. 410–411). Like the woman who loses her coin, the woman who spills her grain, and the woman who overproduces bread, the shepherd is portrayed as incompetent. In Matthew the other sheep are left on the mountains (Matt 18:13), whereas in Luke, they disperse to the desert (Luke 15:4). *Thomas* does not give any location for the other sheep (*Gos. Thom.* 107); the difference in location, however, makes little difference to the interpretation of the parable (Scott, 1989, p. 411). Although interpreters have suggested that the shepherd hands control of the other sheep over to another shepherd or members of the extended family, there is nothing in the extant versions to suggest this (contra Bailey, 1983, p. 149; Jeremias, 1972, p. 133; Linnemann, 1982, p. 65; Scott, 1989, p. 415). That the shepherd has left the rest of the sheep to wander off by themselves in danger from wolves or other predators increases the portrayal of the shepherd as being incompetent in his duties. In Luke the shepherd returns home with the sheep on his shoulders (Luke 15:5). Some interpreters consider this to be normal practice (Jeremias, 1972, p. 134), whereas others consider this to be a secondary trait of the parable (Linnemann, 1982, p. 67). The common representation of a shepherd carrying a sheep in pagan and Christian art may have influenced Luke's performance of the parable (Scott, 1989, p. 411).

The shepherd, given his marginal status in Israel's society of the time, does not represent God. The shepherd is a shepherd (Wilder, 1964, p. 81) and an incompetent one at that. In contrast to God as the shepherd of Israel, this one has attention only for the one, rather than the many, once the sheep are abandoned in a dangerous place (Ezek 34:6; 1 Kgs 22:17; Scott, 1989, pp. 415–416). Further, in Ezekiel 34, God eventually gathers together the flock and vindicates the sheep (34:22–31). In the Gospels, the shepherd does no such thing. He takes a great risk in abandoning the other sheep in search of the one. Thus, the shepherd is a fool and the outcome of the situation is unknown (Bailey, 1983, p. 150; Scott, 1989, p. 417). We do not know what happens to the other sheep. The Gospel versions have made the story come out well, with the "little ones" not perishing and the rejoicing over the sinners who are found. Once taken from its Gospel contexts, however, the parable is more ambiguous. One is left to ponder the significance of the parable, as to whether the kingdom is like gathering the flock together or finding the one that was lost (Scott, 1989, p. 417). Again, the kingdom is not what is expected (the gathering and vindication of all the sheep) but likened to a marginal outcast who loses one sheep and responds by risking the other 99. In any case, the parable does not challenge the gendered role of the man as shepherd, but as with the women characters portrays him as incompetent.

The Lost Son. The parable of the Lost Son is actually a parable about two sons, a younger and an elder. This parable is probably among the most famous of Jesus's parables and has been argued to encapsulate the entire gospel of Jesus in one short story (Bailey, 1983, pp. 188–190; Jeremias, 1972, p. 131). The younger son becomes a figure of repentance, the father the figure of God welcoming an errant "sinner" into the Kingdom (Bailey, 1983, p. 190). Of all the parables, it is the most commonly viewed as having a clear theological meaning. Most scholars agree that the parable was originally addressed to the Pharisees during the life of Jesus (Dodd, 1961, p. 93; Jeremias, 1972, p. 124). Thus, again, the Pharisees, who are identified with the elder son, are invited to join in the open table fellowship of the Kingdom of God with "tax collectors and sinners" (Linnemann, 1982, p. 73). This reading, however, has been clearly influenced by the Lukan setting for the parable, which is fiction (Scott, 1989, p. 101).

In Luke, the Gospel narrative centers on Jesus, sinners, and scribes and Pharisees. Jesus and the sinners are on one side with Jesus as the hero, and the scribes and Pharisees are on the other. The entire chapter (15) is geared toward vindicating Jesus's association with "tax collectors and sinners," especially his practice of eating with them. The other two parables in Luke 15, the Lost Coin and the Lost Sheep, are also interpreted by Luke to vindicate Jesus's association with "sinners" who are lost and then found. The setting of the parable is thus clearly Lukan and should not be assumed to be the setting of the original parable or a clue to its original audience and meaning.

The first part of the parable focuses on the younger son. Here he requests that his father give him his portion of inheritance. The father agrees, and the son takes his inheritance, sells it, and then leaves town for the city. Some suggest such a situation would have been common (Jeremias, 1972, p. 129; Linnemann, 1982, pp. 74–75), but such a request would have shown that the son wished the father dead, as the dispersal of his property assumes that the father is dead (Bailey, 1983, p. 161; Scott, 1989, p. 111). Popular wisdom argued against such early dispersal of a father's wealth (Sir 33:19–23; Scott, 1989, pp. 109–110; contra Bailey, 1983, p. 163), and thus any father who agreed to such a thing was a fool. He was threatening his own livelihood in the future (Scott, 1989, pp. 110–113; cf. Bailey, 1983, p. 166). Like the shepherd in the previous parable, the father is not a sympathetic character. He is disrupting the family honor and threatening the family's relationship to the entire community (Rohrbaugh, 1998, pp. 151–153; Scott, 1989, p. 110). Like the other characters in the story the father is dysfunctional and does not fulfill his obligations to himself, his family, or his community (Rohrbaugh, 1998, p. 151).

However, the younger son is also foolish because by selling his property and leaving for the city, he is cutting himself off from his entire familial and community support network and opening himself up for potential economic disaster (Rohrbaugh, 1998, pp. 151–152). The elder son, who also receives a portion, is equally culpable in the dispersal (Bailey, 1983, p. 168; Rohrbaugh, 1998, p. 151). Following his departure, the younger son is said to squander all his money (15:13) and ends up in poverty. He is forced

to work for a city citizen feeding pigs. Although he is tempted, he does not eat the pigs' food (Jeremias, 1972, p. 129; Linnemann, 1982, p. 152, n. 11; Scott, 1989, p. 114; contra Bailey, 1983, p. 170). Thus, his situation is desperate: in a time of famine, he is forced to work for a foreigner in a despised occupation. The objection to such a job by Jews, for whom pigs were unclean animals, is clear (Rohrbaugh, 1998, p. 153; Scott, 1989, p. 114). The son is clearly degraded and dehumanized (Scott, 1989, p. 115).

To reverse this situation the son decides to come home and be a worker on his father's estate. He does not, however, repent. It is his stomach that urges him home, not his conscience (Bailey, 1983, pp. 173–180; Rohrbaugh, 1998, p. 145). His father's response, to him, however, cuts off his complete request and restores the younger son to his place in the family (Scott, 1989, p. 118; Rohrbaugh, 1998, pp. 156–157). Here the father runs to meet his son and treats him like an honored guest. This surely protects the son from the anger of the rest of the community, who might have gotten to him first (Bailey, 1983, p. 181; Rohrbaugh, 1998, pp. 156–157). For a patriarch to run, although not unheard of, was unusual, and beneath his dignity (Bailey, 1983, p. 181; LaHurd, 2002, p. 70; Rohrbaugh, 1998, p. 156; Scott, 1989, p. 117). The scene is caricature and burlesque. The father even kisses the son with an affection usually expressed by women (contra Bailey, 1983, p. 183; Scott, 1989, p. 117). The scene is using hyperbole, however, and should not be taken as a literal challenge to the gendered role of the father. The scene is supposed to elicit laughter in the audience, not a serious reconsideration of gender roles in the family and community. The father's actions reinstate the son into the honor of the father (Scott, 1989, p. 118), and the subsequent feast, which would have been shared by the rest of the community, shows his reinstatement into the larger community as well (Bailey, 1983, p. 186; Rohrbaugh, 1998, pp. 157–158).

In a contrived opening to the next section of the parable, the elder son is reintroduced (Bailey, 1983, p. 192; Linnemann, 1982, p. 10; Scott, 1989, p. 119). The elder son comes in from the field, learns of the celebration from a servant, and becomes angry. He refuses to come into the house. Such a refusal on his part would have been unusual, since elder sons usually would have helped play the host in a party given by the father. The elder son thus wrongs the father's honor and shames him (Bailey, 1983, p. 195; Rohrbaugh, 1998, p. 160; Scott, 1989, p. 120). As the younger son is separated from his father in the first part of the parable, so now is the elder son estranged (Scott, 1989, p. 120). The elder son complains that he has slaved for his father and yet never has been given even a lesser celebration (15:29). Yet, the response of the father to the elder son is similar to his response to his younger son and is further uncharacteristic and unexpected. He pleads with him and addresses him affectionately as "child" (Bailey, 1983, p. 196; LaHurd, 2002, p. 70; Rohrbaugh, 1998, p. 160; Scott, 1989, pp. 121–122). Again, the story is filled with hyperbole, and this should not be taken as a sign that the father is taking on a maternal role rather than a masculine one (contra Scott, 1989, p. 122). Further, the father affirms the place of his elder son and declares him his heir (15:31). Thus, both sons are affirmed in the story. Neither is rejected; both have their place in the family.

Rather than being an encapsulation of the entire Gospel and a heavily theological story about the actions of God, this story reflects a reversal of a common theme of the Hebrew Bible, that of the two sons. In these stories, there is a younger son and an elder son, and the younger son is a rogue and favored while the older son is denied his inheritance (Scott, 1989, p. 112). Cain and Abel, Ishmael and Isaac, and Esau and Jacob are all sets of brothers whose stories follow this theme. Both brothers in the Lost Son parable thus play stereotypical roles: the younger son is a rogue and favored, and the elder one is dutiful (Scott, 1989, p. 123). This theme also functions to show why God favors Israel over other nations. Israel is always the heir of the younger son (Scott, 1989, p. 124). Here, however, the expected story is not followed. Both younger and elder sons are accepted; both have a share in the father's honor. In fact, the elder son, according to the parable, inherits everything. Thus, the point of the story is that the Kingdom is universal; no one is chosen (Scott,

1989, p. 125). The parable thus has nothing to do with gender or gender roles. The actions of the father, while outlandish for a patriarch, are meant to be hyperbole and comic and do not constitute a challenge to patriarchal family roles.

The Good Samaritan. The Good Samaritan parable is likewise one of the most famous of Jesus's parables. It is only attested by Luke (10:30–35). Luke places the parable within a discussion between Jesus and a lawyer about inheriting eternal life. It falls within the context of Luke's travel narrative, which begins with Jesus sending messengers to a Samaritan village (9:51). When the messengers are rejected and Jesus does not pass judgment on the village, the way is prepared for Jesus's telling of the Good Samaritan parable, which has a Samaritan hero (Scott, 1989, p. 190). In Luke the parable demonstrates neighborliness. Many scholars have assumed that this was the original parable's point (Bailey, 1983, p. 33; Jeremias, 1972, pp. 202–203; Linnemann, 1982, p. 51). However, as the lawyer's question is found also in Mark and Matthew separate from the parable and as the Lukan context shows evidence of Lukan redaction, the parable and the lawyer's question about eternal life no doubt circulated separately in oral tradition (Crossan, 1992, pp. 57–61; Funk et al., 1988, p. 31; Hedrick, 1994, pp. 93–95; Scott, 1989, p. 191). Further, as there are parallels between the first part (the question about eternal life) and the second part (the question about who is my neighbor), the question about neighborliness is also Lukan construction (Crossan, 1992, pp. 57–61; Funk et al., 1988, p. 31; Hedrick, 1994, pp. 93–95; Scott, 1989, pp. 191–192). Thus, the parable also was transmitted apart from the question about neighborliness (Crossan, 1992, pp. 57–61; Funk et al., 1988, p. 31; Hedrick, 1994, pp. 93–95; Scott, 1989, pp. 191–192). From the Lukan perspective, the parable is an example story, "Go and do likewise" (Luke 10:37) (Crossan, 1992, p. 56; Hedrick, 1994, p. 93; Scott, 1989, p. 192). However, the original story does not have this meaning nor demonstrate neighborliness. It is rather a parable of reversal (Crossan, 1992, pp. 63–64; Oakman, 1992, p. 123).

In the story a man is traveling from Jerusalem to Jericho. The road from Jerusalem to Jericho is about seventeen miles. It was known for its rough and rocky terrain and as a hideout for bandits. Thus the robbery of the man on the road is not a surprise to the hearer of the parable (Bailey, 1983, pp. 41–42; Hedrick, 1994, p. 104; Scott, 1989, p. 194). The man is anonymous throughout the parable, although the hearers would have probably thought he was Jewish (Bailey, 1983, p. 42; Scott, 1989, p. 194; contra Hedrick, 1994, p. 103). This makes the contrast with the Samaritan who appears later more pronounced. The bandits strip the man and leave him naked, which would have left the man without identifying clues to his class, village, or ethnicity (Bailey, 1983, p. 42; Hedrick, 1994, p. 104; Scott, 1989, p. 194). He is left "half dead" (Luke 10:30). Peasant hearers of the parable probably did not identify with the half-dead man but with the bandits (Oakman, 1992, p. 121) or an awaited hero (Scott, 1989, p. 194). The secularity of the parable is underscored by the fact that those who travel by the man are only on the road by coincidence. There is no divine plan in the works (Hedrick, 1994, p. 105; Scott, 1989, p. 195). Two men travel by, a priest and a Levite. They are probably on their way home to Jericho from their temple duties in Jerusalem (Hedrick, 1994, p. 105; Scott, 1989, p. 195). Both approach the half dead man and pass by to the other side of the road. They may fear robbers and bandits (Bailey, 1983, p. 47; Hedrick, 1994, p. 106; Scott, 1989, p. 195), or they may have concerns about preserving their ritual purity (Bailey, 1983, pp. 44–45; Hedrick, 1994, pp. 105–106; Scott, 1989, p. 195). However, such prohibitions against touching a corpse were not absolute. The need to care for an abandoned corpse took precedence over concerns for ritual purity (Hedrick, 1994, p. 106; Scott, 1989, pp. 195–196). The priest and the Levite should therefore stop and care for the man (Scott, 1989, p. 197). As priests were from the upper classes and urban elites, rural peasants would have been critical of their behavior in the parable (Scott, 1989, p. 197).

Following the priest and a Levite, a Samaritan comes along the road. Hearers of the parable would have had a negative reaction to his appearance in the story, as the hatred of Jews for Samaritans was proverbial (Bailey, 1983, p. 48; Hedrick, 1994, p. 107; Scott, 1989, p. 197). Further, as it appears the Sa-maritan is a tradesman, he would have been seen as having a despised occupation by a peasant audience (Oakman, 1992, pp. 121–122). The expected triad would have been a priest, a Levite, and then a Jewish layman. The appearance of the Samaritan is therefore a real surprise (Bailey, 1983, p. 47; Jeremias, 1972, p. 204; Scott, 1989, p. 198). The Samaritan binds the man's wounds, gives him medical attention with wine and oil, and placing him on his own mount takes him to an inn where he gives the innkeeper additional funds for the man's care. Further, he tells the innkeeper that he will return and pay the man's debts (Luke 10:34–35). These actions are usually seen as a sign of the Samaritan's great generosity and compassion and are assessed positively (Bailey, 1983, pp. 49–56; Hedrick, 1994, pp. 113–116; Scott, 1989, pp. 200–201). However, from a peasant's perspective, giving aid to those not next of kin was pure folly (Oakman, 1992, pp. 122–123). Further, innkeepers were known for their unsavory reputations (Oakman, 1992, p. 122; Scott, 1989, p. 200, n. 53) and inns were no place to leave a wounded man as they were dirty, noisy, and smelly (Oakman, 1992, p. 122). Finally, giving the innkeeper what amounts to a blank check is also problematic, since the man will be kept hostage until the Samaritan returns (Oakman, 1992, p. 122). Thus the man is left worse off than he started. Thus, for the hearers of the parable, the Samaritan is not only an enemy but he is a fool (Oakman, 1992, p. 123). The story, like other parables, would have evinced laughter (Oakman, 1992, p. 123) and the narrative is caricature. God's kingdom, then, is compared to the actions of a foolish man of hated ethnicity and a despised social occupation. This reverses the expectations of the hearers and locates the kingdom in an unlikely, immoral place (Crossan, 1992, pp. 63–64; Oakman, 1992, p. 123). Further, the parable indicates that the kingdom is about crossing religious boundaries. There are no insiders and outsiders in God's kingdom (Scott, 1989, p. 202). Clearly, the parable has nothing to do with the gender of the character but with his ethnicity and occupation. The point of the parable is that God's kingdom is not what is expected but is located among socio-religious outcasts. Again, as in other parables, the main character of the story is also a fool.

Assessment. The parables of Jesus are remarkably difficult to interpret once they are taken from their Gospel contexts. However, the readings offered here strongly suggest that Jesus had little interest in challenging gender stereotypes in his culture (Levine, 2014). The women characters in his parables serve traditional roles associated with the household: women bake bread, do housework, and carry grain in jars. Men are shepherds and fathers. Both men and women characters, however, are portrayed in negative ways: the women are incompetent and the men are often fools. In this regard, Jesus treats the male and female characters in his stories equally as caricatures. Apart from gender, Jesus did have interest in class and class inequity in his culture. He favors the resistant attitude of the lower classes, imagines a kingdom of God where even the poor gather for a feast, and represents the results of the economic injustices of his society in sometimes shockingly realistic ways. There is no evidence, however, that Jesus transferred this interest in class inequities to an interest in gender inequities. That transference was left to a later generation that declared that in Christ there was "neither slave nor free" and "not male and female" (Gal 3:28). For Jesus, who primarily spoke to peasants, demonstrating the social and economic injustices of first-century Palestine was probably enough. Therefore the reconstruction of Jesus as a gender egalitarian or having a revolutionary feminist vision cannot be sustained on the basis of his most famous parables. Such an egalitarian reading is misguided, in light of the evidence presented in the Gospels and in light of the social and religious environment of Jesus's day. Why so many scholars are so loath to recognize this reality and face an image of Jesus foreign to their own remains a question for further consideration.

Another outstanding question concerns the function of such popular reconstructions of Jesus in scholarly discourse. These readings require a reconstruction of a "gender non-egalitarian" Judaism in order to make its point. Such a reading thus reinforces an anti-Judaic reconstruction of history, objections of Elisabeth Schüssler Fiorenza and others to the contrary notwithstanding. Jesus, rather than blending into his social and religious environment, stands out as extraordinary in terms of his gender critique of his culture. For a truly liberative gender-critical reading of Jesus to emerge, it would seem that scholars must come to terms with the outdated and biased nature of this particular reading of Jesus and his teaching and abandon it for a reading that does not bear false witness against Judaism.

[*See also* Feminism, *subentry* Second-Wave Feminism; Imagery, Gendered, *subentry* Gospels; Masculinity and Femininity, *subentry* New Testament; Religious Participation, *subentry* New Testament; *and* Rhetorical-Hermeneutical Criticism.]

BIBLIOGRAPHY

Bailey, Kenneth E. *Poet and Peasant, and Through Peasant Eyes: A Literary-Cultural Approach to the Parables in Luke.* Grand Rapids, Mich.: Eerdmans, 1983.

Borg, Marcus. *Meeting Jesus Again for the First Time: The Historical Jesus and the Heart of Contemporary Faith.* San Francisco: HarperSanFrancisco, 1994.

Corley, Kathleen E. *Women and the Historical Jesus: Feminist Myths of Christian Origins.* Santa Rosa, Calif.: Polebridge, 2002.

Crossan, John Dominic. *In Parables. The Challenge of the Historical Jesus.* Sonoma, Calif.: Polebridge, 1992.

Dodd, C. H. *The Parables of the Kingdom.* New York: Charles Scribner's Sons, 1961.

Durber, Susan. "The Female Reader of the Parable of the Lost." *Journal for the Study of the New Testament* 45 (1992): 59–78.

Funk, Robert W. *Parables and Presence: Forms of the New Testament Tradition.* Philadelphia: Fortress, 1982.

Funk, Robert W., James R. Butts, and Bernard Brandon Scott. *The Parables of Jesus, Red Letter Edition: A Report of the Jesus Seminar.* Sonoma, Calif.: Polebridge, 1988.

Hedrick, Charles W. *Parables as Poetic Fictions: The Creative Voice of Jesus.* Peabody, Mass.: Hendrickson, 1994.

Jeremias, Joachim. *The Parables of Jesus.* New York: Charles Scribner's Sons, 1972.

LaHurd, Carol Schersten. "Reviewing Luke 15 with Arab Christian Women." In *A Feminist Companion to Luke*, edited by Amy-Jill Levine, pp. 246–268. Feminist Companion to the New Testament and Early Christian Writings 3. Sheffield, U.K.: Sheffield Academic Press, 2002.

Levine, Amy-Jill. "Second Temple Judaism, Jesus and Women: Yeast of Eden." *Biblical Interpretation* 2 (1994): 8–33.

Levine, Amy-Jill. *Short Stories by Jesus: The Enigmatic Parables of a Controversial Rabbi.* San Francisco: HarperOne, 2014.

Linnemann, Eta. *Parables of Jesus: Introduction and Exposition.* London: SPCK, 1982.

Oakman, Douglas E. "Was Jesus a Peasant? Implications for Reading the Samaritan Story (Luke 10:30–35)." *Biblical Theology Bulletin* 22 (1992): 117–125.

Perrin, Norman. *Rediscovering the Teaching of Jesus.* New York: Harper and Row, 1967.

Reid, Barbara E. *Choosing the Better Part? Women and the Gospel of Luke.* Collegeville, Minn.: Liturgical Press, 1996.

Reid, Barbara E. "A Godly Widow Persistently Pursuing Justice." *Biblical Research* 45 (2000): 25–33.

Reid, Barbara E. "Beyond Petty Pursuits and Wearisome Widows: Three Lukan Parables." *Interpretation* 56.3 (2002): 284–294.

Rohrbaugh, Richard. "A Dysfunctional Family and Its Neighbors: Luke 15:11–32." In *Perspectives on the Parables: Images of Jesus in His Contemporary Setting,* edited by V. George Shillington, pp. 141–164. Edinburgh: T&T Clark, 1998.

Schottroff, Luise. *Lydia's Impatient Sisters: A Feminist Social History of Early Christianity.* Louisville, Ky.: Westminster John Knox, 1995.

Schüssler Fiorenza, Elisabeth. *In Memory of Her: A Feminist Theological Reconstruction of Christian Origins.* New York: Crossroad, 1983.

Scott, Bernard Brandon. *Hear Then the Parable. A Commentary on the Parables of Jesus.* Minneapolis: Fortress, 1989.

Slee, Nicola. "Parables and Women's Experience." *Modern Churchman* 26 (1984): 20–31.

Waller, Elizabeth. "The Parable of the Leaven: Sectarian Teaching and the Inclusion of Women." *Union Seminary Quarterly Review* 35 (1979): 99–109.

Wilder, Amos N. *The Language of the Gospel: Early Christian Rhetoric.* New York: Harper and Row, 1964.

Kathleen E. Corley

L

LEGAL STATUS

This entry contains six subentries: Ancient Near East; Hebrew Bible; Roman World; New Testament; Early Judaism; *and* Early Church.

Ancient Near East

The world's oldest laws are found in the ancient Near East. Dating from the twenty-sixth century until the fourth century B.C.E., abundant corpora of laws, the products of numerous societies, languages, cultures, and political systems, widely dispersed chronologically and geographically, attest to a long-standing concern regarding legal status and societal issues throughout ancient Near Eastern history. Though scholars debate whether one can speak of "ancient Near Eastern law" as a meaningful academic endeavor, others argue that despite the nearly three thousand years of history the commonalities in the laws were so great that these ancient Near Eastern societies belonged to a common legal culture (Westbrook, 2003). Whether these laws were actually practiced or whether they were simply products of a scribal intellectual activity, they offer valuable insight into the societal concerns of the ancient world.

Sources. While the canonical cuneiform law collections provide the majority of information regarding legal status and gender, they are supplemented by a myriad of records of daily life, such as letters, contracts, administrative and economical documents, and trial records of civil disputes. Gender ideology and status are also revealed throughout the literary and mythical texts, as characteristics and actions of the gods and goddess tend to mirror societal norms. In addition to the laws found in the Hebrew Bible, seven surviving collections of cuneiform laws are the benchmark for any scholarly study of the ancient Near Eastern law. Concentrated mainly in two historical periods: the Old Babylonian period (nineteenth to sixteenth century B.C.E.) and the Neo-Babylonian/ Persian period (sixth to fourth century B.C.E.), these collections of texts enable an understanding of the fundamental legal concerns of the peoples in the ancient Near East. A chief responsibility of the king was to uphold the laws with principles of justice and equality; therefore many of the law collections are attributed to various kings.

The earliest two law collections, the Sumerian Laws of Ur-Namma (LU), dated to 2112–2095 B.C.E., and the Laws of Lipit-Ishtar (LL), dated to 1932 B.C.E., are from the cities Ur and Isin in southern Mesopotamia respectively. Written in Old Babylonian Akkadian and stemming from a similar cultural milieu, the Laws of Ešnunna (LE), dated to ca. 1770 B.C.E., and the Laws of Hammurabi (LH) written within the same century (ca. 1750 B.C.E.) suggest that the law collections may have been meant as supplementary to one another. Later Akkadian law compositions include a collection of fourteen fragmentary tablets from 1076 B.C.E., called the Middle Assyrian Laws (MAL) and the Neo-Babylonian Laws (NBL), a school tablet containing an excerpt from a larger collection, dated to approximately 700 B.C.E. A Hittite collection of laws (HL) from Anatolia, dated to the sixteenth and the twelfth centuries B.C.E., parallels many of the Mesopotamia laws. Documents from Nuzi, an administrative center in northeastern Mesopotamia (1450–1340 B.C.E.), also contribute to our knowledge of legal status. These formal law collections, however, are often incomplete and were not likely intended as exhaustive or comprehensive sources for all legal situations.

Of all the cuneiform laws the most famous collection and one that garners the greatest attention from biblical scholars is the Babylonian Laws of Hammurabi. The longest continuous cuneiform inscription in the ancient Near East, the text is inscribed on a large diorite stela in three sections. The first section, a poetic prologue, describes Hammurabi's military conquests, his divine selection as king, and his role as champion of social justice as one who will "crush the evil-doer and protect the weak from the strong." A formulaic prose section of approximately 282 casuistic law stipulations follows, and the stela concludes with an epilogue. These laws draw upon earlier legal traditions and establish ancient Near Eastern societal norms that later find commonalities in the writings of the neighboring cultures and the Hebrew Bible. The written laws followed a standard format: they are stated in a casuistic (if/then) formula that contains a protasis (a conditional clause) followed by apodosis (stating the penalty if the condition in the protasis was met).

Gender and Legal Status. The subject of the laws is the adult male of the free citizen class. Though each gender had distinctive rights and responsibilities, the laws generally protect and reinforce the privilege of the male citizenry. The father and husband were authoritative as the heads of the household and managed the family's estates. Female heads of household, especially among royal families, were well-attested in the Neo-Assyrian period (Radner, 2003).

Women had no special status under the law but were considered subordinate members of a household; their status is designated in relation to a male family member. A woman remained legally as the "daughter of a (free) man" until she was betrothed, when she then assumed the status of the "wife of a (free) man." Women's rights and legal obligations were restricted within their statuses of wives, mothers, and daughters. Women who did not legally belong to a man—widows, divorcées, prostitutes, and priestesses such as the *nadītu* (women dedicated to a god)—were in a special legal category and were granted greater autonomy. In many cases, they were afforded rights that married women lacked. They could manage the household and own property until their sons were old enough. A man could award his wife property with a sealed document, so that, after his death, the sons could not claim it. The widow, then may bestow her estate to whichever son she chooses (LH 150). A widow could also collect the amount of her dowry and her bride price from her husband's property. If she had no dowry, a judge appraised the property and awarded her an equivalent value (NBL 12). Some texts mention women other than widows as property owners. If a daughter became a priestess during her father's lifetime, she had an equal share along with her brothers in her father's estate (LL 22; LH 180–181). A slave, whether male or female, was considered chattel, but in the case of a female slave, her owner could sexually exploit her, sell her, or put her in concubinage. In general, however, most women were subject to legal control by a male. Husbands had exclusive financial, sexual, and legal jurisdiction over their wives and fathers over their daughters.

In addition to binary male/female gender categories, legal status was also determined by age, marital status, family position, wealth, class, and citizenship. Motherhood, for example, had social implications resulting in a wife's higher position inside the family hierarchy. A native born citizen had more rights than a foreigner. All of these multiple factors, which must be taken into consideration, produce complex understandings when determining one's individual's legal status (Roth, 1998). The law codes of Hammurabi denote social stratification, detailing three types of statuses in Babylonian society: the *awīlu*, a free citizen, normally native born, and a member of one of the landholding families; the *muškenu*, a commoner or a free citizen who did not possess land; and the *ardu* and *amtu*, male and female slave. The Middle Assyrian laws also reveal a similar tripartite division of society. Remedies and punishments fluctuated greatly according to social standing. Persons of the free citizen class abided by a different standard than one of the commoner or the slave classes. Despite this stratification, there is some evidence that the classes were not always rigidly separated as one could presumably suffer a hardship, a loss of land, or be sold in debt slavery and therefore descend to a lower social class. Other than a free citizen marrying his slave woman and raising her status to a concubine, there was little opportunity of upward social mobility.

Family Laws: Betrothal, Marriage, and Divorce. The basic unit of society was the patriarchal household, structured around the "father's house," the paternal estate. The household might consist of up to three generations of family, along with slaves, apprentices, and indentured servants. Familial laws covering marriage, divorce, widowhood, incest, adultery, dowries, and inheritance practices were therefore indispensable for the proper functioning of the social order.

Marriage and betrothal in the ancient Near East were legal contracts, often made for economic reasons. Almost all the law collections include provisions regarding marriage, betrothal, and divorce. Marriages were arranged by the father (or eldest male relative) of each family. The bride was not a party to the contract but rather was the object of the transaction. The agreement between the two families included formal contracts and financial exchanges. In most cases, the groom's family paid a bridal gift (*terhātu*) and often a marriage-settlement (*nudunnû*) to the bride's father. Once the *terhātu* was exchanged, the woman's legal status changed and the betrothed was then called a wife, even though the marriage was not yet completed. Though not a legal requirement and varying in amount depending on a number of factors—family wealth, class standing, and historical period—the bride's father usually bestowed upon his daughter's husband a dowry (*šeriktu* in LE, LH and *širku* in MAL).

This dowry, though administered by the husband and subsumed into the husband's property during the marriage, remained the legal property of the bride to be returned to her in the case of divorce or widowhood. A married woman's property consisted of her dowry, personal possessions, and other items given to her by her father-in-law at her marriage. Though inheritances passed through sons as male heirs, daughters received a share of the paternal estate through their dowries upon marriage. Legally speaking, the dowry is an advanced form of inheritance, and this property given to a woman was protected to keep it within the family.

The laws also detail provisions for failed or broken troths. Some allow the father to nullify his daughter's betrothal and/or give her to another man (LH 160, LH 161, LU 15–16, LE 25). In situations of a broken betrothal, like any other contractual argument, financial compensation to the injured party was warranted. If the father broke the engagement, he was required to pay back the *terhātu*, often at twice the price. LE 25 reads, "If a man claims his bride at the house of the father-in-law and his father-in-law rejects him and gives his daughter to another, the daughter's father shall return double the bridal payment that he received." The fiancé can also break the agreement. LH 159 discusses a situation of a betrothed man whose attention has been diverted to another woman. He must declare to his father-in-law, "I will not marry your daughter," and then forfeit all claims to the *terhātu*. The daughter's legal status reverts back to the control of her father.

Polygamy was legal in the ancient Near East, though for economic reasons monogamy was more likely the norm among the everyday citizen. A man might take a second wife if his first wife was barren. He could also marry his female slave and procure children by her. Several laws stipulate protections for the first wife when a man marries a second. LH 148 refers to the first wife suffering a (presumably incurable) disease. The husband may take a second wife, but he is obligated to continue to support the first one and keep her in his household for as long as she lives. LL 28 provides a similar safeguard for first wife who has become blind or paralyzed.

Marriages could be terminated by the death of one of the spouses, desertion, and divorce. Just as the establishment of marriage was a legal proceeding, divorce required the legal dissolution of contractual agreements. The husband possessed the right to initiate divorce on any grounds. Declaring a formulaic statement, "you are/she is not my wife," effectively dissolved the marriage. Some texts also mention the divorcing husband as "cutting the (wife's) hem," possibly a symbolic ritual action to end the marriage.

If a husband divorced his wife for reasons other than adultery, he was normally required to provide economic support to his wife, either in the return of the dowry or another stipulated price. In the laws of Ur Namma (LU 9, 10) the husband paid her sixty shekels of silver, or, if she was a former widow, thirty shekels. In the Hammurabi laws, a childless wife was entitled to the full amount of the *terhatu* and her *šeriktu* at the divorce (LH 138). However, this is not consistent, as in the Middle Assyrian laws, a man could divorce his wife without grounds and was not obliged to pay her any compensation (MAL A37).

Though divorce initiated by a wife was legal, it was dangerous and often came with harsh punishments—the forfeiting of her children, loss of her dowry, substantial financial penalty, and in some situations, her death. A man could divorce his wife without any reasons, but a woman's case for divorce must be justified, investigated by authorities, and proven to be truthful or she risked her life with her claim. If the outside authorities determine that her accusations are warranted and that she is without any fault, her divorce is granted. She is allowed to take her dowry and return to her father's house (LH 142). However, if her charges are gratuitous, she has disparaged her husband. She is "cast into the water" and dies (LH 143). An Old Babylonian marriage agreement contains a comparable situation. If the wife says (to her husband), "You are not my husband," she is bound and thrown into the water (Westbrook, 2003). These cases indicate that female-initiated divorce was probably not very common as the consequences for the wife could be severe.

Laws of Adultery, Incest, and Rape. The ancient Near Eastern laws regulating the sexual conduct of women are numerous and precisely detailed (LH 129; MAL A13–14; 22–23; HL 198; cf. Deut 22:22; Lev 20:10). Adultery was generally described as consensual sexual relations between a married woman and any man other than her husband. A man could legally have sexual relations outside of marriage with any woman who was not betrothed or married to another man, including prostitutes, female slaves, and in some cases, widows. Even the (unwarranted) accusation of a woman's extramarital relations could be grounds for severe punishment. As a wife's sexual rights were the exclusive property of her husband, adultery was regarded as a grave offense against the husband, allowing the wronged husband to inflict, control, or even waive his wife's punishment. He was entitled to divorce her and penalize her in a variety of manners. In the Middle Assyrian laws, he could physically assault her by such means as striking her, mutilating her, or plucking out her hair, in addition to any other punishments required (MAL A57, 58, 59). In committing adultery both the wife and her lover have committed an offense against the woman's husband. MAL requires death for both parties, especially if the accused man knew the woman was married (MAL A13 and 15). If he did not know, he is innocent (MAL A14). In some cases, especially if the lovers are caught in the act, the husband retained the right to have them both killed, provided the same level of punishment was inflicted on both of them. If the husband allows the wife to live, he also must allow her lover to live and be spared any further penalty (LH 129; HL 198). Some of the earlier laws, however, impose a death sentence for the unfaithful wife alone. In the Laws of Ur-Namma, only the woman was put to death, whereas the man received no punishment (LU 7). Similarly, if the husband catches the wife "in the lap of (another) man," she is killed. There is no mention of penalty to the man (LE 28). A woman could be accused of adultery by her husband or by a third party (LU 11; LH 131,132; MAL A17, 18). A false accusation of adultery penalized the person making the claim, as the accusation is legally considered slander against the husband. In the Laws of Lipit-Ishtar, a false accusation against the daughter of a free man was remedied by a fine of ten shekels of silver (LL 33). Other times, the punishment was more severe. MAL A18 prescribes forty blows with a rod, a month's conscription in the corvée, a slave mark, and a fine of 3,600 shekels of lead to the accuser. If the husband accused his wife of adultery but she was not caught in the act, she could make an exculpatory oath proclaiming her innocence and then return to her house (LH 131, cf. Num. 5:11–31). If a wife is accused of adultery by a third party, but there was neither evidence nor was she caught *in flagrante delicto*, there were methods to ascertain her innocence or guilt. Often she had to vindicate herself by submitting to an ordeal. In Mesopotamia and Anatolia, the River Ordeal was known. Used particularly for accusations of witchcraft (LH 2) and adultery (LH 132, MAL A17 and 22) in the absence of witnesses or solid evidence, the river meted out divine justice. The details of the procedure are not completely known. Likely it involved one or both of the accused parties undergoing something in the water, such as swimming a distance or floating. If the accused person was innocent of the charge he or she floated, but if deemed guilty by the river, then the person drowned. Known also from court cases from Mari, the River Ordeal may have functioned as a last resort when other attempts at verification of the charges had failed.

Common taboos against incest were widespread throughout the ancient Near East law collections. Sexual relations between a son and his natural mother were strictly prohibited (LH 157; HL 189 cf. Lev 18:7), even if the father was already deceased. In LH 157, both the mother and the son were burned to death. This prohibition extended to sexual relations between a son and his father's wife; however, the penalties were less severe, such as disinheritance from the father's house (LH 158). No penalty is stipulated for the woman. Sexual relations between other close relatives such as a father with a daughter (LH 154) and daughter-in-law (LH 155) were also forbidden.

Like adultery, rape was also considered a serious offense against the husband (or father), and further demonstrates how a woman's body is subject to male authority. Several factors were weighed regarding a rape. First it had to be determined if the sexual act was consensual. If not, then the marital status of the woman as well as the location of the rape was considered. Rape of a virgin or an unmarried woman was an offense against her father. "If a man raped a free man's virgin daughter, then her father could then take the wife of the rapist and give her to be ravished." He did not have to return her to the rapist but could keep her as his own (MAL A55). Here the rapist's wife was just as victimized as the raped daughter herself. The wife of the rapist is only protected if the rapist swears that the daughter gave herself willingly to him. His word was taken over the young woman's. His penalty was payment in silver to the father equal to the value of the daughter, and he was free to keep his wife (MAL A56). The rape of a betrothed virgin daughter brought the death penalty for the man, but the woman was to go free (LH 130; LU6.). Location of the rape also mattered. If the rape occurred in a remote location such as in the mountains, or away from the city, where the woman could presumably cry out for help and not be heard, penalty is exacted on the man. For example, Hittite law states that if a man rapes a women in the mountains or open country, he is executed and she is blameless. But if she is raped in her house, it is her crime and she will be killed (HL 197; cf. Deut 22:23–27). In MAL A12, a woman who is walking along a main throughway must "protect" herself (possibly by screaming out for help) against a man who attempts to rape her.

Conclusion. As the legal system is concerned with societal order, several laws specifically deal with the social, familial, economic, and status of persons. Gender roles were strictly divided in the patriarchal and patrilineal society of the ancient Near East, but a women's legal status or treatment was not stagnant or uniform throughout history. While changes in the laws display the societal value placed upon women during various historical periods, some general similarities are apparent. First, the very fact of being female makes the woman dependent upon a male, regulating and restricting her societal roles to a far greater extent than that of a man's. Laws regulated women's sexuality with harsh penalties for violations.

Women were economically dependent on males, but in some cases, such as with widows, priestesses, and abandoned wives, women could control their own means.

[*See also* Economics, *subentry* Ancient Near East; Gender and Sexuality: Ancient Near East; Marriage and Divorce, *subentry* Ancient Near East; *and* Religious Leaders, *subentry* Ancient Near East.]

BIBLIOGRAPHY

Chavalas, Mark W. *Women in the Ancient Near East: A Sourcebook.* New York: Routledge, 2013.

Driver, Godfrey, and John Miles. *The Assyrian Laws.* Oxford: Oxford University Press, 1935.

Driver, Godfrey, and John Miles. *The Babylonian Laws.* Oxford: Oxford University Press, 1956.

Frymer-Kensky, Tikva. "Patriarchal Family Relationships and Near Eastern Law." *Biblical Archaeologist* 44 (1981): 209–214.

Greengus, Samuel. "Legal and Social Institutions of Ancient Mesopotamia." In *Civilizations of the Ancient Near East*, Vol. 1, edited by Jack M. Sasson, pp. 469–484. New York: Scribner, 1995.

Hoffner, Harry A., Jr. *The Laws of the Hittites.* Leiden, The Netherlands: Brill, 1997.

Matthews, Victor H., Bernard Levinson, and Tikva Frymer-Kensky. *Gender and Law in the Hebrew Bible and the Ancient Near East.* Journal for the Study of the Old Testament. Supplement Series 262. Sheffield, U.K.: Sheffield Academic Press, 1998.

Radner, Karen. "Neo-Assyrian Period." In *A History of Ancient Near Eastern Law*, Vol. 1, edited by Raymond Westbrook, pp. 883–910. Leiden, The Netherlands: Brill, 2003.

Roth, Martha T. *Law Collections from Mesopotamia and Asia Minor.* 2d ed. Writings from the Ancient World. Atlanta: Scholars Press, 1997.

Roth, Martha T. "Gender and Law: A Case Study from Ancient Mesopotamia." In *Gender and Law in the Hebrew Bible and the Ancient Near East*, edited by Victor H. Matthews, Bernard M. Levinson, and Tikva Frymer-Kensky, pp. 174–184. Sheffield, U.K.: Sheffield University Press, 1998.

Wells, Bruce. "Law and Practice." In *A Companion to the Ancient Near East*, edited by Daniel Snell, pp. 183–195. Malden, Mass.: Blackwell, 2007.

Westbrook, Raymond. *Studies in Biblical and Cuneiform Law.* Cahiers de la Revue Biblique 26. Paris: Gabalda, 1988.

Westbrook, Raymond. "Adultery in Ancient Near Eastern Law." *Revue Biblique* 97 (1990): 542–580.

Westbrook, Raymond. *A History of Ancient Near Eastern Law.* 2 vols. Leiden, The Netherlands: Brill, 2003.

Westbrook, Raymond, F. Rachel Magdalene, and Bruce Wells. *Law From the Tigris to the Tiber: The Writings of Raymond Westbrook.* Winona Lake, Ind.: Eisenbrauns, 2009.

Julye Bidmead

Hebrew Bible

This entry considers ways in which gender and sex functioned in the social realm of ancient Israel to grant or deny various legal rights and duties. After addressing overarching issues in defining legal status, it then turns to specific legal statuses of various classes of people, demonstrating that women of whatever class were under more legal strictures than men.

Ascribed Characteristics and Legal Status. Persons may be granted power and status in a society based on ascribed characteristics, which are determined by circumstances beyond one's control such as race, ethnicity, gender, citizenship, class, caste, kinship, legitimacy of birth, religion, and physical abilities or disabilities (Kemper, 1974, pp. 845, 848). Achieved characteristics and status, on the other hand, are earned (Davis, 1950, p. 96). Inequitable stratification in a given society is often related to ascribed characteristics (Kemper, 1974, p. 852; Parsons, 1951, p. 96). Gender is one of the primary ascribed characteristics that determine one's social and legal status.

Ancient Israel was a patriarchal, patricentric, and patrilinear culture (Block, 2003, pp. 40–45) with a patrimonial government (Schloen, 2001). The patriarch had authority (*patria potestas*) within his household. Patriarchs were chosen not by personal charisma but through traditional rules of inheritance (Weber, 1947, p. 328). In ancient Near Eastern patrimonialism,

the entire social order is viewed as an extension of the ruler's household—and ultimately of the god's household. The social order consists of a hierarchy of sub-households linked by personal ties at each level between individual "masters" and "slaves" or "fathers" and "sons." There is no global distinction between the "private" and "public" sectors of society because governmental administration is effected through personal relationships on the household model rather than through an impersonal bureaucracy. (Schloen, 2001, p. 51)

The fundamental social ranking in the Hebrew Bible begins with a male God, to whom the male king is subordinate, to whom, in turn, each male householder is subordinate, to whom, in turn, every person in that male's household is subordinate. Biblical laws support the authority of the deity, king, and individual male householder in that order; all others are subordinate to them. Thus, gender was a significant feature of the structure of ancient Israelite society. Cheryl Anderson argues that gender is the "master-status" identity because laws regarding women "assume the perspective of the free, privileged, Israelite males" and disadvantage women (Anderson, 2004, pp. 74–75). Gender was more than simply legal asymmetry (as articulated by Pressler, 1993) but of such import that cross-dressing was prohibited (Deut 22:5).

Though critical in determining social and legal status, gender was not the only distinguishing feature of status in ancient Israel. Whether one is free or slave, or emancipated or unemancipated also contributes to one's position in society. "Emancipation," its meaning derived from Roman law, refers to releasing a person from the *patria potestas*, while "manumission" refers to release from slavery. One is free if born to free parents or if a manumitted chattel slave. Unemancipated persons exist under the authority of the head of household and are legally incapacitated in important regards (Wunsch and Magdalene, 2014). Through marriage or betrothal a woman was transferred from her father's *potestas* to that of husband or father-in-law (Driver and Miles, 1952, pp. 248–249; Westbrook, 1990, p. 570; see Gen 24:50–60), and adultery provisions apply to both. Within each social and legal category of free or slave, emancipated or unemancipated, married or unmarried, the female ranked lower than the male.

Legal Statuses by Class of Person. In the next section, the legal status of various classes of persons in the Hebrew Bible is discussed.

Free male householders. Free male householders (sometimes "elder," *zāqēn*, lit. "bearded one") held the highest legal status (McKenzie, 1959, p. 522); nobles and officers ("elders of [the king's] house" [e.g., 2 Sam 12:17; cf. Ps 105:22]) emerged from their ranks (Willis, 2001,

p. 8). Such householders could serve in a judicial capacity within an assembly, reflecting their superior legal standing (Willis, 2001, p. 8). The male head-of-household held legal authority and reported only to those superior in rank. He provided for and protected those living in his household, including wives, free concubines, children, daughters-in-law, other relatives (such as a widowed mother, unmarried sisters, and young brothers), and manumitted slaves unless they were emancipated (Wunsch and Magdalene, 2014). The *paterfamilias* was expected to be a religious man, instruct his family in the laws, uphold their reputation, and represent them in public and legal spheres (Block, 2003, pp. 47–48, 99–100; van der Toorn, 1996, p. 21). He exercised power over those in his household, able to place them under the control of another individual or institution (e.g., in adoption, as an apprentice, for temple services, for sexual purposes [e.g., Gen 19:8; Judg 19:24; cf. Lev 19:29]) or pledge or sell them in times of need (Exod 21:7–11; Neh 5:5, 8). He determined inheritance (Gen 27:1–40; 49:1–28) and dowry amounts (Gen 29:24, 29; 1 Kgs 9:16; Mic 1:14) for children, although some strictures applied to inheritance (e.g., Deut 21:15–16). He held powers of life and death over household members (Gen 22; 38:24; Judg 11; cf. Deut 21:18–21).

This power over persons was so great that it may appear that everyone in the *paterfamilias*'s household was his property (e.g., Pressler, 1993, pp. 90–91; Wegner, 1988, pp. 12–13). Such may not be the case, however. Even though the Decalogue includes wives in a list of property that one might covet (Exod 20:17; cf. Deut 5:21 [MT 5:18]), free persons living under the householder's *potesta* were not property from a legal standpoint. Only chattel slaves were human property (Wunsch and Magdalene, 2014). Unemancipated persons were, rather, legal "infants" and incapacitated in numerous regards (Wunsch and Magdalene, 2014). Gender affected the type and extent of their incapacity. Gender also affected how and when emancipation occurred and what duties were owed the household while unemancipated.

Sons and daughters. In the case of free sons, emancipation occurred automatically on their father's death (Westbrook, 2003, p. 39). Until then, their legal rights were limited. Sons were expected to work for the household. They could not litigate in court. A son's marriage plans had to meet his father's approval, and marriage did not change his legal status. His wife usually joined his father's household (Gen 24:51–67); Jacob (Gen 29) and Moses (Exod 2:21) were exceptions to the rule, residing in their father-in-laws' homes. Sons owed duties of support (*kabbēd* "to honor"; Exod 20:12; Deut 5:16; Westbrook, 2008, p. 114) and respect (Exod 21:15, 17; Lev 20:9; Deut 21:18–21; 27:16) to parents. They also performed mourning rituals for parents (Deut 21:13). A son was not to humiliate his father by having sexual relations with his father's wife or concubine (Gen 35:22; Deut 23:1; 2 Sam 16:21–22; 1 Kgs 2:17–25). Sons could disgrace the householder by being a *nabal*, one who willfully ignores general rules of propriety (Prov 15:20), or a drunkard and glutton (Deut 21:20; Bellefontaine, 1979).

Daughters born to free parents were generally free, but they could lose that status by being taken into captivity during war (e.g., Lev 25:44; Num 31:9–18; Deut 20:14; 1 Kgs 9:20–21) or given over to debt slavery (Exod 21:7; Lev 25:47; Neh 5:5, 8; cf. Deut 28:68; cf. Lev 25:39–43). Free women were rarely emancipated from a male *potestas*. Women who never married generally remained unemancipated in the household of their father or oldest surviving male relative until death, although they could inherit (Num 26:33–27:11; 36). When the woman moved to her husband's or father-in-law's home, she was not emancipated; instead, the *potestas* under which she lived transferred from her paternal household to that of her husband or his family (cf. Westbrook, 2003, pp. 39–40). As long as a daughter lived with her father, she had no right to sue and could not serve as a recording witness. Unemancipated daughters were dependent on their fathers and could be treated harshly (Gen 19:8; Judg 11; 19:24). A father could repudiate any vow of his daughter if he did so on the same day he heard of it (Num 30:3–5 [MT 30:4–6]). Women's legal inferiority is also seen in the valuation of a vow: e.g., 30 shekels for a woman and 50 for a man (Lev 27:3–4). Single daughters existed to assist the family until marriage (and were equal to sons in terms of duties of respect and parental

burial) and to form bonds between their father's family and that of their husband at marriage (e.g., 1 Kgs 3:1; Matthews, 2002, p. 294), especially in the case of royal daughters (e.g., 1 Kgs 3:1; cf. 1 Kgs 16:31).

Marriages were typically arranged by the father or eldest surviving male (e.g., Gen 24; 29). The bride, as unmarried daughter, was expected to be a virgin (e.g., 2 Sam 13:1–13); unmarried women dishonored their fathers by being unchaste (e.g., Deut 22:13–21). Priests could only marry a virgin (Lev 21:13; Ezek 44:22). Non-virgins were marriageable, if less desirable (Matthews, 2003, p. 9). The bride's family was given some property as a bride-price (better "bride-wealth") to replace her services to the family and not as a purchase price, as is commonly suggested. The betrothed bride was given a dowry by her father (e.g., Gen 29:24, 29; 1 Kgs 9:16). The dowry was generally considered to be a portion of the inheritance, although it was more in the nature of a gift, the amount of which was at the father's discretion. The dowry, except for slaves and personal items, was usually controlled by the woman's husband or his family during the marriage, but technically it remained her property. It was to be returned to her in any divorce in which she had no fault (Frymer-Kensky, 2003, p. 1010); it was for her support in case of widowhood (cf. Judg 17:1–4) and was to be inherited by her children at the time of her death (Westbrook, 1991, pp. 154, 156).

Married women. Married women were not emancipated, lived under the *potestas* of their father-in-law or husband, and did not generally hold and manage property. A woman was expected to be subservient to the male head of household, although occasional narratives report that wives took initiative without their husbands' consent (e.g., 1 Sam 25; 2 Kgs 4:8–47). They were responsible for domestic chores of the household, and their ideal traits are set forth in Proverbs 31:10–31.

A married woman was expected to provide exclusive sexual and reproductive services to her husband (cf. Judg 19:25). Adultery was defined as illicit sexual intercourse between a married or betrothed woman and a man other than her husband or intended. The female focus of this law is evident, since a husband was not bound to monogamy. He could marry other women and have sexual liaisons with prostitutes and concubines as long as they were not married or betrothed to another man (e.g., Gen 38:15–16; 1 Sam 1:1–8; 2 Sam 19:5 [MT 2 Sam 19:6]). These provisions are extended to inchoately married women in Exodus 22:16–17 (MT 22:15–16) and Deuteronomy 22:23–25, 28–29. These verses instruct that to avoid capital punishment a betrothed woman must cry out that she is being taken by force, although her attacker is guilty of adultery whether or not she cried out. If she is not betrothed, however, her attacker need only pay the bride-wealth and marry her; neither shall die. Genesis 38:24, where Tamar is subject to the death penalty for being pregnant, also recognizes adultery by an inchoately married woman, because she is inchoately married under levirate marriage law.

Adultery was absolutely prohibited (Exod 20:14 [MT Exod 20:13]; Lev 18:20; 20:10; Deut 5:18 [MT 5:17]; 22:22). It was a capital crime (e.g., Gen 20:9; 39:9; Ezek 22:11) and subject to divine punishment (Ezek 16:38; Mal 3:5). The community was understood to be adversely impacted by adultery and expected to intervene (Deut 22:22; cf. Lev 18:24–30). Whether lesser punishments were allowed by the cuckold husband is debated (pro: e.g., Lowenstamm, 1980; McKeating, 1979; contra: e.g., Otto, 2000; Phillips, 1981); in these cases, divorce seems likely (Deut 24:1; Jer 3:8; Hos 2:4–6; Prov 6:33) as well as monetary damages (Lev 19:20–22; Prov 6:35; see also Job 31:11). If lesser punishments were allowed, the wife and paramour would suffer the same punishment to avoid collusion of wife and husband against a paramour (Wells, 2005; Lev 20:10; Deut 22:22).

The gravity of adultery is reflected in biblical narratives (e.g., Gen 12; 20; 26; 38; 39; 2 Sam 11), in prophetic texts as a metaphor for disobedient Israel (Jer 3:8 passim; Ezek 16; 23; Hos 2—4), and in the wisdom literature (e.g., Prov 5, 6—7; Job 24:15; 31:1, 9–12). This evidence demonstrates that adultery was understood to have significance beyond injury to the cuckold male: it also was an affront to Yahweh. Women's obedience to their husbands was one of the standards by which men's obedience to Yahweh was measured (Mernissi, 1986, pp. 98–99).

Because ancient Near Eastern societies favored procreation to pass on land through inheritance and to make one's mark on the world, women were expected to have and raise children, especially sons. Procreation was a sign of divine blessing (e.g., Gen 1:28; 12; 15; 17; Exod 23:26; Deut 7:14; Ps 127:3–4). Infertility was deemed a tragedy (e.g., Gen 16:1–4; 30:1; 1 Sam 1–2), while births were a cause for rejoicing (Jer 20:15). Contraception by coitus interruptus was unacceptable (Gen 38:8–10). Miscarriage was understood as the result of divine curse (Hos 9:14; cf. Exod 23:26), and involuntary miscarriage that resulted from the violence of another was an actionable crime (Exod 21:22–25).

A child conceived in marriage was legally protected, presumed to be the husband's as a matter of law, and under the *potestas* of the husband. This status is reflected in the laws of adultery, especially the "ordeal" of Numbers 5:11–30. The ritual involves a husband who suspects his wife of adultery but has no concrete evidence. Some scholars suggest that the husband has no reasonable grounds for suspicion (e.g., McKane, 1980, p. 474), but others argue that he believes she is pregnant (e.g., Levine, 1993, pp. 201–204). During the ordeal, she takes an oath and ingests a bitter potion of holy water, tabernacle earth, and ink from a written oath, mixed in an earthen vessel. If she is guilty, Yahweh will make her "womb discharge, [her] uterus miscarry" (author's translation; vv. 21b–22a; cf. Ps 58:8 [MT 58:9]; Isa 26:18–19). Most scholars argue that she suffers something like a prolapsed uterus and infertility (e.g., Frymer-Kensky, 1984, pp. 468–469), but others argue that the potion is an actual or mystical abortifacient, meant to rid the wife of the illicitly conceived fetus and make her again fertile to her husband in case he did not wish to kill her (Levine, 1993, pp. 192–210; Magdalene, 2009, pp. 139–140; cf. Brenner, 1997, pp. 69–70; Stol, 2000, p. 32). It appears, then, that if a woman conceived a child by her paramour the husband had the right to kill her and the fetus with her. The fetus was under the *potestas* of the male head-of-household. A husband could abort the fetus of another man gestating in his wife's womb because it violated his right to use his wife's womb.

Divorced and widowed women. Divorce was the prerogative of the husband, although Deuteronomy 24:1–2 requires a bill of divorce so the wife could marry again (cf. Jer 3:8; Isa 50:1). A husband who raped his wife before marriage could not divorce her (Deut 22:28–29). In other cases, a husband might divorce his wife with fault (Deut 24:1–2) or without (*śānēʾ*, lit.: he "hates" her; Mal 2:16; Westbrook, 1986, pp. 401–403). If he had cause for divorce, she would forfeit her dowry. If he had no cause, she could take her dowry and be emancipated. In most cases, she returned to the house of her father or oldest living male relative and submitted to his *potestas*.

Financially, a widow received her dowry but no inheritance (Num 27:8–11; Pressler, 1993, pp. 69–71; Westbrook, 1991, p. 145). Her life could be precarious. If she had sufficient funds or no family, she would be emancipated at widowhood (1 Kgs 17:9–24). A widow might return to her father's house (Lev 22:13). A young widow with small children might remain with the husband's family as an unemancipated daughter-in-law. If the widow was childless and fertile, she might have been expected to remain in the husband's family and marry another son (Gen 38:6–11; Deut 25:5–6) or next of kin (Gen 38:12–26; Ruth 3–4) through the operation of the levirate, although a man might be released from this duty (Deut 25:7–10; Ruth 4:1–7). If the widow was older with adult children and unable to support herself, she often remained with her eldest son, who inherited the bulk of his father's estate. The possible emancipated status of widows and divorcees is acknowledged by the fact that their vows are binding (Num 30:9 [MT 30:10]).

Women's nondomestic roles. Some women in the Hebrew Bible also took on nondomestic roles. Many of these appear in narrative or prophetic texts, including Israelite queen consorts and queen mothers (1 Kgs 18–19; 2 Kgs 9:30–35; 11:1–20; 2 Chr 22:10—23:21; 24:7; 1 Kgs 15:13; 2 Chr 15:16); queens of foreign nations (1 Kgs 10:1–13; 2 Chr 9:1–12; Esther); women in other political and religious capacities (Judg 4–5; Exod 15:19–21; Mic 6:4; 2 Kgs 22:12–20; Neh 6:14; 2 Sam 14:1–24; 20:16–22), singers (Neh 7:67; 2 Chr 35:25); weavers (cf. 2 Kgs 23:7); midwives (Gen 35:17; 38:28; cf. Exod 1:15–21); and wet-nurses (Exod 2:7–9; cf. Num 11:12).

Prostitutes (*iššâ zonāh* and other terms) were emancipated but socially marginalized (Lev 19:29; Amos 7:17; Matthews, 2003, pp. 2–3). Priests could not marry them (Lev 21:7), and a priest's daughter who was a prostitute could be burned (Lev 21:9). Both men and women could be illegally involved in so-called black arts (e.g., Lev 19:31; Deut 18:10–12) and could be expelled (e.g., 1 Sam 28:3; cf. Kiboko, 2010) or put to death (e.g., Lev 20:27; cf. Exod 22:18 wherein only women are put to death).

Freed slaves and temple oblates. Based on comparison with other ancient Near East cultures, women might have also been freed slaves or temple oblates (*nᵉtînîm*). Freed slaves remain members of, and are expected to work for, the household unless also emancipated at the time of manumission or a later date (Wunsch and Magdalene, 2014). Temple oblates, mentioned fifteen times in Ezra-Nehemiah (Ezra 2:43 passim) and in 1 Chronicles 9:2, are similar to the Mesopotamian temple *širkū*: they are free but unemancipated and permanent dependents of the temple (Wunsch and Magdalene, 2015).

Female chattel slaves and debt-slaves. Because of their sexual and reproductive capacity, female slaves were governed by special rules (Westbrook, 1998, p. 215). As property, they were subject to both sale and sexual exploitation. If taken as concubines to produce children for their master, they were given limited protections. In Mesopotamia, the Laws of Hammurabi indicate that they were freed upon their master's death (LH §171) and that if given by their mistress to the master they maintained dual status in regard to husband and wife (LH §§146–147). If a slave woman bore a child, she might be demoted in the household but not sold. Such regulations parallel Genesis 16, where Hagar is treated harshly by Sarah and returned by Yahweh when she flees.

Even if fathered by the master, children of slave women were considered house-born slaves and generally deemed fatherless, without the right of inheritance. Abraham goes beyond these rules, claiming Ishmael by naming him (Gen 16:15) as he does Isaac (Gen 21:3). Sarah recognizes Ishmael's inheritance right in Genesis 21:10, which leads her to cast out Hagar and Ishmael (Gen 21:9–21). Adultery laws do not apply in the same way to betrothed slave women (Lev 19:20–22). In such cases, neither the man nor the woman would be executed but the paramour instead paid the owner compensation and brought a guilt offering (cf. Exod 21:8).

When free daughters were given in concubinage, they lost rights (implied by Exod 21:7–11) and were given the normal protection for concubines (Westbrook, 1998, p. 219). Nevertheless, where a woman displeased her master, she could not be set free and emancipated, as could male slaves, but rather was redeemed by her family. She could not be sold to a foreign people where no one could redeem her. If the master gave the woman to his son, the husband was required to treat her as wife and the master to treat her as daughter-in-law. If not provided for as wife, she was set free without payment of the redemption price.

Other Indices of Women's Lower Status. Women were deemed unclean for a substantial portion of their adult lives because of the rules surrounding menstruation and childbirth. Women were isolated for seven days during their menstrual period or as long as they bled, plus an additional seven days (Lev 15:19–29), and for seven days after birth of a male child and fourteen after the birth of a female child (Lev 12:1–5). After intercourse, women were required to wash and remained unclean until evening, similar to their partner (Lev 15:18). Those who touched her in this unclean state were also unclean (e.g., Gen 31:35; Lev 15:19; 33). Sexual relations during menses were a crime (Lev 20:18).

The Hebrew Bible reports many incidents of violence against women, which reveals further their lesser social and legal status. Rape, both within and beyond the context of war, is a common theme throughout the Hebrew Bible (Magdalene, 1995; Scholz, 2010). Women lived under the constant threat of sexual and physical violence.

Despite their inferior legal status, however, women were required to learn and uphold the law in a manner equal to men (e.g., Num 5:6; Deut 17:2, 5; 29:18; 31:12; Neh 8:3). Rules of negligence and homicide apply equally whether men or women were victims (e.g., Exod 21:18–21). Both men and women could take the Nazirite vow (Num 6:2). Nevertheless, given the manifest lesser legal status of women attested throughout the Hebrew Bible, these few instances of equality should not be overrated.

[*See also* Family Structures, *subentry* Hebrew Bible; Imagery, Gendered, *subentry* Prophetic Literature; Male-Female Sexuality, *subentry* Hebrew Bible; Marriage and Divorce, *subentry* Hebrew Bible; Race, Class and Ethnicity, *subentry* Hebrew Bible; Religious Participation, *subentry* Hebrew Bible; *and* Sexual Transgression, *subentry* Hebrew Bible.]

BIBLIOGRAPHY

Anderson, Cheryl B. *Women, Ideology, and Violence: Critical Theory and the Construction of Gender in the Book of the Covenant and the Deuteronomic Laws.* Journal for the Study of the Old Testament, Supplement Series 394. London: T&T Clark, 2004.

Bellefontaine, Elizabeth. "Deuteronomy 21:18–21: Reviewing the Case of the Rebellious Son." *Journal for the Study of the Old Testament* 13 (1979): 13–31.

Block, Daniel I. "Marriage and Family in Ancient Israel." In *Marriage and Family in the Biblical World*, edited by Ken M. Campbell, pp. 33–102. Downer's Grove, Ill.: InterVarsity Press, 2003.

Branch, Robin Gallaher. *Jeroboam's Wife: The Enduring Contributions of the Old Testament's Least-Known Women.* Peabody, Mass.: Hendrickson, 2009.

Brenner, Athalya. *The Intercourse of Knowledge.* Leiden, The Netherlands: Brill, 1997.

Davis, Kingsley. *Human Society.* New York: Macmillan, 1950.

Driver, Godfrey R., and John C. Miles, *The Babylonian Laws.* Vol. 1. Oxford: Clarendon, 1952.

Frymer-Kensky, Tikva S. "The Strange Case of the Suspected *Sotah* (Numbers V 11–31)." *Vetus Testamentum* 34 (1984a): 11–26.

Frymer-Kensky, Tikva S. "Women." In *Harper's Bible Dictionary*, edited by Paul J. Achtemeier, pp. 1138–1141. San Francisco: Harper & Row, 1984b.

Frymer-Kensky, Tikva S. "Anatolia and the Levant: Israel." In *A History of Ancient Near Eastern Law*, edited by Raymond Westbrook, Vol. 2, pp. 975–1046. Handbuch der Orientalistik 72. Leiden, The Netherlands: Brill, 2003.

Kemper, Theodore D. "On the Nature and Purpose of Ascription." *American Sociological Review* 39 (1974): 844–853.

Kiboko, J. Kabamba. "Divination in 1 Samuel 28 and Beyond: An African Study in the Politics of Translation." Ph.D. diss., University of Denver, 2010.

Levine, Baruch A. *Numbers 1–20: A New Translation with Introduction and Commentary.* Anchor Bible 4. Garden City, N.Y.: Doubleday, 1993.

Loewenstamm, Samuel E. "The Laws of Adultery and Murder in Biblical and Mesopotamian Law." In *Comparative Studies in Biblical and Ancient Oriental Literatures*, pp. 146–153. Kevelaer, Germany: Butzon & Bercker, 1980.

Magdalene, F. Rachel. "Ancient Near Eastern Treaty Curses and the Ultimate Texts of Terror: A Study of the Language of Divine Sexual Abuse in the Prophetic Corpus." In *Feminist Companion to the Latter Prophets*, edited by Athalya Brenner, pp. 326–352. Feminist Companion to the Bible 8. Sheffield, U.K.: Sheffield Academic, 1995.

Magdalene, F. Rachel. "Abortion. I. ANE and Hebrew Bible/OT." In *Encyclopedia of the Bible and Its Reception*, edited by Dale C. Allison et al., Vol. 1, pp. 138–140. New York: Walter de Gruyter, 2009.

Matthews, Victor H. "Family Relationships." In *Dictionary of the Old Testament: Pentateuch*, edited by T. Destmond Alexander and David W. Baker, pp. 291–299. Downer's Grove, Ill.: InterVarsity, 2002.

Matthews, Victor H. "Marriage and Family in the Ancient Near East." In *Marriage and Family in the Biblical World*, edited by Ken M. Campbell, pp. 1–32. Downer's Grove, Ill.: InterVarsity, 2003.

McKane, W. "Poison, Trial by Ordeal and the Cup of Wrath." *Vetus Testamentum* 30 (1980): 474–492.

McKeating, Henry. "Sanctions against Adultery in Ancient Israelite Society, with Some Reflections on Methodology in the Study of Old Testament Ethics." *Journal for the Study of the Old Testament* 11 (1979): 57–63.

McKenzie, J. L. "The Elders in the Old Testament." *Biblica* 40 (1959): 522–540 (= *Analecta Biblica* 10: 388–406).

Mernissi, Fatima. "Femininity as Subversion: Reflections on the Muslim Concept of Nushãz." In *Speaking of Faith: Cross-cultural Perspectives on Women, Religion, and Social Change*, edited by Diana L. Eck and Devaki Jain, pp. 88–100. London: Women's Press, 1986.

Otto, Eckart. *Gottes Recht als Menschenrecht: Rechts- und literaturhistorische Studien zum Deuteronomium*. Beiträge zur Zeitschrift für altorientalische und biblische Rechtsgeschichte 2. Wiesbaden, Germany: Harrassowitz, 2000.

Parsons, Talcott. *The Social System*. Glencoe, Ill.: Free Press, 1951.

Phillips, Anthony. "Another Look at Adultery." *Journal for the Study of the Old Testament* 20 (1981): 3–25.

Pressler, Carolyn. *The View of Women Found in the Deuteronomic Family Laws*. Berlin: Walter de Gruyter, 1993.

Schloen, J. David. *The House of the Father as Fact and Symbol: Patrimonialism in Ugarit and the Ancient Near East*. Studies in the Archaeology and History of the Levant 2. Winona Lake, Ind.: Eisenbrauns, 2001.

Scholz, Susanne. *Sacred Witness: Rape in the Hebrew Bible*. Minneapolis: Fortress, 2010.

Stol, Marten. *Birth in Babylonia and the Bible*. Cuneiform Monographs 14. Groningen, The Netherlands: Styx, 2000.

Van der Toorn, Karel. *Family Religion in Babylonia, Syria, and Israel*. Leiden, The Netherlands: Brill, 1996.

Weber, Max. *The Theory of Social and Economic Organization*. 2 vols. Translated and edited by A. M. Henderson and Talcott Parsons. Oxford and New York: Oxford University Press, 1947.

Wegner, Judith Romney. *Chattel or Person? The Status of Women in the Mishnah*. Oxford and New York: Oxford University Press, 1988.

Wells, Bruce. "Sex, Lies and Virginal Rape: The Slandered Bride and False Accusation in Deuteronomy." *Journal of Biblical Literature* 124 (2005): 41–72.

Westbrook, Raymond. "The Prohibition on Restoration of Marriage in Deuteronomy 24:1–4." In *Studies in Bible*, edited by Sara Japhet, pp. 387–405. Scripta Hierosolymitana 35. Jerusalem: Hebrew University, 1986.

Westbrook, Raymond. "Adultery in Ancient Near Eastern Law." *Revue Biblique* 97 (1990): 542–580. Reprinted in *Law from the Tigris to the Tiber: The Writings of Raymond Westbrook, 1983–2008*, edited by Bruce Wells and F. Rachel Magdalene, Vol 1., pp. 245–287. Winona Lake, Ind.: Eisenbrauns, 2009.

Westbrook, Raymond. *Property and the Family in Biblical Law*. Journal for the Study of the Old Testament, Supplement Series 113. Sheffield, U.K.: JSOT Press, 1991.

Westbrook, Raymond. "The Female Slave." In *Gender and Law in the Hebrew Bible and the Ancient Near East*, edited by Victor Matthews et al., pp, 214–238. Journal for the Study of the Old Testament, Supplement Series 262. Sheffield, U.K.: Sheffield Academic Press, 1998.

Westbrook, Raymond. "Introduction: The Character of Ancient Near Eastern Law." In *A History of Ancient Near Eastern Law*, edited by Raymond Westbrook, Vol. 1, pp. 1–90. Handbuch der Orientalistik 72. Leiden, The Netherlands: Brill, 2003.

Westbrook, Raymond. "The Laws of Biblical Israel." In *The Hebrew Bible: New Insights and Scholarship*, edited by Frederick E. Greenspahn, pp. 99–119. New York: New York University Press, 2008. Reprinted in *Law from the Tigris to the Tiber: The Writings of Raymond Westbrook, 1983–2008*, edited by Bruce Wells and F. Rachel Magdalene, Vol. 1, pp. 317–340. 2 vols. Winona Lake, Ind.: Eisenbrauns, 2009.

Willis, Timothy. *The Elders of the City: A Study of the Elders-Laws in Deuteronomy*. Society of Biblical Literature Monograph Series 55. Atlanta: Society of Biblical Literature, 2001.

Wunsch, Cornelia, and F. Rachel Magdalene. "Freedom and Dependency: Neo-Babylonian Manumission Documents with Oblation and Service Obligation." In *Extraction and Control: Studies in Honor of Matthew W. Stolper*, edited by Michael Kozuh et al., pp. 337–346. Studies in Ancient Oriental Civilizations 68. Chicago: Oriental Institute of the University of Chicago, 2014.

Wunsch, Cornelia, and F. Rachel Magdalene. *Manumission, Emancipation, and Oblation: On Changing Personal Status in Neo-Babylonian Times.* Babylonian Archives. Dresden: ISLET-Verlag, 2015.

F. Rachel Magdalene

Greek World

See Family Structures, *subentry* Greek World; *and* Marriage and Divorce, *subentry* Greek World.

Roman World

Any overview of legal status and gender in the Roman Empire is obliged to acknowledge that in Roman law distinctions between male and female were in some ways outweighed in importance by distinctions between free and enslaved persons and, in the case of free persons, between citizens and noncitizens. This is because Roman law, based on notions of personality, applied only to those who were both free and citizens. Slaves, who were neither free nor citizens, were "nonpersons" with no rights in Roman law. The many inhabitants of the empire who were not citizens also had no rights in Roman law until the granting of universal citizenship by the emperor Caracalla in the third century C.E. Women who were free citizens, meanwhile, had access to law as a means of regulating aspects of social and economic life and often used it to their advantage.

Nevertheless, the law did not grant equal rights to men and women. A focus on legal status and gender helps to demonstrate how granting rights or imposing limitations based on gender-based norms was part of the development of law and public policy in the early Roman Empire. Gender-based assumptions and stereotypes are detectable in the writings of the so-called classical jurists, legal scholars who were active from the first century B.C.E. to the third century C.E. These assumptions, whether encoded in legal rights and restrictions or expressed directly by the jurists, influenced the relationship of Roman citizens to the law and to institutions such as marriage. This overview of legal status and gender focuses on the evidence of the early Imperial period, highlighting both the opportunities and the limitations it created for women.

Sources of Roman Law. The *Digest* of Justinian provides most of the source material for Roman law of the first century B.C.E. to the third century C.E. The *Digest*, a massive text compiled in the sixth century C.E. by legal scholars working under Emperor Justinian, contains excerpts from the Latin works by early Imperial jurists. For ease of reference, Justinian's compilers organized the books of the *Digest* by topic, such as marriage or divorce, with relevant segments of classical juristic works cited. Jurists whose writings are particularly well represented in the *Digest* are Ulpian, Julian, Papinian, Modestinus, and Paul. The jurists, who were neither judges nor lawyers, did not make or enact laws; rather, they worked as a small circle of intellectuals sponsored by the emperor, offering comment and interpretation on how the law should apply and sometimes disagreeing with each other.

Apart from the *Digest,* the *Institutes* of Gaius, a second-century legal handbook that survives in its entirety, provides evidence for certain Roman legal institutions that were keyed to gender roles, such as the guardianship of women, as we will see below. A later source, the *Excerpts from Ulpian's Writings* (*Tituli ex corpore Ulpiani*) was composed in the fourth century C.E. Some written responses, or rescripts, of Roman emperors to legal questions submitted by citizen petitioners also survive. Found in the *Codex* of Justinian, compiled in the sixth century C.E., these second- and third-century rescripts provide insight into how law played a part in the lives of citizens and into how the emperor responded to citizen requests. Finally, documentary papyri that have survived from Roman Egypt, such as records or requests by petitioners to a civic official, are invaluable for revealing how gender-based legal rights and restrictions affected the daily life of citizens.

Legal Capacity: Rights and Restrictions. In the Roman Empire, a free citizen female was likely to be under the legal authority of a male. If her father was alive, she was under paternal power (*patria potestas*). By this power, her father (*paterfamilias*) owned all of her possessions; he also had the traditional "right of life and death" (*ius vitae necisque*), which, although rarely exercised by the early empire, permitted him to end the life of his offspring. His approval was also legally required for her marriage to be valid. It should be noted that these aspects of paternal power, including approval of marriage, applied to male as well as female children. Nor was *patria potestas* eliminated once a child passed the age of puberty and ceased to be a minor; adults with living fathers, too, were under *patria potestas*.

In an early form of Roman marriage, a wife was transferred into the power of her husband (*manus*), at which point she was removed from the power of her father. The legal consequences of *manus* were in some ways similar to the consequences of *patria potestas*, although the evidence for *manus* is scant. As the jurist Gaius notes, a wife in *manus* was held to be "in the position of a daughter" if her husband died without leaving his will, leaving her to inherit a share of the estate equal to that of each of her children (Gaius, *Institutes*, 3.1–3). There is no conclusive evidence, however, that a husband held the right of life and death over his wife who was in *manus*, and thus there is reason to believe that *manus* was a less all-encompassing power than *patria potestas*. By the early empire, moreover, *manus* marriage was not common, and a married woman remained in *patria potestas* as long as her father was alive.

Upon the death of the *paterfamilias*, citizen women as well as men became legally independent, or "in their own power" (*sui iuris*); in this area, the law made an important gender-based distinction. An adult male became a *paterfamilias* when his father died, with *patria potestas* over his offspring; an adult female did not acquire an equivalent legal status. Female children or adults who were *sui iuris* remained under the legal control of an appointed male guardian (*tutor*), in the institution of guardianship (*tutela*). The guardianship of adult women (*tutela mulierum*) brought with it some restrictions on an individual woman's freedom, including the requirement that her *tutor* give approval for major legal transactions, including

entering a marriage, bringing certain types of lawsuits, or writing a will (*Excerpts from Ulpian's Writings*, 11.27).

The limitations, however, on women's freedom to manage their affairs appear to have been limited. Even without a *tutor* women had some ability to alienate property, take up lawsuits, and act as creditors (Gaius, *Institutes*, 2.80–81, 85). The gender-based assumptions behind the institution of guardianship, too, attracted the notice of the jurists. Gaius expressed skepticism at the explanation commonly given for permanent guardianship, women's "weakness of judgment" (*levitas animi*), and observed that in some situations a *tutor* gave permission for a transaction solely as a matter of form and often could be compelled by a civic official, the praetor, to give permission even if unwillingly (Gaius, *Institutes*, 1.190–191).

Although it appears that the constraints of guardianship were gradually eroded or circumvented, there was also a positive legal right granted to women, beginning in the first century C.E. with Emperor Augustus, which explicitly linked legal and economic freedom with successful childbearing. This "right of (three) children" (*ius [trium] liberorum*)—"three" is sometimes, but not always, included in ancient citations of the right—allowed women who had given birth to three children to be freed from guardianship. Although evidence for *ius liberorum* is not plentiful, one surviving third-century C.E. document on papyrus from Roman Egypt attests that some women exercised it. For example, a woman named Aurelia Thasous, from the town of Oxyrhynchus in the Fayyum region of Egypt, undertakes a business transaction independently. She notes, in addressing the prefect, that she manages her own affairs because she possesses the right of three children (*P. Oxy.* XII.1467).

Although the implementation of such a right for women suggests an effort to expand rather than curtail their legal and economic freedom, it also generated worries that women would not be capable of managing their affairs. The perceived need to protect women from financial harm prompted actions by the Roman senate to place limits on their freedom to do business. By the provision of the Velleian senatorial decree (*senatusconsultum Velleianum*) in the first century C.E., women were forbidden from "interceding" on behalf of others, including their husbands, by taking on or guaranteeing their debts. As the jurist Paul notes (*Digest*, 16.1.1), the justification for this restriction was that women should not be allowed to assume too much risk when it came to their family property.

The Velleian senatorial decree addressed a perceived vulnerability faced by inexperienced women who undertook financial transactions. Although this was a valid concern, it is worth noting that disparities between the expertise of men and women in business affairs were primarily a reflection of traditional Roman social values, such as the premium placed on female modesty. Such concerns were pronounced enough to prompt restrictions on the ability of a respectable citizen woman to engage in some activities or types of work. Women's role in politics was extremely limited; for example, women were unable to vote or hold public office. In professional life, they were ineligible for the position of *tutor*, as noted above, and could not take on the position of banker, nor could they represent others in court.

In discussing each of these examples, jurists such as Neratius, writing under Emperor Hadrian, and Ulpian, writing a century later under Emperor Septimius Severus, expressly state that certain careers are more suitable for males (*Digest*, 26.1.16 pr.; 2.13.12; 3.1.1.5). They do not mention women's weakness of judgment as in discussion of the reasons for guardianship, but rather suggest that certain professions or activities bring with them the risk of corruption of female virtue. This is perhaps most evident in Ulpian's mention of the behavior of Carfania, a woman who assumed the role of lawyer, as the initial spur for the prohibition. Ulpian's mention of Carfania's example reveals the discomfort provoked by independent female action in the world of the courtroom. A similar concern for virtuous femininity is implied in the prohibition on banking (*Digest*, 2.13.4), a semipublic activity. Ultimately, these restrictions imply an additional assumption about women's lives, namely that respectable women would occupy themselves in the private, domestic sphere and have little need to enter the public world. The

vision of a respectable woman as playing the role of household manager likely explains an exception to one of the gender-based restrictions on guardianship: a woman could seek permission from the emperor to assume the role of *tutor* for her minor-age children and thus to manage their estate (*Digest*, 26.1.18).

Marriage. The jurist Modestinus (*Digest*, 23.2.1) described marriage as "the union of a male and a female," and Roman law emphasizes procreation as the purpose of marriage, implying that heterosexual unions were envisioned as the norm. Assumptions about gender roles also influenced the legal rules related to marriage and divorce. In Roman legal thought, marriage was based on the agreement of the partners; valid matrimony required initial and ongoing consent and "marital affection" (*affectio maritalis*), as Ulpian calls it, of both husband and wife. The requirement of mutual consent meant, too, that divorce could be achieved by either spouse unilaterally, as we will see below.

Although consent and affection appear to endorse marriage as a voluntary union, the state, beginning with Emperor Augustus, also undertook to compel citizens of childbearing age to marry and reproduce. The emphasis on procreation is most evident in the legislation enacted by Augustus in 18 B.C.E. and 9 C.E., the *Julian and Papian Laws*. One part of this legislation required male citizens ages 25 to 60 and female citizens ages 20 to 50 to marry and have children or be penalized in their ability to inherit from persons to whom they were not closely related. Those married couples who did not have children, for example, could inherit only one tenth of each other's property (*Excerpts from Ulpian's Writings*, 15.1–2, 16.1–2). The laws also for the first time made adultery a criminal offense to be adjudicated in the court system rather than in the household.

The state's emphasis on reproduction as the purpose of marriage prompted the Roman jurists to consider how the ability to procreate should affect eligibility for marriage. The minimum age for entry to marriage, around the age of puberty for both boys and girls, suggests that sexual maturity was a criterion (*Excerpts from Ulpian's Writings*, 5.2). Occasionally, a jurist's consideration of a problem related to procreation and eligibility for marriage will offer insight into Roman cultural perceptions of gender categories. In one case, Ulpian considers the question of whether a eunuch (*spado*), who was incapable of fathering children, should be able to marry. Given the emphasis placed by the state on procreation, a negative answer might be expected. Ulpian suggests otherwise, however, noting that a eunuch should be eligible to marry as long as his condition is congenital and not the result of castration (*Digest*, 23.3.39.1). This interpretation of the law appears to imply an objection to castration rather than a worry about infertility; that it does so underscores the notion that concerns about status could occasionally overwhelm concerns about the proper fulfillment of reproductive roles.

In Ulpian's view, a couple need not be able to procreate to be married, yet it is clear that once a husband and wife had children, the patriarchal structure of the Roman family had an effect on the relationship of the father and mother to their children. Because the Roman family (*familia*) was based on a model of agnatic kinship, with emphasis on the male line and *patria potestas*, a wife was technically not in the *familia* of her children—she remained in the power of her father for as long as he lived and then was in her own power. This had some legal consequences for women, as we will see below, in the case of child custody upon divorce.

Divorce and Remarriage. The Augustan legislation makes clear that the Roman state was willing to use law to usher citizens into marriage, but this legislation did not encourage marriage by prohibiting or restricting divorce. Roman law, more generally, took a surprisingly hands-off approach to divorce, which could be achieved by either spouse—sometimes, it appears from juristic discussion, without even notifying the affected spouse. Some literary sources indicate that divorced women, especially, could be socially marginalized, but there is little sign of this in the discussion of the jurists. "No-fault" divorce was the accepted model, in which the divorcing spouse was not required to prove that an offense had been committed against the marriage by the other spouse.

Divorce may have been easy to initiate, but a wife undergoing divorce could also confront a challenge in regard to the dowry she had brought to the marriage, and this challenge reflects gender-based norms. Her dowry, although recoverable upon divorce (or death) of her husband, presumably to facilitate remarriage, was under her husband's control for the duration of the marriage. If the marriage ended in divorce, a portion of the dowry—which could be made up of a number of elements, including slaves, land, and cash—could be retained by the husband if he could prove his wife had committed a moral offense; a portion could also be kept for the children if he could show that he had committed no moral wrong. The deductions that might be taken from the dowry for the support of children also highlight that in cases of divorce, the children of the union typically went with the father, as an opinion of Ulpian makes clear (*Digest*, 43.30.3.5). In the case of child custody, it appears that *patria potestas* was privileged over the maternal relationship.

Extramarital and Illegal Sexual Relations. Beginning with the legislation of Emperor Augustus in 18 B.C.E., the state enforced marital fidelity by punishing the offense of adultery, which was defined in terms of the status of the woman who was involved. Specifically, adultery was defined as extramarital sexual relations by or with a married woman. Although concerned with the conduct of men as well as women, the criminal charge of adultery largely focused on women, since uncertainty about paternity could lead to offspring being deemed illegitimate. The legislation served to distinguish married women from prostitutes, with whom sexual relations were not illegal. From this feature of the law, it is clear that the ideologies of status as well as those of gender were of interest to the emperor in its creation.

Likewise, questions about the proper punishment for adultery centered, in juristic discussion, on women. A father who apprehended a daughter in the midst of adulterous behavior was granted a very limited "right to kill" (*ius occidendi*) (*Digest*, 48.5.21–22; 48.5.24 pr., 4). A husband was permitted to kill an adulterer discovered with his wife in their home (*Digest*, 48.5.25 pr., 1) and might have his punishment mitigated if he overstepped this right, as a rescript of third-century Emperor Alexander Severus suggests (*Codex of Justinian*, 9.9.4.1). He was, however, as the jurist Papinian wrote, prohibited from killing his wife (*Digest*, 48.5.39.8). These efforts to delineate and restrict the right to kill an adulterous woman speak to the juristic interest in limiting it. The alternative punishment, however, could be severe and lasting. A woman convicted of adultery could face a range of punishments, including loss of a portion of her dowry and the inability to remarry (*Excerpts from the Writings of Ulpian*, 13.2; *Digest*, 23.2.43.12–13).

The hard line taken against female adultery is made in an extraordinary case discussed by Ulpian, in which a girl who has not yet turned 12, the minimum age of marriage, can be accused of adultery as a fiancée (*Digest*, 48.5.14.8). This categorization of a betrothed girl as an adulteress vividly illustrates how gender-based ideology could exert a strong influence on decisions about legal status, with potentially serious consequences for young women. Meanwhile, assumptions about women's proper place in relation to legal procedure are implied in the restriction on their bringing an accusation of adultery to court. A rescript of the emperors Septimius Severus and Caracalla, from the third century C.E., states that in a public trial women were not permitted to bring an accusation of adultery, even against their husbands (*Codex of Justinian*, 9.9.1).

Although women were punished harshly for adultery, the high value placed on modesty meant that they were also protected by the law against sexual assault or harassment of respectable women. The punishment of this assault or harassment, which is labeled *stuprum*, or "illicit sexual activity," similarly seems pointed toward protecting male interests. In the case of an unmarried virgin, the interests of her *paterfamilias* are being protected; in the case of a wife, the interests of her husband are central.

Recent Debates. Contemporary studies of women's role in Roman law and society have taken up the question of whether gender-based categories in legal and nonlegal texts show points of contact with each other and what this might imply about the interplay between Roman law and social norms. Using the evidence of the *Digest* and other legal and nonlegal texts, scholars have attempted to evaluate the extent to which Roman law responded to social attitudes toward gender; on the other side, scholars have asked whether law acquired a normative dimension, shaping assumptions and expectations in society as much as being influenced by them.

These lines of inquiry raise related questions about the level of contact the inhabitants of the Roman Empire had with the institution of the law. Among the citizenry, how far up and down the social ladder, for example, were Roman legal rules observed and enforced? Moreover, although female Roman citizens in Asia Minor or Egypt were subject to the same set of laws as were their counterparts in Rome itself, the unevenness of the evidence—apart, perhaps, from papyrological evidence in Egypt—prevents us from concluding much about the impact of law on the daily lives of citizens across the geographically expansive empire. The debate on these topics is ongoing, and many of the secondary sources listed are engaged in it.

[*See also* Economics, *subentry* Roman World; Family Structures, *subentries on* New Testament *and* Roman World; Legal Status, *subentry* New Testament; *and* Marriage and Divorce, *subentries on* New Testament *and* Roman World.]

BIBLIOGRAPHY

Primary Sources

The Commentaries of Gaius and the Rules of Ulpian. Translated by J. T. Abdy and B. Walker. Cambridge, U.K.: Cambridge University Press, 1885. Reprint, Clark, N.J.: Lawbook Exchange, 2006.

The Digest of Justinian. Rev. ed. 4 vols. Edited by A. Watson. Philadelphia: University of Pennsylvania Press, 2009.

The Institutes of Gaius. Translated by W. M. Gordon and O. F. Robinson. Ithaca, N.Y.: Cornell University Press, 1988.

The Oxyrhynchus Papyri. London: Egypt Exploration Society, 1898.

Tituli ex corpore Ulpiani. In *Fontes Iuris Romani Antejustiniani* II, 2d ed., pp. 261–301, edited by J. Baviera. Florence: Barbera, 1968.

Secondary Sources

Arjava, A. *Women and Law in Late Antiquity*. Oxford: Clarendon, 1996.

Evans Grubbs, J. *Women and Law in the Roman Empire: A Sourcebook on Marriage, Divorce and Widowhood*. New York: Routledge, 2002.

Frier, B. W., and Th. A. J. McGinn. *A Casebook on Roman Family Law.* New York: Oxford University Press, 2004.

Gardner, J. F. *Women in Roman Law and Society.* London: Croom Helm, 1986.

Gardner, J. F. "Gender-Role Assumptions in Roman Law." *Echos du Monde Classique/Classical Views* 39, no. 14 (1995): 377–400.

McGinn, Th. A. J. *Prostitution, Sexuality, and the Law in Ancient Rome.* New York: Oxford University Press, 1998.

Rowlandson, J. *Women and Society in Greek and Roman Egypt: A Sourcebook.* Cambridge, U.K.: Cambridge University Press, 1998.

Treggiari, S. *Roman Marriage: "Iusti Coniuges" from the Time of Cicero to the Time of Ulpian.* Oxford: Clarendon, 1991.

Lauren Caldwell

New Testament

Gender has to do with how bodies are configured and scripted to perform in certain ways. Gender, therefore, is about identity, about identifying with and being identified by a certain bodily configuration or performance. The law, however, is concerned with regulating and disciplining bodies. It is an important, sometimes dominant, script in this process of shaping and scripting bodies—individual and communal, male and female, free and slave. Legal texts, therefore, offer insight into the complex negotiation involved in identity construction.

Pursuing the question of gender and legal status in the New Testament provides a window into how the ancients engaged in this complex negotiation of identity and, more tellingly, how the early Christ-follower communities both mimicked and resisted the dominant scripts (and scripting) of the ambient cultures of the Mediterranean. Although the influence of a Greco-Roman and Jewish scripting on the body—the *ekklesia*—of Christ-followers is clearly evident, it is equally important to note that this body negotiated a new ethnic identity. The New Testament is thus both a product of a scripting influence and itself engaged in rescripting and reconfiguring the bodies comprised therein.

Reading the New Testament with a view toward tracing how legal status and gender intersect is to read how gendered bodies are regulated and disciplined to perform in certain normative ways and how this happens through law, both narrowly and broadly defined. Such a reading requires careful consideration for how gender and law are but parts of a more thickly layered interplay of social categories. This entry seeks to navigate the confluence and contestation of these social categories, the connective tissue that holds together the concrete setting within which the early Christ-follower communities negotiated identity in the shadow of the empire.

Intersectionality: Overlapping Social Categories. The tendency to treat topics such as gender and legal status or law as mutually exclusive social categories results in a "single-axis framework" (Crenshaw, 2011, p. 25) that does not do justice to how law actively engages in an act of gender scripting. It is necessary, therefore, to approach the topic intersectionally, reading gender and law within a multiaxial framework that wrestles with the interplay and overlapping of these categories, as well as a range of others (Kartzow, 2012). These overlapping and interlocking systems play a significant role in the scripting of identity in general and of gendered identity in particular.

When applied to the New Testament, intersectionality draws attention to the reality of overlapping arenas and enables a more thickly textured reading of gender, or power, confirming that "gender is the primary way of signifying relations of power" (Scott, 1999, p. 48). This approach presupposes that gender (identity) is constructed (Lieu, 2004) and that such construction reflects the overlapping of social, economic, ethnic, political, and religious scripts that inform and shape bodily performance—that is, the continuous rehearsal of certain behaviors, traits, and expectations that constitute femininity and masculinity.

The regulation and scripting of gendered bodies raises several key questions with which we must wrestle: (1) How was the regulating and scripting achieved? (2) Who constructed and controlled the means by which that regulating and scripting took place? (3) To what degree was the regulating and scripting effective; that is, is there evidence of resistance?

Legal Status and Gender. Regulating and scripting bodies was achieved by means of a complex web of texts. The word "texts" here refers both to actual texts (literary sources) and to the mass media of the Mediterranean world (a range of images). The literary data include extant legal texts (e.g., *The Institutes of Gaius*, Justinian's *Digest*, *Code of Justinian*, and *Theodosian Code*). Although these literary texts give us access to a particular vantage point from which to view the role of the law in regulating and scripting bodily performance, their angle of vision is narrow. The textual data alone can obscure the more complex machinations of gender construction and legal status, precisely because the authors of texts are engaged in an act of constructing. They control what (or who) is made visible and what (or who) is kept from view.

To fill out the picture, the broader material culture (graffiti, reliefs, inscriptions, friezes, etc.) must figure in our reconstruction of how bodies were regulated, not only by legislation, but also by authoritative (normativizing) texts and images. Material culture illuminates those aspects that texts tend to hide from plain view. This is particularly important when studying legal texts since they provide only the perspective of the elite for whom the legal codes are put into service. Furthermore, the legal codes obscure any evidence of resistance because they seek to effect conformity to particular norms.

Gender and identity: Text and image. Identity in the ancient world was actively constructed (Punt, 2012) and its construction was achieved through both text (as a crystallization and reproduction of memory) and image.

The early Christ-follower communities of the first century C.E. were rooted within a rich textual tradition and were themselves developing a textual tradition of their own, which served as a way of both reflecting and constituting a particular identity. These texts were a crystallization of the cultural memory of the Christ communities and served "to stabilize and convey that society's self-image" (Punt, 2012, p. 30).

Since texts have "both a 'life' and an 'effect' " (Vander Stichele and Penner, 2009, p. 83), they give us access to "how *the shaping of a body of literature has a correlating effect on the formation of early Christian identity*" (p. 83, italics added). So while the early Christ-follower communities were engaged in an exercise of scripting bodies through the development of a body of texts, the enterprise was, in macrocosm, being undertaken by the empire, where the role of texts as a reproduction of memory, even mythical memory, in the construction of social identity can be seen as, for example, in Virgil's *Aeneid*.

To read a body of texts is to read the body of a community, and to do so is to read how bodies, individual and collective, were visually (re-)presented and (re-)imaged in the first century. In this setting, the gendered bodies of women and men become the social and political sites for regulating and disciplining social norms and conventions and for re-inscribing the deeply entrenched hierarchy of the Greco-Roman world. The physical body, however it is (re-)presented, is a symbol of the social body, the body politic—and in the case of the New Testament, the Roman imperial body politic.

Although bodies became sites for imaging the social structuring of society, it is important to note that not all bodies were the same. Some bodies mattered more than others. Some bodies were merely scaffolding for the construction of identity for bodies that really mattered (e.g., slave bodies and the bodies of conquered nations were all textually represented to underwrite the identity of those in power).

The intersection of textual representation with art, architecture, and sculpture becomes an important intertext for making sense of how bodies were being configured and often disfigured (Kahl, 2010). Engagement with texts and the broader material culture enables a more complex picture of how bodies were constructed to emerge. Furthermore, such engagement also enriches the interplay between text and image in the construction of identity. This is critical to the question of gender and legal status since in many ways the images we have to work with often provide evidence of how identity was in fact constructed quite apart from the ideals expressed in some of the texts.

In addition to a sculptural program that depicted conquered nations as female bodies (e.g., the many friezes of the Sebasteion at Aphrodisias; see Lopez, 2008), we may note too how women's bodies became the site of Roman imperial ideology, with emperors using their wives to persuade other women, especially those of higher social rank, to conform to the normativizing script of the empire. This illustrates the use of women's bodies for political and social ends and functioned as the means by which a normative sense of gender distinction and place in society was inculcated. Bruce Winter (2003) frames the matter this way: "The imperial clothing and hairstyles of wives were meant to make them icons and trendsetters and…were deliberately used to counter influences in society which were judged detrimental to its well-being" (p. 176).

Legislation in the Roman period. Within the classical period of Roman history (ca. 200 B.C.E.–300 C.E.), it is important to note that the ancient legal system of the Romans reflects the intersection of social coding (honor/shame, belonging, status, etc.) and legislation. The legal system, established by the social elite, reflected the attempt of the elite to both prop up a particular social hierarchy and, through social coding, maintain and exercise control (Knapp 2011, p. 34). Thus, at both the implicit and the explicit level, the Roman legal system was not simply a matter of regulating through legal prescription or sanction. Instead, a more complex notion of social conditioning emerges. This is evident in the legislation governing dress and adornment and reinforces the notion that "Roman jurisprudence distinguished between them [respectable married women and high-class prostitutes and others] by means of their appearance which was defined in terms of apparel and adornment" (Winter, 2003, p. 4). By projecting the ideal imperial family onto society, Augustus (and some who would come after him), for whom appearance was critically important, was engaging in a normalizing scripting of the ideal woman, of the ideal family.

In the Roman legal system, then, we find legal sanction intermingled with social conditioning, which, despite its potency, failed on one level to curtail certain behaviors, particularly as it related to gender. On this, Winter's (2003) study on the emergence of "new women" who resisted the traditional roles assigned to them by actively participating in public life and by pushing the boundaries around sexual propriety is particularly instructive, especially for our reading of the New Testament.

Roman law and the family. The Roman family reflected a strong bias toward men, establishing the *pater* (father) as the head of the *familia*, "the basic Roman social and property-owning unit" (Gardner, 2009, p. 4). In this role, the *pater* exercised almost omnipotent power and authority over the members of the household, which included wives, children, grandchildren, and slaves (and often their children, claimed as property of the estate). This power and control, known as the *patria potestas*, over the household was a legal right of the *pater* and is noted by Gaius, a mid-second-century jurist who comments on its uniqueness: "Again, we have in our power our children, the offspring of a Roman law marriage. This right is one which only Roman citizens have; there are virtually no other people who have such power over their sons as we have over ours" (*Institutes*, 1.55). The *pater* would exercise this control for as long as he lived, regardless of the whether "his descendants matured and established independent households" (Arjava, 1998, p. 148). This had far-reaching implications for the legal status of the family members, the *filius familias* (male children) and *filia familias* (female children).

Under the *potestas* of the *pater*, adult children were not in any position to engage in economic transactions without the consent of the *pater*, could not own property, and were often at the mercy of the *pater* when it came to marriage. When adult children did engage in economic transactions, with consent, all acquisitions were accrued to the *pater*. Thus adult children could make their way through life (at least for the duration of the *pater's* life) with either an allowance or a sum of money (or property), known as a *peculium*. Adult children were therefore nothing more than an extension of the *pater* and lived under his *potestas*.

The family served as an overlay for the empire and the Roman family as a microcosm of the empire. Structured as a larger family with a *pater* (caesar) in place, the empire was constructed to make a clear distinction between those who belonged to the family, Roman citizens, and those who did not. At this juncture we have a very interesting interplay, legally speaking.

Some recent interpreters have illustrated the legal semiotics attached to Roman imperial ideology. As a means of analyzing social codes and structures, semiotics is concerned with "how, and in whose interests, reality is constructed" (Lopez, 2008, p. 20). In her analysis of the Great Altar of Pergamon, Brigitte Kahl (2010) attempts to trace out a series of binaries that reflect how Roman imperial ideology sought to construct the *other* visually: "rationality versus stupidity, true manliness and courage versus self-destructive fearlessness and rashness, moderation and self-discipline versus excessive emotion and brainless action, righteousness versus lawlessness" (p. 103). The ubiquity of images such as these illustrate how the Romans sought to define themselves over against the other, and of particular interest is how this lawless other is so often cast in gendered terms as a woman's body. We will note this tendency again in our section on slavery.

Roman law and marriage. Marriage becomes one more site for the intersection of legal status and gender. Under Augustus three important pieces of legislation, designed to promote the particular vision of the empire, come into play: *lex Iulia de maritandis ordinibus* (18 B.C.E.), the *lex Iulia de adulteriis* (18 B.C.E.), and the *lex Papia Poppaea* (9 B.C.E.). Each of these laws reflects the attempt of the powerful to construct identity through legal sanction (and incentive). And although these laws were designed to promote marriage and childbearing, they carried specific gendered implications for Roman women in particular and likely much wider since, as Winter notes, the influence of Roman law and Roman society was not restricted to Roman citizens (Winter, 2003, p. 2).

For example, the *lex Iulia de adulteriis* granted the *pater* the right to impose "summary justice on a daughter caught in the act of adultery in his son-in-law's house" (Gardner, 2009, p. 6). This piece of legislation is clearly directed against women and seeks to curtail certain behaviors deemed out of place or inappropriate for women. And although it is evident that during the time of Augustus women charged with adultery were charged criminally, rather than capitally (Winter, 2003, p. 20), penetration of women's bodies and not penetrating men becomes the real issue. The sexual act is "about social and economic relations," and thus penetration was understood as a "social act that maps dominant and subordinate

relationships in the ancient world" (Vander Stichele and Penner, 2009, p. 45).

Likewise, women "were for their entire lives subject to some degree of limitation on their capacity for independent legal action" (Gardner, 1986, p. 4). Throughout their lives girls and women were under some form of guardianship. Even in marriage, women were restricted legally. Whether with their husband or, in his absence through death, an assigned tutor, women could only operate with reference to their guardian. The *lex Papia Poppaea*, however, did make provision for manumission from tutelage if women had three children.

Judaism and gender in the shadow of the empire. The presence and influence of Roman ideology was felt across the empire. Visually, conquered nations were constantly reminded (through architecture, coinage, art, etc.) of Rome's power to monopolize, control, and define the *other*. The extent of this presence meant that "There was no 'Rome-free' zone" (Kahl, 2010, p. 218). Jews, like the peoples of all other conquered nations, were eventually thoroughly integrated into the imperial mind-set (Pucci Ben Zeev, 2010, p. 351). Consequently, Jewish notions of gender, family, slavery, etc., were "virtually identical with those of its ambient culture(s)" (Cohen, 1993, p. 2).

In this contestational space, the right to claim bodies, to construct them, becomes a hard-fought battle. The negotiation of identity in the Roman Empire can be traced in the complex relationship between conqueror and conquered. This relationship allowed for a kind of flexibility in the exercise of Jewish rights, and although these were "neither permanent nor inherently stable" (Pucci Ben Zeev, 2010, p. 351), Jews were in some measure free to construct identity around specifically Jewish distinctives. Josephus notes this freedom in his *Jewish Antiquities* (11.338, also 12.142, 12.150), indicating that Jews were granted the right "to observe their country's laws." However, things are never quite so straightforward. We also have evidence to support the curtailment of such freedoms, which was always dependent "on the personal goodwill of the ruler who happened to be in power" (Pucci Ben Zeev, 2010, p. 368).

The active construction of identity, especially as it relates to the role of legal texts, defined broadly—the regulating role of sacred texts, and narrowly—the actual codification of legislation, in gender identity, meant that while the empire exerted its influence in such construction, Jews themselves actively engaged in this task. As Helena Zlotnik (2002) notes, "to be a Jew involves a complex series of prescriptive and preventive injunctions, do's and don'ts. To be a Jewess primarily means the latter" (p. 1). So although the Hebrew Bible and its interpretations, as regulating canon, present a general frame for what it meant to be Jewish, it did so in ways that cast women, in particular, by means of a series of negative examples. Women's bodies become sites for articulating boundary crossing. And where this is not the case, women's bodies are employed as exemplars of virtue (Zlotnik, p. 2). We must, however, be careful not to overstate the case and play into the notion that an absence of evidence of more positive examples of women and their roles necessarily implies "the male distortion of women's lives" (Kraemer, 1993, p. 101).

Slavery, gender, and legal implications. The intersection of slavery and gender constitutes another avenue to pursue when exploring the question of legal status and gender. Here again, bodies are at stake.

In ancient slaveholding cultures, slaves were considered commodities, rather than fully valorized human persons. This meant that slaves did not qualify as legal persons since they were objects, instruments, or, in Aristotle's terms, "tools that breathe" (*Politics*, 1.1252a–1256a). According to ancient political and religious scripts, slave bodies belonged to their masters, and slaves could not legally form families of their own.

The category of slaves was nuanced enough to recognize how gender difference played out in bodily ways, that is, in how such gendered bodies were utilized by their masters. Commenting on slaves' bodies as surrogates for the elite, Kartzow (2012) notes that slaves "could be imprisoned or beaten on behalf of their owners, and *both male and female slaves were sexually available for both their owners and others.* The most important sign of free male status was bodily integrity, that is, that they were not subject to sexual penetration or corporal punishment, a privilege also held by the poorest among free men, in contrast to slaves" (p. 38, italics added).

Although J. Albert Harrill (2006) notes that the physiognomic distinction between slaves and free bodies was a literary construction, these distinctions carried massive practical implications for notions of masculinity. Effectively, the literary distinctions served to construct a particular configuration of what it meant to be male, especially as it relates to the ability to exercise *auctoritas*, domination over others (Harrill, p. 36). The distinction, thus, had little to do with the relationship between free and slave. Instead, it had to do with how the free employed servile descriptions as invective against other free men. In other words, the slave physiognomics serves as just one more example of how the bodies of slaves were used in the construction of manhood (for the free).

Navigating Law, Gender, and the New Testament. This entry has attempted to provide a basic road map for reading gender and law or legal status in the New Testament. It has mapped out some key hermeneutical ideas that show the connection between bodies and gender, bodies and law, and has done so intersectionally. The navigational points sketched above may provide directionality for reading, for example, the *Haustafeln* in Paul, or the way in which Mark's Gospel seems to foreground women in discipleship. But perhaps most importantly, this entry has attempted to sensitize contemporary readers to the ways in which our engagement with authoritative texts—"legal" in the broad sense—continue to be put into the service of those at the center to script normative gender discourses. If in our reading of these sources, textual and visual, we do not see our own proclivities toward constructing identity—and gendered identity in particular—in restrictive ways, then we might be implicated in perpetuating exclusionary discourses. Ultimately, this entry signposts a journey toward much deeper wrestling with how legal status intersects gender and what the implications of that intersection are for our reading of New Testament texts.

[*See also* Family Structures, *subentries on* New Testament *and* Roman World; Gender Transgression, *subentry* New Testament; Intersectional Studies; Legal Status, *subentry* Roman World; Race, Class, and Ethnicity, *subentry* Roman World; *and* Rhetorical-Hermeneutical Criticism.]

BIBLIOGRAPHY

Arjava, Antti. "Paternal Power in Late Antiquity." *Journal of Roman Studies* 88 (1998): 147–165.

Cohen, Shaye J. D., ed. *The Jewish Family in Antiquity.* Atlanta: Scholars Press, 1993.

Crenshaw, Kimberlé W. "Demarginalising the Intersection of Race and Sex: A Black Feminist Critique of Anti-Discrimination Doctrine, Feminist Theory, and Anti-Racist Politics." In *Framing Intersectionality: Debates on a Multi-faceted Concept in Gender Studies*, edited by Helma Lutz, Maria Teresa Herrera Vivar, and Linda Supik, pp. 25–43. Aldershot, U.K.: Ashgate, 2011.

Gardner, Jane F. *Women in Roman Law and Society.* Bloomington: Indiana University Press, 1986.

Harrill, J. Albert. *Slaves in the New Testament: Literary, Social, and Moral Dimensions.* Minneapolis: Fortress, 2006.

Kahl, Brigitte. *Galatians Re-imagined: Reading with the Eyes of the Vanquished.* Paul in Critical Contexts. Minneapolis: Fortress, 2010.

Kartzow, Marianne Bjelland. *Destabilizing the Margins: An Intersectional Approach to Early Christian Memory.* Eugene, Ore.: Pickwick, 2012.

Knapp, Robert. *Invisible Romans: Prostitutes, Outlaws, Slaves, Gladiators, Ordinary Men and Women—The Romans That History Forgot.* London: Profile Books, 2011.

Kraemer, Ross S. "Jewish Mothers and Daughters in the Graeco-Roman World." In *The Jewish Family in Antiquity*, edited by Shaye J. D. Cohen, pp. 89–112. Atlanta: Scholars Press, 1993.

Lieu, Judith M. *Christian Identity in the Jewish and Graeco-Roman World.* Oxford: Oxford University Press, 2004.

Lopez, Davina C. *Apostle to the Conquered: Reimagining Paul's Mission.* Paul in Critical Contexts. Minneapolis: Fortress, 2008.

Pucci Ben Zeev, Miriam. "Jews among Greeks and Romans." In *Early Judaism: A Comprehensive Overview*, edited by John J. Collins and Daniel C. Harlow, pp. 367–389. Grand Rapids, Mich.: Eerdmans, 2010.

Punt, Jeremy. "Identity, Memory and Scriptural Warrant: Arguing Paul's Case." In *Early Christianity and Its Literature, Paul and Scripture: Extending the Conversation*, edited by Christopher D. Stanley, pp. 25–54. Atlanta: Society of Biblical Literature, 2012.

Scott, Joan Wallach. *Gender and the Politics of History.* Rev. ed. New York: Columbia University Press, 1999.

Vander Stichele, Caroline, and Todd Penner. *Contextualizing Gender in Early Christian Discourse: Thinking Beyond Thecla.* New York: Continuum, 2009.

Winter, Bruce W. *Roman Wives, Roman Widows: The Appearance of New Women and the Pauline Communities.* Grand Rapids, Mich.: Eerdmans, 2003.

Zlotnik, Helena. *Dinah's Daughters: Gender and Judaism from the Hebrew Bible to Late Antiquity.* Philadelphia: University of Pennsylvania Press, 2002.

Robert N. Stegmann

Early Judaism

The Talmud, a key text of Judaism, is composed of two distinct strata: the Mishnah, published orally ca. 200 C.E., and the Gemara, a wide-ranging commentary on the Mishnah, also published orally, circa 650 C.E. The Talmud addresses and analyzes a wide range of subjects, from Jewish ritual practice to civil and criminal law to interpretation of biblical passages. The spokespeople, all men, are called rabbis, or teachers. Women played no role in composing or compiling this literature, although they are frequently mentioned in it. The Talmud is a layered text, with each generation of rabbis interpolating its comments into the discussion units transmitted from the previous generation.

The Dead Sea Scrolls, a collection of materials dating to the first century C.E., also comment on women's legal status. However, since they are sectarian writings, their rules apply only to members of the group. The Tosefta and the Halakic Midrashim, rabbinic texts from the same time period as the Mishnah, are likely to have influenced the thinking of the rabbis of the Talmud but did not themselves become normative works.

There are two Talmuds. The Babylonian Talmud is the product of study houses in Babylonia, today Iraq, the place to which many Jews relocated in the centuries following the destruction of the Second Temple in 70 C.E. The Jerusalem Talmud, produced by rabbis living in the land of Israel, was completed ca. 425 C.E. Much material is common to both Talmuds because teachings were transmitted from one country to the other.

The two Talmuds do not describe how most Jews lived in the first five or six centuries of the first millennium. They focus on rabbis and their families and those individuals who associated themselves with the rabbinic movement. As time passed, rabbis gained in influence and became religious and political leaders of the Jewish community in both Babylonia and the land of Israel.

Rabbinic society, as portrayed in the many laws and anecdotes, was patriarchal. Men controlled women, first as fathers and later as husbands. Women were dependent on men for financial support, social standing, and physical protection. Although women functioned primarily in the domestic sphere, they were not isolated from contact with the outside world. A home in the rabbinic period was not private, as it is today, but rather open to vendors and service providers of all sorts. It follows that women at home regularly interacted with a wide variety of tradespeople.

A dominant feature of rabbinic life, as suggested by the Talmud, is participation in Torah discussions. The study venue, or *bet midrash*, was sometimes a physical structure but often was the home or courtyard of a rabbinic master. It was thus possible for rabbinic wives, daughters, and even mothers to overhear and occasionally participate in Torah discussions, as evidenced by anecdotes scattered throughout the Talmud (see, for example, *b. Qidd. 12b*). Women did not formally participate in study sessions, however.

One of the six main orders of the Mishnah is Nashim, which is usually translated as women, but more accurately means married women or wives, for this order deals with a wide variety of rules governing Jewish marriage. The volumes that constitute this order are rich in information on gender relations.

Marriage. According to both the Bible (Deut 22:13ff.) and the Talmud, women were expected to be virgins at the time they married. The Mishnah places a premium on virginity, stipulating a 200-zuz marriage settlement for virgins but only 100 zuz for nonvirgins (*m. Ketub. 1:2*). Men favored virgins for the obvious reason of knowing with certainty the lineage of their children. They also wished to avoid a woman who was "used goods." The Talmud adds another reason: marrying a virgin meant that a wife would not be able to compare her husband's sexual performance to that of another man (*b. Pesaḥ. 112b*). It is clear that a husband's emotional, social, and sexual needs were viewed as paramount.

Some marriage rules appearing in the Talmud are the same as those in the Bible: it is he who betroths

her, not she who betroths him; he may take more than one wife, but she may not be married to more than one husband; he may divorce her, but she may not divorce him.

Other marriage rules changed. According to the Torah (Deut 22:29), a prospective husband pays 50 pieces of silver to the bride's father to "purchase" a virgin. According to the Talmud, a husband does not deal with the father of the bride but rather hands a symbolic payment of one penny (*perutah*) or more, or an object worth a penny or more, to the bride herself (*m. Qidd. 1:1*). Unlike marriage in the Torah, she must consent to the match. Income from a wife's assets accrues to the husband for the duration of the marriage. He, in return, is required to feed and clothe her and provide her with a home, both in his lifetime and after his death. She is expected to perform a variety of household tasks for him.

The rabbis instituted a ketubah, a marriage contract, which stipulated that should the husband predecease or divorce the wife, he or his estate would pay her a lump sum of money (*b. Ketub. 82b*). The ketubah also stated that whatever assets she brought into the marriage would accompany her when she exited. Viewed together, all of these rules transformed marriage from the purchase of a bride from her father into a negotiated relationship between a man and a woman.

Did women in the ancient world have ketubot? Were they drawn up in accordance with rabbinic law? The evidence so far suggests that women entered into marriage with various kinds of financial arrangements, but not exactly the same ones established by the rabbis. The documents left by Babatha, a wealthy woman who lived in the first part of the second century C.E., show both similarities and differences between common practice and rabbinic law. Her marriage document contains a number of the clauses stipulated by the rabbis as well as a number of other clauses. Her documents also show that women were able to buy and sell goods and petition the court to approve their requests.

Procreation. Other than the blessing "be fruitful and multiply" (Gen 1:28), the Torah does not view procreation as a commandment. The rabbis do. They assume that women will be sexually available to their husbands and bear children for them. However, they require only men, not women, to procreate, in particular to produce two children (*m. Yebam.* 6:6). Since women are of necessity drawn by men into fulfillment of this requirement, women do behave as if obligated. If a woman does not succeed in becoming pregnant, her husband may divorce her. The rabbis recognized that men, too, could be the infertile partner and therefore allowed a woman to sue for divorce in a rabbinic court if she claimed her husband was impotent (*b. Yebam. 65a*). Women could also ask the rabbinic court to assist them in obtaining a divorce if they did not produce a child after years of trying to do so (*b. Yebam. 65b*). Although the letter of the law did not grant women the right to a divorce in such circumstances, the Talmud presents cases in which the rabbinic judges found in their favor.

Levirate Marriage. Levirate marriage is another patriarchal institution of the Bible that was modified by the rabbis. According to Deuteronomy 25:5–10, should a man die childless, his wife must marry his brother (i.e., her levir). The couple is expected to produce a child who will carry on the name of the deceased. If the brother of the deceased does not want to marry the widow, he may choose to undergo a *halizah* (release) ceremony with her. Its purpose is to shame a man who refuses to keep his brother's memory alive.

The most significant change that the rabbis introduced into the institution of levirate marriage is that they permit a daughter to count as offspring, although she will not prevent her father's name from being blotted out. It is possible that in the time of Josephus (first century C.E.) this change had already been adopted. The rabbis also developed a series of cases in which levirate marriage would not be permitted, such as when the surviving brother shares a mother with the deceased but not a father. As for the widow, she was not given a choice. Upon her husband's death, she was considered already betrothed to her brother-in-law.

The Menstruant (*Niddah*). As stated in the Torah, genital discharges lead to ritual uncleanness for both men and women (Lev 15:1–33). In particular, menstrual blood conveys impurity (vv. 19–24). The Torah does not prescribe a purification ritual for the menstruant, but the rabbis do: immersion in a ritual bath (*mikvah*). The Torah elsewhere proscribes sex with a *niddah* during her seven "blood days" (Lev 15:19; 18:19). Later rabbis added seven "white days" to the ban on intimacy (*b. Nid. 67a*). Rabbinic law places the *niddah* in her own home, performing household tasks (*b. Ketub. 61a*). She is not sent away for the duration of her period of menstrual uncleanness.

Divorce. To divorce a wife the Torah requires the husband to prepare a bill of severance and put it into her hand (Deut 24:1). Just as a slave needs a writ of manumission to prove he is a free man, a divorcée needs a *get*, a writ of divorce, to prove she is free to remarry. The rabbis later standardized the language of the *get*, reducing the likelihood of forgeries and simplifying verification, thereby benefiting women.

The Mishnah pays little attention to grounds for divorce. The last paragraph of *m. Gittin* (9:10), which deals with bills of divorce, suggests that a husband has the right to divorce a wife for any reason whatsoever or even for no reason. As for a wife, the Mishnah lists a number of grounds on which she may ask the rabbinic court to assist her in getting a divorce from her husband. They include cruel treatment of the wife by the husband, such as denying her the freedom to visit family or attend weddings or refusing to have sexual relations with her for a period of time (*m. Ketub.* 7:1–5). Rabbinic divorce remained an asymmetrical institution: by withholding a *get*, a husband could stop a wife from remarrying; she could not prevent him from taking a second wife. A woman no longer living with her husband but unable to obtain a writ of divorce from him is called an *agunah*, an anchored woman.

Sotah. According to the Torah, if a husband suspects a wife of infidelity but lacks evidence of her alleged misbehavior, he may nonetheless require her to go with him to the Kohen, apparently to the cultic center, and subject her to a trial by ordeal (Num 5:11–31). If the waters she is forced to drink show her to be innocent, the husband's suspicions would be allayed. If they show her to be guilty, she would suffer physical deterioration.

Following the destruction of the Second Temple the ordeal could no longer be administered. The entire discussion of the errant woman, called a *sotah*, is hypothetical and hence revealing of rabbinic attitudes to women. A review of the tractate shows that, on one hand, the rabbis added pornographic details to the ordeal, saying, for instance, that when she is forced to drink the waters her hair should be loosened and her garments ripped, and a crowd should gather to view her debasement (*m. Soṭah* 1:5, 6). On the other hand, these same rabbis introduced legislation that made it nearly impossible to carry out the ordeal. The Mishnah states that two men must witness her husband issuing a warning to her not to talk to a particular man, and two witnesses must then see her closet herself with that very man (*m. Soṭah* 1:1, 2). Requirements like these show that the rabbis oppose the biblical institution, probably because they object to both trial by ordeal and abusive treatment of women.

Rape and Seduction. The Bible regards the rape and seduction of a virgin not as a crime but as a means of contracting marriage. If a man engages in forced sex with an unbetrothed virgin, he has thereby taken her to be his wife and must pay her father the bride price (Exod 22:15, 16; Deut 22:29). Unlike the Torah, rabbinic law treats these instances of forced sex as cases of assault and battery and hence punishable. The rapist or seducer is required to pay for injury, pain, medical expenses, and shame (*m. Ketub.* 3:4). The moneys go to the victim's father since it is he who suffers financial loss. Most important, marriage is not forced on the rape victim. She (or her father) may opt out (*b. Ketub. 39b*).

Forbidden Marital Unions. The Torah mentions a number of prohibited marital unions, and the rabbis add many more. For instance, the Torah says that a Kohen may not marry a *zonah* (Lev 21:7), a prostitute, but the rabbis interpret that word as referring to any woman who had sex prior to marriage. They thus further limit the marital choices of a Kohen. They define *mamzer*, a word left unclear by the Torah (Deut 23:3), as the product of an incestuous or adulterous relationship. Such a person, according to the rabbis, could only marry another *mamzer* or a convert (*m. Qidd.* 4:1). They also decided that the Jewishness of a child was to be determined solely by his or her mother; only if the mother were Jewish could the child be Jewish by birth (*m. Qidd.* 3:12). The Jewishness of the father played no role. This is not necessarily an affirmation of women but a consequence of not knowing with certainty who the father is.

Inheritance. Perhaps the clearest deviation of rabbinic law from Torah law appears in conjunction with inheritance. The Torah relates that when the daughters of Zelophehad approached Moses and requested to be assigned their father's parcel of land in Israel, he turned to God to find out the laws of inheritance (Num 27:1–11). The main principle is that sons—not daughters—inherit their father's estate. Only if a father leaves no sons do daughters inherit. The Torah later reports that in response to a complaint by the men of Zelophehad's tribe, Moses had to stipulate further that when daughters inherit their father's parcel of land, they must marry within the tribe (Num 36:1–9). The underlying patriarchal assumption is that sons identify with their father's tribe, not their mother's. When the mother dies and the sons inherit her land, the land passes from her tribe to their father's, thus diminishing her tribe's holdings.

The rabbis included women in the laws of inheritance. They incorporated into Jewish law the Roman institution of gifts in contemplation of death and in this way made it possible for a father to give his daughter on his deathbed whatever share of his estate he wished (*m. B. Bat.* 8:5). The rabbis also inserted a clause into the marriage contract, called the "ketubah of male offspring," which stated that a woman's sons would inherit her entire dowry and not have to share it with their half-brothers. In this way, fathers of daughters were encouraged to give them a generous dowry on the day they married because the fathers could be sure that the assets would remain in the family. Dowry, in other words, is the way that daughters "inherit" a share of their father's wealth (*b. Ketub. 52b*).

Civil and Criminal Law. In nonmarital areas women fare better than in marital areas. In most matters of civil and criminal law, women are treated in the same way as men. The Talmud states in several places that the Torah's phrase "a man *or a woman*" (Num 5:6), appearing in the context of making restitution for robbery, implies that all are equal before the law in civil cases (*b. B. Qam. 15a*). Even in criminal cases, women are to be treated like men, with only minor differences. If a man is convicted of a capital crime, he is executed and then hanged; a woman is executed but not hanged (*m. Sanh.* 6:4). The reason, it seems, is to prevent men from gazing upon a woman's body.

A key procedural difference between men and women, however, is that a woman may not serve as a witness or judge in either civil or criminal cases. The Torah does not explicitly exclude women from giving testimony, but the rabbis interpret the Torah as doing exactly that (*b. Šebu. 30a*). Even so, they provide exceptions to their own rule by permitting women to testify in a number of critical cases, such as allowing a female witness to establish a man's death, which would then permit his widow to remarry (*m. Yebam.* 16:7). The Talmud says that the rabbis relaxed their own restrictions to avoid creating a situation in which a woman would remain an *agunah*, chained to a dead husband (*b. Yebam. 88a*).

Ritual Acts. The Torah does not require women to perform ritual acts. For instance, only men are expected to show up at the cultic center on the three pilgrimage holidays (Exod 23:17). The rabbis regard women as independent religious personalities and require them to perform ritual acts, but not as many as men. According to *m. Qiddushin* 1:7, all Torah prohibitions apply to men and women equally, for instance, not eating leavened products on Passover (Exod 13:7) or not working on the Sabbath (Exod 20:10). However, key religious acts, like hearing the shofar blown on the New Year or dwelling in a booth on the festival of Sukkot, are incumbent on men only. A number of remarks in the Talmud suggest that it was women's second-class social status that led to their lower level of obligation (*b. Meg. 23a*). Men did rely on women to perform rituals in the home, such as separating a portion of the dough for the Kohen or designating a tithe from produce grown on their own fields (*m. Ketub.* 7:6).

Relations between the Sexes. The Torah portrays men as having sexual needs that they seek to satisfy, inside or even outside of marriage. For example, the Torah relates that Judah, whose wife had died, had sex with a woman he thought was a prostitute (Gen 38:15, 16). The Talmud similarly holds that men's libido pushes them to act out sexually in any situation in which it is possible to do so. The Mishnah says that a man may not be alone with two women lest he engage first one and then the other in sex (*m. Qidd.* 4:12). Two men, it goes on to say, may be alone with one woman because each will restrain the other from having sex with her. One might have thought that in a situation of this sort a woman is vulnerable to rape. But no, says the Mishnah, each man will protect her from his fellow man, for her sake, one imagines, but also to stop a man from committing an immoral act. In this pair of scenarios, it is the men who are making overtures to the women. The Talmud's view of women is that they can be seduced or overpowered by men, but the average woman is not portrayed as a temptress.

The Talmud has little to say about women's libido. It understands that women have sexual needs. Rabbinic rules of marriage require that a man engage his wife sexually. If not, she can sue for divorce. Lesbian relations among women are tolerated. How women behave with each other does not seem to be of interest to the rabbis. As for same-sex relations among men, the Torah forbids them (Lev 18:22).

The Torah knows of only two genders, male and female. The Talmud recognizes four—male, female, androgyne, and *tumtum* (a person of indeterminate gender). In matters of civil and criminal law, all four genders are treated equally. In ritual matters, anyone who is not fully male is regarded as lower on the scale of religious obligation.

Summary. The Torah's rules are the basis of rabbinic legislation. Even so, there is no doubt that the practices of surrounding cultures also entered into rabbinic thinking, as did evolving ethical sensibilities. Overall, the rabbis did not view women as deserving of equality with men before the law, in particular in the areas of marriage and religious ritual. Like most men in the ancient world, they saw themselves as occupying the highest social status and regarded women, who occupied lower social standing, as in need of men's care and protection. In summary, the rabbis changed women's status from chattel, as in the Torah, to second-class citizen in their legislative scheme.

Scholarly Debates. There are not many scholarly debates regarding women's legal status in ancient

Judaism. One topic that arouses dispute is whether the rabbis of the Talmud improved women's legal status relative to the Bible or worsened it. Those who argue that the rabbis worsened women's legal status usually cite biblical narratives to support their view, not biblical legislation. As shown above, when the two legal systems are set side by side, changes for the better characterize rabbinic legislation about women. Another debate is whether the small legal anecdotes in the Talmud are literary constructions for the purpose of making a point or whether they reflect, albeit in an edited version, the actions of real women. Either way, the anecdotes, which are often at odds with the rule they come to illustrate, indicate that women carried out the law but tweaked it somewhat.

[*See also* Children, *subentry* Early Judaism; Gender Transgression, *subentry* Early Judaism; Male-Female Sexuality, *subentry* Early Judaism; Marriage and Divorce, *subentry* Early Judaism; *and* Sexual Violence, *subentry* Early Judaism.]

BIBLIOGRAPHY

Biale, Rachel. *Women and Jewish Law*. New York: Schocken, 1984.

Boyarin, Daniel. *Carnal Israel: Reading Sex in Talmudic Culture*. Berkeley: University of California Press, 1995.

Fonrobert, Charlotte Elisheva. *Menstrual Purity: Rabbinic and Christian Reconstructions of Biblical Gender*. Stanford, Calif.: Stanford University Press, 2002.

Friedman, Mordechai A. *Jewish Marriage in Palestine: A Cairo Geniza Study*. Vol. 1, *The Ketubba Traditions of Eretz Israel*; Vol. 2, *The Ketubba Texts*. Tel Aviv: Tel Aviv University; New York: Jewish Theological Seminary of America, 1980–1981.

Hauptman, Judith. *Rereading the Rabbis: A Woman's Voice*. New York: Perseus, 1998.

Hauptman, Judith. "Women and Torah Study in the Talmudic Period." *Jewish Studies Internet Journal* 9 (2010): 249–292. http://www.biu.ac.il/JS/JSIJ/9-2010/Hauptman .pdf

Hezser, Catherine. *The Oxford Handbook of Jewish Daily Life in Roman Palestine*. New York: Oxford University Press, 2010.

Ilan, Tal. *Jewish Women in Greco-Roman Palestine*. Tübingen, Germany: Mohr Siebeck, 1995.

Labovitz, Gail. *Marriage and Metaphor: Constructions of Gender in Rabbinic Literature*. Lanham, Md.: Lexington, 2012.

Peskowitz, Miriam. *Spinning Fantasies: Rabbis, Gender, and History*. Berkeley: University of California Press, 1997.

Valler, Shulamit. *Women and Womanhood in the Talmud*. Atlanta: Scholars Press, 1999.

Wegner, Judith. *Chattel or Person?: The Status of Women in the Mishnah*. New York: Oxford University Press, 1988.

Weisberg, Dvora. *Levirate Marriage and the Family in Ancient Judaism*. Waltham, Mass.: Brandeis University Press, 2009.

Judith Hauptman

Early Church

In the pre-Constantinian era, the legal status of Christians was not well defined. Nevertheless, it is still common for scholars to assert that the Romans classified Christianity as an illegal religion (*religio illicita*). This belief apparently stems from two passages in Tertullian's *Apology*. In the first, Tertullian complains that the Romans unfairly classify Christianity as unlawful (4.4; cf. 38.1), while in the second he refers to Judaism as a legitimate religion (*religio licita*), implying that Christianity was not (21.1). The silence of Roman sources, however, makes this reconstruction difficult to sustain: not only is there no evidence that the Romans distinguished religions with the categories *licita* or *illicita*, but there is also no indication that imperial authorities—whether the senate or emperor—ever issued a judicial proclamation outlawing the faith (Barnes, 1968, pp. 32–33; Millar, 1973, p. 145). Indeed, the earliest Roman source on Christianity comes from a governor who admits that he was unfamiliar with Christianity and uncertain of the methods he should use to judge Christians (Pliny the Younger, *Letter* 10.96.1). The emperor's response that there is no "general rule" or "fixed standard" for dealing with Christians only confirms the absence of formal legislation against the movement (Pliny the Younger, *Letter* 10.97).

Instead of imagining that an official law guided the Romans in their evaluation of Christianity, it is more probable that imperial officials exercised considerable latitude in their approach to the religion.

Their primary goal was to maintain the "peace of the gods" (*pax deorum*), a concept that relied on a well-regulated social order. Because this idea undergirded the legitimacy of the empire, how administrators preserved the peace was less important than their success in ensuring that it was a palpable reality. To gain the gods' favor, Roman officials insisted on fidelity to the time-honored religious traditions of their ancestors (*mos maiorum*). The performance of sacrificial rites was the primary mechanism to ensure peace, and thus these practices constituted *religio*, true religion (Cicero, *On the Nature of the Gods* 1.117; 2.72). The threat to *religio*, and thus the compact with the gods, was superstition (*superstitio*), a term used to classify foreign cults that exhibited a "foolish fear of the gods" and extreme displays of emotion, and that engaged in false prophecy, astrology, soothsaying, and magic (Cicero, *On Divination* 2.149; Seneca, *On Superstition*, fr. 34–35; Janssen, 1979). Imperial officials were thus deeply suspicious of groups that promoted such activities, not only because they refused to honor the (Roman) gods but also because they preyed on weak minds and upset one's mental tranquility (Cicero, *On the Nature of the Gods* 1.117; Cicero, *On Divination* 2.81; Horace, *Satires* 2.3.79–80; Seneca, *On Mercy*, 2.5.1). Fearing that these mental disturbances could lead to seditious thoughts, the Romans exercised vigilance in monitoring the activities of these associations (Livy, *The History of Rome* 39.8.1–19.7; Valerius Maximus, *Memorable Doings and Sayings* 1.3; Tacitus, *Annals* 2.85; Suetonius, *Tiberius* 36; Cassius Dio, *Roman History* 52.35–36).

Roman Representations of Early Christianity and Ancient Gender Codes. Not surprisingly, when Roman writers encountered Christianity they saw *superstitio*. Pliny the Younger (*Letter* 10.96.8), Tacitus (*Annals* 15.44), and Suetonius (*Nero* 16.2) all adopt this category and modify the term with pejorative adjectives— "depraved and excessive" (*pravam et immodicam*); "pernicious" (*exitiablilis*); and "novel and mischievous" (*novae ac maleficae*)—that register their derision and contempt. As members of this type of association, Christians suffered under the weight of a variety of other abusive labels, the three most popular being atheism, immorality, and misanthropy. The failure to

acknowledge Roman divinities meant that Christians were "godless and impious" and guilty of worshiping a corpse (Justin Martyr, *2 Apology* 3; Athenagoras, *Plea Regarding the Christians* 4; Origen, *Against Celsus* 7.68). Connecting these defective judgments with intellectual weakness allowed Roman writers to expand their negative evaluation of Christianity into the realm of ethics. Charges of cannibalism and incest (Athenagoras, *Plea Regarding the Christians* 3; 31; Minucius Felix, *Octavius* 8–9) and contempt for the human race (Tacitus, *Annals* 15.44; Origen, *Against Celsus* 1.1; 3.5) feature prominently in these discussions. Perhaps the most visible sign of Christian irrationality, however, was the Christians' stubborn rejection of Roman *religio*: by refusing to demonstrate their loyalty to the emperor through sacrifice, even at the cost of their lives, Christians presented Roman writers with an irrefutable sign of their "madness" (Epictetus, *Discourses* 4.7.6; Pliny, *Letter* 10.96.3; Galen, *Plato Arabus* 1.99; Marcus Aurelius, *Meditations* 11.3; Origen, *Against Celsus* 8.65).

Such descriptions are part of a larger collection of stereotypes that ancient writers employed when they sought to define or "know" the "other." Through these acts of representation, the writers were also advancing their own self-understanding ("we" are unlike "them"), a strategy designed to establish a hierarchical power relationship between themselves and Christians/ity (Foucault, 1995, pp. 27–29). In antiquity, these power/knowledge formulations were produced through a linguistic system that was both produced and informed by patriarchal cultural patterns that privileged masculinity over femininity (Conway, 2008; Laqueur, 1992; Marín, 2006; Montserrat, 2000). The result was the development of a language permeated by phallogocentric thinking: man/woman; universal/derivative; perfect/deficient; reason/emotion; self-control/passions; active/passive; mind/sense perceptions; spirit/flesh; soul/body are just a few of the binary "truths" these writers created and assumed (Diogenes, *Thales* 1.33; Ovid, *Metamorphoses* 3.316–338; Philo, *Questions in Genesis* 1.33, 37, 43; Galen, *On the Usefulness of the Parts of the Body* 2.630; 14.6–7; Dio Chrysostom, *Oration* 74.9–10; Apuleius, *Metamorphoses* 9.14). Because gendered thinking is embedded in language, gender criticism may elucidate a text even when bodies, human anatomy, or sex and gender roles are not explicitly discussed therein. It is a distinct "ideological apparatus" that targets the production of identities, boundary formations, and power relationships (Clark, 1991).

This insight is especially relevant when studying antiquity, which did not think of gender as a fixed essence or a predetermined "fact" that derived from a person's biological sex. Instead, the ancients believed that gender was fluid and processual, the product of stylized "performances," and that these acts in turn determined one's sexual identity (Laqueur, 1992). A person's gendered identity could thus shift along a masculine–feminine axis based on the person's self-presentation and the public reception of these performances. This sliding gender scale provided writers with considerable freedom to make judgments about a person's physical and moral worth based upon visual inspections (Polemo, *Physiognomy* 2.1.192–194F; Dio Chrysostom, *Oration* 33.51–61). For ancient writers, the ideal male demonstrated virtues such as reason, self-control, justice, prudence, courage, excellence, and domination. Ideal femininity consisted of displays of modesty, obedience, chastity, and faithfulness (Cobb, 2008, pp. 18–32). "Slippage" from one pole to the other could provoke a variety of reactions, from shame and reproach to amazement or outrage.

When viewed through the lens of gender criticism, Christianity failed to achieve masculine status in the eyes of the Romans. From their predilection for sexual deviance to their excessive obsession with death, Christians consistently demonstrated an inability to master their emotions. A further indication of Christianity's lack of manliness stemmed from the fact that the people who joined the movement—women, children, and slaves—were notable for their undeveloped or defective intellectual capacities (Aristotle, *Politics* 1260a). Celsus, for instance, mocks the Christian recruiters for strategically targeting people incapable of exercising reasoned judgments: "Their injunctions are like this. 'Let no one educated, no one wise, no one sensible draw near. For these abilities are thought by us to be evils. But as for anyone ignorant (*amathēs*), anyone stupid, anyone uneducated (*apaideutos*), anyone who is a child, let him come

boldly.'…they want and are able to convince only the foolish (*ēlithious*), dishonorable (*agenneis*), and stupid (*anaisthētous*), and only slaves, women, and little children" (Origen, *Against Celsus* 3.44). Lucian too satirizes their mental deficiencies by marveling at how quickly a charlatan like Peregrinus managed to infiltrate a Christian community and become revered as a god. In this story, Lucian singles out gullible Christians—again women and children—who were so impressed with Peregrinus that they hailed him as "the new Socrates" (*The Passing of Peregrinus* 11–12). Both of these portraits engage in self-definition and the formation of power relationships: as the authors denigrate Christian femininity they simultaneously preserve masculine honor for the intellectual elite.

Gender in Early Christian Rhetoric. Of course, early Christians refused to accept such characterizations. To counter the negative impressions that dominated the Roman record, they became active agents in their own self-presentation. To rehabilitate their image, Christian authors turned to the rhetoric of gender to attack their opponents and defend themselves. Early Christian identity formation was thus firmly anchored in and informed by a critical engagement with the gendered discourses of the age.

Christians on Christians on trial: Apologies and martyrologies. Although the Romans did not officially proscribe Christianity, their negative impressions of the group left its members vulnerable to abuse during moments of acute social pressure. When such situations arose, Christians were brought before the authorities for interrogation. In these exchanges, the accused who acknowledged their Christian status were subject to execution, even if they had not been definitively linked to any criminal activity (Pliny the Younger, *Letter* 10.96.2–3; Justin Martyr, *1 Apology* 4; *2 Apology* 2; Athenagoras, *Plea Regarding the Christians* 2; Eusebius, *Ecclesiastical History* 5.1.10, 20–22; Tertullian, *Apology* 1–3; cf. Hadrian's rescript in Justin Martyr, *1 Apology* 68). In an environment when confrontations could erupt with little warning, Christian anxieties were understandably high. Constructing arguments that were aligned with Greco-Roman gender codes was one strategy for defusing social tensions.

For Christian writers, the notion that a person could receive a capital sentence simply for acknowledging his religious identity seemed capricious and cruel, especially since this practice had no history in Roman jurisprudence (traditionally, the courts established guilt by weighing evidence of a crime). Apologists attempted to solve this problem by linking Christianity with rational beliefs and virtuous practices, and castigating Rome for its folly (Knust, 2006, pp. 89–112). To develop this idea, they insisted that Christians could hardly be atheists when they worship the true God "in reason and truth" and live according to the *logos*, the rational principle of the cosmos (Justin Martyr, *1 Apology* 6; 13; *2 Apology* 6; 8; 10). Moreover, their fidelity to reason prohibited them from participating in depraved behaviors. Instead, in a world dominated by lust and violence, they distinguished themselves by their commitment to chastity and their refusal to murder or even attend the public games (Athenagoras, *Plea Regarding the Christians* 33; 35; Tertullian, *Apology* 45.3). In their thoughts and deeds, then, the apologists maintained that Christians were "men" whose performance of *virtus* was noble because it sustained the social order (Tertullian, *Apology* 32.1; 39.2, 21).

Identifying Christianity as the true religion leads to the conclusion, found most forcefully in Tertullian's *Apology*, that Roman religion and its cultural institutions were in fact grounded in superstition (24.2; 38.4; 40.1; 41.1; Clement of Alexandria, *Miscellanies* 7.1). Roman persecution of Christianity was thus explained as a mistake made by people who lived according to irrationality and willful ignorance (Athenagoras, *Plea Regarding the Christians* 4; 13; Tertullian, *Apology*, 1.4). Many apologies thus begin with an exhortation to their addressees (usually emperors and other high-ranking officials) to reject this anti-intellectual stance and embrace reason. When Christians came to trial, the authors assert, truth, piety, and justice should guide Roman deliberations (Justin Martyr, *1 Apology* 2–3; Athenagoras, *Plea Regarding the Christians* 2). The apologists are critical, however, of previous hearings in which judges failed to uphold these masculine attributes and instead practiced violence and tyranny. As Justin Martyr exclaims, these leaders did not investi-

gate the charges carefully, but "giving in to unreasoning passion" they exacted punishments "without trial or consideration" (*1 Apology* 5; *2 Apology* 1). In this the apologists simply followed their accusers whose irrational opinions and love of rumor instigated the proceedings (Justin Martyr, *1 Apology* 2; Athenagoras, *Plea Regarding the Christians*, 11; Tertullian, *Apology* 7.8–14). The outlandish charges they leveled at Christians were the result of "madness" and "unsound judgment" and proved their mental weakness (Athenagoras, *Plea Regarding the Christians* 4; 35). Complementing the opponents' feminine intellect is a corresponding lack of control over the passions: greed, violence, and lust, so the apologists maintain, are the hallmarks of a corrupt Roman society (Justin Martyr, *1 Apology* 14; Tertullian, *Apology* 40.1).

Christian martyr narratives dramatize the arguments found in the apologies. Staging public punishment is a way for rulers to reinscribe social hierarchies: the judge and executioner, symbolizing state power, use the criminal to reinforce political and juridical authority and discipline the crowds (Foucault, 1995). Yet by employing a series of literary reversals and inversions, the martyrologies reject imperial scripts (Castelli, 2004). In these texts the martyrs—elderly men, women, youths, and slaves—refuse to accept their assigned role as condemned criminals in the emperor's spectacle. Rather, they comport themselves as hypermasculine heroes who display courage, endurance, military valor, rhetorical skill, and athletic prowess, traits that stand in stark contrast to their effeminate opponents. Polycarp and Pothius (eighty-six and ninety years old, respectively), for instance, face their arrests and trials with stoic fortitude, deliver unwavering testimony on trial, and die with noble resolve (*Martyrdom of Polycarp* 5.1; 7.2; 9.1–12.1; 13.3–15.1; Eusebius, *Ecclesiastical History* 5.1.29–31). Similarly, when the Romans parade martyrs in the amphitheater, the martyrs rejoice in the battle: as they become transformed into gladiators and noble athletes, their heroic endurance enables them to overcome their torturers and claim the crown of immortality (Eusebius, *Ecclesiastical History* 5.1.7, 17, 19, 24, 36, 40–61; *Martyrdom of Perpetua and Felicitas* 10; 18–21; cf. Tertullian, *To the Martyrs* 2–3).

Predictably, the authors denigrate the Romans (and occasionally the Jews) for their feminized characteristics. The authorities exhibit unreasonable judgment, are ineffectual in speech-making, and respond to Christian oratory with amazement and shame (Eusebius, *Ecclesiastical History* 5.1.9; *Martyrdom of Polycarp* 8.2; 12.1; *Martyrdom of Perpetua and Felicitas* 16.3–4). The mobs too show none of the characteristics of masculine honor; on the contrary, they are irrational, demonically inspired beasts who misunderstand Christianity and rage at the righteous martyrs (*Martyrdom of Polycarp* 17.2; Eusebius, *Ecclesiastical History* 5.1.7, 15, 38, 50). Most notably, the tortures of the executioners fail to have their intended effect: rather than reinscribing imperial *auctoritas* by triumphing over the helpless criminal, they either rely on the martyr to finish the job and thus assume the role of the heroic gladiator (*Martyrdom of Perpetua and Felicitas* 21.9–10; cf. Seneca, *Letter* 30.8), or they become physically exhausted by the suprahuman stamina of the martyrs whose bodies not only withstand the pain but are even invigorated by it (Eusebius, *Ecclesiastical History* 5.1.17–19, 21–26). In these passages it becomes clear that Roman *imperium* cannot dominate the Christian body, whose tortured and punished frame discloses the cracks in the empire's ideology, strikes a blow against demonic power, and testifies to Christian truth, represented most forcefully in the words of Justin Martyr, "you are able to kill us, but you cannot hurt us" (*1 Apology* 2; cf. Origen, *Against Celsus* 8.44).

Cultivating a masculine community. When Polycarp arrives at the stadium for his trial, he hears a voice from heaven exhorting him to "be strong" and "act like a man" (*ischue…andrizou*) (*Martyrdom of Polycarp* 9.1). This statement highlights both the separation between sex and gender in antiquity (one does not necessarily follow the other) and the performative aspects of gender. Early Christians were sensitive to these issues and expended considerable energy delineating and cultivating masculine gendered identities that were consistent with Greco-Roman mores. Ignatius's *Letter to Polycarp* and *The Shepherd of Hermas* both posit that manly presentations of Christianity begin with its officers. Drawing from the tropes of Roman *virtus*, Ignatius advises the young bishop to clothe himself in the weapons of faith and become a "perfect athlete" in order to exhort others to salvation, bear the burdens of those who suffer, and endure the wiles of false teachings (1.2–3; 3.1–2; 6.6.2). *The Shepherd of Hermas* too offers instructions for enacting masculine Christian leadership. In this text, Hermas, who had been struggling to guide his community, receives a heavenly command to "act like a man" (*andrizou*) (*Herm. Vis.* 1.4.3). A series of visions unfold that detail Hermas's journey from an ineffectual leader into an authoritative *paterfamilias* who demonstrates mastery over himself and his community (*Herm.* 10.4.1; Young, 1994). Critical in this gender transformation are the appearance of female virgins whose embodiment of self-control (*enkrateia*) and related virtues (*Herm. Vis.* 3.8.1–8; *Herm.* 9.2.5) are instrumental for Hermas in the management of his own desire (*epithumia*) and self-fashioning as a man (*Herm. Vis.* 1.1.8; *Herm.* 5.6–7; 9.11.1–8; 9.15.1–3; Lipsett, 2011, pp. 19–53).

Other texts target the larger community in an attempt to regulate the proper performance of gender. In *Christ the Educator*, for example, Clement of Alexandria presents a discourse on Christian education (*paideia*) that offers instruction on living that would distinguish members of the true faith from outsiders (Buell, 1999, p. 108). The counsel he delivers repeatedly underscores the importance of exhibiting self-control, especially in one's approach to food, alcohol, and sexual relationships (2.1–34, 40–44, 83–102). By encouraging his audience to adopt a moderate stance on these topics, one that resists acting on impulse (2.90), Clement promotes a masculine Christianity directed by reason, a tactic designed to counter attempts to link the Christian behaviors with feminine excess.

Clement's manual includes discussions of the proper comportment of men and women. On this topic he displays an interest in maintaining social conventions that correspond to Greco-Roman values. Thus, men should utilize their "natural" proclivities (wisdom, temperance, and the exercise of bodily control), while women should conform their lives to the virtues peculiar to their sex (silence and modesty)

(Clement of Alexandria, *Christ the Educator* 2.1, 33, 46, 110). Deviations from these patterns, such as men who pay too much attention to their appearance or women who assume the active role in sex, represent shameful, unnatural behaviors deserving of censure (2.68; 3.15–25). This thinking reaches a more strident register in the writings of Tertullian, whose insistence that male and female gender roles remain distinct dominates a number of his moral treatises (*On the Veiling of Virgins*; *On the Apparel of Women*).

Gender transgressions and polemics. The variety of approaches to self-definition in early Christianity helps explain the church fathers' relatively conservative stance on gender. While they promoted the fiction that gender distinctions were fixed and grounded in natural law, many other Christians were busy experimenting with new forms of gendered behaviors that reconfigured masculine *virtus*. For instance, in some texts the call to make oneself male or to "flee femininity" may be read as a metaphor to encourage all people to seek spiritual perfection (*Gospel of Thomas* 114; *Second Treatise of the Great Seth* 65.24–30; *Zostrianos* 131.5–12; Clement of Alexandria, *Miscellanies* 6.12.100; cf. Philo, *Questions in Exodus* 1.8; Meyer, 1985). Yet it is only a short step to link this metaphor to chastity, so that femininity becomes shorthand for the rejection of "polluted intercourse" and continence a requirement for attaining salvation (*Book of Thomas the Contender* 144.8–10; *Acts of Peter* 34; *Acts of Thecla* 5–6; 12; *Acts of Thomas* 12–15). Encratite and Marcionite theologies appear to have developed their theologies around these ideas (Tatian, *Oration to the Greeks*, 8.1; 33.2; Tertullian, *Against Marcion* 1.29). Authors supportive of this ascetic discipline exploited the fluidity of gender categories to attribute a masculine ethos to the men and women who practiced these behaviors. In the *Apocryphal Acts of the Apostles*, for example, celibacy among the apostles and their converts exemplifies an intensified commitment to self-control, while characters such as Thecla, Cleopatra, and Mygdonia signified "manly" women whose commitment to sexual renunciation was, along with their other masculine attributes (rational comportment, public ministry), a clear indication that they had transcended the "natural" weakness of their sex.

The rejection of marriage and sexuality conflicted with mainstream pagan philosophy, which identified the genitalia as a locus of masculine honor and considered celibates as enemies of civilization (Epictetus, *Discourses* 1.2.25–28; Musonius Rufus 14; cf. *Acts of Thecla* 9). Emerging proto-orthodox writers also found this practice objectionable because it upset the divinely ordained gender distinctions found in the Bible (Gen 2—3; 1 Cor 11:2–16). Moreover, these biblical passages anchored the sociocultural "fact" of patriarchy. The thought of men rejecting their honored status as progenitors and women assuming roles normally ascribed to men represented threats to a carefully calibrated society whose foundations rested on the fiction of stable gender identities (Upson-Saia, 2011). It is thus not surprising that effeminate men and masculine women cause these writers anxiety (Clement of Alexandria, *Christ the Educator* 3.15; Tertullian, *On Baptism* 17.4).

Early Christian debates over identity reveal the prominent role that gendered rhetoric played in the formation of the categories "orthodoxy" and "heresy." Examinations of the polemics that survive (mainly from the proto-orthodox writers) have revealed that Christian writers slandered their opponents using many of the same tactics that the Romans deployed against Christianity. The goal is the same too; namely, to classify and denigrate the "other" as morally deviant and to produce a true Christian moral identity, one that is superior to both heretical Christianities and Rome's ethical traditions (Knust, 2006, pp. 1–13). Clement of Alexandria's typology that classifies all heresies as either libertine or ascetic illustrates this power/knowledge dynamic. In his *Miscellanies*, he uses these two categories as a foil to illustrate the proper attitude toward marriage. After demonstrating that neither extreme leads to knowledge of God, he positions his moderate approach to marriage, one that teaches a mastery of desire through self-control, as the true form of Christianity (*Miscellanies* 3.40–60).

Similarly, the heresiological technique of establishing genealogical trees to identify groups within and outside the family of God is dependent upon gendered language. Justin and Irenaeus are the primary proponents of this strategy: in their writings neither the

Jews nor the heretics can claim a place in the divine economy because of their enslavement to desire (Knust, 2006, pp. 143–63). A number of overlapping strategies for exclusion emerge from heresiologists' accounts: the founder is a charlatan who pronounces blasphemous doctrines and trades in magic (*superstitio!*); the group places women in leadership roles but their teachings are not grounded in reason or they introduce innovative, deviant practices; the heretic and its members participate in sexual perversion (Irenaeus, *Against the Heresies* 1.13, 22, 25; Hippolytus, *Refutation of All Heresies* 1.9; Tertullian, *Against Marcion* 1.1; Stratton, 2007). Such portraits thus enable the authors to introduce their own understandings of Christianity as normative and authentic (Irenaeus, *Against the Heresies* 1.10).

[*See also* Gender Transgression, *subentry* Early Church; Legal Status, *subentries on* New Testament *and* Roman World; Masculinity and Femininity, *subentry* Early Church; Popular Religion and Magic, *subentry* Early Church; *and* Sexual Transgression, *subentry* Early Church.]

BIBLIOGRAPHY

Barnes, T. D. "Legislation against the Christians." *Journal of Roman Studies* 58 (1968): 32–50.

Buell, Denise Kimber. *Making Christians: Clement of Alexandria and the Rhetoric of Legitimacy.* Princeton, N.J.: Princeton University Press, 1999.

Castelli, Elizabeth A. *Martyrdom and Memory: Early Christian Culture Making.* Gender, Theory, and Religion. New York: Columbia University Press, 2004.

Clark, Elizabeth. "Sex, Shame, and Rhetoric: En-gendering Early Christian Ethics." *Journal of the American Academy of Religion* 59 (1991): 221–245.

Cobb, L. Stephanie. *Dying to Be Men: Gender and Language in Early Christian Martyr Texts.* Gender, Theory, and Religion. New York: Columbia University Press, 2008.

Conway, Colleen M. *Behold the Man: Jesus and Greco-Roman Masculinities.* New York: Oxford University Press, 2008.

Foucault, Michel. *Discipline and Punish: The Birth of the Prison.* 2d ed. Translated by Alan Sheridan. New York: Vintage, 1995.

Janssen, L. F. "'Superstitio' and the Persecution of the Christians." *Vigiliae Christianae* 33 (1979): 131–159.

Knust, Jennifer Wright. *Abandoned to Lust: Sexual Slander and Ancient Christianity.* Gender, Theory, and Religion. New York: Columbia University Press, 2006.

Laqueur, Thomas. *Making Sex: Body and Gender from the Greeks to Freud.* Cambridge, Mass.: Harvard University Press, 1992.

Lipsett, B. Diane. *Desiring Conversion: Hermas, Thecla, Aseneth.* New York: Oxford University Press, 2011.

Marín, Moisés Mayordomo. "Construction of Masculinity in Antiquity and Early Christianity." *lectio difficilior* 2 (2006). http://www.lectio.unibe.ch/06_2/marin_construction.htm

Meyer, Marvin W. "Making Mary Male: The Categories 'Male' and 'Female' in the Gospel of Thomas." *New Testament Studies* 31 (1985): 554–570.

Millar, Fergus. "The Imperial Cult and the Persecutions." In *Le Culte des souverains dans l'Empire romaine*, edited by Willem den Boer, pp. 145–165. Geneva: Vandoeuvres-Genève, 1973.

Montserrat, Dominic. "Reading Gender in the Roman World." In *Experiencing Rome: Culture, Identity and Power in the Roman Empire*, edited by Janet Huskinson, pp. 153–181. New York: Routledge, 2000.

Stratton, Kimberly B. "The Rhetoric of 'Magic' in Early Christian Discourse: Gender, Power, and the Construction of Heresy." In *Mapping Gender in Ancient Religious Discourses*, edited by Todd Penner and Caroline Vander Stichele, pp. 89–114. Biblical Interpretation Series 87. Leiden, The Netherlands: Brill, 2007.

Upson-Saia, Kristi. *Early Christian Dress: Gender, Virtue, and Authority.* Routledge Studies in Ancient History 3. New York: Routledge, 2011.

Young, Steve. "Being a Man: The Pursuit of Manliness in *The Shepherd of Hermas*." *Journal of Early Christian Studies* 2 (1994): 237–255.

David M. Reis

LINGUISTIC TURN APPROACHES

While the term "turn" has become a popular way of designating academic trends (cultural turn, corporeal turn), what has come to be known as the "linguistic turn" has had much more profound ramifications for the study of texts and gender, and our understanding of the "external world," than other so-called turns. Concepts such as discourse, representation, gender, agency, essentialism, and palimpsest have entered the parlance of biblical studies and changed, for many people, the ways in which we read and understand the Bible in the modern world.

However, defining what the "linguistic turn" is, and what exactly is to be included under its purview, is somewhat of a challenge. One reason is that the label itself is a later consolidation of several decades of developments in methods, including semiotics and literary criticism, new historicism, gender theory, and various forms of ideological critique. Another challenge is that the term has become partially synonymous with poststructuralism, which is understandable, given that the canonical poststructuralist thinkers are also part of the "linguistic turn" group. It is nevertheless also imprecise, given that the turn to language cannot be reduced simply to poststructuralism. At the intersection of biblical and gender studies, however, it is with few exceptions the poststructuralist linguistic turn that has come to prevail and, consequently, will be the main focus of this essay.

A significant point of origin for charting the linguistic turn is the work of the semiotician Ferdinand de Saussure and his understanding of language as a system of signs, which arbitrarily link the signified with the signifier. Known as "structural linguistics" or "structuralism" because of its insistence that all of language, and life, is unintelligible without understanding the system of relationships embedded in its structure, this epistemological shift unsettled the presupposed reliability of the relationship between the word and external world. As a methodological framework, Saussure's structuralism had a tremendous impact beyond the narrow area of linguistics through such seminal thinkers as Roland Barthes, Claude Levi-Strauss, Louis Althusser, and Jacques Lacan, whose work in turn informed a whole generation of critical theorists, including Luce Irigaray, Jacques Derrida, Hélène Cixous, Julia Kristeva, Michel Foucault, Clifford Geertz, and Monique Wittig.

The application of linguistic analysis as a means to critically engage various areas of human life and activity meant a shift in our relation to "reality" as well as an expansion in the notion of "text," and gave special prominence to the concept of discourse. Broadly put, the linguistic turn enabled scholars to regard a text as a representation or mediation of reality and thus examine how it contributes to producing what we perceive to be reality. Reality is always mediated by language, and we are unable to access it in its "pure" prelinguistic form, and consequently we view this reality as discursively constructed. This then has obvious implications for the ideology of representation and the specific point of view of the text as well as the reader. Given that the basic presupposition of the linguistic turn is that reality is only attainable through language, then historical contexts, archaeological remains, or rituals are also always already shaped, understood, and presented, and not merely just "out there" to be discovered.

The Linguistic Turn and Gender: History and Issues. Feminist and gender-critical analysis would also be reshaped by the epistemological shifts entailed by the linguistic turn, as well as contribute to them. Examples include the work of Luce Irigaray and Julia Kristeva on phallogocentrism, abjection, and the representation of women within the universe of men; Simone de Beauvoir's inquiries into women's subjectivity; Genevieve Lloyd's re-presentation of the man of reason through the history of philosophy; and Denise Riley's interrogation of the category of woman. From a genealogical point of view, Joan W. Scott's seminal article on gender as a useful category of historical analysis represents the shift from feminism/woman to gender, a shift that refracted not only the questions but also the way of posing questions. Here a divide developed between what has come to be known as "social constructionist" and "essentialist" forms of feminist analysis. The category of essentialism, for example, was introduced initially to counter arguments based on biological determinism, but is now used to dismiss arguments that do not operate on the basis of discourse. By contrast, social constructionism functions as a catchall category for that which is cultural in origin and functions as the "nurture" area of the so-called nature/nurture divide. A basic controversy that has precipitated from the epistemological shift from women to gender is the contention that such a shift renders impotent any historical reconstructive efforts, or efforts to locate "real women" in history. If all of life is to be located discursively, and not materially, and if texts are not reliable as reflections of some kind of historical reality, then where might we "find" women in the past—and particularly in the ancient past? For biblical scholars who front gender concerns, and particularly for those who are concerned with how biblical literature has been used to support or deny women's agency in "real life," this is no small matter.

Elizabeth Clark has provided the most cogent analysis of implications of the linguistic turn for biblical scholars and historians of early Christianity. Not only has she written a full introduction to the linguistic turn and the discipline of history (Clark, 2004), but she also has shown in her work in the field of early Christianity how the theoretical insights from the linguistic turn may be profitable; as such, her work deserves serious consideration. Clark identifies two major challenges to feminist historians by literary theorists: (1) that there is an unsurmountable chasm between the poststructuralist critique of objectivity and the disciplinary standards of history, and that representation risks severing the peoples of the past from the description of them in the texts; and (2) that the fracturing of categories makes it impossible to speak of women, and the decentering of the male subject problematizes the notion of a female subject (Clark, 1998, p. 416).

One group of problems afforded by the linguistic turn relates to the issue of representation and reality, the other to the question of subjectivity. Clark notes that while feminist historians are hesitant to take the full consequence of the epistemological shift, they are nevertheless reluctant to return to earlier views on representation and reality, and thus explore ways of combining the emphasis on language's role in the shaping of reality with "more traditional historical concerns for the extratextual world" (Clark, 1998, p. 417). Thus, Clark proposes a "third way" of negotiating the linguistic turn wherein feminist and gender-critical scholars might add discursive analysis to their methodological toolbox.

A seminal issue of the Scandinavian journal *Studia Theologica* illustrates how these issues come to the fore. Edited by Halvor Moxnes, this 1989 collection of essays was the result of a 1988 Nordic conference named "Feminist Reconstruction of Early Christian History: Methodological and Hermeneutical Questions." Moxnes notes in his introduction that this gathering was the first of its kind, and the nature of the participants revealed that feminist biblical scholarship was not "an established area of study" at the theological faculties of the Nordic universities. Apart from being an attempt at building a feminist network, the conference also engaged in dialogue with Elisabeth Schüssler Fiorenza's feminist theological reconstruction of Christian origins. Schüssler Fiorenza argues for a feminist reconstruction of Christian origins rather than a male-oriented or "male-stream" reading, and endeavors to highlight as central historical actors those whom the androcentric text marginalizes or excludes. Interestingly, Schüssler Fiorenza notes that theory that eschews any historical reconstruction reinforces the androcentric text's rhetorical world. Instead, she argues, it is necessary to develop a theory and method of interpretation that integrates both sociohistorical and literary criticism. She outlines four points that show the difference between postmodernism and feminist criticism, which she sees as pertinent to reconstructing Christian origins: (1) the realization that scientific theories and totalizing articulations of the world are not objectively true opens up possibilities of empowerment; (2) it is possible to give a truer account of the world; (3) there is no abandonment of women as subjects—women must be constituted as historical subjects; and (4) there is no rejection of the humanistic values of the Enlightenment. All of this means, then, that the agenda for feminist and gender-critical interpreters should be one of hermeneutics of suspicion, or a reading against the grain in order to grant agency to those the text has overwritten.

Here we find positions that express anxiety about the first set of problems and positions that attempt to address the middle way articulated by Clark but dismiss or overlook the issues raised in the second set of problems. Linguistic turn approaches enabled scholars to push further in answering questions and addressing issues that had already been raised, rather than a revolution of Copernican dimensions. For example, Lone Fatum's article in the issue of *Studia Theologica* discussed above serves as a response to Schüssler Fiorenza's influential feminist theological reconstruction efforts. She accuses the feminist reconstruction project of wanting to "achieve two different results through one analytical process, namely exposing the suppression of women by the biblical material and, at the same time, seeking the affirmation of women by the biblical material" (Fatum, 1989, p. 61). Fatum points out that to the feminist reconstructionists it seemed that certain texts were above and beyond criticism, such as Galatians 3:28. If a feminist reconstruction is necessary, then it must occur on the other side of a deconstruction process that reveals the androcentrism and patriarchal values in the New Testament texts. In terms of questions of subjectivity, Fatum insists that the feminist confrontation with the objective interpreter is not only critically justified and "of great hermeneutical importance" but that it does not lend legitimacy to feminist subjectivity "as an aim in itself" (p. 64). Because the women in the texts are not granted subject status by the texts, then any attempt at breaking that silence will be on the conditions and with the voices of present day Christian feminists.

From the standpoint of linguistic turn approaches, one of the things that were problematic in both Schüssler Fiorenza and Fatum was the static notion of "woman," as Jorunn Økland has shown. While it was more obvious that Schüssler Fiorenza subscribed to such a position, in Fatum's work it was more in the background, yet assumed as a subject position and a point of view in reading of the Corinthian situation (Økland, 2004, pp. 18–19). Økland uses Irigaray to introduce the concept of phallogocentrism, which is an ideological position that regards the male as norm and subsumes the female under its categorizations and places it in relation to the male through likeness, opposition, or complementarity. Thus "woman" within phallogocentric discourse functions as "an empty category with changing content" (p. 17). This argument is undergirded by reference to Denise Riley, who, as mentioned above, argued that "woman" is historically and discursively constructed, and thus must always be analyzed in its particularity. Økland then uses the work of Joan

Scott to show how feminist interpreters are forced to simultaneously accept and refuse static and dichotomized notions of gender. These two moves underpin Økland's analysis of the production of sanctuary space in 1 Corinthians.

This particular moment in the history of feminist and gender-critical biblical scholarship draws out broader contested issues facing discussions of method: subjectivity or agency, representation or discourse, and, somewhere in between the two, the politics of identity. These issues will serve as signposts through the next two sections, which outline the linguistic turn and gender in the study of the Hebrew Bible and New Testament, respectively.

Linguistic Turn, Gender, and the Study of the Hebrew Bible. While the example from the above discussion is from the discipline of New Testament studies, the developments regarding the linguistic turn and gender in the study of the Hebrew Bible have proceeded similarly, most notably in turning around the question of historical presence and subject status of women. On the other hand, the Hebrew Bible has, due to its scope and variety in material, ambivalences, and editions (and undoubtedly a host of other reasons), proven to be exceptionally fertile soil for all kinds of readings that deploy, in more direct measures, the various theorists of the linguistic turn.

One particular feature of the Hebrew Bible that has been extremely important in feminism and gender studies is the excessive violence against women in these texts. This has led some feminists, such as Mary Daly, to dismiss the text as patriarchal and oppressive and to search elsewhere for spirituality for women. Other scholars, such as Phyllis Trible, have set out to reclaim the biblical text. In her seminal article from 1973, "Depatriarchalizing in Biblical Interpretation," Trible endeavors to recover "a depatriarchalizing principle at work in the Hebrew Bible," which she defines as "a hermeneutic operating within Scripture itself" (Trible, 1973, p. 49). This principle she identifies in Song of Songs as well as Genesis 2–3 and is consonant with what she understands to be the "intentionality of biblical faith," which is not to perpetuate patriarchy but "to function as salvation for both women and men" (p. 31).

Of course, such a proposal is not universally accepted, even by female scholars. As a reaction to this earlier work from a perspective formed by the linguistic turn, we may look at Yvonne Sherwood's study on Hosea, which uses both reader-based theories and text-based theories (semiotics and deconstruction) to analyze the first three chapters of Hosea and their interpretations. The final chapter stages a reading from a woman's point of view and argues, by way of deconstruction, how objectification is a struggle in process: the woman is in the course of the text transformed from subject to object, increasingly restricted by the language and structure of the text, carefully displaying the mechanisms of objectification (Sherwood, 1996, p. 310), but also how the mechanisms hold the seeds of their own deconstruction, and reveals a covert desire for male objectification (p. 311). For Sherwood, the problem with depatriarchalizing readings such as the one advanced by Trible is that the principle is seen as being at the level of the text and consequently it is ascribed to authorial intent. Sherwood sees this as an effort to salvage the text at the expense of the woman in it (pp. 274–275).

The question of subjectivity has also been an issue in studies of the Hebrew Bible, as is indicated by the efforts of Sherwood, and scholars have used various theoretical approaches to bring out what are thought to be submerged subjectivities in the texts and their histories of interpretation. The work of Athalya Brenner (2005), for example, "fleshes out" the biographies of female characters in the Hebrew Bible who did not die and are able to live on—not only in Brenner's text, but also in the traditions that lie in between. Brenner uses the Talmud, the Mishnah, present day politics, and feminist scholarship to reconstruct the submerged subjectivities of figures like Dinah, Huldah, and Zipporah, granting them the voice that the texts of the Hebrew Bible has denied them. Similarly, Julie Kelso uses Luce Irigaray's work to analyze how the production of the coherent imaginary world of Chronicles relies on the exclusion and repression of the maternal body. Kelso, however, also argues that Irigaray enables a mode of reading differently, reading and listening to the silences in order to "write ourselves into the symbolic" (Kelso, 2007, p. 97). Erin Runions makes

use of postcolonial theory (Homi Bhabha), psychoanalysis (Jacques Lacan, Slavoj Žižek), and Marxism (Louis Althusser) to engage and develop Žižek's understanding of interpellation, that is, the subjectification process in Althusser's work. By using Bhabha to unsettle the fixed and determined nature of Žižek's interpellated subject, Runions demonstrates how the text plays with readers, and how taking the shifts in the text seriously, rather than glossing them over as textual deviants or corruptions, obstructs any attempt to approach and depart from the text with a fixed sense of gendered subjectivity.

Such a reading is enabled by close attention to the shifting signifiers of the text and the text's practice of slippery repetition with respect to gender and tense, which was also a significant feature in Sherwood's reading of Hosea.

Negotiating what seems to be the chasm between suppressed voices and subjectivities, the work of Russian philosopher Mikhail Bakhtin has proven to be quite fruitful, especially for Hebrew Bible scholars. Although Bakhtin did not deploy gender as a category of analysis, his work still has turned out to possess possibilities for gender-critical approaches, a feature he has in common with Derrida and Foucault. Barbara Green (2000) has demonstrated how Bakhtin may be appropriated and developed by feminists to present a reading that is attentive to questions of gender. While many facets of Bakhtin have been taken up in biblical studies (chronotope, the carnivalesque, grotesque), it could be said that his notion of monologic and dialogic language has the most potential for countering dominant readings and patriarchal/androcentric texts. Scholars who use Bakhtin form a bit of a subgroup due to specialized language and terms, which are not as fluid and malleable as the broader theoretical concepts of agency, space, and subversion. However, Carleen Mandolfo's study of Lamentations and Bakhtin succeeds in showing how fruitful the encounter is, as through a dialogic reading she enables the Daughter of Zion to emerge from the text (Mandolfo, 2007).

Narratology is another area that falls under linguistic turn approaches as they have been used in studies of the Hebrew Bible, most notably through the work of the literary scholar Mieke Bal. One of Bal's analytical techniques is that of narrative subjectivity, or examining who speaks, who sees, and who acts; how direct speech is distributed; and how readers through these effects are urged to comprehend the events in the text. A particularly cogent combination of gender theory, critical narratology (especially Bal's work), psychoanalysis and economics is represented by David Jobling's study on 1 Samuel (Jobling, 1998).

Some of the most thought-provoking and transgressive work that the linguistic turn has enabled in studies of the Hebrew Bible does not adopt any one approach in an exclusive manner. Such scholarship stands at the intersection where the identities of biblical characters and modern readers might be constructed and negotiated in the same space. There scholars might explore the relation between biblical bodies, cultural criticism, and politics of identity in order to challenge the concept of the "biblical" in culture (for a North American example, see Beal and Gunn, 1997).

Linguistic Turn, Gender, and the Study of the New Testament and Early Christianity. Since the late twentieth century, the linguistic turn has had a similarly complex methodological impact on the study of the New Testament, Christian origins, and early Christian literature. While the agenda set by scholars such as Elisabeth Schüssler Fiorenza was predominantly that of theological and historical reconstruction, others focused on literary strategies and narrative representation in the New Testament and early Christian literature. Within the field of New Testament studies as related to lenses that focus on gender as a category of analysis, the influence of the linguistic turn is intertwined with the contributions of second-wave feminism. Both methodological trajectories acknowledge the ideological nature of interpretive acts, and both claim to represent departures from those hermeneutical strategies and methods whose practitioners claim neutrality and/or an apolitical stance.

Given the complexity of the issues in this area, referencing several signal moments, rather than sweeping linear narratives, where we might detect the influence of the linguistic turn through the themes and questions raised in several important anthologies and special journal issues assists in charting and navigating this history of scholarship. Most notably,

the 1980s saw an interest in a turn to gendered discourse at the same time as historical reconstruction efforts that fronted women were under discussion. For example, the journal *Semeia*, dedicated to cutting-edge biblical scholarship that emphasized theoretical contributions and interdisciplinary exploration, published the first of several issues devoted to feminist interpretation in 1983, and featured signal essays from Elizabeth Struthers Malbon, Janice Capel Anderson, Cheryl Exum, Sharon H. Ringe, Toni Craven, William A. Walker, and Mary Ann Tolbert. Within this collection, second-wave feminist reconstruction efforts were in dialogue with literary approaches indebted to the linguistic turn, a conversation that continued in subsequent *Semeia* volumes devoted to the intersection of gender and critical theory in biblical interpretation. Such endeavors proved to be thoroughly interdisciplinary in nature, a feature that would define the linguistic turn's influence in New Testament studies, and particularly its "textualization" of oral traditions, rituals, anthropological observation, and so on.

During the 1990s, linguistic turn approaches shifted more clearly in the direction of addressing issues of representation and textual analyses of the discursive formations of texts, that is, examining the interaction between language and power as it is enacted in particular biblical texts. A seminal example of this shift is Elizabeth Castelli's *Imitating Paul: A Discourse of Power* (1991), which was one of the first studies of the New Testament to make sustained use of Michel Foucault's observations on power relationships to analyze Paul's patriarchal rhetoric of imitation in 1 Thessalonians, Philippians, and 1 Corinthians. Similarly, the publication of the Bible and Culture Collective's *Postmodern Bible* (1995), along with monographs from Dale Martin (1995), Stephen Moore (1996), and Daniel Boyarin (1994), continued deepening the relationship between critical theoretical approaches and the study of the New Testament. Martin explores the debates in 1 Corinthians related to the body in Greco-Roman thought, and discusses how the ideological construct of the body is useful for articulating issues of power and status, contagion and pollution. Moore appraises male bodies and masculine perfectibility in the New Testament, reading the biblical texts and their commentaries alongside personal narratives and various medical textbooks. Boyarin reads Paul from a Jewish perspective, and deconstructs the binary opposition between flesh and spirit in Galatians through the study of gender and ethnicity in Paul. While Moore is greatly influenced by Michel Foucault, Boyarin is more indebted to Derrida, and Martin to rhetorical criticism. However, they all focus on the gendered body, which represents one of the privileged topoi of the linguistic turn. Tina Pippin's work on apocalyptic literature (1999) also models this kind of analysis, which in addition to the multidisciplinary readings of biblical apocalyptic texts is also an early example of how reception history—in this case, of apocalyptic imagery—can play a vital role in the interpretive enterprise.

The above-mentioned publications mark the first generations of the linguistic turn as it relates to gender in New Testament studies. Like in earlier forms of scholarship, the focus remains on the text itself. However, instead of focusing on the production process of the text, which was so important to historical-critical research, attention shifted to how the text produced or constructed agents, symbols, and ideologies, as well as their afterlives. Instead of regarding the texts as transparent sources for reconstructions of antiquity, focus had moved to how the texts represented and produced reality and its effects. Furthermore, the shift to focusing on the production of patriarchal power, phallic symbolism, and masculinity meant widening the agenda of feminism and women's studies and deploying the broader and more constructivist concept of gender and the workings of gender relations in the texts.

As explored in the Hebrew Bible section of this entry, the linguistic turn also had an impact on understandings of the readers in the study of the New Testament and early Christian literature. Herein the textualization of the biblical characters may also be noted at the level of the interpreter herself or himself. The person carrying out the analysis inserts herself in the text, as a text. This can range from deployments of what has become a usual litany of self and privilege (white, Western, middle class, male) at the beginning of the study to long narratives of self, interwoven with

analysis, such as the style of Moore (in the New Testament) or Brenner (in the Hebrew Bible).

More recently, New Testament scholars who make use of linguistic turn approaches to analyze and address gender concerns have contributed to expanding the field through interacting with postcolonial criticism and queer theory (as with Runions in the Hebrew Bible). For example, Joseph Marchal (2008) has offered a feminist study of the language of power, transculturalism, and empire in Pauline interpretation and Paul's letter to the Philippians. Drawing on cultural studies, Marchal not only shows the limitations of earlier interpretive strategies for dealing with such complex issues but also offers ways of negotiating them. Caroline Vander Stichele and Todd Penner (2009) have proposed an analysis of early Christian discourse that moves outside the boundaries of the New Testament canon, as well as the incorporation of intersectionality, race-critical, and queer approaches, to articulate a gender-critical companion to the primary source texts. This work also makes use of an ideological-critical lens to engage the politics of the guild and of the interpretative process itself.

Emerging Questions. Approaches indebted to the linguistic turn have enabled new vocabularies, new frameworks, and new discussions in biblical scholarship and gender through three key, interrelated factors: ambivalence/polyvalence, representation, and agency.

Various influences within the linguistic turn have precipitated a focus on the ambivalence or polyvalence of the biblical texts, as well as how the absence of a singular meaning, or the basic instability of meaning-making as a process, has been suppressed in traditional analyses. Thus, maintaining the instability of meaning has meant a flourishing of multiple voices and interpretations that draw on a range of theories and practices to generate ever new combinations. In terms of gender, this has meant an extension of the agenda of feminism, which sought to make women more visible in the biblical texts and as interpreters of those texts. But the emphasis on the reader has also entailed a proliferation of readers, and a recognition of the reality that readers may feel freer to engage with the texts from particular individual and contingent standpoints, instead of having to conform to universal, traditional, and/or institutional values.

Representation has also generated a wide range of possibilities for biblical interpretation in a linguistic turn. Because the meaning of the text is no longer tied to a specific historical approach, such interpretation has also opened up for analyses the reception history of the texts in arts and popular culture, as well as the history of effects in the use of the Bible in missionary and other colonizing endeavors. For gender-critical approaches this has meant not only dissolving the links between historical figures and biblical women and men but also questioning the ideology of the representations and their role in the overall power mechanisms of the text. The linguistic turn has opened up ways of analyzing and tracing the biblical understandings of women and men, which then can be used to understand the operations and effects of gender in contemporary societies.

Finally, whereas feminism was concerned with restoring agency to women in the texts, the linguistic turn has also sought to make visible not only the other marginalized people in the texts (for example slaves, disabled bodies, prostitutes, LGBTI) but also the readers. For example, Averen Ipsen (2009) reads passages from the Bible with sex workers to bring out different interpretations of figures such as Rahab, the Whore of Babylon, Solomon and the two prostitutes, and the anointing women in the Gospels. Along similar lines, Musa Dube has examined how African women read, understood, and, above all, used the biblical texts in their own contexts—and more recently with emphasis on the AIDS/HIV epidemic.

There is no denying that the approaches comprising the linguistic turn have challenged biblical studies in a profound manner and reconfigured our views of biblical texts. Historical-critical approaches that focused on the production of the text, as well as social-scientific supplementary approaches, have tended to view the texts from antiquity as reliable sources for reconstructing and understanding antiquity. The linguistic turn has shifted the line of questioning, focusing on the production of meaning and (the effects of) representation. This has carried gender into newer fields of study, such as autobiog-raphy and postcolonialism, intersectional studies, queer and disability studies, ecological and affect studies, and so on.

Nevertheless, there are also caveats. Returning to some of the initial discussions in this essay, the consolidation of various standpoints into "the linguistic turn" warrants consideration. Theoretical developments preceding the linguistic turn, including psychoanalytical, feminist, and Marxist approaches, as well as liberation theology, contributed significantly to its articulation. It could be said that in a somewhat cannibalistic way, the linguistic turn has swallowed these approaches, digested them, and regurgitated them as critical or high theory, gender theory, and postcolonial theory. On the one hand the shift from feminism to gender theory has produced greater awareness of how gender is constructed, extending analysis to include the constructions of masculinity and nonbinary understandings of gender, but on the other it has failed to examine the assumptions of the theories deployed. For biblical scholarship, various engagements of historical-critical discourse with newer theoretical approaches such as postcolonialism might criticize "the masters" of traditional scholarship on the one hand but on the other hand also might reify the likes of Derrida, Foucault, and Bakhtin into new tools for the old toolbox (see Penner and Vander Stichele, 2005).

Finally, many of the theorists whose ideas are enthusiastically employed in approaches indebted to the linguistic turn are male, and do not have an explicit gender-critical perspective. How can we avoid reproducing an even more clandestine masculine ideology by not questioning the assumptions—historical, economic and ideological—that govern not only the emergence of these theories but also their astounding success in an epistemological paradigm shift? How is seeking agency and identity from dialogic spaces, the instability of language and meaning, and discerning counter-discourses, cracks, fissures, and tensions different from, or more sophisticated than, seeking agency and identity in the cracks and fissures in the patriarchal biblical texts? As Lone Fatum warns, in respect to the New Testament texts, that in order to be "saved," women must count as male by being asexual and nonfemale; Stephen Moore has referred to this conundrum as a "soteriological sex-change." In unhesitatingly and uncritically embracing theoretical tools that could—in theory—be just as androcentric as what we are combating, have we committed ourselves to a theoretical sex-change? Or perhaps the question is whether, in our rush to commit theoretical acts of interpretation, we could in the process also be committing ourselves to a theoretical sex change.

[*See also* Feminism, *subentries on* Second-Wave Feminism *and* Third-Wave Feminism; Gender; Historical-Critical Approaches; Intersectional Studies; Reader-Oriented Approaches; *and* Rhetorical-Hermeneutical Criticism.]

BIBLIOGRAPHY

Beal, Timothy K., and David M. Gunn, eds. *Reading Bibles, Writing Bodies: Identity and the Book.* London: Routledge, 1997.

Boyarin, Daniel. *A Radical Jew: Paul and the Politics of Identity.* Contraversions 1. Berkeley: University of California Press, 1994.

Brenner, Athalya. *I Am…: Biblical Women Tell Their Own Stories.* Minneapolis: Fortress, 2005.

Castelli, Elizabeth A. *Imitating Paul: A Discourse of Power.* Literary Currents in Biblical Interpretation. Louisville, Ky.: Westminster John Knox, 1991.

Clark, Elizabeth A. "Holy Women, Holy Words: Early Christian Women, Social History, and the 'Linguistic Turn.'" *Journal of Early Christian Studies* 6, no. 3 (1998): 413–430.

Clark, Elizabeth A. *History, Theory, Text: Historians and the Linguistic Turn.* Cambridge, Mass.: Harvard University Press, 2004.

Fatum, Lone. "Women, Symbolic Universe, and Structures of Silence: Challenges and Possibilities in Androcentric Texts." *Studia Theologica: Nordic Journal of Theology* 43, no. 1 (1989): 61–80.

Green, Barbara. *Mikhail Bakhtin and Biblical Scholarship: An Introduction.* Semeia Studies 38. Atlanta: Society of Biblical Literature, 2000.

Ipsen, Avaren. *Sex Working and the Bible.* Bible World. London: Equinox, 2009.

Jobling, David. *1 Samuel.* Berit Olam. Collegeville, Minn.: Liturgical Press, 1998.

Kelso, Julie. *O Mother, Where Art Thou? An Irigarayan Reading of the Book of Chronicles.* Bible World. London: Equinox, 2007.

Mandolfo, Carleen R. *Daughter Zion Talks Back to the Prophets: A Dialogic Theology of the Book of Lamentations.* Semeia Studies 58. Atlanta: Society of Biblical Literature, 2007.

Marchal, Joseph A. *The Politics of Heaven: Women, Gender, and Empire in the Study of Paul.* Paul in Critical Contexts. Minneapolis: Fortress, 2008.

Martin, Dale B. *The Corinthian Body.* New Haven, Conn.: Yale University Press, 1995.

Moore, Stephen D. *God's Gym: Divine Male Bodies of the Bible.* London: Routledge, 1996.

Økland, Jorunn. *Women in Their Place: Paul and the Corinthian Discourse of Gender and Sanctuary Space.* Journal for the Study of the New Testament Supplement Series 269. London: T&T Clark, 2004.

Pippin, Tina. *Apocalyptic Bodies: The Biblical End of the World in Text and Image.* London: Routledge, 1999.

Runions, Erin. *Changing Subjects: Gender, Nation and Future in Micah.* Playing the Texts 7. London: Sheffield Academic Press, 2001.

Sherwood, Yvonne. *The Prostitute and the Prophet: Hosea's Marriage in Literary-Theoretical Perspective.* Journal for the Study of the Old Testament Supplement Series 212; Gender, Culture Theory 2. Sheffield, U.K.: Sheffield Academic Press, 1996.

Trible, Phyllis. "Depatriarchalizing in Biblical Interpretation." *Journal of the American Academy of Religion* 41, no. 1 (1973): 30–48.

Vander Stichele, Caroline, and Todd Penner, eds. *Her Master's Tools? Feminist and Postcolonial Engagements of Historical-Critical Discourse.* Global Perspectives in Biblical Scholarship 9. Atlanta: Society of Biblical Literature, 2005.

Vander Stichele, Caroline, and Todd Penner. *Contextualizing Gender in Early Christian Discourse: Thinking beyond Thecla.* London: T&T Clark, 2009.

Christina Petterson

MALE-FEMALE SEXUALITY

This entry contains six subentries: Hebrew Bible; Greek World; Roman World; New Testament; Early Judaism; *and* Early Church.

Ancient Near East

See Gender and Sexuality: Ancient Near East.

Hebrew Bible

Male-female sexuality in the Hebrew Bible is embedded in a larger network of power relations. Incorporating institutions such as marriage and the family as well as economies of exchange, especially the exchange of women, male-female sexuality is a fundamental part of larger Israelite social structures. It also encompasses individual bodies and the sexual acts they may or may not perform.

Sexuality in the Hebrew Bible is normatively heterosexual; the creation stories in Genesis 1 and 2—3 establish the male-female sexual pairing as paradigmatic. The proper domain of this heterosexual sexuality is marriage, although the biblical texts include many examples of extramarital sexuality (for example, David and Bathsheba, 2 Sam 11). Procreation is an important aim of sexuality, although the texts also frame sexu-ality as desire. The texts also include a large number of stories concerning transgressive sexuality, including incest, sexual violence, and homosexual rape.

Like other forms of sexuality in the Hebrew Bible, male-female sexuality takes shape through relations of penetration and power. These relations are both literal (who sexually penetrates whom) and symbolic (who has power and of what sort). In the case of sexual acts, what is most important is not the gender or sex of the participants, but rather the relative status of the penetrating and penetrated bodies. The salient feature of the penetrated body is not biological sex but relative status. In the words of Daniel Boyarin (1995), "Permitted and tabooed sexual behavior was completely a function of status. The world was divided into the screwers—all male—and the screwed—both male and female" (p. 333). Thus male-female sexuality is a subset of a larger set of sexual acts.

The emphasis on domination and penetration assumes a model of gender not as two separate categories ("male" and "female"), but as a continuum of relative masculinities. This spectrum of masculinities is linked to what the historian Thomas Laqueur (1990) terms the "one sex model" of the body. Laqueur demonstrates convincingly that ancient people organized the world into one body (better or worse, which is to say more or less masculine) but two genders. Under this one-sex system, sexuality is what "genders" the body by marking it as more or less masculine.

Relevant Hebrew Vocabulary. There is no word in biblical Hebrew that corresponds to the contemporary term "sexuality." Instead, the language and texts employ a range of terms to describe sex, sexuality, and the sexed and sexualized body. More than a dozen verbs are used in Hebrew to describe sexual intercourse. The sexual act is clearly described with the verb "to penetrate sexually" (*b'l*, in Qal; Niphal, "to be penetrated sexually"), a term that is linked to the word for "master" or "husband" and thus encodes relations of power. This term, however, is not frequently used; the texts prefer idiomatic or euphemistic formulations such as "to know" (*yd' 'ēt*), "to come into" (*bw' 'al*), "to come near to" (*qrb 'al*), "to approach" (*ngš*), or "to lie with" (*škb 'im* or *škb 'ēt*), all of which mean "to have sex with" or "to penetrate sexually." Other verbs mean "to laugh" or "to play (sexually)" (*śḥq, ṣḥq 'im*, or *ṣḥq 'ēt*) and "to make sexual advances" or "to play sexual games" (*'gb 'al*). Legal texts often use "to uncover the nakedness" (*glh 'erwâ*) or "to use one's penis for sex" (*ntn šĕkōbet*). "To love" (*'hb*) covers a spectrum of meanings, encompassing divine love, familial love, erotic love, and the suzerain relationship; its meaning can be either sexual or nonsexual. When "to love" describes erotic or sexual love, the subject is normally masculine; Michal is the only named female character to love (*'hb*) a man (1 Sam 18:20). Several verbs mean "to desire," including *ḥpṣ, 'wh*, and *ḥšq*, but their meaning tracks closer to love than to sexual desire. The text also has a specific verbal root meaning "to engage in sexual relations outside of marriage or to fornicate" (*znh*) to describe the Israelites' sexual relations with the Moabites; the verb is related to the noun "prostitute" (*zônāh*).

The sexual organs of the body entail their own set of terms. Although the Hebrew Bible is deeply phallocentric, the penis almost never receives a textual name of its own. Instead, it is referred to as "flesh" (*bāśār*) or identified, through contiguity or metonymy, as "feet" (*raglāyim, margĕlôt*), "loins" (*ḥălāṣayim*), "thigh" (*yārēk*), "heel" (*'āqēb*), or "hand" (*yād*). "Rib/side" (*ṣēlā'*) may also possibly indicate the penis, as in the second creation story (Gen 2:21). In Deuteronomy 25:11, the text refers to the male genitals as "shameful parts" (*mĕbûšîm*), but also associates male sexuality

with virility in *'āwen*, "virility, male generative power." "Testicle" (*'ešek*) occurs once in Leviticus 21:20, in the context of men with crushed testicles being prohibited from the community; Deuteronomy 23:1 likewise refers to "crushed testicles" (*pĕṣûa' dakkā'*) or a severed "penis" (*šāpĕkâ*) as disqualifications for entry into the assembly. The term "foreskin" (*'orlā*) occurs repeatedly in the context of circumcision.

The female genitals are described with greater visual detail in the text; the exposure of female nakedness is both a threat and a titillation. As with male bodies, "nakedness" (*'erwâ*) indicates the genitals. The term "womb" (*reḥem*) occurs frequently. The vulva and vagina are referred to as a "hole" (*ḥōr*, Song 5:4) or "opening" (*petaḥ*, Song 7:13 [7:14 in Hebrew]). The "navel" (*šorĕr*) may also more properly refer to the vulva (Song 7:3). "Female" (*nĕqēbâ*), used for humans and animals alike, comes from a root meaning "hole," "cavity," or "opening" (*nqb*); thus femaleness itself is linguistically constituted through the receptive sexual function (see further Brenner, 1997). The word "masculine" (*zākār*), in distinction, suggests a social function of remembrance through its connection to the verb "to remember" (*zkr*) (p. 12). For a more detailed discussion of vocabulary, see further Brenner (1997) and Davidson (2007).

Male Sexuality. Male sexuality in the Hebrew Bible is a practice of power. Male sexual relations with, and control of, women figure into a larger economy of masculinity and domination. The male sexual role is normatively the active one; men are tasked with seeking out sexual and marital partners and with initiating the social negotiations that lead to marriage. The stories of the patriarchs as well as those of Moses offer examples of this sort of marriage negotiation. Although monogamy is the norm, multiple wives also appear without judgment in the text, as in the case of Jacob's wives, Leah and Rachel. As Jacob's story also demonstrates, male control over a wife's sexuality extends to the sexuality of her maids, although always, in the text's account, with the wife's permission.

The "house of the father" (*bêt 'āb*) is an important organizing metaphor that brings together sexuality, the family, and social power. Fathering children, especially sons, is an important part of masculinity.

The house of the father reinforces the cultural importance of heterosexuality and heterosexual marriage under the overarching framework of patriarchy and patrilocality.

Sexual relations with women are frequently used to negotiate relations between men. Marriage, for example, constitutes an exchange of women between men. Abraham, fearing for his own safety, twice passes his wife Sarah off as his sister (Gen 12, 20); Isaac does the same (Gen 26:7–11). In his revolt, Absalom demonstrates his power over his father David by sleeping with the latter's concubines (2 Sam 16:22). Related to this use of women to negotiate between men, adultery, in the biblical definition, rests entirely upon the marital status of the woman; the extramarital sexual activities of a man do not disturb the social order, so long as they do not involve a married woman. There is likewise no textual emphasis placed on male virginity. Nevertheless, the text disapproves of sexual excess in men as well; Reuben's sexual encounter with his father's concubine Bilhah (Leah's maidservant) is used to discredit him (Gen 35:22; 49:3–4). There are likewise a number of additional sexual prohibitions, including against excess, in Leviticus 18 and 20.

Male sexuality is also a crucial part of Israelite religious experience. The covenant, the core of the relationship between God and Israel, is represented bodily through modification of the male genitals via circumcision. Scholars have analyzed this emphasis on modification of the penis as the bodily sign of the covenant, indicative of the phallocentrism of Israelite religion and the biblical texts (see further Rashkow, 2000; Brenner, 1997). Although circumcision emphasizes the importance of male sexuality to the divine-human relation, it also contains, according to scholars such as Rashkow and Howard Eilberg-Schwartz (1995), a threat of castration. The sexed male body stands in ambivalent relation to the male deity. The relationship between a male God and the male Israelites also complicates male-female sexuality by threatening to displace either heteronormativity or male privilege in religious relations.

Female Sexuality. In the Hebrew Bible, female sexuality is strongly linked to fertility and reproduction. The biblical command to "be fruitful and multiply" (Gen 1:28), although directed at men and women alike, becomes, in practice, a female domain. The narratives of the matriarchs are, emphatically, narratives of fertility. The fate of a barren woman in ancient Israel was bleak; Rachel's demand "Give me children or I will die" (Gen 30:1) is less an impetuous statement than a stark recognition of the cultural value of procreation and its consequences for women. At the same time, the stories of barrenness and conception in the Hebrew Bible emphasize the role of Yahweh in opening and sealing the womb. Embodied sexuality represents the closest form of contact for women with the divine. Women also exert proxy control over the sexuality of other women, as in the matriarchs' relations with their handmaids (Sarah and Hagar [Gen 16, 21], Rachel and Bilhah [Gen 29—30], Leah and Zilpah [Gen 29—30]).

The emphasis placed on female sexuality is linked, as well, to a larger textual emphasis on female sexuality as a commodity controlled and exchanged by men. The institution of Levirite marriage (Deut 25:5–6) is perhaps the most pronounced example of the textual insistence on female sexuality in the service of men. Female sexuality is controlled by men: first fathers and brothers, then husbands. As a result, many of the narratives involving female sexuality are stories of rape. The rape of Dinah (Gen 34) offers a clear example of what Gayle Rubin (2009) calls "the traffic in women" as Dinah's father, brothers, and Shechem compete over her sexuality. Rape likewise figures in the narrative of David's daughter Tamar, whose violation by her half-brother Amnon leads, in part, to Absalom's revolt (2 Sam 13). In each of these stories, female sexuality—and violated female sexuality in particular—becomes the grounds of negotiation between men. The exchange of female sexuality provides the groundwork for what Rubin names "the sex-gender system," defined as "the set of arrangements by which a society transforms biological sexuality into products of human activity, and in which these transformed sexual needs are satisfied" (p. 88). Nowhere is this more apparent than in the book of Judges and especially in chapter 19, where the raped body of the Levite's unnamed concubine is cut into twelve pieces and sent to the twelve tribes as a summons to war.

Although procreation and virginity are highly valued in the Hebrew Bible, female sexual agency is not. The book of Proverbs warns young men against the seductions of the strange woman, whose active solicitations are in contrast to the passive wife who represents wisdom and prudence (Prov 5:3). And female promiscuity and sexual agency are repeatedly linked with objectionable religious practice, most prominently in the Prophets, where an anthropomorphized female Israel is represented as lusting after, and engaging in intercourse with, rival gods. The text also links foreignness to female promiscuity, as in the representation of Potiphar's wife (Gen 39) and the foreign woman in Proverbs (Prov 1—9).

A partial exception to this condemnation of female sexuality is the figure of the prostitute. Although prostitutes are generally viewed negatively, they play important narrative roles, such as the prostitute Rahab, who saves the Israelite spies in the city of Jericho (Josh 2). There is some evidence, moreover, that the term "prostitute" may simply refer to a woman who lives independently of the house of her father or husband and not to a woman who exchanges sex for money.

Incest, Sexuality, and the Family. Sexuality frequently figures in the construction and policing of identity boundaries in the Hebrew Bible. The exchange of women, discussed briefly above, is a key domain in negotiating the boundaries of national and familial identity. The rape of Dinah (Gen 34) is not simply a story about the relations of sexuality in the family and the competing demands of the paternal, filial, and marital orders. It is also a narrative about the boundary between Israelite identity, represented by the family of Jacob/Israel, and ethnic otherness, represented by Shechem. Dinah's punishment—Shechem is killed, Dinah is left childless—signals the punishments levied on intermarriage, which is prohibited in Exodus 34 and again in Deuteronomy 7. The text repeatedly uses violence to reinforce sexual and national boundaries, as in the rape and murder of the Midianite woman Cozbi in Numbers 25. And yet there is also tension surrounding this boundary, as a number of foreign women enter into the Israelite genealogy—Rahab (Josh 2), Ruth (Ruth), Tamar (Gen 38), and so forth

(this motif is thematized in the New Testament as well; see further Matt 1).

The narratives of rape and abduction of women—which include, as well, the rape of the Levite's concubine (Judg 19), the abduction of the women of Shiloh (Judg 21:19–24), and the near rape of Lot's daughters (Gen 19)—also offer a point of continuity with other rape-oriented foundation myths, such as the rape of Lucretia and the rape of the Sabine women. Lot's story also points to a second important thematics of sexuality as boundary: the issue of incest. Most forms of incest are explicitly prohibited by biblical law (Lev 18, 20), with incest between a brother and a full sister or between a father and a daughter forming the notable exceptions. However, there are also significant narrative moments of incest, including not only Lot and his daughters (Gen 19:8) and Tamar and Amnon (2 Sam 13), but also Judah and Tamar (Gen 38) and perhaps Noah and Ham (Gen 9:20–27; see further Rashkow, 2000) and Abraham and Sarah (Gen 12). Furthermore, Reuben and Absalom each sleep with their fathers' concubine or concubines, a violation of family boundaries that also shows the use of sexuality as a power play.

Other forms of sexuality that violate power structures of the family are regulated and punished in the text. The imbalance in sexual relations is clear in the biblical definition of adultery as between a married woman and a man (married or unmarried) who is not her husband; as the asymmetrical definition makes clear, adultery threatens the value of the woman as commodity. Adultery is prohibited in Exodus 5:18 and 20:14 and in Leviticus 18:20, as well as in the Prophets and wisdom literature; it is punished by stoning, as with other crimes against the community (see Rashkow, 2000). Numbers 5 prescribes a ritual for determining whether charges of adultery are valid. Because female sexuality is given its significance in relation to men, there is also a certain overlap between rape and adultery (for a married woman) or consensual sex (for a virgin). Deuteronomy 22:23–27 provides mitigating circumstances in the case of a betrothed virgin who is raped "in the open country" (Deut 22:25) and whose cries for help thus cannot, presumably, be heard; in such cases, the raped woman is not punished. There is no such mitigation, however, for married women who are raped outside the city.

Male-Female Sexuality and Foreignness. In addition to the boundaries of the family and the community, sexuality is used to thematize national difference. The origin myths of the Moabites and the Ammonites as descendants of Lot's incestuous relations with his daughters (Gen 19) also exemplify the tendency, found in the biblical text but hardly limited to it, to associate foreignness with sexual depravity. The sex laws in Leviticus 18 open with an injunction on the Israelites: "You shall not do as they do in the land of Egypt, where you lived, and you shall not do as they do in the land of Canaan, to which I am bringing you" (Lev 18:3). Elsewhere, in both the Pentateuch and the prophetic marriage metaphor texts, Canaanite and Egyptian sexuality are linked to sexual depravity.

The licentious sexuality of the Canaanites is a repeated theme in the Prophets. Hosea and Ezekiel treat non-Yahwistic religious practice as adultery; Hosea describes Israel as "playing the whore" (Hos 2:5). The Prophets' vigor for describing Canaanite licentiousness is so pronounced that it led a generation of biblical scholars to hypothesize the existence of a Canaanite sex cult (see, for example, Hans Walter Wolff's 1973 commentary on Hosea), complete with temple prostitutes. This theory, however, has been widely rejected by contemporary scholarship (see further, Stone, 1997).

Egypt, too, is described as a place of sexual temptation and excess. It is in Egypt that Abraham first passes off Sarah as his sister (Gen 12) and that Joseph faces the advances of Potiphar's wife (Gen 39). Egypt is a place of fecundity and excess in the biblical imagination; the Israelites reproduce excessively while in Egypt and then long for (a word used as well for sexual desire) the meat and melons of the nation after they have left. The sexualization of Egypt extends to its people. Ezekiel, for example, describes the Egyptians in hypersexualized terms, directing particular attention to their genitals and their appeal to Israel (Ezek 23:20). This hypersexualization is a strategy of othering that plays on the social role of sexuality.

Male-Female Sexuality and Desire. Sexual desire has an ambivalent status in the Hebrew Bible. Sexual relations are generally framed through power and privilege, not desire. Thus marriage, for example, is as much a negotiation between men as it is the outgrowth of sexual attraction and desire. This is not to say that desire never figures into sexual or marital relations. David desires Bathsheba (2 Sam 11:2–3) and Jacob works for fourteen years out of his desire for Rachel (Gen 29:18–30). Desire also does not always end in marriage, as in Amnon's desire for Tamar, which leads to rape and, through Absalom's revenge, the near collapse of a family. In addition to positioning individual desire in a larger network of family politics and concern, both the Tamar/Amnon and the Rachel/Jacob stories share a linking of male desire to female beauty. Although the Bible is notoriously reticent in its descriptions, the visual seems to be the most important sense in engendering desire (this is the case, as well, in the woman's desire for the fruit of the tree of knowledge of good and evil in Gen 3:6).

Desire is most frequently the purview of men. Female desire is rarely mentioned in accounts of marriages, for example, although Eve is cursed with (heterosexual) desire in the scene of expulsion from Eden (Gen 3:16). Female sexuality is represented most positively in the Song of Songs, a text that seems to embrace female desire and sexual pleasure. In the Song, the Shulamite praises her own beauty and describes her intimate pleasures with her lover (Song 1:5–7; 2:3–7; *ff.*); these sexual pleasures are not censored but rather celebrated by the text. There are, however, some suggestions of a more complex representation of female sexual pleasures beyond procreative heterosexual sex, as in the possible references to masturbation and to masochism and sadism (see further, Burrus and Moore, 2003). The Song also embraces male sexuality and male sexual pleasure. As in other biblical texts, sexual desire is linked to the visual sense—much is made of the sight of the body of the lover—but here the other senses also come into play, including taste, touch, and smell. The account of desire and sexual pleasure between a man and a woman, specifically but not exclusively heterosexual, contrasts with the rhetoric of exchange, idolatry, and condemnation elsewhere in the text.

[*See also* Creation; Marriage and Divorce, *subentry* Hebrew Bible; Race, Class and Ethnicity, *subentry* Hebrew Bible; *and* Sexual Transgression, *subentry* Hebrew Bible.]

BIBLIOGRAPHY

Bal, Mieke. *Death and Dissymmetry: The Politics of Coherence in the Book of Judges.* Chicago: University of Chicago Press, 1988.

Bird, Phyllis. "'To Play the Harlot': An Inquiry into an Old Testament Metaphor." In *Gender and Difference in Ancient Israel*, edited by Peggy Day, pp. 75–94. Minneapolis: Fortress, 2009.

Boer, Roland. *The Earthy Nature of the Bible: Fleshly Readings of Sex, Masculinity, and Carnality.* New York: Palgrave Macmillan, 2012.

Boyarin, Daniel. "Are There Any Jews in 'The History of Sexuality'?" *Journal of the History of Sexuality* 5, no. 3 (1995): 333–355.

Brenner, Athalya. *The Intercourse of Knowledge: On Gendering Desire and Sexuality in the Hebrew Bible.* Biblical Interpretation Series 26. Leiden, The Netherlands: Brill, 1997.

Burrus, Virginia, and Stephen Moore. "Unsafe Sex: Feminism, Pornography, and the Song of Songs." *Biblical Interpretation* 11, no. 1 (2003): 24–52.

Davidson, Richard M. *Flame of Yahweh: Sexuality in the Old Testament.* Peabody, Mass.: Hendrickson, 2007.

Eilberg-Schwartz, Howard. *God's Phallus: And Other Problems for Men and Monotheism.* Boston: Beacon, 1995.

Laqueur, Thomas. *Making Sex: Body and Gender from the Greeks to Freud.* Cambridge, Mass.: Harvard University Press, 1990.

Penner, Todd C., and Caroline Vander Stichele. *Mapping Gender in Ancient Religious Discourses.* Biblical Interpretation Series 84. Leiden, The Netherlands: Brill, 2007.

Rashkow, Ilona. *Taboo or Not Taboo: Sexuality and Family in the Hebrew Bible.* Minneapolis: Fortress, 2000.

Rubin, Gayle. "The Traffic in Women: Notes on the Political Economy of Sex." In *Feminist Anthropology*, edited by Ellen Lewin. Hoboken, N.J.: Blackwell, 2009. Essay first published in 1975 in *Toward an Anthropology of Women*, edited by Rayna R. Reiter (New York: Monthly Review), pp. 157–210.

Stone, Ken. "The Hermeneutics of Abomination: On Gay Men, Canaanites, and Biblical Interpretation." *Biblical Theology Bulletin* 27, no. 2 (1997): 36–41.

Wolff, Hans Walter. *Hosea: A Commentary on the Book of Hosea.* Hermeneia: A Critical and Historical Commentary on the Bible. Philadelphia: Augsburg Fortress, 1973.

Yee, Gale A. *Poor Banished Children of Eve: Woman as Evil in the Hebrew Bible.* Minneapolis: Augsburg Fortress, 2003.

Rhiannon Graybill

Greek World

"Greek love" evokes for us erotic exchanges between males, but the main object of ancient Greek fictional representation, normative arrangements, and theoretical inquiry was sexuality between women and men. This begins with the Homeric epics. The most valiant of Greek warriors at Troy, Achilles, and his friend Patroklos were passionate lovers Plato tells us (*Symposium* 179e–180b), but the poems (as we know them) fail to mention their passion. Zeus burned with love (*amore arsit*) for the son of the founder of Troy, Ganymede, and abducted him on Mount Olympus, Ovid tells us (*Metamorphoses* 15.155–156). But, in the *Iliad*, it is (all) the gods who, moved by the divine beauty of this young man, took hold of him, so that he could serve as Zeus's cupbearer and live forever with the Immortals (20.232–235). This does not mean that love between men and boys was absent from archaic poetry: in the *Homeric Hymn to Aphrodite*, Zeus's rape of Ganymede appears in an erotic context (201–218; cf. Theognis, 2.1345–1350). It simply means that the predominant focus of the *Iliad* and the *Odyssey* was on sexuality involving women and men.

"Sexuality" is a controversial term. In *The Use of Pleasure*, Michel Foucault defined sexuality as an experience, in a culture, at the intersection of normative discourses, domains of knowledge, and forms of subjectivity (1984, p. 9). Sexuality is a complex experience, I would add, but one of desire, pleasure, the body, and institutions (laws and mores) that frame sexual activity and, crucially, sexual interactions (Sissa, 2008). The latter definition allows for more analytical attention to the texts and demands a keener account of legal norms and social settings. Moreover, "heterosexuality" is a contested and misleading category. In opposition to "homosexuality," it implies that one significant antithesis—*same/other*—organizes sexual preferences. Love for individuals of the same (*homoios*) sex—females or males—is set against love for individuals of the other (*heteros*). But, in Greek culture, the prime criterion for mapping desire, pleasure, and the body was gender. Gender commanded the logic of sexuality. And the standpoint was generally men's desire. As we can see in comparative and contrasting arguments, in praise of boys versus females (Plato, Plutarch, or the novel), ancient texts insist on the superior qualities of male and manly partners—not on the dilemma of sameness/otherness. Women's love for women is also seen through the prism of beauty, not similarity. Sexual orientation is a matter of competitive attractiveness between aesthetically different bodies. It is more appropriate, therefore, to speak about female–male sexuality.

Epic and Mythological Traditions. In all human societies, men exchange women. Marriage is a basic factor of civilization. Kinship systems regulate the formation of households, and the creation of bonds of alliance and affinity. In the fictional society projected by the epics, sexuality between women and men provides a unique source of narrative developments and powerful characters. Since this kind of intercourse results in procreation, it brings to life generations of gods, human beings, demigods, and heroes. Since this sexual activity has to be disciplined and ritualized through marriage, the wedding, and family connections, it provides the building blocks of the social world. Since this erotic interaction involves both genders, it brings into the picture a dramatic depiction of the aristocratic, heroic world: warlike masculinity (strong, courageous, aggressive, mobile), versus pleasurable femininity (weak, cowardly, soft, domestic). Since societal values represented in the poems hinge on honor, and honor is inseparable from sexual pride, this sexuality can also cause offensive transgressions, revenge, and blood shedding.

The cause of the Trojan War was the seduction of Helen, a beautiful woman married to Menelaus, the king of Sparta. Her husband wanted to retrieve her and thus initiated a Panhellenic expedition to this end. The *Iliad*'s plot is set in motion when King Agamemnon deprives his best warrior, Achilles, of a female captive, Briseis. This was a "wife who suited his heart" (*alochon thymarea*), Achilles lamented, and

whom he "loved passionately" (*ek thymou phileon*: 9.336–342). It was not rapturing, earth-shattering, romantic love, perhaps, but it was love, and it was significant enough to cause anger and revenge. Honor was at stake, precisely because Menelaus "lovingly cared" (*philéei kai kēdetai*) for Helen, as Achilles did for Briseis. The language of love, passion, and care (*philein, thymos, kēdos*) conveys an attachment that is personal, special, affective, and that goes beyond the intent of mere social reproduction or property rights. A woman is not a tripod.

In the *Odyssey*, one of the Greek princes surviving the Trojan carnage, Odysseus, travels home, eager to be reunited with his beloved wife, Penelope. Along the way, he encounters a goddess, Calypso, and a magician, Circe, with whom he makes love. Penelope remains sexually faithful, but, meanwhile, she keeps waiting the best young men from Ithaca, who patiently woo her. They have sex with the maids. Once home, Odysseus exterminates the men who have besieged his wife and has the promiscuous servants hanged. Again, it is a matter of honor, but *eros* is not absent. Quite the contrary: Penelope's suitors cause offense because they want to marry her without knowing whether Odysseus is dead, and they do so not in order to succeed Odysseus, settle into his house, and take over his position of power. Should Penelope choose a new spouse, she would follow him to *his* home, exactly as she did when marrying Odysseus (18.269–270; 19.572; 579; 20.328–337). In this virilocal society, the wife joins the husband's residence. The winning suitor would not occupy Odysseus's bed. The Ithacan youths, therefore, compete for her: for Penelope, that is, as an object of erotic interest. When Penelope appears before her admirers, they feel their knees go soft (*lyto gounata*), while *eros* enchants their hearts and they pray to be in bed with her (*lechéessi klithēnai*: 18.211–212; 1.366). When Odysseus is finally ready to rest, the couple celebrates for three days, in bed.

The master plots of the Homeric poems intertwine the aspirations of Hellenic and Trojan warriors, who fight for sovereignty, status, power, and glory, with their experience of marriage, pleasure, and desire. But there are also episodic storylines, scenes, and details that reveal the omnipresence of erotic images and feelings. Think of Helen, whose sensual splendor justifies the war (*Iliad* 3.156–160), and of Hera's successful attempt to distract Zeus from the battlefield by luring him to make love in a golden cloud (14.153–351). Think of Calypso's attachment to Odysseus and their ambivalent relationship. For years, they sleep together, Odysseus being "unwilling beside the willing nymph" (*par' ouk ethelōn ethelousē*: 5.155) but, on the eve of Odysseus's departure toward Ithaca (and his spouse), "they sleep with each other enjoying love" (*terpesthēn philotēti, par' allēloisi menontes*: 5.227). Think of Hephaestus, the lame metal smith to the gods, who entraps his wife, Aphrodite, in bed with a much fitter Olympian male, Ares, the god of war. All the Olympians enjoy the spectacle (*Odyssey* 266–366). Gods seduce human virgins, and the seduction is usually followed by the birth of heroes: think of Hermes and Polymele, Poseidon and Tyro. The *Hymns* also narrate erotic tales, e.g., Zeus's love for Maia (*Hymn to Hermes*) and Aphrodite's infatuation with Anchises (*Hymn to Aphrodite*). Aphrodite is proud to subdue mortals and immortals, but Zeus makes her feel what she usually inflicts upon others: to be taken by irresistible desire at the sight of a beautiful young person. It is her turn to fall for a mortal, and to have to seduce him. Then she will stop boasting about her power over the Olympians! Since the issue of this erotic experiment is Aeneas, the Trojan hero who will ultimately found Rome, this is no inconsequential affair.

In Homer, sexuality involving women and men is pervasive. The poetry we conventionally attribute to "Homer" was a crucial component of classical, Panhellenic culture and played a unique role in the official self-representation of Athens. Hipparchos (sixth century B.C.E.) instituted the Panathenaia, a sumptuous festival in which Athens celebrated its own accomplishments under the auspices of a powerful goddess, the virgin Athena. The festivities included the recitation of the *Iliad* and the *Odyssey*, the text of which was now fixed and regulated. The theater also re-enacted incessantly the vicissitudes of the heroes involved in the Trojan War. This monumental legacy framed the mainstream representations of Greek culture at large. Hence, the literature's depiction of male–female sexuality had far-reaching influence.

Hesiod the other archaic (and probably legendary) poet and theologian, who flourished in eighth–seventh century B.C.E., but remained a well-known reference in the classical period, placed great emphasis on women and their relations with men. Hesiod tells the story of the creation of Woman. In the *Theogony* two gods clash over a matter of honor: Prometheus deceives Zeus in the distribution of the portions of an ox. He offers him the inedible parts, the bare bones, hidden under a slice of glittering fat. This is insulting. Zeus gets frightfully angry and starts a series of retaliations that culminate with the confection of a "beautiful evil" (*kalon kakon*) in the likeness of immortal goddesses: the first mortal woman, *gynē*. Woman will now share the life of all men, introducing "women's baneful deeds" (*mermera erga gunaikōn*) into their existence. Woman will be idle and yet avid for wealth. She will make possible, however, the procreation of children. Men will face a new dilemma: either produce offspring but bear life in the company of a seldom-tolerable wife or be lonely in their old years (570–612). In *Works and Days*, the first woman is called Pandora, "all gifts." By opening a jar that she had been ordered to keep closed, Pandora lets "painful cares" (*kēdea lygra*) swarm into the world (53–105).

Hesiod's narratives create a paradigmatic train of thought: the first "mortal human beings" (*thnētoi t' anthropoi*) were of one gender, male; females were accidentally added to the world, as a supplement to that original humanity; as soon as there are two genders, they interact sexually; the sexual act is fecund; for humankind, sexuality is the condition of survival; the whole interaction is narrated from men's standpoint, and in view of its consequences for men. Female-male sexuality is a by-product of the division (by addition) between the sexes, which is but a fatal misstep.

Mortals mate, for Hesiod, like the primordial, divine powers did at the beginning of the world. In the *Theogony, Eros* was there at the outset. In the opening lines of the genealogy of the gods, there is Chaos and then Gaia/Earth. Out of nowhere, Eros springs into life as the most beautiful of all the gods, the one who melts the limbs (*lysimelēs*) and who subdues the mind and counsel of mortals and immortals (120–122). Then black Night comes to be; joining in love (*philotēti migeisa*) with Erebos, she engenders Aether (the upper atmosphere), and Day. All by herself, Earth generates Sky; through intercourse (*eunētheisa*) with him, she gives birth to generations of beings out of which the rest of the cosmos comes into existence. Female–male sexuality is foundational and cosmogonic. And yet the human female is not part of nature, but a work of art. Once the artisan god Hephaestus has fashioned Woman's body, the goddess Athena clothes her, wraps her in an embroidered veil, and places wreaths of flowers and a crown of gold on her head. She is now "a wonder to see" (*thauma idesthai*; 570–584). In *Works and Days*, Athena adorns Pandora with the help of the Graces, Persuasion, and the Hours. Hermes equips her with lies, crafty words, and a deceitful nature (60–82). Statuesque and bejewelled, elaborately ornate and skilled in sly speech, Woman is unnatural.

This sequence—male gender, unfortunate addition of the female, coition, and generation—resurfaces in Plato's *Timaeus*. Medieval and Renaissance artists will perceive the potential for a comparison with the biblical narrative about the belated creation of Eve, after Adam; original sin; and expulsion from the earthly Paradise. Hence *Eva Prima Pandora* as an enduring poetic and iconographic theme.

Sexuality on Stage. In classical Greece, the erotic interaction between women and men finds its most significant expression in the Theater. Theater was not just a literary genre but also a cultural event. Performances of tragic and comic plays were part of yearly religious festivals honoring the god Dionysos. An Athenian official, the Archon, oversaw the competitive submission of scripts, their selection, and their production, which wealthy citizens financed. To attend, spectators received an allowance, the *theorikon*. The theater was not a private, marginal, or elitist form of entertainment, therefore, but an official occasion meant for a vast, inclusive, general audience. The visibility and potential impact of the characters, plots, and ideas were unique. Since playwrights had to compete, year after year, for prizes, success, and celebrity, they had to choose popular topics. Drama reveals less the intentions of the authors, than the taste of the public.

Women, and their loves, take the stage. Greek tragedy offers the most complex representation of couples of husbands and wives, and of adulterous lovers. That complexity arises first of all from the fact that the plays revisit mythological and epic traditions and thus represent the vicissitudes of large networks of genealogically connected individuals such as the descendants of Atreus, Labdacos, Peleus, or Cadmos. Kinship, marriage, rape, and adultery provide the poets with an inexhaustible repertoire of characters, emotions, and canvasses. The poets re-write and magnify intricate situations in which relations meant to entail solidarity, attachment, and affection turn into conflict, murder, betrayal, and retaliation. Tragedy, Aristotle tells us, is about unexpected violence among friends (*Poetics* 14.1453b.19–22).

As sexual partners, siblings, and mothers, women are protagonists. First, they belong in a remote, princely society, in which their role as passionate agents or insightful advisors was prominent. The tragic focus on the aristocratic heroic past instead of the contemporary democratic *polis*, allows for unique attention to the feminine. Second, women live their sexuality—their experience of desire, pleasure, the body, and the institutions that frame that experience, such as marriage and the family—in ways that create suspense. When we think of the striking figures in tragic dramas, we must make sense of their agency and intentions by placing them against the background of contemporary Greek culture, but we must also appreciate the unforeseeable twists that the genre imposes upon conventional expectations. Third, it is in tragedy and particularly in Euripides's plays that we find representations of female actions and passions, of male misunderstandings and trite projections, and of conflicting negotiations between women and men. Thus, when reading Greek tragedy, static notions of gender as social construction of roles and characters become insufficient. We must capture new definitions of female–male sexuality that are unexpected, unstable, and, above all, dynamic. The expression "difference *between* the sexes" is more suitable. Such difference is not just biological dimorphism. It is a cultural artefact shaped by language, laws, mores, and different domains of knowledge, but, precisely because there are so many layers, we should be careful not to flatten the texture. The dichotomy of two finite genders generates the illusion that female/

male might be a simple binary opposition, coherent with others such as passive/active, natural/cultural, emotional/rational. But Greek theater plays with the templates of binary logic. Tragedy reassigns qualities, behaviors, and intents in surprising ways. To speak of difference *between* the sexes, furthermore, keeps us alert to the relevance of the body and its erotic experience. Sexuality on stage is a cultural, personal, and sexual dialectic. It is drama.

A paradigmatic play, Euripides's *Medea* (431 B.C.E.), illustrates this dialectic. Medea, a princess from the Black Sea and grandchild of the Sun, is in love with her Greek husband, Jason, a man for whom she has left her homeland, betrayed her father, and killed her brother. The couple live in Corinth. Jason decides to abandon his wife in order to marry another woman, the daughter of the local king. Hurt and furious, Medea plans revenge: she will kill him, together with his new household. In a shocking dialogue, however, Jason refuses to acknowledge what Medea has done for him. All she has accomplished, he claims, is not even her doing but what a divinity has made her do. Jason upholds the archaic conception of *eros* as overcoming mortals and immortals. There is no human love; there is just Aphrodite. By the same logic, Jason defends his defection as a reasonable project for the sake of his children. Unlike Medea, he does not care for *eros*, he claims, but only for the boys—who, once included in the royal family, will live a better life. Crushed by Jason's failure to recognize who she is—a loving woman, in action— Medea changes her mind: she will spare Jason and kill the children instead. Jason will suffer as a father, mourning what allegedly matters most to him.

In cultural terms, we can explain Jason's mistake as an attempt to appropriate the children as his own offspring, obliterating their mother. This is not just an act of individual bossiness but a significant miscalculation. It is contrary to the Athenian system of filiation, which is asymmetrical (the paternal line prevails) but bilateral (the maternal line is acknowledged). This principle inspired Pericles's decree on the transmission of citizenship through both parents (451 B.C.E.) and is embedded in the laws regulating adoptions. It is not a couple who adopts, but

a man; women cannot adopt. A child, therefore, can acquire a different father, but "it happens that the mother is just the same" (*all' homoiōs hyparchei tēn autēn einai mētera*: Iseus 7.25; cf. 10.10). The maternal line, therefore, could not possibly be ignored: it cannot be erased, not even through a proper adoption. From the standpoint of Athenian legal culture, Jason commits a serious blunder, followed by an even more foolish error.

Aristotle's theory of emotions guides our interpretation of the play. We may receive an undeserved offense, either from someone who unduly disrespects us or from an ungrateful person we have benefitted. This causes anger. Anger (*orgē*) is a justified response to an unjustified slight. It is a desire to take revenge, This definition fits the scenarios of noble, heroic, and divine irascibility found in the epic tradition, the theater and political rhetoric. Aristotle is an excellent interpreter of his own culture. In Euripides's *Medea*, it is precisely the language of anger that expresses what we would call the "jealousy" of this proud woman. Medea is the victim of contempt. She feels aggrieved; she must retaliate. The retaliation will have to strike the most appropriate target. This is heroic and just. The chorus (but also the Nurse and the king of Athens, Aegeus, who promises to help her) readily sides with Medea. Until she resolves to murder her children, which is indefensible, she is absolutely right. Everybody agrees—except Jason.

Jason is unable to predict the inexorable logic of anger, as well as the compelling logic of kinship. Filiation, for him, is malleable and can be adjusted to individual interests; *orgē*, as the sequence of an unjustified injury, ensuing excruciating pain, followed by the wish to react, comes as a total surprise to him. He is Greek but behaves like an alien. Cultural incompetence goes with his deafness to Medea's self-representation: he fails to acknowledge Medea's agency or to understand the nature of *eros*. He does not even fear his wife's tremendous expertise in magic. He is a man but is completely thoughtless. Euripides places in his mouth a collection of banalities about women: they only care about the bed; they are obsessed with erotic passion; they serve the purpose of begetting children, but what a pity that men cannot do so by a different means, such as buying babies. His prejudices toward women clash with Medea's awareness of the Greek female condition: we are obliged to buy a master (a bitter allusion to the dowry), she claims; we cannot really choose our husbands; are stuck in marriage; must be faithful whereas men are not; and must suffer pregnancy and labor. Medea knows the experience of love and marriage. Woman is concrete and rational, even in situations in which it is difficult to make decisions. Woman suffers but perseveres. In contrast, from the male character we hear frivolous wishful thinking, fickle and disloyal infatuation, opportunism, and sheer ungratefulness. Jason is supposed to be a successful hero, but Euripides makes of him a shallow buffoon. This is the moral assessment that emerges from the many voices in the drama. Whereas Medea (before she kills the children) has everyone on her side, nobody shows the slightest respect for Jason. It is this dissonance that, in this play, shapes the difference between the sexes. In the end, Medea will destroy all the good will she once enjoyed. But the tragedy shows a struggle for recognition that is cultural, personal, and sexual. The failure of recognition defines tragedy. The inability to acknowledge their antagonists' agency and their ethical reasons prevents tragic figures from overcoming disagreements. Hegel had a fundamental intuition. Not only did he identify this deadlock, as essential to the genre (in his interpretation of Sophocles's *Antigone*), but he also saw that what lies at the core of tragedy is a particular kind of frozen dialectic: the collision of the sexes.

Ancient comedy is also full of sexuality. The comic stage exposed sexual urges, pleasures, and fantasies. It exhibited, above all, the erotic body in extra-large scale and hyper-realistic features. Sexual activity is a matter of endless allusion, from costumes and props, to gestures and language (in crude descriptions, word-plays, or metaphors), to plots, action, and characters. Male characters were equipped with huge, fake phalluses; penetration, vaginal and anal, was their obsession. Female characters (impersonated by male actors) wore costumes that enhanced anatomical attributes such as the breasts, and were both sexy and sexually avid. Comedy represented

a caricature of both genders. In jest, comedic performance initially blurred social expectations, but always reconfirmed mainstream conventions by the end of the story. The typical happy ending (e.g., in *Acharnians, Peace, Birds, Thesmophoriazusae, Ecclesiazusae, Lysistrata, Wealth*) was euphoric female–male intercourse or a cheerful wedding.

Legal and Medical Discourses. Although fictional discourses such as archaic poetry and theater reveal cultural representations and values, law and medicine decisively shaped ancient Greek views of female–male sexuality. Athenian laws required that to be recognized as a citizen one had to be born of properly wedded Athenian parents. Marriage was the condition of an individual's membership in society. Proper marriage consisted of the transfer of a young woman from her paternal family to her husband. Consistently, the law on adultery stipulated that seducing a married woman was a serious crime, justifying the murder of an adulterous man caught *in flagrante* and even obliging the wronged husband to divorce his consenting wife. Marriage legislation was based on a systematic asymmetry and a double standard. Virginity was expected from brides but not grooms. Fidelity was required from women but not from men—who could have sex with lovers, concubines, and prostitutes of both genders (but not married women) with impunity. To initiate a divorce was easier, and more frequent, for men than women. As Xenophon's *Oeconomicus* (fourth century B.C.E.) and Plutarch's *Advice to the Bride and Groom* (first to second century C.E.) relay, the ideal life of a conjugal couple was polarized between the feminine role (domesticity, compliance, faithfulness, and tolerance for spousal infidelity) and the male one, focused on extra domestic, and extramarital, activities. Marriage was intended for the procreation of legitimate children, but maternity defined women's lives in a much more compelling manner than paternity did for men. Men cared about generating children, but women took care of them.

Medical discourse was a benchmark for conceptions of gendered bodies and their physical relations. A collection of treatises, conventionally entitled the *Hippocratic Corpus* (fifth century B.C.E.), includes works on female anatomy, physiology, and pathology.

A central tenet of these texts is that vaginal intercourse, followed by pregnancy, was healthy—even therapeutic—for the female body. Although Hippocratic writers thought that women produced a seminal fluid analogous to sperm, they saw the womb not only as an internal phallus, capable of ejaculating, but also and primarily as a container, a receptive cavity. The uterus's ability to take in semen, close down, and shelter a growing fetus was to be maintained. Whenever the proper function of the womb was impaired, a physician (sometimes assisted by a female helper) had to intervene to restore the correct position, elasticity, humidity, or perviousness of the womb.

Remedies included aromatic (evil-smelling or fragrant) fumigations applied through the vagina and/or nostrils to attract, or repel, the uterus, thus bringing it back to its natural site; pessaries made of relaxing, irritating, or constricting ingredients, inserted into the genitals; elaborate mixtures and concoctions, administered orally; or, in extreme cases, surgery. The purpose of these treatments was to re-establish the conditions propitious to fruitful sexual activity. Special attention was paid to the *stoma*, the "mouth" of the cervix, which could be too lax and dilated, too hard and contracted, or imperforated. "When a woman is unable to receive the semen, there is every possibility that a membrane (*mēnigks*) has grown in the mouth of the uterus. You must take some verdigris, bull's gall and snake oil, mix these together, and then take a piece of wool and soak it with the mixture." The patient had to place this suppository inside her vagina at night; then she had to take a bath in warm water and myrtle the day after, and, finally, she should have intercourse (Hippocrates, *Barrenness*, 11; cf. *Nature of Women*, 67; *Diseases of Women*, 1.20; trans. Potter, modified).

The sexual act itself was considered to be a natural therapy. Whenever prolonged chastity or other abnormal conditions caused the occlusion of the cervix, coition was recommended. The author of *Diseases of Virgins* writes that "whenever the mouth of the exit is not open" (*hokotan oun to stoma tēs exodou mē ē anestomōmenon*), a virgin might suffer pain and suffocation. Since "more blood would flow into the uterus,

due to the food and the growth of the body," this blood rushes to the heart and the diaphragm. The physician recommends that those who suffer these crippling symptoms should "cohabit with a man" as soon as possible. "If they conceive, they become healthy" (Hippocrates, *Diseases of Virgins* 8.466–468 L.). This theory of male–female sexuality is consistent with the fact that ancient Greek medicine ignored the existence of a natural and normal membrane closing the vagina (or womb) in healthy virgins (Soranus, *Gynecology* 1.17).

Philosophers such as Plato and Aristotle offer theories of female/male sexuality, which circulated in restricted circles. In visible public venues, poets and playwrights were culturally significant, and, perhaps, influential. Physicians examined their patients, touched their body, prescribed medications, and probably explained the logic of what they were doing. Medical texts convey empirical and normative knowledge, which must have had a unique impact upon people's lives.

[*See also* Legal Status, *subentry* Greek World; Male-Female Sexuality, *subentry* New Testament; Marriage and Divorce, *subentry* Greek World; Masculinity and Femininity, *subentry* Greek World; Sexuality; *and* Sexual Transgression, *subentry* Greek World.]

BIBLIOGRAPHY

Primary Works

Aristotle. *Poetics; Longinus: On the Sublime; Demetrius: On Style.* Edited and translated by D. A. Russell et al. Loeb Classical Library. Cambridge, Mass.: Harvard University Press, 1995.

Euripides. *Fabulae.* Vol. 1: *Cyclops, Alcestis, Medea, Heraclidae, Hippolytus, Andromacha, Hecuba.* Edited and translated by J. Diggle. Oxford Classical Texts. Oxford: Oxford University Press, 1984.

Hesiod. *Hesiod.* Vol. 1: *Theogony; Works and Days; Testimonia.* Edited and translated by G. W. Most. Cambridge, Mass.: Harvard University Press, 2007.

Hippocrates. *Hippocrates.* Vol. 10: *Generation; Nature of the Child; Nature of Women; Barrenness; Diseases 4.* Edited and translated by P. Potter. Loeb Classical Library. Cambridge, Mass.: Harvard University Press, 2012.

Homer. *The Iliad.* 2 vols. Edited and translated by T. W. Allen and D. B. Monro. Oxford Classical Texts: Homeri Opera 1–2. Oxford: Oxford University Press, 1920.

Homer. *The Odyssey*. 2 vols. Edited and translated by T. W. Allen and D. B. Monro. Oxford Classical Texts: Homeri Opera 3–4. Oxford: Oxford University Press, 1922.

Homeric Hymns. *Homeric Hymns; Homeric Apocrypha; Lives of Homer*. Edited and translated by M. L. West. Loeb Classical Library. Cambridge, Mass.: Harvard University Press, 2003.

Ovid. *Metamorphoses*. Edited and translated by R. J. Tarrant. Oxford Classical Texts. Oxford: Oxford University Press, 2004.

Plato. *Opera*. Vol. 2: *Parmenides, Philebus, Symposium, Phaedrus, Alcibiades I and II, Hipparchus, Amatores*. Edited and translated by J. Burnet. Oxford Classical Texts. Oxford: Oxford University Press, 1922.

Plutarch. *Plutarch's Advice to the Bride and Groom and A Consolation to His Wife: English Translations, Commentary, Interpretive Essays, and Bibliography*. Edited and translated by S. B. Pomeroy. New York: Oxford University Press, 1999.

Soranus. *Soranus' Gynecology*. Edited and translated by O. Temkin. Baltimore: Johns Hopkins University Press, 1991.

Xenophon. *Oeconomicus: A Social and Historical Commentary*. Edited and translated by S. B. Pomeroy. New York: Oxford University Press, 1995.

Secondary Works

Agacinsky, Sylviane. *Femmes entre sexe et genre*. Paris: Editions du Seuil, 2012.

Beachy, Robert. "The German Invention of Homosexuality." *Journal of Modern History* 82 (2010): 801–838.

Boehringer Sandra. *L'Homosexualité féminine dans l'Antiquité Gréco-Romaine*, Paris: Belles Lettres, 2007.

Flemming, Rebecca, and Ann Ellis Hanson. "Hippocrates' *Peri Parthenion* (Diseases of Young Girls): Text and Translation." *Early Science and Medicine* 3 (1998): 241–252.

Foley, Helene. *Female Acts in Greek Tragedy*. Princeton, N.J.: Princeton University Press, 2001.

Foucault, Michel. *The History of Sexuality*. Vol. 2: *The Use of Pleasure*. Translated by Robert Hurley. New York: Vintage, 1990.

Goldhill, Simon. *Foucault's Virginity. Ancient Erotic Fiction and the History of Sexuality*. Cambridge, U.K.: Cambridge University Press, 1995.

Hanson, Ann Ellis. "Hippocrates: Diseases of Women 1." *Signs* 1 (1975): 567–584.

Holmes, Brooke. *Gender: Antiquity and its Legacy*. Oxford: Oxford University Press, 2013.

King, Helen. *Hippocrates' Woman: Reading the Female Body in Ancient Greece*. London and New York: Routledge, 1998.

Leduc, Claudine. "Marriage in Ancient Greece." In *A History of Women in the West*. Vol. 1: *From Ancient Goddesses to Christian Saints*, edited by P. Schmitt Pantel and translated by A. Goldhammer, pp. 233–295. Cambridge, Mass.: Belknap, 1992.

Panofsky, Dora, and Erwin Panofsky. *Pandora's Box: The Changing Aspects of a Mythical Symbol*. New York: Pantheon, 1956.

Sissa, Giulia. *Sex and Sensuality in the Ancient World*. Translated by George Staunton. New Haven, Conn.: Yale University Press, 2008.

Sissa, Giulia. "Agathon and Agathon: Male Sensuality in Aristophanes' *Thesmophoriazusae* and Plato's *Symposium*." *EuGeStA: Journal on Gender Studies in Antiquity* 2 (2012): 25–70.

Sissa, Giulia. "The Hymen Is a Problem, Still: Virginity, Imperforation, and Contraception, from Greece to Rome." *EuGeStA: Journal on Gender Studies in Antiquity* 3 (2013): 67–123.

Zeitlin, Froma. *Playing the Other. Gender and Society in Classical Greek Literature*. Chicago: University of Chicago Press, 1996.

Giulia Sissa

Roman World

Romans felt the sharp sting of desire and knew the satisfaction of a longed-for tryst and the joys and challenges of bearing children. For sexuality, as for so much else of Roman life, what was acceptable was defined by the *mos maiorum*—the way things were done and had always been done. That which was new was instantly suspect, while that which was traditional had made the Roman state and its citizens strong. Within this framework, other cultures were viewed as dangerous or corrupting. Romans distinguished themselves in the early period from the Etruscans and in later times had a fascination with and revulsion for Greek sexuality. For Romans, one's sexuality was a defining feature of an individual and could typify praiseworthy or contemptuous qualities in both men and women.

Male–female sexuality separates into three major categories: sex for procreation within marriage; sex for the satisfaction of personal (almost always male) desire; and sex for reinforcing mutual intimacy and lasting emotional attachment. Procreative sex within marriage was a common topic and informed the sharp disparity between male and female sexuality. Most Roman sources focused on the second category of satisfying personal and male desire. An author like Ovid praised the mutual satisfaction of man and woman in the sexual act (*Art of Love* 2.725–728) and Pliny the Younger expressed ongoing desire for his wife Calpurnia (*Letters* 7.5.1), but these expressions were unusual for Romans. The sources for all three categories are limited, however, and almost all of the evidence preserves elite male perspectives. When other groups and individuals are addressed, it is by elite males who place upon them their desires, fears, and expectations. The genre of each source is also essential to its interpretation.

Male and Female Sexuality. The ideal elite man demonstrated *virtus* (roughly manliness or masculinity) in all of his sexual actions. He was the dominant partner, showing the same mastery in sexual action as in all of his affairs. For a male to be passive or overly concerned for another's pleasure was dangerously weak and degrading. Elite men availed themselves of a range of sexual partners. Wives were for procreation, but marriage did not carry with it any assumption of male sexual fidelity. A young and particularly attractive wife could be praised as a cause for sexual desire and satisfaction. Greek-style poems for the bridal chamber that celebrated a bride's beauty and fertility were developed in Latin by Catullus and later authors (Catullus, *Songs* 61). Generally speaking, any women who were not married or potentially marriageable were fair game for sexual pursuit. Men regularly satisfied their sexual desires on slaves (their personal property) be they female or male, prostitutes, or others of lower class. Male attitudes toward these sexual actions ranged widely—with expressions of longing and pursuit (as in Roman love elegy) or simply grabbing whomever was available (Horace, *Satires* 1.2.114–119). Another man's slaves were that man's personal property and sexual use of them was treated as an invasion of his property rights unless approved by the slave's owner. Men were expected to have decorum in their sexual pursuits and to practice appropriate moderation and self-restraint.

Sexuality between men and women was expressed especially in terms of dominance and submission.

Romans lived within a highly stratified world of social hierarchy. Citizens, freeborn, freedmen, and slaves were each distinct categories with particular privileges and protections (or lack thereof). One's status determined appropriate sexual opportunity and availability. The complex system of patronage further nuanced this social landscape with clients looking to patrons for support and protection while reinforcing the patron's power. Both elite men and women had clients that could include a range of other citizens, freeborn men and women, and freed men and women. Within this system, citizen males had diverse sexual opportunity while all other categories of people were often objects for sexual use or had at best more limited sexual choices.

Roman elites. Elite Roman women were consistently praised for their *pudicitia*—a woman's modesty or chastity was one of her foremost virtues. It was a wife's duty to her husband, family, and the state to bear legitimate children. A young woman's virginity was closely guarded by her family and on marriage her continuing fidelity was of vital concern. There was significant age disparity in marriage, with women marrying at an average age of thirteen to fourteen and men at twenty-two to twenty-three. For a man to have sexual relations with a marriageable young woman outside of marriage was unacceptable. A marriage created a vital link between two families. Typically the woman remained under the protection and oversight of her family of origin. Only in a less common *manus* marriage did the wife and her property pass fully into the control of her husband. Women could have significant personal wealth that they managed separate from their husbands (especially in the late republic and after). The wealth, combined with less direct oversight, created opportunities for a range of sexual activity and accusation. Divorce was common as families realigned their interests through marriage. Unless there was wrongdoing, divorce did not negatively reflect on either husband or wife. However, it was considered highly praiseworthy and a statement of devotion for a woman to be married to a single man her whole life—an *univira*, a one-man woman—as evident on tomb inscriptions (parallel praise appears rarely for men).

Adultery was a form of *stuprum* (sexual misconduct) and legally was classed alongside seduction/forced sex with an unmarried virgin or male citizen youth as a grave offense. In the early periods of Roman history, a woman's father retained the right to kill both her and the adulterous male if they were discovered (part of his *patria potestas*). A husband likewise could kill a male of lower status but had no right to harm his wife. Under later state supervision (starting in 18 B.C.E.), an accused male adulterer could be tried and if he was found guilty the woman was then tried. Financial penalties resulted along with a loss in status for both men and women. Under the new early Imperial laws, husbands were also forced to stop adulterous wives or face charges themselves. The state-controlled system removed the flexibility of earlier familial handling of *stuprum* and also created a system that could reward outside accusers.

A broad range of professions carried the designation of *infamia* with sexuality protected by neither state nor custom. Actors, dancers, gladiators, and prostitutes all were *infamia*. Gladiators with their remarkable *virtus* were renowned for their sexual appeal, especially to women (see CIL 4.4342 and 4353). How often they created marital challenges is unclear but Juvenal describes a senator's wife running away with a gladiator (Juvenal 6.82–113). Prostitutes were frequently slaves and most lived in extremely unpleasant circumstances in cramped brothels. High-class companions like the Greek *hetaira* were very different from most Roman prostitutes.

Non-elite sexualities. The sexuality of the larger populace, removed as they were from the interest of male elites, is difficult to analyze. Literature and the law pay limited attention to their lives—sexual or otherwise. Inscribed grave markers provide one source for this population. The inscriptions are often brief and formulaic but sometimes include praise for sexual virtues and happy marriages as well as longing for the deceased. Most sexualized art—like wall paintings, mirrors, and cups—was produced for the wealthy and reflected their tastes. Arretine-ware pottery, which spread across the empire in the first to the third centuries C.E., provides a rare example that permeated a range of classes. Molded pottery,

especially in the form of lamps, included sexualized images of romance, tenderness, and pleasure (see Clarke, 2001).

Medical and Philosophical Understanding of Sexuality. Roman medical understandings focus on the role of men and women in procreation, how to procreate successfully, the physiological responses leading to sexuality, and the value of sexual activity for men and women. Medical works, with their close attention to biology, can offer an "essentialist" approach to sexuality. They are, however, closely intertwined with cultural assumptions and reinforce expected Roman sexual practice. Philosophers also addressed the value and dangers of sexuality for men and women and grounded their ideas in medical terms.

For men, sexual intercourse was tied especially to the release of semen. Lucretius (*On the Nature of Things* 4) described how seed is stirred up and gathers in the groin, straining to reach the object that awakened its desire. In seeking to satisfy this insatiable and self-perpetuating need, according to Lucretius, young men waste their energies and weaken the state. An Epicurean, Lucretius solves the problem by encouraging the wide dispersion of their seed, rather than allowing it to fixate as Venus directs. Galen (*On Semen* 1.16) is more strictly clinical in his description of semen and employs dissection to support his ideas. Noting that semen is held in the testicles and drawn from the blood, Galen is concerned that over-use of semen draws out the vital spirit from one's blood, leaving a man weak and tired, even unto death. Consequently, Galen encouraged a moderation in the emission of semen that fit well with Roman attitudes towards the importance of self-restraint. Similarly, Musonius Rufus, a Stoic philosopher, opined on the appropriate limits for sexual activity. Highly restrictive, he argued that sexual pleasure should not be pursued and was permissible only within the legal context of marriage and only then for procreation. For Musonius Rufus, the pursuit of any sexual pleasure outside of procreative marriage resulted in a loss of honor and self-discipline. In opposition to Galen and Rufus's concern over semen control, however, is Diogenes Laertius's (third century C.E.) implicit approval of the Cynic Diogenes's public masturbation.

Digoenes wishes he could rub his stomach and get rid of his hunger as easily (*Lives of Eminent Philosophers* 6.2.46). Semen, its preservation or wide dispersion, was clearly central to philosophers' views on male–female sexuality.

Building on Greek thought, Romans writers often presented a woman as being like a fertile field. Within this framework, a man's job was to plough the field and to plant his seed. Whether the male or female essences were dominant in the act of procreation could determine whether the child developed into a male or female. Soranus (*Gynecology* 1.8–10) emphasized the importance of a woman's sexual maturity for procreation to occur. The woman's body needed to possess a full-sized uterus and to have menstruated. Soranus set fourteen as the correct age for sexual maturity (an age that corresponds with Roman practice) and noted that waiting too long after could create physical challenges for the unmarried teen. Soranus argued that a woman must have the urge and appetite for sexuality before conception could take place. Otherwise the semen would not be successful. Whether this medical view emphasizing a woman's desire for successful procreation shaped sexuality within marriage and fostered intimacy is unclear. Regular sexual intercourse was sometimes advised by authors as necessary for women to remain healthy and to control both the uterus and menstrual fluid (see Soranus, *Gynecology* 1.7).

All of these medical and philosophical perspectives informed Roman attitudes toward sexuality. How representative and persuasive they were is less clear. Certainly marriage with its established restraints continued despite odd examples like the Stoic Cato the Younger allowing his friend Hortensius to marry his own wife Marcia to procreate with her or Diogenes's idea that wives should be held in common (6.2.72). Nor did Musonius Rufus's Stoic ideals of sexual pleasure only for procreation in marriage supplant the established system for Roman sexuality.

Magic and Sexuality. Diverse corpora of magical spells include a type that has been described as "love magic." These erotic spells are typically employed to accomplish sexual ends when all other means have failed. Forcing desired lovers to come under the spell-caster's power, the spells describe how every part of the lover will now be available for penetration and satisfaction. Incorporating Roman ideas of dominance in sexuality taken to an extreme these spells probably have little to do with "love." Romans understandably viewed as powerful and dangerous such magic with its limited concern for societal expectations and intentional destruction of marital and familial bonds.

Sexuality over Time. Despite attempts to appeal to the *mos maiorum* and hold to an imagined continuity in Roman sexual behavior, the changing place of Rome in the larger world brought changes for male–female sexuality. If, as many scholars in the field have contended, sexuality is culturally constructed, rather than "essential" to human nature, then these shifts are of decisive importance.

Early republic. During the early republic, Romans defined their sexuality especially in relation to Etruscan practices. Sixth-century B.C.E. Etruscan funerary urns depicted husband and wife sharing couches at banquets with close and affectionate physical contact. Fourth-century B.C.E. sarcophagi took this intimacy further with husband and wife in their marriage bed facing one another or in close embrace. Livy's later depiction of early Romans emphasized their comparably chaste behavior. The story of Lucretia was in part a statement of the sexual license of kings in general and Etruscan practice in particular. Even with the "Rape of the Sabine Women," Livy presented Roman men as less motivated by uncontrollable sexual desire than by a need to procreate and to create interconnected (if initially challenging) bonds with their neighbors (Livy, *History* 1.9–13). Although through this early period, Greek colonies in the Italic peninsula were a source of ongoing contact and trade was widespread, any Greek influence on sexuality in the early period drew little attention.

Middle and late republic. The middle and late republics were periods of rapid political and social change. Emerging out of wars with Carthage, Rome became undisputed master of its region and then expanded into the Greek East. Enormous wealth and increased contact with foreign cultures brought rapid changes to society and to sexual perspective and opportunity. Cato the Elder decried this new wealth and sexual license as a certain path to Rome's decline. Polybius presented Greek sexuality and licentiousness as particularly threatening. "Greek" sexuality was variously reacted to by Republican Romans who embraced or feared its possibilities. The early second-century B.C.E. playwright Plautus's adaptation of Greek New Comedy, with its bawdy sexuality, found a ready Roman audience despite moralizing that opposed theater in general and Greek sexuality in particular. By the end of the republic, Roman exposure to Greek culture in all of its forms was widespread and the vast wealth that Cato had feared was a common feature of Roman aristocracy.

Early empire. The early empire followed a period of rapid social change and widespread civil war. Augustus attempted to create a new foundation looking back to an idealized past. The long period of civil war was blamed on the arrogance of powerful men and typified by the immorality of the elite. Augustus placed new emphasis on "family values" with accompanying piety to the gods (the Ara Pacis provides one visual representation of this ideal). Augustus reinforced this emphasis on family with new marriage and adultery laws in 18 B.C.E. (added to with the *Lex Papia Poppaea* in 9 C.E.). The results of these new laws included rewarding of women (and men) who bore three or more children, punishment of young men and women who did not marry, and prohibiting senators from marrying freed-women and those branded *infamia*. Adultery was criminalized and prosecuted publicly. Developments such as Augustus's attachment to Venus Genetrix situated her inviting sexuality into a fitting Roman context of fertility and nurture. Such domestication of Venus's sexuality was offset by the phallic figure of Priapus and by the provocative poetry of Ovid, with its mix of erotic seduction (in his *Art of Love*) and sexualized violence (rape in his *Metamorphoses*).

The early empire (and very late republic) included a range of literature idealizing Roman sexuality. Roman love elegy (by such authors as Catullus, Propertius, Tibullus, and Ovid) cherished the beloved and described longing and the fear of rejection. Directed toward a range of individuals—from elite wives and widows to women who were *infamia*—the literature reflects a world where females may have chosen their lovers, or may simply reflect another form of male fantasy. Within this corpus, the preserved writings of Sulpicia provide a rare female voice. Ideals of mutual romantic love and affection also find clear expression in the late first and second century C.E. Greek romance novels. Young lovers torn apart by fate engage in searches filled with longing for their beloved and threats to their chastity only to be reunited with divine assistance. Apuleius's *Metamorphoses* offers an often less romantic, if even more sexual, Latin novel.

The sudden destruction of Pompeii and Herculaneam in 79 C.E. preserved a rich corpus of visual evidence for the period. A wide array of explicitly sexual wall paintings decorate buildings. Baths, brothels, and wealthy homes displayed sexualized art. Precisely how this art is to be understood is still a matter of debate. But clearly Roman elites enjoyed viewing a wide array of sexuality in diverse contexts. Sexually explicit graffiti gives voice to less wealthy, if still literate, individuals.

Later empire. The later empire continued many of the earlier themes of Roman sexuality. Stoic philosophers were increasingly critical of what they saw as sexual excess, while romantic ideals of sexuality also persisted. Dramatic change, when it did come, appeared with Christian attitudes that favored chastity and idealized virginity and self-renunciation. Martyrs and monks presented very different attitudes toward the body and sexuality. But even as Christians challenged established Roman sexual practice and further criminalized elements of it, they also could find in Roman longing for an idealized past and philosophical critique of sexual license a language to reinforce their own understandings of sexuality.

Historiographical Issues. Roman sexuality has been a long-standing source of fascination for Western culture. Christian authors, drawing on Roman self-critique of excess, emphasized extremes of debauchery finding particularly rich examples in such hated emperors as Nero, Caligula, and Domitian. Hollywood did little to correct such images, finding in the Roman world an opportunity to depict lavish excess to a hungry audience. Throughout most of the twentieth century, the best scholarly treatments worked closely with the rich array of ancient sources. Despite useful collection of sources and commentary, the dominant interpretation remained moralizing, seeing in Roman lasciviousness the need for Christianity's rise (Kiefer, 1934, is a good example). Starting in the 1970s the study of ancient sexuality changed dramatically. The close study of women in the classical period made the topic of sexuality a central, rather than peripheral topic. Feminist interpretation of classical texts brought the position of women into sharp focus and challenged the simplistic acceptance of ancient male perspective. The study of homosexuality added further fuel to this careful reexamination and reinterpretation of the sources. Modern assumptions of homo- and heterosexuality were made increasingly problematic in the study of ancient literature and the construction of gender and sexuality underwent considerable reevaluation. For sexuality in general, and particularly for homosexuality, study of ancient Greece and especially of classical Athens often dominated the field. Roman sexuality, except with the study of particular canonical literature, was often less developed and received less sustained attention until the late 1990s and after (Richlin, 1983, is a rare exception). Roman sexuality is increasingly being addressed with greater appreciation in current scholarship for distinctive aspects and attention to less canonical sources. Foucault's work long dominated the discussion of sexuality throughout, especially with conceptual terms and categories. Foucault's lasting impact endures but there is also critical perspective of his work especially with the severe limitations of his androcentric focus.

Assessment. Roman sexuality remains a lively topic within the vibrant field of social history with feminist treatment of women and study of homosexuality/gender construction two of the most ongoing and productive areas. The least studied and understood areas remain non-elite culture and heterosexual affection within marriage. Non-elite sexuality is particularly hard to capture as so little evidence remains and what is preserved brings with it challenges of interpretation. Affectionate sexual relations within marriage are challenging to recover because they were largely considered private and if done properly are simply noted as praiseworthy asides for both parties. It is when such relations become more problematic or challenged that Roman literature finds such delight in depicting them in loving detail.

[*See also* Male-Female Sexuality, *subentries on* Greek World *and* New Testament; Marriage and Divorce, *subentry* Roman World; Popular Religion and Magic, *subentry* Roman World; Same-Sex Relations, *subentry* Roman World; *and* Sexual Transgression, *subentry* Roman World.]

BIBLIOGRAPHY

Adams, James Noel. *The Latin Sexual Vocabulary.* Baltimore: Johns Hopkins University Press, 1982.

Clarke, John R. *Looking at Lovemaking: Construction of Sexuality in Roman Art 100 B.C.–250 A.D.* Berkeley and Los Angeles: University of California Press, 1998 [reprint 2001].

Clarke, John R. *Roman Sex: 100 B.C. to A.D. 250.* New York: Abrams, 2003.

Edwards, Catherine. *The Politics of Immorality in Ancient Rome.* Cambridge, U.K., and New York: Cambridge University Press, 1993.

Foucault, Michel. *The History of Sexuality.* 3 vols. Translated by Robert Hurley. New York: Vintage, 1988–1990.

Hallett, Judith P., and Marilyn B. Skinner, eds. *Roman Sexualities.* Princeton, N.J.: Princeton University Press, 1997.

Kiefer, Otto. *Sexual Life in Ancient Rome.* London: Routledge and Kegan Paul, 1934.

Langlands, Rebecca. *Sexual Morality in Ancient Rome.* Cambridge, U.K.: Cambridge University Press, 2006.

Larson, Jennifer. *Greek and Roman Sexualities: A Sourcebook.* London and New York: Bloomsbury, 2012.

McClure, Laura, ed. *Sexuality and Gender in the Classical World: Readings and Sources.* Oxford and Malden, Mass.: Blackwell, 2002.

McGinn, Thomas. *Prostitution, Sexuality and the Law in Ancient Rome.* New York: Oxford University Press, 1998.

McGinn, Thomas. *The Economy of Prostitution in the Roman World.* Ann Arbor: University of Michigan Press, 2004.

Richlin, Amy. *The Garden of Priapus: Sexuality and Aggression in Roman Humor.* New York: Oxford University Press, 1983 [rev. 1992].

Richlin, Amy, ed. *Pornography and Representation in Greece and Rome.* New York: Oxford University Press, 1992.

Skinner, Marilyn. *Sexuality in Greek and Roman Culture.* Malden, Mass.: Blackwell, 2005 [rev. 2013].

Younger, John G. *Sex in the Ancient World from A to Z.* London and New York: Routledge, 2005.

Bradford A. Kirkegaard

New Testament

After briefly introducing general, ancient conceptions of sexuality and marriage, this article is divided into the treatment of sexuality in Greco-Roman, Jewish, and New Testament sources.

Ancient Constructions. Ancient Mediterranean peoples understood male–female sexuality not as "heterosexual" (versus "homosexual"), but rather as one of a range of possible sexual relationships, the legitimacy of which was determined by social and legal status and active–passive roles. Rather than a dichotomy of male and female, there existed a "sliding scale" of sex and gender. Sexual anatomy and physical appearance were only some of the factors that determined one's masculinity and femininity. Gestures, speech, dress, rank, class, citizenship, and region of origin all played a role in one's identification as an active, powerful, penetrating, dominant man or as less than a man, characterized by greater passivity, weakness, penetrability, and submissiveness. With this understanding, all penetrative (or phallocentric) sexual acts involved masculine and feminine (less masculine) roles.

Broadly speaking, male–female sexuality was legitimated through the institution of marriage in Greco-Roman and Jewish society. From one perspective, marriage may be understood as a way by which sexual love and desire (*eros*) could be controlled and used for society. But ample evidence shows that *eros* consistently transgressed the confines of marriage and that marriage, at least in Greco-Roman culture, was not seen as a chiefly or even as a likely conduit for *eros*. It is more accurate to say that marriage was understood and used as a way to control male–female sexuality (mainly its reproductive aspect) for the purposes of organizing society into units for the transmission of property after death.

Legitimate relationships established by marital sexual reproduction served as the basis for inheritance; confining female sexuality, particularly the activities and desires of free, elite women, was therefore of utmost importance. A woman might produce illegitimate heirs by adultery and therefore was subject to divorce or punishment if discovered; a girl's virginity had to be policed for the same reason and to convince suitors that her chastity would be guaranteed in marriage. A man, on the other hand, might have extramarital relations without legal or societal consequences so long as he did not violate another man's wife. Male virginity was not a social preoccupation, and prostitution and the exploitation of the lower classes, including slaves, provided easily available (and expected) ways for a boy or man to gain sexual experience.

In both Greco-Roman and Judaic cultures, a man demonstrated his own power and identity as a full participant of society through marriage and the production of heirs. The maintenance and control of his household further evinced masculine dominance. In this dynamic, women (to varying degrees) were mainly a part of the production of male identity and mastery on a social-political level.

This introductory discussion does not discount the existence of love, passion, and desire between men and women in the ancient world (see below) but modern readers should be aware that male-female sexuality was always primarily understood as a means of production to be harnessed and controlled through marriage.

Greco-Roman World. The following discusses, in necessarily generalizing terms, the attitudes and beliefs about sexual desire and passion in Greco-Roman literature, philosophy, and medical texts.

Literature. Some of the most detailed descriptions of love and longing between men and women are given in the Greek novels (first three centuries C.E.). In these stories, a young man and woman fall in love but, through some misfortune, are separated and must endure numerous adventures before they are reunited. During these travails, the lovers experience sexual desire and urgency, fits of passionate despair, doubts, jealousy, and romantic rapture. Quintessential to the plot is the tension over whether the lovers will remain faithful to each other, despite impossible odds and numerous rival suitors.

The inviolability of the man and the chastity of the woman are a major preoccupation and plot device as numerous powerful men lust for and seek to own and transgress women's beautiful bodies.

The romantic relationships of the Greek novels portray idealized betrothed or marital love, with an emphasis on protecting chastity, so that sexual faithfulness is the source of all longing, desire, and fear. Roman poetry, such as that of Catullus (ca. 84–54 B.C.E.) and Ovid (43 B.C.E.–17/18 C.E.), however, describes the pleasure and passion of illicit sexual love between men and women outside of marriage. The art of seduction, its frustrations, and jealousy serve as major themes. Although generally the male lovers in these poems still consistently play the active role of the seducer, a mistress of elite status, such as Catullus's Lesbia, could wield considerable power in her choice of lover and even in her taking on of several lovers. This could in part reflect slightly greater agency on the part of elite Roman women at the time, who could inherit their father's property, initiate divorce, and have significant influence as the wives (or widows) of powerful men.

Although dating from the fourth century B.C.E., Apollodorus's statement regarding the "use" of women of different status, legitimate or illegitimate, elite or slave, encapsulates first-century C.E. views: "[m]istresses (*hetairas*) we keep for pleasure, concubines for daily attendance upon our person, but wives for the procreation of legitimate children and to be faithful guardians of our households" (*Against Neaera*, 122).

Philosophy. All philosophical schools regarded sexual desire and passion (*epithymia* and *pathos*) warily as potentially dangerous to the (masculine) body, soul, and mind, partly because the act of ejaculation was understood as an emission of a vital substance, full of spirit (*pneuma*) (see *Medical understandings*). Epicurus warned against having sexual intercourse at all and advised against marriage and producing children, with few exceptions. For the Pythagoreans, Plato, and the later Stoics, sex belonged within marriage strictly for procreation (although in the *Republic* Plato advocates nonexclusive communal sex to stave off the distractions and territoriality of marriage). In almost all philosophical

thought, sexual desire and passion were to be mastered and controlled—always on the assumption that the philosophical subject is an elite male intent on masculine self-mastery.

Medical understandings. Ancient assumptions regarding masculine strength and feminine weakness supported the medical understanding that men, on one end of the spectrum, were stronger, hotter, drier, and more full of *pneuma*, whereas females, on the other end, were weaker, colder, wetter, and containing less *pneuma*. According to the second-century C.E. medical doctor and philosopher Galen, the genitalia of a fetus are determined by the combination and unequal contributions of male and female seed at conception. If more male seed is contributed, enough *pneuma* pushes the developed genitals outward, forming the penis and scrotum outside the body; if more female seed exists, the *pneuma* is weak and flagging, and the genitals remain within (*On Semen*, 2.5.48ff). In this way, masculinity and femininity were separated by degrees, and females and the feminine were viewed, ultimately, as deformed males and less than masculine. It is also significant that, according to this conception of genitalia, females (having an internal penis) also experience sexual pleasure, which is as necessary as male pleasure for reproduction. Indeed, feminine sexual desire (including that in all less than men, such as eunuchs) was seen as far more wanton and irrational (lacking masculine reason) and, therefore, dangerous.

Jewish Society. One marked difference between first-century Jewish and Greco-Roman constructions of marriage was the strong legacy of polygyny and levirate marriage (a widowed woman being taken in marriage by her husband's brother) in Jewish history and literature. The figures of Sarah and Hagar (the wives of Abraham) and Rachel and Leah (the wives of Jacob), along with many others, loomed large in the Jewish imagination of marital love and discord, even as monogamy became standard in Hellenistic Judaism. Central to these storied marriages are key elements of Jewish constructions of marriage and sexual desire: an emphasis on endogamy, the production of heirs, sexual passion for procreation, and a celebration of marital love.

Genesis. The marriages of the patriarchs were used as metaphors by Second Temple Jewish writers and the authors of the New Testament to illustrate a variety of concepts. The story of Jacob, Rachel, and Leah (Gen 29:1—30:24), for example, presents typical literary elements and concepts later used in allusions and allegory. The couple meets at a well (similar to Isaac and Rebekah, Moses and Zipporah), where the love story begins. Jacob eventually marries both Rachel and her sister, Leah, and although both vie for sexual intercourse with Jacob, their desire is centered on their competition in producing heirs. This story highlights the well as a site for romantic encounters, the importance of endogamous marriage, the wedding banquet, and the affirmation of marital love, although always tempered by the imperative to produce heirs.

Second Temple literature and Philo. Sexual desire and love, most explicitly celebrated in the Song of Songs, is also affirmed in wedding celebrations, descriptions of faithful betrothals, and the pleasures of the marriage bed in works such as the book of Tobit, Joseph and Asenath, and the Book of Wisdom. The beauty of the bride on her wedding night is often allegorized—always, however, with the ever-present theme of male domination and control of the household, whether it is the bride's father's or the groom's. Philo (first century C.E.) gives a positive description of the sexual passion and union of Adam and Eve in Eden and of Abraham and Sarah, but he does so to emphasize that their union is for the sake of procreation within the confines of marriage and enjoys divine blessing. In keeping with his contemporaries, Philo warns against uncontrolled or inappropriate passion and the chaos it could cause in the mind and body.

The New Testament: Key Passages. The following section covers major New Testament passages. Those passages dealing specifically with marriage and divorce, as well as their social and legal implications, may be found in other entries.

The Gospels. In the Gospels there are both dire warnings against sexual lust and acknowledgement of sexual desire.

Desire and adultery. Various passages in the gospels address male–female desire.

Matthew 5:27–30. In the Sermon on the Mount, Jesus states, "You have heard that it was said, 'You shall not commit adultery.' But I say to you that everyone who looks at a woman with lust has already committed adultery (*emoicheusen*) with her in his heart." The seventh of the Ten Commandments (Exod 20:1–17; Deut 5:6–21), forbidding adultery, is here intensified so that what takes place in a man's thoughts is as incriminating as the physical consummation of sexual desire. Contextually, these verses refer to a man's desire for a married woman, since that is the only action on the part of the man that qualifies as adultery (it was not considered adultery for a married man to have sex with an unmarried woman). Some translate the prepositional phrase *pros to epithymēsai autēn* as "with a view to lusting after her," with *pros* indicating purpose so that the condemned behavior is not mere sexual attraction, arousal, or desire itself but the intent to look in order to lust (Loader, 2012, p. 119), but the immediate context suggests the more radical warning against inappropriate sexual desire itself. Immediately following this antithesis (Matt 5:27–28), Jesus states, "If your right eye causes you to sin, tear it out and throw it away; it is better for you to lose one of your members than for your whole body to be thrown into hell" (5:29). So also should a hand be cut off if it causes one to sin (5:30). These "excision" verses together with the antithesis on adultery constitute a warning about sexual desire and its destructive and damning potential, in keeping with the general views of the time.

Matthew 18:8–9; Mark 9:43–48. The excision sayings are repeated in Matthew and are redacted from Mark, with the addition of cutting off a foot. The sinning by eye, hand, and foot may come from a tradition of formulaic warnings against lustful gazing (by the eye), masturbation (by hand), and adultery (by "foot," the Hebrew euphemism for genitalia) (Deming, 1990). Again, the radical instruction to suffer such violence rather than risk damnation for desire gone awry points toward a highly skeptical view of sexual desire.

John 7:53–8:11. The passage on the woman caught in adultery provides a counterpoint to the condemnation of inappropriate sexual desire. Although absent from many ancient manuscripts, the story nevertheless forms an important part of the tradition of Jesus's character. The main point of the passage does not revolve around adultery but rather Jesus's ability to avoid the trap of the Pharisees' question: "Now in the law Moses commanded us to stone such women. Now what do you say?" (John 8:5). Rather than reject or advocate stoning, Jesus deflects the question by focusing on the sin of all present: "Let anyone among you who is without sin be the first to throw a stone at her" (8:7). Jesus does not deny that the woman has committed a wrong, for he instructs her not to sin again (8:11), but his treatment of her sexual deviance acknowledges the shortcomings of all while offering the woman—exposed to public humiliation and violence—compassion. Thus while verses such as the excision passages highlight the danger of sexual desire, this story concedes the common reality of passion out of bounds.

The eschatological wedding banquet and Jesus the bridegroom. The kingdom of heaven is compared twice in Matthew (22:1–14; 25:1–13) to a wedding banquet, evoking celebration and the anticipation of the arrival of the groom. Jesus himself is described as the bridegroom, whose arrival inaugurates feasting and joy (Mark 2:19–20; Matt 9:15; Luke 5:34–35). The metaphor of the wedding banquet serves both to indicate the exceptional time of Jesus's ministry, wherein fasting and mourning are inappropriate, and the coming of the eschaton, for which all must be prepared. Those awaiting Christ's return do so as a bride, eagerly anticipating the wedding feast and night, as is also described in the book of Revelation, where the new Jerusalem is adorned as a bride, waiting for her husband (Rev 19:7; 21:9–10; 22:17). Although the anticipation of Christ's return may signal to some the need for ascetic devotion (see *Pauline epistles* below), in the Gospel tradition it is understood through the metaphor of sexual desire and anticipation.

John 4:1–26. This passage may be read as an oblique reference to Jesus as the coming groom, having already turned water into wine during the wedding feast in Cana (John 2:1–11) and closely following John the Baptist's pronouncement of Jesus as the bridegroom (3:29). Here, his meeting with the Samaritan woman at Jacob's well and asking her for a drink of water alludes to the romantic encounters in Genesis and Exodus (see above). The story, however, works in ironic opposition to the tales of Isaac and Rebekah, etc., because (1) rather than being a kinswoman, the woman represents a group shunned by the Jews, (2) rather than being a virgin, she has had five husbands and is with a man who is not her husband, and (3) she does not, in the end, give Jesus a drink but he instead offers her "living" water. This offer could be read as an alternative marriage proposal, which is in keeping with the themes of the Gospel that use the metaphor of marriage and sexual union but refer to *spiritual* betrothal, feast, conception, and birth, because the children of this marriage are "not of blood or of the will of the flesh (*sarkos*) or of the will of man, but of God" (1:13) and are born not of flesh but of the spirit (3:6). The living water disregards the physical realities of thirst, desire, and the woman's sexual past and replaces it with spiritual desire and consummation.

Pauline epistles. Though not an instigator of radical social change, Paul views marriage and social-sexual roles as secondary given Christ's imminent return. Paul concedes that marriage is useful as a preventative measure against sexual passion.

No male or female. Paul's statement that "there is no longer male and female; for all of you are one in Christ Jesus" (Gal 3:28), has been interpreted to mean either that Paul advocates total equality between men and women or that Paul believes in the equal standing of men and women in terms of salvation ("in Christ Jesus") but was not proposing equality in church or societal roles. The first interpretation is difficult to reconcile with passages where Paul explicitly distinguishes between the ontological nature of men and women ("a husband is the head of his wife") and addresses the behavior of women in church—instructing them, for example, to wear head coverings while praying or prophesying (1 Cor 11:3–16). The latter interpretation may present a more historically accurate reading of Paul, who does not appear to advocate radical social change in other passages. Proponents of both interpretations, however, usually work from the assumption that Paul is speaking with a stark gender dichotomy in mind. This may not be the case, given the "one-sex" model of human anatomy contemporary with Paul (see *Medical understandings*). Furthermore, there existed an understanding that the first human was an androgyne, and, given Paul's belief that the eschaton was near, he could be describing a return of all those saved to that original, androgynous state (not to be understood, however, as a "mixture" of male and female equally but a return to the default, perfected, most masculine state).

Paul and passion. Recent scholarship has pointed to the many parallels between Paul's use of vocabulary, metaphors, and rhetoric and that of contemporary philosophers, particularly the Stoics. The current debate regarding Paul's attitude toward sexual passion and desire does not, therefore, revolve around whether Paul uses philosophical concepts in his writings but whether the philosophical milieu he drew on advocated the extirpation of sexual passion. Scholars who argue that Paul and the philosophers were not against passion but against *excess* passion believe that both affirmed sexual desire within the confines of marriage. On the opposite side of the debate are those who propose that Paul and the philosophers (particularly the Stoics Musonius and Seneca) viewed passion as dangerous and believed that desire, even within marriage, was damaging.

1 Thessalonians 4:3–8. The first of a brief set of instructions here prohibits fornication (*porneia*), a term that should be understood to encompass all sexual activities considered deviant at the time. It is difficult to give a single translation to the second instruction: "that each one of you know how to control (*ktasthai*) your own body (*skeuos*) in holiness and honor, not with lustful passion (*mē en pathei epithumias*), like the Gentiles who do not know God." The meanings of *skeuos* in the context of sexual matters ranges from "wife" or "woman" (as a vessel that may contain seed) to one's own body (by default male) to one's penis. Arguments can and have been made for each of these three translations, with the meaning of the verb *ktasthai* translated to mean "take" (understood sexually) when *skeuos* is "wife" or "control" if *skeuos* is translated as "body" or "penis." However one trans-

lates the verse, it is hard to argue for any affirmation of sexual passion here since Paul distinctly associates it with pagan gentiles. Whether the instruction concerns marital sexual relations or sexual activity in general, it seems clear that Paul takes a highly negative view of sexual desire.

I Corinthians 7. This chapter follows on the heels of Paul's prohibition of visiting prostitutes, reminding the Corinthians that such unions pollute their bodies and, in turn, pollute the body of the community (1 Cor 6:15–20). He then addresses a concern that the Corinthians had apparently written to him about, the statement, "It is well for a man not to touch a woman" (7:1). Paul affirms this saying but throughout the chapter expresses concerns for those who lack the self-control to avoid *porneia* if they have no outlet for sexual activity. As a concession, then, Paul advocates marriage for those who would otherwise "be aflame with passion" (*purousthai*, literally "to burn") (7:9). Husbands and wives therefore are not to deny each other "conjugal rights" (*tēn opheilēn apodidotō*, literally "pay what is due") (7:3). This is far from a concept of marriage that celebrates sexual desire and passion; in fact, this portrayal of marital sex is based on notions of debt, power, and obligation: "For the wife does not have authority over her own body, but the husband does; likewise the husband does not have authority over his own body but the wife does" (7:4). In this last verse, both wife and husband are included in the equation as having authority, but it does not include descriptions of mutual desire or any sense of partnership.

Paul's recommendations for virgins and the unmarried are consistent with the theme of concession: he urges the Corinthians—in light of the approaching eschaton—to remain unmarried (1 Cor 7:25–30; 32–38) *unless*, without the legitimate outlet of conjugal sex, they are too weak to control their passions. In light of these verses, it is difficult to interpret Paul's conception of sexual desire as anything other than something to be eradicated and for which marriage functions as a legitimate outlet. Some scholars insist that because Paul makes no mention of childbearing here, he affirms sexual intercourse for pleasure and must have a more positive view of mutual, marital sex. These are, however, arguments from silence, and the overall, consistent depiction of marriage given by Paul is one of functionality based on a concession to weakness.

[*See also* Male-Female Sexuality, *subentries on* Early Judaism *and* Roman World; Marriage and Divorce, *subentry* New Testament; Same-Sex Relations, *subentry* New Testament; Sexuality; *and* Sexual Transgression, *subentry* New Testament.]

BIBLIOGRAPHY

Aune, David Charles. "Passions in the Pauline Epistles: The Current State of Research." In *Passions and Moral Progress in Greco-Roman Thought*, edited by John T. Fitzgerald, pp. 221–237. London: Routledge, 2008.

Deming, William. "Mark 9.42–10, Matthew 5.27–32, and *B. Nid.* 13b: A First Century Discussion of Male Sexuality." *New Testament Studies* 36 (1990): 130–141.

Deming, William. *Paul on Marriage and Celibacy: The Hellenistic Background of 1 Corinthian 7.* 2d ed. Grand Rapids, Mich.: Eerdmans, 2004.

Flemming, Rebecca. *Medicine and the Making of Roman Women: Gender, Nature, and Authority from Celsus to Galen.* Oxford: Oxford University Press, 2000.

Gaca, Kathy L. *The Making of Fornication: Eros, Ethics, and Political Reform in Greek Philosophy and Early Christianity.* Berkeley: University of California Press, 2003.

Halperin, David M., John J. Winkler, and Froma I. Zeitlin, eds. *Before Sexuality: The Construction of Erotic Experience in the Ancient Greek World.* Princeton, N.J.: Princeton University Press, 1990.

Laqueur, Thomas. *Making Sex: Body and Gender from the Greeks to Freud.* Cambridge, Mass.: Harvard University Press, 1990.

Loader, William. *The New Testament on Sexuality.* Grand Rapids, Mich.: Eerdmans, 2012.

Martin, Dale. *Sex and the Single Savior: Gender and Sexuality in Biblical Interpretation.* Louisville, Ky.: Westminster John Knox, 2006.

Meeks, Wayne. "The Image of the *Androgyne*: Some Uses of a Symbol in Earliest Christianity." *History of Religions* 13 (1974): 165–208.

Muchow, Michael David. *Passionate Love and Respectable Society in Three Greek Novels.* Baltimore: Johns Hopkins University Press, 1988.

Satlow, Michael L. *Jewish Marriage in Antiquity.* Princeton, N.J.: Princeton University Press, 2001.

Wyke, Maria. *The Roman Mistress: Ancient and Modern Representations.* Oxford: Oxford University Press, 2002.

Yii-Jan Lin

Early Judaism

Early Jewish literature derives several principles of heterosexuality from the biblical creation stories. According to *Midrash Rabbah* (Gen 8:1), the first creation story (Gen 1:27–28) describes the creation of an androgynous being, later separated into male and female halves. "And God created the person and His image, in the image of God He created him; male and female He created them God blessed them and God said to them, 'Be fertile and increase, fill the earth and subdue it.'" God subsequently split the double-faced androgynous creature, making two backs for the two faces and separate genitalia.

According to *Alphabet of Ben Sira* 47 (Eisenstein, 1915), the female creature split from the androgyne was called Lilith. A conflict arose between Lilith and Adam over who would assume the top and the bottom sexual positions. Because they were both created from the earth, Lilith claimed equality and refused to be on the bottom. Adam, in turn, claimed that he was inherently destined to be on the top. Lilith fled from Adam and refused to return, even after God sent angels to bring her back. As punishment, Lilith became a demoness who attacks children. Practices of protecting children from Lilith arose from this story, including amulets and letting little boys' hair grow so they resemble girls, who are at less risk from Lilith. Although the story seems to advocate for the missionary position, rabbinic literature more broadly permitted a variety of sex acts and sexual positions.

Another view of sexuality derived from Genesis 1:28 is based on the word *vekhivshuha*, וכבשה, "*and subdue it*," where the pronominal suffix is feminine and the verb form is singular according to the written text, with only the vocalization indicating the plural form. One Midrash (*Bereishit Rabbah* Theodor-Akbeck, Bereishit *paresha* 8:28) states, "The man subdues his wife that she not go out to the marketplace, for the end of every woman who goes out to the marketplace is to fail. From where? From Dinah as it is written *And Dinah went out* (Gen 34:1)." An alternate Midrash in *b. Yebam.* 65b on the spelling of this word actually attributes domination to males: "*And they subdue it*, a man's manner is to subdue, but it is not a woman's manner to subdue." In a similar manner, *b. Qidd. 2b* asks why the Torah stated, "When a man takes a woman" (Deut 22:13) when it could have said when a woman is taken to a man. It answers, "because it is the nature of a man to search out a woman and it is not the nature of a woman to search out a man. Like a man who has lost an object, who searches out the object? The one who lost it searches out his lost object." The lost object is a reference to the man's missing side in the second creation story (*b. Nid. 31b*).

The missing side is, in part, restored during coitus. Genesis 2:24–25 states, "Hence a man leaves his father and his mother and clings to his wife, so that they become one flesh. They were both naked and not ashamed." Although *Midrash Rabbah* attempts to harmonize the second creation story (Gen 2:24–25) with the first by claiming that the Hebrew word *tzalotav* refers to a side of the sanctuary rather than Adam's rib, this notion of creation informed the normative rabbinic understanding of creation. This view of creation advocated heterosexuality and supported a hierarchal relationship between the sexes. God is said to prefer the commandment of procreation, requiring sexual relations, over the temple (*y. Ketub.* 5:7, *30b*).

The suggestion of sexual relations between Eve and the snake (*b. Šabb. 145b–146a*, parallels, *Yalqut Shimoni* Genesis *remez* 28) appears in some rabbinic explanations of the Garden of Eden story. The snake infected Eve with lust, which was transferred to all of humanity through her. Only removed from Israel because of the giving of the Torah at Mt. Sinai, the woman's desire for her husband is part of Eve's curse. *ʾAbot R. Nat.* (version A, ch. 1) and *b. ʿErub. 100b* explain that a woman's desire for her husband is strong when he is about to leave for a journey. A particular kind of uterine blood, the so-called blood of desire (*dam himud*), was attributed to some women when they longed for their absent husbands. It appears that the rabbinic construction of this fictitious blood is based on a male paradigm of semen leakage or ejaculation and perhaps refers to spotting in mid-cycle because of ovulation, which is one of the high points of desire in women. Another source (*b. Ned. 20b*) states that when women initiate sexual relations, the resulting children will be especially beautiful.

Love. Love between couples is rarely expressed in the Bible. The lovers in Song of Songs speak of mutual love, love sickness, and erotic interest. Jacob loves Rachel (Gen 29:11) in the one-sided manner more common in the Bible, but readers never know her feelings. Shechem loved Dinah, spoke to her heart, and sought to marry her (Gen 34). Most commentators read this text as a rape story, but Tzemah Yoreh (2010) sees it as a story of love and seduction in which the resulting genocide caused embarrassment to the biblical editors. As a result, they presented Shechem's actions as rape to justify the genocide.

Marriage. The rabbis expanded the list provided in Leviticus 18 and 20 of prohibited marriage partners. Women born Jewish were forbidden to marry bastards (a child who was conceived from adultery) but converts were allowed to do so. Men were also forbidden to marry bastard women. Marriages in the rabbinic period were not generally the result of romance and love. They were contractual connections enacted by presenting the woman with money or a deed or by having sexual intercourse (*m. Qidd.* 1:1).

Several models of marriage existed prior to the rabbinic period, but the one that became normative in the rabbinic period was unilateral acquisition of the woman by the man. Thus only the man could divorce his wife. This left many women stranded in unsatisfactory marriages, a problem that is deeply felt today. The rabbis felt that it would be preferable for women to be with anyone than to remain single (*b. Yebam. 118b*, *b. Ketub. 75a*, and parallels). Marriage was the preferable state for men as well and it was stated that an unmarried man was excommunicated by heaven (*b. Pesaḥ. 113b*). Unmarried men were said to live without joy, blessing, peace, or goodness (*b. Yebam. 62b*).

Although some scholars hold that the age of marriage was well past puberty even for girls, there is ample evidence in the legal literature that girls were frequently married off before puberty. The sprouting of two pubic hairs and attaining the age of twelve years, six months, and one day constituted legal adulthood for girls. A minor girl who was married was obligated to use a contraceptive absorbent (*mokh*) (*t. Nid.* 2:6). The age of eighteen is recommended for the marriage of boys in *m. ʾAbot.* 5:21, although ages varying from sixteen to twenty-four are also mentioned in the Talmud (*b. Qidd. 29b–30a*). *Shulhan Arukh Even HaEzer* 1:7 sets the minimum age at thirteen and the preferred age at eighteen. At twenty a boy is strongly encouraged to marry, unless supporting his wife along with his Torah study would be too difficult. Marriage also allowed men to study Torah with purity of thought (*b. Yebam. 62b*).

Conjugal Rights and Duties. In addition to clothing and food, regular sexual relations were part of a woman's marital rights. The frequency of sexual relations depended on the occupation of the husband (*b. Ketub. 61b*), but rabbinic sages held that Friday night was a particularly efficacious moment to fulfill the mitzvah of conjugal duty (*onah*) and procreation (*periya ureviah*) (*y. Ketub. 5:11, 30b*). If a man vowed not to have sexual relations with his wife, Shammai limited the vow to two weeks, whereas Hillel limited it to only one week. Beyond that, the man was required to divorce his wife (*m. Ketub. 5:6*). Rabbis were allowed to leave their homes without permission for the purpose of Torah study for a month despite the obligation of conjugal duty. There are several stories in which sages left home for months and years at a time, often with negative repercussions to their families. Rabbi Akiva left home twice for twelve years to study.

Menstrual Impurity. Sexual relations, and even touching, were prohibited during the time the woman was ritually impure (during menstruation, during abnormal uterine bleeding, in the seven days after the birth of a male child and during the fourteen days after the birth of the female child). Sexual relations during the postpartum bleeding beyond the seven or fourteen days were permitted after ritual immersion. In the Tannaitic period (until approximately 220 C.E.) and for some of the amoraic period, the biblical menstrual laws requiring a seven-day separation were preserved. Rabbi Zeira in the name of the daughters of Israel conflated the biblical menstrual laws with the biblical laws for abnormal uterine bleeding, which required seven clean days after the cessation of bleeding (*b. Nid. 66b*). This resulted in a minimum of twelve days of abstinence each cycle. Currently a growing number of Orthodox couples are returning to observance of the biblical seven days or to allowing some level of nonsexual contact (as in the film *Purity*). Some even take hormones to reduce the frequency of menstrual periods so as not to have to bother with the abstinence, internal examinations, and ritual immersion that menstrual impurity imposes.

Sexual relations, which include ejaculation of semen, cause impurity to both the man and the woman (Lev 15:18). Men who are ritually impure because of semen were not supposed to pray in the normal manner or to study Torah. The requirement for ritual immersion after seminal emission and sexual relations was canceled in Babylon (*b. Ber. 22a*). A woman also became impure when she expelled semen up to three days after conjugal relations (*m. Šabb. 9:3*).

Procreation. Procreation, although not the sole purpose for marriage, was considered extremely important and a blessing. Procreation honors the biblical commandment to have children (based on Gen 9:1, 7 and Gen 35:11), as well as the rabbinic commandments to continue to procreate (*la'erev*) and to cause the world to become inhabited (*lashevet*). The commandment of *la'erev* is based on Ecclesiastes 11:16, which states that one should sow seed in the morning and continue to sow in the evening because it is unknown which will be successful. This was interpreted by Rabbi Yehoshua (*b. Yebam. 62a*) to mean that one should marry and have children in one's youth as well as in one's old age. Menopause makes this unlikely to refer to women. The commandment of *lashevet* is based on Isaiah 45:18 that God did not create the world to be a void, but to be inhabited. Only males were obligated in procreation though Rabbi Yohanan ben Beroqa held that women were also obligated to reproduce due to the plural form in Genesis 1:28 (*b. Yebam. 65b*). Very few *posqim* consider women obligated in *lashevet*.

The rabbis considered procreation a base necessity, animal-like, although it became a commandment for men. Refraining from procreation was equated with bloodshed and diminishing God's image, according to *t. Yebam.* (Lieberman) 8:7. Ben Azai excused himself because his love for the Torah was so great that others would have to fill the world with people.

Men were forbidden to marry a congenitally infertile woman (*ailonit*), a minor, or a menopausal woman unless they had already fulfilled the commandment of procreation (Rambam, *Ishut* 16:7). Men were also obligated to divorce wives who had not given birth after ten years of marriage if they did not already have children. Using very delicate language, a woman married to an impotent man could request that the court compel him to divorce her. A woman could not sue for divorce to fulfill the commandment of procreation because she was not obligated to procreate. However, she could claim that she wanted someone to lean on in her old age and to bury her (*b. Yebam. 65b*).

There was a strong desire for male children. The Talmud suggests various ways to facilitate having male children:

1. Orienting one's bed in a north-south direction (*b. Ber. 5b*, which also aids in preventing miscarriage);
2. Giving charity;
3. Gladdening one's wife to fulfill the commandment (presumably of procreation, *b. B. Bat. 10b*);
4. Separating from one's wife near her menstrual period;
5. Reciting *havdala* over wine to make the separation between impure and pure or between the holy and the common;
6. Sanctifying oneself (Rashi—by modesty) (*b. Šebu. 18b*);
7. Marrying a suitable woman;
8. Praying/sanctifying oneself during intercourse; and
9. Restraining oneself from ejaculating until the woman emits her seed first (*b. Nid. 31a*).

"Gladdening one's wife" may mean arousing her desire for intercourse. "Restraining oneself from ejaculating until the woman emits her seed" may refer to female orgasm. This latter statement is based on a male paradigm according to which male ejaculation of seed is simultaneous with male orgasm. This is most likely based on the Greek idea about the relative strengths of the seed and that whoever emits his or her seed last will determine the sex of the fetus (Laqueur, 1990). In an era before ovulation was known, this model was one logical possibility. It was challenged, however, when a woman became pregnant without an orgasm or had an orgasm without conceiving. Modern rabbis use this reference as the source that Jewish men should be considerate lovers.

Refusal of Sexual Relations. Refusal to have sexual relations on a regular basis places the woman in the category of a rebellious wife, *moredet*. If after public notification the woman continues to refuse to have sexual relations, seven dinars were subtracted from the value of her *ketubah* each week until the *ketubah* was diminished completely. A man who refuses to have sexual relations is considered a rebellious husband, *mored*, and must add to his wife's *ketubah* three dinars per week (*m. Ketub. 5:7*). The difference in payment reflects the fact that the rabbis held that the man suffers more than the woman by not having sexual relations. For this reason, men seek out prostitutes and there is an external manifestation of their passion, via an erection, whereas women have only an internal manifestation (*b. Ketub. 64b*). In Babylon some rabbis permitted temporary marriage, a form of prostitution (*b. Yebam. 37b*). Married men could fornicate with an unmarried prostitute without repercussion, whereas a married woman having sexual intercourse with someone other than her husband was considered adulterous; the husband was obliged to divorce her. Married women's sexual feelings and needs were not allowed the same expression as men's.

Sexual Acts and Practices. According to Rabbi Yohanan ben Dahabai (*b. Ned. 20a*) people are born lame because "the table is overturned" (presumably referring to rear-entry vaginal intercourse), people are born mute because the man kisses "that place" (cunnilingus), people are born deaf because the parents converse during sexual relations, and people are born blind because the man looks at the woman's genitalia. The euphemism "that place" is used exclusively for female genitalia. There is no direct statement about fellatio. Anal intercourse may have been seen in a negative light as well.

The sages, however, reject the restrictive opinion of Rabbi Yohanan ben Dahabai by saying, "Whatever a man wants to do with his wife, he does." This is compared to the ability to choose how one's meat or fish is prepared and eaten, a sexual metaphor. Other references to food and drink as metaphors for sex are found in the continuation of the discussion in *b. Ned. 20b* in which women came to Rabbi [Yehuda the Patriarch] and Rav to complain that their husbands overturned their set table. Rabbi stated that the Torah permitted him, but Rav simply said, "How does this differ from fish?" It is unclear whether the women are asking Rabbi this question because they disliked rear-entry vaginal intercourse and hoped in vain for rabbinic prohibition or whether they sought clarification because they wanted sexual relations to be according to rabbinic rules. Rabbi also prohibits drinking from one cup [having sexual relations with one woman] while thinking of another, but Ravina says that this holds only when he has two wives. Rambam and other legal experts accept the opinion of the sages who allow a variety of sexual acts but prohibit ejaculation in these other sexual acts as wastage of seed. A bride may be acquired by vaginal intercourse, but a levirate wife may be acquired by any kind of sexual act. It is significant that we hear no female voices expressing desire, a state attributed as noted to the curse of Eve.

Imma Shalom, the spouse of Rabbi Eliezer ben Hyrkanus, refers to sexual relations as "conversing." The commentators Ritva and Ran understand the conversation to be about how to satisfy or stimulate the desire of the woman. Imma Shalom's description of sexual relations includes timing (middle of the night so that there are no distractions, particularly women walking by in the street), uncovering of a small area of her body by her husband and covering it again (for the sake of modesty), and haste, as if her husband were compelled by a demon. A later commentary explains that Rabbi Eliezer ben Hyrkanus hurried his intercourse so that no thoughts of other women would come to him. Imma Shalom does not state her feelings about her husband's sexual relations with her or whether she enjoyed them.

There are several Talmudic statements warning that sexual intercourse at certain times will have an effect on the children conceived: after bloodletting of the man (weaklings), after bloodletting of both spouses (skin disease), immediately after returning from a journey (weaklings), immediately after using the privy (epilepsy) (*b. Giṭ. 70a*), during menstruation (leprosy) (*Tanhuma Metzora 3*), or by lamplight (epilepsy) (*b. Pesaḥ. 112b*). Children will be rebellious transgressors if they are conceived from intercourse under certain conditions: the woman consents only because of fear or force; the man hates her or he is excommunicated; he is thinking of his other wife; the couple is fighting; he is drunk; he intends to divorce her; she has had intercourse with other men or has not waited sufficiently after her previous marriage; or she demands intercourse (*b. Ned. 20b*).

Certain positions during intercourse also affected the man's well-being: intercourse while standing (the man will be liable to convulsions); intercourse while sitting (liable to spasms); and the woman above and he below (diarrhea) (*b. Giṭ. 70a*). The text does not describe the effects of these positions on the woman. If the woman is injured during sexual relations, the man was liable for her injuries because, even if the act were consensual, the man is considered the active party (*b. B. Qam. 32a*).

Desire, Pleasure, and Arousal. Coitus, like bathing and anointing, is considered one of the three things that do not enter the body but from which the body benefits (*b. Ber. 57b*). Rabbi Yitzhaq claims that genuine legitimate pleasure from coitus diminished after the destruction of the Temple except for sinners (*b. Sanh. 75a*). A number of texts describe stages of male arousal and types of sex acts but are nearly silent about stages of arousal for women. The only text that mentions female arousal claims that if she emits her seed first, the child conceived by that sexual act will be male (*b. Nid. 31a*). Nakedness in women is often attributed to harlots. It was considered appropriate to have sexual relations in the dark and in a private room. Even candlelight in the bedroom was considered immodest (*b. Nid. 17a*).

Moderation in the frequency of sexual relations was desirable because too much sex could cause weakness (*b. Ber. 57b*), especially in old age (*b. Šabb. 152a*).

Virginity. The bride price for a virgin was double (200 *maneh*) that of a nonvirgin. If a girl were married with the understanding that she is a virgin, then a claim could be made against her if she does not bleed as a result of intercourse. Deuteronomy 22:15–17 shows that the bride's parents kept the tokens of her virginity, the bloodied sheets, in case the groom slandered her. Bleeding on first intercourse is often more than hymeneal tearing, particularly for prepubertal girls: without proper lubrication a vaginal tear may result. According to the rabbis, if the bride is an adult, there can be no claim about her virginity because it is assumed that the hymen wore away as she grew and was active. In Judah, the groom was allowed to be alone with the bride to become intimate (according to one source) so that the Roman governor could not claim first-night privileges with the virgin bride (*b. Ketub. 12a*).

Women's voices are notably absent in the classical rabbinic texts on marriage and sexuality, as they are in all literature produced by the rabbinic elite. Although Rav Kahana hid under Rav's bed to learn how to behave during sexual relations, the practice was considered rude (*b. Ber. 62a*). Rabbinic discussions of ways to arouse women were very limited, which may not have boded well for an atmosphere of joyful and satisfying sex.

[*See also* Creation; Legal Status, *subentry* Early Judaism; Marriage and Divorce, *subentries* on Early Judaism *and* Hebrew Bible; *and* Sexual Transgression, *subentry* Early Judaism.]

BIBLIOGRAPHY

Biale, David. *Eros and the Jews: From Biblical Israel to Contemporary America*. Berkeley: University of California Press, 1997.

Boyarin, Daniel. *Carnal Israel: Reading Sex in Talmudic Culture*. Berkeley: University of California Press, 1993.

Boyarin, Daniel. "Are There Any Jews in 'The History of Sexuality'?" *Journal of the History of Sexuality* 5, no. 3 (1995): 333–355.

Boyarin, Daniel. *Unheroic Conduct: The Rise of Heterosexuality and the Invention of the Jewish Man*. Berkeley: University of California Press, 1997.

Eisenstein, Julius, ed. *Otzar Midrashim*. 2 vols. New York: Grossman's, 1915.

Elman, Pearl. "Deuteronomy 21:10–14: The Beautiful Captive Woman." In *Vixens Disturbing Vineyards*, edited by Tzemah Yoreh, Aubrey Glazer, and Justin Lewis, pp. 208–218. Boston: Academic Studies Press, 2010.

Feldman, David. *Birth Control in Jewish Law: Marital Relations, Contraception, and Abortion as Set Forth in the Classic Texts of Jewish Law*. New York: New York University Press, 1995.

Fox, Harry. "Biblical Recognition: Separation from Bestiality and Incestuous Relationships." In *Anagnorisis as Mode of Knowledge: Recognition after Aristotle*, edited by Teresa Russo, pp. 77–100. Calgary: University of Alberta Press, 2012.

Irshai, Ronit. *Fertility and Jewish Law: Feminist Perspectives on Orthodox Responsa Literature*. Waltham, Mass.: Brandeis University Press, 2012.

Kriger, Diane. *Sex Rewarded, Sex Punished: A Study of the Status "Female Slave" in Early Jewish Law*. Edited and prepared for publication by Tirzah Meacham (leBeit Yoreh). Boston: Academic Studies Press, 2011.

Laqueur, Thomas. *Making Sex: Body and Gender From the Greeks to Freud*. Cambridge, Mass.: Harvard University Press, 1990.

Meacham (leBeit Yoreh), Tirzah. "*Dam Himud*—Blood of Desire." *Koroth* 11 (1996): 82–89. In Hebrew.

Meacham (leBeit Yoreh), Tirzah. "Marriage of Minor Girls in Jewish Law: A Legal and Historical Overview." In *Jewish Legal Writings by Women*, edited by M. D. Halpern and Ch. Safrai, pp. 23–37. Jerusalem: Urim, 1998.

Meacham (leBeit Yoreh), Tirzah. "An Abbreviated History of the Development of Jewish Menstrual Laws." In *Women and Water: Menstruation in Jewish Life and Law*, edited by Rahel Wasserfal, pp. 23–39, 255–261. Hanover, Mass.: University Press of New England, 1999.

Meacham (leBeit Yoreh), Tirzah. "From Heaven They Punished Her." In *Studies in Memory of Professor Ze'ev Falk*, edited by Michael Corinaldi, Moshe David Herr, Rivka Horwitz, and Yochanan Silman, pp. 71–88. Jerusalem: Mesharim Schechter Institue of Jewish Studies, 2005a. In Hebrew.

Meacham (leBeit Yoreh), Tirzah. "Hebrew Prayers for Women in Italy: Transgendered Spirituality." In *To Be a Jewish Woman, Proceedings of the Third International Conference: Woman and Her Judaism*, edited by Tova Cohen and Aliza Lavie, pp. 23–41. Jerusalem: Kolech—Religious Women's Forum, 2005b.

Meacham (leBeit Yoreh), Tirzah. "Contraception," "Female Purity," "Legal and Religious Status of the Female According to Age," "Legal and Religious Status of the Female," "Legal and Religious Status of the Married Woman," "Legal and Religious Status of the *Moredet* (Rebellious Wife)," "Legal and Religious Status of the Suspected Adulteress (*Sotah*)," "Legal and Religious Status of the Virgin." In *Jewish Women: A Comprehensive Historical Encyclopedia*. Edited by Paula E. Hyman and Dalia Opher. Philadelphia: Jewish Publication Society, 2006. On CD-ROM.

Meacham (leBeit Yoreh), Tirzah. "On the Margins of Jewishness: The Ambivalent Status of the Convert." In *From Antiquity to the Postmodern World: Contemporary Jewish Studies in Canada*, edited by Daniel Maoz and Andrea Gondos, pp. 18–37. Newcastle upon Tyne, U.K.: Cambridge Scholars, 2011.

Meacham (leBeit Yoreh), Tirzah. "Women Are Not Susceptible to Arousal." In *To Be a Jewish Woman*, vol. 6, edited by Tova Cohen, pp. 153–167. Jerusalem: Kolech, 2013. In Hebrew.

Meacham (leBeit Yoreh), Tirzah, ed. *Sefer haBagrut leRav Shmuel ben Hofni Gaon veSefer haShanim leRav Yehuda ben Yosef Rosh haSeder*. Introduction and notes by Tirzah Meacham (leBeit Yoreh). Translated from Judeo-Arabic to Hebrew by Miriam Frankel. Jerusalem: Yad haRav Nissim, 1998. In Hebrew.

Meacham (leBeit Yoreh), Tirzah, and Harry Fox. "Holiness in Jewish Marriage: The Apologetics of Acquisition." In *To Be a Jewish Woman*, edited by Tova Cohen, pp. 325–345. Jerusalem: Kolech, 2007. In Hebrew.

Rubenstein, Jeffrey. *Rabbinic Stories*. Mahwah, N.J.: Paulist, 2002.

Satlow, Michael. *Tasting the Dish: Rabbinic Rhetorics of Sexuality*. Atlanta: Scholars Press, 1995.

Satlow, Michael. *Jewish Marriage and Antiquity*. Princeton, N.J.: Princeton University Press, 2001.

Satlow, Michael. "Marriage, Sexuality and the Family." In *Cambridge History of Judaism*, vol. 4, edited by Steven Katz et al., pp. 612–626. Cambridge, U.K.: Cambridge University Press, 2006.

Shremer, Adiel. *Male and Female He Created Them: Jewish Marriage in Late Second Temple, Mishnah and Talmud Periods*. Jerusalem: Zalman Shazar Center, 2003. In Hebrew.

Yoreh, Tzemah. "Shekhem and the So-Called Rape of Dina." In *Vixens Disturbing Vineyards*, edited by Tzemah Yoreh, Aubrey Glazer, and Justin Lewis, pp. 67–78. Boston: Academic Studies Press, 2010.

Yoreh, Yoam. "The Beautiful Woman in Sifrei and Early Commentary." In *Vixens Disturbing Vineyards*, edited by Tzemah Yoreh, Aubrey Glazer, and Justin Lewis, pp. 627–635. Boston: Academic Studies Press, 2010. In Hebrew.

Zuria, Anat, dir. *Purity* (*Tehora*). DVD. New York: Women Make Movies, 2002.

Tirzah Meacham (leBeit Yoreh)

Early Church

Despite Paul's formative role in shaping many another Jewish-derived Christian norm in the early church, the Jewish heritage of performing conjugal sexual duties in heterosexual marriage as reworked by Paul in 1 Corinthians 7:2–5 did not find a happy home in early church doctrine. Instead, partly in light of 1 Corinthians 7:1, the status of perpetual virginity and celibacy is regularly elevated over Christian marriage by early church fathers, Jerome and Augustine noteworthy among them. Although Michel Foucault is correct that persons in antiquity did not identify themselves as heterosexual or homosexual in their personal identity and orientation, the appellation "heterosexuality" remains a reasonable synonym for "male-female sexuality" in the early Christian church.

Paul's Formulations of Marriage. Paul develops an ideology of reinforced reciprocality in 1 Corinthians 7:2–5, insisting that in Christian marriage the woman and man must each "have" (*echetô*) each other sexually. The man does not simply have the woman. The woman has mastery (*exousiazei*) over the man's body and the man has mastery over the woman's body, depending on who takes the lead in performing the shared Christian marital duty (*opheilê*) to sustain these sexual practices in which she is in charge of him and he is in charge of her in their shared sexual effort to keep religiously rebellious acts of sexual fornication (*tas porneias*) at bay.

In Paul's view, the reason for this shared mastery and obligation is that Satan (*ho Satanas*) is an inimical adversary regularly testing and trying to lure married Christians into religiously alienating sexual fornication (*porneia*), to which the spouses succumb if they deviate from making love to anyone but each other in a fully Christian or sufficiently Christian marriage. Here, the word "sufficiently" refers to an already formed marriage that promises to become fully Christian through the conversion of one spouse to Christianity before the other. The Christian husband and wife pairs in turn are powerless in their inability (*akrasia*) to withstand Satan's lure of religiously alienating fornication unless they remain sexually active with each other as a shared prophylactic against succumbing to Satan's powers. Thus, rather as condoms keep sex safe nowadays, and diaphragms, condoms, and medications fend off unwanted pregnancies, so too the above sexual marital workout is needed in Christian marriage in order to keep the sexually fornicating ways of the devil out of the union, as far Paul was concerned in his mission to Greeks and other gentiles. For that purpose the wife wields sexual power over her husband and he over her.

This sexual norm allows for only relatively short periods of sexual abstinence to pray (1 Cor 7:5). How short these time periods are Paul does not say, but according to Matthew, Christians should keep their prayers succinct, unlike gentiles whose prayers and hymns to the gods go on at length (Matt 6:7). By this principle it is not viable to become married Christian celibates in a state of extended or perpetual prayer. Christian wives and husbands are to refrain from sexual activity together to say the Lord's Prayer or the like, and then they are promptly to return to their sexually active guard duty performed on and with each other. Thus, even though Paul may have regarded perpetual Christian virginity and celibacy as the preferred but rare human condition (1 Cor 7:1 interpreted as Paul's own view, cf. 7:7), he not only allows but expects Christian spouses to engage in plenty of sexual activity with each other, seeing that this is what it takes to keep each other protected from the sexually fornicating ways of Satan.

Thanks to the integration of gender and sexuality studies with biblical studies over the last few decades, it has now become possible to appreciate Paul's striking teaching in 1 Corinthians 7:2–5. Especially noteworthy is his strong affirmation of the wife taking a sexually assertive role when it is her turn to take on her man, all as part of her religious marital duty to keep her husband and herself safe. Further, it has also become possible to appreciate that Paul here is voicing his distinctively emphatic take on the sexual norms of Jewish marriage that were part of his culture, in which the husband must honor his wife, and she him, by performing their conjugal sexual duties with each other.

Departures from Paul in the Early Church. In the emergent church, Paul's basic homiletic fare about appropriate Christian marital sexual norms became disconnected from the apostle's fervent teaching that Christian spouses need to make love together frequently. In its stead was favored a sexually restrictive rule that is Pythagorean in origin. This rule gained normative sway in the early church through Pythagorean-imbued Hellenistic Judaism, which is now found primarily in the works of Philo of Alexandria but had many other proponents beyond Philo. This is the teaching that sexual relations should be marital, and that husbands and wives should make love for procreation only, a view now known as "procreationism." In and through Pythagoreanizing Judaism, procreationism took on the aura of being the canonical word of the LORD and grew distant from its original Pythagorean rationale and motivation. As Pythagorean doctrine, the rule was geared toward bringing immortal souls responsibly and carefully into a reincarnated embodiment by elevating marital sexual intercourse as the "right" way to make love, insisting that this copulation be restrained and focused strictly on the goal of conception. This was motivated by the belief that like any other careful craftwork, this particular sexual technique was necessary to enable newborn infants to be born with their embodied souls in good harmonic working order: this so that the children can grow up and become morally good rather than corrupt and dissolute adults. Conversely, human and social corruption derives from unrestrained and non-purposive sexual conduct, especially when it leads to procreation by chance, which seriously damages the souls being embodied, throws them out of tune, and ruins their condition for the duration of their embodiment: thus this ruin manifests itself as moral and social corruption.

Partly under the influence of Pythagorean-imbued Hellenistic Judaism as expressed in Philo, early church fathers such as Clement of Alexandria attributed procreationism to Genesis 1:28 ("grow and multiply"). Similar biblical sentiments are understood to be a direct Pythagorean order from the Old Testament that Christians who wish to be sexually active must marry and make love in Christian marriage for no reason other than strictly to multiply. But for the church fathers, the stakes for Christian deviance from this rule, be it within or outside of heterosexual Christian marriage, changed considerably. Now Christians were under penalty of the Lord's retaliatory wrath for failing to restrict their lovemaking strictly within the procreationist limit, even when the sexual activity remained in Christian marriage: this deviance was rebellious sexual fornication. To make love within Christian marriage for any non-procreationist reason was highlighted as a major problem in the early church by being identified with the dread succumbing to Satan that Paul makes clear Christians must avoid at all costs: "flee sexual fornication" (*pheugete tên porneian*, 1 Cor 6:18).

The early church step of identifying non-procreationist Christian marital sexual relations as sexual fornication is directly at odds with Paul's teaching in 1 Corinthians 7:2–5, which is neither procreationist nor Pythagorean-influenced, but seeks to have Christian husbands and wives making love together regularly precisely to keep Satan and sexual fornication out of Christian marriage. Paul's position is consonant with Genesis 1:28 and like biblical sentiments, for these biblical proof texts are not procreationist, voicing as they do nothing more than the widespread ancient view that childbearing is a basic purpose of heterosexual copulation within marriage, not the Pythagorean-influenced early church inference that Christian marital conception and childbearing are the only allowable function of Christian sexual activity according to Genesis 1:28 and the like. The Jewish and Pauline view that spouses in the Lord must fulfill marital sexual duties for reasons beyond reproduction are fully consonant with "grow and multiply."

By contrast, early church sexual morality is a much more restrictive, sober, and repressed affair by virtue of being imbued with procreationism treated as the LORD's inflexible word. Further, when conjoined with the Gospel teachings of Jesus against divorce (Matt 19:4–6; Mark 10:6–9; cf. 1 Cor 7:10; cf. Eph 5:25–33), Christian procreationism leads to this restrictive signature of early church sexual morality: once married man to woman and woman to man, you cannot change your mind, leave the union, and remarry. Second, when making love with your one and only spouse, the copulating must be restrained and goal-directed toward procreating—or at least not contraceptive of this end. This rules out Paul's directive that Christian wives and husbands must engage in frequent sexual relations together so as to keep the danger of extramarital sexual fornication at bay, even though Paul urges this directive with no little vehemence. In its stead arises the early church doctrine that Christian husbands and wives must limit

their copulating to strictly reproductive aims as the only way to avoid the rebellious sexual fornication.

Definitions of Sexual Transgression in Antiquity. To better understand this gulf between the early church's view of Christian marital sexual morality and that advocated by Paul it is important to consider the ways in which definitions of rebellious sexual fornication were shaped by the biblical heritage and by the gendered dimensions of ancient religion.

Biblical backgrounds. In the Old Testament, to sexually fornicate in a rebellious or apostate way primarily signifies that persons who were supposed to be devoted solely to the LORD, Israelites and Jews historically, allegedly turned away from the LORD by engaging in religiously mixed, and religiously mixing, heterosexual marriages and childrearing. This practice involved worshipping, within the family, gods other than or in addition to the LORD. This transgresses the first commandment in the Decalogue to worship the LORD alone and thereby alienates the Israelite or Jewish spouses and their children and children's children from the LORD. Practices of this sort are so strong an emblem of religiously alienating danger as to seem the epitome of Satan and his doings for Paul and other Christians, Israelites, and Jews of like mind.

Because religiously mixed marriages are understood to elicit the LORD's wrath against both the apostates and communities tolerating this practice, an alarmist condemnation of such sexual fornication recurs in many Old Testament books, with the Prophets presenting the most fearsome and graphic imagery of the LORD's fury. Hence, sexual fornication is so fearsome and evil-seeming in its origins because religiously mixed marriage and childrearing are apostate rebellion against the LORD, and as such elicits the LORD's wrath against the perpetrators and their fellow community members at large.

In 1 Corinthians 7:2–5 and elsewhere (e.g., 2 Cor 6:14–7:1; Ignatius, *Pol.* 5.2), Paul and his followers accept the dangers associated with sexually fornicating apostasy in the Old Testament as a Christian marital norm by insisting on the need to keep religiously mixed and mixing sexual practices out of early Christianity. Christian marital lovemaking is a prophylactic affirmation of this need for Paul.

Further, according to Paul, all gentiles belong to a universal gentile Israel that must become Christian Israel, which means that the worship of Christ the Lord is universally required. Paul alleges in Romans 1:18–32 that a group of gentiles who are nebulous in their specific ethnic identity, but most likely Greeks, once recognized but later abandoned the LORD, on the model of sexually fornicating Israel in the Prophets. Although these apostate gentiles are a fabrication—a fabrication Paul evidently believed—to Paul and many church fathers this apostate culture was real, Greek exclusively or mainly, and needed to be retrieved from its ancestral gods, starting with the Greek gods of sexuality and marriage, Aphrodite foremost. It would be hard to overstate the normative impact of this innovative Pauline notion of religiously rebellious sexual fornication. The enforced conversion of gentiles to norms of Christian marriage and reproduction derived to a large degree from Paul's revolutionary new teaching that religiously alien and alienating sexual fornication must be driven from the midst of Christian Israel.

Gender in ancient religion. In the ancient world, the powers of human and other animal sexuality and procreation were strongly vested in deities, especially but not only those in female form or goddesses, who were thought to preside over and to be immanent in the powers of sexual arousal and activity. Further, women and girls in the Near East and ancient Mediterranean were strongly acculturated to worship these female deities in ways intimately bound up with their sense of themselves and their community roles as sexual and reproductive agents. These goddesses include the nude Ishtar or queen of heaven (Greek Astarte) in the Near East and, on the Greek side, her Greek counterpart Aphrodite, as well as goddesses dating to the second-century Bronze Age in Mycenaean Linear B (the first Greek writing system), which include Eileithyia, Potnia, Artemis, and Hera, and, to an extent, perhaps dating before the Bronze Age in the prehistory of Old World antiquity.

Because of the long-standing strength of this religious sexual devotion in the largely separate social domain of women and girls in antiquity, female deities central to their sexual and procreative lives, and to the well-being of their people, proved especially difficult to eradicate once their social groups came to be claimed strictly for the biblical LORD. In one striking instance of this problem, Jeremiah singles out the queen of heaven for condemnation. In a confrontational interchange in Egypt with women in Jewish marriages, the women refuse to follow Jeremiah's command to turn away from the queen of heaven and to follow the LORD God alone. With the support of their husbands, they insist, "We will carry out our vows to burn sacrifices to the queen of heaven and pour drink-offerings to her," practices that they saw as critical for sustaining the well-being of their community (Jer 44:17–19, 25). Jeremiah, by contrast, retorts that the LORD's wrath will destroy them and their families, and that this devastation will demonstrate that the LORD's word will prevail (Septuagint [LXX] Jer 51:1–28). It is not clear from Jeremiah whether these wives were raised as Ishtar worshippers and living in religiously mixed marriages with Jewish husbands or already self-identified as Jewish adherents of the Lord, but still worshipping Ishtar in their women's social world.

To devotees of the LORD like Jeremiah, these questions about the wives' religious derivation and social identity as spouses did not matter. In the LORD's domain, which included this diaspora settlement in Egypt, no marriage, whatever its socially formative basis, could rest content being only partly in the LORD: it needed to be fully and solely in the LORD to avert his wrath and keep his protection. This meant that the worship of Ishtar and her kind, goddesses like Aphrodite, especially had to be driven out of their female strongholds in communities claimed for the LORD, marriage by marriage, family by family, generation after generation until goddesses of human sexuality became a defunct and distant memory.

From a Greek and Hellenized perspective, by contrast, to make love for any reason, even to procreate, meant the pleasurable act of giving Aphrodite her due. "Each and every mortal being is attentive to the works of Aphrodite with the shapely crown," as stated in the *Homeric Hymn to Aphrodite* (5.1–6). From this perspective "golden Aphrodite" prevails universally over sexuality, sexual desire, sexual activity, and its inherent delight and pleasures (Mimnermus 1.1). Notwithstanding the allure of her sexual gifts to humanity, Aphrodite can bring torments along with the excitement of falling into passionate love. In pre-Christian antiquity the Greeks accordingly trembled with sexual arousal and more when worshipping Aphrodite as the preeminent deity in the erotic domain, built temples to her, sculpted statues to embody her presence, and composed Muse-inspired hymns and poetry in her honor. From this long-standing Greek perspective, it was impossible to imagine being sexually aroused or making love without Aphrodite, for sexual arousal and activity were the "works of Aphrodite."

By contrast with the apostle Paul's Jewish-informed belief that marital sexual activity fully and strictly in the Lord was an eminently viable practice, the popular and deep-rooted Greek beliefs about Aphrodite and her sexual powers made it very difficult for Greek and Hellenized Christians to reject Aphrodite without either renouncing sexual activity altogether, as Encratite Christians like Tatian did, or believing, as did Clement of Alexandria and other early church fathers, that Christ saved Christians from the religiously alienating ways of Aphrodite only so long as they remained soberly procreationist and strictly goal-oriented toward reproduction when copulating. From this perspective, there was nothing sweet about the desire Aphrodite provoked universally in humans, as there was for the Greeks. True life and immortality belonged to Christ the Lord, while the Lord's wrath incarnate, sexual pleasure and eternal death belonged to Aphrodite.

Athanasius (ca. 296–373) accordingly finds Aphrodite brazenly culpable for having instigated the sexually fornicating mores by which Greek polytheism was sustained, and he forthrightly declares that he considers Greek "women gods" more intolerable than Greek male gods (*Contra gentes* 26.1–3). From this ecclesiastical viewpoint, Aphrodite was not a sensuous nude or demi-nude deity using her arms, hands, and garments to disclose a sexually grounded spirituality through female allure, as she was in Greek and Hellenized society. No, she was a "whore" who "shamelessly bared the unseeable parts of her body for all to view," as Cyril of Alexandria puts it (*In duodecim prophetas*, Pusey 1868, 1.111).

In this guise, the "naked so-called goddess" was a blazing emblem of the religiously dangerous "female" who "provokes the pleasure that trips up males into apostasy from God, as declared by a follower of Athanasius (ps.-Athan. *On the Deception of the Devil* [*De fallacia diaboli*], 8, 10). This follower accordingly urges his listeners to stop bowing down to this naked woman god in reverence, and joyously celebrates each Christian conversion as a victory over this practice: "Let us not stop giving thanks, ... for the one who yesterday was bowing down to a naked woman now professes belief in God!"

Further, as Gregory of Nazianzus asserts (ca. 329–389), Aphrodite, "shamelessly a whore," was "one who services shameful unions" that are best termed "whorish initiations" (*Orat. 5*, PG 35.704–705, *Orat. 35*, PG 36.337). These "shameful unions" and "whorish initiations" were mainly traditional non-Christian Greek weddings, practices that were still being celebrated in late antiquity, as John Chrysostom (ca. 347–407) notes with strong disapproval. In his day in Antioch, non-Christian Greek families were still dancing and singing hymns for Aphrodite at their daughters' weddings. To Chrysostom, this was a religious outrage: The hymns teem with shameful sexual contents that are not even "appropriate for earnest slaves to hear," let alone the virgin in her bridal procession. Her father and mother protected their daughter from debauchery, only to waste this upbringing by subjecting her to it on her wedding day and making her shameless from then on (*Propter fornicarios*, PG 51.211).

With authoritative agreement, the church fathers urged their congregations and new converts to cast Aphrodite down and to praise the LORD for this accomplishment. To prepare the way of a gentile-turned-Christian Israel, the LORD as reworked into Christ the Lord required begetting children strictly for him, and that meant the religiously alien worship of Aphrodite needed to be banished from Christian marriage. Where Paul and the church fathers differ is in the Christian marital sexual code they thought was needed to keep the female satanic force away from Christian marriage. For Paul, Christian husbands and wives are free in the LORD to make love together frequently and must do so, and this not for procreation alone. By contrast, this Pauline teaching was far too redolent of Aphrodite worship for the early church fathers. Hence their receptivity to, and advocacy of, a Pythagorean-indebted Christian procreationism to keep rebellious sexual fornication out of the Christian marriage bond by allowing lovemaking therein for no reason other than to procreate, generation after generation.

[*See also* Masculinity and Femininity, *subentries on* Early Church *and* Greek World; Paul; Sexuality; *and* Sexual Transgression, *subentry* Early Church.]

BIBLIOGRAPHY

Brown, Peter. *The Body and Society: Men, Women, and Sexual Renunciation in Early Christianity.* New York: Columbia University Press, 1988.

Clark, Anna. *Desire: A History of European Sexuality.* New York: Routledge, 2008.

Cooper, Kate. *The Virgin and the Bride: Idealized Womanhood in Late Antiquity.* Cambridge, Mass.: Harvard University Press, 1996.

Corrington Streete, Gail. *The Strange Woman: Power and Sex in the Bible.* Louisville, Ky.: Westminster John Knox, 1997.

Elm, Susanna. *Virgins of God: The Making of Asceticism in Late Antiquity.* Oxford: Oxford University Press, 1994.

Gaca, Kathy L. "Paul's Uncommon Declaration to the Greeks: Romans 1:18–32 and Its Problematic Legacy for Pagan and Christian Relations." *Harvard Theological Review* 92 (1999): 165–198.

Gaca, Kathy L. *The Making of Fornication: Eros, Ethics, and Political Reform in Greek Philosophy and Early Christianity.* Berkeley: University of California Press, 2003.

Pirenne-Delforge, Vinciane. *L'Aphrodite grecque: Contribution a l'étude de ses cultes et de sa personnalité dans le pantheon archaïque et classique.* Liège, Belgium: Centre International d'Étude de la Religion Grecque Antique, 1994.

Sfameni Gasparro, Giulia, Cesare Magazzu, and Concetta Aloe Spada, ed. *The Human Couple in the Fathers.* Translated by Thomas Halton. New York: Pauline, 1998.

Kathy L. Gaca

MARRIAGE AND DIVORCE

This entry contains seven subentries: Ancient Near East; Hebrew Bible; Greek World; Roman World; New Testament; Early Judaism; *and* Early Church.

Ancient Near East

Most of the evidence for marriage and divorce in the ancient Near East (ANE) comes from legal collections such as the Laws of Hammurabi (LH) and from private legal contracts. Because this material focuses on specific legal issues that may arise in various cases, it provides a rather narrow view of the topic that perhaps overrepresents certain kinds of concerns. It likely also overrepresents certain kinds of families, as the codes and contracts were mostly drawn up with the interests of middle- and upper-class city-dwellers in mind (Roth, 1989, p. 25). The evidence also comes primarily from the Old Babylonian (OB) and Neo-Babylonian (NB) periods, meaning that it is somewhat geographically and chronologically limited. Nevertheless, the texts do provide a picture of many of the finer points of how marriages might be formed and dissolved, and the similarities between the material over time and in different regions also suggest that there was considerable continuity, despite certain changes.

Marriage. Because the relevant material focuses on technical legal aspects for the most part, we can reconstruct little of how marriage functioned on a personal level or what the day-to-day relationship of a married couple would have looked like. Occasionally a source will mention some detail of the relationship; for example, LH 142 and 143 mention marital discord and suggest that a couple was expected to behave in an appropriate fashion toward one another, though some of this may have had to do with outward appearances rather than private behavior.

Despite this general blindness about the inner workings of the marital relationship, we know what many of the technical and legal aspects of a marriage were, and we also know something about how a marriage was contracted—that is, what steps were involved in a couple becoming married. Though the selection process—what factors went into the decision for two people to marry—is opaque, some contracts suggest that the couple being married may have played a role, though their families were usually also involved. Spousal selection by parents cannot be ruled out. In particular, this seems to be the case for women; the bride is seldom the subject of any action in the contracts. In a few exceptional cases from the NB period, women appear to have played an active role in contracting their own marriages, occasionally even providing their own dowries (Roth, 1989, pp. 5–6; Westbrook, 1988, pp. 43–44). This seems most often to be the case with widows and divorced women (Roth, 1989, p. 7; Westbrook, 1988, pp. 61–62). Whereas men married at a later age, never-married women were likely to be younger and still living with their families, who would have taken the lead in arranging their marriages. Thus the bride's lack of a role in her marriage could be a function as much of her age as of her gender (Roth, 1998, p. 182), and later in life, were she to remarry, she might find these circumstances changed and the details of the marriage within her own control. Brothers and mothers could be involved in the arrangements, alongside fathers. In the case that a girl's father was dead or otherwise absent, it was often her brothers who stepped in to play the role of the *paterfamilias*, arranging the dowry, receiving the bridewealth, and generally being in a position of authority over their sister.

The ANE legal texts relating to marriage display a general lack of concern with the bride's virginity, despite the likelihood that female virginity was valued in Mesopotamia (Marsman, 2003, p. 256). Discussion of the topic is largely lacking in the laws. Terms that seem to indicate that a bride is a virgin appear in marriage contracts, especially from the NB period, though these terms may have more to do with age than with sexual history (Roth, 1989, p. 7). This apparent lack of concern could be the result of the legal material's focus on other matters, though it could also indicate that less control was placed on this aspect of women's lives. Nevertheless, some degree of sexual control was certainly still exerted

on Mesopotamian women, as their roles and rights in marriage were more restricted than were men's, especially where adultery, polygamy, and divorce were concerned.

Marriage laws and contracts use a variety of terms that, though common in other senses, constitute a technical vocabulary when they are used specifically for marriage. The verb *aḫāzum*, "to take," with the groom as the subject and the bride as the object, is the basic verb for marrying (Westbrook, 1988, pp. 10–11). The term is used alone and in variants of the phrase *ana aššūtim u mutūtim aḫāzum* (lit. "to take for wifeship and husbandship"). A bride can also be "given in marriage" (*ana aššūtim nadānum*). The fuller forms appear especially in OB contracts; in OB law collections, *aḫāzum* alone or the shortened form *aššatam aḫāzum* ("to take a wife") appears instead (Westbrook, 1988, p. 12). These terms continue to be used in later periods as well (Westbrook, 1988, p. 16).

Marriage in the ANE took place in stages. The first stage was betrothal, at which point the groom or his family usually gave a gift of bridewealth (*terḫatum*) to the bride's family. The *terḫatum* might become part of the dowry or it might remain with the bride's family. The bridewealth might be a small amount, or be omitted entirely, especially if the bride was arranging her own marriage, an indicator that she had no family to receive the gift. Payment of the *terḫatum* initiated the process of marriage and established the groom's right to marry the bride, usually at some time in the future, though it is not clear how long this betrothal period usually lasted. The practice of giving the *terḫatum* disappears in the NB period, coinciding with an increased emphasis on dowry and likely indicating increased social stratification (Lemos, 2010, pp. 149, 158; Westbrook, 1988, p. 7).

After the betrothal, the bride continued to live in her father's home in most cases. In some instances, though, the betrothed bride might move to the groom's father's household, a state called *kallūtum*, literally "daughter-in-law-ship," in which male authority over the daughter was transferred from her own father to her future father-in-law rather than her husband (Westbrook, 1988, pp. 36–37). From the family's perspective, the betrothed couple, living in the same household or not, were not yet married, and thus the penalties for breaking the arrangement off at this stage were less severe than they would be if the marriage had been finalized. However, any infidelity by the betrothed bride was considered the same as adultery and evoked the same harsh punishment that an adulterous married woman would have received (Lemos, 2010, p. 142). Though there might be penalties for breaking off the marriage at this point, they were less severe than the penalties once the marriage was consummated and especially once the marriage had produced offspring.

The marriage was considered final when the husband "took" (*aḫāzum*) the bride, usually indicating that she now took up residence in her husband's household (or in the case of *kallūtum*, that authority over her shifted from her father-in-law to her new husband). Though *aḫāzum* suggests physical action, it does not necessarily correspond to consummation of the marriage, though in most cases that is likely what it did mean. The term refers more concretely to the transfer of authority over the woman from her father (or her father-in-law) to her husband.

Children and inheritance were the main purposes of marriage, and the law collections and contracts are especially geared toward protecting inheritance rights within the marriage. The majority of the estate that children would inherit came from their fathers, but dowry (*nudunnûm*, *šeriktum*), property that the bride brought into the marriage with her, was another important piece of the inheritance and was a key aspect of the marriage. Dowry served as a means of inheritance from the maternal grandfather, conveyed through his daughter. Whereas men often did not marry until after their fathers had died and thus they had inherited their portion of the paternal estate, women married much younger. Because marriage involved the woman's departure from her father's household, she received her portion of his estate through the institution of dowry at the time of her marriage (Roth, 1989, p. 9). Unlike a son's inheritance, a daughter had no right to a dowry protected by law; dowry was considered a voluntary donation, though it functioned nonetheless as a form of inheritance. Her children would inherit whatever was left

of her dowry on the woman's death. Given the importance of the dowry, which could be of considerable value, most of the marriage contracts are really about disposition of the dowry and what would happen to it if the wife was divorced or widowed.

The dowry might include usable goods such as oil or grain, durable goods such as furniture and utensils, and items such as cattle and slaves. In some cases it could also include property. In the earlier periods, the dowry was a gift from the bride's father to the bride, and in the OB period it was her property even after the marriage. In the NB period, the dowry became the husband's property, though it passed through the husband to the wife's children alone, not to any children he might have had through other wives (Marsman, 2003, p. 97; Roth, 1989, pp. 7–8). In both periods, the dowry was a means for the woman's support if she was divorced or widowed, even if she was childless. However, if the woman died childless, the dowry reverted to her father.

The details of the dowry and its disposition were often spelled out in the marriage contract, and these dowry provisions may have been the most important features of the marriage contracts, especially in the NB period (Roth, 1989, pp. 8, 25–27). Though some laws state that a marriage was not valid without a written contract (Westbrook, 1988, p. 33), the overall underrepresentation of such contracts in the vast collection of cuneiform sources indicates that in fact most marriages were probably concluded without written contracts. In addition, clauses about children in some marriage contracts indicate that sometimes contracts for dowry and inheritance were drawn up well after the couple began cohabiting and having children (Roth, 1989, pp. 17–18).

Polygamy. Polygamy—or more accurately, polygyny, marriage to multiple wives—was practiced in the ANE. As is nearly universal in societies practicing a form of plural marriage, polyandry—the practice of one woman having multiple husbands—was not allowed. Polygyny seems to have been somewhat circumscribed, usually being a means of securing heirs when a couple was childless or when a woman, because of her status as a *nadītu* priestess, could not bear children. A man seems to have had the right to marry a second wife if he wanted one, but a first wife could object to her husband doing so in certain circumstances (Westbrook, 1988, p. 109). According to LH 144, for example, if the aforementioned *nadītu* provided her husband with a slave woman who produced offspring, then the husband was forbidden from marrying another wife.

Wives could also be of different status: primary and secondary wives, and slave-wives and concubines, in addition to primary wives. These distinctions in status were at times protected by stipulations in the laws, indicating that they had real effects on the places and roles of women within their marriages. More so, these rules protected the status of the children of these marriages, so that the children of the primary wives, who would have been the primary heirs, could not be disinherited because their mother fell out of favor or was supplanted by another wife. Slave wives and concubines were in the most vulnerable position; the children of slave wives could be legitimated through special action, but the children of concubines could not (Westbrook, 1988, p. 107).

Adultery. Husbands had relative impunity in how they treated wives guilty, or even suspected, of adultery, though it also seems to have been a private matter that left some discretion to the husband in how he handled the situation (Roth, 1988, p. 204). Although there is limited evidence for the handling of adultery, the husband who caught his wife and her lover in the act was justified in killing them both, though other options for retaliation were available to him. Both the law collections and the contracts assume that the husband has some right to punish his adulterous wife and her lover, though the punishment of the former may be more severe than that of the latter. The disproportionate punishment of the woman versus her male lover may be a function of the woman's status as an insider and the man's as an outsider in a case of family law (Roth, 1998, p. 183). In addition, wives had some protections against unsubstantiated accusations or suspicions of adultery. In OB law, the woman accused of adultery is submitted to a trial by ordeal, but her husband does not have the authority to kill her based only on his own suspicion. If there is no formal accusation but only

the husband's suspicion, then the wife must swear an oath that she is innocent, but the husband is allowed no further action.

Divorce. A marriage could be ended at any time, though not necessarily for any reason. The primary term for divorce is *ezēbum* (Westbrook, 1988, pp. 20–21), and the divorce settlement is referred to by the related term *uzzubûm* (Westbrook, 1988, p. 23). The divorce was usually effected through the husband's pronouncement; in the case that the woman did not take her dowry with her, the act of divorce was accompanied by the symbolic cutting (*sissiktum*) of the hem of the woman's garment (Westbrook, 1988, pp. 69–70).

During the betrothal stage either party could break off the arrangement; if the father of the woman decided to break the agreement and give his daughter to another, he had to repay the *terḫatum* (Westbrook, 1988, pp. 41–42). If the groom broke the agreement, then he forfeited the *terḫatum* that he had already given. Once the marriage had been finalized, the husband could decide to terminate it, and the wife had few means to protect herself from divorce. However, if the wife was deemed not to be at fault, regardless of whether the marriage had produced children, she was given a divorce settlement, consisting of her dowry and an amount equal to her bridewealth, or of another stipulated amount. If the woman was deemed to be at fault in some way, she did not receive any settlement. In some cases, women seem to have had a right to initiate a divorce, particularly in cases of misconduct or abandonment by the husband (Westbrook, 1988, pp. 80–81).

In the case that the marriage had produced children, there were additional safeguards to keep the wife from being cast aside. A man could not always marry another woman over his wife's objections, especially if the new woman was not a slave or concubine and would have had full status as a wife, even if a secondary one. If a wife became ill and could not bear children, she was also protected from divorce, though her husband was permitted to take a second wife in order to produce children.

The divorced woman, like the widow, could remarry, though there appear to have been some restrictions. The restrictions have more to do with disposition of her dowry and differentiating the inheritance rights of the children from the first marriage and any from the subsequent marriage. Divorced women and widows, especially if they had no living male relatives, most likely were able to arrange their own remarriages. The limited evidence in contracts in which women seem to provide their own dowries appear to have been cases in which the women were not entering their first marriages.

[*See also* Children, *subentry* Ancient Near East; Legal Status, *subentry* Ancient Near East; *and* Religious Leaders, *subentry* Ancient Near East.]

BIBLIOGRAPHY

Friedl, Corinna. *Polygynie in Mesopotamien und Israel: Sozialgeschichtliche Analyse polygamer Beziehungen anhand rechtlicher Texte aus dem 2. und 1. Jahrtausend v.Chr.* Alter Orient und Altes Testament 277. Münster, Germany: Ugarit Verlag, 2000.

Grosz, Katarzyna. "Bridewealth and Dowry in Nuzi." In *Images of Women in Antiquity*, edited by Avril Cameron and Amelie Kuhrt, pp. 193–206. Detroit: Wayne State University Press, 1983.

Holtz, Shalom E. "'To Go and Marry Any Man That You Please': A Study of the Formal Antecedents of the Rabbinic Writ of Divorce." *Journal of Near Eastern Studies* 60 (2001): 241–258.

Lemos, T. M. *Marriage Gifts and Social Change in Ancient Palestine, 1200 B.C.E. to 200 C.E.* Cambridge, U.K.: Cambridge University Press, 2010.

Marsman, Hennie J. *Women in Ugarit and Israel: Their Social and Religious Position in the Context of the Ancient Near East.* Oudtestamentische Studiën 49. Leiden, The Netherlands: Brill, 2003.

Matthews, Victor H. "Marriage and Family in the Ancient Near East." In *Marriage and the Family in the Biblical World*, edited by Ken M. Cambell, pp. 1–32. Downers Grove, Ill.: IVP Academic, 2003.

Roth, Martha T. "'She Will Die by the Iron Dagger': Adultery and Neo-Babylonian Marriage." *Journal of the Economic and Social History of the Orient* 31 (1988): 186–206.

Roth, Martha T. *Babylonian Marriage Agreements: 7th–3rd Centuries B.C.* Alter Orient und Altes Testament 222. Neukirchen-Vluyn, Germany: Neukirchener Verlag, 1989.

Roth, Martha T. *Law Collections from Mesopotamia and Asia Minor.* 2d ed. SBL Writings from the Ancient World. Atlanta: Scholars Press, 1997.

Roth, Martha T. "Gender and Law: A Case Study from Ancient Mesopotamia." In *Gender and Law in the Hebrew Bible and the Ancient Near East*, edited by Bernard M. Levinson, Tikva Frymer-Kensky, and Victor H. Matthews, pp. 173–184. Journal for the Study of the Old Testament, Supplement Series/Library of the Hebrew Bible/Old Testament Studies 262. Sheffield, U.K.: Sheffield Academic Press, 1998.

Toivari-Viitala, Jaana. "Marriage and Divorce." In *UCLA Encyclopedia of Egyptology*, edited by Elizabeth Frood and Willeke Wendrich. Los Angeles, 2013. http://digital2.library.ucla.edu/viewFile.do?contentFileId=2181363

Westbrook, Raymond. *Old Babylonian Marriage Law.* Archiv für Orientforschung 23. Horn, Germany: Verlag Ferdinand Berger, 1988.

Sarah Shectman

Hebrew Bible

The institution of marriage, as well as its ramifications and possible consequences such as divorce, is evidenced throughout the Hebrew Bible, although the most extensive data are provided through legal material and the patriarchal narratives. Although many see Genesis 2:24 as presenting the ideal of marriage as between one man and one woman, the passage does not mention the institution per se; the interpretation is mostly grounded in the use of the term *'iššah* with a possessive suffix, suggesting the translation "wife" rather than "woman." The verse, however, is presented as descriptive rather than prescriptive (Trible, 1973), although it does not reflect the sociohistorical reality of biblical marriage: the scenario represented would suggest biblical marriage to be matrilocal, whereas the marriages represented in the Hebrew Bible are mostly patrilineal, patrilocal, and polygynous.

Agency. Within the basic familial institution, the *bet 'ab* ("father's house"), a man had sexual access to and agency over more than one woman in his household, whereas women were not legally allowed agency over their bodies. Women's sexuality was under the legal authority of their father (or occasionally brothers) before marriage and their husband after marriage. This is evidenced by the language of marriage in the Hebrew Bible, where the most common expressions to indicate marriage include verbs such "to give" and "to take," with the wife as an object. Although other terms, such as *ḥtn* (always in the *hithpaʿel*), *nśʾ*, *yšb* (in the *hiphʿil*), and *bʿl*, are occasionally used, they appear to be used only under specific circumstances (Guenther, 2005). Clear examples of a woman's lack of legal agency over her sexuality also appear in the legal material, where a daughter can be sold as a servant by her father but, unlike other servants, cannot leave after seven years. Her owner cannot sell her to a foreigner but can choose to keep her or give her to his son, in which case she will be treated as a daughter and therefore have the right of a wife. If the husband fails to abide by these rules, she will go free without money (Exod 21:7–11). Although it can be said that under the circumstances the woman's rights are preserved, it is clear here, as elsewhere, that whereas the men have choices and agency, women do not.

Polygyny. Throughout the patriarchal narratives, the Hebrew Bible describes many instances of bygynous or polygynous marriages, although not all instances of continued sexual relations of a man with a woman within his household necessarily constitute "marriage." Various Hebrew words are used for women of different status within the household. A man could marry more than one wife (*iššah*), such as Jacob marrying the sisters Leah and Rachel (Gen 29) and Esau marrying multiple women (Gen 26:34; 28:9). A man also could have access to other women within the household, usually described as "concubines." This English term is misleading, since it is used to translate various Hebrew words without elucidating their nuances. In some instances a man had sexual intercourse and possibly children with a household servant, *šipḥah*, who in most cases is described as belonging to the man's wife (*iššah*). Although a *šipḥah* does not only belong to a wife (Gen 29:24, 29), in cases such as the one described for Sarah and Hagar (Gen 16:1–4) as well as the case of Jacob's wives (Gen 30), the wife offers her servant to her husband to procure offspring. Although she gives the *šipḥah* to him to be "his wife," Leviticus 19:20 indicates that a *šipḥah* was not exactly the same as a wife: a man who engages in carnal intercourse (*šikvat zeraʿ*) with a *šipḥah* designated for another

man will be subject to punishment but not the expected capital punishment (Lev 20:20; Deut 22:22), since the woman is not a free woman. Another term for concubine is *pilegeš*, occasionally but not always synonymous with *šipḥah*, as is the case for Bilḥah, who is described with both terms (Gen 29:29; 35:22). Conversely, the *šipḥah* and the *pilegeš* were expected to engage in sexual intercourse with only one man, just as wives, but their roles were clearly secondary and their offspring would not necessarily be entitled to inheritance (Gen 25:6). Given all the above examples, marriage in the Hebrew Bible cannot be described as being between one man and one woman, but instead between a man and all the women sexually available to him in his household. Furthermore, adultery was only punishable in the case in which a man infringed upon another man's wife or concubine, implying that adultery only pertained to the status of a woman. Polygyny and concubinage are also attested in accounts of royal marriages, where the narrators address further considerations such as dynastic succession (as in the case of David and Michal, 1 Sam 18:21) or diplomatic concerns (as in the case of Solomon's marriage to Pharaoh's daughter, 1 Kgs 3:1).

Endogamy. The narratives of the Hebrew Bible most often promote (e.g., Gen 24 and 28) endogamous marriage. Exceptions appear in the patriarchal narratives (e.g., Gen 26:34; 38:2; 41:45) as well as in the narratives about Moses (Exod 2:21; Num 12:1) and Ruth. Some unions are even consanguineous (Gen 20:12; 24:16; 29:12). Exogamy is specifically prohibited in legal codes (Exod 34:16; Num 25:1–9; Deut 7:1–4). In Deuteronomy 23:7–8, however, exceptions are allowed for Edomites and Egyptians, in contrast to Ammonites and Moabites, because of Israel's kinship with Edom and its temporary residence in Egypt. Third-generation children of these marriages could be admitted into the congregation. The prophetic materials and Proverbs reflect a deeply seated distaste for marrying foreigners, particularly women, who are portrayed as responsible for promiscuous sexual practices and idolatrous rites, thereby threatening the religious stability of the people. Whereas the book of Malachi simply makes a pejorative reference to Judah's marriage to the daughter of a "foreign god" (Mal 2:11), the books of Ezra and Nehemiah exhibit a strong abhorrence of exogamous marriages. Various scholars stress the impact of socioeconomic factors in determining the preference for endogamous marriages in different periods of Israelite history, but the language for such justification in the Hebrew Bible is deeply ideological and religious. This negativity culminates in the disturbing expulsion of foreign wives and their children in Ezra 9—10 and the purging of foreign elements in Nehemiah 23:23–31. Most scholars agree that during the Persian period "religious" concerns about exogamy as a temptation to worshiping foreign gods shifted toward a concern for "purity" related to the preservation of the holy seed. For example, the author of the book of Ezra laments that "the holy seed have mingled themselves with the people of the land" (Ezra 9:2).

Virginity. Various passages in the Hebrew Bible express the expectation that a bride be a virgin. The term representing this concept is *betulim*, an abstract variation of the term *betulah*, which, however, does not always mean "virgin" but often simply refers to a young woman of marriageable age. In some instances an expression such as "a man did not know her" is necessary to further clarify the issue (Gen 24:16). A major concern about virginity is the higher brideprice, or *mohar*, that would be paid to her father: for example, in Exodus 22:16–17, a man who seduces an unbethrothed virgin has to pay the *mohar* and make her his wife. Should the father refuse to give her in marriage to the man, the latter would have to pay a *mohar* equal to that of virgins (in Exod 22:28–29 the amount is specified as 50 shekels), presumably because it would be impossible to request it from the husband she would eventually marry.

A bride's virginity could be challenged by the groom, as is envisioned in the case of the "Slandered Bride" (Deut 22:13–21), in which a man "hates" his bride and, in front of the elders, accuses her of not having been a virgin. Since the bride cannot act *sui juris* (although she can be punished), the responsibility of proving her innocence falls on her father, ultimately responsible for her virginity, who should produce a presumably bloodied "cloth" as proof. If the woman is cleared, the accusing husband will be chastised (*ysr*) by the elders, pay a fine of 100 shekels, and marry her without possibility of divorce. However, if her innocence cannot be proven, she shall be stoned to death.

Marriage Preliminaries. Courtship is not often described in the patriarchal narratives, but perhaps a kind of example can be seen in Genesis 24 in the well scene of Rebekah and Abraham's servant. A man may have had a say with regard to the choice of bride, as attested in the narratives where a smitten son asks his parents to give him a specific woman as wife (Gen 34; Judg 14:2). In the majority of cases, marriages were arranged by parents (Gen 27:46—28:2), the father (Gen 38:6), the father through a trusted mediator (Gen 24), or possibly the mother, as in the case of Hagar choosing a wife for Ishmael (Gen 21:21). In this last case, however, it is likely that his removal from the Abrahamic line made his mother, de facto, Ishmael's guardian. This is not uncommon for children of slaves, who are often identified by a matronymic rather than a patronymic (unless the father recognizes or adopts them as his own). Although the narratives attest to the possibility of choice for the groom, the lack of sexual agency makes it impossible from the legal standpoint for a woman to choose her husband. However, a case of assent is possibly detailed in the laconic expression "I will go" from Rebekah in Genesis 24:58. In one specific case, the "rape" of Dinah in Genesis 34, her "going out" may be an instance of a woman voluntarily asserting her sexual agency, yet her choice in this regard seems to be ignored or addressed in a negative tone by the narrator. As elsewhere, regardless of her will, the improper sexual act is registered as an offense against the males in her family. Scholars debate the verb used here (*'nh*, in the *pi''el*), which connotes sexual impurity but not necessarily force (van Wolde, 2002).

Betrothal. A preliminary stage of marriage is represented by the betrothal, which was reached when the brideprice had been paid; this is evidenced by other ancient Near Eastern sources, as well as in the betrothal of David and Michal by the price of 100 foreskins of the Philistines (2 Sam 3:14). The act of betrothal can be represented by the verb *'rš*, where the wife is the object and the brideprice is the means; in this stage a woman already legally belongs sexually to her future husband, as evidenced by the laws regulating other men's access to her (Deut 22:23–27). It is likely that the marriage gift known as *mohar* was, as in other ancient Near Eastern sources, a required condition for the marriage to take place, although it is only attested in a few instances (Gen 34:12; Exod 22:16; 1 Sam 18:25). A form of *mohar*, although not monetary, may be reflected in the seven-year labor offered by Jacob to Laban in Genesis 29.

The evidence is not conclusive about another type of marital gift, the dowry, given to the bride by her paternal family. In some of the instances in which a wife was given a *šiphah*, she may have received her as a dowry even when the term is not specifically attested (Gen 29:29). Betrothal is not always necessary or documented, and in many cases it may have overlapped or coincided with the stage called inchoate marriage. Marriage was presumably marked by a ceremony and the cohabitation of the couple in the patriarchal home. As to the specifics of the ceremony, the evidence is scant. The anointing of the woman, attested in neighboring cultures, may be suggested in Ezekiel 16:9. The possibility of *verba sollemnia* is presumed but not clearly attested.

Divorce. Legal and other texts in the Hebrew Bible indicate that a husband had the right to divorce his wife, apparently with or without a cause. A description and possible instance of divorce is described in Deuteronomy 24:1–4, where a wife falls into her husband's disfavor for some unspecified indecency (literally *'erwah*, "nakedness") and he writes for her a document of *keritut* (a term usually translated as "divorce" and etymologically related to the verb *krt*, "to cut off") and sends her away (*šlḥ*). A woman in possession of such a document could enter into marriage with another man, but if he should divorce her too, she would not be able to return to her previous husband. *Šlḥ* is also used in Deuteronomy 22 to indicate divorce, although in this case cause is not clearly mentioned. Another verb with similar meaning is *grš*, "to cast out," which is the basis of the technical term *gerušah*, meaning *divorcée* (Lev 21:7). The *gerušah* is paired in some instances with the widow (Lev 21:14; Ezek 44:22) as a common category, probably related

to the fact that, since both had belonged to the sexual sphere of a man, there may be restriction to their remarrying (for example, in cases where priestly husbands were involved), or as women whose vow shall stand (Num 30:10) since there is no husband to annul it. Finally, the expulsion of the wives in Ezra 10:3, 13 is expressed through the verb *yṣ'* (in the *hiph'il*), indicating a forced exit. Although in most cases divorce is indicated by a description of separation, the term *śn'*, "to hate," is used occasionally to denote the change of heart of the husband (Deut 22:13) and should also be considered in the vocabulary of divorce (Botta, 2013).

Widowhood. The state of widowhood is complicated by the fact that a widow (*'almanah*), having lost a husband, does not immediately fall under the authority (often described as protection) of a man, particularly if her children have not yet reached adulthood. Although there are various examples of wealthy widows (Judg 17:1–4; 1 Sam 25:2), the Hebrew Bible as well as other ancient Near Eastern sources most often portrays the widow as vulnerable and needy, often in association with the orphan and the poor (Deut 16:14; 24:17; Jer 7:6; 22:3). Failure to provide them justice is seen as evidence of social decay (Isa 10:2). The depiction of the widow as in need of protection, rather than as independent and possibly wealthy, may have been a social strategy to neutralize her, as she deviates from the norm for women, who should always be under the authority of a man in a patriarchal home (van de Toorn, 1995).

Levirate Marriage. Within the context of widowhood, textual evidence illuminates the peculiar practice usually described as levirate marriage (derived from the Latin *levir*, "brother-in-law," which translates the Hebrew *yabam*, literally "husband's brother"). The legal prescription regarding this practice is detailed in Deuteronomy 25:5–10, and a paradigmatic example is found in Genesis 38 and possibly, although debated, in Ruth 4. The Deuteronomy and Genesis sources portray men as reluctant to implement the practice, although ultimately accepting its necessity to address the problem raised by the untimely death of a childless married man, which could result in his name being "blotted out" from Israel (Deut 25:6). To avoid such a dismal fate, one of his brothers would take his wife as his own, avoiding the possibility of her marrying an outsider and assuring that the firstborn shall rise into the name of the deceased. Deuteronomy 25 envisions the possibility of a refusal, which it remedies with the widow performing a public shaming of the reluctant brother in front of the elders, combined with pulling away his shoe and spitting on his face. The narrative in Genesis 38 describes the trials of the widow Tamar who, through no fault of her own, becomes a widow when her husband Er, son of Judah, apparently is "evil in the eyes of the Lord" (Gen 38:7) and dies. Er's brother Onan's reluctance to completely perform his levirate duty results also in his untimely death. Because Judah hesitates to give her in marriage to his third son, who is also his last, even when the time is right, Tamar ultimately tricks Judah into having intercourse with her and thus providing her a child. Her desperate act is ultimately vindicated by the narrative and represents one of the few examples of a woman acting with agency in the sexual sphere. A similar scenario is also present in Genesis 19:31–36, where the desperation of Lot's daughters brings them to have intercourse with their father after having inebriated him to secure progeny and the continuation of his seed. In both instances the narratives ascribe the sexual initiative to the women in violation of incest laws, so that the men, one unaware and the other under a drunken stupor, obtain the desired result, progeny, without guilt. In the case of Ruth 4, although the scenario is not that of levirate marriage, the episode closely reflects the practice as it is described in Deuteronomy 25 and thus is often cited as another example, reflecting the complexity of the practice through time.

Marriage Metaphor. Despite the complex depictions of marriages detailed above, marriage in the Hebrew Bible is generally described by scholars as a covenant between one man and one woman, bridegroom and bride (e.g., Marsman, 2003), although in only one instance is the term *berit* unequivocally associated with marriage (Mal 2:14). This notion is mostly derived from the metaphorical representation of the covenantal relationship of Yahweh with Israel as a marriage. Scholars agree that the language of covenant between Yahweh and Israel finds its an-

tecedents in the suzerain treaties between unequal partners, where the suzerain offers protection in exchange for absolute loyalty. Although echoes of it are represented in the legal materials in the portrayal of Yahweh as a "jealous" deity (Exod 20:5; 34:14), the development of the equation of breaching of the covenantal loyalty in terms of *zonim* (sexual impropriety) is already present in Exodus 34:15 and 16, always attributed to Israel as the unfaithful wife and widely attested in the books of Jeremiah, Isaiah, Hosea, Ezekiel, and Malachi. Certain passages underscore the violent public shaming (Hos 1—3; Jer 2—3; Ezek 16, 23) of Israel as a woman. A number of modern scholars have highlighted the intrinsic problems arising from such violent descriptions and the almost sole focus on the sexuality of the woman. Also troublesome is the notion that this example should be elevated as the ideal of biblical marriage. For the modern reader, it is important to underscore the consequences of the violent descriptive language focusing on female sexuality (e.g., Weems, 1995). It is also difficult to maintain that the prophetic marriage metaphor provides an example of monogamous marriage (with the possible exception of Ezek 23). Although sharing some of the language and a general and unavoidable patriarchal bent, it does not match the vision of marriage as portrayed in the legal material and in the narratives and should not be viewed as a model for the relationship envisioned in human marriages (Frymer-Kensky, 1992).

[*See also* Family Structures, *subentry* Hebrew Bible; Imagery, Gendered, *subentry* Prophetic Literature; *and* Legal Status, *subentry* Hebrew Bible.]

BIBLIOGRAPHY

Bal, Mieke. *Lethal Love: Feminist Literary Readings of Biblical Love Stories*. Bloomington: Indiana University Press, 1987.

Ben Zvi, Ehud. "Observations on the Marital Metaphor of YHWH and Israel in Its Ancient Israelite Context: General Considerations and Particular Images in Hosea 1.2." *Journal for the Study of the Old Testament* 28, no. 3 (2004): 363–384.

Botta, Alejandro F. "Hated by the Gods and Your Spouse: Legal Use of שׂנה in Elephantine and in Ancient Near Eastern Context." In *Law and Religion in the Eastern Mediterranean*, edited by Reinhard G. Kratz and

Anselm C. Hagedorn, pp. 105–127. Oxford: Oxford University Press, 2013.

Frymer-Kensky, Tikva. *In the Wake of the Goddesses: Women, Culture, and the Biblical Transformation of Pagan Myth*. New York: Maxwell Macmillan International, 1992.

Guenther, Allen. "The Typology of Israelite Marriage: Kinship, Socio-economic, and Religious Factors." *Journal for the Study of the Old Testament* 29, no. 4 (2005): 387–407.

Levine, Étan. "Biblical Women's Marital Rights." *Proceedings of the American Academy for Jewish Research* 63 (1997–2001): 87–135.

Marsman, Hennie J. *Women in Ugarit and Israel: Their Social and Religious Position in the Context of the Ancient Near East*. Leiden, The Netherlands, and Boston: Brill, 2003.

Meyers, Carol. *Discovering Eve: Ancient Israelite Women in Context*. Oxford and New York: Oxford University Press, 1988.

Trible, Phyllis. "Eve and Adam: Genesis 2–3 Reread." *Andover Newton Quarterly* 13, no. 4 (1973): 251–258.

Van der Toorn, Karel. "Torn between Vice and Virtue: Stereotypes of the Widow in Israel and Mesopotamia." In *Female Stereotypes in Religious Traditions*, edited by Ria Kloppenborg and Wouter J. Hanegraaff, pp. 1–13. Leiden, The Netherlands: Brill, 1995.

van Wolde, Ellen. "Does *'innâ* Denote Rape? A Semantic Analysis of a Controversial Word." *Vetus Testamentum* 52, no. 4 (2002): 528–544.

Weems, Renita J. *Battered Love: Marriage, Sex, and Violence in the Hebrew Prophets*. Minneapolis: Fortress, 1995.

Annalisa Azzoni

Greek World

As is all the information concerning the Greek world, the sources on marriage and divorce in Greek society and law are incomplete. The data registered in the Linear B tablets concern only the financial and administrative life of the Greek Mycenaean kingdoms, and do not contain information concerning the marriage system of the Greeks who lived in the centuries preceding the period once called the Dark Age of Greece. The oldest data about marriage goes back to the Homeric poems where, at the beginning of *Odyssey*, book 4, we read that a feast was being held in Sparta for Hermione (the daughter of Helen and Menelaus) before her departure for Phthia, where she would become the wife of Achilles's son, to whom Menelaus had betrothed her during the war of Troy. This shows that the Homeric rites were already composed of two ceremonies (as in the following classical times): the promise made by the father of the bride-to-be to the father of the husband-to-be, and the following transfer of the bride into the house of the groom, accompanied by the transfer of "gifts" (*hedna*) from the groom's family to the bride's one.

Starting in the eighth century B.C.E. (luckily much more documented) in the Greek territory, many cities (*poleis*) were born, each of them autonomous and sovereign and each with its own laws, according to the different ethnic origins. Each *polis* was so different from the others that some legal historians prefer to speak of "Greek laws" instead of a "Greek law," a difference that raises a methodological problem concerning the sources. The information about Sparta, the most important and famous Doric city (and Athens's mortal enemy) comes from Athenian authors and is ideologically biased, in some cases in favor of Spartan ideology, organization, and way of life (as Xenophon and Plutarch), and in others against that ideology (as Aristotle). In the case of Gortyn (the other important Cretan Doric polis whose institutions are sufficiently documented), the related sources, although coming from the same city, consist exclusively of a series of legal rules. Because we do not have other documents, it is impossible to know the distance between the law and social ideology and behavior. Athens is the only Greek polis whose matrimonial institutions may be reconstructed with a certain completeness, I will start with the exposition of Athenian marriage laws.

Ionic Cities: Athens. In Athens, the legal age for contracting a valid marriage was twelve years for women and fourteen for men. The choice of the groom was made by the father of the bride-to-be and was decided in many cases when she was much younger. In one of Demosthenes's speeches, for example, the orator's sister was promised to a future husband when she was only five (Demosthenes 27.4 ff.). But even when the bride-to-be was an adult woman (widow or divorced), the choice of her husband was not in her charge. Athenian women were for their entire life under the control of a *kyrios* (guardian), whose powers included the right to decide the terms of their marriage. At birth the *kyrios* was their father; after the father's death a homopatric brother; in case a brother did not exist it was the paternal grandfather or an uncle. Upon marriage the husband became the *kyrios*, and in case of dissolution of the marriage, the rights of the former *kyrios* revived.

Men (who were usually some fifteen years older than their wives) upon reaching the age of majority (eighteen years) were freed from paternal power and legally entitled to choose a bride-to-be (unless, albeit legally free, they still depended economically on their fathers and consequently were dependent on his will).

The moment a woman was promised to a man was called *eggue* or *egguesis* (betrothal). The ceremony consisted in the promise made by the woman's *kyrios* to grant his daughter (or sister, or niece). The presence of the bride at the *eggue*, as well as her consent, were not legally required, and often she was not even aware of the promise. No legal action was considered if the promise was broken. If the marriage did not follow, the only legal consequence was the groom's duty to return the dowry if it had already been handed over. However, the *eggue* was necessary for the existence of the marriage. In other words only a woman who had been *egguetheisa* (promised with an *eggue*) to the man in whose house she was transferred during the wedding ritual had the *status* of a wife (*damar* or *gyne*) and that distinguished a marital cohabitation (indicated as *sunoikein* "live in," "participate in the same household") from concubinage (indicated by the verb *suneinai*, "to be together"). The wedding rituals usually lasted three days. On the first day the bride consecrated her toys to the goddess Artemis and took a ritual bath with the groom in water coming from a sacred source. On the second day, after a nuptial banquet, the woman was *ekdotheisa* (given away) with an act called *ekdosis* ("delivery"), that combined with the earlier *eggue* initiated the conjugal bond. The other rites had no legal value; along with the dowry they were only social indicators of the existence of the marriage. The unique exception to the above quoted rules was the case of the marriage of the *epikleros*, that is the daughter of a man

who died without a male heir. According to Athenian law, this women (ironically called "heiress") could not inherit her father's patrimony but was only the instrument that could transmit the patrimony to a male of the family. Because of this, she was bound to marry *ho eggutata genous*, her nearest kin in the masculine line (usually her paternal uncle). Since official civic records did not exist in Athens, if the heiress were very rich two or more relatives might claim to be entitled to marry her. In this case the decision was made by a judge at the end of a trial called *epidikasia* that, combined with the following *ekdosis*, would give legal effects to the union in the place of the *eggue*.

The offspring born outside of a legitimate union did not have the legitimate status (*gnesioi*). They were considerate *nothoi*, a word usually translated as "bastard," recently at the center of a debate whose solution is tied to the interpretations of a famous decree enacted by Pericles (451–450 B.C.E.). According to this decree (usually quoted as Pericles's citizenship law), citizenship would be granted only to children born from both an Athenian father and an Athenian mother, and not to all the children of an Athenian father, as it had been up to that moment (Aristotle, *Ath. Pol.* 42, 1–2; cf. Aristotle, *Pol.* 1278a 26–34; 131b 8–10). The interpretation of the decree is in fact controversial; some scholars maintain that it implicitly included the prohibition to marry foreigners (a prohibition explicitly expressed in 403 B.C.E., when Pericles's decree was reenacted), while others maintain that Pericles's earlier decree did not include this prohibition. Consequently, according to the second opinion, in the period between 451 and 450 and 403, children born from a legitimate marriage with a foreign woman would have been *nothoi*.

Marriage was forbidden with a direct ancestor or descendant, and between uterine brothers and sisters (born from the same mother), while it was allowed between consanguineous brothers and sisters (born from the same father). In the second half of the eighteenth century and until the second half of the nineteenth century, some scholars considered the prohibition of marriage between uterine siblings as proof of an archaic period of matriarchy, or at least of a matrilineal system in which the children of the same mother could not marry because they belonged to the same family. According to a more recent explanation, the differences in incest taboo were tied to the different economic consequences of marriages between consanguineous and uterine siblings: in the first case the dowry stayed in the family, which did not suffer an economic loss, while in the second the family lost the dowry.

Regarding the relationship between husband and wives, wives were bound to the strictest sexual fidelity, while husbands were allowed to have sexual relations with more than one woman. A famous passage in a speech attributed to Demosthenes describes the three kinds of woman an Athenian man might have: a wife (*damar*) "for the birth of legitimate children"; a concubine (*pallake*) "for the care of the body" (an expression referring to the possibility of having regular sexual relations); and a companion (*hetaira*) "for the pleasure." *Hetairai* were specialized prostitutes, very different from the ones of lower level called *pornai*. They received a professional education that made them more capable of accompanying men on social occasions, such as the banquets (*symposia*) where wives were not admitted, and they entertained their clients with sexual relations that might be more than merely occasional, albeit more than exclusive.

Athenian husbands, then, enjoyed a remarkable sexual liberty, while their wives were strictly bound to be sexually faithful. Wives' infidelity fell under the crime called *moicheia*, usually translated as "adultery," that encompassed any sexual relations between a woman (married or unmarried) and a man who was not her husband. The *moicheia*, then, not only protected the certainty of paternity (as in the case of married women), but more generally the honor of the family offended, as in other ancient and contemporary cultures, by the sexually incorrect behavior of the women of the group. These values were confirmed by the first Athenian law, enacted by Draco in 621–620 B.C.E., that generally prohibited killing for revenge but granted some exceptions such as *phonos dikaios* (legitimate homicide). For example, a man who killed another man caught in his house while having a sexual encounter with his wife, mother, daughter,

sister, or free concubine (i.e., all the women belonging de iure or de facto, as the concubines, to the family group) was granted total impunity. This impunity was still granted in the fourth century B.C.E. when Lysias wrote a speech in defense of a certain Euphiletus who had killed Eratosthenes, his wife's lover, claiming that Euphiletus had killed "lawfully" because, as he said, Eratosthenes "dishonored me and my children, entering my house" (Cantarella, 1976, pp. 131–159).

Adulterers not caught in the act could be prosecuted with a public action (*graphe moicheias*), proposable by any Athenian citizen (Aristotle, *Pol.* 59, 3), which could possibly end with the death penalty. If the adulteress survived, she was prohibited from participating in ceremonies of public cult; if she did not respect the ban, she was punished with a penalty chosen by the person who charged her, with the exclusion of death. In addition, a law quoted in the Pseudo-Demosthenic speech *Against Neaera* (*contra Neaer.*, 87) stated that a husband who had not repudiated his wife prosecuted with a *moichos* was punished with the loss of civic rights (*atimia*).

In Athens both husband and wife could dissolve the marriage. Divorce initiated by the husband was called *apopempsis* (repudiation); divorce initiated by the wife was called *apoleipsis* (abandonment [by the woman] of the conjugal roof). Women, however, were both legally and socially strongly disadvantaged if they initiated the interruption of the marriage. A wife who wanted to abandon the conjugal roof had to record the act in the office of the *archon* (the magistrate in charge of divorces) accompanied by her *kyrios*. In addition, social judgement condemned women who decided to divorce, as denounced in Euripides's tragedy by Medea's famous complaint: a woman is not allowed when and whom to marry. After her father has decided the marriage, she becomes a slave of a man, who has been given a dowry to accept her as a wife. When married, the husband does not lose his freedom: if and when he is tired of staying home, he goes out with a friend; a woman instead, if she decides to divorce her husband, acquires a bad reputation. A marriage could be interrupted with a procedure called *aphaeresis* by a third person, usually the father of the wife, who could do so without the need to obtain the assent of the daughter.

Doric Cities: Sparta. The sources on Sparta, because of their scarcity and the ideological attitude of the authors, need to be treated with the greatest caution. In spite of the impossibility of believing any single fact that they relate, they compose a reliable narrative of the general lines of the related customs and life style.

The customs and the legal rules of the matrimonial system are very different from the Athenian ones because the Dorian cities had different conceptions of the relation between the public and private spheres. According to tradition the first rules concerning this relation are ascribed to Lycurgus, the lawgiver who organized the education system of the Spartiates, the citizens enjoying full rights, also called "the equals" (*homoioi*). This system established that the young Spartiates would be educated by the state, not by the family. Plutarch (*Lives, Life of Lycurgus*, 16) writes that if the newly born male children were found sick or deformed by the elders, they were abandoned on Mount Taygetus; the others, the healthy and strong ones, were assigned a lot of land for their maintenance. When they were seven years old, the Spartiates went to live in groups (*agelai*) under the guidance of an older youth, learning to face every type of difficulty, in order to become the best of soldiers. When they were twenty years old, they became *eirenes* and started, in their turn, to train the younger boys for war. In Sparta, Plutarch observes, the sons "were not private possession of fathers, but common possession of the state" (Plut. *Lyc.*, 15, 8); Xenophon adds that in the other *poleis* each father exercised control over his children. Lycurgus instead gave to every man the authority over his sons and over the sons of others (Xen. *Lac. Pol.* 6, 1).

Equally strong were the powers of the state over the conjugal life of the Spartiates: in the first instance, marriage was obligatory, and those who did not marry were punished by *atimia* (Plut, *Lyc.*, 15, 1–2). Husbands, upon reaching the age of thirty and until sixty years (the age in which military obligations ceased), were bound to participate every night in the *syssitia*, common banquets reserved for men. According to Xenophon (Xen., *Lac. Pol.*, 14, Lycurgus imposed restrictions also on young couples'

sexual life, because he thought that sons conceived during passionate sexual intercourse were stronger than those born from a non-passionate marital lovemaking routine. To increase matrimonial sexual desire, Plutarch writes that the husband had to leave his wife after the wedding and then participate in a common banquet before going back home and making love to his wife (Plut., *Lyc.* 15, 3–5).

An interesting feature of the Spartan marriage (and a further proof of the prevalence of city interests over familial ones) was the custom of trading wives, in order to beget the maximum number of children. In a passage of the *Lives of Lycurgus and Numa* (*Lyc. Numa*, 3, 1) Plutarch writes that both these lawgivers

> with a healthy politics convinced the husbands to liberate themselves from egotistic jealousy. Nevertheless their methods were not the same: if a Roman husband had a sufficient number of sons, another that did not have children could convince him to give him his wife for good or only for a season; a Spartan husband instead could consent to sharing his wife with another man, while his wife remained in his house and the marriage maintained its rights and its original duties.

Scholarship has often challenged the reliability of this information as far as the Roman matrimonial customs are concerned, but its reliability as far as Sparta is concerned is confirmed by Xenophon (Xen. *Lac. Pol.* 1, 2–10 and Plut. *Lyc.*, 15, 6–8) and is today commonly acknowledged as a historical fact (see Lacey, 1968, 199; Thomas, 1986). Plutarch claims that in Sparta adultery or sexual violence did not exist (*Lyc.* 15, 9–10), but he could simply mean that laws on these matters did not exist. The sources concerning Spartan life cannot be read critically, but beyond the details that clearly seem to reflect an idealized reality (such as the rules dictating the state control, as in the details, on the wedding night), they are sufficient to give a picture of the relations between public and private spheres and of the familial organization.

Gortyn. The so-called Great Epigraph, known as the *Law Code of Gortyn*, is a document of extraordinary importance and interest; it enables us to reconstruct in an organic way the normative system of a polis. The information contained in this document concerning marriage and divorce is particularly interesting because it shows, on one side, the analogies with the Ionic poleis that allow us to speak of a common basic "Greek" legal identity; on the other side, it shows the peculiarities of the Gortynian system.

Among the peculiarities, one is unique, even among the other Dorian cities. In Gortyn marriage was permitted not only between free persons but also between free people and slaves (*douloi* or *oikeis*, apparently without distinction), and between two slave persons.

Marriage between a free and a slave person was allowed, according to Col. 6, 55–7, 10 of the Code, but only if the free person were the woman: "If the slave going to the free woman marries her, free are to be the children. If the free woman goes to the slave, slaves are to be the children. If from the same mother free and slave children are born, if the mother dies, if there is property, the free are to have it, but if there be not free, those with a claim (*epiballontes*) are to take it over." What kind of free woman would decide to go live with a slave, bearing slave children? Could she decide to marry without the permission of her family? How would her family accept a slave as husband of one of the group? And why would the owner of a slave man allow him to leave and move to the house of a free woman? Besides losing the services of the slave, he would lose the property of his children, who would be freeborn. It has been suggested that the free woman was the *patroiochos*, the Gortynian equivalent of the Athenian *epikleros* (and of the Spartan *patroukos*). In contrast to the Athenian "heiress," the Gortynian one was not bound to marry the closest relative. She was a single woman relatively free from family constraints, who perhaps could make (for love?) some life choices otherwise inconceivable. But this is only a speculation.

As far as marriage between free persons, the law recognized the capacity to contract it with women at age twelve, and with men upon reaching puberty (12, 17–19). The marriage rites are unknown: the law code does not mention them but simply indicates a legitimate union with the verb *opuein* for men and *opuesthai* in the middle voice for women. Children born from a matrimonial union had the status of legitimate children (*gnesioi*) if the father accepted them into the family, exactly as in Athens. Besides these similarities, in Gortyn (where women were economically more empowered than in Athens) the relationship between husband and wife was different than in Athens. In Gortyn, if a woman gave birth to a son after divorce, she had to present the newborn to the house of the former husband, who could decide whether to accept him in the family. If he refused, the former wife had the power to decide to bring him up or to abandon him to his fate (3, 44–52). This complex of rules clearly shows that wives, in Gortyn, enjoyed with their husbands relationships if not egalitarian then at least not as subordinated as those of the Athenian ones.

[*See also* Children, *subentry* Greek World; Legal Status, *subentry* Roman World; *and* Sexual Transgression, *subentry* Greek World.]

BIBLIOGRAPHY

Cantarella, E. *Studi sull' omicidio in diritto greco e romano*. Milan: Giuffrè, 1976.

Cantarella, E. *Pandora's Daughters: The Role and Status of Women in Greek and Roman Antiquity*. Translated by M. Fant. Baltimore and London: Johns Hopkins University Press, 1993.

Cantarella, E. "Gender, Sexuality, and Law." In *The Cambridge Companion to Ancient Greek Law*, edited by Michael Gagarin and David Cohen, pp. 236–254. Cambridge, U.K.: Cambridge University Press, 2005.

Carey, C. "Rape and Adultery in Athenian Law." *Classical Quarterly* 45, no. 2 (1995): 407–417.

Carlier, P. "Observations sur le nothoi." In *L' Etranger dans le Mond Grec*, II (Actes Deuxieme Colloque sur l' Etranger), edited by R. Lonis, pp. 107–125. Nancy, France: Presses Universitaires de Nancy, 1992.

Gagarin, M. "The Economic Status of Women in the Gortyn Code: Retroactivity and Change." *Symposion* (1993): 61–71.

Hansen, M. H. *Polis: An Introduction to the Ancient Greek City-State*. Oxford: Oxford University Press, 2006.

Harrison, A. R. W. *The Law of Athens*. Vol. 1: *The Family and Property*. Oxford: Clarendon, 1968.

Karabelias. E. *L'epiklerat attique*. Athens, Greece: Academie d'Athenes, 2002.

Lacey, W. K. *The Family in Classical Greece*. London: Thames and Hudson, 1968.

MacDowell, D. M. *The Law in Classical Athens*. London: Thames and Hudson, 1978.

Modzejewski, J. "La structure juridique du mariage grec." In *Scritti in onore di Orsolima Montevecchi*, pp. 221–268. Bologna, Italy: CLUEB Editrice, 1981.

Patterson, C. *The Family in Greek History*. Cambridge, Mass.: Harvard University Press, 1998.

Thomas, Y. "'Le ventre': Corps maternel, droit paternel." *Le genre humain* 14 (1986): 211–236.

Eva Cantarella

Roman World

In comparison to modern romantic ideals, the Romans had a utilitarian approach to marriage and divorce, especially in the noble families for whom evidence is most abundant. The purpose of a marriage was widely considered to be the production of children. Indeed, the etymology of the Latin word for marriage, *matrimonium*, literally means to "lead a woman into motherhood." Legitimate children were considered an obligation that the couple owed to their families in order to ensure the legitimate transfer of property from one generation to the next. At least among the nobility, family members and friends scrutinized potential brides and grooms with an eye to the family's political, social, and financial advantage. These considerations demonstrate that the choice of partner, the bond of marriage, and even its dissolution were often dominated by family interests. Though genuine affection between couples came to be a sentimental ideal in the late republic, demographic studies have shown that in elite circles, men and women could expect several marriages in their lifetimes, often created and dissolved for reasons that had little to do with romantic attachment. The familial manipulation of marriages and divorces for political and dynastic advantage is nowhere more visible than in the imperial households.

Type of Evidence. There are three main types of evidence for marriage and divorce in Rome: literary, legal, and epigraphic. Each type of evidence presents challenges for scholars who interpret them. Descriptions of marriage, divorce, and weddings appear in many different genres from the middle republic to late empire, in Greek and Latin sources. The demands of the genre often dictate the depictions of weddings; *epithalamia* ("wedding songs"), for instance, cast the bride, groom, wedding, and marriage in rosy hues while historians or orators may denigrate the same scene as incestuous or unnatural. Literary authors have specific agendas and the evidence culled from these works must be treated with an eye to the rhetoric they employ.

Many scholars see law codes or jurists' interpretations of law as a useful corrective to the problems inherent with literary evidence. Legal evidence, however, is also problematic. Although seemingly abundant, legal evidence is chronologically spotty. The speeches and dialogues of Cicero are our best legal sources for the republican period, while legal handbooks date from the late empire (namely, the *Institutes* of Gaius [second century C.E.], and the *Rules of Ulpian* and *Opinions of Paul* [fourth century C.E.]). In the sixth century C.E., Justinian I commissioned the *Digest*, a massive collection of legal opinions from second- and third-century Roman jurists. The jurists' love for theoretical legal issues makes it difficult for family scholars to distinguish whether a case was constructed as an intellectual exercise or a reflection of a real case with real litigants. Likewise, it is often unclear whether the laws that jurists discuss are descriptive of legal precedents or proscriptive.

Since the 1980s some scholars of the Roman family have turned to epigraphic evidence in funerary contexts, especially tombs and altars, in an attempt to address questions of demography. Though these studies have met with some success, the accidental nature of surviving inscriptions and the suspicion that the sample size is unrepresentative necessarily mean that the conclusions are hesitant and often problematic.

The Age at Roman Marriage. Modern scholars are divided concerning the ages at which men and women undertook their first marriages. In the late republic, the legal age for women to marry was twelve, fourteen for boys. Using the epigraphic evidence on tombstones, Richard P. Saller (1987) suggested that men married in their mid- to late twenties, though senatorial men married slightly younger, in their early twenties. Using literary evidence, however, Lelis Percy, and Verstraete placed the first marriage for men in their early to mid-twenties, with senatorial men marrying earlier still, between sixteen and twenty. In the wake of Saller, Brent D. Shaw (1987) employed epitaphs to conclude that girls married in their late teens, while Lelis, Percy, and Verstraete insisted that evidence pointed toward women, especially senatorial women, marrying between twelve and sixteen years old. Both assessments emerge, however, from evidence produced by or about the nobility or the relatively wealthy since they were both the subject of literature and most likely to erect tomb inscriptions. Our knowledge of the age at which lower class men and women married is even more sketchy and impressionistic.

Arrangements and Negotiations. Among the nobility, parents, guardians, or friends often arranged engagements after protracted examinations of potential partners that might well include endorsements of individuals by family friends and even negotiations concerning the transfer or maintenance of family property. Negotiations often took place between men, but evidence shows that women (usually mothers or aunts, less commonly prospective brides) sometimes influenced the choice of partners and the terms of the marriage. If the groom were under his own legal power (*sui iuris*) he theoretically had more control over whom he courted, but if not, both he and his bride were expected to accept the mate chosen by their families. Though authors vary in their list of the most desirable traits in a bride or a groom, the qualities change little over the centuries of Rome's empire. In the seventh century C.E., Isadore of Seville listed some of the more common ideal qualities in a groom: manliness or courage (*virtus*), high birth (*genus*), good looks (*pulchritudo*), and pleasant speech (*oratio*), whereas women ought to possess beauty, family, wealth (*divitiae*), and good character (*mores*, i.e., she should be chaste). A formal engagement or betrothal (*sponsalia*) was agreed on by two men, one of whom was the prospective bride's *paterfamilias*, or guardian, whose permission was required for anyone in his household to enter a legal or financial contract, including marriage. Some ancient jurists opined that a *paterfamilias* had the right to compel his child into an unwanted marriage, but nearly all agreed that the father had

an obligation to find a suitable match. The *sponsalia* was a legally binding agreement that could be dissolved with a *repudium*, a verbal or written notice terminating the engagement.

One of the terms of the betrothal negotiations, at least into the late republic, was the question of whether the marriage would be *sine manu* or *cum manu*. (This is not ancient terminology but modern clarifications of longer Latin periphrases concerning the presence or absence of *manus* in marriage.) The oldest forms of marriage, and those most closely associated with the passing down of elite priesthoods, required a *cum manu* marriage. In this schema, a woman left the *potestas* or power of her own *paterfamilias* when she entered into her husband's home and thus became the ward of her husband, or her husband's *paterfamilias*. In relinquishing a daughter *cum manu*, the family surrendered to her husband's family the right to any property the bride owned. Though this form of marriage was required to hold certain priesthoods, its obvious disadvantages for families with economic and political aspirations caused its popularity to fade in the late republic.

In *sine manu* marriages, the bride would continue to be under the control (*patria potestas*) of her own father or *paterfamilias*, which also demanded that if a dissolution of the marriage were to occur either due to death or divorce, the dowry of the bride and her possessions would be returned to her *paterfamilias*. Because marriage involved the transfer of a woman into her husband's home, any children produced from a marriage would remain with the father or his family in case of divorce or death. His children would in turn be subject to their father's *patria potestas*, under which they would remain until he died or emancipated them. For this reason, any children from a marriage would thus stay with their father and his family. If marriages did not produce children or meet familial expectations, the *paterfamilias* had the power to initiate a couple's divorce, even without the consent of his child. Likewise, though ancient jurists insist that the consent of both the bride and groom was required to form a legal union, a bride's *paterfamilias* outweighed his daughter's objection, or at least was an acceptable substitute for her consent if she were to remain silent.

Marriage Rituals. There appears to have been no particular set of religious, political, or social rituals that were demanded in order to bind a couple together. Wedding ceremonies varied considerably in terms of pomp and circumstance, the timing of delivering the bride to the groom's household, or the involvement of priestly figures. The one constant was the veiling of the bride and some sort of public pronouncement of the union. This pronouncement could be as simple as publicly escorting the veiled bride through the streets so that the community could witness the union. Ulpian famously noted that all that was required to consider a marriage intact was the *affectio maritalis* (a desire to be married) between bride and groom (*Digest* 24.1.32.13). One must exercise caution in applying this notion too broadly, however. Ulpian's larger questions concern whether a man and woman were still considered married despite a long separation. To what extent one may apply his pronouncement to the initiation of marriages remains an open question.

Types of Legally Recognized Unions. There were several types of unions that were recognized by Roman jurists, characterized by the social status, citizenship, and the legal emancipation of the bride and groom. *Matrimonium iustum* or *nuptiae iustae* endowed automatic legitimacy upon the couple's children and thus guaranteed them security in the transfer of their father's name, status, and family property. This privilege, however, subjected the descendants to the *patria potestas* of the *paterfamilias*. Since this type of marriage provided the most secure path for inheritance, it also had the most legal requirements. According to Ulpian, both bride and groom had to be Roman citizens, meet the minimum age and physical requirements, and be able to consent to the union (*Digest* 5.2). The consent of the *paterfamilias* was also required should either the bride or groom be under his power, regardless of their ages. The prospective couple should be no more closely related than within six degrees (i.e., second cousins could not marry). But exceptions to each of these rules abound. As seen previously, some jurists considered the consent of a *paterfamilias* sufficient for a non-emancipated youth to be married—no need to consult the bride or groom. Non-citizens sometimes received *conubium*, the right to marry a Roman citizen and once granted, it allowed them to enter into a *matrimonium iustum*. Likewise, the age limit could be circumvented if the girl were physically mature. Additional conditions came to be required in order to be married under this most legitimate form of marriage, especially with Augustan legislation. For instance, certain professions were dubbed socially unrespectable and thus it was forbidden for senatorial ranks to marry gladiators, pimps, prostitutes, actors, and undertakers. Senatorial elites were likewise forbidden to marry freedmen.

However, there were other types of legally recognized unions, especially the *concubinatus* and the *contubernium*. The definition of *concubinatus* is not altogether clear, but it seems to have been a union in which one or both members of the couple lacked Roman citizenship or the right to marry a citizen (*conubium*). This does not mean, however, that *concubinatus* was necessarily considered socially inferior to *matrimonium iustum*. By contrast, *contubernium* was a committed relationship either between a master and his slave or between freed slaves. Strikingly, couples entering into less privileged unions than the *matrimonium iustum* often mimicked elements of that ceremony, especially in terms of bridal costume, and they employed the same marriage vocabulary such as "spouse" or "wife" in funerary epitaphs as did those who enjoyed *matrimonium iustum*.

Dissolution of Marriage. Dissolution of marriages was common in ancient Rome due to divorce or death. Because personal law governed marriage and divorce, neither required state authorization. A statement of divorce (*repudium*) required no particular verbal formulation and could be delivered verbally or in writing. In some instances, a divorce was recognized even without a *repudium*, especially if the erstwhile husband remarried. In the early days of the republic, only men could divorce their wives unilaterally. If the wife had participated in extramarital affairs or otherwise misbehaved, the husband was entitled to keep a portion of her property; likewise, if the husband divorced a worthy and well-behaved wife, the husband might be required to return the dowry in within a very short and thus inconvenient timeframe.

Roman women did not earn the right to unilateral divorce until the first century C.E. In the republic, punishments for a woman's infidelities or other breaches of the marriage contract were meted out by the *paterfamilias* in consultation with family councils. These family councils often comprised senior male and female members of the family, and the punishments varied considerably up to and including death. Augustan marriage legislation criminalized infidelity, however, removing these decisions from family councils and locating them instead in the praetor's court.

The rate of divorce continues to be a matter of scholarly interest, though compelling statistics are lacking. The same demographic and epigraphic evidence is used to support scholarly arguments both for and against the frequency of divorce. The sentimental ideal, however, of a *univira*, literally a "one-man woman," loomed large in the Roman imagination. Only *univirae* were eligible to hold certain religious offices, and they were lauded in funerary epitaphs and literature for their idealized loyalty, devotion, and chastity.

Assessment. Although much information about Roman marriage and divorce is generalizable, the procedural and social parameters varied widely over time and space, often accompanying major political and social change. Customs of marriage and divorce in the provinces sometimes differed significantly from the descriptions given above, for example. For the majority of Roman rule over the Mediterranean, subject peoples were allowed to retain local traditions in legal and social institutions unless they proved to be somehow politically subversive or destabilizing. Thus, relationships that were considered taboo in Rome, such as brother–sister unions, were nonetheless legal among non-elites and soldiers in Egypt. In areas culturally dominated by Rome, however, some important watershed moments stand out in the legal history of Roman marriage and divorce. These largely concern the rights of inheritance, eligibility for marriage, and redefinitions of citizenship and moral norms. Among the most important are the Twelve Tables (mid-fifth century C.E.), the Licinian reforms (fourth century C.E.), Augustan marriage legislation (first century B.C.E. and C.E.), and Severan laws on the military and citizenship (third century C.E.). Scholars continue to disagree about the extent to which marriage and divorce changed under Christian emperors, though it is clear that unilateral "no fault" divorce for women was rescinded after Constantine's ascension (fourth century C.E.). It is wise to consider these changes, however, in terms of a continuum rather than an abrupt break from tradition.

[*See also* Children, *subentry* Roman World; Family Structures, *subentries on* New Testament *and* Roman World; Legal Status, *subentry* Roman World; *and* Marriage and Divorce, *subentries on* Early Church, Greek World, *and* New Testament.]

BIBLIOGRAPHY

Arjava, Antti. *Women and Law in Late Antiquity.* New York: Oxford University Press, 1996.

Frier, Bruce Woodward, and Thomas A. J. McGinn. *A Casebook on Roman Family Law.* New York: Oxford University Press, 2004.

Gardner, Jane F. *Family and Familia in Roman Law and Life.* Oxford: Clarendon, 1998.

Grubbs, Judith Evans. "'Pagan' and 'Christian' Marriage: The State of the Question." *Journal of Early Christian Studies* 2.4 (1994): 361–412.

Hersch, Karen K. *The Roman Wedding: Ritual and Meaning in Antiquity.* New York: Cambridge University Press, 2010.

Phang, Sara E. *The Marriage of Roman Soldiers (13 B.C.– A.D. 235): Law and Family in the Imperial Army.* Columbia Studies in the Classical Tradition 24. Boston: Brill, 2001.

Rawson, Beryl. *Marriage, Divorce and Children in Ancient Rome.* Oxford: Clarendon, 1991.

Saller, Richard P. "Men's Age at Marriage and Its Consequences in the Roman Family." *Classical Philology* 82.1 (1987): 21–34.

Shaw, Brent D. "The Age of Roman Girls at Marriage: Some Reconsiderations." *Journal of Roman Studies* 77 (1987): 30–46.

Treggiari, Susan. "Divorce Roman Style: How Easy and How Frequent Was It?" In *Marriage, Divorce, and Children in Ancient Rome*, edited by Beryl Rawson, pp. 31–46. New York: Oxford University Press, 1991.

Treggiari, Susan. *Roman Marriage: "Iusti Coniuges" from the Time of Cicero to the Time of Ulpian*. Oxford: Clarendon, 1991.

Julie Langford

New Testament

Christianity emerged at a time when Augustus's legal measures and Roman moral discourse had made marriage, divorce, adultery, illicit sex, and child-rearing central topics in imperial politics (Severy, 2003; Milnor, 2005). Yet the earliest Christian texts supply little in the way of explicit directives or reflection on marriage. References to marriage in the New Testament fall into three categories: strictures on divorce, remarriage, and sexual asceticism; directives to wife and husband in the household codes; and metaphorical uses of marriage and weddings.

Some interpretive problems require preliminary attention. Greek commonly uses the same words for "man" and "husband" (*anēr*), and for "woman" and "wife" (*gunē*). Therefore, the exact status of a partner is not always clear, and early communities are likely to have included slaves, some freedpersons, non-citizens, and others whose unions lacked some or all legal or social protections. Thus, when Paul condemns the man who has sex with his father's *gunē*, the woman in question may be his father's (second) wife, his concubine, or his slave (1 Cor 5:1–11). The use of euphemisms introduces further ambiguities. For instance, when Paul declares it God's will that "each one of you possess his own vessel in holiness and honor" (1 Thess 4:4, lit.), it could mean "control his sexual member" (NRSV) or "acquire his own wife" (Yarbrough, 1986, pp. 68–76).

Divorce and Remarriage. The first group of texts addresses the issue of divorce and remarriage, and their contexts suggest ambitions of renouncing sex and the family. This section will treat the texts in roughly chronological order, beginning from the un-disputed letters of Paul as the earliest texts in the New Testament, and then treating the Gospel of Mark and its interpretation by Matthew and Luke.

Undisputed Pauline letters. In two consecutive and interrelated sections of 1 Corinthians, Paul discusses issues that appear to have been raised by the Corinthians. In 1 Corinthians 7:1, Paul cites, from an earlier letter he received, a principle he seems to share: "Concerning what you have written: 'it is good for a person [*anthrōpōi*] not to touch a woman'"—that is, it is good to abstain from sex. In 1 Corinthians 7:25–40, he addresses the issue of whether a man should marry "his virgin."

Paul's response to the praise of celibacy is ambivalent; he first insists that the danger of "fornication" (*porneia*) requires that everyone has his or her own spouse, and have sex (1 Cor 7:2–4), allowing only for occasional, mutually agreed abstinence for prayer (1 Cor 7:5–6). The affirmation of sex and marriage as an antidote to immorality may have been Paul's standard counsel, if 1 Thessalonians 4:4 is rightly translated: "that each one of you know how to obtain a wife in holiness and honor." This androcentric articulation of marital morality differs from 1 Corinthians 7:2–4, where Paul takes pains to counsel women on the same terms as men. After acknowledging his own preference for celibacy (1 Cor 7:7), Paul recommends continued celibacy to "unmarried men and widows" (1 Cor 7:8–9). He then commands "a woman not to separate from her husband, and if she does to remain unmarried or to be reconciled to her husband." Correspondingly, a man is told "not to leave a wife." It is unclear whether the alternatives of celibacy or reconciliation that Paul stipulates for a woman who separates from her husband also apply to a man leaving his wife. Attributed to "the Lord," this command is widely connected to Mark 10:10–12 and Matthew 19:9 and identified as a tradition from the historical Jesus, but Paul may also have received this "command of the Lord" through the prophetic activity he promotes in 1 Corinthians 14 (D'Angelo, 1990a, pp. 86–94).

Paul proceeds to both affirm and modify the command in the case of an unbelieving partner, again attending to both partners (1 Cor 7:12–16). His counsel depends on the will of the unbelieving partner:

if the unbeliever wishes to separate, the brother or sister "is not enslaved" (*ou dedoulōtai*). The verb used here is significant for Paul's understanding of sex and marriage, which, to him, enable the partner to exercise power or dominion (*exousiazei*, 1 Cor 7:4) over one's body. Paul will not submit to dominion (*ouk exousiasthēsomai*, 1 Cor 6:12) from anyone or anything. Marriage is a form of bondage for both a man (1 Cor 7:27) and a woman (1 Cor 7:39). To be unmarried or released from marriage is analogous to emancipation from slavery (1 Cor 7:21–24, 27, 39). Even so, for Paul marital bondage seems more closely associated with women (1 Cor 7:39; Rom 7:1–6), not only submitting them to the distractions of the world whose form is passing away (1 Cor 7:31), but also hindering them from being "holy in both body and spirit" (1 Cor 7:34). For Paul and the Corinthians, the ambition of freedom may derive not only from prudence in the face of "the impending necessity" (1 Cor 7:26) and the conviction that sex and marriage belong to a world that is passing away (1 Cor 7:29–31) but also from a popularized version of Stoicism's ambition of extirpating the passions. Philo also manifests veneration for sexual abstinence (*De vita contemplativa* 18–20, 30–32, 67–68).

While Paul addressed both men and women in regard to ending a marriage for celibacy, his treatment of a virgin—a girl, apparently betrothed, who had never been married—differs. In 1 Corinthians 7:25–38 he assumes that the decision to marry rests entirely with the man, interrogating his male interlocutor and reassuring him that neither he nor the virgin sins if they marry (1 Cor 7:27). In contrast, he declares that a widow is free to marry whomever she wishes, "but in the Lord" (1 Cor 7:39–40). Marriage frequently constituted a passage to adulthood for women in antiquity, who typically first married between the legal age (twelve) and twenty. Adult women, especially widows, could often arrange their own lives.

Paul's counsel to marry "in the Lord" and his observation that marriage "sanctifies" the unbelieving partner and produces "holy" children suggest that marriage played a role in communal identity. The greetings in Romans name male/female pairs as missionary partners: Prisca and Aquila, Junia and

Andronicus, Rufus and his mother, Philologus and Julia, and Nereas and his "sister" (Rom 16:3–5, 7), as well as one pair of two women and another of two men (Rom 16:9, 12; see D'Angelo, 1990b). Clearly not all of these pairs are husband and wife, although they have usually been interpreted as marriages, in part because Acts 18:2 names Prisca ("Priscilla") as Aquila's wife. The reference to a sister-woman in 1 Corinthians 9:4 is usually read as "wife." Paul's observation that the unmarried woman is concerned only with "how to be holy in body and soul" stands in some tension with this development. Paul's strictures on divorce betray some sense of pragmatic considerations, as divorce from a reluctant partner, especially followed by remarriage, was likely to attract suspicion and hostility that could fall on the community, particularly if the first partner was an unbeliever and the new partner was "in the Lord."

Gospels. Divorce and remarriage seem to become an issue in the Gospels partly to curb rejection of marriage. Mark 10:2–12, in which Jesus repudiates divorce and remarriage, consists of two scenes, a public debate initiated by "Pharisees" (Mark 10:2–9) and a private exchange with the disciples (Mark 10:10–12). First the interlocutors test Jesus, asking whether it is permitted for a husband to dismiss a wife; when they offer Deuteronomy 24:1–4 as a warrant for divorce, Jesus overrides Moses's permission by reading Genesis 1:27 and 2:24 as expressing an original intention for a permanent bond. The private teaching identifies remarriage after divorce as adultery, whether for a man or a woman. Mark 10:2–12 and 13–16, in which he welcomes little children (*paidia*), serve to limit the radical demand to leave all and follow Jesus in Mark 10:17–31: disciples may leave "houses and brothers and sisters and parents and [grown] children [*tekna*] and fields" but not a spouse or little children (D'Angelo, 2010). These sayings modify the call to itinerant preaching and protect against the anti-familial character of some of the other sayings (e.g., Mark 3:31–35; Matt 8:19–22//Luke 9:57–60; Matt 10:37//Luke 14:25–27).

While affirming marriage as ordained at the creation, Mark, like Paul, sees marriage as belonging to the transient order. When the Sadducees question

Jesus about the ultimate partner of a hypothetical woman who underwent levirate marriages to seven successive husbands, he responds that marriage will have no place in the resurrection, "when they will be like the angels in heaven" (Mark 12:25; cf. Matt 22:30). In 6:15–17 Mark attributes the arrest of John the Baptist to his challenge to Antipas's marriage to his brother Philip's wife, but the issue there seems to be forbidden relations rather than divorce (Loader, 2005).

Matthew also excludes marriage from the angelic life of the resurrection (Matt 20:23–33); counsels on divorce and remarriage are integrated into emerging ascetic ambitions. Matthew 19:2–12 revises the form and content of Mark 10:2–12, dropping the distinction of public and private scenes and clarifying the Pharisees' question and Jesus's exegesis (Matt 19:3–8). The case of a woman who divorces disappears, and "except on account of fornication" is added to the pronouncement that a man who divorces and remarries commits adultery (Matt 19:9). For Jesus's disciples, the prohibition of remarriage suggests that it would be better not to marry (Matt 19:10). Jesus affirms this observation, for those "to whom it is given," describing them as having "made themselves eunuchs for heaven's reign" (Matt 19:11–12).

The prohibition of remarriage also appears in the Sermon on the Mount; Jesus offers "greater justice" by revising Deuteronomy 24:1 with the pronouncement that "one who divorces his wife, except for fornication, makes her an adulterer, and one who marries a divorced woman commits adultery" (Matt 5:31–32). The preceding antithesis reinterprets "You shall not commit adultery" by reapplying warnings against apostasy from Mark 9:43–48 to lust, creating a sexual discipline (Matt 5:27–29). These counsels are addressed only to men.

Matthew's exception for fornication (*porneia*) might refer to forbidden relations, as is the case in John the Baptist's objection to Herod's marriage (Matt 14:3–14). However, the author probably views divorcing a wife for a sexual offense as an imperative, consonant with the Roman legal requirement that a husband divorce an adulterous or suspect wife. Joseph is characterized as "just" in feeling obligated to divorce Mary and avoid disgracing her (Matt 1:19).

Ascetic concerns also impact Luke–Acts. Jesus's response to the Sadducees implies that not only in the future but even now "those made worthy to attain that age and the resurrection of the dead do not marry nor are they given in marriage" (Luke 20:35). Although the prohibition of divorce makes no appearance, Luke does provide a version of the saying that identifies remarriage with adultery (Luke 16:18). "A wife" (but not a husband) is now among those that one may leave for God's reign (Luke 18:29). Despite the androcentric articulations of these ideals, Luke–Acts credits sexual abstinence to women, at least in the case of Anna (Luke 2:36–38) and the prophetic virgin daughters of Philip (Acts 21:9).

Behind Paul and the Gospels. Scholarly discussions of these prohibitions of divorce and remarriage tend to explain them as originating with Jesus—in part on the grounds that a prohibition of divorce and remarriage is attributed to Jesus, and in part on grounds of multiple attestation (1 Cor 7:9–10; Mark 10:11–12; and Matt 5:32//Luke 16:18). Scholars evoke passages from the Dead Sea Scrolls as testimony that another Jewish sectarian movement rejected divorce and offers a precedent for Jesus's prohibition. On the other hand, it is not clear that the *Damascus Document* refers to divorce; it enjoins monogamy on the basis of Genesis 1:27, but lacks reference to Deuteronomy 24:1 (CD 4.20–5.1). The *Temple Scroll* requires monogamy of the king (11QT 56:17–19). Furthermore, the case for multiple attestation is not as certain as is usually supposed. Matthew 5:32 and Luke 16:18 do not differ consistently enough from Mark 10:11–12 to definitively indicate derivation from Q. The form and vocabulary of 1 Corinthians 7:9–10 differ from the Synoptic sayings, and the claim that remarriage is adultery is lacking.

Scholars also disagree on the marital status of Jesus. Some claim that no first-century Jewish male would have been unmarried at "about thirty" (Luke 3:23), while others read antifamilial and ascetic sayings as evidence of Jesus's celibacy. The canonical Gospels give no information on whether or not Jesus married. The *Gospel of Philip* (second/third century refers to Mary Magdalene as Jesus's companion (*koinōnos*, 59.8–9, 63.34) and celebrates marriage as a *mysterion* (64.31–35), but the significance of these references is unclear.

Some scholars have suggested that Jesus prohibited divorce to protect women, or to equalize their status, on the mistaken view that Jewish women were not allowed to initiate a divorce in this period. Elisabeth Schüssler Fiorenza offers a more comprehensive liberationist view in proposing that Mark 10:2–12 attested an end to patriarchal marriage in the Jesus movement. She further argues that Galatians 3:28 proclaimed an end of patriarchal marriage among Paul's contemporaries (Schüssler Fiorenza, 1983). Such claims illuminate the comprehensive nature of problem. Gender roles and marriage have been mutually defining; without radical revision of gender expectations equal to "the end of patriarchal marriage," both divorce and its unavailability disadvantage women.

House Churches and Household Codes. Evidence suggests that early Christians met in and were organized around households or similar groupings. Missionary partners like Prisca and Aquila, Tryphaena and Tryphosa (Rom 16:3–5, 12),; individuals like Philemon (Phlm 1) and Nympha (Col 4:15); and groups like Philologus and Julia, Nereas and his "sister," and Olympas hosted these small assemblies, possibly in their own living space. Enhanced by the use of familial language and imagery, household settings appear to have combined with the role of the Roman *matrona* to enable some form of women's leadership in the communities (Osiek and MacDonald, 2006).

This household base, together with occasional conflicts with the empire (Pliny, *Letters* 10.94–95) and a desire for respect from "those outside," bestowed moral weight on good behavior according to one's role. Early Christians drew on philosophical treatments of "household management," producing a subgenre of moral exhortation referred to as "household codes" (Balch, 1981). The most stylized are those of the deutero-Pauline letters Colossians (3:18—4:1) and Ephesians (5:21—6:9), which prescribe appropriate asymmetrical relations between the

paterfamilias (husband, father, owner) and his subjects (wife, children, slaves). Some scholars observe that Colossians and Ephesians require submission from wives but obedience from children and slaves. They then suggest that this recognizes differences between the status of wives and that of slaves, and use Ephesians 5:21 to argue that submission between spouses was to be mutual. But Ephesians 5:33 underscores disparities between the partners: "Let each of you love his own wife as himself, but let the wife fear [NRSV: "respect"] the husband" (cf. Eph 5:21; Col 3:22).

Such idealizations of imperial masculinity should be seen as prescriptive rather than descriptive. The codes ignore the complexities of actual households, as in Colossians 4:15, which greets a woman householder as host of a church. They do not reference household freedpersons, that wives and children might also be enslaved, or that slaves might have or be partners or children. They also leave unclarified whether obedience owed to masters required the sexual submission of slaves, which would fall under the condemnation of participating in *porneia* (Glancy, 2002; MacDonald, 2007).

The pressures of imperial order and the views of outsiders are even more evident in 1 Peter, wherein the code begins with the counsel to submit to human structures, starting with the emperor (1 Pet 2:13–14); addressees are urged to suffer as Christians rather than as malefactors (1 Pet 4:15, 16). Wives are urged to try to convert their unbelieving husbands "without a word," using only their submissive behavior and aversion to the feminine display of wealth targeted by Roman sumptuary laws and ideology (1 Pet 3:1–6). The brief counsel to husbands urges wise behavior toward a woman as the "weaker vessel," according them "honor as also co-heirs of the gift of life, so that your prayers not be hindered" (1 Pet 3:7), which may encourage allowing wives to abstain from sex for prayer, or may simply encourage harmony.

The Pastoral Epistles represent a different stage of household codes; 1 Timothy might be identified as a letter combined with a household code for "the household of God, which is the church." It prescribes "how to conduct oneself" according to one's role (1 Tim 3:15)—men and women, overseers (*episkopoi*) and ministers (*diakonoi*), elders and widows all come in for counsel. Marriage is expected of all; overseers must be "husband of one wife" and display their control of their own households and children as a qualification of office (1 Tim 3:2–4); ministers are held to the same obligations (1 Tim 3:12); their wives, or perhaps women ministers, are to be sober and not quarrelsome (1 Tim 3:11). A first obligation is prayers for emperors and those in high places (1 Tim 2:2); men are to pray without quarreling (1 Tim 2:8). Women are of particular concern: they must avoid conspicuous consumption, learn in quiet, and not teach or act independently. Secondary and gullible like Eve, women attain salvation by childbearing (1 Tim 2:9–15). Young widows are to be excluded from communal support; they must remarry, raise children, and do good works. Widows must be over sixty, and be the wife of one husband. This effectively excludes all women who follow the first counsel, to marry and remarry while young, and echoes the double bind constructed by the Julian law's requirement to remarry until fifty and the Roman adulation of the *univira*, the one-man woman. Titus similarly combines letter form with household code for communal living (1 Tim 1:5—2:10); the counsel to "woman elders" exhorts them to be teachers of younger women in virtue, and the hostility to women who learn or teach in 1 Timothy 2:14 and 2 Timothy 3:6–7 is not evident.

Marriage and Wedding Imagery. New Testament literature evokes imagery from marriage and weddings in two ways that are frequently combined. First, female personification of cities, nations, and peoples from Israelite, Greek, and Roman traditions contribute to depictions of Christ as husband/bridegroom and a community as wife/bride; second, the wedding as a time of fulfillment and festivity is a way to distinguish a time of fulfillment and joy. In these cases, marital or nuptial imagery is formed (or distorted) by the point the author seeks to communicate. What seems consistent is the subordination of the woman/wife/bride to the man/husband/groom.

An early illustration comes from the undisputed Pauline letters. In 2 Corinthians 11:2, Paul complains:

"I espoused you to one husband, to present you to Christ as a pure virgin." He then voices his fear that the Corinthians' thoughts have been corrupted "as the serpent deceived Eve" (2 Cor 11:3; Gen 3:4).

The Gospels also employ marriage imagery. Identifying Jesus's ministry as the time when the groom is with his companions marks it as a season for celebration, not fasting (Mark 2:17–20; Matt 9:14–15; Luke 5:33–35). Matthew compares heaven's reign to "a human king who gave a wedding for his son" (Matt 22:1–14); a parable in the eschatological discourse makes an analogy between the *parousia* and the arrival of a bridegroom (Matt 25:1–13). The wedding setting collaborates with the abundance of excellent wine produced in Jesus's first "sign" in the Gospel of John to suggest that this miracle anticipates Jesus's hour that "has not yet come" (John 2:1–12). In John 3:29, the Baptist uses the groom and groom's friend as an analogy for the distinction between himself and Jesus.

Revelation similarly evokes the festival character of the eschatological future under the image of the "wedding of the Lamb" and celebrates the purity and splendor of the new Jerusalem as a bride (Rev 19:7–9; 21:2; 22:17) contrasted with "the great Babylon, the mother of harlots" (Rev 17–18).

In Ephesians, commands to husband and wife are warranted by an analogy with Christ and the church: "The husband is the head of the wife as Christ is the head of the church, the body of which he is the savior" (Eph 5:23). The husband's love is to be modeled on Christ who "handed himself over for" the church, sanctifying and cleansing her from spot and blemish (Eph 5:25–27). This example evokes prophetic personifications of Israel and Judah, Samaria and Jerusalem, as straying wives whom the deity calls to repentance and restoration (e.g., Ezek 16). Applying body imagery to Genesis 2:24, the author identifies the wife with body and flesh (Eph 5:29–32)—the husband's own flesh, to be fostered, not hated.

Conclusion. In the New Testament, attention to marriage and divorce is scattershot and limited. To some extent, marriage is assumed as part of the structures of this world; in the undisputed Pauline letters and the Gospels it is addressed for the purpose of ending or avoiding marriage, for freedom from sexual and social bonds, or in pursuit of the angelic life. In the household codes, marital relations are among those that affirm Christian moral probity, including gender conformity, as an asset in imperial order. Some women and men were able to use renunciation of sex, and some women to use the household role of the *matrona*, to carve out a place for themselves in the leadership of early Christianity. Some same-sex missionary pairs mimicked marriage. But where marriage was concerned, the gender expectations of the first-century empire had to be either satisfied or addressed.

[*See also* Family Structures, *subentries on* New Testament *and* Roman World; Jesus; Legal Status, *subentry* New Testament; Male-Female Sexuality, *subentry* Roman World; Paul; *and* Religious Leaders, *subentry* New Testament.]

BIBLIOGRAPHY

Balch, David L. *Let Wives Be Submissive: The Domestic Code in 1 Peter*. Monograph Series, Society of Biblical Literature 26. Chico, Calif.: Scholars Press, 1981.

D'Angelo, Mary R. "Remarriage and the Divorce Sayings Attributed to Jesus." In *Divorce and Remarriage: Religious and Psychological Perspectives*, edited by William P. Roberts, pp. 78–106. Kansas City, Mo.: Sheed & Ward, 1990a.

D'Angelo, Mary R. "Women Partners in the New Testament." *Journal of Feminist Studies in Religion* 6 (1990b): 65–86.

D'Angelo, Mary R. "Roman Imperial Family Values and the Gospel of Mark: The Divorce Sayings (Mark 10:2–12)." In *Women and Gender in Ancient Religions: Interdisciplinary Approaches*, edited by Stephen P. Ahearne-Kroll, Paul A. Holloway, and James A. Kelhoffer, pp. 57–81. Wissenschaftliche Untersuchungen zum Neuen Testament. Tübingen, Germany: Mohr Siebeck, 2010.

Glancy, Jennifer A. *Slavery in Early Christianity*. Oxford: Oxford University Press, 2002.

Loader, William. *Sexuality and the Jesus Tradition*. Grand Rapids, Mich.: Eerdmans, 2005.

MacDonald, Margaret Y. "Slavery, Sexuality, and House Churches: A Reassessment of Colossians 3:18–4:1 in Light of New Research on the Roman Family." *New Testament Studies* 53 (2007): 94–113.

MacDonald, Margaret Y. "Beyond Identification of the Topos of Household Management: Reading the Household Codes in Light of Recent Methodologies and Theoretical Perspectives in the Study of the New Testament." *New Testament Studies* 57 (2011): 65–90.

Milnor, Kristina. *Gender, Domesticity and the Age of Augustus: Inventing Private Life*. Oxford: Oxford University Press, 2005.

Osiek, Carolyn, and Margaret Y. MacDonald. *A Woman's Place: House Churches in Earliest Christianity*. Minneapolis: Fortress, 2006.

Satlow, Michael L. *Jewish Marriage in Antiquity*. Princeton, N.J.: Princeton University Press. 2001.

Schüssler Fiorenza, Elisabeth. *In Memory of Her: A Feminist Theological Reconstruction of Christian Origins*. New York: Crossroad, 1983.

Severy, Beth. *Augustus and the Family at the Birth of the Roman Empire*. New York: Routledge, 2003.

Treggiari, Susan. *Roman Marriage: "Iusti Coniuges" from the Time of Cicero to the Time of Ulpian*. Oxford: Clarendon, 1991.

Yarbrough, O. Larry. *Not Like the Gentiles: Marriage Rules in the Letters of Paul*. Atlanta: Scholars Press, 1986.

Mary Rose D'Angelo

Early Judaism

This article deals first with marriage and then with divorce (according to the order of these procedures in real life).

Marriage. Among the Jews, as among the Greeks and Romans, marriage was considered an important commandment because it was a necessary condition for the framework of fertility and procreation. However, whereas for the Greeks and Romans the purpose of procreation was to produce citizens and soldiers, according to the Jewish view the purpose was to maintain the world and to do God's will. Although marriage in Jewish society was considered an important commandment, it was not raised to the level of a religious law where the person who refrains from performing it is considered a sinner, and it was not even considered an institution sanctified to the point of being indissoluble, as in Christianity. Marriage was seen as a contractual agreement between individuals whose success was associated with divine intervention as reflected in R. Akiva's adage: "When husband and wife are worthy, the *Shechinah* [divine presence] abides with them; when they are not worthy fire consumes them" (*b. Soṭah 17a*).

The Mishnah in Pirkei Avoth (5:21) which says "eighteen years old, to the wedding canopy" is more of a suggestion than a religious law. In a source from the Mishnaic period (*baraitha*) cited in the Babylonian Talmud, harsher things are said of one who did not marry by the age of twenty: "Until the age of twenty, the Holy One, blessed be He, sits and waits. When will he take a wife? As soon as one attains twenty and has not married, He exclaims, 'Blasted be his bones!'" (*b. Qidd. 29b*). However, other sources from the Mishnaic period quoted in the Babylonian Talmud present a diametrically opposed view: "The Torah has thus taught a rule of conduct: that a man should build a house, plant a vineyard and then marry a wife" (*b. Soṭah 44a*) and "Our Rabbis taught: If one has to study Torah and to marry a wife, he should first study and then marry. But if he cannot [live] without a wife, he should first marry and then study" (*b. Qidd. 29b*). Second Temple sources document cases of marriage at a later age, and an Eretz Israel Midrash claims, "The common practice is to marry at the age of 30, have a child at 40" (*Song Rab. 7:7*).

In cases where the members of the couple were young, negotiations around the issue of the dowry were conducted between their fathers. The negotiations were called *Shiddukhin* and the Talmud says that the Babylonian sage Rav would punish anyone who married a woman without previous *Shiddukhin* (*b. Qidd. 12b*). The amount of the dowry according to Babylonian sages Abaye and Rava might be up to one tenth of the father's assets and was meant to help his daughter get married and compensate her for the fact that if she had brothers, she had no chance of receiving a share in her father's inheritance (*b. Ketub. 52b*).

Kiddushin is the purposeful agreement of a man and woman to live together and have marital relations. This act of betrothal by the man can be done in one of three ways: by money, by deed, or by intercourse (*m. Qidd. 1:1*). It is valid only if the woman agrees to it: "'A woman is acquired,' implying only with her consent, but not without her consent" (*b. Qidd. 2b*). The act of acquisition is called *kiddushin* because the man consecrates the women to himself exclusively, and from that point onward, she is forbidden to any other man—she is consecrated to him. The purpose of her being ascribed exclusively to a certain man was to give security that the woman is pregnant by him and that her children are from him, so that he will not evade the responsibility to maintain them on the claim that they are not his. The man is not consecrated to the woman since there is no fear that the children she gives birth to are not hers.

A woman attests to her consent to the *kiddushin* by means of accepting a nominal sum of money—according to Shammai's school of thought one *dinar*, and according to Hillel's one *pruta*. The *kiddushin* procedure takes place in the presence of two witnesses and includes a declaration (*b. Qidd. 5b*). A man was free to betroth a woman using words he chose himself, on condition that his utterance express his affiliation with the woman (*b. Qidd. 6a*). Before the *kiddushin* and sometimes after, the man would send his bride gifts known as *siblonot* (*b. Qidd. 50b*). In addition the man wrote a *ketuba* writ that included his declaration of betrothal and his obligations, should the marriage come to an end due to death or divorce. There is one opinion that the *ketuba* is a development of the dowry mentioned in the Bible that evolved from a payment made by the groom to the father of the bride to a debt the groom paid the bride herself.

According to another opinion, the *ketuba* is an innovation of the rabbis that was designed to make it harder for men to divorce their wives and to protect women in the event that nevertheless they were divorced. In several sources the formulation of the custom of the *ketuba* into law was attributed to Simeon ben Shetah in the first century B.C.E. (*t. Ketub. 12:1; y. Ketub. 32:2; b. Ketub. 82b; b. Šabb. 14b*). In any case, the most important part of the *ketuba* is the husband's undertaking to pay the major sum written in it—a sum of 200 zuz for a virgin and 100 for a divorcee or widow, as well as the additional amount that he pledged in the event that the marriage ends (*m. Ketub. 1:2*) and additional monetary undertakings even if not written specifically into the *ketuba* (*m. Ketub. 4:7–12*). After the *kiddushin* the betrothed woman remains with her parents and is forbidden to her future husband. The maximal engagement period is twelve months for a virgin and thirty days for a widow. This timeframe allows them to prepare what they will need for their livelihood (*m. Ketub.* 5:2).

The *nisu'in* (marriage) begins with entering the wedding canopy (or chamber). In the Jerusalem Talmud we find a description of the wedding canopy: "These were wedding canopies of painted sheets and gold-embroidered ribbons hanging from them" (*y. Soṭah* 23:3 lit.). However, we do not find in the Mishnah or the Talmud a clear definition of the role and function of the canopy. In the Babylonian Talmud it is said: "What is festive building? If one builds a wedding residence for his son [on the occasion of his marriage]" (*b. Meg. 5b*). Rashi comments that the father would build for his first son a house and a wedding canopy inside it. According to this, the canopy was the place where the bride and groom sat during the wedding celebration (*b. Sukkah 25b*), which lasted seven days if the bride was a virgin and three days if she was a widow. When accompanying the bride to the wedding canopy, they would dance in front of her and praise her (*b. Ketub. 16b*), and during the wedding celebration itself, they would participate in a wedding feast prepared by the groom, drink wine, and recite the wedding benedictions (*b. Ketub. 8a*). According to the language of the early *ketubot*, which according to the Talmud were from the time of Hillel, "When thou art taken for the canopy, be thou my wife" (*B. Meṣi'a 104a*), he led her into the wedding chamber, which denoted that the *kiddushin* had begun, and the beginning of their married life.

The husband undertakes ten responsibilities toward his wife. Three of them are mandated by the Torah and seven by the rabbis. According to the Torah he owes her food, whose quality and quantity are determined by his standard of living; clothing, which means apparel including jewelery, housing, and household amenities according to his financial ability (*m. Ketub.* 5:8–9); and marital duty, namely marital relations whose frequency is determined by his occupation, which dictates how long he is at home.

A man or woman who does not want to fulfill the commandment of marital duty is called a *mored* or *moredet* and is fined. The man is fined by the addition of three dinars a week to his wife's *ketuba*, and the woman by the deduction of seven dinars a week.

According to the rabbis, the man owes his wife: the main part of the *ketuba* which is 200 zuzim for a virgin and 100 for a widow or divorcee and the addition to it—the sum he pledged at the time of the marriage. He also undertakes to pay her medical expenses if she is ill, to ransom her from captivity and return her to his home, and if he is a priest to return her to her city, also to pay her burial expenses. He further pledges that after his death, she and her daughters will continue to live in his house and receive maintenance; she, until she demands the amount of her *ketuba*, and the daughters until they are betrothed. Finally, he must guarantee that if she dies during her husband's lifetime, her sons will inherit their mother's *ketuba* and the dowry that she brought with her to the marriage (*m. Ketub.* 4:7–12).

The responsibilities that the wife owes her husband are not written in the Torah but were instituted by the rabbis in exchange for his responsibilities toward her. She owes him the profits of her handiwork and whatever she finds, in exchange for his providing her maintenance (*b. Yebam. 90b*). She also owes him the profits of her assets (usufruct). The bride brings to the marriage a dowry—money and assets that she received from her father and the groom benefits from the profits and guarantees in the *ketuba* to return them to her, with an additional third, if the marriage ends. This relates to that part of her assets that the woman defined as *tzon barzel*, i.e., property made over to the absolute responsibility of the husband to use during their marriage. The part of her dowry that the wife kept as her own responsibility is called *nikhsei melog*. They are not written in the *ketuba* and the husband benefits only from the profits (usufruct) and is not allowed to sell it. The husband also benefits from any profit in property that the wife receives after they are married. According to the Babylonian Talmud, the husband enjoys the fruits of his wife's assets in exchange for his obligation to ransom her from captivity (*b. Ketub. 47b*). The husband is also entitled to inherit from his wife, and he has precedence over everyone else.

Divorce. Usually the man is sovereign in the matter of divorce. If he wishes to divorce his wife, he is allowed to do so, even if she is opposed. According to the disputes cited in the Mishnah around the issue of what constitutes a legitimate reason for divorce, it appears that some of the Mishnaic sages did not see divorce as a serious matter. According to the School of Shammai, he may divorce her only if he discovered that she was unfaithful. But the School of Hillel thought he could divorce her for a trivial matter, e.g., if she spoiled a dish for him. Rabbi Akiba went so far as to say: "Even if he found another that is more beautiful than his wife" (*m. Giṭ.* 9:10). It might be that the rabbis' seemingly frivolous view of divorce was influenced by the view of divorce in Greece and Rome.

In Greece, a man could divorce his wife without any particular reason (in contrast, the woman could demand a divorce only if she supported her claim by a charge of cruelty or neglect by her husband). In Roman law there was no need for legal or governmental intervention, and divorce would take place by itself if one or both members of the couple reached the conclusion that their affection for each other had come to an end. Despite the opinions that made it easy for a man to divorce his wife which were expressed by the schools of Hillel and Shammai, a man divorcing his first wife was perceived by the sages of the Mishnah as a difficult thing and the R. Eliezar was quoted in the Talmud as saying: "For him who divorces the first wife, the very altar sheds tears" (*b. Sanh.* 22a). The Talmudic sages expressed their reservations about a hasty divorce that was decided without proper consideration by saying that the purpose of the *ketuba* was to make it hard for a man to divorce his wife.

According to the Mishnaic sages, a woman also had to agree in order to give validity to the divorce even though she is not the one carrying it out, and they ruled that if she did not receive the bill of divorce (*get*) into her hands, or possession, the divorce is not valid. For the Torah said "it comes to pass that she finds no favour in his eyes, then let him write her a bill of divorce and put it **in her hand**" (Deut 24:1). On this basis, the Mishnah ruled "If a man throws a *get* to his wife while she is in her house or in her courtyard, she is thereby divorced. If he throws it to her into his house or into his courtyard, even though he is with her on the same bed, she is not thereby divorced. If he throws it into her lap or into her work-basket, she is thereby divorced" (*m. Giṭ.* 8:1). And further: "If she was standing on public ground and he threw it to her, if it lands nearer to her she is divorced, but if it lands nearer to him she is not divorced" (idem 8:2).

Divorce usually depends on the husband's volition. However, there are cases where the Mishnah ruled that the court of law can force him to divorce her. Sometimes coercion is exercised because of matters related to him and sometimes because of matters related to her. Things related to him are bodily defects or diseases that arose after the marriage that the wife cannot tolerate; the wife's claim that he is sterile; his refusal to move with her to the Land of Israel, as well as his unpleasant behavior toward her, e.g., not allowing her to maintain family relationships or excluding her from benefits or from marital relations with him. In all of these cases, he must divorce her with a bill of divorce and pay her *ketuba*. In matters that relate to her, there are cases where it says, "He should send her away and give her the *ketuba*"; for example, if she is barren for ten years. There are cases where she is sent away without a *ketuba*, such as bodily defects that appeared in her after they were married that he cannot tolerate, or negative behavior toward him or in general (*m. Ketub.* 7:6). The bill of divorce must be written exclusively for the woman and be signed by two expert witnesses and must be handed over to the woman in the presence of two witnesses. It must be stated explicitly in the bill of divorce that the husband wrote it of his free will, and it must be written explicitly that it is made out between the two members of the couple. The Mishnah was meticulous about everything connected to the writing of the bill of divorce and its delivery to the woman, even to the point of the writing materials so that there would be no doubt whatsoever that the woman was truly free and available to marry whichever man she might choose. All of this was done to cancel out any possibility of a suspicion of *mamzerut* that might threaten the children who were later born to the woman from a remarriage after she is divorced.

[*See also* Family Structures, *subentry* Early Judaism; Legal Structures, *subentry* Early Judaism; *and* Marriage and Divorce, *subentries on* Greek World *and* Roman World.]

BIBLIOGRAPHY

Albeck, Shalom. *The Principles of Marriage and Family Law in the Talmud.* Ramat-Gan, Israel: Bar-Ilan University Press, 2010 (Hebrew).

Baron, Salo W. *Social and Religious History of Israel.* Ramat-Gan, Israel: Massada, 1968 (Hebrew).

Falk, W. Ze'ev. *The Law of Marriage.* Jerusalem: Meisharim, 1983 (Hebrew).

Gafni, I. "The Institution of Jewish Marriage in Rabbinic Times." In *The Jewish Family: Metaphor and Memory*, edited by D. Kraemer, pp. 13–30. Oxford and New York: Oxford University Press, 1989.

"T'shut, Get." In *Encyclopedia Hebraica*, Vol. 7. Tel Aviv: Encyclopedia Pub. Co., 1959 (Hebrew).

Katzoff, Ranon. "The Age at Marriage of Jewish Girls during the Talmudic Period." In *Teuda* 13. pp. 9–18. Tel Aviv: Tel Aviv University Press, 1997 (Hebrew).

Neubauer, Jacob. *The History of Marriage Laws in Bible and Talmud: Comparative Historical Study.* Jerusalem: Hebrew University–Magnes Press, 1999 (Hebrew).

Rabello, A. Mordecai. "Patria Potestas in Roman and Jewish Law." In *Dinei Israel: Annual of Jewish Law and Israeli Family Law*, Vol. 5, pp. 85–153. Tel Aviv: Tel Aviv University, Faculty of Law, 1974.

Satlow, Michael L. "Reconsidering the Rabbinic Ketubah Payment." In *The Jewish Family in Antiquity*, edited by Shaye J. D. Cohen, pp. 133–151. Atlanta: Scholars Press, 1993.

Satlow, Michael L. *Jewish Marriage in Antiquity.* Princeton, N.J.: Princeton University Press, 2001.

Schremer, Adiel. *Male and Female He Created Them: Jewish Marriage in the Late Second Temple, Mishnah and Talmud Periods.* Jerusalem: Zalman Shazar Center, 2003 (Hebrew).

Shulamit Valler

Early Church

In the second and early third centuries C.E., Christian churches were characterized by vigorous diversity and their leaders by varied opinions about marriage and divorce. In this period—before church institutions became central or broadly unifying, before Christians could influence state marriage laws, and before full theologies of marriage had been articulated—Christian discourse about marriage also conveyed multiform understandings of gender, community, and even salvation.

Selected texts from this period help illuminate a range of early Christian social ideals, rhetorical goals, and theological investments relating to marriage and divorce. Describing social realities, however, is difficult: identifying how, why, or when early Christians married or how they experienced married life or divorce. No early Christian writing offers plain descriptions of social experience. Mostly, texts come from male authorities, so women's views and experiences remain more oblique, as do those of the non-literate or otherwise silent majority. Yet social historians of early Christian marriage benefit from and contribute to a recent flourishing of interdisciplinary study of the ancient family (Balch and Osiek, 2003; Dixon, 2011).

Members of early Christian groups seem to have entered and experienced marriage in ways that resembled their non-Christian contemporaries. Nevertheless, some Christian teachings and concerns stand out as distinctive. Ancient Christians seem to have differed from their contemporaries, for example, in more strictly prohibiting divorce and in negotiating an ascetic and anti-family strand of Christian teaching along with the valuation and experience of marriage.

Social Conventions, Ideals, and Benefits. In the ancient Mediterranean, marriage was a union for the production of legitimate heirs. The stability and strength of marriages and households were deemed crucial to the health of cities and states. By the Roman imperial period, moral philosophers also celebrated marriage as the sharing of a common life marked by harmony and friendship between spouses. The Stoic Musonius Rufus remarks, "But in marriage there must be above all perfect companionship and mutual love of husband and wife, both in health and in sickness and under all conditions, since it was with desire for this as well as for having children that both entered upon marriage" (13A, Lutz, 1947). The Platonist Plutarch urges that in a marriage marked by unity, a wife should worship and recognize only her husband's gods (*Advice to the Bride and Groom*, 19).

Some early Christian writers echo such conventions and ideals. Though neither Jesus nor Paul makes procreation the end of marriage, some second- and third-century Christians do. Clement of Alexandria (ca. 150–ca. 215 C.E.) remarks, "The goal of marriage is procreation, and its end is fair children" (*The Instructor* 2.10.83, Wood, 1954, p. 173). Clement notes that couples marry for the sake of their country, the succession of children, and "the perfection of the world" (*Miscellanies* 2.23). Tertullian (ca. 160–ca. 225 C.E.) in his treatise "To His Wife" describes an idealized communion of Christian spouses. Urging his "dearest companion" not to remarry after his death, and most crucially, not to marry a pagan, he offers a lovely vignette as one persuasive element in his sharp argument about monogamy: "Side by side in the church of God and at the banquet of God, side by side in difficulties, in times of persecution and in times of consolation. Neither hides anything from the other, neither shuns the other, neither is a burden to the other. They freely visit the sick and sustain the needy. They give alms without anxiety, attend the sacrifice without scruple, perform their daily duties unobstructed" (2.8; Hunter, 2001, p. 38).

Tertullian also succinctly describes what women and men might typically seek in marriage, even as, paradoxically, he argues fiercely against such reasons compelling *second* marriage. For a widow, a husband may provide strength and comfort, protection for her good name, necessities of life, or children and the hope of posterity (*To His Wife* 1.4). A man may seek a wife not only to provide children but also to govern a household: managing slaves and servants, overseeing household accounts and keys, supervising spinning, managing the kitchen,

and sharing cares and responsibilities (*Exhortation to Chastity* 1.12). Or men may seek remarriage due to infirmity, poverty, or loneliness (*On Monogamy* 16). Sarcastically dismissing such necessities but implicitly granting the importance of the household, Tertullian proposes that a widower take in a Christian widow (or a group of them) to do a wife's work. Despite his aims, Tertullian's polemic details discrete gender-differentiated benefits of marriage widely recognized and lauded in his culture.

Law and Custom. Under Roman law, a valid marriage had two requirements: the legal *capacity* to marry (Roman citizenship and proper age) and the *consent* or intent of the parties (the husband and wife, and, unless they were legally independent of paternal authority, the father or other ascendant male of each family). Marriage was a private arrangement; the state did not ratify or register marriages, nor were public or religious ceremonies required (though marriage celebrations were socially important events). Divorce was also accomplished primarily by the intent of one or both spouses and was, by the second century C.E., relatively easy and possibly common. After legislation introduced by the emperor Augustus (27 B.C.E.–4 C.E.), Roman marriage law included complex incentives and penalties generally aimed at encouraging the production of new generations of Roman citizens, particularly among the propertied elite. The laws convey social values—for example, discouraging both adultery and celibacy—relevant to how Christians articulated their ethics and theologies of marriage. Yet Roman marriage laws' effects on non-citizens, on lower strata of society, or on those in the broad reaches of the Roman Empire where Christianity spread are difficult to trace (Osiek and Balch, 1997, p. 62).

For most early Christian groups, local marriage laws or customs were most likely more pertinent (Osiek and MacDonald, 2006, p. 23). Indeed, one mid- to late-second century apologist argues that Christians are understandable precisely because they are typical, though morally superior: "For Christians differ from other people neither in country, nor language, nor customs.... They marry like everyone else and have children, but they do not cast them out once born" (*Epistle to Diognetus*, 5.1, 6). In some regions and periods, church authorities may have taken (or wanted) a role akin to familial or paternal involvement in granting consent to marry. For instance, Ignatius, early second-century bishop of Antioch, urges Polycarp, bishop of Smyrna: "It is proper for men and women who marry to make their union with the approval of the bishop, so that the marriage may be for the Lord and not for passion" (*To Polycarp*, 5.2c, author's trans.). Tertullian complains about "counselors" or "spiritual directors" who have recently allowed a Christian woman to marry a pagan (*To His Wife*, 2.2, 2.8). Both urge that the church have a role in consent to marriage; whether others heeded their arguments remains unknown.

Common marriage practices, at least among elites, included formal betrothal. Tertullian notes betrothal rituals in Carthage, such as an exchange of hands and a kiss, the giving of a ring to the woman, and (a key concern) the veiling of virgins (*Apology* 6.4; *On the Veiling of Virgins*, 11.4–5). Negotiations of dowry may have accompanied betrothals. Dowry was the wealth a woman brought into a marriage, available for her husband's use during the marriage, yet under Roman law remaining hers, recoverable by her or her family in the case of divorce or her husband's death. Typical ages at marriage were for men, after twenty-five; for women, after fifteen (or somewhat older among lower classes; Treggiari, 1991, pp. 400–401). Given age differences between husband and wife, average lifespans, and the dangers of childbirth, men and women frequently experienced the death of a spouse. Remarriage was common, resulting in complex relations among parents, children, stepchildren and siblings.

Early churches likely included members whose unions were respected despite lacking the legal status of marriage. Concubinage could function as a social equivalent of marriage. A man might take a concubine if the two were of unequal social status. Such unions could be public and honorable, sometimes lasting and monogamous, though without legal marriage benefits such as rights of inheritance or legitimacy of children. Augustine of Hippo's relationship with his concubine provides one well-known example from late ancient Christianity. Slaves had no legal capacity to marry, though lasting unions in which one or both spouses were enslaved did occur, vulnerable to consent of the slaveowner(s). Children born to such a union followed the mother's status. If both partners were freed, a recognized marriage could follow.

Marriage, Gender, Sexuality, and Virtue. Just as Greco-Roman moral philosophy and political rhetoric linked the stability of cities to the orderliness of households, some early Christian writers connected church unity with harmonious marriages and households. Several second-century Apostolic Fathers instruct men (husbands or church leaders) in how to guide wives and other subordinate household members, reinforcing the norm that governance of the home manifests masculinity. Directives for wives reflect culturally typical markers of female virtue (and corresponding worries about arenas for female transgression): chastity, affection for husbands, control of speech, discipline of children, and moderation of desires (*1 Clement* 21.6–8; Ignatius, *To Polycarp* 5.1; Polycarp, *To the Philippians* 4.2–3). In the *Shepherd of Hermas*, similar concerns are conveyed in narrative and dialogue. The protagonist Hermas (married householder, freed slave, prosperous businessman, and prophet to the church in Rome) encounters a series of heavenly revealers. They diagnose his shortcomings, including that his household (which seems paradigmatic of the church) needs reform. His children are rebellious (*Vis.* 2.2.2) and his talkative wife perpetrates evil with her speech (*Vis.* 2.2.3). Hermas himself is guilty of excessive affection for, neglect of, and grudges against his wife and children (*Vis.* 2.3.1) and of desire for another kind of wife (*Vis.* 1.1.2; *Mand.* 4.1.1). Hermas, his household, and the church require self-control (*enkrateia*) and repentance from the whole heart (*Vis.* 2.2.4).

The emphasis on chastity and control of desire expressed in early Christian household instructions reflects a broader ancient moral discourse about the regulation of the passions, including sexual self-control. Married women were expected to be sexually faithful to their husbands. Elite men were often presumed to have broader sexual prerogatives, including the right to make sexual use of slaves, yet lack of self-control could bring dishonor. Still sterner notes on male sexual virtue were sounded. A philosophic stream represented by Musonius Rufus argued against the sexual double standard and for a strict restriction of sex to procreative purposes. Musonius writes: "Men who are not wanton or immoral are bound to consider sexual intercourse justified only when it occurs in marriage and is indulged in for the purpose of begetting children, since that is lawful, but unjust and unlawful when it is mere pleasure-seeking, even in marriage" (12, Lutz, 1947).

When second- and third-century Christian apologists refuted pagan charges that Christians were engaged in sordid sexual acts, they did so in part by recommending the sexual self-restraint and exemplary marriages of Christians. Justin Martyr (ca. 155) and Athenagoras (ca. 176) both claim that Christians limit sex to marriage, only for procreation, and only in one marriage, rejecting remarriage after the death of a spouse (*1 Apology* 29; *Plea for the Christians* 33; see Aristides, *Apology* 9.15; Minucius Felix, *Octavius* 28–31). The apologists evoke no sexual double standard. Rhetorical claims may, however, disclose little about the sexual practices of ancient church members. To name one troubled issue, given that neither hortatory nor apologetic texts specify Christian difference on the question of sex with slaves, some scholars question whether Christian slave-owners did renounce the sexual use of slaves (Glancy, 2006, pp. 130–156; Osiek and MacDonald, 2006, pp. 103–111).

Apologists such as Justin and Athenagoras do claim that many admirable Christians have altogether renounced marriage and sexuality (*1 Apology* 15, 29; *Plea* 33). Earlier in the century, Ignatius and 1 Clement also allude to some who choose to remain in "purity," though both caution such persons against boasting or arrogance (*To Polycarp* 5.2; *1 Clement* 38.2). The strong Christian valuation of celibacy begins in the New Testament (Matt 19:12; 1 Cor 7:8; Luke 18:29–30). Some second- and third-century groups, however, advanced forms of asceticism that denied any positive value to marriage and procreation.

Ascetic Challenges to Marriage. Sharp challenges to marriage came from leaders and groups who urged not discipline but renunciation of sexuality, and not by some but by all baptized Christians. Lumped together as heretics by their opponents, leaders such as Marcion, Tatian, and Valentinus held distinctive teachings, yet drew some comparable conclusions for the life of the believer. Marcion, who came from Asia Minor to Rome around 140 C.E., distinguished between the creator God of Genesis and the true God. Holding that the Savior was not manifested in the flesh (a docetic view), Marcionite churches were said to baptize only those who renounced the procreative sexual act associated with the creator god (Tertullian, *Against Marcion*, 1.29.1–9). Valentinus, a sophisticated teacher in Rome around 138 to 166 C.E., also held docetic and dualistic views, and urged more advanced Christians to embrace sexual renunciation as a key to ending inner division. The term "Enkratite" ("continent") is attributed by opponents to Tatian, who moved from Rome to Syria around 172 C.E. For Enkratite Christians, ascetic practices such as sexual renunciation and dietary restriction could enable humanity to escape the bounds of flesh for restoration to a spiritual existence lost in the original fall. According to Irenaeus of Lyon (d. 202 C.E.), Marcion blamed God for the propagation of the human race and Tatian declared marriage "nothing else than corruption and fornication" (Irenaeus, *Against Heresies* 1.28.1; see Brown, 1988, pp. 83–121).

Other challenges to the marriage union and conventional households take lively narrative form in the early Apocryphal Acts of the Apostles. In one common plot line, apostles preach a gospel of sexual renunciation; girls and women respond by abandoning marriage or the marriage bed and adopting changed social roles; households and cities are left in turmoil; and elite males pursue the disruptive apostles. In the *Acts of Thomas*, the apostle travels to India where, in the bridal chamber on the wedding night, he persuades the king's daughter and her bridegroom to renounce "filthy intercourse," with its hazards of children (*Acts of Thomas*, 12). In the *Acts of Andrew*, the female disciple Maximilla joins herself to the apostle, leaves her husband Aegeates's bed (13–16), for a time substituting a slave girl, Eucleia, to disguise her sexual withdrawal (17–21). In the *Acts of Paul and Thecla*, Paul preaches a sermon overheard by Thecla that echoes and extends asceticizing New Testament sayings: "Blessed are those who have wives as though they did not have them, for they shall inherit God [1 Cor 7:29]....Blessed are the bodies of the virgins, for those bodies shall be well-pleasing to God and shall not lose the reward of their purity" (*Acts of Paul and Thecla*, 5–6, author's trans.). Thecla's subsequent devotion to Paul leaves her fiancé Thamyris lamenting, "I am deprived of my marriage" (14, author's trans.) and her mother Theocleia calling for her daughter's execution, "burn the lawless one, burn the one who is no bride" (20, author's trans.). Thecla is transformed from sheltered virgin to bold witness to Christ. Yet households remain significant in the story: that of hospitable Onesiphorus, married and with children; that of the wealthy, elite widow Tryphaena, who shelters and then adopts Thecla, conferring wealth upon her which allows Thecla to become Paul's financial benefactor (39, 41). The Apocryphal Acts present complex challenges to marriage, conventional gender roles, and social order.

The Theological Defense of Marriage. In the face of such challenges, early theologians defended the good of marriage while also advancing the good of sexual renunciation. Tertullian wrote three treatises on marriage: *To His Wife, An Exhortation to Chastity*, and *On Monogamy*. Each text makes similar arguments, though the rhetoric intensifies, possibly due to Tertullian's involvement in the North African Montanist movement. Against "heretics" who repudiate marriage, he insists marriage is "blessed" and "something good," devised by God for procreation and "to set the world in order" (*To His Wife* 1.2–3; *Exhortation* 1.6). Yet while marriage is good, abstinence is better. Drawing on Paul's language in 1 Corinthians 7, Tertullian argues marriage was granted as a "concession" or "permission" (1 Cor 7:7, 9; see Clark, 1999, pp. 267–268, 272–273). Now that the world is sufficiently populated, the "good" of procreative marriage may properly be restricted (*Exhortation to Chastity* 1.6). Freedom to marry is worthy of *respect*, but continence earns *veneration* (*On Monogamy* 1.1).

Origen of Alexandria (ca. 185–254 C.E.) also draws on 1 Corinthians 7:7 to argue that both marriage and celibacy are gifts of God (*Commentary on Matthew* 14.16; *Commentary on 1 Cor* 7:7). Yet, like Tertullian, Origen's esteem for sexual renunciation qualifies his view of marriage. Commenting on Matthew's sayings about eunuchs for the kingdom of God (Matt 19:10–12), Origen acknowledges that absolute chastity is a gift of God, but then weaves a catena of scriptures on prayer that make chastity seem a gift that could be available to anyone who would pray continuously for it (*Comment. Matthew* 14.25).

The most developed pre-Constantinian defense and exposition of marriage comes from Clement of Alexandria, particularly in *Miscellanies* (*Stromateis*) Book 3 and *The Instructor* (*Paedagogos*) Book 2. Clement scorns those who repudiate marriage— Marcionites, Enkratites, and some Gnostics (*Misc* 3.18.109). Unlike Tertullian, Clement considers the Genesis command for humans to "multiply" a continuing imperative. Clement does aim to discipline passion, and he prohibits all non-procreative sex. He urges decorous, restrained married intercourse, avoiding "every indecency in intimate embraces" (*Instructor* 2.10.90, Wood, 1954, p. 174). He specifies for men the hazards of sexual expenditure (*Instructor* 2.10.94). Yet Clement also suggests that nature permits the longing for procreation (*Instructor* 1.10.90). Indeed, married, procreative sex allows participation in the image of God as creator, cooperating with divine purposes in the continuance of humanity (*Instructor* 2.10.83). Writing about and for men, Clement argues that marriage is a fitting preparation for church leadership (*Misc.* 3.12.79). Not only were Peter and Philip married, but also Paul, he surprisingly holds (*Misc.* 3.6.52.4–53.1–2). Rather than ascribing higher masculinity to the ascetic renunciation of marriage, Clement maintains that true manhood is won by the disciplined exercise of the duties of husband, father, and head of household (*Misc.* 7.12.70). The responsible married householder, in Clement's ideal, would then renounce sexual activity once the household is sufficiently populated with children.

Marriage and desire, in Clement's thought, are rooted in sexual difference, which will ultimately be erased (Matt 22:30; Mark 12:25). At times he writes as though the eradication of gender and sexual difference will come about as the female becomes male (*Misc.* 6.12.100.3), at times as though an androgynous, lust-free state of reward awaits both male and female (*Instructor* 1.4.10). For Clement, such a state follows from here honoring the social and holy life based on married union.

Divorce, Death, and Remarriage. Many early Christian writers articulate their understandings of monogamy through their deliberations on divorce and on remarriage for widows or widowers. In a culture where remarriage was the norm for men and women still seeking children, Christian teachings, though not uniform, seem distinctive compared to their contemporaries.

Some writers consider circumstances when divorce might be justified, necessary, or even admirable. In *The Shepherd of Hermas*, the Shepherd (the angel of repentance) enjoins strict marital fidelity upon Hermas (and his church), then instructs divorce in a case when adultery is known (Mandate 4.1.4–6). The offended spouse should not remarry, however, but be willing once (and only once) to reconcile with a repentant partner (Mandate 4.1.8). Similarly, Justin Martyr offers the example of a Roman matron, formerly sexually promiscuous but now converted to Christianity and sexually restrained. Facing her husband's scandalous and continued licentiousness, the matron divorced him, then found her husband denouncing her as a Christian and prosecuting her Christian teacher. Protesting the injustice, Justin makes the divorce an index of the admirable virtue Christianity instills, even in female adherents (*Second Apology* 2; see Kraemer, 2011, pp. 46–54). Righteous causes for divorce emerge also in Origen's exegesis of Matthew's divorce sayings (Matt 19:3–12). Building on Matthew's exception clause (that *porneia* is grounds for divorce), Origen suggests other just causes for a man divorcing a woman: poisoning, infanticide, destruction of the husband's home (*Commentary on Matthew* 14.24). In Origen's reading, Jesus prohibits remarriage after divorce, not divorce itself.

To the question of widows or widowers remarrying, the Shepherd tells Hermas that a second marriage is not sin, but remaining alone is a higher honor (Mandate 4.4.2). Clement of Alexandria likewise concludes that a man who remarries commits no sin (appealing to 1 Cor 7:8–9), but falls short of the higher perfection of the gospel ethic (*Misc.* 3.12.82). Tertullian's position is, as noted earlier, sharper. His more moderate stance is that any remarriage must be to another Christian (*To His Wife* 2.1); his more vehement formulations hold that any deviation from monogamy is degeneracy (*Exhortation* 1.5) and that all intercourse with a second man is adultery (*On Monogamy* 9). Tertullian betrays, however, that remarriage is in fact taking place in third-century Carthage, even and perhaps often between Christians and pagans (Evans Grubbs, 1995, pp. 68–69).

Assessment. As this brief survey of early Christian literature attests, persuasive rhetoric signals not consensus about marriage and divorce, but the untidy but fascinating reality of diverse practices, understandings, and debates in second- and third-century churches.

[*See also* Family Structures, *subentries on* Early Church *and* New Testament; Legal Status, *subentry* Early Church; Male-Female Sexuality, *subentry* Early Church; Marriage and Divorce, *subentries on* New Testament *and* Roman World; *and* Social Interaction, *subentry* Early Church.]

BIBLIOGRAPHY

Primary Sources

Barnard, L. W., ed. *The First and Second Apologies: St. Justin Martyr*. New York: Paulist Press, 1997.

Ehrman, Bart D., ed. and trans. *The Apostolic Fathers*. Vols. 1 and 2. Loeb Classical Library 24 and 25. Cambridge, Mass.: Harvard University Press, 2003.

Hennecke, E., and W. Schneemelcher, eds. *New Testament Apocrypha*. 2 vols. Rev. ed. Philadelphia: Westminster, 1991.

Hunter, David G., ed. and trans. *Marriage in the Early Church*. Minneapolis: Augsburg Fortress, 1992; reprint, Eugene, Ore.: Wipf and Stock, 2001.

Le Saint, William P., ed. and trans. *Tertullian: Treatises on Marriage and Remarriage. To His Wife, An Exhortation to Chastity, Monogamy*. Ancient Christian Writers 13. New York: Newman, 1951.

Lutz, Cora E., ed. and trans. "Musonius Rufus: The Roman Socrates." *Yale Classical Studies* 10 (1947): 3–147.

Wood, Simon P., trans. *Clement of Alexandria. Christ the Educator*. Fathers of the Church 23. New York: Fathers of the Church, 1954.

Secondary Sources

Balch, David L., and Carolyn Osiek, eds. *Early Christian Families in Context: An Interdisciplinary Dialogue*. Grand Rapids, Mich.: Eerdmans, 2003.

Brown, Peter. *The Body and Society: Men, Women, and Sexual Renunciation in Early Christianity*. New York: Columbia University Press, 1988.

Clark, Elizabeth A. *Reading Renunciation: Asceticism and Scripture in Early Christianity*. Princeton, N.J.: Princeton University Press, 1999.

Dixon, Suzanne. "From Ceremonial to Sexualities: A Survey of Scholarship on Roman Marriage." In *A Companion to Families in the Greek and Roman Worlds*, edited by Beryl Rawson, pp. 245–261. Oxford: Wiley-Blackwell, 2011.

Evans Grubbs, Judith. *Law and Family in Late Antiquity: The Emperor Constantine's Marriage Legislation*. Oxford: Clarendon, 1995.

Glancy, Jennifer A. *Slavery in Early Christianity*. Minneapolis: Fortress, 2006.

Kraemer, Ross Shepard. *Unreliable Witnesses: Religion, Gender, and History in the Greco-Roman Mediterranean*. New York: Oxford University Press, 2011.

Osiek, Carolyn, and David L. Balch. *Families in the New Testament World: Households and House Churches*. Louisville, Ky.: Westminster John Knox, 1997.

Osiek, Carolyn, and Margaret Y. MacDonald, with Janet H. Tulloch. *A Woman's Place: House Churches in Earliest Christianity*. Minneapolis: Fortress, 2006.

Treggiari, Susan. *Roman Marriage: "Iusti Coniuges" from the Time of Cicero to the Time of Ulpian*. Oxford: Clarendon, 1991.

B. Diane Lipsett

MASCULINITY AND FEMININITY

This entry contains five subentries: Hebrew Bible; Greek World; Roman World; New Testament; *and* Early Church.

Ancient Near East

See Gender and Sexuality: Ancient Near East.

Hebrew Bible

The texts of the Hebrew Bible span a considerable time period, which complicates analysis of their constructions of masculinity and femininity. Sociopolitical structures and class systems shape different understandings of gender. The texts represent specific strata of society and may be portraying ideal or constructed realities that do not necessarily reflect the lived social experience of gender for the majority of people. With that caveat, this entry explores the portrayal of gender in several genres of texts, examining both rhetorical and descriptive uses of gender. It then considers several major spheres in which gender is portrayed in the texts: family, work, war, ritual, and clothing.

Gender in Biblical Genres. The Hebrew Bible incorporates a variety of biblical genres that reveal a range of constructions of gender. Gender is used by these texts in different ways, from overtly rhetorical to descriptive. Examining each genre separately reveals the complexity of gender in the texts.

Legal texts. Legal texts reflect and shape Israelite identity, although they may not have functioned to regulate daily life. Cheryl Anderson's (2004) examination of femininity and masculinity in the legal material finds three characteristics of femininity. First, women are subordinate to men. Because women and their sexuality are under the control of men, the laws related to sexual assault or extramarital sex focus on the injury to an aggrieved male party and not to the woman. Second, women are meant to have sex with men. Not only do most of the laws concerning women relate to marriage and sexual relations, but low-status women, particularly slaves and foreigners, are implicitly sexualized in the legal material. Third, a woman's function is to reproduce. The laws do not treat women as independent agents but as components within a patrilineal system.

While the law constructs femininity as dependent and oriented toward reproduction, the legal texts construct masculinity as the dominant gender, associated with violence and conquest. According to feminist legal theory, the law itself articulates male experience. It assumes the perspective of a free male subject who can marry a wife and own slaves, while it disregards the experience of a female victim of sexual assault, focusing solely on payment to the male (Exod 22:16; Deut 22). The laws favor male power and oppress women by granting males the right to control female sexuality, either as fathers or husbands. With rare exceptions, daughters cannot inherit, and their control of property is limited (Num 27, 36). Men are exclusively called to pilgrimage festivals (Exod 23:17; Deut 16:16). It is likely that certain laws written in ostensibly gender-neutral terms had a disproportionate negative impact on women. Among these are the laws that ban sorcery and apostasy in the wake of a centralization of worship, which reduced female access to the normative cult. Female medical practices related to fertility and childbirth may have been demonized as sorcery.

Narrative texts. The narrative texts display a broader conception of femininity and masculinity than the legal texts do, with some elements reinforced and others subverted. Athalya Brenner has laid out several roles for women portrayed in the biblical narratives (1985). These include queens, wise women, poets, prophetesses, magicians, sorcerers and witches, and prostitutes. She also describes several female narrative types, including the Hero's Mother, the Temptress, Foreign Women, and the Ancestress. Because women in the narratives are often a combination of an individual character and a literary type, it is difficult to use narratives to determine actual feminine roles, but they do reveal information about cultural gender identity. The paucity of women's roles shows that women were marginalized when it came to political and legitimate religious leadership in Israel. They hint that women had networks of power beyond what is visible in texts written and transmitted by elite males. Carol Meyers observes that Israelite society, especially during the premonarchic period, may be more helpfully categorized as heterarchical than hierarchical. Heterarchy implies that multiple realms of power and networks intersect, rather than there being one direct line of power. Heterarchy would account for women's formal and informal networks, including

guilds of singers and prophetesses, as well as the networks created in communal activities such as bread baking and weaving (in Rooke, 2007).

In the literary type roles, women show strong character and power within the domestic sphere, but they work to further the interests of the male line. Particularly in Genesis and Judges, the women step up to do what is necessary when men falter in their duties (see Sarah in Gen 21, Tamar in Gen 38, Achsah in Judges 1, Deborah in Judges 4—5). Some characteristics of femininity drawn from these portrayals include a strong concern for favored progeny, trickery, resourcefulness, and courage. The women stand up to the men and coerce them into action, but ultimately are not in a position to be independent leaders. While Deborah appears to have a prominent leadership role, she does not actually lead the troops into battle. Jael kills Sisera in the realm of her tent, not on the battlefield (Judg 4—5). In negative portrayals of women, deceitfulness and nagging feature prominently (Gen 39; Judg 16; 1 Kgs 21).

Masculinity is presented much more complexly in the narrative texts than in the legal texts. There is a tension between the dominant masculinity in the larger culture and the masculinity favored for a follower of Yahweh. On one hand, the texts share many characteristics of masculinity with other ancient Near Eastern cultures, such as the importance of military prowess, sexual potency, honor, control of women, and physical strength. On the other hand, the men chosen by God as leaders often do not thoroughly embody these characteristics, because they must agree to submit to God. Isaac is a wimp who avoids confrontation (Gen 26); Jacob is a mama's boy who hangs out in the tents as a young man (Gen 27); Moses speaks poorly (Exod 4); Barak refuses to go into battle without Deborah (Judg 4); and Gideon requires three proofs of God's presence in order to act (Judg 6). Thus the narratives at times reinforce a masculinity based on violent dominance of others, but elsewhere undermine this definition and include more characteristics associated with femininity, such as trickery and submission, in the ideal masculine follower of God.

Poetic texts. Poetic texts offer engaging symbolic gender figures. Song of Solomon has caught the interest of feminist interpreters, because it displays feminine voicing, even if it was not written by a woman (Brenner and van Dijk-Hemmes, 1993). The song expresses a positive view of female sexuality, voicing female desire. This evocative premarital desire is not condemned by the text, although the protagonist does face opposition from her brothers. Her father is notably absent from the text. The text provides a glimpse into idealized feminine physical characteristics. She is described as having lovely eyes, thick hair, matching white teeth, red lips, cheeks like pomegranates, a long neck, and prominent breasts. She wears a veil and necklace.

Lady Wisdom and Lady Folly in Proverbs are literary types that reinforce ideas about chastity in marriage as a high value. They are used as a pedagogical tool to appeal to young men. Folly is compared to an adulterous woman, loud and messy, with poor hygiene, taking over public spaces and luring young men astray (Prov 7). Wisdom also inhabits public spaces, but her activities are not deceitful. The young man is encouraged to be faithful to her (Prov 8). The ideal wife presented in Proverbs 31 runs the home, but goes into public spaces in order to trade and support the family.

The ideal man in Song of Solomon is ruddy with curly black hair, attractive eyes, soft lips, a hard body, and strong legs (5:10–15). He speaks sweetly (5:16). He pursues the woman, but is also pursued by her. The brothers display more typical concern for their sister's chastity (8:8–9). In Proverbs, the implied audience is a young man learning from his wise father and mother. He is seen as vulnerable to the wiles of foreign women, but is implored to uphold the masculine standards of honor, self-restraint, wisdom, and temperance. The Psalms show masculine virtues such as honor, bravery, and faithfulness, but also allow for expression of fear and the request for help from the deity to defeat the psalmist's enemies and vindicate the singer's honor and integrity. Thus, as in the narratives, the picture of ideal masculinity is dominance over fellow humans but submission to God.

Prophetic texts. The prophetic texts present a number of striking images of femininity. The trope of Samaria/Jerusalem as the unfaithful wife of Yahweh features in Hosea, Jeremiah, and Ezekiel. The metaphor of adultery to represent unfaithfulness to Yahweh has implications of political, economic, and religious disobedience. Because it works on the cultural expectation that the wife should be the sexual property of the husband alone, the wife's sexually tinged punishment is portrayed as justified (Hos 2). Ezekiel takes this imagery to an extreme in chapters 16 and 23, showing Jerusalem as a foundling child raised and later wedded by Yahweh, but who yearns for foreign affairs. The image reinforces the portrayal of masculinity as the domination of females and of femininity as submissive and sexually chaste. The imagery also reinforces a stereotype of women as deceitful and ungrateful, not recognizing their true husbands. Elsewhere in the prophetic texts, women are used more generally as a symbol of defeat, especially in the personification of cities as women. Defeated cities are shown as weeping women, lamenting over the loss of their children, and as sexually penetrated women (Lam 1; Mic 1; Nah 3). Childbirth is used as an image of crisis and fear (Mic 4:9–10; Zech 9:5).

Since many of the prophetic texts are indictments of improper political and economic policy decisions, the texts frequently impugn the masculinity of national leaders to get them to submit to Yahweh. As Susan Haddox (2011) discusses, Hosea uses gendered imagery from Assyrian treaty curses to critique his elite male audience. They consider themselves the epitome of masculinity, displaying sexual and military potency, honor, and dominance. Hosea's rhetoric reveals that they are really feminine (as an unfaithful wife) or at the least poor specimens of masculinity: they are impotent with slack "bows," dishonorably engaged in adulterous-type coups, and the pawns of foreign powers. They are not able to provide for their families or to control their wives and children. They are fearful and run away. They are like prey animals, hunted by others. In most of the prophetic texts, Yahweh is portrayed as the ultimate male: a powerful warrior and avenging husband, who will sweep aside the enemies. Humans who think they are in a similar position are disabused of this notion with emasculating rhetoric. As with the other genres of literature, in the Prophets, proper human masculinity is subordinate to God.

Gender Roles and Expectations. Several features of gender cross genre boundaries. Compiling a composite picture can better illuminate the complexity of gender performance in the Hebrew Bible.

Clothing. Clothing serves several social purposes, demarking status, social position, and roles. The prohibition of cross-dressing in Deuteronomy 22:5 reinforces the importance of gender distinctions, though specific items of clothing are not mentioned. Parts of the feminine costume in other texts are veils (Gen 24, 38), headdresses, and robes (Isa 3). Jewelry includes rings, earrings and nose rings, necklaces, and bracelets and ankle bracelets (Isa 3). Clothing may have served a role in marking marital status, as when Rebekah received jewelry upon her engagement (Gen 24). Tamar was marked as a virgin daughter of the king by her robe with long sleeves (2 Sam 13). Widows and prostitutes also had distinctive clothing, though its form is not specified (Gen 38). Special clothing marked life events such as weddings (Judg 14) and mourning, which involved tearing clothing or wearing sackcloth.

The most detailed descriptions of clothing are of the priestly garments in Exodus, which are reserved for males. The high priest's garments set him apart as consecrated and served to protect him from divine power. The garments included a breastplate, an ephod, a robe, a woven tunic, a turban, and a sash woven out of gold, blue, scarlet, and purple threads and decorated with precious stones inscribed with the names of Israel's tribes (Exod 28). The priests' genitalia were covered with undergarments.

Men also donned clothing for battle: helmets, breastplates, swords. A particular act associated with masculinity was "girding one's loins." The phrase generally indicates a preparation for exertion. In Job 38:3 and 40:7, God tells Job to gird his loins like a man. The only woman who girds her loins is the intrepid wife in Proverbs 31.

Family. One of the most important gendered institutions in ancient Israel was the family. The family was the center of gender performance for most women, where they were expected to be chaste daughters, then faithful wives and fruitful mothers in their husbands' families. Family life was generally patrilocal, although a few texts indicate possible competing matrilocal systems (Judg 19; Gen 28). Women seemed to be the primary caregivers for children, although the fathers were also involved, particularly with respect to teaching ritual (Gen 17; Gen 22). Both parents seemed to be sources of authority for education (Proverbs). Although femininity is constructed as subordinate to masculinity, within the household women could hold considerable power. Sarah determined the reproductive and inheritance future of the family, although Abraham ostensibly had the final say (Gen 16, 21). Similarly, Rebekah determined which son received the blessing, even tricking Isaac to do so (27). In both cases, God took the side of the mother, not the father. Legally, however, the father had the authority to discipline and punish the women under his control (Gen 38; Deut 22). Judah had the right to burn his daughter-in-law for fornication, as a widow within his family, but again this narrative shows that the woman was able to control the situation through her use of clever manipulation. Thus there is tension between articulated legal gender roles and flexible power situations within the individual family dynamic. The text itself often condones these uses of trickery and manipulation, but the end of such activities is the furtherance of the patriarchal lineage. While the women determine the particular direction of the lineage, the focus remains on the sons; the women factor as mothers only. Barren women feature prominently, but their situations highlight the importance of the sons they finally bear through divine intervention. Within the family, males compete with their brothers. The firstborn son, whose legal rights are protected in the Deuteronomic law (Deut 21:15–17), often loses out in the narrative texts to the manipulation of younger sons. Daughters seldom thrive in narrative texts; their appearance furthers a masculine story line. Dinah (Gen 34) and Tamar (2 Sam 13) are raped, which violations function as catalysts for power struggles involving their brothers. Jephthah's sacrifice of his daughter serves narratively to impugn his character (Judg 11).

Work. Work is another realm in which gender-role differentiation is clear. Typically, women's work roles center in the household, whereas men's work roles often extend into the public sphere. Cross-cultural studies, supported by hints in the biblical text, indicate that in pastoral and agrarian situations, both men and women contributed to the work as necessary, whereas in urban settings greater differences in gendered work arose. Genesis, which describes a pastoral context, has more balanced work roles. Daughters can have the task of watering the flocks (Gen 24, 29; Exod 3), though when the flocks are pastured in distant fields, shepherding is a role for sons and slaves (Gen 30, 34, 37). Women typically prepared the food, though men also cooked (Gen 25, 27). Both men and women were subject to enslavement. For both genders, but for women especially, sexual servitude and reproduction appear to be possible components of slavery (Gen 16; Gen 30; Exod 21).

As society became more centralized, more role differentiation appears. Men predominated in public positions such as leadership roles, though a few women came to power. Deborah is a judge in Judges 4—5 and Athaliah is a queen in 2 Kings 11, though her portrayal is very negative. Men are much more frequently named as prophets and scribes, but the prophetess Huldah was consulted to verify the scroll discovered by Josiah's servants, indicating that some women were also prophets (2 Kgs 22).

Warfare. Warfare is closely associated with masculinity in the Hebrew Bible. Successful kings and leaders display the ability to conquer enemies and protect their families and lands. This association starts as early as Abraham, who made short work of the Canaanite kings who kidnapped Lot (Gen 13). Weapons are used metonymically to describe men, such as David's lament for Saul and Jonathan, entitled "Bow," in which he decries the loss of the weapons of war (2 Sam 1). Lack of military bravery or success is equated with a lack of manliness. Thus

the timorous Philistine soldiers in 1 Samuel 4 are instructed to "be men and fight." Being killed by a woman is a worse fate, such that Abimelech requests that his sword bearer kill him lest he be remembered as one killed by the woman who dropped the millstone on his head (Judg 9). God is frequently portrayed as a warrior, fighting the enemy with storms and lightning. Keeping with the characteristic submission to God, the text often undermines typical masculine achievements in war, attributing them to God, such as in the story of Gideon (Judg 6—8) and the defeat of Jericho (Josh 6).

While warfare and conquest is intertwined with masculinity, defeat is frequently described with feminine images. Cities are personified as female and their captures represented as rape. Nahum taunts the soldiers of Nineveh, saying they have become women in her midst, unable to fight (Nah 3). Because defeat is gendered as female, the masculine is firmly associated with violence and victory, as being the penetrator and the destructor, never the penetrated and victim, even when it is actual men who are dying.

Religious roles. The religious sphere significantly shapes the construction of gender in ancient Israel. Certain religious practices, such as praying, are shared by both genders. Women are portrayed mostly as mothers praying for the sake of children (Gen 25, 29; 1 Sam 1), a task also undertaken by Isaac (Gen 25). Abraham speaks repeatedly to God, in person and in prayer. Within the official cult, women have little place. Sacrificial worship is largely in the male realm. While God promises offspring to Hagar and Sarah, the covenant is made only with Abraham, ratified through animal sacrifice and circumcision, a practice limited by definition to males. The cultic laws in Exodus and Leviticus set up the purity system for priests and those entering the presence of the Lord. One ritual marker is bathing. Nicole Ruane (in Rooke, 2007) observes that with only a few exceptions, bathing is specified as a means to mark entry into a purified state only for men. The effect of this specification is that men have a higher cultic status than women. Howard Eilberg-Schwartz (1994) notes that submitting to a male God raises difficulties for men. Men are required to take the feminine, subordinate role with respect to the deity. One way to deal with that gender inversion is to exclude women, the natural complements of a male god, from the cult entirely. With the centralization of the cult, the separation of women from the official activities became even more pronounced.

In much of the Deuteronomistic History, women, particularly foreign women, are associated with improper worship. The identification of apostasy with women is solidified through the use of the term *znh* (fornicate) as a dead metaphor (the Israelites "whoring after" other gods). Figurines of female figures found in archaeological sites dating from before the Exile indicate that worship of goddesses may have occurred alongside that of Yahweh in the household. Jeremiah's condemnation of the women who bake cakes to the "Queen of Heaven" provides textual evidence for these practices (Jer 7, 44). Men's ritual practice was codified as official and acceptable, whereas women's ritual practice was excluded and made illicit.

Troubling the Categories. The Hebrew Bible presents constructions of masculinity and femininity that in many ways correspond with others found in the ancient Near East and in patriarchal agrarian cultures elsewhere. Because a key theme in the biblical texts is human submission to God, however, there are subversive factors and alternate framings present in the text, particularly with regard to masculinity. A few examples of femininity contest the standard portrayal, but in general women are shown with little public, political, or ritual power, although they have power in the household. The range of masculinity displayed, however, is broader than a simple hegemonic model. While the mode of male dominance and potency is present, the top of the spectrum is reserved for God. The ideal human male, while still exhibiting masculine characteristics, should also acknowledge his subordination to God, thus incorporating some more stereotypically feminine traits in the construction of masculinity. While many of the elite leaders of Israel resist the subordinate masculinities, those favored by God embody them.

[*See also* Imagery, Gendered, *subentries on* Deuteronomistic History, Prophetic Literature, *and* Wisdom Literature; Legal Status, *subentry* Hebrew Bible; Masculinity Studies; *and* Religious Participation, *subentry* Hebrew Bible.]

BIBLIOGRAPHY

Anderson, Cheryl B. *Women, Ideology, and Violence: Critical Theory and the Construction of Gender in the Book of the Covenant and the Deuteronomic Law.* Journal for the Study of the Old Testament Supplement Series 394. London: T&T Clark, 2004.

Bird, Phyllis A. *Missing Persons and Mistaken Identities: Women and Gender in Ancient Israel.* Overtures to Biblical Theologies. Minneapolis: Fortress, 1997.

Brenner, Athalya. *The Israelite Woman: Social Role and Literary Type in Biblical Narrative.* Biblical Seminar 2. Sheffield, U.K.: JSOT Press, 1985.

Brenner, Athalya, and Fokkelien van Dijk-Hemmes. *On Gendering Texts: Female and Male Voices in the Hebrew Bible.* Biblical Interpretation 1. Leiden, The Netherlands: Brill, 1993.

Chapman, Cynthia R. *The Gendered Language of Warfare in the Israelite-Assyrian Encounter.* Harvard Semitic Monographs 62. Winona Lake, Ind.: Eisenbrauns, 2004.

Clines, David J. A. *Interested Parties: The Ideology of Writers and Readers of the Hebrew Bible.* Journal for the Study of the Old Testament Supplement Series 205. Gender, Culture, Theory 1. Sheffield, U.K.: Sheffield Academic Press, 1995.

Creangă, Ovidiu, ed. *Men and Masculinity in the Hebrew Bible and Beyond.* Bible in the Modern World 33. Sheffield, U.K.: Sheffield Phoenix, 2010.

Eilberg-Schwartz, Howard. *God's Phallus, and Other Problems for Men and Monotheism.* Boston: Beacon, 1994.

García Bachmann, Mercedes L. *Women at Work in the Deuteronomistic History.* International Voices in Biblical Studies 4. Atlanta: Society of Biblical Literature, 2013.

Haddox, Susan E. *Metaphor and Masculinity in Hosea.* Studies in Biblical Literature 141. New York: Peter Lang, 2011.

Matthews, Victor H., Bernard M. Levinson, and Tikva Frymer-Kensky, eds. *Gender and Law in the Hebrew Bible and the Ancient Near East.* Journal for the Study of the Old Testament Supplement Series 262. Sheffield, U.K.: Sheffield Academic Press, 1998.

Pressler, Carolyn. *The View of Women Found in the Deuteronomic Family Laws.* Beihefte zur Zeitschrift für die Alttestamentliche Wissenschaft 216. Berlin: Walter de Gruyter, 1993.

Rooke, Deborah W., ed. *A Question of Sex? Gender and Difference in the Hebrew Bible and Beyond.* Hebrew Bible Monographs 14. Sheffield, U.K.: Sheffield Phoenix, 2007.

Stone, Ken. "Gender Criticism: The Un-Manning of Abimelech." In *Judges and Method: New Approaches in Biblical Studies*, 2d ed., edited by Gale A. Yee, pp. 183–201. Minneapolis: Fortress, 2007.

Yee, Gale A. *Poor Banished Children of Eve: Woman as Evil in the Hebrew Bible.* Minneapolis: Fortress, 2003.

Susan E. Haddox

Greek World

(Early) Christian writings show significant interest in masculinity and femininity, whether as related to diseases of a female (Luke 8:40–48) or a male body (Luke 9); or as related to Paul, who describes in 1 Thessalonians 4:4 a wife as a vessel; or the author of 1 Peter 3:7, who describes women as "weaker vessels"; or to the author of Ephesians 5:22–33, who describes a husband as head of a wife; as to the phrase *to logikon gala* "logical milk" in 1 Peter 2:2; or as to childbearing for salvation (1 Tim 2:12). The arguments used here are entangled into deeper ancient concept, well-known as *oikonomia*, the household codes, which gives an outline how gender-roles and social distinctions shall behave inside and outside the house. Therefore the category of male and female nature interacts with other categories like disease, religion, and social distinctions.

Terminological and Methodological Problems. Thinking about femininity and masculinity in Greece is complicated in three ways.

The categories of sex and gender. Judith Butler and other gender theorists have challenged the earlier feminist distinction between gender as a social construct and sex as a biological matter, arguing that this disjunction remains rooted in the dualism of mind and body established by Descartes. According to Butler, biological sex itself is a social construction, a cultural interpretation of the physical body. This insight—that what one lives as gender is dependent on the interpretation of the physical construct—illumines a great deal of ancient terminology on sex and gender.

Uncertain ancient terminology. Ancient Greeks had no specific terms for either gender or sexuality. While the term *genos* denotes biological sex as a class, the terms *arrēn* (male) and *thēlus* (female) delineate the sexes, and Greek also distinguishes between *anēr* and *gynē, andrēiēs* (manliness) and *gynaikos* (womanly). The designation *anthropos*, human being, is found only very rarely with a feminine definite article (*hē*; see e.g. Pindar, *Pythia* 4.98; Herodot 1.60). According to Plato the Greeks considered biological sex differences prior to other characteristics (*Symposium* 189e) when he writes, "For at that time one was androgynous [*androgynon*] in form and shared its name with both the male [*arrenos*] and female [*thēleos*]." The verb *andron* means "to alter someone into a man" (active) and "to become a man" (passive). Masculinity must be permanently proven (Corpus Hippocraticum [CH], *De diaeta* 1.28). *Andreia* (manliness) is performed in the gymnasium, palaestra, and, as a citizen, in the polis (King, 2004, p. 123). Thomas Laqueur caused a stir with his book *Making Sex*, in which he declared that the idea of the body in antiquity was in fact what he called the "one-sex model." For Laqueur, Aristotle represents this way of thinking, in which each body exists as male and female, differentiated only through greater or lesser "rendition." In Aristotle's works on biology the body takes the form of an investigation into specific morphological and physiological differences, and a discussion of the individual contributions each sex makes to procreation and heredity; his metaphysics explores the question of the relation of the characteristics *male* and *female* to the characteristic *human*. In his writings on ethics and politics, the focus is on the relationship between man and woman in their individual and public contexts. In all these discussions there is one constant: the inequality of the sexes on a social level is clear, while on a physiological level he assumes only one sex, namely, the male with the female as a deviation from the male. In the Hippocratic treatise *De genitura* (1.8–20), the term *aidoion* refers first to the entire genital area and is correlated with the class of humans (*to anthropou*); later however, the term refers only to the penis, since it is contrasted with the testicles.

Private and public space. Space in Greek houses is often designated by three terms defined by the sex of their uses: while the *andron* was a separate area for males in formal dining parties and the *andronitis* was a specific male area, the *gynaikonitis* refers to an area for women in the house that some scholars assumed to be situated upstairs (Xenophon, *Oeconomicus* 9; Vitruvius 6.7.1–2). But this practice of reading strict sex/gender boundaries in Greek house plans was criticized in modern scholarship. Domestic space was not specialized in function and was therefore flexible. Several scholars argue that the *gynaikonitis* and *andronitis* should be considered as men's and women's social spheres and conceptual boundaries rather than an absolute border limiting men's and women's movement in the house (Nevett, 1994). The *oikos* (house) was a structure with fluid boundaries, based on the household proper, the extended family (*anchisteia*), and pseudo-kinship (phratry, e.g., courtesans, slaves, and foreigners). Studies have shown that in the Hellenistic era, elite families considered the entire city to be a part of their house. We know of Archippe in Kyme who twice provided money for sacrificial acts and for the tribes of the city, the resident aliens (*metoikoi*), and the freedmen (Bielman, 2002). Since sacrificial acts were central to all forms of both private and public life and all political, military, and judicial activities were conducted with reference to the gods, it is better to describe the polis as a "sacrificial community" (Burkert, 1985, p. 256). Women participated in sacrifices (Aristophanes, *Acharnians* 253), organized the Thesmophoria including the election of officials (Isaeus 8.19–20, 3.80), participated in public funeral orations (Thucydides 2.46), attended wedding feasts where bridesmaids danced and male guests might talk with other female guests (Isaeus 8.18; Aristophanes, *Acharnians* 1056). Scholars argue that this pattern replicates family relations characteristic of ancient social life. Women could also function as patrons donating money for civic buildings (Archippe restored the *bouleuterion* in Kyme, 130–100 B.C.E.; further examples in Bielman, 2002). In the *Politeia* Aristotle says that in a democracy it is impossible to prevent the women (and men) of the poor from going out to work (1300a, 1323a). Several textual and visual sources indicate that women and men worked in the fields (Aristophanes, *Pax* 535; Demosthenes 57.45), sold produce in the market (Demosthenes 57.30–31; Aristophanes, *Acharnenses* 478), and engaged in many other activities including acting as a nurse or midwife (Plato, *Theaetetus* 149; several times in Soranus and CH).

Physical Constitution of Female and Male. In central passages in the Hippocratic Corpus, the physical constitution of the female body is differentiated from that of the male body, the former being described as porous (*araios*) and soft, while the latter is seen as compact and firm. The female body is porous and soft because of its high moisture content, as a result of women's lack of activity, just as physical labor makes the male body muscular, compact, dense and nonabsorbent, making the absorption of excess fluid difficult. The idea that the nourishment ingested by the woman reaches the breasts by way of the uterus and is turned into milk there can be found in the Hippocratic Corpus (*De natura pueri* 21 [VII 510 Littré]; *De muliebribus* 1.73 [VIII 156 Littré]); Aristotle on the other hand explains that milk can also be produced by men (*Historia animalium* 1.12 493a, 3.20 522a). The author of *De muliebribus* demonstrates this fact by means of an experiment (CH, *De muliebribus* I 1.24–37 [VIII 12.6–19 Littré]): a piece of wool or a cloth is laid on top of a wide-lipped container filled with water in order to illustrate the porousness of the body tissue of women. The ancient writer sees distinct variation within the category of "women," however. The body of a woman who has not yet given birth is strong, firmer, and more compact, and her bleeding is more painful, while a woman who has given birth has more porous veins, because childbirth stretches and loosens the body.

Medical treatises of antiquity describe pregnancy and birth as a sign of health or even healing for women, although these are not the only such signs. Their explanations make it clear that women's health always also involves more than pregnancy and birth, such as bringing the fluids in the body into equilibrium, or a well-regulated dietetics. Many texts explain that the body must manage nourishment instead of being managed by it, which is why the verb *kra-teein* is used often in connection with men as well as women. In addition, it is not the doctor who is responsible for the health of the family, but instead the *paterfamilias*, as an example from Cato shows.

In *De muliebribus* 2 one finds variations of the expression *meladainein*, "if she is cared for," which leads to health, which is in opposition not to illness but rather to death: "If she is not cared for, she will die" (CH, *De muliebribus* 1.4 [VIII 26 Littré]). Clearly, this is true for men as well as for women. There-fore, one thing is certain: health and intervention go hand in hand. This holds regardless of any differ-ence in sex, with one qualification: the definition of health for a woman is closely bound to her ability to have children and not doing physical work. Here, monthly bleeding in sufficient amounts is of central importance, and sexual intercourse is also vitally important for female health. Finally, pregnancy is a sign of female health: "if she conceives," "if she bears a child," and "if she carries a child the full term, she evacuates everything and becomes healthy" (CH, *De muliebribus* 1.37 [VIII 92 Littré]).

The physiological difference between the sexes according to which men were thought to be more rational than women is demonstrated in a few pas-sages, along with support from the study of anatomy, meant to show that women are more inclined to madness than men. In this context, *De morbis popu-laribus* II 6.19.1–2 (V 136.12–13 Littré) is remarkable: "A thick vein is in each breast. These [*tauta*] parts contain the greatest portion of understanding." The gender of *tauta* is neuter and not—as one would expect—female because of the mixed genders of its antecedents. Therefore the remark belongs to female and male.

The Womb. The author of Hippocratic texts com-pares the womb with a jar, a storage pot (CH, *De mu-liebribus* 33; *De genitura* 9.3; *De morbis popularibus* 6.5.11), and a suction cup (CH, *De vetere medicina* 22; cf. also Soranus 1.9). Especially in the Hippo-cratic Corpus, it seems that the uterus is seen as a second body in addition to the body of the woman, "the health of the body and of the womb" (CH, *De muliebribus* 217 [VIII 418 Littré]). Some manuscripts

of the Latin translation of Soranus (Bibiliothèque Royale de Belgique) preserve late antique illustra-tions of the womb as a jar that is labeled with medical vocabulary: the top of the uterus is described as *fundus*, "bottom"; beneath is the *cervix*, the neck, and finally the *orificium/os*, the mouth of the uterus that opens, closes, and conceives the seed (Soranus 1.9, 1.36, 1.43). Some sources maintain the idea that the womb communicated with the mouth via a tube or direct connection between the upper mouth and lips (*labia*) and the lower mouth (womb) and lips (*labia*, the vagina). This idea is related to some ex-periments testing the fertility of a woman and can be found in different works and authors like the *Corpus Hippocraticum* (*Aphorismi* 5.59; *De muli-ebribus* 46; *De superfetatione* 24), Aristotle (*Genera-tione animalium* 747a7–15), and Soranus (in Aëtius 16.7; but Soranus criticized this idea in *Gynaikeia* 1.35). And the womb wanders in the female body (CH *De muliebribus* 123–131; *De locis homine* 47; Are-tius 2.11; Aëtius 16.67ff.). If the womb gets thirsty and needs moisture it rises; if it is hungry it needs sperm (Aristotle, *Historia animalium* 634b33–35, 643b35a25). Both an insufficient flow of blood to the uterus in younger and older women and a lack of sexual intercourse are named as possible causes of lightness, which could result in other organs such as the liver, heart, or brain exerting a pull on the uterus, causing a woman to lose her voice, or even lose con-sciousness (CH *De muliebribus* I 125.1–9 [VIII 268.10–18 Littré]). The text describes various methods by which doctors could bring the uterus back into the correct position: sweet or foul-smelling substances, breathed in through the nose or placed at the vagina, could cause the uterus to move—the sweet-smelling substances moving the uterus back into the correct place, the foul-smelling ones inducing it simply to move from the incorrect position it had taken up. In essence a woman was "an uninterrupted vagina from nostrils to womb" (Manuli, 1983, p. 157).

Embryology. A number of Hippocratic writings, in particular *De genitura* and *De victu*, proceed from the two-seed doctrine, meaning that in addition to the male seed they recognize the existence of a female seed containing the mother's hereditary information;

according to this view, menstrual blood is responsible for the nourishment of the embryo. Sex determination is seen as based on the characteristics of the female and male seed. The writer of *De genitura* even assumes the existence of a seed of both sexes. The consistency of the seed determines the sex: a weaker, moister seed creates a female body, while a stronger, more compact seed generates a male body. Therefore hot, cold, dry, and wet are seen not as physical characteristics but rather as essential characteristics. Diet can also influence the sex of the child. Differences in sex result in differing processes of development within and outside the womb. Female offspring develop more slowly in the womb than male offspring. Outside of the womb, the woman's weaker physiology causes her to age more quickly.

The human soul consists of water and fire and, therefore, of the four qualities of warm, cold, moist, and dry (*De victu* 25) and the human soul stems from the seed. The four qualities are also responsible for the development of embryos. These qualities create the differences between the genders and arbitrarily influence the sex/gender of embryos by means of a particular way of life (cold/moist or warm/dry).

In addition to the condition of the uterus, the will of the mother is also an important factor in this process, indicating the woman's self-aware handling of her own sexuality (CH *De genitura* 5.1–9 [VII 476.18–26 Littré]): "Whenever the woman engages in intercourse and if she should not intend to receive the seed in herself, the seed from both male and female must evacuate to the outside in the customary way whenever the woman desires." This idea is further reinforced here by the use of the expression *methiei* ("set one free to do one's will"), otherwise used to refer to the man's ejaculation. Examples of an experienced woman's ability to determine the exact moment of conception or even initiate a miscarriage are found in *De carnibus* 19. This notion is also reinforced by the conditional sentences indicating that the woman has control of the seed and not the other way around. The seed must evacuate or remain as she desires. A woman's receptivity to becoming pregnant is a determining factor in her retention of the seed.

The pangenetic theory, however, does not by itself fully explain the formation of the sexes or the existence of similarities, or especially the existence of mixed gender and secondary sexual characteristics; therefore it is accompanied by a second theory that postulates that the woman contributes her own seed and thereby has a part in procreation. Both theories are linked to a further idea, which Lesky calls the sexual bipotence of the seed: men and women each have male and female seed, so that in the formation of the sex of the child, there are three alternatives: if both parents contribute a strong seed, a boy will be produced; if both contribute a weak seed, a girl; and if they contribute seeds of differing quality, the sex resulting from the seed represented in a greater amount in the total emission from both partners will be produced.

The Virgin: *Parthenos*. The treatise *De virginibus* in the Hippocratic Corpus offers a description of the physiological consequences for young girls of being unmarried, linking sociological events to a description of the physiology of the female body. Thus the document has been called an "instrument of socialization" (Pinault, 1992, p. 129). The author links his physiological interpretation of the nature of the female body with what we know as the "epileptic phenomenon," which in his opinion affects young women more often and more acutely than young men because young women have a weaker physical constitution and are less courageous than young men. On this basis, the author cannot be said to describe epileptic phenomena as we know them from the document *De morbo sacro*. The term *phronēsasēs* designates the stage in a female's life when she ceases to be a child without understanding and becomes a woman with understanding. This shift occurs at puberty when the channels of the body become large enough to carry reproductive fluid throughout the body. These enlarged channels enhance the communicative abilities within the body and thus permit an increase in understanding. This change is often explained as a result of an excess of blood common among women at this age. According to the author, the woman's diet and her body's growth are the cause of this excess blood. As it does in all women, the excess blood flows to the uterus and from there out of the body. When this discharge is not possible, the reason given is that the "opening/mouth" that is normally open is closed. In this connection, King points to a girl's first menses, which signals the readiness or maturity of the body (King, 2004, p. 20): menstrual blood is on the one hand a sign of the body's readiness to create a fetus, as well as its ability to receive the seed. Because its passage downward is blocked, the blood travels upward in its search for a way out, becoming concentrated in the vicinity of the heart and stagnating because the veins around the heart are "at an angle," causing the pressure on the heart to increase. At this point the issue arises: because the heart is the site of reason, the pressure on the heart caused by the stagnation of blood gives rise to mental disorders. The patient may suffer from hallucinations or a longing for death, along with the desire to strangle herself.

The only possible cure the author offers is marriage, which, he says, allows the blood to be discharged and the young woman to become pregnant, after which she is healed. The danger remains, however, for married women who do not bear children. Turning to classical mythology, one encounters numerous virgins, one of the best examples perhaps being Artemis, in whose cult young women similarly avoided the passage from the state of a young girl to that of a young woman—one would describe this phenomenon, however, as "active virginity" (Sissa, 1990, p. 112). King points out that *parthenos* does not mean a virgin, because the inviolability of the hymen was not definitive in antiquity (King, 2004, p. 51); *parthenos* is therefore a social status of living a celibate life.

Hermaphrodites. In the ethnographic portion of *De aere, aquis, loci* (CH *Aer.*) the author shows some interest in the roles of the sexes: the female Sauromatian warriors and the persons referred to as Scythian eunuchs (*De aere aquis locis* 17, 22). Both are relevant to a medical discussion, the eunuchs being impotent for organ-related pathological reasons and the Sauromatians for reportedly burning away the right breasts of their daughters in order to channel all of their strength into their right arms. Chapter 22 of

de aere auqis locis is dedicated to the discussion of individuals the author calls Scythian eunuchs, who are called *anarieis* or *andrieis*. Recent scholarship show that families of the Scythian upper class were genetically predisposed to a disease inhibiting the body's ability to break down iron, which was triggered by the high iron content of the drinking water, especially in the Dnieper region. The author of the document points in particular to excessive riding and bloodletting as triggers of the illness. Bleeding is more significant for the Scythians because the Scythian practice of bleeding damaged the veins next to the ears, to which the author ascribes a central significance in the transport of semen. The Scythians themselves interpret the disease in terms of divine influence, which has consequences for gender roles: affected men put on women's clothing, perform women's tasks together with women, and speak like women. It remains unclear, however, what this actually means. The author's evaluation of this choice of sex/gender role is rather negative, his view being that the Scythians ruined their health in general and their reproductive power in particular. The long passage dealing with male sterility is especially significant, as it is one of the only mentions of male sterility in the entire Hippocratic Corpus. The barbarian thereby becomes an example of the impotent man, his impotence being the result of a misguided lifestyle (riding, wearing trousers, bleeding), the cold climate of his country, and feminized nature.

[*See also* Family Structures, *subentry* Greek World; Gender; Gender Transgression, *subentry* Greek World; *and* Social Interaction, *subentry* Greek World.]

BIBLIOGRAPHY

Bielman, Anne. *Femmes en public dans le monde hellénistique: IVe–Ier s. av. J.-C.* Paris: Sedes, 2002.

Burkert, Walter. *Greek Religion.* Cambridge, Mass.: Harvard University Press, 1985.

Butler, Judith. *Gender Trouble: Feminism and the Subversion of Identity.* Thinking Gender. New York: Routledge, 1990.

Cox, Cheryl Anne. *Household Interests: Property, Marriage, Strategies, and Family Dynamics in Ancient Athens.* Princeton, N.J.: Princeton University Press, 1998.

King, Helen. *The Disease of Virgins: Green Sickness, Chlorosis, and the Problems of Puberty.* London: Routledge, 2003.

Laqueur, Thomas. *Making Sex: Body and Gender from the Greeks to Freud.* Cambridge, Mass.: Harvard University Press, 1990.

Lesky, Erna. *Die Zeugungs- und Vererbungslehren der Antike und ihr Nachwirken.* Wiesbaden, Germany: Steiner, 1951.

Manuli, Paola. "Donne mascoline, femmine stirili, vergini perpetue: La ginecologia greca tra Ippocrate e Sorane." In *Madre materia: Sociologia e biologia della donna greca*, edited by Silvia Campese, Paola Manuli, and Giulia Sissa, pp. 161–179. Turin, Italy: Boringhieri, 1983.

Nevett, Lisa C. "Separation or Seclusion? Toward an Archaeological Approach to Investigating Women in the Greek Household in the Fifth to Third Century B.C." In *Architecture and Order: Approaches to Social Space*, edited by Michael Parker Pearson and Colin Richards, pp. 98–112, London: Routledge, 1994.

Pinault, Jody Rubin. "The Medical Case for Virginity in the Early Second Century C.E.: Soranus of Ephesus, *Gynecology* 1.32." *Helios* 19 (1992): 123–139.

Sissa, Giulia. *Greek Virginity.* Translated by Arthur Goldhammer. Cambridge, Mass.: Harvard University Press, 1990.

Annette Weissenrieder

Roman World

Like the Greeks, the Romans had clearly defined boundaries that designated the spheres of masculinity and femininity. These boundaries were marked by socially constructed patterns of behavior that incorporated cultural expectations pertaining to service to the state (in political, military, and religious arenas), spousal and familial relationships, and sexual propriety.

Masculinity. In relation to the aristocratic patricians and the *nobiles* (plebeians with a consular family member), Roman masculinity was governed by a strict value-system that involved a code of honor and behavior. This system was structured within a set of linguistic and behavioral paradigms, and included various terms, among which the most important was *virtus* (manliness, bravery, excellence).

Cicero (106–43 B.C.E.) defines *virtus* via an etymological discussion of its connection with the word for man, *vir*: "For the word *virtus* is from *vir*; in fact, the main quality of men is fortitude [*fortitudo*], to which there are two main duties: contempt of death and personal suffering. Therefore, these must be employed, if we wish to be able to possess *virtus* or, since the word *virtus* has been borrowed from *vir*, if we wish to be men" (*Tusculan Disputations* 2.43; all translations by author). Cicero emphasizes that *virtus* is connected with *fortitudo* (translated here as "fortitude," but close to *virtus* in meaning, embracing concepts of manliness, bravery, endurance). He also reveals that to possess *virtus* is to demonstrate or perform it, namely, to undergo personal suffering—even to the point of death—without faltering.

Other important terms related to Roman conceptions of masculinity include *pietas* (dutiful conduct in relation to the gods, the state, and the family); *fidelitas* (trustworthiness, loyalty); and *dignitas* (worthiness, the ability to garner respect and authority). All of these values were partly inherited from one's ancestors, thus bestowing honor on one's *gens* (family) and oneself, but, more importantly, they had to be enhanced by the individual for his own prestige and, in turn, the ongoing prestige of his heritage. This process of augmentation of a preexisting esteem was encapsulated in the term *gloria* (glory, fame, renown). Thus, a Roman man from the patrician class or from the *nobiles* was expected to actively perform and thus embody these values by service to the state, particularly in the form of military endeavors and/or politics.

Such values and their importance to the Roman concept of acceptable and esteemed masculinity are illustrated in the epitaphs of the Cornelii Scipiones, a branch of the patrician family the *gens Cornelia*; for example, on Publius Cornelius Scipio:

To the one who has worn the honored cap of Jupiter's priest. Death has caused all your honor [*honos*], fame [*fama*], manliness [*virtus*], glory [*gloria*]: and ingrained character [*ingenium*] to have ended. If it had been permitted you to be active over a long life, it would have been an easy thing for you to have exceeded by achievements [*facta*] the glory [*gloria*] of your ancestors [*maiores*]. Joyfully does the earth receive you in her bosom, o Scipio Publius Cornelius, born to Publius. (*Inscriptiones latinae liberae rei publicae* 311)

Publius, possibly the son of Scipio Africanus (236–183 B.C.E.), died before he could accomplish great things as befitting his family. Therefore, the inscription speaks of the possibilities that would have been realized had he lived. The sequence of value terms utilized here highlights some of the most important qualities of a Roman *vir*: *honos* (in this usage, the acquisition of high office), *virtus*, and *ingenium*. These values combine to give the man *fama* and *gloria*, which in turn bestow more grandeur on his family, and thus he has actively paid heed to his *mos maiorum* (ancestral custom).

This epitaph is also indicative of the competitive nature of the Roman elite. The vying for authority in politics, the military, and religious fields was directly related to the attainment of *auctoritas* (the power and right to initiate; the authority and prestige that comes from the capacity to initiate) and external *imperium* (the right to give orders and be obeyed outside the city walls). The familial pride and competition that underscored Roman masculinity are further illustrated by the inclusion of the spoils of military achievements in temples and in the private home (*domus*), where the display of ancestral images (*imagines*) is a feature of the *atrium*. The adornment of homes with weaponry and related accoutrements of defeated enemies was not only a privilege permitted to the patricians and *nobiles*; lower-class citizens could demonstrate their masculine accomplishments in the same way and thereby also set the standard for their sons to follow.

Throughout the republic, the primary means by which a male could serve the state and thus demonstrate his masculinity was through military service and/or leadership. Therefore, from an early age, boys were indoctrinated in the values of soldiery and trained to attain the physical attributes it required. Much of this education no doubt came at the father's instigation, which was part of his responsibilities as one invested with *patria potestas* (fatherly authority or power). After assuming the *toga virilis* (toga of manhood) around the age of fifteen, a young male underwent military training, including time as a reserve soldier. The rewards for military service, for embodying the qualities of *virtus*, were generous for both the average infantryman and his elite leaders. A Roman soldier's bravery ensured he would receive material benefits in the form of booty as well as various honors and military decorations (see Polybius, *The Histories* 6.39). For the elite officers, the rewards were, of course, greater. A commander of victorious military campaigns was honored at a public triumph. Called a *vir triumphalis* (man of triumph) and possessing the power of one holding *imperium*, he would be paraded through the streets of Rome, chariot-borne, preceded by the members of the Senate, various fanfares, animals destined to be sacrificed, the conquered peoples and their leaders, the spoils of war, and his troops (see Plutarch, "Life of Aemilius Paulus" 34). Additional advantages for successful leaders included an increase in their status within senatorial ranks.

There were severe punishments for the citizen who did not adhere to the strict procedures that governed masculinity. In relation to the battlefield, for example, a cowardly or rebellious soldier was subject to a variety of punishments. For groups of mutinous or indolent soldiers, the punishment was often *decimatio* (literally, the removal of a tenth), which involved the choosing by lot of one man in ten, to be beaten to death by his recalcitrant peers (see Livy, *History of Rome* 2.59.9–11).

The essence of Roman masculinity was also expressed through the body. As a Roman citizen did not cede power to another—for that is to assume the role of a woman or slave—his masculinity was inextricably tied to the inviolability and invulnerability of his body. Thus, to be scourged like a cowardly soldier or a slave is have forfeited *virtus* and be subject to intense degradation. Adherence to the code of behavior and honor that regulated the life and reputation of the Roman male also ensured protection of his body—the outward manifestation of his *virtus* and power. As a *vir*, and especially as one who possessed *patria potestas*, the Roman male's sense of authority, self-worth, and respectable disposition were directly allied with control—not only over the members of his household (wife, children, slaves) but over himself, particularly his body. Thus, the Roman male was expected to be vigilant in relation to such matters by avoiding, for example, an indulgent lifestyle that would render his physique flabby, weak, or in some way feminized. A lifestyle marked by temperance also extended to control over one's sexual body, and thus a marker of vigorous masculinity was the assumption of an active role in all sexual activities, be they with females or males. To be in any way passive, specifically in relation to penetration or the performance of acts deemed unmanly (such as oral stimulation), was to betray one's social standing and to lose control.

As Roman masculinity was a precarious condition that was always under threat, so austere and demanding its requisites, it needed to be constantly guarded, acted upon, and monitored—not only by the individual but by his family and associates as well. There were regular external threats to masculinity such as the moral degeneration that arose after the Roman conquests of the second and first centuries B.C.E., particularly after the destruction of Carthage in 146 B.C.E. (see Sallust, *War with Jugurtha* 41). The works of Sallust (86–ca. 35 B.C.E.) discuss the influences of external forces, such as environment, on masculinity; for example, he writes of the effects of the contact with Asia under Sulla's command in the mid-80s B.C.E.:

> In order to ensure the support established of those whom he had led into Asia, Lucius Sulla excessively approved a luxury and freedom against ancestral tradition [*mos maiorum*]. These charming and idyllic lands, during times of leisure [*otium*], easily softened the warlike spirits of the soldiers. There, for the very first time, the soldiery of the Roman people became compelled to participate in erotic activity, to drinking; to admiring statues, paintings, and engraved vases and to stealing them from private and public places; and to desecrating temples and polluting everything sacred and profane....As soon as riches came to be honored, glory [*gloria*], the right to give orders [*imperium*] and power [*potentia*] followed them; manly virtue [*virtus*] began to fade, a moderate lifestyle regarded a disgrace, integrity [*innocentia*] to be taken for malevolence. (Sallust, *War with Catiline* 11.5–12.1)

In this passage, the idyllic, charming lands of Asia, which offered not only temperate climate but a culture of luxury, corrupted Roman soldiers. Here there is a contrast between what the Romans liked to regard as the demanding environment and climate of Italy, which produced strong, hardy peoples—predominantly soldiers and farmers—and the lush climate of Asia, which produced soft effeminates, lacking in physical and moral fiber. Exposure to luxury and leisure time is shown to have clearly affected the soldiers, damaging the value system and increasing the lust for power and authority. Sallust's work, composed after the end of the republic, exemplifies the role of the moral historian as the voice of probity and tradition, an embodiment of a collective social conscience.

The potential vulnerability of this system of gender identity is illustrated, then, in the threats made to it. These threats were increasingly realized as the era of the republic gave way to the imperial age. While the first emperor, Augustus (63 B.C.E.–14 C.E.), vigorously advocated the resurrection and maintenance of the social and moral values of masculinity, particularly in his program of moral reform, the reality was, nevertheless, that a sole ruler represented a significant curtailment of one's access to *virtus, gloria*, and related values. This was because *auctoritas*, once exclusive to the senatorial class, became the prerogative of one man. As "first citizen," or *princeps*, the emperor held not only supreme *auctoritas* over the Senate but supreme *imperium* and *potestas* also. In this way, a Roman man, whose responsibility was to serve the state and augment his own standing and that of his family, saw his freedom to do so—his *libertas*—stifled. This became the case increasingly as subsequent emperors followed and the power of the senatorial elite, and indeed all *liberi* (freeborn men) diminished.

Femininity. While masculinity, particularly in the republic, was marked by a code that governed lifestyle, performance of duty, and morality to ensure the preservation of society, there was a complementary system for women. The poet Statius (ca. 45–ca. 96 C.E.) emphasizes the discrete value systems of men and women when he congratulates Julius

Menecrates on the birth of his third child, noting that *virtus* is expressly suited to sons, so his daughter will serve him best by the provision of a grandson (*Silvae* 4.8). Statius implicitly underlines the gendered roles of Roman society, specifying the values appropriate for both men and women. For a woman to embody *virtus*, for example, is to assume a masculine role, which is inappropriate.

The most important value for women, indeed required of women, was *pudicitia* (an awareness of modesty, chastity, feminine virtue). This value underpinned the life of the Roman female, from her premarital years as a *virgo* (virgin), to her time as a *nupta* (a bride and a new wife), through to her role as a *matrona* (a married woman with a child or children). The essence of *pudicitia* was not only one that a woman had to embrace mentally, but one that was required to be performed. As with masculinity, femininity was inscribed on the body and was thus displayed in a woman's appearance: the way she presented herself in public, her gait, her clothing, the way she communicated her modesty. Indeed, a woman's display of positive values had to be witnessed by others; this would validate her intrinsic goodness and thus bring a form of female *gloria* to her husband and her children—especially her sons—as well as her family and family-in-law. The poet Catullus (84–ca. 54 B.C.E.) captures such an ideal of womanhood in his marriage hymn for Marcus Torquatus and Junia Aurunculeia, which concludes with a wish for a baby boy who will resemble his father and thus prove the *pudicitia* of his mother:

> May he be like his father
> Manlius and easily recognized
> by all who do not know his origin,
> and prove the chastity [*pudicitia*]
> of his mother by his face.
> May such praise of him by reason of a good
> mother establish his descent.
>
> (61.214–220)

One of the archetypal examples of *pudicitia* from the semilegendary history of Rome is the heroine Lucretia. Beautiful, but more importantly chaste, Lucretia was the wife of Lucius Tarquinius Collati-

nus. Livy (59 B.C.E.–17 C.E.) emphasizes her womanly virtues, her *castitas* (chastity), and accentuates her embodiment of *pudicitia*: "Lucretia, in contrast to the daughters-in-law of the king, who had been seen at a luxurious banquet, idling time with their companions, was—though it was late at night—intent upon her weaving, while her handmaidens worked with her in the lamplight as she sat in the hall. The prize of this contest of womanly virtue went to Lucretia" (*History of Rome* 1.57.9–10).

Livy captures Lucretia's *pudicitia* in several ways: she did not indulge in luxurious living by partaking in extravagant banquets or in idleness and gossip; she made effective and appropriate use of her time by working wool late into the night, an activity that was a potent signifier of what constituted dutiful behavior for a *nupta* or *matrona*.

Lucretia's beauty, dutifulness, and purity aroused the lust of Sextus Tarquinius, the son of the tyrannical king of Rome, Lucius Tarquinius Superbus. Sextus violated Lucretia, who, after exacting a promise of revenge from her husband and her father, took her own life. Lucretia's suicide was interpreted by the Romans as evidence of her womanly virtue. Lucretia, though receiving support and absolution from her father and husband, took her own life because she believed her *pudicitia* was irredeemably lost and her husband's *dignitas* impaired: "Although I absolve myself from the transgression, I do not free myself from the penalty; no unchaste [*impudica*] woman shall henceforth live by the example of Lucretia" (*History of Rome* 1.58.10). A martyr to her perfection, Lucretia became a symbol—an almost unattainable ideal—for Roman women of both the elite and plebeian classes.

Funereal monuments of women, which sometimes included statues of the deceased with their bodies covered in the feminine robe (*palla*), an image defined as the pose of *pudicitia*, often had an accompanying epitaph that read: "I kept house. I worked wool." On an inscription dated between 135 and 120 B.C.E. for a woman named Claudia, it reads: "Stranger, the message is short. Stand and read it through. Here is the unlovely tomb of a lovely woman. Her parents called her by the name

Claudia. She loved her husband with her whole heart and she bore two sons, one of whom she leaves on the earth. She was charming in conversation but nevertheless appropriate in disposition. She kept house. She spun wool. I have spoken thus. Go your way" (*Inscriptiones latinae liberae rei publicae* 00973). In an epitaph almost certainly arranged by her husband, Claudia epitomizes the necessary and valued qualities of the *matrona*. Herein we see, some four hundred years after the story of Lucretia, the embodiment of her ideal by a real Roman woman.

The significance of *pudicitia* in Rome is further exemplified by the personification of the concept in the form of a goddess of the same name. Unfortunately, there are no extant sources on how the goddess was worshiped in rituals. Livy provides some interesting insights into the possible origins of the cult in his discussion of an alleged argument between patrician and plebeian women in 296 B.C.E. (see *History of Rome* 10.23.1–10). Livy reveals that there was a sanctuary of patrician Pudicitia, and, owing to its class-based access, plebeian women established their own precinct, naming it the temple of plebeian Pudicitia. In the conclusion to his etiological description of the second precinct, Livy provides a specific qualification for participating in the rites; namely, a woman had to be a *matrona* of obvious *pudicitia* and to have been married to one man only. A "once-married" woman is encapsulated in the term *univira* (literally, "one man woman"), a word that has an unbroken history from early republican texts through to the Christian era (on the term in the early empire, see Propertius 4.11). The *univira* was a special and revered woman, and while the epithet was used of women from the upper echelon, like so many value terms, it was also adopted by those of less elite status. This appropriation of ideals, values, and role modeling exemplifies the social diffusion that characterized, in particular, the late republican and imperial ages.

Like masculinity, idealized forms of femininity in ancient Rome were vulnerable states that could be destabilized and were thus in need of constant vigilance and protection. Female beauty, for example, was potentially dangerous, stimulating lust and thereby placing a woman like Lucretia in a vulnerable position regarding her *castitas*. A woman's reputation was easily sullied and, once tarnished, was almost impossible to restore. Women who challenged the socially constructed boundaries of femininity were liable to public condemnation, as evidenced in Ovid's portrait of Claudia Quinta (fl. late third century B.C.E.), ancestor of the aforementioned Claudia:

> Claudia Quinta traced her bloodline [*genus*] from lofty Clausus,
> nor was her outward appearance at odds with her nobility [*nobilitas*].
> Chaste [*casta*] indeed, but not also credited as such: an unjust rumor
> had afflicted her, and she was made a defendant on a false charge.
> Her refinement [*cultus*] and the fact of her stepping out with her hair variously adorned
> stood against her, and a ready tongue aimed at straitlaced old men.
> A conscience aware of what was true laughed off the mendacities of gossip;
> but we are a credulous mob when it comes to vice [*vitium*].
>
> (*Fasti* 4.305–312)

The patrician Claudia Quinta was a famous example of perfect femininity: a *matrona* par excellence and a devout woman who served her family. Nevertheless, Ovid is at pains to stress that she was also a woman who took pride in her appearance, styled her hair, and spoke her mind. These characteristics, which countered the strict code of *pudicitia* in its external manifestation, thereby cast doubt on Claudia's reputation, and thus, whether she deserved it or not, she was the subject of *infamia* (ill repute).

Conclusion. The Roman republican period, from earliest times until its late period, had a clearly prescribed set of boundaries that defined the expression of masculinity and femininity. While the values that underscored the gender dynamics of the republic were initially prescribed for the elite members of society, they were the models that plebeians and, later, non-Roman members of the empire aspired to emulate. The imperial age saw the rise of individual men as sole rulers; thus masculine values and the avenues in which to express them may be regarded as having been limited, as the emperor and his *auctoritas* undermined the voice and influence of the Senate, and the magisterial roles of individual men. Nevertheless, the drive to possess, augment, and express one's masculinity was still an imperative. Likewise, while the late republic saw an increasing freedom for women, traditional ideals of femininity were still extolled and indeed reinforced by Augustus (although, at times, with limited success). Monuments, epitaphs, and literature of all genres consistently reflect traditional gender binaries and expectations despite, at times, a contested, complex, and shifting sociopolitical environment.

[*See also* Gender; Gender Transgression, *subentries on* Greek World *and* Roman World; Masculinity and Femininity, *subentry* Greek World; Sexual Transgression, *subentry* Roman World; *and* Social Interaction, *subentry* Greek and Roman Worlds.]

BIBLIOGRAPHY

D'Ambra, Eve. *Roman Women.* Cambridge, U.K.: Cambridge University Press, 2007.

Degrassi, Attilio. *Inscriptiones latinae liberae rei publicae.* 2 vols. Florence: La Nuova Italia. 1957–1963.

Dixon, Suzanne. *Reading Roman Women: Sources, Genres, and Real Life.* London: Duckworth, 2001.

Edwards, Catharine. *The Politics of Immorality in Ancient Rome.* Cambridge, U.K.: Cambridge University Press, 1993.

Foxhall, Lin, and John Salmon, eds. *When Men Were Men: Masculinity, Power, and Identity in Classical Antiquity.* London: Routledge, 1998.

Gardner, Jane F. *Being a Roman Citizen.* London: Routledge, 1993.

Hallett, Judith P. *Fathers and Daughters in Roman Society: Women and the Elite Family.* Princeton, N.J.: Princeton University Press, 1984.

Langlands, Rebecca. *Sexual Morality in Ancient Rome.* Cambridge, U.K.: Cambridge University Press, 2006.

Lightman, Majorie, and William Zeisel. "*Univira*: An Example of Continuity and Change in Roman Society." *Church History* 46, no. 1 (1977): 19–32.

McDonnell, Myles. *Roman Manliness:* Virtus *and the Roman Republic.* Cambridge, U.K.: Cambridge University Press, 2006.

Olson, Kelly. *Dress and the Roman Woman: Self-Presentation and Society.* Milton Park, U.K.: Routledge, 2008.

Skinner, Marilyn B. *Sexuality in Greek and Roman Culture.* Malden, Mass.: Blackwell, 2005.

Walters, Jonathan. "Invading the Roman Body: Manliness and Impenetrability in Roman Thought." In *Roman Sexualities*, edited by Judith P. Hallett and Marilyn B. Skinner, pp. 29–46. Princeton, N.J.: Princeton University Press, 1997.

Williams, Craig A. *Roman Homosexuality.* 2d ed. Oxford: Oxford University Press, 2010.

Marguerite Johnson

New Testament

Before specifically addressing the New Testament, this entry first considers the Greco-Roman context.

Masculinity and Femininity in the Greco-Roman World. Studies of masculinity and femininity in the Greco-Roman world—the conceptual matrix of the New Testament—underwent a revolution in the 1980s and 1990s after the work of Michel Foucault's *History of Sexuality.* As outlined in *The Use of Pleasure* and *Care of the Self*, Foucault argued that unlike biologically determined sex, gender is a cultural construction whose norms and practices are collectively established, situational, and not driven exclusively by genetic or reproductive difference. His work converged with long-standing research on the New Testament, principally driven by debates over the role of women in ecclesiastical and liturgical practices, and by the rising numbers of women among the professional guilds of biblical interpreters and church historians. Many of Foucault's individual arguments have been modified by later scholarship; his fundamental assumptions about the relationship of gender and hierarchy, however, have been used with profit, generating readings whose fundamental plausibility seem to confirm his theses. Other scholarship has revealed a complicated and nuanced picture of cultural norms for gender description and behavior in antiquity (not necessarily at odds with Foucault's fundamental assumptions) by exposing and elaborating on the diverse and variegated practices actually found in the texts.

Gender and hierarchy. Perhaps Foucault's most fundamental insight was that gender in Greco-Roman literature, roughly contemporary with the New Testament, was intractably woven together with construction(s) of hierarchy. Roman political, economic, and social culture were stratified. Issues such as family of origin, ethnicity, and wealth complicated social status, but a fundamental assumption was that altern social groups, individuals, customs, social norms, and even traits were defined as more "masculine" but not as sexual preference(s). One performed gender by articulation or demonstration of one's social and economic power. Further, gender, like alterity or hierarchy, was a continuous scale or spectrum. One might be "masculine" in one context, yet "feminine" in another. Gender, Foucault argued, was a performed identity and was somewhat plastic and malleable, resulting in both potential and risk. Gender "maintenance" was a constant concern and was intrinsically tied to social privilege and status.

Gender and public/private space. Gender description in the Greco-Roman world largely conceded, at least in the articulation of the ideal-type, long-standing Western ideas that divided the spheres of public and private life into masculine and feminine realms, respectively, for the "proper" performance of gender. Public activities (economic, political, academic, martial, civic, etc.) were the privilege of men. Women were consigned to private or domestic activity (food preparation, care of children, household management, etc.). These ideas were attended by belief that women needed strict management, lacking "male" self-control, discernment, logic, or self-discipline. Infantilized, women were, in extreme cases such as in classical Athens, actually physically confined to the interior of the house for much of their adult lives.

Variations in practice. Recent scholarship, while generally confirming Foucault, has complicated some of his arguments. While gender was deeply intertwined with hierarchy and social division, scholars such as Sarah Pomeroy and Elisabeth Schüssler Fiorenza have evidence from antiquity and nascent Christianity in which the expression of norms was often "violated" or nuanced. In some cases, women violated expectations and taboos

without undue public censure and, occasionally, commentary.

Given its reliance on political monument or the haphazard remains of public literature, most evidence from antiquity is remarkably limited and overwhelmingly skewed toward the educated and economic elite. In reality, however, the Roman Empire was remarkably diverse, so that we cannot assume that what was true for one region or social class was true generically or that what one text argues or asserts was universally conceded. Given these variations, evidence exhibiting the highest geographic and chronological parity with the New Testament provides our best information. Prior scholarship, for example, often constructed ideas of women's opportunity in communities contemporary with Paul (mostly Western Turkey during the mid-first century C.E.) by using evidence of gender expectations from literature written in fifth century B.C.E. Athens. Aware of this dubious practice, Ross Kraemer Shepherd and Sarah Pomeroy have argued that while general trends and conventions may have existed, individual norms and activity for men and women could, and did, vary. Social norms for strict division of gender in terms of domestic verses public activity varied by socioeconomic status, ethnicity, and by geopolitical needs.

Masculinity and Femininity in the New Testament. Because the texts of the New Testament only rarely address masculinity and femininity in theoretical terms, our study must (re)construct values and assumptions by what the texts imply, either in argument or in examples of performed roles. Nevertheless, a general pattern emerges: in general, the canonical New Testament equates gender with hierarchy (where "masculinity" is dominant) and a nod toward division of public and private spheres. We also have conflicting data regarding expectations and potential in the construction of masculinity and femininity. Much of the latter is the result of the compositional process of the New Testament and the complexity of the history of nascent Christianity. Many scholars argue that the movement following Jesus in the first two centuries C.E. was more varied than uniform in terms of ethnicity, socioeconomic status, and even confession. Furthermore, the documents preserved in the New Testament were composed in a variety of contexts (say, Palestinian versus Diaspora Judaism, Jewish versus gentile community) over a period of about 150 years. Some were written, some were initially oral, some were combinations of the two.

The Synoptic Gospel traditions. Matthew, Mark, and Luke present a largely male world that conforms to both aspects of Greco-Roman gender construction. Jesus's genealogy is (largely) given in patriarchic terms (Matt 1:1–16; Luke 3:23–38). Gospel lists of the apostles are male, despite other gospel evidence that women were part of Jesus's inner circle (Matt 10:1–4; Mark 3:13–19; Luke 6:12–16). His parables tend to feature male protagonists and reflect male, public concerns (commercial activity, governance, agricultural work). His disputes are among other males. Marriage and divorce policies are oriented toward male prerogative and desire, not female needs or reality; the afterlife will not be gender-differentiated (Matt 5:27–32; 19:3–9; Mark 10:2–11; 12:18–27).

There are some notable exceptions. Several stories, among the most popular, feature Jesus healing women (Matt 9:18–26; Mark 5:21–43; 12:41–44, 47; Luke 7:11–17; 8:40–56). Women are particularly drawn to displays of devotion to Jesus, washing his feet and anointing his hair (Matt 26:6–13; Luke 7:36–50). In one confrontation, Jesus is persuaded to heal a non Jewish woman (a "Syrophonician" or a Canaanite woman) who out-duels him in word play, even after he insultingly compares her to a (female) dog (Matt 15:21–28; Mark 7:24–30). Women are occasionally protagonists in parables, but usually confined to domestic activity (Matt 25:1–13; Luke 21:1–4). Mary Magdalene is a significant figure in the synoptic Passion traditions (Matt 27:55; 28:1, 5, 10; Mark 16:1–8; 15:40, 41; Luke 23:55–56). In Luke, she is a financial backer of Jesus (along with Joanna who leaves her husband to follow Jesus, Luke 8:1–3). In all Gospels, women followers are the first to declare an empty tomb and a risen Jesus; in all Gospels, Mary Magdalene is among the most prominent of these women.

Women fare best in the Gospel of Luke, which notes the impressions of Mary, the mother of Jesus, during Mary's pregnancy and Jesus's childhood, the only account to do so. Luke also presents the character of Elizabeth, Mary's cousin and mother of John the Baptist, and Anna, a prophetess who recognizes the infant Jesus (Luke 1:1–23, 26–56, 57; 2:36–38). Luke notes that women, particularly Mary Magdalene and others, followed Jesus and financially supported him (Luke 8:2). Luke contains some key healing stories and parables where women are protagonists (Luke 15:8–10; 18:1–8). Luke mentions the characters of Mary and Martha: Martha displays typical domestic-oriented femininity; Mary "prefers the better" as she sits at Jesus's feet (Luke 10:38–42). The author of Luke continues this attention on women in his second volume, the Acts of the Apostles, noting women among the apostles (Acts 1:13–14), the conversion (or resistance) of prominent women (Acts 5:14; 13:50; 17:12), early women prophets (Acts 21:8–9), and several strong female characters, some of whom are partners in early mission work (Acts 9:36–41; 12:12; 16:11–15; 18:2, 18, 26).

The pauline traditions. Scholars do not unanimously concede that all thirteen letters attributed to Paul were actually composed by him. In general, scholarship agrees seven are authentically Pauline without serious question (Rom, 1—2 Cor, Gal, Phil, 1 Thess, and Phlm). Gender construction plays a role in these debates. The seven undisputed letters reflect a community with comparatively egalitarian gender opportunity. Later traditions suggest a clear inscription of gender difference and reassertion of more traditional norms.

In the undisputed letters, Paul acknowledges women as equal partners in his ministry, regarding some as deacons, some as co-workers (fellow missionaries), and one (Junia) as an "apostle" (Rom 16:1, 3, 6, 7, 12, 15; 1 Cor 1:11; 16:19; Phil. 4:2–3; Phlm 1:2; Col 4:15). In places, Paul is explicit that in the new community of followers of Jesus, gender, like ethnicity, does not matter as all are equal before God (Gal 3:28). The Pauline letters, like the Pauline traditions in Acts, recognize women prophets, teachers, deacons, evangelists, and, perhaps, apostles. Ephesians

4:10–12 provides a listing of some ancient Christian "vocations" or offices of service; there are explicit (often named) examples of women fulfilling each of these offices in the canonical literature associated with Paul. Paul does not seem to concede a normative bifurcation between public and private domains and gender activity, at least not when it comes to the opportunity to spread the teachings of/about Jesus.

Paul, however, does not argue for absolute gender equality. For example, he asserts women are to keep their heads covered in public prayer and prophecy (1 Cor 11:2–16; men are not so restricted). Paul sees his views as confirmed by nature (1 Cor 11:14–15). Paul opposes divorce but not marriage (1 Cor 7:1–40; he also observes that it is good for a man not to touch a woman). For Paul, God is the apex of order; failure to recognize the real God (or God's messiah, Jesus) is a violation of cosmic order. This abrogation of order results in sexual and gender disruption (Rom 1:22–27). Though still granting conventional notions of gender and hierarchy, Paul does allow for more activity of women beyond the domestic field.

The disputed epistles complicate this idea. Both Colossians and Ephesians present household codes that reestablish male domination within the home (Col 3:18–20; Eph 5:22–33). Women are subordinate to men in ways equivalent to the believer's subordination to Jesus. They are not to value "outward adornment" but to cultivate inner (domestic?) beauty. In the Pastorals women are forbidden, explicitly, from roles in public teaching (at least of men) and are restricted from having any authority over a man (1 Tim 2:13–15). Female deacons (or the wives of deacons; the text is not clear) must be temperate and not given to gossip (1 Tim 3:11). This subordination is grounded in the "natural" order, with the clear assumption that women are easily duped or deceived and lack appropriate discipline. Women's sexuality is a temptation to men, which should be controlled and avoided (1 Tim 5:2, 11–15). Women are weaker intellectually and readily duped by false teachers (2 Tim 3:6). The Pastorals declare women will be saved "through childbirth" and are to keep, otherwise, silent, given their flawed natures (1 Tim

2:15; as exhibited by Eve). In other words, the Pastorals conform to elite male Greco-Roman prejudices about women and reaffirm these gender norms. This tendency to restore conservative views on women vis-à-vis a curtailing of public activity may well have spilled back into the conventional Pauline letters. Scholars of the text tradition of 1 Corinthians have noted that 14:33b–36's injunction to women's complete silence and submission (a position diametrically at odds with Paul's other remarks in the same letter that women are to have covered heads when speaking in Christian assemblies) is a later insertion, bringing 1 Corinthians into harmony with the Pastorals. Many scholars argue that the Pauline tradition began with a cautiously open attitude toward greater gender equality. Even here, though, Paul assumes fundamental gender frames from Roman culture. Later Pauline traditions rein in this trend toward equality and reinscribe (elite) Roman convention restricting women onto Pauline traditions.

The Catholic epistles. These five epistles (Hebrews, James, 1–2 Peter, Jude) say little about gender, explicitly or implicitly. The book of Hebrews does not address the issue at all, although it focuses upon the masculinity of Jesus (stressing his status as "son of God"), presents only male exemplars of faith (11:1–40) and generally focuses upon masculine metaphors (12:1–7). James addresses gender only in its calls for compassion for the widows and the fatherless. Jude and 2 Peter exclusively address false teaching regarding, as one of many elements for condemnation, the "lasciviousness" of false teachers and their tendency to confuse women and the simple-minded (2 Pet 2:2, 10, 14, 18; Jude 1:7). The Petrine letters have a brief moment in 1 Peter 3:1–7 where attention is given to household administration. Slaves are told to be submissive; "in the same way" wives are called upon to be submissive to their husbands. Their status is decidedly domestic and subordinate; women are not to speak in public.

In other words, women do not appear at all in the public vision of the Catholic epistles save for a few remarks that conform to traditional ideas of women's intellectual inferiority and adjurations for women to remain within their submissive, domestic spheres.

The Catholic epistles famously (e.g., 1 Pet 4:12–19) appeal to general social conservativism. Largely thought to address Diaspora and gentile audiences, a typical theme is to eschew not only false teaching (i.e., to present a united front) but also to avoid engagement with social issues, which would cause further division or outsider suspicion. This general tendency toward social conservatism mirrors the epistles' views on gender. Though saying little specifically about the matter, these documents, in many ways, most demonstrate typical Greco-Roman gender ideology.

The Johannine literature (and Revelation). In John's Gospel, the sisters Mary and Martha appear again, but interest now is upon their brother Lazarus (John 11:1–44); Mary anoints Jesus's feet (John 12:1–8). Returning, and also more vibrant, is the character of Mary Magdalene (John 19:25; 20:1–18). These figures seem to be followers of Jesus at least as dynamic, if not more, than most of the apostles. Later manuscript traditions of John have stories of Jesus in private conversation with a Samaritan woman (a violation, some argue, of multiple gender taboos) and as a defender of a woman caught in adultery (John 4:7–30; 7:53—8:11). The Gospel Passion narratives present a problem for the masculinity of Jesus in terms of Greco-Roman norms. In essence, Jesus as God (hierarchy of hierarchies) is murdered by the state, penetrated, and beaten. The Gospels all "reframe" this narrative by showing the intentionality of Jesus in suffering. Defeat now becomes an expression of (ideologically driven) disciplined defiance. In an argument advanced by Colleen Conway, Jesus in John is at his most masculine when "controlling" the events of his trial and execution. Jesus (and his followers) become masculine in defeat by employing the trope of the martyr.

The Johannine epistles all address questions of early Christian missionary work. They refer to the church as "the elect lady," but consistently use masculine metaphors for God and believers (2 John 1:2, 5, 13; 2 John 2:1, 12–14). In the *Apocalypse of John*, women prophets are viciously condemned with overtly sexualized gender-slurs (Rev 2:20–23). The reserves of the Kingdom of God are men who have

avoided "defilement" by women (14:4). Sin is metaphorically equal to contact with women (Rev 18:3, 7–10). The city of Rome is personified, famously, as a whore; she will be condemned to brutal public rape before she is eaten alive (Rev 17:1–18). The one female protagonist is cast aside on her own once she has delivered her child (Rev 12:1–6, 13–17). The "Bride of Christ" turns out to be a city (Rev 21:1ff). In John's Gospel, the interest is in a mystic and clearly masculine Jesus. Men and masculine activities dominate the account. There is, however, interest in key women, and there are suggestions of a feminine element within God as well. The Apocalypse, however, is bitterly angry at women, first sexualizing, then dismissing them. The Apocalypse is also deeply invested in structures of sociopolitical—indeed, even cosmic hierarchies. In its hierarchical worldview, women are debased and devalued (very much in keeping with Greco-Roman conventions).

To summarize: the New Testament generally conforms to Greco-Roman conventions on the enmeshment of gender difference and hierarchy and to conventions that divide public and private spheres into gendered spaces. The New Testament also contains diverse ideas on gender performance. Some parts of the text seem more open to gender-egalitarianism. Some moments forcefully reassert and defend conservative Greco-Roman norms. The New Testament seems to reflect a trajectory of change. Earlier followers of Jesus were more egalitarian in their construction of gender norms and their tolerance for women's violation of the domestic/public bifurcation. Later traditions become more socially conservative, in extreme cases arguing that women have no voice in public or leadership roles.

Disputes and Debates. This variation is root cause for much scholarly debate regarding New Testament texts. While clearly the gender-norms of the Roman World (and, by extension, the New Testament) were more restrictive in many ways than present American or British norms, it does appear that there are moments reflected within the New Testament that argue for a greater degree of gendered, egalitarian communities. Yet there are also moments within the New Testament that implicitly and explicitly reinscribe conventional norms. Scholarship remains skewered on the various horns of this dilemma, with some scholars arguing that the New Testament promotes gender egalitarianism, while others argue that it does not. Most likely, it does both: some voices resist convention, others reinscribe or assume it.

Much of the scholarship on gender in the New Testament from the second half of the twentieth century was working to unveil the actual complexity of the New Testament writings about women, revealing the moments of women's activity, explicit language for gender-equality, and attempting to contextualize the later restrictions. This data has provoked substantial debate among Christian communities that regard biblical text as ground for faith and practice, as well as among groups who tend to see the narratives of the first centuries of Christianity as etiological. Other scholars have argued for a much more dynamic view of ancient Christianity, noting that its variety vis-à-vis gender occurs as a result of a community that is evolving in its self-description while also influenced by various cultural voices. Still other scholars have regarded the New Testament as a historically and culturally bound document; seeing particulars in terms of argument as sometimes culturally dictated, they seek out the larger, essential, ideological argument, often abandoning language on gender difference all together. Scholars further debate whether figures such as Jesus or Paul were more or less inclusive of women. Once again, these arguments tend to eventually become intertwined with arguments constructing etiological narratives of nascent Christianity or inter-related with constructions of gender found in late Second-Temple Judaism.

Until very recently, scholarship did not regularly attend to the ways that the New Testament grounds its construction of gender norms in hierarchical structures. Contemporary criticism, largely by feminist and queer-theory scholars, has worked to reveal the way the New Testament assumes fundamentally hierarchical structures argued in terms of gender, but actually articulating norms of domination. Such moments have become, in later communities influenced by the Bible, the basis for social structures that preserve (if not perpetuate) social imbalance, and present gender distinction and roles as essentialist and "natural"—indeed, more than just natural but also decreed and inscribed by divinity. Implicit in such arguments is that modern gender construction rests, knowingly or not, upon these biblical texts and their long history in establishing cultural norms, taboos, and ideal-types. Revealing that the arguments of the New Testament reflect a (now debatable) infatuation with domination would, some hope, result in both reassessment of these hierarchies in modern society and reorient debates about the arbitrariness of gender differentiation. To date, this scholarship is regarded by many as hostile to traditional Christian theology and community.

[*See also* Family Structures, *subentry* New Testament; Gender; Jesus; Paul; Masculinity Studies; Masculinity and Femininity, *subentries on* Greek World *and* Roman World; *and* Religious Leaders, *subentry* New Testament.]

BIBLIOGRAPHY

Conway, Colleen. *Behold the Man: Jesus and Greco-Roman Masculinity.* New York: Oxford University Press, 2008.

Foucault, Michel. *The History of Sexuality.* Vol. 2 : *The Use of Pleasure.* Translated by Robert Hurley. New York: Viking, 1985.

Foucault, Michel. *The History of Sexuality.* Vol. 3: *The Care of the Self.* Translated by Robert Hurley. New York: Viking, 1986.

Gaventa, Beverly Roberts. *Our Mother Saint Paul.* Louisville, Ky.: Westminster John Knox, 2007.

Gleason, Maud W. *Making Men: Sophists and Self Presentation in Ancient Rome.* Princeton, N.J.: Princeton University Press, 2008.

Kraemer, Ross Shepherd. *Her Share of the Blessings: Women's Religions Among Pagans, Jews and Christians in the Greco-Roman World.* New York: Oxford University Press, 1994.

Martin, Dale. *Sex and the Single Savior.* Louisville, Ky.: Westminster John Knox, 2006.

Moore, Stephen D. *God's Gym: Divine Male Bodies of the Bible.* New York: Routledge, 1996.

Moore, Stephen D. *God's Beauty Parlor: And Other Queer Spaces in and around the Bible.* Stanford, Calif.: Stanford University Press, 2001.

Moore, Stephen D., and Janice Capel Anderson, eds. *New Testament Masculinities*. Semeia Studies, 45. Atlanta: Society of Biblical Literature, 2003.

Newsom, Carol A., and Sharon H. Ringe, eds. *Women's Bible Commentary*. Rev. ed. Louisville, Ky.: Westminster John Knox, 2012.

Pomeroy, Sarah B. *Goddesses, Whores, Wives and Slaves: Women in Classical Antiquity*. New York: Schocken, 1975.

Pomeroy, Sarah B., and Lin Foxhall, eds. *When Men Were Men: Masculinity, Power and Identity in Classical Antiquity*. New York: Routledge, 2010.

Schüssler Fiorenza, Elisabeth. *In Memory of Her: A Feminist Theological Reconstruction of Christian Origins*. New York: Crossroad, 1983.

Robert Seesengood

Early Judaism

See Gender Transgression, *subentry* Early Judaism.

Early Church

The English terms "masculinity" and "femininity" refer to cultural designations for gender roles for men and women. Although it has become commonplace among scholars to differentiate sex (a biological category) from gender (a culturally constructed category) there was significant overlap in the ancient world; clear-cut distinctions are, therefore, anachronistic when thus applied. Taking into consideration the intersections between sex and gender, the following discussion is divided into four main sections: common terminology; sex and gender construction; gender roles in the early church; and discursive appropriations of the categories of "masculinity" and "femininity" in early Christian literature.

Common Terminology. Common Greek and Latin terms for male/masculinity and female/femininity include *gunē/femina/mulier* (woman), and *anēr/vir/homo* (man). As Kraemer discusses, the Greek terms *gunē* and *anēr* are used to denote adult females and males, but the terms may also indicate that a woman or man is married (2010, p. 12). The terms,

therefore, relate either to sex assignment or to marital status. Latin terminology is somewhat more precise: "woman" (*femina/mulier*) is differentiated from "wife" (*uxor*). But *vir* denotes either maleness or married status. Corbeill notes that the Latin pair *vir/femina* are used in prose works to signify elite members of society, while *homo/mulier* denote nonelites (2010, p. 223). Two Latin terms were used to indicate perceived gender deviance, which some scholars suggest may reflect a third gender category: *tribades* refers to a woman assuming the dominant role (i.e., the male role) in a homoerotic relationship. The *cinaedus* is a man who is the recipient—rather than the penetrative agent—of a sexual act in a homoerotic relationship. To understand gender categories and their attendant virtues, we must understand constructions of sex in the ancient world.

Sex and Gender Construction. Scholars commonly describe the differences between male and female in antiquity as a difference of degree rather than of kind or type. Maleness was the *telos* of a hierarchy of perfection, and any particular individual could be "mapped" along a vertical axis between perfect maleness on one end and imperfect maleness (or femaleness) on the other. Burrus describes the ancient system as "a dynamic spectrum or gradient of relative masculinities" (2007, p. 4). Greek and Roman medical and philosophical traditions regularly assert the perfection of the male and thus the flawed nature, or imperfection, of the female. Philo, for instance, states that "the female is nothing else than an imperfect male" (*Questions and Answers on Exodus* 1.7). Likewise, Aristotle understood the female to be "like a mutilated male" (*Generation of Animals* 737a). Expressing the relative perfection of male to female, Galen explains that "within mankind the man is more perfect than the woman" (*On the Usefulness of the Parts of the Body* 14.7).

Not all males, of course, could be placed at the pinnacle of maleness—nor females at the nadir—so ancient medical theories had to explain cases where men and women acted in unexpected ways. Sometimes men were unmanly and women were unwomanly. Hippocratic traditions suggest that both males and females produce sperm that varies in strength. If both sexual partners emit strong sperm, a male is conceived; if both partners emit weak sperm, a female is conceived; if sexual partners produce different strengths of sperm, the sex of the fetus is determined by numerical superiority (*On Generation* 6.2). The masculinity or femininity of an individual was related—in this theory—to both the quality and quantity of male/female sperm. Thus it was possible for a male to exhibit feminine qualities and a female to exhibit masculine ones; both would be abhorrent, unnatural. Heat was another common explanatory factor for both sex and gender differences. Galen explains the inferiority—indeed, the very existence—of the female by appealing to her "lack of heat"; conversely males are perfected through their "excess of heat" (*On the Usefulness of the Parts of the Body* 14.7).

Claims to the biological superiority and perfection of maleness have direct implications for understandings of virtue. As the male was the perfect sex, so males, likewise, were expected to embody the more perfect, more desirable, traits. Among the male virtues in the ancient world were justice, self-control, wisdom, and "manliness" (*andreia*) (Plato, *Phaedrus* 69C; Plutarch, *On the Advantage to Be Derived from One's Enemies*, 88C). After Philo asserts the relative perfection of the male, he continues by identifying male and female characteristics. Femaleness is in all ways opposite to maleness: it is "material, passive, corporeal and sense-perceptible," while maleness is "active, rational, incorporeal and more akin to mind and thought" (*Questions and Answers on Exodus* 1.7). The relationship of maleness to perfection of virtue is clear in the language: *virtus*, "virtue," is reminiscent of—if not etymologically derived from—*vir*. Indeed, Cicero claims the etymological derivation as an explanation of inherent male superiority (*Tusculan Disputations* 2.18.43). Males who exhibit cowardice, lack of self-control, emotionality or who act in other nonmasculine ways are described as "unmanly" (*anandros*). Women who display unexpected courage or rationality are described as men (*Passion of Perpetua* 10.7; Pliny the Elder, *Natural History* 7.4.36–39). Ancient medical literature, importantly, institutionalizes women's inferiority, not

only biologically but also socially since virtue, in this system, is inextricably linked to nature.

Gender is always relationally constructed. Femininity, as we have seen, is defined over against masculinity. Masculinity is equally relational: a person is understood to be more or less masculine in comparison to another person or being. Thus all relationships require mapping of relative masculinity and femininity, which takes into consideration not only biological sex but—even more importantly— social status. Defining masculinity and femininity relationally allows authors to portray individuals as displaying ideal virtue regardless of their biological sex. In other words, various ideal virtues associated with masculinity and femininity may be utilized in ancient discourse apart from a person's sex, either with an intent to praise or to shame individuals or groups.

Gender Roles in the Early Church. Reconstructing gender roles in the early church is a difficult task that is complicated by the prescriptive literature that emerges from Christian circles. Establishing the range of appropriate gender roles, especially for women, has occupied scholars since the emergence of the feminist movement within biblical and early Christian studies. Although scholarship is generally moving more toward analyzing literary representations of gender (see discussion later) and what they tell us about early Christian social concerns, there are, nevertheless, some conclusions that may tentatively be posited regarding possibilities for service within the early church.

On occasion, issues of dress—largely concerned with women's dress—are addressed in early Christian literature. Paul, famously, exhorts the women in the Corinthian church to cover their heads when they pray and prophesy (1 Cor 11:6). Why Paul requires this—and even what he implies by it—remains the subject of scholarly dispute. Ross Kraemer (2011) argues that contemporary art suggests Roman matrons did not always cover their hair and, thus, for women to show their hair was not a transgression of gender expectations. Nonetheless, head coverings, when worn, signify a woman's submission to a man's authority (p. 137). In the third century C.E.,

Tertullian underscored Paul's teachings on veiling in a treatise that criticized virgins who defied the scriptural mandate ("On the Veiling of Virgins," 10). For Tertullian, at least part of the problem with unveiled women was related to sexual temptation; reminding the women of his congregation that they were the "devil's gateway," he insisted they be modest in dress ("On the Apparel of Women," 1.1).

Varieties of gender roles in the early church may be traced to New Testament texts. On the one hand, the Pauline epistles are often read as reflecting a rather egalitarian stance. Romans 16 lists a number of women who appear to have held important roles in the local churches and who presumably served alongside men. So also 1 Corinthians 11 indicates that women pray and prophesy in worship settings, as do men. On the other hand, later texts associated with the Pauline school restrict women's roles. 1 Timothy 2 teaches that women are to be silent in church; they may not teach. That some early Christians drew on Pauline support to establish public leadership roles for women is clear from Tertullian's outrage: he asserts that the Apocryphal *Acts of Paul and Thecla*—on the basis of which, he says, women were asserting the power to baptize—was not authentic ("On Baptism," 18.5). In making the case against women's leadership roles in Christian ritual, Tertullian appealed to 1 Timothy.

Within proto-orthodox circles of the second century and beyond, traditional Roman gender roles seem to have prevailed. Churches, for example, were led by male bishops (see 1 Tim 3: 1–7). Groups that come to be labeled "heretical," such as Montanism, may earn that title, in part, because they promulgate alternative gender norms: scholars have traditionally seen Montanism—at least in its roots in Asia Minor, though most likely not in its North African iteration—as promoting women's leadership in the church. Two of the three prophets associated with the earliest days of the movement were women (Epiphanius, *Panarion* 1.3).

There is, however, some evidence for a female diaconate in the proto-orthodox church—at least through the sixth century C.E.—predominantly, but not exclusively, in the Greek East, which suggests that memories of women's clerical and ordained roles in the church were lost sometime thereafter. Evidence for female presbyters is also extant, though less prevalent. The sources gathered by Madigan and Osiek indicate that a female diaconate may have been charged, especially, with assisting at the baptism—and attendant rituals—of women. The earliest Latin attestation for a female diaconate comes from Pliny the Younger's account of his prosecution of Christians. He mentions choosing two female slaves "who were called deacons (*ministrae*)" ("Epistle to Trajan," 10.96). Several influential Christian writers of the patristic period—John Chrysostom (e.g., *Letter* 96; 103; 191), Severus of Antioch (e.g., *Letter* 69–72), and Theodoret (e.g., *Letter* Patmos 48)—address letters to women with the title "deacon"; ascetic *vitae* also refer to female deacons (e.g., *Life of Macrina* 29). The widespread employment of the title "deacon" for women in the Greek East and, somewhat less often, in the Latin West, requires scholars to nuance previous views of women's subordination in the clerical hierarchy of the Late Antique church.

The ascetic movement provided some Christian women with opportunities for independence that were otherwise difficult to attain. Ascetic women are referred to as "manly" by ascetic authors, an appellation that may reflect a measure of equality in opportunity available through asceticism, as Elizabeth Clark has argued (1981, p. 245). Through asceticism, women might avoid unwanted marriages—including attendant problems such as abuse—dangerous pregnancies, and might control the distribution of their wealth (Clark, 1981, pp. 253–254; Kuefler, 2001, p. 223). Indeed, in form—particularly in the Latin West— women's and men's monasticism were similar: both were often set in homes (as opposed to the wilderness of Eastern monasticism) and both centered on spiritual—rather than physical—labors. The freedom accorded ascetic women in contradistinction to their matron contemporaries is seen in their ability to travel for pilgrimages (e.g., Palladius, *Lausiac History* 46) and their instruction in—and teaching of—scripture and doctrine (e.g., *Life of Melania the Younger*, 54).

Gendered Discourse in Early Christian Literature. Literary interests in gender roles in the early church reflect specific social and ecclesiastical settings; they are not fixed or consistent across time and space, and thus there is no single early Christian view of gender roles. Rather, early Christians employed gender expectations to particular ecclesiastical, doctrinal, and apologetic ends. Colleen Conway (2008) argues that scholars must take into account not merely hegemonic masculinity but also competing alternative masculinities that may either support or subvert the dominant model (p. 11). From this perspective, it is clear that Christian literature sometimes employed gendered language in terms that appear to align with normative Roman gender expectations, but at other times it subverted larger cultural gender assignments. In both cases, of course, Christian discourse is drawing on—either in support of or in rejection of—the dominant constructions of gender. In acknowledgment of these differences, the following discussion will categorize various types of Christian literature in terms of their relationships to dominant Roman models of masculinity and femininity rather than making generalized claims. The discussion cannot, of course, be exhaustive of types of Christian literature or their constructions of gender; rather, it is suggestive of approaches to gender in the literature of early church.

Two genres of literature that emerge within a milieu of persecution are martyr literature and apologetics. Both of these sets of texts draw on constructions of hegemonic masculinity to paint Christianity as nonthreatening and, thus, Christians as innocent victims of persecution; they also present Christians as ideal models of masculinity—along with its attendant virtues—in comparison to their Jewish and pagan persecutors. Such a depiction is important because it maps masculinity onto Christianity as a whole, as Caroline Vander Stichele and Todd Penner (2009) have demonstrated: "the characteristics thus attributed to a group are in turn believed to be present in all of its members" (p. 73).

Martyr literature regularly portrays faithful Christians as reasonable, rational, courageous, and self-disciplined—in short, as men. Thus, it appeals to hegemonic constructions of gender to portray Christianity as embodying ideal masculinity while pagans, Jews, and apostate Christians are mapped lower on the scale. The *Martyrdom of Polycarp*, for instance, demonstrates Christian masculine self-control by asserting that Christians remain steadfast during torture. Polycarp, for instance, is "not troubled" (5.1) when he is arrested, and when the proconsul threatens him with death, the martyr "did not collapse in terror" (12.1). The author juxtaposes Christian self-control with pagan emotionality, a signal of pagan non-manliness: the pagan bystanders "were brought to pity and mourning" at the sight of torture (2.2). While the Christians in the text embody all of the qualities of normative masculinity, their opponents are depicted as embodying feminine qualities and ideals. In addition to being emotional, Christian opponents are irrational, unjust, and out of control. But only one character in this narrative is described with the Greek term *anandros*, "unmanly," and he is an apostate Christian. Thus, in this text masculinity is mapped from the zenith of the martyr downward, through the pagan persecutors and the pagan and Jewish crowds, to the nadir, the apostate Christian who is the most unmanly of them all (Cobb, 2008, pp. 60–91).

The *Martyrdom of Polycarp* does not narrate stories of female Christians, so it is to the *Passion of Perpetua* that we turn to glimpse gender constructions for female martyrs. In this text, Perpetua is described as separating herself from worldly concerns (that is, femininity) and concentrating on heavenly concerns (that is, masculinity). She miraculously stops lactating (6.8), a sign of her physical movement toward a drier, hotter, male body (Cobb, 2008, pp. 102–107). Before her martyrdom, she receives a vision in which she prepares for a battle with Satan. Her assistants remove her robe for battle and the martyr declares, "I became a man" (10.7). The transformation from femininity to masculinity is complete and Perpetua dies a faithful martyr. Martyr texts' claims to masculinity function as shaming mechanisms for Christianity's opponents: even Christian women and slaves are more manly than pagans and Jews. Importantly, however, these texts do not subvert Roman constructions of gender; rather, they appropriate them. These texts, in other words, draw on the discourses of masculinity to claim superior rationality, courage, and justice for Christianity as a whole.

As martyr texts claim hegemonic masculinity—in spite of the realities of persecution—to depict faithful Christians as self-controlled, self-possessed, and reasonable, while the persecutors are depicted as unmanly, so also apologetic literature makes similar claims, and to similar ends. Justin's *Apologies* may be taken as illustrative of the representation of gender in apologetic literature with the aim of shaming the narrative—though most likely not "real"—audience, the emperor. Justin's rhetoric emphasizes pagan profligacy and immorality in comparison to Christian self-mastery, a "sexual slander," as Jennifer Wright Knust (2006) demonstrates, that is gendered. Christians are portrayed as exhibiting masculine qualities while pagans embody feminine qualities.

Ascetic literature provides an interesting case for gender analysis in early Christianity because—from the perspective of traditional constructions of masculinity that focus on power and penetration—*askesis* itself is a feminizing practice. Late-ancient Christianity, however, reformulated the discourse surrounding *askesis* such that it became a central element in the construction of a masculinized Christianity. As Matthew Kuefler (2001) observes, emphasizing the strength and steadfastness required of asceticism masculinizes it; so also, appropriating Roman gendered associations of femininity with sexuality allowed Christian authors to paint women as temptresses (pp. 170–178). Women who excelled at the ascetic life, however, were portrayed as "manly."

Asceticism champions submission to divine power rather than assertion of self-will and continence rather than sexual prowess. The case of the young virgin martyr Agnes reflects the gender-bending so often seen in ascetic literature. On the one hand, as Burrus demonstrates, Prudentius's Agnes is feminized in that she "is penetrated by sacrifice or Christ" but masculinized in relation to the "feminized executioner" (1995, p. 45). Two types of literature emerging from the ascetic movement in early Christianity are the *Apocryphal Acts* and ascetic *Vitae*. Although both genres may be understood as challenging normative constructions of gender, they may also, at times, be understood as shifting claims to masculinity away from the human realm into the divine realm. That is, as Conway (2008) notes, "Rather than transcending gender, God is the perfect example of masculinity" (p. 36). Taken from this perspective, the ubiquitous feminizing of the ascetic—both male and female alike—may reflect a (traditional) mapping of gender, one that sees God as residing at the zenith of masculinity.

Gender reversal is a common motif in *Apocryphal Acts*. A conversion scene in the *Acts of Andrew*, for example, casts the male disciple Andrew as midwife and the male convert Stratocles as both the laboring mother and the fetus. The women who observe the conversion are cast as guarantors of the conversion moment, a masculinizing role (Schwartz, 2007, pp. 298–299). After the conversion, Andrew is recast in a masculine role, as father to the new convert. The female protagonist, Maximilla, is called a "wise man" (*andros*; 41), thus confirming a gender reversal for her. Nonetheless, the *Acts* finally conform to normative gender constructions, even if they are momentarily queered for narrative effect. As Saundra Schwartz (2007) notes, Maximilla's actions propel the plot, but it is Stratocles "who emerges from the narrative as the focalizer" (p. 310). The female convert may function as a role model for female Christians, but she is ultimately subordinated to the male convert, in whom the disciple finds the one he loves and desires (43.2–3). Stories such as these, offering complex gender descriptions of the narrative heroes and heroines, endorse the gender hierarchies prevalent in the Roman world: male power is confirmed, often by means of female participants (Cooper, 1996).

Hagiographical accounts of ascetic women's lives often describe their heroines' pious achievements in masculine terms. Palladius states that the accomplishments of his female exemplars are "equal to those of men" (*Lausiac History* 41), but he goes on to indicate that these women had achieved glory in asceticism because they had "masculine and perfect mind[s]" ("Introduction," 1). It was problematic to refer to Melania the Elder as female—"if one can call so manly a Christian a woman" (Paulinus, *Letter* 29.6)—for she was, in fact, a "female man of God" (Palladius, *Lausiac History* 9). The complex relationship of feminine sexuality to masculine piety is apparent also in Palladius's description of Olympius: "not a woman but an *anthropos*, a manly creature: a man in everything but body" (Palladius, *Dialogue* 16.179–90; cf. description of Macrina in *Life of Macrina* 960; Nonna in Gregory of Nazianzus, *Concerning Himself* 116; Melania the Younger in *Life of Melania the Younger* prologue; 39). Gillian Cloke (1995) argues that such designations of ascetic women may serve as shaming mechanisms for less pious men (p. 132); such descriptors might also indicate the equality of struggle in which male and female ascetics engaged (p. 133). Ultimately, as Cloke argues, the language of masculinity in hagiographies of female ascetics underscores the understanding that in the early church, femaleness was a condition to be surpassed: "anyone holy enough to be an exemplar of the faith could not be a woman" (p. 135). By contrast, Nonna Verna Harrison (1994) argues that the gendered rhetoric in asceticism does not indicate a need for female transformation into the perfect male but, instead, a Christian understanding of the soul as incorporating both masculine and feminine qualities. Ascetic literature, from this perspective, imagines the transcendence of gender altogether. In this reading, it is especially the alignment of the feminine with values such as receptivity and interiority that are utilized in the construction of the ideal ascetic individual (p. 67).

Assessment. The terms "masculinity" and "femininity" as used and performed in the early church may serve diverse discursive needs. At times they are used to subvert dominant hegemonic gender constructions, while at other times early Christian authors appropriate—and claim—the dominant model for the Christian community. Sustained attention to patterns in the literature reveals a diversity of such appropriations and claims, rendering it impossible to maintain that the early Christians inhabited a single model or view.

[*See also* Gender Transgression, *subentries on* Early Church *and* Roman World; Male-Female Sexuality, *subentry* Early Church; Masculinity and Femininity, *subentries on* New Testament *and* Roman World; *and* Religious Participation, *subentry* Early Church.]

BIBLIOGRAPHY

Burrus, Virginia. "Reading Agnes: The Rhetoric of Gender in Ambrose and Prudentius. " *Journal of Early Christian Studies* 3 (1995): 25–46.

Burrus, Virginia. "Mapping as Metamorphosis: Initial Reflections on Gender and Ancient Religious Discourse." In *Mapping Gender in Ancient Religious Discourses*, edited by Todd Penner and Caroline Vander Stichele, pp. 1–10. Biblical Interpretation Series 87. Leiden, The Netherlands: Brill, 2007.

Clark, Elizabeth A. "Ascetic Renunciation and Feminine Advancement: A Paradox of Late Ancient Christianity." *Anglican Theological Review* 63 (1981): 240–257.

Cloke, Gillian. *This Female Man of God: Women and Spiritual Power in the Patristic Age, A.D. 350–450*. London: Routledge, 1995.

Cobb, L. Stephanie. *Dying to Be Men: Gender and Language in Early Christian Martyr Texts*. New York: Columbia University Press, 2008.

Conway, Colleen M. *Behold the Man: Jesus and Greco-Roman Masculinity*. New York: Oxford University Press, 2008.

Cooper, Kate. *The Virgin and the Bride: Idealized Womanhood in Late Antiquity*. Cambridge, Mass.: Harvard University Press, 1996.

Corbeill, Anthony. "Gender Studies." In *The Oxford Handbook of Roman Studies*, edited by Alessandro Barchiesi and Walter Scheidel, pp. 220–233. Oxford: Oxford University Press, 2010.

Harrison, Nonna Verna. "The Feminine Man in Late Antique Ascetic Piety." *Union Seminary Quarterly Review* 48 (1994): 49–71.

Knust, Jennifer Wright. *Abandoned to Lust: Sexual Slander and Ancient Christianity*. New York: Columbia University Press, 2006.

Kraemer, Ross. *Unreliable Witnesses: Religion, Gender, and History in the Greco-Roman Mediterranean*. New York: Oxford University Press, 2011.

Kuefler, Mathew. *The Manly Eunuch: Masculinity, Gender Ambiguity, and Christian Ideology in Late Antiquity*. Chicago: University of Chicago Press, 2001.

Madigan, Kevin, and Carolyn Osiek. *Ordained Women in the Early Church: A Documentary History*. Baltimore: Johns Hopkins University Press, 2005.

Schwartz, Saundra. "From Bedroom to Courtroom: The Adultery Type-Scene and the *Acts of Andrew*."

In *Mapping Gender in Ancient Religious Discourses*, edited by Todd Penner and Caroline Vander Stichele, pp. 267–312. Biblical Interpretation Series 87. Leiden, The Netherlands: Brill, 2007.

Vander Stichele, Caroline, and Todd Penner. *Contextualizing Gender in Early Christian Discourse: Thinking Beyond Thecla*. New York: T&T Clark, 2009.

L. Stephanie Cobb

MASCULINITY STUDIES

Masculinity studies is an interdisciplinary academic field spanning the humanities and social sciences. It flourishes in such disciplines as anthropology, sociology, history, literary studies, and cultural studies (Adams and Savran, 2002). Most often, masculinity studies is the analysis of how masculinity is represented, constructed, or performed in specific cultural contexts (Simpson, 2011; Watson and Shaw, 2011). For most practitioners of masculinity studies, masculinity—or masculinities—are not innate, invariable, or inevitable. They are not anatomically or biologically predetermined or otherwise hard-wired, but are rather the complex products of interlocking systems of stylized behaviors and symbolic practices that are historically contingent and culturally variable (Reeser, 2010). The term "hegemonic masculinity," popularized by the sociologist R. W. Connell in his seminal study *Masculinities* (1995), is frequently employed in masculinity studies. It refers to the mode of masculinity idealized or exalted in a given culture and used to legitimate patriarchy within it (p. 77). Hegemonic masculinity is realized by relatively few males, but is sustained through the complicity of many more. It emerges co-constitutively against *subordinated masculinities*, such as male homosexuality in many contemporary cultures (pp. 78–79). Masculinity is plural, then, not just across cultures (many cultures, many masculinities) but also within cultures (many masculinities within a single culture).

Masculinity Studies and the Hebrew Bible. According to Björn Krondorfer (2009), "An early interest in men and religion by religious studies scholars is already discernible in the 1980s, though it took about ten more years before these scholars began to identify themselves—albeit often tentatively and loosely—as belonging to a group working on common themes" (p. xiv). This was the general context in which the first monograph on biblical masculinity appeared. Howard Eilberg-Schwartz's *God's Phallus and Other Problems for Men and Monotheism* (1994) argued that the maleness of the biblical God is a problem for ancient Israelite men, ancient Jewish men, and Jewish men of any age. The Hebrew Bible enjoins love for a male God on its male audiences and that divine-human relationship is described in erotic terms through metaphors of marriage and sexual intimacy. Men can assume their assigned role in this sexualized relationship only by imagining themselves as wives of the male God, notwithstanding the taboo against homoeroticism. The problem of Yahweh's maleness is also the reason why his body is an object of concealment: this divine cover-up is designed to mitigate the conundrum that the injunction to human males to love a male God would create for a culture centrally preoccupied with procreation. Whereas numerous feminist studies have demonstrated how "a divine male both legitimates male authority and deifies masculinity" (p. 2), Eilberg-Schwartz demonstrates how that ideology is fractured and destabilized by anxious contradictions.

Two essays from the following year sought to show not how biblical masculinity comes apart but rather how it coheres. David Clines's "David the Man" (1995) had as its immediate focus the construction of masculinity in the David story (1 Sam 16—1 Kgs 2), but argued that the six masculine traits discernible in that story reflected the cultural norms of ancient Israelite masculinity more broadly. Being a formidable warrior, capable of deadly violence against other males, was the foremost masculine characteristic. Being "intelligent in speech" (1 Sam 16:18), an eloquent and persuasive speaker, was a second masculine trait; being beautiful or comely in form was a third; being a male who bonds intensely (but perhaps not emotionally) with other males was a fourth; being a male who does not bond with women was a fifth; and being a skillful musician was a sixth. Clines's essay may be seen as an early attempt to rough out a "grammar" of ancient Israelite masculinity—an account of the codes and conventions that determined the performance of hegemonic masculinity in that culture. Relatedly, John Goldingay's "Hosea 1—3, Genesis 1—4 and Masculist Interpretation" (1995) isolated three prime masculine traits in Genesis 1—4. Men are constituted differentially in relation to women; men possess authority; and men have a capacity for violence. Goldingay analyzed the character of Yahweh in Hosea 1—3 in terms of these three traits, arguing, for example, that "Yahweh is incomplete without Israel as men are incomplete without women" (p. 165) and that he fully displays the male propensity for violence. Yahweh, however, is caught in contradiction. As Hosea 11 indicates, even God does not possess the hypermasculine omnipotence that God is supposed to possess. Stephen Moore's *God's Gym: Divine Male Bodies of the Bible* (1996) also analyzed Yahweh's masculinity (pp. 75–102), but in a cultural studies mode. Noting that Yahweh is predominantly represented as corporeal, perfect, and male and, as such, is implicitly a physically perfect male, Moore appealed to contemporary bodybuilding culture to decrypt and deconstruct Yahweh's masculinity. Yahweh is massively encompassed by the defensive trappings of hegemonic hypermasculinity. This excessive masculinity, however, queerly teeters over into its opposite, femininity, thereby explaining both Yahweh's application of female metaphors to himself/herself and his/her misogyny.

This modest flurry in the mid-1990s of studies of Hebrew Bible masculinities was followed by a ten-year hiatus in which relatively little work centrally devoted to the topic appeared (see Stone, 2001, 2007; Clines, 2002; Sawyer, 2004; Haddox, 2006; Olson, 2006; cf. Chapman, 2004). The year 2010 saw the publication of Ovidiu Creangă's edited collection, *Men and Masculinity in the Hebrew Bible and Beyond*. Many of its essays ventured generalizations on ancient Israelite masculinity. Independently yet cumulatively, the twelve main essays built up a multifeatured sketch of the ideal Israelite man. This man differentiates himself sharply and self-constitutively from all that is female or feminine. He does not dress like a woman nor act like a woman. He avoids unnecessary association with, and emotional attachment to, women. He disdains the feminine, asserting or assuming the inferiority of women. Yet he also needs women as producers of (male) progeny to perpetuate his name. This hyperhegemonic man also constitutes himself over against other males. He is able to dominate other males physically. He is skilled in weapons and warfare. He unleashes lethal aggression against male enemies. His honor is his most precious possession. It entails guarding the chastity of his women. It is also tied to such traits as generosity, hospitality, and integrity. Additionally, he is wise, articulate, and persuasive, able to exchange the sword for the word as an instrument to control lesser males.

Several of the contributors to *Men and Masculinity* were drawn to emasculating moments in the biblical texts. Brian DiPalma, for instance, argued that the opening chapters of Exodus deconstruct masculine values and begin to construct a reconfigured gender identity for Moses, whereas Creangă argued that Joshua's masculinity in the conquest narrative is destabilized by ambiguity and the absence of definitive masculine traits. For still other contributors, Israel's God is the principal (and paradoxical) source of deconstructive destabilization or complication of Israel's masculine values. Submission, for example, runs counter to those values—to be a man is to refuse to submit—yet Yahweh demands absolute submission from his male subjects. This leads to contradictions comparable to those earlier explored by Eilberg-Schwartz (1994). The ideal masculinity of the Hebrew Bible is at once a hegemonic masculinity and a subordinated masculinity.

In 2011, Susan Haddox's monograph *Metaphor and Masculinity in Hosea* appeared. She noted that whereas the female imagery in Hosea has received much attention, the more extensive male imagery has not. She identified seven linguistic markers of masculinity in Hosea, including military might, honor, virility, and the ability to provide for a household. Unlike earlier exercises of this kind, however, Haddox's markers of masculinity were not drawn solely from the Hebrew Bible. Building on the work of Cynthia Chapman (2004), Haddox also extracted masculine traits from Assyrian textual and iconographic sources, such as royal inscriptions. She argued that Hosea's audience is composed primarily of elite males whose social persona was hypermasculinized, and Hosea's rhetoric aims to erode this masculinity. More specifically, Hosea employs the imagery of Assyrian treaty curses to reinforce Yahweh's hegemonic masculinity while undermining the masculinity of the audience. This is where Hosea's infamous female imagery comes into play. Haddox argues that Hosea treats his opponents not as rival men but as emasculated males, representing them as a whoring wife who has aroused the punitive wrath of her lord and husband, Yahweh.

Masculinity Studies and the New Testament. Single-minded studies of masculinity in the New Testament began in 1994 with Eilberg-Schwartz's *God's Phallus* and Jennifer Glancy's "Unveiling Masculinity: The Construction of Gender in Mark 6:17–29." *God's Phallus* dealt briefly (Eilberg-Schwartz, 1994, pp. 223–237) with the infancy narratives of Matthew and Luke, arguing, for example, that Matthew relativizes physical descent by dissociating Jesus's paternity from Joseph or any human father. Matthew "contests the Jewish conception of paternity" (p. 233) and effects "a transformation of the meaning of masculinity" (p. 234), since "the male organ of generation" now "begin[s] to lose [its] positive value" (p. 235). Glancy's methodology was also broadly psychoanalytic. Taking her inspiration from prominent female Freudians, she approached Mark's tale of the imprisonment and execution of John the Baptist "with the assumption that masculinity is a front to disguise vulnerability and weakness" (Glancy, 1994, p. 36). Her analysis of the gender relations between Herod, Herodias, the dancing daughter, the all-male audience of the dance, and the (soon beheaded) Baptist yielded such conclusions as that "active voyeurism is a prerogative of masculinity" in the narrative; "that masculinity is vulnerable before the expression of female desire…; and perhaps that the bond between a mother and her daughter is threatening to men who encounter them" (p. 42).

Moore's "The Beatific Vision as a Posing Exhibition: Revelation's Hypermasculine Deity" (1995) focused on the hyperhegemonic, phallic male form that is the object of unceasing adoration in Revelation and the central fixture of its throne-room spectacle. As in his related study of Yahweh's body, Moore utilized the contemporary cultural spectacle of male bodybuilding to defamiliarize this queer scene of mass worship. It is Jesus and Paul, however, who have been the principal foci of New Testament masculinity studies. Clines's "*Ecce Vir*, or, Gendering the Son of Man" (1998) tackled the masculinity of the Jesus who emerges from the composite portrait of the canonical gospels (cf. Ward, 1999, which also dealt with the masculinity of the composite Christ). Clines employed an adapted version of his model of ancient Israelite masculinity to analyze the gospel Jesus(es). The essay's conclusions may be relayed by listing the titles of the six subsections that make up its central section: "Jesus the Strong"; "Jesus the Violent"; "Jesus the Powerful and Persuasive Speaker"; "Jesus the Male Bonder"; "Jesus the Womanless"; and "Jesus the Binary Thinker." Moore pondered Paul and masculinity in "Que(e)rying Paul" (1998), first parsing out certain of the fundamental traits of hegemonic masculinity in the ancient Mediterranean world, such as self-mastery (see also Moore and Anderson, 1998), and then turning to Romans and using the gender logic encrypted in 1:26–27 to decode the letter's soteriology. Implicitly for Paul, Jesus is a paragon of masculinity and the salvation celebrated in Romans amounts to the attainment of true manhood. Righteousness in Romans, conceived as self-mastery, is essentially a masculine trait, whereas unrighteousness or sin, conceived as lack of self-mastery, is essentially a feminine trait. Brigitte Kahl also tackled Paul in "No Longer Male: Masculinity Struggles behind Galatians 3:28?" (2000). The burning issue in Galatians, that of circumcision, is, as Kahl notes, exclusively a male issue. Paul's critique of circumcision in Galatians amounts to a radical reconception of Israel as no longer defined or determined by male descent, fathers begetting sons who become fathers in turn. Since circumcision was the physical token of the covenant with Abraham and hence of the patrilineal concept of Israel, Paul's reconception of Israel as no longer centered on physical fatherhood also entailed a decentering of maleness. According to Kahl, "The male Galatians' wish to get circumcised then would indicate a profound desire to return to a less confusing understanding of what it meant to be a Jew, free, and, on top of all that, a man" (p. 49).

Two other early studies in New Testament masculinity focused on Luke–Acts. Abraham Smith's "'Full of Spirit and Wisdom': Luke's Portrait of Stephen (Acts 6:1—8:1a) as a Man of Self-Mastery" (1999) first tracked the topic of self-mastery, or control of the passions, through Greco-Roman moral discourse. It "was defined in androcentric terms, and even the women who possessed it were considered not 'feminine'" (p. 99). Smith argued that Stephen is presented as an exemplar of self-mastery, as are the other "witnesses" in Acts and Jesus in the Gospel of Luke. Smith ended by addressing the question, "Given the way self-mastery is constructed as a masculine trait, what are the ethical implications of embracing Luke's acceptance of this philosophical ideal?" (p. 106). Mary Rose D'Angelo's "The ANHP Question in Luke–Acts: Imperial Masculinity and the Deployment of Women in the Early Second Century" (2002) argued that masculine authority is deployed in Luke–Acts against a backdrop of unassertive feminine deportment to represent Christians as models of Roman imperial values, which were also gender values. The Lukan Jesus is an ideal man in the Roman mold—heroic, educated, and a skilled orator, whereas "Paul the Roman citizen is the climactic paradigm of elite Christian masculinity; his Jewishness guarantees the authentic antiquity of the Christian message; his citizenship its safety in the imperial world" (D'Angelo, p. 68). Meanwhile, the deference and devoted service the Lukan women lavish on its leading men "testifies to the rightness of early Christian gender arrangements" (p. 68).

In 2003, *New Testament Masculinities*, edited by Moore and Janice Capel Anderson, appeared. The volume's ten main essays analyzed the construction and performance of masculinity in Matthew, Mark, John, and Luke–Acts; the Pauline and deutero-Pauline letters; and the book of Revelation and the *Shepherd of Hermas*. Representative arguments advanced in the essays include the following. Matthew enshrines multiple contradictory assumptions regarding masculinity, sometimes reifying the dominant ancient Mediterranean codes of masculine behavior, sometimes challenging them. Mark's Jesus also embodies competing conceptions of masculinity, at once a victim and an agent of patriarchal gender norms. He is a vehicle of Mark's conflicted attempt to resist Roman colonialism while mimicking Roman imperial and masculinist authority. The high Johannine Christology is intimately intertwined with the superior masculinity of the Johannine Jesus—although even he is necessarily feminine in relation to God, the gospel's supreme embodiment of hegemonic masculinity. Paul's masculinity, as cumulatively constructed in his letters, displays marked continuities with the model of masculinity enshrined in the Hebrew Bible. Unrelatedly, Romans 1:18—2:16 is permeated by the topos of the emasculated Stoic ruler, and that charge of effeminacy is leveled by Paul against the stoicized magistrates of Rome. The Pastoral Epistles seek to cultivate an elite masculine self and, as such, a model for Christian masculinity that is at odds with the more anomalous models represented by John the Baptist, Jesus, and Paul. The Pastorals, Luke–Acts, and the *Shepherd of Hermas* all affirm male household government as a measure of manly virtue and engage in a dialectic of resistance to, and accommodation with, the "family values" promoted by Trajan and Hadrian. The intimately interrelated Roman themes of masculinity and activity/passivity illuminate Revelation's slain lamb, which although initially feminized is subsequently masculinized through a commanding performance of virility.

Colleen Conway's monograph, *Behold the Man: Jesus and Greco-Roman Masculinity*, appeared in 2008. It began with a chapter titled "How to Be a Man in the Greco-Roman World" and moved to an examination of how the masculinities of three "divine men" were constructed: Caesar Augustus, Philo's Moses, and Philostratus's Apollonius. Successive chapters then treated the construction of Jesus's masculinities in the Pauline letters, Mark, Matthew, Luke–Acts, John, and Revelation. Throughout, Conway was attentive to the intersection of New Testament masculinities and New Testament Christologies. One important contribution of the book was that it accorded unprecedented attention to Jesus's crucifixion as a problem for ancient hegemonic conceptions of masculinity (for previous treatments, see esp. Liew, 2003; Thurman, 2003, 2007). Mark's narrative, for example, from 8:31 onward, seems to prepare the audience to construe Jesus's impending demise as a heroic and noble death, as Conway notes, fully in accord with the canons of masculine honor in the ancient Mediterranean world. The passion narrative, however, muddies the clean lines of this noble death portrait. How is Jesus's anguish in Gethsemane to be construed? As erosion of his masculinity or confirmation of it through an exemplary performance of self-control? And what of his silence in his trial before Pilate? Submissive posture or manly self-restraint? Most of all, what of his cries from the cross? Conway's reflections end on a psychological note: "Perhaps at some unconscious level, there is genuine resistance to hegemonic masculinity to be found…in the cry of anguish from the cross," even if only for "a brief moment," since "the narrative soon moves to the rewards of the manly death represented by the empty tomb" (p. 106). In the narration of Jesus's death, nonetheless, "the grueling cultural demand[s] of hegemonic masculinity are exposed" (p. 106).

Paul's lash- and rod-scarred body (2 Cor 11:23–25a; cf. Gal 6:17) earlier provoked related reflections by Glancy. In "Boasting of Beatings (2 Cor 11:23–25)," Glancy (2004) argued that, contrary to what scholars have tended to imagine, beholders of Paul's scars would not have been culturally predisposed to see them as marks of courage so much as "markings of a servile body, insignia of humiliation and submission" (p. 99). Paul's paradoxical boast is "not of his *andreia* [manly courage] but of his humiliating corporal vulnerability" (p. 101). In a related article, "Paul's Masculinity," Jennifer Larson (2004) proposed that Paul's Corinthian critics appeal to cultural canons of masculinity: "Rhetorical skills were inextricably

tied to virility and manhood" (p. 87). To denigrate Paul's speaking skills, therefore, was to question his masculinity. Paul's response to his opponents, with its unabashed embrace of "weakness," is "a rejection of certain traditional standards of masculinity" (Larson, 2004, p. 94). Moisés Mayordomo Marin (2006), in "Construction of Masculinity in Antiquity and Early Christianity," a wider-ranging study of the Corinthian correspondence, also argued that the masculinity espoused by Paul is counterhegemonic—but not consistently so: Paul shares the hegemonic disdain for "unmanly," "effeminate" males (see also Ivarsson, 2007).

Bonnie Flessen's *An Exemplary Man: Cornelius and Characterization in Acts 10* (2011) shifted the spotlight from Jesus, Paul, and other towering New Testament men to a lesser character. Flessen argued that the elite protocols of Greco-Roman masculinity do not apply to Lukan characters like Cornelius who are not elite men and who therefore exhibit alternative masculinities. Cornelius is a multiply anomalous man, on Flessen's reading. As a nonviolent, pious centurion he does not match stereotypical representations of Roman military personnel. Yet he *is* a centurion and so embodies the power of the Roman Empire within the narrative. He even acts like a centurion to a degree, issuing orders to those under him. But Cornelius is also a centurion who acts like a pious Jew, submitting himself through prayer and almsgiving to the God of Israel. That submission also extends to God's human agents. The centurion paradoxically prostrates himself before Peter, a member of a subject people. If Cornelius is a Lukan model for Roman military masculinity, he must be deemed a counterhegemonic model of the first order.

Challenges for Biblical Masculinity Studies. The relationship of masculinity studies to feminist studies was once a controversial issue. Before the term "masculinity studies" began to circulate in the late 1990s, there was "men's studies." One end of the men's studies spectrum was staunchly pro-feminist, but the other end shaded over into masculinist men's movements that resisted feminism, waxed nostalgic for traditional masculinities, "and gathered men into supportive enclaves" (Gardiner, 2002,

p. 4). It was a time when embarking on the study of biblical masculinities required autobiographical explanations (Clines, 1998, p. 353), assurances that masculinity studies meant feminist studies no harm (Goldingay, 1995, pp. 161–163), or apologias designed to fold masculinity studies into feminist studies altogether (D'Angelo, 2002, p. 44; Moore and Anderson, 2003, pp. 2–3). These tensions have not vanished entirely. Yet many feminist biblical scholars seem less suspicious of masculinity studies than in the past. Symptomatic of this increased acceptance is the introduction to the latest edition of the *Women's Bible Commentary*: "As we decided to do a third edition… we realized that a wholesale revision was needed, for several reasons. First, the field of feminist biblical criticism has developed in profound ways in the last twenty years. Issues that were just beginning to be explored in 1989—the hermeneutical significance of sexual identity, analysis of masculinity, and postcolonial positioning—were, by 2009, very much a part of feminist criticism" (Lapsley et al., 2012, p. xxii).

By then, too, biblical masculinity studies was also very much a part of historical criticism. Early investigations of biblical masculinities were variously fueled by psychoanalytic theory (Eilberg-Schwartz, 1994; Glancy, 1994), sociology (Clines, 1995), cultural studies (Moore, 1995, 1996, pp. 75–102), autobiographical criticism (Parsons, 1995), queer theory (Moore, 1998), and French critical theory (Ward, 1999). But on the New Testament side in particular, methodological eclecticism soon reduced to a standard method or interpretive strategy, for which the field of classics was the enabling interdiscipline. One proceeded deductively, first homing in on key aspects of ancient Mediterranean masculinity, which were handily prepackaged in various works of classical scholarship (e.g., Gleason, 1995; Williams, 1999), and then measuring selected New Testament males against these masculine yardsticks. This is the version of masculinity studies that has caught on in New Testament studies, one that requires engagement with no extradisciplinary field other than classics, the privileged interdiscipline for New Testament scholarship since its inception.

Masculinity studies of the Hebrew Bible has been a less formulaic enterprise. Practitioners do not have the luxury of proceeding deductively for the most part, since the relevant comparative literature is more scant and there are no encyclopedic profiles of ancient Near Eastern masculinities on hand. Yet most of the work on Hebrew Bible masculinities has been thoroughly historical-critical in at least one respect. In his response essay in *Men and Masculinities*, Clines (2010) expresses dismay that the essays in the collection appear to have "no agenda…other than intellectual curiosity" (p. 238). That may be why biblical masculinity studies has only made modest inroads into feminist studies: much of masculinity studies appears to lack political passion.

The missing political agenda might be supplied using analyses of ancient masculinities—especially the counterhegemonic masculinities now commonly identified in biblical texts—to critique contemporary expressions of hegemonic masculinity—especially those that appeal to biblical texts for legitimation. A further opening up of biblical masculinity studies to queer theory (see Moore, 2001; Stone, 2001, 2007, 2011; and esp. Burke, 2013, which follows a chapter on queer theory with a chapter on ancient masculinities) might serve such a critique. Deryn Guest (2012), for instance, writing from a queer/LGBT perspective, questions the tendency in biblical masculinity studies "to think in terms of gender reversals"—the feminization of males, the masculinization of females—rather than to consider how the ostensibly feminized male, say, "may be better understood in liminal terms as gender indeterminate," which is "a better way forward than concentrating solely on gender reversals which do not question the two-sex, two-gender fiction" (p. 142). Such an analysis might still "be labelled a study in masculinity, but it will be so much more for it will come from a place informed by feminist, queer, trans theory that…sees its contemporary political import" (p. 142). A widespread turn of this sort in biblical masculinity studies would also entail, on the New Testament side, a recovery of the frequently forgotten origins of classical masculinity studies in the work of three politicized gay men—

Michel Foucault (1985, 1986), David Halperin (1990), and John Winkler (1990)—and a rediscovery that the concept of gender as performance, commonplace in both classical and biblical masculinity studies, derives from queer theory (Butler, 1990) and contains much largely untapped subversive potential.

[*See also* Gender; Imagery, Gendered, *subentries on* Deuteronomistic History *and* Prophetic Literature; Masculinity and Femininity, *subentries on* Hebrew Bible *and* New Testament; *and* Queer Theory.]

BIBLIOGRAPHY

Adams, Rachel, and David Savran, eds. *The Masculinity Studies Reader.* Oxford: Blackwell, 2002.

Burke, Sean D. *Queering the Ethiopian Eunuch: Strategies of Ambiguity in Acts.* Minneapolis: Fortress, 2013.

Butler, Judith. *Gender Trouble: Feminism and the Subversion of Identity.* New York: Routledge, 1990.

Chapman, Cynthia R. *The Gendered Language of Warfare in the Israelite-Assyrian Encounter.* Winona Lake, Ind.: Eisenbrauns, 2004.

Clines, David J. A. "David the Man: The Construction of Masculinity in the Hebrew Bible." In *Interested Parties: The Ideology of Writers and Readers of the Hebrew Bible*, pp. 212–243. Sheffield, U.K.: Sheffield Academic Press, 1995.

Clines, David J. A. "*Ecce Vir*, or, Gendering the Son of Man." In *Biblical Studies/Cultural Studies*, edited by J. Cheryl Exum and Stephen D. Moore, pp. 352–375. Sheffield, U.K.: Sheffield Academic Press, 1998.

Clines, David J. A. "Final Reflections on Biblical Masculinity." In *Men and Masculinity in the Hebrew Bible and Beyond*, edited by Ovidiu Creangă, pp. 234–239. Sheffield, U.K.: Sheffield Phoenix, 2010.

Clines, David J. A. "He-Prophets: Masculinity as a Problem for the Hebrew Prophets and Their Interpreters." In *Sense and Sensitivity: Essays on Reading the Bible in Memory of Robert Carroll*, edited by Alastair G. Hunter and Philip R. Davies, pp. 311–328. Sheffield, U.K.: Sheffield Academic Press, 2002.

Connell, R. W. *Masculinities.* Cambridge, U.K.: Polity, 1995.

Conway, Colleen M. *Behold the Man: Jesus and Greco-Roman Masculinity.* Oxford: Oxford University Press, 2008.

Creangă, Ovidiu, ed. *Men and Masculinity in the Hebrew Bible and Beyond.* Sheffield, U.K.: Sheffield Phoenix, 2010.

D'Angelo, Mary Rose. "The ANHP Question in Luke-Acts: Imperial Masculinity and the Deployment of Women in the Early Second Century." In *A Feminist Companion to Luke*, edited by Amy-Jill Levine with Marianne Blickenstaff, pp. 44–72. Sheffield, U.K.: Sheffield Academic Press, 2002.

Eilberg-Schwartz, Howard. *God's Phallus and Other Problems for Men and Monotheism.* Boston: Beacon, 1994.

Flessen, Bonnie J. *An Exemplary Man: Cornelius and Characterization in Acts 10.* Eugene, Ore.: Pickwick, 2011.

Foucault, Michel. *The History of Sexuality.* Vol. 2: *The Use of Pleasure.* Translated by Robert Hurley. New York: Random House, 1985.

Foucault, Michel. *The History of Sexuality.* Vol. 3: *The Care of the Self.* Translated by Robert Hurley. New York: Random House, 1986.

Gardiner, Judith Kegan. "Introduction." In *Masculinity Studies and Feminist Theory: New Directions*, edited by Judith Kegan Gardiner, pp. 1–29. New York: Columbia University Press, 2002.

Glancy, Jennifer A. "Unveiling Masculinity: The Construction of Gender in Mark 6:17–29." *Biblical Interpretation* 11 (1994): 34–50.

Glancy, Jennifer A. "Boasting of Beatings (2 Corinthians 11:23–25)." *Journal of Biblical Literature* 123 (2004): 99–135.

Gleason, Maud W. *Making Men: Sophists and Self-Representation in Ancient Rome.* Princeton, N.J.: Princeton University Press, 1995.

Goldingay, John. "Hosea 1–3, Genesis 1–4 and Masculist Interpretation." In *A Feminist Companion to the Latter Prophets*, edited by Athalya Brenner, pp. 161–168. Sheffield, U.K.: Sheffield Academic Press, 1995.

Guest, Deryn. *Beyond Feminist Biblical Studies.* Sheffield, U.K.: Sheffield Phoenix, 2012.

Haddox, Susan E. "(E)Masculinity in Hosea's Political Rhetoric." In *Israel's Prophets and Israel's Past*, edited by Brad E. Kelle and Megan Bishop Moore, pp. 174–200. New York: T&T Clark International, 2006.

Haddox, Susan E. *Metaphor and Masculinity in Hosea.* New York: Peter Lang, 2011.

Halperin, David M. *One Hundred Years of Homosexuality: And Other Essays on Greek Love.* New York: Routledge, 1990.

Ivarsson, Fredrik. "Vice Lists and Deviant Masculinity: The Rhetorical Function of 1 Corinthians 5:10–11 and 6:9–10." In *Mapping Gender in Ancient Religious Discourses*, edited by Todd Penner and Caroline Vander Stichele, pp. 163–184. Leiden, The Netherlands: Brill, 2007.

Kahl, Brigitte. "No Longer Male: Masculinity Struggles behind Galatians 3:28?" *Journal for the Study of the New Testament* 79 (2000): 37–49.

Krondorfer, Björn. "Introduction." In *Men and Masculinities in Christianity and Judaism: A Critical Reader*, edited by Björn Krondorfer, pp. xi–xxi. London: SCM Press, 2009.

Lapsley, Jacqueline E., Carol A. Newson, and Sharon H. Ringe. "Introduction to the Twentieth-Anniversary Edition." In *Women's Bible Commentary*, 3d ed., edited by Jacqueline E. Lapsley et al., pp. xxi–xxiii. Louisville, Ky.: Westminster John Knox, 2012.

Larson, Jennifer L. "Paul's Masculinity." *Journal of Biblical Literature* 123 (2004): 85–97.

Liew, Tat-siong Benny. "Re-Mark-able Masculinities: Jesus, the Son of Man, and the (Sad) Sum of Manhood?" In *New Testament Masculinities*, edited by Stephen D. Moore and Janice Capel Anderson, pp. 93–136. Atlanta: Society of Biblical Literature, 2003.

Marin, Moisés Mayordomo. "Construction of Masculinity in Antiquity and Early Christianity." *lectio difficilior* 2 (2006). http://www.lectio.unibe.ch/06_2/marin_construction.htm.

Moore, Stephen D. "The Beatific Vision as a Posting Exhibition: Revelation's Hypermasculine Deity." *Journal for the Study of the New Testament* 60 (1995): 27–55.

Moore, Stephen D. *God's Gym: Divine Male Bodies of the Bible*. New York: Routledge, 1996.

Moore, Stephen D. "Que(e)rying Paul." In *Auguries: The Jubilee Volume of the Sheffield Department of Biblical Studies*, edited by David J. A. Clines and Stephen D. Moore, pp. 250–274. Sheffield, U.K.: Sheffield Academic Press, 1998.

Moore, Stephen D. *God's Beauty Parlor: And Other Queer Spaces in and around the Bible*. Stanford, Calif.: Stanford University Press, 2001.

Moore, Stephen D. "'O Man, Who Art Thou...?': Masculinity Studies and New Testament Studies." In *New Testament Masculinities*, edited by Stephen D. Moore and Janice Capel Anderson, pp. 1–22. Atlanta: Society of Biblical Literature, 2003.

Moore, Stephen D., and Janice Capel Anderson. "Taking It Like a Man: Masculinity in 4 Maccabees." *Journal of Biblical Literature* 117 (1998): 249–273.

Moore, Stephen D., and Janice Capel Anderson, eds. *New Testament Masculinities*. Atlanta: Society of Biblical Literature, 2003.

Olson, Dennis T. "Untying the Knot? Masculinity, Violence, and the Creation-Fall Story of Genesis 2–4." In *Engaging the Bible in a Gendered World*, edited by Linda Day and Carolyn Pressler, pp. 73–86. Louisville, Ky.: Westminster John Knox, 2006.

Parsons, Mikeal C. "Hand in Hand: Autobiographical Reflections on Luke 15." *Semeia* 72 (1995): 125–152.

Reeser, Todd W. *Masculinities in Theory: An Introduction*. Oxford: Wiley-Blackwell, 2010.

Sawyer, Deborah F. "Biblical Gender Strategies: The Case of Abraham's Masculinity." In *Gender, Religion, and Diversity: Cross-Cultural Perspectives*, edited by Ursula King and Tina Beattie, pp. 162–171. New York: Continuum, 2004.

Simpson, Mark. *Male Impersonators: Men Performing Masculinity*. London: Cassell, 2011.

Smith, Abraham. "'Full of Spirit and Wisdom': Luke's Portrait of Stephen (Acts 6:1—8:1a) as a Man of Self-Mastery." In *Asceticism and the New Testament*, edited by Leif E. Vaage and Vincent L. Wimbush, pp. 97–114. New York: Routledge, 1999.

Stone, Ken. "Gender Criticism: The Un-manning of Abimelech." In *Judges and Method: New Approaches in Biblical Studies*, 2d ed., edited by Gale A. Yee, pp. 183–201. Minneapolis: Fortress, 2007.

Stone, Ken. "Lovers and Raisin Cakes: Food, Sex and Divine Insecurity in Hosea." In *Queer Commentary and the Hebrew Bible*, edited by Ken Stone, pp. 116–139. Sheffield, U.K.: Sheffield Academic Press, 2001.

Stone, Ken. "Queer Reading between Bible and Film: *Paris Is Burning* and the 'Legendary Houses' of David and Saul." In *Bible Trouble: Queer Reading at the Boundaries of Biblical Scholarship*, edited by Teresa Hornsby and Ken Stone, pp. 75–98. Atlanta: Society of Biblical Literature, 2011.

Thurman, Eric. "Looking for a Few Good Men: Mark and Masculinity." In *New Testament Masculinities*, edited by Stephen D. Moore and Janice Capel Anderson, pp. 137–162. Atlanta: Society of Biblical Literature, 2003.

Thurman, Eric. "Novel Men: Masculinity and Empire in Mark's Gospel and Xenophon's *An Ephesian Tale*." In *Mapping Gender in Ancient Religious Discourses*, edited by Todd Penner and Caroline Vander Stichele, pp. 185–229. Leiden, The Netherlands: Brill, 2007.

Ward, Graham. "The Displaced Body of Jesus Christ." In *Radical Orthodoxy: A New Theology*, edited by John Milbank, Catherine Pickstock, and Graham Ward, pp. 163–181. New York: Routledge, 1999.

Watson, Elwood, and Marc E. Shaw, eds. *Performing American Masculinities: The 21st-Century Man in Popular Culture*. Bloomington: Indiana University Press, 2011.

Williams, Craig A. *Roman Homosexuality: Ideologies of Masculinity in Classical Antiquity*. Oxford: Oxford University Press, 1999.

Winkler, John J. *The Constraints of Desire: The Anthropology of Sex and Gender in Ancient Greece*. New York: Routledge, 1990.

Stephen D. Moore

MUJERISTA CRITICISM

Mujerista criticism is the practice of analyzing, interpreting, and evaluating biblical texts from the perspective of Latinas' religious faith and the role it plays in their daily life experiences, in *lo cotidiano* ("everyday life"). This critical approach, also known as *mujerista* biblical interpretation, is grounded in Latinas' struggle for survival and their conviction that reading the Bible must contribute to their liberation. *Mujerista* criticism draws on the insights of *mujerista* theology—a liberation theology that uses as its theological source the lived experience of Latinas living in the United States—to explore the biblical text as a resource for Latinas' liberation. Ultimately, the goal of *mujerista* criticism and *mujerista* theology is the liberation and fullness of life of Latinas and of all poor and oppressed people. Therefore, any interpretation of the Bible that does not contribute to this goal is not accepted as valid, and any biblical text that impedes this goal is denounced.

Doing *Mujerista* Criticism. Since *mujerista* criticism is grounded in Latinas' religious faith and the role it plays in *lo cotidiano*, the first move of *mujerista* criticism, before exploring the biblical text, is to perform a critical cultural, sociohistorical, political, and economic analysis of Latinas' reality. Such analysis should also include a careful understanding of their worldview, namely the values and goals that guide them and the hopes and dreams that inspire them. This critical analysis is done in two stages, first the internal understanding of themselves and then the external understanding of their cultural, sociohistorical, political, and economic reality. This analysis seeks to help Latinas and society at large to understand what changes are needed to enable the struggle for liberation.

After the analysis of Latinas' reality, the second move of *mujerista* criticism is to go to the Bible and find a text that matches the issues that are being addressed by the community or can speak about their reality. *Mujerista* criticism is highly suspicious of traditional interpretations and biblical texts that can obstruct liberation for Latinas; therefore *mujerista* criticism is very intentional about seeking and highlighting biblical texts that deal with *lo cotidiano* and using only biblical interpretations that give attention to the importance and centrality of everyday experience.

Mujerista criticism highlights texts that can be used to empower Latinas and give them strength as they live every day. Key passages are those that characterize women taking control of their lives or making their own decisions, particularly when they go against the systems of power that are oppressive and unjust. These biblical stories do not need to be exclusively about women, since gender is not the only identity marker that speaks of oppression. *Mujerista* criticism acknowledges the multidimensionality of the lived experiences of marginalized subjects who are excluded not only because of gender but also because of ethnicity, economic status, and sexual orientation.

Some of the favorite passages in *mujerista* theology include the stories of (1) Shiphra and Puah (Ex. 1:15–21), two simple midwives who defied the king by disobeying his orders; (2) the young women of Israel who refused to let history forget Jephthah's daughter by commemorating her life every year (Judg 11); (3) Ruth and Naomi, joined in faithfulness and relationship (Ruth 3:13–17); (4) the woman who washed Jesus's feet with her tears (Luke 7:36–59), a story demonstrating Jesus's vulnerability, expressed in his need to be touched and be taken care of; (5) Jesus's sharing with others his self-understanding and his mission, which expressed inclusivity (Luke 9:28–36); (6) Matthew's description of the kin-dom of God as including human needs and care for the body (Matt 25:31–46); and (7) day workers who are treated unfairly and struggle for justice (Matt 20:1–16). All of these passages highlight the biblical *cotidiano*, which is central to a *mujerista* reading and interpretation of the Bible.

The third move in *mujerista* criticism is to analyze the context of the selected biblical text. As a mode of inquiry, *mujerista* criticism positions itself within the interpretive paradigm of cultural criticism because of its particular interest in *lo cotidiano*. *Mujerista* criticism is mostly attracted to this mode of critical discourse because it explores the biblical texts as sociocultural products emerging from their social and cultural context; the texts are inscribed with the codes from a particular world. The analysis of cultural criticism calls for an examination of social institutions, values, behaviors, class, and class conflict. What attracts *mujerista* criticism to this interpretive approach is its focus on the economic and sociocultural context of the text. This critical approach highlights the biblical *cotidiano* of the text—the cultural values and behaviors and the cultural matrix behind the text—rather than the religious and theological aspects of the text. This approach is interested in understanding the world behind the text.

Mujerista criticism listens to the voice of grassroots Latinas whose readings may not be scholarly but are valid because they are life-giving to themselves and to their communities. This recognition of the authority of Latinas to interpret the Bible is intrinsic to a *mujerista* praxis of liberation that seeks to contribute to the strengthening of these women's moral agency and self-definition. Ultimately, theological and religious meaning of the text is not determined by the church or traditional interpretations but by the religious value that the text itself may have for Latinas given their experience in their individual reality, subjectivity, and everyday life.

Key Concepts in *Mujerista* Criticism. In *mujerista* theology, liberation is understood as *la lucha*, the daily struggle for the flourishing of lives and fullness of life, for Latinas and for all. Therefore, *mujerista* criticism is guided by *la lucha*: it must contribute to liberation of Latinas and all.

Lo cotidiano is one of the core elements of *mujerista* theology. It is a complex term that goes beyond the everyday life experiences. For *mujerista* criticism, *lo cotidiano* means the immediate spaces of Latina lives, the first horizon of their experiences, which are the experiences that constitute their reality. *Lo cotidiano* is the cultural space of encounter where Latinas face the material world and interact with it; it is made up not only of physical realities but also of the relationship of Latinas with reality and their understanding and evaluation of such reality. *Lo cotidiano* is what grounds and situates the expe-

riences of Latinas, what gives structure and limits to their social relations; it is constituted by the habitual way of judging reality, the usual tactics used to interact in life, and the practices and beliefs that have been inherited.

This way of being in the world and interacting with reality is not an uncritical act. *Lo cotidiano* is a way of interacting and negotiating everyday life in a critical and conscious way.

It refers to the lived experiences that have been analyzed and are now part of Latina identity, how Latinas understand reality and how they act. In and from *lo cotidiano*, Latinas engage in multifaceted dimensions of humanity. *Lo cotidiano* refers to the ways that they express themselves and the interplay of their multidimensionality—how they negotiate economic status, race, ethnicity, and gender. The scope of *lo cotidiano* goes beyond the personal and private world; it encompasses the public arena, the social system with which they interact every day, and the relations they have with friends, family, and community.

Mujerista criticism is unapologetically and radically subjective. It responds to the personal, which is understood by the social and human ability to discern and establish criteria that resonates with others. Radical subjectivity is about taking a stand and being grounded in Latinas' interests and commitments, which are also accountable to the existence of others. It is the tension between the personal interest and the interest of others that makes it possible to be open to others for the sake of the common good. Radical subjectivity validates the claims that emerge from daily experience rather than from abstract ideas; it acknowledges the particularity and contextuality of all human knowledge.

Approaches to Biblical Texts. Liberation and the promotion of liberation are the criteria for accepting or rejecting biblical interpretations and biblical texts. Biblical texts and interpretations are both validated and accepted as long as they help in the struggle for liberation. From that standpoint the biblical message is considered as the Word of God by *mujerista* criticism when it brings light and support to the process of liberation.

The text (or image), selected as analogy to help in moral decision-making, has to be consistent with the central biblical message. The biblical text has to be consistent with a theologically sound concept of God based on the understanding of the community. The text should be measured against the perspective of the whole life of Jesus.

Particular biblical and theological presuppositions undergird *mujerista* criticism.

First, the God of the Gospels is understood to have a preferential option for the poor and the marginalized. Second, the main message that Jesus preaches in the Gospels is understood as the establishment of the Kin-dom of God, where the hungry are fed, the homeless receive shelter, and the naked are clothed. This focus on *kin-dom* rather than *king-dom* is central to *mujerista* understanding.

While during the first-century Jewish world the metaphor of kingdom was probably the best way Jesus and his early followers found to indicate God's benevolence, in today's world the metaphor of the kingdom has become irrelevant; kingdoms rarely exist anymore. The metaphor of kingdom has lost much of the positive meaning it had for Jesus and his followers, and now often promotes decidedly anti-kingdom values. In *mujerista* theology the metaphor of the kingdom is now seen to refer only to male sovereigns and to reinforce a male image of God, still very prevalent in the church; it is seen as an ineffective and dangerous metaphor, suggesting an elitist, hierarchical, patriarchal structure that supports all sorts of systemic oppressions.

Exploring the context of the original metaphor provides a way forward. For Jesus and his early followers, speaking of the "Kingdom of God" was a way of speaking about shalom, about fullness of life. Shalom was not a private reality that each individual had to find or construct but a reality for which people needed to work together. Jesus made love of neighbor central to life in the Kingdom of God: love is communal, the task of a people and not solely of individuals. Shalom—fullness of life—is the value at the heart of the kingdom metaphor that Jesus used; today in *mujerista* theology, shalom goes by the name of liberation—a holistic liberation that happens at all levels of life: social, political, personal, spiritual.

The idea of kin-dom of God, of the family of God, is a much more relevant and effective metaphor today to communicate what Jesus lived and died for. It also serves as response to the ongoing concern for the loss of family values and the loss of a true sense of family in present day society. Kin-dom of God as the core metaphor for the goal of Jesus's life helps to reconstitute the sense of family, as a family united not by ties of blood but by bonds of friendship, love, care, and community. This new family is an inclusive one, not constrained by the patriarchal structure of a ruling father with a submissive mother but inviting different structural configurations and a value on belonging, being safe, and becoming fully oneself.

Third, Latinas' beliefs about *Jesucristo* come out of their reality as marginalized persons who struggle for fullness of life. Seeking to answer the question Jesus posed to his disciples, "who do you say that I am?," *mujerista* criticism follows the tradition of the Gospel writers who created narratives about Jesus that responded to the questions and issues alive in the communities for which they wrote. Its struggle for liberation is a call for creative explanations of who *Jesucristo* is for them in ways that have a certain logical flow and coherence. Listening carefully to the voices of grassroots Latinas, *mujerista* Christology treats belief about Jesus as a mirror for conscience: Latinas know Jesus is with them because he joins them in their struggle for liberation—fullness of life.

***Mujerista* Theology.** *Mujerista* theology emerged in the late 1980s from the work of activist and theologian Ada María Isasi-Díaz. Committed to the struggle for justice and peace, she began developing *mujerista* theology in the company of and in conversation with grassroots Latinas using ethnomethodology, an approach to sociological inquiry interested in the study of the everyday routines that people use to produce social order. The goal of ethnomethodology is to document the methods and practices used by the members of society to make sense of their world. As such, *mujerista* theology emerged as a forum for the voices of Latinas in their daily struggle for liberation and survival, and it continues to offer them the opportunity to confront oppressive religious teachings and practices as it seeks to empower Latinas to become agents of radical change in order to transform society and eliminate oppression.

Mujerista theology draws from three central elements of the reality of grassroots Latina women. First, *mujerista* theology is based on a *mestiza* and *mulata* Christianity, a mixture of religious practices and contents that come from the Catholicism of the Spaniard conquistadores, the African and Amerindian religions, and the Protestant and evangelical traditions. Within this Latino/a Christianity, influenced and shaped by different religious understandings and practices, the importance and use of the Bible offers a wide spectrum that goes from nonexistent for some Latinas to highly authoritative for others. Mindful of the wide spectrum, *mujerista* criticism seeks to help Latinas to appropriate the Bible in a liberative way.

Second, the source of *mujerista* theology is the experience of Latina women and their struggle for survival, not the Bible. Equally, the starting point for interpreting the Bible from a *mujerista* perspective is the experience of Latina women. Third, *mujerista* theology operates under the critical lens of liberation, a liberation that has to do with physical and cultural survival. Reading the Bible from this perspective means that the Bible can be accepted as divine revelation and as authoritative for life only as long as it contributes to the liberation of Latina women.

Out of the three foundational elements of *mujerista* theology emerge three guiding principles for doing *mujerista* biblical criticism: (1) the criterion for using the Bible is the need for liberation. Latina grassroots women use the Bible when they need it, for what they need from it, and in the manner in which they need it; (2) the central lens in *mujerista* criticism is the struggle for liberation, a hermeneutics of *la lucha*; and (3) Latinas' interpretation of the Bible is central for identifying and struggling for their *proyecto histórico*, their preferred future.

The implementation of the *proyecto histórico* shapes *mujerista* biblical interpretation in four concrete ways. First, biblical exegesis is praxis. It is a communal task where all participants have a voice and it is a way to claim their right to think. Second, Latinas live their faith within a functional religious pluralism, a "grassroots ecumenism," which Isasi-Díaz takes as an invitation to read the Bible beyond traditional doctrinal purity and in solidarity with Latinas, bringing to the text whatever tool is necessary from their diverse religious practices in order to understand the text in a liberative way. Third, the Bible should be read in ways that confront and defy elitism, demanding the elimination of its hierarchical understandings, structures, and ecclesiastical privileges. Fourth, *mujerista* criticism should reject the split between the personal and the political, respect the self-determination for the person, analyze and redefine power for a just society, respect the right of all groups to struggle and achieve liberation, and achieve the common good.

Influenced by her Roman Catholic background as a former novice, Isasi-Díaz's main concern about the Bible is the exclusivist way in which it has been read and used to control women and prevent them from appropriating the text from their own views. Operating from a hermeneutics of suspicion, Isasi-Díaz seeks to subvert the patriarchal power of the Bible by questioning its authority and accepting it only as a liberating and authoritative text in as far as it enables and advances the liberation and survival of Latina women. By empowering Latina women to use their experience as the entry point into the Bible and by opening a forum where Latina women can read the Bible the way in which they need to in order to survive, Isasi-Díaz challenges the elitist views and hierarchical readings of those in power to authorize the correct interpretation of the Bible. By subverting all the authorized ways of reading the Bible, Isasi-Díaz de-patriarchalizes the biblical text and calls into question the solidarity of the church with women who have to find their own liberative ways of reading the Bible in order to survive and struggle for a better world. *Mujerista* theology affirms that without liberation there cannot be justice and peace. Liberation is a communal endeavor, and no one can find liberation in isolation or at the expense of others. *Mujerista* criticism, therefore, is a communal endeavor that seeks the liberation of all.

In the process of finding a name for the theological work of Latinas and their commitment to liberation, Isasi-Diaz was inspired by the work of black feminists who preceded Latinas in the struggle to name themselves and was immensely influenced by their use of the term "womanist." The name *mujerista* is derived from the Spanish word *mujer*, which means woman. The name *mujerista* was inspired by the songs of women from Isasi-Diaz's Latina community, who sing about strong women who struggle for equality, particularly "Cántico de Mujer" written by Latina activist Rosa Marta Zárate Macías.

Who Is a *Mujerista*? *Mujerista*s are persons who opt for Latinas, who have Latinas' liberation and fullness of life as their goal because they are convinced that no one can be fully liberated unless all are liberated. Men can be *mujerista*s; non-Latinas or non-Latinos can be *mujerista*s. Professional theologians can be *mujerista*s, in the same way that grassroots Latinas are theologians. Also, Latinas with some training in religious studies such as catechists, pastoral workers, or ordained Latina women in Protestant churches can be *mujerista* theologians. All those who see themselves interconnected in the struggle for liberation can be *mujerista*s, for everyone can take part of it as *mujerista*s themselves. The struggle for liberation is an option for life and a rejection of untimely and unjust death.

Doing *mujerista* theology is a praxis of liberation, a way of making a contribution to the struggle for fullness of life for Latinas in the United States. Doing *mujerista* theology is a way of contributing to the church and to its theological understandings, enriching what it teaches about the divine and about Latinas' relationship with the divine. Doing *mujerista* theology is way of influencing society, a call for all to be concerned about others and for others, particularly those who are oppressed—the poor, marginalized, exploited, abused, and victims of discrimination. Doing *mujerista* theology is a way of bringing joy to others, of contributing to their fullness of life. Doing *mujerista* theology is life-giving, particularly when it is life-giving to others.

[*See also* Intersectional Studies; Reader-Oriented Criticism; *and* Womanist Criticism.]

BIBLIOGRAPHY

Isasi-Diáz, Ada María. *Hispanic Women: Prophetic Voice in the Church: Toward a Hispanic Women's Liberation Theology.* San Francisco: Harper & Row, 1988.

Isasi-Diáz, Ada María. "The Bible and *Mujerista* Theology." In *Lift Every Voice*, edited by Susan B. Thistlethwaite and Mary Potter Engle, pp. 261–269. San Francisco: Harper & Row, 1990.

Isasi-Diáz, Ada María. "Defining Our Proyecto Histórico: *Mujerista* Strategies for Liberation." *Journal of Feminist Studies in Religion* 9, no. 1–2 (Spring–Fall 1993): 17–28.

Isasi-Diáz, Ada María. "La palabra de Dios en nosotras—The Word of God in Us." In *Searching the Scriptures*, Vol. 1, edited by Elisabeth Schussler Fiorenza, pp. 86–97. New York: Crossroad, 1993.

Isasi-Diáz, Ada María *En la lucha = In the Struggle: A Hispanic Women's Liberation Theology.* Minneapolis: Fortress, 1993.

Isasi-Diáz, Ada María. "*Mujerista* Theology's Method: A Liberative Praxis, a Way of Life." In *Mestizo Christianity*, edited by Arturo J. Banuelas, pp. 175–190. Maryknoll, N.Y.: Orbis, 1995.

Isasi-Diáz, Ada María. Mujerista *Theology: A Theology for the Twenty-first Century.* Maryknoll, N.Y.: Orbis, 1996.

Isasi-Diáz, Ada María. *La lucha Continues:* Mujerista *Theology.* Maryknoll, N.Y.: Orbis, 2004.

Isasi-Diáz, Ada María. "Communication as Communion: Elements in a Hermeneutic of *Lo cotidiano*." In *Engaging the Bible in a Gendered World*, edited by Linda Day and Carolyn Pressler, pp. 27–36. Louisville, Ky., and London: Westminster John Knox, 2006.

Isasi-Diáz, Ada María. "*Mujerista* Theology: A Praxis of Liberation—My Story." In *Shaping a Global Theological Mind*, edited by Darren C. Marks, pp. 77–87. Aldershot, U.K., and Burlington, Vt.: Ashgate, 2008.

Isasi-Diáz, Ada María. "A *Mujerista* Hermeneutics of Justice and Human Flourishing." In *Bible and the Hermeneutics of Liberation*, edited by Alejandro F. Botta and Pablo R. Andiñach, pp. 181–195. Atlanta: Society of Biblical Literature, 2009.

Isasi-Diáz, Ada María. "Identificate con nosotras: A *mujerista* Christological Understanding." In *Jesus in the Hispanic Community*, edited by Harold J. Recinos and Hugo Magallanes, pp. 38–57. Louisville, Ky.: Westminster John Knox, 2009.

Isasi-Diáz, Ada María. "An Interview with Ada María Isasi-Díaz (Interviewee); Isherwood, Lisa (Interviewer)." *Feminist Theology* 20, no. 1 S (2011): 8–17.

Leticia Guardiola-Saenz